SALMOND AND HEUSTON

ON THE

LAW OF TORTS

TWENTIETH EDITION

by

R. F. V. HEUSTON, D.C.L., F.B.A.
Honorary Fellow of Pembroke College, Oxford
Honorary Bencher of Gray's Inn, and of the King's Inns, Dublin

and

R. A. BUCKLEY, M.A., D.PHIL.
Fellow of Mansfield College, Oxford
Of Lincoln's Inn, Barrister

LONDON
SWEET & MAXWELL LTD.
1992

First Edition	(1907) The Author
Second Edition	(1910) The Author
Third Edition	(1912) The Author
Fourth Edition	(1916) The Author
Fifth Edition	(1920) The Author
Sixth Edition	(1924) The Author
Seventh Edition	(1928) W. T. S. Stallybrass
Eighth Edition	(1934) W. T. S. Stallybrass
Ninth Edition	(1936) W. T. S. Stallybrass
Tenth Edition	(1945) W. T. S. Stallybrass
Eleventh Edition	(1953) R. F. V. Heuston
Twelfth Edition	(1957) R. F. V. Heuston
Second Impression	(1959)
Thirteenth Edition	(1961) R. F. V. Heuston
Second Impression	(1962)
Fourteenth Edition	(1965) R. F. V. Heuston
Second Impression	(1967)
Fifteenth Edition	(1969) R. F. V. Heuston
Sixteenth Edition	(1973) R. F. V. Heuston
Seventeenth Edition	(1977) R. F. V. Heuston
Eighteenth Edition	(1981) R. F. V. Heuston and R. S. Chambers
Nineteenth Edition	(1987) R. F. V. Heuston and R. A. Buckley
Twentieth Edition	(1992) R. F. V. Heuston and R. A. Buckley

Published by
Sweet & Maxwell Ltd.
South Quay Plaza
183 Marsh Wall, London E14 9FT

Computerset by Promenade Graphics Limited, Cheltenham
Printed in Great Britain by
Richard Clay (The Chaucer Press) Ltd.
Bungay, Suffolk.

*A CIP catalogue record
for this book is available
from the British Library*

ISBN 0 421 45980 8

PREFACE TO THE TWENTIETH EDITION

The scope and object of this 20th edition of Sir John Salmond's textbook remains as stated by the author in his preface to the 1st edition. But 85 years on the complexity of life has made it impossible for us to imitate completely his admirable brevity and clarity.

As the 21st century comes into view, probably the most important fact to record about the law of torts is that it is still in existence—and in a form which Salmond would at once recognise. In other words, tort has not been replaced by a system of no-fault insurance such as that recommended by the Pearson Commission nearly 15 years ago. Nor, if we interpret the political scene correctly, will it be replaced during the lifetime of this edition.

On the other hand, there are many signs that the European dimension of torts will increase significantly. In particular, if it becomes possible to recover damages from a government for loss caused by the non-implementation of an EC Directive, an explosion in litigation is likely, which will require the brief section now devoted to Eurotorts to be expanded into a chapter.

In the Anglo-American dimension close links will no doubt continue. But, as the leading authority in this area has remarked, English lawyers will continue to be surprised by "the abrasive, prominent and controversial role played by the tort process in American public life" (Fleming, *The American Tort Process* (1988), p. v).

There are two major changes of structure or arrangement. First, we have abandoned the former system of numbering the sections consecutively throughout the book, and followed the general practice of numbering (and so cross-referencing) by chapters and sections within each chapter.

Secondly, there is now a distinct chapter on New and Emergent Torts (No. 3), as there are also on Vicarious Liability (No. 21) and Damages for Personal Injuries (No. 24). The chapter on Defamation (No. 8) remains over-long, despite all our efforts. The basic problem here is that Parliament has refused to attend to the many calls for reform of this part of the law. In addition we have had to deal with four major appellate decisions—on publication (*Slipper* v. *B.B.C.*), on privilege and fair comment (*Kingshott* v. *Associated Kent Newspapers*, and *Telnikoff* v. *Matusevitch*), and damages (*Sutcliffe* v. *Pressdram*).

Other, more minor, changes include the rearrangement of the material on statutory authority and reversionary interests. We are not sure that we have always found the best places for developments relating to unborn children, rape and AIDS, but we resisted the temptation to have a new section entitled Sex and Torts.

So far as changes of substance are concerned, the last 20 years have been dominated by the problem of economic loss in negligence. At one stage it seemed as if it would be impossible to produce a coherent account of the law within a reasonably brief chapter. Fortunately the decision of the House of Lords in *Murphy* v. *Brentwood D.C.* [1991] 1

A.C. 398, whatever else may be said about it, has eased the editorial task, in that it enabled us to treat as legal history many appellate court judgments (lengthy and learned though they were) of the eighties.

The Table of Statutes has been carefully checked, and obsolete citations accordingly deleted. It is interesting to note that only 34 pre-1900 statutes are cited in this edition in comparison with 162 dating from post-1900.

It would have involved a disproportionate amount of effort to make a similar count for the Table of Cases. But the footnotes have been carefully combed for obsolete decisions, and a surprising number detected and quietly deleted.

The text has been revised in the light of the material available to us on October 31, 1991, but it has occasionally been possible to insert brief references to later developments. Readers may be glad to know that the text is approximately 100 pages shorter than the previous edition. Although we jointly share editorial responsibility for the whole work, the preparation of Chapters 5 and 24, along with Chapters 9–13 inclusive, was undertaken primarily by R.A.B. and that of all the remaining chapters by R.F.V.H. We are grateful to Professor E. M. Barendt and Mr. P. B. Carter for help with the complex material on social security benefits and conflict of laws respectively. We are also indebted to our publishers for their support and encouragement.

R. F. V. Heuston
R. A. Buckley

June, 1992

PREFACE TO THE FIRST EDITION

I have endeavoured in this book to set forth the principles of the law of Torts with as much precision, coherence, and system as the subject admits of, and with as much detailed consideration as is necessary to make the work one of practical utility. No book is justified by the good intent of its author: but I hope that the present work will be found of use to lawyers and to students of law as a general exposition, in moderate compass, of an extensive and in some respect difficult and imperfectly developed department of our legal system.

J.W.S.

WELLINGTON, NEW ZEALAND,
August 5, 1907

CONTENTS

7. TRESPASS TO THE PERSON

8. DEFAMATION

9. NEGLIGENCE

14. LIABILITY FOR ANIMALS

15. DOMESTIC RELATIONS

16. THE ECONOMIC TORTS

17. TRADE DISPUTES

18. DECEIT AND INJURIOUS FALSEHOOD

19. WRONGFUL PROCESS OF LAW

20. PARTIES

21. VICARIOUS LIABILITY

22. MISCELLANEOUS DEFENCES

23. DAMAGES: GENERAL PRINCIPLES

24. DAMAGES FOR PERSONAL INJURY AND DEATH

25. REMEDIES: MISCELLANEOUS MATTERS

26. EXTRAJUDICIAL REMEDIES

TABLE OF CASES

xvii

TABLE OF STATUTES

CHAPTER 1

INTRODUCTORY

§ 1.1. The Forms of Action

In the fourteenth century remedies for wrongs were dependent upon writs. No one could bring an action in the king's common law courts without the king's writ and the number of writs available was very limited. Where there was no writ there was no right. One of Sir Henry Maine's most famous generalisations explains our early law: "So great is the ascendancy of the law of actions in the infancy of courts of justice, that substantive law has at first the look of being gradually secreted in the interstices of procedure."[1] Every plaintiff had to bring his cause of action within a recognised form of action, and "the key-note of the form of action is struck by the original writ, the writ whereby the action is begun."[2] Although modern research is inclined to minimise the importance of the writ system, it can be said that for five hundred years the writ determined the right. After some preliminary amendments of the law in 1832 and 1833, the Common Law Procedure Act 1852, s.3, provided that "it shall not be necessary to mention any form or cause of action in any writ of summons." Yet the most recent version of the Rules of Court[3] has been interpreted to mean that even if it is not necessary to state the cause of action in the writ it is very desirable to do so.[4] Today "a cause of action" means a factual situation which entitles one person to obtain a remedy from another person in the courts.[5] So that it is unnecessary to attach a specific label such as "conversion" or "trespass," if the pleaded facts sufficiently support either claim.[6] It is sufficient for the pleader to state the material facts: he need not state the result.[7] Today the fundamental principle is that whenever a person has a right the law should give a remedy.[8] "This principle enables us to step over the tripwires of previous cases and to bring the law into accord with the needs of to-day."[9] The absence of a remedy is evidence, but no more than evidence, that no right exists.[10] Finally, it is interesting to

---

[1] *Early Law and Custom*, p. 389.

[2] Maitland, *Forms of Action*, p. 299. For 800 years the writ contained a command by His Majesty to enter an appearance; "this was dignified but was, perhaps, obscure and peremptory to persons abroad; it has now been omitted": Note to Ord. 6, r. 1 in *Supreme Court Practice* (1985).

[3] Ord. 18, r. 15(2).

[4] *Sterman* v. *E. W. and W. J. Moore Ltd.* [1970] 1 Q.B. 569, 603–604.

[5] *Letang* v. *Cooper* [1965] 1 Q.B. 232, 242–243.

[6] *Hesperides Hotels* v. *Aegean Turkish Holidays Ltd.* [1979] A.C. 508, 538.

[7] *Metall und Rohstoff A.G.* v. *Donaldson Lufkin and Jennette Inc.* [1990] 1 Q.B. 391, 436.

[8] *Letang* v. *Cooper* [1965] 1 Q.B. 232, 239. But see the criticism of this case below, § 25.4.

[9] *Hill* v. *Parsons (C.A.) & Co. Ltd.* [1972] Ch. 305, 316, *per* Lord Denning, M.R.

[10] *Dies* v. *British and International Mining Corporation* [1939] 1 K.B. 724, 738–739; *Sales Affiliates Ltd.* v. *Le Jean* [1947] Ch. 295, 305; *Nelson* v. *Larholt* [1948] 1 K.B. 339, 343; *Abbott* v. *Sullivan* [1952] 1 K.B. 189, 200.

note that it is exceptional for a writ to lead to a contested judicial hearing. The annual Civil Judicial Statistics show that judgment by default is given in over 90 per cent. of actions begun by writ.

The forms of action

"An English lawsuit is not a moot or a debate, but an attempt to arrive at a result on the facts before the court: broad academic arguments are quite unsuited to the processes of the English law."[11] So it is still necessary to know something of the nature and scope of the forms of action. "The forms of action," said Maitland at the beginning of this century[12] "we have buried, but they still rule us from their graves"— perhaps less imperiously today than when Maitland wrote, for Lord Atkin said[13] that "When these ghosts of the past stand in the path of justice clanking their medieval chains the proper course for the judge is to pass through them undeterred." A knowledge of the forms of action is necessary for the following three reasons.

First, to one who is wholly ignorant of the old learning many of the older authorities on liability for civil injuries are unintelligible, especially those which deal with the difference between trespass and case.

Secondly, questions as to the existence, nature, and extent of liability depend even yet in some instances on the particular kind of writ or remedy that would have been available for the plaintiff under the old practice.[14] An illustration is *Esso Petroleum Co. Ltd.* v. *Southport Corporation.*[15] The defendants' oil tanker *Inverpool* ran aground on a revetment wall in the Ribble estuary. There was a danger that she might break her back, with the probable loss of the ship herself and the lives of her crew. In order to prevent this the master decided to lighten the ship by jettisoning some of her cargo. The 400 tons of oil so discharged were carried by the action of the wind and tide on to the premises of the Southport Corporation. "Gratitude for deliverance, apart from other instincts, might have inspired a desire to reimburse the Corporation of Southport the amount of the expense to which they were put in cleaning the oil which came unwanted and unwelcome to their shore and to their lake."[16] Esso Petroleum took a different view. As events turned out they were legally justified in doing so. For although the plaintiffs alleged that the deposit of oil on the foreshore gave rise to three distinct causes of action—trespass, nuisance, and negligence—the trial judge decided each one of these allegations adversely to them and his judgment was approved by the House of Lords. A second illustration is the litigation arising out of another escape of oil at sea, this time from the *Wagon Mound* in Sydney Harbour. In one action the owners of a damaged

---

[11] *Duple Motor Bodies* v. *I.R.C.* [1960] 1 W.L.R. 510, 526, *per* Harman L.J.
[12] *Forms of Action*, p. 296. See (1905) 21 L.Q.R. 43 for similar remarks by Salmond.
[13] *United Australia Ltd.* v. *Barclays Bank* [1941] A.C. 1, 29.
[14] Sutton, *Personal Actions*, pp. 58–62, gives some practical illustrations.
[15] [1956] A.C. 218 (H.L.).
[16] [1954] 2 Q.B. 182, 203, *per* Morris L.J.

wharf failed to recover,[17] but in another action, differently framed, the owners of ships moored to that wharf did recover.[18] Again as the same facts may support an action either in tort or in contract, and as there are different periods of limitation for tort and contract, the choice of remedy may be of great practical importance.[19]

Thirdly, as Maitland pointed out, a lawyer can still "do his client a great deal of harm by advising a bad or inappropriate course of procedure, though it is true he cannot bring about a total shipwreck of a good cause so easily as he might have done some years ago."[20] The Esso Petroleum case again provides an example. The plaintiffs' case before and at the trial was that the defendants were vicariously responsible for the negligent conduct of the master of the *Inverpool* in his navigation of the vessel. As the master was acquitted of negligence it logically followed that the defendants also went free. The House of Lords (reversing the Court of Appeal) held that it was not then open to the Southport Corporation to allege that Esso Petroleum must discharge the onus of showing that they had not negligently sent the vessel to sea in an unseaworthy condition. Adherence to the pleadings is not "pedantry[21] or mere formalism."[22] It is bad law and bad practice to shrug off a criticism as "a mere pleading point."[23] These statements are of particular importance today, when the expansion of the tort of negligence, with its emphasis on the foresight of the hypothetical reasonable man, has tended to emphasise vagueness, informality and imprecision in the law. So it has been necessary to state that "the tort of negligence has not yet subsumed all torts and did not supplant the principles of equity, or contradict contractual promises or complement the remedy of judicial review or supplement statutory rights."[24] To put it in another way, the structured principles of an established tort such as defamation[25] or malicious prosecution[26] cannot be evaded by suing in negligence.

Justice according to law

"The law of tort has fallen into great confusion, but, in the main, what acts and omissions result in responsibility and what do not are matters defined by long-established rules of law from which judges ought not wittingly to depart and no light is shed upon a given case by large

---

[17] [1961] A.C. 388.

[18] [1967] 1 A.C. 617.

[19] See below, § 2.1. and § 25.4.

[20] *Forms of Action*, p. 303.

[21] It should be remembered that a pedant may be right: *The Merak* [1965] P. 223, 260.

[22] [1956] A.C. 218, 241, *per* Lord Radcliffe. In general it is not possible to raise on appeal a point not taken in the court below: *Perkowski* v. *Wellington Corporation* [1959] A.C. 53. Yet in *Carmarthenshire C.C.* v. *Lewis* [1955] A.C. 549 the House of Lords appears to have allowed the appeal on a ground which was not argued at the trial.

[23] *Farrell* v. *Secretary of State* [1980] 1 W.L.R. 172, 180.

[24] *China & South Sea Bank Ltd.* v. *Tan* [1990] 1 A.C. 536, 543, *per* Lord Templeman.

[25] *Bell-Booth Group Ltd.* v. *Att.-Gen.* [1989] 3 N.Z.L.R. 148. But see below, § 9.7 n. 39 and cases there cited.

[26] *McDonagh* v. *Metropolitan Police Commissioner* [1991] C.L.Y. 4315.

generalisations about them."[27] It is better that the law should be clear than that it should be clever.[28] As it was put in an American case, "rather than add to the already existing confusion with the formulation of a new rule, we conclude that the wisest approach is to return to the traditional principles, theories and standards of tort law."[29] For it must always be borne in mind that justice according to law is the common law ideal. "The qualities that saved English law when the day of trial came in the Tudor age were not vulgar common sense and the reflection of the layman's unanalysed instincts: rather they were strict logic and high technique, rooted in the Inns of Court, rooted in the Year Books, rooted in the centuries."[30] Sentiment is a poor guide to decision. So when in 1401 the defendant was about to be held liable for the escape of his fire, his counsel argued that he would be "undone and impoverished all his days if this action is to be maintained against him; for then twenty other such suits will be brought against him," but was met with the reply: "What is that to us? It is better that he should be utterly undone than that the law should be changed for him."[31] The same answer would be given today. So it is not open to a modern judge to create a new remedy, and accordingly a new right, simply on the grounds of economy or convenience,[32] although sympathy for a morally meritorious plaintiff is sometimes judicially expressed, especially when he is a workman injured in the course of his employment.[33] On the other hand, a court should try not to be influenced against the plaintiff by the fact that he is a disagreeable person standing on his legal rights,[34] and adopting a "dog in the manger" attitude,[35] or has made a grossly exaggerated claim.[36]

§ 1.2. TRESPASS AND CASE[37]

The term "trespass" has been used by lawyers and laymen in three senses of varying degrees of generality. (1) In its widest and original

---

[27] *Victoria Park Racing and Recreation Grounds Co. Ltd.* v. *Taylor* (1937) 58 C.L.R. 479, 505, per Dixon J.

[28] *Parsons* v. *B.N.M. Laboratories Ltd.* [1964] 1 Q.B. 95, 102.

[29] *Hunsley* v. *Giard* 553 P.(2d) 1096, 1102 (1976).

[30] Maitland, Selden Society, Vol. 17, p. xviii. After several decades of so-called realism, it is worth noting that in the 1970s, "Comprehensive, abstract, generalised theory has reappeared in torts literature" (G. Edward White, *Tort Law in America* (1980), p. 155).

[31] *Beaulieu* v. *Finglam* (1401) Y.B. 2 Hen. IV, f. 18, pl. 6 (reprinted in Baker and Milson, *Sources*, p. 588).

[32] *Re Wykeham Terrace* [1971] 1 Ch. 204, 213.

[33] *Chapman* v. *Oakleigh Animal Products Ltd.* (1970) 8 K.I.R. 1063, 1067.

[34] As in *Withers* v. *Perry Chain Co. Ltd.* [1961] 1 W.L.R. 1314, 316, or in some of the leading cases of wrongful imprisonment (see below, § 7.2).

[35] As in *Anchor Brewhouse Developments Ltd.* v. *Berkley House Ltd.* [1987] 2 E.G.L.R. 173.

[36] "Parties who open their mouths far too wide may still be entitled to a cut off the joint, even if they are clearly not entitled to the joint itself." *R.* v. *Take-Over Panel, ex p. Guinness plc., per* Lord Donaldson M.R. [1990] 1 Q.B. 146, 180.

[37] See Winfield and Goodhart, "Trespass and Negligence" (1933) 49 L.Q.R. 359; Prichard, "Trespass, Case, and the Rule in *Williams* v. *Holland*" [1964] C.L.J. 234; Trindade, "Some Curiosities of Negligent Trespass to the Person" (1971) 20 I.C.L.Q. 706; Fridman, "Trespass or Negligence" (1971) 9 Alberta L.Rev. 250.

signification it includes any wrongful act—any infringement or transgression of the rule of right. This use is common in the Authorised Version of the Bible, and was presumably familiar when that version was first published. But it never obtained recognition in the technical language of the law,[38] and is now archaic even in popular speech. (2) In a second and narrower signification—its true legal sense—the term means any legal wrong for which the appropriate remedy was a writ of trespass—*viz.* any direct and forcible injury to person, land or chattels. (3) The third and narrowest meaning of the term is that in which, in accordance with popular speech, it is limited to one particular kind of trespass in the second sense—*viz.* the tort of trespass to land (trespass *quare clausum fregit*).

Under the old practice the remedies for torts were in general two in number—namely, the action of trespass and that of trespass on the case[39] (commonly called by way of abbreviation "case" simply). Trespass—"that fertile mother of actions"[40]—was the remedy for all forcible and direct injuries, whether to person, land, or chattels. Case, on the other hand, provided for all injuries not amounting to trespasses—that is to say, for all injuries which were either not forcible or not direct, but merely consequential.[41] An *injury* is an actionable wrong, in contrast to *damage* which means loss or harm occurring in fact, whether actionable as an injury or not.[41]

"Forcible"

The term "forcible" is used in a wide and somewhat unnatural sense to include any act of physical interference with the person or property of another. To lay one's finger on another person without lawful justification is as much a forcible injury in the eye of the law, and therefore a trespass, as to beat him with a stick. To walk peacefully across another man's land is a forcible injury and a trespass, no less than to break into his house *vi et armis*. So also it is probably a trespass deliberately to put matter where natural forces will take it on to the plaintiff's land.[42] But when there is no physical interference there is no trespass and the proper remedy is case: as, for example, in libel, malicious prosecution or deceit.

---

[38] But Professor Milsom has contended ((1958) 74 L.Q.R. 407) that "had there been a medieval Salmond or Winfield trespass would have been the title, not of a chapter, but of the book."

[39] The action on the case (*super casum*), so called because the particular circumstances of the case are set out in the writ, goes back at least to the thirteenth century. For its relation to the Statute of Westminster II—a controversial matter—see Plucknett, *Concise History*, pp. 372–373.

[40] Maitland, *Forms of Action*, p. 342. The importance of the distinction was that in trespass if the plaintiff recovered less than 40 shillings he was entitled to no more costs than damages, whereas nominal damages in case carried costs with them.

[41] See the authoritative statement by Viscount Simon L.C. in *Crofter Handwoven Harris Tweed Co. Ltd.* v. *Veitch* [1942] A.C. 435, 442.

[42] See below, § 4.1.

"Direct"

To constitute a trespass, however, it is not enough that the injury should be forcible; it must also be direct and not merely consequential. An injury is said to be direct when it follows so immediately upon the act of the defendant that it may be termed part of that act; it is consequential, on the other hand, when, by reason of some obvious and visible intervening cause, it is regarded, not as part of the defendant's act, but merely as a consequence of it. In direct injuries the defendant is charged in an action of trespass with having done the thing complained of; in consequential injuries he is charged in an action of case with having done something else, by reason of which (*per quod*) the damage complained of has come about.[43] "And the distinction is well instanced by the example put[44] of a man throwing a log into the highway: if at the time of its being thrown it hit any person, it is trespass; but if after it be thrown, any person going along the road receive an injury by falling over it was it lies there, it is case. Neither does the degree of violence with which the act is done make any difference: for if the log were put down in the most quiet way upon a man's foot it is trespass; but if thrown into the road with whatever violence, and one afterwards falls over it, it is case and not trespass."[45]

This distinction between direct and consequential injury is not identical with that between intentional and accidental or negligent injury. These are cross-divisions. Trespass lies for all direct injuries, whether wilful or merely negligent. Case is the appropriate remedy for all consequential injuries. This was settled by *Leame* v. *Bray*,[46] in which it was held that the act of the defendant in negligently driving his carriage so as to bring it into collision with that of the plaintiff was actionable in trespass. In trespass the defendant's state of mind is irrelevant: the law looks only to the results of his conduct. Wilfulness is not necessary to constitute trespass. But if it is sought to make a master vicariously liable for the acts of his servant, case and not trespass is the proper form of remedy—unless, indeed, the particular act complained of is done by the command of the principal.[47]

"Damage"

In case, damage is the gist of the action, and the plaintiff will fail if he cannot prove it. But in trespass it is not necessary to prove actual damage. Trespass is actionable *per se*. This may be important when a remedy is sought for the infringement of personal liberty[48] or privacy.[49]

---

[43] *Hutchins* v. *Maugham* [1947] V.L.R. 131, 133.
[44] By Fortescue J. in *Reynolds* v. *Clarke* (1725) 1 Str. 634, 636.
[45] *Leame* v. *Bray* (1803) 3 East 593, 602, *per* Le Blanc J.
[46] (1803) 3 East 593. Even today intentional trespass is not equivalent to negligence; *Long* v. *Hepworth* [1968] 1 W.L.R. 1299, 1302.
[47] *Esso Petroleum Co. Ltd.* v. *Southport Corporation* [1956] A.C. 218, 244.
[48] See below, § 7.4.
[49] As in *Kaye* v. *Robertson* (1991) F.S.R. 62 (below § 3.1).

Conversely, a successful plaintiff in trespass may be deprived of his costs if his action was "oppressive to the last degree."[50]

Is trespass preferable to case?

At the present day trespass has been somewhat eclipsed by the growth of the action on the case for negligence, and it has even been suggested in the Court of Appeal that the time has come to abolish the difference between them.[51] This is partly because most actions for personal injuries are brought against an employer vicariously liable for the torts of his servant[52]; partly because of the growth of the rule that the plaintiff must prove negligence when damage has been caused to his person or chattels as a result of the defendant's conduct on the highway, or where his property adjacent to the highway has been injured in consequence of the defendant's conduct on the highway[53]; and partly because the courts insist that actions against physicians or surgeons should be in negligence and not in trespass.[54] Further, it has even been held that in an action for personal injuries, whether on or off the highway, the onus is always on the plaintiff to prove intention or negligence in the defendant.[55] But the authority of this decision is doubtful, and many think that there is still a difference between trespass and case,[56] and that that difference has important practical consequences—for example, in relation to the burden of proof,[57] or inevitable accident,[58] or the limitation of actions,[59] or the place where the tort was committed when an action is brought upon a foreign tort,[60] or remoteness of damage,[61] or the granting of an injunction to restrain the commission of an act which does not cause actual damage.[62] In Australia it has been asserted that "The two causes of action are not the same now and they never were,"[63] and "Despite many attacks by judges and scholars, the trespass action has survived in Canada."[64] Modern English statutes

---

[50] As in *Fielden* v. *Cox and Brook* (1906) 22 T.L.R. 411.
[51] *Berry* v. *British Transport Commission* [1962] 1 Q.B. 307, 339; *Letang* v. *Cooper* [1965] 1 Q.B. 232, 238.
[52] The Civil Judicial Statistics for 1985 revealed that 73 per cent. of defendants in tort actions are corporations. The same statistics reveal the overwhelming preponderance of negligence actions for personal injuries—there were 33,880 such claims, but only 880 for all other torts.
[53] See below, § 7.4.
[54] *Chatterton* v. *Gerson* [1981] Q.B. 432, 443.
[55] *Fowler* v. *Lanning* [1959] 1 Q.B. 426; see below, § 7.4.
[56] See Buckley L.J. in *S.C.M. Ltd.* v. *Whittall Ltd.* [1971] 1 Q.B. 337, 357, and Croom-Johnson L.J. in *Wilson* v. *Pringle* [1987] Q.B. 237, 247.
[57] See below, § 7.4
[58] See below, § 2.4.
[59] See below, § 25.4.
[60] See below, § 25.8.
[61] See below, § 23.5.
[62] *Patel* v. *W.H. Smith Ltd.* [1987] 1 W.L.R. 853, 858.
[63] *Williams* v. *Milotin* (1957) 97 C.L.R. 465, 474, *per curiam*.
[64] *Bell Canada Ltd.* v. *Cope (Sarnia) Ltd.* (1980) 11 C.C.L.T. 170, at 180, *per* Linden J.

have also recognised the continued existence of trespass as a distinct concept. So the Theft Act 1968, s.9(1) refers to entry "as a trespasser," and the Family Law Reform Act 1969, s.8 permits a minor to give a valid consent to acts which would otherwise "constitute a trespass to his person."[65]

---

[65] See, conversely, the Justices of the Peace Act 1979, s.44 for recognition of "a tort, in the nature of an action on the case."

CHAPTER 2

GENERAL PRINCIPLES OF LIABILITY

§ 2.1. The Nature of a Tort

(1) Tort and crime[1]

There are several connections. Historically tort had its roots in criminal procedure. Even today there is a punitive element in some aspects of the rules on damages. Analytically some distinctions must be made.

A tort is a species of civil injury or wrong. The distinction between civil and criminal wrongs depends on the nature of the appropriate remedy provided by law. A civil wrong is one which gives rise to civil proceedings—proceedings, that is to say, which have as their purpose the enforcement of some right claimed by the plaintiff as against the defendant. Criminal proceedings, on the other hand, are those which have for their object the punishment of the defendant for some act of which he is accused. It is settled that not every breach of a criminal statute gives rise to an action in tort.[2] But it is often the case that the same wrong is both civil and criminal—capable of being made the subject of proceedings of both kinds. Assault, libel, theft and malicious injury to property, for example, are wrongs of this kind. Speaking generally, in all such cases the civil and criminal remedies are not alternative but concurrent, each being independent of the other. The wrongdoer may be punished criminally by imprisonment or otherwise, and also compelled in a civil action to make compensation or restitution to the injured person.[3]

Damages essential mark of tort

Although a tort is a civil injury, not all civil injuries are torts, for no civil injury is to be classed as a tort unless the appropriate remedy for it is an action for damages. Such an action is an essential characteristic of every true tort.[4] Thus a public nuisance is not a tort merely because the civil remedy of injunction may be obtained at the suit of the Attorney-General, but only in those exceptional instances in which a private per-

---

[1] See Winfield, *The Province of the Law of Tort* (Cambridge, 1931), Chap. 8; Williams, "The Definition of Crime" [1955] C.L.P. 107; Linden, "Tort Law as Ombudsman" (1973) 51 Can. Bar Rev. 150.

[2] *Lonrho Ltd.* v. *Shell Petroleum Co. Ltd.* (*No. 2*) [1982] A.C. 173. For this case, see below, § 10.01.

[3] A criminal court may order a convicted person to pay a sum of money to the injured party by way of compensation: see the Powers of Criminal Courts Act 1973, ss.35–38, as amended by the Criminal Justice Act 1988, ss.104–105. These compensatory sums are unliquidated, but (unlike damages in tort) are not claimable in the first instance, but only in addition to some punishment. Yet increasing use is made of them, and a court is under a statutory duty to give reasons for *not* making an order. But the average amount of the order is only £100.

[4] *Gouriet* v. *Union of Post Office Workers* [1978] A.C. 435, 459; *Garden Cottage Ltd.* v. *Milk Board* [1984] A.C. 130, 136.

son may recover damages for loss sustained by him in consequence thereof. Again, the infringement of a statutory right to hold a fair on a common is not a tort, for it is remediable only by a declaratory judgment and an injunction when action is brought by the minority of the inhabitants of a parish.[5] Nor is any wrong a tort if the appropriate remedy is an action, not for unliquidated damages but for a liquidated sum of money—e.g. an action for money paid by mistake, or due under a judgment, or paid to the use of another without contract.[6] Such claims are classed by our law as quasi-contractual, but in truth they belong neither to contract nor tort, but to the distinct category entitled restitution.

The fact that damages are small does not necessarily mean that the case is unimportant, as it might in an action of contract, for the action may have been brought to establish a point of principle,[7] even of a dubious kind[8] or to vindicate wounded feelings or character.[9] An unsolved problem is whether there can be a tort without damages being available to the party injured. It is usual to say that a person is liable in tort irrespective of whether or not a judgment for damages has been given against him.[10] He is liable from the moment he commits the tort.[11] But sometimes a party is under a duty but has some peculiar immunity from suit—e.g. the immunity from suit possessed by a spouse before 1962.[12] It has been said that in such a case the immunity is purely procedural[13]—there is a tort but the defendant cannot be sued for it. But this view has been strongly denied[14] and it may therefore be concluded that the existence of a sanction by way of damages is an essential mark of a tort.

But other remedies are important

Although an action for damages is the essential mark of and the characteristic remedy for a tort, there may be and often are other remedies also. An injunction is often the first remedy which the practitioner thinks of in a case of nuisance or trespass to land, and the only one which is of any real value to the plaintiff.[15] So, despite the large number of statutory controls, the riparian owner's action in nuisance is still the

---

[5] *Wyld* v. *Silver* [1963] Ch. 243.
[6] *Att.-Gen.* v. *Canter* [1939] 1 K.B. 318.
[7] A tort action may channel unfavourable publicity towards a powerful defendant—e.g. the actions by the thalidomide children against the manufacturers of the drug.
[8] *Hunter* v. *Chief Constable of the West Midlands* [1982] A.C. 529, in which a convict brought an action for assault with the object of securing early release from a life sentence.
[9] *Steljes* v. *Ingram* (1903) 19 T.L.R. 534.
[10] *Roberts* v. *Roberts* [1962] P. 212, 217–218.
[11] *Wah Tat Bank* v. *Kum* [1975] A.C. 507, 518.
[12] See below, § 20.8.
[13] *Broom* v. *Morgan* [1953] 1 Q.B. 597.
[14] *Tooth & Co. Ltd.* v. *Tillyer* (1956) 95 C.L.R. 605, 615 ("metaphysical unreality"); *Auten* v. *Rayner, The Times*, March 15, 1960. In the difficult area of trade disputes, the H.L. has held that "not actionable in tort" means "not unlawful in tort": *Hadmor Productions Ltd.* v. *Hamilton* [1983] 1 A.C. 191, 229.
[15] *Warder* v. *Cooper* [1970] 1 Ch. 495, 501.

most effective means of stopping pollution.[16] Again, in the emergent wrong of breach of confidence,[17] an injunction is the main remedy to prevent the disclosure of confidential information.[18] Although an injunction is a discretionary remedy, the plaintiff need only show that there is a serious issue to be tried,[19] not that he has a prima facie case, as was once thought.

(2) Tort and contract[20]

The distinction between tort and contract is that the duties in the former are primarily fixed by the law, while in the latter they are fixed by the parties themselves. Further, in tort the duty is towards persons generally; in contract it is towards a specific person or persons. Until the abolition of the forms of action confusion was often caused by the fact that it was possible to sue in tort for causes of action which were really contractual. It may still be of practical importance to determine whether an action is in substance contractual or for a tort—*e.g.* when damages are sought for mental distress,[21] or when the defendant is a minor,[22] or in relation to the running of time under the Limitation Act 1980[23]—in contract time runs from the breach of warranty, in tort from the occurrence of the damage.[24] There is also a difference in relation to remoteness of damage.[25] If the plaintiff's claim can be said to be equally poised as between tort and contract he can at least rely upon that aspect which puts him in the more favourable position.[26]

Privity of contract and tortious liability[27]

At one time it seems to have been thought that if A undertook a contractual obligation towards B, and his non-performance or mis-performance of that obligation resulted in damage to C, then C could not sue A unless he could show that A had undertaken towards him the same obligation as he had assumed towards B. Thus in *Winterbottom* v. *Wright*[28] Lord Abinger C.B., speaking of a contract of repair, said "Unless we confine the operation of such contracts as this to the parties

---

[16] See Newsom Q.C. in (1971) 2 Otago L.R. 383 ("I have never known a case of industrial pollution where the evil was not cured in consequence of the injunction").

[17] See below, § 3.1.

[18] *Woodward* v. *Hutchins* [1977], 1 W.L.R. 760.

[19] *American Cyanamid Co.* v. *Ethicon Ltd.* [1975] A.C. 396.

[20] Markesinis, "An Expanding Tort Law—The Price of a Rigid Contract Law" (1987) 103 L.Q.R. 354.

[21] See below, § 9.6.

[22] Below, § 20.5.

[23] See *Bell* v. *Peter Browne & Co.* [1990] 3 W.L.R. 510, 524 ("an anomaly which our law could well do without": *per* Mustill L.J.).

[24] This is a legitimate difference, for as contract is concerned to protect the expectations of the parties, it is right that the limitation period should run from the date when the contract is made.

[25] See below, § 23.3.

[26] *Chesworth* v. *Farrar* [1967] 1 Q.B. 407, 416; *Coupland* v. *Arabian Gulf Oil Co.* [1983] 1 W.L.R. 1136, 1153.

[27] See Palmer, "Why Privity Entered Tort" (1983) 27 Am.Jo. of Legal History 85.

[28] (1842) 10 M. & W. 109, 114.

who entered into them, the most absurd and outrageous consequences, to which I can see no limit, would ensue." Enlightenment came only when it was realised that the duty (if any) which A owed to C in such circumstances was not only referable to a legal origin distinct from that of the contractual obligation assumed towards B but also might well be framed in different terms. The "privity of contract fallacy" (as it has been conveniently called) was at last exploded by the House of Lords in *Donoghue* v. *Stevenson*,[29] in which it was held that a manufacturer of products was under a duty to the ultimate user or consumer even though there was no contractual relationship between them. This duty had its origin in the law of tort and not in the law of contract; nor did it amount to a warranty that care had been taken to see that the article was sound—an obligation appropriate only to the contractual relationship of vendor and purchaser: the duty was no more than to take reasonable care to protect the consumer.

It has been more difficult to understand that a professional man such as an architect or banker might owe a duty to care of someone other than the other party to the contract. But even here liability has been imposed, whether the damage caused to the plaintiff has been physical,[30] or financial.[31] The duty is imposed not because he has made a contract, but because he has undertaken the work.[32] So the present position is that the "privity of contract fallacy" has disappeared.[33] The matter is open: the absence of a contract between the parties is but one of the factors to be considered in determining whether liability in tort exists. It is of course also necessary to avoid the converse fallacy of assuming that C will automatically have a good cause of action against A merely because A's failure to perform his contract with B has resulted in damage to C.

In the immediate aftermath of the decision of the House of Lords in *Junior Books Ltd.* v. *Veitchi Co. Ltd.*,[34] in which a sub-contractor was held directly liable in tort to a building owner with whom he had no direct contractual relationship but for whom he had provided a floor which was defective but not dangerous, some thought the courts were about to hold that every breach of contract was a tort. But it was quickly held that, "If the principle does not have certain limits, it will come perilously close to abrogating completely the concept of privity of contract."[35] Then the Privy Council halted this movement by holding[36] that

---

[29] [1932] A.C. 562.

[30] *Clay* v. *A.J. Crump & Son Ltd.* [1964] 1 Q.B. 533.

[31] *Hedley Byrne & Co. Ltd.* v. *Heller and Partners Ltd.* [1964] A.C. 465. See below, § 9.6.

[32] *Voli* v. *Inglewood Shire Council* (1963) 110 C.L.R. 74, 85.

[33] *Candler* v. *Crane, Christmas & Co.* [1951] 2 K.B. 164, 177; *Greene* v. *Chelsea B.C.* [1954] 2 Q.B. 127, 138.

[34] [1983] 1 A.C. 520. This case is fully considered below, § 9.5.

[35] *Balsamo* v. *Medici* [1984] 1 W.L.R. 951, 959, *per* Walton J. Would not the solution be for the main contractor to assign to the building owner any rights of action against sub-contractors?

[36] *Tai Hing Cotton Mill* v. *Liu Chong Hing Bank Ltd.* [1986] 1 A.C. 801, 807. (Two of the Law Lords in *Tai Hing* (Lords Roskill and Brandon) had sat in *Junior Books*). The C.A. decided against the plaintiff for similar reasons in *Greater Nottingham Co-Op* v. *Cementation Ltd.* [1989] Q.B. 71, and the H.L. refused leave to appeal. A similar case is *Simaan Contracting Co. Ltd.* v. *Pilkington Ltd.* (*No. 2*) [1989] Q.B. 758.

there is no advantage in searching for a liability in tort when the parties are in a contractual relationship. It was also held that the mutual obligations in tort cannot be any greater than those to be found expressly or by necessary implication in the contract.[37] There is good sense in this. Parties to a contract should not be denied their reasonable expectations that their relationships will be governed by the legal structure which they have themselves created, and not by some parasitic tortious duty.[38] In such a case if the plaintiff fails in contract he must necessarily fail in tort.[39] So the time-honoured common-law concepts of tort and contract have not been displaced by an amorphous continental-style concept entitled obligation.

Concurrent liability

The former rule that an action by a client against a solicitor for damages for breach of his professional duty of care is necessarily and exclusively one in contract is incompatible with modern developments in the law of torts, and has therefore been over-ruled in Ireland,[40] and in England.[41] It is the general proximity relationship, and not any particular manifestation in a contract, which founds the duty between the parties. Presumably other professional men who once claimed to be in the same position as solicitors—*e.g.* architects[42]— are now subject to the same duty to take reasonable care.

Some questions remain to be answered. One is whether a solicitor owes a similar duty to any person for whom he acts professionally without reward. According to *Hedley Byrne*[43] such a duty is owed unless there is a disclaimer. This may put those who act for neighbourhood law centres and similar bodies in a difficult position, and the wisdom of thus suppressing charitable instincts and undermining professional responsibility may be doubted.[44]

Secondly, does this duty extend to anyone who may have been damaged by the solicitor's want of skill, such as beneficiaries under a will or an intestacy? Again the *Hedley Byrne* principle points to liability, at least if the third party has changed his position in reliance on the defendant's professional skill—*e.g.* a home-purchaser who has relied on an achitect's certificate.[45] But more recently the requirement of reliance has been discarded, and a solicitor may be liable to one who has merely failed to obtain a benefit—*e.g.* a disappointed legatee.[46] The solicitor in such cases knows that one specified person will suffer loss of a calcu-

---

[37] A point confirmed by *Reid* v. *Rush & Tompkins plc* [1990] 1 W.L.R. 212.
[38] *Pacific Associates Inc.* v. *Baxter* [1990] Q.B. 993.
[39] *National Bank of Greece S/A* v. *Pinios Shipping Co.* [1990] 1 A.C. 637.
[40] *Finlay* v. *Murtagh* [1979] I.R. 249.
[41] *Midland Bank* v. *Hett, Stubbs & Kemp* [1979] Ch. 384.
[42] *Bagot* v. *Stevens Scanlon & Co. Ltd.* [1966] 1 Q.B. 197.
[43] See below, § 9.7.
[44] Jolowicz, Note, [1979] C.L.J. 54, 56.
[45] As in *Clay* v. *A.J. Crump & Son Ltd.* [1964] 1 Q.B. 533.
[46] *Ross* v. *Caunters* [1980] Ch. 297.

lable amount[47] if reasonable care is not taken in the drafting or execution of the document. A duty may even be owed to the spouse of a client.[48]

(3) Tort and equity[49]

No civil injury is to be classed as a tort if it is only a breach of trust or some other merely equitable obligation. The reason for this exclusion is historical only. The law of torts is in its origin a part of the common law, as distinguished from equity, and it was unknown to the Court of Chancery.[50] There is no need to regard the procurement of breach of trust as a tort,[51] for the good reason that for centuries equity has protected the beneficiary by treating the procurer as a wrong-doing trustee.

(4) Tort and bailment

An action in bailment is distinct from one in either tort or contract. It has the advantage that it shifts the burden of proof to the defendant to explain how the loss occurred.[52]

(5) Tort and delict

In Scotland and on the Continent the name given to what we call tort is delict, with the adjectives delictual or delictal.[53]

Tort defined[54]

Summing the matter up, we have seen that there are four classes of wrongs which stand outside the sphere of tort:
- (1) Wrongs exclusively criminal;
- (2) Civil wrongs which create no right of action for unliquidated damages, but give rise to some other form of civil remedy exclusively;
- (3) Civil wrongs which are exclusively breaches of contract;
- (4) Civil wrongs which are exclusively breaches of trust or of some other merely equitable obligation.

We may accordingly define a tort as *a civil wrong for which the remedy*

---

[47] There is thus no fear of liability in an indeterminate amount to an indeterminate class: see below, § 9.5.

[48] *Al-Kandari* v. *J.R. Brown & Co.* [1987] Q.B. 514 (but the facts were very unusual).

[49] See the question discussed at length, Winfield, *Province*, Chap. 6.

[50] The two preceding sentences were approved by the C.A. in *Metall & Rohstoff* v. *Donaldson Inc.* [1990] 1 Q.B. 391, 474.

[51] "Nothing is gained by creating an unnecessary tort": *Metall & Rohstoff A.G.* v. *Donaldson Inc.* [1990] Q.B. 391, 409, *per* Gatehouse J.

[52] *American Express Co.* v. *British Airways Board* [1983] 1 W.L.R. 701, 705.

[53] "The form 'delictal' is not given in the O.E.D. but it is a pleasantly clean word which seems to have been invented by Salmond": Williams and Hepple, *Foundations of the Law of Tort* (2nd ed.), p. 11, n. 1. (The 2nd (1989) ed. of the O.E.D. recognises the word.)

[54] The terms *tort* and *wrong* were originally synonymous. *Tort* is derived from the Latin *tortum*, while *wrong* is in its origin identical with *wrung*, both the English and the Latin terms meaning primarily, therefore, conduct which is crooked or twisted, as opposed to that which is straight or right (*rectum*). The first reported use of the word tort is in *Boulston* v. *Hardy* (1597) Cro.Eliz. 547, 548. *Tort*, however, has become specialised in its application, while *wrong* has remained generic.

is a common law action for unliquidated damages, and which is not exclusively the breach of a contract or the breach of a trust or other merely equitable obligation.[55]

§ 2.2. GENERAL CONDITIONS OF LIABILITY

In general, a tort consists in some act done by the defendant whereby he has without just cause or excuse caused some form of harm to the plaintiff.[56] The law of torts exists for the purpose of preventing men from hurting one another, whether in respect of their property, their persons, their reputations, or anything else which is theirs.[57] The fundamental principle of this branch of the law is *alterum non laedere*—to hurt nobody by word or deed. An action of tort, therefore, is usually a claim for pecuniary compensation in respect of damage suffered as the result of the invasion of a legally protected interest. An interest is a claim or demand or want or desire put forward by man in a civilised society. The task of the courts is first, to decide which interests should receive legal protection, and secondly, to hold the balance between interests which have received protection. It is obvious that not all objects of human desire can or should receive legal protection. The law began by affording protection against invasion of interests in bodily security, integrity of land or chattels, and freedom of reputation. In the course of time it has recognised other and less obvious (but perhaps equally valuable) interests. Thus interests in the security of domestic or contractual relationships have been protected, and in recent years considerable advances have been made in the direction of protecting interests in emotional security,[58] and in protecting financial or pecuniary interests against careless invasions.[59]

Damnum sine injuria[60]

There are many forms of harm of which the law takes no account. Damage so done and suffered is called *damnum sine injuria*, and the reasons for its permission by the law are various and not capable of exhaustive statement. For example, the harm done may be caused by some person who is merely exercising his own rights; as in the case of the loss inflicted on individual traders by competition in trade,[61] or when the damage is done by a man acting under necessity to prevent a greater evil,[62] or in the exercise of statutory authority.[63] Or the courts

---

[55] This definition was approved in *Anglo-Saxon Petroleum Co. Ltd.* v. *Damant* [1947] K.B. 794, 796, and in *Philip Morris Ltd.* v. *Airley* [1975] V.R. 345, 347.

[56] "Harm is the tort signature": Seavey, "Principles of Torts" (1942) 56 Harv.L.Rev. 72, 73. We shall see later (§ 3.1) that it is easier to explain the objects of the law of torts than to define a tort.

[57] *Lee Cooper Ltd.* v. *Jeakins (C.H.) & Sons Ltd.* [1967] 2 Q.B. 1, 8.

[58] See below, § 9.8.

[59] See below, § 9.7.

[60] The term *injuria* is here used in its original and proper sense of *wrong* (*in jus*, contrary to law). See *Crofter Hand Woven Harris Tweed Co.* v. *Veitch* [1942] A.C. 435, 442.

[61] See below, Chap. 16.

[62] See below, § 22.1.

[63] See below, § 22.7.

may hold, on balancing the respective interests of the parties, that sound policy requires that the interests of the defendant should prevail over those of the plaintiff. So the natural right to support of a landowner is subordinate to the natural right of his neighbour to exploit his property by the extraction of underground water not percolating through defined channels, whether the defendant has acted intentionally[64] or carelessly.[65] Other examples may be found in the law relating to damage caused by defamatory statements made on a privileged occasion.[66] Or the harm complained of may be too trivial, too indefinite, or too difficult of proof for the legal suppression of it to be expedient or effective. Thus no action will lie for mere mental suffering unaccompanied by physical harm, though caused by the wilful act or carelessness of the defendant.[67]

So also the harm done may be of such a nature that the law considers it inexpedient to confer any right to pecuniary compensation upon the individual injured, but provides some other remedy, such as a criminal prosecution. Such is the case, for example, with the harm which an individual suffers in common with the public at large by reason of the existence of a public nuisance.[68] So a landlord who cuts off his tenant's supply of gas and electricity without entering the premises is liable only for a breach of contract: there is no separate tort entitled "eviction,"[69] though there may be criminal as distinct from civil[70] liability under the Protection from Eviction Act 1977, s.1. So too a landlord who serves a valid notice to quit cannot be held liable in tort because his motive was the vindictive one of punishing the tenant for having given evidence against him in other proceedings. There is no right of action for damages for contempt of court.[71] So also there are no torts entitled "breach of trust,"[72] or "harassment,"[73] or "unlawful trading."[74] For sometimes the imposition of tortious liability may have undesirable downstream effects—*e.g.* leading doctors to take unnecessary X-rays ("defensive medicine").[75]

Injuria sine damno

Just as there are cases in which damage is not actionable as a tort (*damnum sine injuria*), so conversely there are cases in which behaviour

---

[64] *Bradford Corporation* v. *Pickles* [1895] A.C. 587.

[65] *Stephens* v. *Anglian Water Authority* [1987] 1 W.L.R. 1381. (The H.L. refused leave to appeal.)

[66] Below, § 8.11.

[67] See below, § 9.8.

[68] See below, § 5.9.

[69] *Perera* v. *Vandiyar* [1953] 1 W.L.R. 672. But see Housing Act 1988, s.27.

[70] *McCall* v. *Abelesz* [1976] Q.B. 585.

[71] *Chapman* v. *Honig* [1963] 2 Q.B. 502.

[72] See *Metall* [1990] Q.B. 391, 409.

[73] *Patel* v. *Patel* [1988] 2 F.L.R. 179.

[74] *Associated Newspapers plc* v. *Insert Media Ltd.* [1990] 1 W.L.R. 908, 909.

[75] For the "overkill" problem, see dicta in *Caparo Industries plc* v. *Dickman* [1989] Q.B. 653, 688–689, and *Murphy* v. *Brentwood D.C.* [1991] 1 A.C. 378, 472.

is actionable as a tort, although it has been the cause of no damage at all (*injuria sine damno*). Torts are of two kinds—namely, those which are actionable *per se*, and those which are actionable only on proof of actual damage resulting from them. Thus the act of trespassing upon another's land is actionable even though it has done the plaintiff not the slightest harm.[76] This is in essence the distinction between Trespass and Case which has already been considered.[77]

The importance which the law places upon the security of the plaintiff's interests in such a case can be seen from the fact that the onus lies on the defendant to justify his conduct—*e.g.* in an action of libel the defendant must show that the statement is true or privileged or protected by whatever other defences may be available. On the other hand, in torts such as negligence or malicious prosecution the onus lies on the plaintiff to show that the conduct of the defendant is legally unjustified.

Is there any general principle of liability?[78]

The basic question is: Does the law of torts consist of a fundamental general principle that it is wrongful to cause harm to other persons in the absence of some specific ground of justification or excuse, or does it consist of a number of specific rules prohibiting certain kinds of harmful activity, and leaving all the residue outside the sphere of legal responsibility? The first alternative is supported by a number of dicta[79] going back for at least a century,[80] which assert that an unlawful, intentional and positive act which inevitably causes damage to the plaintiff is prima facie actionable, at least if the damage is to the plaintiff's person or tangible property as distinct from economic interests.[81]

Salmond's view

Salmond argued that the second of these alternatives, which is supported by decisions and dicta going back for six centuries,[82] was that

---

[76] *Nicholls* v. *Ely Beet Sugar Co.* [1936] Ch. 343, 350–351.

[77] See above, § 1.2.

[78] Williams, "The Foundation of Tortious Liability" (1939) 7 Camb.L.J. 111; Dworkin, "Intentionally Causing Economic Loss" 1974 1 Mon.L.R. 4.

[79] Also an emphatic Scottish dictum. "There is no such thing as an exhaustive list of named delicts in the law of Scotland. If the conduct complained of appears to be wrongful, the law of Scotland will afford a remedy . . . ": *The Mihalis* [1984] 2 Lloyd's Rep. 525, 543, *per* Lord Ross.

[80] See, *e.g. Mogul Steamship Co.* v. *McGregor, Gow & Co.* (1889) 23 Q.B.D. 598, 613; *J. Bollinger* v. *Costa Brava Wine Co. Ltd.* [1960] Ch. 262, 283; *Rookes* v. *Barnard* [1964] A.C. 1129, 1216. See further, below, § 3.2.

[81] *Home Office* v. *Dorset Yacht Co. Ltd.* [1970] A.C. 1004, 1027. So the 18th Report of the Law Reform Committee (Cmnd. 4774 (1971)), para. 25 recommended that an intentional act done without lawful justification involving interference with a chattel should be actionable as a new tort which will supersede conversion, detinue and trespass, but Parliament did not go as far as this when it enacted the Torts (Interference with Goods) Act 1977 (see below, Chap. 6).

[82] *Associated Newspapers Group plc* v. *Insert Media Ltd.* [1988] 1 W.L.R. 509, 511. And see below, § 2.10.

which had been accepted by our law. "Just as the criminal law consists of a body of rules establishing specific offences, so," Salmond said, "the law of torts consists of a body of rules establishing specific injuries. Neither in the one case nor in the other is there any general principle of liability. Whether I am prosecuted for an alleged offence, or sued for an alleged tort, it is for my adversary to prove that the case falls within some specific and established rule of liability, and not for me to defend myself by proving that it is within some specific and established rule of justification or excuse." For Salmond there was no English law of tort; there was merely an English law of torts, that is, a list of acts and omissions which, in certain conditions, were actionable. This book is entitled the *Law of Torts*, not the *Law of Tort*. We still approach the law of torts as if it were a law of crimes.[83]

Invention of new torts

Although "most legal writers have come back to Sir John Salmond's conclusion"[84] that there is no law of tort, it must be admitted that there is not a single case[85] in the reports in which an action has been refused on the sole ground that it was new. It has been clearly established ever since the memorable judgment of Sir John Holt C.J. in *Ashby* v. *White*[86] that mere novelty is no bar to an action. "I wish never to hear this objection again," said Sir Charles Pratt C.J. 60 years later.[87] Similar statements may be found in more modern cases.[88] The novelty of a claim may indeed raise a presumption against its validity. So a court may remark: "It is enough to say that the world has gone on very well without such actions as these; and I doubt whether it would continue to do so if such things were allowed,"[89] or "I would not exclude the possibility of such an action; but none as yet has ever appeared in the books. And this will not be the first."[90] But there is undoubtedly power to rec-

---

[83] "This can be demonstrated quite simply by asking a class: 'Is blackmail a tort?' and watching their faces as the better students tick alphabetically through the index in their skulls: assault, battery, conversion, defamation. . . . It takes them ages to get to the delict quaintly called *Wilkinson* v. *Downton* [see below, § 9.8], and even there they are (rightly) unhappy about the fit": Rudden, Book Review (1984) 33 I.C.L.Q. 247, 248.

[84] *International Encyclopaedia of Comparative Law* (1983) Vol. xi, § 18.

[85] Possible exceptions are *Barnardiston* v. *Soame* (1676) 6 St.Tr. 1063; *Hunt* v. *Damon* (1930) 46 T.L.R. 579.

[86] (1702) 2 Ld.Raym. 938; 14 St.Tr. 695. The question was whether an action lay against a returning officer for refusing to accept the vote of an elector. The Chief Justice, against the opinion of his three puisnes, held that it did, and his dissenting judgment was upheld in the H.L.

[87] *Chapman* v. *Pickersgill* (1762) 2 Wils. 145, 146.

[88] *Best* v. *Samuel Fox Ltd.* [1950] 2 All E.R. 798, 800; *Abbott* v. *Sullivan* [1952] 1 K.B. 189, 216; *Malone* v. *Police Commissioner* (No. 2) [1979] Ch. 344, 372; *Banque Keyser Ullman S/A* v. *Skandia Insurance Co. Ltd.* [1990] 1 Q.B. 665, 802.

[89] *Revis* v. *Smith* (1856) 18 C.B. 126, 141, *per* Cresswell J., cited with approval in *Marrinan* v. *Vibart* [1963] 1 Q.B. 234, 239. The "thing" was an action for damages in respect of perjured evidence.

[90] *Wheeler* v. *Somerfield* [1966] 2 Q.B. 94, 104, *per* Lord Denning M.R.

ognise a novel claim if justice so requires,[91] although the process may take time.[92]

We can trace back to particular decisions the origin of many torts which are recognised as such at the present day, of malicious prosecution,[93] of deceit in *Pasley* v. *Freeman*,[94] of inducement of breach of contract in *Lumley* v. *Gye*,[95] and of negligence in *Donoghue* v. *Stevenson*.[96] Again, it was only in 1964 that the existence of the tort of intimidation was definitely established,[97] the House of Lords affirming that it had power to adapt the common law to changing social circumstances.[98] Again, although in 1888 a claim for damages for a careless statement causing economic loss was dismissed as "an attempt to manufacture a new action which the court would not sanction,"[99] yet in 1963 the House of Lords recognised such a tort.[1] In 1979 the House of Lords recognised a great expansion in the tort of passing-off.[2]

But there are limits, difficult to state, but understood by most practitioners, "to what we can or should do. If we are to extend the law it must be by the development and application of fundamental principles. We cannot introduce arbitrary conditions or limitations: that must be

---

[91] So in *Brightside and Carbrook (Sheffield) Cooperative Society Ltd.* v. *Phillips* (1963) *The Times*, November 26, Sellers L.J. said: "I should be astounded if there was no cause of action in circumstances like these. It's high time there was one" (not reported in [1964] 1 W.L.R. 185).

[92] "The creation of a new tort is now very rare and takes a long time. It is rather like the process of canonisation. The cause is first of all fostered by academic well-wishers and then promoted in the lower courts. Eventually, if things prosper, the tort will be beatified by the Court of Appeal and then, probably after a long interval, it will achieve full sainthood in the House of Lords" (Lord Devlin in *The Listener*, December 12, 1968).

[93] Winfield, *History of Conspiracy*, Chap. 5.

[94] (1789) 3 T.R. 51.

[95] (1853) 2 E. & B. 216. In the light of these cases, it is difficult to support the statement that by 1806 "practically the only tort that was known was the tort of trespass": *Gardiner* v. *Moore (No. 2)* [1969] 1 Q.B. 55, 73 *per* Thesiger J.

[96] [1932] A.C. 562. "If you read the great cases of *Ashby* v. *White*, *Pasley* v. *Freeman* and *Donoghue* v. *Stevenson* you will find that in each of them the judges were divided in opinion. On the one side there were the timorous souls who were fearful of allowing a new cause of action. On the other side there were the bold spirits who were ready to allow it if justice so required. It was fortunate for the common law that the progressive view prevailed": *Candler* v. *Crane, Christmas & Co.* [1951] 2 K.B. 164, 178 *per* Denning L.J. As Bingham L.J. said in *The Goring* [1987] Q.B. 687, 717: "The law, happily, develops. If novelty itself were a sufficient objection, the claim of Mrs. Donoghue (or Miss M'Alister) might have been summarily struck out, to the great impoverishment of the law." But it is worth recalling what Sir Francis North C.J. said in *Barnardiston* v. *Soame* (1676) 6 St.Tr. 1063, 1115: "My brother Atkyns said, the common law complied with the genius of the nation; I do not understand the argument. Does the common law change? Are we to judge of the changes of the genius of the nation? Whither may general notions carry us at this rate?"

[97] *Rookes* v. *Barnard* [1964] A.C. 1129.

[98] *Rookes* v. *Barnard* [1964] A.C. 1129, 1169.

[99] *Priestley* v. *Stone* (1888) 4 T.L.R. 730, *per* Lord Esher M.R.

[1] *Hedley Byrne & Co. Ltd.* v. *Heller and Partners Ltd.* [1964] A.C. 465.

[2] *Erven Warnink BV* v. *Townend & Sons Ltd.* [1979] A.C. 731. Note that Lord Diplock (at p. 744) expressly rejected the argument that to do so "would open the floodgates, or, more ominously, a Pandora's box of litigation." For "the floodgates argument" in the context of Negligence, see below, Chap. 9.

left to legislation."[3] No English court would, or perhaps could, utter such a statement as "The law is what the law should be."[4] The English view is that a tort must have been committed "within the legal landscape."[5] So when the issue was whether emotional distress caused by watching the death of a near relation on television was actionable, the trial judge said: "No case in any common law jurisdiction has yet had to grapple with the question. . . . It is therefore necessary to approach the new question from old principles."[6] The judge's conclusion against liability was upheld by the House of Lords.[6a]

Conclusion

To some extent the critics seem to have misunderstood Salmond. He never committed himself to the proposition, certainly untenable now, and probably always so, that the law of torts is a closed and inexpansible system. "To say that the law can be collected into pigeon-holes does not mean that those pigeon-holes may not be capacious, nor does it mean that they are incapable of being added to."[7] Salmond merely contended that these changes were not exclusively referable to any single principle. In this he was probably right. The factors relevant to a decision to impose, or not to impose, liability are many and varied.[8]

§ 2.3. INTENTION AND MALICE[9]

The term malice, as used in law, is ambiguous, and possesses two distinct meanings which require to be carefully distinguished. It signifies either (1) the intentional doing of a wrongful act, without just cause or excuse; or (2) action determined by an improper motive. To act maliciously means sometimes to do the act intentionally, while at other times it means to do the act from some wrong and improper motive, some motive of which the law disapproves. This motive need not be that of spite or ill-will—that is to say, it need not amount to malice in the narrow and popular sense of the term. Any motive is malicious in the second sense which is not recognised by law as a sufficient and proper one for the act in question.

(1) Wilful and conscious wrongdoing

It is to malice in the first sense that the well-known definition in *Bromage* v. *Prosser*[10] is exclusively applicable: "Malice in common

---

[3] *Myers* v. *D.P.P.* [1965] A.C. 1001, 1021, *per* Lord Reid.
[4] *Williams* v. *State*, 260 N.Y.S. 2d 953, 955 (1965), *per curiam*.
[5] *Dunlop* v. *Woollahra Council* [1982] A.C. 158, 163. See *R.C.A.* v. *Pollard* [1983] Ch. 135, 148 ("It is for Parliament, not the judges, to provide new remedies for new wrongs").
[6] *Jones* v. *Chief Constable of Yorkshire* [1991] 1 All E.R. 353, 378.
[6a] [1991] 3 W.L.R. 1057.
[7] Williams (1939–41) 7 Camb.L.J. 111, 114.
[8] See below, § 3.2.
[9] Gutteridge, "Abuse of Rights" (1935) 5 Camb.L.J. 22; Fridman, "Malice in the Law of Torts" (1958) 21 M.L.R. 484; Devine, "Some Comparative Aspects of the Doctrine of Abuse of Rights" (1964) *Acta Juridica* 48.
[10] (1825) 4 B. & C. 247, 255, *per* Bayley J., who was "a judge of outstanding quality" (Lord Edmund-Davies in *Hoskyn* v. *Metropolitan Police Commissioner* [1979] A.C. 474, 502).

acceptation means ill-will against a person, but in its legal sense it means a wrongful act, done intentionally, without just cause or excuse." But the use of the term malice in this technical sense merely befogs the issue. It is true that sometimes the conservatism of pleaders has retained in statements of claim the allegation that the defendant "maliciously" or "falsely and maliciously" did the acts complained of[11]; but it was recognised as long ago as 1674 that these allegations were mere verbiage, which could not affect the legal characteristics of the act.[12]

(2) Improper motive

Clearly to be distinguished from the first sense of the term malice is the second sense, in which it signifies the existence of an improper motive. Thus, malicious prosecution does not mean the intentional and wrongful prosecution of an innocent man; it means that prosecution inspired by an improper motive, for example, the extortion of money.[13] A prosecution so inspired may be actionable even though there was an honest belief in the guilt of the accused. Nuisance, conspiracy, and injurious falsehood are other torts in which malice is on occasion relevant.[14] Similarly, defamation which is inspired by malice, *i.e.* an improper motive, loses the protection which the law normally affords to defamatory statements made on occasions of qualified privilege. An improper motive may also be relevant in the assessment of damages. The arrogant, wicked, or spiteful conduct of the defendant may inflame the damages awarded against him for an otherwise ordinary libel, assault, or trespass.[15]

Save in such exceptional cases malice in the sense of improper motive is entirely irrelevant in the law of torts. The law in general asks merely what the defendant has done, not why he did it. A good motive is no justification for an act otherwise illegal, and a bad motive does not make wrongful an act otherwise legal. The rule is based partly on the danger of allowing such a tribunal as a jury to determine the liability of a defendant by reference to their own opinions and prejudices as to the propriety of his motives, and partly on the difficulty of ascertaining what those motives really were.[16] So it has been held that a landlord who maliciously serves a valid notice to quit on a tenant commits no

---

[11] As in actions for defamation.

[12] "If we should make the words *falso et malitiose* support an action without a fit subject matter, all the actions of mankind would be liable to suit and vexation: they that have the cooking (as we call it) of declarations in actions of the case will be sure to put in the words, let the case be what it will; they are here pepper and vinegar in a cook's hand, that help to make sauce for any meat, but will not make a dish of themselves": *Barnardiston* v. *Soame* (1676) 6 St.Tr. 1063, 1114, *per* Sir Francis North C.J. See Sharwood, "Barnardiston v. Soame; A Restoration Drama" (1964) 4 *Melbourne University Law Review* 502.

[13] *Mitchell* v. *Jenkins* (1833) 5 B. & Ad. 588, 595.

[14] See *Chapman* v. *Honig* [1963] 2 Q.B. 502, 520.

[15] Below, § 23.1.

[16] *Allen* v. *Flood* [1898] A.C. 1, 118–119, 153.

civil wrong,[17] also that the inhabitants of a parish are entitled to exercise a long-defunct right to hold a fair solely to prevent another erecting buildings for which planning permission had been given.[18]

The leading case is *Bradford Corporation* v. *Pickles*,[19] in which the defendant was held not liable for intentionally intercepting, by means of excavations on his own land, the underground water that would otherwise have flowed into the adjoining reservoir of the plaintiffs, although his sole motive in so doing was to coerce the plaintiffs to buy this land at his own price. It was already settled law that the abstraction (as distinct from the pollution) of underground water not flowing in defined channels is not an actionable wrong, even though done intentionally,[20] but in this case an attempt was made to establish an exception to this rule when the damage was caused not merely intentionally but also maliciously. This contention, however, was rejected by the House of Lords. Yet the limits of the decision in *Bradford* v. *Pickles* should be noted.[21] The respondent's conduct was not malicious in the sense of being actuated by spite or ill-will towards the appellants. His position was simple. He had something to sell and he did not see why the appellants should not pay the price he asked: it was an attitude with which they, as representatives of one of the great commercial communities of Yorkshire, must have been perfectly familiar.[22] In short, his motive was not an improper one in the eyes of the common law, which has never recognised as an illegal motive the instinct of self-advancement and self-protection, which is the very incentive to all trade. When a judge was told that there was, or should be, a tort of unfair competition, he replied that "I would only cite my nanny's great nursery proposition: 'The world is a very unfair place and the sooner you get to know it the better.' "[23] The selfish and anti-social use of resources is a matter which may well be better regulated by some breach of public law than by the law of tort. Thus an indictment for public nuisance or conspiracy may lie against those who use their property or economic power to the detriment of the community; or powers to inspect, regulate or license may be given to some administrative authority, as under the Town and Country Planning Acts and the Restrictive Practices Act. The doctrine of "Abuse of Rights" recognised by some Continental systems seems too vague to serve as a useful legal principle in the common law.

---

[17] *Chapman* v. *Honig* [1963] 2 Q.B. 502.

[18] *Wyld* v. *Silver* [1963] Ch. 243.

[19] [1895] A.C. 587.

[20] *Chasemore* v. *Richards* (1859) 7 H.L.C. 349, "which shows that if a man has the misfortune to lose his spring by his neighbour digging a well, he must dig his own well deeper": *Ibbetson* v. *Peat* (1865) 3 H. & C. 644, 650, *per* Bramwell B. Strangely enough, in *Bradford* v. *Pickles* the rights arising from the pollution of the water, though clearly established, were not discussed.

[21] [1895] A.C. 587, 600, *per* Lord Macnaghten.

[22] Yorkshire "is a county not only of broad acres but of great manufacturing cities": *Yorkshire Copper Works Ltd.* v. *Registrar of Trade Marks* [1954] 1 W.L.R. 554, 557, *per* Lord Simonds.

[23] *Swedac Ltd.* v. *Magnet Southerns* [1989] F.S.R. 243, 249, *per* Harman J.

§ 2.4. FAULT

Arguments in Favour of Fault

Salmond said that a second condition usually demanded by the law for liability in an action of tort was the existence of either wrongful intention or culpable negligence on the part of the defendant. Salmond wrote as follows: "Pecuniary compensation is not in itself the ultimate object or a sufficient justification of legal liability. It is simply the instrument by which the law fulfils its purpose of penal coercion. When one man does harm to another without any intent to do so and without any negligence, there is in general no reason why he should be compelled to make compensation. The damage done is not thereby in any degree diminished. It has been done, and cannot be undone. By compelling compensation the loss is merely shifted from the shoulders of one man to those of another, but it remains equally heavy. Reason demands that a loss shall lie where it falls, unless some good purpose is to be served by changing its incidence; and in general the only purpose so served is that of punishment for wrongful intent or negligence. There is no more reason why I should insure other persons against the harmful results of my own activities, in the absence of any *mens rea* on my part, than why I should insure them against the inevitable accidents which result to them from the forces of nature independent of human actions altogether."[24] More recently a Canadian judge has reasserted the point. "One value at the heart of tort law is the notion of individual responsibility, something that is central to Western civilisation."[25] In the 1980s various dicta by Law Lords can be cited to show that individual moral responsibility is still a relevant factor in a marginal case.[26]

Hence Salmond was logically compelled to say[27] of the decision in *Rylands* v. *Fletcher*,[28] which is founded upon a theory of strict liability: "No decision in the law of torts has done more to prevent the establishment of a simple, uniform, and intelligible system of civil responsibility." It must be admitted that fault somehow tends to re-appear even in areas of strict liability. So the Criminal Injuries Compensation Board has held that the claimant's anti-social conduct is a reason for reducing his compensation.

Arguments Against Fault

Three objections may be raised to Salmond's powerful argument. They may be summarised briefly, if cynically, by saying that in England today "the real wrongdoer hardly ever pays for the damage he does. He

---

[24] 6th ed., pp. 12–13. It is odd that Salmond, who endeavoured to force the law of torts into the strait-jacket of "no liability without fault,", should have denied the existence of a law of tort.

[25] Linden, *Canadian Tort Law* (1978), p. 13.

[26] *e.g.* Lord Bridge of Harwich in *McLoughlin* v. *O'Brian* [1983] A.C. 410, 441.

[27] 6th ed., vii.

[28] See below, Chap. 13.

is usually not worth suing. The payer is either his employer or an insurance company."[29]

(1) Fault never essential

Fault has never been, and is not today, an essential element in tortious liability.[30] There are two main theories of the history in English law of the relations between blameworthiness and civil responsibility. According to Holmes,[31] the law began with liability based upon actual intent and actual personal culpability and tended, as it grew, to formulate external standards which might subject an individual to liability though there was no fault in him. According to Wigmore,[32] the law began by making a man act at his peril and gradually became more moralised until liability was connected with fault. Time out of mind there has been strict liability for innkeepers and common carriers—they are "quasi-insurers."[33] It was perhaps only natural that the beginning of the twentieth century should have found Salmond writing as he did in support of the school of Wigmore. For by that date the courts had largely abandoned the distinction between direct and indirect damage so familiar in the medieval common law. Instead the emphasis had shifted to the distinction between intentional and negligent conduct, which is now regarded as all-important.[34] In particular, the growing importance of the tort of negligence, with its familiar test of asking what a reasonable and prudent man would have done in the circumstances, had brought the question of fault to the forefront. But today we can say that neither view seems to be entirely correct.[35] The law has moved in cycles. A period of strict liability, an "unmoral" period, is succeeded by a period of fault liability, a "moral" period, and then the pendulum swings back again. So in 1953 Lord Goddard's Committee on Civil Liability for Animals[36] argued strongly in favour of replacing strict liability by negligence. But in 1967 the Law Commission,[37] after a further investigation, concluded that there were considerable advantages in retaining some forms of strict liability.

---

[29] Devlin, *Law and Morals* (Oxford, 1965), p. 39. The relationship of torts and insurance is discussed below, § 2.5.

[30] "As an English lawyer, I can only say that we never heard of it here. Stated as a general proposition, it is contrary to the whole law of trespass, to much of the law of nuisance, to the whole law of defamation, and to the responsibility of principals for their agents": Pollock, "A Plea for Historical Interpretation" (1923) 39 L.Q.R. 164, 167.

[31] *Common Law*, Lects. III and IV.

[32] Wigmore, "Responsibility for Tortious Acts" (1893) 7 Harv.L.Rev. 315, 383, 441.

[33] *Fletcher* v. *Rylands* (1865) H. & C. 774, 793, *per* Martin B.

[34] *Long* v. *Hepworth* [1968] 1 W.L.R. 1299.

[35] In *Read* v. *Lyons* [1947] A.C. 156, 180, Lord Simonds, after referring to this "age-long conflict of theories which is to be found in every system of law," says that "It will not surprise the students of English law or of anything English to find that between these theories a middle way, a compromise, has been found. . . . For somewhere the line must be drawn unless full rein be given to the doctrine, that a man acts always at his peril, that 'coarse and impolitic idea' as Holmes J. somewhere [*Common Law*, p. 163] calls it."

[36] Cmd. 8746 (1953).

[37] Law Commission Published Working Paper No. 13 (H.M.S.O., 1967).

(2) Fault judged by an objective standard

It is clear that to Salmond, with his emphasis on *mens rea*, fault was a matter of personal shortcoming. But the "fault" upon which liability may rest is social fault, which may but does not necessarily coincide with personal immorality.[38] The law finds "fault" in a failure to live up to an ideal standard of conduct which may be beyond the knowledge or capacity of the individual. Conversely, it is worth remembering that one who is under no legal liability for damage caused to another may yet think it right and proper to offer some measure of compensation.[39]

(3) Punishment not main object of law of torts

Since he held that wrongful intention or culpable negligence was a condition of civil liability in tort, it is natural that Salmond should have considered pecuniary compensation, not as in itself the ultimate object or a sufficient justification of legal liability, but as a means of punishment. But this was not the original conception of English law, nor is it generally considered to be the conception of English law today.[40] The object of a civil inquiry into cause and consequence is to fix liability on some responsible person and to give reparation for damage done, not to inflict punishment for duty disregarded.[41] So a series of decisions has emphasised that damages in actions for personal injuries are compensatory[42]: damages are to compensate the victim, not to reflect what the wrongdoer ought to pay.[43] On the other hand, the House of Lords has re-affirmed that punitive or exemplary damages, imposed to show a wrongdoer that tort does not pay, have a limited but definite place in the law.[44]

The main weakness of Salmond's theory lies in the fact that compensation payable in civil proceedings is often in no way commensurate either with the fault of the defendant or with his financial resources. A moment's inadvertence may result in personal injuries for which damages amounting to thousands of pounds can be recovered.[45] It is worth noting that a different principle prevails in admiralty, whereby shipowners who have caused loss or damage to any other vessel by

---

[38] See further on this topic, below, § 9.8, and *Workington Dock and Harbour Board* v. *SS. Towerfield (Owners)* [1951] A.C. 112, 160; *Gollins* v. *Gollins* [1964] A.C. 644, 664.

[39] As Pufendorf (*De Jure*, III 1.6) remarked: "Should some poverty-stricken man, in a mere accident, be injured by a man of means, it will be seemly in a man of such station to confer some kindness upon the poor man." This was the attitude of the successful appellants in *Bolton* v. *Stone* [1951] A.C. 850 ("The cricket clubs of this country who supported the appeal to the House of Lords have done everything that they can to see that Miss Stone does not suffer financially": (1952) 68 L.Q.R. 3).

[40] But if a plaintiff who has been deprived of all normal senses is entitled to substantial damages, although he can neither enjoy them in his lifetime nor bequeath them by will, as the House of Lords has affirmed in *Lim* v. *Camden Health Authority* [1980] A.C. 174, how can it be said that the aim of torts is compensation rather than punishment?

[41] *Weld-Blundell* v. *Stephens* [1920] A.C. 956, 986.

[42] See below, § 24.1.

[43] *Pickett* v. *British Rail Engineering Ltd.* [1980] A.C. 136.

[44] *Cassell & Co. Ltd.* v. *Broome* [1972] A.C. 1027. Note the conflicting dicta by Lords Reid and Wilberforce on the function of compensation in torts. See below, § 23.1.

[45] As in *Winkworth* v. *Hubbard* [1960] 1 Lloyd's Rep. 150.

reason of improper navigation are entitled to limit their liability[46] according to a scale set out in an international convention. This is very rough justice, for a small tug towing a large ship can do immense damage.[47]

Functions of damages

But although the present emphasis may be on compensation rather than punishment, this does not mean that the latter factor can be ignored entirely. It will always remain important so long as there is power to award aggravated or exemplary damages.[48] Again, although damages in libel are mainly compensatory, the sum awarded is not to be reduced by the fact that the judge has in his judgment praised the plaintiff or excoriated the conduct of the defendant.[49] Compliments, even from the Bench, are no substitute for cash. Again, practitioners testify to the importance in popular morality of "making the defendant pay,"[50] and the courts would be unwise to ignore this feeling entirely.[51] For "a tort suit may provide some psychological satisfaction. Instead of demonstrating with a picket sign, an aggrieved individual may begin a law suit."[52] So torts "is sometimes the last resort of the citizen who wishes to bring a serious grievance to the attention of the public. The great advantage is that the levers of the civil action are operated by the citizen himself and are not in the benevolent control of an official such as the Attorney-General, the Ombudsman or the D.P.P. So we cannot afford to let tort law become the victim of a puritan search for adminis-trative efficiency."[53] Further, this admonitory or educational aspect of tort law is meaningful only if the defendant has somehow been morally at fault.[54]

It should also be remembered that the law of torts aims not merely to provide compensation for losses which have occurred already, but also seeks to minimise or prevent entirely the occurrence of such losses in the future. Hence an award of damages may serve to compensate the plaintiff and also to deter the defendant and others from similar conduct in the future. So there is some evidence that the Press (but not, appar-ently, television) has been inhibited in its conduct by large damages in libel actions.[55] Another example is said to occur when an employer is

---

[46] Merchant Shipping Act 1979, ss.17–18.

[47] *The Bramley Moore* [1964] P. 200, 219.

[48] See below, § 23.1.

[49] *Associated Newspapers Ltd.* v. *Dingle* [1964] A.C. 371.

[50] So even supporters of insurance concede that "the social security system is less emotionally satisfying to the injured worker than the old Workmen's Compensation scheme was, since under the latter the employer was seen to pay the price of his wrong-doing": Barrett (1975) 2 Poly. Law Review 22, 25.

[51] So even in a jurisdiction which has a no-fault compensation scheme there is room for tort law: *Re Chase* [1989] 1 N.Z.L.R. 325.

[52] Linden, *Canadian Tort Law* (1978), p. 15.

[53] Harlow, *Compensation and Government Torts* (1982), p. 160.

[54] See White, *Tort Law in America* (1980), p. 239.

[55] See below, § 8.25.

held strictly responsible for breach of a statutory duty designed for the protection of his workmen, but some of the evidence available about employers' liability insurance policies does not support this belief. Some insurance companies take the view that accident prevention is not part of their function, but should be left to the criminal law. Yet this is not very effective—in 1988 the average fine was only £420. This is not an impressive sanction. Again the Food and Drugs Acts 1975–1982 impose criminal penalties for the sale of unfit food, but there are only about 250 convictions each year, though sales of contaminated food have increased dramatically in the past decade. The employer's liability insurance premium may be increased if his safety record is bad, but as the premium is a deductible expense for tax purposes, this too is not a serious sanction. An increase in premiums may also result in attempts to avoid or defeat claims rather than to prevent accidents. Some have argued that fault has little or no relevance to the expectations and claims of accident victims.[56]

§ 2.5. SOME ALTERNATIVE MODES OF COMPENSATION

(1) Insurance

The influence of insurance on the law of torts has been significant, both on a theoretical level and in practice. We shall examine first its influence at a theoretical level. Insurance has undermined one of the two purposes of an award of damages, and it has cast doubt on the value judgments made by the courts in determining which particular test of liability is appropriate in given circumstances.

Regardless of whether in the particular circumstances the appropriate principle of liability is intention, malice, fault, or strict liability, the purpose of common law damages remains the same. The primary purpose of an award of damages is to compensate the victim for his loss, with a view to restoring him as near as possible to the position he would have been in but for the tort of the wrongdoer. But damages have another purpose: by making the *wrongdoer* responsible for meeting the award of damages, the courts are trying to deter others from committing similar tortious wrongs. Insurance[57] vitiates that secondary purpose of damages, at the same time incidentally ensuring that the primary purpose is more often achieved. It can scarcely be realistically asserted that insured defendants are deterred by the prospect of losing a no-claims

---

[56] Harris and others, *Compensation and Support for Illness and Injury* (Oxford, 1984), Chap. 4. But the argument is based on a small sample of accident victims in the mid-1970s.

[57] There are two principal kinds of insurance: liability or third party insurance, which provides compensation to a person injured by the insured if he can establish the insured's liability, and loss or first party insurance, which provides compensation for the insured in the event of certain insured contingencies occurring. First-party insurance is more efficient and cheaper than the other variety—*e.g.* as there is no cover against economic loss (simply because there is no consumer demand for it) premiums are lower.

bonus or by an increase of premium on renewal of their policies. Once it is conceded that insurance renders compensation the sole purpose of damages, then the tort action itself becomes more vulnerable to attack, for there are many ways—some perhaps fairer and administratively cheaper than tort—of compensating a victim for a loss he has suffered.

Prima facie, where a person suffers loss of a recognised kind as the result of another's act, then the latter should have to make good that loss. But, for valid reasons, the courts have held that, in certain circumstances, the actor will have to compensate his victim only if he (the actor) has been at fault. The victim's right to compensation is, therefore, curtailed in an attempt to be fair to both parties. The courts have made a policy decision that, in the circumstances, it is right to reward a defendant who has been careful by protecting him from liability for the consequences of his actions and that, as a corollary, the plaintiff must forgo his compensation. This policy decision is made on the supposition that the wrongdoer would himself have to pay the damages but for this protection; it by no means follows that the same decision would be made if there were no risk of the wrongdoer's having to provide the compensation.[58] It is difficult to judge why the victim's right to compensation should be curtailed when that curtailment is not justified by a corresponding benefit to the wrongdoer. The requirement of fault ceases to play its role as the leveller between the victim's legitimate expectations and the wrongdoer's legitimate expectations, and becomes instead simply a hurdle in the victim's progress to compensation. If it is accepted that one can insure against liability for harm caused intentionally to another,[59] then similar arguments can be made about the inappropriateness of the victim's having, in certain circumstances, to prove an intention to do him harm, when it is irrelevant to the wrongdoer whether he had such an intention or not. Again, the victim's right to compensation is being curtailed without any corresponding benefit to the wrongdoer.

However, insurance has influenced the law of tort on a much more practical level as well. While the fact of insurance is not of itself a reason for imposing liability, or for refusing to permit a defendant to escape from liability,[60] there can be no doubt that it does add "a little extra tensile strength" to the chain which binds a wrongdoer to his responsi-

---

[58] For instance, if Parliament had decided from the start that all motorists should take out liability insurance, then strict liability, rather than fault liability, might well have seemed the fairer test for injuries caused on the highway.

[59] It is well established that those guilty of manslaughter as a result of reckless and drunken driving can still be indemnified by their insurance company: *James* v. *British General Insurance Co. Ltd.* [1927] 2 K.B. 311, unless there is an appropriate exemption clause, as in *Marcel Beller Ltd.* v. *Hayden* [1978] Q.B. 694, 703, but even then the victim will be able to claim on his own policy. Nor can it be realistically asserted that crime would be encouraged if an intentional wrongdoer could rely on his insurers' discharging his civil liability to his victim, because a person who is not deterred by the risk of perhaps long imprisonment for his act is not going to be deterred by the fear of civil liability to his victim: *Hardy* v. *Motor Insurers' Bureau* [1964] 2 Q.B. 745, 770.

[60] *White* v. *Blackmore* [1972] Q.B. 651, 668.

bilities.[61] As well, it has given a new horizon to damages[62]; It is true that traditionally it was considered improper to inform the court that a defendant was insured,[63] but "those days are long past"[64] and now it is frequently openly recognised that the defendant will be insured.[65]

Such a recognition is inevitable in certain areas because Parliament has decreed that insurance must be effected. For instance, the Employers' Liability (Compulsory Insurance) Act 1969 requires each employer to maintain an approved policy of insurance with an authorised insurer against liability for bodily injury or disease sustained by his employees and arising out of and in the course of their employment. Third party insurance cover is also compulsory in respect of nuclear installations, dangerous wild animals, riding establishments, and oil pollution from merchant ships. The most common instance of compulsory insurance is, of course, motorists' third party cover. The Road Traffic Act 1988 (ss.143 and 145) requires every person who uses a vehicle on a road to take out a policy of insurance indemnifying him in respect of the death of or bodily injury to any person caused by, or arising out of, the use of a vehicle on a road. As well, a third person who suffers bodily injury as a result of the tortious act of the insured is given a direct right of action against the insurers, provided that the liability of the insured is first established.[66] Indeed, the real defendants in most tortious litigation are insurance companies, since 70 per cent. of the cases decided annually in the High Court are cases arising from personal injury caused by road accidents.

Insurance has also resulted in a reduction of litigation. As a matter of practice, English insurance companies contest in court only one per cent. of claims made against them; the rest they settle.[67] An uninsured defendant may well consider that he has little to lose by forcing the plaintiff to prove his case in court; even to settle may mean to him

---

[61] *Executor Trustee and Agency Co. Ltd.* v. *Hearse* [1961] S.A.S.R. 51, 54, *per* Chamberlain J.

[62] Indeed, fears have been expressed that damages might become excessively high with the result (a) that insurance premiums would become so heavy that some products and services would simply become unavailable, and (b) that small insurance companies would be ruined. In the 1980s premiums for professional indemnity insurance mounted to exceptionally high levels. In 1987 the two largest medical insurance companies announced premium increases of 80 per cent. Architects in particular complained that as a result of developments in the law relating to latent damage and the limitation of actions (see below, §§ 220–222), they would have to keep up expensive liability policies even after retirement. It was said that an architect would have to live to 102 to avoid defending claims arising out of work for which he was commissioned at the age of 60 (*The Financial Times*, April 25, 1985).

[63] *Davie* v. *New Merton Board Mills Ltd.* [1959] A.C. 604, 627.

[64] *Smith* v. *Eric S. Bush (A Firm)* [1990] A.C. 831, 888, *per* Lord Griffiths.

[65] "Most collision cases are collisions between insurance companies": *The Abidin Daver* [1984] A.C. 398, 420, *per* Lord Templeman.

[66] *Bradley* v. *Eagle Star Insurance Ltd.* [1989] A.C. 957.

[67] Report of the Royal Commission on Civil Liability and Compensation for Personal Injury, Cmnd. 7054 (1978) (hereinafter termed "Pearson Report"), para. 180. Because there is always some risk in any claim, the defendant's insurers often exploit this and make a discount in settlement offers. An interesting account of the settlement process is Genn, *Hard Bargaining* (Oxford, 1987).

financial ruin, and so the risk of going to trial, with the possibility of staving off defeat by some means or other, is often worth running.

Liability insurance provides compensation to a person injured by the insured if he can establish the insured's liability. Thus such insurance is essentially parasitic; nothing is payable until the insured's legal liability in tort is proved. But there is another kind of insurance which is quite independent of tort and which is seen by some as the eventual successor of tort: this is loss insurance, sometimes called self-insurance or first party insurance. A person may take out a policy of insurance providing for benefits in the event of his death or personal injury. In short, liability insurance provides protection for tortfeasors; loss insurance provides protection for those injured. Loss insurance is rarely compulsory. The main exception to that is the national insurance scheme, which provides benefits to those who suffer injuries at work. Each worker pays a contribution to this insurance; his employer and the state provide additional contributions. In practice too, householders with mortgages must insure against damage by fire: the effecting of such a policy is invariably stipulated by mortgagees. New Zealand's accident compensation scheme is in essence a system of compulsory loss insurance of a far-reaching kind. Because of that scheme's pervasiveness, a person's right to sue in tort if he suffers personal injury as the result of an accident was considered superfluous and has been abolished.

The Pearson Commission thought that a scheme of general compulsory insurance would not be feasible. One real practical difficulty is the enforcement of compulsory insurance; all the present requirements for compulsory insurance are linked to a system of licensing or certification. Not all could afford the premiums for compulsory loss insurance; further, objection might justifiably be taken to a person's being compelled to insure against harm from risks caused by others. All-embracing compulsory liability insurance would seem irrational in that it would mean that the primary disadvantage of tort—namely, the enormous cost of operating the system—would remain, while its principal advantage—namely, that the wrongdoer pays for the consequences of his wrong—would disappear. The Pearson Commission did recommend, however, that, where compulsory insurance was now required, it should continue to be so required, and that consideration should be given to its imposition in respect of exceptional risks and private aircraft. Better the Commission thought to develop further the social security system and the relationship with tort than to expand by legislation the role of insurance, other than in certain defined areas posing special risks. In July 1989 it was announced that Government Committees would examine the possibility of no-fault compensation for minor traffic accidents. This was the only sign of official approval of the Pearson Report.

(2) Social security and other forms of state compensation

Of even greater significance than insurance has been the development this century of social security and other forms of state compensation. The breakaway from dependence on tort came in 1897, in the field of industrial accidents. The Workmen's Compensation Act of that year introduced the concept of liability without fault and the provision of cash benefits as of right and without a test of means. From that Act has developed the modern industrial injuries scheme, which provides various state benefits for those unable to work or disabled as a result of an accident "arising out of or in the course of" employment or because of a prescribed disease related to the nature of such employment. Compensation under this scheme is paid each year in over 600,000 new cases of work injury and disease; the total annual cost is about £250 million. By comparison, only £70 million is paid each year in respect of work injuries to some 90,000 people through the tort system.[68]

Criminal injuries

In 1964 Great Britain set up a non-statutory scheme[69] to provide compensation for those who suffer personal injuries[70] which are directly attributable to a crime of violence (including arson and poisoning), or to an arrest or attempted arrest of an offender or suspected offender, or to the prevention or attempted prevention of any offence. If the victim dies, his spouse or dependents may claim. There is no legal claim to a grant of compensation, but the Board[71] which administers the scheme makes awards within the framework laid down by the document establishing the scheme. Rather surprisingly for a body which is regarded as part of the social security system, compensation is assessed in the same way as common law damages, but aggravated and exemplary damages are not permitted. Many awards are for comparatively small sums, but, to avoid trivial claims, no compensation is payable unless the injury was one for which damages of not less than £400 would be awarded. The award may be reduced because of the applicant's conduct, but any immunity of an offender attributable to his youth or insanity is left out of account. There is a right of appeal on points of law, and decisions of the Board are subject to judicial review.

---

[68] Pearson Report, para. 772. The money paid under the tort system will nearly all come from insurance companies for there is now a statutory obligation on employers to insure against their liability for personal injury to their employees: Employer's Liability (Compulsory Insurance) Act 1969. The employer's liability is very wide; he is liable for not only his own negligence, but also the negligence of his employees towards one another, and even now for personal injury to employees caused by defects in equipment provided by him, even if the defect is attributable wholly or partly to the fault of a third party, for example a manufacturer or repairer: Employers' Liability (Defective Equipment) Act 1969. But wide as is the employers' liability it is not all-embracing, and if a gap exists it is for Parliament and not the courts to fill it: *Reid* v. *Rush & Tompkins plc* [1990] 1 W.L.R. 212, 222–223.

[69] Now incorporated in the Criminal Justice Act 1988, ss.109–115. See Duff, Note (1989) 52 M.L.R. 518.

[70] So damage to or loss of property is excluded.

[71] Its address is: 19 Alfred Place, London WC1E 7LG. In 1989/90 it paid out £106 million in compensation. Other E.C. countries are not nearly so generous—Germany and France each paid out about £12 million.

DSS

On top of this, there is the vast network of social security benefits. Measures aiming at no more than the bare relief of extreme poverty have given place to a system in which cash benefits are provided as of right, together with comprehensive medical services and supporting social services to meet a wide variety of contingencies. At any one time, almost 20 million social security benefits, pensions and allowances are being paid in the United Kingdom.

The effect of this cornucopia of state compensation has been fully investigated by the Pearson Commission. The Commission recommended that the tort system should be retained, despite widespread criticisms of its expensiveness,[72] because of its deterrent effect and because "[t]here is an elementary justice in the principle of the tort action that he who has by his fault injured his neighbour should make reparation."[73] Yet, at the same time, it acknowledged that "social security should be regarded as the primary method of providing compensation."[74] The Commission saw the need for an extension of the "no-fault" form of state compensation in certain select areas.[75] For injuries arising in the work-place, it advocated the continuance of the industrial injuries scheme, with higher benefits. It suggested a similar no-fault compensation scheme for injuries caused by motor vehicles; road injuries were singled out largely because they occur on a scale not matched by any other category of accidental injury within the Commission's terms of reference[76] and because they are particularly likely to be serious. At present, only about a quarter of those injured by motor vehicles recover tort compensation.[77] The Commission recommended the retention of the criminal injuries compensation scheme, although it thought it ought to be put on a statutory basis.

The Commission's approach may be criticised on the ground that its preference for one class of beneficiaries is irrational. Why should the cause of the injury be regarded as so important? This is undoubtedly because the report is a compromise: there were three schools of thought within the Commission, one wanting a no-fault scheme covering all accidents, a second looking forward to the eventual disappearance of the tort system once it had been seen how the social security system could cope with the demands which the present recommendations if

---

[72] The operating costs of the tort system amount to about 86 per cent. of the value of tort compensation payments, or about 45 per cent. of the combined total of compensation and operating costs; by comparison, the cost of administering social security benefits for injured people is about 11 per cent. of the value of compensation payments, or 10 per cent. of the cost of payments and administration. Surprisingly, the County Court is more expensive than the High Court, and the saving in time or money from settlements is minimal.

[73] Pearson Report, paras. 245–263.

[74] *Ibid.* para. 275.

[75] The Commission rejected a no-fault scheme covering all injuries as being outside its terms of reference (para. 239).

[76] Accidents in the home (which the Commission did not consider) account for injuries to about a million people in Britain each year.

[77] Pearson Report, para. 994. The Oxford Socio-Legal Study recorded an even smaller percentage.

enacted would put upon it, and the third school hoping that there would always be a place for the tort system, whatever happened to no-fault provision.

On the other hand, the report may be praised for coming to terms with the relationship of tort with social security and other forms of state compensation. For the first time, a clear guideline has been given as to how tort and state compensation should co-exist. At present, certain social security benefits are partially offset against any damages assessed for loss of income due to personal injury, but the general rule remains that benefits accruing to the plaintiff as a result of an accident are not to be deducted from his award of damages. The overall scope for the duplication of compensation is substantial. The principal beneficiaries of double compensation are those who are entitled to industrial injuries benefit, because of all the victims of accident and disease, they are treated most generously by both the tort system and the social security system. The reason for the overlap stems undoubtedly from the fact that tort and social security approach the problem of compensation from different perspectives, and neither has sufficiently taken into account the implications of the other. The Pearson Commission recommended that the full value of social security benefits payable to an injured person or his dependants as a result of an injury for which damages are awarded should be deducted in the assessment of the damages.[78] By a majority, the Commission recommended that social security benefits should be divided into three categories—loss of earnings, expenses, and non-pecuniary loss; the benefits in each category should then be deducted in assessing the corresponding portion of the tort award. As a further recognition of the influence of social security, the Commission recommended that damages for future pecuniary loss should no longer continue to be awarded on a lump sum basis, at least in cases where the accident has caused death or serious and lasting injury; instead, the compensation should be in the form of periodic payments.

Thus, the Commission's Report acknowledged, not only that the social security system was already the main source of compensation, but also that it should play a greater role in the future. The tort system must at last recognise its new neighbour, and tortious damages should be awarded subject to social security benefits, so that duplication of compensation might be prevented. On the other hand, tort should be retained, if only in a reserve capacity as a means of preserving the common law principle of *restitutio in integrum*.[79] In the final analysis, it may be said that the report is a realistic document and that all those in favour of change towards greater justice in compensating the injured should

---

[78] Parliament has followed this recommendation when enacting the Vaccine Damage Payments Act 1979. Section 6(4) provides that the receipt of the £10,000 lump sum payable under the Act does not prejudice the recipient's right to institute or carry on civil proceedings, but the Court must treat that payment as paid on account of any damages which the Court awards in respect of the disablement.

[79] By preserving tort, the Commission thought that it would be assured that the injured received their just deserts, for there would be a separate body—"the independent courts of the realm"—to ensure that any statutory tariff was fair and sufficient in any particular case.

support it, even if on the basis that half a loaf is better than no bread at all. It seems unlikely, however, that there will be any early enactment of the major recommendations of the Commission.

(3) Torts and computers[80]

These share the characteristics of being easier to describe than to define. So their relationship is puzzling. But it seems clear that a computer is not a thing dangerous in itself: it is unlikely to cause physical damage.[81] On the other hand, a computer may be responsible for economic loss on an enormous scale if abused deliberately or recklessly, and problems may soon emerge. The infringement of privacy or copyright by electronic devices has already attracted the attention of Parliament (see, e.g. the Data Protection Act 1984, s.22, which provides a right to claim compensation by one who has suffered from inaccurate data held by a data user) and the courts.[82]

§ 2.6. LIABILITY WITHOUT FAULT

In certain cases, liability is independent of intention or negligence. Liability in libel does not depend on the intention of the defamer, but on the fact of defamation; so too there is strict liability for damage done by a wild animal, or by the escape of dangerous things accumulated for some non-natural purpose (the rule in *Rylands* v. *Fletcher*); again, liability is strict when one is vicariously responsible for the acts of another. In cases such as these the security of the particular interest of the plaintiff is predominant over the defendant's interest in freedom of action. It is a mistake, however, to think of the predominance as complete. In appropriate cases defences such as act of God or act of a third party are available. Liability may be strict but it is never absolute.

The plea of inevitable accident is that the consequences complained of as a wrong were not intended by the defendant and could not have been foreseen and avoided by the exercise of reasonable care and skill.[83]

An accident in its popular sense is any unexpected injury resulting from any unlooked-for mishap or occurrence.[84] In law a happening is only regarded as an accident if it is one out of the ordinary course of things, something so unusual as not to be looked for by a person of ordinary prudence.[85] So an ordinary fall of snow is not an accident, but only an incident which happens in the ordinary course of things.[86] One form of inevitable accident is that which is due to an act of God,[87] as

---

[80] See C. F. Tapper, *Computer Law* (4th ed., 1989), Chap. 3.

[81] But see *The Lady Gwendolen* [1965] p. 294, in which a ship's radar was abused.

[82] See Lord Templeman in *C.B.S. Songs Ltd.* v. *Amstrad plc* [1988] A.C. 1013, 1059, and below, § 3.2.

[83] *McBride* v. *Stitt* [1944] N.I. 7, 10.

[84] *Fenton* v. *Thorley & Co.* [1903] A.C. 443, 451. So Othello (Act I, Scene iii, line 134) refers to "moving accidents by field and flood."

[85] *Makin* v. *L. and N.E. Ry.* [1943] 1 All E.R. 362, 364–365.

[86] *Fenwick* v. *Schmalz* (1868) L.R. 3 C.P. 313, 316.

[87] *Makin* v. *L. and N.E. Ry.* [1943] K.B. 467, 475, 478.

when a car-driver has a sudden affliction, such as a stroke.[88] The driver will not be liable if his actions were wholly beyond his control.[89]

There is no general principle that inevitable accident is a good defence. In actions of trespass it is now settled (after some hesitation) that it may be pleaded as a defence; but it will probably succeed only if the defendant had in truth no control over the act which caused the damage.[90] In torts of strict liability (*e.g.* under the rule in *Rylands* v. *Fletcher*) only the special form of inevitable accident known as act of God (or possibly the uncontrollable act of a third party) affords a good defence. In actions in which negligence has to be proved by the plaintiff, the plea of inevitable accident may sometimes be tantamount to saying that the defendant has not failed to observe the standard of care required of him. Hence a court may well prefer to say that the defendant was not negligent rather than that he has affirmatively proved inevitable accident.[91] So in an action of negligence it is not necessary for the defendant to show that the accident was inevitable in the strictest sense—that is to say, incapable of being prevented at all, or only by the exercise of extraordinary care and skill. If a man drives a motor-car, and in spite of the exercise of all reasonable care on his part an accident happens, he may plead that it was due to inevitable accident; and it will be no answer to this plea to prove that if he had altogether refrained from those dangerous forms of activity it would not have ensued.[92]

Finally, a point of pleading should be noted—in an action of trespass, inevitable accident must be specifically pleaded; but in an action of negligence, evidence of inevitable accident, or the negligence of a third party, may be given when a general denial is pleaded.[93] It is then in substance not a separate defence but merely a denial of negligence.

---

[88] *Waugh* v. *Allan (J.K.) & Sons Ltd.* 1964 S.C. 162.
[89] *Roberts* v. *Ramsbottom* [1980] 1 W.L.R. 823.
[90] See below, § 7.4.
[91] *McBride* v. *Stitt* [1944] N.I. 7, 14.
[92] *Cutler* v. *United Dairies* [1933] 2 K.B. 297, 305.
[93] *MacKnight* v. *McLaughlin* [1963] N.I. 34. See an admirable note in (1963) 15 N.I.L.Q. 571.

CHAPTER 3

NEW AND EMERGENT TORTS

§ 3.1. New and Emergent Torts

There are a number of cases in which the courts have displayed willingness to create new heads of liability. No more can be done here than to indicate the present state of development of six of these doubtful torts: (1) Invasion of privacy; (2) Breach of confidence; (3) Abuse of statutory powers; (4) Infringement of status; (5) Innominate torts; (6) Eurotorts.

(1) Invasion of privacy[1]

English lawyers have always been sceptical about the effectiveness of general declarations for the protection of rights. So English law probably[2] does not, and in the view of the Younger and Calcutt Committees should not, recognise any general right of privacy. But the right to privacy is recognised by the overwhelming majority of American courts, whose decisions were analysed by Prosser under four different headings which are adopted here for the sake of convenience.[3]

First, the tort covers cases in which there has been an intrusion upon the plaintiff's seclusion or solitude, or into his private affairs. This head of liability has obvious affinities with the present law governing trespass to the person or property,[4] or nuisance,[5] or breach of copyright or infringement of patents or trade marks,[6] or the intentional infliction of emotional distress. English law gives an adequate remedy in these cases, usually civil but sometimes criminal,[7] subject to the qualification that the plaintiff must first bring his claim within the four corners of the recognised tort or crime. For example, it may be the tort of nuisance to telephone another unreasonably often,[8] or to subject him to constant aerial surveillance,[9] but as the plaintiff in nuisance must have a pro-

---

[1] See Wacks, *Personal Information* (Oxford, 1989), and the Reports of the Younger (Cmnd. 5012, 1972) and Calcutt (Cm. 1102, 1990) Committees.

[2] See the (regretful) dicta of the C.A. in *Kaye* v. *Robertson* (1991) 18 F.S.R. 62.

[3] The analysis in Harper, James and Gray, *The Law of Torts* (2nd ed.), Chap. 9, is fuller and slightly different.

[4] So in *Sheen* v. *Clegg, Daily Telegraph,* June 22, 1961, damages for trespass were awarded against a defendant who had secretly installed a microphone over the plaintiff's marital bed. But in *Kaye* v. *Robertson* (1991) 18 F.S.R. 62 the C.A. held that the plaintiff, who had been photographed while recovering in hospital from brain surgery, could not sue in trespass as he was not in possession of the hospital bed. (Might not the hospital authority have been joined as co-plaintiff?) But the plaintiff recovered in injurious falsehood (see below, §18.8) for the false and malicious statement that he had consented to being photographed in his sorry state.

[5] See below, § 5.3.

[6] See below, § 18.12.

[7] So the Malicious Communications Act 1988, s.57 makes it an offence to send letters or other objects for the purpose of causing distress or anxiety.

[8] See below, § 5.4.

[9] *Bernstein* v. *Skyviews Ltd.* [1978] Q.B. 479, 489 ("monstrous invasion of privacy").

prietary interest, this means that a guest in a house as distinct from the
occupier could not complain of such conduct. A plaintiff may also
obtain aggravated and, in a few cases, exemplary damages if the conduct of the defendant has been outrageous or disgraceful.[10] But the
common law gives no remedy to one who complains that his neighbours have spied from their windows into his premises, or have cut off
an attractive view from his house by erecting a spite-fence.[11] No recognised tort has been committed. Nor again is any remedy at present
given to one who complains that his photograph (or other likeness) has
been taken and reproduced without his permission[12] unless the publication is defamatory,[13] and it must be remembered that truth is a
defence to an action fo libel.[14] Nor does there seem to be any civil remedy for the interception of telephonic or other conversations,[15] unless
the tapping has resulted in the abuse of confidential information.[16]

There is clearly a need for some development if the right of individual
freedom is to be safeguarded properly in the age of such scientific
achievements as micro-miniature radio transmitters, subliminal and
subaudial projection of images, truth drugs, the tape-recorder, tele-
scopic cameras and television. Indeed the Superior Court of Quebec
awarded damages on the following facts. The plaintiff wrote to a television company to complain about the quality of one of their pro-
grammes. The announcer displayed the plaintiff's name and address on
the screen and invited listeners to write or telephone to the plaintiff
saying what they thought of his conduct. The resultant barrage of
offensive letters and telephone calls was so great that the plaintiff was
obliged to disconnect his telephone and suffered severe inconvenience
and worry.[17]

Secondly, there are cases in which complaint is made about the public disclosure of embarrassing private facts about the plaintiff—for
example, that he does not pay his debts. In the leading American case
the defendant published to the world an account of the plaintiff's earlier
career as a prostitute and the accused in a sensational murder trial. The
plaintiff, who had quite left aside her earlier life of shame and now
moved in reputable society, recovered damages.[18] Until the Rehabilitation of Offenders Act, 1974 the defendants would have had the
defence of justification if sued for libel in such a case in England.

Thirdly, there are cases relating to defendants who place the plaintiff
in a false light in the public eye by publishing untrue statements about

---

[10] *Cassell & Co.* v. *Broome* [1972] A.C. 1027.
[11] *Cf.* the Rights of Light Act 1959.
[12] See *Kaye* v. *Robertson* (1991) 18 F.S.R. 62. But a *flashlight* photograph may be a battery.
[13] Tickets to pop concerts often contain a clause whereby the holder consents to being
filmed as one of the audience.
[14] As it was in *Dunlop Rubber Co. Ltd.* v. *Dunlop* [1921] 1 A.C. 367. See below, § 8.8.
[15] *Malone* v. *Metropolitan Police Commissioner* [1979] Ch. 334, 358–360.
[16] *Francome* v. *Mirror Group Ltd.* [1984] 1 W.L.R. 892. The Interception of Communications
Act 1985 creates criminal offences, but does not directly affect the law of tort.
[17] *Robbins* v. *C.B.C.* (1958) 12 D.L.R. (2d) 35.
[18] *Melvin* v. *Reid* (1931) 112 Cal.App. 285, 297 Pac. 91.

him. Here there will sometimes be a remedy under the law of defamation,[19] or copyright,[20] or passing off.[21]

Fourthly, there are cases in which the defendant has appropriated for his own purposes some attribute of the plaintiff's name or identity.[22] The law does not prevent any person from calling himself by the name of another, so long as he has no fraudulent purpose in doing so.[23] There is, however, some protection given in cases where a proprietary interest has been infringed, as when the creator of a work finds that it has been the subject of derogatory treatment,—e.g., where a reputable film director discovers that scenes of explicit sex or violence have been added during editing.[24]

(2) Breach of Confidence[25]

This is now recognised as a distinct tort. It is committed when the person in whom confidential information reposes (the confidant) makes use of or discloses to others the information in question to the detriment of the plaintiff (the confider).[26] Past breaches of confidence may be remedied by an action for damages in tort, or by taking an account of the profits made by the misuse or disclosure. Apprehended future breaches may be restrained by an injunction. This remarkable example of judge-made law has been achieved by borrowing features from contracts, property, equity, bailment and torts.

Th obligation of confidence may arise from an express or implied term in a contract of employment, as when a company discovers that an ex-employee has set up his own company in the same area and appears to be using confidential information (e.g., lists of customers) acquired in his former employment.[27] But more often the obligation arises in a non-contractual fiduciary situation. These situations cannot be catalogued,

---

[19] *Ridge v. The English Illustrated Magazine* (1913) 29 T.L.R. 592.

[20] Copyright, Designs and Patents Act, 1988, s.84, which specifically gives a cause of action for false attribution of authorship.

[21] *Byron v. Johnston* (1816) 2 Mer. 29. As Pollock said (R.R. Vol. 16, Preface, v): "Lord Eldon has been often called hard names (unduly, as most lawyers think) for depriving Shelley of the custody of his truly begotten children: I am not aware that the world of letters has ever given him due credit for helping Byron to repudiate the spurious offspring which some pirate bookseller sought to father on him."

[22] This may be on the verge of recognition as a distinct tort: see Frazer, "Appropriation of Personality—A New Tort" (1983) 99 L.Q.R. 281.

[23] See below, § 18.11.

[24] See the Copyright, Designs and Patents Act 1988, ss.83–84.

[25] The law up to 1981 is exhaustively reviewed in *Breach of Confidence* (Law Com. No. 110). Later developments are surveyed by The Hon. Mr Justice Scott, "Developments in the Law of Confidentiality" [1990] Denning L.J. 77. In the UK the litigation arising out of the publication of Peter Wright's *Spycatcher* culminated in *Att.-Gen v. Guardian Newspapers Ltd (No. 2)* [1990] A.C. 109 (hereafter *Spycatcher*). The many *Spycatcher* judgments in other jurisdictions are conveniently collected in [1988] 2 F.S.R. 1, and reviewed in Gareth Jones, "Breach of Confidence after Spycatcher" [1989] C.L.P. 49.

[26] Normally the information will have been supplied by the confider to the confidant, but in *Argyll v. Argyll* [1967] Ch. 302 the duke's knowledge of the duchess's extra-marital behaviour seems to have been acquired by observation or inference.

[27] See *Faccenda Chicken Ltd. v. Fowler* [1987] Ch. 117.

as the law is developing very rapidly. But marital[28] or other inter-personal relationships[29] are included, as are the secrets of the security services,[30] or the relationship of doctor and patient.[31] But the obligation does not cover criminal or immoral information,[32] or, conversely, information which is trivial or already in the public domain.[33]

Normally the obligation will have been breached by the confidant, but the court can, as it were, trace the breach of confidence into the mind of a third party who has acquired the information with notice of its confidential character.[34] Sometimes the court may have to balance the plaintiff's interest in protecting his commercial secrets as against the defendant's interest in exercising the right of free speech.

(3) Abuse of governmental powers[35]

Today the wrongful exercise of power by an official of the central or local administration can cause harm to a citizen in a way or on a scale which would not be possible for a private defendant. But a citizen so aggrieved cannot recover compensation by the public law remedy of judicial review. Damages can be recovered by the tort which in England has the clumsy title of misfeasance in a public office.[36] The tort is well-established and its existence justifiable in principle.[37]

The tort is committed when damage is caused to the plaintiff by the malicious exercise of power by a public servant[38] or corporation.[39] The plaintiff must prove that the defendant knew he was acting *ultra vires* or maliciously, otherwise every property owner damaged by an invalid planning resolution could sue.[40] Although malice alone is not a suf-

---

[28] An in *Argyll* v. *Argyll* [1967] Ch. 302.

[29] As in *Stephens* v. *Avery* [1988] Ch. 449.

[30] As in *Spycatcher*.

[31] As in *W.* v. *Egdell* [1990] Ch. 359.

[32] It would be indefensible if A could say to B, "This is confidential: I'm going to kill my wife," and then seek an injunction to restrain B from disclosing the information to the authorities. This used to be known as the defence of iniquity.

[33] As in *Spycatcher*.

[34] So as "to include certain situations—beloved of law teachers—where an obviously confidential document is wafted by an electric fan out of a window into a crowded street": *Spycatcher* [1990] A.C. 109, 201, *per* Lord Goff.

[35] See Wade, *Administrative Law* (6th ed., 1988), pp. 779–784.

[36] In Scotland it is called simply the deliberate abuse of statutory powers: *The Mihalis* [1984] 2 Lloyd's Rep. 525.

[37] "The assumptions of honour and disinterest on which the tort of misfeasance in a public office are founded are deeply rooted in the polity of a free society . . . It ought to be unthinkable that the holder of an office of government in this country would exercise a power thus vested in him with the object of injuring a member of that public by whose trust alone that office is enjoyed": *Jones* v. *Swansea City Council* [1990] 1 W.L.R. 54, 85, *per* Nourse L.J. The lengthy judgment of the H.L. turns, exceptionally, on issues of fact, but supports the statements of the law in the C.A.: see [1990] 1 W.L.R. 1453, 1458.

[38] As in *Bourgoin* v. *Ministry of Agriculture* [1986] Q.B. 716.

[39] As in *Jones* v. *Swansea City Council* [1990[1 W.L.R. 1453, in which the power alleged to have been misused was contractual and not statutory. But this was irrelevant: the vital factor was the nature of the office, not the nature of the power.

[40] So the plaintiff failed in *Dunlop* v. *Woollahra Municipal Council* [1982] A.C. 158.

ficient basis for the action,[41] the plaintiff need not prove "targeted malice,"—*i.e.*, an improper motive specifically aimed at the plaintiff.[42]

(4) Infringement of a status

In the modern world a person may suffer serious loss by reason of his expulsion from a trade union or trade association, or the revocation of a licence which is necessary to carry on his trade or profession. The courts are aware of the problem, and over the past few decades there has been a marked trend towards shielding the employee from undue hardships suffered at the hands of those who have power over his livelihood.[43] Therefore on occasion the remedies of damages or injunction or declaratory judgment are available[44] for an improper expulsion in breach of the principles of justice and fairness, even if the rules of the union purport to give an unfettered power of expulsion.[45] Yet no action is given for a refusal to admit to membership, however unreasonable and however productive of loss to the plaintiff,[46] unless perhaps the refusal is by a self-appointed body with a monopoly in that trade or profession. But the Employment Act 1990, s.1 provides that a refusal of employment on grounds related to union membership is unlawful. The remedy is complaint to an industrial tribunal. There may also be remedies for discrimination on the grounds of race or sex under the Race Relations Act 1976, s.57(1) or the Sex Discrimination Act 1975, s.66(1). As damages may be awarded under these sections, there is in effect a statutory tort.[47]

(5) Innominate Torts[48]

Jurists of the eminence of Lord Bowen,[49] Sir Frederick Pollock,[50] and Lord Devlin[51] have suggested that the intentional infliction of temporal damage gives rise to a prima facie cause of action which requires some justification by the defendant if he is to escape liability. In the United States this is called the prima facie tort doctrine.[52] In England the preferred phrase is "innominate torts,"[53] although there has been reluc-

---

[41] *McDonagh* v. *Metropolitan Police Commissioner* [1990] C.L. 400.

[42] *Bourgoin* v. *Ministry of Agriculture* [1986] Q.B. 716, 732.

[43] *Hill* v. *Parsons (C.A.) & Co. Ltd.* [1972] Ch. 305.

[44] *Bonsor* v. *Musicians' Union* [1956] A.C. 105; *Vine* v. *National Dock Labour Board* [1957] A.C. 488.

[45] *Faramus* v. *Film Artistes' Association* [1964] A.C. 925.

[46] *Nagle* v. *Feilden* [1966] 2 Q.B. 633.

[47] *Alexander* v. *Home Office* [1988] 1 W.L.R. 968, 975.

[48] See Cane, "Justice and Justifications for Tort Liability" (1982) 2 Ox.Jo. Legal Stud. 30; Elias and Wallington, "Economic Torts and Labour Law" [1982] C.L.J. 321; Fridman, "The Unmysterious Law of Torts" (1985) 34 Univ. of New Brunswick L.J. 13.

[49] In *Mogul Steamship Co.* v. *McGregor, Gow, & Co.* (1889) 23 Q.B.D. 598, 613.

[50] *The Law of Torts* (15th ed., 1951) pp. 17–18.

[51] Judicially in *Rookes* v. *Barnard* [1964] A.C. 1129, 1216; extra-judicially in *Samples of Law-making* (Oxford, 1962), pp. 11–13.

[52] See the full discussion in Fowler, James and Gray, *Torts* (2nd ed., 1986) §6.4.

[53] See the pleadings in *British Airways Board* v. *Laker Airways* set out in [1984] 1 Q.B. 142, 208, and the judgments in *Dunlop* v. *Woollahra Municipal Council* [1982] A.C. 158, 170, and *Lonrho* v. *Shell Petroleum Ltd.* [1982] A.C. 173, 187–188.

tance on the part of English judges to recognise such a concept, principle or doctrine.[54] This is partly due to an English inability to produce satisfactory generalisations and also partly to the decision of the House of Lords in *Allen* v. *Flood*,[55] which requires that the plaintiff must prove an unlawful act, and not just intention or malice, on the part of the defendant. So the right to make a take-over bid is not a legally protected asset.[56] But it is precedent and not some inherent common law principle which prevents the recognition of the doctrine.[57] If it had been judicially accepted, much of the complex legislation on racial and sexual discrimination would have been unnecessary. The courts would have been provided with a strong yet flexible weapon against outrageous conduct.

It must be conceded that there are authoritative dicta in the House of Lords[58] and the Court of Appeal[59] against the existence of innominate torts. Yet a court which was minded to distinguish these cases could find grounds for doing so without too much difficulty.[60] Finally, appellate tribunals in New Zealand[61] and Canada[62] have recognised that innominate torts exist.

(6) Eurotorts

Under Articles 85 and 86 of the Treaty of Rome conduct constituting undue restriction of competition and abuse of dominant position may be a tort in England, for which damages and not merely a declaration or injunction can be obtained.[63] But an embargo on the importation of goods contrary to Article 30 does not give rise to a remedy in damages, but a right to a declaration or judicial review, as Article 30 is concerned with the discretionary powers of public authorities, and in England no action lies for abuse of such a power unless bad faith is proved.[64] But apparently no such restriction is imposed on a claim for damages for

---

[54] As Fleming comments, "Modest as this may be by the standards of some legal systems accustomed to broad Code formulations, it has yet proved too ambitious for the common law": *Introduction to the Law of Torts* (2nd ed., 1986, p. 214).

[55] [1898] A.C. 1. See below, § 15.1.

[56] *Lonrho plc* v. *Fayed* [1990] 1 Q.B. 490.

[57] There are a number of grounds on which *Allen* v. *Flood* might be distinguished—*e.g.* that the final decision was that of a minority of the judges who heard the case.

[58] Three of them are by Lord Diplock: *Dunlop* v. *Woollahra Municipal Council* [1982] A.C. 158, 170, *Lonrho* v. *Shell Petroleum Ltd.* [1982] A.C. 173, 187–188; *British Airways Board* v. *Laker Airways* [1985] A.C. 58, 79–80. Yet the same Law Lord conceded that there was a new generic economic tort of causing loss by unlawful means: *Merkur Island Shipping Corporation* v. *Laughton* [1983] 2 A.C. 570, 609–610.

[59] *Bourgoin S.A.* v. *Ministry of Agriculture* [1986] Q.B. 775, 777–778, 1075.

[60] *e.g.* in *Woollhara* there was no positive and unlawful trespassory act; in *Lonrho* the acts had that character, but were not aimed at the plaintiff; and in *Laker* and *Bourgoin* there were non-English factors in the litigation.

[61] *Van Camp Chocolates* v. *Aulsebrooks* [1984] 1 N.Z.L.R. 354.

[62] *Canada Safeway* v. *Manitoba Food and Commercial Workers Union Local 832* (1981) 25 C.C.L.T. 1, 10.

[63] *Garden Cottage Foods Ltd.* v. *Milk Marketing Board* [1984] A.C. 130, 141, 144.

[64] *Bourgoin S.A.* v. *Ministry of Agriculture* [1986] Q.B. 716.

breach of a Council Directive imposing a duty on a public body providing a public service under the control of the state.[65]

§ 3.2. PROVINCE AND FUNCTION OF TORTS

Some conclusions are now possible. First, the law of torts is not a static
body of rules, but is capable of alteration to meet the needs of a changing society. Usually such an alteration takes the form of an expansion of
liability, especially within the tort of negligence. But social needs may
require contraction as well as expansion.[66] It may even be necessary to
reverse a process of expansion, as when the House of Lords in *Murphy*
v. *Brentwood District Council*[67] refused to follow a previous decision of
its own[68] which had led to an unacceptably large number of claims
against local authorities and builders. For the expansion of liability may
lead to an undesirable diversification of social resources—doctors may
feel obliged to take unnecessary X-rays ("defensive medicine"), and
builders may pour concrete into foundations on an extravagant scale.[69]
So the courts have been justified in refusing to introduce new heads of
tortious liability to enable a witness to be sued for perjury,[70] or conspiracy to defame.[71] Equally Parliament was justified when it used three
words ("Detinue is abolished") in section 5(2)(i) of the Torts (Interference with Goods) Act 1977 to abolish a tort which had existed for six
centuries.[72] Again a tort may be invented or discovered only to have
little use made of it. So for a century little has been heard of the action[73]
for excluding the plaintiff from a public office to which he is legally
entitled.

Secondly, it is not possible to find a general formula or criterion
which will at once explain all the cases in which liability has been
imposed in the past and also furnish a guide for the decision of doubtful cases in the future. If reasonable foresight was ever believed to provide such a criterion, that belief has now been abandoned.[74] There must
also be abandoned, for the present, in England, the belief that damage-
causing conduct which is unlawful, intentional and positive automatically gives rise to liability.[75] It is now recognised that the decision of a
court to impose liability in tort may be influenced by a number of factors, of which one or more may be of decisive importance in the particu-

---

[65] *Foster* v. *British Gas plc* [1991] 2 W.L.R. 258.
[66] *Gallagher* v. *McDowell Ltd.* [1961] N.I. 26, 44.
[67] [1991] 1 A.C. 398.
[68] *Anns* v. *Merton London Borough Council* [1978] A.C. 728.
[69] For this problem of "overkill," see *Caparo Industries plc* v. *Dickman* [1990] 1 A.C. 605,
616, 618, 633; *Murphy* v. *Brentwood District Council* [1991] 1 A.C. 398, 472.
[70] *Hargreaves* v. *Bretherton* [1959] 1 Q.B. 45.
[71] *Marrinan* v. *Vibart* [1963] 1 Q.B. 528.
[72] "It is not every day that the Lord Chancellor can have the pleasure of abolishing a tort":
378 H.L. col. 1060, *per* Lord Elwyn-Jones.
[73] Recognised in *Lawlor* v. *Alton* (1873) 8 Ir.Rep.C.L. 160. But in *Stoke-on-Trent City Council*
v. *W. J. Wass Ltd.* [1988] 1 W.L.R. 1406 the forgotten medieval tort of levying a rival market was revived.
[74] See below, § 9.3.
[75] See above, § 3.2.

lar case, and that the most profitable inquiry is likely to be into the nature and significance of these factors. The Law Lords have shown themselves increasingly ready and willing to state and assess the various considerations of principle or public policy which influence them in marginal cases.[76] Still, too much reliance should not be placed on isolated dicta[77]: the common law is shaped as much by the way it is practised as by dicta.[78]

Thirdly, it should be remembered that other factors besides the value of the plaintiff's interest and the nature of the defendant's conduct may be relevant. We have already had examples of four such factors: (i) historical development; (ii) vengeance; (iii) deterrence; (iv) ability to bear the loss. A fifth factor is the economic and social background of the case.[79] "In the end one is left in the slack water of first principles."[80]

---

[76] See, e.g. Dorset Yacht Co. Ltd. v. Home Office [1970] A.C. 1104; McLoughlin v. O'Brian [1983] 1 A.C. 410.
[77] West (Richard) and Partners Ltd. v. Dick [1969] 2 Ch. 424, 431–432.
[78] Jayasena v. R. [1970] A.C. 618, 625.
[79] As in Murphy v. Brentwood District Council [1991] 1 A.C. 398, 472, 482 (consumer protection best left to Parliament).
[80] Gunton v. Richmond London Borough Council [1982] Ch. 448, 460, per Shaw L.J.

CHAPTER 4

TRESPASS TO LAND

§ 4.1. The Nature of Trespass to Land

The tort of trespass to land (trespass *quare clausum fregit*) consists in the act of (1) entering upon land in the possession of the plaintiff, or (2) remaining upon such land, or (3) placing or projecting any object upon it—in each case without lawful justification.[1]

(1) Trespass by wrongful entry

The commonest form of trespass consists in a personal entry by the defendant, or by some other person or animal,[2] through his procurement, into land or buildings occupied by the plaintiff. The slightest crossing of the boundary is sufficient—*e.g.* to put one's hand through a window, or to sit upon a fence. Nor, indeed, does it seem essential that there should be any crossing of the boundary at all, provided that there is some physical contact with the plaintiff's property.[3] There may be sufficient physical interference if matter is deliberately placed where natural forces will carry it to the land of the plaintiff—*e.g.* if oil is jettisoned in such circumstances that wind and wave must carry it to the foreshore of the plaintiff.[4] The courts have taken account of scientific developments, and the matter constituting a trespass probably need not be tangible—it may be a gas.[5] But depriving an occupier of facilites—*e.g.* gas and electricity—without interfering with his possession is not a trespass[6] or statutory tort, as distinct from a breach of contract.[7]

Trespass to land, like all other forms of trespass, is actionable *per se* without any proof of damage.[8] "Every invasion of property, be it ever so minute, is a trespass."[9] These principles have been part of English law for centuries. So the fundamental right of privacy of the home has

---

[1] *Barker* v. *The Queen* (1983) 153 C.L.R. 338, 356.

[2] *League Against Cruel Sports* v. *Scott* [1986] Q.B. 240 (dog). But not a bee: *Tutton* v. *Walter Ltd.* [1986] Q.B. 61.

[3] *Gregory* v. *Piper* (1829) 9 B. & C. 591. ("If a single stone had been put against the wall it would have been sufficient.")

[4] *Southport Corporation* v. *Esso Petroleum Ltd.* [1953] 3 W.L.R. 773, 776–777 (Devlin J.); [1954] 2 Q.B. 182, 204 (Morris L.J.); *contra*, [1954] 2 Q.B. 182, 195 (Denning L.J.); [1956] A.C. 242, 244 (Lords Radcliffe and Tucker).

[5] *McDonald* v. *Associated Fuels* [1954] 3 D.L.R. 775.

[6] *Perera* v. *Vandiyar* [1953] 1 W.L.R. 672.

[7] *McCall* v. *Abelesz* [1976] Q.B. 585.

[8] *Ashby* v. *White* (1703) 2 Ld.Raym, 938. But in criminal law actual damage must be shown for a prosecution to succeed under the Criminal Damage Act 1971. Hence the notice "Trespassers will be Prosecuted" is "a wooden falsehood": Maitland, *Justice and Police* (1883), p. 13. But there may be a conviction under the Criminal Law Act 1977: see below, Chap. 26.

[9] *Entick* v. *Carrington* (1765) 19 St.Tr. 1029, 1066.

been re-asserted by the House of Lords.[10] If the entry is intentional, in the sense of being a voluntary act, it is actionable[11] even though made under a mistake and though the defendant honestly believed that the land was his own or that he had a right of entry on it. There is no foundation for the assumption that a man cannot be a trespasser unless he knows he is one.[12] An action of trespass may also be used to determine a disputed title to land, though today a declaratory judgment may be preferred.[13]

Accidental trespasses

Whether an accidental as opposed to a mistaken entry is actionable was once open to doubt. The Statute of Limitations 1623, s.5, enacts that in all actions of trespass *quare clausum fregit* the defendant may plead a disclaimer of any title or claim to the land, that the trespass was by negligence or involuntary, and a tender or offer of sufficient amends before action brought, in which case the plaintiff is barred of his action. This seems to imply that an involuntary trespass is actionable if no amends are tendered. But the better view is that it might be a good defence to prove that the trespass was accidental and involuntary, for example, trespass by one's dog.[14] As it now seems settled that inevitable accident is a defence in actions of trespass to the person and to chattels[15] it would be strange if a different rule governed trespass to land.[16]

Statutory rights of entry

It must not be forgotten that many modern statutes confer a right of entry upon private property,[17] in addition to the older common law powers of entry. Thus the National Parks and Access to the Countryside Act 1949, s.60, provides that "where an access agreement or order is in force as respects any land a person who enters upon land comprised in the agreement or order for the purpose of open-air recreation without breaking or damaging any wall, fence, hedge or gate, or who is on such land for that purpose after having so entered thereon, shall not be treated as a trespasser on that land or incur any other liability by reason only of so entering or being on the land."[18] The Law Commission has recommended that landowners should have a statutory right of access

---

[10] *Morris* v. *Beardmore* [1981] A.C. 446.

[11] But not necessarily a criminal entry "as a trespasser" under the Theft Act 1968, s.9(1): *R.* v. *Collins* [1973] Q.B. 100.

[12] *Conway* v. *Wimpey & Co. (No. 2)* [1951] 2 K.B. 266, 273.

[13] *Acton B.C.* v. *Morris* [1983] 1 W.L.R. 1228.

[14] *League Against Cruel Sports* v. *Scott* [1986] Q.B. 240, 251. So it is not necessary to obtain the occupier's permission to enter to recover a hat which has blown over a fence: *Halliday* v. *Nevill* (1984) 155 C.L.R. 1, 7–8 ("the law must not be seen to be an ass").

[15] *National Coal Board* v. *Evans (J.E.) & Co. Ltd.* [1951] 2 K.B. 861, discussed below, § 7.4.

[16] *Mann* v. *Saulnier* (1959) 19 D.L.R. (2d) 130, 132.

[17] Below, § 11.7.

[18] Such a person may, however, incur liability if he fails to observe any of the 15 restrictions on user set out in the Second Schedule to the Act, or any restriction contained in the access agreement or order itself.

to neighbouring land to do work on their own property.[19] Again the Transport Act 1981, s.25(1) gives a constable power to enter, "if need be, by force" any place where a person suspected of a drink-driving offence may be. Finally, the Police and Criminal Evidence Act 1984, ss.17–18 gives wide powers of entry to effect an arrest, or a search after arrest.

Trespass by abuse of right of entry: highways

Even he who has a right of entry on the land of another for a specific purpose commits a trespass if he enters for any other purpose[20] or under any other claim or title apart from that under which he might lawfully enter.[21] The chief application of this rule is the abuse of a right of way, public or private; but presumably the same principle applies to all rights of entry—for example, to one given by a contract or licence containing conditions[22]—*e.g.* that the entrant should not take photographs. So far as abuse of a right of way is concerned, a public highway is a piece of land vested either in some local authority or in the adjoining landowners and subject to a public right of way. The law vests in the highway authority the top spit, "or perhaps, I should say, the top two spits,"[23] of the road for a legal estate in fee simple determinable on its ceasing to be a highway. Any person who uses a highway for any purpose other than that of passage (including the subordinate purposes reasonably and ordinarily incident to passage, such as sitting down to rest[24] or to photograph or to sketch[25]) becomes a trespasser against the owner[26] of the subsoil.[27] Thus it is a trespass to depasture one's cattle on the highway,[28] or to go there for the purpose of interfering with the adjoining occupier's right of shooting[29] or of persistently watching what is being done on the adjoining land,[30] or of picketing premises,[31]

---

[19] See Working Paper No. 78 (1980).

[20] So a surreptitious entry with T.V. equipment into a bar to check whether short measure is being given may be a trespass: *Savoy Hotel* v. *B.B.C.* (1983) 133 N.L.J. 105.

[21] *Purtill* v. *Athlone U.D.C.* [1968] I.R. 205, 210. See also below, §11.8.

[22] *Barker* v. *The Queen* (1983) 153 C.L.R. 338, and the cases on trespass *ab initio*, below, § 4.5.

[23] *Tithe Redemption Commission* v. *Runcorn U.D.C.* [1954] Ch. 383, 407, *per* Denning L.J.

[24] Or parking a car for some temporary and limited purpose: *Rodgers* v. *Ministry of Transport* [1952] 1 T.L.R. 625; *Randall* v. *Tarrant* [1955] 1 W.L.R. 255.

[25] See *Lincoln Hunt (Aust.) Pty.* v. *Willesee* [1986] N.S.W.R. 457, 462. "I may stoop to tie up my shoe-lace, but I may not occupy a pitch and invite people to come upon it and have their hair cut": *Iveagh* v. *Martin* [1961] 1 Q.B. 232, 273, *per* Paull J.

[26] But it does not follow that other persons using the highway are thereby relieved of any duty to take reasonable care for the trespasser's safety: *Farrugia* v. *G.W. Ry.* [1947] 2 All E.R. 565. Yet see *Young* v. *Edward Box Ltd.* [1951] 1 T.L.R. 789, 793.

[27] *Hickman* v. *Maisey* [1900] 1 Q.B. 752.

[28] *Dovaston* v. *Payne* (1795) 2 H.Bl. 527.

[29] *Harrison* v. *Rutland (Duke of)* [1893] 1 Q.B. 142.

[30] *Hickman* v. *Maisey* [1990] 1 Q.B. 752. It does not seem that the defendant in this case (unlike *Harrison* v. *Rutland*) owned the subsoil of the highway. Cf. *The Carlgarth* [1927] P. 93, 107–108, where Scrutton L.J. said: "There is no right to sit in the middle of a road and say one is exercising a right to use a public roadway."

[31] *Hubbard* v. *Pitt* [1976] Q.B. 142.

unless protected by the Trade Union and Labour Relations Act 1974, s.15.[32]

So it is a trespass to put down permanent moorings in tidal waters.[33] Again it is a trespass against the Crown to use the foreshore for the purpose of bathing in the sea, for the only right of the public on the foreshore is the right to pass over it in boats when it is covered by water for the purposes of fishing[34] and navigating. The public have no general right of way along the foreshore.[35] It is not necessary that the thing so done in abuse of the right of entry should be the cause of any harm to the occupier of the land or to anyone else. It is enough that it falls outside the purpose for which the right is conferred. But if the act done on the land is within that purpose, it does not matter what ulterior object the defendant may have in exercising his right of entry. Thus it is not a trespass to walk along a highway with the object of committing a crime elsewhere.[36] Moreover, even a wrongful act done upon the land itself does not make the defendant a trespasser within the present rule, unless it can be shown that he entered for that purpose. If he entered for a lawful purpose, he is no trespasser unless the case is one to which the doctrine of trespass *ab initio* applies.[37]

(2) Trespass by remaining on land

Even a person who has lawfully entered on land in the possession of another commits a trespass if he remains there after his right of entry has ceased. To refuse or omit to leave the plaintiff's land or vehicle[38] is as much a trespass as to enter originally without a right. Thus any person who is present by the leave and licence of the occupier may, as a general rule, when the licence has been properly terminated, be sued or ejected as a trespasser, if after request and after the lapse of a reasonable time he fails to leave the premises.[39] A reasonable degree of force may be used to control the movements of a trespasser or to eject him.[40] This must be distinguished from the case of a person lawfully in possession of land who refuses or omits to give it up on the termination of his lease or other interest. A lessee holding over is no trespasser until demand made; for a trespass can be committed, as we shall see, only against the person in the present possession of the property.[41]

---

[32] For this, see below, §17.1.

[33] *Fowley Marine Ltd.* v. *Gafford* [1967] 2 Q.B. 808, 823 (not challenged on appeal in [1968] 2 Q.B. 618).

[34] *Beckett Ltd.* v. *Lyons* [1967] Ch. 449.

[35] *Blundell* v. *Catterall* (1821) 5 B. & Ald. 268; *Brinckman* v. *Matley* [1904] 2 Ch. 313, 323 (in which Vaughan Williams L.J. observed that the judgment of Holroyd J. in *Blundell* v. *Catterall* "has come to be regarded as one of the finest examples we have of the way in which the judgment of an English judge ought to be expressed, and the reasons for it given").

[36] *Harrison* v. *Rutland (Duke of)* [1893] 1 Q.B. 142, 158.

[37] *Hickman* v. *Maisey* [1990] 1 Q.B. 752, 757. See § 4.5.

[38] *C.P.R.* v. *Gaud* [1949] 2 K.B. 239 (ship).

[39] *Cottreau* v. *Rodgerson* (1966) 53 D.L.R. (2d) 549, 557. *Cullen* v. *Rice* (1981) 120 D.L.R. (3d) 641, 644.

[40] See below, § 7.4.

[41] *Hey* v. *Moorhouse* (1839) 6 Bing.N.C. 52.

(3) Trespass by placing things on land

It is a trespass to place any thing upon the plaintiff's land,[42] or to cause any physical object or noxious substance[43] to cross the boundary of the plaintiff's land, or even simply to come into physical contact with the land, though there may be no crossing of the boundary: for example, to cause a Virginia creeper to grow upon it,[44] or to lean a ladder, planks or a shed, or to pile rubbish against it.[45]

Trespass and nuisance

In all such cases, in order to be actionable as a trespass, the injury must be direct, within the meaning of the distinction between direct and consequential injuries which has been already explained as determining the line between trespass and case.[46] It is a trespass, and therefore actionable *per se*, directly to place material objects upon another's land; it is not a trespass, but at the most a nuisance or other wrong actionable only on proof of damage, to do an act which consequentially results in the entry of such objects. To throw stones upon one's neighbour's premises is the wrong of trespass; to allow stones from a ruinous chimney to fall upon those premises is the wrong of nuisance.[47]

§ 4.2. CONTINUING TRESPASSES

That trespass by way of personal entry is a continuing injury, lasting as long as the personal presence of the wrongdoer, and giving rise to actions *de die in diem* so long as it lasts, is sufficiently obvious.[48] It is well settled, however, that the same characteristic belongs in law even to those trespasses which consist in placing things upon the plaintiff's land. Such a trespass continues until it has been abated by the removal of the thing which is thus trespassing; successive actions will lie from day to day until it is so removed: and in each action damages (unless awarded in lieu of an injunction)[49] are assessed only up to the date of the action.[50] Whether this doctrine is either logical or convenient may be a question, but it has been repeatedly decided to be the law.[51] It seems that, if things are placed on land under leave and licence and are not removed within a reasonable time after the licence is withdrawn, a continuing trespass is committed.[52] These cases of continuing trespass must be distinguished from cases of the continuing consequences of

---

[42] *Turner* v. *Thorne* (1960) 21 D.L.R. (2d) 29 (parcels delivered in error).

[43] *McDonald* v. *Associated Fuels* [1954] 3 D.L.R. 775 (blowing carbon monoxide into a house is a trespass).

[44] *Simpson* v. *Weber* (1925) 41 T.L.R. 302.

[45] *Westripp* v. *Baldock* [1939] 1 All E.R. 279.

[46] See above, § 1.2.

[47] *Mann* v. *Saulnier* (1959) 19 D.L.R. (2d) 130, 132.

[48] *Winterbourne* v. *Morgan* (1809) 11 East 395, 405.

[49] *Masters* v. *Brent B.C.* [1978] Q.B. 841.

[50] Below, § 25.1.

[51] *Bowyer* v. *Cooke* (1847) 4 C.B. 236.

[52] *Konskier* v. *B Goodman & Co. Ltd.* [1928] 1 K.B. 421. Compare the case of persons entering under licence: below § 5.9.

trespass which is over and done with. If I trespass on another's land, and make an excavation there without leaving any rubbish on the land, the trespass ceases as soon as I leave the land and does not continue until I have filled the excavation up again. Consequently only one action will lie, and in it full damages are recoverable for both the past and the future.[53]

§ 4.3. TRESPASS BENEATH AND ABOVE THE SURFACE[54]

In general he who owns or possesses the surface of land owns or possesses all the underlying *strata* also.[55] Any entry beneath the surface, therefore, at whatever depth, is an actionable trespass.[56] It is commonly said that the ownership and possession of land bring with them the ownership and possession of the column of space above the surface *ad infinitum. Cujus est solum, ejus est usque ad coelum et usque ad inferos.*[57] This is true to this extent, that the owner of the land has in private law the right to use for his own purposes, to the exclusion of all other persons, the air-space above it. Thus he may cut the overhanging branches of a tree growing in his neighbour's land, whether they do him harm or not[58]; yet he has no right of action against the owner of the tree unless he can show actual damage.[59] So he may cut and remove an unauthorised telegraph or other electric wire stretched through the air above his land, at whatever height it may be, and whether he can show that he suffers any harm or inconvenience from it or not.[60] So an injunction can be obtained against the passage of a hammer-head crane through the plaintiff's airspace. Such an "over-sailing" is prima facie a wrong to property remediable by injunction: there is no question of balancing interests, as there may be with intrusions by aircraft.[61]

All entries actionable?

It ought not to follow from this that any entry above the surface is in itself an actionable trespass. Salmond thought[62] that such an extension of the rights of a landowner would be an unreasonable restriction of the right of the public to the use of the atmospheric space above the earth's surface. It would make it an actionable wrong to fly a kite, or send a message by a carrier pigeon, or ascent in an aeroplane, or fire a bullet

---

[53] *Clegg* v. *Dearden* (1848) 12 Q.B. 576.

[54] Wilkinson, "Trespass to Air-Space" (1985) 138 L.J. 161.

[55] *Corbett* v. *Hill* (1870) L.R. 9, Eq. 671, 673.

[56] *Willcox* v. *Kettel* [1937] 1 All E.R. 222 (intrusion of concrete foundation by 20 inches a trespass).

[57] *Corbett* v. *Hill* (1870) L.R. 9 Eq. 671, 673. "Law makes long spokes of the short stakes of men," was the comment of the poet William Empson: *Cambridge Poetry* (1929). But "So sweeping, unscientific and unpractical a doctrine is unlikely to appeal to the common law mind": *Commissioner for Railways* v. *Valuer-General* [1974] A.C. 328, 351, *per* Lord Wilberforce.

[58] *Lemmon* v. *Webb* [1895] A.C. 1.

[59] *Smith* v. *Giddy* [1904] 2 K.B. 448. Below, § 26.3.

[60] *Wandsworth Board of Works* v. *United Telephone Co.* (1884) 13 Q.B.D. 904, 927.

[61] *Anchor Brewhouse Developments Ltd.* v. *Berkley House Ltd.* [1987] 2 E.G.L.R. 173.

[62] 6th ed., p. 226.

across it,[63] even in cases where no actual or probably damage, danger, or inconvenience could be proved by the subjacent landowners. In his submission there could be no trespass without some physical contact with the land (including, of course, buildings, trees, and othe things attached to the soil), and a mere entry into the air-space above the land was not an actionable wrong unless it caused some harm, danger, or inconvenience to the occupier of the surface, when there was a cause of action in the nature of nuisance. Salmond's view received strong support in a case in which the plaintiff unsuccessfully alleged that an intrusion for the purpose of aerial photography was an actionable trespass.[64] So a sensible distinction is now drawn between temporary intrusions at a high level, and more permanent intrusions at a low level.[65] So it has been held that a direct infringement of the air-space over another man's land by a structure attached to the adjoining land is a trespass, so that the owner of a one-storey shop was entitled to a mandatory injunction requiring the removal of an advertising sign protruding by no more than eight inches into the super-incumbent column of air-space.[66] But in that case the sign was at a height at which it might have interfered with the owner's use of his land, and so there was no need to balance the respective interests of the parties.[67]

Aircraft, spacecraft and weather

In respect of aeroplanes and other aircraft this matter is now dealt with by statute. By section 76 of the Civil Aviation Act 1982 it is provided that "no action shall lie in respect of trespass or in respect of nuisance, by reason only of the flight of an aircraft over any property at a height above the ground, which, having regard to wind, weather and all the circumstances of the case, is reasonable, or the ordinary incidents of such flight,[68] so long as" certain provisions of the Act or any orders made hereunder are observed. The Act does not expressly exclude the possibility of damages being recovered for such an invasion of privacy as aerial photography of one's house.[69] The same section of the same Act, however, makes the owner of aircraft liable for all material loss or damage caused by it, or by a person in, or by an article or person falling from it, while in flight, taking off,[70] or landing, whether to person or property, "without proof of negligence or intention or other cause of

---

[63] As in the Tasmanian cat case (*Davies* v. *Bennison* (1927) 22 Tas.L.R. 52) in which the defendant shot a cat on the plaintiff's roof. The plaintiff was held entitled to damages for trespass to land as well as for the value of the cat.

[64] *Bernstein* v. *Skyviews Ltd.* [1978] Q.B. 479, 487, which contains a full review of the authorities.

[65] *Anchor Brewhouse Developments Ltd.* v. *Berkley House Ltd.* [1987] 2 E.G.L.R. 173, which also makes the point that the court should not in effect enable the defendant to expropriate the plaintiff by suspending the injunction. A similar decision is *Didow* v. *Alberta Power Ltd.* (1988) 45 C.C.L.T. 23.

[66] *Kelsen* v. *Imperial Tobacco Co. Ltd.* [1957] 2 Q.B. 334.

[67] *Anchor Brewhouse Developments Ltd.* v. *Berkley House Ltd.* [1987] 2 E.G.L.R. 173.

[68] In short, the Act gives legislative force to Salmond's view, but this implies that the common law did not adopt that view.

[69] Cmnd. 5012 (1972), para. 396.

[70] See *Blankley* v. *Godley* [1952] 1 All E.R. 436n.

action, as if the loss or damage had been caused by the wilful act, neglect, or default of the owner of the aircraft," except where there is contributory negligence, and gives the owner a right of action over against the person whose negligence actually caused the damage.

Liability for damage done by spacecraft is governed by international law, which recognises strict liability.[71]

§ 4.4. THE TITLE OF THE PLAINTIFF

A trespass is actionable only at the suit of him who is in possession of the land, using the word possession in its strict sense as including a person entitled to immediate and exclusive possession.[72] Actual entry by the true owner is not necessary to enable him to bring trespass, for as against a wrongdoer the slightest acts indicating an intention to regain or obtain possession,[73] by the person having title, or his predecessors, will be sufficient.[74] Where it is uncertain which of several claimants has possession, it will be adjudged to be in him who can prove title, *i.e.* the right to possess.[75] This may seem hard on a plaintiff who can show considerable actual use of the premises, but whose paper title is defective, unless the court can interpret the acts done by the party or parties not having the paper title as not amounting to the assertion of a possessory right.[76] This tort is essetially a violation of the right of possession, not of the right of property. Ownership unaccompanied by possession is protected by other remedies.[77] Thus a landlord cannot sue for a mere trespass to land in the occupation of his tenant; such an action can be brought only by the tenant.[78] The landlord has no right of action unless he can prove more than a mere trespass—*viz.* actual harm done to the property, of such sort as to affect the value of his reversionary interest in it.

For the same reason the mere use of land, without the exclusive possession of it, is not a sufficient title to found an action of trespass for the disturbance of that use. Thus, in general a lodger or boarder has no possession of the room in which he is lodged, and cannot sue in trespass for any disturbance of his use of it.[79] So also with the use of a seat in a theatre or a railway carriage[80] or the use of a bed in a hospital.[81] Whether a person having thus the use of land without the possession of it has any remedy at all against a stranger who disturbs him is a ques-

---

[71] See the 1972 Convention on Liability for Space Objects. Liability for damage caused by weather modification is fully discussed by Heilbronn in (1979) 6 Mon.L.R. 122.

[72] *Thompson* v. *Ward* [1953] 2 Q.B. 153, 158–159.

[73] *Ocean Estates Ltd.* v. *Pinder* [1969] 2 A.C. 19.

[74] *Portland Managements Ltd.* v. *Harte* [1977] Q.B. 306.

[75] *Hegan* v. *Carolan* [1916] 2 I.R. 27.

[76] *Fowley Marine (Emsworth) Ltd.* v. *Gafford* [1968] 2 Q.B. 618.

[77] *Wallis* v. *Hands* [1893] 2 Ch. 75.

[78] *Attersoll* v. *Stevens* (1808) 1 Taunt. 183, 190.

[79] *Allan* v. *Liverpool Overseers* (1874) L.R. 9 Q.B. 180, 191–192.

[80] *Lane* v. *Dixon* (1847) 3 C.B. 776, 784.

[81] *Kaye* v. *Robertson* (1991) 18 F.S.R. 62 (see above, § 3.2). A forgotten dictum of Lord Denman C.J. is to the contrary: *Lewis* v. *Ponsford* (1838) 8 C. & P. 687, 690.

tion which we shall consider later.[82] In the meantime it is enough to note that he cannot sue as for a trespass to land, or exercise the rights of self-help available in the case of trespassers.

Jus tertii no defence

The mere *de facto* and wrongful possession of land is a valid title of right against all persons who cannot show a better title in themselves, and is therefore sufficient to support an action of trespass against such persons.[83] Just as a legal title to land without the possession of it is insufficient for this purpose, so conversely the possession of it wihout legal title is enough. In other words, no defendant in an action of trespass can plead the *jus tertii*—the right of possession outstanding in some third person—as against the fact of possession in the plaintiff.[84] It is otherwise, of course, if the defendant is himself the lawful owner[85] or has done the act complained of by the authority, precedent or subsequent, of him who is thus rightfully entitled.

The same rule holds good in an action of ejectment where the defendant has committed a trespass against the plaintiff. If, therefore, the plaintiff is in possession the *jus tertii* will afford the defendant no answer to the action.[86] But usually the plaintiff in an action of ejectment is not in possession: he relies upon his right to possession, unaccompanied by actual possession. In such a case, he must recover by the strength of his own title, without any regard to the weakness of the defendant's. The result, therefore, is that in an action of ejectment the *jus tertii* is in practice a good defence.[87] To the rule that it is in practice a good defence in ejectment there are two exceptions, or rather, applications of the general principle that the *jus tertii* is no defence: (1) Whenever a person has acquired possession through another whose title is defective, he cannot set up this defect against that other or anyone claiming through him,[88] although he may show that such title has since expired or been parted with.[89] This is an application of the principle of estoppel. The commonest instance is that the lessee is estopped from denying his lessor's title. (2) Probably, if the defendant's possession is wrongful as against the plaintiff, the plaintiff may succeed though he cannot himself show a good title.[90] For possession is prima facie evidence of title. If such prima facie evidence is not displaced by proof of title in a third person the plaintiff with prior possession will recover.[91]

---

[82] Below, § 5.9.
[83] *Wellaway* v. *Courtier* [1918] 1 K.B. 200.
[84] *Nicholls* v. *Ely Beet Sugar Factory* [1931] 2 Ch. 84.
[85] *Delaney* v. *T. P. Smith Ltd.* [1946] K.B. 393, 397.
[86] *Davison* v. *Gent* (1857) 1 H. & N. 744.
[87] *Doe* d. *Carter* v. *Barnard* (1849) 13 Q.B. 945.
[88] *Doe* d. *Johnson* v. *Baytup* (1835) 3 A. & E. 188.
[89] *Claridge* v. *MacKenzie* (1842) 4 M. & G. 142.
[90] *Davison* v. *Gent* (1857) 1 H. & N. 744.
[91] *Fowley Marine (Emsworth) Ltd.* v. *Gafford* [1968] 2 Q.B. 618.

Trespass by relation

He who has a right to the immediate possession of land, and enters in the exercise of that right, is then deemed by a legal fiction to have been in possession ever since the accrual of his right of entry, and may accordingly sue for any trespass committed since that time. This is known as the doctrine of trespass by relation, because the plaintiff's possession relates back to the time when he first acquired a right to the possession. So a lessee may sue for a trespass done between the granting of the lease and his entry in pursuance of it. So a landlord entitled to re-enter after the termination of the lease may after re-entry sue for any trespass committed since the lease determined.[92] We shall see how the action for mesne profits in case of dispossession is founded on the same rule of trespass by relation.[93]

Trespass as between co-owners

One tenant in common or joint tenant of land cannot sue his co-tenant in trespass or ejectment unless the act of the defendant amounts either to the total exclusion or ouster of the plaintiff or to destructive waste of the common property.[94] For each of the co-tenants is entitled to the possession of the land, to use it in a proper manner, and to take from it the fruits and profits of that user. If one of the owners receives from the common property a larger share of the profits than that to which he is entitled, this is no tort against the other owner, but the proper remedy is an action for an account.

§ 4.5. TRESPASS AB INITIO

In 1610 six carpenters entered the Queen's Head Inn, Cripplegate, and consumed a quart of wine (7d.) and some bread (1d.), for which they refused to pay. The question for the court was whether their non-payment made the entry tortious, so as to enable them to be sued in trespass *quare clausum fregit*. The court held that[95]: "When entry, authority or licence is given to any one by the law, and he doth abuse it, he shall be a trespasser *ab initio*," but that the defendants were not liable as their non-payment did not constitute a trespass.

The rule is that the authority, having been abused by doing a wrongful act under cover of it, is cancelled retrospectively so that the exercise of it becomes actionable as a trespass. The rule is primarily one of procedure, the effect of it under the old practice being that a writ of trespass would lie for the entry or seizure itself, instead of a writ of trespass or of case for the subsequent abuse only. In this respect the rule has now lost its significance; but its secondary effect upon the substantive law still remains—*viz.* that it enables the plaintiff to recover damages for the entire transaction, and not merely for the wrongful portion of it.[96] The

---

[92] *Elliott* v. *Boynton* [1924] 1 Ch. 236.
[93] Below, § 4.7.
[94] *Murray* v. *Hall* (1849) 7 C.B. 441.
[95] (1610) 8 Co.Rep. 146a. See Williams, *Animals*, pp. 97–100.
[96] *Oxley* v. *Watts* (1785) 1 T.R. 12.

rule has been abolished by statute in the case of distress for rent[97] (but not for distress damage feasant) but otherwise it still exists,[98] though it is regarded with suspicion, the doctrine of relation back not being favoured.[99]

Limits of the rule

(1) The rule applies only to acts done in pursuance of an "entry, authority, or licence given to anyone by the law."[1] (2) The rule applies only when the subsequent abuse amounts to a positive wrongful act, as opposed to a mere omission or non-feasance. Thus in the *Six Carpenters' Case* itself it was resolved that the defendants were not trespassers *ab initio* merely because they refused to pay for the quart of wine and the pennyworth of bread which they bought and consumed in the plaintiff's inn. (3) A lawful entry does not become by abuse a trespass *ab initio*, unless that abuse has reference to and so takes away the entire ground and reason of the entry. If there remains any independent ground or reason of entry, which is unaffected by the abuse, it will suffice to justify the entry and protect it from the rule of trespass *ab initio*.[2] Thus in *Elias* v. *Pasmore*[3] police constables lawfully entered premises to arrest one of the plaintiffs and whilst on the premises took possession of a large number of documents, some rightfully, some wrongfully. It was held that they were trespassers only as to the documents which were wrongfully taken, and that they were not liable as trespassers *ab initio* for damage to the premises which they had lawfully entered for the purpose of the arrest.

§ 4.6. MEASURE OF DAMAGES

Some special rules require to be mentioned.

Trespass to land

When a trespass has caused physical damage to the land, the measure of damages is the loss thereby caused to the plaintiff, which in all ordinary cases is measured by the resulting diminution in the value of the property. This measure of damages is not necessarily the cost of reinstatement—the cost of restoring the land to the condition in which it formerly was—for this is a cost which may greatly exceed the actual

---

[97] Distress for Rent Act 1737, s.19, which creates a new statutory tort of irregular distress, with a penalty of treble damages. Law Com. No. 194 (1991) recommends the repeal of this Act.

[98] *Cinammond* v. *British Airports Authority* [1980] 1 W.L.R. 582, 588.

[99] *Chic Fashions (West Wales) Ltd.* v. *Jones* [1968] 2 Q.B. 299. But the rule was originally designed to provide a remedy against abuses of authority which might lead to the oppression of the subject; and it might still be useful for this purpose: Denning, *Freedom under the Law*, p. 109.

[1] *Six Carpenters' Case* (1610) 8 Co.Rep. 146a.

[2] *Chic Fashions (West Wales) Ltd.* v. *Jones* [1968] 2 Q.B. 299.

[3] [1934] 2 K.B. 164. If such cases are carried out to their logical consequences they cut down considerably the doctrine of trespass *ab initio* as it was understood in the time of the *Six Carpenters*.

diminution in the value of the land.[4] Thus if an old building is pulled down, the plaintiff cannot recover the cost of putting up a new one, but merely the value of the old,[5] unless his house was unique, or the case is in some other way exceptional.[6] But prospective damages can be recovered.[7] When a trespass consists in some beneficial use wrongfully made of the plaintiff's land, even if it causes no damage, the plaintiff is entitled to claim by way of damages a reasonable remuneration for that use, as if it had been had under an agreement.[8] This is an exception to the general rule that only nominal damages can be recovered if no loss has been proved.[9]

Wrongful severance of goods

When part of the land has been wrongfully severed and turned into a chattel, the value of that chattel is sometimes greater and sometimes less than the resulting diminution in the value of the land. In such cases what is the measure of damages—the value of the chattels so taken away, or the resulting diminution in the value of the land? It depends on whether the wrongdoing has been wilful.

(i) Wilful wrongdoing

The rule is that the plaintiff may elect to claim either the one or the other, and he will of course claim the amount which is the larger in the particular case. The chattel, although it has been severed and made into a chattel by the labour and expenditure of the defendant, nevertheless belongs to the plaintiff, who may recover its full value without making any allowance for the fact that part of that value has been given to it by the defendant.[10]

(ii) No wilful wrongdoing

This penal rule[11] by which the plaintiff recovers more than his actual loss does not apply where there is no fraud or conscious wrongdoing on the part of the defendant. In such a case the plaintiff cannot recover the value of the chattel, and is entitled to nothing more than his actual loss—viz. the diminution of the value of the land. So that if the plaintiff's coal is severed and taken by mistake as to title or boundaries, the measure of damages is the value of the coal in the seam, as if it had been bought in situ by the defendant.[12]

---

[4] Nalder v. Ilford Corporation [1951] K.B. 822.
[5] Lodge Holes Colliery v. Wednesbury Corporation [1908] A.C. 323.
[6] Munnelly v. Calcon Ltd. [1978] I.R. 397.
[7] Townend v. Askern Coal Co. [1934] Ch. 463.
[8] Stoke-on-Trent Council v. W. & J. Wass Ltd. [1988] 1 W.L.R. 1406, 1410–1411.
[9] See also The Mediana [1900] A.C. 113, 117, cited below, § 22.1.
[10] Peruvian Guano Co. v. Dreyfus Bros. [1892] A.C. 166, 173–177.
[11] It is an illustration of one of the categories in which an award of exemplary damages is permissible: Cassell & Co. Ltd. v. Broome [1972] A.C. 1027, 1130.
[12] Townend v. Askern Coal Co. [1934] Ch. 463.

§ 4.7. THE ACTION FOR MESNE PROFITS

Any person wrongfully dispossessed of land had, in addition to a right of action for the recovery of the land, a right of action for damages in respect of all loss suffered by him during the period of his dispossession. Such an action is termed an action for mesne profits. A claim for mesne profits is now usually joined with the action for recovery of the land.[13] Whether the dispossession had or had not been effected by way of trespass, the claim for mesne profits was always in form a claim for damages for a continuing trespass upon the land. Such a claim was based upon the doctrine of trespass by relation. It followed that the action would not lie until after the plaintiff had re-entered and recovered the possession of the land. But this requirement of re-entry as a condition precedent to an action for mesne profits is now abolished, to this extent only, that a claim for such profits may in all cases be joined with the action. The law, then, seems to be as follows: A person dispossessed of land may (1) sue for recovery and for mesne profits in one action; (2) sue for mesne profits, if he has already got back into possession; (3) sue for mesne profits without recovery of possession, if his interest in the land has already come to a end.[14] In an action for mesne profits (notwithstanding the name of the action) the plaintiff is not limited to a claim for the profits which the defendant has received from the land, or those which he himself has lost. The plaintiff recovers all the loss which has resulted from the dispossession.[15] Profits are assessable from the date of the writ, not from that of the breach of covenant or other wrongs.[16] It seems not to have been decided whether a defendant in an action for mesne profits can set off the value of improvements made by him to the property in good faith during the period of his possession.

---

[13] R.S.C. Ord. 13, rr. 4, 5.
[14] *Southport Tramways* v. *Gandy* [1897] 2 Q.B. 66.
[15] *Strand Electric Co.* v. *Brisford* [1952] 2 Q.B. 246.
[16] *Elliot* v. *Boynton* [1924] 1 Ch. 236.

CHAPTER 5

NUISANCE

§ 5.1. Three Kinds of Nuisance[1]

(1) Private nuisance

The distinguishing characteristic of private nuisance is the imposition of liability as the result of an act or omission whereby a person is annoyed, prejudiced or disturbed in the enjoyment of land. The disturbance may take the form of physical damage to the land or, more usually, of the imposition of discomfort upon the occupier. Typical situations which may give rise to liability involve incursions by water, smoke, smell, fumes, gas, noise, heat, vibrations, electricity, animals and vegetation. Wrongful interference with the exercise of an easement, profit, or other similar right affecting the use and enjoyment of land also come within the rubric of private nuisance. Nuisance is therefore really a field of tortious liability rather than a single type of tortious conduct: the feature which gives it unity is the interest invaded—that of the use and enjoyment of land.[2] The tort emphasises the harm to the plaintiff rather than the conduct of the defendant.[3] Thus a judicial definition which has often been cited with approval is the following: "private nuisances, at least in the vast majority of cases, are interferences for a substantial length of time by owners or occupiers of property with the use or enjoyment of neighbouring property."[4] In the older cases it was sometimes said that the basis of the law of nuisance is the maxim *sic utere tuo ut alienum non laedas*: a man must not make such use of his property as unreasonably and unnecessarily to cause inconvenience to his neighbour.[5] This maxim has also been called "mere verbiage,"[6]

---

[1] See Buckley, *Law of Nuisance* (London, 1981); Newark, "The Boundaries of Nuisance" (1949) 65 L.Q.R. 480 (an article commended by Lord Simonds in *Jacobs* v. *L.C.C.* [1950] A.C. 361, 374); Tromans, "Nuisance-Prevention or Payment," [1982] C.L.J. 87; McLaren, "Nuisance Law and the Industrial Revolution—Some Lessons from Social History," (1983) 3 O.J.L.S. 155; Gearty, "The Place of Private Nuisance in a Modern Law of Torts," [1989] C.L.J. 214.

[2] " . . . nuisance is one of those areas of the law where the Courts have long been engaged in the application of certain basic legal concepts to a never-ending variety of circumstances; and that will continue to be so, for by its very nature the law of nuisance is intimately involved with the developing use of the environment, both natural and manmade, in which we all live": *Bank of New Zealand* v. *Greenwood* [1984] 1 N.Z.L.R. 525, 530, *per* Hardie Boys J.

[3] *Gertsen* v. *Municipality of Toronto* (1973) 41 D.L.R. (3d) 646, 669.

[4] *Cunard* v. *Antifyre* [1933] 1 K.B. 551, 556–557; *Southport Corporation* v. *Esso Petroleum Co. Ltd.* [1956] A.C. 218, 224.

[5] *Aldred's Case* (1610) 9 Co.Rep. 57b, 59a; *Tenant* v. *Goldwin* (1704) 2 Ld.Raym. 1089, 1092; *Sedleigh-Denfield* v. *O'Callaghan* [1940] A.C. 880, 898.

[6] *Bonomi* v. *Backhouse* (1858) E.B. & E. 622, 643.

however, and there is much in this criticism. The phrase does little to assist in the process of deciding which interferences should be actionable and which should not.

It will be seen that the word "nuisance," even in the private nuisance context, is ambiguous—sometimes it refers to the conduct of the defendant, sometimes to the results of that conduct, and sometimes to such results of that conduct as are actionable.[7] Of course in ordinary speech the expression is used more widely still, and is not confined to contexts relating to land. It is probable that the influence of this looser usage is at least partly responsible in the law itself for the development of the separate concept of public nuisance.[8]

(2) Public nuisance[9]

A public or common nuisance is a criminal offence. It is an act or omission which materially affects the reasonable comfort and convenience of life of a class of Her Majesty's subjects.[10] It is not necessary to establish that every member of the public, as distinct from a representative cross-section, has been affected.[11] The question whether the number of persons affected is sufficient to be described as a class is one of fact. One test is to ask whether the nuisance is so widespread in its range or indiscriminate in its effect that it would not be reasonable to expect one person to take proceedings to stop it as distinct from the community at large.[12] Examples of the crime of public nuisance are organising a festival of pop music which generates large-scale noise, traffic, and apprehension,[13] obstructing a highway,[14] or making it dangerous for traffic. Public nuisances are met by an indictment or by an action by the Attorney-General or a local authority[15] where an injunction is desired to put an end to the public nuisance.

Public and private nuisances are not in reality two species of the same genus at all. There is no generic conception which includes the crime of

---

[7] See the (undelivered) judgment of Erle C.J. in *Brand* v. *Hammersmith Railway* (1867) L.R. 2 Q.B. 223, 247; Keeton, "Trespass, Nuisance and Strict Liability," (1959) 59 Col.L.Rev. 457, 464.

[8] In its origin nuisance was merely a generic expression meaning wrongful harm, and although it subsequently lost this wide signification it was not wholly successful in attaining a specific application instead. The term is derived, through the French, from the late Latin *nocentia*: see Tertull Apol., Cap. 40—*Deus innocentiae magister nocentiae judex*. Chaucer used it in this generic sense, "Helpe me for to weye ageyne the feende . . . Keepe us from his nuisance.": (Mother of God, I, 21). Nuisance appears in the old Latin pleadings as *nocumentum*—*i.e.* harm. The terms trespass and tort, though similarly generic in their original use, have been more successful in the process of specification.

[9] See J. R. Spencer, "Public Nuisance—A Critical Examination" [1989] C.L.J. 55.

[10] *Att.-Gen.* v. *P.Y.A. Quarries Ltd.* [1957] 2 Q.B. 169, 184.

[11] *Att.-Gen. for Ontario* v. *Orange Productions Ltd.* (1971) 21 D.L.R. (3d) 257.

[12] *Att.-Gen.* v. *P.Y.A. Quarries Ltd.* [1957] 2 Q.B. 169, 191.

[13] *Att.-Gen. for Ontario* v. *Orange Productions Ltd.* (1971) 21 D.L.R. (3d) 257.

[14] This is considered in detail below, §§ 5.11 & 5.12.

[15] Local Government Act 1972, s.222; and see *Solihull Metropolitan Borough Council* v. *Maxfern Ltd.* [1977] 1 W.L.R. 127.

making a bomb-hoax[16] and the tort of allowing one's trees to overhang the land of a neighbour.[17] A public nuisance falls within the law of torts only in so far as it may in the particular case constitute some form of tort also. Thus the obstruction of a highway is a public nuisance; but if it causes any special and peculiar damage to an individual, it is also a tort actionable at his suit.

(3) Statutory nuisance

Every statutory nuisance is a criminal offence created by statute. Certain statutory nuisances are defined in Part III of the Environmental Protection Act 1990[18] which gives wide powers to Magistrates' Courts, and in certain circumstances to the High Court,[19] to grant orders putting an end to anti-social conduct amounting to a nuisance. Such enforcement orders may be very effective in practice, but since they do not give rise to claims in tort, they are not considered here. Not every statutory nuisance is a public nuisance[20] or, of course, a private nuisance.

§ 5.2. STATE OF AFFAIRS

Nuisance is commonly a continuing wrong—that is to say, it consists in the establishment or maintenance of some state of affairs[21] which continuously or repeatedly causes the escape of noxious things onto the plaintiff's land (*e.g.* a stream of foul water, or the constant noise or smell of a factory).[22] An escape of something on a single occasion would not ordinarily be termed a nuisance, although there is no reason in principle why it should not be.[23] If a neighbouring occupier's land or the buildings thereon are damaged by an errant cricket ball from a club ground on only a few occasions, the occupier may still maintain an action in nuisance.[24] The gist of the claim in nuisance is not the isolated act of hitting a ball on to the neighbouring land but the organising or carrying on of a game on property adjacent to the neighbouring land whereby the enjoyment of that land is rendered dangerous. The fact that balls reach that land only very occasionally is evidence that no dangerous state of affairs exists in the adjoining field.[25] This approach enables us to explain cases of good authority in which the plaintiff has recovered for damage caused by a single escape of dangerous thing—

---

[16] See *R.* v. *Madden* [1975] 3 All E.R. 155, 157h.
[17] See, *e.g. Lemmon* v. *Webb* [1895] A.C. 1.
[18] See s.81(5).
[19] See especially s.79.
[20] *Salford City Council* v. *McNally* [1976] A.C. 379, 390.
[21] *Bank of New Zealand* v. *Greenwood* [1984] 1 N.Z.L.R. 525, 532.
[22] *Cunard* v. *Antifyre* [1933] 1 K.B. 551, 556.
[23] *S.C.M. (United Kingdom) Ltd.* v. *W. J. Whittall & Son Ltd.* [1970] 2 All E.R. 417, 430.
[24] *Matheson* v. *Northcote College Board of Governors* [1975] 2 N.Z.L.R. 106; *Miller* v. *Jackson* [1977] Q.B. 966.
[25] See *Stone* v. *Bolton* [1950] 1 K.B. 201 in which the Court of Appeal refused to impose liability (affirmed in [1951] A.C. 850, but without nuisance being considered).

water,[26] gas,[27] metal foil,[28] or fire.[29] So it has been rightly pointed out that "an intermittent noise, particularly when it does not come at stated intervals, is likely to be more disagreeable than if it were constant."[30] It has never been seriously suggested that the plaintiff whose house has been flooded or blown up as a result of the defendant's activities can recover only for the second or subsequent but not the first of such incidents.[31] The truth is that all wrongful escapes of deleterious things, whether continuous, intermittent, or isolated, are equally capable of being classed as nuisances. The type of harm caused by the escape[32]; the gravity of that harm, and the frequency of its occurrence are each relevant (but not conclusive) factors in determining whether the defendant has maintained on his premises a state of affairs which is a potential nuisance.[33] This balancing process is the hallmark of the nuisance action, and distinguishes it from trespass as well as negligence.

Nuisance: where created

As nuisance is a tort arising out of the duties owed by neighbouring occupiers, the plaintiff cannot succeed if the act or omission complained of is on premises in his sole occupation.[34] The nuisance must have arisen elsewhere than in or on the plaintiff's premises, whether it is a common law[35] or a statutory[36] nuisance. A nuisance is therefore usually created by acts done on land in the occupation of the defendant, adjoining or in the neighbourhood of that of the plaintiff. Yet this is not invariably the case. A nuisance may be created not on the land of the defendant but elsewhere[37]—e.g. on a highway adjoining the plaintiff's house[38] or business premises,[39] or in a navigable river,[40] or in some place of public resort. Even when it is on adjoining private land, the defendant need not necessarily be the owner or occupier of that land; he may, for example, be a contractor executing works there which make the property defective[41] or otherwise cause a nuisance to adjoining property,[42] or the lessor of the premises.[43]

---

[26] *Rylands* v. *Fletcher* (1866) L.R. 1 Ex. 265 is of course the model of such a case.

[27] *Midwood & Co. Ltd.* v. *Manchester Corporation* [1905] 2 K.B. 597; *Northwestern Utilities Ltd.* v. *London Guarantee and Accident Co. Ltd.* [1936] A.C. 108.

[28] *British Celanese Ltd.* v. *A. H. Hunt (Capacitors) Ltd.* [1969] 1 W.L.R. 959.

[29] *Spicer* v. *Smee* [1946] 1 All E.R. 489.

[30] *Rapier* v. *London Tramways Co.* [1893] 2 Ch. 588, 591, *per* Kekewich J.

[31] Yet see *Att.-Gen.* v. *P.Y.A. Quarries Ltd.* [1957] 2 Q.B. 169, 192.

[32] The law of nuisance has always been more willing to remedy damage to property than personal injuries.

[33] *Matheson* v. *Northcote College Board of Governors* [1975] 2 N.Z.L.R. 106, 111.

[34] For co-occupiers as plaintiffs or as defendants, see *Hooper* v. *Rogers* [1975] Ch. 43.

[35] *Titus* v. *Duke* (1964) 6 W.L.R. 135.

[36] *National Coal Board* v. *Thorne* [1976] 1 W.L.R. 543.

[37] *Paxhaven Holdings* v. *Att.-Gen.* [1974] 2 N.Z.L.R. 185.

[38] *Halsey* v. *Esso Petroleum Co. Ltd.* [1961] 1 W.L.R. 683.

[39] *Hubbard* v. *Pitt* [1976] Q.B. 142.

[40] *Southport Corporation* v. *Esso Petroleum Co. Ltd.* [1954] 2 Q.B. 182, 204.

[41] *Heaven* v. *Mortimer* (1968) 205 E.G. 767.

[42] See below, § 5.6.

[43] See below, § 5.6.

§ 5.3. THE RIGHT TO ENJOYMENT OF LAND

Two kinds of harm

A distinction is traditionally drawn in the cases between two kinds of harm sufficient to found an action of nuisance. It may consist either in (1) some interference with the beneficial use of the premises occupied by the plaintiff, or (2) some physical injury to those premises, or to the property of the plaintiff situated thereon. Thus smells emanating from a pig-farm,[44] or noise causing deprivation of sleep[45] might come within the former category. Indeed any substantial interference with the comfort or convenience of persons occupying or using the premises is a sufficient interference with the beneficial use of them within the meaning of this rule. Damage to the land by causing sewage[46] or flood-water to collect upon it,[47] or vibrations from powerful engines causing structural damage[48] might come within the latter category.

The line thus drawn between two types of harm is not, however, free from difficulty.[49] Indeed it may sometimes be very artificial. Thus land or buildings subjected to noise or smells, on a recurring basis, are unlikely to prove attractive to purchasers if placed on the market, and their owners will accordingly suffer loss through the consequent reduction in value.[50] Nevertheless, provided the distinction is used flexibly, and not permitted to degenerate into a rigid classification likely to cause anomaly in borderline cases, it is useful and promotes clarity. A plaintiff who wishes to establish a nuisance to personal comfort has a heavier burden of proof to discharge than one who seeks to show a nuisance to property.[51]

(1) Interference with beneficial use

The governing principle here is expressed in some constantly cited words of Knight Bruce V.-C. in *Walter* v. *Selfe*[52]: "Ought this inconvenience to be considered in fact as more than fanciful, more than one of mere delicacy or fastidiousness, as an inconvenience materially interfering with the orindary comfort physically of human existence, not merely according to elegant or dainty modes and habits of living, but according to plain and sober and simple notions among the English people?" So a church congregation in a poor part of Brighton disturbed

---

[44] *Bone* v. *Seale* [1975] 1 W.L.R. 797.

[45] *Shelfer* v. *City of London Electric Lighting Co.* [1895] 1 Ch. 287 (engines); *Metropolitan Properties Ltd.* v. *Jones* [1939] 2 All E.R 202, 204 (badly installed heating apparatus).

[46] *Jones* v. *Llanrwst Urban Council* [1911] 1 Ch. 393.

[47] *Sedleigh-Denfield* v. *O'Callaghan* [1940] A.C. 880; *Pemberton* v. *Bright* [1960] 1 W.L.R. 436.

[48] *Meux's Brewery Co.* v. *City of London Electric Lighting Co.* [1895] 1 Ch. 287; *Hoare & Co.* v. *McAlpine* [1923] 1 Ch. 167.

[49] See McLaren, "Nuisance Actions and the Environmental Battle" (1972) 10 Osgoode Hall Law Journal 505, 534.

[50] See Ogus and Richardson, "Economics and the Environment: A Study of Private Nuisance" (1977) 36 C.L.J. 284, 299.

[51] *Gaunt* v. *Fynney* (1872) L.R. 8 Ch. 8, 11–12.

[52] (1851) 4 De G. & Sm. 315, 322. Similar cases are *Jones* v. *Powell* (1628) Palm. 536, 538 ("Si home est cy tendernosed, que no poit indurer sea-cole, il doit lesser son mease"); *Pembroke (Earl of)* v. *Warren* [1896] 1 I.R. 76.

by "a buzzing noise" from a power station was without remedy.[53] But the law judges by no Spartan standards. The loss of even one night's rest is no trivial matter.[54] nor is the loss of the opportunity to lie quietly in bed on Sunday morning.[55] Nor need injury to health be proved.[56] There may often be difficulty in defining precisely what degree of smell or noise or vibration amounts to a nuisance, but the court will look at the substance of the matter, and be "slow to repose on the easy pillow of uncertainty."[57]

The standard of comfortable living which is thus to be taken as the test of a nuisance is not a single universal standard for all times and places, but a variable standard differing in different localities. The question in every case is not whether the individual plaintiff suffers what he regards as substantial discomfort or inconvenience, but whether the reasonable man who resides in that locality would take the same view of the matter. The reasonable man connotes a person whose notions and standards of behaviour and responsibility correspond with those generally obtained among ordinary people in our society at the present time, who seldom allows his emotions to overbear his reason and whose habits are moderate and whose disposition is equable. He is not necessarily the same as the average man—a term which implies an amalgamation of counter-balancing extremes. The result is that he who dislikes the noise[58] of traffic must not set up his abode in the heart of a great city. He who loves peace and quiet must not live in a locality devoted to the business of making boilers or steamships. Thus in *Sturges* v. *Bridgman*,[59] Thesiger L.J. said: "What would be a nuisance in Belgrave Square would not necessarily be so in Bermondsey." In *Polsue and Alfieri Ltd.* v. *Rushmer*[60] this doctrine of the local standard of comfort was definitely accepted by the House of Lords.[61] Changes in standards and expectations in society generally will be reflected in the law itself. It is true that as late as 1965 it was held that "the ability to receive television free from occasional . . . electrical interference is [not] so important a part of an ordinary householder's enjoyment of his property" that it ought to be protected.[62] It may be doubted however, whether this view still represents the law.[63] It may even be that ultimately the courts will recognise a limited right to prospect or view: so far, except in one

---

[53] *Heath* v. *Mayor of Brighton* (1908) 24 T.L.R. 414.

[54] *Andreae* v. *Selfridge & Co.* [1938] Ch. 1, 8, *per* Greene M.R. (This case is also an interesting authority on judicial notice, for Greene M.R. "made considerable use in his judgment of his acquaintance with the *va et vient* of west-end hotels": Landon (1943) 59 L.Q.R. 185.)

[55] *Haddon* v. *Lynch* [1911] V.L.R. 230.

[56] *Crump* v. *Lambert* (1867) L.R. 3 Eq. 409, 412.

[57] *Hampstead and Suburban Properties Ltd.* v. *Diomedous* [1969] 1 Ch. 248, 257, *per* Megarry J.

[58] For noise, see Kerse, *The Law Relating to Noise* (London, 1975).

[59] (1879) 11 Ch.D. 852, 865.

[60] [1907] A.C. 121.

[61] The lowering of the standard of comfort in particular localities does not depend on the existence of prescriptive rights to create nuisances there: *Rushmer* v. *Polsue and Alfieri Ltd.* [1906] 1 Ch. 234, 251.

[62] *Bridlington Relay Ltd.* v. *Yorkshire Electricity Board* [1965] Ch. 436, 447.

[63] cf. *Nor-Video Services Ltd.* v. *Ontario Hydro* (1978) 84 D.L.R. (3d) 221.

dictum,[64] the English courts have not been prepared to acknowledge an impairment of enjoyment in these circumstances.[65] But the aesthetic sensibilities of the public are increasing and the law should keep pace.

(2) Interference with property

The rule that the standard is determined by the locality where the nuisance is created is limited to those cases where the nuisance complained of is productive of sensible personal discomfort. A different principle applies where the nuisance causes a material injury to property, or sensibly reduces its value. The distinction was drawn in the classic judgment of Lord Westbury L.C. in *St. Helens Smelting Co.* v. *Tipping*.[66]

> "It appears to me that it is a very desirable thing to mark the difference between an action brought for a nuisance upon the ground that the alleged nuisance produces material injury to the property, and an action brought for a nuisance on the ground that the thing alleged to be a nuisance is productive of sensible personal discomfort. With regard to the latter, namely, the personal inconvenience and interference with one's enjoyment, one's quiet, one's personal freedom, anything that discomposes or injuriously affects the senses or the nerves, whether that may or may not be denominated a nuisance, must undoubtedly depend greatly on the circumstances of the place where the thing complained of actually occurs. . . . But when an occupation is carried on by one person in the neighbourhood of another, and the result of that trade or occupation, or business, is a material injury to property, then there unquestionably arises a very different consideration. I think, my Lords, that in a case of that description the submission which is required from persons living in society to that amount of discomfort which may be necessary for the legitimate and free exercise of the trade of their neighbours, would not apply to circumstances the immediate result of which is sensible injury to the value of property."

In this case the plaintiff succeeded on proof that his trees and shrubs had been damaged by the fumes from the defendant's smelting works: the plea that the locality in question was devoted to works of this kind was unsuccessful. "It is as though the Westbury proposition had imported into the law of nuisance a doctrine closely akin to *res ipsa*

---

[64] *Thompson-Schwab* v. *Costaki* [1956] 1 All E.R. 652, 654, where Lord Evershed M.R. held that the defendant's use of his house as a brothel forced itself "on the sense of sight" of the plaintiffs and as such interfered with the comfortable enjoyment of their land. See also *Laws* v. *Florinplace* [1981] 1 All E.R. 659 (triable issue whether sex shop in a residential area was an actionable nuisance).

[65] A right to a view was acknowledged in *Lockwood* v. *Brentwood Park Investments Ltd.* (1970) 10 D.L.R. (3d) 143, 166; but *cf. Morris* v. *Dominion Foundries & Steel Ltd.* [1947] 2 D.L.R. 840, 845 (criticised by Silverstone, "Visual Pollution: Unaesthetic Use of Land as Nuisance," (1974) 12 Alta.L.Rev. 542, 545).

[66] (1865) 11 H.L.C. 642, 650.

loquitur in the law of negligence."[67] As has already been pointed out, however, the borderline between these two classes has not been clearly drawn: noise and smoke may not only interfere with personal comfort but also make the premises uninhabitable for the purpose of the business carried on there and so cause "sensible injury to the value of the property."[68] Further, not every injury to the value of the property is an actionable loss. There is no right not to have one's property overlooked by that of one's neighbour.

The temporary nature of the inconvenience or discomfort is a fact to be taken into account in judging whether it is sufficiently substantial to amount to a nuisance.[69] But if it is otherwise substantial, it is nonetheless a nuisance because it is merely temporary, evanescent, fleeting or occasional.[70] It is not time but the effect on the plaintiff which is significant.

Sensitive plaintiffs

No action will lie for nuisance in respect of damage which is due solely to the fact that the plaintiff is abnormally susceptible to interference. "A man cannot increase the liability of his neighbour by applying his own property to special uses, whether for business or pleasure."[71] Thus in *Robinson* v. *Kilvert*[72] the plaintiff could not recover for damage done by heat from the defendants' pipes to his stock of brown paper— "an exceptionally delicate trade"—since it would not have prejudicially affected any ordinary trade.[73] Similarly, the owners of a drive-in cinema could not complain if lights on an adjoining race-course prevented the cinema audience from being able to see the film,[74] and mink farmers could not expect their neighbours to give up all activities which created noise during the whelping season.[75] In short, the plaintiff must not be hypersensitive—he has[76] merely "a right to the ordinary enjoyment of his land."[77]

It has been argued that the principle relating to extraordinary or sensitive use is fully justified both in terms of fairness and on economic grounds.[78] On this view there is indeed no reason why the "normal user," and his consumers, should be penalised by the presence of an

---

[67] *Kent* v. *Dominion Steel and Coal Corporation Ltd.* (1964) 49 D.L.R. (2d) 241, 248, *per* Furlong C.J.

[68] *Russell Transport Ltd.* v. *Ontario Malleable Iron Co. Ltd.* [1952] 4 D.L.R. 719.

[69] *Matania* v. *National Provincial Bank* [1936] 2 All E.R. 633, 644.

[70] *Fritz* v. *Hobson* (1880) 14 Ch.D. 542, 556.

[71] *Eastern and South African Telegraph Co.* v. *Cape Town Tramways* [1902] A.C. 381, 393. *Contra, National Telephone Co.* v. *Baker* [1893] 2 Ch. 186, 202.

[72] (1889) 41 Ch.D. 88.

[73] *Cf. Hoare & Co.* v. *McAlpine* [1923] 1 Ch. 167 (very old but not abnormally unstable house: liability imposed).

[74] *Amphitheaters Inc.* v. *Portland Meadows* (1948) 198 P. 2d 847.

[75] *Grandel* v. *Mason* [1953] 3 D.L.R. 65, as explained in *Rattray* v. *Daniels* (1959) 17 D.L.R. (2d) 134, 138, where mink farming described as "delicate and sensitive" use of land.

[76] *Stretch* v. *Romford Football Club Ltd.* (1971) 115 S.J. 741.

[77] *Backhouse* v. *Bonomi* (1861) 9 H.L.C. 503, 512; 11 E.R. 825, 829.

[78] Ogus and Richardson, "Economics and the Environment: A Study of Private Nuisance," [1977] C.L.J. 284, 303–304.

abnormal neighbour. If individuals require greater protection than is usual, they must procure it through contract or by statute.

However, once it has been established that the right to the ordinary enjoyment has been infringed, the plaintiff can claim protection for his extraordinary or sensitive use. In *McKinnon Industries* v. *Walker*,[79] the plaintiff's enjoyment was impaired by the emission of fumes and sulphur dioxide gas from the defendant's works. The defendant argued that, even if an injunction were granted, it should be modified so as to exclude protection for the plaintiff's orchids, the growing of which is "from the horticultural point of view a particularly difficult and delicate operation." But the Privy Council rejected this argument: once the plaintiff's ordinary enjoyment was affected there was "no reason to treat damage to orchids differently from damage to any other flower plant or shrub."[80]

Actual damage

The damage complained of in an action of nuisance must be actual as distinct from a contingency perceived as a possible occurrence in the future. Until damage is caused or is imminent there is no nuisance, only the potentiality of a nuisance.[81] If the defendant's operations do not now cause harm, discomfort, or inconvenience, they do not constitute a nuisance, even though they would certainly produce such effects were the plaintiff to have occasion in the future to use his land in some other way.[82] Substantial present damage must normally be shown.

> "It would be wrong, as it seems to me, for this court in the reign of Henry VI to have interfered with the further use of sea coal in London, because it had been ascertained to their satisfaction, or predicted to their satisfaction, that by the reign of Queen Victoria both white and red roses would have ceased to bloom in the Temple Gardens."[83]

This does not mean, however, that the plaintiff is always obliged to wait until he has actually suffered damage before bringing proceedings. If damage is clearly imminent as a result of the defendant's activities, but has not yet actually occurred, the court will in suitable cases restrain the defendant by the award of a *quia timet* injunction.[84]

§ 5.4. MALICE

The concept of "reasonableness," for the purposes of the principles relating to unreasonable interference in the law of nuisance, may have to be understood in a subjective as well as an objective sense. Therefore if acts otherwise justified on the ground of reciprocity between neighbours are done wantonly or maliciously the defendant cannot argue

---

[79] [1951] 3 D.L.R. 577 (P.C.).
[80] *Ibid.*, 581.
[81] *Pemberton* v. *Bright* [1960] 1 W.L.R. 436.
[82] *Sturges* v. *Bridgman* (1879) 11 Ch.D. 852.
[83] *Salvin* v. *North Brancepeth Coal Co.* (1874) L.R. 9 Ch. 705, 709, *per* James L.J.
[84] See, *e.g. Hooper* v. *Rogers* [1975] Ch. 43. *cf. Fletcher* v. *Bealey* (1885) 28 Ch.D. 688.

that, *e.g.* the volume of noise created could, from some abstract view-point, be regarded as within the limits of what the plaintiff ought to be expected to tolerate. So in *Christie* v. *Davey*[85] an injunction was granted against hammering and the beating of trays against a party wall and other noises which were maliciously intended to cause discomfort to the occupier of the adjoining house, although, had they been made for a legitimate purpose, the discomfort would not have been sufficiently substantial to be actionable, or at any rate to give grounds for an injunction. Similarly, in *Hollywood Silver Fox Farm Ltd.* v. *Emmett*,[86] damages and an injunction were granted when the defendant ordered his son to fire guns on his own land as near as possible to the plaintiff's breeding pens in order that the latter's vixen might refuse to breed or miscarry, though clearly he was entitled to shoot on his own land to keep down rabbits or for pleasure. Again, although a person who has a telephone may in general use it to call whomsoever he likes, he may be liable if, by way of retaliation for a real or fancied grievance, he persistently and deliberately makes calls for the purpose of disturbing and vexing another.[87] These cases at first sight seem inconsistent with the general principle that the presence of malice does not render that actionable which without malice would not have been actionable.[88] But the inconsistency is apparent rather than real. The infinite variety of situations capable of giving rise to claims in nuisance necessarily means that the question of liability has, in most cases, to be approached via the broad concept of reasonable user rather than in terms of highly detailed rules of law. And to inquire whether a defendant acting maliciously could simultaneously be described as acting "reasonably" would be at best artificial and at worst meaningless.

§ 5.5. Who Can Sue

It follows from what has been said above that the plaintiff must be able to show that he is entitled to the right to enjoyment of land which nuisance protects. That right normally vests in the person in possession of the land injuriously affected.[90] So a weekly tenant[91] or a tenant at will[92] may maintain an action for nuisance, though the duration of the tenancy may be relevant to the question whether and on what terms an injunction should be granted. Conversely, a reversioner has no cause of action unless he can prove a permanent injury to his proprietary right. If the damage is of a continuing nature, such as encroaching roots, an

---

[85] [1893] 1 Ch. 316.
[86] [1936] 2 K.B. 468, more fully reported [1936] 1 All E.R. 825. See also *MacGibbon* v. *Robinson* [1952] 4 D.L.R. 142 ("downright cussedness").
[87] *Stoakes* v. *Brydges* [1958] Q.W.N. 5; *Alma* v. *Nakir* [1966] 2 N.S.W.R. 396.
[88] *Bradford Corporation* v. *Pickles* [1895] A.C. 587 (above § 2.3). For dicta favouring the application of the general principle in an unusual context see *Att.-Gen. of Manitoba* v. *Campbell* (1985) 32 C.C.L.T. 57.
[89] See Kodilinye, "Standing to sue in private nuisance," (1989) 9 L.S. 284.
[90] *Read* v. *Lyons* (J.) & *Co. Ltd.* [1947] A.C. 156, 183.
[91] *Jones* v. *Chappell* (1875) L.R. 20 Eq. 539.
[92] *Burgess* v. *Woodstock* [1955] 4 D.L.R. 615.

occupier can recover for damage inflicted before as well as after he acquired his proprietary and possessory interest.[93]

A licensee with a right to possess land[94] may sue in nuisance, but licensees without exclusive possession cannot sue.[95] It has been suggested that members of the occupier's family should be able to sue, as long as they are resident on the land,[96] but there would seem little justification for that normally as, if the land is interfered with, the occupier himself should sue. However, the inchoate rights in land given to matrimonial partners under modern legislation would perhaps suggest that either spouse should be able to sue, regardless of his or her actual legal or equitable interest in the land.

De facto possession is sufficient[97]; indeed, it would be odd if it were otherwise because even in conversion which, unlike nuisance, necessarily involves a reflection on the plaintiff's title, actual possession is protected against all but the rightful owner.

That the plaintiff must be able to show an entitlement to use and enjoyment in land is not an anomaly but follows from the very nature of the action. The purpose of the action is to protect the right to use and enjoyment of land. Freeholders, licensors, licensees in exclusive occupation, and lessees can show such entitlement. Because a lessor has a definite right to possession in the future, he can sue in nuisance if he can show that, unless something is done, he will suffer an impairment of enjoyment at the time when he does regain possession.

What damage is actionable

Nuisance is primarily a wrong to property, but even when there is no physical damage compensation can be recovered for annoyance and discomfort.[98] Nevertheless the emphasis on the proprietary character of the nuisance action raises doubts as to whether damages can be recovered for personal injuries and damage to chattels as distinct from damage to the plaintiff's land or the enjoyment thereof. But it seems probable that compensation can be recovered for damage to chattels, at least if the chattels belong to the occupier.[99] There seems, however, to be no case which definitely either affirms[1] or denies the right to recover

---

[93] *Masters* v. *Brent L.B.C.* [1978] Q.B. 841.

[94] Although it is not necessary that he have any title in the land: *Newcastle-under-Lyme Corporation* v. *Wolstanton Ltd.* [1947] Ch. 92, 104, 108; on appeal, [1947] Ch. 427. The working of a coal and ironstone mine caused the surface land to move, with the result that the corporation's gas mains and pipes were damaged. Although the corporation had no title to the land, it did have exclusive possession of the area occupied by the pipes.

[95] *Malone* v. *Laskey* [1907] 2 K.B. 141; *Cunard* v. *Antifyre* [1933] 1 K.B. 551; *Masters* v. *Brent L.B.C.* [1978] Q.B. 841.

[96] McLaren, 10 Osgoode Hall L.J. 505, 517.

[97] *Foster* v. *Warblington U.D.C.* [1906] 1 K.B. 648; *Paxhaven Holdings Ltd.* v. *Att.-Gen.* [1974] 2 N.Z.L.R. 185, 189.

[98] *Bone* v. *Searle* [1975] 1 W.L.R. 797 (£1,000 for noxious smell).

[99] *Harris* v. *Carnegies Pty. Ltd.* [1917] V.L.R. 95; *Cunard* v. *Antifyre Ltd.* [1933] 1 K.B. 551, 567; *Halsey* v. *Esso Petroleum Co. Ltd.* [1961] 1 W.L.R. 683, 692–693.

[1] Though see *Cunard* v. *Antifyre Ltd.* [1933] 1 K.B. 551, 567 ("whatever form the injury takes").

for personal injuries in an action of private nuisance, although the well-established right to recover for personal injuries caused by a public nuisance has been criticised as anomalous.[2] One possibility is that a distinction might be drawn between personal injuries suffered by the occupier, which would be remediable, and those suffered by other persons on the premises, which would not.[3] But on the other hand, it is not easy to see why the mere fact of a plaintiff's being injured *qua* occupier of land should relieve him of the burden of proving negligence which normally lies upon victims of personal injury. It is therefore submitted that the better view is that damages for personal injury cannot be recovered in private nuisance. Coherent reform of the general law relating to personal injury, and of the capricious way in which the negligence requirement sometimes operates, can now only be achieved by Parliament.

§ 5.6. WHO IS LIABLE: (1) OCCUPIER[4]

Speaking generally, the occupier of premises is liable for all nuisances which exist upon them during the period of his occupancy. His duty is not merely to refrain from positive acts of misfeasance which cause harm to his neighbours, but also to take care that such harm is not caused by his omission or by third parties or by nature, and to abate it if it does. "I have the control and management," said Sir Charles Abbott C.J.,[5] "of all that belongs to my land or my house, and it is my fault if I do not so exercise my authority as to prevent injury to another." Hence an occupier may be responsible for what is done, not only by his servants or (in some cases) independent contractors,[6] but also by his invitees or licensees.[7] The reason is that an owner of private property, if he likes to take the necessary measures, can prevent people coming on his land and causing harm, because he can shut everyone out if he so wishes.[8] Similarly, an occupier is liable even for a continuing nuisance which already existed on the premises when he first entered into possession of them.[9]

Nature of liability

When the harm flows from a state of affairs which has been created by the defendant himself or by someone for whom he is responsible, it is usually no defence that all possible care and skill have been taken to prevent the operation becoming a nuisance.[10] But when the harm flows

---

[2] See *Dymond* v. *Pearce* [1972] 1 Q.B. 496.

[3] There is some authority for the adoption of this distinction in actions under *Rylands* v. *Fletcher*, *sed quaere*: see below, § 13.3.

[4] See Blundell, "Liabilities of Landlord and Tenant in respect of Non-repair, Nuisance, and Dangerous Premises" (1941) 5 *The Conveyancer* 100, 163, 261; Friedmann, "The Incidence of Liability in Nuisance" (1943) 59 L.Q.R. 63.

[5] *Laugher* v. *Pointer* (1826) 5 B. & C. 547, 576.

[6] *Hughes* v. *Percival* (1883) 8 App.Cas. 443; *Spicer* v. *Smee* [1946] 1 All E.R. 489.

[7] *White* v. *Jameson* (1874) L.R. 18 Eq. 303.

[8] *Hall* v. *Beckenham Corporation* [1949] 1 K.B. 716, 724.

[9] *Broder* v. *Saillard* (1876) 2 Ch.D. 692.

[10] See below, § 5.8(3).

from the act of a trespasser, or otherwise without the act, authority, or permission of the occupier, the occupier is not responsible for that harm unless, with knowledge or means of knowledge of the existence of the state of affairs causing the harm, he suffers it to continue without taking reasonably prompt and efficient means for its abatement.[11]

Five Different Cases

The problems may arise in five different ways.

(i) *The harm may be due to the act of a trespasser or stranger, or to natural causes*

In *Sedleigh-Denfield's* case[12] a trespasser laid a pipe and grating in the defendants' ditch in so inefficient a manner that the grating became choked with leaves, and water overflowed onto the plaintiff's premises. The defendants knew of the existence of the pipe, which drained their own land, and ought to have recognised the possibility of a flood occurring, but (despite the lapse of nearly three years) did nothing to remedy the obstruction. "In my opinion," said Lord Maugham,[13] "an occupier of land 'continues' a nuisance if with knowledge or presumed knowledge of its existence he fails to take any reasonable steps to bring it to an end though with ample time to do so. He 'adopts' it if he makes any use of the erections, building, bank or artificial contrivance which constitutes the nuisance." The defendants were held liable because they had both continued and adopted the nuisance. It has since been held that there is no difference between such a hazard created by a human agency, such as a trespasser, and one arising from natural causes or act of God.[14] It is a logical extension of this reasoning to hold that an occupier who permits gypsies to act on his land in a way which offends all the senses may have adopted the nuisance.[15]

(ii) *The occupier may have taken over the nuisance when he acquired the property*

Instances of this are the cases of a tenant of a house which obstructs the plaintiff's lights,[16] and the purchaser of land on which a nuisance exists.[17]

(iii) *The nuisance may be due to a latent defect*

Here the occupier is not liable if he did not know and could not by the exercise of reasonable care have known of the existence of the nuis-

---

[11] *Sedleigh-Denfield* v. *O'Callaghan* [1940] A.C. 880, 893, 910; *Goldman* v. *Hargrave* [1967] 1 A.C. 645, 660; *Leakey* v. *National Trust* [1980] Q.B. 485.

[12] [1940] A.C. 880.

[13] [1940] A.C. 880, 894.

[14] *Goldman* v. *Hargrave* [1967] 1 A.C. 645; *Leakey* v. *National Trust* [1980] Q.B. 485, 518.

[15] *Page Motors Ltd.* v. *Epsom & Ewell Borough Council* (1980) 78 L.G.R. 505.

[16] *Roswell* v. *Prior* (1701) 12 Mod. 635.

[17] *Penruddock's Case* (1597) 5 Co.Rep. 1006.

ance.[18] It has been said that "the occupier or owner is not an insurer."[19] So in *Noble* v. *Harrison*[20] the occupier of land was held not liable when the branch of a beech tree growing on his land and overhanging a highway suddenly broke off, owing to a latent defect not discoverable by any reasonable careful inspection, and damaged the plaintiff's motor-coach which was passing along the highway.

(iv) *Things naturally on the land*

It is now settled that there may be liability in nuisance for the escape of things naturally on the land, if the occupier has failed to take reasonable care.[21] So the Court of Appeal has held that an occupier was liable when a steep natural hill collapsed as a result of earth movements, as he was well aware of the hazard.[22] But the court, in assessing what is reasonable, cannot disregard the fact that the occupier has had the nuisance thrust upon him through no fault of his own, and must not expect an excessive expenditure of time or money.[23]

(v) *Premises on highways*

It has sometimes been said that the principle that knowledge of the defect must be proved has one exception. In *Wringe* v. *Cohen*[24] the Court of Appeal decided that where premises on a highway became dangerous and constitute a nuisance, so that they collapse and injure a passer-by or an adjoining owner, the occupier or owner of the premises, if he has undertaken the duty to repair, is answerable, whether he knew or ought to have known of the danger or not.[25] Damage due to want of repair was distinguished from damage due to the acts of trespassers or to a latent defect, *e.g.* a secret and unobservable operation of nature[26] such as a subsidence. "Positive act and neglect of duty are thus placed on the same footing."[27] Atkinson J., who had delivered the judgment of

---

[18] *Wilkins* v. *Leighton* [1932] 2 Ch. 106.

[19] *Sedleigh-Denfield* v. *O'Callaghan* [1940] A.C. 880, 897, *per* Lord Atkin.

[20] [1926] 2 K.B. 332. "*Noble* v. *Harrison* saved the beautiful hedgerows of the English Countryside": Landon, (1940) 56 L.Q.R. 144. But the safety of the public must take precedence over the duty of the National Trust to safeguard amenities: *Quinn* v. *Scott* [1965] 1 W.L.R. 1004. See also *Caminer* v. *Northern and London Investment Trust* [1951] A.C. 88 (no duty to lop well grown elm near a highway in absence of anything which would signify danger to the prudent landowner).

[21] *Goldman* v. *Hargrave* [1967] 1 A.C. 645.

[22] *Leakey* v. *National Trust* [1980] Q.B. 485.

[23] *Goldman* v. *Hargrave* [1967] 1 A.C. 645, 661; *Leakey* v. *National Trust* [1980] Q.B. 485.

[24] [1940] 1 K.B. 229. Further discussion of this case: Friedmann, (1943) 59 L.Q.R. 305; Landon, (1940) 56 L.Q.R. 140, and in Pollock, *Torts*, p. 324; Blundell (1941) 5 *The Conveyancer* 100; Treitel, (1951) 14 M.L.R. 347.

[25] This is the essence of the decision as explained in *Jacobs* v. *L.C.C.* [1950] A.C. 361, 373 and *Mint* v. *Good* [1951] 1 K.B. 517, 524. Yet, as Lord Simonds said in the *Jacobs* case (at 373), "the dispute was between adjoining owners, the premises of one having been damaged by the defective condition and collapse of the other, and references to highway and passer-by were alike strictly unnecessary".

[26] This distinction has been drawn in Australia: *Cartwright* v. *McLaine & Long Ltd.* (1979) 53 A.L.J.R. 413.

[27] [1940] 1 K.B. 229, 248.

the Court of Appeal, said in a later case[28]: "A duty to prevent his house from becoming dangerous from want of repair connotes a duty to inspect and examine, and if a landlord fails to do either, it is right that he should not be allowed to rely upon his want of knowledge. There is nothing latent in the premises becoming in such disrepair as to be in danger of collapse. That was the point in *Wringe v. Cohen*." But this begs the question. Is there a duty in the absence of actual or presumed knowledge? The judgment in *Wringe v. Cohen* was delivered before the hearing in the House of Lords of *Sedleigh-Denfield's* case,[29] but it was not referred to either in the arguments of counsel or in any of the opinions delivered by the Law Lords.[30] It is not easy to reconcile with the assumptions underlying the opinions in the later case but has been regarded as binding in some later cases.[31] The judgment is also at variance with *Caminer v. Northern and London Investment Trust Ltd.*[32] where the House of Lords held the respondent not liable when his elm tree fell on the appellants' car because a prudent landowner would not have suspected the danger. The owner of a tree adjoining a highway should be in no different a position from the owner of a house adjoining the highway.

Liability after occupation ceases

Does a person who is in occupation of premises on which there is a nuisance, and who is liable for that nuisance by virtue of his occupation, cease to be so liable when he ceases to occupy? Does a vendor of land, for example, put off his responsibility along with his ownership? Or does the liability of a tenant cease with the assignment, surrender, or determination of the lease? On this point there is little authority, but it is submitted that (except in the case of nuisance by positive misfeasance) liability dependent on occupation lasts only so long as the occupation on which it is based. In the case of positive misfeasance however, this is not so. Liability of this kind is based not on occupancy but on the doing of the act which creates the nuisance; and its continuance, therefore, is independent of the ownership or occupation of the property on which the act is done. Thus he who builds a house which obstructs ancient lights remains liable for the continuance of that obstruction, even after he has sold the property.[33]

---

[28] *Spicer v. Smee* [1946] 1 All E.R. 489, 494.

[29] The Court failed to consider the Court of Appeal's judgments in *Sedleigh-Denfield's* case [1939] 1 All E.R. 725 and *Job Edwards Ltd. v. Birmingham Navigations* [1924] 1 K.B. 341, in which all three Lord Justices considered relevant the defendant's knowledge of the existence of the nuisance.

[30] Presumably because at the time notice of appeal had been given in *Wringe v. Cohen*, which was therefore *sub judice*.

[31] *Heap v. Ind Coope* [1940] 2 K.B. 476; *Cushing v. Walker & Son* [1941] 2 All E.R. 693. It was not followed in *O'Leary v. Meltitides* (1960) 20 D.L.R. (2d) 258, 266–268 and *Brewer v. Kayes* [1973] 2 O.R. 284.

[32] [1951] A.C. 88, 96, 110.

[33] *Roswell v. Prior* (1701) 12 Mod. 635.

§ 5.7. WHO IS LIABLE: (2) NON-OCCUPIERS

We must now examine in detail the liability in nuisance of non-occupiers. For although it is generally true that the person liable is the occupier of the land on which the cause of injury exists, it is not invariably so. There are four categories to be considered.

(1) Liability of creator of a nuisance

He who by himself or by his servants by a positive act of misfeasance (as opposed to a mere non-feasance, such as an omission to repair)[34] creates a nuisance is always liable for it, and for any continuance of it, whether he be the owner, the occupier or a stranger, and notwithstanding the fact that it exists on land which is not in his occupation, and that he has therefore no power to put an end to it.[35] Thus if any building obstructs ancient lights or interferes wih any other servitude, the builder is liable no less than the occupier of the land on which the building stands.[36] Moreover, this liability is a continuing one, extending not merely to the wrongful act itself, but to the continuance of the wrongful state of things which results from it. It is no defence that the defendant has no power to abate or put an end to this state of things, for he ought not to have created it.[37]

(2) Liability of one who authorises another to create or continue a nuisance

On the same principle a lessor, or licensor, of land is liable when he has expressly or impliedly authorised his lessee, or licensee, to create or continue the nuisance, or when it is certain to result from the purposes for which the lease or licence of the property was granted. In *Tetley* v. *Chitty*[38] a local authority which leased land for the purpose of go-kart racing was held liable for a nuisance found in the circumstances to be an ordinary and necessary consequence of that activity. If, however, the purpose for which the lease is granted is not such as necessarily to cause a nuisance,[39] the landlord is not responsible merely because a nuisance is in fact created by the manner in which the tenant chooses to conduct his operations. On this principle in *Smith* v. *Scott*,[40] it was held that a landlord was not responsible for a nuisance caused by the behaviour of tenants known to be unruly, because the lease contained a clause which specifically prohibited the commission of a nuisance.[41] Nor in such a

---

[34] In some cases even an omission to repair may give rise to liability: see *infra*.

[35] *Kraemers* v. *Att.-Gen.* [1966] Tas.S.R. 113.

[36] *Thompson* v. *Gibson* (1841) 7 M. & W. 456; *Dalton* v. *Angus* (1881) 6 App.Cas. 740. See also *Southport Corporation* v. *Esso Petroleum Co. Ltd.* [1953] 3 W.L.R. 773, 776 (Devlin J.); [1954] 2 Q.B. 184, 204 (Morris L.J.). *Contra* [1954] 2 Q.B. 184, 196 (Denning L.J.); [1956] A.C. 218, 242 (Lord Radcliffe).

[37] *Thompson* v. *Gibson* (1841) 7 M. & W. 456.

[38] [1986] 1 All E.R. 663; *Harris* v. *James* (1876) 45 L.J.Q.B. 545.

[39] *Metropolitan Properties Ltd.* v. *Jones* [1939] 2 All E.R. 202.

[40] [1973] Ch. 314.

[41] But *cf. Tetley* v. *Chitty* [1986] 1 All E.R. 663, 671 where it is suggested that foreseeability of nuisance should be the test.

case is the landlord to be deemed to authorise the nuisance simply because, with knowledge of its existence, he refrains from exercising his right of determining the tenancy,[42] or takes no active steps to prevent what is being done.[43] The automatic continuance of a determinable letting is not a re-letting so as to render the lessor liable.[44] It should be observed that even though the landlord is liable for creation or authorisation his liability is concurrent with and not exclusive of that of the tenant.[45]

(3) Liability of lessor or licensor who lets premises with a nuisance on them

A further extension of this principle is that a lessor or licensor is or may be liable when the nuisance existed at the commencement of the lease or licence, and was known or ought to have been known by the landlord to exist.[46] It was once thought that a landlord could exempt himself from liability by taking from the tenant a covenant to repair,[47] but as this would permit the easy evasion of the duty which arises from the ownership or occupation of property, the modern tendency is to hold that an injured third party cannot be adversely affected by the terms of the contract between landlord and tenant.[48] The test of an owner's duty to his neighbour now depends on the degree of control exercised by the owner in law or in fact for the purpose of repairs.[49]

(4) Owner's liability for breach of covenant to repair

This is a branch of the law which has seen some developments.[50] First, it was long ago held in *Payne* v. *Rogers*,[51] that the landlord is liable when the nuisance is due to a breach by him of the covenants of the lease: for example, when the premises are allowed by him to fall into a dangerous state of disrepair, and the duty of repair is cast upon him by the terms of the lease. It may seem anomalous that the terms of the contract between landlord and tenant should operate *inter alios*, so as to determine the liability of either of them to third persons; but the rule can probably be explained as merely a special application of the doctrine of authorisation already considered—that is to say, a landlord who himself undertakes the duty of repair and disregards it must be taken to have authorised his tenant to leave the premises in a state of disrepair, and is to be held liable accordingly.[52]

---

[42] *Bowen* v. *Anderson* [1894] 1 Q.B. 164.
[43] *British Office Supplies Ltd.* v. *Auckland Masonic Institute* [1957] N.Z.L.R. 512, 517.
[44] *Bowen* v. *Anderson* [1894] 1 Q.B. 164.
[45] *Roswell* v. *Prior* (1701) 12 Mod. 635.
[46] *St. Anne's Well Brewery Co.* v. *Roberts* (1928) 140 L.T. 1, 7. See Stallybrass, "The St. Anne's Well Brewery Case" (1929) 45 L.Q.R. 118.
[47] See *Pretty* v. *Bickmore* (1873) L.R. 8 C.P. 401.
[48] *Brew Bros. Ltd.* v. *Snax (Ross) Ltd.* [1970] 1 Q.B. 612.
[49] *Brew Bros. Ltd.* v. *Snax (Ross) Ltd.* [1970] 1 Q.B. 612, 637, 644.
[50] See Law Com. No. 32, paras. 61–64.
[51] (1794) 2 H.Bl. 350.
[52] *St. Anne's Well Brewery Co.* v. *Roberts* (1928) 140 L.T. 1, 8; *Wringe* v. *Cohen* [1940] 1 K.B. 229, 233.

Secondly, in *Wilchick* v. *Marks*,[53] it was held that when there was no agreement between landlords and tenants as to repairs, but the landlords knew that there was adjoining the street a defective shutter on premises over which they had expressly reserved the right to enter and do repairs, they were liable to a passer-by who was injured by the defective shutter. This decision was approved by the Court of Appeal in *Heap* v. *Ind Coope and Allsopp Ltd.*[54]

Thirdly, in *Mint* v. *Good*,[55] the Court of Appeal also held that this principle, applied when the landlord impliedly, as distinct from expressly, reserved the right to enter and do repairs. It was held that such an implication will be easily made in the case of a weekly tenancy: if nothing is said on the matter both parties will be taken to have contemplated that the premises will be kept in a habitable state of repair and that this task will be performed by the landlord,[56] even though the Rent Restriction Acts have given the tenant a certain fixity of tenure. The Housing Act 1985 provides that in a lease of a dwelling-house for a term of less than seven years there shall be implied certain repairing covenants by the lessor, in respect both of the exterior[57] of the premises and certain installations in it. Contracting out of these provisions is forbidden, though the county court may, with the consent of the parties, allow the statutory provisions to be excluded or modified. Thus the law imposes on the owner of property (at any rate if it adjoins a highway) a distinct personal obligation.[58]

§ 5.8. Defences

A number of supposed "defences" to nuisance turn out, on analysis, to be ineffective in most types of situation. Six categories must be considered[59]:

(1) Volenti non fit injuria and contributory negligence

It has long been the law that it is no defence that the plaintiff "came to the nuisance."[60] A person is not denied redress for a nuisance if with full knowledge of its existence he chooses to become the owner or occupier of land affected by it; *e.g.* if he knowingly takes a house close to a noisy factory. The maxim *volenti non fit injuria* is capable of no such application. It would be unreasonable to expect a person to refrain from

---

[53] [1934] 2 K.B. 56.

[54] [1940] 2 K.B. 476. This case extended the principle in *Wilchick* v. *Marks* in one respect, for Goddard J. had confined the landlord's liability to cases where he knew of the defect, and in *Heap's* case he did not. But the Court of Appeal held that the necessity for this limitation had been removed by its own decision in *Wringe* v. *Cohen* [1940] 1 K.B. 229 (*sed quaere*: see criticism of *Wringe* v. *Cohen* in § 5.6., above.) For the position under the Defective Premises Act 1972, see Chap. 11.

[55] [1951] 1 K.B. 517. See also *McAuley* v. *Bristol City Council* [1992] 1 All E.R. 749 C.A.

[56] *Ibid.* at 521–523 (Somervell L.J.) and 527 (Denning L.J.).

[57] See Odgers, Note, (1969) 85 L.Q.R. 333.

[58] See also the Defective Premises Act 1972 (discussed below, Chap. 11.)

[59] For the defences of necessity and statutory authority, see below, Chap. 22.

[60] *Bliss* v. *Hall* (1838) 4 Bing.N.C. 183.

buying land merely because it is already subject to a nuisance.[61] That this principle is still good law was reaffirmed in 1977 by the Court of Appeal,[62] albeit by a majority[63] and with some hesitation, in a case in which damages were awarded to the occupiers of houses newly-built adjacent to a cricket field, which had been in use without complaint for 70 years until the proximity of the houses (which were only 102 feet from the centre of the pitch) meant that escaping balls frequently interfered with the enjoyment of the occupiers. Similar reasoning will normally prevent contributory negligence being successfully relied upon as a defence to a claim in private nuisance, although it is available in cases of public nuisance.[64] In general it may be said that in such cases the standard of care to which the plaintiff in public nuisance is required to conform, if he is not to be found guilty of contributory negligence, is not necessarily as high as that required of the defendant. So a person using a highway which he is entitled to expect will be free from nuisance is in much the same position as a workman in a factory: thoughtlessness or carelessness is not equivalent to contributory negligence.[65] The act of a third party is not necessarily a defence if it is the very kind of act which should have been foreseen when the defendant originally created the nuisance.[66]

(2) Public benefit

It is no defence that the nuisance, although injurious to the individual plaintiff, is beneficial to the public at large. A nuisance may be the inevitable result of some manufacture or other operation that is of undoubted public benefit—a benefit that far outweighs the loss inflicted upon the individual—but it is an actionable nuisance nonetheless.[67] No consideration of public utility can at common law be suffered to deprive an individual of his rights without compensation.[68] Public interest may occasionally, however, be a relevant factor leading the court to deny the plaintiff an injunction, which if granted would have brought about the cessation of an activity otherwise considered desirable. On this ground the Court of Appeal recently refused to order the closure of a cricket field, and awarded damages instead.[69] But such cases are not common. In a subsequent case, also decided by the Court of Appeal, dicta in the earlier case were criticised and an injunction was awarded to a plaintiff who had actually been refused one by the trial judge on the ground of public interest.[70]

---

[61] cf. Sturges v. Bridgman [1879] 11 Ch.D. 852.
[62] See Miller v. Jackson [1977] Q.B. 966.
[63] Lord Denning M.R. dissented on the point.
[64] Dymond v. Pearce [1972] 1 Q.B. 496.
[65] Farrell v. John Mowlem & Co. Ltd. [1954] 1 Lloyd's Rep. 437, 441.
[66] Cunningham v. McGrath Bros. [1964] I.R. 209. See below, Chap. 23.
[67] Shelfer v. City of London Electric Lighting Co. [1895] 1 Ch. 287, 316; and below, Chap. 25.
[68] Bellew v. Cement Ltd. [1948] I.R. 61.
[69] Miller v. Jackson [1977] Q.B. 966 (Geoffrey Lane L.J. dissenting).
[70] Kennaway v. Thompson [1981] Q.B. 88.

(3) Care and skill

In some cases dicta can be found which say that the tendency of modern law is to assimilate nuisance and negligence and to move away from strict liability.[71] The better view[72] is that nuisance is not yet, and perhaps never will be, a branch of the law of negligence.[73] So, in 1979 counsel conceded before the Court of Appeal that a claim in negligence as distinct from nuisance would not be proceeded with because "it would give rise to much difficulty and expense."[74] The focus of nuisance is pimarily on the particular interest of the plaintiff which has been affected, rather than on the nature of the conduct of the defendant responsible. Accordingly, once undue interference is proved, the task of the plaintiff is easier than in negligence. " . . . the great merit of framing the case in nuisance as distinct from negligence," Denning L.J. once observed, is that "it greatly affects the burden of proof. It puts the legal burden where it ought to be, on the defendant, whereas in negligence it is on the plaintiff."[75]

Nevertheless many cases have confused nuisance and negligence. Much of the confusion has been due to equating fault with actionable negligence (the former is usually required,[76] the latter not), or in failing to distinguish between different types of nuisance, or between creating a nuisance and continuing it. In the case of continuing nuisances, where the defendant himself or someone for whom he is responsible has created the nuisance,[77] it is no defence that all possible care and skill are being used to prevent the operation complained of from amounting to a nuisance. If an operation cannot by any care and skill be prevented from causing harm, it cannot lawfully be undertaken at all, except with the consent of those injured by it or by the authority of a statute.[78]

(4) Contributory acts of others

Two or more persons may jointly create or continue a nuisance and then they will be joint tortfeasors.[79] But it is also no defence that the act of the defendant would not amount to a nuisance unless other persons acting independently of him did the same thing at the same time.[80] Thus if 20 factories pour out smoke and fumes into the atmosphere, the

---

[71] *British Road Services Ltd.* v. *Slater* [1964] 1 W.L.R. 498, 504.

[72] *Cunard* v. *Antifyre Ltd.* [1933] 1 K.B. 551, 558; *Sedleigh-Denfield* v. *O'Callaghan* [1940] A.C. 880, 904; *Spicer* v. *Smee* [1946] 1 All E.R. 489, 493; *Jacobs* v. *L.C.C.* [1950] A.C. 361, 374; *Farrell* v. *John Mowlem & Co. Ltd.* [1954] 1 Lloyd's Rep. 437, 440; *Paxhaven Holdings* v. *Att.-Gen.* [1974] 2 N.Z.L.R. 185.

[73] *Klimenko* v. *City of Winnipeg* (1966) 55 D.L.R. (2d) 573, 574.

[74] *Allen* v. *Gulf Oil Refining Co. Ltd.* [1980] Q.B. 156, 164.

[75] *Morton* v. *Wheeler, The Times,* February 1, 1956, per Denning L.J.

[76] *The Wagon Mound (No. 2)* [1967] 1 A.C. 617, 639.

[77] *Gourock Ropework Co. Ltd.* v. *Greenock Corporation* 1966 S.L.T. 125, 128.

[78] *Powell* v. *Fall* (1880) 5 Q.E.D. 597. See also *Adams* v. *Ursell* [1913] 1 Ch. 269 (fried fish shop using "the most approved appliances"), and *Bone* v. *Seale* [1975] 1 W.L.R. 797, (defendant liable for smell, "though he really could not do any more about it").

[79] *Brew Bros. Ltd.* v. *Snax (Ross) Ltd.* [1970] 1 Q.B. 612.

[80] *Lambton* v. *Mellish* [1874] 3 Ch. 163.

contribution of each may be so small and its detrimental effect so inappreciable that it does not *per se* amount to a nuisance. Yet the aggregate quantity may be the cause of serious harm or discomfort. In such a case each of the contributors is liable in nuisance and for his own proportion of the total damage.[81]

(5) Reasonable use of property

He who causes a nuisance cannot avail himself of the defence that he is merely making a reasonable use of his own property. No use of property is reasonable which causes substantial discomfort to other persons or is a source of damage to their property.[82] "If a man creates a nuisance, he cannot say that he is acting reasonably. The two things are self-contradictory."[83] The wrongful character of the defendant's act is not to be tested, as it is in negligence, by asking whether he could have foreseen the damage.[84] The proper angle of approach to a case of alleged nuisance is rather from the standpoint of the victim of the loss or inconvenience than from the standpoint of the alleged offender.[85]

Give and take

The term "reasonable" is, however, sometimes used in a rather confusing fashion in the cases due to a failure to distinguish between the proposition to be proved and the means of proving that proposition. If the defendant has created a nuisance, it is actionable; but the "reasonableness" of his conduct is relevant in determining whether he has in truth created a nuisance. For "a balance has to be maintained between the right of the occupier to do what he likes with his own, and the right of his neighbour not to be interfered with."[86] In this context reasonableness "is a two-sided affair"[87]: it is not enough to ask if the defendant has acted reasonably; it must be asked if he has acted reasonably having regard to the fact that he has a neighbour. So in *Bamford* v. *Turnley*[88] Bramwell B. said:

> "Those acts necessary for the common and ordinary use and occupation of land and houses may be done, if conveniently[89] done, without subjecting those who do them to an action. . . . It is as much for the advantage of one owner as of another; for the very nuisance the one complains of, as the result of the ordinary use of his neighbour's land, he himself will create in the ordinary use of his own, and the reciprocal nuisances are of comparatively trifling

---

[81] *Pride of Derby and Derbyshire Angling Association Ltd.* v. *British Celanese Ltd.* [1952] 1 All E.R. 1326, 1342 (not considered at [1953] Ch. 149). There is no joint liability in such cases; each is severally liable for his own act.

[82] *Vanderpant* v. *Mayfair Hotel Co.* [1930] 1 Ch. 138, 166.

[83] *Att.-Gen.* v. *Cole* [1901] 2 Ch. 205, 207, *per* Kekewich J.

[84] *Kraemers* v. *Att.-Gen.* [1966] Tas.S.R. 113, 122.

[85] *Watt* v. *Jamieson*, 1954 S.C. 56, 57–58.

[86] *Sedleigh-Denfield* v. *O'Callaghan* [1940] A.C. 880, 903, *per* Lord Wright.

[87] *Baylis* v. *Lea* [1962] S.R.(N.S.W.) 521, 529.

[88] (1862) 3 B. & S. 62, 83–84.

[89] *i.e.* not done in an unreasonable manner, or to an excessive degree: *Baylis* v. *Lea* [1962] S.R.(N.S.W.) 521, 540.

character. The convenience of such a rule may be indicated by calling it a rule of give and take, and live and let live."[90]

Activities such as the burning of weeds and the making of noises during temporary repair operations provide examples of this principle.
Thus inconvenience may be caused to adjoining occupiers if a building
is demolished in order to make way for a new one, but this will not constitute an actionable nuisance if all reasonable skill and care is taken to
reduce the annoyance to a minimum.[91]

Relevance of defendant's capacity and resources

A defendant's conduct is likely to be judged reasonable if to hold
otherwise would require from him a degree of effort or expense so great
as to amount to an intolerable burden.[92] In *Goldman* v. *Hargrave* Lord
Wilberforce observed that "what is reasonable to one man may be very
unreasonable, and indeed ruinous, to another."[93] This approach was
recently reaffirmed in *Leakey* v. *National Trust*[94] in which the Court of
Appeal brushed aside the argument that such a subjective approach
would result in delay in reaching decisions, increased complexity, the
necessity for discovery of the defendant's bank account and a detailed
examination of his financial resources. The approach thus adopted contrasts with the objective test which generally prevails elsewhere in tort,
and reflects the special nature of the neighbourhood relationship; it also
resembles that which at common law applied as between occupiers and
trespassers.[95] The *Goldman* and *Leakey* cases both concerned situations
in which the hazard on the defendant's land, which threatened the
plaintiff, had arisen through an act of nature. It is probable, however,
that the subjective test is not limited to such situations but extends to all
cases in which the defendant was not himself responsible for creating
the nuisance.[96]

(6) Prescription

The right to commit a private nuisance may be acquired by prescription. In order to establish such a claim the defendant must show that in
doing the acts complained of he was acting openly and to the knowledge of the owner of the servient tenement.[97] Subject to these conditions, after a nuisance has been continuously in existence for 20 years,
a prescriptive right to continue it is acquired as an easement appurte-
nant to the land on which it exists. On the expiration of this period the
nuisance becomes legalised *ab initio*, as if it had been authorised in its

---

[90] See also *Trevett* v. *Lee* [1955] 1 W.L.R. 113, 122.
[91] *Andreae* v. *Selfridge & Co.* [1938] Ch. 1, 5–6.
[92] *Andreae* v. *Selfridge & Co.* [1938] Ch. 1, 9; *Hargrave* v. *Goldman*, 110 C.L.R. 40, 71, *per*
Windeyer J.
[93] [1967] 1 A.C. 645, 663.
[94] [1980] Q.B. 485.
[95] *British Railways Board* v. *Herrington* [1972] A.C. 877.
[96] See *Page Motors Ltd.* v. *Epsom and Ewell Borough Council* (1980) 78 L.G.R. 505, 516–519,
per Balcombe J.
[97] *Liverpool Corporation* v. *Coghill (H.) & Son Ltd.* [1918] 1 Ch. 307.

commencement by a grant from the owner of the servient land.[98] It is
not sufficient, however, that the operations of the defendant which now
cause the nuisance have been continued for the space of 20 years; they
must have been a *nuisance* for that period. The time runs, not from the
day when the cause of the nuisance began, but from the day when the
nuisance began. In *Sturges* v. *Bridgman*[99] the defendant had for more
than 20 years used certain heavy machinery in his business as a confectioner. His premises in Wigmore Street adjoined the lower end of the
garden of the plaintiff, a physician in Wimpole Street. Some short time
before the action the plaintiff built a consulting room at the foot of his
garden, and then found that in the use of it he was seriously inconve-
nienced by the noise of the defendant's machinery. The defendant
pleaded a prescriptive right, but the defence was held insufficient
because there had been no actual nuisance until the erection of the
plaintiff's consulting room, and until then he had had no right of action.
It follows from the same principle that the nuisance must for 20 years
have been a nuisance to the plaintiff or his predecessors in title, and
that it is not enough that it has been for that period a nuisance to other
people in the occupation of other property. The right can be acquired
only against specific property, not against all the world. Public nuisances cannot be legalised by prescription.[1]

§ 5.9. LICENCES[2]

A licence, in the sense of the term with which we are concerned in this
chapter, is an agreement (not amounting to the grant of a lease or easement or *profit à prendre*) that it shall be lawful for the licensee to enter
upon the land of the licensor or to do some other act in relation thereto
which would otherwise be illegal. The classical description of a licence
was given by Sir John Vaughan C.J. in *Thomas* v. *Sorrell*[3]: "A dispen-
sation or licence properly passeth no interest, nor alters or transfers
property in anything, but only makes an action lawful which without it
would have been unlawful. As a licence to go beyond the seas, to hunt
in a man's park and carry away the deer killed to his own use, to cut
down a tree in a man's ground, and to carry it away the next day after to
his own use, are licences as to the acts of hunting and cutting down the
tree, but as to carrying away the deer killed and the tree cut down, they
are grants."

Lease and licence

Sometimes it is difficult to determine whether the transaction which
has given rise to entry upon the premises of another is lease or a licence.
If the transaction is a lease a proprietary interest passes to the lessee; the
parties must comply with the conditions prescribed by the Law of Prop-

---

[98] *Sturges* v. *Bridgman* (1879) 11 Ch.D. 852, 863.
[99] (1879) 11 Ch.D. 852.
[1] *R.* v. *Cross* (1812) 3 Camp. 224.
[2] On this topic, see Dawson and Pearce, *Licences Relating to the Occupation or Use of Land* (1979).
[3] (1673) Vaugh. 330, 351.

erty Act 1925, s.40; and the lessee may be able to take advantage of the protection afforded by the Rent Restriction Acts. It is quite clear that the difference between a lease and a licence does not depend on any label which the parties themselves have affixed to the transaction but upon the true interpretation in law of what they have done.[4] A vital question is whether the entrant has obtained exclusive possession of the premises; if he has, the transaction is probably a lease and not a licence. There may be cases in which a person with exclusive possession is rightly described as a licensee, but they are exceptional.[5]

We must consider (1) the effect of the licence as between the parties to it, and (2) the extent to which it binds third parties.

(1) The effect of the licence as between the parties

The main distinction drawn here is between licences coupled with the grant of an interest and bare licences. Licences coupled with an interest (as they are often called) are irrevocable.[6] An injunction can be obtained to prevent the wrongful revocation of such a licence.[7] In such a case the licence and the proprietary interest thereby granted are distinct concepts.

It is uncertain whether the term "interest" is confined to interests in land or in goods on the land. It has been held to cover a right to attend a creditors' meeting[8] or a cinema performance,[9] but it is doubtful whether it covers a right to do specified works under a construction contract.[10]

Bare licence prima facie revocable at common law

Under a bare licence no interest in property passes: the licensee is simply not a trespasser. A licence of this kind may be either gratuitous or contained in a contract for valuable consideration: in either case at common law it was revocable at the will of the licensor and was therefore no justification for any act done in exercise of it after revocation. This was laid down in *Wood* v. *Leadbitter*[11] and emphatically reaffirmed by the Court of Appeal in *Thompson* v. *Park*.[12]

In *Wood* v. *Leadbitter* the occupiers of Doncaster racecourse in breach

---

[4] A unanimous House of Lords in *Street* v. *Mountford* [1985] A.C. 800 used almost the same language as Sir John Vaughan C.J. in *Thomas* v. *Sorrell*: "The parties cannot alter the effect of the agreement by insisting that they only created a licence. The manufacture of a five-pronged implement for manual digging results in a fork, even if the manufacturer, unfamiliar with the English language, insists that he intended to make and has made a spade"—*Street* v. *Mountford* [1985] A.C. 800, 819, *per* Lord Templeman.

[5] *Street* v. *Mountford* [1985] A.C. 800, 819, *per* Lord Templeman.

[6] Some statutory licences are also irrevocable—*e.g.* those granted under the Domestic Violence Act 1976.

[7] *Frogley* v. *Lovelace* (1859) John. 333.

[8] *Vaughan* v. *Hampson* (1875) 33 L.T. 15.

[9] *Hurst* v. *Picture Theatres Ltd.* [1915] 1 K.B. 1.

[10] *Hounslow London Borough Council* v. *Twickenham Garden Developments Ltd.* [1971] Ch. 233.

[11] (1845) 13 M. & W. 838.

[12] [1944] K.B. 408.

of their agreement ordered the plaintiff, to whom they had sold a ticket for the races, to leave the premises while the races were going on, and on his refusal to leave they procured his forcible expulsion by their servant, the defendant. In an action for assault the defendant pleaded that the plaintiff was a trespasser. It was held by the Court of Exchequer that the action would not lie. Although the licence had been revoked improperly and in breach of contract its revocation was nonetheless effectual. The plaintiff was a trespasser. It will be noticed that the action was one of tort against the servant of the licensor and not one for breach of contract against the licensor himself. It is well settled[13] that an action for breach of contract will lie in such a case even at common law, and notwithstanding *Wood* v. *Leadbitter*. If, however, the licensee insists, notwithstanding the revocation of his licence (even though it is wrongful as being in breach of contract), in entering or remaining on the land or in otherwise exercising his licence, he becomes at common law a trespasser or other wrongdoer. The rule is an illustration of the difference between a legal power to do a thing effectively and a legal *right* or *liberty* to do it lawfully. A licensor has at common law the power to revoke the licence at any time, but he has no right to revoke it before the expiration of the term.[14]

Exceptions

There are two recognised qualifications to the rule in *Wood* v. *Leadbitter*:

(1) A licensee is entitled to a reasonable time in which to remove himself and his property after the licence has been revoked and he cannot be treated as a trespasser until the expiry of that time.[15] This packing-up period (as it has been usefully called[16]) is available to gratuitous as well as to contractual licensees. It is unnecessary for the licensor in his notice of revocation to specify the period to which the licensee is entitled.[17] If the licensor gives insufficient, or no, notice of revocation, the licensee still cannot ignore the revocation and treat the licence as if it were still subsisting.[18] In some cases it seems that a licensee may be entitled to reasonable notice of the proposed revocation as well as to the packing-up period.[19]

---

[13] *Kerrison* v. *Smith* [1897] 2 Q.B. 445; *King* v. *David Allen & Sons Ltd.* [1916] 2 A.C. 54.

[14] *Thompson* v. *Park* [1944] K.B. 408, 410. But *Thompson* v. *Park* was said to have been decided "quasi in furore" in *Hounslow London Borough Council* v. *Twickenham Garden Developments Ltd.* [1971] Ch. 233, 249, and emphatically dissented from in *Verrall* v. *Great Yarmouth B.C.* [1981] Q.B. 202. In *Thompson* v. *Park* one of the plaintiff's witnesses was a self-confident nine-year-old named Michael Heseltine: J. Critchley, *Heseltine* (1987), p. 1.

[15] *Tool Metal Manufacturing Co. Ltd.* v. *Tungsten Electric Co. Ltd.* [1955] 1 W.L.R. 761. And even a trespasser is not entirely without rights: below, § 11.9.

[16] *Winter Garden Theatre (London) Ltd.* v. *Millennium Productions Ltd.* [1948] A.C. 173, 206.

[17] *Isaac* v. *Hotel de Paris Ltd.* [1960] 1 W.L.R. 239.

[18] *Dorling* v. *Honnor Marine Ltd.* [1964] Ch. 560, 567 (reversed on another point [1965] Ch. 1).

[19] *Winter Garden Theatre (London) Ltd.* v. *Millennium Productions Ltd.* [1948] A.C. 173, 205.

(2) The premature revocation of a licence imposes no obligation upon the licensee to do any act for the purpose of preventing the continuing effect upon the servient land of any act which he may have lawfully done before the revocation.[20]

Wood v. Leadbitter doubted

Since the fusion of law and equity, according to the decision of the majority of the Court of Appeal in *Hurst* v. *Picture Theatres Ltd.*[21] the rule in *Wood* v. *Leadbitter* has to a very large extent become obsolete. In *Hurst's* case the majority held that the plaintiff, who had purchased from the defendants a ticket entitling him to occupy a seat at a cinema, had a good cause of action in *tort* for the act of the defendants in forcibly removing him from the building under the mistaken belief that he had wrongfully obtained admission without payment. Hence the plaintiff recovered substantial damages for battery instead of the merely nominal damages which would have been recoverable in an action for breach of contract.[22] The majority of the court seem to have adopted the view that the decision in *Wood* v. *Leadbitter* turned on the absence of a seal and that since the Judicature Acts this ground of decision had become obsolete for all courts would now treat the plaintiff as being in the same position as if the licence had in fact been under seal. But a seal would have made no difference in *Hurst* v. *Picture Theatres*.[23] The essence of the matter is that the right to enter on premises to see a spectacle is not a interest in land in the ordinary use of legal language: it is not a proprietary interest capable of being the subject-matter of a grant, as is a lease, easement or a *profit à prendre*. The law has always been reluctant to permit the number of proprietary interests in land to be increased beyond the recognised categories of incorporeal hereditaments for fear lest purchasers should find themselves saddled with unknown and perhaps fanciful burdens.[24]

It has been said that the fallacy of this criticism of *Hurst's* case lies in its insistence upon discovering a proprietary right as a condition of

---

[20] *Armstrong* v. *Sheppard and Short Ltd.* [1959] 2 Q.B. 384. But see above, § 4.2.

[21] [1915] 1 K.B. 1, followed in *Whipp* v. *Mackey* [1927] I.R. 372, 387.

[22] It is generally believed that the damages obtainable by such a licensee in an action for breach of contract are limited to the value of his ticket, either because the battery is too remote a consequence of the breach of contract, or because of the rule in *Addis* v. *Gramophone Co.* [1909] A.C. 488, which prohibits the award of damages for mental distress in an action for breach of contract, and which is still binding on the C.A.: *Bliss* v. *South East Thames Regional Health Authority.* [1987] I.C.R. 70.

[23] [1915] 1 K.B. 1, 18, *per* Phillimore L.J. (dissenting). As Alderson B. himself said: "It may further be observed, that a licence under seal (provided it be a mere licence) is as revocable as a licence by parol" ((1845) 13 M. & W. 838, 845).

[24] It is not easy to find authority for this elementary proposition: "But to hold that one of the fundamental doctrines of real property can be called in question because it has not been in terms laid down by a judgment of the House of Lords is, in my opinion, to invest the judicial proceedings of this House with an authority to which they are not entitled. The ABC of the law is generally not questioned before your Lordships, just because it is the ABC"; *Johnston* v. *O'Neill* [1911] A.C. 552, 592, *per* Lord Dunedin.

affording protection to the licensee.[25] Contracts as well as grants may create irrevocable interests, and so the question whether any restrictions exist on the power of a licensor to determine a revocable licence must depend upon the circumstances of each case.[26] This view has received much support[27] since it was adopted by Lord Greene M.R. in the *Winter Garden Theatre* case[28] as a "rather simple way . . . to get round any difficulties which might be felt as to the reasoning in *Hurst* v. *Picture Theatres*."

The present law

It seems, therefore, that the former rule of law that a licence is revocable despite any contract has been converted into a rule of construction that a licence is *prima facie* revocable or variable[29] subject to the terms of any contract between the parties.[30] The extent to which the licensor has disabled himself from exercising his power of revocation will have to be ascertained according to the ordinary principles of construction. It may well be that an injunction could be obtained to restrain the revocation of a licence which is intended to extend over a substantial tract of time—*e.g.* a ticket entitling the holder to admission throughout the season at an open-air racecourse.[31] But the courts will also probably be ready to assume that a licence granted for valuable consideration for a limited time and for a limited purpose was intended to be irrevocable until that purpose has been accomplished in the manner contemplated.[32] If in such a case performance of the act or purpose licensed has actually begun the remedies of declaration or injunction will be available to the licensee to restrain the licensor from either revoking in breach of contract or acting on his purported revocation, as the case may require. So in a proper case a licence[33] or statutory right[34] to go upon or use land may be enforced by way of injunction. But it is still no easier than before to understand what the law is if the licence is not suitable to be specifically enforced by way of injunction (as in *Thompson* v. *Park*[35]), or if the licensee has been actually ejected (as in *Hurst's* case) before the

[25] *Cowell* v. *Rosehill Racecourse Co.* (1937) 56 C.L.R. 605, 651, *per* Evatt J.
[26] *Tool Metal Manufacturing Co. Ltd.* v. *Tungsten Electric Co. Ltd.* [1955] 1 W.L.R. 761.
[27] See, *e.g.* *Hounslow London Borough Council* v. *Twickenham Garden Developments Ltd.* [1971] Ch. 233, and *Verrall* v. *Great Yarmouth B.C.* [1981] Q.B. 202.
[28] [1946] 1 All E.R. 678, 685.
[29] *White* v. *Blackmore* [1972] 2 Q.B. 651.
[30] There is an implied condition in a licence to enter to see a spectacle that the licensee will behave in a reasonable manner: *Duffield* v. *Police* [1971] N.Z.L.R. 378.
[31] Evershed M.R. (1954) 70 L.Q.R. 339–340.
[32] *Duffield* v. *Police* N.Z.L.R. 378, 381.
[33] *Heidke* v. *Sydney City Council* (1952) S.R.(N.S.W.) 143.
[34] *Warder* v. *Cooper* [1970] Ch. 495.
[35] [1944] K.B. 408 (quarrelling schoolmasters: the courts cannot compel two men to be of one mind in a house). If the licence is not fit to be specifically enforced by way of injunction, neither is it fit to be exercised in defiance of the will of the licensor. Yet, until *Hurst's* case is overruled, this cannot be said to be the law.

aid of equity can be invoked,[36] or if he claims only damages and not an injunction. Still, as wrongful acts are no passport to favour in a court of equity, one wrongfully ejected may be put back in possession by a mandatory injunction.[37]

(2) Effects of the licence on third parties

Since a licence is not a legal servitude, it does not run with the servient land at law so as to bind all subsequent owners of it. At law, indeed, it is a mere agreement, which binds no one save the grantor himself. Such an agreement, however, if of such a nature as to be specifically enforceable, amounts to a good equitable servitude—that is to say, it binds and runs with the land in equity so as to be enforceable not merely against the grantor, but also against all subsequent owners and occupiers of the land except purchasers for value without notice of any such equitable right.[38] Thus it has been held that a licence to occupy premises is binding on the devisee of the licensor.[39]

Yet such an "equity" is enforceable against the third party only in the sense that he will be restrained by injunction from acting inconsistently with it. For although a licensee has an action for damages for breach of contract against the licensor for any disturbance of the licence committed by him, he has no remedy at law against any subsequent owner or occupier or any stranger for a disturbance of his right. This seems to follow logically from the fact that he has no legal estate or interest in the servient land, and it is against the policy of the law to create new proprietary interests.[40] Thus in *Hill* v. *Tupper*,[41] in which the plaintiff had acquired by grant under the seal of a canal company an exclusive right of keeping pleasure-boats for hire upon the canal, he unsuccessfully sued at law for damages a stranger who infringed this monopoly.

This absence of a remedy by way of damages available to a licensee against a stranger is an anomalous feature of our law. It seems curious that he who, by agreement with the occupier of a building, has expended money in painting advertisements upon one of its walls should have no civil remedy against a third person who wilfully defaces

---

[36] The suggestion that a judge who happened to pass by such an incident might have been persuaded to grant an *ex parte* injunction is no longer fanciful (as it once was: Megarry, 11 J.S.P.T.L. 181). Under Ord. 29, r. 1, an injunction may be granted in an urgent case before the writ or originating summons is issued: *Re N.* [1967] Ch. 512; and in *Allen* v. *Jambo Holdings Ltd.* [1980] 1 W.L.R. 1252, it would appear that the plaintiff's counsel successfully applied for a *Mareva* injunction by telephoning the judge. Still, "even the longest modern film would not have given Hurst time to get an injunction from a Chancery judge and return with his order to the cinema before the end of the showing": Evershed, (1954) 70 L.Q.R. 333.

[37] *Warder* v. *Cooper* [1970] 1 Ch. 495.

[38] *Bendall* v. *McWhirter* [1952] 2 Q.B. 466, 481. These rights are outside the scope of the Land Registration Act 1925, at any rate when the licensee is in actual possession or occupation of the land: *Binions* v. *Evans* [1972] Ch. 359.

[39] *Errington* v. *Errington* [1952] 1 K.B. 290.

[40] *National Provincial Bank Ltd.* v. *Ainsworth* [1965] A.C. 1175.

[41] (1863) 2 H. & C. 121.

them.[42] There is, however, one important class of licences to which this rule has no application—namely, those in which the licence is of such a nature that it would, if created by deed or prescription, amount to a legal easement or profit. Thus in *Mason* v. *Clarke*[43] the appellant had the benefit of an oral agreement entitling him to catch rabbits on the Hothorpe estate (a *profit à prendre*); the House of Lords held that he could recover damages from the respondent for his interference with the exercise of those rights. The distinction between *Hill* v. *Tupper* and *Mason* v. *Clarke* is that in the former case what the plaintiff was trying to do was set up, under the guise of an easement, a monopoly which had no normal connection with the ordinary use of his land, but which was merely an independent business enterprise.[44] It is also a question whether the power of courts of equity to grant an injunction to a licensee, taken in conjunction with their power to grant damages in lieu of injunction,[45] does not exclude the rule in *Hill* v. *Tupper* in all cases in which an injunction can be granted.

§ 5.10. Rights of Way

Rights of way are either private or public. The former call for no special consideration, for they are governed by the ordinary principles relating to easements in general and are therefore more appropriately dealt with in works on real property.[46] Public rights of way, on the other hand, are not easements and demand more particular examination. They are of two kinds, for they exist either over highways or over navigable rivers.[47] The law as to these two is essentially the same.

A highway (including in that term any public way) is a piece of land over which the public at large possesses a right of way. A highway extends to the whole width of the space between the fences or hedges on either side, and is not confined to the metalled centre strip[48]—partly in order to admit light and air to it, and partly because "Macadam's system of road-making with broken stone was not introduced at the earliest until just before the end of the eighteenth century."[49] At common law the ownership of a highway is in the owner or owners of the land adjoining it on either side, the highway having been made such by an actual or presumed dedication of it to the use of the public by the proprietors of the land over which it runs. By statute certain kinds of highways are now vested in local authorities. These statutes, however, have been so interpreted as to vest in the local authorities not the whole of the land on which the highway lies *usque ad coelum et ad inferos* but only so much of it above and below the surface as is reasonably necess-

---

[42] *King* v. *David Allen & Sons, Billposting Ltd.* [1916] 2 A.C. 54. Perhaps this decision could be limited to cases in which the licence has not yet been acted on.

[43] [1955] A.C. 778.

[44] *Re Ellenborough Park* [1956] Ch. 131, 175.

[45] See below, Chap. 25.

[46] See Megarry and Wade, *The Law of Real Property*. See also the 18th edition of the present work, § 23.

[47] *Tate & Lyle Ltd.* v. *G.L.C.* [1983] 2 A.C. 509.

[48] *Holland* v. *Dublin County Council* (1967) 112 I.L.T.R. 1.

[49] *Harvey* v. *Truro R.D.C.* [1903] 2 Ch. 638, 643, *per* Joyce J.

ary for the efficient construction, care, and use of the highway. The sub-soil below and the space above the limits so defined remain as at common law in the owners of the adjoining lands.[50]

There are at least four distinct kinds of injury which may be committed in respect of a highway:

(1) Trespass and the highway

This has already been considered.[51]

(2) Nuisance to adjoining occupiers

This may arise in several ways—for example, keeping horses or vehicles standing constantly in front of a shop,[52] or watching or besetting premises with a view to compelling the occupier to do, or abstain from doing, what he is entitled to do, at any rate if there is intimidation, violence or obstruction. There is no general right to picket premises,[53] although some protection is given in trade disputes by the Trade Union and Labour Relations Act 1974, s.15 (as substituted by the Employment Act 1980, s.16).

(3) Disturbance of the rights of access to a highway[54]

Every person who occupies land immediately adjoining a highway has a private right of access to the highway from his land and vice versa; and any act done without lawful justification whereby the exercise of this private right is obstructed is an actionable wrong.[55] This right of access is a private right of property, and if what is complained of is sufficiently substantial to constitute an interference with that right, he may recover at least nominal damages, for it is an example of an action on the case succeeding without proof of special damage.[56] This right may indirectly protect the owner's interest in a view from or to his land, interference with which is not otherwise actionable. Interference with a window display may be actionable if it deprives the plaintiff of his own right of access to that window.[57]

At common law a frontager had the right of entrance and exit from his land on to a highway at any point. But this common law right does not mean that the landowner can require that the highway should be in a condition or state, along his whole frontage, most convenient for the exercise of the right.[58] In any event, the common law right of access has been greatly cut down by statutes (see, for example, the Highways Act 1980, s.124), especially since local authorities have had vested in them the surface of the highway.[59] Opening up a new access may also consti-

---

[50] *Tithe Redemption Commission* v. *Runcorn U.D.C.* [1954] Ch. 383.
[51] Above, Chap. 4.
[52] *Benjamin* v. *Storr* (1874) L.R. 9 C.P. 400.
[53] *Hubbard* v. *Pitt* [1976] Q.B. 142. See below, Chap. 16.
[54] See Garner, "Rights in the Highways" (1960) 24 *The Conveyancer* 454.
[55] *Barber* v. *Penley* [1893] 2 Ch. 447.
[56] *Walsh* v. *Ervin* [1952] V.L.R. 361.
[57] *Hall* v. *Jamaica Omnibus Services Ltd.* (1966) 9 W.L.R. 344.
[58] *Holland* v. *Dublin County Council* (1967) 112 I.L.T.R. 1.
[59] Cork, "Right of Access to and from the Highway" [1952] J.P.L. 553.

tute development for which planning permission is required. This right of access to a highway by the occupier of land abutting upon it must be distinguished from the right of passing along the highway.[60] The former is a private and the latter a public right, and for any infringement of the former an action will lie; whereas, as we shall see in the next section, no action will lie for an infringement of the public right of passing except on proof of some special or particular consequential damage suffered by the plaintiff. The private right of access thus protected includes merely the right to get from the highway into the plaintiff's land, and from his land into the highway; and does not include a right to get to and from the plaintiff's land by going along the highway, for this is merely the public right of passage.[61] A disturbance of this private right of access may or may not be at the same time a disturbance of the public right of passage. A man's doorway may be obstructed by an act which in no way obstructs the use of the highway; and conversely the highway may be obstructed, while the right of access remains unaffected.[62]

(4) Public nuisance to a highway

This consists in obstructing the highway or rendering it dangerous.[63] These are two different categories of nuisance, and cases of dangers in the highway are not necessarily authorities on obstruction.[64] For an obstruction, if unreasonable, is a public nuisance in itself, and it is not necessary also to show that it is dangerous. The topic is fully considered in the following section.

§ 5.11. NUISANCE TO A HIGHWAY (1) NATURE OF INTERFERENCE

The term nuisance is here used in the sense of public nuisance—*i.e.* an indictable criminal wrong.[65] "In order to establish nuisance or obstruction in a public highway something which is indictable—a punishable offence—must be established."[66] But the plaintiff must prove that the nuisance was a cause of his injuries, so contributory negligence is a defence.[67]

Obstructions to the highway

Examples of this are stopping or narrowing a highway by erecting a fence, scaffolding or hoarding,[68] or building[69] which projects beyond the boundary line; causing siltation of a navigable river by constructing

---

[60] *Holland v. Dublin Couty Council* (1967) 112 I.L.T.R. 1.
[61] This established principle was re-affirmed in *R. (McCreash) v. Armagh County Court Judge* [1978] N.I. 164.
[62] *Walsh v. Ervin* [1952] V.L.R. 361.
[63] *Trevett v. Lee* [1955] 1 W.L.R. 113, 117; *Dymond v. Pearce* [1972] 1 Q.B. 496, 501.
[64] *Dymond v. Pearce* [1972] 1 Q.B. 496, 502.
[65] The Highways Act 1980, Part IX, creates numerous criminal offences in relation to the obstruction of or damage to highways. See also the Rights of Way Act 1990.
[66] *The Carlgarth* [1927] P. 93, 102, *per* Bankes L.J.
[67] *Dymond v. Pearce* [1972] 1 Q.B. 496.
[68] *Harper v. Haden & Sons* [1933] Ch. 298.
[69] *Black v. Mitchell* [1951] N.I. 145 (projecting sunblind).

badly designed ferry terminals,[70] leaving[71] horses and carts,[72] or motor-vehicles,[73] standing on the highway for an unreasonable time or in unreasonable number,[74] collecting a crowd of people in it, as at the door of a theatre[75] or shop,[76] or holding a picket,[77] demonstration or procession. But the procession must be an unreasonable use of the high-way[78]—it cannot be a nuisance for a number of people to use the highway jointly and contemporaneously, for that is just what the highway is made for.[79] In *Thomas* v. *National Union of Mineworkers*[80] picketing which fell short of obstruction was held to be capable of constituting a tort analogous to an actionable nuisance

> "Suppose an individual were persistently to follow another on a public highway, making rude gestures or remarks in order to annoy or vex. If continuance of such conduct were threatened no one can doubt but that a civil court would, at the suit of the victim, restrain by an injunction the continuance of the conduct."[81]

Dangers to the highway

These may be caused either by something done in the highway itself or by something done on the land which adjoins it. It is now clear that the fact that a vehicle has broken down on the highway in the dark and its lights have gone out without any negligence on the part of the driver does not constitute nuisance (or negligence[82]) immediately and automatically. The driver may, however, be liable if he allows the unlighted vehicle to obstruct the highway without taking reasonable steps to light it or remove it or give warning of its existence,[83] for "any unlighted obstacle on a fast motor-road is a danger to traffic. That is a proposition, not of law, but of common sense."[84] Other examples are keeping in the highway defective and dangerous tramway-lines, coal-plates, or cellar gratings[85]; leaving on the highway or adjacent thereto matter on which

---

[70] *Tate & Lyle Ltd.* v. *G.L.C.* [1983] 2 A.C. 509.

[71] This term connotes some degree of permanence: *Dymond* v. *Pearce* [1972] 1 Q.B. 496.

[72] *Fritz* v. *Hobson* (1880) 14 Ch.D. 542.

[73] *Chesterfield Corporation* v. *Arthur Robinson (Transport) Ltd.* (1955) 106 L.J.(News.) 61 is a good modern example. A main road was obstructed for 76 hours as a result of the defendants' negligent mode of conveying an outsize load of 83 tons. The plaintiffs recovered for the special damage which they had suffered through the diversion of their omnibus service.

[74] "No one can make a stableyard on the King's highway": *R.* v. *Cross* (1812) 3 Camp. 224, 227, *per* Lord Ellenborough C.J.

[75] *Barber* v. *Penley* [1893] 2 Ch. 447 (crowds at *Charley's Aunt*).

[76] *Dwyer* v. *Mansfield* [1946] K.B. 437.

[77] Cf. *Hubbard* v. *Pitt* [1976] Q.B. 142 (picketing premises constituted private nuisance).

[78] *R.* v. *Clark* [1964] 2 Q.B. 315.

[79] *Johnson* v. *Kent* (1975) 132 C.L.R. 164, 176.

[80] [1985] 2 All E.R. 1.

[81] [1985] 2 All E.R. 1, 22.

[82] *Moore* v. *Maxwells of Emsworth Ltd.* [1968] 1 W.L.R. 1077.

[83] *Maitland* v. *Raisbeck* [1944] K.B. 689.

[84] *Hill-Venning* v. *Beszant* (1950) 66 T.L.R. (Pt. 2) 921, 927, *per* Denning L.J.

[85] *Pretty* v. *Bickmore* (1873) L.R. 8 C.P. 401. See also the Highways Act 1980, s.182(6).

passengers are likely to slip[86]; allowing a house, fence, or other structure immediately adjoining the highway to become ruinous and
dangerous[87]; keeping unfenced an excavation so close to the highway
as to be a danger in case of accidental deviation[88]; keeping at a golf-club
a hole where players are in the habit of slicing onto the highway.[89] The
plaintiff's property need not be immediately contiguous to the highway: it is enough if it is sufficiently proximate to the highway to be
affected by the misuse of it.[90]

Existing dangers

When, however, a road is dedicated to the public, it is presumed to be
so dedicated on the terms that the public right of passage is to be subject to all obstructions and dangers which exist at the time of dedication; and the adjoining owners and occupiers are therefore under no
liability for maintaining such obstructions or dangers or for any mischief that may result from them.[91] Nor are they liable for a mere passive
failure to prevent new dangers from arising on the highway or to give
warning of their existence. *A fortiori* when something has been done on
the highway itself which makes it dangerous, there is no obligation on
the occupier of the adjoining land to do away with the danger. Were it
otherwise, an intolerable burden would be put upon the occupiers of
land adjoining highways.[92] In these respects the public must look after
itself.

Unreasonable obstructions

It must be realised that it is not every obstruction of or a danger to the
highway which constitutes a public nuisance. The law has to hold an
even balance between the conflicting claims of those who have an interest in the use of the highway. On the one hand, it has been settled for at
least a century that "traffic on the highways, whether by land or sea,
cannot be conducted without exposing those whose persons or property are near to it to some inevitable risk; and that being so, those who
go on the highway, or have their property adjacent to it, may well be
held to do so subject to their taking on themselves the risk of injury
from that inevitable danger."[93] Hence although a permanent obstruction erected in a highway without lawful authority necessarily constitutes a public nuisance, as it in fact operates as a withdrawal of part of

---

[86] *McGowan* v. *Masterson* (1952) 87 I.L.T.R. 102.
[87] *Harrold* v. *Watney* [1898] 2 Q.B. 320. Contrast *Morton* v. *Wheeler, The Times,* February 1,
1956 (spikes on shop window not a nuisance).
[88] *Jacobs* v. *L.C.C.* [1950] A.C. 361.
[89] *Castle* v. *St. Augustine's Links* (1922) 38 T.L.R. 615.
[90] *Southport Corporation* v. *Esso Petroleum Co. Ltd.* [1956] A.C. 218, 225.
[91] *Fisher* v. *Prowse* (1862) 2 B. & S. 770.
[92] *Nicholson* v. *Southern Ry.* [1935] 1 K.B. 558.
[93] *Fletcher* v. *Rylands* (1866) L.R. 1 Ex. 265, 286, *per* Blackburn J. See the same learned judge
in *River Wear Commissioners* v. *Adamson* (1877) 2 App.Cas. 743, 767.

the highway from the public, a temporary obstruction may be permiss-ible if it is negligible in point of time or authorised by Parliament or occasioned in the reasonable and lawful user of the highway as a high-way.[94] The law relating to the user of highways is in truth the law of give and take.[95] Thus a person has a right to obstruct a highway by the erection of scaffolding and hoardings for the purpose of repairing his house,[96] so long as the inconvenience to the public is necessarily so caused and does not offend either in *quantum* or duration; or he may temporarily obstruct the highway by causing his motor-car to stop out-side his house for the purpose of discharging passengers or goods going into the house.[97] Again a temporary excavation[98] or stoppage[99] may be permissible.

On the other hand, we shall see that any person who procures or authorises the doing in any highway of any dangerous act other than the use of the highway for ordinary purposes of passage has imposed upon him a duty of care so strict that it cannot be discharged by the employment of an independent contractor.[1]

§ 5.12. NUISANCE TO A HIGHWAY (2) DAMAGE

A nuisance to a highway is a criminal offence and may be made the subject of an indictment at common law. It may also be restrained by injunction at the suit of the Attorney-General acting *ex officio* or at the relation of any private person interested in the matter, or by a local authority acting under section 222 of the Local Government Act 1972. But it is not *per se* actionable at the suit of a private person—a rule established for the purpose of preventing oppression by means of a multiplicity of civil actions for the same cause. No such action will lie save at the suit of a person who can show special and particular damage suffered by himself and distinct from the general inconvenience endured by him in common with the public at large.[2] So in this branch of the law it is plain that it is not enough for the plaintiff to show that the damage was reasonably foreseeable.[3] The terms "special" and "par-ticular" are used, apparently indiscriminately, in this field of the law, to describe the nature of the damage which the plaintiff must prove. The latter term is preferable: the plaintiff need not prove that the damage which he has suffered is extraordinary. Indeed it has even been held in an Australian case that the particular damage for which an individual

---

[94] *Buck* v. *Briggs Motor Bodies Ltd.* (1959) *The Times*, April 18 (gate across pavement).

[95] *Harper* v. *Haden (G.N.) & Sons Ltd.* [1933] Ch. 298, 316–317, 320.

[96] *Harper* v. *Haden (G.N.) & Sons Ltd.* [1933] Ch. 298 (in fact in this case the scaffolding was erected for the purpose of adding another storey); *Almeroth* v. *Chivers Ltd.* [1948] 1 All E.R. 53 is on the other side of the line.

[97] *Trevett* v. *Lee* [1955] 1 W.L.R. 113, 118.

[98] *Wall* v. *Morrissey* [1969] I.R. 10.

[99] *Dymond* v. *Pearce* [1972] 1 Q.B. 496.

[1] *Wall* v. *Morrissey* [1969] I.R. 10, 14. See below, Chap. 21.

[2] *Winterbottom* v. *Derby (Lord)* (1867) L.R. 2 Ex. 316, 320, 322.

[3] *The Wagon Mound (No. 2)* [1967] 1 A.C. 617.

can sue in his own name is not limited to special damage in the sense of actual pecuniary loss, but may consist of proved general damage, *e.g.* inconvenience and delay, provided that it is substantial, direct and appreciably greater in degree than any suffered by the general public.[4] The damage must be of a substantial character, not fleeting or evanescent.[5]

Nature of particular damage[6]

The special or particular damage which must be proved may include injury to the plaintiff's person or chattels, depreciation of actual value of property and loss of custom.[7] Costs incurred in actually removing an obstruction to the highway may also be recoverable.[8]

(1) Injury to person

In *Castle* v. *St. Augustine's Links*[9] a taxicab driver[10] who lost his eye from a sliced golf-ball recovered damages from the golf-club whose hole was so near the highway as to be a public nuisance. But it is doubtful whether a plaintiff in *private* nuisance can recover for personal injuries.[11]

(2) Injury to chattels

When oily smuts from the defendant's refinery damaged both the clothes drying in his garden and the paintwork of his car parked in the road outside, the plaintiff recovered for the former in private nuisance but for the latter in public nuisance.[12] The most striking example is *The Wagon Mound (No. 2)*,[13] in which it was conceded that the destruction by fire of two ships was particular damage entitling their owners to sue in nuisance.[14]

(3) Injury to pecuniary interests

This kind of damage may occur when the plaintiff has incurred expense or suffered pecuniary loss by being prevented from using the

---

[4] *Walsh* v. *Erwin* [1952] V.L.R. 361.
[5] *Vanderpant* v. *Mayfair Hotel Co.* [1930[1 Ch. 138, 153; *Harper* v. *Haden (G.N.) & Sons* [1933] Ch. 298, 304, 308.
[6] Prosser, "Private Action for Public Nuisance" (1966) 52 Va.L.Rev. 997; Kodilinye, "Public nuisance and particular damage in modern law" (1986) 6 *Legal Studies* 182.
[7] *Walsh* v. *Ervin* [1952] V.L.R. 361, 368.
[8] *Tate & Lyle Ltd.* v. *G.L.C.* [1983] 2 A.C. 509.
[9] (1922) 38 T.L.R. 615.
[10] Who had been General Plumer's driver throughout the First World War without injury.
[11] See above, § 5.5.
[12] *Halsey* v. *Esso Petroleum Co. Ltd.* [1961] 1 W.L.R. 683.
[13] [1967] 1 A.C. 617.
[14] But not to recover damages in nuisance, because the loss was unforeseeable: see below, Chap. 23.

highway. Thus in *Rose* v. *Miles*[15] the plaintiff, who complained of the obstruction of a navigable canal, was held to have a good cause of action on proving that he had been compelled to unload his goods from barges and carry them overland thereby incurring additional expense. If the requirement of particular damage were carried to its logical conclusion, it would seem to exclude a plaintiff who had merely suffered delay through the nuisance, for his damage would be no different from that of others.[16] But the courts have tended to say that "time is money," and permitted recovery for any delay which is different in degree, and not necessarily in kind, from that suffered by other members of the public.[17] So recovery was permitted when "a medical man in large practice whose time is of substantial value" was delayed for 20 minutes at a level-crossing.[18] An action will lie even if the only special damage proved is an injury to the plaintiff's business, due to the fact that the obstruction to the highway has hindered the public from resorting to his business premises,[19] or the conduct of the business had become more expensive.[20] In other words, it is said that the special damage may be suffered by the plaintiff not because he has been prevented from using the highway as beneficially as heretofore, but merely because other persons have been so hindered, so that the result of their hindrance is a loss suffered by himself.[21] The result would therefore seem to be that damage done to the plaintiff in his trade by the illegal obstruction of a highway is an actionable wrong.[22]

Criticism

These principles are as old as any in the common law[23] and can now be altered only by legislation.[24] In theory the proper remedies for personal injuries caused by such obstructions of the highway as amount to a public nuisance should be the actions of trespass and negligence.[25] But in practice the same result is achieved by the courts requiring proof of negligence in an action for personal injuries caused by an obstruction of the highway.[26]

---

[15] (1815) 4 M. & S. 101. *cf. Tate & Lyle Ltd.* v. *G.L.C.* [1983] 2 A.C. 509.

[16] *Winterbottom* v. *Derby* (*Lord*) (1867) L.R. 2 Ex. 316.

[17] *Smith* v. *Wilson* [1903] 2 I.R. 45 (farmer obstructed on way to market).

[18] *Boyd* v. *G.N.R.* [1895] 2 I.R. 555 (yet the damages were only 10s.).

[19] *Campbell* v. *Paddington Corporation* [1911] 1 K.B. 869.

[20] *Gravesham B.C.* v. *British Rail* [1978] Ch. 379, 398. *cf. Tate & Lyle Ltd.* v. *G.L.C.* [1983] 2 A.C. 509.

[21] *Amalgamated Theatres Ltd.* v. *Charles S. Luney Ltd.* [1962] N.Z.L.R. 226, 229.

[22] *Blundy, Clark & Co.* v. *L. and N.E. Ry.* [1931] 2 K.B. 334; *Harper* v. *Haden* (*G.N.*) & *Sons* [1933] Ch. 298. This particular point was not taken in *Lyons, Sons & Co.* v. *Gulliver* [1914] 1 Ch. 631 (theatre queue obstructing access).

[23] *Hardcastle* v. *South Yorkshire Ry.* (1859) 4 H. & N. 67.

[24] *Mumford* v. *Naylor* [1951] 1 T.L.R. 1068, 1070 (reversed on another point in [1951] W.N. 579). Although the law on the matter is commonly traced back to a dictum of Fitzherbert J. in 1536 (Y.B. 27 Hen. VIII, Mich., pl. 10), there was a divergence of opinion even before that date: *Walsh* v. *Ervin* [1952] V.L.R. 361, 367.

[25] See Newark, "The Boundaries of Nuisance" (1949) 65 L.Q.R. 480.

[26] *Dymond* v. *Pearce* [1972] 1 Q.B. 496.

Plaintiff off highway

The particular damage required to support an action must have been suffered as a result of the use of the highway.[27] Thus in *Jacobs* v. *L.C.C.*[28] the plaintiff, in order to reach a shop, stepped from the highway on to a paved forecourt separating the shop from the public pavement, and tripped over a stopcock about two feet from the boundary line which protruded about an inch and a quarter above the surrounding paving stones. It was held that (even assuming that a stopcock protruding by so little was capable of being a nuisance) the plaintiff had not suffered injury while using the highway and was without remedy.[29] Lord Simonds said that the "House was referred to no case and my researches have led me to none where a plaintiff has deliberately left the highway to go elsewhere, and having left it and having suffered injury upon the adjoining land, has then been held entitled to recover upon a claim of public nuisance in respect of which he suffered special damage. Far as the law of nuisance has travelled beyond its original limits, this further extension appears to me to be justified neither by reason nor by authority."[30] So also if a person climbs upon a stationary vehicle, which is left upon the highway, to see a cricket match and falls off and injures himself, it is not relevant for him to complain that the van was an obstruction to the highway and a nuisance. The accident does not happen because the vehicle is an obstruction to the highway, but because the plaintiff has trespassed upon it.[31] A mere temporary departure from the boundaries of the highway will not always, however, disentitle the plaintiff to recover. He may still be regarded as a user of the highway if he has diverged from it accidentally[32] or by reason of necessity.[33]

§ 5.13. Liability for the Non-Repair of Roads[34]

(1) The common law

The law governing the liability of highway authorities towards individual members of the public exercising the common right of passage over the highway had no similarity or even analogy to the duties of occupiers of property to those permitted or invited to enter the premises.[35] At common law no action lay against any authority entrusted with the care of highways for damage suffered in consequence of the omission of the defendants to perform their statutory duty of keeping the highways in repair. This exemption extended only to cases of pure

---

[27] *Tate & Lyle Ltd.* v. *G.L.C.* [1983] 2 A.C. 509.
[28] [1950] A.C. 361.
[29] A claim founded on the duty owed by an occupier of dangerous premises to those who enter on them also failed: see below, § 11.1.
[30] [1950] A.C. 361, 377.
[31] *Donovan* v. *Union Cartage Co.* [1933] 2 K.B. 71, 78.
[32] *Barnes* v. *Ward* (1850) 9 C.B. 392.
[33] *McKenna* v. *Lewis* [1945] I.R. 66.
[34] See Denning (1939) 55 L.Q.R. 343; Sawer, "Non-Feasance Revisited" (1955) 18 M.L.R. 541.
[35] *Buckle* v. *Bayswater Road Board* (1936) 57 C.L.R. 259, 280.

nonfeasance, and the public authority was responsible for any active misfeasance by which the highway was rendered dangerous.

(2) Reform by statute

The immunity from liability for nonfeasance was, however, swept away by statute in 1961[36] and relevant law (which binds the Crown[37]) is now to be found in the Highways Act 1980.

The Act applies whether the plaintiff is suing in negligence or nuisance or for breach of a statutory duty. But section 58(1) provides that in an action against a public authority for damage resulting from their failure to maintain[38] a highway it shall be a defence to prove that the authority has taken such care as is reasonable in the circumstances to secure that the part of the highway to which the action relates was not dangerous for traffic. Section 58(2) specifically provides that in assessing what is reasonable the court shall have regard to such factors as the character of the highway and the traffic which might reasonably be expected to use it; the standard of maintenance appropriate for a highway of that character and used by that traffic; the state of repair in which a reasonable person would have expected to find the highway; and the authority's knowledge of the danger.[39] Further, the default of an independent contractor is not in general a defence.[40]

It was once held[41] that these sections do not make negligence an essential element in a plaintiff's cause of action, but rather provide a defence to a statutory claim based on strict liability. But in later cases the courts have adopted an interpretation more favourable to highway authorities. So that if a pavement is in continual use, inspected reasonably often, and no complaint has been made by the local inhabitants, the plaintiff may fail to prove that the defendants have not discharged their duty.[42] There is not a cause of action whenever someone trips over an uneven pavement or falls as a result of a fractional difference in levels between flagstones,[43] as distinct from a metal plate which protrudes by $\frac{1}{8}$ inch.[44] Further, there is a distinction between a transient danger due to the elements, e.g. a pool of water or a patch of ice or snow,[45] and a permanent danger due to want of repair.[46] The plaintiff may fail to discharge the burden of proof in the former case.

---

[36] See the Highways (Miscellaneous Provisions) Act 1961, s.1(1) which abrogated "the rule of law exempting the inhabitants at large and any other persons as their successors from liability for non-repair of highways."

[37] Highways Act 1980, s.58(3). This is important, as an increasing number of roads are being vested in the Crown in right of the Minister of Transport.

[38] A duty to maintain may be wider than a duty to repair; *Haydon* v. *Kent C.C.* [1978] Q.B. 343.

[39] Yet another example of the growing tendency, both legislative and judicial, to spell out the factors relevant to the standard of care required, see generally below, Chap. 9.

[40] See below, Chap. 21.

[41] *Griffiths* v. *Liverpool Corporation* [1967] 1 Q.B. 374.

[42] *Pridham* v. *Hemel Hempstead Corporation* (1970) 69 L.G.R. 523.

[43] *Littler* v. *Liverpool Corporation* [1968] 2 All E.R. 343.

[44] *Pitman* v. *Southern Electricity Board* [1978] 3 All E.R. 901.

[45] *Haydon* v. *Kent C.C.* [1978] Q.B. 343.

[46] *Burnside* v. *Emerson* [1968] 1 W.L.R. 1490.

CHAPTER 6

INTERESTS IN GOODS

§ 6.1. INTRODUCTORY

The Torts (Interference with Goods) Act 1977 abolishes the tort of detinue but otherwise neither replaces nor redefines the other relevant torts, though it applies the term "wrongful interference with goods" to all torts which involve lost or damaged goods, and this term has appeared in a few judgments.[1] Another usage is "possessory torts" to include trespass, conversion and detinue. So the old law is still important. "In the development of our law, two principles have struggled for mastery. The first is the protection of property. No one can give a better title than he himself possesses. The second is the protection of commercial transactions. The person who takes in good faith and for value without notice should get a good title."[2] In the course of centuries both common law and statute have created exceptions to the principle that no one can give a better title than he himself has (*nemo dat quod non habet*). The nemo dat principle has been emphatically re-affirmed by the Law Lords.[3]

The common law has always recognised that the title of the true owner[4] may be divested in favour of a bona fide purchaser for value in two cases. One depends upon a peculiarity in the property (*i.e.* money or negotiable instruments); the other upon a peculiarity in the place where the purchaser buys it (*i.e.* markets overt). So every shop in the City of London is a market overt for the sale between sunrise and sunset[5] of goods ordinarily sold in that shop, and the purchaser in good faith will get a good title even though the vendor[6] has none.[7] Parliament has also given further protection to the security of commercial transactions by the Factors Act 1889, and the Sale of Goods Act 1979, which should be construed as one single code. Thus a mercantile agent who has possession of goods in his capacity as mercantile agent[8] has power to pass title under section 2(1) of the Factors Act 1889. Section 27 of the

---

[1] See, *e.g.* the C.A. in *Metall* [1990] 1 Q.B. 391, 479–482.
[2] *Bishopsgate Motor Finance Corporation* v. *Transport Brakes Ltd.* [1949] 1 K.B. 322, 336–337, *per* Denning L.J.
[3] *National Employers' Mutual General Insurance Association Ltd.* v. *Jones* [1989] A.C. 24, 59.
[4] "There is no such thing as a chattel which has never had an owner." *Webb* v. *Ireland* [1988] I.R. 353, 389, *per* Walsh J.
[5] *Reid* v. *Metropolitan Police Commissioner* [1973] Q.B. 551.
[6] To argue that the vendor, who may be the agent of the thief, should be protected by the doctrine of market overt as well as the purchaser "capsizes the intellect": *Ganly* v. *Ledwidge* (1876) I.R. 10 C.L. 33, 36. To avoid misconception, it may be noted that the mere fact that the owner has thus been compulsorily divested of his property does not mean that he must bear the loss. A takes B's goods and sells them to C in market overt: C gets a good title but A is liable to B for the value of the goods.
[7] *Bishopsgate Motor Finance Co.* v. *Transport Brakes Ltd.* [1949] 1 K.B. 322.
[8] *Astley Industrial Trust Ltd.* v. *Miller* [1968] 2 All E.R. 36.

Hire Purchase Act 1964, effected a considerable change in the law by providing that, where a hirer of a motor-vehicle under a hire-purchase agreement wrongfully disposes of that vehicle to a bona fide private purchaser[9] for value who has no notice of any relevant hire-purchase agreement,[10] then a good title to the vehicle is passed, although the hirer may still be liable to the finance company. So the Factors Act 1889, s.2(1) and the Sale of Goods Act 1979, s.25(1) provide that if a mercantile agent is, with the consent of the owner, in possession of goods or the documents of title to goods, any sale, pledge or other disposition made by him when acting in the ordinary course of business of a mercantile agent, shall be effective to pass a good title to a bona fide purchaser for value. It is well settled that consent obtained by fraud is still consent for the purposes of this section,[11] so that when a rogue obtains possession of a motor-car by false pretences and sells it for cash in the Warren Street used-car market the purchaser gets a good title.[12] But those Acts do not enable the bona fide purchaser for value to over-ride the title of the true owner when the factor or agent has been entrusted with the goods by a thief or purchaser from a thief, as distinct from the owner himself.[13]

Some have denied or doubted the existence of a law of property in chattels on the ground that our law recognises no real or proprietary action for the recovery of chattels corresponding to the *vindicatio* of Roman law.[14] But, "as modern experience shows, a very true and intense ownership of goods can be pretty well protected by actions in which nothing but money can with any certainty be obtained."[15] The value of the thing is obtained because the plaintiff shows that it belongs to him. It seems irrelevant that an historical accident denies him recovery *in specie*. Indeed there is reason to believe that in some respects the common law is more favourable to the owner of goods than systems founded on the civil law.[16] For the action of conversion, which is our normal remedy for one deprived of his goods, has features characteristic of both property and tort.[17] In so far as it is a *vindicatio* there is no room for inquiry as to the defendant's state of mind: liability in conversion is strict. In so far as it is an action in tort it lies against anyone who has at any time committed an act which constitutes a denial of the plaintiff's title. "Where there have been successive conversions of the same goods, trover lies against all persons guilty of conversion and recovery of

---

[9] But a trade purchaser is still liable in conversion: *Moorgate Mercantile Co. Ltd.* v. *Twitchings* [1978] A.C. 890.

[10] *Barker* v. *Bell* [1971] 1. W.L.R. 983.

[11] *Du Jardin* v. *Beadman Bros.* [1952] 2 Q.B. 712.

[12] *Newtons of Wembley Ltd.* v. *Williams* [1965] 1 Q.B. 560.

[13] *National Employers' Mutual Insurance Association Ltd.* v. *Jones* [1989] A.C. 24.

[14] This has been a commonplace since the time of Bracton, although now the courts have a discretionary power to order the specific restitution of chattels. This statute has removed the original reason for which we call lands "real" and chattels "personal" property; but the terms were adopted long ago and are likely to endure: For the power to order the plaintiff to accept restitution instead of damages, see below, § 6.12.

[15] Pollock and Maitland, *History of English Law*, Vol. ii, pp. 181–182.

[16] See Lawson, *The Rational Strength of English Law*, pp. 125–131.

[17] This has made for difficulty in the search for the basis of liability in tort: above, § 2.4.

damages against one is no answer by the defendants in subsequent actions, though . . . as soon as full satisfaction has been obtained the plaintiff has exhausted his rights."[18]

The object of the 1977 Act is to create a more general remedy based as far as possible on the existing incidents of the tort of conversion.[19] So we must now consider the details of the four actions which protected property interests in chattels: trespass, conversion, detinue, and replevin.

These were sometimes called "the possessory torts," but now section 1 of the 1977 Act provides a comprehensive description ("wrongful interference") for the tort of conversion and the other torts affecting goods.

§ 6.2. Trespass to Goods

The tort of trespass consists in committing without lawful justification any act of direct physical interference with goods in the possession of another person.[20] Thus it is a trespass to take away goods or to do wilful damage to them. The tort of trespass is wider than conversion in that a mere act of interference is sufficient, special damage need not be proved, and it is not necessary to prove a denial of title; but it is narrower than conversion in that the act of interference must be direct.

The tort may be committed against an animal,[21] e.g. it is a trespass to beat a dog,[22] or to shoot racing pigeons.[23] Even negligent damage, provided that it is direct and not merely consequential, falls within the scope of trespass: as in the case of a negligent collision between two vehicles.[24] Physical interference usually consists in some form of physical contact—some application of force by which the chattel is moved from its place or otherwise affected. So in *Kirk* v. *Gregory*[25] the plaintiff was the executor of one who had died in his own house in a state of *delirium tremens*. The defendant, alarmed by the fact that the servants and others were feasting and drinking in the house, moved certain rings from one room to another, in the mistaken but genuine belief that it was necessary to do so. The defendant was held liable in trespass[26] for the loss of the rings. But it is also presumably a trespass wilfully to

---

[18] *Morris (B.O.) Ltd.* v. *Perrott* [1945] 1 All E.R. 567, 569, *per* Lord Goddard. This is not to say that there may not be claims for contribution or indemnity between the defendants, but the primary concern of the law is to compensate the plaintiff for his loss: his is entitled to sue that person in the chain of converters who seems the most likely to be able to pay, leaving him to collect what he can from anybody else in the chain.

[19] See Palmer, *Bailment* (1979), Appendix One.

[20] *R.* v. *I.R.C., ex p. Rossminster* [1980] A.C. 952, 1000, 1011; *Wilson* v. *New Brighton Panel Beaters Ltd.* [1989] 1 N.Z.L.R. 74, 76.

[21] Or by an animal, *e.g.* if I train my dog to fetch another's golf balls: *Manton* v. *Brocklebank* [1923] 2 K.B. 212, 229.

[22] *Wright* v. *Ramscot* (1667) 1 Wms.Saund. 84.

[23] *Hamps* v. *Darby* [1948] 2 K.B. 311.

[24] *Leame* v. *Bray* (1803) 3 East 593.

[25] (1876) 1 Ex.D. 55.

[26] Nominal damages of one shilling were awarded.

frighten a horse so that it runs away, or to drive cattle out of a field in which they lawfully are,[27] or to kill a dog by giving it poisoned meat.

Trespass actionable per se

A trespass to goods is actionable per se without any proof of actual damage.[28] Any unauthorised touching[29] or moving of an object is actionable at the suit of the possessor of it, even though no harm ensues. So it is a trespass for a shop assistant to snatch a customer's handbag and detain it "for a few moments,"[30] or to erase a tape-recording[31] or show a private letter to an unauthorised person,[32] as distinct from merely looking at the letter when it is in another's possession,[33] or over-hearing a conversation.[34] It may be very necessary for the protection of certain kinds of property, *e.g.* museum or art gallery exhibits, that this should be the law. Hence the successful plaintiff will always be entitled to nominal damages at least,[35] and, if the defendants are persons in authority guilty of outrageous behaviour,[36] to exemplary damages as well.[37] In this way the common law gives an indirect remedy for invasions of privacy.[38]

It was once unnecessary for the plaintiff in an action of trespass to prove intention or negligence in the defendant. But the present position is doubtful in view of the fact that it now seems settled that in an action of trespass for personal injuries the plaintiff must prove intention or negligence,[39] and in practice the courts assume that in trespass to goods intention or negligence must be proved. In any event the general principle that liability in trespass is strict has been much weakened by two admitted exceptions.

(i) *Highway accidents*

A person whose property on or adjoining the highway (*e.g.* a motor-car or house) has been damaged accidentally as the result of the activities of a user of the highway can recover only if he establishes negligence. This rule has been established more by the dicta of eminent judges and the common understanding of the profession than by any

---

[27] R. v. *Riley* (1853) 22 L.J.M.C. 48.

[28] *Leitch & Co.* v. *Leydon* [1931] A.C. 90, 106.

[29] "Scratching the panel of a carriage would be a trespass": *Fouldes* v. *Willoughby* (1841) 8 M. & W. 540, 549, *per* Alderson B. *Everitt* v. *Martin* [1953] N.Z.L.R. 298 suggests that a merely accidental contact without any damage or asportation is not actionable: *sed quaere.*

[30] *White* v. *Brown* (1983) C.L.Y. 972 (damages £775).

[31] *The Times*, October 1, 1966 (damages: £200).

[32] *Thurston* v. *Charles* (1905) 21 T.L.R. 659 (damages: £400).

[33] "The eye cannot by the laws of England be guilty of a trespass": *Entick* v. *Carrington* (1765) 19 St.Tr. 1030, 1066, *per* Lord Camden C.J.

[34] *Malone* v. *Metropolitan Police Commissioner* [1979] Ch. 344, 374–76.

[35] As in *Kirk* v. *Gregory* (1876) 1 Ex.D. 55.

[36] As in the General Warrant Cases in the 1760s, discussed in Heuston, *Essays in Constitutional Law* (2nd ed.), pp. 35–36.

[37] *Cassell & Co. Ltd.* v. *Broome* [1972] A.C. 1027.

[38] See above, § 3.2.

[39] See below, § 7.4.

particular decision,[40] but its authority appears now to be beyond question.[41]

(ii) *Inevitable accident*

In *National Coal Board* v. *Evans*[42] the Court of Appeal held that inevitable accident was a good defence to an action for trespass. The plaintiff's predecessors in title laid an electric cable under the land of a county council without informing it or the defendant contractors, whom it employed to conduct the excavation in the course of which the cable was damaged. It was held that since the accident was mainly attributable to the act of the plaintiffs in wrongfully placing their cable in another's land the defendants were excused as being utterly without fault.

Searches and seizures

Before the Police and Criminal Evidence Act 1984 (PACE) it was settled that a magistrate had statutory power to issue a search warrant for stolen goods and for some other, but by no means all,[43] offences. If property not covered by the warrant was seized, the police might be liable in trespass. But in the interest of repressing crime the courts extended the protection given to the police.[44] So when a police officer entered a house by virtue of a search warrant for stolen goods, he could seize not only the goods which he believed on reasonable grounds to be covered by the warrant, but also any other goods which he reasonably believed to have been stolen and to be material evidence on a charge of receiving, or perhaps of any crime,[45] against the person in possession of them, or anyone associated with him.[46] The police were also justified in seizing, and retaining temporarily, articles or documents which[47] were of evidential value if there was reasonable cause to believe a serious offence had been committed,[48] but not just to meet a possible order of the court for compensation or restitution.[49]

PACE, ss.8–22 replaces the common law by complex statutory provisions. Wide powers of entry, search and seizure are granted, but if they are not exercised in accordance with the relevant statutory conditions, a tort will have been committed. For example, section 8 provides for the issue of warrants to enter and search premises for evidence of serious arrestable offences, but section 16(8) provides that a search under a warrant may be a search only to the extent required for the purpose for which the warrant was issued. So that if the warrant was issued

---

[40] *Gayler and Pope* v. *B. Davies & Son* [1924] 2 K.B. 75, 83.
[41] See also above, § 4.1.
[42] [1951] 2 K.B. 861.
[43] *e.g.* not murder: *Ghani* v. *Jones* [1970] 1 Q.B. 693.
[44] *I.R.C.* v. *Rossminster Ltd.* [1980] A.C. 952.
[45] *Jennings* v. *Quinn* [1968] I.R. 305.
[46] *Chic Fashions Ltd.* v. *Jones* [1968] 2 Q.B. 299.
[47] *Reynolds* v. *Metropolitan Police Commissioner* [1985] Q.B. 881.
[48] *Ghani* v. *Jones* [1970] 1 Q.B. 693.
[49] *Malone* v. *Metropolitan Police Commissioner* [1980] Q.B. 49, 63.

to search for stolen vehicles it would be unlawful to rip up the floor boards of a house—a power which might be permissible if the search warrant was for illegal drugs. But the statutory powers are very wide— *e.g.* the power to seize articles during a valid search is not limited to serious arrestable offences.

The title of the plaintiff

Trespass to goods, like trespass to land, is essentially an injury to possession and not to ownership. The plaintiff, therefore, must have been in actual possession at the time of the interference complained of.[50] So even an owner of goods may be liable in trespass if he seizes those goods from one who has lawful possession of them—*e.g.* as a bailee.[51] The former rule that a defendant could show that a third party had a better title than the plaintiff has been abolished by section 8 of the 1977 Act.[52] On the other hand, the possessor is entitled to the return of his goods, and, in the absence of statute, it is no defence that his prior possession of them was illegal.[53]

§ 6.3. CONVERSION: HISTORY[54]

The wrong of conversion is dependent for an understanding of its true nature upon a knowledge of its origin and historical development. There are three distinct methods by which one man may deprive another of his property, and so be guilty of a conversion and liable in an action of trover—(1) by wrongly taking it, (2) by wrongly detaining it, and (3) by wrongly disposing of it.[55] The term conversion was originally limited to the third of these cases. To convert goods meant to dispose of them, to make away with them, to deal with them, in such a way that neither owner nor wrongdoer had any further possession of them: for example, by consuming them, or by destroying them, or by selling them, or otherwise delivering them to some third person. Merely to take another's goods, however wrongfully, was not to convert them. Merely to detain them in defiance of the owner's title was not to convert them. The fact that conversion in its modern sense includes instances of all three modes in which a man may be wrongfully deprived of his goods, and not of one mode only, is the outcome of a process of historical development whereby, by means of legal fictions and other devices, the action of conversion was enabled to extend its limits and appropriate the territories that rightly belonged to other and earlier forms of action.

---

[50] *Ward* v. *Macauley* (1791) 4 T.R. 489.

[51] *Keenan Bros. Ltd.* v. *C.I.E.* (1962) 97 I.L.T.R. 54.

[52] See also below, § 6.8.

[53] *Gollan* v. *Nugent* (1986) 168 C.L.R. 18.

[54] For the complex history, see Milsom, "Not Doing is no Trespass" [1954] C.L.J. 105; Simpson, "The Introduction of the Action on the Case for Conversion" (1959) 75 L.Q.R. 364.

[55] *Penfolds Wines Pty. Ltd.* v. *Elliott* (1946) 74 C.L.R. 204, 240.

§ 6.4. CONVERSION: DEFINITION

A conversion is an act, or complex series of acts,[56] of wilful interference, without lawful justification, with any chattel in a manner inconsistent with the right of another, whereby that other is deprived of the use and possession of it.[57] Two elements are combined in such interference: (1) a dealing with the chattel in a manner inconsistent with the right of the person entitled to it, and (2) an intention in so doing to deny that person's right or to assert a right which is in fact inconsistent with such right.[58] But the word "intention" refers only to the intentional commission of the act. For where the act done is necessarily a denial of the other's right or an assertion of a right inconsistent with it, the tort may have been committed,[59] though the doer may not know of or intend to challenge the property or possession of that other.[60] If a person, not being an agent or bailee,[61] deals with the goods of another as his own, his intention is irrelevant, for liability in conversion is strict.[62]

Dealing with the chattel

In order to amount to conversion the act done with respect to the chattel must have been one of wilful and wrongful interference. But the "dealing" need not, though it often will, take the form of an interference with possession. There may be "conversion at a distance," if the plaintiff's right to the chattel has been denied, even though the defendant has not taken possession of it as when a vehicle's log-book is deliberately not returned.[63] In the absence, however, of a wilful and wrongful interference there is no conversion, even if by the negligence of the defendant the chattel is lost or destroyed. Thus in *Ashby v. Tolhurst*[64] a car-park attendant allowed a stranger, who had neither the ticket nor the key for a car which had been left in the parking-ground under a contract, to take the car away. His employers were not liable to the owner of the car for conversion.[65] Formerly a bailee who by accident lost the goods entrusted to him was not liable in conversion but merely in detinue.[66] But now section 2(2) of the 1977 Act provides that an action lies in conversion for loss or destruction of goods which a bailee has allowed to happen in breach of his duty to his bailor (that is to say it lies in a

---

[56] *Douglas Valley Finance Co. Ltd.* v. *Hughes (Hirers) Ltd.* [1969] 1 Q.B. 738.
[57] The above definition was cited with approval in *Lewis Trusts* v. *Barrbers Stores* [1983] F.S.R. 453, 459.
[58] *Penfolds Wines Pty. Ltd.* v. *Elliott* (1946) 74 C.L.R. 204, 229.
[59] See *Cuff* v. *Broadlands Finance Ltd.* [1987] N.Z.L.R. 343, 346; *Wilson* v. *New Brighton Panel Beaters Ltd.* [1989] 1 N.Z.L.R. 74, 77. See below, § 6.4.
[60] As in *Moorgate Mercantile Finance Co. Ltd.* v. *Finch* [1962] 1 Q.B. 701.
[61] See below, § 6.5.
[62] See below, § 6.7.
[63] As in *Bryanston Leasings Ltd.* v. *Principality Finance Ltd.* [1977] R.T.R. 45.
[64] [1937] 2 K.B. 242.
[65] In such a case there may be liability for breach of an occupier's duty to his visitors' see below, § 11.4.
[66] *Williams* v. *Gesse* (1837) 3 Bing.N.C. 849. Liability in negligence was imposed in *Fairline Shipping Corporation* v. *Adamson* [1975] Q.B. 180, but the cases cited were not considered.

case which is not otherwise conversion, but would have been detinue before detinue was abolished).[67] But if there has been no loss or destruction of the goods, but simply a detention, without more, it is doubtful if any tort has now been committed. If the plaintiff alleges the conversion of a number of chattels, it is not necessary to particularise them item by item: a general description of their nature and value is sufficient.[68]

(1) Conversion by taking

Every person is guilty of a conversion who, without lawful justification, takes a chattel out of the possession of anyone else with the intention of exercising a permanent or temporary dominion over it, because the owner is entitled to the use of it at all times.[69] It is no defence that restoration has become impossible, even though no permanent taking was intended and the impossibility has resulted from no act or default of the defendant but solely through the loss or destruction of the property by some inevitable accident or the wrongful act of some third person.[70] For he who wrongfully takes possession of another's goods has them at his own risk and must in all events either return them or pay for them.[71] No demand for the return of the chattel is needed.[72]

But a mere taking unaccompanied by an intention to exercise such a dominion is no conversion, though it is actionable as a trespass. So the mere act of wrongfully removing a chattel from one place to another, without intent to assume possession of it or to deprive the owner of possession, is not in itself a conversion, but is a mere trespass.[73] Thus in *Fouldes* v. *Willoughby*[74] the plaintiff went on board the defendant's ferry-boat to cross from Birkenhead to Liverpool, having with him two horses; the defendant wrongfully refused to carry the horses and told the plaintiff that he must take them ashore. The plaintiff refused to do so and the defendant took the horses from him and put them on shore. The plaintiff remained on board the ferry-boat and was conveyed across the river. It was held that the mere act of removing the horses from the boat, although wrongful, and actionable as a trespass, did not amount to the wrong of conversion.[75]

(2) Conversion by detention

The detention of a chattel amounts to a conversion only when it is adverse to the owner or other person entitled to possession—that is to say, the defendant must have shown an intention to keep the thing in

---

[67] This subsection is "an excellent example of how parliamentary drafting may be both crystal clear and quite unintelligible": (1978) 75 *Guardian Gazette* 78.
[68] *Brightside Co-operative Society* v. *Phillips* [1964] 1 W.L.R. 185.
[69] *Fouldes* v. *Willoughby* (1841) 8 M. & W. 540, 548.
[70] *Wellington City* v. *Singh* [1971] N.Z.L.R. 1025, 1027.
[71] See below, § 6.7.
[72] *Cuff* v. *Broadlands Finance Ltd.* [1987] N.Z.L.R. 343.
[73] *Wilson* v. *New Brighton Panel Beaters Ltd.* [1989] 1 N.Z.L.R. 74, 77.
[74] (1841) 8 M. & W. 540.
[75] The principle in *Fouldes* v. *Willoughby* is fully accepted in modern law; *Leitch & Co.* v. *Leydon* [1931] A.C. 90, 103–109; *Beaman* v. *A.R.T.S. Ltd.* [1948] 2 All E.R. 89, 92.

defiance of the plaintiff.[76] Merely to be in possession of a chattel without title is not a conversion,[77] and indeed may not be a tort of any kind. It cannot be detinue since that tort was abolished by section 2(1) of the 1977 Act. Thus if a bailee merely holds over after the end of the period for which the chattel was bailed to him, as distinct from acting in a manner totally repugnant to the terms of the bailment, he may be liable for a breach of contract, but he is not necessarily guilty of conversion.[78] So he who finds a chattel lost cannot be sued in conversion, however long he keeps it, unless by refusing to give it up or in some other way he shows an intention to detail it adversely to the owner. No one is bound, save by contract, to take a chattel to the owner of it; his only obligation is not to prevent the owner from getting it when he comes for it.[79] But a denial of possession does not cease to be a conversion because it is accompanied by some excuse—*e.g.* that delivery will cause "trade union difficulties."[80]

Demand and refusal

The usual method of proving that a detention is adverse within the meaning of this rule is to show that the plaintiff demanded the delivery of the chattel, and that the defendant refused or neglected to comply with the demand.[81] The demand must be unconditional in its terms,[82] specify the goods which the plaintiff requires[83] and be brought to the knowledge of the defendant.[84] But the defendant is entitled to take a reasonable time to verify the title of the person who requires the goods to be handed over to him.[85] Demand and refusal, however, is not the sole method by which an adverse detention may be proved. If wrongful detention can be established without proving a demand there is a good cause of action, as when the defendant has simply taken the plaintiff's goods.[86] Presumably any conduct of the defendant which shows that he not merely possesses the goods, but intends to hold them in defiance of the plaintiff and to deprive him of the possession of them is sufficient to constitute a conversion, even though there has been no formal demand for restitution. Thus if a person is entrusted with a pipe of wine and bottles it there is some evidence of a conversion even though none of the wine be actually drunk.[87]

A failure to deliver up goods on demand is not in itself a conversion if at the time of the demand they are no longer the possession of the defendant: as when they are already destroyed or consumed or have

---

[76] *Clayton* v. *Le Roy* [1911] 2 K.B. 1031, 1052.
[77] *Caxton Publishing Co.* v. *Sutherland Publishing Co.* [1939] A.C. 178, 202.
[78] *Mitchell* v. *Ealing L.B.C.* [1979] Q.B. 1.
[79] *Capital Finance Co. Ltd.* v. *Bray* [1964] 1 W.L.R. 323, 329.
[80] *Howard E. Perry Ltd.* v. *British Railways Board* [1980] 1 W.L.R. 1375, 1384.
[81] *Capital Finance Co. Ltd.* v. *Bray* [1964] 1 W.L.R. 323.
[82] *Rushworth* v. *Taylor* (1842) 3 Q.B. 699.
[83] *Abington* v. *Lipscomb* (1841) 1 Q.B. 776.
[84] *King* v. *Walsh* [1932] I.R. 178.
[85] *Bristol Airport plc* v. *Powdrill* [1990] 2 W.L.R. 1362, 1381.
[86] *London Jewellers Ltd.* v. *Sutton* (1934) 50 T.L.R. 193, 194; *Cuff* v. *Broadlands Finance Ltd.* [1987] N.Z.L.R. 343.
[87] *Philpott* v. *Kelley* (1835) 3 A. & E. 106.

already got into the possession of some other person. No one can convert a chattel by refusing to give it up when he no longer has it; this is so even if it is due to his own act or default that delivery is no longer possible,[88] though he may be liable for some prior act of conversion.

It is possible that in one case there is no conversion even though there is an adverse detention. If A's chattel comes on to B's land neither by accident nor by the act of B nor by the criminal act of a third party, it is probably the law that B is not guilty of a conversion, even though he will not either allow A to retake his chattel or himself restore it, provided that no inference can be drawn from his attitude of an assertion of title or an exercise of dominion over the goods.[89]

(3) Conversion by wrongful delivery

Every person is guilty of a conversion who, without lawful justification, deprives a person of his goods by delivering them to someone else[90] so as to change the possession. The leading case is *Hollins* v. *Fowler*.[91] A rogue obtained Fowler's cotton, and offered it for sale to Hollins, a broker; Hollins sold and delivered it to Micholls & Co., who worked it into yarn. Hollins accounted for the proceeds to the rogue, who disappeared. Hollins was liable in conversion to Fowler, even though he had acted in good faith and obtained only a broker's commission from Micholls & Co. So an auctioneer who sells and delivers[92] stolen property or property subject to a bill of sale is liable to the true owner or to the bill of sale holder, even though ignorant of any such adverse title, and even though he has already paid over the proceeds to his own client.[93] But it is possible that a bailee of goods for safe custody is not liable if he, or his servant, honestly but mistakenly[94] delivers the goods to someone who is not entitled to them, at least if the contract of bailment so provides.

(4) Conversion by wrongful disposition

Every person is guilty of a conversion who, without lawful justification, deprives a person of his goods by giving some other person a lawful title to them. There are certain cases in which a person in possession of goods to which he has no title can nevertheless effectively, though wrongfully, so dispose of them by sale, pledge, or otherwise that he confers a good title to them on someone else. Any such disposition

---

[88] *Williams* v. *Gesse* (1837) 3 Bing.N.C. 849.

[89] See below, § 26.2.

[90] But it is no conversion to give the custody of the goods to your own servant, for legally they still remain in your possession.

[91] (1875) L.R. 7 H.L. 757.

[92] Whether under the hammer or by private treaty: *Willis* v. *British Car Auctions Ltd.* [1978] 1 W.L.R. 438.

[93] *Consolidated Co.* v. *Curtis* [1892] 1 Q.B. 495.

[94] As distinct from dishonestly: *Morris* v. *Martin (C.W.) & Sons Ltd.* [1966] 1 Q.B. 716, see below, § 21.8.

amounts to a conversion as against the true and original owner, for by the creation of this adverse title he has been deprived of his property. This is the case, for example, with a sale in market overt, or with a wrongful disposition made by a vendor of goods who continues or retains possession of them,[95] in whatever capacity,[96] or by one who has a motor-vehicle on hire-purchase.[97] But a bailee of goods may have the express or implied authority of the owner to create a repairer's lien; this is the position of one who has a motor-car or other chattel under a hire-purchase agreement.[98] In most of such cases, indeed, the wrongful disposition is also a wrongful delivery and therefore is a conversion for that reason also, but this coincidence is not essential. It seems, however, that in order to give rise to civil liability it is not enough to attempt to sell another's goods,[99] or even to sell them without delivering them to the purchaser or to his order, for a mere sale or other attempted disposition unaccompanied by delivery and ineffectual to divest the plaintiff's title to the property is not a conversion.[1]

(5) Conversion by wrongful destruction

Every person is guilty of a conversion who, without lawful justification, wilfully consumes or otherwise destroys a chattel belonging to another person.[2] Mere damage, however, which falls short of actual destruction, is not in itself a conversion.[3] The test of destruction, as opposed to mere damage, is presumably the disappearance of the identity of the article. Grapes are presumably destroyed when they are turned into wine, cotton when it is woven into cloth, corn when it is ground into flour.[4]

(6) Conversion of documents and tokens

The difficulty here is that primarily conversion means conversion of goods, and the relation of bank to customer is that of debtor and creditor. As no specific coins in a bank are the property of any specific customer, a bank which pays part of what it owes to its customer to some other person not authorised to receive it is not at first sight converting its customer's chattels. Again, a bank which collects a cheque borrows from its customers the proceeds when collected, and in collecting

---

[95] Sale of Goods Act 1979, ss.22, 24.
[96] *Worcester Works Finance Ltd.* v. *Cooden Engineering Co. Ltd.* [1972] 1 Q.B. 210.
[97] Though the purchaser may get a good title under the Hire-Purchase Act 1965, s.27.
[98] *Tappenden* v. *Artus* [1964] 2 Q.B. 185. *Aliter* if the agreement has been validly determined by the finance company.
[99] But there may be a criminal prosecution in such a case: *Rogers* v. *Arnott* [1960] 2 Q.B. 244.
[1] *Consolidated Co.* v. *Curtis* [1892] 1 Q.B. 495, 498. See below, § 6.4.
[2] *Hollins* v. *Fowler* (1875) L.R. 7 H.L. 757, 768.
[3] Where the chattel continues to exist as such, there may be trespass, but there is no conversion: *Simmons* v. *Lillystone* (1853) 8 Ex. 431.
[4] *Northern Ireland Master Butchers' Wholesale Supply Association* v. *Belfast Corporation* [1965] N.I. 30. See below, § 6.12.

exhausts the operation of the cheque. "The difficulty has been surmounted by treating the conversion as of the chattel, the piece of paper, the cheque under which the money was collected, and the value of the chattel converted as the money received under it."[5] The law regards the substance of the transaction and gives an adequate remedy for the wrong.[6] This principle is not limited to documents which are, or are in the nature of, negotiable instruments: but it may include documents which are evidence of a chose in action—e.g. trading stamps.[7]

It may also be extended to cover the tokens which are such a feature of contemporary life—e.g. cheque cards, credit cards, book tokens, and gaming chips.[8] The measure of damages will usually be the value of the property represented by the token.[9]

If a cheque has been converted, and the collecting bank[10] has acted without negligence, it may be protected under the Cheques Act 1957, s.4. The onus is on the bank to show that it has followed the ordinary practice of careful bankers.[11]

(7) Miscellaneous forms of conversion

Every person is guilty of a conversion who, in any other way than those mentioned in the preceding sections, causes the loss of a chattel by any act of wilful interference without lawful justification. It has even been held that the use of another's motor-car for smuggling, entailing its liability for forfeiture to the Crown, amounts to a conversion.[12] So an innocent infringement of copyright was a conversion.[13] In such a case the plaintiff, in addition to claiming damages and an injunction for the infringement of his copyright, was in effect claiming to be the owner of all the infringing copies of his work, and requiring that he be compensated for the loss of his property. But this severe rule was abolished by the Copyright, Patents and Designs Act 1988, ss.95–100, which instead provide for discretionary judicial orders, injunctions and accounts, and orders for delivery up and seizure. There may also be conversion even though the defendant has never been in physical possession of the goods, if he has dealt with them in such a way as to amount to an absolute denial and repudiation of the plaintiff's rights,[14] as by stripping a commercial vehicle of its A licence, or refusing to return a log-book.[15] But it is now clear that even an absolute denial and repudiation of the plaintiff's right, if unaccompanied by circumstances which make such

---

[5] *Per* Scrutton L.J. in *Lloyds Bank* v. *Chartered Bank, etc.* [1929] 1 K.B. 40, 55–56.
[6] *Morison* v. *London County and Westminster Bank* [1914] 3 K.B. 356, 365–366.
[7] *Building, etc. Holidays Scheme Ltd.* v. *Post Office* [1966] 1 Q.B. 247.
[8] 18th Report of the Law Reform Committee (Cmnd. 4774 (1971)), paras. 90–91.
[9] This has been settled since *Loosemore* v. *Radford* (1842) 9 M. & W. 657 (title deeds).
[10] *Westminster Bank* v. *Zang* [1966] A.C. 182.
[11] *Marfani & Co. Ltd.* v. *Midland Bank Ltd.* [1968] 1 W.L.R. 956.
[12] *Moorgate Mercantile Credit Co. Ltd.* v. *Finch* [1962] 1 Q.B. 701.
[13] *W.E.A. Records Ltd.* v. *King* [1975] 1 W.L.R. 44.
[14] *Douglas Valley Finance Co. Ltd.* v. *Hughes (Hirers) Ltd.* [1969] 1 Q.B. 738, 751.
[15] *Bryanston Leasings Ltd.* v. *Principality Finance Ltd.* [1977] R.T.R. 45.

denial a "dealing" with the goods, does not constitute conversion,[16] although it may amount to injurious falsehood,[17] or else the plaintiff may obtain a declaration that the defendant has no right to the goods.[18]

§ 6.5. ACTS NOT AMOUNTING TO CONVERSION

(1) Mere receipt of chattels no conversion

We have already seen that the mere possession of goods without title is neither a conversion nor any other kind of tort.[19] The only detention that is actionable is adverse detention—a withholding of possession from the person entitled to it. It seems to follow logically from this that merely to receive goods in good faith by way of pledge, sale or otherwise from a person who has no title to them is not a conversion by the recipient, who commits no tort until he refuses to deliver them to the true owner or wrongfully disposes of them. This was once held to be the law in the case of a person taking goods by way of deposit.[20] But the 1977 Act has reversed this decision. Section 11(2) provides, tersely but definitely, that "Receipt of goods by way of pledge is conversion if the delivery of the goods is conversion."

Except on a sale

But even before the 1977 Act the common law recognised that where there is a taking by sale the rule was different, and liability in conversion was imposed.[21] "Certainly a man is guilty of a conversion who takes my property by assignment from another who has no authority to dispose of it; for what is that but assisting that other in carrying his wrongful act into effect."[22] The rule is an illustration of the principle that persons deal with the property in chattels or exercise acts of ownership over them at their peril.[23] Hence one who innocently buys and takes delivery[24] of goods from another who has no authority to sell them is liable in conversion.[25] A familiar situation in which this rule applies is when a banker collects for a customer a cheque to which the customer has no title or a defective title; the banker is liable in conversion to the true owner of the cheque unless he can show that he is pro-

---

[16] See s.11(3) of the 1977 Act, giving effect to the 18th Report of the Law Reform Committee (Cmnd. 4774 (1971)), para. 45.

[17] Below, § 18.8.

[18] A procedure used in *Loudon v. Ryder (No. 2)* [1953] Ch. 423.

[19] See *Lewis Trusts v. Bambers Stores* [1983] F.S.R. 453, 459, and above, § 6.4.

[20] *Spackman v. Foster* (1883) 11 Q.B.D. 99.

[21] Rightly, in the opinion of the 18th Report of the Law Reform Committee (Cmnd. 4774 (1971)), para. 43.

[22] *McCombie v. Davis* (1805) 6 East 538, 549, *per* Lord Ellenborough C.J.

[23] Below, § 6.4.

[24] As the vendor in a contract of sale under which the goods have not been delivered is not liable in conversion the buyer must also escape liability: *Douglas Valley Finance Co. Ltd. v. Hughes (Hirers) Ltd.* [1969] 1 Q.B. 738.

[25] *Hilbery v. Hatton* (1864) 2 H. & C. 822.

tected by the Cheques Act 1957,s.4.[26] Since the 1977 Act it must be doubted whether the exception has not swallowed up the rule.

(2) Redelivery no conversion

It further follows that if he who innocently acquires possession of another's goods by way of deposit redelivers them to him from whom he got them, before he has received notice of the plaintiff's claim to them, he is free from responsibility. He has not deprived the plaintiff of his property, for that property is now in exactly the same position as if the defendant had never interfered with it at all. "A warehouseman," said Blackburn, J.[27] in *Hollins* v. *Fowler*,[28] "with whom goods have been deposited is guilty of no conversion by keeping them or restoring them to the person who deposited them with him, though that person turns out to have no authority from the true owner."[29]

Delivery to third party

What shall be said, however, if the innocent holder has delivered the goods not to the person from whom he received them but at his order to some third person? As when a carrier receives stolen goods from a consignor, and delivers them to the consignee; or a warehouseman delivers such goods to him to whom the delivery warrant has been transferred by the depositor. If in such a case the defendant acts in good faith and without any knowledge that the delivery made by him is in pursuance of some sale or other disposition purporting to affect the title and not merely the possession of the goods, it is probable that he is under no liability. He is a mere conduit-pipe. In a sentence, the carrier is not liable because he merely changes the position of the goods and not the property in them.[30] "On principle, one who deals with goods at the request of the person who has actual custody of them in the bona fide belief that the custodier is the true owner, or has the authority of the true owner, should be excused for what he does if the act is of such nature as would be excused if done by the authority of the person in possession, if he was the finder of goods or entrusted with their custody."[31] Similarly, the solicitor of a bankrupt who receives after-acquired property on behalf of his client and transfers it to another

---

[26] *Lloyds Bank* v. *Chartered Bank* [1929] 1 K.B. 40, 69; *Bute (Marquess of)* v. *Barclays Bank Ltd.* [1955] 1 Q.B. 202. These cases are an interesting illustration of how the usage or practice of a trade or profession can be influenced by judicial decisions, which themselves take account of changing banking practices: *Marfani & Co. Ltd.* v. *Midland Bank Ltd.* [1968] 1 W.L.R. 956.

[27] "A judge who knew more about these matters than anyone else": *Rogers* v. *Lambert* [1891] 1 Q.B. 318, 325, *per* Lord Esher M.R.

[28] (1875) L.R. 7 H.L. 757, 767.

[29] *Aliter* if he has notice of the claim of the true owner. He should interplead. If he does not, he delivers at his peril: *Winter* v. *Bancks* (1901) 84 L.T. 504.

[30] *Barker* v. *Furlong* [1891] 2 Ch. 172, 182.

[31] *Hollins* v. *Fowler* (1875) L.R. 7 H.L. 757, 766, *per* Blackburn J. The 18th Report of the Law Reform Committee (Cmnd. 4774 (1971)), paras. 46–50, reached a substantially similar conclusion after a full review of the problem. The 1977 Act is silent on the matter.

agent (even with knowledge that that agent has been instructed to sell it) is not liable in conversion at the suit of the trustee in bankruptcy.[32]

A doubtful case

If, however, a carrier, warehouseman, agent, or bailee has actual knowledge that his delivery of the goods is part of a transaction affecting the title and not merely the possession, the question of his liability would seem to be still an unsettled point. If *National Mercantile Bank* v. *Rymill*[33] is well decided,[34] there is no liability even under these circumstances. In this case it was held by the Court of Appeal that an auctioneer with whom the goods of the plaintiff had been wrongfully deposited for sale was not liable for a conversion, although he had delivered them at the request of the vendor to a person to whom, as the auctioneer knew, the vendor had sold them by private contract. The defendant had not sold the goods, or authorised their sale, but he had received the purchase price, and passed it on to the plaintiff after deducting commission. It is difficult to reconcile this decision with earlier cases such as *Stephens* v. *Elwall*,[35] and it is contrary to the opinion of Blackburn J. in *Hollins* v. *Fowler*.[36]

§ 6.6. Conversion by Estoppel[37]

A defendant who has in truth committed no conversion may be held liable for one because he is estopped by his own act from alleging the fact which constitutes his defence: for example, that he has never had possession of the goods, or that he is no longer in possession of them, or that the plaintiff has no title to them.[38] Thus a bailee is estopped from denying the title of his bailor, and therefore a refusal to redeliver the property is a conversion, even though in fact the plaintiff has no title to it.[39] Nor does it make any difference whether the plaintiff has no title at the time of the bailment, or has lost his title since the bailment, *e.g.* by re-selling to a third party.[40] But the bailment and also the estoppel of a bailee no longer exist if he has asserted and proved his own title,[41] or,

---

[32] *Re Samuel* (No. 2) [1945] Ch. 408.

[33] (1881) 44 L.T. 767.

[34] It was doubted in *Willis* v. *British Car Auctions Ltd.* [1978] 1 W.L.R. 438, but approved in *Barker* v. *Furlong* [1891] 2 Ch. 173, and *Consolidated Co.* v. *Curtis* [1892] 1 Q.B. 495, and is quite consistent with *Re Samuel* (No. 2) [1945] Ch. 408.

[35] (1815) 4 M. & S. 259. But in this case the defendant had "set the goods afloat upon a sea of strangers" by sending them out of the jurisdiction to the U.S.A., which might well be a conversion even today (18th Report of the Law Reform Committee (Cmnd. 4774 (1971)), para. 41).

[36] (1875) L.R. 7 H.L. 757, 767.

[37] This is a convenient expression, though estoppel is in general only a rule of evidence and not a cause of action.

[38] *Seton, Laing & Co.* v. *Lafone* (1887) 19 Q.B.D. 68.

[39] *Biddle* v. *Bond* (1865) 6 B. & S. 225.

[40] *Rogers, Sons & Co.* v. *Lambert & Co.* [1891] 1 Q.B. 318.

[41] *Webb* v. *Ireland* [1988] I.R. 353.

on the demand of the true owner, given up possession to him, or if he defends the action on his behalf, and by his authority.[42] Conversely, an owner is not estopped by his own negligence from suing in conversion.[43]

§ 6.7. INEFFECTUAL DEFENCES

(1) Mistake

Although a conversion is necessarily an intentional wrong in the sense already explained, it need not be knowingly wrongful. A mistake of law or fact is no defence to anyone who intentionally interferes with a chattel in a manner inconsistent with the right of another.[44] He does so *suo periculo* and takes the risk of the existence of a sufficient lawful justification for the act; and if it turns out that there is no justification, he is just as responsible in an action of conversion as if he had fraudulently misappropriated the property.[45] "Persons deal with the property in chattels or exercise acts of ownership over them at their peril."[46] Thus an auctioneer who honestly and ignorantly sells and delivers property on behalf of a customer who has no title to it is liable for its value to the true owner, even though he has already paid the proceeds of the sale to his own client.[47]

(2) Contributory negligence

At common law there were a number of statements to the effect that contributory negligence was no defence. The majority view[48] was that an owner of property was entitled to be as careless as he liked. As liability in conversion is strict, the strange result was that a person is not bound to look after his own property as carefully as other people are expected to look after it for him. Now in England the 1977 Act confirms the common law. Section 11(1) provides that contributory negligence is no defence in proceedings founded on conversion,[49] or on intentional trespass to goods.[50]

---

[42] *Kahler* v. *Midland Bank Ltd.* [1950] A.C. 24, 38.

[43] *Moorgate Mercantile Co. Ltd.* v. *Twitchings* [1977] A.C. 890. See also below, § 6.7.

[44] Sometimes the defence of agency of necessity may be available: see below, § 22.1.

[45] *Wilson* v. *New Brighton Panel Beaters Ltd.* [1989] 1 N.Z.L.R. 74, 79.

[46] *Hollins* v. *Fowler* (1872) L.R. 7 Q.B. 616, 639, *per* Cleasby B. The facts of this leading case (see above, § 30) well illustrate this principle, which has not been questioned for a century: *Union Finance Ltd.* v. *British Car Auctions Ltd.* [1978] 2 All E.R. 385, 387.

[47] *Consolidated Co.* v. *Curtis* [1892] 1 Q.B. 495. "That is one of the risks of their profession"; *Sachs* v. *Miklos* [1948] 2 K.B. 23, 37, *per* Lord Goddard C.J.

[48] See, *e.g. Moorgate Mercantile Co. Ltd.* v. *Twitchings* [1977] A. C. 890, 925.

[49] But in relation to a bank which is relying on s.4 of the Cheques Act 1957, s.47 of the Banking Act 1979 provides that "a defence of contributory negligence shall be available to the banker notwithstanding the provisions of s.11(1) of the Torts (Interference with Goods) Act 1977."

[50] See below, § 22.13. But perhaps this defence is available if the action is framed in negligence.

(3) Remoteness of damage

If the defendant has thus intentionally interferred with a chattel without lawful justification and loss of the chattel does in fact result from the interference, it is no defence that such a loss was not intended, or even that it was not the natural or probable result.[51] In *Hiort* v. *Bott*[52] the plaintiffs, by a mistake fraudulently induced by their own agent, consigned certain barley to the defendant which he had not ordered. They also sent him a delivery order which made the barley deliverable "to the order of consignor or consigee" to enable him to obtain it from the carrier. The plaintiffs' agent thereupon informed the defendant that the consignment was a mistake and induced him to indorse and hand over the delivery order to him (the agent) in order that the goods might be obtained by him from the carrier and redelivered to the plaintiffs. The agent thus obtained possession of the barley, sold it, and absconded with the proceeds; and the defendant was held liable in conversion for its value. It will be noted that the defendant in this case, although he had never come into possession of the goods, had done an act which affected the title in them which he was not obliged to do at all—for if he had done nothing the terms of the delivery order would have ensured that the barley would have stood at the order of the plaintiff consignors. His position is thus clearly distinguishable from that of an involuntary bailee, who is in general liable only if the unauthorised act which has deprived the plaintiff of his property is also a negligent one.[53]

(4) Defendant acting for account of another

It is not necessary that the defendant should have acted on his own account, or have converted the goods to his own use. He is equally liable if he has acted on behalf and for the benefit of some other person as his agent or servant.[54] On the other hand, a merely ministerial dealing with the goods at the request of an apparent owner having the actual control of them is not a conversion.[55] Even when the act is done for the supposed benefit of the true owner and with the honest intention of preserving or restoring the property, it will amount to a conversion if done without lawful justification and if it results in fact in a loss of the property.[56]

(5) Loss not permanent

The loss or deprivation of possession suffered by the plaintiff need not be permanent. The duration of the dispossession is relevant with

---

[51] *Wilson* v. *New Brighton Panel Beaters Ltd.* [1989] 1 N.Z.L.R. 74, 80.
[52] (1874) L.R. 9 Ex. 86.
[53] *Elvin & Powell Ltd.* v. *Plummer, Roddis Ltd.* (1933) 50 T.L.R. 158; Burnett, "Conversion by an Involuntary Bailee" (1960) 76 L.Q.R. 364. See also below, § 26.2.
[54] *International Factors Ltd.* v. *Rodriguez* [1979] Q.B. 351.
[55] See above, § 6.4.
[56] See *Consolidated Co.* v. *Curtis* [1892] 1 Q.B. 495.

respect to the measure of damages, but makes no difference to the nature of the wrong.[57]

§ 6.8. The Title of the Plaintiff[58]

Whenever goods have been converted, an action will lie at the suit of any person in actual possession or entitled at the time of the conversion to the immediate possession of them.[59] It is not necessary for the plaintiff to show that he is the owner of the goods.[60] Hence not merely can a bailee at will sue,[61] but also his bailor,[62] and also one who has a lien over goods,[63] or has an equitable title to them, as distinct from a more contractual right.[64] Conversely a person not so entitled cannot sue in conversion, even though he is the owner of the property. So a bailor for a fixed term, or the buyer of goods which remained in the possession of the seller until his lien for the unpaid purchase price had been discharged could not sue a third party.[65] In such a case the remedy of the plaintiff was not conversion but a special action on the case for the injury to his reversionary interest. As this action has not been specifically abolished by the 1977 Act, presumably it still exists.

In certain cases, however, a person who has a merely reversionary interest is remitted to the right of immediate possession by the very act of conversion itself, which causes in certain circumstances a forfeiture and determination of the particular interest in possession.[66] "Any act or disposition which is wholly repugnant to or as it were an absolute disclaimer of the holding as bailee revests the bailor's right to possession, and therefore also his immediate right to maintain trover or detinue even where the bailment is for a term or is otherwise not recoverable at will, and so *a fortiori* in a bailment determinable at will."[67] Thus if the hirer under a contract of hire-purchase sells the article bailed to him, the lessor accordingly becomes entitled to immediate possession and can therefore sue either the hirer or the auctioneer who has effected the sale or the purchaser in conversion and not merely for an injury to his reversionary interest.[68]

---

[57] *Penfolds Wines Pty. Ltd.* v. *Elliott* (1946) 74 C.L.R. 204, 243.

[58] Warren, "Qualifying as Plaintiff in an Action for a Conversion" (1936) 49 Harv.L. Rev. 1084.

[59] *Winkworth* v. *Christie, Manson & Woods Ltd.* [1980] Ch. 496.

[60] *Bute (Marquess of)* v. *Barclays Bank Ltd.* [1955] 1 Q.B. 202.

[61] *Burton* v. *Hughes* (1824) 2 Bing. 173, 175.

[62] *U.S.A.* v. *Dollfus Mieg et Cie* [1952] A.C. 582.

[63] *Rogers* v. *Kennay* (1846) 9 Q.B. 592.

[64] *International Factors Ltd.* v. *Rodriguez* [1979] Q.B. 351.

[65] *Lord* v. *Price* (1874) L.R. 9 Ex. 54.

[66] *Citicomp Australia Ltd.* v. *Stillwell Fund Ltd.* (1979) 21 S.A.S.R. 142, 144.

[67] Pollock and Wright, *Possession*, pp. 132–133. This passage was approved in *Penfolds Wines Pty. Ltd.* v. *Elliott* (1946) 74 C.L.R. 294, 227; in *North General Wagon and Finance Co. Ltd.* v. *Graham* [1950] 2 K.B. 7, 15; in *Alexander* v. *Railway Executive* [1951] 2 K.B. 882, 888, and in *Union Finance Ltd.* v. *British Car Auctions Ltd.* [1978] 2 All E.R. 385, 391.

[68] *North General Wagon and Finance Co. Ltd.* v. *Graham* [1950] 2 K.B. 7. The position may be different if the contract provides that the finance company may only terminate the hire in some particular way, *e.g.* by giving notice to the hirer.

Finders[69]

The true owner of an object, if he is discoverable, has a better title to that object than its finder, or the occupier of the land where it is found.[70] The finder is in the position of a sub-bailee, and owes to the owner a duty to take reasonable care of the chattel and to return it to him, if it is possible to do so.[71] But if the true owner is not discoverable the finder has title as against all other persons, and it has been settled for over three centuries that the measure of damages is the same as if the plaintiff's title was indisputable. So a chimney sweeper's boy who had found a jewel recovered its full value in trover from a jeweller to whom he gave it to value but who refused to return it.[72] Although the report is silent on the point, it seems legitimate to assume that the jewel had been found in a chimney.[73] The principle has been followed ever since. Thus in *Parker v. British Railways Board*[74] the Court of Appeal held that one who found a gold bracelet lying on the floor of an airport lounge was entitled to keep it. But to these authorities an exception, easily stated but difficult to explain, has been developed. If the article found is attached to or lying under the surface of the land, the owner of the land is entitled to in in priority to the finder, unless it is treasure trove, when it goes to the Crown.[75] Thus in *London Corporation v. Appleyard*[76]; a safe containing banknotes was found by two workmen in the basement wall of a house which they were demolishing. The lessee of the premises was held to have priority over the workmen.[77] Yet it is hard to see why a trespasser who finds an article should be in a better position as against the occupier merely because he can say "I did not dig it up—I picked it up,"[78] and it has been suggested that the finder of unattached articles should have priority over the occupier only when

---

[69] See Goodhart, *Essays*, Chap. 4; 18th Report of the Law Reform Committee (Cmnd. 4774 (1971)), (Annex 1).

[70] *Moffat v. Kazana* [1969] 2 Q.B. 152.

[71] *Webb v. Ireland* [1988] I.R. 353.

[72] *Armory v. Delamirie* (1722) 1 Str. 505. The defendant, now better known as Paul de Lamerie, was silversmith to George I. Note that the jury was directed to award the plaintiff the value of the finest jewel which the socket would hold, not the finest jewel that had ever been known.

[73] Note that the owner of the chimney was not a party to the proceedings.

[74] [1982] Q.B. 1004. Lord Donaldson M.R. later commented extra-judicially:

> "We found there was no authority binding on the Court of Appeal at all, and that there were quite interesting policy considerations. If you said it was to be the property of the finder, people would be very much happier to admit to finding something. On the other hand, if you said it belonged to British Airways, it would be very much easier for the unfortunate owner to track down lost items."

(*Judging the World*, ed. G. Sturgess and P. Chubb (London, 1988), p. 292).

[75] Treasure trove comprises articles of gold or silver, which have not been abandoned, but whose (undiscoverable) owner intends to return to them: *R. v. Hancock* [1990] 2 Q.B. 242.

[76] [1963] 1 W.L.R. 982.

[77] The men were given rewards of £500 each by the London Corporation: *The Times*, April 5, 1963.

[78] *Byrne v. Hoare* [1965] Qd.R. 135, 168.

the premises are of a public character.[79] It is not clear whether it makes any difference in what mode the plaintiff obtained the possession on which he relies, but probably he must be an innocent finder.[80] It should not be the policy of the law to encourage people to pry on other persons' property, especially with such devices as metal detectors.[81]

Possessory title: the jus tertii

At common law it was settled that mere *de facto* possession is, as against a stranger, a sufficient title to support an action for a conversion, for as against a wrongdoer possession is title, and the defendant cannot plead the *jus tertii* unless he defends on behalf and by the authority of the true owner, or has already made satisfaction to him.[82]

The *jus tertii* rule was much criticised. There was something unjust, and indeed absurd, about a legal system which refused to listen to a defendant's incontrovertible proof that the plaintiff had no title to the goods whose value he nevertheless claimed from the defendant.[83] So section 8 of the 1977 Act abolishes the *jus tertii* and enables a defendant in an action for wrongful interference to defend the action on the grounds that a third party has a better right to the goods, or part of them, than the plaintiff. Rules of Court[84] prescribe a procedure whereby (a) the plaintiff must give particulars of his title to the goods and specify any other person with an interest in them; and (b) the defendant will be then able to join any other such person in the proceedings. This section does not abolish or alter the relative strength of the different titles. But it prevents a defendant being faced successively with a finder and an owner, and having to pay twice. A consequential change is made by section 7, which modifies the law whereby a person may be required to pay damages more than once in respect of the same act of wrongful interference and may thereafter have no recourse against anyone. Under the Act, where both claimants are parties, subsection (2) will avoid double liability. Where one claimant only is a party, and receives more from the wrongdoer than he would have received had all claims been considered at once, he is, by subsection (3), made liable to account over to the other possible claimants; and, under subsection (4), the wrongdoer can recover any amount which he has overpaid.

§ 6.9. CONVERSION AS BETWEEN CO-OWNERS[85]

The 1977 Act, in section 10(1)(a), restates the common law on this topic. The basic principle is that when a chattel is held in common ownership,

---

[79] 18th Report of the Law Reform Committee (Cmnd. 4774 (1971)), (Annex 1). The Act of 1977 is silent on the whole matter.
[80] *Buckley* v. *Gross* (1863) 3 B. & S. 566, 574.
[81] See *Webb* v. *Ireland* [1988] I.R. 353, 378.
[82] There is a full discussion of this difficult topic in the 18th Report of the Law Reform Committee (Cmnd. 4774 (1971)), paras. 51–78.
[83] See 378 H.L. Deb., col. 1062 (16 December 1976).
[84] See S.I. 1978 No. 579.
[85] Derham, "Conversion by Wrongful Disposal as between Co-owners" (1952) 68 L.Q.R. 507.

one of the owners cannot sue another of them in conversion unless the act of the defendant amounts to the destruction of the chattel or otherwise permanently destroys the right of the plaintiff to the possession thereof—*e.g.* a sale in market overt. Each of the co-owners is equally entitled to the possession and use of the chattel, and neither therefore commits any wrong as against the other by taking or retaining possession of it and using it for the purposes for which it is designed, even if the other is thereby prevented from making the like use of it. But if one co-owner does an act which can be justified only by claiming a right to exclusive possession, then he commits an act of conversion. Section 10(1)(*f*) of the 1977 Act extends the common law by providing that a sale or purported sale by one co-owner can consent to a conversion.[86] If any co-owner acquires from the use of the common property a greater share of the profits derived therefrom than that to which he is entitled, he does not thereby commit any tort against the other owner, whose proper remedy is an action of account.[87]

§ 6.10. Conversion and Limitation of Actions

The Limitation Act 1980, s.3(2) provides in effect that theft and allied offences shall be "imprescriptible" so that the thief or any person claiming through him cannot set up section 2 of the Act. It often happens that two or more successive acts of conversion are committed in respect of the same property, either by the same person or by different persons, and difficult questions formerly arose as to the date from which in such cases the period of limitation began to run. Section 3 of the Limitation Act 1980 deals with both cases. Before the 1939 Act the only effect of the expiry of the period of limitation was to bar the plaintiff's right of action. Now under section 3(2) of the Act of 1980 not only his right of action but his title to the chattel converted is extinguished as it had previously been, and still is, in the case of land. The Act of 1980, s.3(1) further provides: "Where any cause of action in respect of the conversion of a chattel has accrued to any person and, before he recovers possession of the chattel, a further conversion takes place, no action shall be brought in respect of the further conversion after the expiration of six years from the accrual of the cause of action in respect of the original conversion." So (1) where there are successive acts of conversion by the same person, as where, for example, the defendant wrongfully takes a chattel, and on a subsequent date wrongfully consumes it, or refuses to restore it on demand, or (2) where there are successive conversions by different persons, as where, for example, A wrongfully disposes of the plaintiff's chattel to B who subsequently refuses to deliver it up on demand, the cause of action is extinguished after six years from the original conversion.

But Parliament decided that time should not run against an owner in respect of the theft of his chattel or any subsequent conversion other

---

[86] The N.Z.C.A. re-stated the common law so as to achieve the same result in *Coleman* v. *Harvey* [1989] 1 N.Z.L.R. 723.

[87] See *Jacobs* v. *Seward* (1872) L.R. 5 H.L. 464.

than a purchase in good faith. The complex provisions of section 4 in effect provide that a purchase in good faith starts time running against the owner, as distinct from the thief and other converters who preceded the purchase in good faith.

§ 6.11. Detinue

The common law was that a claim in detinue lay at the suit of a person who had an immediate right to the possession of the goods against another who is in actual possession of them, and who, upon proper demand,[88] failed or refused to deliver them up without lawful excuse.[89] But now section 2(1) of the 1977 Act provides tersely that "Detinue is abolished."[90] The action is now framed as one for wrongful interference with goods.

Section 3 of the 1977 Act provides in effect that if the plaintiff in such an action is successful he obtains a judgment which may take one of three different forms[91]: (i) for the value of the chattel as assessed[92] and also for damages for its detention: (ii) for the return of the chattel or recovery of its value as assessed, and also for damages for its detention; or (iii) for return of the chattel and damages for its detention. Form (i) is appropriate for ordinary articles of commerce, or for cases in which the plaintiff does not, or cannot, claim the return of the goods[93]; in such a case the judgment itself deprives both parties of the right to insist on a return of the chattel. Forms (ii) and (iii) are appropriate where damages would not be a suitable remedy and specific restitution is desirable.[94] If there is an order for return or delivery up of the chattel, the defendant is not entitled to remain inert, but should take positive steps to return it, or the plaintiff may levy execution.[95]

§ 6.12. Specific Restitution

We have already seen that at common law the owner of chattels had no absolute right to the specific recovery of them.[96] The form of the judgment in detinue gave the defendant the choice whether he would deliver up the chattels or pay their assessed value. Later the law was altered by empowering the court after judgment in an action of detinue to make on the application of the plaintiff an order for specific delivery

---

[88] *Alicia Hosiery Ltd.* v. *Brown Shipley Ltd.* [1970] 1 Q.B. 195, 207.

[89] *Garrett* v. *Arthur Churchill Ltd.* [1970] 1 Q.B. 92.

[90] This must be one of the shortest sections on the statute-book: see *Howard E. Perry Ltd.* v. *British Railways Board* [1980] 1 W.L.R. 1375, 1378, and above, § 6.4.

[91] See the full discussion by Diplock L.J. in *General and Finance Facilities Ltd.* v. *Cooks Cars (Romford) Ltd.* [1963] 1 W.L.R. 644, 648–652 and by the 18th Report of the Law Reform Committee (Cmnd. 4773 (1971)), paras. 92–97.

[92] The value was assessed at the date of the judgment: *Malhotra* v. *Choudhury* [1980] Ch. 52, 79.

[93] *e.g.* because they have been sold to a third party *pendente lite*.

[94] For these circumstances, see § 6.9.

[95] *Metals & Ropes Co. Ltd.* v. *Tattersall* [1966] 1 W.L.R. 1500.

[96] Above, § 6.1.

of the property, enforceable by way of execution. This jurisdiction is preserved by the Torts (Interference with Goods) Act 1977 and the Rules of the Supreme Court made under it.[97] The power of the court to order the specific restitution of chattels is discretionary.[98] Such an order, therefore, may be either refused altogether, or made only on such terms as to the court seems necessary to do complete justice between the parties.[99] This being so, it may be assumed that one or other of these courses will be adopted in all cases in which the value of the chattel exceeds the amount of damages to which the plaintiff is entitled. But when the chattel is an ordinary article of commerce of no special value or interest and not alleged to be of any special value to the plaintiff,[1] and damages will fully compensate, the court will not normally order specific restitution.[2] If the defendant has, since taking the property, increased the value of it by his own labour or expenditure, the plaintiff is entitled to recover as damages only its original and not its present value.[3] This being so, it is clear that if the plaintiff seeks specific restitution instead of damages the court must either refuse this remedy altogether or grant it only on the terms that the plaintiff shall make to the defendant a fair allowance in respect of the increased value of the property.[4]

Accessio, specificatio, and confusio[5]

It is in this circumstance that specific restitution is a matter of judicial discretion and not of right that we must find the solution in English law of all those puzzles concerning *accessio*, *specificatio*, and *confusio* which we find discussed with such unsatisfactory results in Roman law and the Continental systems founded upon it. *Accessio* is the combination of two chattels belonging to different persons into a single article: as when a vehicle let on hire-purchase has new accessories fitted to it. *Specificatio* is the making of a new article out of the chattel of one person by the labour of another—as when A.'s corn is ground into flour by B. Unless there is a contract governing the matter,[6] English law, like Roman law,

---

[97] Ord. 45, r.4.
[98] Except when s.10 of the Contempt of Court Act 1981 applies: the return of a document which may disclose the source of confidential information can be ordered only in exceptional cases: *Defence Secretary* v. *Guardian Newspapers* [1985] A.C. 339.
[99] See the various relevant factors considered in *Howard Perry & Co. Ltd.* v. *British Railways Board* [1980] 1 W.L.R. 1375. In 1966/78 only 19 Writs of Delivery were issued in Greater London—two for Rolls-Royce cars.
[1] As distinct from the MS of a play by Dylan Thomas: *Thomas* v. *Times Book Co. Ltd.* [1966] 1 W.L.R. 911.
[2] *Whiteley Ltd.* v. *Hilt* [1918] 2 K.B. 808, 819.
[3] See below, §§ 6.13 and 6.14.
[4] *Webb* v. *Ireland* [1988] I.R. 353.
[5] See Slater, "Accessio, Specificatio, and Confusio" (1957) 37 Can.Bar Rev. 597, Guest, "Accession and Confusion in the Law of Hire Purchase" (1964) 27 M.L.R. 505; Matthews, "Specificatio in the Common Law" Anglo-American Law Review 121. All the authorities are reviewed in McCormack "Mixture of Goods," (1990) 2 L.S. 293.
[6] As under the reservation of title clause so familiar in modern commercial practice—see *Clough Mill Ltd.* v. *Martin* [1985] 1 W.L.R. 111, 119, 124.

awards ownership to B.[7] *Commixtio* occurs when articles belonging to different persons are mixed together, as with items for a jumble sale piled up on the floor of a community centre. Here there is no practical or legal problem: the articles can be separated again. *Confusio* is the mixture of things of the same nature but belonging to different owners so that the identification of the things is no longer possible: as when motor-vehicles are "cannibalised," and their parts used to build a new machine. In all these cases there are two distinct questions to be asked. The first, which is of subordinate importance, is: In whom is the ownership of the new article so created? the second is: Who is entitled to the possession of the new article, and on what terms will he be permitted to retain or recover it? As to the first question Salmond thought that a person's property was not divested by any such event. "If my tree is cut down and sawn into timber, the timber is mine."[8] But there are dicta going back over four centuries[9] against Salmond's view, and there are now two clear decisions[10] adopting the principle that the mixture is held in common, so that the innocent party is entitled to receive from it a quantity equal to that of his goods which went into it in the first place. (This is the same principle as that adopted in Roman law.) Any doubt as to the quantity or quality of the innocent party's goods should be resolved in his favour according to the principle in *Armory* v. *Delamirie*.[11]

Over and above the question of ownership, however, there arises the question of the right of possession. Here English law avoids all difficulties by making the matter one of judicial discretion. It may be assumed that in all ordinary cases the court will be guided by the relative values of the interests of the rival claimants. Possession will be awarded to him whose interest is the more substantial, on the terms that he pays the value of the other's interest.

§ 6.13. Damages in Trespass and Conversion[12]

If a plaintiff relies upon a right of possession he can recover only according to the amount of his interest.[13] But it has long been settled that a plaintiff who has actual possession of goods is entitled, in an action for conversion, to recover their full value as damages, even though he is not the owner, but has merely a limited interest, such as that of a bailee, agent or pledge. In other words, the plaintiff in conver-

---

[7] *Northern Ireland Master Butcher's Wholesale Supply Association* v. *Belfast Corporation* [1965] N.I. 30, 33 ("To clarify the concepts of trespass and conversion, and in default of illumination from the conventional legal lamps, the shadowy figures of the Roman jurists Gaius and Justinian with their torches still alight walked in the detention and condemnation rooms of the Corporation abattoir, no doubt much to the astonishment of those who work there—and the word on their lips was 'specificatio.' ")

[8] 6th ed., p. 406.

[9] To *Stock* v. *Stock* (1594) Poph. 37.

[10] *Indian Oil Corporation Ltd.* v. *Greenstone Shipping S.A.* [1988] Q.B. 345, 370; *Coleman* v. *Harvey* [1989] 1 N.Z.L.R. 723.

[11] (1722) 1 Str. 505. See above, § 6.8.

[12] See Palmer, *Bailment* (1979), Appendix I.

[13] *Bloxam* v. *Hubbard* (1804) 5 East 407.

sion is entitled either to the property or to its precuniary equivalent.[14] The law seems to have assumed that the value of the goods must always represent the plaintiff's actual loss. But there are cases in which this is far from being the truth, and to permit the plaintiff to recover more than his actual loss is a significant departure from the principle, which in general governs the award of damages, that compensation of the plaintiff is the object of the law. The leading case is *The Winkfield*,[15] in which the Postmaster-General was held entitled as bailee to recover the whole value of certain mails which were lost through a collision at sea caused by the negligence of the defendants, although the Postmaster-General was, as the law then stood,[16] under no liability to the parties interested in the lost letters and parcels.

The damages so recovered by the plaintiff above the value of his own interest are held by him on account of the other persons interested in the property, and he is liable to those others in an action for money had and received to their use.[17] The rule in *The Winkfield* has been cut down when the plaintiff is a finance company, whose right of action as a bailor would not have accrued but for the conversion. Therefore, if one who is the bailee of a motor-car under a contract of hire-purchase with a finance company sells or pledges it to a third party, the damages payable by that third party to the finance company for the conversion of its property are limited to the value of the plaintiff's interest, that is, the amount of the unpaid instalments, or the value of the car, whichever is the less.[18] There is no reason why the third party purchaser should be liable for the market value of the chattel if it is more than the total of the unpaid instalments. Similarly an unpaid vendor who wrongly disposes of the goods,[19] and is then sued in conversion by the purchaser, is entitled to deduct the price for which the purchaser is no longer liable.[20]

Although it has never been decided, it is presumably the law that a plaintiff entitled under the rule in *The Winkfield* to recover the whole value of the property on account of himself and all other persons interested can do so only if these others stand by and make no objection. Therefore if the bailor or principal has already received with or without an action the value of his interest from the defendant, it is impossible for the bailee to recover more than his own interest. It seems also to follow that, even though no such prior satisfaction has been made, it is a good defence to an action brought by a plaintiff with a limited interest that a claim has been already made on the defendant by another person interested in the property, and that the action is defended on that person's behalf and by his authority. It is settled that this is a good plea in

---

[14] *Chabbra Corporation Ltd.* v. *Jag Shaki (Owners)* [1986] A.C. 337, 346–348.

[15] [1902] P. 42.

[16] For the present law, see § 20.1.

[17] *A. Tomlinson (Hauliers) Ltd.* v. *Hepburn* [1966] A.C. 451.

[18] *Chubb Cash Ltd.* v. *John Crilley & Son* [1983] 1 W.L.R. 599. If the hire-purchase agreement has been terminated by the company, the hirer will have no right to the goods unless he has paid one-third of the purchase price.

[19] As distinct from re-possessing them: *Healing Ltd.* v. *Inglis Electrix Ltd.* (1968) 42 A.J.L.R. 280.

[20] *Chinery* v. *Viall* (1860) 5 H. & N. 288.

an action brought by a plaintiff with a merely possessory interest,[21] and there seems no reason why it should be less effective in a claim by a plaintiff with a limited interest for damages in excess of that interest.

When a defendant has, in accordance with the rule in *The Winkfield*, paid the full value of the property to a claimant with a limited interest, he is probably thereby discharged from all liability to any other person interested in the property.[22] This rule was first put forward in 1374[23] and has never since been disputed, but the matter has been very little considered and involves serious difficulties.[24] The rule is clearly otherwise in the case of payment to a wrongdoer having a merely possessory title; payment to him, even by compulsion of the law, is no defence against a subsequent claim by the true owner.[25]

§ 6.14. ASSESSMENT OF VALUE

In all actions for a conversion the plaintiff may recover, in addition to the value of the property or of his interest in it, any additional damage which he may have sustained by reason of the conversion which is not too remote.[26] Primarily the value of an article is its market price, or if there is no market in such goods, the cost of replacement.[27] Damages in conversion may be reduced by the return of the property converted[28] and sometimes the plaintiff may be compelled to accept the return of the property. Further, where the defendant is able to prove that the plaintiff has got back part of the proceeds of the property wrongfully converted he is *pro tanto* excused.[29] But mere receipt of moneys from the wrongdoer will not go in diminution of damages unless the plaintiff has received the benefit of the sum in question and has received it with knowledge of the conversion.[30] When there is a doubt about the value of a chattel which has been converted the defendant must either produce it or account for its non-production. If he does not do so, it will be assumed against him that it was of the highest possible value. *Omnia praesumuntur contra spoliatorem*.[31]

Value assessed as at date of conversion

The value recoverable in an action for conversion is in general the value of the property at the date of the conversion, and not its value at any earlier or later date,[32] together with any consequential damage

---

[21] *Biddle v. Bond* (1865) 6 B. & S. 255.

[22] *Eastern Construction Co. v. National Trust Co.* [1914] A.C. 197, 210.

[23] Holdsworth, H.E.L., vii, pp. 461–462.

[24] *Morrison Steamship Co. v. Greystoke Castle (Cargo Owners)* [1947] A.C. 265, 278, 298.

[25] *Attenborough v. London and St. Katherine's Dock Co.* (1878) 3 C.P.D. 450, 454. See above, § 6.8.

[26] *Hillesden Securities Ltd. v. Ryjack Ltd.* [1983] 1 W.L.R. 959, 963.

[27] *J. E. Hall Ltd. v. Barclay* [1937] 3 All E.R. 620.

[28] *U.S.A. v. Dollfus Mieg* [1952] A.C. 582, 619.

[29] *Liggett (Liverpool) Ltd. v. Barclays Bank* [1928] 1 K.B. 48.

[30] *Lloyds Bank v. Chartered Bank* [1929] 1 K.B. 40.

[31] *Armory v. Delamirie* (1721) 1 Stra. 505.

[32] *Caxton Publishing Co. v. Sutherland Publishing Co.* [1939] A.C. 178, 192–193.

which is not too remote to be recoverable.[33] This general rule, which has been affirmed by high authority,[34] may be subject to an exception when the depreciation of property has only been temporary and not permanent.

Effect of rise or fall in value

If the property falls in value after the date of the conversion, as may happen with shares, even without any act or default of the defendant, he is nevertheless liable to account for its original value.[35] For *non constat* that the plaintiff would not, before such a loss occurred, have sold the property and so obtained the value of it at the time of the sale. If, on the other hand, the property increases in value after the date of the conversion, a distinction has to be drawn. If the increase is due to the act of the defendant, the plaintiff has no title to it, and his claim is limited to the original value of the property.[36] So indirectly the improver is compensated for the value of his improvement.

The 1977 Acts section 6(1) specifically re-states this common law principle, although limiting its operation to cases in which the defendant improver has acted in the honest but mistaken belief that he had a good title to the goods. A purchaser from an improver is also protected. But it is doubtful whether the section covers one who has only maintained the goods without improving them.

If, however, the subsequent increase of value is not due to the act of the defendant, but would have occurred in any case, even had no conversion been committed, the plaintiff is entitled to recover it as special damage resulting from the conversion, in addition to the original value of the property converted: as when goods taken or detained have risen in value by reason of the fluctuation of the market.[37] But if the plaintiff knew or ought to have known of the conversion he cannot claim the benefit of the subsequent rise in value, for he is under a duty to mitigate his damages.[38]

§ 6.15. EFFECT OF JUDGMENT IN ACTION OF CONVERSION

A mere judgment for the value of the property without actual satisfaction does not in any way affect the plaintiff's title to the property.[39] Therefore he may exercise all his rights as owner notwithstanding the judgment, *e.g.* he may seize the chattel either from the defendant or from anyone else in whose hands it is. Yet in no case can be by the exercise of such concurrent remedies obtain a double satisfaction. If he actually recovers the property his judgment for its value becomes

---

[33] *General and Finance Facilities Ltd.* v. *Cooks Cars (Romford) Ltd.* [1963] 1 W.L.R. 644, 649.

[34] *BBMB Finance Ltd.* v. *EDA Holdings Ltd.* [1990] 1 W.L.R. 409, 411.

[35] *Solloway* v. *McLaughlin* [1938] A.C. 247, 258.

[36] In trespass the result is otherwise: see above, § 4.6.

[37] *Aitken* v. *Gardiner* (1956) 4 D.L.R. (2nd) 119, 138.

[38] *Sachs* v. *Miklos* [1948] 2 K.B. 23.

[39] The judgment may be either for the value alone or for the value with an alternative provision for the return of the property. The rule is the same in either case: *Ellis* v. *John Stenning & Son* [1932] 2 Ch. 81, 90.

inoperative; and if he actually receives its value he cannot exercise his right of recaption or enforce his judgment for specific restitution. And if he receives its value from one defendant he cannot enforce his judgment against another.[40]

Although judgment without satisfaction has thus no effect upon the property or upon the rights of the owner of it, a defendant who satisfies a judgment in damages representing the value of goods detained or damages for their conversion acquires thereby such title to the goods as was vested in the plaintiff whose judgment has been satisfied.[41] It is in effect a compulsory purchase of the goods by the defendant. After such satisfaction, therefore, the former owner is deprived of all his rights of recaption and specific restitution. This principle has been confirmed by section 5 of the 1977 Act.

Power to order plaintiff to accept restitution instead of damages

When property has once been converted there is a vested right of action which is not divested by the fact that the owner subsequently accepts restitution of the property. Such a recovery of possession goes merely in mitigation of damages and not in bar of the action. Therefore the plaintiff may still commence or proceed with his action for the recovery of such damages as are due in respect of his temporary dispossession.[42] But is the plaintiff bound to accept such a restitution of converted property; or can he refuse a tender of it, and insist on his right to sue for its value? After some hesitation the courts finally consented to stay the action in cases in which it was just to the parties that the plaintiff should be thus compelled to accept the property.[43] In other words the courts do not give the plaintiff a right to enforce a sale and so recover the full value of his property. Were the rule otherwise, much hardship might be caused to innocent defendants who have converted in good faith and are entirely willing to return the property.

§ 6.16. Replevin[44]

Whenever chattels are taken by one person out of the possession[45] of another, whether by way of distress[46] or otherwise, the latter may by way of proceedings in replevin recover immediate and provisional possession of them, pending the result of an action brought by him to determine the rights of the parties. The right to replevy goods is a right to get them back at once and provisionally, on giving security to bring an action of replevin, instead of having first to establish one's title to

---

[40] *Ellis* v. *John Stenning & Son* [1932] 2 Ch. 81, 90.
[41] *U.S.A.* v. *Dollfus Mieg* [1952] A.C. 582, 622.
[42] *Moon* v. *Raphael* (1835) 2 Bing.N.C. 310.
[43] *U.S.A.* v. *Dollfus Mieg* [1952] A.C. 582, 619.
[44] See Williams, "A Strange Offspring of Trespass *ab initio*" (1936) 52 L.Q.R. 106.
[45] So that a bailee can claim: *Swaffer* v. *Mulcahy* [1934] 1 K.B. 608.
[46] The best short account is in Chapman, *Statutes*, pp. 318–320.

them in an action of conversion, detinue, or trespass. The plaintiff must prove that at the commencement of the action he was the owner or entitled to possession of the chattel in question and that it was at that time being unjustly detained from him.[47]

Replevin is allowable only when the chattels have been taken by a trespass by the defendant out of the plaintiff's possession. It is not available for a mere detention or for any other dispute as to the title or right of possession. The process is based on the presumption that the possessor of goods is the owner of them, and that a seizure of them is illegal, conferring therefore upon the possessor a right to their provisional restoration pending an inquiry into the title.[48] The right of replevin is usually exercised only in cases of distress, whether for rent, for rates,[49] damage feasant, or otherwise, though it is legally available for all forms of taking whether under colour of distress or not.[50] If the plaintiff succeeds in an action of replevin he keeps the property which has been thus provisionally restored to him and has judgment for all damage (for example, annoyance in his trade) resulting from the defendant's seizure of it.[51] If the defendant succeeds, he has judgment for the restitution of the property, or in the alternative (when his claim is one of distress for rent), if he so requests, for payment of the amount claimed by him or (where the claim is one of distress damage feasant), if the plaintiff so requests, for the amount of the damages sustained by him.[52] Under section 4 of the 1977 Act a procedure for interim custody pending trial has been provided. The relationship to replevin is obscure.

§ 6.17. RESCOUS AND POUND-BREACH

Rescous involves the rescue of distrained goods before they reach the pound; pound-breach arises after they have been impounded. Anyone who commits either tort is liable to a statutory action for treble damages.[53] Once goods are impounded they are *in custodia legis*, and if a pound has been created it must be respected not merely by the tenant but by strangers as well. It was no defence that the defendant did not know that the goods were impounded. Liability was therefore strict. With the increase in the practice of "walking possession" by bailiffs this caused difficulties, and the law has now been modified. A defendant is not liable unless he has a guilty mind, that is, unless he knows that the goods which he took had been impounded.[54] But it is uncertain

---

[47] *MacKenzie* v. *Somers* [1954] 1 D.L.R. 421.
[48] *Mennie* v. *Blake* (1856) 6 E. & B. 842.
[49] As when a tram-car was seized in *L.C.C.* v. *Hackney B.C.* [1928] 2 K.B. 588.
[50] *Shannon* v. *Shannon* (1804) 1 Sch. & Lef. 324.
[51] *Smith* v. *Enright* (1893) 69 L.T. 724.
[52] County Court Rules, 1936, Ord. 33, rr. 1–3.
[53] Distress for Rent Act 1689, s.3. But the Law Commission has recommended the abolition of these torts: Law. Com. No. 194 (1991)
[54] *Abingdon R.D.C.* v. *O'Gorman* [1968] 2 Q.B. 811.

whether goods have been impounded if they have not been the subject of a distinct act which makes it obvious that they are not to be taken away but are *in custodia legis*. For although it was asserted that "walking possession" was valid as against strangers as well as the tenant,[55] this has been doubted.[56]

[55] *Lavell & Co.* v. *O'Leary* [1933] 2 K.B. 200.
[56] *Abingdon R.D.C.* v. *O'Gorman* [1968] 2 Q.B. 811.

CHAPTER 7

TRESPASS TO THE PERSON

§ 7.1. BATTERY

The torts known as assault, battery and false imprisonment are based on the ancient action of trespass.[1] So any direct and immediate interference with personal liberty is actionable without proof of damage.[2] "English law goes to great lengths to protect a person of full age and capacity from interference with his personal liberty. We have too often seen freedom disappear in other countries not only by coups d'état but by gradual erosion; and often it is the first step that counts. So it would be unwise to make even minor concessions."[3] Therefore all, or nearly all, medical treatment, and all surgical treatment of an adult administered without consent is tortious. "This is incontestable."[4]

The application of force to the person of another without lawful justification amounts to the wrong of battery.[5] This is so, however trivial the amount or nature of the force may be, and even though it neither does nor is intended nor is likely or able to do any manner of harm.[6] Even to touch a person without his consent or some other lawful reason is actionable.[7] Nor is anger or hostility essential to liability: an unwanted kiss may be a battery.[8] For the interest that is protected by the law of assault and battery is not merely that of freedom from bodily harm, but also that of freedom from such forms of insult as may be due to interference with his person.[9] In respect of personal dignity, therefore, a man may recover substantial damages for a battery which has done him no

---

[1] *Collins* v. *Wilcock* [1984] 1 W.L.R. 1172, 1177. The criminal offences of false imprisonment and kidnapping are surprisingly obscure in comparison with "the steady well-documented development" of the torts: see Napier, "Detention Offences at Common Law," in *Reshaping the Criminal Law* (ed. Glazebrook 1978), p. 190, and Lambert (1979) Cambrian L.Rev. 20.

[2] See above § 1.2.

[3] *S.* v. *McC.* [1972] A.C. 24, 43, *per* Lord Reid. See also Lord Griffiths in *Murray* v. *Ministry of Defence* [1988] 1 W.L.R. 692, 703.

[4] *Re F. (Mental Patient: Sterilisation)* [1988] 2 W.L.R. 1025, 1034, *per* Lord Donaldson of Lymington M.R. For reality of consent see below, § 22.3. See now, however, the emphatic dicta in *Re F.* [1990] 2 A.C. 1, 73–75.

[5] *Eisener* v. *Maxwell* [1951] 1 D.L.R. 816, 832.

[6] *Donselaar* v.*Donselaar* [1982] 2 N.Z.L.R. 97, 110.

[7] *Cole* v. *Turner* (1704) 6 Mod. 149; but not for him to invite you to touch him in an indecent manner: *D.P.P.* v. *Rogers* [1953] 1 W.L.R. 1017 (though it may be a criminal offence: Indecency with Children Act 1960).

[8] *R.* v. *Chief Constable of Devon and Cornwall* [1982] Q.B. 458, 471. *Wilson* v. *Pringle* [1987] Q.B. 237 seems to require hostility. Rape is, of course, a battery. But, in practice, claims for damages are rare, although the Criminal Injuries Compensation Board often make awards. (The starting figure in 1985 was £2,750—a figure produced after "an assessment exercise in which there were 41 participants, female as well as male": *The Times*, December 20, 1985). Murder is also a battery, but the first claim by the estate of the victim was in *Halford* v. *Brookes*, *The Times*, October 3, 1991.

[9] *Collins* v. *Wilcock* [1984] 1 W.L.R. 1172, 1177.

physical harm whatever,[10] as when finger-prints are taken without observing the statutory[11] requirements,[12] *e.g.* that the prints be taken in the building which houses the court which made the order.[13]

It is certainly clear that consent is implied to such physical contacts as are a reasonably necessary consequence of social life, *e.g.* touching another on the shoulder to attract his attention,[14] and in the crowded conditions of modern England there is a judicial tendency to widen this exception.[15] A defence is therefore available for "the jostler, the back-slapper, and the hand-shaker,"[16] or the person who swats a horsefly on a friend's thigh.[17] Consent may also be implied to harm suffered in the course of some lawful game.[18] But footballers have been ordered to pay substantial damages for deliberately fouling an opponent.[19]

Battery[20]

Intentionally to bring any material object into contact with another's person is a sufficient application of force to constitute a battery; for example, to throw water upon him,[21] or to pull a chair from under him whereby he falls to the ground[22] or to apply a "tone-rinse" to his scalp.[23] So it is a battery forcibly to take from him some object which he holds[24] or wears.[25] It is also probably a battery to project heat, light, noise, or vapours onto another person in such a manner as to cause physical injury or personal discomfort.[26] But the appropriate tort for personal injuries resulting from medical treatment is not battery but negligence.[27]

It is a disputed question how far the term "battery" was, or is now, confined to cases of wilful or intentional acts.[28] As the line of division between trespass and case depended on whether the damage was direct

---

[10] *Stewart* v. *Stonehouse* (1926) 2 D.L.R. 683, 684.

[11] Magistrates' Courts Act 1952, s.40.

[12] *Callis* v. *Gunn* [1964] 1 Q.B. 495.

[13] *R.* v. *Jones* [1978] 3 All E.R. 1098.

[14] *Collins* v. *Wilcock* [1984] 1 W.L.R. 1172.

[15] *Wilson* v. *Pringle* [1987] Q.B. 237, 252, *per* Croom-Johnson L.J. "A modern instance is the batsman walking up the pavilion steps at Lords after making a century. He receives hearty slaps of congratulation on his back. He may not want them. Some of them be too heavy for comfort."

[16] Lord Devlin, *Samples of Lawmaking* (1962), p. 85.

[17] Lucas, in *Law, Morality and Society* (ed. Hacker), p. 87.

[18] See below, § 22.3

[19] *Lewis* v. *Brookshaw*, The Times, April 10, 1970; *Manning* v. *Shilson*, The Times, February 15, 1980.

[20] See Trindade, "Some Curiosities of Negligent Trespass to the Person" (1971) 20 I.C.L.Q. 706.

[21] *Pursell* v. *Horn* (1838) 8 A. & E. 602.

[22] *Hopper* v. *Reeve* (1817) 7 Taunt. 698.

• [23] *Nash* v. *Sheen* [1953] C.L.Y. 3726.

[24] *Green* v. *Goddard* (1704) 2 Salk. 641.

[25] *Humphreys* v. *Connor* (1864) 17 Ir.C.L.R. 1 (Orange lily).

[26] Although taking a photograph without consent is not usually a tort (see above, § 3.2) a flashlight photograph may be a battery: *Kaye* v. *Robertson* (1991) 18 F.S.R. 62.

[27] *Sidaway* v. *Governors of Bethlem Hospital* [1985] A.C. 871; *T.* v. *T.* [1988] Fam. 52.

[28] *Long* v. *Hepworth* [1968] 1 W.L.R. 1229.

or indirect and not on whether it was intentional or negligent,[29] a long series of cases affirmed that a battery did not necessarily involve intention.[30] It is the act and not the injury which must be intentional. Fear in the sense of alarm is not an essential ingredient of the tort of battery. Indeed, not even apprehension of the infliction of force is required: a blow from behind is a battery. The position is very different in assault, in which fear or apprehension must be proved. On the other hand, in popular speech "assault" includes a battery, and Salmond himself[31-32] thought that the legal and the popular terminology should coincide. His view has been greatly strengthened by *Fowler v. Lanning*,[33] in which it was held that in an action of trespass to the person intention or negligence must be shown. But the status of this decision is still somewhat doubtful, and until it has been definitely approved on appeal[34] it is better to adhere to the traditional common law.

Assault

The act of putting another person in reasonable fear or apprehension of an immediate battery by means of an act amounting to an attempt or threat to commit a battery amounts to an actionable assault.[35] The tort is remarkable, for it "remains the only instance in English jurisprudence of a mere offensive sensation unaccompanied by any untoward psychosomatic symptoms, let alone external trauma, giving a cause of action for damages."[36] Probably mere words do not constitute an assault,[37] however insulting or even menacing[38]; the intent to do violence must be expressed in threatening acts, not merely in threatening speech.[39] But most of the cases come from an age when the means of communication and of inflicting violence were less developed than today, and so a modern court might hold some oral threats actionable.[40] Contrariwise words accompanying an act may render harmless what might otherwise be an assault.[41] Even threatening acts do not constitute an assault unless they are of such a nature as to put the plaintiff in fear or apprehension

---

[29] See above, § 1.2.
[30] *Eisener v. Maxwell* [1951] 1 D.L.R. 816, 827 (approving the views of Stallybrass in earlier editions), reversed [1951] 3 D.L.R. 345; *Mantey v. Spanks* [1952] 3 D.L.R. 783.
[31] *Wilson v. Pringle* [1987] Q.B. 237.
[32] 6th ed., s.117.
[33] [1959] 1 Q.B. 426. See below, § 7.4.
[34] It was approved, *obiter*, in *Letang v. Cooper* [1965] 1 Q.B. 232.
[35] *Stephens v. Myers* (1830) 4 C. & P. 349.
[36] Fleming, *Introduction to the Law of Torts*, p. 3.
[37] They may be actionable on other grounds: below, § 7.4.
[38] Handford, "Tort Liability for Threatening or Insulting Words" (1976) 54 Can. Bar Rev. 563.
[39] *Meade's and Belt's Case* (1823) 1 Lew. 184. "For Meade's case proves, or my Report's in fault, that singing can't be reckoned an assault": Adolphus, "The Circuiteers" (1884) 1 L.Q.R. 232. *Contra*, Lord Goddard C.J. in *R. v. Wilson* [1955] 1 W.L.R. 493, 494. But the traditional view is impliedly supported by *Wilkinson v. Dowton* [1897] 2 Q.B. 57, in which the defendant had only spoken, and not acted (see below, § 9.8).
[40] *Barton v. Armstrong* [1969] 2 N.S.W.R. 451, 454.
[41] *Tuberville v. Savage* (1669) 1 Mod. 3.

of immediate violence. To shake one's fist in a man's face is an assault; to shake it at a man who by his distance from the scene of action is inaccessible to such violence is not an assault.[42]

There need be no actual intention or power to use violence, for it is enough if the plaintiff on reasonable grounds believes that he is in danger of it.[43] Thus it is actionable to point a gun at a man in a threatening manner, even though to the knowledge of the defendant, but not to that of the plaintiff, it is unloaded.[44] But if there is no reasonable fear there is no assault: as, for example, when a gun is pointed at a man behind his back.[45] Mere passive obstruction does not constitute an assault,[46] although if the plaintiff is thereby hindered from going about his lawful occasions he may use reasonable force by way of self-help.[47]

Criminal law[48]

An assault is not merely a tort, but also a criminal offence, and the civil and criminal remedies are in general concurrent and cumulative. It is provided, however, by the Offences against the Person Act 1861, ss.44 to 45, that summary criminal proceedings, whether they result in a conviction or an acquittal (after an actual hearing on the merits, as distinct from a plea of guilty[49]), are a bar to any subsequent civil proceedings for the same cause.

§ 7.2. FALSE IMPRISONMENT

The wrong[50] of false[51] imprisonment consists in the act of arresting or imprisoning any person without lawful justification, or otherwise preventing him without lawful justification from exercising his right of leaving the place in which he is.[52] It may also be committed by continuing a lawful imprisonment longer than is justifiable.[53] But the essence of the tort is the imprisonment of someone who is otherwise free. As a convicted prisoner is already in prison, he cannot sue in this tort for interference with his "residual liberty."[54] As it is derived from the action of trespass there is no need to prove actual damage or bad faith.

---

[42] *Thomas* v. *N.U.M.* [1986] Ch. 20, 62.
[43] *Bruce* v. *Dyer* (1966) 58 D.L.R. (2d) 211, 216.
[44] *R.* v. *St. George* (1840) 9 C. & P. 483, 493.
[45] *Osborn* v. *Veitch* (1858) 1 F. & F. 317.
[46] *Innes* v. *Wylie* (1844) 1 C. & K. 257 (defendant "like a door or wall").
[47] See below, § 7.4.
[48] North, "Civil and Criminal Remedies for Assault" (1966) 29 M.L.R. 16.
[49] *Ellis* v. *Burton* [1975] 1 W.L.R. 386.
[50] For the crime, see above, § 7.1.
[51] The term false is here used not in the ordinary sense of mendacious or fallacious, but in the less common though well-established sense of erroneous or wrong; as in the phrases false quantity, false step, false taste, etc.
[52] *Weldon* v. *Home Office* [1990] 3 W.L.R. 465, 470.
[53] *Mee* v. *Cruikshank* (1902) 86 L.T. 708.
[54] *R.* v. *Deputy Governor of Parkhurst Prison, ex p. Hague* [1991] A.C. 58, 162–165.

In any event, when the liberty of the subject is at stake questions as to the damage sustained become of little importance.[55] Aggravated damages may be awarded in a proper case,[56] as when the imprisonment, although in itself of a nominal character, is offensive or hurtful to the plaintiff's feelings.[57] In some circumstances exemplary damages may also be awarded, as when there has been an abuse of power by the state.[58] The wrong of false imprisonment is in most cases that of assault also, but not necessarily so[59]; locking a man up in a room in which he already is by his own act amounts to false imprisonment but is no assault. Even if the plaintiff fails to prove some of the ingredients of this tort he may have a special action on the case for the infringement of his liberty,[60] or an action for defamation, malicious prosecution, misfeasance in a public office, or the intentional infliction of mental distress. He can also recover his liberty by a writ of habeas corpus.

The imprisonment

To constitute the wrong in question there need be no actual imprisonment in the ordinary sense—*i.e.* incarceration.[61] It is enough that the plaintiff has been in any manner completely deprived of his personal liberty, for any time, however short. A mere unlawful arrest, for example, amounts in itself to false imprisonment, and so does any act whereby a man is unlawfully prevented from leaving the place in which he is: for example, a house[62] or a motor-car,[63] or a ski-lift,[64] or the common travel area at a port by refusing to allow him to enter immigration control.

An arrest is complete if a person is touched and informed of the reason for his arrest; it is not necessary for him to be brought under physical control.[65] Whether a person has been arrested depends not on the legality of the arrest but on whether he has been deprived of his liberty to go where he pleases.[66] An arrest is a state of fact and not a legal concept.[67] A threat of force, whereby the submission of the person threatened is procured, is sufficient: for example, showing a man a warrant for his arrest and thereby obtaining his submission is itself an arrest if it amounts to a tacit threat to execute the warrant by force if

---

[55] *John Lewis & Co.* v. *Tims* [1952] A.C. 676, 680; *Murray* v. *Ministry of Defence* [1988] 1 W.L.R. 692, 703.
[56] See below, § 22.15.
[57] *Fogg* v. *McKnight* [1968] N.Z.L.R. 330.
[58] *Cassell & Co. Ltd.* v. *Broome* [1972] A.C. 1027.
[59] *Willis* v. *Att.-Gen.* [1989] 3 N.Z.L.R. 574, 579.
[60] *Bird* v. *Jones* (1845) 7 Q.B. 742, 752.
[61] *R.* v. *Deputy Governor of Parkhurst Prison* [1991] A.C. 58, 173–174. *Blundell* v. *Att.-Gen.* [1967] N.Z.L.R. 492, 503–504.
[62] *Warner* v. *Riddiford* (1858) 4 C.B.(N.S.) 180.
[63] *Burton* v. *Davies*, 1953 St.R.Qd. 26.
[64] *The Times*, June 26, 1963.
[65] *Hart* v. *Chief Constable of Kent* [1983] R.T.R. 484.
[66] *Spicer* v. *Holt* [1977] A.C. 987, 1000.
[67] *Lewis* v. *South Wales Chief Constable* [1991] 1 All E.R. 206.

necessary[68] "In such cases . . . though little may be said, much is meant and perfectly understood."[69] It is enough if the plaintiff shows that he has submitted to restraint because of moral pressure exerted by the defendants, *e.g.* if the plaintiff goes to answer a charge in order to avoid an embarrassing scene in a public place.

What is the position if a police officer invites a suspect against whom no charge has yet been made to accompany him to the police station for an interview? The law draws a very sensible distinction between one who goes to the police station voluntarily in the first instance[70] and one who, having had a charge made against him, goes voluntarily to meet it.[71] The second person may be able to sue for false imprisonment, but the first cannot: his liberty has not been interfered with, as he can leave the police station at any time.[72] The common law has never encouraged notions such as "preventive custody," which are familiar elsewhere.[73]

It has now been held that a person may be imprisoned without knowing it.[74] In many such cases the plaintiff might obtain only nominal damages. But it is not difficult to think of cases in which justice would require a substantial award—*e.g.* when an infant is kept in solitary confinement, or the victim of kidnappers is kept under sedation.

To constitute imprisonment the deprivation of the plaintiff's liberty must be complete—that is to say, there must be on every side of him a boundary drawn beyond which he cannot pass. That boundary may be very narrowly,[75] or quite broadly,[76] drawn, but it must be complete and definite. It is no imprisonment to prevent the plaintiff from going in some directions while he is left free to go as far as he pleases in others. Thus no action for false imprisonment[77] will lie for unlawfully preventing the plaintiff from going along one part of the highway and compelling him to go round or back.[78] But the means of escape available must be such as are reasonable in all the circumstances of the case. Probably the means of escape are unreasonable if they involve exposure of,[79] or danger to,[80] the person, or material harm to the clothing, or damage to the person (as distinct from a mere trespass against the property[81]) of another.

---

[68] *Warner* v. *Riddiford* (1858) 4 C.B.(N.S.) 180. It is doubtful whether the signing of the charge-sheet is sufficient: *Clubb* v. *Wimpey* [1936] 3 All E.R. 148.

[69] *Bird* v. *Jones* (1845) 7 Q.B. 742, 748, per Williams J.

[70] This is not so unlikely as might appear at first sight; a man often prefers to answer police inquiries at the station rather than at home within sight of curious neighbours: Devlin, *The Criminal Prosecution in England* (1960), p. 68.

[71] *Peters* v. *Stanway* (1835) 6 C. & P. 737.

[72] *Dunne* v. *Clinton* [1930] I.R. 366, 372. See, further, below § 7.4.

[73] For the distinction between arrest and custody, see below, § 7.4.

[74] *Meering* v. *Grahame-White Aviation Co.* (1919) 122 L.T. 44, 53, per Atkin L.J., whose opinion was unanimously affirmed by the H.L. in *Murray* v. *Ministry of Defence* [1988] 1 W.L.R. 692, 701.

[75] *e.g.* the cubicle in a public lavatory: *Sayers* v. *Harlow U.D.C.* [1958] 1 W.L.R. 623.

[76] *e.g.* the perimeter of airport buildings: *Kuchenmeister* v. *Home Office* [1958] 1 Q.B. 496.

[77] But an action may lie for assault or intimidation.

[78] *Bird* v. *Jones* (1845) 7 Q.B. 742.

[79] As where the plaintiff is bathing and the defendant removes his clothes.

[80] As in *Sayers* v. *Harlow U.D.C.* [1958] 1 W.L.R. 623.

[81] So ruled by Sir John Holt C.J. at Nisi Prius: *Wright* v. *Wilson* (1699) 1 Ld.Raym. 693.

Failure to afford facilities for leaving premises[82]

One who has lawfully entered premises is therefore entitled to leave them; but it is not clear whether he is entitled to leave by the same gate or door as that by which he entered. Such a right might be very inconvenient if exercised at, say, a crowded sporting event. So an occupier is entitled to stipulate that a visitor shall leave by some gate or door other than that by which he entered the premises.[83] An occupier of premises (a term which includes a vehicle) may also be entitled to stipulate that a visitor shall not leave except after the expiry of a reasonable time: a passenger on an express train is not entitled to get out at an unscheduled stop.[84]

But there is no positive duty to assist another to obtain his liberty. Towards persons who are upon his premises and who are unable to leave them unless active measures are taken by him in that behalf, an occupier owes no duty to take such measures. If my neighbour falls down a pit upon my land I am under no obligation to pull him out. In *Herd* v. *Weardale Steel Coke and Coal Co.*[85] certain miners, having been lowered down the defendants' mine, wrongfully refused to continue their work, and demanded that they should at once be taken to the surface. The defendants, however, refused to do so, and stopped the working of the cage, by reason of which the miners were compelled to remain for some little time in the mine against their will. In an action for false imprisonment it was held by the House of Lords that it was a case of *volenti non fit injuria*. Even if the motive was to punish the plaintiffs,[86] there was no cause of action, though it might have been otherwise if it had been a case of sudden illness, or if the mining company had been in breach of contract.

§ 7.3. FALSE IMPRISONMENT AND ABUSE OF PROCESS[87]

No action for false imprisonment will lie against a person who has procured the imprisonment of another by obtaining against him a judgment or other judicial order of a court of justice, even though that judgment or order is erroneous, irregular, or without jurisdiction. The proper remedy in such a case is an action for malicious prosecution or other malicious abuse of legal process.[88] In an action of that description that plaintiff can succeed only if he proves both malice and the absence of any reasonable and probable cause for the proceedings complained of; whereas in an action for false imprisonment, just as in all other cases of trespass to person or property, liability is created, in general, even by

---

[82] Williams, "Two Cases on False Imprisonment," in *Law, Justice and Equity* (ed. Holland and Schwarzenberger) (1967).

[83] This is perhaps the best explanation of the difficult case of *Robinson* v. *Balmain New Ferry Co. Ltd.* [1910] A.C. 295.

[84] *Herd* v. *Weardale Steel, Coke and Coal Co. Ltd.* [1915] A.C. 67, 71.

[85] [1915] A.C. 67.

[86] As in *Burns* v. *Johnston* [1917] 2 I.R. 137; (1916) 50 I.L.T.R. 224.

[87] See Kodilinye, "False Imprisonment through Ministerial Officers" (1979) 28 I.C.L.Q. 766.

[88] See below, § 16.2.

honest and inevitable mistake. The rule, therefore, that no action for false imprisonment will lie against a litigant in respect of judicial imprisonment procured by him is a valuable protection against liability for error in the course of legal proceedings.[89] Accordingly, if the plaintiff has been wrongly arrested without warrant and taken before a magistrate, who remands him in custody, he must sue in respect of his imprisonment before the remand in an action for false imprisonment, but in respect of that which is subsequent to the remand in an action for malicious prosecution.[90] The reason for this distinction is that a man cannot be sued in trespass (and so not for false imprisonment) unless he himself, whether personally or by his agent, has done the act complained of. A court of justice, however, is not the agent of the litigant but acts in the exercise of its own independent judicial discretion. The litigant can be charged only with having maliciously and without reasonable cause exercised his right of setting a court of justice in motion.[91] This exemption of the litigant from any liability for false imprisonment extends even to cases in which the court ordering the imprisonment has acted without jurisdiction. It is the right of every litigant to bring his case before the court, and it is for the court to know the limits of its own jurisdiction and to keep within them.[92]

Ministerial officers

If, however, the litigant, after procuring a judicial order of imprisonment, proceeds to execute it by means of some ministerial officer whom he thereby makes his agent, he may thereby make himself responsible in an action for false imprisonment if the order was one which ought not to have been made.[93] Whether he will be so responsible or not depends on whether the order is of such a nature as, even though wrongful, to be a protection to those who act in reliance on it. If he makes that ministerial officer his agent he is responsible for any arrest or detention so procured or authorised. It is necessary to prove actual direction or authorisation; mere information given to such an officer, on which he acts at his own discretion, is no ground for liability.[94]

§ 7.4. DEFENCES[95]

The following eight defences are available: (1) consent; (2) contributory negligence; (3) self-defence; (4) that the defendant was acting to prevent a trespass or ejecting a trespasser; (5) that the defendant was acting in support of the criminal law to secure the public peace; (6) that the defendant was exercising parental or other authority; (7) inevitable accident; (8) statutory authority.

---

[89] *Austin* v. *Dowling* (1870) L.R. 5 C.P. 534, 540, *per* Willes J.
[90] *Lock* v. *Ashton* (1848) 12 Q.B. 871.
[91] *Lea* v. *Charrington* (1889) 23 Q.B.D. 45.
[92] *Brown* v. *Chapman* (1848) 6 C.B. 365.
[93] *Painter* v. *Liverpool Gas Light Co.* (1836) 3 A. & E. 433.
[94] *Grinham* v. *Willey* (1859) 4 H. & N. 496.
[95] See Beale, "Justification for Injury" (1928) 41 Harv.L.Rev. 553.

(1) Consent

This is considered elsewhere, as is the allied defence of necessity.[96]

(2) Contributory negligence

Contributory negligence is generally assumed to be a defence to assault and battery[97] or false imprisonment,[98] but there is authority the other way.[99]

(3) Self-defence

It is lawful for any person to use a reasonable degree of force for the protection of himself or any other person against any unlawful use of force. In the older books a distinction is drawn between the defence of oneself and of certain persons with whom one is closely connected (such as a wife, child, or master), and the defence of a mere stranger. It may be safely assumed, however, that at the present day all such distinctions are obsolete and that everyone has the right of defending any person by reasonable force against unlawful force,[1] even if he has made a genuine mistake about the perilous position of that other.[2] Still, the relationship of the parties may be relevant to the reasonableness of force used.

Force is not reasonable if it is either (i) unnecessary—*i.e.* greater than is requisite for the purpose—or (ii) disproportionate to the evil to be prevented. In order that it may be deemed reasonable within the meaning of this rule, it is not enough that the force was not more than was necessary for the purpose in hand. For even though not more than necessary it may be unreasonably disproportionate to the nature of the evil sought to be avoided.[3] It must also be noted that the law changes with differing social conditions. Once it was held "that if an author is to go and give a beating to a publisher who has offended him, two or three blows with a horse-whip ought to be quite enough to satisfy his irritated feelings,"[4] but today those ideas no longer prevail.[5] Still, "If you are attacked with a deadly weapon you can defend yourself with a deadly weapon or with any other weapon which may protect your life. The law does not concern itself with niceties in such matters. If you are attacked by a prize-fighter you are not bound to adhere to the Queensberry rules in your defence."[6] He on whom an assault is threatened or committed is not bound to adopt an attitude of passive defence: "I am not bound to wait until the other has give a blow, for perhaps it will come too late afterwards," it was said in the *Chaplain of Gray's Inn's Case*

---

[96] Below, §§ 22.1–22.5.
[97] *Lane* v. *Holloway* [1968] 1 Q.B. 379; *Murphy* v. *Culhane* [1977] Q.B. 94.
[98] See Hudson, "Contributory Negligence as a Defence to Battery" (1984) 4 L.S. 332.
[99] *Hoeberger* v. *Koppens* [1974] 2 N.Z.L.R. 597.
[1] *The People* v. *Keatley* [1954] I.R. 12, 17: *Goss* v. *Nicholas* [1960] Tas.S.R. 133.
[2] *R.* v. *Fennell* [1971] 1 Q.B. 428.
[3] *Cook* v. *Beal* (1697) 1 Ld.Raym. 176, 177, *per curiam.*
[4] *Fraser* v. *Berkeley* (1836) 7 C. & P. 621, 626, *per* Lord Abinger C.B.
[5] *Lane* v. *Holloway* [1968] 1 Q.B. 379, 392.
[6] *Turner* v. *M.-G.-M. Pictures Ltd.* [1950] 1 All E.R. 449, 471, *per* Lord Oaksey.

in 1400.[7] The defendant will be justified so long as he does not go beyond what is reasonable as a measure of self-defence. Nor need he make any request or give any warning, but may forthwith reply to force by force.[8] Provocation by the plaintiff may wipe out the element of aggravated damages but cannot be used to reduce the real damages for the harm done.[9]

(4) Prevention of trespass or ejection of a trespasser

It is lawful for any occupier of land, or for any other person with the authority of the occupier, to use a reasonable degree of force in order to prevent a trespasser[10] from entering or to control his movements[11] or to eject him after entry.[12] So reasonable force may be used to control or eject a trespasser taking part in a demonstration[13] on private premises.[14] This right of using force against trespassers is conferred only on the occupier of the land (or his agents), for it is only the occupier who is entitled to complain of a trespass and to take legal proceedings in respect thereof.[15] This right must be distinguished from forcible re-entry upon land of which possession has been wrongfully taken or detained[16] and from the right of an occupier to justify his acts on the ground of necessity.[17] Presumably any person entitled to the possession of a chattel may also defend his possession by the use of reasonable force.[18]

Previous request necessary

A trespasser cannot be forcibly repelled or ejected until he has been requested to leave the premises and a reasonable opportunity of doing so peaceably has been afforded to him.[19] But as against him who enters or seeks to enter by force, "I need not request him to be gone, but may lay hands on him immediately, for it is but returning violence with violence. So if one comes forcibly and takes away my goods, I may oppose him without any more ado, for there is no time to make a request."[20] As

---

[7] Y.B. 2 Hen. IV, fo. 8, pl. 40.

[8] *Cottreau* v. *Rodgerson* (1965) 53 D.L.R. (2d) 549, 554.

[9] *Lane* v. *Holloway* [1968] 1 Q.B. 379.

[10] In 178 H.L.Deb., cols. 421–442 (July 29, 1952), there is a statement by Lord Simonds on the position of a householder in relation to a person who has a statutory right of entry but does not produce a search warrant.

[11] *Harrison* v. *Rutland (Duke of)* [1893] 1 Q.B. 142 (trespasser on grouse-moor held down by keepers until the drive was over).

[12] *Green* v. *Goddard* (1704) 2 Salk. 641.

[13] In *Ball* v. *Manthorpe* (1970) 15 D.L.R. (3d) 99, 100, a demonstration was judicially defined as "a noisy mob scene of the sort which until recently occurred only in countries inhabited by excitable foreigners who live under bizarre constitutions."

[14] *R.* v. *Chief Constable of Devon and Cornwall* [1982] Q.B. 458, 478.

[15] *Dean* v. *Hogg* (1834) 10 Bing. 345; *Holmes* v. *Bagge* (1853) 1 E. & B. 782. As against a mere wrongdoer, however, actual possession without title is doubtless sufficient, just as in an action of trespass: *Brett* v. *Mullarkey* (1873) Ir.Rep. 7 C.L. 120.

[16] Below, § 26.1.

[17] Below, § 22.1.

[18] For forcible recaption of chattels, see below, § 26.2.

[19] See above, § 6.3.

[20] *Green* v. *Goddard* (1702) 2 Salk. 641, *per curiam*.

to the amount of force that may be used, it must amount to nothing more than forcible removal and must not include beating, wounding, or other physical injury. Thus in *Collins* v. *Renison*[21] the plaintiff sued for the assault of throwing him off a ladder. It was held a bad plea that the plaintiff was trespassing and refused after request to leave the premises, and that the defendant thereupon "gently shook the ladder, which was a low ladder, and gently overturned it, and gently threw the plaintiff from it upon the ground, thereby doing as little damage as possible to the plaintiff." Sir Dudley Ryder C.J. held that such force was not justifiable in defence of the possession of land. In any event, as he very sensibly observed, "The overturning of the ladder could not answer the purpose of removing the plaintiff out of the garden; since it only left him upon the ground at the bottom of the ladder, instead of being upon it." Nor may an occupier do indirectly what he is prohibited from doing directly: he cannot eject the trespasser if his removal from the premises would expose him to serious risk of physical injury.[22]

There are two exceptions to this rule:

(1) If the trespasser in the course of eviction makes or threatens to make an assault upon the person evicting him, the case becomes one of the defence of the person, and thereafter any force may be used which is reasonable within the rule as to self-defence already considered, even though it involves beating or physical harm.

(2) If the trespasser enters or seeks to enter by means of a forcible offence the case falls within the rule that any force is justifiable which is necessary to prevent the commission of such an offence.[23]

(5) Defendant acting in support of the law

Sometimes an assault or imprisonment may be justified on the ground that the defendant was acting in support of the law. But the courts are anxious to see that the liberty of the subject is not invaded except under due process of law and the onus of proving a legal justification lies on the defendant.[24] The plea of public interest or act of state is not enough.[25] So one who relies upon a statutory power of entry for

---

[21] (1754) Sayer 138.

[22] *Depue* v. *Flateau* (1907) 100 Minn. 299 (sick trespasser turned out into snow).

[23] The criminal law on the matter is not as clear as might be wished. In Dicey, *Law of the Constitution* (8th ed.), p. 494 (the passage is not in the current edition), the following remarkable opinion of Willes J. is given as related by "an ear-witness." "The judge was asked: 'If I look into my drawing-room, and see a burglar packing up the clock, and he cannot see me, what ought I to do?' Willes replied, as nearly as may be: 'My advice to you, which I give as a man, as a lawyer, and as an English judge, is as follows: In the supposed circumstances this is what you have a right to do, and I am by no means sure that it is not your duty to do it. Take a double-barrelled gun, carefully load both barrels, and then, without attracting the burglar's attention aim steadily at his heart and shoot him dead.' " It cannot be supposed that Sir James Shaw Willes meant this to be taken seriously: he may have been answering a fool according to his folly.

[24] *Christie* v. *Leachinsky* [1947] A.C. 573, and *Re F. (Mental Patient: Sterilisation)* [1990] 2 A.C.I. are two cases in which The Law Lords emphasised this basic principle.

[25] See below, § 20.2.

public health[26] or mental health[27] purposes must prove that all the statutory conditions precedent to entry have been complied with, or else an assault upon him may be justifiable. At one time the "breath-alyser"[28] legislation was also very strictly construed, but in view of the great social evil of drunken driving, and of the increasing number of unmeritorious technical defences, it has been held that a lawful arrest is no longer a condition precedent to a breath test.[29]

(i) Breach of the peace

The common law has not been affected by the Police and Criminal Evidence Act 1984 (PACE). At common law it is the right, and indeed the duty,[30] of every subject[31] to arrest without warrant any person for a breach of the peace continuing in his presence or if there is a well-founded apprehension of its renewal.[32] An arrest after the breach of the peace is over is in general unjustifiable: a warrant should be obtained. A breach of the peace takes place when harm is actually done or likely to be done to a person, or in his presence to his property. A breach of the peace may occur on private premises, at least if a member of the public is likely to be disturbed, but a purely domestic dispute will not often attain such dimensions as to amount to a breach of the peace.[33] Mere annoyance or insult is not enough.[34] It is the particular duty of a magistrate or police officer to preserve the peace unbroken; hence if he has reasonable cause to believe that a breach of the peace is imminent he may be justified in committing an assault[35] or effecting an arrest.[36] But there is no power to arrest and detain a person merely because it is apprehended that he may be in danger some time in the future.[37] "If that were so, the adventurous spirits that sought the North Pole, or the interior of Africa, or that conquered the Atlantic in flight, might have been locked up for their own good. Nor does the fact that the supposed danger arises from the designs of wicked men warrant interference with the wish of him who desires to brave it. If it were otherwise, every informer in Irish history could have been locked up for life."[38] The Criminal Law Act 1967, s.3(1), provides that a person may use such force as is reasonable in the prevention of crime, or in effecting or assisting the arrest of offenders or suspected offenders, or of persons unlawfully at large. By section 3(2) the provisions of section 3(1) replace the rules of

---

[26] *Stroud* v. *Bradbury* [1952] 2 All E.R. 76.

[27] *Townley* v. *Rushworth* (1963) 62 L.G.R. 95.

[28] The Road Traffic Act 1972, s.6, as amended by Transport Act 1981, s.25(2).

[29] *Fox* v. *Chief Constable of Gwent* [1986] A.C. 281.

[30] *R.* v. *Brown* (1841) C. & M. 314.

[31] There is no recent example of such a prosecution against a private person, but a constable was convicted in *R.* v. *Dytham* [1979] Q.B. 723.

[32] *Albert* v. *Lavin* [1982] A.C. 546, 565.

[33] *McConnell* v. *Chief Constable of Greater Manchester* [1990] 1 W.L.R. 364.

[34] *Bryan* v. *Robinson* [1960] 1 W.L.R. 506 (smiling and beckoning by Soho hostesses).

[35] *Humphreys* v. *Connor* (1864) 17 Ir.C.L.R. 1 (removal of Orange lily from lady).

[36] *Duncan* v. *Jones* [1936] 1 K.B. 218.

[37] *Connors* v. *Pearson* [1921] 2 I.R. 51.

[38] *Ibid.* 91, *per* O'Connor L.J.

the common law on the question of the use of justifiable force in such circumstances.

(ii) *Arrestable offences*

The law relating to arrest is complex and badly in need of reform. The need has been accentuated and not diminished by the Criminal Law Act 1967, ss.1 and 2, which abolished the traditional distinction between felonies and misdemeanours and created a new category entitled "arrestable offence." As amended by section 21 of PACE, this statutory distortion of the English language is defined to mean an offence for which the punishment is fixed or for which the law authorises imprisonment for five years, and also attempts to commit such offences.

PACE, s.24(4) provides that any person may arrest without warrant any person who is, or whom he suspects with reasonable cause to be, in the act of committing an arrestable offence. It also provides (s.24(5)) that any person who has reasonable cause to believe that a particular person is guilty of an arrestable offence may arrest him without warrant if that arrestable offence has in fact been committed. Further, section 24(6) provides that when a constable with reasonable cause, suspects that an arrestable offence has been committed, he may arrest without warrant anyone whom he suspects, with reasonable cause, to be guilty of the offence. These provisions preserve the rule in *Walters* v. *W. H. Smith & Son Ltd.*[39]—one of the strangest of common law rules, and a dangerous trap for the public-spirited citizen. The rule draws a distinction between arrest by a private person (a "citizen's arrest") and arrest by a constable or other peace officer. A private person justifying an arrest must prove that the offence has actually been committed, whether by the person arrested or someone else, and if in fact that offence has not been committed it is no defence that there was reasonable and probable cause for believing the person arrested to be guilty. On the other hand, it is enough for the constable to show that there was reasonable and probable cause for suspicion even though no offence had in fact been committed.[40] Further, reasonable suspicion is not the same as prima facie proof. Suspicion can take into account matters which could not be given in evidence at all—*e.g.* previous convictions. Also the constable can take the arrested person to a police station for interrogation.[41]

It will be seen that the legality of the arrest by a private person is therefore made to depend not on the presence or absence of reasonable cause in the mind of the citizen at the moment when he effects the arrest, but on the outcome of the eventual prosecution—an event for which he is in no way responsible, and which he cannot control. A

---

[39] [1914] 1 K.B. 595.

[40] *Christie* v. *Leachinsky* [1947] A.C. 573, 1602. As Lord du Parcq remarked, this is one of the few privileges which the common law confers on the police constable, "who may be described as a private person paid to perform as a matter of duty acts which, if so minded, he might have done voluntarily."

[41] *Mohammed-Holgate* v. *Duke* [1984] A.C. 437, which holds that the validity of the constable's discretion may be judged by the *Wednesbury* principles of public law.

prosecution may break down for a variety of reasons, some creditable, some not, but on this may depend the liability of the honest arrestor to pay damages.

At the time of arrest. As the common law is always solicitous for the freedom of the individual, the subject who is arrested is entitled to know the reason for his arrest so that he may know at once whether he is bound to submit.[42] This principle was clearly established by the House of Lords in *Christie* v. *Leachinsky*.[43] So a constable is not entitled to keep the reason to himself or give a reason which is not the true one: if he does so he will in general be liable for false imprisonment. These rules have been confirmed by PACE, s.28, which also requires the reason to be given even if the ground for arrest is obvious. It is enough, however, if the substance of the matter is conveyed to the person arrested—precise legal language need not be used.[44] So if a person is told he is being arrested for handling stolen drugs he cannot complain if the charge ultimately brought is one of unauthorised possession of drugs.[45] The constable must do the best he can in the circumstances and if it is what a reasonable man would have done he will be protected: if he is arresting a deaf person he is not bound to use a speaking-trumpet,[46] and if he is arresting someone who cannot speak English he is not obliged to find an interpreter.[47] But it is irrelevant that the offence is apparently trivial or the person arrested of doubtful character.[48]

After the arrest. There is no intermediate position between liberty and detention. The law does not recognise any such procedure as "holding for questioning."[49] An arrested person cannot be detained whilst investigations are carried out,[50] but must be brought with reasonable expedition before the next sitting of a court.[51] It is unfortunately uncertain whether a failure to comply with the latter condition renders unlawful an arrest which was originally lawful, or whether it makes any difference that the arrested person is later acquitted as distinct from

---

[42] But statute may derogate from this common law right—see *Murray* v. *Ministry of Defence* [1988] 1 W.L.R. 692.

[43] [1947] A.C. 573.

[44] *Abbassy* v. *Metropolitan Police Commissioner* [1990] 1 W.L.R. 385, 392–394, 399.

[45] *R.* v. *Kulyncz* [1971] 1 Q.B. 367.

[46] *Tims* v. *John Lewis & Co.* [1951] 2 K.B. 459, 467.

[47] *Wheatley* v. *Lodge* [1971] 1 W.L.R. 29.

[48] *McElduff* v. *Att.-Gen.* [1972] N.I. 1 *R.* v. *Purdy* [1975] Q.B. 288. These rules apply to arrest by a private person as well as by a constable: [1947] A.C. 573, 588.

[49] "You may sometimes read in novels and detective stories, perhaps written by people not familiar with police procedure, that persons are sometimes taken into custody for questioning. There is no such power in this country. A man cannot be detained unless he is arrested": *R.* v. *Roberts* (unreported), *Manchester Guardian*, March 25, 1953, *per* Devlin J. The same point is made in Devlin, *The Criminal Prosecution in England* (1960), p.68, and s.29 of PACE specifically recognises that a person attending voluntarily at a police station is entitled to leave at will unless he has been arrested.

[50] But a limited power to arrest for questioning was recognised in *Holgate-Muhammed* v. *Duke* [1984] A.C. 437, and approved by Parliament in s.37(2) of the 1984 Act.

[51] *Dunne* v. *Clinton* [1930] I.R. 366, 372; *R.* v. *Brown (Michael)* (1976) 64 Cr.App.R. 231.

being convicted.[52] But it is certain that an arrest which was originally unlawful becomes lawful once reasons are given.[53] A person arrested should be brought before a magistrate or possibly handed over to a police officer not necessarily immediately or by the most direct route but within a reasonable time.[54] Thus in *John Lewis & Co.* v. *Tims*[55] a regulation of the appellants' department store provided that only a managing director or general manager was authorised to institute a prosecution. The respondent, having been arrested by the appellants' servants on suspicion of larceny, was accordingly brought back to the office and detailed there for a short time while the necessary authority was obtained. The House of Lords refused to accept the contention that the defendants were guilty of false imprisonment because the plaintiff had not been taken before a magistrate or to the police station forthwith. "There are advantages in refusing to give private detectives a free hand and leaving the determination of whether to prosecute or not to a superior official."[56] PACE provides elaborate rules for detention in a police station, if the suspect is to be held for more than six hours.

(iii) *General arrest conditions*

Except in the case of a breach of the peace there was no power at common law to arrest without warrant on suspicion of an offence other than an arrestable offence (formerly a misdemeanour).[57] But statutes gave very extensive powers of arrest in such circumstances. What is the position if the constable honestly and on reasonable grounds believed that the person he has arrested has committed such an offence when in fact he has not? There has been an unfortunate difference of opinion on the matter for over a century. Finally, in *Wills* v. *Bowley*[58] a bare majority of the House of Lords held that an honest suspicion based on reasonable grounds is a defence. Now section 25(1) of PACE provides a constable with a general power of arrest for non-arrestable criminal offences if at least one of "the general arrest conditions" specified in section 25(3) is satisfied. These conditions are, for example, that the name of the relevant person is unknown to, and cannot be readily ascertained by, the constable, or that the constable has reasonable grounds for believing that arrest is necessary to prevent the relevant person causing physical harm to himself or another. The Act (s.26(1)) repeals nearly all other statutory powers of arrest without warrant.

(6) Parental and other authority

A parent is not guilty of an assault if he physically interferes with his child by way of reasonable restraint or chastisement, or for therapeutic

---

[52] See *R.* v. *Brown (Michael)* (1976) 64 Cr.App.R. 231.
[53] *Lewis* v. *South Wales Chief Constable* [1990] W.L.R.
[54] PACE, s.46 requires a person *charged* to be brought before a magistrates' court as soon as practicable.
[55] [1952] A.C. 676.
[56] [1952] A.C. 676, 691, *per* Lord Porter.
[57] *Wershof* v. *Metropolitan Police Commissioner* [1978] 3 All E.R. 540.
[58] [1983] A.C. 57.

reasons—*e.g.* to take a blood test.[59] If the child is sent away to school, the schoolmaster is entitled to administer reasonable chastisement to the child,[60] or to expel him for reasonable cause.[61] According to the older authorities, the schoolmaster's power arose from a delegation to him of the parental authority; but the modern view is that the schoolmaster has his own independent authority to act for the welfare of the child.[62] Hence an education authority which has removed a child from its parents' care for the purposes of instruction is entitled to punish it. The schoolmaster's authority is not confined to the four walls of the school: it has been held that a schoolmaster was justified in administering five strokes of a cane to a boy under 16 who had, contrary to the rules, been smoking in the street during term after having returned home.[63]

Similarly the master of a ship has statutory[64] and common law[65] powers of arrest to preserve good order and discipline on board. The commander of an aircraft has similar powers.[66] There is one decision, much criticised, that it is not an assault for prison officials to take reasonable steps to preserve the health of those in custody—*e.g.* by forcible feeding.[67]

(7) Inevitable accident[68]

Inevitable accident provides a good excuse for a prima facie trespass which is otherwise actionable. An inevitable accident has been defined as an event over which the defendant had no control, and the effects of which could not have been avoided by the exercise of the greatest care and skill.[69] This may be said to be the generally accepted view since *Stanley* v. *Powell.*[70] In that case the defendant whilst firing at a pheasant accidentally and without negligence shot the plaintiff, who was employed to carry cartridges for a shooting party, with a pellet which ricochetted from a tree at a considerable angle. *Stanley* v. *Powell* might have been decided on the ground that the plaintiff had voluntarily

---

[59] *S.* v. *McC.* [1972] A.C. 24. The right is recognised by s.1(7) of the Children and Young Persons Act 1933.

[60] *Ryan* v. *Fildes* [1938] 3 All E.R. 517. But see s.47 of the Education (No. 2) Act 1986 which effectively outlaws the practice of corporal punishment in the state sector of education.

[61] *Fitzgerald* v. *Northcote* (1865) 4 F. & F. 656 (in which the successful plaintiff was the son of Fitzgerald J. of the Irish Queen's Bench).

[62] *Ramsay* v. *Larsen* [1965] A.L.R. 121.

[63] *R.* v. *Newport (Salop) J.J.* [1929] 2 K.B. 416.

[64] Merchant Shipping Act 1970, s.79.

[65] *Hook* v. *Cunard Steamship Co. Ltd.* [1953] 1 W.L.R. 682.

[66] Civil Aviation Act 1982, s.94.

[67] *Leigh* v. *Gladstone* (1909) 26 T.L.R. 139. See below, §§ 22.1.

[68] See Fridman, "Trespass or Negligence" (1971) 9 Alberta L.Rev. 250; Trindade, "Some Curiosities of Negligent Trespass" (1971) 20 I.C.L.Q. 706; Bates, "Accident, Trespass and Burden of Proof." (1976) 11 Ir.Jur.(N.S.) 88.

[69] *The Albano* [1892] P. 419, 429.

[70] [1891] 1 Q.B. 86. For criticisms of this case, see Landon's vigorous onslaught in Pollock, *Torts*, pp. 128–134 (of *National Coal Board* v. *Evans* he says: "all one can do is to wring one's hands and to note this recent case as a striking illustration of the old maxim *communis error facit jus*. And the point is still an open one for the House of Lords").

accepted the risk by joining the party,[71] but Denman J.[72] based his decision on the ground that even if the action was in trespass, not case, the injury being accidental the defendant could not be liable. In *National Coal Board* v. *Evans*[73] the Court of Appeal, holding inevitable accident to be a good defence in an action of trespass to to chattels, approved the reasoning in *Stanley* v. *Powell*.

Intention or negligence must now be shown

In so far as *Stanley* v. *Powell* decided that inevitable accident was a good defence to an action of trespass it probably cannot now be questioned. But in recent years a series of decisions by puisne judges in England,[74] the West Indies,[75] British Columbia,[76] and New Zealand[77] have extended *Stanley* v. *Powell* so far as to hold that a plaintiff in an action of trespass for injuries to the person must always prove intention or negligence on the part of the defendant. It is submitted that these decisions are open to review in an appellate court[78] on the ground that they confuse the distinction between trespass and case which has been part of the common law "from the time whereof the memory of man runneth not to the contrary." In this context the distinction has, or until very recently had, six important consequences. First, it has always been the understanding of the profession[79] that in trespass the defendant has to prove affirmatively that he was not negligent; in case for injuries to the person the plaintiff had to prove affirmatively intent or negligence in the defendant.[80] Hence when the plaintiff was injured by force applied directly to him by the defendant, his case was made by this fact and the onus then lay on the defendant to prove that the trespass was

---

[71] Winfield (1939) 55 L.Q.R. 451 makes the point that in such a case it would be unnecessary for the defendant to disprove negligence. But surely the plaintiff takes upon himself the risk of careful, not of careless, shooting. And, even if that is not so, the difference in no way invalidates the suggestion that the case might have been decided on that ground.

[72] Landon (Pollock, *Torts*, p. 133) went too far in describing Denman J. as "an undistinguished puisne judge" who had obtained his position on the bench "*per stirpes* and not *per capita*." He was indeed one of the sons (for another, see § 20.2) of Lord Denman C.J. (and as the son of a peer was one of the few High Court judges permitted to decline the customary knighthood), but in his youth he "had been Senior Classic and a Fellow of Trinity, but had other and perhaps greater titles to fame: he had been Captain of the Trinity Boat Club, not the Sculls, and had 'polished off a college porter at his gate.' Thus he was emphatically an all-round man and a popular character:" Winstanley, *Early Victorian Cambridge* (1955), p. 419.

[73] [1951] 2 K.B. 861.

[74] *Fowler* v. *Lanning* [1959] 1 Q.B. 426. In effect, this converted the exception into the general rule. The exception was the rule as to proof of negligence in actions arising out of highway accidents, which had become established in the nineteenth century (see below, § 22.3).

[75] *Robley* v. *Placide* (1966) 11 W.L.R. 58.

[76] *Walmsley* v. *Humenick* [1954] 2 D.L.R. 232. But not Ontario: *Bell Canada Ltd.* v. *Cope (Sarnia) Ltd.* (1980) 11 C.C.L.T. 170, or Novia Scotia: *Larin* v. *Goshen* (1975) 56 D.L.R. (3d) 719.

[77] *Beals* v. *Hayward* [1960] N.Z.L.R. 131; Davis, Note, (1965) 28 M.L.R. 674.

[78] The High Court of Australia avoided ruling on the point in *Hackshaw* v. *Shaw* (1984) 155 C.L.R. 614, 619, 670.

[79] See the vivid illustration in Sutton, *Personal Actions*, pp. 56–63.

[80] *Exchange Hotel Ltd.* v. *Murphy* [1947] S.A.S.R. 112, 117.

utterly without his fault.[81] This distinction may have great practical importance when the defendant is a young child, against whom it will be difficult to establish intent or negligence,[82] or one who, having denied fault in the pleadings, fails to appear at the trial.[83] "The trespass action, though somewhat anomalous, may thus help to smoke out evidence possessed by the defendants."[84] As juries have disappeared in civil cases, the risk of confusion between different burdens in different actions[85] is minimal. Secondly, there is a difference in relation to the proper test for remoteness of damage: in trespass it is probably directness, in negligence it is foreseeability.[86] Thirdly, until recently,[87] there was a difference in relation to the running of time under the Limitation Act 1980. Fourthly, there may still be a difference as to the date of the accrual of the cause of action.[88] Fifthly, trespass is actionable *per se*; in case, actual damage must be shown.[89] Sixthly, it is uncertain whether contributory negligence is a defence[90] to an action for a negligent trespass.

(8) Statutory authority

Apart from statutory powers of arrest, Parliament has authorised medical examinations or tests which would otherwise constitute a serious battery—*e.g.* breath tests under the Road Traffic Act 1988, s.6, or blood tests under sections 20 to 23 of the Family Law Reform Act 1969.

---

[81] Amongst the many cases which support this are: *Hall* v. *Fearnley* (1842) 3 Q.B. 919; *Sadler* v. *South Staffs. Steam Tramways Co.* (1889) 23 Q.B.D. 17; *Blacker* v. *Waters* (1928) 28 S.R.(N.S.W.) 406; *Cook* v. *Lewis* [1952] 1 D.L.R. 1, 15; *Southport Corporation* v. *Esso Petroleum, Ltd.* [1953] 3 W.L.R. 773, 781; *Joyce* v. *Bartlett* [1955] 1 D.L.R. 615; *O'Brien* v. *McNamee* [1953] I.R. 86; *McHale* v. *Watson* (1964) 111 C.L.R. 384; *Dahlberg* v. *Naydink* (1968) 67 D.L.R. (2d) 31.

[82] *Tillander* v. *Gosselin* (1966) 60 D.L.R. (2d) 18, 25.

[83] *Tsouvalla* v. *Bini* [1966] S.A.S.R. 157.

[84] *Bell Canada* v. *Cope (Sarnia) Ltd.* (1980) 11 C.C.L.T. 170, 180.

[85] Which caused worry in *Hackshaw* v. *Shaw* (1984) 155 C.L.R. 614, 619.

[86] See below, § 23.2

[87] *Long* v. *Hepworth* [1968] 1 W.L.R. 1299. See below, § 25.3

[88] See below, § 25.4.

[89] See above, § 1.2.

[90] See below, § 22.13.

CHAPTER 8

DEFAMATION

§ 8.1. Defamation Defined

The English law of defamation has often been criticised for its complexity, both substantive and procedural, but it has probably passed beyond the stage when it could be improved by the courts.[1] Perhaps in the hope of stirring the legislature into action, the courts have refused to permit the well-settled rules on defamation to be by-passed by actions in negligence.[2] The tort consists in the publication of a false and defamatory statement concerning another person without lawful justification. So if an entity has no legal personality it cannot sue for defamation.[3] Hence not only does an action of defamation not survive for or against the estate of a deceased person,[4] but a statement about a deceased or unborn person is not actionable at the suit of his relatives, however great their pain and distress, unless the statement is in some way defamatory of them.[5] But although a corporate public authority certainly exists it cannot sue for defamation.[5A]

Libel and slander[6]

A defamatory statement is not necessarily made in words, either written or spoken. A man may defame another by his acts no less than by his words. To exhibit an insulting picture[7] or effigy[8] holding up the plaintiff to ridicule or contempt is an actionable libel.

---

[1] See Lloyd, "Reform of the Law of Defamation" (1976) 29 C.L.P. 183. The report of the Committee on the Law of Defamation (Cmd. 7536 (1948)), of whom Lord Porter was chairman, is invaluable, as is that presided over by Faulks. J. Cmnd. 5909, 1975). The Report of the Porter Committee was followed by the Defamation Act 1952, but "well-nigh total apathy has reigned" since the Faulks Committee reported: see *Gleaves* v. *Deakin* [1980] A.C. 477, 493. This is "the greatest pity" (*Blackshaw* v. *Lord* [1984] 1 Q.B. 1, 40), but the Government has no intention of introducing legislation: H.L.Deb. Vol. 429, col. 1298 (May 1982). In 1990, however, the C.A. obtained new powers to contol awards of damages, and the complexities of pleading in defamation cases were brought under review by the Lord Chancellor.

[2] *Bell-Booth Group Ltd.* v. *Att.-Gen.* [1989] 3 N.Z.L.R. 148. But two High Court judgments permit a person damaged by a false character reference to sue in negligence: see below, § 9.7, n. 39.

[3] *EETPU* v. *Times Newspapers Ltd.* [1980] Q.B. 585.

[4] See below, § 20.10.

[5] Report of the Faulks Committee, para. 421. For the interesting steps taken by the relatives of Mr. Gladstone to defend his honour against the disgraceful aspersions of Captain Wright, see Symmons, "Libel on the Dead" (1980) 18 Univ. of W. Ontario L.R. 521.

[5A] *Derbyshire County Council* v. *Times Newspapers Ltd.*, *The Independent*, February 21, 1992.

[6] See Kaye, "Libel and Slander—Two Torts or One" (1975) 91 L.Q.R. 524.

[7] *Garbett* v. *Hazell, Watson and Viney Ltd.* [1943] 2 All E.R. 359 (juxtaposition of pictures with captions). One may "Convey a libel in a frown. And wink a reputation down": Swift, *Journal of a Modern Lady.*

[8] *Monson* v. *Tussauds Ltd.* [1894] 1 Q.B. 671.

The wrong of defamation is of two kinds—namely, libel and slander.[9] In libel the defamatory statement is made in some permanent and visible form, such as writing, printing, pictures, or effigies.[10] In slander it is made in spoken words or in some other transitory form, whether visible or audible, such as gestures or inarticulate but significant sounds. It is not always easy to determine whether in a particular case the proper cause of action is libel or slander. Is the true difference between the two that slander is addressed to the ear, libel to the eye?[11] Or is it that libel is defamation crystallised into some permanent form, while slander is conveyed by some transient method of expression? The Court of Appeal in *Youssoupoff* v. *Metro-Goldwyn-Mayer Pictures*[12] did not have much difficulty in holding that defamation in a "talking" film was libel. But there is no authority as to whether defamatory matter recorded on a gramophone disc (unaccompanied by any pictorial or other matter) is libel or slander. It is addressed to the ear, not to the eye, but it is in permanent, not in transient form. It is submitted that the correct answer is that to utter defamatory words with the intention that they shall be recorded is slander only, but that when the record has been made, if it is published, the manufacturer is responsible for libel. In such a case the person whose voice is recorded might be responsible on the ordinary principles of vicarious liability, and presumably those who distribute or play the record to third persons are in the same position as the disseminators of a written libel. The Defamation Act 1952, apparently[13] settles a disputed point by providing[14] that the broadcasting of words[15] by means of wireless telegraphy[16] shall be treated as publication in permanent form. The Theatres Act 1968, s.4, makes a similar provision for words published during the public performance of a play.

Although libel and slander are for the most part governed by the same principles, there are two important differences:

    (1) Libel is not merely an actionable tort, but also a criminal offence; whereas slander is a civil injury only. It was once thought that the likelihood of a breach of the peace was a vital factor in criminal libel, but this is now only one relevant factor.[17] But the prosecution must prove that the libel is serious and not trivial, and

---

[9] Libel and slander give rise to distinct causes of action even if the nature of the defamation is the same in both: libel is one genus, slander a different genus: *Weber* v. *Birkett* [1925] 2 K.B. 152.

[10] *Monson* v. *Tussauds Ltd.* [1894] 1 Q.B. 671, 692.

[11] So held in *Mitchell* v. *Australian Broadcasting Commission* (1958) 60 W.A.l.R. 38.

[12] (1934) 50 T.L.R. 581.

[13] *Church of Scientology* v. *Anderson* [1980] W.A.R. 71.

[14] s.1.

[15] Defined by s.16(1) to include pictures, visual images, gestures and other methods of signifying meaning.

[16] As defined by s.16(3), means publication for general reception by means of wireless telegraphy within the meaning of the Wireless Telegraphy Act 1949, 2.19.

[17] *Gleaves* v. *Deakin* [1980] A.C. 477. The topic is fully surveyed in the Law Commission's Working Paper No. 84 (1982).

the leave of a High Court judge is required before proceedings can be begun against a newspaper.[18]

(2) Libel is in all cases actionable *per se*: but slander is, save in special cases, actionable only on proof of actual damage. This distinction has been severely criticised. It is indeed odd that the maker of a deliberately false and malicious public speech may not be liable in damages, but that a journalist who innocently reports it may be.[19] It was recognised by the Porter Committee to be "arbitrary and illogical,"[20] but a majority of the Committee[21] was not willing to recommend, or Parliament to enact, that libel and slander should be assimilated.

The different rules applicable to the wrongs of libel and slander are due to the different historical origin of the two actions.[22] The rules relating to slander derive from the common law action on the case, the rules relating to libel from criminal proceedings in the Star Chamber.

§ 8.2. Nature of a Defamatory Statement

A defamatory statement is one which has a tendency to injure the reputation of the person to whom it refers; which tends, that is to say, to lower him in the estimation of right-thinking members of society generally[23] and in particular to cause him to be regarded with feelings of hatred, contempt, ridicule, fear, dislike, or disesteem.[24] The statement is judged by the standard of an ordinary, right-thinking member of society. Hence the test is an objective one, and it is no defence to say that the statement was not intended to be defamatory, or uttered by way of a joke.[25] A tendency to injure or lower the reputation of the plaintiff suffices, for "If words are used which impute discreditable conduct to my friend, he has been defamed to me, although I do not believe the imputation, and may even know that it is untrue."[26] Hence it is settled[27] that a statement may be defamatory although no one to whom it is published believes it to be true.[28]

Injurious falsehood[29]

A defamatory statement must be distinguished from one which is merely injurious. Both are falsehoods told by one man to the prejudice of another, and both are on certain conditions actionable; but they are to a large extent governed by different rules. An injurious statement is a falsehood told about another which in no way affects his reputation,

---

[18] *Desmond* v. *Thorn* [1983] 1 W.L.R. 163.
[19] See the Faulks Report, § 81.
[20] Cmd. 7536 (1948), para. 38.
[21] The Faulks Committee (§ 91) recommends the assimilation of libel and slander.
[22] See O'Sullivan, "Evolution of the Law of Libel" [1950] C.L.P. 84.
[23] *Sim* v. *Stretch* (1936) 52 T.L.R. 669, 671, *per* Lord Atkin.
[24] *Vander Zalm* v. *Times Publishers* (1980) 109 D.L.R. (3d) 531, 535, 543.
[25] *Capital and Counties Bank* v. *Henty* (1882) 7 App. Cas. 741, 772.
[26] *Hough* v. *London Express* [1940] 2 K.B. 507, 515, *per* Goddard L.J.
[27] *Morgan* v. *Odhams Press Ltd.* [1971] 1 W.L.R. 1239.
[28] As in *Theaker* v. *Richardson* [1962] 1 W.L.R. 151.
[29] See Chap. 18 for a fuller discussion of this tort (sometimes called malicious falsehood).

but nevertheless in some other manner causes loss to him. Thus it is not defamatory to state that a certain tradesman has ceased to carry on business; yet if this statement is wilfully false, an action will lie for it. There are many cases on the question whether defamation of goods involves defamation of the trader who sells those goods, but no clear test has yet emerged.[30]

Abuse

Mere insult or vulgar abuse does not amount to defamation[31] whether it be spoken or written. Defamation is a false statement or suggestion of fact to the prejudice of a man's reputation; insult consists in words or conduct offensive to a man's dignity. Insult in itself seems to be no cause of action by the law of England, though particular forms of insult may be actionable if accompanied by other facts which confer a right of action. Assault, false imprisonment, and certain kinds of wilful and wanton trespasses to property amount to insults, as being attacks upon the dignity of the plaintiff as well as upon his person or property; and aggravated damages may accordingly be obtained for them.[32] Insulting threats not amounting to assault are not actionable at all,[33] unless they fall under the rubric of intentional infliction of emotional distress.[34] But persons given to using abusive language may be required to enter into sureties to be of good behaviour under the Justices of the Peace Act 1361, or prosecuted under the Public Order Act 1986, sects. 4–5, or the Race Relations Act 1976, s.57(1).

Hatred, ridicule, and contempt

The test of the defamatory nature of a statement is its tendency to excite against the plaintiff the adverse opinions or feelings of other persons. The typical form of defamation is an attack upon the moral character of the plaintiff, attributing to him any form of disgraceful conduct, such as crime, dishonesty, untruthfulness, ingratitude, or cruelty. But a statement may be defamatory if it tends to bring the plaintiff into ridicule or contempt even though there is no suggestion of any form of misconduct. An action will lie, therefore, for the publication of a caricature of his personal appearance or manners.[35] In some circumstances it might even be defamatory to say of a man that his acts were legally justified. Rightminded men sometimes think the less of one who has successfully pleaded a technical defence—e.g. the Gaming Acts or the Statute of Limitations. Successful litigants have in the past been booed on leaving the court. Again a statement is defamatory if it amounts to a reflection upon the fitness or capacity of the plaintiff in his profession

---

[30] *Drummond-Jackson* v. *British Medical Association* [1970] 1 W.L.R. 688.

[31] *Parkins* v. *Scott* (1862) 1 H. & C. 153 ("You have been a whore from your cradle").

[32] Below, § 23.1.

[33] *Lane* v. *Holloway* [1968] 1 Q.B. 379 ("Shut up, you monkey-faced tart").

[34] Below, § 9.6.

[35] *Dunlop Rubber Co.* v. *Dunlop* [1921] 1 A.C. 367. (Mr. Dunlop, the inventor of the pneumatic tyre and "a plain and ordinary citizen of Dublin," depicted in advertisements in "absurd or unsuitable costumes or attitudes.")

or trade, or in any other undertaking assumed by him.[36] So a novelist recovered damages against the publishers of a magazine for publishing under his name a story of which he was not the writer, on the ground that anyone reading the story would think him a mere commonplace scribbler.[37] But a statement is not defamatory if it merely alleges a breach of conventional etiquette[38]—presumably because that does not lower the plaintiff in the estimation of right minded people—as distinct from an allegation that a business man was "not conversant with ordinary business ethics."[39] Still, what is not defamatory today may be defamatory tomorrow, or vice-versa, for the political and social ideas of the reasonable man alter with the times.[40] Thus the appellations German,[41] Czech,[42] "Jewish international financier,"[43] and Communist[44] have all at different times been held capable of a defamatory meaning. Conversely, "the word 'ruthless,' which businessmen two decades ago regarded as libellous, is now used as a compliment."[45]

A statement is not defamatory merely because it excites hatred, contempt, ridicule, or other adverse feelings in some particular class of the community whose standard of opinion is such that the law cannot approve of it. Words are only defamatory if they impute conduct to the plaintiff which would tend to lower him in the eyes of a considerable and respectable class of the community though not in the eyes of the community as a whole.[46] Thus in *Byrne* v. *Deane*[47] the plaintiff complained of a typewritten piece of doggerel on the notice-board of a golf club which suggested that he had been guilty of disloyalty to his fellow-members by reporting to the police that there were some "diddler" (gambling) machines kept on the premises.[48] Although it is clear that any such charge would lower the plaintiff in the estimation of most of his fellow-members it was held that it cannot be defamatory to say of a man that he has put in motion the proper machinery for suppressing crime, whether in his own country or another.[49]

---

[36] *Capital and Counties Bank* v. *Henty* (1882) 7 App. Cas. 741.

[37] *Ridge* v. *The English Illustrated Magazine* (1913) 29 T.L.R. 592. *Cf. Archbold* v. *Sweet* (1832) 5 C. & P. 219, where the defendants published a third edition of the plaintiff's work on criminal law (with "many errors and mistakes") without stating that it had not been edited by the plaintiff.

[38] *Sim* v. *Stretch* (1936) 52 T.L.R. 669, 672.

[39] *Angel* v. *Bushell & Co. Ltd.* [1968] 1 Q.B. 813.

[40] But even today an allegation of homosexuality is probably defamatory: *R.* v. *Bishop* [1975] Q.B. 274.

[41] *Slazengers Ltd.* v. *C. Gibbs & Co.* (1916) 33 T.L.R. 35.

[42] *Linklater* v. *Daily Telegraph Ltd.*, *The Times*, November 11, 1964.

[43] *Camrose* v. *Action Press Ltd.* (1937) *The Times*, October 14 (damages: £12,500, Hilbery J. emphatically refusing a stay of execution). The report in the *Daily Telegraph* makes it quite clear that it was not alleged that the appellation "Jew" alone was defamatory. The innuendo was that the plaintiff was unscrupulous and unpatriotic.

[44] *Braddock* v. *Bevins* [1948] 1 K.B. 580; *Lewis* v. *Smith* (1959) *The Times*, July 10.

[45] A. Sampson, *The Changing Anatomy of Britain* (1983), p.360.

[46] *Quigley* v. *Creation Press Ltd.* [1971] I.R. 269, 272.

[47] [1937] 1 K.B. 818. See also *Fraser* v. *Kemsley Newspapers Ltd.* (1959) *The Times*, June 2.

[48] The words were: "But he who gave the game away May he byrnn in hell and rue the day."

[49] *Berry* v. *Irish Times Ltd.* [1973] I.R. 368.

§ 8.3. PROOF OF REFERENCE TO THE PLAINTIFF[50]

It is essential in every action for defamation that the defamatory statement should be shown to refer to the plaintiff. A court has power in
interlocutory proceedings[51] to dismiss the action on the ground that no
reasonable person could conclude that the plaintiff should be identified
with the person named in the matter complained of as defamatory.[52] At
the trial the judge may also withdraw the case from the jury.[53] It is never
necessary, however, that the reference to the plaintiff should be express.
It may be latent; and it is sufficient in such a case that it should have
been understood even by one person, although it remained hidden
from all others.[54]

But the defendant must himself have published the statement complained of by the plaintiff.[55] A defendant is not responsible for statements made by third parties unless he has expressly or impliedly
adopted them as his own.[56] Nor is a defendant responsible to the plaintiff for statements made about third parties, unless those statements are
also in themselves defamatory of the plaintiff.[57]

Innocence no defence

At common law it was not necessary that the defendant should have
intended the defamatory statement to refer to the plaintiff.[58] The question was not whether the defendant intended any such reference, but
whether any person[59] to whom the statement was published might
reasonably think that the plaintiff was the person referred to. Nor was it
any defence that the defendant had no reason to suppose that any such
reference would be attributed to his words, or even did not know that
any such person as the plaintiff existed. This application or extension of
the doctrine that a man publishes defamatory statements at his peril
was established by the House of Lords in *Hulton & Co., v. Jones*.[60] A
newspaper published an article descriptive of life in Dieppe, in which
one Artemus Jones, described as a churchwarden at Peckham, was
accused of living with a mistress in France. The writer of the article was
ignorant of the existence of any person of the name of Artemus Jones
and invented the name as that of the fictitious character in his narrative.
Unfortunately, however, the name so chosen was that of a real person, a
barrister and journalist, and those who knew him supposed the news-

---

[50] See Symmons, "Proof of Reference to the Plaintiff" (1974) Anglo-Am.L.Rev. 98.
[51] See *Keays* v. *Murdoch Magazines Ltd.* [1991] 1 W.L.R. 1184.
[52] *Morgan* v. *Odhams Press Ltd.* [1971] 1 W.L.R. 1239.
[53] See below, § 8.4.
[54] *Hayward* v.*Thompson* [1982] Q.B. 47.
[55] For publication, see § 8.7.
[56] *Astaire* v. *Campling* [1966] 1 W.L.R.34.
[57] *Wheeler* v. *Somerfield*[1966] 2 Q.B. 94.
[58] The Defamation Act 1952, s.4 may now provide a defence. See § 8.6 below.
[59] It need not be a reasonable person: a hasty but sensible reader is the norm since *Morgan*
v. *Odhams Press Ltd.* [1971] 1 W.L.R. 1239.
[60] [1910] A.C.20.

paper article to refer to him. It was held by a majority of the Court of Appeal that the newspaper was responsible for a libel and decision was unanimously affirmed (in an unreserved judgment[61]) by the House of Lords.[62] The point was crisply put during argument. Counsel for the appellant asserted "The question is, who was meant", but Lord Loreturn L.C. interjected "Is it not rather who was hit?"[63]

It has also been held by the House of Lords[64] that there is no rule that before the publisher of a defamatory statement which identifies no definite person can be held liable, there must be found in the statement some key or pointer or peg which refers to the plaintiff. Extrinsic evidence[65] is admissible to show that some people, perhaps with knowledge of special facts, thought the statement referred to the plaintiff.

Even if the defamatory words are true of some other person it was not impossible for them to be at the same time defamatory of the plaintiff, for they might be understood by reasonable persons to refer to him.[66] Thus in *Newstead* v. *London Express Newspaper Ltd.*[67] the defendants published an account of a trial for bigamy of "Harold Newstead, 30-year-old Camberwell man." It was a true account of the trial of one Harold Newstead, a Camberwell barman, but not of Harold Newstead, a Camberwell hairdresser, of about the same age. The Court of Appeal held that the jury would have been justified in finding that reasonable persons would have understood the words complained of to refer to the latter. Where the words complained of are *ex facie* defamatory the hardship is not so serious as might appear. Writers who publish such statements may not unreasonably be expected to identify the person described so closely that the words cannot reasonably be capable of referring to someone else.[68]

---

[61] Lord Uthwatt told the present editor that after *Hulton* v. *Jones* The House of Lords had made it a rule of practice never to deliver an unreserved judgment—though there is at least one reported exception to this: see below, § 11.9, n. 12. Lord Denning "would like to see the House of Lords take *Hulton* v. *Jones* by the scruff of the neck and thrown out of the courts, and start afresh": *Landmarks in the Law* (1984), p.296.

[62] There is some evidence that the decision may have been based on the recklessness or even spite of the defendants. Stallybrass always said that this was the opinion of Lord Hewart, who was counsel for the plaintiff at all three stages of the action. The plaintiff had been a contributor to the defendants' paper for 12 years and his name was well known in their office, although not to the actual writer of the article. The managing director admitted in cross-examination that he had read the article in proof and thought at first reading that it referred to the plaintiff. See letters to *The Spectator* of November 5 and 12, 1948, from Lady Artemus-Jones and C.K. Allen. The point is still important, for if the actual facts in *Hulton* v. *Jones* recurred today, the defendants might be held to have failed to establish reasonable care under s.4 of the Defamation Act 1952: see below, § 8.6.

[63] [1910] A.C. 20, 22.

[64] *Morgan* v. *Odhams Press Ltd.* [1971] 1 W.L.R. 1239.

[65] See below, § 8.5.

[66] Robert Graves had taken the point in 1936: see his admirable novel, *Antigua, Penny Puce*, p. 252.

[67] [1940] 1 K.B. 377.

[68] See the caustic judgment of MacKinnon L.J. [1940] 1 K.B. 377, 391–393. It is significant that the Faulks Committee recommend no change.

Defamation of a class of persons

In every case where the plaintiff is not named the test whether the words used refer to him is the question whether the words are such as would reasonably lead persons acquainted with the plaintiff to believe that he was the person referred to. If the words can be regarded as capable of referring to the plaintiff, the jury still have to decide the question of fact—Do they lead reasonable people who know him, to the conclusion that they do refer to him.[69] The reason why a libel published of a large or indeterminate number of persons described by some general name generally fails to be actionable is the difficulty of establishing that the plaintiff was, in fact, included in the defamatory statement for the habit of making unfounded generalisations is ingrained in ill-educated or vulgar minds, or the words are occasionally intended to be facetious exaggeration.[70] Thus no action would lie at the suit of anyone for saying that all mankind is vicious and depraved, or even for alleging that all clergymen are hypocrites or all lawyers dishonest.[71] For charges so general in their nature are merely vulgar generalisations.

But if the class is so small or so completely ascertainable that what is said of the class is necessarily said of every member of it, then a member of the class can sue.[72] Again, although the words purport to refer to a class, if in fact in the particular circumstances of the case they point to one or more individual persons, those persons will have an action.[73] In deciding the question, the size of the class, the generality of the charge and the extravagance of the accusation may all be elements to be taken into consideration.[74]

§ 8.4. PROOF OF DEFAMATORY MEANING

Although the proper interpretation of a statement alleged to be defamatory may give rise to difficult questions of construction, there is one point which is perfectly clear and unquestioned: a statement is none the less defamatory because the defendant did not intend to bring the plaintiff into hatred, ridicule or contempt. The meaning to be attached to it is not necessarily the meaning with which the defendant published it but that which is, or may be presumed to be, reasonably given to it by the person to whom it is published. A defamatory purpose will not render the defendant liable if the statement has for others no libellous significance[75]; conversely, an innocent intention will be no defence for a person who makes a statement which has a defamatory meaning for

---

[69] Knupffer v. London Express Newspaper [1944] A.C. 116, 121.

[70] Knupffer v. London Express Newspaper [1944] A.C. 116, 122, per Lord Atkin.

[71] E.E.T.P.U. v. Times Newspapers Ltd. [1980] Q.B. 585, 595–596. No doubt the criminal law of seditious libel might be invoked in serious cases. Neither the Porter Committee nor (after much discussion) Parliament could find a suitable remedy for "group defamation." For a curious unreported case in which a newspaper thought it prudent to settle an action brought by the 134 valuers employed by the L.C.C. see 682 H.C. Deb. 5, s., cols. 456–463, and 776 H.C. Deb., col. 1764.

[72] Browne v. D.C. Thomson & Co. 1912 S.C. 359.

[73] Le Fanu v. Malcolmson (1848) 1 H.L.C. 637.

[74] Knupffer's Case [1944] A.C. 116, 124.

[75] Sadgrove v. Hole [1901] 2 K.B.1.

those to whom he makes it,[76] though the fact that his intention was innocent may be given in evidence in mitigation of damages.[77] Something may depend on the nature of the publication. The ordinary sensible man reading an article in a popular newspaper is not expected to analyse it like a Fellow of All Souls.[78] The general impression on such a reader is what counts.[79]

Functions of judge and jury

The interpretation of a defamatory statement is a question of fact for a jury or for a judge if sitting without a jury.[80] Since the Libel Act 1792 (usually called Fox's Act), "libel or no libel" has always been essentially a question for the jury.[81] It is true that the Act of 1792 is in terms limited to criminal proceedings, but it has always been regarded as merely declaratory of the common law.[82] The right of the jury in this matter in this matter is subject, however, to one limitation. The judge must first be satisfied that there is sufficient evidence to go to the jury—that is to say, he must be satisfied that the statement is reasonably capable of the meaning which the plaintiff alleges and complains of, and if he considers that it is not so capable, the case must be withdrawn from the jury altogether.[83] In a clear and obvious case the plaintiff's statement of claim may also be struck out under R.S.C., Ord. 18, r.19.[84] If more than one defamatory meaning is alleged, then the judge must rule whether the words are capable of bearing each, and if so, which, of those meanings.[85] It is not certain whether the plaintiff is confined to the defamatory meanings or inferences alleged in his statement of claim.[86]

In *Capital and Counties Bank* v. *Henty*[87] the defendants, having had a dispute with one of the branch managers of the plaintiff bank, sent a circular notice to their own customers[88] in these words: "Henty and Sons hereby give notice that they will not receive in payment cheques drawn on any of the branches of the Capital and Counties Bank." An action for libel was thereupon brought by the bank, alleging that the notice was defamatory, inasmuch as it amounted to an imputation of insolvency. It was held, however, by the House of Lords that the statement was not reasonably capable of such a meaning, and that there was no case fit to be left to a jury, although the notice resulted in a run of a quarter of a million pounds on the bank immediately it was issued, and

---

[76] *Hulton & Co. Ltd.* v. *Jones* [1910] A.C. 20, 23. For the innuendo, see below, § 8.5.

[77] See below, § 8.25.

[78] *Morgan* v.*Odhams Press Ltd.* [1971] 1 W.L.R. 1239, 1246, 1254, 1264.

[79] *Bookbinder* v. *Tebbitt* [1988] 1 W.L.R. 640, 651.

[80] *Slim* v. *Daily Telegraph Ltd.* [1968] 2 Q.B. 157.

[81] *Broome* v. *Agar* (1928) 138 L.T. 698.

[82] *Truth (N.Z.) Ltd.* v. *Holloway* [1960] N.Z.L.R. 69, 92.

[83] *Lewis* v. *Daily Telegraph Ltd.* [1964] A.C. 234.

[84] *Drummond-Jackson* v. *British Medical Association* [1970] 1 W.L.R. 688.

[85] *Lewis* v. *Daily Telegraph Ltd.* [1964] A.C. 234, 286.

[86] *Slim* v. *Daily Telegraph Ltd.* [1968] 2 Q.B. 157. The conflicting dicta are assessed in the Faulks Report, § 112.

[87] (1882) 7 App.Cas. 741.

[88] This was an important point: see *Tolley* v. *Fry* [1931] A.C. 333, 342; *Lewis* v. *Daily Telegraph Ltd.* [1964] A.C. 234, 246.

the bank's customers were presumably ordinary men who believed the statement had the meaning alleged.[89] *Henty's* case has often been cited by defendants seeking to contend that if one non-defamatory meaning can be found the plaintiff cannot succeed, but it does not mean that.[90] It is more difficult to say positively what it does mean, for there are a large number of different judicial interpretations, particularly in cases involving innuendoes.[91] The most simple test[92] is that in deciding whether the words are capable of a defamatory meaning the court will reject those meanings which can emerge only as the product of some strained or forced or utterly unreasonable interpretation.

On the other hand, the words may be so plainly and necessarily defamatory that the judge should instruct the jury that they are calculated to bring the plaintiff into hatred or contempt, and should forthwith proceed to direct their attention to the question of damages. If a jury find a plain and obvious defamation, incapable of any innocent explanation, to be non-libellous, their verdict may be set aside.[93] But in England[94] and in Ireland[95] the circumstances must be very exceptional to justify such a course. There appear to be only two reported cases in which a verdict of a jury in favour of a defendant,[96] and none in which such a finding of a judge sitting alone,[97] has been reversed on appeal.

§ 8.5. The Innuendo

It is clear then that no statement is necessarily and in all circumstances defamatory. There is no charge or imputation, however serious on the face of it, which may not be explained away by evidence that in the special circumstances of the case it was not made or understood in a defamatory sense. It may be shown to have been made in jest, or by way of irony, or in some metaphorical or secondary innocent sense,[98] and that it was or ought to have been understood in that sense by those as to

---

[89] There are several statements to the effect that the law and the facts got pretty far apart from each other in *Henty's* case: *Youssoupoff* v. *M.-G.-M. Pictures Ltd.* (1934) 50 T.L.R. 581, 584; *Slim* v. *Daily Telegraph Ltd.* [1968] 2 Q.B. 157, 187. But in *Sim* v. *Stretch* [1936] 2 All E.R. 1237 the H.L. held the words in question incapable of a defamatory meaning, though three judges below had held they were so capable, and a jury that they were in fact defamatory.

[90] *Lewis* v. *Daily Telegraph Ltd.* [1964] A.C. 234, 246. It was held that the words "R.D." (or their equivalent) on the cheque of a non-trader were incapable of a defamatory meaning: *Plunkett* v. *Barclays Bank Ltd.* [1936] 2 K.B. 107, but now it is a question for the jury in each case: *Jayson* v. *Midland Bank Ltd.* [1968] 1 Lloyd's Rep. 409.

[91] For these, see below, § 8.5.

[92] *Jones* v. *Skelton* [1963] 1 W.L.R. 1362, 1370.

[93] *Lockhart* v. *Harrison* (1928) 139 L.T. 521, 523, 524 (see the amusing explanation of this case given by Norman Birkett, K.C., the plaintiff's counsel, in 76 L.J. (News.) 366).

[94] *Lockhart* v. *Harrison* (1928) 139 L.T. 521, 524, where Lord Dunedin Regretted the result: "I think the letter in question the mean letter of a coward . . . That it was a libel has been the opinion of every judge who has had the case before him; but, of course, that is not the question. The question is whether it is a verdict at which 12 reasonable men could possibly have arrived."

[95] *Barrett* v. *Independent Newspapers Ltd.* [1986] I.R.13.

[96] *Lockhart* v. *Harrison* (1928) L.T. 521, 523.

[97] *Dingle* v. *Associated Newspapers Ltd.* [1964] A.C. 371, 376.

[98] *Grubb* v. *Bristol United Press Ltd.* [1963] 1 Q.B. 309, 328, 339.

whom it was made.[99] Conversely, no statement is necessarily and in all circumstances innocent. An allegation which on the face of it contains no imputation whatever against the plaintiff may be proved from the circumstances to have contained a latent and secondary defamatory sense. So the plaintiff must bring evidence to establish slang or cant meaning which he attaches to an apparently innocent word such as "pansy."[1] Although no statements are necessarily defamatory or necessarily innocent, yet all statements are divisible into two classes, according as they are (1) prima facie defamatory, or (2) prima facie innocent.

(1) Statements prima facie defamatory

A statement is prima facie defamatory when its natural, obvious, and primary sense is defamatory: such a statement is actionable unless its defamatory significance is successfully explained away; and the burden of such an explanation rests upon the defendant. In determining whether the words in their natural and ordinary meaning are defamatory the jury may have regard to the mode and occasion of the publication,[2] for example, that they were published in large italicised block type in a popular newspaper.[3]

(2) Statements prima facie innocent

When a statement is prima facie innocent, the plaintiff must expressly and explicitly[4] set forth in his pleadings the defamatory meaning which he attributes to it.[5] That defamatory meaning may not be the ordinary meaning, or it may be one of two or more ordinary meanings. In the first case the plaintiff must,[6] and in the second case the plaintiff should,[7] set out the meaning which he says the words bear. Such an explanatory statement is called an innuendo.[9] It is not a true innuendo to repeat the obvious meaning of defamatory words in other language, or in an embroidered or exaggerated way.[8] Otherwise an ingenious pleader could perplex the judge and jury and harry the defendant[9] by ringing

---

[99] *Australian Newspaper Co.* v. *Bennett* [1894] A.C. 284.

[1] *Thaarup* v. *Hulton Press* (1943) 169 L.T. 309. ("I personally was not alive to the slang meaning of the word, nor I think, was my brother MacKinnon, but my brother Goddard fortunately was quite alive to it, having had judicial experience as a result of which he had come to know about it": *per* Scott, L.J. 169 L.T. 310.)

[2] *Capital and Counties Bank* v. *Henty* (1882) 7 App.Cas. 741, 744.

[3] *English and Scottish, Co-op. Society* v. *Odhams Press* [1940] 1 K.B. 440, 452-453.

[4] *Polly Peck Ltd.* v. *Threlford* [1986] Q.B. 1000.

[5] The plaintiff must also "give particulars of the facts and matters on which he relies in support of such sense": Ord. 82, r.3(1). Conversely, a defendant who pleads justification must state the meaning which he seeks to justify: *Prager* v. *Times Newspapers Ltd.* [1988] 1 W.L.R. 77.

[6] *Lewis* v. *Daily Telegraph Ltd.* [1964] A.C. 234.

[7] *Allsop* v. *Church of England Newspapers Ltd.* [1972] 2 Q.B. 161.

[8] *Lewis* v. *Daily Telegraph Ltd.* [1964] A.C. 234.

[9] In particular, by preventing him from obtaining particulars under Ord. 82, r. 3(1) of the extrinsic facts necessary to support a true innuendo. *Loughans* v. *Odhams Press Ltd.* [1963] 1 Q.B. 299, which seemed to permit such ingenuity, did not really do so: *Lewis* v. *Daily Telegraph Ltd.* [1964] A.C. 234, 273, 280.

the changes on the same words,[10] creating numerous different causes of action, each requiring a separate verdict. A true innuendo relies on a conjunction of the words used and some extrinsic fact or facts,[11] which are known to the person to whom the words are published at the date of publication.[12] Thus the statement "X is a good advertiser" is innocent in itself, but carries a libellous innuendo if published to persons who know the extrinsic fact that X is an eminent member of the Bar.

Although each innuendo gives rise to a distinct cause of action, the court can look at the substance of the matter, and ask the jury to give one verdict and make one award of damages, or permit the defendant to pay one single sum into court.[13] The plaintiff is probably bound by his own innuendo and must prove the meaning as so alleged by him.[14] He cannot at the trial fall back upon some other secondary and latent sense, instead of that which he himself alleged in his pleadings, although he may fall back on the primary defamatory sense of the statement[15] if it is not worse than the meaning alleged.[16]

A striking example of an innuendo being successfully pleaded can be found in *Tolley* v. *J. S. Fry & Sons Ltd.*[17] In that case an amateur golf champion sued the defendants, a firm of chocolate manufacturers, who had published an advertisement in the middle of which "there appeared a caricature of Mr. Tolley hitting one of this most vigorous drives, with a carton of Fry's chocolate sticking prominently out of his pocket and comic caddy dancing with another carton of Fry's chocolate in his hand, and comparing in doggerel verse the excellence of the drive with the excellence of the chocolate. Mr. Tolley was, as most people would be, much annoyed at this piece of offensive vulgarity, which reflects very little credit on the good taste of those who control the advertising of Messrs. Fry. He does not eat Fry's chocolate, and his permission for the appearance of the cartoon had not been asked."[18] The innuendo alleged was in effect that he had consented to the use of his portrait as an advertisement for reward and had prostituted his reputation as an amateur golfer.[19] The House of Lords held that there was evidence on which a jury would be entitled to find the advertisement to be defamatory of the plaintiff,[20] but ordered a new trial on the issue of damages.[21]

---

[10] As in *Grubb* v. *Bristol United Press Ltd.* [1963] 1 Q.B. 309.

[11] *Lewis* v. *Daily Telegraph Ltd.* [1963] 1 Q.B. 340, 364.

[12] *Grappelli* v. *Derek Block (Holdings) Ltd.* [1981] 1 W.L.R. 822.

[13] *Pedley* v. *Cambridge Newspapers Ltd.* [1964] 1 W.L.R. 988.

[14] *"Truth" (N.Z.) Ltd.* v. *Holloway* [1960] 1 W.L.R. 997.

[15] *Sim* v. *Stretch* (1936) 52 T.L.R. 669, 671.

[16] *Slim* v. *Daily Telepgraph Ltd.* [1968] 2 Q.B. 157.

[17] [1931] A.C. 333.

[18] [1930] 1 K.B. 467, 472, *per* Scrutton L.J.

[19] In England 60 years ago sportsmen played for sport, not for money.

[20] Lord Blanesburgh dissenting on the ground that it was just because the publication was so offensive that no reasonable man could be assumed to have taken it seriously: to him, it was ([1931] A.C. 333, 347) "only another instance of the toll levied on distinction for the delectation of vulgarity." We have already seen (above, § 3.2. that the infringement of privacy is not yet a recognised tort.

[21] A jury had awarded the plaintiff £1,000.

Cassidy's case

When the law relating to proof of an innuendo is combined with the rule that the test of the defamatory nature of a statement is objective and not subjective, it may well be asked whether it is not a necessary conclusion that a person is responsible for a statement which he believes to be innocent, but which is in fact defamatory by reason of facts unknown to him but known to the persons to whom he makes it. To this question the majority of the Court of Appeal gave an affirmative answer in *Cassidy* v. *Daily Mirror Newspapers Ltd.*[22] "The facts in this case are simple. A man named Cassidy, who for some reason also called himself Corrigan and described himself as a General in the Mexican Army, was married to a lady who also called herself Cassidy or Mrs. Corrigan. Her husband occasionally came and stayed with her at her flat, and her acquaintances met him. Cassidy achieved some notoriety in racing circles and in indiscriminate relations with women, and at a race meeting he posed, in company with a lady, to a racing photographer, to whom he says he was engaged to marry the lady and the photographer might announce it."[23] The defentants accordingly published the photograph with the following words underneath: "Mr. M. Corrigan, the racehorse owner, and miss 'X', whose engagement has been announced." The innuendo placed upon these words by the plaintiff was that she was an immoral woman who had cohabited with Corrigan without being married to him, and some female acquaintances of the plaintiff gave evidence that they had formed a bad opinion of her on that ground as a result of the publication. The jury found that the words did reasonably bear a defamatory meaning, and awarded the plaintiff £500 damages. A majority of the Court of Appeal held that their verdict could not be disturbed. Further, it has since been laid down[24] that where words are capable of being understood in a defamatory sense by persons to whom special facts are known, it is unnecessary to prove more than that there are people who knew those special facts and so might reasonably[25] understand the words in a defamatory sense. One way of proving this proposition is to call witnesses with such knowledge and such understanding, but to say it is the only way would be to fall into the elementary error of confusing the proposition to be proved with the means of proving that proposition.

§ 8.6. THE DEFAMATION ACT 1952: s.4

Hulton v. *Jones* added "a terror to authorship."[26] That terror was intensified by the decisions of the Court of Appeal in *Cassidy's* case, *Newstead's*

---

[22] [1929] 2 K.B. 331.

[23] [1929] 2 K.B. 331, 337, *per* Scrutton L.J. In 1946 Corrigan, aged 49, was found hanged in his cell in Brixton Prison where he was awaiting trial for obtaining money by false pretences.

[24] *Hough* v. *London Express Newspaper Ltd.* [1940] 2 K.B. 507.

[25] *Morgan* v. *Odhams Press Ltd.* [1971] 1 W.L.R. 1239.

[26] *Knupffer* v. *London Express Newspaper Ltd.* [1943] K.B. 80, 89.

case and *Hough's* case.[27] "Liability for libel," said Russell L.J.,[28] "does not depend on the intention of the defamer; but on the fact of defamation." Hence there was much complaint by authors, printers and publishers. On the other hand writers who publish statements which are *ex facie* defamatory may not unreasonably be expected to identify the party described so closely that the words cannot reasonably be interpreted as capable of referring to anyone else. If there is a risk of coincidence why should it not be borne by the party who put the mischievious statement in circulation rather than by the innocent person to whom the words are taken to refer?[29] So after full consideration the Porter Committee,[30] and the Faulks Committee,[31] decided to retain the principle in *Hulton* v. *Jones,* subject to a major qualification. The major qualification is a new defence of Unintentional Defamation.

Unintentional defamation

The Act of 1952, s.4, provides that a person who has published words[32] alleged to be defamatory of another person may, if he claims that the words were published by him innocently in relation to that other person, make an offer of amends. Such an offer must be expressed to be made for the purposes of this section, and must be accompanied by an affidavit specifying the facts relied upon by the person making it to show that the words in question were published by him innocently in relation to the party aggrieved. An offer of amends shall be understood to mean an offer (i) in any case, to publish or join in the publication of a suitable correction of the words complained of, and a sufficient apology to the party aggrieved in respect of those words,[33] and (ii) where copies of a document or record containing the said words have been distributed by or with the knowledge of the person making the offer, to take such steps as are reasonably practicable on his part for notifying persons to whom copies have been so distributed that the words are alleged to be defamatory of the party aggrieved.

Such an offer may be either accepted or rejected. We shall indicate the statutory solution for either alternative.

---

[27] Yet it is easy to exaggerate the hardships; a jury is quick to detect a "gold-digging" action. It is sometimes forgotten that the jury in *Newsteads'* case gave the plaintiff one farthing damages and the C.A. refused to interfere with its verdict. See, too, *Blennerhassett* v. *Novelty Sales Services Ltd.* (1933) 175 L.T.J. 393 (*The Yo-yo* case) and *Progress Bars Ltd.* v. *Associated Newspapers Ltd., The Times,* June 9, 1950 (*The Moo-Cow Milk Bar* case), each a case where plaintiffs theoretically within the protection of *Hulton* v. *Jones* were laughed out of court.

[28] *Cassidys'* case [1929] 2 K.B. 331, 354.

[29] *Newsteads'* case [1940] 1 K.B. 377, 388.

[30] Pars. 55, 73.

[31] Faulks Committee Report (Cmnd. 5909, §§ 121, 281).

[32] This includes pictures, visual images, gestures and other methods of signifying meaning: s.16(1).

[33] Note (1) that the apology need not apparently be brought to the notice of any person to whom the words complained of were published, and (2) that there must be an offer of such an apology in the offer of amends even though there has been an apology in earlier correspondence.

(1) If the offer of amends is accepted

If the offer is accepted and duly performed, no proceedings for libel or slander shall be taken or continued by the party aggrieved against the person making the offer. This, however, is without prejudice to any cause of action against any other person jointly responsible for that publication. Any question as to the steps to be taken in fulfilment of the offer as so accepted shall in default of agreement be determined by the High Court, whose decision shall be final. Whether or not such proceedings are taken, the High Court has power, on the application of the party aggrieved, to order the person making the offer to pay to the party aggrieved costs "on an indemnity basis[34] and any expenses reasonably incurred or to be incurred by that party in consequence of the publication in question."

(2) If the offer of amends is rejected

If the offer is not accepted by the party aggrieved, then it shall be a defence, in any proceedings for libel or slander by him against the person making the offer, to prove that the words were published by the defendant innocently in relation to the plaintiff and that the offer was made as soon as practicable after the defendant received notice that there were or might be defamatory of the plaintiff,[35] and has not been withdrawn. But this provision does not apply in relation to the publication by any person of words of which he is not the author unless he proves that the words were written by the author without malice. This preserves (and indeed extends) the common law rule that the malice of one defendant infects his co-defendants.[36] It seems that if the editor of a newspaper publishes an anonymous letter containing statements *ex facie* innocent, but in fact not so by reason of the fact that the writer is secretly actuated by malice, the editor cannot make use of this statutory defence.

In the normal case the vital question will be whether the words have been published innocently. The Act provides that words shall be treated as having been published innocently only if either of the following conditions is satisfied:

   (i) that the publisher[37] did not intend to publish them of and concerning the party aggrieved, and did not know of circumstances by virtue of which they might be understood to refer to him[38]; or
   (ii) that the words were not defamatory on the face of them and the

---

[34] For the intended meaning of these words, see Report of Proceedings in H.C. Sel. Cttee. B, March 4, 1952.

[35] See *Ross* v. *Hopkinson* [1956] C.L.Y. 5011 (six weeks may be too long).

[36] See below, § 8.18.

[37] This includes "any servant or agent of his who was concerned with the contents of the publication"—not, be it noted, "with the publication."

[38] This meets the problem of statements not intended to refer to the plaintiff at all, as in *Hulton* v. *Jones* and the *Newstead* case.

publisher did not know of circumstances by virtue of which they might be understood to be defamatory of the party aggrieved,[39] and in either case that the publisher exercised all reasonable care in relation to the publication.[40]

Finally, it must be noticed that the facts which the publisher may adduce as evidence that the words were published innocently by him are restricted to those which he had set out in the affidavit accompanying his original offer of amends. It is therefore clear that a person who wishes to claim the protection of the Defamation Act 1952, s.4, must ensure that the affidavit is drafted with care. For if the party aggrieved should refuse to accept the offer of amends the defendant will be severely hampered at the trial if some of the facts upon which he relies to establish his innocence have been omitted from the affidavit. In practice these pit-falls are such that little use is made of the statutory defence.

§ 8.7. PUBLICATION

(1) Mode of publication

Publication of the defamatory statement is an essential element of the cause of action.[41] It is the publication, not the composition or subsequent circulation of a libel which is the actionable wrong.[42] Often the person sued for publishing is not the writer. Publication means the act of making the defamatory statement known to any person or persons other than the plaintiff himself.[43] It is not necessary that there should be any publication in the popular sense of making the statement public. A private and confidential communication to a single individual is sufficient. Nor need it be published in the sense of being written or printed; for we have seen that actions as well as words may be defamatory.[44] The liability of the publisher (in this narrow sense of the word) is strict: it does not matter how careful he has been.[45] A communication to the person defamed himself,[46] however, is not a sufficient publication on which to found civil proceedings[47]; though it is otherwise in the case of a criminal prosecution, because such a communication may provoke a breach of the peace.[48] Nor does a communication between husband

---

[39] This meets the problem of statements which are intended to refer to an existing person and are *ex facie* harmless, but by reason of facts unknown to the author or publisher are defamatory, either of the person intended to be referred to, or of some other person, as in *Cassidy's* case.

[40] See *Ross* v. *Hopkinson* [1956] C.L.Y. 5011. It is by no means clear that the defendants in *Hulton and Cassidy* would be held to have taken all reasonable care: see above, § 8.3.

[41] *Powell* v. *Gelston* [1916] 2 K.B. 615, 619.

[42] *Grappelli* v. *Derek Block Ltd.* [1981] 1 W.L.R. 822.

[43] *Pullman* v. *Hill* [1891] 1 Q.B. 524, 527.

[44] Above, § 8.2.

[45] *Paterson Zochonis Ltd.* v. *Merfarken Packaging Ltd.* [1983] F.S.R. 273, 296 ("a thoroughly healthy restraint upon the activities of printers").

[46] As when a credit agency gives a customer a copy of his file under the Consumer Credit Act 1974, s.158.

[47] *Powell* v. *Gelston* [1916] 2 K.B. 615.

[48] *R.* v. *Adams* (1888) 22 Q.B.D. 66

and wife amount to publication[49]; domestic intercourse of this kind is exempt from the restrictions of the law of libel and slander. But a statement by the defendant to the wife or husband of the plaintiff is a ground of action.[50] It may even be reasonable to foresee that the spouse of the plaintiff will open a letter addressed to the plaintiff.[51]

The contents of a written document may be published either by allowing someone to read the document for himself or by reading it out to him. It is submitted, however, that this latter mode of communication amounts to slander only, and not to libel. A defamatory statement may be published by being dictated to a secretary, typist, or other reporter who reduces it to writing, but it is submitted in this case also that such a publication amounts to slander only. There are dicta to the contrary, indeed, in certain cases[52] in which dictation to a secretary is said to be the publication of libel to the secretary; but it is difficult to see how A can publish to B a document which is written by B himself.[53]

Publication need not consist of a positive or overt act. If a man deliberately refrains from removing or obliterating defamatory matter on premises under his control, he may make himself responsible for its continued presence in the place where it was put. If removal or obliteration was reasonably easy he will be held to have published it. But he will not be responsible if a stranger has made it impossible or very difficult for him to put an end to the libel, as where the objectionable words have been carved deep into the stone-work of his house.[54]

Every publication a new libel

When there are several publications of the same libel a separate action lies for each publication.[55] The actions may, however, be consolidated.[56] If they are not consolidated, but tried separately, there may be difficulties about the assessment of damages.[57] This power of consolidation extends to actions for slander and for slander of title and other form of injurious falsehood.[58]

(2) Persons to whom published

A publication is not sufficient unless it is made to a person who understands the defamatory significance of the statement, and who also understands that it refers to the plaintiff.[59] Publication will be presumed and the burden of disproving it lies upon the defendant, in all

---

[49] *Wennhak v. Morgan* (1888) 20 Q.B.D. 635. See below, § 8.18.
[50] *Wenman v. Ash* (1853) 13 C.B. 836.
[51] *Theaker v. Richardson* [1962] 1 W.L.R. 151.
[52] *Pullman v. Hill* [1891] 1 Q.B. 524, 527, 529, *Boxsius v. Goblet Frères* [1894] 1 Q.B. 842, 844; *Marbé v. George Edwardes (Daly's Theatre) Ltd.* [1928] 1 K.B. 269, 277.
[53] *Osborn v. Thomas Boulter & Sons* [1930] 2 K.B. 226, 237.
[54] *Byrne v. Deane* [1937] 1 K.B. 818, 838.
[55] *"Truth" (N.Z.) Ltd. v. Holloway* [1960] 1 W.L.R. 997. For the "single-publication" rule, see the Faulks Report (Cmnd. 5909, § 289).
[56] Law of Libel Amendment Act 1888, s.5.
[57] See below, § 8.25.
[58] Defamation Act 1952, s.13.
[59] *Sadgrove v. Hole* [1901] 2 K.B.1.

cases in which the document is so put in the way of being read and understood by someone that it is probable that he actually read and understood it. Thus it is a sufficient proof of publication to prove that a letter was posted and therefore probably read by the person to whom it was addressed or by his clerks,[60] or his wife,[61] but not his butler[62]; or that a postcard was posted and therefore probably read by the post office officials or by the family of him to whom it was sent.[63]

(3) Who is liable for publication

Where defamatory matter is contained in a book, periodical, or newspaper, there are normally a series of publications each of which constitutes a separate tort. First, there is a publication by the author to the publisher, for which the author is solely liable. Secondly, there is the publication by the author and publisher jointly to the printer, for which the author and publisher are jointly liable. Thirdly, there is the publication of the printed work to the trade and the public, for which the author, publisher, and printer are jointly liable. It is normally in respect of this last publication that proceedings for libel are brought, although it is open to the plaintiff to sue in respect of the separate publications set out above.[64] A publication to the wrong person by mistake is a ground of action: as when a document is meant to be sent to the plaintiff himself, or to some person privileged to receive it and it is sent to someone else[65] or when a man making charges against the plaintiff to his very face or whilst talking scandal to his wife negligently allows what he says[66] to be overheard by a third person.

(4) Innocent dissemination

The law adopts a more lenient attitude, however, towards him who is not the printer or the first or main publisher of a libel, but has taken only a subordinate part in its dissemination—for example, a newspaper distributor or librarian or a bookseller.[67] Such a person, sometimes called "a mechanical distributor," may be held not to have published the work if he can prove that (1) he disseminated the work without knowing that it contained a libel; (2) there was nothing in the work or in the circumstances in which it came to him or was disseminated by him which ought to have led him to suppose that it contained a libel; (3) when the work was disseminated by him, it was not by any negligence

---

[60] *Warren* v. *Warren* (1934) 1 C.M. & R. 250.
[61] *Theaker* v. *Richardson* [1962] 1 W.L.R. 151.
[62] *Huth* v. *Huth* [1915] 3 K.B. 32.
[63] *Robinson* v. Jones (1879) 4 L.R.Ir. 391. *Aliter* In the case of a letter in an unclosed envelope: *Huth* v. *Huth* [1915] 3 K.B. 32.
[64] Porter Committee Report, s.116.
[65] *Hebditch* v. *MacIlwaine* [1894] 2 Q.B. 54, 64.
[66] *White* v. *Stone Ltd.* [1939] 2 K.B. 827, 836. But it seems that if he has no reason to suspect that his words will be overheard there is no publication.
[67] There is a striking contrast between the recognition of negligence in this part of the law of libel and its non-recognition in *Hulton* v. *Jones* (above, § 8.2.).

on his part that he did not know that it contained a libel.[68] It is not very easy to see the difference between the second and the third of these questions, and Scrutton L.J. expressed the opinion[69] that in order to avoid confusing the jury, "the safest course for a trial judge is to follow Bowen L.J.,[70] who is a very good man to follow," and ask the jury simply: (1) whether the defendant knew, and (ii) whether he would have known if he had carried on his business properly.[71]

Defences and Remedies

We shall consider in detail the following six defences: (1) Justification; (2) Absolute Privilege; (3) Qualified Privilege; (4) Fair Comment; (5) Consent; (6) Apology. We have already considered the defence provided by the Defamation Act 1952, s.4 for cases of "unintentional defamation." The question of what may be given in evidence in mitigation of damages will be considered later.[72] The remedies of damages and an injunction are also considered later. These defences are of crucial importance in the law of defamation because of the low level of the threshold which a statement must pass in order to be defamatory.

The threshold of liability in libel is very low, because as a result of *Hulton* v. *Jones* it is easy for a plaintiff to get his case before the jury. On the other hand, the balance is tipped in favour of the defendant by the number and complexity of the defences. Nevertheless, this very complexity, and the fact that legal aid is not available for defamation means that,

> "It is only the very rich, the very foolish, the very malicious or the very dedicated who will knowingly put themselves in a position in which they have to defend a libel action, even with the benefit of qualified privilege as a possible defence. The anxieties would be enormous and, even if ultimately successful, the difference between actual and recoverable costs would be very substantial indeed."[73]

§ 8.8. JUSTIFICATION

No action will lie for the publication of a defamatory statement if the defendant pleads and proves that it is true. "For the law will not permit a man to recover damages in respect of an injury to a character which he

---

[68] *Bottomley* v. *Woolworth & Co.* (1932) 48 T.L.R. 521 (American magazines sold by multiple store). The defence, although commonly called "innocent dissemination," is strictly a defence of "never published": Porter Committee Report, s.112. The defence is also available in proceedings for contempt of court: Administration of Justice Act 1960, s.11.

[69] In *Sun Life Assurance Co.* v. *W.H. Smith & Son Ltd.* (1933) 150 L.T. 211, 214.

[70] In *Emmens* v. *Pottle* (1885) 16 Q.B.D. 354, 358.

[71] In *Goldsmith* v. *Sperrings Ltd.* [1977] 1 W.L.R. 478, in which 37 distributors of *Private Eye* were sued, a majority of the C.A. (Lord Denning M.R. dissenting) seem to have thought that the liability of a subordinate distributor was strict, and the H.L. refused the defendants leave to appeal.

[72] See below, § 8.25.

[73] *Hasselblad Ltd.* v. *Orbinson* [1985] Q.B. 475, 502, *per* Sir John Donaldson M.R.

either does not, or ought not, to possess."[74] This is so even though the defendant is proved to have been actuated by malicious and improper motives. In this part of the law the interest in free speech prevails completely over the interest in security of reputation. The common law affords no protection to the man who has led a blameless and worthy life for many years but finds his youthful follies published to the world at large in gloating and accurate detail by some malicious enemy.[75] The only exception is that under the Rehabilitation of Offenders Act 1974, s.8, a plaintiff who proves that the defendant has maliciously published details of a spent conviction[76] may recover damages.[77] But this section does not affect the defences of absolute[78] or qualified privilege and fair comment. So that an employer will (in the absence of malice) still be protected if he writes a reference which mentions a spent conviction. The policy of the complex Act is open to question. It is strange that those who have been convicted should be better protected by Parliament than those who have been acquitted.

In a criminal prosecution for libel the rule is different. At common law the truth was no defence at all on an indictment[79]; but by the Libel Act 1843, s.6, the publication of the truth, however defamatory, is no longer a criminal offence if the jury is of opinion that the publication of it was for the public benefit. The onus is on the defendant of proving justification and public benefit. In the last century there has been only one prosecution in which the defence was unsuccessfully raised.[80] It has often been suggested that this requirement of public interest should be extended to civil proceedings, but the Faulks Report did not recommend such a change.[81]

Pleading

The defence that the statement is true is termed a plea of justification, the defendant being said to justify the publication. The burden of proof rests upon the defendant; it is for him to prove that the statement is true, not for the plaintiff to prove that it is false.[82] So the hallowed phrase in the statement of claim that the words were published "falsely

---

[74] *McPherson* v. *Daniels* (1829) 10 B. & C. 263, 272, *per* Littledale J.

[75] For the suggested tort of infringement of privacy, see above, § 3.2.

[76] In short, one imposed more than ten years ago which resulted in a non-custodial sentence or a custodial sentence of not more than 30 months.

[77] An interlocutory injunction can be obtained only if the evidence of malice—*i.e.* some spiteful or improper motive—is overwhelming: *Herbage* v. *Pressdram Ltd.* [1984] 1 W.L.R. 1160.

[78] For an exception, see § 8.10. below.

[79] "Dost know that old Mansfield Who writes like the Bible, Says the more 'tis a truth, sir, The more 'tis a libel" (Burns, *The Reproof*). This familiar maxim is usually explained on the ground that the more truthful the statement the more likely is the person defamed to commit a breach of the peace.

[80] Law Commission Working Paper No. 84, §§ 3.18–3.2

[81] Cmnd. 5909, § 144.

[82] *Beevis* v. *Dawson* [1957] 1 Q.B. 195 (which see also for the practice when the plaintiff intends to give evidence in rebuttal of the plea of justification).

and maliciously" is illogical and bad pleading.[83] The defence is a dangerous one, for an unsuccessful attempt to establish it may be treated as an aggravation of the original injury.

It is not necessary to prove that the statement is literally true; it is sufficient if it is true in substance, if the essence of the imputation is true and if the erroneous details in no way aggravate the defamatory character of the statement or alter its nature.[84] Thus in *Alexander v. N.E. Ry.*,[85] a statement that the plaintiff had been convicted of travelling in a train without a ticket, and had been fined one pound with *three weeks'* imprisonment in default of payment, was held capable of being sufficiently justified by proof that he had been fined one pound for that offence with a *fortnight's* imprisonment in default of payment. Today, the Defamation Act 1952, s.5, provides that in an action for libel or slander in respect of words[86] containing two or more distinct charges against the plaintiff, a defence of justification shall not fail by reason only that the truth of every charge is not proved, if the words not proved to be true do not materially injure the plaintiff's reputation having regard to the truth of the remaining charges. But the defendant will be in a difficult position if the plaintiff disregards some of the charges and sues in respect only of those which are most favourable to his case, as he is still entitled to do, at least if the charges are distinct and severable.[87]

Rumours

When the defamatory statement is put forward by way of rumour or report only, it is not sufficient to prove that the rumour or report really existed; it is necessary to prove that it was true. For to give it further currency is to suggest that it may be well founded, and it is this suggestion that must be justified. Were it not for this rule every man could escape the consequences of publishing libels and slanders by adopting the simple precaution of stating them as matters of rumour or suspicion, instead of as matters of fact.[88] On the other hand, a statement that the Fraud Squad of the police were inquiring into the affairs of the plaintiff has been held incapable of supporting the meaning that he was guilty of fraud,[89] as distinct from being suspected of it, but the statement in this case was not put forward by way of rumour.

---

[83] Faulks Report, § 143.
[84] *Sutherland v. Stopes* [1925] A.C. 47, 78–81.
[85] (1865) 6 B. & S. 340.
[86] As defined by s.16(1); see above, § 8.2.
[87] *Bookbinder v. Tebbitt* [1989] 1 W.L.R. 640, 646. So in *Polly Peck (Holdings) plc v. Threlford* [1986] Q.B. 1000 it was held that a defendant may justify all the allegations in a publication if a jury find they have a "common sting." Any unjustified specific acts of misconduct may be used in mitigation of damages: *Pamplin v. Express Newspapers Ltd.* [1988] 1 W.L.R. 116, 119–120.
[88] *Watkin v. Hall* (1868) L.R. 3 Q.B. 396.
[89] *Lewis v. Daily Telegraph Ltd.* [1964] A.C. 234. Awards of damages amounting to £217,000 were set aside by the House of Lords as being out of all proportion, and a new trial ordered. The defendants later paid £22,000 in settlement: *The Times*, December 18, 1964.

Convictions and expulsions

It is not certain whether it is sufficient to justify a statement that a man has been warned off the turf or a boy expelled from school to prove that he has been so warned off or expelled. It has been said that "It would be an extraordinary result . . . that if you said that a properly constituted tribunal had found a man guilty of some wrongful act you could be sued for libel unless you could prove that the properly constituted tribunal had rightly decided that he was guilty."[90] But persons may be warned off or expelled for a variety of reasons, and it seems possible to place an actionable innuendo upon such a statement—e.g. that he has been rightly expelled for disgraceful conduct.[91] It is in any event clear that to say a man has been rightly convicted is quite different from saying simply that he has been convicted: so until the law was changed by the Civil Evidence Act 1968, s.13, someone who published the former statement found himself under the heavy burden of fighting a criminal trial over again.[92]

§ 8.9. PRIVILEGE[93]

We have seen that in general he who publishes a defamatory statement does so at his peril, and is liable if this statement turns out not to be true, however honestly and carefully he may have acted, and however inevitable his mistake. This rule is subject to a number of important exceptions which are grouped together under the title of Privilege. A privileged statement[94] may be defined as one which is made in such circumstances as to be exempt from the rule that a man attacks the reputation of another at his own risk. In other words, privilege includes those exceptional cases in which it is not enough, in order to create liability, to prove that the defendant has published a false and defamatory statement. The defendant, being privileged[94] is not responsible for this alone, but is either wholly free from responsibility or is liable only on proof that he was animated by a malicious motive and not by any genuine intention to use his privilege for the purpose for which the law gave it to him. It is common to speak of the statement as being privileged, but the better view[94] is that it is the occasion and not the statement which is privileged.[95]

The cases in which privilege exists are, speaking generally, those in which there is some just occasion for publishing defamatory matter in the public interest or in the furtherance or protection of the rights or

---

[90] *Cookson* v. *Harewood* [1932] 2 K.B. 478, 485, *per* Greer L.J.

[91] *Lewis* v. *Daily Telegraph Ltd.* [1963] 1 Q.B. 340, 372–373 (not considered in H.L.).

[92] See *Hinds* v. *Sparks, The Times,* July 27, 1964. For a curious converse case, see *Loughans* v. *Odhams Press Ltd., The Times,* February 14, 1963. The Civil Evidence Act 1968, s.13 provides that if it is relevant in defamation proceedings whether a person committed a criminal offence, proof of conviction is conclusive evidence that he did commit that offence. But note that proof of an acquittal is not conclusive evidence of innocence.

[93] The argument of Holmes, K.C., in *Perera (M.G.)* v. *Peiris* [1949] A.C. 1 reviews the history of the defence.

[94] *Minter* v. *Priest* [1930] A.C. 558, 571–572.

[95] *Angel* v. *Bushell Ltd.* [1968] 1 Q.B. 813.

lawful interests of individuals. In such cases the exigency of the occasion amounts to a lawful excuse for the attack so made upon the plaintiff's reputation. The right of free speech is allowed wholly or partially to prevail over the right of reputation. If the defamatory statement can be shown to be true, the defence of privilege is not required; for it is allowable to publish the truth on all occasions, privileged or not, and from all motives, good or bad, that it is necessary to fall back upon the plea of privilege, and to prove that the occasion of the publication was such as to exempt the defendant from the consequences of his error. It has been held however, that a defendant may plead that the occasion on which he published the words was privileged, even though he also denies that he ever published the words in question.[96]

§ 8.10. Absolute Privilege

Privilege is of two kinds, distinguished as absolute and qualified. A statement is said to be absolutely privileged when it is of such a nature that no action will lie for it, however, false and defamatory it may be, and even though it is made maliciously—that is to say, from some improper motive. The right of free speech is allowed to prevail wholly over the right of reputation. As may be expected, the cases in which the right of free speech can be placed at so high a level are few in number and quite exceptional in character.

They are the following:

(1) Any statement made in the course of and with reference to judicial proceedings by any judge, juryman, party, witness, or advocate;
(2) Fair, accurate, and contemporaneous reports of public judicial proceedings published in a newspaper;
(3) Any statement made in Parliament by a member of either House;
(4) Parliament papers published by the direction of either House, and any reputation thereof by any person in full;
(5) Certain statements made by one officer of State to another in the course of official duty;
(6) Communications between husband and wife.

(1) Judicial privilege

"The authorities establish beyond all question this: that neither party, witness, counsel, jury, nor judge can be put to answer civilly or criminally for words spoken in office; that no action of libel or slander lies, whether against judges, counsel, witnesses, or parties, for words written or spoken in the course of any proceedings before any court recognised by law, and this though the words written or spoken were written or spoken maliciously without any justification or excuse, and from personal ill-will and anger against the person defamed. This absolute privilege has been conceded on the grounds of public policy to ensure freedom of speech where it is essential that freedom of speech should exist, and with the knowledge that courts of justice are presided

---

[96] *Kirkwood Hackett* v. *Tierney* [1952] I.R. 185.

over by those who from their high character are not likely to abuse the privilege, and who have the power and ought to have the will to check any abuse of it by those who appear before them."[97]

The privilege extends to all courts, superior and inferior, civil and military.[98] If the privilege is abused the remedy is removal from office rather than the harassment of an action. But if the court is an inferior one privilege probably attaches only when the court has acted within jurisdiction.[99] The privilege also extends to tribunals acting in a manner similar to courts of justice, even though they are purely domestic bodies not established by statute.[1] so that Jasper Addis unsuccessfully argued that an order of the Disciplinary Committee of the solicitors' profession was not absolutely privileged.[2] But the privilege does not extend to officials possessing merely administrative as opposed to genuine judicial functions, as with an investigation by the Commission of the European Communities under Art. 29 of the Treaty of Rome.[3]

The privilege extends not merely to judges[4] but witnesses,[5] parties,[6] advocates,[7] and court welfare officers[8] it includes not merely statements made by a witness in court but also statements made by him to a party, or to the party's solicitor, in the course of preparation for trial.[9] For it would not be of much use to grant absolute privilege to what is said in court, if a plaintiff could say: "I cannot sue you for what you said in the witness-box, but I am going to sue you for what you told your solicitor you were going to say in it."

The statement, in order to be privileged, need not be relevant, in the sense of having a material bearing upon the matter in issue in the case. Thus the statement of a witness is privileged, even though inadmissible as evidence, and even though so immaterial that no prosecution for perjury would be possible in respect of it. Nevertheless the statement, though it need not be relevant in this sense, must, it would seem, be

---

[97] *Royal Aquarium and Summer and Winter Garden Society Ltd.* v. *Parkinson* [1892] 1 Q.B. 431, 451, *per* Lopes L.J.

[98] *Scott* v. *Stansfield* (1868) L.R. 3 Ex. 220 (county court); *Thomas* v. *Churton* (1862) 2 B. & S. 475 (coroner); *Dawkins* v. *Rokeby (Lord)* (1873) L.R. 8 Q.B. 255 (court-martial), *Law* v. *Llewellyn* [1906] 1 K.B. 487 (magistrate); *Bottomley* v. *Brougham* [1908] 1 K.B. 584 (official receiver).

[99] See below, § 19.2.

[1] *Trapp* v. *Mackie* [1979] 1 W.L.R. 377, in which the House of Lords identified no fewer than ten characteristics which entitled a tribunal to the cloak of absolute privilege.

[2] *Addis* v. *Crocker* [1961] 1 Q.B. 11 But a complaint to the Bar Council (as distinct from the Benchers of an Inn) has only qualified privilege: *Lincoln* v. *Daniels* [1962] 1 Q.B. 237.

[3] *Hasselblad Ltd.* v. *Orbinson* [1985] Q.B. 475.

[4] In the case of judges, however, this is simply a special instance of a much more general rule of exemption from civil liability for judicial acts. As to this, see below, §19.1. For an attempt to outflank the judicial privilege by using "every trick of the administrative law trade," see Beck, "Trial of a High Court Judge for Defamation" (1987) 103 L.Q.R. 461, 482.

[5] *Seaman* v. *Netherclift* (1876) 2 C.P.D. 53, Nor will an action for perjury lie against a witness: *Hargreaves* v. *Bretherton* [1959] 1 Q.B. 45, See above, §2.2.

[6] *Kennedy* v. *Hilliard* (1859) 10 Ir. C.L.R. 195.

[7] *Munster* v. *Lamb* (1883) 11 Q.B.D. 588.

[8] *Brown* v. *Matthews* [1990] 2 W.L.R. 879, 887.

[9] *Watson* v. *M'Ewan* [1905] A.C. 480.

made in the course of and with reference to the case in hand. A judge who from the Bench made a defamatory observation in respect of some entirely extraneous matter would no longer be speaking in his capacity as a judge, and would have no privilege.[10]

(2) Privileged reports

By the Law of Libel Amendment Act 1888, s.3, it is provided that "A fair and accurate[11] report in any newsaper[12] of proceedings publicly heard before any court exercising judicial authority[13] shall, if published contemporaneously with such proceedings, be privileged: provided that nothing in this section shall authorise the publication of any blasphemous or indecent matter." The report need not be a verbatim one; it is enough if it is in substance a fair account of what took place; a few slight omissions or inaccuracies are immaterial[14] Nor is a newspaper obliged to verify whether what counsel or a solicitor or a witness has said is accurate; a fair and accurate report of counsel's opening address in (say) a fashionable libel action is just as much entitled to privilege as such a report of the judge's summing-up.[15] "Proceedings" covers anything done in the course of the proceedings which is in any way related to them,[16] but not an intervention in court which is wholly irrelevant to anything before the tribunal,[17] or evidence about a spent conviction which a court has ruled to be inadmissible under section 4(1) of the Rehabilitation of Offenders Act 1974.[18]

It is generally understood that the word *privileged* in section 3 of the Act of 1888 means absolutely privileged.[19] If one of the statutory conditions has not been fulfilled it may be that the report has qualified privilege at common law.[20]

---

[10] *More* v. *Weaver* [1928] 2 K.B. 520, 525.

[11] It is no defence that the omission of a material statement during the proceedings was due to its not being heard by the reporter owing to inattention: *Mitchell* v. *Hirst, Kidd and Rennie Ltd.* [1936] 3 All E.R. 872. Lawrence J. there suggested during argument that it would have been otherwise if the omitted statement *could* not have been heard.

[12] As defined in s.1 A broadcast report is also protected: the Defamation Act 1952, s.9(2).

[13] Within the United Kingdom only: the Defamation Act 1952, s.8. Reports of proceedings before foreign and Commonwealth tribunals may be the subject of qualified privilege: see below, § 8.14.

[14] *Kimber* v. *Press Association* [1893] 1 Q.B. 65.

[15] *Burnett and Hallamshire Fuel Ltd.* v. *Sheffield Telegraph & Star Ltd.* [1960] 1 W.L.R. 502.

[16] *Farmer* v. *Hyde* [1937] 1 K.B. 728.

[17] *Lynam* v. *Gowing* (1880) 6 L.R.Ir. 259.

[18] Unless, according to s.8(7), the report in question is in a bona fide series of law reports, or has been published for bona fide educational purposes Lecturers and students who refer to spent convictions in other ways—*e.g.* in seminars—may find themselves paying damages to rehabilitated persons.

[19] See *McCarey* v. *Associated Newspapers Ltd.* [1964] 1 W.L.R. 855 (not discussed on appeal in [1965] 2 Q.B. 86) and Spencer Bower, *Actionable Defamation*, pp. 406–408 ("anything more unjust or pernicious or inimical to public welfare cannot well be imagined"). This seems to be the assumption of the Defamation Act 1952, s.8, although it was probably not what Parliament intended in 1888 (Faulks Report, § 189).

[20] *Thom* v. *John Fairfax & Sons Pty. Ltd.* [1964] N.S.W.R. 396.

(3) Parliamentary privilege

It is clear that statements made by members of either House of Parliament in their places in the House, though they might be untrue to their knowledge, cannot be made the foundation of civil or criminal proceedings, however injurious they might be to the interest of a third person.[21] The privilege is based on the Bill of Rights 1688, Article 9, which provides that 'the freedom of speech and debates on proceedings in Parliament ought not to be impeached or questioned in any court." The courts have always been sensitive to claims of parliamentary privilege, so the width of terms such as "proceedings" and "questioned" is still unclear.[22]

(4) Parliamentary papers

By the Parliamentary Papers Act 1840, s.1, absolute privilege is conferred upon the publication[23] by order of either House of Parliament of the reports, papers, votes, or proceedings of either House, and also upon the republication in full of any documents of this nature which have been already published by such authority. The publication of extracts or abstracts of a parliamentary paper is the subject of qualified privilege[24] under section 3 of the 1840 Act. At common law the protection accorded to statements made in Parliament did not extend to the publication of defamatory documents elsewhere, even by order of one of the Houses,[25] for one House cannot by its own resolution alter the law of the land. For that a statute is required.

(5) Official privilege

At common law no action will lie against an officer of State for any defamatory statement made by him to another officer of State in the course of his duty.[26] It has not been established clearly what classes of public servants are officers of State. Protection has ben extended to official reports made by a military officer to his superior,[27] by a Minister to a subordinate official,[28] and by the High Commissioner of a Commonwealth country to his Prime Minister,[29] but it is doubtful whether it extends to a report made by a police-inspector to his superior officer,[30]

---

[21] Ex p. Wason (1869) L.R. 4 Q.B.573, 576;

[22] Rost v. Edwards [1990] 2 Q.B. 460.

[23] A term which now includes broadcasting: Defamation Act 1952, s.9(1).

[24] Associated Newspapers Ltd. v. Dingle [1964] A.C. 371, 407.

[25] Stockdale v. Hansard (1839) 9 A. & E. 1. Lord Denman's was an "admirable judgement than which a finer never was delivered within these walls, and in which the spirit of Holt is combined with the luminous reasoning of a Mansfield": Wason v. Walter (1868) L.R. 4 Q.B. 73, 91, per Cockburn C.J.

[26] Chatterton v. Secretary of State for India [1895] 2 Q.B. 189.

[27] Dawkins v. Lord F. Paulet (1869) L.R. 5 Q.B. 94. The authority of the case is weakened by Cockburn C.J's powerful dissenting judgement.

[28] Peerless Bakery Ltd. v. Watt [1955] N.Z.L.R. 339. But see Szalatnay-Stacho v. Fink [1946] 1 All E.R. 303, 305 (the point was not discussed in the C.A.).

[29] Isaacs & Sons Ltd. v. Cook [1925] 2 K.B. 391.

[30] Merricks v. Nott-Bower [1965] 1 Q.B. 57.

or to reports made by the security service of a foreign Power,[31] as distinct from communications between members of the same foreign embassy.[32] Probably this absolute immunity is given only where upon clear grounds of public policy a remedy must be denied to private injury because complete freedom from suit appears indispensable to the effective performance of judicial, legislative, or official functions.The presumption is against such a privilege and its extension by the courts is not favoured.[33]

On the other hand, parliament has been liberal in granting absolute privilege to certain reports and statements made to and by the Parliamentary Commissioner for Administration (Ombudsman),[34] the Local Commissioner,[35] Director-General of Fair Trading,[36] and the Lord Chancellor and designated judges while performing statutory functions.[37]

(6) Statements between husband and wife

A defamatory statement made by one spouse to the other, as distinct from a statement made to the spouse of the plaintiff, cannot be the subject of an action. The older authorities put this upon the ground that there has been no publication; but it seems preferable today, when the fiction of the unity of husband and wife has been discarded, to say that it is an instance of absolute privilege, the reason for which is the highly confidential character of the relationship.

Consequential Communications

If the occasion be covered by absolute privilege then consequential communications also are privileged in the same way. So, in *Isaacs & Sons Ltd.* v. *Cook*,[38] the publication of the report to the clerks and servants through whom the production and issue of the report were arranged was privileged along with the report itself.[39]

§ 8.11. QUALIFIED PRIVILEGE

When an occasion of qualified privilege exists a person (provided he is not actuated by malice) is entitled to make defamatory statements about another. The right of freedom of speech prevails over the right of reputation, but only to a limited extent. The statement must be made honestly and without any indirect or improper motive. Qualified privilege, therefore, is an intermediate case between total absence of privi-

---

[31] *Richards* v. *Naum* [1967] 1 Q.B. 620.
[32] *Fayed* v. *Al-Tajir* [1988] Q.B. 712.
[33] *Gibbons* v. *Duffell* (1932) 47 C.L.R. 520, 528. This privilege must be distinguished from the evidentiary privilege which enables a Minister to refuse to produce a document if it would be contrary to the public interest to do so.
[34] Parliamentary Commissioner Act 1967, s.10(5).
[35] Local Government Act 1974, s.32.
[36] Competition Act 1980, s.16(2).
[37] Courts and Legal Services Act 1990, s.69(2).
[38] [1925] 2 K.B. 391.
[39] As in cases of qualified privilege, below, § 8.17.

lege and the presence of absolute privilege. The principle is that the
statement is protected if it is fairly made by a person in the discharge of
some public or private duty, whether legal or moral, or in the conduct of
his own affairs, in matters where his interest is concerned.[40] No complete list of such occasions is possible or desirable,[41] but it is generally
agreed that the chief instances are the following:

   (1) Statements made in the performance of a duty;
   (2) Statements made in the protection of an interest;
   (3) Reports of parliamentary, judicial, and certain other public pro-
        ceedings;
   (4) Professional communications between solicitor and client.
   We shall now consider each in turn.

§ 8.12. STATEMENTS IN PERFORMANCE OF A DUTY

A statement is conditionally privileged if it is made in the performance
of any legal or moral duty imposed upon the person making it.[42] The
privilege is that of the publisher; the person to whom the statement is
published needs no privilege, because he commits no tort.[43] Nevertheless it is essential[44] that the person to whom the statement is made has a
corresponding interest or duty to receive it. This is not to say that both
parties must have a duty or both an interest: one may have an interest
and the other a duty, as in the common case of a servant's character.[45]
The duty need not be, and indeed seldom is, one enforceable at law.[46] It
is sufficient that by the moral standard of right conduct prevalent in the
community the defendant lay under an obligation to say what he did. It
is not enough that he believed himself to be under such an obligation.[47]
It is for the judge, and not for the jury, to decide whether on the facts as
proved such a duty existed.[48] The judge will have to estimate the value
of and make a choice between the various interests—of life, family,
reputation, or property—involved in the case. It is plain that no universally valid criterion is possible. "Would the great mass of right-minded
men in the position of the defendant have considered it their duty,
under the circumstances, to make the communication?"[49] is one test
often cited.

Voluntary communications

   A communication which is volunteered, without any inquiry on the
part of anyone possessing a lawful interest, is unprivileged, unless

---

[40] *Toogood* v. *Spyring* (1834) 1 C.M. & R. 181, 193.

[41] *London Association for Protection of Trade* v. *Greenlands* [1916] 2 A.C. 15, 23.

[42] *Stuart* v. *Bell* [1891] 2 Q.B. 341.

[43] *Bryanston Finance Ltd.* v. *de Vries* [1975] 1 Q.B. 703, 726.

[44] *Watt* v. *Longsdon* [1930] 1 K.B. 130.

[45] *Phelps* v. *Kemsley* (1942) 168 L.T. 18, 21.

[46] There is a legal duty to make certain entries in a ship's log book under the Merchant
Shipping Act 1970, s.68.

[47] *Phelps* v. *Kemsley* (1942) 168 L.T. 18.

[48] *Watt* v. *Longsdon* [1930] 1 K.B. 130.

[49] *Watt* v. *Longsdon* [1930] 1 K.B. 130, 153, *per* Greer L.J.

there is some such confidential or other relation between the parties as creates a duty to speak without being asked. Thus a father or other near relative may warn a woman as to the character of the man whom she proposes to marry.[50] It would seem that there may even be circumstances in which a duty lies upon a third party to communicate to one spouse the delinquencies of the other, but in such cases the judge would be "much influenced by the consideration that as a general rule it is not desirable for anyone, even a mother-in-law, to interfere in the affairs of man and wife."[51] Again, a host owes a duty to his guest which will justify him in warning his guest against a servant suspected of dishonesty.[52] On the same principle, in the case of a trade protection association which makes on behalf of its members inquiries into the financial position of persons with whom they propose to deal, communications made by the association or its agents to a member who has requested this information, and who has a lawful interest in obtaining it, are privileged,[53] at least if the association has not been created solely for the purpose of gain.[54]

§ 8.13. Statements in Protection of an Interest

Even when there is no duty to make the statement, it is nevertheless privileged if it is made in the protection of some lawful interest of the person making it: for example, if it is made in the defence of his own property or reputation.[55] But here also there must be reciprocity. There must be an interest to be protected on the one side and a duty to protect it on the other.[56] Thus in *Adam* v. *Ward*[57] the plaintiff, in the House of Commons, had made against General Scobell charges of the most wounding character. General Scobell, as he was compelled to do by King's Regulations, referred the matter to the Army Council, which after investigation found that the attack was unjustifiable. It ordered the defendant, its secretary, to publish in the newspapers a letter to General Scobell vindicating him and also containing statements defamatory of the plaintiff. The House of Lords held that the occasion of this publication was privileged.[58] and that the privilege was not destroyed either

---

[50] *Todd* v. *Hawkins* (1837) 8 C. & P. 88.
[51] *Watt* v. *Longsdon* [1930] 1 K.B. 130, 150, *per* Scrutton L.J.
[52] *Stuart* v. *Bell* [1891] 2 Q.B. 341.
[53] *London Association for Protection of Trade* v. *Greenlands Ltd.* [1916] A.C. 15.
[54] See the Younger Committee on Privacy (Cmnd. 5012 (1972) paras. 273–275.
[55] *Turner* v. *M.-G.-M. Pictures Ltd.* [1950] 1 All E.R.449, 470.
[56] *White* v. *Stone Ltd.* [1939] 2 K.B. 827, 835.
[57] [1917] A.C. 309.
[58] "Every subject of the Crown, whatever position of our far-flung Empire he may inhabit has, and must have, an interest in the British Army, its courage, the confidence of its men in their officers, its discipline and efficiency . . . It would be a disgrace and injury to the service if a man, publicly accused of the shameful breach of duty of which General Scobell was accused, was allowed to continue in command of a brigade in the Army unless and until he had been cleared of the accusation made against him. Every subject, therefore, who had an interest in the Army had an interest in being by a public communication informed of General Scobell's acquittal": *per* Lord Atkinson, [1917] A.C. 309, 343.

by the number of pople whom the publication might reach,[59] or by reason of the fact that it contained matter defamatory of the plaintiff, for where the defendant's character has been publicly attacked by the plaintiff, the courts will not be over-nice in their scrutiny of the language which he uses in his defence, although a counter-attack which makes irrelevant and spiteful allegations will not be privileged.[60] But no privilege attaches when the sender of the document makes a mistake, however honest or reasonable, about the nature of the occasion[61] or the interest of the recipient.[62]

There may sometimes be a common interest and a reciprocal duty in respect of the subject-matter of the communication.[63] Thus a master has a sufficient interest in the honesty of his servants to be privileged in warning them against the character of their associates.[64] So a tenant may make a complaint to his landlord of the conduct of persons engaged by the latter to effect repairs to the premises.[65] Conversely, a landlord may complain to his tenant of the conduct of the latter's lodgers at the windows of the house as having a tendency to bring the house into disrepute.[66]

Charges against public persons

The same principle is applicable even when the interest of the defendant is merely the general interest which he possesses in common with all others in the honest and efficient exercise by public officials of the duties entrusted to them. Thus any member of the public may make charges of misconduct against any public servant and the communication will be privileged[67] but the charge must be made to the proper persons—that is to say, to those who have a corresponding interest. Otherwise there would be a startling licence to defame on a grand scale.[68] So a constituent may write to his Member of Parliament asking for his assistance to bring to the notice of the appropriate Minister or other person a complaint of improper conduct on the part of a public officer, for example, a police officer or a justice of the peace, acting in his constituency in relation to his office.[69] If this were not the law, a Member of Parliament would act at his peril if he extended his activities beyond the Palace of Westminster.[70] But a communication to the wrong person,[71] and a fortiori a publication of the complaint to the world at

---

[59] See below, § 8.17.
[60] News Media Ownership v. Finlay [1970] N.Z.L.R. 1089.
[61] Pyke v. Hibernian Bank Ltd. [1950] I.R. 195.
[62] Beach v. Freeson [1972] 1 Q.B. 14, 24.
[63] Watt v. Longsdon [1930] 1 K.B. 130, 147.
[64] Hunt v. G.N.Ry. [1891] 2 Q.B. 189.
[65] Toogood v. Spring(1834) 1 C.M. & R. 181.
[66] Knight v. Gibbs (1934) 1 Ad. & E. 43.
[67] Harrison v. Bush (1855) 5 E. & B. 344.
[68] London Artists Ltd. v. Littler [1968] 1 W.L.R. 607, 615.
[69] Beach v. Freeson [1972] 1 Q.B. 14.
[70] Beach v. Freeson [1972] 1 Q.B. 14, 22.
[71] Hynes-O'Sullivan v. O'Driscoll [1988] I.R. 436.

large in a newspaper or otherwise, is an excess of privilege, and the privilege will be thereby forfeited.[72] On the other hand, the Defamation Act 1952, provides[73] that a defamatory statement published by or on behalf of a candidate in any election to a local government authority[74] or to Parliament shall not be deemed to be published on a privileged occasion on the ground that it is material to a question in issue in the election, whether or not the person by whom it is published is qualified to vote at the election.

Privilege distinguished from fair comment

This privilege of making complaints against public persons must not be confounded with the right to make fair comments on matters of public interest, which will be discussed in a later section.[75] Privilege deals with false and defamatory statements of fact, not with defamatory comment on proved or admitted facts. A comment may be published to all the world; a specific charge of misconduct may be published only to the persons in authority over the offender.

§ 8.14. Privileged Reports

Fair and accurate reports, whether in a newspaper or elsewhere, of the public proceedings of any municipal court of justice are conditionally privileged by the common law. "Fairness and accuracy are factual matters eminently suited for decision by a jury".[76] The privilege extends to all courts, whether superior or inferior, and whether courts of record or not.[77] It makes no difference whether the proceedings are preliminary or final,[78] or whether they are taken *ex parte* or otherwise. The privilege is not excluded by the fact that the matter is one over which the court has no jurisdiction, provided that it has jurisdiction to inquire whether the matter is one which it could properly entertain.[79] A fair and accurate contemporaneous report of judicial proceedings before a foreign tribunal is also privileged (by judicial decision[80] in England, by statute[81] in Ireland), at least if the matter is of legitimate and proper interest to the public. It seems, however, that no privilege attaches if the proceedings take place in a court to which the public are not admitted,[82]

---

[72] *Truth (N.Z.) Ltd.* v. *Holloway* [1960] N.Z.L.R. 69 (not discussed on appeal, [1960] 1 W.L.R. 997).

[73] s.10.

[74] *Plummer* v. *Charman* [1962] 1 W.L.R. 1469.

[75] Below, § 8.20.

[76] *Kingshott* v. *Associated Kent Newspapers Ltd.* [1991] 1 Q.B. 88, 101, *per* Bingham L.J.

[77] *e.g.* a coroner's court: *McCarey* v. *Associated Newspapers Ltd.* [1964] 1 W.L.R. 855.

[78] *Kimber* v. *Press Association* [1893] 1 Q.B. 65.

[79] *Allbutt* v. *General Council of Medical Education* (1889) 23 Q.B.D. 400.

[80] *Webb* v. *Times Publishing Co. Ltd.* [1960] 2 Q.B. 535. See the interesting Note on this case in (1964) 64 Col.L.Rev. 1102.

[81] Defamation Act 1961, Sched. 2.

[82] *Kimber* v. *Press Association* [1893] 1 Q.B. 65.

or in a domestic tribunal, *e.g.* the Stewards of the Jockey Club,[83] nor where the subject-matter of the publication is an obscene or blasphemous libel.[84] As has been already indicated[85] a *newspaper* report of judicial proceedings is the subject of a statutory privilege, probably absolute, if it fulfils the requirements of section 3 of the Law of libel Amendment Act 1888. If any of those requirements are not satisfied, the report is subject to the common law rule of qualified privilege only. Fair and accurate reports of parliamentary debates are covered by qualified privilege at common law,[86] whilst the publication of extracts from or abstracts of reports or papers ordered by Parliament to be published is the subject of qualified privilege by statute.[87]

Reports of public meetings

At common law the reports, whether in a newspaper or elsewhere, of the proceedings of public meetings possessed no privilege.[88] Then the Law of Libel Amendment Act 1888, s.4, gave a limited measure of protection to newspapers which published fair and accurate reports of certain meetings. The Porter Committee recommended,[89] that the defence should be extended, both by widening the definition of "newspaper" to include monthly journals as well as those published at shorter intervals and by extending the categories of reports entitled to such privilege so as to give effect to the changes in social, economic, and political conditions which had occurred during the preceding 60 years.

Two classes of reports

Accordingly the Defamation Act 1952, s.7, provides that the publication in a newspaper[90] of the reports[91] or other matters about to be mentioned shall be the subject of qualified privilege. The reports and matters concerned fall into two categories:

(1) Statements privileged without any explanation or contradiction.

(2) Statements privileged subject to explanation or contradiction.

The defence of qualified privilege is not available to an action brought in respect of the publication of any of the statements mentioned in this second category if it is proved that the defendant had

---

[83] *Chapman* v. *Ellesmere (Lord)* [1932] 2 K.B. 431, 475. But privilege attaches to the publication of a decision of such a tribunal, in the terms in which the tribunal bona fide embodied it, in the publication chosen by the parties as the means of communication between the tribunal and the section of the public interested. This is merely an application of the rule *volenti non fit injuria*. In such a case the plaintiff cannot rely upon an innuendo: *ibid.* [1932] 2 K.B. 431.

[84] *R.* v. *Carlile* (1819) 3 B. & Ald. 167.

[85] Above, §8.10.

[86] *Wason* v. *Walter* (1868) L.R. 4 Q.B. 73.

[87] Parliamentary Papers Act 1840, s.3. Above § 8.10.

[88] *Purcell* v. *Sowler* (1877) 2 C.P.D. 215.

[89] Paras. 95–111.

[90] Means any paper containing public news or observations thereon, or consisting wholly or mainly of advertisements, which is printed for sale and is published in the U.K. either periodically or in parts or numbers at intervals not exceeding 36 days. Broadcast statements are also protected: s.9(2).

[91] Note that it is the report which is protected, as distinct from the original statement.

been requested by the plaintiff to publish in the newspaper in which[92] or, in the case of a broadcast statement, in the manner in which,[93] the original publication was made a reasonable letter or statement by way of explanation or contradiction,[94] and has refused or neglected to do so, or has done so in a manner not adequate or reasonable having regard to all the circumstances.[95] The Act does not protect the publication of any matter the publication of which is prohibited by law, or of any matter which is not of public concern and the publication of which is not for the public benefit.[96] This limitation is important: the legislature never intended to extend protection to reports of defamatory remarks which have no relevance to the objects of the meeting.[97] Although the report must be fair and accurate it need not be verbatim; nor, provided it is substantially accurate, will minor errors deprive it of protection.[98]

(1) Statements privileged without any explanation or contradiction

    (i) A fair and accurate report of any proceedings in public of the legislature of any part of Her Majesty's dominions outside Great Britain.

    (ii) A fair and accurate report of any proceedings in public of an international organisation of which the United Kingdom or Her Majesty's Government in the United Kingdom is a member, or of any international conference to which that Government sends a representative.

    (iii) A fair and accurate report of any proceedings in public of an international court.

    (iv) A fair and accurate report of any proceedings before any court exercising jurisdiction throughout any part of Her Majesty's dominions outside the United Kingdom or of any proceedings before a court-martial held outside the United Kingdom.

    (v) A fair and accurate report of any proceedings in public of a body or person appointed to hold a public inquiry by the government or legislature of any part of Her Majesty's dominions outside the United Kingdom.

---

[92] This must mean an issue of the newspaper subsequent to that in which the original publication was made.

[93] If the libel was contained in a variety sketch, or interview, it would hardly be necessary to reassemble the original cast: Chapman *Statutes*, p. 295.

[94] A general demand by the plaintiff for an apology is not a request within the meaning of this section: *Khan* v. *Ahmed* [1957] 2 Q.B. 149.

[95] The reason for the distinction has been explained by E. C. S. Wade (1950) 66 L.Q.R. 35): "It is surely not appropriate to require of editors when reporting overseas news . . . that they should throw their columns open to overseas statesmen or litigants, say in Australia or the United States, who may claim the right to refute or explain derogatory statements made in the English press. On the other hand, in the case of statements falling into the second category, especially reports of proceedings of domestic tribunals and meetings of local authorities, a correction or explanation may go a long way towards meeting any slur which may have been cast upon the plaintiff." See *Khan* v. *Ahmed* [1957] 2 Q.B. 149.

[96] Public concern and public benefit are questions of fact for the jury: *Kingshott* v. *Associated Kent Newspapers Ltd.* [1991] 1 Q.B. 88.

[97] *Pankhurst* v. *Sowler* (1887) 2 T.L.R. 193.

[98] *Nowlan* v. *Moncton Publishing Co.* [1952] 4 D.L.R. 808.

(vi) A fair and accurate copy of or extract from any register kept in pursuance of any Act of Parliament which is open to inspection by the public, or of any document which is required by the law of any part of the United Kingdom to be open to inspection by the public.

(vii) A notice or advertisement published by or on the authority of any court within the United Kingdom or any judge or officer of such a court.

(2) Statements privileged subject to explanation or contradiction

    (i) A fair and accurate report of the findings or decision of any of the following associations, or any committee or governing body thereof, that is to say—

        (a) an association formed in the United Kingdom for the purpose of promoting or encouraging the exercise of or interest in any art, science, religion or learning, and empowered by its constitution to exercise control over or adjudicate upon matters of interest or concern to the association or the association or the actions or conduct of any persons subject to such control or adjudication;

        (b) an association formed in the United Kingdom for the purpose of promoting or safeguarding the interests of any trade, business, industry or profession, or of the persons carrying on or engaged in any trade, business, industry or profession, and empowered by its constitution to exercise control over or adjudicate upon matters connected with the trade, industry, business or profession, or the actions or conduct of those persons;

        (c) an association formed in the United Kingdom for the purpose of promoting or safeguarding the interests of any game, sport or pastime to the playing or exercise of which members of the public are invited or admitted, and empowered by its constitution to exercise control over or adjudicate upon persons connected with or taking part in the game, sport or pastime,

being a finding or decision relating to a person who is a member or is subject by virtue of any contract to the control of the association.

    (ii) A fair and accurate report of the proceedings at any public meeting held in the United Kingdom, that is to say, a meeting bona fide and lawfully held for a lawful purpose and for the furtherance or discussion of any matter of public concern, whether the admission to the meeting is general or restricted.[99]

    (iii) A fair and accurate report of the proceedings at any meeting or sitting in any part of the United Kingdom of—

        (a) any local authority or committee of a local authority or local authorities;

---

[99] See *Khan* v. *Ahmed* [1957] 2 Q.B. 149.

(b) any justice or justices of the peace acting otherwise than as a court exercising judicial authority;

(c) any commission, tribunal, committee or person appointed for the purpose of any inquiry by Act of Parliament, by Her Majesty or by a Minister of the Crown;

(d) any person appointed by a local authority to hold a local inquiry in pursuance of any Act of Parliament;

(e) any other tribunal, board, committee or body constituted by or under, and exercising functions under, an Act of Parliament,

not being a meeting or sitting admission to which is denied to representatives of newspapers and other members of the public.

(iv) A fair and accurate report of the proceedings at a general meeting of any company or association constituted, registered or certified by or under any Act of Parliament or incorporated by Royal Charter, not being a private company

(v) A copy or fair and accurate report or summary of any notice or other matter[1] issued for the information of the public by or on behalf of any Government Department, officer of state, local authority or chief officer of police.[2] This privilege protects only the newspaper publishing the notice and does not cover the source from which the newspaper obtained its information.[3]

§ 8.15. PROFESSIONAL COMMUNICATIONS

Confidential communications between solicitor and client are privileged. The foundation of the privilege is the importance in the interests of justice that such communications should be free and unfettered by any fear of the consequences. The privilege is limited to the legal profession and covers all professional communications passing for the purpose of getting or giving professional advice,[4] and exists even if the solicitor does not accept the retainer.[5] The communication must be such as, within a very wide and generous ambit of interpretation, is fairly referable to the relationship of solicitor and client.[6] Thus the privilege is not confined to litigation: even conversations between a solicitor and client relating to the business of obtaining a loan for the deposit on the purchase of property are protected, as the business is professional business within the ordinary scope of a solicitor's employment.[7] It is probable that this is an instance of qualified, not absolute, privilege, though

---

[1] *Blackshaw* v. *Lord* [1984] 1 Q.B. 1, 23, 37.
[2] As in *Boston* v. *Bagshaw & Sons Ltd.* [1966] 1 W.L.R. 1126 ("wanted" notice on TV).
[3] *Foster* v. *Watson* (1944) 44 S.R. (N.S.W.) 399.
[4] *Minter* v. *Priest* [1930] A.C. 558, 581.
[5] *Minter* v. *Priest* [1930] A.C. 558, 584.
[6] *Minter* v. *Priest* [1930] A.C. 558, 568.
[7] *Minter* v. *Priest* [1930] A.C. 558, 584.

in *More* v. *Weaver*,[8] where the plaintiff was not repesented by counsel, the Court of Appeal held it to be absolute. But in *Minter*, v. *Priest*[9] the House of Lords expressly reserved opinion upon the point. This privilege must be distinguished from the privilege in the law of evidence which entitles a litigant, or a party to impending litigation, to object to an order for the production on discovery of a document on the ground that it is a professional communication.

§ 8.16. MALICE

The defence of qualified privilege is not available if the defendant was actuated by malice.[10] Malice means the presence of an improper motive, or even gross and unreasoning prejudice.[11] It does not necessarily mean personal spite or ill-will, though a desire to injure the plaintiff will usually be present. A statement is malicious when it is made for some purpose other than the purpose for which the law confers the privilege of making it. If the occasion is privileged it is for some reason, and the defendant is only entitled to the protection of the privilege if he uses the occasion for that reason. He is not entitled to the protection if he uses the occasion for some indirect and wrong motive.[12] It is neither necessary nor sufficient to constitute liability that the statement was made without reasonable and probable cause. Not necessary—for if the statement is made maliciously, and is in fact false, the defendant is liable for it although he had good grounds for believing it to be true; malice destroys the privilege, and leaves the defendant subject to the ordinary law by which a mistake, however reasonable, is no defence. Neither is the absence of reasonable and probable cause sufficient in itself to constitute liability. The law requires that a privilege shall be used honestly but not that it shall be used carefully. Negligence in making defamatory statements on a privileged occasion is not actionable.[13] The absence of any positive or honest belief in the truth of the statement is conclusive proof of malice, for the defendant cannot have had a proper motive in saying what he did not believe to be true.[14] On the other hand, a genuine belief in the truth of the statement is quite consistent with the existence of malice. If he uses the occasion for an improper motive he will be liable, even though he said what he believed to be true: to avoid liability he must have said it for the purpose of which the law allows

---

[8] [1928] 2 K.B. 520. In *Groom* v. *Crocker* [1939] 1 K.B. 194, the C.A. treated the privilege as qualified.

[9] [1930] A.C. 558.

[10] *Horrocks* v. *Lowe* [1975] A.C. 135, 138.

[11] *Horrocks* v. *Lowe* [1975] A.C. 135.

[12] *Horrocks* v. *Lowe* [1975] A.C. 135, 149.

[13] *Moore* v. *Canadian Pacific S.S. Co.* [1945] 1 All E.R. 128, 133.

[14] *Stewart* v. *Biggs* [1928] N.Z.L.R. 673. Save, indeed, in those exceptional cases in which a man may be under a duty to make some statement or communication, irrespective of whether he personally believes it to be true or not. His duty may make the truth of the matter no concern of his: *British Railway Traffic Co.* v. *The C.R.C. Co.* [1922] 2 K.B. 260, 271.

such a statement to be made.[15] But a court should be slow to draw such an inference.[16]

Onus of proof

The burden of proof lies upon the plaintiff, and the judge has to be satisfied that there is some reasonable evidence of malice to go to the jury. The law presumes honest belief in the truth of the statement unless the contrary is proved.[17] The rule is now the same in the defence of fair comment.[18] "If, however, the plaintiff can show any example of spite or indirect motive, whether before or after the publication, he will establish his case provided that the examples given are so connected with the state of mind of the defendant as to lead to the conclusion that he was malicious at the date when the libel was published . . . each piece of evidence must be regarded separately, and even if there are a number of instances where a favourable attitude is shown, one case tending to establish malice would be sufficient evidence on which a jury could find for the plaintiff. Nevertheless, each particular instance of alleged malice must be carefully analysed, and if the result is to leave the mind in doubt, then that piece of evidence is valueless as an instance of malice whether it stands alone or is combined with a number of similar instances."[19] But the judge may be entitled to leave the issue of malice generally to the jury.[20]

Evidence of malice

This may be either intrinsic or extrinsic. Intrinsic evidence consists in the contents of the statement itself. Its language, for example, may be so violent or insulting—it may go far beyond the just requirements of the occasion—as to amount in itself to sufficient evidence of malice.[21] But when considering whether the actual expressions used can be held as evidence of express malice no nice scales should be used.[22] The defendant will be protected even though his language should be violent or excessively strong or prejudiced,[23] if, having regard to all the circumstances of the case, he might honestly and on reasonable grounds have believed that what he wrote or said was true and necessary for his pur-

---

[15] *Horrocks* v. *Lowe* [1975] A.C. 138, 146, 149.

[16] *Horrocks* v. *Lowe* [1975] A.C. 138, 150.

[17] *Horrocks* v. *Lowe* [1975] A.C. 138, 149. The plaintiff may find the task of proving malice a difficult one since R.S.C., Ord. 82, r. 6, abolished (on the recommendation of the Porter Committee) the power to administer interrogatories as to the sources of the defendant's information or belief. See below, § 8.20.

[18] *Telnikoff* v. *Matusevitch* [1990] 3 W.L.R. 725, 737.

[19] *Turner* v. *M.-G.-M. Pictures Ltd.* [1950] 1 All E.R. 449, 455, *per* Lord Porter. If the case is tried with a jury the judge has a discretion to entertain and rule on a submission made by the defendant at the close of the plaintiff's case that there is no evidence to go to the jury without putting him to his election whether he will or will not call evidence: *Young* v. *Rank* [1950] 2 K.B. 510.

[20] *Boston* v. *Bagshaw & Sons Ltd.* [1966] 1 W.L.R. 1126.

[21] *Laughton* v. *Bishop of Sodor and Man* (1872) L.R.4 P.C. 495, 505.

[22] *Turner* v. *M.-G.-M. Pictures Ltd.* [1950] 1 All E.R. 449, 470.

[23] *Horrocks* v. *Lowe* [1975] A.C. 138.

pose, even though in fact it was not so.[24] Otherwise the protection which the law throws over a privileged occasion would be largely defeated. For the fact that the defendant has been unreasonable does not mean that he has been malicious.[25]

Extrinsic evidence consists in the circumstances under which the statement was made—circumstances which go to show that the statement, even though moderate and justifiable in its language, was in reality animated by some improper motive. It is not necessary that the plaintiff should prove affirmatively what this improper motive really was; it is sufficient to disprove the existence of a proper motive: for example, by showing that the defendant had no genuine belief in the truth of the statement.[26] Again, the behaviour of the defendant or his witnesses at the trial may be some evidence of malice.[27] A failure to apologise combined with a persistence in a plea of justification is not necessarily evidence of malice.[28]

§ 8.17. EXCESS OF PRIVILEGE

Privilege is forfeited if it is exceeded—that is to say, if the publication of the defamatory statement is more extensive than the occasion of the privilege requires and justifies. The question whether privilege has been exceeded seems to be distinct from the question of whether there is evidence of malice.[29] It is also a question of law for the court and not of fact for the jury.[30] Certain forms of privilege, indeed, permit of publication to the whole world: for example, the reports of judicial proceedings. Privilege such as this cannot be exceeded in the sense now under consideration.[31] But in other cases the privilege is limited to publication to certain persons only; and any mistake as to the limits of the privilege[32] is termed an excess of privilege, and deprives the defendant of the benefit of it.[33]

Newspapers in no special position

This question often arises in relation to charges made in newspapers against public men. If such a charge is solely an assertion of fact, so that

[24] *Adam* v. *Ward* [1917] A.C. 309, 339.
[25] *Turner* v. *M.-G.-M Pictures Ltd.* [1950] 1 All E.R. 449, 463. See the similar rule in Fair Comment, below, § 8.20.
[26] *Clark* v. *Molyneux* (1877) 3 Q.B.D. 237, 245; *Watt* v. *Longsdon* [1930] 1 K.B. 130.
[27] *Turner* v. *M.-G.-M. Pictures Ltd.* [1950] 1 All E.R. 449, 469.
[28] *Broadway Approvals* v. *Odhams Press Ltd.* [1965] 1 W.L.R. 805, which also see on proof of malice if defendant is a corporation.
[29] *Horrocks* v. *Lowe* [1975] A.C. 138, 151.
[30] *Adam* v. *Ward* [1917] A.C. 309, 318, 320–321, 327, 348.
[31] *Adam* v. *Ward* [1917] A.C. 309, 343.
[32] As in *Hynes-O'Sullivan* v. *Driscoll* [1988] I.R.436.
[33] There is another use sometimes made of the phrase "excess of privilege" in which it means, not an excessive publication of a privileged statement, but the improper and malicious use of that privilege. In this latter sense evidence of excess means merely evidence of malice: see Lord Porter in *Turner* v. *M.-G.-M. Pictures Ltd.* [1950] 1 All E.R. 449, 462.

the defence of fair comment is not open,[34] a defendant newspaper which is unable or unwilling to justify its allegations sometimes pleads privilege. The privilege is said to exist at common law, as distinct from that given by the Defamation Act 1952, s.7,[35] and to be created by the interest which the public at large have in hearing the details of such a charge against such a person. But the common law does not recognise any special privilege as attaching to the profession of journalism.[36] A journalist, like everyone else, is subject to the ordinary law: even a famous film critic may have her criticisms commented on by her victims.[37] A journalist who obtains information reflecting on a public man has no more right than any other private citizen to publish his assertions to the world at large.[38] Such assertions are not privileged merely because the general topic developed in the article is of public interest.[39] It will be otherwise, of course, if the assertion is contained in a fair and accurate report of a public meeting or judicial proceedings.[40] "It may be true in one sense to say that [newspapers] owe a duty to their readers to publish any and every item of news that may interest them. But his is not such a duty as makes every communication in their paper relating to a matter of public interest a privileged one. If it were, the power of the press to libel public men with impunity would in the absence of malice be almost unlimited."[41] So in *Chapman* v. *Lord Ellesmere*[42] it was held that, as the law then stood,[43] *The Times* newspaper (as distinct from the Racing Calendar) was not protected by privilege when it published a decision of the Stewards of the Jockey Club, although it was an accurate report of the decision.

It is not necessarily in the public interest to publish what interests the public.[44] A laxer view is taken in the United States, where public officials,[45] or even persons in the public eye,[46] must prove actual malice in an action for a libel on their public life. In England a Report published by Justice,[47] and written by a sub-committee of lawyers and journalists,[48] proposed that the Press should be given a new qualified privilege for statements based upon information which might reason-

---

[34] If fair comment can be pleaded, the widest latitude is given to the critic: *Doyle* v. *Economist Newspaper* [1980] N.I. 171, 179.

[35] As to which, see above, § 8.15.

[36] *Truth (N.Z.) Ltd.* v. *Holloway* [1960] N.Z.L.R. 69, 83.

[37] *Turner* v. *M.-G.-M. Pictures Ltd.* [1950] All E.R. 449, see Also R. Churchill, *What I Said About the Press* (London, 1957).

[38] *Loveday* v. *Sun Newspapers Ltd.* (1938) 59 C.L.R. 503, 513.

[39] *Truth (N.Z.) Ltd.* v. *Holloway* [1960] N.Z.L.R. 69. (The ruling was not challenged on appeal to the J.C: [1960] 1 W.L.R. 997.); *Doyle* v. *Economist Newspaper Ltd.* [1980] N.I. 171, 179.

[40] See *Russell* v. *Norfolk (Duke of)* [1949] 1 All E.R. 109; *Green* v. *Blake* [1948] I.R.R. 242; Lloyd, "The Disciplinary Powers of Professional Bodies" (1950) 13 M.L.R. 281, 297–299.

[41] *Chapman* v. *Ellesmere (Lord)* [1932] 2 K.B 431, 474–475, *per* Romer L.J.

[42] [1932] 2 K.B. 431.

[43] The report would now be privileged under the Defamation Act 1952; see above § 8.12.

[44] *London Artists Ltd.* v. *Littler* [1968] 1 W.L.R. 607, 615.

[45] *New York Times* v. *Sullivan*, 376 U.S. 245 (1964).

[46] *Curtis Publishing Co.* v. *Butts*, 87 S.Ct. 1975 (1967).

[47] *The Law and the Press* (London, 1965).

[48] One of whom later changed his mind.

ably be believed to be true, provided that the defendant published a reasonable statement from the plaintiff by way of explanation if so requested, and, if necessary, an apology. Outside the media the Report was not well received either in Parliament,[49] or by the Faulks Committee.[50]

Presence of uninterested persons

No publication, however, which is reasonably necessary for the effective use of the defendant's privilege amounts to an excess of it. Another way of putting this point is to say that there is an ancillary privilege for such incidental but necessary publications.[51] So as under current business practice the reasonable and ordinary way of getting a document written and despatched to its addressee is to dictate it to a typist, the publication of its defamatory contents to the typist attracts the same privilege as its subsequent publication to the addressee.[52] But in a business communication containing a very serious allegation against a man's character more care ought to be taken in limiting the communication to the higher officials of a firm than in writing an ordinary business letter.[53] The business of life could not well be carried on if unnecessary restraints were imposed on these communications. As the plaintiff has an interest in hearing the charges made against him there can be no doubt that the occasion is privileged, even though the statement is made to the plaintiff himself and so could not by itself have given him a cause of action.[54]

§ 8.18. JOINT LIABILITY

It is clear that the agents through whom a person properly publishes a privileged communication are themselves covered by the like privilege: for example, a printer who prints a privileged document, the printing of which is not an excess of privilege, or a solicitor who in the course of his duty towards his client publishes a statement which that client is privileged to publish.[55] It is not so clear what the position is if one (or more) of the co-defendants is inspired by malice. Does this defeat the privilege of his co-defendants? The earlier case of *Smith* v. *Streatfield*,[56] in which it was held that it did, was overruled by *Egger* v. *Chelmsford (Vis-*

---

[49] In 274 H.L.Deb., col. 1371 Lord Goodman said that "the frequent assertion that newspapers have in their archives hundreds of files which would reveal dreadful goings-on has never been established to the satisfaction of any conscientious witness."
[50] Cmnd. 5909, § 211.
[51] *Bryanston Finance Ltd.* v. *de Vries* [1975] 1 Q.B. 703.
[52] *Bryanston Finance Ltd.* v. *de Vries* [1975] 1.Q.B. 703, 727.
[53] *Roff* v. *British and French Chemical Co.* [1918] 2 K.B. 677, 684.
[54] It is submitted that the decision of the Court of Appeal to the contrary in *White* v. *Stone (J. & F.) Ltd.* [1939] 2 K.B. 827, is based upon a mistaken view of the authorities: see Goodhart, "Defamatory Statements and Privileged Occasions" (1940) 56 L.Q.R. 262.
[55] *Baker* v. *Carrick* [1894] 1 Q.B. 838.
[56] [1913] 3 K.B. 764.

count),[57] in which four of the 11 defendants to a libel action against whom malice had not been found appealed successfully against a judgment that they were infected by the malice of the other seven defendants. Three of the four successful appellants each had an original privilege of his own, distinct from that of the others, and so far the decision can hardly be criticised. But the fourth appellant was the secretary of the defendants' committee. He too was successful, either on the narrow ground that such a person has an independent privilege, which arises whenever the official mouthpiece of a quasi-judicial body communicates its decisions, or on the wider ground that no man ought to be responsible for the malice of another except in cases of vicarious liability.[58] It is not easy to reconcile this broad ground with the view that it is the occasion, rather than the person, which is the subject of privilege,[59] but *Egger* v. *Chelmsford* has been followed.[60] It is uncertain whether the principle in *Egger* v. *Chelmsford* extends to Fair Comment as well as Privilege, but probably it does.[61]

§ 8.19. FAIR COMMENT[62]

A fair comment on a matter which is of public interest or is submitted to public criticism is not actionable. This right is one of the aspects of the fundamental principle of freedom of expression, and the courts are zealous to preserve it unimpaired.[63] "It must not be whittled down by legal refinements."[64] The jury are the guardians of the freedom of public comment as well as of private character. It is only on the strongest grounds that a court will set aside a verdict for a defendant when fair comment is pleaded.[65]

Comment or criticism must be carefully distinguished from a statement of fact. The former is not actionable if it relates to a matter which is of public interest; the latter is actionable, even though the facts so stated would, if true, have possessed the greatest public interest and importance. Comment or criticism is essentially a statement of opinion as to

---

[57] [1965] 1 Q.B. 248. Yet it is worth noting that the House of Commons specifically refused to accept the recommendation of the porter Committee (paras. 127–132) to absolish the rule in *Smith* v. *Streatfield*: see H.C.Deb. Stdg. Ctee. B., March 6, 1952. But "we have come after several years to find that the law is as Lord Porter's Committee recommended it should be": [1965] 1 Q.B. 248, 265, *per* Lord Denning M.R., although the Porter Committee (para. 132) (unlike Lord Denning) insisted that there must not be negligence in failing to know of the other's malice.

[58] The view favoured by Lord Denning and Harman L.J. (but not Davies L.J.) in *Egger* v. *Chelmsford* [1965] 1 Q.B. 248, 263.

[59] See above, §8.9.

[60] *Riddick* v. *TBM* [1977] Q.B. 881.

[61] Faulks Report, §261.

[62] See Johnston, "Uncertainties in the Defence of Fair Comment" (1978) 8 N.Z.U.L.R. 359 (one of the few academic articles on this topic).

[63] *Kemsley* v. *Foot* [1951] 2 K.B. 34, 45–47. See the history of the defence discussed by Diplock, K.C., in [1952] A.C. 345, 349.

[64] *Slim* v. *Daily Telegraph Ltd.* [1968] 2 Q.B. 157, 170, *per* Lord Denning M.R.

[65] *Odger* v. *Mortimer* (1873) 23 L.T. 472.

the estimate to be formed of a man's writings or actions.[66] Being therefore a mere matter of opinion, and so incapable of definite proof, he who expresses it is not called upon by the law to justify it as being true, but is allowed to express it, even though others disagree with it, provided that it is honest.

Nature of defence

Salmond held the view that fair comment is simply an instance of qualified privilege.[67] Although this view has the support of Willes J.,[68] there is considerable authority in favour of another view, which may be expressed as follows: The defence of fair comment is a denial of the libel, a traverse of the allegation in the statement of claim[70] the defence of privilege is an admission of the libel, but a claim that it was published in such circumstances as afford the defendant an immunity from the ordinary consequences of publishing a libel, a plea in confession and avoidance. "A privileged occasion is one on which the privileged person is entitled to do something which no one who is not within the privilege is entitled to do on that occasion. A person in such a position may say or write about another person things which no other person in the kingdom can be allowed to say or write. But, in the case of a criticism upon a published work, every person is entitled to do and is forbidden to do exactly the same things, and therefore the occasion is not privileged."[71] Therefore, the question to be put to the jury is, not whether the article is privileged, but whether it is or is not libel.

Yet if there are two criticisms of a book by different writers, both couched in similar terms, and each being on its face fair comment, it seems difficult to say that one exceeds the limit of fair comment, if the writer of it is actuated by malice against the author, whereas the other does not exceed those limits because the writer is not so actuated. But this is the law. For the Court of Appeal held in *Thomas v.Bradbury, Agnew & Co. Ltd.*,[72] and it has since been accepted in the House of Lords,[73] that express malice will destroy a plea of fair comment. In any event there are two admitted differences between the defence of fair comment and the defence of qualified privilege. If the publication was upon a privileged occasion, the burden is upon the plaintiff to prove express malice; the defendant, on the other hand, has first the burden of showing that a comment is fair before the burden of proving malice is cast back upon the plaintiff.[74] On the other hand, the plaintiff who has

---

[66] Exceptionally, an inference of fact may be capable of being a comment: *Jeyeretnam* v. *Goh Chok Tong* [1989] 1 W.L.R. 1102.

[67] 6th ed., s.145(9).

[68] *Henwood* v. *Harrison* (1872) L.R. 7 C.P. 606, 625.

[69] *Telnikoff* v. *Matusevitch* [1990] 3 W.L.R. 725, 737.

[70] *Peter Walker & Son Ltd.* v. *Hodgson* [1909] 1 K.B. 239, 250.

[71] *Merivale* v. *Carson* (1887) 20 Q.B.D. 275, 280, *per* Lord Esher.

[72] [1906] 2 K.B. 627. This was the only successful libel action ever brought against the publishers of *Punch*. See the interesting account of the case by the defendants' counsel, A. Birrell, *Things Past Redress* (1937), pp. 161–162.

[73] *Sutherland* v. *Stopes* [1925] A.C. 47, 63–64.

[74] *Telnikoff* v. *Matusevitch* [1991] 3 W.L.R. 952, 959–962.

submitted his work or his acts to public criticism bears the onus of proving that a prima facie protected occasion is not in fact protected, whereas the defendant who relies upon a qualified privilege has affirmatively to prove the existence of the privilege.[75] Again, some instances of abuse of privilege (*e.g.* excessive publication) can have no application to the defence of fair comment.

§ 8.20. ELEMENTS OF FAIR COMMENT

The defence has three elements. It must be shown that the words complained of are (1) comment, (2) fair comment, and (3) fair comment on a matter of public interest.

(1) Comment and fact

It is essential to the plea of fair comment that the defamatory matter must appear on the face of it to be a comment and not a statement of fact. To come within a plea of fair comment the facts on which the comment is based must be stated or referred to and the imputation must appear as an expression of the defendant's opinion on those facts. It is a question for the jury (subject to the direction of the judge) whether the words, on their true construction in their context, amount to a positive statement of fact or an expression of opinion or an inference.[76] If they are the former they must be justified. If the defendant cannot justify them, then the only issue for the jury is the amount of damages.[77] Sometimes it is difficult to distinguish fact from comment or to decide how far the facts upon which comment is made have been set out or referred to in the alleged libel. In *Kemsley* v. *Foot*[78] the respondents had published an attack upon the conduct of one of Lord Beaverbrook's newspapers, with which the appellant, also a newspaper proprietor, had no connection, under the heading "Lower than Kemsley." It was argued that the plea of fair comment (as distinct from justification) was not open to the respondents because the subject-matter on which the comment "Lower than Kemsley"[79] was made was not indicated with sufficient particularity. But the House of Lords held that a sufficient substratum of fact could be found or indicated in the words complained of, namely, that Lord Kemsley was the active proprietor of and responsible for the Kemsley Press, which had a wide public circulation.[80]

The task of the critic in such a case would be impossible if he had to set out in detail the facts upon which his criticism was based.[81] It is true

---

[75] *Thomas* v. *Bradbury, Agnew & Co.* [1906] 2 K.B. 627, 640.
[76] *Jeyaretnam* v. *Goh Chok Tong* [1989] 1 W.L.R. 1109, 1113.
[77] As in *London Artists Ltd.* v. *Littler* [1969] 2 Q.B. 375.
[78] [1952] A.C. 345.
[79] "It is not in my opinion a statement of fact that a newspaper is low: it is a comment. It may be a statement of fact to say that a man is fraudulent, for there is a legal sanction for fraud, but there is no legal sanction for publishing low newspapers": [1952] A.C. 345, 361, *per* Lord Oaksey.
[80] The proceedings were eventually compromised: *The Times*, June 26, 1952.
[81] But in *Telnikoff* v. *Matusevitch* [1991] 3 W.L.R. 952, a majority of the H.L. interpreted *Kemsley* in a restrictive way.

that not all of those to whom the libel has been published will have read for themselves the issues of the periodical in question, but "its contents and conduct are open to comment on the ground that the public have at least the opportunity of ascertaining for themselves the subject-matter on which the comment is founded."[82] A similar principle applies to literary and artistic works submitted to the public: a critic is not shut out from the defence of fair comment because he has confined his remarks on, say, the first night of a new play to the words "This is a disgraceful production."[83] Although it is therefore not necessary for the defendant to have all the facts at the forefront of his mind, no man can comment upon future facts. The facts which form the basis of the comment must be in existence when the comment is made.[84]

(2) Fair comment on facts truly stated

Here there are three points to be considered: (i) the facts must be truly stated; (ii) the comment must be fair; (iii) imputations of corrupt or dishonourable motives must be warranted by the facts.

(i) The facts must be truly stated

The comment must not misstate facts: no comment can be fair which is build upon facts which are invented or misstated.[85] As Sir Alexander Cockburn C.J. once said: "To say that you may first libel a man, and then comment upon him is obviously absurd."[86] So when in a review of a play the defendant stated falsely that it contained an incident of adultery, his plea of fair comment failed.[87] originally it was necessary to show that every statement of fact in the words complained of (however minor or unimportant) was true. But now the Defamation Act 1952, s.6, provides that in an action for libel or slander in respect of words[88] consisting partly of allegations of fact and partly of expressions of opinion, a defence of fair comment shall not fail by reason only that the truth of every allegation of fact is not proved if the expression of opinion is fair comment having regard to such of the facts alleged or referred to in the words complained of as are proved. So now it is enough for the commentator to get his basic facts right.[89] It has been argued that this section has made a radical change in the law by conferring immunity in respect of unproved allegations of fact if the allegations of fact which are proved are sufficient to support the comment.[90] This was certainly not what the Porter Committee intended,[91] but it may well be what Parlia-

---

[82] [1952] A.C. 345, 355–356, *per* Lord Porter.
[83] *McQuire* v. *Western Morning News* [1903] 2 K.B. 100.
[84] *Cohen* v. *Daily Telegraph Ltd.* [1968] 1 W.L.R. 916.
[85] *Jeyaretnam* v. *Goh Chok Tong* [1989] 1 W.L.R. 1109, 1113.
[86] *R.* v. *Carden* (1879) 5 Q.B.D. 1, 8.
[87] *Merivale* v. *Carson* (1887) 20 Q.B.D. 275.
[88] As defined in s.16(1): see above, § 8.5.
[89] *London Artists Ltd.* v. *Littler* [1969] 2 Q.B. 375, 391.
[90] Gatley, *Libel*, p. 332.
[91] See para. 89 of the Report.

ment intended,[92] although whether it has succeeded in carrying that intention into effect is another matter. It is submitted that it has not,[93] and the defence of fair comment still protects only the comment, and not unjustified statements of fact.

The rolled-up plea. In view of the distinction thus drawn between comment and matter of fact, and in view of the circumstances that comment and fact are so frequently combined in the same statement, the plea of fair comment used to be formulated as to justify at the same time the statements of fact thus included in the allegations complained of. The usual form of such a plea was that "in so far as the statements complained of are statements of fact they are true in substance and in fact, and in so far as they consist of comment they are fair comment on a matter of public interest." Such a plea, known as the "rolled-up plea," was a plea of fair comment only, and not of justification coupled with a plea of fair comment.[94] Although this plea was not regarded by the courts with favour it was much used, for the defendant could not be compelled to give particulars of the facts which he proposed to prove at the trial in support of his plea.[95] But now the defendant may be required to furnish "particulars stating which of the words complained of he alleges are statements of fact and of the facts and matters he relies on in support of the allegation that the words are true."[96] But the plaintiff is not entitled to such particulars if the defendant does not plead the "rolled-up plea" but only the general plea of fair comment.[97] Then the defendant is only obliged to give particulars of the basic facts on which he relies in support of his plea.[98]

Comment and privileged statements of fact. If a statement of fact is itself privileged, and the subject-matter is one which is open to comment, the plea of fair comment is not excluded by the circumstance that the statement of fact on which the comment proceeds is erroneous. So it has been held that he who comments on the statements made by a witness in the box,[99] or contained in a parliamentary paper,[1] may plead fair comment, although the original statements are mistaken. But there is

---

[92] See Standing Committee B., H.C.Deb., March 6, 1952, cols, 846–855, and 500 H.C.Deb., col. 794.

[93] *London Artists Ltd.* v. *Littler* [1969] 2 Q.B. 375, 391.

[94] *Sutherland* v. *Stopes* [1925] A.C. 47, 62–63.

[95] For this would have been an indirect way of compelling him to specify which of the statements complained of were statements of fact and which expressions of opinion, and this is a question to be decided by the jury.

[96] R.S.C., Ord. 82, r.3.

[97] *Lord* v. *Sunday Telegraph Ltd.* [1971] 1 Q.B. 235.

[98] The defendant is not required to prove the truth of every fact so adduced; it is enough if he can establish sufficient facts to support the comment to the satisfaction of the jury: *Kemsley* v. *Foot* [1952] A.C. 345. "It is one thing to publish a defamatory statement of fact; it is quite another to allege a defamatory statement of fact in a pleading in order to show that a public comment was fair": *Kemsley* v. *Foot* [1952] A.C. 345, 361, *per* Lord Oaksey.

[99] *Grech* v. *Odhams Press Ltd.* [1958] 2 Q.B. 275, 285.

[1] *Cook* v. *Alexander* [1974] 1 Q.B. 279.

now a tendency to protect the public from irresponsible journalism, so that a court should be slow to permit such a plea,[2] and may even require the re-publisher to prove that his re-publication is fair and accurate.[2A]

(ii) The comment must be fair

It is settled since the decision of the Court of Appeal in *Thomas* v. *Bradbury, Agnew & Co.*[3] that a comment which is objectively and prima facie fair may become unfair if made with a malicious motive. The absence of any genuine belief in the truth of the comment is the strongest possible evidence of malice[4], for no man can have a proper motive for making defamatory statements which he does not believe to be justified. Even a comment genuinely believed to be true, however, will be actionable as unfair if it is inspired by any improper and malicious motive, though a court should be slow to draw such an inference.[5] It is sometimes said that comment is also to be classed as unfair, even in the absence of any dishonesty or malice, if the critic fails to show a certain degree of moderation, judgment and competence.[6] It is said that there is a certain measure of violence or perverseness on the part of a critic which will itself condemn his criticism as unfair and actionable. But this is not so. To apply any such test would mean that any jury would be at liberty to find a comment unfair simply because they did not agree with it and thought it unduly severe: it is of the highest importance to the community that the critic of literary or artistic matters should not have his work judged by the standard of "the man on the Clapham omnibus."[7] The violence, exaggeration or perverseness of a critic has not in itself any operation in making his criticism unfair, but is merely evidence that his criticism is not honest or that it is inspired by malice.[8] In *Turner* v. *M.-G.-M. Pictures Ltd.*[9] Lord Porter said he would adopt these words, "except that I would substitute 'honest' for 'fair' lest some suggestion of reasonableness instead of honesty should be read in." Perhaps it would be better if the defence was simply called Comment,[10] or if it were appreciated "that the question is not whether the comment

---

[2] *Austin* v. *Mirror Newspapers Ltd.* [1986] A.C. 299, 318.

[2A] *Brent Walker Group plc.* v. *Time Out Ltd.* [1991] Q.B. 33, 45.

[3] [1906] 2 K.B. 627. See above, § 8.19.

[4] *Telnikoff* v. *Matusevitch* [1991] 3 W.L.R. 959, 962.

[5] *Horrocks* v. *Lowe* [1975] A.C. 135, 150.

[6] *Wason* v. *Walter* (1868) L.R.4 Q.B. 73, 96.

[7] *McQuire* v. *Western Morning News* [1903] 2 K.B. 100, 109; *Turner* v. *M.-G.-M. Pictures Ltd.* [1950] 1 All E.R. 449, 475.

[8] *Merivale* v. *Carson* (1887) 20 Q.B.D. 275, 281, *per* Lord Esher. See also *Silkin* v. *Beaverbrook Newspapers Ltd.* [1958] 1 W.L.R. 743; the Faulks Report, § 177 and Duncan and Neill, *Defamation* (2nd ed.), § 12.4

[9] [1950] 1 All E.R. 449, 461. In *Lea* v. *Justice of the Peace Ltd.* (*sub nom. Privacy and the Press*, Butterworths, 1947) there is a valuable discussion between Hilbery J. and Sir Valentine Holmes, K.C., on the scope of the defences of justification and fair comment."*Holmes*: I have always thought that it is a tremendous misfortune, especially when you are trying to deal with lay clients, that a plea of fair comment is called fair comment, because it is so difficult to make a person understand that a comment which they think is grossly unfair may nevertheless be pefectly fair comment for the purpose of establishing a defence. *Hilbery*: It is easy for the lay mind to think that by 'fair comment' you mean 'moderate comment.' *Holmes*: Quite, my Lord."

[10] Faulks Report, § 177.

is fair in the ordinary sense of that word, but whether the words complained of can fairly be regarded as comment."[11]

(iii) Imputations of corrupt motives

A man's moral character is not a permissible subject of adverse comment, and this is so even though the person attacked occupies some public position which makes his character a matter of public interest. He who says or suggests that a person is dishonest, corrupt, immoral, untruthful, inspired by base and sordid motives, must either justify his accusation by proving it to be true, or show that the imputation is a correct inference from the facts commented on. It may be fair comment mistakenly to accuse an author of folly, but not to accuse him of vice; of want of dignity, but not of want of honesty; of incapacity, but not of corruption; of bad taste, but not of mendacity.[12] This important limitation upon the right of criticism was established in *Campbell* v. *Spottiswoode*,[13] in which it was held actionable to suggest, however honestly, that the editor of a religious magazine, in advocating a scheme for missions to the heathen, was in reality an imposter inspired by motives of pecuniary gain. Such comment goes outside the realm of criticism of the plaintiff in relation to the book, its subject-matter, or the plaintiff as an author.[14] "A writer in a public paper," said Sir Alexander Cockburn C.J.,[15] "may comment on the conduct of public men in the strongest terms; but if he imputes dishonesty, he must be prepared to justify."[16] Such a personal attack, therefore, is to be regarded as a defamatory statement of fact, and not as a mere comment. It is true that there is some authority for the view that it is enough for the defendant to prove that the attack was a reasonable inference from the proved facts,[17] but such a view runs counter to the whole nature of the defence.[18] If reasonableness is irrelevant in assessing the fairness of the comment, it should also be irrelevant here.

(3) What matters may be commented on

The right of comment is universal; there is full liberty to criticise all men and things of public interest, provided that the criticism is honest. Further, everyone is entitled to comment. A newspaper reporter or editor has the same rights as a private citizen, neither more nor less, so it does not matter whether the comment appears in a Sunday newspaper

---

[11] *Telnikoff* v. *Matusevitch* [1990] 3 W.L.R. 725, 734, *per* Lloyd L.J.

[12] But the "private life of a Member of Parliament may be material to his fitness to occupy his public office": *Lyle-Samuel* v. *Odhams Ltd.* [1920] 1 K.B. 135, 146, *per* Scrutton L.J. And literary productions can be criticised for their treatment of life and morals as freely as for bad writing: *Kemsley* v. *Foot* [1952] A.C. 345, 356.

[13] (1863) 3 B. & S. 769; 32 L.J.Q.B. 185.

[14] *Wilson* v. *Manawatu Daily Times Co. Ltd.* [1957] N.Z.L.R. 735, 742.

[15] *Campbell* v. *Spottiswoode* (1863) 32 L.J.Q.B. 185, 196, 199.

[16] Approved in *Greville* v. *Wiseman* [1967] N.Z.L.R. 795, 800.

[17] *Porter* v. *Mercury Newspapers Ltd.* [1964] Tas.S.R. 279.

[18] *Dakhyl* v. *Labouchère* [1908] 2 K.B. 325n., 329. See Duncan and Neill, *Defamation*, §§ 12, 25.

with an enormous circulation or in a private letter.[19] But it is only in a limited class of cases that there is any right to express one's own opinion honestly and fearlessly regardless of whether others can be induced to agree with it or not. The cases in which this right exists may be divided into two classes—namely, (i) matters of public interest or concern[20]; and (ii) matters which, although of no public interest, have been submitted to criticism by the persons concerned. In all other cases the defendant will be liable unless he can prove that the alleged libel is true not only in its allegations of fact but also in any comments made thereon.[21] He must justify both the facts and the comment.

(i) Matters of public interest or concern

For example, the administration of justice,[22] the conduct of the government and of public servants,[23] the mode in which local authorities and other public bodies perform their functions,[24] the management of public institutions,[25] or of a private business of large extent.[26] It makes no difference that the public interest in the matter in question is limited to a particular locality, instead of extending throughout the realm. That which is primarily of public interest to the citizens of Manchester is indirectly of public interest to all England.[27]

(ii) Matters submitted to public criticism by the persons concerned

He who voluntarily gives up his right of privacy by submitting himself or his deeds to public scrutiny and judgment must submit to the exercise of a right of public comment. This right, therefore, extends to books and every form of published literature, works of art publicly exhibited, and public musical or dramatic performances.[28] It should be noted that works of criticism are themselves submitted to public scrutiny and their subject-matter and style may thus in turn be criticised.[29]

Burden of proof

The burden of proving that a comment is fair is on the defendant. He must establish that the facts upon which the comment is based are true, and that the comment thereupon is warranted in the sense that it is

---

[19] *Silkin* v. *Beaverbrook Newspapers Ltd.* [1958] 1 W.L.R. 743, 746, See also above, § 8.11.

[20] *London Artists Ltd.* v. *Littler* [1969] 2 Q.B. 375.

[21] *Sutherland* v. *Stopes* [1925] A.C. 47, 62. "But that is not very good English, because I do not think a comment can ever be said to be true. It can only be said to be justified": Holmes, K.C., *arguendo* in *Lea* v. *Justice of the Peace Ltd.* (1947), *sub nom. Privacy and the Press*, 165. "True comment" presumably means comment which in the opinion of the court is warranted by the facts and well founded.

[22] *Hibbins* v. *Lee* (1864) 4 F. & F. 243 (conduct of magistrates). The law relating to contempt of court should here by borne in mind.

[23] *Henwood* v. *Harrison* (1872) L.R. 7 C.P. 606.

[24] *Purcell* v. *Sowler* (1877) 2 C.P.D. 215.

[25] *Cox* v. *Feeney* (1863) 4 F. & F. 13, 20.

[26] *London Artists Ltd.* v. *Littler* [1969] 2 Q.B. 375 (four West End theatres).

[27] *Purcell* v. *Sowler* (1877) 2 C.P.D. 215, 218.

[28] *Turner* v. *M.-G.-M. Pictures Ltd.* [1950] 1 All E.R. 449 (insensitive but honest comment on broadcast by film critic).

[29] *Turner* v. *M.-G.-M. Pictures Ltd.* [1950] 1 All E.R. 449.

such as might be made by a reasonable man. Once the defendant has established that in this sense the comment is fair, the onus is shifted to the plaintiff if he wishes to prove that the prima facie protection is displaced by the presence of malice in the defendant.[30] In other words, there is a two-stage test, the first being objective and the second subjective.[31]

It is a question for the jury whether the words are statements of fact or expressions of opinion, and, if the latter, whether they are fair or not. But it is for the judge to decide in the first place (1) whether the words are capable of being statements of fact, (2) whether the subject is one which is in law open to comment, and (3) whether there is any reasonable evidence to go to the jury that the comment is unfair.[32]

Effect of malice of writer on printer[33]

We have seen that the printer of a privileged document may not be protected if the writer was actuated by malice.[34] The same rule applies to one who prints comment on a matter of public interest. Hence the editor of a literary journal who publishes a contributed article containing criticisms of the works of a living writer which he honestly agrees with may yet be liable for the malice which, unknown to him, has actuated the author of the article.[35] In practice, however, this will probably only occur when the plaintiff is aware of the identity of the contributor. For the Rules of Court,[36] provide that where a defendant, whether a newspaper or any ordinary person, pleads fair comment or qualified privilege no interrogatories as to the defendant's source of information or grounds of belief shall be allowed.[37] This "newspaper rule," as it has been called, is limited to interlocutory proceedings in actions for defamation, and does not extend to actions for breach of confidence.[38]

§ 8.21. Consent[39]

It is a defence that the plaintiff has expressly or impliedly consented to the publication complained of[40]—for example, in cases of slander the aggrieved party sometimes, perhaps rashly, invites the speaker "to repeat that before witnesses."

---

[30] *Jones* v. *Skelton* [1963] 1 W.L.R. 1362, 1378.

[31] *Telnikoff* v. *Matusevitch* [1990] 3 W.L.R. 725, 740, 743.

[32] *London Artists Ltd.* v. *Littler* [1969] 2 Q.B. 375.

[33] See Heeney, "Publishing the Defamatory Statements of Others" (1985) 59 A.L.J. 371.

[34] Above, § 8.17.

[35] See the example given by the Porter Committee, s.130.

[36] R.S.C., Ord. 82, r. 6. But note that a journalist has no general evidential privilege entitling him not to answer questions: *X Ltd.* v. *Morgan-Grampian (Publishers) Ltd.* [1991] 1 A.C. 1, 47.

[37] This also prohibits interrogatories as to the defendant's actual information and knowledge: *Adams* v. *Sunday Pictorial Newspapers (1920) Ltd.* [1951] 1 K.B. 354.

[38] *British Steel Corporation* v. *Granada Television* [1981] A.C. 1096.

[39] See Boberg, "Defence of Consent in a Defamation Action" (1961) 78 S.A.L.J. 54.

[40] *Collerton* v. *Maclean* [1962] N.Z.L.R. 1045.

§ 8.22. APOLOGY[41]

The offer or the making of an apology is in general no defence to an action for libel, although it may be given in evidence in mitigation of damages.[42] But by section 2 of the Libel Act 1843, in actions for a libel contained in a public newspaper or periodical the defendant may plead that it was inserted without actual malice and without gross negligence and that before the commencement of the action or at the earliest opportunity afterwards he inserted in the newspaper or periodical a full apology, or, if the periodical is ordinarily published at intervals exceeding one week, had offered to publish such apology in any newspaper or periodical selected by the plaintiff. Every such defence must be accompanied by a payment of money into court by way of amends.[43] Although neither the fact nor the amount of the payment into court must be disclosed to the jury,[44] it seems to be the practice to disclose both in the pleadings. But in practice little use is made of this defence, for if any branch of it fails, the plaintiff must succeed in the action, damages are assessed without regard to the payment into court and the defendant is liable for the whole costs of the action.[45] In any event, the provisions of section 4 of the Defamation Act 1952, now afford wider protection in appropriate cases.

§ 8.23. SLANDER ACTIONABLE PER SE[46]

In the following cases slander is actionable *per se* without proof of special damage:
    (1) An imputation that the plaintiff has committed a criminal offence;
    (2) An imputation that the plaintiff suffers from an existing contagious or infectious disease;
    (3) An imputation of unchastity against a woman;
    (4) An imputation against the plaintiff in the way of his business or office.

(1) Imputation of criminal offence

An imputation of a criminal offence to be actionable *per se* must amount to a direct charge, and must not be a mere suggestion or statement of suspicion.[47] The crime charged need not be indictable; but it must amount to an offence punishable with imprisonment in the first instance and not be an offence punishable by fine merely, even though

---

[41] See Fleming, "Retraction and Reply" (1978) 12 U.B.C. Law Rev. 15.
[42] See below, § 8.25.
[43] Libel Act 1845, s.2.
[44] *Joyce* v. *Beaverbrook Newspapers Ltd.* [1959] Ir.Jur.Rep.20.
[45] See *Bell* v. *Northern Constitution* [1943] N.I. 108. The better procedure is to pay a sum of money into court and plead the apology in mitigation of damages: Duncan and Neill, *Defamation*, § 16.09.
[46] See above, § 8.1.
[47] *Simmons* v. *Mitchell* (1880) 6 App. Cas.156.

there is power to imprison in default of payment of the fine.[48] It seems[49] that the basis of this rule is not that the words put the person defamed in jeopardy of a criminal prosecution, but that other people are likely to shun and avoid a person guilty of the conduct alleged.[50] So it is actionable *per se* to say of a man that he is "a convicted person," even though such an allegation does not put him in jeopardy of a prosecution.[51] It would seem to follow that a slander imputing to a corporation the commission of a criminal offence which in the case of a natural person would be punishable with imprisonment is actionable *per se*.[52]

(2) An imputation that the plaintiff suffers from an existing contagious or infectious disease

Here again the basis of the rule is that the imputation is likely to cause other persons to shun the plaintiff. The diseases included are veneral disease.[53] leprosy or plague,[54] and probably any contagious skin complaint caused by personal uncleanliness.[55] Perhaps today AIDS is included.

(3) Accusation of unchastity

At common law a verbal imputation of unchastity was not actionable *per se*, but it is now provided by the Slander of Women Act 1891, s.1 that words spoken and published which impute unchastity or adultery to any woman or girl shall not require special damage to render them actionable.[56] The plaintiff cannot recover more costs than damages unless the judge certifies at the end of, or after[57] the trial that there was reasonable ground for bringing the action.

(4) Imputations in respect of profession, business, or office

Any defamatory imputation upon a man in the way of his profession, business, or office is actionable *per se*: for example, a charge of insolvency against a trader,[58] of incompetence against a surgeon, of ignorance against a lawyer. This is so however humble the profession or calling. A defamatory charge, however, against a man in respect of a business in which he is no longer engaged, or in respect of an office

---

[48] *Ormiston* v. *G.W. Ry.* [1917] 1 K.B. 598, 601. ("You have been travelling First Class with a Third Class ticket.")

[49] *Gray* v. *Jones* [1939] 1 All E.R. 798.

[50] Gatley *Libel*, p.84.

[51] *Gray* v. *Jones* [1939] 1 All E.R. 798.

[52] The point was left open by the C.A. in *D. & L. Caterers Ltd.* v. *D'Ajou* [1945] K.B. 364.

[53] *Houseman* v. *Coulson* [1948] 2 D.L.R. 62.

[54] See the old cases cited in Gatley, *Libel*, p. 90.

[55] Porter Committee's Report, para. 45.

[56] In *Youssoupoff* v. *Metro-Goldwyn-Mayer Pictures* (1934) *The Times*, March 6, p.5, Avory J. said *obiter* that it was an attack upon a woman's chastity to say that she had been raped. And in the C.A. Scrutton L.J. seems to have been of the same opinion, but Slesser L.J. expressed no opinion: (1934) 50 T.L.R. 581, 584, 587. Unchastity includes lesbianism: *Kerr* v. *Kennedy* [1942] 1 K.B. 409.

[57] *Russo* v. *Cole* [1966] 1 W.L.R. 248.

[58] *Brown* v. *Smith* (1853) 13 C.B. 596.

which he no longer holds, is not actionable *per se*.[59] At common law a charge was not actionable *per se* merely because it tended to injure the plaintiff in the way of his business or office; it must have amounted to a charge against him in relation to his business or office. Thus, it was not actionable *per se* to impute dishonesty to a solicitor, unless he was alleged to be dishonest towards his clients.[60] Nor was it actionable *per se* to impute immoral conduct to a schoolmaster except in the way of his business.[61] These cases show that the common law was capable of giving rise to serious injustice.[62] But now the Defamation Act 1952, s.2, in accordance with the recommendation of the Porter Committee, provides that in an action for slander in respect of words[63] calculated to disparage the plaintiff[64] in any office, profession, calling, trade or business held or carried on by him at the time of the publication,[65] it shall not be necessary to allege or prove special damage, whether or not the words are spoken of the plaintiff in the way of his office, profession, calling, trade or business. It was once thought not[66] actionable *per se* to say of a workman that he is not a member of a trade union, but today a different view might be held.

§ 8.24. SLANDER: SPECIAL DAMAGE

In all other cases of slander the plaintiff must plead and prove that he has suffered special damage as the natural and probable result of the publication of the defamatory matter. This is so, however disgraceful the imputation and however certain it may be that it will damage the reputation of the plaintiff.[67] The special damage required in actions for slander must be the loss of some definite material advantage; it must not consist merely in the loss of reputation itself.[68] Actual damage might be a more accurate term. A loss of the voluntary hospitality of friends is sufficient, however,[69] and so also in all probability is a resulting separation between husband and wife.[70] Further, when special damage is proved, damages can be recovered not merely for it but for the injury to the plaintiff's reputation generally—*i.e.* compensation is

---

[59] *Hopwood* v. *Thorn* (1849) 8 C.B. 293. A man may conduct several professions simultaneously: *Bull* v. *Vazquez* [1947] 1 All E.R. 334.

[60] *Hopwood* v. *Muirson* [1945] K.B.313.

[61] *Jones* v. *Jones* [1916] 2 A.C. 481.

[62] See also the examples given by Earl Jowitt in 177 H.L.Deb. 5s., col. 1103.

[63] As defined in s.16(1): see above, §8.1.

[64] This will include a corporation (*D. & L. Caterers Ltd.* v. *D'Ajou* [1945] K.B. 210, 364).

[65] These words seem wide enough to include offices of honour as well as offices of profit. Before 1952 words imputing unfitness for (as distinct from lack of integrity in) an office of honour were not actionable *per se* unless, if true, they would be a ground for removal from the office. This distinction still exists: Gatley, *Libel*, p.94.

[66] *McMullan* v. *Mulhall* [1929] I.R. 470.

[67] *Jones* v. *Jones* [1916] 2 A.C. 481 (immoral conduct in a schoolmaster). But an allegation of cheating at cards imputes a criminal offence: hence the plaintiff in the *Baccarat* case did not have to show special damage: *Gordon-Cumming* v. *Green* (1891) 7 T.L.R. 408.

[68] *Roberts* v. *Roberts* (1864) 5 B. & S.384.

[69] *Davies* v. *Solomon* (1871) L.R. 7 Q.B. 112. But not loss merely of the society of one's friends: *Palmer* v. *Solmes* (1880) 30 U.C.C.P. 481.

[70] *Best* v. *Samuel Fox & Co. Ltd.* [1952] A.C. 716, 732.

not limited to the amount of actual loss proved, although proof of some actual loss is an essential foundation for a claim for general damages.

Special damage must not be too remote. But the law of causation in defamation does not differ from that in other torts.[71] It was once thought that damage immediately caused by the illegal act of a third party—*e.g.* his dismissal of the plaintiff from his employment was too remote. But it is submitted that today the test is whether the consequences in question is the natural and reasonable result of the defendant's words,[72] so that the dismissal of the plaintiff may in an appropriate case constitute special damage, whether it be wrongful or not.[73] Again, although it was once held[74] that illness resulting from mental trouble produced by slander was too remote, now the decision is questionable in view of modern developments in the law relating to nervous shock.[75]

There was one thought to be a rule that special damage is too remote if it is due not to the original slander, but to a repetition of it by other persons.[76] But it is now held that it is always a question of fact whether the repetition was the intended or foreseeable result of the original publication.[77]

§ 8.25. DAMAGES

(1) General principles of assessment

The spectrum of awards ranges from contemptuous damages of $\frac{1}{2}$p[78] to exemplary damages of scores of thousands of pounds.[79] In the 1980s juries began to award very large sums, mainly against media defendants.[80] The amount of money at stake, combined with the complexity of the law of libel, has resulted in some lengthy trials.[81] Some material injury to reputation must be proved: mere mental suffering is not an object of compensation.[82] Otherwise almost the only guidance is the vague principle that the award must be reasonable and moderate.[83] A jury is the constitutional tribunal for assessing the proper sum to be paid for an attack on the reputation of a fellow-citizen, particularly on

---

[71] *Slipper* v. *British Broadcasting Corporation* [1991] 1 Q.B. 283.
[72] *Chamberlain* v. *Boyd* (1883) 11 Q.B.D. 407.
[73] *Speake* v. *Hughes* [1904] 1 K.B. 138; *Longdon-Griffiths* v. *Smith* [1950] 2 All E.R. 662, 678 (not in [1951] 1 K.B. 295).
[74] *Allsop* v. *Allsop* (1860) 5 H. & N. 534.
[75] *Rigby* v. *Mirror Newspapers Ltd.* [1964] S.R. (N.S.W.) 34.
[76] *Weld-Blundell* v. *Stephens* [1920] A.C. 956.
[77] *Slipper* v. *British Broadcasting Corporation* [1991] 1 Q.B. 283.
[78] As in *Bloom* v. *News of the World* (1977), *Daily Telegraph*, March 11.
[79] As in *Cassell & Co. Ltd.* v. *Broome* [1972] A.C. 1027.
[80] But the highest award of £1.5 million was against non-media defendants: *Aldington* v. *Tolstoy and Watt, The Times*, December 1, 1989.
[81] So in *Gee* v. *Rantzen & B.B.C.* the trial lasted 87 days before the defendants agreed to pay the plaintiff £75,000 in damages and estimated costs of £1 million (*The Times*, February 21, 1986). But in *Warren* v. *Daily Mirror, The Times*, June 26, 1990, the trial lasted only two hours, and the jury retired for only 25 minutes before awarding £10,000.
[82] *Wheeler* v. *Somerfield* [1966] 2 Q.B. 94, 104.
[83] *Lewis* v. *Daily Telegraph Ltd.* [1964] A.C. 234.

one in a public position, such as a politician,[84] and within wide limits its award will not be interfered with by an appellate court.[85] All matters relating to the mode of publication, the circumstances of the parties, and the conduct of the defence (e.g. a failure to apologise, or bullying tactics by counsel[86]) can be considered. If the trial is before a judge without a jury, it was once thought that the award could be reduced by reason of the fact that the judge could use his tongue to exonerate the plaintiff or excoriate the defendant, but this is no longer the law.[87] The plaintiff may recover not only the estimated amount of his past and future losses but also, "in case the libel, driven underground, emerges from its lurking place at some future date, he must be able to point to a sum awarded by a jury sufficient to convince a bystander of the baselessness of the charge."[88]

There is power to award exemplary damages when the defendant has calculated that the publication of the libel will bring him in a profit which will exceed any damages which a court may order him to pay to the plaintiff.[89] This does not mean that a newspaper will be liable to have punitive damages awarded against it merely because its circulation increases after an attack on a public figure, but only if there is evidence of a cold and cynical[90] or reckless[91] attempt to increase circulation at the expense of the plaintiff's reputation. But in practice the scope of compensatory damages is wide enough to permit them to be aggravated by the wounding, insulting or outrageous circumstances surrounding the publication of the libel.[92] In this way a remedy can be given for hurt feelings, although they are not a primary object of compensation.[93] There is, therefore, in England a distinction between conduct which shocks the plaintiff (aggravated damages) and conduct which shocks the jury (exemplary damages).[94] This is not an example of parasitic damages: the award is permissible simply because the real damages are at large.[95]

---

[84] *Snyder* v. *Montreal Gazette Ltd.* (1978) 87 D.L.R.5 (which has three useful appendices, listing awards in different jurisdictions).

[85] See the emphatic judgments of the C.A. in *Sutcliffe* v. *Pressdram Ltd.* [1991] 1 Q.B. 153. But it was also held that an award of £600,000 "simply cannot be justified." The jury should have been given some guidance about the real value of such very large sums. In the Supreme Court Act 1981 s.69 Parliament impliedly recognised the sacrosanct nature of the jury's verdict in defamation cases, but s.8 of the Courts and Legal Services Act 1990 now provides for the Court of Appeal to be empowered by rules of court to substitute its own sum for the sum awarded by the jury instead of ordering a new trial.

[86] See *Greenlands Ltd.* v. *Wilmhurst* [1913] 3 K.B. 507, 532.

[87] *Associated Newspapers Ltd.* v. *Dingle* [1964] A.C. 371.

[88] *Cassell & Co. Ltd.* v. *Broome* [1972] A.C. 1027, 1071, *per* Lord Hailsham of St. Marylebone L.C.

[89] See below, §23.1.

[90] *Manson* v. *Associated Newspapers Ltd.* [1965] 1 W.L.R. 1038, 1043.

[91] *Cassell & Co. Ltd.* v. *Broome* [1972] A.C. 1027, 1079.

[92] *Ley* v. *Hamilton* (1935) 153 L.T. 384, 386.

[93] *Wheeler* v. *Somerfield* [1966] 2 Q.B. 94. As Tennyson wrote in *Locksley Hall*, "But the jingling of the guinea helps the hurt that Honour feels."

[94] *Broadway Approvals Ltd.* v. *Odhams Press Ltd.* [1965] 1 W.L.R. 805, 822.

[95] See below, § 23.1.

(2) Mitigation of damages

Several matters may be given in evidence in mitigation of damages.

1. Although an apology is no defence,[96] section 1 of the Libel Act 1843 provides that in any action for defamation the defendant may, provided he gives notice at the time of delivering his defence, give in evidence in mitigation of damages that he made or offered an apology before the commencement of he action or at the earliest opportunity afterwards if he had no opportunity before. No payment into court need be made.

2. The defendant, even though he does not plead justification, is entitled to adduce in mitigation of damages evidence of the plaintiff's general bad reputation prior to the publication of the libel. For since the plaintiff sues for an injury to his reputation, it is permissible for the defendant to prove in this way that such reputation was of little value. But the evidence is limited to general evidence as to the plaintiff's reputation, and to that reputation in the same sector of life; it does not include specific evidence of disreputable conduct or of rumours of such conduct, otherwise the position of the plaintiff would be intolerable. In other words, the defendant may prove that the plaintiff did have a bad reputation, not that he ought to have had one. The law is concerned with the plaintiff's reputation rather than with his disposition.[97] Yet the dividing line may be a fine one,[98] for sometimes a man's reputation rests upon specific incidents of some notoriety.[99] More often, however, a man's reputation is based upon the judgment of his fellows on his general life over a period of time before the publication of the libel in suit.[1] It also follows that a defendant cannot give in evidence in mitigation of damages the repetition of the same defamatory words by other persons contemporaneously with his publication.[2]

There is an exception to the general rule in the case of previous convictions, which are admissible provided that they are recent and relevant to the sector of the plaintiff's life which has been attacked. It would be outrageous if a person serving a sentence of 30 years' imprisonment for robbery should be able to sue for libel as if his character were unblemished.[3]

In the absence of any plea of justification, notice must be given to the plaintiff before trial of the defendant's intention to adduce such evidence in mitigation of damages and the particulars thereof.[4] If the plaintiff in a libel action gives evidence, he is, of course, subject to cross-examination as to credit like any other witness; but if he is cross-examined as to specific incidents, not mentioned in the particulars, and denies them, no further evidence can be called to rebuild his denials,

---

[96] Above, §8.22.
[97] *Plato Films Ltd.* v. *Speidel* [1961] A.C. 1090, 1131.
[98] See Faulks Report (Cmnd. 5909). § 365.
[99] *Waters* v. *Sunday Pictorial Newspapers Ltd.* [1961] 1 W.L.R. 967.
[1] *Associated Newspapers Ltd.* v. *Dingle* [1964] A.C. 371, 399, 406.
[2] *Associated Newspapers Ltd.* v. *Dingle* [1964] A.C. 371.
[3] *Goody* v. *Odhams Press Ltd.* [1967] 1 Q.B. 333 See now Civil Evidence Act 1968, s.13.
[4] Ord. 82, r.7.

and the cross-examination is not admissible to mitigate damages.[5] Where the plaintiff's own evidence or answers elicited in cross-examination show him to have been guilty of malpractices which are completely unconnected with the defamatory statement, the damages will not be reduced on the ground that his reputation is not all that it might have been.[6]

3. It is provided by the Defamation Act 1952, s.12, that in any action for libel or slander the defendant may give evidence in mitigation of damages that the plaintiff has recovered damages, or has brought actions for damages for libel or slander in respect of the publication of words to the same effect as the words on which the action is founded, or has received or agreed to receive compensation in respect of any such publication. But the defendant cannot get relief unless the plaintiff has chosen to sue more than one publisher: in this respect the ordinary law relating to joint tortfeasors[7] has not been followed. The jury should be told to consider how far the plaintiff's loss can be attributed solely to the libel with which they are concerned, and how far to the joint result of the two libels. They must be reminded that the plaintiff is not to be compensated twice for the same loss.[8] But it is irrelevant that the libel has been published elsewhere on a privileged occasion.[9]

4. Facts which tend to disprove malice may also be given in evidence.[10] Thus, the defendant may prove any facts which show that he never intended to refer to the plaintiff or did not intend the words to be understood in a defamatory sense,[11] or honestly believed that the statement was true,[12] or (conversely) that the statement was vague and sensational and believed by few or none of its readers.[13]

---

[5] *Scott* v. *Sampson* (1882) 8 Q.B.D. 491. "In the result, a libel action may resolve itself into a tactical battle in which the defendant adopts such manoeuvres as are likely to force the plaintiff into a position where he is compelled to go into the box and give some evidence—however little—in chief, so that there may be put to him in cross–examination as to credibility the very questions which are inadmissible in cross-examination on mitigation of damages under the rule in *Scott* v. *Sampson*". So the Porter Committee in para. 151, and lso Earl Jowitt, 178 H.L. Deb. 5s., col. 340. Parliament, however, did not change the law, (see Faulks Report, § 368) though the judge at the trial may discourage cross-examination of this kind: see Lord Denning in [1961] A.C. 1090, 1143.

[6] *Hobbs* v. *Tinling* [1929] 2 K.B.1.

[7] See below, §20.11.

[8] *Lewis* v. *Daily Telegraph Ltd.* [1964] A.C. 234, 261.

[9] *Associated Newspapers Ltd.* v. *Dingle* [1964] A.C. 371.

[10] Provided that the terms of Ord. 82, r. 7 are complied with.

[11] *Jones* v. *Hulton* [1909] 2 K.B. 444, 479.

[12] *Campbell* v. *Spottiswoode* (1863) 3 B. & S. 769, 781.

[13] *Morgan* v. *Odhams Press Ltd.* [1971] 1 W.L.R. 1239.

CHAPTER 9

NEGLIGENCE[1]

§ 9.1. INTRODUCTORY

Intention and negligence

In the law of torts, negligence has two meanings: (1) an independent tort, with which we shall deal in the succeeding sections of this chapter; (2) a mode of committing certain other torts—*e.g.* trespass or nuisance. In this latter sense negligence is carelessness. In some cases either negligence or wrongful intent is required by law as a condition of liability. Each involves a certain mental attitude of the defendant towards the consequences of his act. He intends those consequences when he foresees and desires them, has a reasonable prospect of being able to bring them about through his own volition, and therefore does the act in order that they may happen.[2] He is guilty of negligence, on the other hand, when he does not desire the consequences, and does not act in order to produce them, but is nevertheless indifferent or careless whether they happen or not, and therefore does not refrain from the act notwithstanding the risk that they may happen.[3] The wilful wrongdoer is he who desires to do harm; the negligent wrongdoer is he who does not sufficiently desire to avoid doing it. Negligence and wrongful intent are inconsistent and mutually exclusive states of mind. He who causes a result intentionally cannot also have caused it negligently, and vice versa.[4] The difficulty of this topic is due to some extent to the reluctance of English lawyers to generalise about their basic conceptions. There is no General Part in the common law as in the civil law. Three other factors have increased the confusion. First, the action of trespass today lies only if either intention or negligence is shown.[5] But secondly, the action of negligence lies not only for careless but also for intentional conduct[6] it would be no defence to such an action to plead that the conduct causing the harm amounted to a serious crime.[7] Thirdly, there is the constant citation of the misleading maxim, "a man must be taken to intend the natural and probable consequences of his act." The maxim is misleading because it confuses the proposition to be proved with the means of proving that proposition. "In fact people often intend some-

---

[1] See J. C. Smith, *Liability in Negligence* (1984): R. A. Buckley, *The Modern Law of Negligence* (1988); Charlesworth and Percy, *Negligence* (8th ed., 1990). The best historical account is in Baker, *Introduction to English Legal History*, Chap. 17.
[2] *Betty's Cafés Ltd.* v. *Phillips Furnishing Stores Ltd.* [1959] A.C. 20, 34.
[3] *Grill* v. *General Iron Screw Collier Co.* (1860) L.R. 1 C.P. 600.
[4] *Re Armstrong and State Rivers and Water Supply Commission* [1952] V.L.R. 187, 197. The judgment further explains that a man may intend consequences without desiring them, and contrariwise.
[5] See above, Chap. 7.
[6] *Paterson Zochonis Ltd.* v. *Merfarken Packaging Ltd.* [1986] 3 All E.R. 522.
[7] The habit of using "negligence" to describe a deliberate act is well established: *I.C.I. Ltd.* v. *Shatwell* [1965] A.C. 656, 672.

thing quite different from what they know to be the natural and probable result of what they are doing. To take a trivial example, if I say I intend to reach the green, people will believe me although we all know that the odds are ten to one against my succeeding; and no one but a lawyer would say that I must be presumed to have intended to put my ball in the bunker because that was the natural and probable result of my shot."[8] So also Lord Hailsham of St. Marylebone L.C. has expressed "the pious hope that your Lordships will not again have to decide that foresight and foreseeability are not the same thing as intention, although either may give rise to an irresistible inference of such."[9]

Inadvertence

Negligence is usually accompanied by inadvertence, but it is not the same thing, and this coincidence is not invariable.[10] Carelessness as to possible consequences very often results in a failure to bring those consequences to mind—*i.e.* inadvertence. Commonly, therefore, the careless person not only does not intend the consequence but does not even advert to it; its possibility or probability does not occur to his mind. But it is not always so, for there is such a thing as wilful—*i.e.* conscious and advertent—negligence. The wrongdoer may not desire or intend the consequence but may yet be perfectly conscious of the risk of it. He does not intentionally cause the harm but he intentionally and consciously exposes others to the risk of it. This has been described[11] as "an attitude of mental indifference to obvious risks."

Recklessness

The ordinary meaning of the word in the law of torts is a high degree of carelessness. It is the doing of something which in fact involves a grave risk to others, whether the doer realises it or not.[12] The test is therefore objective and not subjective, as it is in criminal law.[13]

§ 9.2. THE TORT OF NEGLIGENCE[14]

The decision of the House of Lords in *Donoghue* v. *Stevenson*[15] treats negligence, where there is a duty to take care, as a specific tort in itself,[16] and not simply as an element in some more complex relationship or in

---

[8] *Gollins* v. *Gollins* [1964] A.C. 644, 664, *per* Lord Reid.

[9] *R.* v. *Moloney* [1985] A.C. 905, 913.

[10] *Hicks* v. *British Transport Commission* [1958] 1 W.L.R. 493, 503.

[11] *Hudston* v. *Viney* [1921] 1 Ch. 98, 104, *per* Eve J. The attitude of the defendant in *Vaughan* v. *Menlove* (1837) 3 Bing. N.C. 468 (see below, § 9.11) is a very good example of this.

[12] *Shawinigan* v. *Vokins* [1961] 1 W.L.R. 1206, 1214; *Donovan* v. *Landy's Ltd.* [1963] I.R. 441, 461 ("the best and most realistic test").

[13] *R.* v. *Lawrence* [1982] A.C. 510.

[14] See Pritchard, "*Scott* v. *Shepherd* and the Emergence of the Tort of Negligence" (Selden Society, 1976).

[15] [1932] A.C. 562.

[16] It may be asked why Intention is not a tort if Negligence is one. The answer is that some forms of intentional harm have already been given specific names—*e.g.* trespass, deceit, conspiracy. But general liability for Intention has been suggested: above, Chap. 3

some specialised breach of duty.[17] Actions do not lie for a state of mind. Negligence is conduct, not a state of mind—conduct which involves an unreasonably great risk of causing damage. There is no necessary element of "fault" in the sense of moral blameworthiness involved in a finding that a defendant has been negligent.[18] It is negligence in the objective sense that is referred to in the well-known definition of Alderson B.[19]

> "Negligence is the omission to do something which a reasonable man, guided upon those considerations which ordinarily regulate the conduct of human affairs, would do, or doing something which a prudent and reasonable man would not do."[20]

So also Lord Wright said[21]:

> "In strict legal analysis, negligence means more than heedless or careless conduct, whether in omission or commission: it properly connotes the complex concept of duty, breach and damage thereby suffered by the person to whom the duty was owing."

It is worth noting that it is erroneous, although usual, to speak of injuries being caused by negligence: injuries do not result from legal concepts, but from acts or omissions which may involve or constitute negligence.[22]

Carelessness and negligence

Lord Wright's analysis is logically correct, but it does not avoid the need for looking at the tort of negligence as a whole: the three elements of duty, breach and damage may penetrate one another.[23] But it is clear that it is not enough for the plaintiff to establish that the defendant has been careless: he must establish that the defendant has been careless in breach of a specific legal duty to take care. "In most situations it is better to be careful than careless, but it is quite another thing to elevate all carelessness into a tort."[24] It is "a most vicious and elliptical habit,"[25] but one which it is only too easy to acquire, "by transporting the word 'car-

---

[17] *Grant* v. *Australian Knitting Mills* [1936] A.C. 85, 103.
[18] *Workington Harbour and Dock Board* v. *SS. Towerfield (Owners)* [1951] A.C. 112, 160. See also above, Chap. 2.
[19] *Blyth* v. *Birmingham Waterworks Co.* (1856) 11 Exch. 781, 784.
[20] "The avalanche of cases since then has not buried that simple statement: and nothing that has been said in them has bettered it": *Munnings* v. *Hydro-Electric Commission* [1971] A.L.R. 609, 622, *per* Windeyer J.
[21] *Lochgelly Iron and Coal Co.* v. *M'Mullan* [1934] A.C. 1, 25.
[22] *Central Asbestos Co. Ltd.* v. *Dodd* [1973] A.C. 518, 546–547.
[23] *Dorset Yacht Co. Ltd.* v. *Home Office* [1970] A.C. 1004, 1052.
[24] *Moorgate Mercantile Co. Ltd.* v. *Twitchings* [1977] A.C. 890, 919, *per* Lord Edmund-Davies.
[25] *Jones* v. *Vauxhall Motors* [1955] 1 Lloyd's Rep. 152, 153, *per* Stable J.

eless' into 'negligent' to dismiss from one's mind the essential problem—namely, whether or not there was in any particular case a failure
of duty."[26]

Duty of care and standard of care

The concept of reasonable foresight is used in seeking the answer to
at least two distinct questions: was the defendant under any duty of
care at all, and, if so, did he observe the standard required in the circumstances of the case? It is not surprising, therefore, to find some confusion in the language of the cases—one judgment describing as breach
of a duty the identical conduct which another judgment described as
breach of the requisite standard of care.[27] Sometimes this can be
explained by a difference of approach.[28] On the whole it seems preferable to reserve the term "duty" for the relation between parties which
imposes on one a legal obligation for the benefit of the other and to deal
with particular conduct in terms of a legal standard of what is required
to meet the obligation.[29] Confusion has also been caused by semantic
refinements of the concept of foreseeability—"very likely," "not
improbable", etc.

Duty of care and remoteness of damage

Confusion has also arisen from the fact that the concept of reasonable
foresight is relevant not only in testing the existence of a duty, *i.e.* to the
question of culpability and not of compensation, but also in cases of
admitted negligence (when the duty and its breach are admitted) to the
question of remoteness of damage, *i.e.* of compensation and not of culpability. This source of confusion was particularly prevalent when the
test of remoteness was directness and the test of duty was reasonable
foresight.[30] But it is now settled that foresight is the test both for duty
and for remoteness.[31] There may be difficulty in deciding whether the
events which have occurred differ in kind or only in degree from those
which ought reasonably to have been foreseen and guarded against,[32]
but this is a question of fact and not of law.

---

[26] *Sharp* v. *Avery* [1938] 4 All E.R. 85, 88, *per* Slesser L.J.
[27] As Holmes long ago pointed out (*Common Law*, p. 111) "the featureless generality, that
the defendant was bound to use such care as a prudent man would do under the circumstances, ought to be continually giving place to the specific one, that he was bound
to use this or that precaution." Hence the temptation to say that he is under a duty to
take such a precaution. The Occupiers' Liability Act 1957 (below, Chap. 11) imposes a
"common duty duty of care" which is really a standard.
[28] *Insurance Commissioner* v. *Joyce* (1948) 77 C.L.R. 39, 57, *per* Dixon J.
[29] Prosser, *Torts* (4th ed.), p. 334.
[30] See *Woods* v. *Duncan* [1946] A.C. 401.
[31] *The Wagon Mound (No. 1)* [1961] A.C. 388; *The Wagon Mound (No. 2)* [1967] 1 A.C. 617.
[32] The contrast between *Hughes* v. *Lord Advocate* [1963] A.C. 837 and *Doughty* v. *Turner
Manufacturing Co. Ltd.* [1964] 1 Q.B. 518 is a good example: see below, § 9.12.

Two functions of reasonable foreseeability

Some confusion has also arisen from a failure to distinguish clearly between two very different functions of the concept of reasonable foreseeability. First, it may be used as a test of whether a new duty should be added to the existing list of admitted duties; secondly, it may be used as a test of the scope or extent of an admitted duty.[33] It is particularly important to make this distinction as it does not follow that because the neighbour principle[34] is adopted in admitting a new duty into the law that the duty itself must be phrased in terms of reasonable foreseeability. The simplest illustration of this point is Lord Atkin's own judgment in *Donoghue* v. *Stevenson*: he created a new duty and adduced the neighbour principle as his authority for doing so; but the duty itself is, as we shall see, formulated in language chosen with the greatest precision. It would be a strange reasonable man who could comprehend all its implications without instruction from a lawyer.[35] In comparatively straightforward cases of negligence, however, the scope or extent of the duty of care which the defendant admittedly owes to the plaintiff is often formulated simply in terms of reasonable foreseeability. This is the duty owed, for example, by those who operate motor-vehicles on the highway.[36]

Nature of the interest infringed

It is a characteristic of the definition of the tort of negligence that it does not refer to the scope of the protection it affords to the plaintiff but rather to the qualities of blameworthiness or fault to be attributed to the conduct of the defendant. The position is precisely the reverse in torts such as defamation or conversion: the mere enunciation of the name at once indicates the nature of the interest which the plaintiff claims to have been invaded by the defendant's conduct. A failure to remember that the nature of the plaintiff's interest is a relevant factor has been responsible for some confusion, as we shall see when we consider liability for economic loss, and for nervous shock. Yet a moment's reflection shows how vital this factor is in a legal system which retains the concept of duty of care. For a duty is a notional pattern of conduct,[37] and such a pattern can take shape in the mind only after a consideration of the person on whom the obligation is imposed, the mode of its performance, the person to whom it is owed, and the nature of the interest protected.[38]

---

[33] See *McPhail* v. *Lanarkshire C.C.* 1951 S.C. 301, 319; *Ward* v. *McMaster* [1985] I.R. 29, 43.

[34] See below, § 9.3.

[35] So Denning L.J. in his well-known dissenting judgment in *Candler* v. *Crane, Christmas & Co.* [1951] 2 K.B. 164, invoked the neighbour principle for the purpose of showing that the court should admit a new duty into the law—but he was careful to formulate the duty itself in terms which owe little or nothing to reasonable foreseeability.

[36] See below, § 9.12.

[37] Dias [1955] C.L.J. 198, 202.

[38] It should be noted that a negligent act may infringe two distinct interests of the one plaintiff, as in *Brunsden* v. *Humphrey* (1884) 14 Q.B.D. 141 (see below, Chap. 25).

§ 9.3. NATURE OF THE DUTY OF CARE

It is a question of law whether in any particular circumstances a duty of care exists. Before 1932 there was no general principle.[39] The law had been built up in disconnected slabs[40] exhibiting no organic unity of structure.[41] In 1932 an attempt was made in the House of Lords in *Donoghue* v. *Stevenson*[42] to formulate some general criterion for the existence of the proximity which would give rise to a duty of care. The pursuer, Mrs May Donoghue, averred that she had suffered injury as a result of seeing and drinking the contaminated contents of a bottle of ginger beer manufactured by the respondent and bought from him by Minghella, the owner of the Wellmeadow Cafe, Paisley, from whom in turn it had been bought by a friend of the pursuer. The House of Lords, by a bare majority, held that if the pursuer could prove that which she averred she would have a good cause of action. We have already seen that the decision is an authority for two distinct propositions; (1) that negligence is a distinct tort[43] and (2) that the absence of privity of contract between plaintiff and defendant does not preclude liability in tort.[44] It is also of course an indisputable authority for the proposition that manufacturers of products owe a duty of care to the ultimate consumer or user.[45] Although it was sometimes said that the *ratio decidendi* of the case was limited to this proposition,[46] it became clear[47] that the case was authority for something more than the proposition that a duty of care is owed to consumers of snails in ginger-beer bottles.[48] This was implicit in the famous passage in which Lord Atkin formulated "the neighbour

---

[39] The 1889 edition of Beven on *Negligence* lists 56 separate duties of care.

[40] "Few can go back 50 years as I can. Few can appreciate the law as to negligence as it then stood." Lord Denning, *The Discipline of Law* (1979), p. 229.

[41] *Candler* v. *Crane, Christmas & Co.* [1951] 2 K.B. 164, 188, *per* Asquith L.J. The passage continues: "These categories attracting the duty had been added to and subtracted from time to time. But no attempt had been made in the past to rationalise them; to find a common denominator between road users, bailees, surgeons, occupiers, and so on, which would explain why they should be bound to a duty of care and some other classes who might be expected equally to be so bound should be exempt—no attempt, that is, save that of Lord Esher M.R. (from which his colleagues dissociated themselves) in *Heaven* v. *Pender* (1883) 11 Q.B.D. 503, 510." Green, *Traffic Victims*, pp. 52–53, says that the statement by Lord Esher (Sir Baliol Brett at the date of the judgment) was "a brilliant generalisation" which "comes close to generalising English tort law for the first time." But nowadays pre–1932 decisions are only of historic interest: *Hurley* v. *Dyke* [1979] R.T.R. 265, 303, *per* Lord Hailsham of St. Marylebone L.C.

[42] [1932] A.C. 562. See Smith and Burns, "*Donoghue* v. *Stevenson*—the Not So Golden Anniversary" (1983) 46 M.L.R. 147. See also *The Paisley Papers* Burns ed. (Vancouver, 1991) and two articles by Alan Rodger QC: "Mrs. Donoghue and Alfenus Varus" (1988) C.L.P. 1; "Lord Macmillan's speech in *Donoghue* v. *Stevenson*" (1992) 108 L.Q.R. 236.

[43] See above, § 9.1.

[44] See above, Chap. 2.

[45] This aspect of the case is considered fully below, Chap. 12.

[46] See the authorities collected in the 17th ed. § 73.

[47] *London Graving Dock Co.* v. *Horton* [1951] A.C. 737, 757.

[48] *Central Asbestos Co. Ltd.* v. *Dodd* [1973] A.C. 518, 550. See also Lords Roskill and Brandon in the *Junior Books* case: [1983] A.C. 510, 539, 540.

principle."[49] By the beginning of the 1970s it was said[50] that *Donoghue v. Stevenson* was an authority for opening up new categories of liability,[51] with caution,[52] not disregarding existing categories, or treating the law of negligence as entirely "open-ended."[53] But by the end of the 1970s the Law Lords had moved so far as to hold that public policy primarily required the imposition of liability unless there was some other and secondary policy demanding a total or partial immunity from suit.[54]

In *Anns v. Merton London Borough Council*, a case concerned with failure to inspect defective houses, this two-tier approach was clearly expounded by Lord Wilberforce[55] whose exposition was initially greeted with enthusiasm and seemed to herald a major advance in the field of economic loss.[56] But after some years doubts were expressed. So in 1984 the tendency to impose liability in building cases on some party outside the construction team (specifically the local authority as distinct from the architect and builders) was halted,[57] and it was stated that the Wilberforce judgment did not contain a test which was universally valid for all cases.[58] This restrictive approach was followed by the Court of Appeal in two more building cases.[59] Outside the area of building cases a restrictive approach was also adopted in 1986 by the Court of

---

[49] "In this way it can be ascertained at any time whether the law recognises a duty, but only where the case can be referred to some particular species which has been examined and classified. And yet the duty which is common to all the cases where liability is established must logically be based upon some element common to the cases where it is found to exist. To seek a complete logical definition of the general principle is probably to go beyond the function of the judge. . . . There must be, and is, some general conception of relations giving rise to a duty of care, of which the particular cases found in the looks are but instances. . . . The liability for negligence, whether you style it such or treat it as in other systems as a species of *culpa*, is no doubt based upon a general public sentiment of moral wrongdoing for which the offender must pay. But acts or omissions which any moral code would censure cannot in a practical world be treated so as to give a right to every person injured by them to demand relief. In this way rules of law arise which limit the range of complainants and the extent of their remedy. The rule that you are to love your neighbour becomes in law, you must not injure your neighbour; and the lawyer's question, Who is my neighbour? receives a restricted reply. You must take reasonable care to avoid acts or omissions which you can reasonably foresee would be likely to injure your neighbour. Who, then, is my neighbour? The answer seems to be— persons who are so closely and directly affected by my act that I ought reasonably to have them in contemplation as being so affected when I am directing my mind to the acts or omission which are called in question."

[50] *Dorset Yacht Co. Ltd. v. Home Office* [1970] A.C. 1004.

[51] *Hedley Byrne & Co. Ltd. v. Heller and Partners Ltd.* [1964] A.C. 465, 482, 524.

[52] *Weller v. Foot and Mouth Disease Research Institute Ltd.* [1966] 1 Q.B. 569, 577.

[53] *Dorset Yacht Co. Ltd. v. Home Office* [1970] A.C. 1004, 1011.

[54] *Arenson v. Casson, Beckman, Rutley & Co.* [1977] A.C. 405, 419.

[55] [1978] A.C. 728–752 (hereinafter *Anns*).

[56] See *Junior Books Ltd. v. Veitchi Co. Ltd.* [1983] 1 A.C. 520 (hereinafter *Junior Books*).

[57] See *Peabody Donation Fund Governors v. Sir Lindsay Parkinson & Co. Ltd.* [1985] A.C. 210 (hereinafter *Peabody*), holding, two years after *Junior Books*, that a property developer, as distinct from a building owner, was not owed a duty by a local authority. See also *Curran v. Northern Ireland Housing Association Ltd.* [1987] A.C. 718.

[58] *Peabody* [1985] A.C. 210, 240.

[59] *Investors in Industry Ltd. v. South Bedfordshire District Council* [1986] Q.B. 1034; *Jones v. Stroud District Council* [1986] 1 W.L.R. 141.

Appeal,[60] and by the Privy Council in two cases in 1985.[61] In *The Mineral Transporter* it was held that the time charterer of a ship could not recover for economic loss caused by damage done to the chartered vessel, for his only right in relation to it was a contractual right to control its use. In *Tai Hing* it was held that a customer does not owe to his bank a general duty of care in tort: his only duty was the specific one of drawing his cheques with reasonable care to prevent forgery. In 1986 the House of Lords affirmed[62] a restrictive rule which had existed for over a century limiting the scope of recovery by a consignee of goods which have been damaged in transit at sea. Shortly thereafter the final phase of the retreat from *Anns* took place.

Murphy v. Brentwood District Council

In 1988, this time in another building case[63] the House of Lords cast doubt on the correctness of the actual decision in *Anns*. Finally in 1990, in *Murphy v. Brentwood District Council*,[64] a seven-member House of Lords invoked the 1966 *Practice Statement* to overrule it.[64a] The plaintiff in *Murphy* was the purchaser of one of a pair of semi-detached houses. The foundations of the houses were defective but the plans and calculations on which they were based had been passed by the Council, due to the carelessness of their engineers, when submitted for building regulation approval prior to construction. The plaintiff lost a substantial sum in selling the house, subject to the defect, at less than its market value in sound condition. The House of Lords emphasised that this was pure economic loss and, as such, was not recoverable in an action in negligence against the local authority.[65] The Council owed no duty to protect building owners or occupiers against such loss when carrying out its statutory functions of building control. The House also confirmed the repudiation of Lord Wilberforce's generalised approach to determination of the existence of a duty of care. The current judicial attitude was expressed by Lord Keith in the form of a quotation from the judg-

---

[60] *Muirhead* v. *Industrial Tank Ltd.* [1986] Q.B. 507 (hereinafter *Muirhead*). The House of Lords (Lord Keith presiding) refused leave to appeal: [1986] 1 W.L.R. 1380.

[61] *Candlewood Navigation Corporation Ltd.* v. *Mitsui O.S.K. Lines Ltd.* [1986] A.C. 1 (hereinafter *The Mineral Transporter*); *Tai Hing Cotton Mill Ltd.* v. *Liu Chong Hing Bank* [1986] A.C. 80 (hereinafter *Tai Hing*).

[62] *Leigh and Sillivan Ltd.* v. *Aliakmon Shipping Co. Ltd.* [1986] A.C. 785 (hereinafter *The Aliakmon*).

[63] *D & F Estates* v. *Church Commissioners for England* [1989] A.C. 177.

[64] [1991] 1 A.C. 398. See Cooke, "An Impossible Distinction" (1991) 107 L.Q.R. 46; Duncan Wallace, "Anns Beyond Repair" (1991) 107 L.Q.R. 228; Howarth, "Negligence after Murphy: Time to Re-think" [1991] 50 C.L.J. 58.

[64a] Markesinis and Deakin have pointed out that in the space of thirteen years which separated *Anns* from *Murphy* the House of Lords considered the various issues involved on at least twelve different occasions producing "298 pages of law reports or (approximately) 180,000 words, or the equivalent of two average-size Oxbridge doctoral theses.": Modern Law Review (forthcoming).

[65] Nor against those primarily responsible, such as builders: see *Department of the Environment* v. *Thomas Bates & Son* [1991] 1 A.C. 499 in which the House of Lords immediately applied its own decision in *Murphy*. See, further, below, § 9.5.

ment of Brennan J. in *Sutherland Shire Council* v. *Heyman*,[66] a case in which the High Court of Australia had itself declined to follow *Anns*:

"It is preferable, in my view, that the law should develop categories of negligence incrementally and by analogy with established categories, rather than by a massive extension of a prima facie duty of care restrained only by indefinable considerations which ought to negative, or to reduce or limit the scope of the duty or the class of person to whom it is owed."

§ 9.4. CONCEPTS NOW USED TO DETERMINE THE EXISTENCE OF A DUTY

Foresight

At the outset, it should be noticed that there are many torts to which the *Donoghue* v. *Stevenson* neighbour principle can, in the nature of things, have no application—for example, defamation, inducement of breach of contract, and conspiracy. The interests of the individual are here protected in other ways. Nobody has seriously suggested that the whole law of tort should be reduced to a question of what the defendant ought reasonably to have foreseen in the circumstances of the particular case.[67] The foresight of the reasonable man, or reasonable foreseeability, to use the customary but inelegant phrase, is not the necessary and sufficient condition of liability in tort such as a whole[68]—not necessary, because it has no place in torts of strict liability; not sufficient, because even within the field of negligence as such, there are cases in which the defendant will escape liability although it is clear that he must have foreseen the likelihood of harm to the plaintiff. The demise of the *Anns* prima facie duty of care approach has been accompanied by renewed emphasis upon the concepts used to narrow the potentially wide scope of the tort.

Reliance

This term first became prominent in legal usage when it was decided that one who had relied to his detriment upon a statement made to him by another could recover in negligence.[69] Its use ensured that liability for careless statements was more limited than unrestricted adoption of the foreseeability test would have produced. The term clearly has significance in cases in which the parties are very close to a contractual situation.[70] Then the term was extended to cases in which there was no real analogy to contract but one party could be said to be relying on another to act in a lawful manner—*e.g.* not to disrupt a commercial con-

---

[66] (1985) 60 A.L.R. 1 at 43–44.

[67] *Lowry* v. *Buchanan* [1982] N.I. 243, 246. "Authority for that proposition is both ample in quantity and exalted in status": *McLoughlin* v. *O'Brian* [1983] A.C. 410, 426, *per* Lord Edmund-Davies.

[68] *Muirhead* [1986] Q.B. 507, 511.

[69] *Hedley Byrne & Co. Ltd.* v. *Heller and Partners Ltd.* [1964] A.C. 465 (hereinafter *Hedley Byrne*).

[70] So in *Junior Books* the parties were "only just short of a direct contractual relationship": [1983] 1 A.C. 520, 533.

tract for the carriage of goods by colliding with the carrier. But it always seems to have been accepted that the concept of reliance has no place in ordinary actions for personal injuries. Finally there may be confusion when the concepts of reliance, proximity and causation run into one another.[71]

Proximity

This term, apparently invented by Lord Esher,[72] was used by Lord Atkin himself to describe the nature of the neighbour principle, and has since been frequently adopted.[73] But in *Murphy* v. *Brentwood District Council*[74] Lord Oliver referred to it as that "elusive element" which "persistently defies definition," and unless the sense in which it is used is understood it may be misleading. It is essentially a short-hand expression to encapsulate the relevant existence of other factors.[75] On the one hand it is clear that geographical proximity between the parties is not of itself sufficient to establish liability,[76] although it may be an important factor.[77] On the other hand it is also clear that the absence of proximity in time or space will not prevent the establishment of liability; the manufacturer of poisonous tinned food is liable although his product has been shipped to the other side of the world and consumed months later.[78] Proximity is therefore a convenient expression "so long as it is realised that it is no more than a label which embraces not a definable concept but merely a description of circumstances from which, pragmatically, the courts conclude that a duty of care exists."[79] It is worth noting once again that the difficulties raised by terms like "reasonable foreseeability" and "proximity" really arise only within the field of negligence. For many other torts have, in a useful phrase,[80] "built-in" proximity rules—*e.g.* in trespass the damage must be direct, and in deceit the statement must have been known to be relied upon. The concept of proximity does not necessarily require that the identity of the plaintiff should be known at the time of the negligent act, although this has been treated as important in some cases of pure economic loss.

---

[71] So in *J.E.B. Fasteners Ltd.* v. *Marks, Bloom and Co.* [1981] 3 All E.R. 289 it was said that although the plaintiff had relied upon the defendant's statement, that statement had not caused the plaintiff's loss.

[72] *Thomas* v. *Quartermaine* (1887) 18 Q.B.D. 685, 688.

[73] See, *e.g.* Lord Keith in *Yuen Kun-Yeu* v. *Att.-Gen. of Hong Kong* [1988] A.C. 175.

[74] [1991] 1 A.C. 398, 487.

[75] Lord Roskill once listed no less than eight factors which established proximity: *Junior Books* v. *Veitchi* [1983] 1 A.C. 520, 533; *Muirhead* v. *Industrial Tank Ltd.* [1986] Q.B. 507, 528.

[76] A shop keeper finds that a shop has been erected next door to him, the second shop-keeper selling the same class of goods at half the price charged by the first. The second man intends to injure the first, but the latter has no cause of action, though the two are physically neighbours. See below, Chap. 16.

[77] So in *Dorset Yacht Co. Ltd.* v. *Home Office* [1970] A.C. 1004 it was thought significant that the property damaged was in the vicinity of the place of detention of the Borstal boys.

[78] See below, Chap. 12.

[79] *Caparo Industries* v. *Dickman* [1990] 2 A.C. 605, 633, *per* Lord Oliver.

[80] See James, "The Fallacies of *Simpson* v. *Thomson*" (1971) 34 M.L.R. 149, 159.

"Just and reasonable"

Lord Keith in *Peabody Donation Fund* v. *Parkinson*[81] said that in determining the existence of a duty of care it was "material to take into account whether it is "just and reasonable" that one should be imposed. So far this potentially wide-ranging concept has been used mainly to deny liability in circumstances in which another defendant, or the plaintiff himself, is regarded as the more appropriate bearer of the relevant loss,[82] or where alternative remedies exist with which a negligence action could undesirably be in conflict.[83] The underlying idea is also reflected in the proposition, unanimously and emphatically upheld by the House of Lords recently, that no duty exists in a situation in which precedents of good authority, supported by convincing reasons, have consistently denied the existence of one.[84] Some of these exceptions to the neighbour principle were established in the law before 1932, and their existence reaffirmed since on the express ground that they had not been affected by *Donoghue* v. *Stevenson*. Obvious examples of this class are the absence of any duty to prevent the subsidence of one's neighbour's premises by the abstraction of underground water in undefined channels[85] and the immunity given to the vendor of defective premises.[86] Others have been established since 1932. Examples are the refusal of the English courts to hold that a finance company is under a duty to a later purchaser to register a hire-purchase agreement[87] or that a university or its examiners owe any duty to its students in respect of examinations[88] or that a judge owes any duty to the litigants before him,[89] or that those taking part in a joint criminal venture are neighbours.[90]

Policy

A consequence of the abandonment of the *Anns* prima facie duty doctrine has been that overt consideration of policy issues, as such, by the judiciary has become less likely. One of the purposes of emphasising the language of "proximity," and phrases such as "just and reasonable," seems to have been to incorporate, at an early stage in the determination of liability, issues which the superseded approach dealt with rather later as a means of rebutting a notional presumption of liability raised by the defendant's carelessness. Lord Keith has said that where "negligence is made out on the proximity basis" it would only be in "rare cases" that public policy would require that there should be no

---

[81] [1985] A.C. 210, 240.
[82] As in *Peabody*.
[83] *Jones* v. *Department of Employment* [1989] Q.B. 1; *Mills* v. *Winchester Diocesan Board* [1989] Ch. 428.
[84] *The Aliakmon* [1986] A.C. 785.
[85] *Stephens* v. *Anglian Water Authority* [1987] 1 W.L.R. 1381.
[86] By *Cavalier* v. *Pope* [1906] A.C. 428. See below, Chap. 11.
[87] *Moorgate Mercantile Co.* v. *Twitchings* [1977] A.C. 890.
[88] *Thorne* v. *University of London* [1966] 2 Q.B. 237.
[89] *Arenson* v. *Casson Beckman Rutley and Co.* [1977] A.C. 405. An advocate also enjoys total immunity in respect of his work in court: see below, § 9.7.
[90] *Marshall* v. *Osmond* [1982] Q.B. 857; *Pitts* v. *Hunt* [1990] W.L.R. 542.

liability.[91] Nevertheless the same Law Lord has affirmed that in such cases public policy is still "capable of constituting a separate and independent ground for holding that the existence of liability in negligence should not be entertained."[92] Thus in *Hill* v. *Chief Constable of West Yorkshire*[93] it was held that it would be contrary to public policy for negligence in the detection of crime to give rise to liability against the police. Another example is the immunity of barristers from liability for negligence in the conduct of proceedings in court.[94] A special area in which overt consideration of fundamental policy questions has been inevitable is that of negligently performed sterilisation operations. After some uncertainty it has been beld by the Court of Appeal that claims by parents who conceive after such operations, for the cost of bringing up the child, are *not* contrary to public policy.[94a]

§ 9.5. ECONOMIC LOSS: THE BACKGROUND[95]

The general rule is that the common law duty to take care to avoid causing injury to others is restricted to physical injury either to person or to property, and to financial losses consequent upon such injury. In the early 1980s a controversial decision of the House of Lords[96] appeared to raise the possibility of the recovery of economic losses, unrelated to physical injury or damage, on a much wider basis than hitherto. But more recent cases, including further decisions of the House of Lords itself, have confirmed the validity of the principle that such losses are only recoverable in negligence in exceptional cases and not as a general rule. This does not mean that the law refuses to protect a person's financial or pecuniary interests.

The existence of the whole law of contract and of such torts as intimidation, deceit, injurious falsehood, inducement of breach of contract and conspiracy sufficiently demonstrates the wide degree of protection afforded—and a person can always protect those interests still further by making an express contract. But the reluctance to grant a remedy in tort for the merely careless invasion of financial or pecuniary interests is long-standing, deep-rooted and not unreasonable.[97] So one who suffers precuniary loss as the result of an inaccurate or false statement made either to himself (deceit) or to others (injurious falsehood) may have a

---

[91] *Yuen Kun-yeu* v. *Att.-Gen. of Hong Kong* [1988] A.C. 175, 193.

[92] *Hill* v. *Chief Constable of West Yorkshire* [1989] A.C. 53, 63.

[93] [1989] A.C. 53. See also *Hughes* v. *National Union of Mineworkers* [1991] 4 All E.R. 278.

[94] *Rondel* v. *Worsley* [1969] 1 A.C. 191; *Yuen Kun-yeu* v. *Att.-Gen. of Hong Kong* [1988] A.C. 175, 193.

[94a] *Emeh* v. *Kensington and Chelsea A.H.A.* [1985] Q.B. 1012 C.A. See Symmons, "Policy Factors in Actions for Wrongful Birth" (1987) 50 M.L.R. 269.

[95] See Cane, *Tort Law and Economic Interests*, (Oxford, 1991). See also Stapleton, "Duty of Care and Economic Loss: a Wider Agenda" (1991) 107 L.Q.R. 249; McGrath, "The Recovery of Pure Economic Loss in Negligence" (1985) 3 Oxford Journal of Legal Studies 350; Bishop, "Negligent Misrepresentation through Economists' Eyes" (1980) 96 L.Q.R. 360.

[96] *Junior Books* v. *Veitchi* [1983] 1 A.C. 520.

[97] *Furniss* v. *Fitchett* [1958] N.Z.L.R. 396, 401; *Spartan Steel and Alloys* v. *Martin and Co. (Contractors) Ltd.* [1973] 1 Q.B. 27, 42.

remedy—but in each case the law requires that he should prove dishonesty and not merely carelessness.

Although the landmark case of *Hedley Byrne & Co.* v. *Heller & Partners*[98] widened the tort of negligence to bring economic loss within its scope, the extent of liability for such loss remains limited. Of course foreseeability is not a sufficient condition of liability even in cases of physical injury or damage, but liability for economic loss is even more restricted in this respect.[99] "There comes a point where the logical extension of the boundaries of duty and damage is halted by the barrier of commercial sense and practical convenience."[1] So it is not enough for a plaintiff to prove that he has been prevented from doing something which previously he had done lawfully,[2] or that he has suffered loss in his trade or business as a foreseeable consequence of the defendant's activities. As a future Lord Chief Justice observed.

> "[In] an agricultural community the escape of foot and mouth disease virus is a tragedy which can foreseeably affect almost all businesses in that area. The affected beasts must be slaughtered, as must others to whom the disease may conceivably have spread. Other farmers are prohibited from moving their cattle and may be unable to bring them to market at the most profitable time; transport contractors who make their living by the transport of animals are out of work; dairymen may go short of milk, and sellers of cattle feed suffer loss of business."[3]

It is therefore necessary to look for some control device, or safety-valve, or modifier (to use some of the phrases to be found in the cases). Traditionally this was done in a pragmatic and contextual fashion, distinguishing between loss caused by careless acts and loss caused by careless statements. But this approach was questioned for a time after the decision in *Junior Books*, a case which continues to be of some (albeit now limited) significance.

Junior Books v. Veitchi[4]

The claim of the pursuers (respondents in the House of Lords) was for the cost of remedying defects in the floor of their factory which had been laid by the defenders (appellants). The defenders were specialists in that work. There was no contractual link between the pursuers and the defenders although the latter were subcontractors nominated under the contract between Junior Books and Ogilvie (Builders) Ltd., the main contractors. It was specifically averred that the pursuers' architects relied on the defenders as flooring specialists to recommend a suitable material for the floor, to arrange the appropriate mix of composition material and to follow the appropriate procedures for laying the floor.

---

[98] [1964] A.C. 465.
[99] *Candlewood Corporation* v. *Mitsui Ltd.* [1986] A.C. 1, 19, 21.
[1] *Lambert* v. *Lewis* [1982] A.C. 225, at 267, *per* Stephenson L.J.
[2] See *Tate and Lyle Ltd.* v. *G.L.C.* [1983] 2 A.C. 509.
[3] *Weller and Co.* v. *Foot and Mouth Disease Research Institute* [1966] 1 Q.B. 569, 577, *per* Widgery J.
[4] [1983] 1 A.C. 520.

The action was brought after cracking had occurred in the surface layer of the flooring. By the time that the action was brought certain areas had lifted and required replacement. It was averred that the entire floor surface required replacement at as early a date as possible to avoid the necessity of continual maintenance, which would be more expensive than immediate replacement or treatment. The total claimed, over £200,000, fell under a number of heads, but all were aspects of the cost of putting right the floor produced by the defenders which had turned out to be defective. A majority of the House of Lords allowed the case to go to trial. They held that there was a sufficient degree of proximity to give rise to a duty of care, and that that duty was not limited to a duty to avoid causing foreseeable harm to persons or property other than the subject-matter of the work.

Although in a later case the House of Lords apparently sought to treat *Junior Books* as a case where the plaintiff had suffered actual damage to property,[5] it is generally thought to have related to pure economic loss divorced from physical damage (the cost of repairing the defective floor).

Return to orthodoxy: the primacy of contract

In three subsequent decisions of the Court of Appeal[6] *Junior Books* v. *Veitchi* was treated as a decision on its own special facts in that the nominated sub-contractor had voluntarily assumed a direct responsibility to the building owner. Finally Lord Bridge, in the House of Lords, observed that *Junior Books* had been "so far dependent on the unique, albeit non-contractual relationship between the pursuer and the defender in that case and the unique scope of the duty of care owed by the defender to the pursuer arising from that relationship that the decision cannot be regarded as laying down any principle of general application in the law of tort"[7] Given that *Junior Books* v. *Veitchi* is taken to have been decided on the special closeness of the relationship between the parties in the case, the extreme narrowness of any principle which might be thought to survive from the decision is illustrated by the fact that plaintiffs may fail in situations in which the relevant relationship was, in a sense, even *closer*. That is to say if the relationship was *actually* contractual the terms of the agreement will govern, and they may preclude liability.[8] Contract therefore remains the primary route for the recovery of pure economic loss: the law of negligence will rarely provide a substitute for the assistance of third parties or those

---

[5] See *Tate and Lyle Ltd.* v. *Greater London Council* [1983] 2 A.C. 509, 530, *per* Lord Templeman. But as was said in *Muirhead* v. *Industrial Tank Specialities* [1986] Q.B. 507, 516, "What matters is what *Junior Books* did decide, not what Lord Templeman said it decided."

[6] *Muirhead* v. *Industrial Tank Specialities* [1986] Q.B. 507; *Simaan General Contracting Co.* v. *Pilkington Glass Ltd. (No. 2)* [1988] Q.B. 758; *Greater Nottingham Co-operative Society* v. *Cementation Piling and Foundations Ltd.* [1989] Q.B. 71.

[7] *D & F Estates Ltd.* v. *Church Commissioners* [1989] A.C. 177, 202.

[8] *Greater Nottingham Co-operative Society* v. *Cementation Piling and Foundations Ltd.* [1989] Q.B. 71.

whose contracts do not provide for recovery.[9] Thus in *D. & F. Estates* v. *Church Commissioners*,[10] and also in the subsequent case of *Department of the Environment* v. *Thomas Bates & Son*,[11] the House of Lords has emphatically reaffirmed that the cost of repairing a defect in a chattel or structure is not recoverable in a tort claim in the absence of actual physical injury or damage to other property. A purchaser of an ordinary article of commerce disappointed by the quality of what he has obtained should look to the vendor for redress, not to the manufacturer. This marks a return to the orthodoxy reflected in the principles set out in the next section.

§ 9.6. ECONOMIC LOSS CAUSED BY CARELESS ACTS

The careless act of the defendant may cause economic loss to the plaintiff either directly or indirectly. If it is caused directly, the principle now established in England is that there is no liability for economic loss unless there is also proved loss to the plaintiff's person or property. Thus in the *Spartan Steel* case,[12] when the defendants negligently cut a cable carrying electric power to the plaintiffs' factory, thereby interrupting the supply for 14 and a half hours, the plaintiffs were held entitled to damages for physical damage to the metal in their furnace (£368), and also for the loss of profit on the sales of that metal (£400), but could not recover for the loss of profit in four further melts (£1,767), which could have been completed but for the power cut.[13] The requirement of the interposition of physical damage between the negligent act and the plaintiff's economic loss has been criticised as an illogical and capricious exception to the principle of reasonable foreseeability,[14] but it is defensible on grounds of policy. It prevents the defendant's insurers being overwhelmed by claims arising out of an open-ended catastrophic risk, for example, a national power cut.[15] But the limits of this principle have not yet been fixed. If the defendant carelessly damages the plaintiff's piece of paper, is there to be liability up to £100,000 because it is a pools ticket?[16]

If the loss has been caused indirectly, it will usually have been through the acts or omission of a third party. In such a case liability is

---

[9] *Reid* v. *Rush and Tompkins* [1990] 1 W.L.R. 212.

[10] [1989] A.C. 177. See Duncan Wallace, "Negligence and Defective Buildings: Confusion Confounded ?" (1989) 105 L.Q. R. 46; Cane, "Economic Loss in Tort: Is the Pendulum out of Control?" (1989) 52 M.L.R. 200.

[11] [1991] 1 A.C. 499 (applying *Murphy* v. *Brentwood District Council* [1991] 1 A.C. 398).

[12] *Spartan Steel and Alloys Ltd.* v. *Martin and Co. (Contractors) Ltd.* [1973] 1 Q.B. 27.

[13] So economic loss resulting from the interruption of the telephone service is not recoverable: *Elliott* v. *Sir Robert McAlpine and Sons Ltd.* [1966] 2 Lloyd's Rep. 482. *Cf.* the Electricity Act 1989, s. 21, which authorises a public electricity supplier to exclude by contract liability for economic loss resulting from negligent disruption of the supply.

[14] See the dissenting judgment of Edmund-Davies L.J. in *Spartan Steel*, which clearly attracted Lord Roskill in *Junior Books*.

[15] See Oliver L.J. in his pamphlet *The Green Saga* (Petersfield, 1983), p. 18 ("Indeed the whole trend of the law in the area of negligence, foreseeability and remoteness of damage must be to reduce insurers to a state of hollow-eyed misery from lack of sleep").

[16] *Bart* v. *B.W.I.A.* [1967] 1 Lloyd's Rep. 239, 267.

even more restricted. There are undoubtedly many situations in which the negligent act or omission of A causing injury to B may deprive C of valuable economic benefits. Thus B may have been made incapable of furnishing the contractual benefit which (unknown to A[17]) he is bound to render to C,[18] or C may be the charterer of B's ship which has been damaged by A's negligence,[19] or he may be the prospective purchaser of part of the damaged cargo in that ship,[20] or C may be the wife or child or servant of B and obliged in consequence to nurse an irritable invalid or to seek new employment.[21] But in none of these cases is C, the third party, thereby invested with any right of action against the wrongdoer. Within the space of one year both the Privy Council[22] and the House of Lords[23] emphatically reaffirmed these principles.

§ 9.7. CARELESS STATEMENTS

Hedley Byrne v. Heller

In 1951 the Court of Appeal had held[24] that the law distinguished between the negligent circulation of chattels and the issue of negligent misrepresentations. There was liability in the former case but not in the latter, and the distinction had not been affected by *Donoghue* v. *Stevenson*. But in 1963 a unanimous House of Lords in *Hedley Byrne and Co. Ltd.* v. *Heller and Partners Ltd.*[25] held that in principle there was no difference between physical loss and financial loss,[26] and that a duty to take care in making statements existed whenever there was a special relationship and there had not been a disclaimer of responsibility. Although there has never been much difficulty in holding that there is liability for careless statements causing physical loss,[27] it was novel to impose liability when such statements caused economic loss.

The facts in *Hedley Byrne* were that the appellants, advertising agents, were anxious to discover the creditworthiness of Easipower Ltd., who had instructed the appellants to arrange substantial advertising contracts. Hedley Byrne asked their bank, the National Provincial, to make inquiries. National Provincial on two separate occasions made these inquiries of Hellers, a firm of merchant bankers, who were financing Easipower as well as being their bankers. The first inquiry was specifically stated by National Provincial to be "without responsibility" on the part of Hellers, and the second inquiry, asking whether Easipower was "trustworthy, in the way of business, to the extent of £100,000 per annum" was answered by Hellers stating, "without responsibility on

---

[17] If A does know, he may be liable for inducement of breach of contract.
[18] *The Mineral Transporter* [1986] A.C. 1, 12.
[19] *The Mineral Transporter* [1986] A.C. 1.
[20] *The Aliakmon* [1986] A.C. 785.
[21] *Best* v. *Samuel Fox and Co. Ltd.* [1952] A.C. 716, 731, 734.
[22] *The Mineral Transporter* [1986] A.C. 1.
[23] *The Aliakmon* [1986] A.C. 785.
[24] *Candler* v. *Crane, Christmas and Co. (A Firm)* [1951] 2 K.B. 164, Denning L.J. dissenting.
[25] [1964] A.C. 465.
[26] A point also emphasised in *Rookes* v. *Barnard* [1964] A.C. 1129. See below, Chap. 16.
[27] *Clayton* v. *Woodman & Sons (Builders) Ltd.* [1962] 2. Q.B. 533.

the part of the bank or its officials," that Easipower was a respectably constituted company, considered good for its ordinary business engagements. Your figures are larger than we are accustomed to see."[28] This reference was passed on to Hedley Byrne, who relied upon it, and suffered loss to the extent of £17,000 when, as *del credere* agents, they had to pay the sums due on the advertising contracts when Easipower went into liquidation.

The House of Lords did not actually impose liability on Hellers, holding that the "without responsibility" disclaimers had been sufficient to protect them from the liability to which, assuming that a special relationship had existed between the parties, any carelessness on the defendants' part would have given rise.

Special relationships

Hedley Byrne affirms and extends the principle that a duty to be careful (as distinct from a duty to be honest) may exist in situations other than those in which there is a contract between the parties. What can be deduced from the case[29] is that the necessary relationship between the maker of a statement and the recipient who acts in reliance on it will normally exist where the statement is required for a purpose which is known to the person making it who also knows that it will be communicated to, and acted upon, by the recipient either specifically or as a member of an ascertainable class, without further independent inquiry. These conditions are neither conclusive nor exclusive. Liability has, for example, been imposed in the absence of any reliance by the plaintiff upon the defendant.[30] It is important to remember that, as Denning L.J. recognised in his famous dissenting judgment in *Candler*,[31] at bottom the problem is one of exclusion: negligence in word cannot in all respects be treated like negligence in act, for that would open up too wide an arc of liability.[32] Even more than in the context of careless deeds, use of reasonable foresight as the only criterion of liability would bring in persons who, it is generally agreed, should be excluded—*e.g.* the solicitor giving casual advice during a railway journey,[33] or the marine hydrographer whose misplaced rock on a chart causes an ocean liner

---

[28] Bankers normally and naturally use careful terms when giving these references, but Heller's language was so guarded that only a very suspicious inquirer might have appreciated he was being warned not to give credit to the extent of £100,000. One week after the reference was given Heller began to press Easipower to reduce their overdraft.

[29] See *Caparo Industries* v. *Dickman* [1990] 2 A.C. 605, 638, *per* Lord Oliver.

[30] See *Ross* v. *Caunters* [1980] Ch. 297 and *Ministry of Housing* v. *Sharp* [1970] 2 Q.B. 233; "cases which give rise to certain difficulties of analysis": *Caparo Industries* v. *Dickman* [1991] 2 A.C. 605, 636, *per* Lord Oliver.

[31] [1951] 2 K.B. 164; a "masterly analysis [requiring] little, if any, amplification or modification in the light of later authority": *Caparo Industries* v. *Dickman* [1990] 2 A.C. 605, 623, *per* Lord Bridge.

[32] [1964] A.C. 465, 482–483, 494, 510, 534.

[33] Which worried Byles J. as long ago as *Fish* v. *Kelly* (1864) 17 C.B.(N.S.) 194. But see *Chaudry* v. *Prabhakar* [1989] 1 W.L.R. 29 (liability for advising a friend on the purchase of a second-hand car).

to go aground.[34] It is important to avoid "liability in an indeterminate amount for an indeterminate time to an indeterminate class."[35] But it also "has to be recognised that to search for any single formula which will serve as a general test of liability is to pursue a will-o'-the wisp."[36] In particular, the belief that the concept of "voluntary assumption of responsibility" could provide such a formula has been doubted since, in appropriate cases, the law may *impose* liability in a manner inconsistent with the subjectivity implied by that concept.[37]

Purposes and circumstances

"[B]efore the existence and scope of any liability can be determined, it is necessary first to determine for what purposes and in what circumstances the information in question is to be given"[38] The authorities suggest that the courts will require a high degree of specificity both with respect to the *purpose* for which the statement was made and the *identity* of those likely to suffer loss in the event of its being made carelessly.[39] In *Smith v. Eric S. Bush*[40] the House of Lords found in favour of the plaintiffs because they satisfied both requirements. In this case it was held that surveyors who valued houses for mortgagees, at the lower end of the market, also owe a duty of care to the mortgagors to whom such reports are usually shown and by whom they are normally relied upon. On the other hand in *Caparo Industries v. Dickman*[41] the purpose for which the information was prepared proved fatal to the imposition of liability. In this case the House of Lords held that those who audit the accounts of public companies, to fulfil the statutory requirements intended to facilitate the control of the companies by their shareholders, do not owe a duty of care to investors in their capacity as such.[42] By contrast representations made with a view deliberately to influencing the conduct of the plaintiff may apparently give rise to liability even if the plaintiff is a bidder in a contested take-over situation and the defend-

---

[34] The possible misfortunes of this possible defendant have been much discussed. Although most cartographers are Admiralty officials for whom the Crown would be vicariously liable, private chart producers still exist: see the definitive work by A. H. W. Robinson, *Marine Cartography in Britain* (Leicester, 1962), Chap. 7.

[35] *Ultramares Corporation v. Touche*, 255 N.Y. 170, 179; 174 N.E. 441, 450 (1931), *per* Cardozo C.J.

[36] *Caparo Industries v. Dickman* [1990] 2 A.C. 605, 633 *per* Lord Oliver.

[37] See *Smith v. Eric S. Bush* [1990] 1 A.C. 831, especially, *per* Lord Griffiths at p. 862.

[38] *Caparo Industries v. Dickman* [1990] 2 A.C. 605 at 629, *per* Lord Roskill.

[39] *Quaere* whether the giving of character references on former employees (which would seem to satisfy these criteria) can give rise to liability notwithstanding a possible conflict with the scope of the defence of qualified privilege in the tort of defamation. Liability has been imposed in two English decisions at first instance: *Lawton v. B.O.C. Transhield* [1987] I.C.R. 7 and *Spring v. Guardian Assurance*, *The Times* February 10, 1992. But *cf.* the decision of the New Zealand in *Bell-Booth Group Ltd. v. Att.-Gen.* [1989] 3 N.Z.L.R. 148.

[40] [1990] 1 A.C. 831; "no decision of this House has gone further than *Smith v. Eric S Bush*": *per* Lord Oliver in *Caparo Industries v. Dickman* [1990] 2 A.C. 605, 642.

[41] [1990] 2 A.C. 605. See also *McNaughton (James) Papers Group v. Hicks Anderson* [1991] 2 Q.B. 113.

[42] See also *Al Saudi Banque v. Clark Pixley* [1990] Ch. 313; *Al-Nakib Investments (Jersey) Ltd. v. Longcroft* [1990] 1 W.L.R. 1390.

ants are the directors and advisers of the target company.[43] Satisfaction of the requirements of purpose and identity will also normally be evident if the parties are in a pre-contractual situation, and the mere fact that the parties are in such a situation will not necessarily prevent a special relationship from arising.[44] The *Hedley Byrne* principle is capable of covering statements made to induce one to enter into a contract with the maker of the statement, or with a third party.[45] Nevertheless the cases in which liability is imposed in such circumstances are rare. This is because the courts are anxious not to allow the law of negligence to outflank established principles of the law of contract, *e.g.* the rule that mere non-disclosure does not normally constitute misrepresentation.[46] At the other extreme from cases where the parties are in a pre-contractual situation are those in which the plaintiff never relied upon the defendant at all. In some circumstances liability can apparently arise in such cases. Thus it has been held that a solicitor's duty of care extends beyond his clients to those whom he knows may suffer loss as a result of his carelessness,[47] as when a will is defectively executed[48] so that a prospective beneficiary loses a legacy.[49] But the scope of this liability is limited and does not, for example, imply that the solicitor owes a duty of care to potential beneficiaries whenever he advises the testator on subsequent transactions involving assets which happen to be included in the will.[50]

Need for profession or skill?

The Privy Council once held,[51] in a controversial majority decision, that the defendant should be a person whose profession or trade it is to make statements or give information or advice; or who has a financial interest in the transaction in question.[52] It may be conceded that it would hardly be desirable to impose liability on a bystander who carelessly misdirected one on his way to an important appointment[53]; but it is very difficult to see how a company can authorise the giving of advice except as part of its business activities, so that it seems hard to hold that an insurance company is not liable for misleading advice about invest-

---

[43] See *Morgan Crucible Co.* v. *Hill Samuel Bank* [1991] Ch. 295, C.A.
[44] *Howard Marine Ltd.* v. *Ogden & Son Ltd.* [1978] Q.B. 574.
[45] *McInerney* v. *Lloyd's Bank Ltd.* [1974] 1 Lloyd's Rep. 246.
[46] *Banque Financière de la Cité S.A.* v. *Westgate Insurance Co.* [1989] 2 All E.R. 952, C.A. (affmd. on other grounds in [1990] 2 All E.R. 947).
[47] See *Al-Kandari* v. *J R Brown* [1988] Q.B. 655, C.A.
[48] As in *Ross* v. *Caunters* [1980] Ch. 297.
[49] As in *Gartside* v. *Sheffield* [1983] N.Z.L.R. 37, where the defendant had delayed preparing a will for an 89-year-old testatrix.
[50] See *Clarke* v. *Bruce Lance & Co.* [1988] 1 W.L.R. 881.
[51] *Mutual Life and Citizens' Assurance Co.* v. *Evatt* [1971] A.C. 793. The force of the decision is much weakened by the powerful dissenting judgments of Lords Reid and Morris, who had themselves sat in *Hedley Byrne.*
[52] As in *Anderson (W. B.) & Sons Ltd.* v. *Rhodes* [1967] 2 All E.R. 850, when one businessman carelessly misstated the creditworthiness of another.
[53] [1964] A.C. 465, 495, 502, 510, 539. *Contra*, Lord Devlin in [1964] A.C. 465, 529.

ments given to a policy-holder.[54] It is also hard to see how the defendant's financial interest can cause the plaintiff to trust the statement made to him.

Immunities

It has been settled for a century that a barrister cannot be sued by his client for breach of contract.[55] The fees which he receives are an honorarium. But there was doubt as to the barrister's liability in negligence as a result of *Hedley Byrne*. These doubts were nearly all quietened when in *Rondel* v. *Worsley*[56] the House of Lords unanimously held that an advocate could not be sued by his client in respect of alleged negligence in the conduct of a criminal trial. It should be noted that *Rondel* v. *Worsley* does not lay down the rule that a barrister cannot be sued in negligence by his client. In fact the case lays down that as between barrister and client there is a special relationship giving rise to a duty of care, unless the barrister can bring himself within the exceptional immunity of an advocate. This immunity is quite distinct from the rule that there is no contractual relationship between barrister and client and is justifiable for a number of reasons on grounds of public policy—because there is a general public interest in a free and independent Bar and a barrister, who owes a duty to the court for the true administration of justice, cannot pick and choose his clients as a solicitor can,[57] or because an action for negligence against a barrister would inevitably involve the re-trial of the original proceedings,[58] or because the barrister shares in the general immunity which is given to all those taking part in the judicial process. But the Law Lords in *Saif Ali* v. *Mitchell & Co.*[59] cut down the extent of the immunity, holding that a barrister was liable when he carelessly failed to advise re-settling the plaintiff's claim so as to add another defendant. So there might well be liability for an opinion given in chambers on a point of law, or for "paperwork" which was unconnected with litigation.[60] And a barrister voluntarily giving his services in a law centre may be liable in tort. A solicitor is in contractual relationship with his client, but is now apparently liable in tort as well as in contract.[61] In his capacity as advocate the solicitor is entitled to the same immunity as the barrister.[62] An arbitrator is generally thought to

---

[54] As was done in *Mutual Life and Citizens' Assurance Co.* v. *Evatt* [1971] A.C. 793, 811. The decision may not be followed: *Howard Marine Case* [1978] Q.B. 574, 600.

[55] *Kennedy* v. *Broun* (1863) 13 C.B.(N.S.) 677.

[56] [1969] 1 A.C. 191. See Sir Ronald Roxburgh, "*Rondel* v. *Worsley*: the Historical Background" (1968) 84 L.Q.R. 178, and 513.

[57] For the "cab-rank" rule, see W. W. Boulton, *Conduct and Etiquette at the Bar*.

[58] See *Somasundaram* v. *Melchior* [1988] 1 W.L.R. 1394.

[59] [1980] A.C. 198. Yet it by no means follows that there is liability in negligence if an error takes place outside the area of immunity. A barrister must be careful: he need not be right.

[60] The result of Saif Ali seems to be that advice not to sue is unprotected. Yet it can hardly be in the public interest to protect barristers who launch unnecessary litigation.

[61] *Midland Bank* v. *Hett, Stubbs & Kemp* [1979] Ch. 384. *Cf. Bell* v. *Peter Browne & Co.* [1990] 3 All E.R. 125. See also below, Chap. 23.

[62] Courts and Legal Services Act 1990, s.62.

enjoy the same immunity as a judge,[63] at any rate when he is exercising the judicial function of deciding a dispute rather than of answering a question. A valuer may also, if the parties who appoint him so agree, enjoy the same immunity: otherwise, he is liable in negligence.[64] Judicial immunity is an exception which is not to be extended.

The disclaimer[65]

It is not entirely clear whether the effect of the disclaimer in *Hedley Byrne* was to exempt the bank from a duty which already lay upon it or to prevent any duty from arising. The latter view seems to be based upon the "voluntary assumption of responsibility" analysis which may be considered artificial and has been criticised in the House of Lords.[66] In any event it is now clear that the Unfair Contract Terms Act 1977 can apply to such disclaimers.[67] In some cases the duty may even be statutory in origin and incapable of being disclaimed.[68] On the other hand it appears that a disclaimer can sometimes now be effective even if it is included in a contract to which the person adversely affected by it is not a party, provided that contract forms part of the background and structure of the situation which the person affected chose to enter.[69]

§ 9.8. PSYCHIATRIC DAMAGE[70]

Scope of liability

The confusion between the three related but distinct concepts of duty, standard of care, and remoteness of damage can be clearly seen in the law relating to emotional disturbance. Nervous shock is "the hallowed expression"[71] by which "lawyers quaintly persist in calling psychiatric illness."[72] Psychiatric damage is now the preferred term.[73]

First, no action lies for mere mental suffering.[74] It was once thought that the defendant was immune even if the mental suffering had resulted in physical lesion or disturbance.[75] But "The crude view that the law takes cognisance only of physical injury resulting from actual impact has been discarded, and it is now well recognised that an action will lie for injury by shock sustained through the medium of the eye or

---

[63] *Sutcliffe* v. *Thackrah* [1974] A.C. 727.

[64] *Arenson* v. *Casson, Beckman, Rutley & Co.* [1977] A.C. 455.

[65] For disclaimers in general, see below, Chap. 22.

[66] See *Smith* v. *Eric S. Bush* [1990] 1 A.C. 831.

[67] *Ibid.*

[68] *Ministry of Housing* v. *Sharp* [1970] 2 Q.B. 223.

[69] *Pacific Associates* v. *Baxter* [1990] 1 Q.B. 993.

[70] See Teff, "Liability for Negligently Inflicted Nervous Shock" (1983) 99 L.Q.R. 100.

[71] *McLoughlin* v. *O'Brien* [1983] A.C. 410, 418, *per* Lord Wilberforce.

[72] *Ibid.* at p. 432, *per* Lord Bridge of Harwich.

[73] *Attia* v. *British Gas* [1988] Q.B. 304, 317. But in a later decision the Court of Appeal appeared to favour the traditional terminology: *Jones* v. *Wright* [1991] 3 All E.R. 88, especially at p. 123, *per* Stocker L.J.

[74] This interest is not given independent protection: it is "parasitic" upon the violation of some other legally recognised interest: see below, Chap. 23.

[75] *Victorian Railways Commissioners* v. *Coultas* (1888) 13 App.Cas. 222. This case is now completely discredited.

the ear[76] without direct contact. The distinction between mental shock and bodily injury was never a scientific one, for mental shock is presumably in all cases the result of, or at least accompanied by, some physical disturbance in the sufferer's system."[77] Proof of physical disturbance prevents the courts from having to deal with frivolous or fanciful claims. In one case it was argued that the plaintiff was exceptionally susceptible to shock, and so outside the law's protection, but the plea was rejected.[78]

Secondly, it has long been settled that one who by extreme and outragous conduct intentionally or recklessly causes severe emotional distress to another is liable for such emotional distress, provided that bodily harm results from it.[79] In *Wilkinson* v. *Downton*[80] the defendant, a licensed victualler, after going to the races, by way of a perverted practical joke had told the plaintiff that her husband was lying injured at a public-house in Leytonstone as the result of an accident, and that she was to go at once in a cab with two pillows to fetch him home. The resultant shock to the plaintiff's nervous system produced severe and permanent physical consequences for which the defendant was held liable in damages[81] by R. S. Wright J.[82]

Thirdly, it has also long been settled that an action lies for shock resulting in physical injury when the plaintiff has been placed in reasonable fear of immediate injury to himself as the result of the negligence of the defendant. The principle is that if the plaintiff has been put in peril of physical impact, it is immaterial that the impact did not materialise if physical injury is in fact caused by shock arising from the peril.[83] So in *Dulieu* v. *White & Sons*,[84] the defendants were held liable by a strong court (Kennedy and Phillimore JJ.) when their servant negligently drove a pair-horse van into the front of a public-house, with resultant shock and illness to the plaintiff, who was standing behind the bar.

Fourthly, an action lies for shock caused by the apprehension or the actual sight or sound of immediate physical injury to a close relative or

---

[76] *Boardman* v. *Sanderson (Keel and Block Third Party)* (1961) [1964] 1 W.L.R. 1317.

[77] *Bourhill* v. *Young* [1943] A.C. 92, 103, *per* Lord Macmillan. Prosser, 44 Calif.L.Rev. 40, 43, says that emotional distress "includes all highly unpleasant mental reactions, such as fright, horror, grief, shame, humiliation, anger, embarrassment, chagrin, disappointment, worry and nausea."

[78] *Chadwick* v. *British Railways Board* [1967] 1 W.L.R. 912. The plaintiff had led the "normal busy life" of a modern Englishman, having "on one occasion been attacked by a gang of youths armed with bicycle chains."

[79] Restatement, Second, Torts § 46.

[80] [1897] 2 Q.B. 57. *Janvier* v. *Sweeney* [1919] 2 K.B. 316 is a similar case.

[81] In all the plaintiff recovered £100 1s. 10½d.—£100 for emotional distress, and 1s. 10½d., the cost of a railway ticket to Leytonstone, for the distinct tort of deceit (see below, Chapter 18). A false statement had been made with the object and effect that she should act on it to her detriment.

[82] "The most learned and accurate lawyer": *Peters* v. *Prince of Wales Theatre Ltd.* [1943] K.B. 73, 77, *per* Goddard L.J.

[83] *Hambrook* v. *Stokes Bros.* [1925] 1 K.B. 141, 162.

[84] [1901] 2 K.B. 669.

just possibly in exceptional cases, any person or object.[85] And substantial damages may sometimes be warranted.[86]

It must be noted that Kennedy J. in *Dulieu* v. *White* did not say that the only sense which the law would recognise as the medium for conveying the impression of fear to the mind was the sense of sight. "I cannot imagine that Kennedy J. would ever have said anything so foolish."[87] So the Court of Appeal[88] held the defendant liable when he ran over an infant while negligently backing a car belonging to the infant's father out of a garage, knowing that the father was in earshot in another part of the garage, and the father suffered nervous shock as a result of hearing his son's screams. There had been a direct perception of the accident as an entire event.

So by the end of the 1970s it appeared to be settled that an action lies if the injury apprehended or actually seen or heard is to a close relative such as a spouse or a child,[89] or (in certain circumstances) a fellow-workman,[90] or even to a third party if the plaintiff was a rescuer.[91] Protection may even be extended to one who has witnessed some unnerving or ghastly spectacle, though neither the life nor limb of any third party has been imperilled.[92] Thus in *Attia* v. *British Gas*[93] the Court of Appeal refused to strike out a claim by a plaintiff who had witnessed the destruction of her home by fire.

Fifthly, it is now clear since the decision of the House of Lords in 1982 in *McLoughlin* v. *O'Brian*[94] that there is no principle or policy or rule of law which prevents damages being awarded to a plaintiff who has not seen or heard the accident in question, but who has suffered reasonably foreseeable nervous shock by experiencing its immediate aftermath.[95]

It is easier to state the effect of *McLoughlin* in this negative way. For although all the Law Lords were clear that reasonable foresight of nervous shock was a necessary condition of liability, some of them also thought that something more was required to establish the necessary proximity. The whole question was again considered by the House of Lords in *Copoc* v. *Wright*,[96] a case which arose out of the 1989 Hillsborough football stadium disaster. Their Lordships once more emphasised that the factors of time, space, and relationship between the parties will

---

[85] *Owens* v. *Liverpool Corporation* [1939] 1 K.B. 394; *Attia* v. *British Gas* [1988] Q.B. 304.

[86] *Hinz* v. *Berry* [1970] 2 Q.B. 40.

[87] *Bourhill* v. *Young*, 1941 S.L.T. 364, 385, *per* Lord Justice-Clerk Aitchinson.

[88] *Boardman* v. *Sanderson* (1961) [1964] 1 W.L.R. 1317.

[89] *Currie* v. *Wardrop*, 1927 S.C. 538 (fiancé); *Turbyfield* v. *G.W. Ry.* (1938) 54 T.L.R. 221 (sister).

[90] *Dooley* v. *Cammell Laird Ltd.* [1951] 1 Lloyd's Rep. 271.

[91] *Chadwick* v. *British Railways Board* [1967] 1 W.L.R. 912 (railway accident).

[92] *Owens* v. *Liverpool Corporation* [1939] 2 K.B. 394 (hearse containing relative's coffin overturned). But this decision was doubted by Lords Thankerton, Wright and Porter in *Bourhill* v. *Young*. Cf. *Attia* v. *British Gas* [1988] Q.B. 304.

[93] [1988] Q.B. 304.

[94] [1983] A.C. 410. This decision sweeps away the confusing dicta to be found in the earlier H.L. decision of *Bourhill* v. *Young* [1943] A.C. 92, and cases which followed it.

[95] The plaintiff was at home when her husband and four children were involved in a horrible car accident some miles away. Two hours later she was told of the disaster, and taken to the hospital, where she saw what had happened to her family.

[96] [1991] 4 All E.R. 907.

all be important. The shock must be caused by the actual sight or sound of the accident or its immediate aftermath, and not by the result of a communication from a third party. There is a real distinction between shock and grief.[97] The House held that even the watching of live television broadcasts would not normally satisfy the sight or sound requirement, at any rate if in accordance with current guidelines which prohibit the transmission of pictures of the death and suffering of recognisable individuals. On the question of the relationship between the parties involved their Lordships declined to specify particular relationships which automatically would, or would not, give rise to liability. While there would be what amounted to a rebuttable presumption that the requirement was satisfied in situations involving spouses or parents every case would ultimately depend on its own facts; and in cases of other family relationships the closeness and intimacy of the parties would have to be examined. In *Copoc* v. *Wright* itself a plaintiff who was himself present at the football ground failed to recover in respect of the loss of his two brothers.[98] But if the circumstances are sufficiently horrific, such as "a petrol tanker careering out of control into a school in session and bursting into flames"[99] the possibility of even bystanders recovering is not completely ruled out. Although in some cases the alarming prospect of open-ended liability has been painted in bright colours,[1] the difficulties of proving the constituent elements of the cause of action impose their own appropriate limitation on its scope. Lord Bridge of Harwich said in *McLoughlin* v. *O'Brian* that "if asked where the thing is to stop, I should answer, in an adaption of the language of Lord Wright[2] and Stephenson L.J.[3] 'where in a particular case the good sense of the judge, enlightened by progressive awareness of mental illness, decides.' "[4]

Conclusion

In *Copoc* v. *Wright* Lord Oliver said that he could not "regard the present state of the law as entirely satisfactory or as logically defensible" and concluded that only "considerations of policy" made it explicable.[5] For whether a person outside the area of physical impact has a legally protected right to be free from the emotional distress occasioned by the sight of the peril in which others have been placed by the defendant's negligence is really a question which each legal system must decide for itself after due consideration of the various social interests involved.[6] While some, including Lord Oliver himself, have sug-

---

[97] *Ravenscroft* v. *Rederiaktiebolaget Transatlantic The Times*, April 6, 1992 C.A. applying observations in *Copoc* v. *Wright*.
[98] "The quality of brotherly love is well known to differ widely—from Cain and Abel to David and Jonathan.": *Copoc* v. *Wright* [1991] 4 All E.R. 907, 921 (Lord Ackner).
[99] *Ibid.* at p. 919.
[1] A phrase used by Lord Wilberforce in *McLoughlin* v. *O'Brian*.
[2] In *Bourhill* v. *Young* [1943] A.C. 92, 110.
[3] In *McLoughlin* v. *O'Brian* [1981] Q.B. 599, 612.
[4] [1983] A.C. 410, 436.
[5] [1991] 4 All E.R. 907, 932.
[6] *Marx* v. *Att.-Gen.* [1974] 1 N.Z.L.R. 164, 176.

gested that that decision should be taken by the legislature, it can powerfully be argued that it is one better left to the pragmatic judicial technique of the courts.[7]

§ 9.9. SCOPE OF THE DUTY OF CARE

Unforeseeable plaintiffs

There is no liability for negligence unless there is in the particular case a legal duty to take care, and this duty must be one which is owed to the plaintiff himself and not merely to others.[8] This duty of carefulness is not universal; it does not extend to all occasions, and all persons, and all modes of activity. So Lord Esher M.R. once uttered the characteristic remark that: "If a man is driving on Salisbury plain, and no other person is near him, he is at liberty to drive as fast and as recklessly as he pleases."[9] So a man may be under a duty of care towards one person, and yet in the same matter and on the same occasion under no duty of care towards another.[10]

In *Palsgraf* v. *Long Island Railroad Co.*[11] two servants of the defendants, while helping a passenger to board a train, negligently dislodged a parcel carried by the passenger: the parcel fell and its contents (assumed to be fireworks) exploded. The shock of the explosion knocked over some scales about 25 feet away, which in turn struck and injured the plaintiff. A majority of the New York Court of Appeals held that she could not recover. Cardozo C.J. said:

> "The conduct of the defendants' guard, if a wrong in its relation to the holder of the package, was not a wrong in its relation to the plaintiff standing far away. Relative to her it was not negligence at all. Nothing in the situation gave notice that the falling package had in it the potency of peril to persons thus removed. . . . The law of causation, remote or proximate, is thus foreign to the case before us."

Scope of the risk or hazard

The harm to the plaintiff's interest which has in fact occurred must be of a kind against which it was the duty of the defendant to take precautions. So, although a peculiar duty to take care is imposed on those who send firearms out into the world, nobody would contend that an action would lie if A lent a loaded gun to B, who dropped it onto C's toes.[12]

---

[7] As all the Law Lords (except Lord Scarman) thought in *McLoughlin* v. *O'Brian* [1983] A. C. 410.

[8] *Palsgraf* v. *Long Island R.R. Co.* (1928) 284 N.Y. 339; 162 N.E. 99.

[9] *Le Lievre* v. *Gould* [1893] 1 Q.B. 491, 497. Lord Esher was not considering criminal liability.

[10] See also above, §§ 9.2–9.3.

[11] (1928) 284, N.Y. 339; 162 N.E. 99.

[12] The well-known case of *Gorris* v. *Scott* (1874) L.R. 9 Ex. 125 (see below, Chap. 10) is perhaps the best example of this point. See also *Jones* v. *Livox Quarries Ltd.* [1952] 2 Q.B. 608 (below, Chap. 22).

Omissions and commissions[13]

In the absence of some existing duty the general principle is that there is no liability for a mere omission to act.[14] There is a basic distinction between causing something and failing to prevent it happening. There may be liability if the defendant is in the position of an employer or invitor, or the risk has resulted from the use of some instrumentality under his control, or from an obvious danger such as fire on land occupied by him,[15] or he has voluntarily intervened to render help. "The result of all this is that the good Samaritan who tries to help may find himself mulcted in damages, while the priest and the Levite who pass by on the other side go on their cheerful way rejoicing."[16] So a doctor who gives first aid to the victim of a traffic accident, although he has a statutory right to recover the cost of his treatment from the person using the vehicle at the time of the event out of which the bodily injury arose,[17] may in theory find himself sued for negligence by the victim. But the courts are unlikely to look with favour upon such a claim, and would be understandably reluctant to find on the facts that the defendant had been careless.[18]

Volunteers

It is well established that in general one who has full knowledge of the nature and extent of the risk and is entirely free to avoid it, but nevertheless voluntarily goes on and is injured, cannot recover.[19] This may either be because the defences of *volenti non fit injuria*[20] or contributory negligence[21] have been raised successfully or because the defendant's duty in the particular relationship under consideration is held to have been discharged. The latter view has been adopted in cases dealing with the liability of drunken drivers of vehicles to their passengers.[22] This has been said to be a more satisfactory manner of ascertaining their respective rights than by opposing to a fixed measure of duty exculpatory considerations, such as the voluntary assumption of

---

[13] See J. C. Smith, *Liability in Negligence* (1984), Chap. 3, cited with approval in *Sutherland Shire Council v. Heyman* (1985) 59 A.L.J.R. 564. See also Logie, "Affirmative Action in the Law of Tort: the Case of the Duty to Warn" [1989] 48 C.L.J. 115; Markesinis, "Negligence, Nuisance and Affirmative Duties of Action" (1989) 105 L.Q.R. 104.

[14] *Smith v. Littlewoods Organisation* [1987] A.C. 241, 271, *per* Lord Goff.

[15] *Goldman v. Hargrave* [1967] 1 A.C. 645.

[16] Prosser, *Torts* (4th ed.), p. 344.

[17] Road Traffic Act 1988, s.158.

[18] *Cf. F. v. West Berkshire Health Authority* [1990] 2 A.C. 52 (Lord Bridge), 68 (Lord Brandon), 73–78 (Lord Goff).

[19] See below, Chap. 22.

[20] See, *e.g. Morris v. Murray* [1991] 2 Q.B. 6, C.A. (no liability to passenger injured during joyride in light aircraft when he knew the pilot was drunk).

[21] Although findings of 100 per cent. contributory negligence, which have sometimes been made, have been criticised as self-contradictory in that they imply that the claimant was solely responsible for his own loss rather than a contributor to it: see *Pitts v. Hunt* [1990] 1 Q.B. 302. For contributory negligence see, generally, below Chap. 22.

[22] *Insurance Commissioners v. Joyce* (1948) 77 C.L.R. 39. See also *Pitts v. Hunt* [1990] 1 Q.B. 302.

risk or contributory negligence,[23] but it is open to the serious objection that it infringes the general principle[24] that the standard of care is an objective one.[25]

Abnormal plaintiffs

Once a breach of duty has been established, the defendant must take his victim as he finds him.[26] In determining whether a duty exists, however, the law will not take account of abnormal susceptibilities or infirmities in the person[27] or property[28] of the plaintiff which the defendant neither knew nor could reasonably be taken to have foreseen. But if the defendant knows that the plaintiff has some characteristic or incapacity which will increase the risk of harm, the court may hold that the defendant owes a proportionately higher degree of care.[29] So the House of Lords has held[30] that persons carrying out excavations in a London street ought to foresee the presence of blind persons (of whom there are some 7,000 in London) and protect them by some better device than a punner hammer[31] with a handle sloping at a height of two feet. This does not place an undue burden on defendants, for they are entitled to assume that there are places to which the blind will not go unaccompanied, and that they will take reasonable care of their own safety—e.g. by using a white stick.[32]

Liability for third parties

In general there is no liability for the acts or omissions of others unless there is some special relationship, (e.g. vicarious liability) between the parties.[33] So business life would be impossible if there was a general duty on traders to satisfy themselves that the goods which they sell will not be used to facilitate some dishonest purpose which will damage others.[34] But situations involving a right to *control* the activities of third parties may give rise to a special relationship. Thus in *Home Office* v. *Dorset Yacht*[35] the House of Lords imposed liability on the Crown when juvenile delinquents escaped from a penal institution on an island and by careless handling of the boat in which they had escaped, damaged the plaintiff's yacht. In the previous year there had been 172 escapes from the institution, but on this occasion the guards

---

[23] *Insurance Commissioners* v. *Joyce* (1948) 77 C.L.R. 39, 59, *per* Dixon J.

[24] See below, § 9.10.

[25] *Nettleship* v. *Weston* [1971] 2 Q.B. 691.

[26] See below, Chap. 23.

[27] *McLaughlin* v. *Trimmer* (1946) 79 L1.L.R. 649 (decayed tooth).

[28] *Nova-Mink Ltd.* v. *Trans-Canada Airlines* [1951] 2 D.L.R. 241 (extra-sensitive mink).

[29] See, *e.g. Kirkham* v. *Chief Constable of Greater Manchester* [1990] 3 All E.R. 246, C.A. (duty to prisoner with suicidal tendencies). *cf. Knight* v. *Home Office* [1990] 3 All E.R. 237.

[30] *Haley* v. *London Electricity Board* [1965] A.C. 778.

[31] A hammer for beating down earth.

[32] *Haley* v. *London Electricity Board* [1965] A.C. 778, 795.

[33] *Smith* v. *Littlewoods Organisation* [1988] A.C. 241, 272, *per* Lord Goff.

[34] *Paterson Zochonis Ltd.* v. *Merfarken Packaging Ltd.* [1986] 1 All E.R. 522, *per* Robert Goff L.J. (as he then was). But it might be different if, say, counterfeit currency was handed to an innocent dupe for circulation, or a car was hired to a person known to be drunk.

[35] [1970] A.C. 1004.

were all asleep. The defendants had a right of control which had not been properly exercised. Attempts to extend the *Dorset Yacht* case to situations not involving so immediate a relationship of control have been unsuccessful. Thus the police will not be liable for damage caused by offenders whom they have carelessly failed to apprehend.[36] Occupiers of property who fail to take or maintain adequate precautions against vandals damaging empty property or using that property as a base from which to attack the premises of others have also generally avoided liability. Some familiar judicial techniques have been employed. It has been said that even though the damage may unfortunately sometimes be foreseeable in contemporary English life, there is still no duty of care in the absence of a right of control,[37] or else that even if there is a duty the damage is too remote.[38] The House of Lords has confirmed the general reluctance to find for plaintiffs in such cases,[39] although the differing reasons given by their Lordships reflects the variety of approaches in the earlier cases.[40]

§ 9.10. STANDARD OF CARE[41]: (1) THE REASONABLE MAN

Standard is objective

The standard of conduct required by the common law is that of the reasonable man. This has been settled ever since *Vaughan v. Menlove*.[42] The plaintiff had an interest in certain cottages on land adjoining that on which the defendant had erected a haystack which was not properly ventilated. The plaintiff's cottages were damaged by a fire which had spontaneously ignited in the haystack, which was insured. "When the condition of the stack, and the probable and almost inevitable consequence of permitting it to remain in its then state were pointed out to him, he abstained from the exercise of the precautionary measures that common prudence and foresight would naturally suggest, and very coolly observed that 'he would chance it'; it was manifest that he adverted to his interest in the insurance office."[43] The argument for the defendant that it was enough if he had acted bona fide to the best of his judgment was rejected.[44] A modern example is *The Lady Gwendolen*.[45]

---

[36] *Hill v. Chief Constable of West Yorkshire* [1989] A.C. 53.

[37] *King v. Liverpool City Council* [1986] 1 W.L.R. 890. So also *P. Perl Exporters Ltd. v. Camden L.B.C.* [1984] Q.B. 342 where it was said (p. 360) that "the contrary proposition would lead to the most starling and far-reaching results"—*e.g.* the more valuable the plaintiff's property, the more precautions his neighbours would have to take.

[38] As in *Lamb v. Camden L.B.C.* [1981] Q.B. 625, distinguished on the facts in *Ward v. Cannock Chase Council* [1986] 2 W.L.R. 660, 679 ("The likelihood of unoccupied property receiving the attention of vandals was very much higher at The Mossley in Rugeley than in Hampstead").

[39] *Smith v. Littlewoods Organisation* [1987] A.C. 241.

[40] It is instructive to contrast the speech of Lord Mackay with that of Lord Goff.

[41] See Kidner, "The variable standard of care" (1991) 11 L.S. 1.

[42] (1837) 3 Bing.N.C. 468; 4 Scott 244.

[43] (1837) 4 Scott 244, 254, *per* Vaughan J. This must be the earliest, and one of the most interesting, judicial references to the impact of insurance on torts: see above, Chap. 2.

[44] (1837) 3 Bing.N.C. 468, 475.

[45] [1965] P. 294.

The directors of Guinness's Brewery sent stout from Dublin to Liverpool in a ship whose captain relied entirely on radar when going up the Mersey at full speed. The directors were held guilty of "actual fault" under the Merchant Shipping Act 1894, s.503, in failing properly to supervise the captain. "The law must apply a standard which is not relaxed to cater for their factual ignorance of all activities outside brewing: having become owners of ships, they must behave as reasonable ship-owners"[46]

"The standard of foresight of the reasonable man," said Lord Macmillan,[47] "eliminates the personal equation and is independent of the idiosyncrasies of the particular person whose conduct is in question. Some persons are by nature unduly timorous and imagine every path beset with lions. Others, of more robust temperament, fail to foresee or nonchalantly disregard even the most obvious dangers. The reasonable man is presumed to be free from both over-apprehension and from over-confidence." "A reasonable man does not mean a paragon of circumspection."[48] So the judges recognise that even a housewife with young children cannot be in two places at once.[49] But the reasonable man or woman is also cool and collected and remembers to take precautions for his or her own safety even in an emergency.[50] So, while on the one hand adoption of a course subsequently seen to have been unfortunate may not necessarily amount to negligence,[51] on the other hand the fact that "it might happen to anyone" is not necessarily a defence[52]—even the most careful are sometimes careless. So the case for wearing seat belts is so strong that forgetfulness will not be accepted as an excuse.[53] A number of judicial metaphors or analogies are now firmly embedded in the law. "The person concerned is sometimes described as 'the man in the street,' 'the man on the Clapham omnibus,' or, as I recently read in an American author, 'the man who takes the magazines at home and in the evening pushes the lawn mower in his shirt sleeves.' "[54]

Different degrees of negligence not recognised

The law of torts[55] does not recognise different standards of care or different degrees of negligence in different classes of case. The sole stan-

---

[46] [1965] P. 294, 305, *per* Winn L.J.

[47] *Glasgow Corporation* v. *Muir* [1943] A.C. 448, 457.

[48] *Billings & Son* v. *Riden* [1958] A.C. 240, 255, *per* Lord Reid.

[49] *Carmarthenshire County Council* v. *Lewis* [1955] A.C. 549, 566.

[50] *Ghannan* v. *Glasgow Corporation*, 1950, S.C. 23.

[51] *Latimer* v. *A.E.C. Ltd.* [1953] A.C. 643, 656.

[52] *Lewis* v. *Carmarthenshire County Council* [1953] 1 All E.R. 1025, 1028.

[53] *Froom* v. *Butcher* [1976] Q.B. 286, 295.

[54] *Hall* v. *Brooklands Auto-Racing Club* [1933] 1 K.B. 205, 224, *per* Greer L.J. Yet "God forbid that the standard of manners should be taken from the man on the Clapham omnibus": *Lea* v. *Justice of the Peace Ltd.* (reported *sub nom. Privacy and the Press*, London, 1947), p. 156, *per* Hilbery J. This mythical figure goes back to the years before the Kaiser's War: after 1914 the omnibus service between Clapham and Knightsbridge ceased to run. See Kahn (1985) 102 S.A.L.J. 18.

[55] *Pentecost* v. *London District Auditor* [1951] 2 K.B. 759, 764. *Aliter* in other branches of law, *e.g.* trusts and criminal law.

dard is the care that would be shown in the circumstances by a reasonably careful person, and the sole form of negligence is a failure to use this amount of care. It is true, indeed, that this amount will be different in different cases, for a reasonable person will not show the same anxious care when handling an umbrella as when handling a loaded gun.[56] Thus a manufacturer of carcinogens must take such a high degree of care as to be almost under strict liability.[57] On the other hand there is a growing tendency in the field of occupiers' liability to expect more of a wealthy company or public authority than of a private individual.[58] But arguments that police officers[59] or sequestrators[60] should for reasons of public policy be held to a lower standard of care have been rejected.

It is commonly a negligent act voluntarily to undertake the doing of any act which can be safely done only through the possession of special skill, unless the doer possesses, or believes on reasonable grounds that he possesses, the requisite skill.[61] The negligence does not consist in the lack of skill but in undertaking the work without skill. It may be quite reasonable for a householder to do his own carpentry or plumbing or painting, but this does not of itself protect him.[62] So a high standard of skill and care is demanded of the driver of a motor-car—since the motor-car has become a lethal weapon.[63] So in some circumstances the reasonable driver will take all possible care.[64] But this is a different thing from recognising different legal standards of care; the test of negligence is the same in all cases.[65] So a learner driver must comply with the same objective and impersonal standard as any other driver.[66] So also must a driver who is old or infirm, as distinct from totally unconscious.[67] But, perhaps illogically, it has been held that an unusually expert rally-driver must display towards a passenger in his car the skill of such a driver,[68] and it has been suggested that a client who employs a solicitor of high standing and great experience is entitled to expect more than ordinary competence.[69]

---

[56] *Beckett* v. *Newalls Insulation Co. Ltd.* [1953] 1 W.L.R. 8, 17.

[57] *Wright* v. *Dunlop Rubber Co. Ltd.* (1972) 13 K.I.R. 255, 273.

[58] *Goldman* v. *Hargrave* [1967] 1 A.C. 645.

[59] *Marshall* v. *Osmond* [1982] Q.B. 857.

[60] *I.R.C.* v. *Hoogstraten* [1985] Q.B. 1007.

[61] See *The Lady Gwendolen* [1965] P. 294.

[62] *Wells* v. *Cooper* [1958] 2 Q.B. 265.

[63] *Daly* v. *Liverpool Corporation* [1939] 2 All E.R. 142, 144.

[64] *Randall* v. *Tarrant* [1955] 1 W.L.R. 255, 259.

[65] Nevertheless, in *Coggs* v. *Bernard* (1704) 2 Ld.Raym. 909, an unfortunate attempt was made to introduce into English law the Roman doctrine. According to this doctrine there are three different kinds or degrees of negligence—ordinary, gross and slight. There are no authorities which compel us to admit that distinctions so vague and impracticable in their nature, so unfounded in principle, and so clearly rooted in historical error as to the rules of Roman law, form any genuine part of the law of England, particularly as the judges have often said they do not understand the expression "gross negligence": *Houghland* v. *R. R. Low (Luxury Coaches) Ltd.* [1962] 1 Q.B. 694, 697–698.

[66] *Nettleship* v. *Weston* [1971] 2 Q.B. 691.

[67] *Roberts* v. *Ramsbottom* [1980] 1 W.L.R. 823.

[68] *McComiskey* v. *McDermott* [1974] I.R. 75.

[69] *Argyll* v. *Beuselinck* [1972] 2 Lloyd's Rep. 172.

Defendant's incapacity irrelevant

The law "does not attempt to see men as God sees them, for more than one sufficient reason. . . . If, for instance, a man is born hasty and awkward, is always having accidents and hurting himself or his neighbours, no doubt his congenital defects will be allowed for in the courts of Heaven, but his slips are no less troublesome to his neighbours than if they sprang from guilty neglect."[70] The foolish and the forgetful are judged by the same external standard as other defendants. An apparent exception to this principle may be found in the case of a minor: it is accepted that the standard of care required is only that which would reasonably be expected of a child of the defendant's age.[71] But the exception is apparent only, for the true question is: what is normal conduct in a child of this age, not this child?

Difficulties of reasonable foresight

The advantage of the test of reasonable foresight is that it keeps the law in touch with the needs of the ordinary person. The disadvantage is that in a complex society ordinary people may have insufficient knowledge or experience of the activity under consideration to entitle them to set the appropriate standard of care. The result may be confused and contradictory decisions which lay down no clear guide for conduct. The best example is the *Wagon Mound* litigation. The facts were that the steamship Wagon Mound was taking in bunkering-oil some 600 feet away from a wharf in the harbour of Sydney. As a result of the carelessness of the seamen, a large quantity of oil spilt into the bay. Some 60 hours later that oil ignited and a fire spread rapidly and did considerable damage to the wharf and also to ships adjoining that wharf. The outbreak of fire was due to the fact that wind and tide had together carried under the wharf some inflammable debris, on top of which lay some cotton waste which was then set alight by molten metal falling from the wharf as a result of welding operations being carried out on it. These flames in turn set the floating oil afire. The Judicial Committee in an action brought by the owners of the wharf held that the damage in question was not reasonably foreseeable at all.[72]

In *The Wagon Mound (No. 2)* a different action was launched by different plaintiffs, the owners of the ships adjoining the wharf which had been damaged in the fire. The trial judge held that the plaintiffs were not entitled to recover in negligence, for although the damage was foreseeable, the risk was so remote that it could be disregarded and was therefore not *reasonably* foreseeable. A reasonable ship's officer would have appreciated, it was said, that there was some possibility of fire from floating oil on the sea water, but that possibility was so remote that he would be justified in disregarding it under the principles set out

---

[70] Holmes, *The Common Law*, p. 108. See also *McGrath* v. *National Coal Board* (unreported), H.L., May 4, 1954, *per* Lord Reid.

[71] See *Gough* v. *Thorne* [1966] 1 W.L.R. 1387 (Contributory negligence).

[72] [1961] A.C. 388.

in *Bolton* v. *Stone*.[73] On appeal the Judicial Committee held[74] that on the facts the defendants ought reasonably to have foreseen damage by fire against which precautions should have been taken, and so they were liable in negligence. The court "based liability on more factors than mere foreseeability; it also assessed the following considerations: the size of the risk, the social utility and legality of the risk-creating activity, the degree to which the defendant is felt to be at fault, and the cost of eliminating the risk."[75]

§ 9.11. STANDARD OF CARE: (2) THE CONCEPT OF RISK

There is now a tendency to expound the standard of care required in any particular case more in terms of risk than in terms of reasonable foreseeability. A risk is a chance of harm to others which the party whose conduct has been called in question should have recognised. Hence negligence is conduct which falls below the standard established by the law for the protection of others against unreasonable risk of harm. (The risk or hazard in question must, as we have already seen, be to a legally protected interest of the plaintiff.[76]) There are three factors for consideration. First, the magnitude of the risk to which the defendant exposes other persons by his action; secondly the importance of the object to be attained by the dangerous form of activity; and thirdly the burden of adequate precautions.[77] We shall consider each separately.

(1) The magnitude of the risk to which others are exposed

The law in all cases exacts a degree of care commensurate with the risk created.[78] There are two factors in determining the magnitude of a risk—the seriousness of the injury risked, and the likelihood of the injury being in fact caused.[79]

Gravity of the injury

In *Paris* v. *Stepney Borough Council*[80] the plaintiff, who had only one good eye, was blinded in the course of his employment. He contended

---

[73] [1951] A.C. 850.

[74] [1967] 1 A.C. 617.

[75] J. C. Smith, *Liability in Negligence* (1984) p. 108.

[76] See above, § 9.2.

[77] *Hicks* v. *British Transport Commission* [1958] 1 W.L.R. 493, 505. This approach has been adopted in many other English cases: see *McCarthy* v. *Coldair Ltd.* [1951] 2 T.L.R. 1226; *Watt* v. *Hertfordshire C.C.* [1954] 1 W.L.R. 835; *Jones* v. *Vauxhall Motors* [1955] 1 Lloyd's Rep. 152; *Morris* v. *West Hartlepool S.N. Co.* [1956] A.C. 552; *Videan* v. *B.T.C.* [1963] 2 Q.B. 650.

[78] *Read* v. *J. Lyons & Co.* [1947] A.C. 156, 173; *Lloyds Bank* v. *Railway Executive* [1952] 1 All E.R. 1248, 1253.

[79] *Paris* v. *Stepney B.C.* [1951] A.C. 367, 381. A vivid summary has been given by Judge Learned Hand: "The duty . . . is a function of three variables: (1) the probability that she [defendant's ship] will break away; (2) the gravity of the resulting injury, if she does; (3) the burden of the adequate precautions. Possibly it serves to bring this notion into relief to state it in algebraic terms: if the probability be called P; the injury L; and the burden B; liability depends upon whether B is less than L multiplied by P, *i.e.* whether $B < PL$": *United States* v. *Carroll Towing Co.* (1947) 159 F. (2d) 169, 173.

[80] [1951] A.C. 367.

successfully that his employers, by omitting to provide him with goggles, were in breach of their duty to take reasonable care of his safety because, though it was not the practice to provide goggles for that class of work, they must have known that the consequences of an accident to his good eye would be particularly disastrous. In the Court of Appeal Asquith L.J.[81] had said[82] that "A greater risk of injury is not the same thing as a risk of greater injury; the first alone is relevant to liability." This neatly phrased apophthegm was disapproved in the House of Lords. The duty of an employer to take reasonable care to protect his servant is owed to each individual workman and a reasonable and prudent employer would be influenced not only by the greater or lesser probability of an accident occurring to the workman in question but also by the gravity of the consequences to him if an accident did occur.[83] Protection in the way of goggles should be provided for two-eyed men as well as for one-eyed men if the risk is sufficiently great.[84]

But if an employee has some special susceptibility to harm it does not follow that his employers are guilty of negligence merely because they know of this and yet permit him to continue with the only work which they can offer him.[85]

Likelihood of injury

The general principle is that before negligence can be established it must be shown not only that the event was foreseeable but also that there is a reasonable likelihood of injury. To base liability upon foreseeability alone would be too severe, for, "foreseeability does not include any idea of likelihood at all."[86] So "people must guard against reasonable probabilities, but they are not bound to guard against fantastic possibilities."[87] Thus in *Blyth* v. *Birmingham Water Works Co.*[88] the defendants were held not guilty of negligence "because their precautions proved insufficient against the effect of the extreme severity of the frost of 1855, which penetratd to a greater depth[89] than any which ordinarily occurs south of the polar regions." Again, in *Bolton* v. *Stone*,[90] the plaintiff, while standing in the quiet suburban highway outside her house, was struck by a cricket ball[91] from the defendant's ground, the batsman "having received the right kind of ball and dealt with it in the

---

[81] "Than whom there have been few greater masters of the English language in judicial interpretation or exposition": *Betty's Cafes Ltd.* v. *Phillips Furnishing Stores Ltd.* [1959] A.C. 20, 34, *per* Viscount Simonds.

[82] [1950] 1 K.B. 320, 324.

[83] *Smith* v. *Howdens Ltd.* [1953] N.I. 131. The difficulty of these cases is shown by the fact that although all the members of the House agreed on the law, two (Lord Simonds and Lord Morton of Henryton) dissented on its application to the facts.

[84] *Nolan* v. *Dental Manufacturing Co. Ltd.* [1958] 1 W.L.R. 936.

[85] *Withers* v. *Perry Chain Co. Ltd.* [1961] 1 W.L.R. 1314.

[86] *Chapman* v. *Hearse* (1961) C.L.R. 112, 155, *per* Dixon C.J.

[87] *Fardon* v. *Harcourt-Rivington* (1932) 146 L.T. 391, 392, *per* Lord Dunedin.

[88] (1856) 11 Ex. 781.

[89] Unstated, but the mains were laid more than 18 inches down.

[90] [1951] A.C. 850. See Goodhart (1951) 67 L.Q.R. 461; Lloyd (1951) 14 M.L.R. 499.

[91] Preserved in the museum at Lord's.

right kind of way."[92] The plaintiff was 100 yards from the batsman and the ball had cleared a 17-foot fence 78 yards from the batsman. Similar hits had occurred only about six times in the previous 30 years. The House of Lords held that the plaintiff had not established such a likelihood of injury as to convict the defendants of negligence in falling to take precautions against it. It was improbable that the ball would be hit out of the ground or would cause personal injuries if it was.[93] The case may be said to have established that, if an event is foreseeable, the antithesis of its being reasonably probable is that the possibility of its happening involves a risk so small that a reasonable man would feel justified in disregarding it.[94] No doubt if cricket cannot be played on a ground without creating a substantial risk it must not be played there at all,[95] but in this case the facts showed no substantial risk.[96] So again defendants who did nothing were held to be justified in their attitude when a man was electrocuted in a way which was "most unexpected" in that particular trade[97] or when every witness said that "he had never heard of an accident of this kind before."[98] But it is not always justifiable to neglect a risk of small magnitude simply because it is small—the difficulty, expense and advantages of eliminating the risk must also be considered,[99] as well as the general practice in such cases.[1] It may well be that defendants are in a stronger position if the risk was so small that they had never thought about it but merely followed the usual practice than if they had considered it and decided that the risks were very small, and so could be disregarded.[2]

Unlikely hazards

On the other hand, it is certainly not necessary that the chances that damage will result should be greater than the chances that no damage will occur.[3] The fire in *The Wagon Mound (No. 2)*[4] was "extremely unlikely" but yet a real danger which should have been reasonably foreseeable. So the fact that the injury which has occurred is unique in character, or has happened previously on a minimal number of occasions, or to a very few people, does not necessarily prove that the defendant is under no duty to take precautions against it. Thus the fact that five million similar objects have been put in circulation without

---

[92] *Booker v. Wenborn* [1962] 1 W.L.R. 162, 168, *per* Lord Evershed M.R.

[93] A claim in nuisance also failed; above, Chap. 5.

[94] *Carmarthenshire County Council v. Lewis* [1955] A.C. 549, 565.

[95] *Stone v. Bolton* [1950] 1 K.B. 201, 212; [1951] A.C. 850, 867.

[96] "It seems to me that a reasonable man, taking account of the chances against an accident happening, would not have felt himself called upon either to abandon the use of the ground for cricket or to increase the height of his surrounding fences. He would have done what the appellants did: in other words, he would have done nothing": [1951] A.C. 850, 869, *per* Lord Radcliffe.

[97] *Cilia v. James (H.M.) & Sons (A Firm)* [1954] 1 W.L.R. 721, 728.

[98] *Cuttress v. Scaffolding (G.B.) Ltd.* [1953] 1 W.L.R. 1311, 1316.

[99] *Goldman v. Hargrave* [1967] 1 A.C. 645.

[1] Below, § 9.13.

[2] *Morris v. West Hartlepool SN. Co. Ltd.* [1956] A.C. 552, 568.

[3] *The Wagon Mound (No. 2)* [1967] 1 A.C. 617.

[4] [1967] 1 A.C. 617. See below, Chap. 23.

complaint is not conclusive[5]; nor is the fact that thousands of persons have safely passed over the premises in question.[6] But, as we have just seen, *Bolton* v. *Stone*[7] holds that such a foreseeable risk may sometimes be disregarded by a reasonable man.

What exactly must be foreseen?

It is not necessary to show that the particular accident which has happened was foreseeable, any more than it is necessary to show that the particular damage was foreseeable[8] or that the particular plaintiff was foreseeable.[9] It is enough if it was reasonable in a general way to foresee the kind of thing that has occurred.[10] If it were necessary for the plaintiff to prove that the defendant ought to have foreseen the particular harm which in the event occurred, few actions for negligence would be successful. "The history of negligence is the history of the unexpected. The books are full of odd occurrences, strange conjunctions, and unpredictable contingencies."[11]

Thus in *Hughes* v. *Lord Advocate*[12] a small boy interfered with a paraffin lamp marking a manhole cover in a street, and was severely burned when the lamp exploded. It was argued for the defendants that they were not responsible for a fire caused by explosion as distinct from conflagration, but the House of Lords held that on the facts this was too fine a distinction. The cause of the accident was a known source of danger behaving in an unpredictable way.[13] *Hughes* v. *Lord Advocate* was distinguished in *Doughty* v. *Turner Manufacturing Co. Ltd.*[14] An asbestos cover was inadvertently knocked into a cauldron containing molten liquid at a temperature of 800 degrees centigrade. The asbestos suffered a chemical change causing the eruption of liquid which burned the plaintiff workman. This was an unforeseeable risk, and not a variant of the perils of splashing—a foreseeable risk. All earlier cases must now be read in the light of *Hughes* and *Doughty*.[15]

Again, although damage from frostbite is unusual in England, a defendant was held liable because he ought to have foreseen the type,

---

[5] *Grant* v. *Australian Knitting Mills* [1936] A.C. 85.

[6] *Protheroe* v. *Railway Executive* [1951] 1 K.B. 376, 379; *Caminer* v. *Northern and London Investment Trust* [1951] A.C. 88, 111.

[7] [1951] A.C. 850.

[8] *Draper* v. *Hodder* [1972] 2 Q.B. 556, 573.

[9] It is not necessary that there should be a specific person to whom the duty is owed at the time of the negligence: the duty may be potential or contingent or owed to a class—*e.g.* new customers as distinct from *this* new customer: *Grant* v. *Australian Knitting Mills* [1936] A.C. 85, 104: *Watson* v. *Fram Reinforced Concrete Co. Ltd., and Winget Ltd.* 1960 S.C. 100, 116; *Chapman* v. *Hearse* (1961) 106 C.L.R. 112, 120.

[10] *Stewart* v. *West African Terminals Ltd.* [1964] 2 Lloyd's Rep. 371, 375.

[11] *Bourhill* v. *Young*, 1941 S.L.T. 364, 387, *per* Lord Justice-Clerk Aitchison.

[12] [1963] A.C. 837.

[13] The principle in *Hughes* is applicable also to cases of economic loss; the precise manner in which the loss occurred does not need to be foreseeable: *Banque Financiere* v. *Westgate Insurance* [1989] 2 All E.R. 952 at p. 986, *per* Slade L J (not considered in [1990] 2 All E R 947 H L).

[14] [1964] 1 Q.B. 518. Note that the leading judgment was given by Lord Pearce, who had been a member of the H.L. in *Hughes* v. *Lord Advocate*.

[15] See *The Wagon Mound (No. 2)* [1967] 1 A.C. 617, 636.

kind or order of harm in question—namely, damage from exceptionally cold weather. It was not required that he should foresee the degree of damage which in fact occurred.[16] So if a road accident is of a type which one would expect on a sub-standard road in bad weather, that ends the matter.[17] But when the plaintiff, a farm-worker, contracted a very rare disease as a result of contract with the urine of rats, as distinct from being bitten by those rats, the defendant escaped liability.[18]

(2) The importance of the object to be attained

The reasonableness of the defendant's conduct will also depend upon the proportion which the risk bears to the object to be attained. To expose others to a risk of harm for a disproportionate object is unreasonable, whereas an equal risk for a better cause may be lawfully run without negligence. By running trains at the rate of 50 miles an hour railways have caused many fatal accidents which could quite easily have been avoided by running at ten miles an hour. But this additional safety would be attained at too great a cost of public convenience, and therefore, in neglecting this precaution, the companies do not fall below the standard of reasonable care and are not guilty of negligence.[19] Similarly, when it was suggested that a bank, which is under a duty to pay on demand a cheque which is in proper form, owed a duty to its customer to investigate all the indorsements, Lord Macnaghten said, "A banker so very careful to avoid risk would soon have no risk to avoid."[20] A different approach may be required if the object in view is of importance only to the defendant himself and not to the public. The saving of life or limb justifies taking risks which would not be permissible in the case of an ordinary commercial enterprise.[21]

(3) The burden of adequate precautions

The general principle is that the risk has to be weighed against the measures necessary to eliminate it. So the occupier of a small property on which a hazard arises which threatens a neighbour with substantial interests should not have to do as much as one with larger interests of his own at stake and greater resources to protect them.[22] If the risk is very remote, it is material to consider the degree of security which the suggested measures would afford: if in such a case the suggested measures are of an elaborate nature and would result only in a possibility that the accident would have been prevented or its consequences

---

[16] *Bradford* v. *Robinson Rentals Ltd.* [1967] 1 W.L.R. 337. See below, Chap. 23.
[17] *Levine* v. *Morris* [1970] 1 W.L.R. 71.
[18] *Tremain* v. *Pike* [1969] 1 W.L.R. 1556.
[19] *Daborn* v. *Bath Tramways Motor Co.* [1946] 2 All E.R. 333, 336. No doubt it was a relevant (if unexpressed) consideration in *Bolton* v. *Stone* that the activity promoted by the defendants was the English national game of cricket. As Goodhart observed ((1951) 67 L.Q.R. 463), if a man reading in his chambers at midnight were to throw his book—or a cricket ball—out of the window in a fit of irritation he could hardly defend himself against an injured passer-by by alleging that such an injury was extremely unlikely.
[20] *Bank of England* v. *Vagliano Bros.* [1891] A.C. 107, 157.
[21] *Watt* v. *Hertfordshire County Council* [1954] 1 W.L.R. 835 (fireman).
[22] *Goldman* v. *Hargrave* [1967] 1 A.C. 645.

mitigated, then the defendants may be justified in doing nothing.[23] It is also relevant to consider the degree of risk (if any) which taking the precautionary measures may involve.[24] But the greater the risk the less should be the weight given to questions of the cost of precautionary measures in time, trouble or money.[25] If the risk to life or property is really substantial, and no precautions would avail against it, it may be the duty of the defendants to cease to carry on the particular activity in question.[26]

If the defendant is held to be under a duty to take certain precautions for the safety of the plaintiff he may be permitted to excuse his failure to take those precautions by alleging that the accident would have happened even if he had fulfilled his duty. For even if he had taken the necessary precautions (*e.g.* provided a safety belt in the case of an industrial accident) the plaintiff might have refused to co-operate with his employer and failed to wear the belt. In such a case the plaintiff has in truth failed to prove that the defendant's breach of duty is causally relevant to the accident.[27]

§ 9.12. PARTICULAR CASES OF NEGLIGENCE

At one time it was regarded as well established that the only use of cases was for the propositions of law which they contained, and that it was no use to compare the facts of one case with those of another to see what decision should be arrived at in the latter. But this simple view became obscured as the law of negligence grew increasingly complicated. In particular, the disappearance of the civil jury meant that trials before a judge sitting alone became longer and more elaborate, and the judgments themselves correspondingly lengthier. A judge sitting alone feels obliged, unlike a jury, to explain why he is accepting or rejecting each of the arguments of counsel. Hence there was a natural but erroneous tendency to think when a judge gave reasons for his decision he was laying down rules of law.[28] But the House of Lords called a welcome halt to this process. In *Qualcast Ltd.* v. *Haynes*[29] it was emphatically reaffirmed that reasons given for decisions on questions of fact are not binding on future judges. The reports should not, therefore, be ransacked to discover isolated sentences with which to support an argument,[30] for owing to the great number of cases on negligence the "tests

---

[23] *Marshall* v. *Gotham Co. Ltd.* [1954] A.C. 360, 376.

[24] *Morris* v. *West Hartlepool S.N. Co. Ltd.* [1956] A.C. 552, 574, 579; *Hicks* v. *British Transport Commission* [1958] 1 W.L.R. 493, 505.

[25] *Morris* v. *Luton Corporation* [1946] 1 All E.R. 1, 4; *Edwards* v. *National Coal Board* [1949] 1 K.B. 704, 710; *Marshall* v. *Gotham Co. Ltd.* [1954] A.C. 360.

[26] *Stone* v. *Bolton* [1950] 1 K.B. 201, 212; [1951] A.C. 850, 867.

[27] *McWilliams* v. *Sir William Arrol & Co. Ltd.* [1962] 1 W.L.R. 295.

[28] It is instructive to compare the judgments on torts of a century ago with those of today. It is not only that Erle or Blackburn or Willes were right in the result—but their reasons were expressed with a clarity, simplicity and brevity rarely found today. Yet these judges had been trained under a system of pleading notorious for its verbosity and complexity.

[29] [1959] A.C. 743.

[30] *Teubner* v. *Humble* (1963) 108 C.L.R. 491, 503.

have been examined, discussed, and described in language either sober or picturesque."[31]

With these warnings in mind, we may consider some of the cases in which the courts have considered the duties owed by those engaged in particular professions, trades, or activities. We may take as examples professional people, schoolteachers, and users of the highway.

Professional people[32]

When the exercise of some special skill or competence, such as that of an architect, or doctor,[33] is in question, the test of the man on the Clapham omnibus is somewhat unreal. It is expected of such a professional person that he should show a fair, reasonable and competent degree of skill;[34] it is not required that he should use the highest degree of skill, for there may be persons who have higher education and greater advantages than he has, nor will he be held to have guaranteed a cure.[35] Thus a barrister is not expected to be right: it is enough that he exercises reasonable care.[36] So a medical practitioner should not be found negligent simply because one of the risks inherent in an operation of that kind occurs, or because in a matter of opinion he legitimately took a view which unfortunately happened to produce an adverse result in the particular circumstances.[37] A leading case is *Roe* v. *Minister of Health*.[38] In 1947 the plaintiff had been injected with nupercaine, a spinal anaesthetic, by a specialist anaesthetist in order to undergo a minor operation. The nupercaine was contained in glass ampoules, which were in turn kept in a jar of phenol. Some of the phenol percolated through cracks in the ampoules and contaminated the nupercaine. As a result the plaintiff was permanently paralysed below the waist. The cracks in the ampoules were not detectable by ordinary visual or tactile examination. This was a risk which was first drawn to the attention of the profession in 1951: it would not have been appreciated by an ordinary anaesthetist in 1947. "Nowadays it would be negligence not to realise the danger, but it was not then."[39]

For over 30 years the standard of care in England has been that of the ordinary skilled person exercising and professing to have that special

---

[31] *Booker* v. *Wenborn* [1962] 1 W.L.R. 162, 172, *per* Danckwerts L.J.

[32] See R. M. Jackson and J. L. Powell, *Professional Negligence* (2nd ed., 1987); A. M. Dugdale and K. M. Stanton, *Professional Negligence*, (2nd ed., 1989).

[33] The duty is also owed by an unqualified person who undertakes to cure another: *Brogan* v. *Bennett* [1955] I.R. 119.

[34] The obligation "to exercise proper skill and judgment in his profession" applies as fully to professional people employed "in house" by organisations as to independent practitioners. There is "no difference" between the two groups in this respect: *Smith* v. *Eric S. Bush* [1990] 1 A.C. 831, 865 (Lord Griffiths). This is an important point when employed professional people are becoming increasingly common.

[35] *Challard* v. *Bell* (1959) 18 D.L.R. (2d) 150, 152.

[36] *Saif Ali* [1980] A.C. 198, 231.

[37] *Whitehouse* v. *Jordan* [1981] 1 W.L.R. 246.

[38] [1954] 2 Q.B. 66.

[39] *Per* Denning L.J. [1954] 2 Q.B. 66, 68. For the defence of general practice, see below, § 9.13.

skill, and a doctor or surgeon was not to be held negligent if he acted in accordance with the practice accepted at that time as proper by a responsible body of medical opinion, notwithstanding that other doctors adopted different practices.[40] This *Bolam* test has twice been emphatically approved by the House of Lords in relation to diagnosis and treatment.[41] The law imposes the duty of care: but its standard is a matter of medical judgment. In *Sidaway* v. *Governors of Bethlem Royal Hospital*[42] the appellant argued that while the *Bolam* test might be correct with regard to diagnosis and treatment it was not correct with regard to warnings of the risk inherent in a course of proposed treatment, and that the courts should adopt instead the doctrine of "informed consent," which had been favoured in some jurisdictions in North America. But the House of Lords again affirmed the *Bolam* test. So in effect a doctor has the right to withhold information from the patient. Therefore the doctrine of "informed consent" has no place in English law, save to the extent that there may be cases in which the proposed treatment involves a substantial risk of grave consequences to this particular patient so that a prudent medical man would give a warning.[43]

The *Bolam* test has been applied to other advisory professions—*e.g.* lawyers[44] and accountants.[45] It has also been applied to a firm of auctioneers valuing a painting for a client prior to sale.[46]

Parents and schoolteachers

A schoolteacher is bound to take such care of his pupils as a careful parent would take care of his or her children.[47] This is generally known as the "careful parent test,"[48] but in the same family one parent might be so prudent as to be criticised for fussiness whereas the other might be too anxious to encourage self-reliance in the child.[49] The "careful parent test" is also hardly appropriate in some circumstances—*e.g.* very large schools[50]—and it is simpler to say that the duty of a schoolteacher is to take such care as is reasonable in the circumstances. This duty is somewhat higher than the common duty of care under the Occupiers'

---

[40] *Bolam* v. *Friern Barnet Hospital Management Committee* [1957] 1 W.L.R. 582.

[41] *Whitehouse* v. *Jordan* [1981] 1 W.L.R. 246; *Maynard* v. *West Midlands Regional Health Authority* [1984] 1 W.L.R. 634. The test also applies to advice given in a "non-therapeutic" context such as contraception: *Gold* v. *Harringey Health Authority* [1988] Q.B. 481.

[42] [1985] A.C. 871.

[43] [1985] A.C. 871, 895, 900, 913. Lord Bridge of Harwich added that if questioned specifically about risks involved in a particular proposed treatment, the doctor is under a duty to answer both truthfully and fully.

[44] *Saif Ali* v. *Sydney Mitchell & Co.* [1980] A.C. 198.

[45] *Mutual Life Assurance Co. Ltd.* v. *Evatt* [1971] A.C. 793.

[46] *Luxmoore-May* v. *Messenger May Baverstock* [1990] 1 All E.R. 1067. As a firm of provincial auctioneers the defendants in this case were treated as "general practitioners" and escaped liability (for failing to identify a painting as being by Stubbs) in circumstances in which it is possible that a major "specialist" London firm would have been held liable: see *ibid.* at p. 1076, *per* Slade L.J.

[47] *Rich* v. *L.C.C.* [1953] 1 W.L.R. 895, 900, 902.

[48] *Durham* v. *Public School Board of North Oxford* (1960) 23 D.L.R. (2d) 711, 717.

[49] *Peters* v. *Hill, The Times*, March 29, 1957.

[50] *Beaumont* v. *Surrey C.C.* (1968) 66 L.G.R. 580, 585.

Liability Act 1957.[51] It is necessary to strike a balance between the meticulous supervision of children every moment of the time they are under the care of their teachers and the very desirable object of encouraging the sturdy independence of children as they grow up.[52] It is not practicable to require constant supervision of children; only such supervision as is reasonable in the circumstances is required.[53] So the defendants were held liable when they failed to provide a guard for a gas stove at a cookery school attended by a girl of 11.[54] But when the plaintiff, a schoolboy of 14 years, was injured by a clod of earth thrown by another boy whilst they were "ragging"when helping a local farmer on a half-holiday, the defendant escaped liability.[55] "If every master is to take precautions to see that there is never ragging or horseplay among his pupils, his school would be indeed too awful a place to contemplate."[56] So there is no obligation to supervise children running races in playgrounds: that is what playgrounds are for.[57] A prudent teacher should also take precautions against children causing injury to persons unconnected with the school.[58] There is not, however, any general duty on a school to have regard to the *economic* welfare of pupils. Thus in *Van Oppen* v. *Bedford Charity Trustees*,[59] in which a pupil suffered very serious injury while playing rugby football, a school was held to be under no duty to take out personal accident insurance for pupils playing rugby or to advise their parents to do so.

Users of the highway[60]

Since the dawn of the motoring age it has been axiomatic that the operation of vehicles on the highway does not give rise to strict liability: the plaintiff must prove negligence.[61] But in some cases a high standard of care is exacted.[62] An underlying principle is that all those using the highway, or land adjacent to it, must show mutual respect and forbearance.[63] The duty of a driver of a vehicle is to use proper care not to cause injury to persons on the highway or in premises adjoining the

---

[51] *Reffell* v. *Surrey C.C.* [1964] 1 W.L.R. 358. This case also establishes that an action lies for breach of the statutory duty of care under s.10 of the Education Act 1944. See below, Chap. 10.

[52] *Jeffery* v. *L.C.C.* (1954) 52 L.G.R. 521.

[53] *Clark* v. *Monmouthshire C.C.* (1954) 118, J.P. 244 (knives in playground). It may be otherwise if the child is very young: *Carmarthenshire C.C.* v. *Lewis* [1955] A.C. 549.

[54] *Fryer* v. *Salford Corporation* [1937] 1 All E.R. 617.

[55] *Camkin* v. *Bishop* [1941] 2 All E.R. 713.

[56] [1941] 2 All E.R. 713, 716, *per* Goddard L.J. This case well illustrates the tendency to run together the questions of duty and standard of care. The Court of Appeal held that the defendant was under no duty to see that the boys whilst engaged upon such work were under supervision. It might as well or better have been held that the defendant was under a duty to take reasonable precautions for the safety of his pupils but that there was no evidence of failure to perform that duty.

[57] *Ward* v. *Hertfordshire C.C.* [1969] 1 W.L.R. 790.

[58] *Carmarthenshire C.C.* v. *Lewis* [1955] A.C. 549.

[59] [1990] 1 W.L.R. 235.

[60] Further information: Bingham, *Motor Claims Cases.*

[61] *Wing* v. *London General Omnibus Co.* [1909] 2 K.B. 652.

[62] *Worsfold* v. *Howe* [1980] 1 W.L.R. 1175, 1178.

[63] *Searle* v. *Wallbank* [1947] A.C. 347, 361.

highway.[64] Proper care connotes avoidance of excessive speed, keeping a good look-out, observing traffic rules and signals and so on.[65] But there is no duty to foresee the driving of an insane person.[66] Highway authorities also owe to motorists a duty of reasonable care.[67] The duty is owed to persons so placed that they may reasonably expect to be injured by the omission to take such care.[68] In actions for personal injuries arising out of highway accidents it is particularly important to remember that the decision in every case turns upon its own facts—*e.g.* there is no rule of law that a person driving in the dark is negligent if he cannot stop within the limit of his lights,[69] or that the vehicle which has the other on its right-hand side is the one to give way,[70] or that a driver is entitled to emerge blind from a minor road onto a major road provided he does so very slowly.[71] The presence of an unlighted vehicle on a highway after dark is evidence of negligence, especially if that vehicle is large and dark-coloured,[72] as also is the presence of a vehicle which has been badly parked.[73] But the defendant may be able to rebut the presumption of negligence which arises in such a case.[74] Further, the standard expected may alter from time to time. In 1964 it was not negligence to fail to wear a safety-belt, but today it is held to be negligent for drivers and passengers to fail to do so, save in such exceptional cases as pregnant women. It is not an exception that the journey was not one which involved a high degree of risk.[75] Finally, there is no absolute right to enter a road junction merely because the lights are green[76]; another vehicle may be lawfully on the intersection.[77]

A failure on the part of any person to observe any provision of the Highway Code may in any civil proceedings be relied upon by any party to the proceedings as tending to establish or to negative any liability which is in question in those proceedings.[78] It has been held that failure to observe the provisions of delegated legislation relating to the lighting of motor-vehicles will not of itself give rise to a remedy to the injured party,[79] nor will a breach of the regulations relating to the construction and use of motor-vehicles,[80] or the prohibition of parking on "clearways"[81] (Although in each case breach of the regulations may be

---

[64] *Bourhill v. Young* [1943] A.C. 92.
[65] [1943] A.C. 92, 104.
[66] *Challoner v. Williams & Croney* [1975] 1 Lloyd's Rep. 124, 128.
[67] *Levine v. Morris* [1970] 1 W.L.R. 71.
[68] *Bourhill v. Young* [1943] A.C. 92.
[69] *Morris v. Luton Corporation* [1946] K.B. 114.
[70] *MacIntyre v. Coles* [1966] 1 W.L.R. 831.
[71] *Worsfold v. Howe* [1980] 1 W.L.R. 1175.
[72] *O'Reilly v. Garvey* [1973] I.R. 89.
[73] *Chop Seng Heng v. Thevannasan* [1975] 3 All E.R. 572.
[74] *Moore v. Maxwells of Emsworth Ltd.* [1968] 2 All E.R. 779.
[75] *Froom v. Butcher* [1976] Q.B. 286.
[76] *Radburn v. Kemp* [1971] 1 W.L.R. 1502.
[77] *Ramoo v. Gan Soo Swee* [1971] 1 W.L.R. 1014.
[78] Road Traffic Act 1988, s.38(7).
[79] *Clarke v. Brims* [1947] K.B. 497.
[80] *Barkway v. South Wales Transport Co. Ltd.* [1950] 1 All E.R. 392.
[81] *Coote v. Stone* [1971] 1 W.L.R. 279.

relied upon as evidence of negligence.) On the other hand an action lies against a party in breach of the regulations governing pedestrian-crossings[82] which impose an absolute statutory duty on the motorist to be able to stop in the event of any conceivable use of a crossing by any conceivable pedestrian, other than a suicide.[83] The Road Traffic Regulation Act 1984, s.86 provides that the speed limit on motor-vehicles shall not apply to any vehicle used for police purposes: but this does not exempt the driver of such a vehicle from civil liability for negligence.[84] Finally, it should be remembered that a pedestrian owes a duty of care to other users of the highway,[85] such as the driver of a motor-scooter[86]; and a passenger in a vehicle, although no longer identified with the contributory negligence of his driver,[87] may himself be guilty of negligence—*e.g.* by opening a door which knocks over a pedestrian.[88]

§ 9.13. General Practice as a Defence[89]

The general rule is that a defendant charged with negligence can clear himself if he shows that he has acted in accordance with the general and approved practice.[90] So a person whose calling in life involves him in creating situations of danger will usually be justified in following the practice which his trade or profession has adopted or approved for dealing with such situations,[91] and he will not be convicted of negligence merely because he has failed to make use of every precaution which ingenuity might suggest.[92] But when there is developing knowledge of new risks he must make reasonable efforts to keep abreast of it. "The employer must keep up to date but the court must be slow to blame him for not ploughing a lone furrow."[93] Yet in medical cases it should be remembered that the mere fact that the defendant has deviated from the normal practice is not enough: many advances in medical science have been due to such deviations.[94] So it is probably not necessary for the defendant to show that the circumstances of his own case are precisely similar to those of the general practice.[95] The common law has been approved by Parliament. The Congenital Disabilities (Civil Liability) Act 1976, s.1(5) provides that a defendant is not liable "if he took

---

[82] *London Passenger Transport Board* v. *Upson* [1949] A.C. 155.
[83] *Kozimor* v. *Adey* (1962) 106 S.J. 431.
[84] *Gaynor* v. *Allen* [1959] 2 Q.B. 403.
[85] *Nance* v. *British Columbia Electric Ry.* [1951] A.C. 601, 611.
[86] *Barry* v. *McDonald* (1966) 110 S.J. 56.
[87] See below, Chapter 22.
[88] *Curley* v. *Mannion* [1965] I.R. 543.
[89] See Holyoak, "Raising the standard of care" (1990) 10 L.S. 201.
[90] *Vancouver General Hospital* v. *McDaniel* (1934) 152 L.T. 56, 57.
[91] Unless the common practice is inherently defective: *O'Donovan* v. *Cork County Council* [1967] I.R. 173.
[92] *Whiteford* v. *Hunter* [1950] W.N. 553 (surgeon).
[93] *Thompson* v. *Smiths Shiprepairers Ltd.* [1984] Q.B. 405, 416, *per* Mustill J.
[94] *Hunter* v. *Hanley*, 1955 S.C. 200, 206.
[95] *Cavanagh* v. *Ulster Weaving Co. Ltd.* [1960] A.C. 145, 158, 167.

reasonable care having due regard to then received professional opinion."

Faults of omission

When the negligence complained of consists of what may be called a fault of omission,[96] the governing principle was stated by Lord Dunedin in a passage which has often been cited.

> "I think it is absolutely necessary that the proof of that fault of omission should be one of two kinds, either to show that the thing which he did not do was a thing which was commonly done by other persons in like circumstances, or to show that it was a thing which was so obviously wanted that it would be folly in anyone to neglect to provide it."[97]

"The rule is stated with all the Lord President's trenchant lucidity. It contains an emphatic warning against a facile finding that a precaution is necessary when there is no proof that it is one taken by other persons in like circumstances. But it does not detract from the test of the conduct and judgment of the reasonable and prudent man. If there is proof that a precaution is usually observed by other persons, a reasonable and prudent man will follow the usual practice in the like circumstances. Failing such proof the test is whether the precaution is one which the reasonable and prudent man would think so obvious that it was folly to omit it."[98] The formulation of the law by Lord Dunedin has been applied for many years in scores of cases against employers in England, Scotland[99] and Ireland.[1] It should not be discarded in favour of some milder version,[2] as there might be a temptation to do if the word "folly" is thought to be equivalent to "ridiculous." But really it means no more than "imprudent" or "unreasonable."[3] Lord Dunedin was in truth laying down no new principle of law but simply stating the factual framework within which the law must be applied[4]—and the law is contained in the proposition that a master must take reasonable care for the safety of his servant.[5] The oft-cited formula does not mean that if a plaintiff calls no evidence of practice he must establish folly in order to make out a prima facie case.[6] Neither does it mean that if a practice is averred and proved

---

[96] The distinction between acts of commission and acts of omission may be a fine one: *Cavanagh v. Ulster Weaving Co. Ltd.* [1960] A.C. 145, 165.

[97] *Morton v. William Dixon Ltd.*, 1909 S.C. 807, 809.

[98] *Paris v. Stepney Borough Council* [1951] A.C. 367, 382, *per* Lord Normand. Some judgments state that Lord Normand did not intend in any way to qualify Lord Dunedin's formula: *Cavanagh v. Ulster Weaving Co. Ltd.* [1960] A.C. 145, 165–166. Others assume that some gloss or qualification was intended: *Bradley v. C.I.E.* [1976] I.R. 217, 221.

[99] *Gallagher v. Balfour Beatty & Co. Ltd.*, 1951 S.C. 712, 717.

[1] *Bradley v. C.I.E.* [1976] I.R. 217.

[2] See *Gallagher v. Balfour Beatty & Co. Ltd.*, 1951, S.C., 712, 717.

[3] *Cavanagh v. Ulster Weaving Co. Ltd.* [1960] A.C. 145, 162.

[4] *Ibid.*

[5] The duty does not extend to protection of the employee's economic interests: *Reid v. Rush & Tompkins Group* [1990] I.W.L.R. 212. On employers' liability generally see below, Chap. 21.

[6] *Cavanagh v. Ulster Weaving Co. Ltd.* [1960] A.C. 162.

which might have averted the accident, this is necessarily conclusive of negligence on the part of an employer who has not followed the practice.[7]

Wisdom after the event

But the general practice itself may not conform to the standard of care required of a reasonably prudent person. In such a case it is not a good defence that the defendant acted in accordance with the general practice.[8] Neglect of duty does not cease by repetition to be neglect of duty.[9] One does not have to wait for an accident or series of accidents before a system can be condemned as unsafe.[10] On the other hand, the fact that experience subsequent to the alleged negligence proves that some additional precaution was necessary does not in itself prove negligence at the earlier date.[11] "People do not furnish evidence against themselves simply by adopting a new plan in order to prevent the recurrence of an accident. I think that a proposition to the contrary would be barbarous. It would be, as I have often had occasion to tell juries, to hold that, because the world gets wiser as it gets older, therefore it was foolish before."[12] For it is easy to be wise after the event,[13] and nothing is so perfect that it cannot be improved.[14]

§ 9.14. Statutory Powers[15]

In *Home Office* v. *Dorset Yacht*[16] the House of Lords held that existence of a statutory power could give rise to liability in the tort of negligence on the part of those on whom the power was conferred, in the event of their being careless in the discharge of their statutory responsibilities. *Dorset Yacht* concerned physical damage to property; but in *Anns* v. *London Borough of Merton*[17] the principle was extended to facilitate recovery by those who suffered pure economic loss as a result of the failure of local authorities to exercise adequately their statutory powers of supervision over building activity. In the 1990 case of *Murphy* v. *Brentwood District Council*,[18] however, a seven-member House of Lords invoked the 1966 *Practice Statement* unanimously to overrule *Anns* v. *London Borough of Merton* on the ground that its imposition of liability for pure economic loss had been contrary to general principle. But the

---

[7] *Brown* v. *Rolls Royce Ltd.* [1960] 1 W.L.R. 210, 214.
[8] *Donovan* v. *Cork County Council* [1967] I.R. 173.
[9] *Carpenters Co.* v. *British Mutual Banking Co.* [1937] 3 All E.R. 811, 820.
[10] *Atkinson* v. *Tyne-Tees Steam Shipping Co. Ltd.* [1956] 1 Lloyd's Rep. 244.
[11] *Philpott* v. *British Railways Board* [1968] 2 Lloyd's Rep. 495, 502.
[12] *Hart* v. *L & Y. Ry.* (1869) 21 L.T. 261, 263, *per* Bramwell B.
[13] *The Wagon Mound* [1961] A.C. 388, 424.
[14] *Pipe* v. *Chambers Wharf and Cold Stores Ltd.* [1952] 1 Lloyd's Rep. 194, 195.
[15] See also below, § 22.7.
[16] [1970] A.C. 1004.
[17] [1978] A.C. 728.
[18] [1991] 1 A.C. 398.

House left open the question whether the statutory power in fact gave rise to *any* duty of care on the part of the local authority, *e.g.* where an inadequately supervised building collapses causing personal injury.[19] The fact that the overruling of *Anns* was confined to the economic loss point, and that the authority of the earlier case of *Dorset Yacht* has apparently never been questioned, means that it is still the law that, in an appropriate case, carelessness in the exercise of a statutory power may give rise to actual negligence liability.[20] Nevertheless such cases are likely to be few, for at least three reasons.

First, although it is important to distinguish common law negligence from liability in the tort of breach of statutory duty,[21] there is an understandable degree of overlap in the approach of the courts to the two areas.[22] Thus the perceived underlying *purpose* of the statute in question will be a major factor in both torts; and a statutory power concerned with the promotion of health and safety, for example, will not provide an appropriate basis for protecting the financial interests of property developers.[23] Secondly, the courts will lean against holding that statutory regulatory agencies, charged with the exercise of wide responsibilities in the general public interest, owe duties of care to individual aggrieved citizens.[24] Thus in *Yuen Kun-yeu v. Att.-Gen. of Hong Kong*[25] the Privy Council denied that licensing authorities could be liable to investors for the default of a licensed investment company.[26] Thirdly, since the law does not, in general, impose liabilities for the acts of third parties defendants alleged to have been careless in a statutory context will need to have had the capacity to exercise a high degree of *control* if liability is to be imposed on them for harm caused by others. This requirement was satisfied in *Dorset Yacht* where prison officers were assumed to have been careless in allowing inmates to escape and cause damage; but it was not satisfied in *Hill v. Chief Constable of West Yorkshire*[27] where the police simply failed to apprehend a criminal as rapidly as it was alleged they should have done.

In accordance with the current fashionable approach the various factors relating to claims based upon carelessness in the exercise of statutory powers are likely to be subsumed under the general requirement of "proximity." While the existence of a statute may occasionally be held to create a relationship of proximity between the parties which would not otherwise have existed, it would appear that full satisfaction of that

---

[19] See [1991] 1 A.C. 398, 463 (Lord Keith), 492 (Lord Jauncey).
[20] " . . . of course I accept that duties at common law may arise in respect of the exercise of statutory powers": *per* Lord Mackay of Clashfern L.C. in *Murphy* v. *Brentwood District Council* [1991] 1 A.C. 398, 457. See also, *Lonrho plc.* v. *Tebbit* [1991] 4 All E.R. 973.
[21] See *Murphy* v. *Brentwood District Council* [1991] 1 A.C. 398, 483, *per* Lord Oliver.
[22] On breach of statutory duty see, generally, Chap. 10, below.
[23] *Peabody Donation Fund* v. *Sir Lindsay Parkinson & Co.* [1985] A.C. 210. See also *Curran* v. *Northern Ireland Co-ownership Housing Association* [1987] A.C. 718.
[24] *Rowling* v. *Takaro Properties* [1988] A.C. 473.
[25] [1988] A.C. 175. Applied in *Davis* v. *Radcliffe* [1990] 2 All E.R. 536.
[26] See also *Minories Finance* v. *Arthur Young* [1989] 2 All E.R. 105.
[27] [1989] A.C. 53.

requirement, and hence the imposition of actual liability, is unlikely to be a frequent occurrence in this context.

§ 9.15. THE PROOF OF NEGLIGENCE

The burden of proving negligence is on the plaintiff who alleges it—or as practitioners often put it, the plaintiff must prove causation.[28] It is not for the doer to excuse himself by proving that the accident was inevitable and due to no negligence on his part; it is for the person who suffers the harm to prove affirmatively that it was due to the negligence of the defendant.[29] Unless the plaintiff produces reasonable evidence that the accident was caused by the defendant's negligence, there is no case to answer, and it is the duty of the judge to enter judgment for the defendant. It is not necessary for the plaintiff to show that the defendant must be found guilty of negligence, or to eliminate every conceivable possibility by which the accident may have been caused without negligence on the defendant's part.[30] This rule is particularly important when the injured person has either been killed in the accident or has no recollection of it. But the plaintiff's evidence must pass beyond the region of pure conjecture into that of legal inference.[31] The dividing line between conjecture and inference is often a very difficult one to draw. A conjecture may be plausible, but it is of no legal value, for its essence is that it is a mere guess. An inference in the legal sense, on the other hand, is a deduction from the evidence, and if it is a reasonable deduction it may have the validity of legal proof.[32] It follows that there can be no inference unless there are objective facts from which to infer the other facts which it is sought to establish.[33] It is to be noticed that this question is to be decided not by weighing the evidence of the plaintiff against the defendant but by disregarding altogether the evidence of the defendant, and by asking whether that of the plaintiff is, *per se* and apart from any contradiction, sufficient or insufficient to bring conviction to a reasonable mind.[34]

Causation

It is difficult to prove causation when the breach of duty alleged consists in the failure to take some precaution prescribed by statute—*e.g.* under the Health and Safety at Work Act 1974. At one time the courts required the plaintiff to prove that the precaution in question would have been effective if it had been taken,[35] but it was subsequently held by the House of Lords to be enough for the plaintiff to prove that the defendants' omission materially increased the risk of the harm occur-

---

[28] *Kay v. Ayrshire and Arran Health Board* [1987] 2 All E.R. 417.
[29] *Wilsher v. Essex Area Health Authority* [1988] A.C. 1074.
[30] *Horabin v. B.O.A.C.* [1952] 2 All E.R. 1016.
[31] *Jones v. G.W. Ry.* (1930) 144 L.T. 194.
[32] *Union Steamship Co. of N.Z. Ltd. v. Wenlock* [1958] N.Z.L.R. 173, 177.
[33] *Caswell v. Powell Duffryn Collieries* [1940] A.C. 152, 169.
[34] *Bill v. Short Bros. and Harland Ltd.* [1963] N.I. 1.
[35] *McWilliams v. Sir William Arrol & Co. Ltd.* [1962] 1 W.L.R. 295.

ring.[36] This considerable extention of the law in favour of plaintiffs[37] appears, however, largely to be confined to the field of industrial accidents.[38] In particular, attempts to apply it in the field of medical negligence have not met with success. In *Wilsher v. Essex Area Health Authority*[39] the House of Lords held that where a patient's injury had been attributable to a number of possible causes, only one of which was the defendants' carelessness, there was no presumption in favour of the patient that the breach of duty was the cause. Nor are the courts able to award the plaintiff a percentage of his loss on the basis that the breach of duty *might* have caused the harm. Thus in *Hotson v. East Berkshire Area Health Authority*[40] the House of Lords reversed a decision of the trial judge and the Court of Appeal to the effect that a careless delay in medical treatment entitled the plaintiff to 25 per cent of his loss in circumstances in which the delay was considered to have deprived him of a 25 per cent chance of making a full recovery following an accidental injury. Their Lordships held that causation is a question of fact to be determined one way or the other at the trial; and that permanent disability would be regarded as having been inevitable from the moment of the accident so that the plaintiff would receive no damages for the delay.[41]

Submission of no case to answer

In cases which are tried by a judge sitting alone the judge is bound to put counsel who has submitted that there is no case to answer to his election whether he wants to stand on the submission or call his evidence before a ruling on the submission is given.[42] If the judge rules in favour of the defendant, but on the appeal the plaintiff establishes that there was a case to answer, he is entitled to judgment and the court has no power to order a new trial. "That follows logically from the principle that the defendant, having elected to call no evidence, is bound by that election, and therefore cannot be given a new trial at which to call evidence that he ought to have called at the hearing."[43] Conversely, if the judge rules against the defendant, but the latter elects to give evidence and has judgment given against him, he cannot ask the Court of Appeal

---

[36] *McGhee v. National Coal Board* [1973] 1 W.L.R.1, in which a failure to take precautions against brick dust causing dermatitis was followed by dermatitis caused by brick dust. It was held (surely correctly) that the trial judge was entitled to draw the inference that the defendants had been negligent.

[37] *Thompson v. Smiths Shiprepairers* [1984] Q.B. 405, 442.

[38] It was applied by the Court of Appeal in a road-accident case in *Fitzgerald v. Lane* [1987] Q.B. 781 (affmd. on other grounds in [1989] A.C. 328) but the correctness of this decision is open to question after the decision of the House of Lords in *Wilsher v. Essex Area Health Authority* [1988] A.C. 1074.

[39] [1988] A.C. 1074.

[40] [1989] A.C. 750. See Stapleton, "The Gist of Negligence: Part II" (1988) 104 L.Q.R. 389; Hill, "A Lost Chance for Compensation in the Tort of Negligence by the House of Lords," (1991) 54 M.L.R. 511.

[41] See Fleming, "Probabilistic Causation in Tort Law" (1989) 68 Can. Bar. Rev. 661.

[42] *Young v Rank* [1950] 2 K.B. 510; *Storey v. Storey* [1961] P. 63.

[43] *Goulding v. Ministry of Works* (unreported) 1955 C.A. 175A, *per* Jenkins L.J. But in *Portland Managements Ltd. v. Harte* [1977] 1 Q.B. 306 an exception is suggested.

to disregard the evidence so given.[44] But in a jury action the judge probably has a discretion whether he will put counsel to his election, which he need not exercise until all the evidence is concluded.[45]

Onus of proof when several defendants[46]

The rule that the plaintiff must prove that the defendant's negligence was the cause of the accident may cause difficulties if the acts of two or more defendants are involved. While it is plain that the trial judge is entitled to dismiss the claim if there is no evidence from which negligence can be inferred on the part of one or the other or both of the defendants, it has also been held in a Canadian case that if A has been injured in circumstances which must have been due to the negligence of B or C, but he is unable to establish which of them is responsible, then the onus of proof is on the defendant to exculpate himself. If he fails to do so, the plaintiff may recover against both defendants.[47] But this principle might cause great hardship to an innocent defendant in a case in which the damage must have been caused by one or other of the defendants, but could not possibly have been caused by both.[48] Hence it may apply only when the defendants are joint tortfeasors, either as being engaged on a concerted common design, or as persons of whom one is vicariously liable for the acts of the other.[49] Thus when the plaintiff has suffered harm as a result of a negligent system of manufacture, inspection or repair adopted by the defendant, he is not required to lay his finger on the exact person in the whole chain who is responsible.[50]

Traffic accidents

The Court of Appeal constantly reminds trial judges that decisions on questions of fact do not lay down legal propositions.[51] When there is a highway collision between two motor-cars in circumstances which give rise to a prima facie case of negligence against each (*e.g.* a head-on collision in broad daylight), in the absence of any evidence enabling the court to distinguish between them, the proper course is for the court to say: both to blame and equally to blame.[52] But it is not easy to see the logic, as distinct from the utility, of this rule, for if a judge does not feel able to give judgment against one of the parties, he should hardly feel able to do the opposite and give judgment against both of them.[53]

---

[44] *Payne* v. *Harrison* [1961] 2 Q.B. 403.

[45] *Payne* v. *Harrison* [1961] 2 Q.B. 403.

[46] See Hogan, "Cook v. Lewis Re-examined" (1961) 24 M.L.R. 331.

[47] *Cook* v. *Lewis* [1952] 1 D.L.R.1. The parties in this case "on what Canadians are pleased to call a 'hunting' trip, though we should perhaps call it a shooting holiday": *Re T. (Infants)* [1968] 1 Ch. 704, 713, *per* Harman L.J.

[48] *Power* v. *Bedford Motor Co. Ltd* [1959] I.R. 391, 418–420.

[49] *Cassidy* v. *Ministry of Health* [1951] 2 K.B. 343, 359; *Roe* v. *Minister of Health* [1954] 1 Q.B. 66, 80, 82, 88; *Walsh* v. *Holst & Sons Ltd.* [1958] 1 W.L.R. 800, 804.

[50] *Grant* v. *Australian Knitting Mills* [1936] A.C. 85, 101.

[51] *Worsford* v. *Howe* [1980] 1 All E.R. 1028 is one in a long series of such decisions.

[52] *Baker* v. *Market Harborough Co-operative Society Ltd.* [1953] 1 W.L.R. 1472. The drivers are not, of course, joint tortfeasors.

[53] *Nesterczuk* v. *Mortimore* [1966] A.L.R. 163.

Appeals

The powers of the Court of Appeal are wider in the case of an appeal from a judge of the High Court sitting alone than in the case of an appeal from the verdict of a jury. The vast majority of civil actions are today tried by a judge alone. It has been held that in a personal injuries claim a jury should be ordered only in very exceptional circumstances,[54] even if the injury is serious.[55] In *Benmax v. Austin Motor Co. Ltd.*[56] the House of Lords pointed out that on an appeal it is necessary to distinguish between the finding of a specific fact and a finding of fact which is really an inference from facts specifically found or, as has sometimes been said, between the perception and evaluation of facts. Thus an appellate court will be reluctant to reject a finding of specific fact which may be founded on the credibility of a witness; but in cases where the point in dispute is the proper inference to be drawn from proved facts,[57] an appeal court is generally in as good a position to evaluate the evidence as the trial judge, and ought not to shrink from the task,[58] though it ought, of course, to give weight to his opinion.[59] While it is useful to have such clear and authoritative guidance, it may perhaps be regretted that the law should have been laid down in such very wide terms. The reports contain many cases in which judges of the greatest eminence have differed as to the evaluation of admitted facts[60] and if appellate tribunals were to make full use of the powers given to them by *Benmax v. Austin Motor Co. Ltd.* the uncertainty of the law would greatly increase.

§ 9.16. Res Ipsa Loquitur[61]

The rule that it is for the plaintiff to prove negligence, and not for the defendant to disprove it, is in some cases one of considerable hardship to the plaintiff, because it may be that the true cause of the accident lies solely within the knowledge of the defendant who caused it. The plaintiff can prove the accident, but he cannot prove how it happened so as to show its origin in the negligence of the defendant. This hardship is avoided to a considerable extent by the principle of *res ipsa loquitur*. "There must be reasonable evidence of negligence," said Sir William

---

[54] *Ward v. James* [1966] 1 Q.B. 273. The Pearson Report (§ 734) recommended that jury trial should not be reintroduced for personal injury litigation.

[55] *Watts v. Manning* [1964] 1 W.L.R. 623. See also *H. v. Ministry of Defence* [1991] 2 Q.B. 103.

[56] [1955] A.C. 370.

[57] "If it could be shown that the course of events affirmed by the learned judge could not have occurred, that would be an excellent reason for reversing his view—in these mundane happenings there is no more conclusive argument than *non est credendum quia impossible*": *The Eurymedon* (1942) 73 L1.L.R. 217, 219, *per* Viscount Simon L.C.

[58] So in *Whitehouse v. Jordan* [1981] 1 W.L.R. 246 the House of Lords reversed a finding by a trial judge that a surgeon had been negligent.

[59] *Benmax v. Austin Motor Co. Ltd.* [1955] A.C. 370, 376.

[60] e.g. *Carmarthenshire C.C. v. Lewis* [1956] A.C. 552; *Ross v. Associated Portland Cement Manufacturers Ltd.* [1964] 1 W.L.R. 768.

[61] See Ayitah, "*Res Ipsa Loqitur* in England and Australia" (1972) 35 M.L.R. 337.

Erle C.J., delivering the judgment of the Court of Exchequer Chamber[62] in the leading case of *Scott v. London and St. Katherine Docks Co.*,[63] "but where the thing is shown to be under the management of the defendant or his servants, and the accident is such as in the ordinary course of things does not happen if those who have the management use proper care, it affords reasonable evidence, in the absence of explanation by the defendant, that the accident arose from want of care." It is characteristic of the great Victorian masters of the common law who framed these limpid sentences (which constitute the whole of the relevant part of the court's judgment) that they should have avoided both lengthy elaboration of the obvious and the use of the Latin maxim *res ipsa loquitur*.[64] These temptations have not always been resisted by their successors, with the result that the law on this topic is still curiously complex and open to review in the House of Lords.[65] First, it should be observed that when all the facts are known there is no room for the application of the maxim: in such a case the only question is whether an inference of negligence becomes practically certain or practically impossible.[66] Secondly, when all the facts are not known the maxim helps the plaintiff to discharge the onus which lies upon him of proving negligence. So two distinct questions arise: (1) what are the conditions for the operation of the principle contained in the maxim? and (2) what is the effect of the operation of the principle, once it has been properly invoked?

(1) Conditions for operation of principle

The court in *Scott v. London and St. Katherine Docks Co.*[67] stipulated (i) that "the thing is shown to be under the management of the defendant or his servants," and (ii) that "the accident is such as in the ordinary course of things does not happen if those who have the management use proper care." As to (i), it is sufficient here to note that the driver of a motor-vehicle is now held to have sufficient control over his vehicle and its surrounding circumstances to attract the operation of the principle in a suitable case.[68] So an unexplained and violent skid is evidence of negligence.[69] But if an object or operation is under the control of two (or more) persons not legally responsible for the acts of each other it is probable that the principle does not apply.[70] As to (ii), it is part of the common experience of mankind that if those who have control are exercising reasonable care, it is not usual for bags of flour to fall from ware-

---

[62] Erle C.J. Crompton, Byles, Blackburn, Keating and Mellor JJ.

[63] (1865) 3 H. & C. 596, 601 (six bags of sugar falling from warehouse onto passer-by).

[64] "If it had not been in Latin nobody would have called it a principle": *Ballard* v. *N.B. Ry.*, 1923, S.C. 43, 56, *per* Lord Shaw.

[65] *Colvilles Ltd.* v. *Devine* [1969] 1 W.L.R. 475, 478. But the paragraph in the text above has been said to be the classical account of the doctrine: *Moorgate Mercantile Co. Ltd.* v. *Twitchings* [1977] A.C. 890, 900.

[66] *Barkway* v. *South Wales Transport Co.* [1950] 1 All E.R. 392, 395; *Bolton* v. *Stone* [1951] A.C. 850, 859.

[67] (1865) 3 H. & C. 596.

[68] *Halliwell* v. *Venables* (1930) 99 L.J.K.B. 353.

[69] *Richley* v. *Faull* [1965] 1 W.L.R. 1454.

[70] See above, § 9.15.

house windows[71] or for stones to be found in a bun[72] or for slippery matter to be left lying on the floor of a shop[73]—to mention only a few of the many cases in which the doctrine has been held to apply. On the other hand, "Everybody knows fires occur through accidents which happen without negligence on anybody's part,"[74] so there was no liability when an ordinary domestic fire was left burning in a grate and the room was set on fire in some unexplained way. Finally, it is not necessary that the doctrine should be pleaded. If the accident is proved to have happened in such a way that prima facie it could not have happened without negligence on the part of the defendants, then it is for the defendants to explain how the accident could have happened without negligence.[75]

A difficulty has arisen where negligence is alleged against surgeons or doctors, for it has been said that as a judge can have no personal knowledge of "the ordinary course of things" in, *e.g.* a complex abdominal operation, the maxim cannot apply in such cases.[76] But the better view is that, properly understood, the maxim may be of help even when the exercise of professional skill is under consideration.[77]

Effect of operation of the principle

In a case in which the operation of the principle contained in the maxim *res ipsa loquitur* has been properly invoked the primary and fundamental effect is that the plaintiff cannot be defeated simply by a plea of no case to answer, so that if he has been non-suited by the trial judge a new trial will be ordered on appeal.[78] The secondary effect is the mere happening of the accident affords "reasonable evidence, in the absence of explanation by the defendant," that it was due to the defendant's negligence. Hence if the defendant gives no evidence a judgment for the plaintiff will stand. So clearly a prudent defendant will feel obliged to offer an "explanation." Opinions have differed as to the nature of the onus which rests upon him.

In the first place, it is well settled that the defendant is entitled to succeed even though he cannot explain exactly how the accident happened if he establishes that there was no lack of reasonable care on his part.[79]

---

[71] *Byrne* v. *Boadle* (1863) 2 H. & C. 722 (perhaps the first case in which the phrase *res ipsa loquitur* occurs). From a practical point of view, the importance of such a decision is that it dispenses the plaintiff from the necessity of calling witnesses from inside the warehouse to prove negligence.

[72] *Chapronière* v. *Mason* (1905) 21 T.L.R. 633.

[73] *Ward* v. *Tesco Stores Ltd.* [1976] 1 W.L.R. 810

[74] *Sochacki* v. *Sas* [1947] 1 All E.R. 344, 345, *per* Lord Goddard C.J.

[75] *Bennett* v. *Chemical Construction (G.B.) Ltd.* [1971] 1 W.L.R. 1571, 1575.

[76] *Mahon* v. *Osborne* [1939] 2 K.B. 14, 23.

[77] *Cassidy* v. *Ministry of Health* [1951] 2 K.B. 343.

[78] *Davies* v. *Bunn* (1936) 56 C.L.R. 246, 268–269. This was precisely the course of events in both *Byrne* v. *Boadle* and *Scott* v. *London, etc. Docks Co.*—though the difficulty of these matters is shown by the fact that in the latter case Erle C.J. dissented from his brethren on the application of the principle to the facts. In fact, when the case was re-tried, the verdict was for the defendants (13 L.T.(N.S.) 148)—which shows very clearly that when the maxim applies the plaintiff is entitled to have a trial, but is not entitled to win it.

[79] *Ludgate* v. *Lovet* [1969] 1 W.L.R. 1016.

But it may be difficult for him to show that he took reasonable care if the disaster was caused by a latent defect.[80]

Difficulty arises when the defendant is still unable to explain the accident and his conduct is open to more than one interpretation. The Privy Council emphasised in a 1988 case that there is *not*, even where *res ipsa loquitur*, any legal presumption of negligence which would effect the putting of the legal burden of disproving negligence on the defendant.[81] Therefore if the defendant produces a reasonable explanation, equally consistent with negligence and no negligence, the burden of proving the affirmative, that the defendant was negligent and that his negligence caused the accident, still remains with the plaintiff.[82] For the scales which have been tipped in the plaintiff's favour by the doctrine of *res ipsa loquitur* would be once more in balance, and the plaintiff would have to begin again and prove negligence in the usual way.[83]

On the other hand, it has been held by the Court of Appeal,[84] and also, apparently, by the Privy Council,[85] and the House of Lords,[86] that the onus of disproving negligence lies on the defendant, at least in the sense that it is not sufficient for him to show that there were several hypothetical causes consistent with an absence of negligence, but he must go further and show either that the accident was due to a specific cause which does not connote his negligence, or that he had used all reasonable care in the matter. But this would mean that a plaintiff who establishes a prima facie case by invoking the maxim would be in a stronger position than one who made out a prima facie case in another way.[87]

Much of the confusion is due to a failure to appreciate that cases where *res ipsa loquitur* applies may vary enormously in the strength, significance and cogency of the *res* proved. There are many cases in which the most eminent judges have been divided on the question whether an inference of negligence could properly be drawn from the facts proved or admitted. Looked at in this light, it is not easy to see why the maxim should be treated as a special part of the law of evidence.[88]

---

[80] *Henderson* v. *Jenkins & Sons* [1970] A.C. 282.

[81] *Ng Chun Pui* v. *Lee Chuen Tat* [1988] R.T.R. 298.

[82] *The Kite* [1933] P. 154. See also the case cited in the previous note.

[83] *Colvilles Ltd.* v. *Devine* [1969] 1 W.L.R. 475.

[84] *Moore* v. *Fox (R.) & Son Ltd.* [1956] 1 Q.B. 596.

[85] *Swan* v. *Salisbury Construction Co. Ltd.* [1966] 1 W.L.R. 204.

[86] *Henderson* v. *Jenkins & Sons* [1970] A.C. 282.

[87] It would really put the plaintiff in the same position as if the action were one of trespass, in which the defendant would have to plead and prove inevitable accident, whereas the general rule in negligence is that the plaintiff must establish his case and the defendant need do no more than plead a general denial: see Devlin J. in *Southport Corporation* v. *Esso Petroleum Co. Ltd.* [1953] 3 W.L.R. 773, 781 (the point is not discussed in the H.L.)

[88] *Lloyde* v. *West Midlands Gas Board* [1971] W.L.R. 749.

CHAPTER 10

STATUTORY DUTIES

§ 10.1. General Principles[1]

The common law was once willing to adopt the simple principle that the breach of a duty created by statute, if it results in damage to an individual, is a tort for which an action for damages will lie at his suit, if no, or no adequate, remedy is provided by the statute itself.[2] "It would be a fine thing," said Sir John Holt C.J., "to make a law by which one has a right but no remedy but in equity."[3] But this principle has not been followed in England[4] for at least a century.[5] The modern approach is to limit the extent of liability by treating the question in each case as one relating to the intention of the legislature in creating the duty. No action for damages will therefore lie if, on the construction of the statute, the intention is to be inferred that some other remedy, civil or criminal, should be the only one available.[5A] A formulation sometimes adopted, in attempting to determine the intention of the statute, is to ask whether the duty is owed primarily to the state or community and only incidentally to the individual, or primarily to the individual and only incidentally to the state or community.[6] This test is also sometimes put in the form of a distinction between the public at large, on the one hand, and a "class" of individuals on the other. So there is no civil remedy if a statute merely prohibits or makes conduct criminal without imposing a duty to a specific class.[6A] Accordingly, in *Lonrho* v. *Shell Petroleum*[7] the House of Lords held that commission of the criminal offence of supplying oil to Rhodesia, in breach of the sanctions order then in force which was intended purely to undermine the illegal regime, did not give a right of action to those who suffered loss due to the prolongation of the regime facilitated by the unlawful trading. But in *R.* v. *Deputy Governor of Parkhurst Prison Ex p. Hague*[8] the House of Lords emphasised that the notion of protection of a class cannot be

---

[1] See Stanton, *Breach of Statutory Duty in Tort* (London, 1986). See also Buckley, "Liability in Tort for Breach of Statutory Duty" (1984) 100 L.Q.R. 204.

[2] See, *e.g.* *Couch* v. *Steel* (1854) 3 E. & B. 402.

[3] *Anon.* (1704) 6 Mod. 32.

[4] *Aliter* in Ireland: *Meskell* v. *C.I.E.* [1973] I.R. 121, 138.

[5] *Atkinson* v. *Newcastle Waterworks* (1877) 2 Ex.D. 441 is often regarded as marking the turning-point.

[5A] See, *e.g.* *Scally* v. *Southern Health and Social Services Board* [1991] 4 All E.R. 563 (no action for damages for breach of statutory duty to provide employee with written particulars of terms of employment: recourse to industrial tribunal as provided in the legislation is the only remedy).

[6] *Solomons* v. *Gertzenstein (R.) Ltd.* [1954] 2 Q.B. 243, 265.

[6A] Even a person within a protected class will be unable to sue in the absence of "loss or injury of a kind for which the law awards damages": *P* v. *Liverpool Daily Post* [1991] 2 A.C. 370, 420, *per* Lord Bridge.

[7] [1982] A.C. 173.

[8] [1992] 1 A.C. 58.

invoked conversely so as to produce an irresistable inference of liability in other cases and thereby escape "the fundamental question: 'Did the legislature intend to confer on the plaintiff a cause of action for breach of statutory duty?' "[9] This question was given a positive answer in *Groves v. Wimborne (Lord)*[10] in which the defendant, a manufacturer, was held liable in damages to one of his employees, who had sustained personal injuries through a failure by the defendant to perform his statutory duty of fencing dangerous machinery. Nevertheless it is not self-evident that the logical basis for the compensation of an injured workman should be the commission of a criminal offence by his employer.[11] Indeed it is not easy to generalise about the circumstances which will give rise to liability since much depends in each case upon the context of the statute and the court's perception of the policy considerations involved. Lord Diplock was once moved to observe that: "The statutes say nothing about civil remedies for breaches of their provisions. The judgment of the courts say all."[12] Thus while the courts lean in favour of conferring on workmen a right to claim damages for breach of statutory duty imposed on their employers or the occupiers of factories in which they work,[13] unlawful segregation of prisoners in breach of rule 43 of the Prison Rules 1964 does not give rise to an action.[14]

In determining the intention of the legislature, the courts consider three different factors:

(i) *The context and object of the statute*

In some situations legislation is passed to promote the provision of facilities, or general protective measures, for the benefit of the public as a whole, and the scheme of the Act is geared more to providing instructions and guidance to those responsible, who will often enjoy considerable discretion, than to the formulation of precise legal rights which could appropriately be made the subject of enforcement by means of damages awards. The statutory duty is then a duty towards the public at large, and not towards individuals, and the correlative right is vested in the public and not in private persons, even though they may suffer loss.[15]

But the Land Charges Act 1925 was passed for the benefit of incumbrancers and purchasers and intending purchasers, and these are a definite group distinct from the public generally.[16] It has also been held that

---

[9] *R. v. Deputy Governor of Parkhurst Prison, Ex p. Hague* [1992] 1 A.C. 58, 159 *per* Lord Bridge.

[10] [1898] 2 Q.B. 402. This was one of the important decisions for the protection of workmen given by the late nineteenth-century courts. For other examples, see §§ 22.3–22.4 below.

[11] *F. E. Callow (Engineers) Ltd.* v. *Johnson* [1971] A.C. 335, 342.

[12] *Boyle* v. *Kodak Ltd.* [1969] 1 W.L.R. 661, 672.

[13] *Groves* v. *Wimborne (Lord)* [1898] 2 Q.B. 402.

[14] *R.* v. *Deputy Governor of Parkhurst Prison, Ex p. Hague* [1992] 1 A.C. 58.

[15] *cf. Watt* v. *Kesteven County Council* [1955] 1 Q.B. 408.

[16] *Ministry of Housing* v. *Sharp* [1970] 2 Q.B. 223.

homeless persons are a distinct class for this purpose.[17] Since Britain's entry into the European Economic Community it may be the case that actions for damages for breach of statutory duty can, in appropriate circumstances, be based upon breaches of articles of the EEC Treaty.[18]

(ii) *The nature and precision of the relevant provisions*

The legislature, even while recognising a private right vested in the injured individual, may intend that it shall be maintained solely by some special remedy provided for the particular case, and not by the ordinary method of an action for damages. Thus, in *Atkinson v. Newcastle and Gateshead Waterworks Co.*[19] it was held by the Court of Appeal that the defendant company was not liable in damages for the destruction of the plaintiff's house by fire, although its destruction was directly due to the failure of the defendants to perform the duty laid upon them under the Waterworks Clauses Act 1847[20] to maintain a certain pressure of water in their water-pipes for the purpose of extinguishing fires. The statute in question provided that any breach of this duty should be an offence punishable by a fine of £10, and the court came to the conclusion that on the true interpretation of the statute this was the sole remedy available, and that there was no intention of imposing on the waterworks company any such heavy civil liability as the opposite interpretation would have subjected them to. Indeed it is sometimes suggested that the courts invariably lean against the grant of civil actions for damages if the Act does, as in *Atkinson's* case, make express provision for a particular penalty; and conversely that an action is more likely to arise if the statute does not include provision for any criminal or other sanction, since otherwise the Act would be a mere "pious aspiration."[21] In practice, however, it is clear that at any rate provision for the imposition of a fine does not give rise to any general presumption against civil liability.[22] Moreover even cases of the opposite kind, where no penalty is provided and the suggested presumption would point the other way, may very often *not* give rise to civil liability despite the supposed reluctance of the courts to hold that an Act of Parliament has no effective legal force. Statutes which do not expressly provide for sanctions are in fact quite likely to be those aimed at promoting general public objectives or services, and which therefore do not readily lend themselves to the creation of individual rights of action.[23] *Atkinson v. Newcastle Waterworks* itself is perhaps better seen as being in principle a case of this type, despite the £10 fine provision.

---

[17] See *Thornton v. Kirklees B.C.* [1979] Q.B. 626.
[18] See *Garden Cottage Foods v. Milk Marketing Board* [1984] A.C. 130. But *cf. Bourgoin S.A. v. Ministry of Agriculture* [1986] Q.B. 716.
[19] (1877) 2 Ex.D. 441.
[20] s.42. But a breach of the duty under s.35 of the same Act to provide a supply of pure and wholesome water gives a right of action for damages to a ratepayer injuriously affected: *Read v. Croydon Corporation* [1938] 4 All E.R. 631. For corresponding provisions see now the Water Act 1989, Part II, Chapter II.
[21] *Cutler v. Wandsworth Stadium* [1949] A.C. 398, 407, *per* Lord Simonds.
[22] See, *e.g.* the numerous cases decided under the Factories Acts.
[23] See, *e.g. Watt v. Kesteven County Council* [1955] 1 Q.B. 408.

One factor which does appear to provide some indication of whether or not civil liability will be imposed, even though not stated in terms in any judicial pronouncement,[24] is that provisions which are highly specific and detailed in laying down the precise content of the duty are more likely than are others to lend themselves to enforcement by way of an action for damages. For example it has been settled ever since *Monk* v. *Warbey*[25] that when a person uninsured against third party risks is permitted by the owner to use his car, and injury is caused by the borrower's negligent driving, the injured third party may, if the borrower is without means,[26] sue the owner of the car directly for breach of his statutory duty,[27] without first suing the uninsured driver. Otherwise the express object of the Act, namely, to give a remedy to third persons who might suffer injury by the negligence of the impecunious driver of a car, would have been defeated. The decision in *Monk* v. *Warbey* has at all times been judicially accepted without comment, and has been affirmed by the Privy Council.[28] The relevant duty upon car-owners is clear and straightforward: not to allow uninsured persons use of the vehicle. By contrast, some other provisions relating to motor vehicles are couched in much more general terms, often simply requiring owners to ensure that the vehicles are properly maintained[29] and not in a defective condition.[30] General provisions of this kind do not lend themselves so readily to enforcement by civil actions for damages.[31]

(iii) *Damage suffered not of kind to be guarded against*

An action for damages will not lie at the suit of an injured person if the damage suffered by him is not of the kind intended to be guarded against. In *Gorris* v. *Scott*[32] the plaintiff sued the defendant, a shipowner, for the loss of sheep which had been swept overboard in consequence of the failure of the defendant to supply certain pens and other structures on the deck of his ship for the accommodation of sheep, as required by Act of Parliament. It was held, however, that the defendant was not liable, because the purpose of the statute in question was to make provision against the spread of contagious disease among the animals, and not to prevent such accidents as the plaintiff complained of.[33] The principle in *Gorris* v. *Scott*[34] has since been approved by the House

---

[24] But see *Cutler* v. *Wandsworth Stadium* [1949] A.C. 398, 417, *per* Lord Reid for *dicta* which would seem to lend some support to the proposition.

[25] [1935] 1 K.B. 75.

[26] *Martin* v. *Dean* [1971] 2 Q.B. 208.

[27] Now s.143 of the Road Traffic Act 1988. But there is no statutory duty to insure against the third party liability of passengers in, but not controlling the use of, the car: *Brown* v. *Roberts* [1965] 1 Q.B. 1.

[28] *Tan Chye Choo* v. *Chong Kew Moi* [1970] 1 W.L.R. 147, 152.

[29] *cf*. Road Traffic Act 1988, s.75.

[30] See, generally, the Road Vehicles (Construction and Use) Regulations 1986 (S.I. 1986 No. 1078).

[31] See, *e.g. Badham* v. *Lambs Ltd.* [1946] K.B. 45; *Phillips* v. *Britannia Hygienic Laundry Co.* [1923] 2 K.B. 832.

[32] (1874) L.R. 9 Ex. 125.

[33] *Sparrow* v. *Fairey Aviation Co. Ltd.* [1962] 1 Q.B. 161, 174.

[34] See n. 32, above.

of Lords, although the decision went the other way on the interpretation of the relevant statute.[35] Again, when the object of a statutory regulation was to prevent men working on a roof from falling to the ground, it was immaterial that the plaintiff was injured by falling through a hole in the roof rather than by falling through fragile roofing material.[36] The distinction is clear and simple: if the damage which in fact occurs is within the risk, it is immaterial that it did not happen in precisely the way contemplated when the duty was imposed. It is the same distinction which caused the decision in *The Wagon Mound (No. 1)*[37] to go one way, and the decision in *Hughes* v. *Lord Advocate*[38] to go the other way.

Finally it should be noted that even when the breach of the statute does not in itself give a right of action to an individual damnified thereby the right of action for breach of any common law duty to conduct oneself with reasonable care so as not to injure those persons likely to be affected by want of care is not excluded.[39] The statutory duty does not extinguish the common law duty unless there is an express provision or necessary implication to that effect.[40] There is no need to strain the statute if the common law can deal with the matter.[41]

Need for a simplified approach

It will be apparent that this is a branch of the law in which a degree of uncertainty is inevitable. Much will depend upon the nature of the particular statute and upon the context in which the claim is made. No general rule can be stated for all cases. Nevertheless some of the obscurity could be eliminated if the courts accepted overtly that the matter is not purely one of statutory interpretation, emphasis upon which has overtones of fiction in this area. It needs to be recognised that the courts themselves in fact exercise an element of decision in these cases; and the various "tests" and concepts which they use in so doing ought preferably to be simplified and reduced in number. It is sometimes suggested that Parliament should itself provide in each statute whether or not an action for breach of statutory duty was intended.[42] Parliament has begun to attend to this complaint, and some statutes now state explicitly that a breach of duty thereby created is actionable. So the Sex Discrimination Act 1975, s.66(1), and the Race Relations Act 1976, s.57(1), provide that discriminatory acts "may be made the subject of civil proceedings in like manner as any other claim in tort . . . for breach of statutory duty." Another particularly important provision is the Consumer Protection Act 1987, s.41 which enables contravention of consumer safety regulations to be actionable as breaches of statutory

---

[35] *Grant* v. *National Coal Board* [1956] A.C. 649.
[36] *Donaghey* v. *Boulton and Paul Ltd.* [1968] A.C. 1.
[37] [1961] A.C. 388.
[38] [1963] A.C. 837. See above, Chap. 9.
[39] *East Suffolk Catchment Board* v. *Kent* [1941] A.C. 74, 89.
[40] *Read* v. *Croydon Corporation* [1938] 4 All E.R. 631, 654.
[41] *Smith* v. *N.C.B.* [1967] 1 W.L.R. 871, 875.
[42] *Cutler* v. *Wandsworth Stadium Ltd.* [1949] A.C. 398, 410, *per* Lord du Parcq.

duty.[43] Conversely, a statute may expressly provide that breach of a duty which it creates is not actionable.[44]

§ 10.2. ABSOLUTE STATUTORY DUTIES

When a duty is created by statute, the breach of which is an actionable tort, it is a question of construction whether the liability is absolute, or depends on wrongful intent or negligence on the part of the defendant. In other words, when a statute provides that a certain thing must be done, it is a question of interpretation whether this means that the thing is to be done in all events, or merely that the person upon whom the duty is imposed is to use due care and diligence in the endeavour to perform it, and that if he fails to perform it through no fault of his he shall be free from liability.[45] The reports contain many cases where actions have been brought for breach of the absolute duty to fence dangerous machinery imposed by the Factories Act 1961.[46] It may be wrong to describe the nature of the duty in these cases as "absolute," for that is a term which signifies a duty which exists independently of fault, and in these cases there has often been an intentional or negligent failure to comply with the statutory duty.[47]

Relationship with negligence

Statutory negligence

The standard of care (or duty) prescribed by the statute may be set out in minute detail (as under the Factories Act), or else merely phrased in general terms (as under the Occupiers' Liability Act). It seems that the decision of the House of Lords in *Lochgelly Iron and Coal Co.* v. *M'Mullan*[48] has settled that an action for breach of a statutory duty which involves the notion of taking care not to injure[49] is for the purposes of an action for damages equivalent to negligence.[50] Lord Wright said[51] that breach of such a duty had been "correctly described as statutory negligence." But in a later case[52] the same Law Lord expressed a contrary view. It is submitted that here second thoughts are best. There are obvious differences between the two claims: in one the standard of care is fixed by the legislature, in the other by the court[53]; in one the defence

---

[43] See also the Resale Prices Act 1976, s.25(3), the Health and Safety at Work Act 1974, s.72, the Petroleum and Submarine Pipe-lines Act 1975, s.30, the Copyright, Designs and Patents Act 1988, s.194.

[44] As with the Safety of Sports Grounds Act 1975, s.13, or the Guard Dogs Act 1975, s.5(1).

[45] *Greenwood* v. *Central Service Co.* [1940] 2 K.B. 447, 461. See also below, § 10.04.

[46] See below, § 10.03.

[47] Williams (1960) 23 M.L.R. 233, 238.

[48] [1934] A.C. 1.

[49] In some cases (*e.g. Monk* v. *Warbey* [1935] 1 K.B. 75) the statutory duty in issue has nothing to do with negligence.

[50] So the statutory precautions must be carried out, even though some other precaution might be equally effective: *Stein & Co. Ltd.* v. *O'Hanlon* [1965] A.C. 890.

[51] [1934] A.C. 1, 23.

[52] *London Passenger Transport Board* v. *Upson* [1949] A.C. 155, 168.

[53] See above, Chap. 9.

of *volenti non fit injuria* is applicable whereas in the other, except in rare cases,[54] it is not.[55] Again negligence and breach of statutory duty are usually treated as separate causes of action from a pleading point of view.[56] Further, a breach of statutory duty does not automatically throw on the defendant the onus of proving he was not in breach of his common law duty.[57] But although the causes of action are separate there is really only one head of damage for which redress is sought, so that satisfaction of one cause of action ends the whole claim.[58] Moreover the fact that breach of statutory duty cannot be equated with negligence, or any other particular tort, does not prevent it from coming under the same general heading. So in *American Express Co.* v. *British Airways Board*[59] the action was held to have been excluded by statutory wording conferring immunity from "proceedings in tort."[60]

§ 10.3. STATUTORY DUTIES IN FACTORIES, MINES AND SHOPS

Probably the most significant area in which breaches of statutory duty have been held to give rise to actions for damages is that involving the protection of employees at their places of work. Indeed claims for damages incurred through the breach of these duties are commonly joined with a claim for negligence at common law.[61] Thus it has been settled for many years that a civil action for damages can be brought by a workman injured as a result of a breach of the safety provisions of the Factories Act and Mines and Quarries Act.[62] Breach of the duties imposed renders the occupier liable to criminal proceedings. But "The real incentive for the observance by employers of their statutory duties under Railway Acts, Factory Acts, Dock Acts, and similar legislation is not their liability to substantial fines, but the possibility of heavy claims for damages."[63] Prosecutions in this area remain much less common than civil claims.[64]

The principal statute is the Factories Act 1961, consolidating the previous legislation. Its provisions will be replaced by regulations issued

---

[54] See *Imperial Chemical Industries* v. *Shatwell* [1965] A.C. 656.

[55] See below, Chap. 22.

[56] *Murfin* v. *United Steel Companies Ltd.* [1957] 1 W.L.R. 104.

[57] *Davis* v. *Everard (F.T.) & Sons, Ltd.* [1960] 1 Lloyd's Rep. 59.

[58] *Graham* v. *C.E. Heinke & Co. Ltd.* [1958] 1 Q.B. 432.

[59] [1983] 1 W.L.R. 701, 708.

[60] *i.e.* in s.29(1) of the Post Office Act 1969.

[61] The imposition of a statutory duty (other than by the Occupiers' Liability Act 1957) does not free the occupier of premises from his common law obligations; but if he complies with the statutory code of conduct it may be difficult to convict him of negligence: *Chipchase* v. *British Titan Products Co. Ltd.* [1956] 1 Q.B. 545.

[62] It does not follow that the person injured can sue every person in breach of those provisions: *Biddle* v. *Truvox Engineering Co. Ltd.* [1952] 1 Q.B. 101 (supplier of defective machinery, as distinct from occupier of factory, not liable under the statute).

[63] *Hutchinson* v. *L. & N.E. Ry.* [1942] 1 K.B. 481, 488, *per* Goddard L.J. But *cf.* the Robens Committee on *Safety and Health at Work*, which suggested that the availability of the action for breach of statutory duty in factory accident cases had actually hindered accident prevention. Cmnd. 5034, pp.144–147; 185–187.

[64] For a reported example of a prosecution see *R.* v. *Swan Hunter Shipbuilders Ltd.* [1981] I.C.R. 831.

under the Health and Safety at Work Act 1974. This Act lays down the general legal obligations relating to employed persons, and provides for enforcement through a Health and Safety Commission. The general duties contained in sections 2 to 9 of the Act will be supplemented by Regulations and Codes of Practice. By section 47 the breach of these general statutory duties is not *per se* actionable. Meanwhile the law is based upon the Act of 1961, which imposes duties relating, *inter alia* to the fencing of dangerous machinery and the construction and maintenance of factory premises themselves. For detailed exposition of the law in this area specialist works should be consulted.[65]

§ 10.4. NATURE OF STATUTORY DUTIES

(1) Absolute

Some statutory duties are absolute in the sense that the obligation, whatever its meaning and effect, must be actually fulfilled and not merely that the person subject to the duty must do his best to fulfil it.[66] The code of conduct required is conclusively fixed by the statute. In such a case there is not so much a duty to perform as responsibility for circumstances.[67] At first sight, therefore, it might seem that these duties have little or nothing in common with the common law obligation to take reasonable care, which is in general measured by what is reasonably foreseeable in the circumstances. But the tendency of the decisions has been to introduce the notion of reasonable foreseeability in determining the true construction of the statutory obligation. So that whether part of a machine is "dangerous" so as to require it to be "securely" fenced, or placed in a "safe" position, or whether a floor is "maintained in an efficient state," involves a consideration of what ought reasonably to be foreseen.[68] But it is well settled that careless as well as careful conduct may have to be foreseen.[69]

(2) "Practicable"

Other duties are not absolute, in the sense that the statute only requires what is "practicable" or "reasonably practicable" to be done. This is often treated as closely analogous to the common law obligation of an employer to his employee,[70] but something more than reasonable care is required,[71] and what is "practicable" may require a higher standard than what is "reasonably practicable,"[72] although not as high a standard as "possible."[73] In general it may be said that the risk has to be balanced against the time, cost, efficiency, and trouble of remedial

---

[65] *e.g.* Munkman, *Employers' Liability at Common Law.*
[66] *Carroll* v. *Andrew Barclay & Sons Ltd.* [1948] A.C. 477, 487.
[67] *Brown* v. *National Coal Board* [1962] A.C. 574, 592.
[68] *John Summers & Sons Ltd.* v. *Frost* [1955] A.C. 740.
[69] *John Summers & Sons Ltd.* v. *Frost* [1955] A.C. 740.
[70] See below, Chap. 21.
[71] *Edwards* v. *National Coal Board* [1949] 1 K.B. 704, 709.
[72] *Sanders* v. *F. H. Lloyd & Co.* [1982] I.C.R. 360, 365.
[73] *Jayne* v. *National Coal Board* [1963] 2 All E.R. 220.

measures,[74] but, under "practicable," questions of cost may be eliminated, though what is done must still be possible in the light of the relevant knowledge and resources at the time of the breach.[75]

Onus of proof

The plaintiff must prove (i) breach of duty, and (ii) that such breach caused the injury complained of. The ordinary standard of proof in civil actions applies: the plaintiff must make it appear that at least on a balance of probabilities the breach of duty caused or materially contributed to his injury.[76] The House of Lords has emphasised the need for the plaintiff to prove causation,[77] but it has also said that this must not impose too severe a burden on him,[78] especially if the fault complained of is one of omission rather than commission.[79] The onus of proving that safety measures were not reasonably practicable rests on the defendant, who must plead the defence and adduce evidence at the trial to support it.[80]

§ 10.5. DEFENCES

(1) Volenti non fit injuria

Consent is no defence when the defendant is an employer who is himself under a statutory duty to the plaintiff.[81] The reason for this rule is that it is contrary to public policy that where there is a statutory obligation on the employer the workman should contract out of it.[82] Hence to give statutory force to a common law obligation is by no means an otiose procedure.[83]

But consent is a defence to an employer when two workmen, each of whom is under a particular statutory duty, embark upon a joint enterprise in breach of that duty and then seek to hold the employer vicariously responsible for the resulting damage.[84] In such a case public policy requires that a workman in breach of his statutory duty should not be entitled to recover damages by luring a fellow-workman to join him[85] in the breach.[86]

---

[74] *Jenkins* v. *Allied Ironfounders Ltd.* [1970] 1 W.L.R. 304.
[75] *Adsett* v. *K. and L. Steelfounders and Engineers Ltd.* [1953] 1 W.L.R. 137, 773; *Richards* v. *Highways Ironfounders (West Bromwich) Ltd.* [1955] 1 W.L.R. 1049; [1957] 1. W.L.R. 781.
[76] *Bonnington Castings Ltd.* v. *Wardlaw* [1956] A.C. 613.
[77] *McWilliams* v. *Arrol (Sir William) & Co. Ltd.* [1962] 1 W.L.R. 295.
[78] *Nicholson* v. *Atlas Steel Ltd.* [1957] 1 W.L.R. 613.
[79] *McGhee* v. *National Coal Board* [1973] 1 W.L.R. 1.
[80] *Bowes* v. *Sedgefield District Council* [1981] I.C.R. 234.
[81] *Wheeler* v. *New Merton Board Mills* [1933] 2 K.B. 669.
[82] *I.C.I. Ltd.* v. *Shatwell* [1965] A.C. 656.
[83] *Alford* v. *National Coal Board* [1952] 1 All E.R. 754, 757. The person on whom the obligation is laid will also usually be liable to criminal proceedings.
[84] *I.C.I. Ltd.* v. *Shatwell* [1965] A.C. 656.
[85] If he acted alone, he would be met by the defence of delegation.
[86] [1965] A.C. 656.

(2) Contributory negligence

In *Caswell* v. *Powell Duffryn Collieries, Ltd.*[87] the House of Lords unanimously, though *obiter*, held that the contributory negligence of the plaintiff provides a good defence to the employer. Today the damages may be apportioned under the Law Reform (Contributory Negligence) Act 1945. But in the case of breach of provisions designed for the protection of workmen, too high a standard of care must not be demanded.[88] The standard to be applied is that of the ordinary prudent workman, and the court must "take into account all the circumstances of work in a factory, and that it is not for every risky thing which a work-man in a factory may do in his familiarity with the machinery that a plaintiff ought to be held guilty of contributory negligence."[89] Again, a workman may be entitled to assume that statutory duties have been complied with.[90]

Although on the whole the courts thus favour the injured workman, when the plaintiff began to repair a scaffolding in a way described as "fantastically wrong," he was held solely responsible for his conse-quent injuries.[91] But the employer is not relieved of liability merely because the workman at the time of the accident was also guilty of a breach of his own duty under the statute, although the workman's breach may be such as to provide evidence of his negligence.[92] Finally, if it has been established that the injury would not have been caused if the employer's statutory duty had been performed, the onus is on the defendant to prove that the plaintiff's contributory negligence was a substantial or material co-operating cause.[93] It is not for the plaintiff to show exactly how the accident happened.[94]

(3) Delegation or co-terminous fault

In some cases it may be a defence to an action for breach of statutory duty that the employer has delegated the performance of that duty to the plaintiff himself, who is then without remedy if he is injured, for he

---

[87] [1940] A.C. 152. For this purpose there is not any difference between the duty imposed by one statute and another: *Sparks* v. *Edward Ash* [1943] K.B. 223, 239, 240.

[88] *Lewis* v. *Denye* [1940] A.C. 921, 931. "The Factories Act is there not merely to protect the careful, the vigilant and the conscientious workman, but, human nature being what it is, also the careless, the indolent, the inadvertent, the weary, and even, perhaps, in some cases, the disobedient": *Carr* v. *Mercantile Produce Co.* [1949] 2 K.B. 601, 608, *per* Stable J. In *Harrison* v. *Metropolitan-Vickers Electrical Co. Ltd.* [1954] 1 W.L.R. 324, 328, the same learned judge said that to attribute to such acts "the rather grim description of contributory negligence is like using an elephant rifle to shoot a rabbit."

[89] *Flower* v. *Ebbw Vale Steel Co.* [1934] 2 K.B. 132, 140, *per* Lawrence J.; approved in *John Summers & Sons Ltd.* v. *Frost* [1955] A.C. 740. This lenient standard, however, does not necessarily apply to simple cases of common law negligence: *Staveley Iron and Chemical Co. Ltd.* v. *Jones* [1956] A.C. 627; *Smith* v. *National Coal Board* [1967] 1 W.L.R. 871.

[90] *Westwood* v. *Post Office* [1974] A.C. 1.

[91] *Norris* v. *W. Moss & Sons Ltd.* [1954] 1 W.L.R. 346; *Rushton* v. *Turner Bros. Asbestos Co. Ltd.* [1960] 1 W.L.R. 96 ("a crazy thing to do").

[92] *Ross* v. *Associated Portland Cement Manufacturers Ltd.* [1964] 1 W.L.R. 768. *A fortiori* where the employee in breach is acting under the employer's orders: *Laszcyk* v. *National Coal Board* [1954] 1 W.L.R. 1426 (plaintiff held five per cent. responsible).

[93] *Caswell's case* [1940] A.C. 152, 172.

[94] *Smithwick* v. *National Coal Board* [1950] 2 K.B. 335.

is held to be the author of his own misfortune.[95] The doctrine appears to have been invented in order to enable an employer to escape liability to an employee if the sole reason for the breach of statutory duty was the employee's own disobedience.[96] For it must be conceded that the doctrine of absolute liability could lead to absurd results when combined with the doctrine of vicarious liability.[97] But the principle of delegation fell into disfavour and now is probably obsolete.[98] It has been abolished by statute in Ireland.[99] The proper approach to the problem is to combine the rule that the plaintiff must prove causation[1] with the principles of contributory negligence.[2] The question is whether there has been some fault on the part of the employer which goes beyond or is independent of the fault on the part of the employee which as a result of the doctrine of vicarious liability constitutes a breach of statutory duty by the employer.[3] Were the faults of the employer and the employee simply co-extensive or co-terminous? If so, the plaintiff is without remedy,[4] at any rate if the statutory duty is imposed on him alone and not on his employer as well. In short, the fundamental question is: Whose fault was it?[5]

---

[95] *Smith* v. *Baveystock & Co.* [1945] 1 All E.R. 531.
[96] For the position when two (or more) employees are jointly disobedient, see *I.C.I. Ltd.* v. *Shatwell* [1965] A.C. 656.
[97] *Boyle* v. *Kodak Ltd.* [1969] 1 W.L.R. 661.
[98] *Ross* v. *Associated Portland Cement Manufacturers Ltd.* [1964] 1 W.L.R. 768.
[99] Civil Liability Act 1961, s.57(2).
[1] See above, Chap. 9.
[2] See below, Chap. 22.
[3] *Quinn* v. *Green* [1966] 1 Q.B. 509.
[4] *Leach* v. *Standard Telephones and Cables Ltd.* [1966] 1 W.L.R. 1392.
[5] *Ross* v. *Associated Portland Cement Manufacturers Ltd.* [1964] 1 W.L.R. 768.

CHAPTER 11

DANGEROUS PREMISES

§ 11.1. Introduction[1]

The principles discussed in sections 11.1 to 11.13 of this chapter apply only to persons who suffer injury while on another's[2] premises. Injuries suffered as a result of the dangerous state of another's premises by persons who have not entered thereon are governed by the Defective Premises Act 1972[3] and the tort of public nuisance.[4] It is essential to keep in mind where the accident takes place and why the plaintiff is in that place, because the duty of the occupier of dangerous premises to the plaintiff who is injured on the highway or on adjoining land may differ materially from his duty to the plaintiff who suffers damage from the defective state of the premises after having entered upon them. "It does not escape me," Lord Simonds said,[5] "that in the result a distinction which may appear capricious will exist between two cases . . . But, my Lords, such distinctions must exist in the law so long at least as a distinction exists between public and private property, and it is ultimately upon that distinction, perhaps, that the different fates of my hypothetical victims depend." But this does not mean that an unlawful entrant is without protection: occupation of property is now increasingly regarded as a ground of liability, not of exemption, both in England[6] and in Ireland,[7] and the Occupiers' Liability Act 1984, s.1 gives parliamentary recognition to this tendency.

What are premises

The principles which follow apply not only to real property but also to appliances or objects upon it of which the plaintiff has been invited or allowed to make use—for example, grandstands,[8] stagings,[9] diving-boards,[10] ships in dry dock,[11] ladders,[12] and electricity pylons.[13] These

---

[1] The main work is North, *Occupiers' Liability* (1971). See also Report of the Law Reform Committee (Cmd. 9305 (1954)); Law Commission Report on Liability for Damage or Injury to Trespassers and related questions of Occupiers' Liability (Law Com. No. 75., Cmnd. 6428 (1976)); Report of the Pearson Commission (Cmnd. 7054 (1978)), Chap. 28

[2] Accidents in one's own home constantly occur. Usually there is no remedy, but it may be possible to sue a builder or decorator. The law relating to liability for defective products (see below, Chap. 12) may also sometimes be relevant.

[3] See below, § 11.14.

[4] See above, Chap. 5.

[5] *Jacobs* v. *L.C.C.* [1950] A.C. 361, 377.

[6] *British Railways Board* v. *Herrington* [1972] A.C. 877, 913.

[7] *McNamara* v. *E.S.B.* [1975] I.R.I., 13, 23.

[8] *Francis* v. *Cockrell* (1870) L.R. 5 Q.B. 501.

[9] *Heaven* v. *Pender* (1883) 11 Q.B.D. 503.

[10] *Perkowski* v. *Wellington Corporation* [1959] A.C. 53.

[11] *London Graving Dock Co. Ltd.* v. *Horton* [1951] A.C. 737.

[12] *Wheeler* v. *Copas* [1981] 3 All E.R. 405, 408.

[13] *McLaughlin* v. *Antrim Electricity Supply Co.* [1941] N.I. 23.

principles may also apply to movables such as ships,[14] lifts,[15] and aeroplanes,[16] in so far as the injury complained of has arisen from the dangerous structural condition of the conveyance. But they do not govern an act of negligence by the driver of it in the course of transit,[17] for it has been settled that the driver of a vehicle owes his passengers the same duty to take reasonable care for their safety whether they are gratuitous or fare-paying,[18] while the common law duty of an occupier of premises was elaborately graduated according to the character of the entrant.

These principles have been confirmed by the Occupiers' Liability Act 1957, s.1(3), which provides that the rules thereby enacted[19] in relation to an occupier of premises and his visitors shall also apply, in like manner and to the like extent as the principles applicable to an occupier of premises and his invitees and licensees would apply, to regulate the obligations of a person occupying or having control over any fixed or movable structure,[20] including any vessel, vehicle or aircraft. But an occupier of premises does not necessarily occupy a chattel on them so as to render him liable for the use made of it by a contractor, e.g. a ladder not integrated into a scaffolding[21] as distinct from a large digging machine in a tunnel.[22]

Who is responsible

In dealing with dangerous premises it is necessary to distinguish between the responsibilities of the owner, those of the occupier or possessor, and those of third parties on the premises. Generally speaking, liability in such cases is based on occupancy or control, not on ownership. The person responsible for the condition of the premises is he who is in actual occupation or possession of them for the time being, whether he is the owner of them or not. For it is he who has the immediate supervision and control and the power of permitting or prohibiting the entry of other persons.[23] It is a question of fact in each case whether the defendant has such control, but the courts look at the matter broadly. So a local authority which has served both a notice to treat and a notice of entry before making a compulsory purchase order may be an occupier,[24] as also indeed may be a tenant who has left the

---

[14] *London Graving Dock Co. v. Horton* [1951] A.C. 737, 750.
[15] *Haseldine v. Daw* [1941] 2 K.B. 343, 358.
[16] *Fosbroke-Hobbes v.Airwork Ltd.* [1937] 1 All E.R. 108.
[17] *Haseldine v. Daw & Sons Ltd.* [1941] 2 K.B. 343, 373; Occupiers' Liability Act 1957, s.5(3).
[18] Kahn-Freund, *The Law of Inland Transport* (4th ed., 1965), p. 503.
[19] See § 11.4.
[20] *Kearney v. Eric Waller Ltd.* [1967] 1 Q.B. 29 (scaffolding).
[21] *O'Malley v. Sheppard and Son Ltd.* [1962] 2 Lloyd's Rep. 221.
[22] *Bunker v. Charles Brand & Son Ltd.* [1969] 2 Q.B. 480.
[23] *Hartwell v. Grayson, Rollo and Clover Docks* [1947] K.B. 901, 917; *Napier v. Ryan* [1954] N.Z.L.R. 1234, 1242; *Nicholls v. Lyons* [1955] N.Z.L.R. 1097, 1106; *Wheat v. Lacon & Co. Ltd.* [1966] A.C. 552, 574, 578; *Holden v. White* [1982] Q.B. 679, 687.
[24] *Harris v. Birkenhead Corporation* [1976] 1 W.L.R. 279.

premises but has retained the keys.[25] To this general principle there are two qualifications. First, there may be more than one occupier of property at the same time liable in respect of the same damage,[26] as when an occupier engages a head contractor to do repairs,[27] or when an employer remains in occupation through his employee or other licensee,[28] as he must if a corporate entity. In such a case each occupier owes, or may owe, a separate duty to the visitor,[29] who may be a trespasser in relation to one of the occupiers, but not in relation to the other.[30] Secondly, it may be that if A invites B onto the premises of C in pursuance of some common material interest, he must either take reasonable care to ensure that C's premises are reasonably safe for the purpose in view or else warn B that he has not done so.[31]

There may be difficulty in distinguishing between a lease, under which exclusive possession passes to the lessee,[32] and a licence, under which it does not,[33] but some courts have been reluctant to permit an occupier to divest himself or his responsibilities by creating a lease for an artificially short period. So the occupiers were held liable when they had "hired" out premises for a dance for four hours, but had retained the right to supply refreshments.[34] "Dancing is hungry and thirsty work. A dance without refreshments would be what Lord Bowen called 'a melancholy spree.' The restaurant keepers were to supply the necessary restoratives in what had been, at all events up to 8 p.m., their own restaurant."[35] So a licensor may, unlike a lessor, be regarded as still in occupation if the terms of the licence permit or require such a conclusion.[36] Primarily, then, liability rests on the occupier, or the occupiers, and we will postpone until later consideration of the liabilities of the owner not in occupation[37] and of third parties.[38]

Who may claim

The position at common law was concisely summarised as follows: "Where a question arises, not between parties who are both present in the exercise of equal rights *inter se*, but between parties of whom one is the owner or occupier of the place and the other, the party injured, is

---

[25] *Morrison Holdings Ltd.* v. *Manders Property Ltd.* [1976] 1 W.L.R. 533, 542.

[26] *Fisher* v.*C.H.T. Ltd.* 1 W.L.R. 1093, *Harris* v. *Birkenhead Corporation* [1976] 1 W.L.R. 279, 286.

[27] *Ferguson* v. *Welsh* [1987] 1 W.L.R. 1557.

[28] *Wheat* v. *Lacon & Co. Ltd.* [1966] A.C. 552.

[29] [1966] A.C. 552, 581, 585, 587.

[30] *Ferguson* v. *Welsh* [1987] 1 W.L.R. 1557, 1563.

[31] *Hartwell* v. *Grayson, Rollo and Clover Docks Ltd.* [1947] K.B. 901, 913.

[32] Although the lessor may also have duties imposed on him by the Defective Premises Act 1972, s.4.

[33] See above, § 5.8

[34] *Kelly* v. *Woolworth & Co.* [1922] 2 I.R. 5.

[35] [1922] 2 I.R. 5, 8, *per* Ronan L.J.

[36] *Wheat* v. *Lacon & Co. Ltd.* [1966] A.C. 552.

[37] See below, § 11.13.

[38] See below, § 11.12

not there as of right,[39] but must justify his presence there if he can, the law has long recognised three categories of obligaton."[40] Such a person may go to the premises (i) by the invitation, express or implied, of the occupier; (ii) with the leave and licence of the occupier; (iii) as a trespasser. These three categories were exhaustive; the temptation to introduce further sub-divisions, (*e.g.* a category of persons who enter as of right) was resisted.[41] The categories were also quite inappropriate for dealing with the incursions of animals such as bees.[42]

§ 11.2. NATURE AND VALUE OF COMMON LAW RULES

It was settled that the rules on this topic were a special subhead of the general doctrine of negligence as expounded in *Donoghue* v. *Stevenson*.[43] Thus the plaintiff must establish that the defendant was an occupier,[44] and not just a licensee who might reasonably have had the plaintiff in contemplation. Although there is proximity between the occupier and his visitors, the Atkinian neighbour principle does not exclusively define or describe that relationship.[45] It may be that if it had been earlier and more generally recognised that the topic was only one branch of the law of negligence it might have been seen that the occupier's duties could not conveniently be put into strait-jackets to fit the character in which the plaintiff came on the premises, and the law would then have been freed of some needless refinements and profitless distinctions.[46] Yet even if this method of approach had been adopted some distinctions between the various classes of entrants would probably have been necessary, for they correspond to real differences in the nature of the user of property and in the reasonable claims to protection of those who are permitted such use.

Need for reform

Various reasons may be assigned for the state of confusion into which the law fell. One significant reason may be found in the rule which before 1966 prohibited the House of Lords from reversing one of its own previous decisions. It was thus necessary for the legislature in the Occupiers' Liability Act 1957 to reverse at least three decisions of the House of Lords,[47] although this is a task which many felt that the Law

---

[39] *i.e.* either a right arising under a contract (for which, see § 11.5) or a right conferred by some rule of statute or common law (for which, see § 11.8).

[40] *Latham* v. *Johnson (R.) & Nephew Ltd.* [1913] 1 K.B. 398, 410, *per* Hamilton L.J. (An "exceedingly comprehensive and able judgment": *Robert Addie & Sons (Collieries) Ltd.* v. *Dumbreck* [1929] A.C. 358, 370, *per* Lord Dunedin.)

[41] *London Graving Dock Co.* v. *Horton* [1951] A.C. 737, 764.

[42] *Tutton* v. *A. D. Walker Ltd.* [1986] Q.B. 61.

[43] *London Graving Dock Co.* v. *Horton* [1951] A.C. 737, 766; *British Railways Board* v. *Herrington* [1972] A.C. 988, 912.

[44] See above, § 11.1.

[45] *Commissioner for Railways* v. *McDermott* [1967] A.C. 169, 186.

[46] See the Third Report of the Law Reform Committee (Cmd. 9305 (1954), s.44).

[47] *Cavalier* v. *Pope* [1906] A.C. 428; *London Graving Dock Co.* v. *Horton* [1951] A.C. 737; *Thomson* v. *Cremin* [1956] W.L.R. 103n.

Lords themselves would be better fitted to perform.[48] The Pearson Commission concluded that a no-fault scheme would not be appropriate for this area of the law: it should continue to be based on negligence.[49] The Occupiers' Liability Act, as interpreted by the courts, has been a noticeably successful piece of law reform.[50]

§ 11.3. Current Operations[51]

Apart altogether from the Occupiers' Liability Act, the strictness of the common law was mitigated by cases in which the courts held that an entrant who is injured as a result of current operations conducted on the premises by the occupier need not bring his claim within the established invitee-licensee-trespasser categories but might have a remedy on the simple ground that the defendant has not fulfilled his duty to take reasonable care for the safety of the plaintiff.[52] In one of the most authoritative of these cases the court stated that its task was to choose between competing categories of the law of torts and to select one of them to the exclusion of the other.[53] In this case, in which a child had been electrocuted while climbing on the defendants' pylon (and so committing a technical trespass), the High Court of Australia selected as the basis of its decision the rule which imposes a high standard of care on those who carry on a dangerous activity (*i.e.* the supply of high-voltage electricity) in preference to the rule which exempts an occupier from any duty of care to a trespasser.[54] Again, in relation to a licensee, in *Slater* v. *Clay Cross Co. Ltd.*[55] the Court of Appeal held the defendants liable to the plaintiff (subject to a reduction of damages on the ground

---

[48] See the remarks of Lord Reid on the Second Reading of the Occupiers' Liability Bill: 203 H.L.Deb. 5s., col. 262. Scottish lawyers always felt aggrieved by the decision in *Robert Addie & Sons* (*Collieries*) v. *Dumbreck* [1929] A.C. 358, which replaced the primitive simplicity of the law of delict by the more elaborate English doctrine. But as the Court of Session also felt itself unable to escape from the "doctrine of the categories" by accepting an invitation to hold that it had been impliedly overruled by *Donoghue* v. *Stevenson* [1932] A.C. 562 (see *Stewart* v. *Glasgow Corporation*, 1958 S.C. 28), it was necessary to enact the Occupiers' Liability (Scotland) Act 1960, which should be studied for its significant differences from the English statue.

[49] Cmnd. 7054, 1978, § 1550.

[50] So Lord Hailsham of St. Marylebone L.C. called it "a little gem of a statute" (H.L.Deb., Vol. 443, col. 720), and even Lord Diplock, who had opposed reform by legislation, later conceded that "it has worked like a charm" (1971) 45 Austn.L.J. 531, 569).

[51] See North, *Occupiers' Liability*, Chap. 6.

[52] *Miller* v. *South of Scotland Electricity Board*, 1958 S.C.(H.L.) 20, 37–38. The distinction is between the occupier's "activity duty" and his "occupancy duty": Newark, "*Twine* v. *Bean's Express Ltd.*" (1954) 17 M.L.R. 102, 109. But note that the occupier has been held entitled to exclude even his "activity duty" by a notice in adequate terms which have been sufficiently brought to the attention of the visitor: *White* v. *Blackmore* [1972] 2 Q.B. 651. See below, § 11.4

[53] *Thompson* v. *Municipality of Bankstown* (1952) 87 C.L.R. 619, 623.

[54] The decision in *Thompson* v. *Bankstown* was expressly approved in *Commissioner for Railways* v. *Quinlan* [1964] A.C. 1054, and in *Munnings* v. *Hydro-Electric Commission* [1971] A.L.R. 609

[55] [1956] 2 Q.B. 264, followed in *McGinlay* v. *British Railways Board* [1983] 1 W.L.R. 1427, 1429.

of her contributory negligence) when she had been knocked down by a train on the defendants' narrow gauge railway line.[56]

On one view the distinction between the occupier's "activity duty" and his "occupancy duty" has been abolished by the Occupiers' Liability Act.[57] This emphasises section 1(1) which provides that the rules enacted by the Act shall have effect, *in place of the rules of the common law*, to regulate the duty which an occupier of premises owes to his visitors in respect of dangers due to the state of the premises or to things done or omitted to be done on them. On this view the only duty which the occupier today owes to his lawful visitors is the common duty of care. *Obiter dicta* in the House of Lords also deny that the distinction between the activity duty and the occupancy duty is relevant to the relationship of occupier and trespasser.[58] Nevertheless the majority of commentators,[59] relying in part on the general background and context of the legislation, apparently incline to the view that activities wholly unrelated to the particular land in question, but which just happen to be carried on there, are governed by ordinary Atkinian negligence as far as non-trespassers are concerned. In practice, however, it is unlikely that the outcome of any case will ever turn on the point. In the one area in which a difference between the two approaches might perhaps have been expected to appear, that of exclusion of liability, it does not in fact seem to have done so.[60]

§ 11.4. GENERAL PRINCIPLES OF THE OCCUPIERS LIABILITY ACT 1957

The degree of criticism to which the state of the common law relating to the liability of occupiers of premises to their visitors had given rise induced the Lord Chancellor to refer the matter to the Law Reform Committee. The Report of the Committee,[61] which contains a full and valuable survey of the common law, made a number of recommendations which were in substance adopted by Parliament in the Occupiers' Liability Act 1957. The first and main change effected by the Act is that the rules which it contains replace the rules of the common law under which the duty of an occupier differs according as the visitor is an invitee or a licensee. Section 2(1) provides that an occupier of premises[62] owes the same duty, "the common duty of care," to all his lawful

---

[56] The Judicial Committee seem to have approved the distinction between the activity and the occupancy duties in *Perkowski* v. *Wellington Corporation* [1959] A.C. 53, 67, and *Commisioner for Railways* v. *McDermott* [1967] 1 A.C. 169, 186–187, but to have disapproved it in *Commissioner for Railways* v. *Quinlan* [1964] A.C. 1054, and *Cooper* v. *Southern Portland Cement Ltd.* [1974] A.C. 623. The Court of Appeal has recognised that the distinction may be a fine one: *Videan* v. *British Transport Commission* [1963] 2 Q.B. 650, 664–665.

[57] See, *e.g.* the Report (1969) of the Alberta Law Reform Institute, p. 48.

[58] *British Railways Board* v. *Herrington* [1972] A.C. 877, 929, 942.

[59] See Odgers, [1957] C.L.J. 39–40; North, *Occupiers' Liability* pp. 80–82; Winfield and Jolowicz, *Tort*, 13th edn. pp. 208–209.

[60] *i.e.* liability can, in certain circumstances, apparently be excluded in respect of both the activity and the occupancy duties: see below, § 11.4.

[61] Cmd. 9305 (1954). See Hutton, "Mechanics of Law Reform" (1961) 24 M.L.R. 18.

[62] Which includes any fixed or movable structure, including any vessel, vehicle or aircraft: s.1(3).

visitors, except in so far as he is free to and does extend, restrict, modify or exclude his duty to any visitor or visitors by agreement or otherwise. The common duty of care is not owed to trespassers under the 1957 Act, but a somewhat analogous duty has in effect been extended to them by the Occupiers' Liability Act 1984.[63]

Common duty of care

The common duty of care is defined (Occupiers' Liability Act 1957, s.2(2)) as a duty to take such care as in all the circumstances of the case is reasonable to see that the visitor will be reasonably safe in using the premises for the purpose for which he is permitted or invited to be there.[64] At common law it was not settled whether it is the particular visitor or the class to which he belongs who must be made safe, but the Act's reference to "the visitor" and "that person"[65] makes it plain that the law is now concered with the particular plaintiff. Therefore it is the visitor who has to be made safe and not the premises.[66] But it is important to note that the Act (s.1(2)) does not alter the common law as to the person on whom such a duty is imposed[67] or to whom it is owed; accordingly the persons who are to be treated as an occupier and as his visitors are the same[68] as the persons who would at common law be treated as an occupier and as his invitees or licensees. The common duty of care is also owed to persons visiting the premises under a contractual right (s.5), or in exercise of a right conferred by law[69] (s.2(6)). In short, the effect of the Act is not to enlarge the class of persons to whom a duty is owed[70] but to reduce the number of categories of visitors to two—lawful visitors and trespassers—and to provide that only one duty is owed to all lawful visitors.

Area of lawful visit. The common duty of care is owed only to a visitor who is "using the premises for the purpose for which he is invited or permitted to be there." If a visitor exceeds the area of invitation or permission he becomes a trespasser, and is owed a lesser duty.[71] It is a question of fact whether in all the circumstances of the case the occupier has taken reasonable steps to warn his visitor of the existence and scope

---

[63] See below, § 11.10.

[64] s.2 proceeds to deal in greater detail with some of the circumstances which may be relevant in any particular case—*e.g.* that the plaintiff is a child, or has knowledge of the danger, or that the occupier has employed an independent contractor to repair the premises. These points are considered fully later.

[65] *McGinlay* v. *British Railways Board* [1983] 1 W.L.R. 1427, 1432.

[66] *Roles* v. *Nathan* [1963] 1 W.L.R. 1117, 1122.

[67] The Act binds the Crown: s.6.

[68] But a person entering any premises in exercise of rights conferred by virtue of an access agreement or order under the National Parks and Access to the Countryside Act 1949, is not, for the purposes of that Act, a visitor of the occupier of those premises: s.1(4). Such entrants are now protected by the Occupiers' Liability Act 1984.

[69] This does not include persons exercising a right of way: below, § 11.8.

[70] *Holden* v. *White* [1982] Q.B. 679, 687.

[71] "When you invite a person into your house to use the staircase, you do not invite him to slide down the bannisters": *The Carlgarth* [1927] P. 93, 110, *per* Scrutton L.J.

of the prohibited area.[72] For if a person has entered on an area to which he was clearly invited, and if he has strayed from that area, the question is not so much whether he has been invited to stray but whether there was anything to delimit the area of invitation.[73] The cases on delimitation of the area by the occupier apply also to delimitation of the invitation by time.[74]

Nature of the duty

As the duty is imposed by a statute it is arguable[75] that this branch of the law is now no longer part of the law of negligence, but should be considered under the heading of actions for breach of statutory duty.[76] Even if this is so, the duty in question differs considerably from the ordinary statutory duty as it is phrased in such wide and general terms.[77] "It is in effect hoping to replace a principle of the common law with a new principle *of the common law*: instead of having the judgment of Willes J. being construed as if it were a statute, one is to have a statute which can be construed as if it were a judgment of Willes J."[78] So the House of Lords has emphasised that the occupier is not an insurer.[79]

Nature of damage recoverable[80]

At common law the better view was that the invitor's duty was to prevent damage not only to the person but also to the goods of an invitee.[81] The Occupiers' Liability Act 1957, s.1(3)(b), affirms[82] and extends the common law by enacting that the common duty of care which an occupier owes to his lawful visitors covers the obligations of a person occupying or having control over any premises or structure in respect of damage to[83] property, including the property of persons who are not

---

[72] So in the bannisters case (previous note), the host is not obliged to put up a notice: the lay-out of the premises speaks for itself: *O'Keefe* v. *Irish Motor Inns Ltd.* [1978] I.R. 83, 101.

[73] *Reaney* v. *Thomas Lydon & Son Ltd.* [1957] Ir.Jur.Rep. 1, 3.

[74] *Stone* v. *Taffe* [1974] 1 W.L.R. 1575, 1580.

[75] See *British Railways Board* v. *Herrington* [1972] A.C. 877, 941.

[76] See above, Chapter 10.

[77] A large number of cases have been reported in *Lloyd's Reports*, but they mostly seem to be on questions of fact.

[78] So the chief parliamentary draftsman: (1961) 24 M.L.R. 18, 28–29. (The reference is to the judgment of Willes J. in *Indermaur* v. *Dames* (1866) L.R. 1 C.P. 274 (below, § 11.6)).

[79] *McGinlay* v. *British Railways Board* [1983] 1 W.L.R. 1427, 1432.

[80] North, *Occupiers' Liability*, Chap. 7.

[81] *The Cawood III* [1951] P. 270; *Workington Harbour and Dock Board* v. *Towerfield (Owners)* [1951] A.C. 112; *Drive-Yourself Lessey's Pty. Ltd.* v. *Burnside* [1959] S.R.(N.S.W.) 390. Contra, *Edwards* v. *West Herts Group Hospital Management Committee* [1957] 1 W.L.R. 415, 417, 422; Goodhart (1957) 73 L.Q.R. 313.

[82] But note that under the Occupiers' Liability Act 1984, s.1(8) there is no liability to trespassers for loss or damage to property: see below, § 11.10.

[83] It is still uncertain whether these words cover loss of property due to theft, or some other wrongful act of a third party: *AMF International Ltd.* v. *Magnet Bowling Ltd.* [1968] 1 W.L.R. 1028.

themselves his visitors.[84] The words "damage to property" are not limited to damages in respect of physical damage but cover damages in respect of subsequent financial loss,[85] provided that the normal rules of remoteness of damage[86] are satisfied.

Can the common duty of care be excluded or modified?[87]

It is necessary first to see how the law stood before the Occupiers' Liability Act 1957. If the visitor had entered under contract there was no doubt that the occupier could modify or exclude the duty which he would otherwise have owed by the insertion of appropriate terms in the contract. But if the visitor had entered by the invitation or licence of the occupier the position was not so clear. It was only on the eve of the passing of the Act that the Court of Appeal in *Ashdown* v. *Samuel Williams & Sons Ltd.*[88] approved the view that it is competent to an occupier of land to restrict or exclude any liability he might otherwise be under to any licensee of his, including his liability for his own or his employee's negligence, by conditions framed and adequately made known to the licensee.[89]

Section 2(1) of the 1957 Act provides, as we have seen, that an occupier of premises owes the same duty, the "common duty of care," to all his lawful visitors, except in so far as he is free to[90] and does extend, restrict, modify or exclude his duty to any visitor or visitors by agreement or otherwise.[91] It is difficult to resist the conclusion that Parliament authorised occupiers of premises to exempt themselves from the duty which they would normally owe to their lawful visitors by the simple device of exhibiting a notice which contains terms suitably framed for this purpose.[92] In other words, Parliament approved the decision in *Ashdown*.[93] But in two later statutes Parliament has limited the right to exclude so that it is now only possible for non-business occupiers, or

---

[84] This would protect the interest of, say, a company which hired out a motor-vehicle which was lawfully brought on to the occupier's premises by the hirer: *Drive-Yourself Lessey's Pty. Ltd.* v. *Burnside* (1959) S.R.(N.S.W.) 390. So an entity which is physically incapable of entering, and does not in fact enter, is yet protected by the Occupiers' Liability Act.

[85] *AMF International Ltd.* v. *Magnet Bowling Ltd.* [1968] 1 W.L.R. 1028.

[86] See below, Chapter 23.

[87] See Symmons, "How Free is the Freedom of the Occupier?" (1974) *The Conveyancer* 253.

[88] [1957] 1 Q.B. 409. See below, Chapter 22, for exemption clauses and disclaimers in general.

[89] [1957] 1 Q.B. 409, 421, *per* Jenkins L.J. See also Parker L.J. p.427. (It should be noted that both these L.JJ. were members of the Law Reform Committee which produced the Report on Occupiers' Liability.)

[90] The occupier is probably not free in respect to visitors entering in pursuance of a contract between the occupier and a third party (see below, § 11.5).

[91] When the Bill was in Committee a proposal to delete the words "or otherwise" was defeated on the advice of Hylton-Foster, S.-G.: H.C. Standing Committee A, March 26, 1957, col. 30.

[92] But observe the significant difference in the wording of s.2(1) of the Occupiers' Liability (Scotland) Act 1960, which makes it plain that Parliament has given no such freedom to the Scottish occupier.

[93] *White* v. *Blackmore* [1972] 2 Q.B. 651, 674.

business occupiers who allow visitors to enter free of charge, (*e.g.* to scenic or historic sites), to exempt themelves from liability.[94]

Contributory negligence. Although the Act does not specifically deal with the point, it has been assumed both in the Court of Appeal[95] and the House of Lords[96] that the defence of contributory negligence is available.

Effect of knowledge of danger. Even if the occupier has not exempted himself from liability by means of "agreement or otherwise" under section 2(1) of the Act, he may still be exonerated from liability in whole or in part by reason of the visitor's knowledge of the danger. This may happen in three ways.

(1) Section 2(5) of the Act provides that the common duty of care does not impose on an occupier any obligation to a visitor in respect of risks willingly accepted as his by the visitor, as when rugby football is played on a ground which complies with the appropriate by-laws.[97] The question whether a risk was so accepted is to be decided on the same principles[98] as in other cases in which one person owes a duty of care to another.[99] Knowledge by the plaintiff is not to be treated without more as absolving the occupier from liability unless in all the circumstances it was enough to enable the visitor to be reasonably safe.[1]

(2) The Act recognises the common law principle that a danger may cease to be a danger to those who know of it. But in each case it is to be a question of fact whether the visitor's knowledge of the danger relieves the occupier from liability, for section 2(4) provides that in determining whether the occupier of premises has discharged the common duty of care to a visitor, regard is to be had to all the circumstances, so that (for example), where damage is caused to a visitor by a danger[2] of which he has been warned by the occupier, the warning is not to be treated without more as absolving the occupier[3] unless in all the circumstances[4] it was enough[5] to enable the visitor to be reasonably safe.[6]

---

[94] See Unfair Contract Terms Act 1977, ss.1 and 2, as amended by the Occupiers' Liability Act 1984, s.2.

[95] *Roles* v. *Nathan* [1963] 1 W.L.R. 1117.

[96] *McGinlay* v. *British Railways Board* [1983] 1 W.L.R. 1427, 1434.

[97] *Simms* v. *Leigh Rugby Football Club Ltd.* [1969] 2 All E.R. 923.

[98] For these principles, see below, Chapter 22.

[99] See *White* v. *Blackmore* [1972] 2 Q.B. 651.

[1] *Bunker* v. *Charles Brand & Son Ltd.* [1969] 2 Q.B. 480, 489.

[2] Does this mean the peril itself or the facts of events which have created that peril?

[3] What is the effect of a warning given by a stranger?

[4] See the cogent example given in *Horton* v. *London Graving Dock Co. Ltd.* [1950] 1 K.B. 421, 428–429.

[5] As it was in *Roles* v. *Nathan* [1963] 1 W.L.R. 1117.

[6] Distinguish the warning which discharges the common duty of care (s.2(4)(a)) from the notice which excludes it (s.2(1)). A notice may be sufficient for the latter purpose even if, considered merely as a warning, it would have been inadequate, which is certainly an odd result: see *White* v. *Blackmore* [1972] 2 Q.B. 651.

(3) Knowledge of a danger may be evidence of contributory negligence on the part of a person injured by it.

§ 11.5. Contractual Entrants

At common law there was much dispute about the scope and nature of the term to be implied in a contract relating to entry upon premises in favour of the entrant. But now Parliament has considerably simplified the law: it has provided that visitors under contract shall be entitled to the common duty of care in the absence of any express provision in the contract governing the matter. Such a visitor may sue in contract or in tort at his option. Whichever is chosen, a successful plaintiff may have his damages reduced if contributory negligence is present: while the apportionment provisions of the Law Reform (Contributory Negligence) Act 1945 do not apply to situations where liability is purely contractual they *do* apply in cases where the defendant's liability in contract is the same as his liability in tort.[7]

Section 5(1) of the Act provides that when persons enter or use, or bring, or send goods[8] to, any premises[9] in exercise of a right conferred by contract with a person occupying or having control of the premises, the duty he owes them in respect of dangers due to the state of the premises or to things done or omitted to be done on them, in so far as the duty depends on a term to be implied in the contract by reason of its conferring that right, shall be the common duty of care. The section does not affect the obligations imposed on a person by or by virtue of any contract for the hire of, or for the carriage for reward of persons or goods in, any vehicle, vessel, aircraft or other means of transport, or by virtue of any contract of bailment.

Effect of contract on occupier's liability to third party. The Occupiers' Liability Act 1957, s.3(1), provides that where an occupier of premises is bound by contract to permit persons who are strangers to the contract[10] to enter or use the premises, the duty of care which he owes to them as his visitors cannot be restricted or excluded by that contract,[11] but (subject to any provision of the contract to the contrary) shall include the duty to perform his obligations under the contract,[12] whether undertaken for their protection or not, in so far as those obligations go beyond the obligations otherwise involved in that duty. So a visitor to a tenant will always be entitled at least to the benefits of the common duty of care; he will also be entitled to the benefit of any additional obli-

---

[7] See *Forsikringsaktieselskapet Vesta* v. *Butcher* [1989] A.C. 852 C.A. (this point was not challenged in the H.L.) and below § 22.11. *Cf. Sole* v. *Hallt Ltd.* [1973] 1 Q.B. 574.

[8] For damage to property, see § 11.4 above.

[9] A term which includes fixed and movable structures: s.5(2). See above, § 11.01

[10] Defined by s.3(3) to mean persons not for the time being entitled to the benefit of the contract as parties to it or as the successors by assignment or otherwise of a party to it.

[11] *Quaere* whether it could be excluded by a notice of disclaimer. Perhaps this is an area in which the occupier is not "free to" exclude his liability in the wording of s.2(1).

[12] Note that an occupier who has taken all reasonable care is not responsible for the defaults of an independent contractor unless the contract expressly provides otherwise: s.3(1).

gation undertaken by the lessor towards the lessee, unless the former has expressly excluded such an obligation. Section 3(4) also provides that the same principles shall apply when by the terms or conditions governing any tenancy (including a statutory tenancy) either the landlord or the tenant is bound, though not by contract, to permit persons to enter or use premises of which he is the occupier.

§ 11.6. VISITORS

(1) Common law: invitees and licensees

At common law entry by permission of the occupier was of two kinds. The permission amounted either to an invitation or to a mere licence. A person invited to enter was commonly referred to as an invitee,[13] or a licensee with an interest, while he who was merely licensed to enter was distinguished as a licensee, or bare licensee. The leading case was *Indermaur* v. *Dames*,[14] in which the occupier of a factory was held liable to the plaintiff, who was the employee of a gasfitter who had contracted to do certain work for the defendant, and who, while testing certain gas-fittings on the defendant's premises, fell through an unfenced opening in one of the upper floors. Willes J.[15] said:

> "The class to which the customer belongs includes persons who go not as mere volunteers, or licensees, or guests, or servants, or persons whose employment is such that danger may be considered as bargained for, but who go upon business which concerns the occupier and upon his invitation, express or implied."

The judgment of Willes J. in this case was discussed in scores of cases and the law became subtle and confused in many respects before the Occupiers' Liability Act 1957. Now, however, the Act specifically provides, in section 1(1), that the rules which it enacts shall have effect "in place of the rules of the common law," and in section 1(3) that those rules shall apply equally to both invitees and licensees: who in effect merge to become "visitors". It follows that the common law position is now only of historical interest.[16] It is enough to say that the leading distinction between an invitor and licensor was that the former was liable not only for dangers of which he knew but also for those which he ought to have known.

---

[13] "To use a non-English word made common, if not invented, by our judges": *Haseldine* v. *Daw (C.A.) & Son Ltd.* [1941] 2 K.B. 343, 350, *per* Scott L.J. But, as Lord Eldon once said, it is "an expression which, though it should never have come into this court, cannot now be thrown out of it.": *Davies* v. *Marlborough (Duke of)* [1814–23] All E.R.Rep. 13, 17.

[14] (1866) L.R. 1 C.P. 274; 2 C.P. 311. The case was decided on February 26, 1866, and the judgment appeared in the part of the *Law Reports* published on April 1—"a speed of reporting which would these days fill us with amazement": *Wanless* v. *Piening* (1967) 68 S.R.(N.S.W.) 249, 256, *per* Jacobs J.A.

[15] "One of the greatest jurists of this or any other time": *Bowen* v. *Hall* (1881) 6 Q.B.D. 333, 342, *per* Lord Coleridge C.J.

[16] The distinction between "licensees" and *trespassers*, however, remains important since it delineates the still separate category of "trespasser": see below § 11.9.

(2) Statutory duty

The duty which an occupier now owes to a visitor is, under the Occupiers' Liability Act 1984, s.2(2), the common duty of care—*i.e.* a duty to take such care as in all the circumstances of the case is reasonable to see that the visitor will be reasonably safe in using the premises for the purposes for which he is invited or permitted to be there. The Occupiers' Liability Act, s.2(3), by way of affirming the common law, also provides that the circumstances relevant to an assessment of the common duty of care owed in any particular case include the degree of care, and of want of care, which would ordinarily be looked for in such a visitor, so that (for example) in proper cases an occupier (1) must be prepared for children to be less careful than adults, and (2) may expect that a person, in the exercise of his calling, will appreciate and guard against any special risks ordinarily incident to it, so far as the occupier leaves him free to do so. "For example, if a window-cleaner (not being an employee of the occupier) sustains injury through the insecurity of some part of the exterior of the premises which he uses as a foothold or handhold for the purpose of cleaning the outside of the windows, the occupier merely as such should not be liable. *Aliter*, if the widow-cleaner is injured through some defect in the staircase when going upstairs in the ordinary way to reach the windows on an upper floor."[17] An occupier is entitled to assume that a chimney-sweep will guard against dangers from or in the flues which he is employed to sweep.[18] But in an important decision the House of Lords affirmed that fire-fighters injured in the course of their duties can sue those whose negligence was responsible for starting the fire.[19]

A visitor is entitled to assume that the premises are in a fit state for his reception: he need not adopt the wary attitude which a prudent licensee at common law needed to assume in self-protection—unless, indeed, the nature of the premises would warn a prudent person to do so.[20] So as it is usual to descend a ladder feet first the opportunities for seeing a defective rung are almost nil.[21] On the other hand, the House of Lords has held that one using unlit back stairs in a public-house must proceed with great caution.[22] The courts are readier today than in the past to find that the plaintiff was not taking reasonable care for his own safety since they now have the power to apportion the loss in cases of contributory negligence. If the visitor is aware of the danger he may be

---

[17] Third Report of the Law Reform Committee, para. 77. See *Bates v. Parker* [1953] 2 Q.B. 231. If the window-cleaner were the employee of a contractor he might have an action against his employer: see below, Chapter 21.

[18] *Roles v. Nathan* [1963] 1 W.L.R. 117. This is one of the few reported cases on the Act which raises a point of law.

[19] *Ogwo v. Taylor* [1988] A.C. 431 (This case was in fact decided on common law principles, but the result would undoubtedly be the same under the Act.) Successful claims were made by firefighters involved in the disaster at Kings Cross underground station.

[20] *Reaney v. Thomas, Lydon & Sons Ltd.* [1957] Ir.Jur.Rep. 1, 3.

[21] *O'Krane v. Alcyon Shipping Co. Ltd.* (1960) 24 D.L.R. (2d) 119, 123.

[22] *Wheat v. Lacon & Co. Ltd.* [1966] A.C. 552. See the criticism of this decision in [1966] A.S.C.L. 251. There is much to be said for the argument that "The greatest danger to which a publican can submit his customers is that of darkness. Any and every danger awaits the unwary in darkness": *Ryan v. Cullen* [1957] Ir.Jur.Re. 65, 66.

defeated for other reasons,[23] but the knowledge is no more than evidence of contributory negligence.

Effect of knowledge

The duty owed at common law to invitees under *Indemaur v. Dames* was really founded, not on the existence of the danger but on the failure of the occupier to prevent damage from it. In some cases such damage might have been prevented by giving notice of the danger to the invitee; in other cases the notice or knowledge might not have enabled the invitee to avoid the danger if he was effectively to accomplish the purpose for which he had entered the premises. In the latter case the better view[24] was that the invitor's duty was not discharged by the mere fact that the invitee knew as much (or more) about the danger as the invitor did. It was a question of fact whether in all the circumstances he had taken reasonable care for the safety of the entrant.[25] So the Occupiers' Liability Act, s.2(4), now provides, as we have seen,[26] that where damage is caused to a visitor by a danger of which he has been warned by the occupier, the warning is not to be treated without more as absolving the occupier from liability, unless in all the circumstances it was enough to enable the visitor to be reasonably safe.

Liability for third parties[27]

The occupier's duty most commonly has reference to the structural condition of the premises, but it may also be extended to include the use which he (or whoever has control so far as is material) permits a third party to make of the premises.[28] The occupier has the power of immediate supervision and control and the power of permitting or prohibiting the entry of other persons and he is under a duty to take reasonable care to prevent damage, at least from unusual danger, arising from such acts of third parties as could reasonably be foreseen.[29] So the occupier of a theatre has been held liable at common law for a dangerous show put on by an independent contractor,[30] and the occupiers of a vehicle, club or restaurant for assaults committed by intoxicated passengers[31] or guests.[32] There is no reason to suppose that these cases would be decided any differently under the Act. But the occupier of a camp-site was not liable when one visitor injured another in the

---

[23] *e.g.* because of *volenti non fit injuria*, or because the invitor's duty is discharged.
[24] The heavily criticised decision of the House of Lords to the contrary in *Horton's* case [1951] A.C. 737 was reversed by the Act: see the Report of the Law Reform Committee Cmd. 9305, ss.77–78.
[25] *O'Donoghue v. Green* [1967] I.R. 40.
[26] Above, § 11.4.
[27] North, *Occupiers' Liability*, pp. 82–84.
[28] *Glasgow Corporation v. Muir* [1943] A.C. 448, 463.
[29] *Simons v. Winslade* [1938] 3 All E.R. 774 (vomit in yard of public-house); *Hobson v. Bartrams Ltd.* [1950] 1 All E.R. 412 (sailors leaving hatch-covers off).
[30] *Cox v. Coulson* [1916] 2 K.B. 177.
[31] *Cf. Adderley v. Great Northern Ry.* [1905] 2 I.R. 378 (assault by drunken fellow-passenger).
[32] *Jordan House Ltd. v. Mennon* (1974) 38 D.L.R. (3d) 105.

course of giving a driving lesson.[33] Nor was the occupier of a public-house liable when an unknown third party removed an electric bulb over a dark staircase, although experience shows that this kind of behaviour is not uncommon.[34]

Independent contractors[35]

In *Thomson v. Cremin* in 1941[36] it was said in the House of Lords by Lord Wright that at common law an invitor's duty to his invitee was personal in the sense that it could not be discharged merely by entrusting its performance to an independent contractor, however competent he appeared to be and however technical the nature of the work which he was employed to do. This was generally thought to interpret the occupier's duty to take reasonable care of his invitee's safety in too severe a sense and the courts interpreted *Thomson v. Cremin* restrictively.[37] Now in accordance with the recommendation of the recommendation of the Law Reform Committee[38] the Occupiers' Liability Act, s.2(4)(*b*), provides that where damage is caused to a visitor by a danger due to the faulty execution of any work of construction, maintenance or repair[39] by an independent contractor employed by the occupier, the occupier is not to be treated without more as answerable for the danger if in all the circumstances he had acted reasonably by entrusting the work to him and had taken such steps (if any) as he reasonably ought in order to satisfy himself that the contractor was competent and that the work had been properly done. So sometimes the law requires an occupier to exercise reasonable supervision over the work done by his independent contractors, as when he constructs a substantial building or a ship. Then he should call in a properly qualified professional person to supervise the contractor. But in other cases, as when a domestic building is re-wired, the occupier is entitled to trust the contractor: otherwise there would be "an almost endless retrogression."[40] The contractor may himself be liable to the plaintiff, either if he is regarded as himself an occupier,[41] or under the general principles of negligence.[42] The occupier will not usually owe a duty under the Act to the independent contractor's own servants for their employer's failure to provide them with a safe system of work.[43]

---

[33] *Crickmar* v. *Cleaver, The Times*, October 8, 1964.

[34] *Wheat* v. *Lacon & Co. Ltd.* [1966] A.C. 552.

[35] See also below, Chapter 21.

[36] [1953] 2 All E.R. 1185; [1956] 1 W.L.R. 103n; *sub nom. Cremin* v. *Thomson* (1941) 71 L.1.L.R. 1.

[37] *Davie* v. *New Merton Board Mills Ltd.* [1959] A.C. 604, 644.

[38] Cmd. 9305, p. 34.

[39] This phrase covers demolition (*Ferguson* v. *Welsh* [1987] 1 W.L.R. 1553), but not careless stowage by stevedores: (*Gaffney* v. *Aviation and Shipping Co. Ltd.* [1966] 1 Lloyd's Rep. 249). It would be paradoxical if *Thomson* v. *Cremin* itself (a stowage case) had not been affected by the Act.

[40] *A.M.F. International Ltd* v. *Magnet Bowling Ltd.* [1968] 1 W.L.R. 1028, 1045.

[41] See above, § 11.1.

[42] *Ferguson* v. *Welsh* [1987] 1 W.L.R. 1553.

[43] *Ferguson* v. *Welsh* [1987] 1 W.L.R. 1553.

§ 11.7. CHILDREN

Children naturally less careful than adults

The Occupiers' Liability Act, section 2(3), provides that in assessing the common duty of care an occupier must be prepared for children to be less careful than adults. This probably does no more than re-enact the common law.[44] So a small child was able to claim when he fell through a gap in some railings which would not have been dangerous to an adult.[45] Many dangers which would be open and obvious to the adult may be concealed and secret traps for the child.[46] "In the case of an infant, there are moral as well as physical traps. There may accordingly be a duty towards infants not merely not to dig pitfalls for them, but not to lead them into temptation."[47] Although an occupier is not bound to make his premises as safe as a nursery, most of the articles on which children come to grief are not such as are commonly found in nurseries, and this is to be borne in mind in considering whether they amount to a trap.[48] "While it is very plain that temptation is not invitation, it may be held that knowingly to establish and expose, unfenced, to children of an age when they follow a bait as mechanically as a fish, something that is certain to attract them, has the legal effect of an invitation to them although not to an adult."[49] It is a question of law whether a given object can be a trap in the double sense of being fascinating and fatal[50]: the mere fact that a child has been lured or tempted into disaster is not enough, for a child can hurt itself on anything. No exhaustive catalogue of "allurements" has been established. "Turntables, escalators and paddling pools have been held to 'allure.' Rivers, ponds and piles of paving stones have been held 'insufficiently seductive.'"[51] The tendency appears to be against extending the category. So chutes in recreation grounds[52] and low-loaders[53] have been held to be unalluring. So for obvious dangers, such as unguarded fire[54] or water

---

[44] *Martin* v. *Middlesbrough Corporation* (1965) 63 L.G.R. 385, 386.

[45] *Moloney* v. *Lambeth B.C.* (1966) 64 L.G.R. 440.

[46] *Williams* v. *Cardiff Corpn.* [1950] 1 K.B. 514 (a grassy slope with tins and broken glass at the bottom is a trap to a child of 4½ years).

[47] *Latham* v. *Johnson* [1913] K.B. 398, 415, *per* Hamilton L.J.

[48] It is better not to use "allurement" to signify the circumstances under which a child enters premises: it remains a trespasser, however natural it may have been for it to enter. But once it has entered with permission it may find on the premises some attractive object which tempts it to meddle when it ought to abstain. This is an "allurement": a "trap" is something defective in the state of the premises themselves: see *Latham* v. *Johnson (R.) & Nephew Ltd.* [1913] 1 K.B. 398, 415–416; *Addie (R.) & Sons (Collieries)* v. *Dumbreck* [1929] A.C. 358, 376; *Williams* v. *Cardiff Corporation* [1950] 1 K.B. 514; *Edwards* v. *Railway Executive* [1952] A.C. 747, *Commissioner for Railways* v. *Cardy* (1961) 104 C.L.R. 274, 321.

[49] *Per* Holmes J. in *United Zinc and Chemical Co.* v. *Britt* (1922) 258 U.S. 268, 275, quoted by Scrutton L.J. in [1934] 2 K.B. 101, 110.

[50] *Latham* v. *Johnson (R.) and Nephew Ltd.* [1913] 1 K.B. 398, 411.

[51] *Sutton* v. *Bootle Corporation* [1947] K.B. 359, 368, *per* Asquith L.J.

[52] *Dyer* v. *Ilfracombe U.D.C.* [1956] W.L.R. 218.

[53] *O'Leary* v. *Wood* [1964] I.R. 269.

[54] *Bohane* v. *Driscoll* [1929] I.R. 428, 436.

(natural or artificial), an occupier will not be liable[55] "If a landowner permits children to pick sticks or flowers in his woods, he is not bound to provide keepers to protect them against the 'allurements' of wasps' nests or poisonous toad-stools."[56]

Very young children

The statement that an occupier is not liable for obvious dangers must be read subject to some qualification if the infant visitor is so young that it cannot really take care of itself at all. There is nothing upon which a toddler cannot hurt itself: the danger may be obvious to its eyes but concealed from its understanding. In *Phipps* v. *Rochester Corporation*[57] Devlin J. was able to formulate a "duty so as to compromise between the robustness that would make children take the world as they found it and the tenderness which would give them nurseries wherever they go."[58] Devlin J. held that although an occupier who tacitly permits the public to use his land wihout discriminating between its members must assume that the public will include little children, as a general rule he will have discharged his duty towards them if the dangers which they encounter are only those which are obvious to a guardian or of which he has given a warning comprehensible by a guardian.[59]

§ 11.8. PERSONS ENTERING AS OF RIGHT[60]

Persons entering as of right but not in pursuance of any contract between the parties are not a separate category: at common law they were either invitees or licensees, and so classified as lawful visitors since 1957. But it may be convenient, for the purpose of assessing the common duty of care, to distinguish between at least two distinct classes of such persons: (1) officials or others who in the exercise of a legal power or duty enter premises; (2) members of the public, who, as such, exercise their rights of using land or premises dedicated to public use such as highways, recreation grounds, lavatories, libraries, museums, and so forth.

It is possible that wives constitute a third class. A wife is on the matrimonial premises as of right, by virtue of her status,[61] but the

---

[55] *Simkiss* v. *Rhondda B.C.* (1983) 81 L.G.R. 460.

[56] *Bohane* v. *Driscoll* [1929] I.R. 428, 436, *per* FitzGibbon J.

[57] [1955] 1 Q.B. 450, approved by the Court of Appeal in *Simkiss* v. *Rhondda B.C.* (1983) 81 L.G.R. 460.

[58] [1955] 1 Q.B. 450, 459.

[59] [1955] 1 Q.B 450, 472. This general rule would not apply to a place where, to the knowledge of the licensor, little children are permitted by their parents to go unaccompanied in the reasonable belief that they will be safe, *e.g.* a recognised playground. An alternative approach was rejected by Devlin J., *viz* that a licence to a young child is conditional on its being accompanied by a competent guardian. This approach was adopted in some cases (*e.g. Bates* v. *Stone Parish Council* [1954] 1 W.L.R. 1249), but Devlin J.'s reasons for rejecting it seem conclusive.

[60] See Paton, "The Liability of an Occupier to Those Who Enter as of Right," (1941) 19 Can. Bar Rev. 1; Prosser, "Business Visitors and Invitees," *Topics* Chap. 5; Wallis-Jones, "Liability of Public Authorities as Occupiers of Dangerous Premises," (1949) 65 L.Q.R. 367; Waters, 'Public Rights of Entry" [1958] C.L.P. 132.

[61] *National Provincial Bank* v. *Ainsworth* [1965] A.C. 1175.

possibility of a wife suing her husband for breach of the common duty care has not been explored in England.[62]

(1) Persons entering in exercise of a power or duty

Modern statutes have vastly increased the numbers of those authorised to enter premises (whether public or private) for some official purpose: thus, to take only a couple of examples, there are powers of entry and inspection under the Factories Act 1961, and the Atomic Energy and Radioactive Substances Acts 1946 to 1959.[63] The position of such persons at common law was not entirely clear, but the balance of opinion was in favour of treating them as invitees and not as licensees,[64] even though their right to enter by no means depended on any invitation issued by the occupier.[65] But now section 2(6) of the Occupiers' Liability Act provides that persons who enter premises for any purpose in the exercise of a right conferred by law[66] are to be treated as permitted by the occupier to be there for that purpose, whether they in fact have his permission or not. They will, therefore, be entitled to the benefits of the common duty of care which the occupier now owes to all lawful visitors—namely, to take reasonable care to see that the premises are reasonably safe for the purpose in hand.[67]

(2) Persons entering on public premises

Those who make use of premises such as public libraries, churches[68] and recreation grounds appear to be in a different category, for the occupier in such a case is normally a public authority empowered but not obliged by statute to devote its premises to the purpose in question for the general benefit of society, whose members in turn are entitled but not in general specifically empowered or obliged to use the premises. At common law the balance of authority was in favour of treating such persons as licensees,[69] although there were weighty arguments in favour of regarding them as invitees.[70] The terms of section 2(6) of the Occupiers' Liability Act, which have been set out in the previous paragraph, appear to place persons entering on public premises into the

---

[62] See below; Chap. 15.

[63] See Stone, *Entry, Search and Seizure* (2nd ed., 1989). 5s, col.

[64] This was the opinion of the Law Reform Committee: 3rd Report, ss.37–38.

[65] A person who exceeds his statutory or common law power of entry is a trespasser and may be dealt with accordingly: *Darling* v. *Att.-Gen.* [1950] 2 All E.R. 793; *Stroud* v. *Bradbury* [1952] 2 All E.R. 76.

[66] With the exception of those entering by virtue of an access agreement or order under the National Parks and Access to the Countryside Act 1949, who were not to be treated as trespassers (s.60(1)). Also excluded from the category of visitors were users of a private right of way: *Holden* v. *White* [1982] Q.B. 679, because the right is conferred by dedication and not by law. But both these categories are now protected by the Occupiers' Liability Act 1984, s.1.

[67] See above, § 11.4.

[68] *Kirwan* v. *Representative Church Body* [1959] I.R. 215.

[69] *Pearson* v. *Lambeth B.C.* [1950] 2 K.B. 353, 367.

[70] *Plank* v. *Stirling Magistrates*, 1956 S.C. 92.

category of licensees. As such they are owed the common duty of care, the nature of which has already been explained.[71]

Passengers on a highway

Passengers on a highway across land in private ownership stand in a class apart. Apart from statutory modifications of the common law, a highway is merely a public right of way over land which remains in the occupation of the owner of that land. Such an occupier is under no responsibility under the Act towards users of the highway for its safety and is not liable for dangers thereon whether they exist at the time of dedication or come into existence later.[72] The occupier is liable, of course, for acts of positive misfeasance whereby he obstructs the highway or renders it dangerous, and he is also apparently liable for maintaining his adjoining premises in such a dangerous condition as to constitute a nuisance to the highway.[73]

§ 11.9. PERSONS OTHER THAN VISITORS

It will be apparent that by no means all entrants upon dangerous premises fall within the category of "visitors" to whom the common duty of care is owed under the Occupiers' Liability Act 1957. The most important category of entrants not dealt with in that Act is that of trespassers. The judge-made law on this point was left untouched, probably because Parliament in 1957 could not make up its mind what to do, and not because Parliament impliedly approved of that law. The matter was, however, subsequently referred to the Law Commission, whose 1975 report[74] helped to prepare the way for the Occupiers' Liability Act 1984 which reforms the law on liability to trespassers and complements the Act of 1957. The new Act is not confined to trespassers, however, but is of wider application. Indeed the word "trespasser" appears nowhere in the Act, which refers instead to "persons other than . . . visitors."[75] The significance of this wider formulation is that it also includes users of private rights of way,[76] and persons who enter pursuant to an access agreement or order made under the National Parks and Access to the Countryside Act 1949.[77] Nevertheless trespassers constitute the main category with which the Act is intended to deal.

Who are trespassers

The word "trespasser" has an ugly sound, but it covers the wicked and the innocent. The burglar and the arrogant squatter are trespassers,

---

[71] See above, § 11.4.

[72] *Greenhalgh* v. *British Railways Board* [1969] 2 Q.B. 286, 294.

[73] *Wringe* v. *Cohen* (1940) 1 K.B. 229, 241.

[74] Law Com. No. 75: Cmnd. 6428.

[75] s.1(1)(a).

[76] Thus reversing *Holden* v. *White* [1982] Q.B. 679. But users of public rights of way not maintainable at public expense are not protected: *Greenhalgh* v. *British Railways Board* [1969] 2 Q.B. 286 and s.1(7) of the Act.

[77] See s.60(1) of the Act of 1949 and paras. 37–41 of the Law Commission's Report, Cmnd. 6428.

but so are all sorts of comparatively innocent people such as walkers in the countryside who stroll unhindered across an open field. It has been suggested that much of the difficulty in this area has arisen from "the simplistic stereotype" of the concept of the trespasser.[78] Indeed it is sometimes difficult to distinguish between a trespasser and a person entering lawfully by the tacit permission of the occupier. Thus the occupier tacitly invites and permits any member of the public coming on lawful business to enter his garden gate and come to the door.[79] If his dog bites a person so entering, liability may depend on whether that person falls within the class of persons so tacitly invited; for otherwise he will be a mere trespasser. Who, then, are thus entitled to enter, and to complain of injuries received? What shall be said, for example, of hawkers, beggars, tract distributors, canvassers,[80] or persons in a shop who are not genuine purchasers but "hostile or at any rate competitive observers"?[81] There is even some authority for the proposition that an entrant may be a trespasser if the ostensible purpose for his being on the premises is not his real purpose, which was unlawful.[82] The acceptable conclusion would seem to be that no person is to be accounted a trespasser who enters in order to hold any manner of communication with the occupier or any other person on the premises, unless he knows or ought to know that his entry is prohibited.[83] So police officers, like any member of the public, have an implied licence to open the garden gate and walk up to the front door of a private house. But an implied licence to approach the front door does not give a right to enter the house itself.[84] Still, it should be remembered that the acquiescence of the occupier in habitual trespasses may be evidence of tacit leave and licence,[85] so as to transform the trespasser into a licensee.[86]

Implied licences

A licence may be granted either expressly or impliedly, but one who claims that he is an implied licensee must show that the occupier has permitted his presence and not merely tolerated it. This is a question which most often arises in relation to children,[87] but the principles apply also to adult visitors. An occupier who resigns himself to the occasional and perhaps inevitable presence of trespassers on his property does not thereby take upon himself the obligations of a licensor.[88] "Permission must be proved, not tolerance, though tolerance in some circumstances may be so pronounced as to lead to a conclusion that it

---

[78] *McNamara* v. *E.S.B.* [1975] I.R. 1, 22.

[79] *Robson* v. *Hallett* [1967] 2 Q.B. 393 (police officers).

[80] See *Dunster* v. *Abbott* [1954] 1 W.L.R. 58.

[81] *Chaytor* v. *London, etc., Fashion Ltd.* (1961) 30 D.L.R. (2d) 527, 534.

[82] *Purtill* v. *Athlone U.D.C.* [1968] I.R. 205, 210–211.

[83] *Christian* v. *Johannesson* [1956] N.Z.L.R. 664, 666. See also *R.* v. *Jones* [1976] 1 W.L.R. 672.

[84] *Robson* v. *Hallett* [1967] 2 Q.B. 393.

[85] See below.

[86] *Rich* v. *Commissioner for Railways (N.S.W.)* (1959) 101 C.L.R. 135; 143; *Commissioner for Railways* v. *Quinlan* [1964] A.C. 1054; 1082.

[87] See below.

[88] *Phipps* v. *Rochester Corporation* [1955] 1 Q.B. 450, 455; *Koehler* v. *Pentecostal Assemblies* (1957) 7 D.L.R. (2d) 616, 621.

was really tantamount to permission," *e.g.* "a mere putting up of a notice 'No Trespassers Allowed' or 'Strictly Private,' followed, when people often come, by no further steps, would, I think, leave it open for a judge or jury to hold implied permission."[89] But it is not sufficient to make the plaintiff a licensee merely to prove that the occupier has not taken such measures as effectually to stop trespass.[90] There is no duty on a proprietor to fence his land against the world under sanction that, if he does not, those who come over it become licensees.[91] An unauthorised invitation by an employee of the occupier, acting outside the scope of his authority, to enter upon the premises will not prevent the person who accepts the invitation from being a trespasser.[92] For this reason it is submitted that a plaintiff who is on premises in breach of some by-law imposing penalties can never plead that he is there by leave and licence[93]: it is against the policy of the law to permit anyone to license another to commit a crime.[94] For a man (or a child) is none the less a trespasser because he does not realise that he is a trespasser.[95]

Infant licensees

When an occupier habitually and knowingly acquiesces in the trespasses of children, these children cease to be trespassers and become licensees, and the occupier owes to them a certain duty of care and protection accordingly.[96] In *Cooke* v. *Midland Great Western Railway of Ireland*[97] the plaintiff was a child between four and five years of age who was injured while playing with his companions on a turntable on the defendant company's railway premises. The turntable was kept unlocked and was close to a public road. The company's employees knew that children were in the habit of entering on the premises from the road for the purpose of playing with the turntable but no precautions were taken by the company, either to exclude the children or to

---

[89] *Addie & Sons* v. *Dumbreck* [1929] A.C. 358, 372 *per* Lord Dunedin. But "an open gate or an unfenced field does not amount to an invitation or licence *urbi et orbi* to enter upon private property": *Kenny* v. *Electricity Supply Board* [1932] I.R. 73, 84, *per* FitzGibbon J.

[90] See *Edwards* v. *Railway Executive* [1952] A.C. 737, 746, *per* Lord Goddard C.J.: "But repeated trespess of itself confers no licence; the owner of a park in the neighbourhood of a town knows probably only too well that it will be raided by young and old to gather flowers, nuts or mushrooms whenever they get an opportunity. But because he does not cover his park wall with a *chevaux de frise* or post a number of keepers to chase away intruders how is it to be said that he has licensed what he cannot prevent?"

[91] *British Railways Board* v. *Herrington* [1972] A.C. 877, 914.

[92] *Hillen* v. *I.C.I. (Alkali)* [1936] A.C. 65; *Conway* v. *Wimpey Ltd.* [1951] 2 K.B. 266.

[93] *Rich* v. *Commissioner for Railways (N.S.W.)* (1959) 101 C.L.R. 135, 143.

[94] See below, Chap. 22.

[95] *Conway* v. *Wimpey Ltd.* [1951] 2 K.B. 266, 273. But involuntary trespassers sometimes have a right of action where voluntary trespassers have not (*Dean* v. *Clayton* (1817) 7 Taunt. 489, 519; *Braithwaite* v. *South Durham Steel Co. Ltd.* [1958] 1 W.L.R. 986) and an occupier may be liable in nuisance to those who accidentally deviate from a highway when he would not be liable to one who did so intentionally: *Barnes* v. *Ward* (1850) 9 C.B. 392.

[96] *Adams* v. *Naylor* [1944] K.B. 750, 761.

[97] [1909] A.C. 229.

lock the turntable,[98] so as to prevent it from being an instrument of mischief. It was held by the House of Lords that there was evidence for a jury of negligence on the part of the railway company—not on the ground that there is any duty of care towards trespassing children, but on the ground that the habitual acquiescence of the company was sufficient evidence to entitle the jury to find that the plaintiff was not a trespasser, but was on the railway premises with the leave and licence of the company.[99] But in these cases the onus is on the plaintiff to establish his licence, and "to find a licence there must be evidence either of express permission or that the landowner has so conducted himself that he cannot be heard to say that he did not give it."[1] Real acquiescence or permission must be shown: tolerance is not acquiescence though it may be evidence of it.[2] The most recent *dicta* in the House of Lords are hostile to the concept of an imputed or implied or fictitious licence.[3] It may indeed be predicted that the courts will now be less ready to accept the concept since trespassers themselves are now treated by the law much less harshly than formerly.[4] In any event it is clear that a licence ought not to be inferred merely because every possible step to keep out intruders has not been taken: a landowner is under no obligation at common law[5] to fence his property against trespassers or to put up warning notices, however attractive his premises may be to trespassers.[6] Our law does not recognise the existence of a class of persons who, though not licensees, must be effectively prevented from becoming trespassers.[7]

---

[98] Which was still in existence in 1953, when one of the present editors saw at least half a dozen children playing on it.

[99] See the explanation of *Cooke's* case in *Corporation of Glasgow* v. *Taylor* [1922] 1 A.C. 44; *Liddle* v. *Yorkshire C.C.* [1934] 2 K.B. 101; *Edwards* v. *Railway Executive* [1952] A.C. 737. Beven attacked the decision in *Cooke's* case with great vigour: his description of the infant plaintiff as one of "a rabble of Irish ragamuffin raiders" moved Mr. Bryne, the editor of the 4th edition of his work to protest that "the child—whom the editor chanced to see while the case was in the Irish courts—was the quite presentable little son of a respectable chemist" (*Negligence*, vol. i, p. 216). Some criticism of *Cooke's* case has ignored the fact that while the H.L. held there was sufficient evidence to go to the jury they did not indicate that they would have reached the same conclusion as the jury did. This point was made in *Smyth* v. *Keys* (1912) 46 I.L.T.R. 68, 69, the court emphasising that it would "not be guilty of the bad taste of criticising a decision of the House of Lords."

[1] *Edwards* v. *Railway Executive* [1952] A.C. 737, 747, *per* Lord Goddard C.J. If a statute makes it a criminal offence to trespass on premises it may be that such permission can never be lawfully given: *Reardon* v. *Att.-Gen.* [1954] N.Z.L.R. 978.

[2] See above.

[3] *British Railways Board* v. *Herrington* [1972] A.C. 877, 899, 934.

[4] See below.

[5] Even if there is a statutory duty to fence (as under the Railways Clauses Consolidation Act 1845, s.68) the duty is no more than to keep the premises shut off by a fence which is duly repaired when broken and obviously intended to keep intruders out: *Edwards* v. *Railways Executive* [1952] A.C. 737, 744.

[6] *British Railways Board* v. *Herrington* [1972] A.C. 877, 920.

[7] *Adams* v. *Naylor* [1944] K.B. 750, 765. This is particularly important if the plaintiff is a child: for "children, small boys especially, resemble burglars; if they want to get in they will, take what precautions you may": *Edwards'* case [1952] A.C. 737, 747, *per* Lord Goddard C.J.

Technical trespasses may be disregarded. If a child has a licence, express or implied, to enter upon the premises of the defendant, he does not necessarily become a trespasser merely because he moves to a place or onto an object outside the strict limits of the licence, especially if the object is known to be an allurement.[8]

The duty of common humanity

The common law relating to liability to trespassers was put on a new footing in 1972 by the decision of the House of Lords in *British Railways Board* v. *Herrington*.[9] Prior to that case the much criticised decision of the House 40 years before, in *Robert Addie & Sons (Collieries) Ltd.* v. *Dumbreck*[10] had laid it down that he who entered wrongfully entered at his own risk. Under *Addie* the occupier owed no duty to a trespasser other than that of not inflicting damage intentionally,[11] or recklessly[12] on one known to be present. In *Herrington* a six-year-old boy suffered injuries when a gap in a fence, which the defendant's employees had left unrepaired, enabled him to get on to an electrified railway track. The House of Lords affirmed a judgment in the boy's favour and refused to follow *Addie,* which it held to have been rendered obsolete and anomalous by changing social condiions. Nevertheless all the Law Lords considered that it was not appropriate simply to adopt a test of reasonable foreseeability,[13] even though such a test is applied in Scotland.[14] The trespasser had no right to be on the premises and so could not force a neighbour relationship on the occupier.[15] Liability would therefore still be the exception rather than the rule. A sentence of Lord Reid's[16] provided a clue to the new approach. The trespasser had to take the occupier, rather than the land, as he found him.

This implied a subjective test rather than the objective test which is so familiar in the tort of negligence. The new approach enabled weight to be given to such factors as the occupier's wealth and resources. Less would be expected of the impecunious suburban householder than of a large industrial concern or a public or local corporation. It was also important to consider whether the occupier had himself created the danger: if he had, more might be expected of him.[17] Other relevant factors included the gravity of the danger and the degree of likelihood of the trespasser's presence. His characteristics might also be relevant. The squatter who fell down a defective staircase could still find himself

---

[8] *Glasgow Corporation* v. *Taylor* [1922] 1 A.C. 44 (child of seven eating poisonous berry in botanic garden).

[9] [1972] A.C. 877.

[10] [1929] A.C. 358.

[11] See, *e.g. Bird* v. *Holbrook* (1820) 4 Bing. 628.

[12] *Excelsior Wire Rope Co.* v. *Callan* [1930] A.C. 404: a rare example of an unreserved judgment (delivered without hearing counsel for the respondent) by the House of Lords; for another example see the libel case of *Hulton* v. *Jones* [1910] A.C. 20 (above Chap. 8).

[13] [1972] A.C. 877, 898, 919.

[14] See the Occupiers' Liability (Scotland) Act 1960, s.2.

[15] [1972] A.C. 877, 899, 920.

[16] [1972] A.C. 877, 899.

[17] *Southern Portland Cement* v. *Cooper* [1974] A.C. 623, 644.

remediless, as distinct from a child with nowhere else to play.[18] The duty was one, in all the circumstances, "to take such steps as common sense or common humanity would dictate."[19] Although later decisions did provide some guidelines, this new formulation of the law was considered to be unsatisfactory as unduly vague and potentially uncertain in its application.[20] In consequence Parliament eventually legislated in an attempt to remove these defects.

§ 11.10. The Occupiers' Liability Act 1984[21]

In order to delineate its sphere of operation the new Act borrows the language and concepts of the Occupiers' Liability Act 1957. Thus "occupier" and "visitor" have the same meaning as in that Act[22] and, similarly, the new duty is owed in respect of injuries suffered "due to the state of the premises or to things done or omitted to be done on them."[23]

The duty

If the occupier has reasonable grounds to believe that a danger exists on his premises,[24] and the consequent risk is one against which in all the circumstances he may reasonably be expected to offer some protection,[25] then he will owe a duty to trespassers, and other uninvited entrants, whom he has reasonable grounds for supposing may be in the vicinity.[26] The duty is one to take such precautions as are reasonable in all the circumstances to see that they do not suffer injury.[27] The intention is clearly to replace the subjective test applied in *Herrington* with an objective one in which the resources or competence of the individual occupier will cease to be relevant. It would be wrong, however, to suppose that the precautions which the new duty will require of occupiers will necessarily be indistinguishable in any given case from those required by the common duty of care owed to lawful visitors. The Act's insistence upon the need to take all the circumstances into account in evaluating reasonableness means that the fact that the presence of trespassers is not always readily foreseeable will still be significant, as well as the circumstances and characteristics of different kinds of trespass. Thus although the nature of the duty is laid down in general terms, there can be no doubt that its content may differ radically in the case of a small child, for example, from that of a burglar. But in perhaps the

---

[18] *McNamara* v. *E.S.B.* [1975] I.R. 1, 24.

[19] [1972] A.C. 877, 909 (Lord Morris).

[20] See Law Com. No. 75: Cmnd. 6428.

[21] Jones (1984) 47 M.L.R. 713; Buckley [1984] Conv. 413. The Act is confined to England and Wales: s.4(3).

[22] See s.1(2) of the 1984 Act.

[23] See s.1(1)(a) of the 1984 Act.

[24] s.1(3)(*a*).

[25] s.1(3)(*c*).

[26] s.1(3)(*b*). See *White* v. *St. Albans City and District Council, The Times*, March 12, 1990, C.A. (recognition of the need to prevent trespass not to be taken as in itself constituting reasonable grounds for believing trespassers to be in the vicinity).

[27] s.1(4).

majority of cases, where the precautions which would be appropriate are obvious, and the presence of trespassers is not significantly less foreseeable than that of lawful visitors, there will in practice be no difference in content between the duty owed to lawful visitors under the 1957 Act and that owed to persons other than visitors under the Act of 1984. It should be noted, however, that only damages for death or personal injury can be awarded under the 1984 Act: unlike the position of visitors under the 1957 Act, damage to property is not recoverable.[28]

Discharge of duty

The Act provides that the duty it imposes may be discharged, in an appropriate case, by taking reasonable steps to warn of the danger or to discourage persons from incurring the risk.[29] Unlike the Occupiers' Liability Act 1957, however, it does not sanction the exclusion of liability by mere disclaimer, and it is submitted that this will not be permitted. But it does provide that the defence of assumption of risk will be available to the occupier if the circumstances so warrant.[30]

§ 11.11. OTHER JURISDICTIONS

Even where it has not been abrogated by statute, the harsh old rule which allowed trespassers to recover only in respect of intentional or reckless conduct, appears progressively to have been whittled away in common law jurisdictions elsewhere. For example the decision of the Privy Council in *Southern Portland Cement* v. *Cooper*,[31] an appeal from New South Wales, imposed a duty determined by considerations of humanity broadly in line with that propounded by the House of Lords in *British Railways Board* v. *Herrington*.[32] In *Veinot* v. *Kerr-Addison Ltd.*[33] the Supreme Court of Canada also adopted a similar approach. These developments have reduced the need for the process, once favoured as a means of circumventing the old law,[34] of seeking to identify other relationships existing between the parties in addition to that of occupier and trespasser.[35]

§ 11.12. LIABILITY OF NON-OCCUPIERS

It must not be supposed that the occupier of dangerous premises is the only person who can be responsible for dangers which there exist.

---

[28] s.1(8).

[29] s.1(5).

[30] s.1(6). *cf. Titchener* v. *British Railways Board* [1983] 1 W.L.R. 1427.

[31] [1974] A.C. 623. This case explained and distinguished the Privy Council's own earlier decision in *Commissioner for Railways* v. *Quinlan* [1964] A.C. 1054, which was widely interpreted as having lent support to the traditional narrow formulation of an occupier's duty to trespassers.

[32] [1972] A.C. 877.

[33] (1975) 51 D.L.R. 533.

[34] See *e.g. Commissioner for Railways* v. *Cardy* (1961) 104 C.L.R. 274, 297; *McCarthy* v. *Wellington City* [1966] N.Z.L.R. 481.

[35] But this technique can still prove useful in some cases: for an example see *Hackshaw* v. *Shaw* [1984] 56 A.L.R. 417.

Whoever actually creates a source of danger, even on premises not in his own occupation, is bound to use reasonable care by guiding, warning or otherwise to preserve from resulting harm persons who enter thereon. The status which the entrant enjoys *vis-a-vis* the occupier is not conclusive of any issue which may arise as between the entrant and some other party whose activities on the premises have created a source of danger, although it may well be relevant in an assessment of the standard of care appropriate to the circumstances.[36] Many cases may be found in which the fact that the injury has occurred on premises occupied by a third party has been treated as irrelevant. Thus in *Billings (A.C.) & Sons Ltd.* v. *Riden*[37] the House of Lords held that a contractor working on premises owes a duty to take reasonable care to prevent damage to persons whom he may reasonably expect to be affected by his work. The case is also a leading authority on the question how far the plaintiff's knowledge of the danger so created will bar his claim entirely or merely be a ground for reduction of his damages under the Law Reform (Contributory Negligence) Act 1945.[38] A non-occupier does not necessarily discharge this duty simply by warning the visitor: he may be under a duty to make the premises reasonably safe.[39] So an invitee may recover against another invitee,[40] or a licensee against another licensee[41] on the broad ground that the defendant has failed to take such care as was reasonable in the circumstances.

Similarly a trespasser may have a successful claim against a non-occupier.[42] In *Buckland* v. *Guildford Gas Light and Coke Co.*[43] an active schoolgirl of 13 years who climbed an attractive oak tree was electrocuted when she came into contact with the defendant's high-voltage electric wires, which were hidden in the foliage at the top. The defendants were held liable because they were in breach of their duty to take reasonable care for the safety of someone who might reasonably have been contemplated as likely to be affected by their want of care.[44] Normally a non-

---

[36] *Miller* v. *South of Scotland Electricity Board*, 1958, S.C. 20, 37.

[37] [1958] A.C. 240.

[38] See below, Chap. 22.

[39] *Johnson* v. *Rea Ltd.* [1962] 1 Q.B. 373.

[40] *Canter* v. *Gardner & Co. Ltd.* [1940] 1 All E.R. 325 (servant of the sub-contractor injured by another sub-contractor). So in *Cleghorn* v. *Oldham* [1927] 43 T.L.R. 465 the plaintiff was on a golf-links with her brother and the defendant ("as a chaperone" the report says) when she was struck by a club owing to the defendant's negligence. The plaintiff recovered on the broad ground of negligence. Similar decisions are *Keegan* v. *Owens* [1953] I.R. 237; *Whitehorn* v. *Port of London Authority* [1955] 1 Lloyd's Rep. 54. Note that an invitee may owe a duty of reasonable care to his invitor: *Lomas* v. *Jones & Son* [1944] K.B. 4.

[41] *Waring* v. *East Anglian Flying Services Ltd.* [1951] W.N. 55.

[42] This rule seems to have survived the Occupiers' Liability Act 1984.

[43] [1948] 2 All E.R. 1086.

[44] Although this doctrine (in so far as it affords protection to a trespasser) may perhaps be traced back to *Latham* v. *Johnson (R.) and Nephew Ltd.* [1913] 1 K.B. 398, the more recent cases are founded directly upon the neighbour principle of *Donoghue* v. *Stevenson*. They appear to represent the law, although critical dicta may be found in *Kenny* v. *Electricity Supply Board* [1932] I.R. 92; *Creed* v. *McGeoch & Sons Ltd.* [1955] 1 W.L.R. 1005, 1008; *Miller* v. *South of Scotland Electricity Board*, 1958 S.C. 20, 36, and (most importantly) in *British Railways Board* v. *Herrington* [1972] A.C. 877, 914, 929, 942.

occupier will be entitled to assume that the premises will be free from trespassers, but on the facts of this case the defendant ought to have foreseen their presence. The fact that the girl might have been a trespasser *vis-a-vis* the owner of the tree did not protect the defendant, for the plaintiff was able to point to some source of obligation other than the relation which the trespass itself created.

§ 11.13. LIABILITY OF LESSORS OR VENDORS AT COMMON LAW[45]

It is necessary to deal separately with the common law and with the Defective Premises Act 1972. In some situations the common law remains effective in its own right but, in any event, the Act cannot be understood without reference to its background.

(1) Liability of landlord to tenant and others

Who is a lessor

It is important to distinguish between an occupier and a lessor: the former owes many duties, the latter very few. A lessor is usually one who transfers to another the exclusive occupation of premises for a definite period. If that other does not obtain exclusive possession, he is only a licensee.[46] Hence the question has arisen whether an owner of premises can avoid his responsibilities by creating a lease of a few days, or even a few hours. There has naturally been a reluctance to permit him to do so, particularly if he is the owner of premises continually used for public purposes at a profit to himself. This has been the approach in two Irish cases, in which the premises were "let" for a dance[47] and a whist drive.[48] These cases have been followed in Australia, although "there are some not inconsiderable, differences between a whist drive and dance in Dublin and a meeting of tobacco growers in Texas, Queensland."[49]

Duty of lessor

Apart from any express or implied contract[50] to that effect, at common law a landlord owes no duty in his capacity as such, either towards his tenant or towards any other person who enters on the premises during the tenancy, to take care that the premises are safe either at the commencement of the tenancy or during its continuance.[51] The rule was so

---

[45] See North, *Occupiers' Liability*, Chap. 12; *Civil Liability of Vendors and Lessors for Defective Premises* (Law Com. No. 40, 1970).
[46] See above, § 5.9
[47] *Kelly* v. *Woolworth Ltd.* [1922] 2 I.R. 5.
[48] *Boylan* v. *Dublin Corporation* [1949] I.R. 60.
[49] *Voli* v. *Inglewood Shire Council* (1963) 110 C.L.R. 74, 92, *per* Windeyer J.
[50] See *Barrett* v. *Lounova* (1982) *Ltd.* [1989] 1 All E.R. 351 C.A.
[51] *MacDonald* v. *Goderich* [1949] 3 D.L.R. 788, 793; *Collins* v. *Torresan* [1956] 3 D.L.R. 740, 743; *Titus* v. *Duke* (1963) 6 W.I.R. 135, 137.

laid down in *Robbins* v. *Jones*.[52] Sir William Erle C.J., in a judgment prepared by Willes J., said: "A landlord who lets a house in a dangerous state is not liable to the tenant's customers or guests for accidents arising during the term; for, fraud apart, there is no law against letting a tumbledown house; and the tenant's remedy is upon his contract, if any." One exception to the general rule has been the decision that a covenant to keep the common parts of the premises in repair could be implied into a lease of a high-rise block of flats.[53] Another exception is the letting of furnished houses or flats. Such agreements contain an implied warranty that the premises and the furniture are at the commencement of the tenancy fit for immediate occupation or use. If they are not so fit, the tenant may determine the tenancy or sue for damages in respect of any injury suffered.[54] But the letting of an unfurnished flat probably[55] falls wihin the general rule and not the exception.[56]

(2) Liability of landlord to third parties

The landlord's exemption from liability for dangers existing on premises in the occupation of his tenant extended not merely to injuries suffered by the tenant himself but to those suffered by other persons entering on the premises during the tenancy.[57] At common law the lease transferred all obligations towards such persons from the landlord to the tenant. This was so even if the landlord had by contract with the tenant taken upon himself the duty of keeping the premises in repair. Such a contract was *res inter alios acta*, and conferred upon strangers no rights against the landlord which they would not have had without it.[58] This was clearly established in *Cavalier* v. *Pope*.[59] The landlord of a defective house contracted with the plaintiff's husband to repair it. Nothing was done and one day the plaintiff fell through the floor and was injured. A common jury awarded her £75 damages and her husband £25. The House of Lords set aside the award in favour of the plaintiff. "There was but one contract and that was made with the husband. The wife cannot sue upon it."[60] But this principle was much criticised,

---

[52] (1863) 15 C.B. (N.S.) 221, 240.
[53] *Liverpool C.C.* v. *Irwin* [1977] A.C. 399.
[54] *Collins* v. *Hopkins* [1923] 2 K.B. 617 (house recently occupied by person suffering from tuberculosis). This warranty does not extend to defects arising after the commencement of the tenancy: *Sarson* v. *Roberts* [1895] 2 Q.B. 395. Another exception is the implied warranties relating to houses of low rateable value established by s.6 of the Housing Act 1957, and s.32 of the Housing Act 1961 (now the Housing Act 1985). But the lessor must have knowledge of the defect: *O'Brien* v. *Robinson* [1973] A.C. 912. A lessor of defective premises may also be required to repair them by the local authority under the Housing Act 1985. On these statutory warranties, see Robinson, "Social Legislation and the Judges" (1976) 39 M.L.R. 43.
[55] See North (1965) 29 *The Conveyancer* 207, 219.
[56] *Cruse* v. *Mount* [1933] Ch. 278; *Davis* v. *Foots* [1940] 1 K.B. 116.
[57] *Bromley* v. *Mercer* [1922] 2 K.B. 126; *Travers* v. *Gloucester Corporation* [1947] K.B. 71.
[58] *MacDonald* v. *Goderich* [1949] 3 D.L.R. 788, 893; *Collins* v. *Torresan* [1956] 3 D.L.R. 740, 743.
[59] [1906] A.C. 428.
[60] *Per* Lord James of Hereford.

and the actual decision in *Cavalier* v. *Pope*, in so far as it related to situations in which the landlord was under an obligation to repair, was reversed by the Occupiers' Liability Act 1957, s.4(1). Now the Defective Premises Act 1972, s.4 has repealed section 4 of the 1957 Act and substituted provisions of even wider scope.[61] Even at common law the *Cavalier* v. *Pope* principle has been confined to "bare landlords": so a landlord who is his own builder or designer may owe a duty of reasonable care to the tenant.[62] It is now settled in England and Ireland that he immunity of a builder/vendor has disappeared.[63]

(3) Liability for landlord's own premises

In all these cases the plaintiff suffered damage while on the premises demised as a result of some defect in the condition of those premises. We have also already considered the position when the plaintiff suffers damage while on premises retained by the lessor in his own occupation (*e.g.* a common stairway).[64] Here there is a liability under the 1957 Act.[65] But what is the position when, as a result of the defective condition of the portion of the premises retained in the landlord's occupation, the tenant or one of the tenant's invitees or licensees is injured while on the portion of the premises demised? In *Cheater* v. *Cater*[66] the Court of Appeal held that a landlord who let a part of his land overhung by yew trees growing upon the land retained by him was not responsible to his tenant[67] for the loss of cattle which were poisoned by eating the overhanging branches. This was carried further in *Shirvell* v. *Hackwood Estate Ltd.*,[68] in which a branch fell from a beech tree, which the occupying owner of the land knew to be in a defective condition, upon the employee of a tenant to whom he had leased the adjoining land. It was said that even if the defendant was negligent there was no liability: but it is probable that those statements were only *obiter dicta*[69] In any case it seems clear that the principle laid down in these cases is confined to situations where the danger existed and was apparent at the date of the demise.[70]

But although it may be assumed that the lessee takes his land subject to the inconvenience and detriment of an overhanging projection, such as a branch, or roof, or cornice, is he really presumed to agree that he will accept the risk of the projection falling on his premises? There is

---

[61] See below, § 11.14.
[62] *Rimmer* v. *Liverpool City Council* [1984] Q.B. 1, 9.
[63] *Ward* v. *McMaster* [1985] I.R. 29, 39.
[64] See above, § 11.4.
[65] *Wheat* v. *Lacon & Co. Ltd.* [1966] 1 Q.B. 335, 366.
[66] [1918] 1 K.B. 247.
[67] If the parties in *Cheater* v. *Cater* had been adjoining owners the defendant would have been liable: *Crowhurst* v. *Amersham Burial Board* (1879) 4 Ex.D. 5.
[68] [1938] 2 K.B. 577. See Hamson in (1938) 2 M.L.R. 215.
[69] *Taylor* v. *Liverpool Corporation* [1939] 2 All E.R. 329, 339.
[70] In *Shirvell* v. *Hackwood Estates* the risk of the branches of the dying tree falling had not become substantially greater after the date of the lease: [1938] 2 K.B. 577, 595, 602.

very persuasive authority to the contrary. In *Cunard v. Antifyre Ltd.*[71] the plaintiffs were tenants in the defendants' block of flats. The defendants retained the possession and control of the roof, from which a piece of guttering fell through the glass roof of a kitchen and injured the plaintiff's wife. A Divisional Court held the defendants liable. Talbot J. said[72] "The plaintiffs' true cause of action (if they have one) is for negligence, for failure by an occupier of property to take reasonable care that his property does not get into such a state as to be dangerous to adjoining property or persons lawfully thereon."[73]

(4) Liability of vendors, builders and others

It was well established[74] that the immunity of a lessor extended to a vendor, and that this immunity had escaped the flood-tide of liability released by *Donoghue v. Stevenson*,[75] so that at common law the vendor of a completed house which turned out to be dangerous was under no liability to the purchaser in the absence of an express or implied warranty that the house was reasonably sound and fit for habitation.[76] But if the defendant is not *merely* the lessor or vendor of the premises in question, but also their builder or designer, it is now clear that ordinary negligence principles apply in place of the immunity.[77]

§ 11.14. LIABILITY OF LESSORS OR VENDORS UNDER STATUTE[78]

The Defective Premises Act 1972, which came into force on January 1, 1974, was passed as a result of recommendations made by the Law Commission.[79] The Act has four main effects. First, the creation of a statutory duty to build dwellings properly, which is to be owed to any person who acquires an interest in the dwelling. Secondly, restriction of the common law immunity. Thirdly, the imposition on a landlord of a wider statutory duty of care in virtue of his obligation or right to repair the premises demised. Fourthly, the exclusion or restriction of any of the dutes imposed by the Act is expressly prohibited.

---

[71] [1933] 1 K.B. 551.
[72] [1933] 1 K.B. 551, 557, 562. Of whom Sir Frank MacKinnon wrote: "On the bench he displayed every quality of the ideal judge. He had learning, dignity, industry, patience, and courtesy: his decisions were invariably right, and on most occasions were thought to be so by the Court of Appeal": *Dictionary of National Biography*, 1931–1940, p. 846. Sir George Talbot was directly descended from Littleton J. (1422–1481), Bromley L.C. (1530–1587), and Talbot L.C. (1685–1737).
[73] The fact that the defendant is in occupation distinguishes this from the line of cases based on *Cavalier v. Pope* [1906] A.C. 428.
[74] *Bottomley v. Bannister* [1932] 1 K.B. 458.
[75] [1932] A.C. 562.
[76] *Perry v. Sharon Development Co. Ltd.* [1937] 4 All E.R. 390. When, however, the contract is for the sale of a house *when completed*, there is an implied contract that the house shall be completed in such a way that it is fit for human habitation: *Lynch v. Thorne* [1956] 1 W.L.R. 303.
[77] *Rimmer v. Liverpool City Council* [1984] Q.B. 1.
[78] See Spencer, "The Defective Premises Act" [1974] C.L.J. 307; [1975] C.L.J. 48.
[79] *Civil Liability of Vendors and Lessors for Defective Premises* (Law Com. No. 40, 1970).

(1) Duty to build dwellings properly

Section 1(1) provides that,

A person taking on work[80] for or in connection with the provision of a dwelling (whether the dwelling is provided by the erection or by the conversion or enlargement of a building) owes a duty—

    (a) If the dwelling is provided to the order of any person, to that person; and

    (b) without prejudice to paragraph (a) above, to every person who acquires an interest (whether legal or equitable) in the dwelling; to see that work which he takes on is done in a workmanlike or, as the case may be, professional manner, with proper materials and so that as regards that work the dwelling will be fit for habitation when completed.

The reference to the dwelling being "fit for habitation when completed" is not part of the duty itself. Rather it refers to the intended consequence of the proper performance of the duty, so that relief can be claimed before the dwelling is completed.[81] It will be noted that the statutory duty is limited to dwellings, so that the situation with respect to other buildings is still governed by the common law.

But subsection (2) safeguards the position of those persons who take on work of the nature described on terms that shall be done in accordance with instructions. It provides that a person who takes on any such work for another on terms he is to do it in accordance with instructions given by or on behalf of that other shall, to the extent to which he does it in accordance with those instructions, be treated for the purposes of this section as discharging the duty imposed on him by subsection (1) above, except where he owes a duty to that other to warn him of any defects in the instructions and fails to discharge that duty.

On the other hand, by subsection (3) a person shall not be treated as having given instructions for the doing of work merely because he has agreed to the work being done in a specified manner, with specified materials or to a specified design. So a builder or developer who offers plans or specifications on a "take it or leave it" basis to a prospective purchaser will continue to be liable.[82]

Subsection (4) extends the statutory duty imposed by subsection (1) on builders and the like to others, such as developers and local authorities who, in the course of a business or in the exercise of statutory powers, provide or arrange for the provision of dwellings, and who accordingly arrange for others to take on such work.

Subsection (5) provides that the period fixed by the Limitation Act[83] runs from the completion of the building. This date might well be months, or even years, before the completion of the purchase.

It should be noted that although the statutory duty cannot be

---

[80] For the meaning of this curious phrase, see *Alexander* v. *Mercouris* [1979] 1 W.L.R. 1270. See also *Andrews* v. *Schooling* [1991] 3 All E.R. 723 (s.1 is not confined to acts of misfeasance, but also applies to nonfeasance.

[81] *Alexander* v. *Mercouris* [1979] 1 W.L.R. 1270.

[82] But a careless valuer is not liable under the Act: he does not provide a dwelling.

[83] See below, Chap. 25.

excluded or restricted by any term of an agreement (s.6(3)), it does not, by section 2, apply at all when the dwelling is constructed or first sold with the benefit of a scheme approved by the Secretary of State—and at present a high proportion of new houses are so protected. The approved scheme is that of the National House-Builders Registration Council (N.H.B.R.C.).[84] The result is that at present few houses seem to be within the scope of the 1972 Act.[85]

(2) Restriction of common law immunity

This is done in a complex way. The Act does not state in a positive way what are the responsibilities of the vendor or lessor. Instead, it assumes that the immunity of the lessor or vendor is due, not to his status as such as had hitherto been thought, but to the transaction of sale or letting. It is therefore, in effect, provided that such a transaction shall not have such an effect, so that the general principles of negligence will apply to work done before the transaction. Therefore section 3 provides that:

(1) Where work of construction, repair, maintenance or demolition or any other work[86] is done on or in relation to premises, any duty of care owed, because of the doing of the work, to persons who might reasonably be expected to be affected by defects in the state of the premises created by the doing of the work shall not be abated by the subsequent disposal[87] of the premises by the person who owed the duty.

(2) This section does not apply—

(a) in the case of premises which are let, where the relevant tenancy[88] of the premises commenced, or the relevant tenancy agreement of the premises was entered into, before the commencement of this Act;

(b) in the case of premises disposed of in any other way, when the disposal of the premises was completed, or a contract for their disposal was entered into, before the commencement of this Act; or

(c) in either case, where the relevant transaction disposing of the premises is entered into in pursuance of an enforceable option by which the consideration for the disposal was fixed before the commencement of this Act.

In a case which is not covered by these complex provisions it is possible that there will be a remedy under the common law,[89] for section 6(2) of the Act expressly provides that any duty which it imposes is in addition to any duty which is otherwise owed.

---

[84] See S.I. 1979 No. 381.

[85] Although it should be noted that the Council now no longer seeks to obtain Government approval for its schemes.

[86] Presumably this covers mere omissions: see *Andrews* v. *Schooling* [1991] 3 All E.R. 723 (decided on s.1)

[87] As defined in s.6(1).

[88] As defined in s.6(1).

[89] As in *Rimmer* v. *Liverpool City Council* [1985] Q.B. 1, where the events had occurred in 1959.

(3) Landlord's duty of care

It has already been noted[90] that the severity of the rule in *Cavalier* v. *Pope*[91] had been mitigated by section 4 of the Occupiers' Liability Act 1957. That section has now been repealed and replaced by wider provisions in section 4 of the 1972 Act, which in effect gives a remedy for an omission to carry out repairs, as distinct from the liability for careless repairs imposed by section 3.

(1) Where premises[92] are let under a tenancy[93] which puts on the landlord an obligation to the tenant for the maintenance or repair of the premises, the landlord owes to all persons who might reasonably be expected to be affected by defects in the state of the premises a duty to take such care as is reasonable in all the circumstances to see that they are reasonably safe from personal injury[94] or from damage to their property caused by a relevant defect.

(2) The duty is owed if the landlord knows (whether as the result of being notified by the tenant or otherwise) or if he ought in all the circumstances to have known of the relevant defect.[95]

The section applies to tenancies existing at the commencement of the Act as well as to future tenancies, and the duty which it imposes cannot be excluded or restricted by any agreement.

The section changes the previous law in three respects, namely:

(i) The duty of care imposed in replacement of the similar duty imposed by section 4 of the 1957 Act is to be owed not merely to visitors to the premises but to all those who might reasonably be expected to be affected by defects in the state of the premises, *e.g.* a passer-by on the highway or a neighbour in his garden, or perhaps even a trespasser.

(ii) Liability for breach of the duty of care imposed will no longer depend upon whether or not the landlord has been notified of the relevant defect in the premises, for subsection (2) provides that he owes the duty not only when he knows, but also when he ought to have known of the defect.

(iii) The duty thus imposed on the landlord is to be extended, by virtue of subsection (4), to apply in cases where the landlord has a right (expressed or implied) to enter the premises to carry out any description of maintenance or repair but no obligation to do so.[95A]

But it should be noted that this section has not been adopted by the Defective premises (Northern Ireland) Order 1975, which in other respects changed the law in that jurisdiction to correspond with the English law. It was thought unfair to impose such a burden on land-

---

[90] See above, § 11.13.
[91] [1906] A.C. 428.
[92] See *Hopwood* v. *Cannock Chase R.D.C.* [1975] 1 W.L.R. 373.
[93] As defined in ss.4(6) and 6(1).
[94] As defined in s.6(1).
[95] As defined in s.4(3).
[95A] See *McAuley* v. *Bristol City Council* [1992] 1 All E.R. 749 C.A.

lords in view of the amount of bomb damaged property in Northern Ireland.

(4) Exclusion prohibited

Section 6(3) provides that—

Any term of an agreement which purports to exclude or restrict, or has the effect of excluding or restricting, the operation of any of the provisions of this Act, or any liability arising by virtue of any such provision shall be void.

§ 11.15. The Overruling of Anns v. Merton London Borough Council

In 1977 the House of Lords handed down its controversial decision in the well-known case of *Anns* v. *Merton London Borough Council*.[96] The precise scope of this case was notoriously difficult to determine. Nevertheless it was widely regarded as having had the effect of imposing liability upon builders, along with local authorities as a result of their statutory powers of building control, with respect to losses flowing from any defects in the buildings themselves even if those losses were in substance purely economic as being merely the cost of repair or replacement. By seeming to permit recovery in *tort* for the mere reduction *in value* of a building or chattel, as distinct from compensation for personal injury or for damage caused by the defective object to *other* property, this interpretation of *Anns* went well beyond the scope of the law as formerly perceived.[97] Moreover it also went significantly further than the statutory protection afforded by section 1 of the Defective Premises Act 1972. As explained above,[98] that section is limited to *dwellings*[99] and is also subject to a limitation period, in favour of the builder, of six years *from the completion of the building*.[1] The *Anns* principle would have been subject to neither restriction[2] and in two subsequent cases the House of Lords indicated that this judicial outflanking of the limited scope of the legislation with respect to defective premises was unacceptable. These two cases, *D & F Estates* v. *Church Commissioners*,[3] which concerned a builder, and *Murphy* v. *Brentwood District Council*,[4] which concerned a local authority, marked a return to orthodoxy by denying the possibility of recovering in a common law tort action, in all but the most exceptional circumstances,[5] pure economic losses resulting from negligence in the construction of buildings. *Murphy's* case indeed expressly overruled *Anns* and in *Department*

---

[96] [1978] A.C. 728.
[97] See above, Chap. 9.
[98] See § 11.14.
[99] s.1(1)
[1] s.1(5).
[2] For Limitation of Actions see, generally, below Chap. 25.
[3] [1989] A.C. 177.
[4] [1991] 1 A.C. 398.
[5] See *Junior Books* v. *Veitchi* [1983] 1 A.C. 520 and above, Chap. 9.

of the Environment v. *Thomas Bates & Son*,[6] in which judgment was handed down on the same day as in *Murphy*, the House of Lords applied that decision directly to a case involving a builder so as further to confirm the denial of a remedy in tort for remedial work carried out on defective buildings.[7] Whatever the social desirability of the outcome, the law is therefore now much simpler. Unless they have a contractual, or analogous, relationship, which furnishes them with a separate cause of action, owners of property which is merely defective will now only find a remedy, if at all, within the confines of the Defective Premises Act 1972.

---

[6] [1991] 1 A.C. 499.
[7] For the law relating to economic loss generally after *Murphy* see above, Chap. 9.

CHAPTER 12

DEFECTIVE PRODUCTS[1]

§ 12.1. Sources of Liability

In 1987 Part I of the Consumer Protection Act of that year introduced a regime of strict liability for damage caused by defective products. This legislation, the precise effect of which is somewhat controversial, did not replace the fault-based common law tortious liability, but expressly preserved existing remedies. It is therefore necessary to consider both the common law and statutory regimes even though the practical importance of the former is now somewhat reduced. Moreover it is important to remember that contractual liability is now not infrequently regulated by statute. Thus defective products may fall under the Sale of Goods Act 1979, the Fair Trading Act 1973, the Unfair Contract Terms Act 1977, or the Supply of Goods and Services Act 1982. The more recent statutes draw a distinction between consumer contracts and business contracts, and impose tighter controls on the former category. In addition Parts II and III of the Consumer Protection Act 1987 enact, respectively, provisions with respect to consumer safety and misleading price indications. The duties thus imposed are enforced primarily by criminal rather than civil proceedings brought by the Trading Standards Departments of local authorities. Nevertheless the Consumer Protection Act 1987, s.41 specifically provides that a civil action lies for breach of safety regulations made under the Act. Little use does, however, seem to have been made of this provision which dates back to the Consumer Safety Act 1978.

§ 12.2. Duty to Immediate Transferee[2]

(1) Transfer under contract

Where a dangerous product is delivered by the defendant to the plaintiff, the liability of the defendant depends on the terms, express or implied, of the contract between them. The extent of responsibility varies in different classes of contract.[3] Thus in a contract of sale there is in many cases an implied condition that the goods are fit for the purpose for which they were bought.[4] In such cases the seller is responsible in damages for any injury caused by a dangerous imperfection in the goods, apart altogether from any negligence.[5] Statutorily implied terms similar to those relating to contracts of sale also apply to other contracts

---

[1] See the full survey in Miller, *Product Liability and Safety Encyclopaedia*.
[2] Whincup, "Reasonable Fitness of Cars" (1975) 38 M.L.R. 660.
[3] *Taylor & Sons* v. *Union-Castle S.S. Co.* (1932) 48 T.L.R. 249, 250.
[4] Sale of Goods Act 1979, s.14.
[5] As *Grant* v. *Australian Knitting Mills* [1936] A.C. 85 clearly shows.

involving the transfer of property in goods as well as to contracts of hire and certain contracts for the supply of services.[6]

(2) Transfer by way of gift

It was once observed that gifts "have furnished very little occasion for the interposition of judicial tribunals, for reasons equally honourable to the parties and to the liberal spirit of polished society."[7] Indeed it was formerly thought to be settled that in the case of a gratuitous loan or gift of a thing there was not even the duty of reasonable care. The donor or lender owed no duty except to give warning of any dangers actually known to him.[8] In short, the transferee could not complain if he knew as much about the state of the article as did the transferor himself.[9] The only exception to this principle arose when the article belonged to the category of things dangerous *per se*: liability in such a case did not depend on the donor's knowledge of the defect. It is now thought to be clear, however, that the decision in *Donoghue* v. *Stevenson* makes the earlier cases on gifts quite out of date.[10] So there may now be a duty to take reasonable care in the case of a gratuitous bailment, as when a ladder[11] or a lawn-mower is lent to a neighbour, at least if the object is used for the purpose contemplated.[12]

§ 12.3. Duty to Ultimate Transferee

It remains to consider the liability of him who delivers a dangerous article for damage suffered, not by the recipient himself, but by some third person. When A, for example, sells or gives a defective gun to B, who gives or sells it to C, who is injured by the bursting of it: is A under any liability to C? Although there is no liability in such cases merely on the ground of the defendant's breach of contract with the immediate recipient of the dangerous thing,[13] there are certain other circumstances which may create a good cause of action. It is necessary to consider both the traditional approach of the common law and, in a subsequent section, the impact of *Donoghue* v. *Stevenson*.

(1) Fraud

The defendant is responsible if he fraudulently represents the articled to be safe, and so misleads the recipient into causing damage to the plaintiff. Thus in *Langridge* v. *Levy*,[14] the defendant sold to the plain-

---

[6] Supply of Goods and Services Act 1982, ss.1–5 (supply of goods); ss.6–10 (hire of goods); ss.12–16 (supply of services).
[7] Story, *Commentaries on the Law of Bailments*, s.285.
[8] *Coughlin* v. *Gillison* [1899] 1 Q.B. 145, 147.
[9] *Fraser* v. *Jenkins* [1968] N.Z.L.R. 816, 824.
[10] *Hawkins* v. *Coulsdon and Purley U.D.C.* [1954] 2 Q.B. 319, 333.
[11] *Wheeler* v. *Copas* [1981] 3 All E.R. 405.
[12] *Campbell* v. *O'Donnell* [1967] I.R. 226.
[13] See Chap. 2.
[14] (1837) 2 M. & W. 519.

tiff's father for the use of the plaintiff a gun which he fraudulently stated to be of good construction, and the plaintiff, having been injured by the bursting of the weapon, was held entitled to sue the seller for damages although there was no contract between them.

(2) Negligence

The defendant is liable if he has been guilty of a breach of a duty of care owed to the plaintiff. Such a duty of care may arise in three cases.

(i) *Things dangerous in themselves*[15]

A distinction was originally drawn between things classed as dangerous in themselves and things dangerous in the particular case or *sub modo*. "It has, however, again and again been held that in the case of articles dangerous in themselves, such as loaded firearms, poisons, explosives, and other things *ejusdem generis*, there is a peculiar duty to take precaution imposed upon those who send forth or install such articles when it is necessarily the case that other parties will come within their proximity. The duty being to take precaution, it is no excuse to say the accident would not have happened unless some other agency than that of the defendant had intermeddled with the matter. A loaded gun will not go off unless someone pulls the trigger, a poison is innocuous unless someone takes it, gas will not explode unless it is mixed with air and then a light is set to it. Yet the cases of *Dixon* v. *Bell*,[16] *Thomas* v. *Winchester*[17] and *Parry* v. *Smith*[18] are all illustrations of liability enforced. On the other hand, if the proximate cause of the danger is not the negligence of the defendant, but the conscious act of another volition, then he will not be liable."[19] It was considered to be a question of law whether a particular object was capable of coming within the category of things dangerous *per se* and a question of fact whether it was dangerous in all the circumstances of the case.[20] The following objects, amongst others, were held to be dangerous: loaded guns,[21] petrol,[22] explosives,[23] noxious hair-dye,[24] and earthenware jars containing sulphuric acid.[25] On the other hand, the following were not

---

[15] Stallybrass, "Dangerous Things and the Non-Natural User of Land" (1929) 3 Camb.L.J. 376; Goodhart, "Dangerous Things and the Sedan Chair" (1949) 65 L.Q.R. 518; Waddams, "The Strict Liability of Suppliers of Goods" (1974) 37 M.L.R. 154.
[16] (1816) 5 M. & S. 198.
[17] (1852) 6 N.Y. 397.
[18] (1879) 4 C.P.D. 325.
[19] *Dominion Natural Gas Co.* v. *Collins* [1909] A.C. 640, 646, *per* Lord Dunedin. In *Donoghue* v. *Stevenson* [1932] A.C. 562, 596, Lord Atkin said this statement "exactly summed up the position."
[20] *Blacker* v. *Lake and Elliot Ltd.* (1912) 106 L.T. 533.
[21] *Sullivan* v. *Creed* [1904] 2 I.R. 317, 340.
[22] *Jefferson* v. *Derbyshire Farmers Ltd.* [1921] 2 K.B. 281, 290.
[23] *Rainham Chemical Works* v. *Belvedere Fish Guano Co.* [1921] 2 A.C. 465.
[24] *Watson* v. *Buckley* [1940] 1 All E.R. 174.
[25] *Adelaide Chemical Co. Ltd.* v. *Carlyle* (1940) 64 C.L.R. 514.

dangerous *per se*: an oil-can,[26] a domestic boiler,[27] a catapult[28] and an air-gun.[29]

The distinction doubted. Over the years, however, a large number of judicial statements accumulated casting doubt upon the validity of the distinction between things dangerous *per se* and things dangerous *sub modo*. The distinction is certainly difficult to support in principle. There is nothing which is at all times and in all circumstances dangerous; there is an element of danger in every object.[30] The following passage from the argument of Sir Hartley Shawcross, Att.-Gen., in *Read v. J. Lyons & Co.*[31] summarises the argument well[32]: "The true question is not whether a thing is dangerous in itself but whether, by reason of some extraneous circumstances, it may become dangerous. There is really no category of dangerous things; there are only some things which require more and some which require less care." In other words, the measure of care increases in proportion with the danger involved in the custody or control of an agency potentially harmful, that is to say, the danger should the safeguards employed, if any, prove insufficient or unsuccessful.[33] In such a case not only the degree of care but also the range of persons to whom a duty is owed may be extended.[34] So the duty owed by those who store explosives is not limited to those who enter the premises but extends to all who have been foreseeably injured by them—*e.g.* children to whom they have been distributed by those who have entered.[35] Even if the category of things dangerous *per se* does exist, the liability of the owner of such an object is not absolute: he is not an insurer.[36] The case of dangerous things is really "a special instance of negligence where the law exacts a degree of diligence so stringent as to amount practically to a guarantee of safety."[37] In truth, the time has surely come[38] to recognise clearly that since the decision in *Donoghue v. Stevenson*[39] the category of things dangerous *per se* has become unnecessary: the sole question is now whether the degree of care appropriate to the circumstances has been exercised. The fact that there is a special duty to take precautions does not mean that there is a special category in which alone the duty exists.[40]

---

[26] *Wray v. Essex C.C.* [1936] 3 All E.R. 97.

[27] *Ball v. L.C.C.* [1949] 2 K.B. 159.

[28] *Smith v. Leurs* (1945) 70 C.L.R. 256.

[29] *Donaldson v. McNiven* [1952] 2 All E.R. 691.

[30] *Oliver v. Saddler* [1929] A.C. 584, 599.

[31] [1947] A.C. 156, 161.

[32] *Beckett v. Newalls Insulation Co. Ltd.* [1953] 1 W.L.R. 8, 15.

[33] *Swinton v. The China Mutual Steam Navigation Co. Ltd.* (1951) 83 C.L.R. 553, 566–567.

[34] *Donoghue v. Stevenson* [1932] A.C. 562, 596.

[35] *McCarthy v. Wellington City* [1966] N.Z.L.R. 481.

[36] *Adelaide Chemical Co. v. Carlyle* (1940) 64 C.L.R. 514.

[37] *Donoghue v. Stevenson* [1932] A.C. 562, 611–612.

[38] As Goddard L.J. affirmed as long ago as *Paine v. Colne Valley Electricity Supply Co. Ltd.* [1938] 4 All E.R. 803, 808.

[39] [1932] A.C. 562. See below, § 12.4.

[40] *Rae v. Eaton & Co. Ltd.* (1958) 28 D.L.R. (2d) 522, 529–530; *Tanner v. Atlantic Bridge Co. Ltd.* (1966) 56 D.L.R. (2d) 162, 163.

(ii) *Non-disclosure of known dangers*

If the defendant has actual knowledge of the dangerous nature of the thing delivered by him, and gives no warning of it to the recipient, he may be liable for resulting injury to third persons even though the thing is not within the category of things dangerous *per se*,[41] as where a valve was reassembled with the bridge upside down so that steam escaped and scalded the plaintiff.[42]

Scope of the duty. If A places in the hands of B a thing which belongs to the category of things dangerous *per se*, or if A actually knows of some dangerous defect, a duty of care rests upon A, not only towards the recipient, but also towards all such persons as may reasonably be contemplated as likely to be endangered.[43] Thus in *Farrant v. Barnes*[44] the defendant delivered to a carrier a carboy of nitric acid without informing him of the dangerous nature of its contents, and was held liable in damages to the carrier's servant who was injured by the bursting of the carboy while he was carrying it on his shoulders.

But there is a genuine demand for "seconds," "and the law would be encouraging waste if it categorically condemned any distribution of defective goods as negligent *per se*."[45] So in some cases the duty of the transferor may be discharged if he delivers the article to a competent person who knows of the danger already or is given an adequate warning about it.[46] It is a question of fact whether the warning is adequate: the transferor need not take the transferee by the hand or the ear, and show or tell him exactly what is wrong.[47] The transferor may be entitled to assume that the recipient will pass on the warning to the ultimate transferee, or will so act as to minimise or nullify the danger. So in *Holmes v. Ashford*[48] the manufacturer of hair-dye was held not liable to one who had contracted dermatitis after the dye had been applied by a hairdresser, for it was shown that the dye had been delivered to the hairdresser by the manufacturer with an adequate warning of its potential dangers. Yet a warning is not a sufficient discharge of the duty if the person to whom the thing is delivered is not a competent person—*e.g.* a child to whom a defective "safety-pistol"[49] or petrol[50] is sold.

---

[41] *Barnes v. Irwell Valley Water Board* [1939] 1 K.B. 21, 44, 46.

[42] *Howard v. Furness Houlder Ltd.* [1936] 2 All E.R. 781, 792.

[43] *Anglo-Celtic Shipping Co. Ltd. v. Elliott* (1926) 42 T.L.R. 297; *Adelaide Chemical and Fertiliser Co. Ltd. v. Carlyle* (1940) 64 C.L.R. 514; *Robinson v. Technico Ltd.* (1953) (unreported) (see (1954) 70 L.Q.R. 170).

[44] (1862) 11 C.B. (N.S.) 533.

[45] J. G. Fleming, *An Introduction to the Law of Torts* (2nd ed.), p. 83.

[46] It may even be that neither the warning nor the knowledge need be of the exact amount of the danger: *Bottomley v. Bannister* [1932] 1 K.B. 458, 473.

[47] *Hurley v. Dyke* [1979] R.T.R. 265.

[48] [1950] 2 All E.R. 76. Yet it may be asked why a person who has created a dangerous situation should be held not liable on the ground that it has not been abated by another whose duty it was to do so: Goodhart (1941) 57 L.Q.R. 163, and see cases cited below, § 12.4.

[49] *Burfitt v. Kille* [1939] 2 K.B. 743, 748.

[50] *Yachuk v. Oliver Blais Co.* [1949] A.C. 386.

(iii) *Negligence with respect to unknown dangers*

Before 1932 it was extremely doubtful whether there was any liability on the part of a manufacturer of goods to the ultimate consumer or user with whom there was no contractual relationship, when there was no fraud, when he did not know the article to be dangerous, and when it did not belong to the category of things dangerous *per se*. But in that year the decision of a majority of the House of Lords in *Donoghue v. Stevenson*,[51] an appeal from the Court of Session, established that in such circumstances the manufacturer might owe a duty to the ultimate consumer. We shall proceed to discuss this great case in fuller detail.

§ 12.4 DONOGHUE V. STEVENSON[52]

The question for the House of Lords in this appeal was whether the averments made by the pursuer in her pleadings, if true, disclosed a good cause of action. The pursuer's averments were that in August 1928 she had entered the Wellmeadow cafe in Paisley occupied by one Minghella, and that a friend[53] who accompanied her had bought from Minghella some refreshment for both of them. The refreshment consisted of two slabs of ice-cream, each of which was placed in a tumbler, and over which was then poured part of the contents of a bottle of ginger-beer. The ginger-beer had been manufactured by the defender Stevenson, and bought from him by Minghella.[54] It was contained in a stoppered bottle made of dark opaque glass. When the pursuer had partly finished the confection, her friend attempted to replenish her glass by pouring into it the remains of the contents of the bottle. As she was doing this the remains of a decomposed snail floated out. The appellant averred that as a result of the nauseating sight of the snail and the impurities in the ginger-beer which she had already consumed, she had suffered from shock and severe gastroenteritis. A majority of the House of Lords (Lords Atkin, Macmillan, and Thankerton) held that if the pursuer could prove that which she averred she would have a good cause of action.[55]

---

[51] [1932] A.C. 562.

[52] See Heuston, "Donoghue v. Stevenson in Retrospect" (1957) 20 M.L.R. 1; Heuston, "Donoghue v. Stevenson: A Fresh Appraisal" [1971] C.L.P. 37; Smith and Burns, "Donoghue v. Stevenson: the Not-So-Golden Anniversary" (1983) 46 M.L.R. 147; "The Good Neighbour on Trial: Good Neighbours Make Bad Law." (1983) 17 U.B.C.L.Rev. 93.

[53] Who seems to have been female and not male: see Lord MacMillan's speech.

[54] At a conference held in Paisley, attended by the Lord Chancellor, to commemorate the sixtieth anniversary of the events which gave rise to one of the most famous cases in the common law world, those attending were served ginger-beer by a descendant of Minghella. The conference gave rise to a book of essays: *The Paisley Papers*, Peter Burns ed. (Vancouver, 1991).

[55] There has been a persistent rumour (which has found support in the courts: *Adler v. Dickson* [1954] 1 W.L.R. 1482, 1483); *Freeman v. Home Office* [1984] 1 Q.B. 524, 556, and in the House of Commons (958, H.C.Deb., col. 820, November 17, 1978)) that when the case was tried it was discovered that there never had been a snail in the bottle at all. This is not so. The truth is that the issue of fact was never decided: the defender died before proof and the pursuer in consequence compromised the action and received £200 in settlement of her claim.

"If your Lordships," said Lord Atkin,[56] "accept the view that this pleading discloses a relevant cause of action you will be affirming the proposition that by Scots and English law alike a manufacturer of products, which he sells in such a form as to show that he intends them to reach the ultimate consumer in the form in which they left him with no reasonable possibility of intermediate examination and with the knowledge that the absence of reasonable care in the preparation or putting up of the products will result in an injury to the consumer's life or property, owes a duty to the consumer to take that reasonable care. It is a proposition which I venture to say no one in Scotland or England who was not a lawyer would for one moment doubt. It will be an advantage to make it clear that the law in this matter, as in most others, is in accordance with sound common sense."

Whatever hesitations may have been felt about Lord Atkin's attempt to formulate a general criterion of the duty of care[57] this exposition of the obligation owed by a manufacturer of products in the circumstances mentioned has never been questioned. Indeed, in the years since 1932 it has been adopted and expanded in over one hundred reported cases throughout the common law world.[58] It will be convenient to discuss briefly some of the more significant phrases in this passage.[59]

(1) "A manufacturer"

The principle has been extended to include repairers,[60] assemblers,[61] erectors[62] and builders.[63] Inspectors and certifiers are also included.[64] Those who let out goods on hire are probably also included.[65] So it might be better to refer to producers rather than to manufacturers. It was once argued that the principle should not include vendors, bailors, or donors of articles not dangerous *per se*, who know nothing of the defect, have not created it, and do not fraudulently or carelessly[66] rep-

---

[56] [1932] A.C. 562, 599.
[57] See above, § 9.1.
[58] See 36 *English and Empire Digest* 458, and add to the cases there cited *Kirby* v. *Burke* [1944] I.R. 207, and *Campbell* v. *O'Donnell* [1967] I.R. 226.
[59] This mode of exposition is adopted simply for the sake of clarity and simplicity: no countenance is intended to be given to the heresy of treating the words of a famous judgment as if they were a passage in statute.
[60] *Malfroot* v. *Noxal* (1935) 51 T.L.R. 551; *Stennet* v. *Hancock* [1939] 2 All E.R. 578; *Herschtal* v. *Stewart and Ardern* [1940] 1 K.B. 155; *Haseldine* v. *Daw* [1941] 2 K.B. 343; *Power* v. *Bedford Motor Co. Ltd.* [1959] I.R. 391.
[61] *Howard* v. *Furness Houlder Ltd.* [1936] 2 All E.R. 781.
[62] *Brown* v. *Cotterill* (1934) 51 T.L.R. 21.
[63] *Sharpe* v. *E.T. Sweeting & Sons Ltd.* [1963] 1 W.L.R. 665.
[64] *Anns* v. *Merton London Borough Council* [1978] A.C. 728.
[65] *White* v. *Steadman* [1913] 3 K.B. 340; *Astley Industrial Trust Ltd.* v. *Grimley* [1963] 1 W.L.R. 584.
[66] The distributors in *Watson* v. *Buckley and Osborne, Garrett & Co. Ltd.* [1940] 1 All E.R. 174 were liable on this ground: they had distributed to the hairdressing trade with laudatory advertisements a dye which they had not tested at all and which had been made by "a gentleman who had emerged quite unexpectedly from Spain."

resent that the article is harmless on the ground that they have done nothing to create the danger. To hold such persons responsible would come very near to imposing liability for mere omissions on persons who are simply distributors and not producers.[67] But liability has been imposed[68] upon a dealer in second-hand motor-cars who supplied the plaintiff[69] with a vehicle containing a latent defect, and upon a store which sold defective cleaning fluid to the plaintiff's husband.[70] The defect would have been discoverable by a reasonable examination, but the defendants neither carried out such an examination nor warned the plaintiff that it had not been done.

(2) "Of products"

This term is no longer limited to articles of food or drink. It includes, for example, underwear,[71] tombstones,[72] motor-cars,[73] lifts,[74] hair-dye[75] and ships' telegraphs.[76] It also covers cases in which the injurious element is not a foreign body but something intrinsically part of the commodity itself.[77] It may cover cases in which there is no allegation that the product has been carelessly made, but it is dangerous to use in the absence of proper warnings or directions.[78] The principle has also been extended, after earlier doubts, to cover buildings,[79] although the vendor or lessor of premises may still enjoy certain immunities.[80] Careless statements were once also excluded, but there may now be liability for them under a distinct head of negligence.[81]

(3) "Which he sells in such a form as to show that he intends them to reach the ultimate consumer in the form in which they left him"

First, it should be noted that "consumer" has been extended to include the ultimate user of the article,[82] or, indeed, anyone through

---

[67] See the Pearson Report, § 1238. The liability of donors or gratuitous bailors is also considered above, § 12.2.
[68] *Andrews* v. *Hopkinson* [1957] 1 Q.B. 229.
[69] By way of a hire-purchase transaction—*i.e.* the dealer sold the car to a finance company, who in turn leased it to the plaintiff under a hire-purchase agreement. In strict legal analysis, therefore, the relationship of vendor and purchaser did not exist between the plaintiff and the dealer.
[70] *Fisher* v. *Harrods Ltd.* [1966] 1 Lloyd's Rep. 500.
[71] *Grant* v. *Australian Knitting Mills* [1936] A.C. 85.
[72] *Brown* v. *Cotterill* (1934) 51 T.L.R. 21.
[73] *Herschtal* v. *Stewart and Ardern* [1940] 1 K.B. 155.
[74] *Haseldine* v. *Daw* [1941] 2 K.B. 343.
[75] *Watson* v. *Buckley* [1940] 1 All E.R. 174.
[76] *Hindustan S.S. Co. Ltd.* v. *Siemens Bros. & Co. Ltd.* [1955] 1 Lloyd's Rep. 167. (In this case the article was defective because of its design.)
[77] *Tarling* v. *Noble* [1966] A.L.R. 189 (bone in chicken sandwich).
[78] *Distillers Co. (Biochemicals) Ltd.* v. *Thompson* [1971] A.C. 458.
[79] *Rimmer* v. *Liverpool City Council* [1984] Q.B. 1.
[80] *Ibid.*, 16.
[81] See above, Chap. 9.
[82] *Grant* v. *Australian Knitting Mills* [1936] A.C. 85.

whose hands the article may pass,[83] and perhaps even anyone who is in physical proximity to it.[84] Equally, liability is no longer limited to one who sells, but extends to any distributor, including donors.[85]

Secondly, it is not of the essence of this principle that the article should reach the consumer or user in the same sealed package or container in which it left the manufacturer: it is enough to show that it reached him subject to the same defect. This was made clear in *Grant* v. *Australian Knitting Mills*.[86] In this case the plaintiff contracted dermatitis as a result of wearing woollen underwear containing an excess of sulphites. The underwear had been sent out by the defendant manufacturers in paper packets containing six sets of which two were sold by retailers to the plaintiff: yet the manufacturers were held liable.

Thirdly, the use of the article for a purpose materially different from that for which the maker designed it or which he might reasonably be taken to have contemplated may afford an answer to a claim[87] based on the article's defective condition.[88] Further, it may well be that after the article has left the manufacturer's hands it has been exposed to vicissitudes which render it defective and for which the manufacturer is in no way to blame: in such a case the plaintiff will have failed to prove that the cause of the damage was the negligence of the manufacturer.[89] Fourthly, and conversely, the mere fact that the damage is foreseeable will not make for liability. The purpose of making cigarettes is that they should be smoked: but that does not automatically give one who develops lung-cancer a remedy.

(4) "With no reasonable possibility of intermediate examination"

Here three different situations have given rise to difficulty. First, there may have been an opportunity for examination, but that opportunity has not been taken; secondly, such an opportunity may have been taken, but without success, so that the defect is still unrevealed; thirdly, the opportunity may have been taken successfully, and the defect revealed, but the plaintiff has nevertheless used the article in its defective condition.

---

[83] *Barnett* v. *Packer* [1940] 3 All E.R. 575 (shop-assistant laying out chocolates for display injured by protruding wire).
[84] *Brown* v. *Cotterill* (1934) 51 T.L.R. 21 (child on tombstone); *Stennett* v. *Hancock* [1939] 2 All E.R. 578 (pedestrian hit by lorry-wheel). Yet see the doubts of Lord Goddard C.J. in *Shave* v. *Rosner* [1954] 2 All E.R. 280, 282 (a passage not reported in [1954] 2 Q.B. 113).
[85] See above § 12.2.
[86] [1936] A.C. 85.
[87] As when a step-ladder is used as a working platform (*Campbell* v. *O'Donnell* [1967] I.R. 226), or a fishing vessel as an excursion boat for children (*Conole* v. *Red Bank Oyster Co. Ltd.* [1976] I.R. 191).
[88] *Davie* v. *New Merton Board Mills Ltd.* [1957] 2 Q.B. 368 (Ashworth J.—the point was not considered on appeal in either the C.A. or the H.L.).
[89] In *Donoghue* v. *Stevenson* [1932] A.C. 562, 622, Lord Macmillan suggested that "it may be a good general rule to regard responsibility as ceasing when control ceases," but in *Grant's* case [1936] A.C. 85, 104, Lord Wright showed that this test might sometimes prove unhelpful. This is important, because Lord MacMillan was a member of the Judicial Committee in *Grant's* case and would hardly have accepted an incorrect interpretation of his judgment in *Donoghue* v. *Stevenson*.

(i) *Opportunity not used*

Does the mere existence of an opportunity for intermediate examin-ation, even if it is not used, or indeed expected by anyone that it could or would be used, suffice to exonerate the defendant? In *Donoghue* v. *Stevenson* itself it was of course unnecessary for Lord Atkin to consider anything else than a "reasonable possibility," for the facts were of a nature which not merely precluded examination by any person inter-posed between the manufacturer and the consumer but also made it unlikely in the extreme that the consumer would discover the defect for himself. After an initial period of uncertainty,[90] it is now fairly[91] plain[92] that the mere existence of such an opportunity will not exonerate the defendant[93]: the proper question is whether he should reasonably have expected that the plaintiff would use the opportunity for inspection in such a way as to give him warning of the risk.[94] In short, the decision in *Donoghue* v. *Stevenson* did not depend on the bottle being stoppered and sealed.[95] Thus in *Grant* v. *Australian Knitting Mills*[96] the manufac-turers' contention that the purchaser could have protected himself by washing the underwear before use[97] was answered by Lord Wright in one sentence: "It was not contemplated that they should be first washed." "If there was any doubt about the governing principle of *Donoghue* v. *Stevenson*, Lord Wright has dissipated it."[98]

Warning notices. One way in which the manufacturer could show that he reasonably expected intermediate examination would be by show-ing that he had attached to the article a warning notice which was adequate in all the circumstances of the case to give effective protec-tion.[99] In such an event, it would be the retailer and not the manufac-turer who would in general be responsible to the ultimate user. It should be noticed that it is not necessary for the defendant to prove that the plaintiff consumed or used the article with full knowledge of the risk; it is enough if examination and consequent knowledge are to be

---

[90] *Dransfield* v. *British Insulated Cables Ltd.* [1937] 4 All E.R. 382. See Goodhart, "*Dransfield* v. *British Insulated Cables Ltd.*" (1938) 54 L.Q.R. 59.

[91] *Taylor* v. *Rover Co. Ltd.* [1966] 1 W.L.R. 1491 adopts the older view.

[92] *Shields* v. *Hobbs, etc. Co.* (1962) 34 D.L.R. (2d) 307; *Cathcart* v. *Hull* [1963] N.Z.L.R. 333.

[93] So in *Paine* v. *Colne Valley Electricity Co.* [1938] 4 All E.R. 803, 808, Goddard L.J. sug-gested that Lord Atkin meant "possibility in a business sense," for a "person who buys 100 cases of tinned salmon from the packers has a physical opportunity of examining each tin. Commercially speaking it would be impossible for him to do so." As Finne-more J. remarked, many reputable manufacturers would be insulted at the suggestion that inspection of their products was necessary before use: *Mason* v. *Williams and Wil-liams Ltd.* [1955] 1 W.L.R. 549, 551.

[94] This sentence was approved in *Cathcart* v. *Hull* [1963] N.Z.L.R. 333, 346, and, with reser-vations in *Jull* v. *Wilson and Horton* [1968] N.Z.L.R. 88, 92, and in *Bowen* v. *Paramount Builders Ltd.* [1977] 1 N.Z.L.R. 394, 412, and in *Griffiths* v. *Arch Engineering Co. Ltd.* [1968] 3 All E.R. 217, 222.

[95] *Clay* v. *Crump & Co. Ltd.* [1964] 1 Q.B. 533, 558.

[96] [1936] A.C. 85, 105.

[97] A practice adopted by "some rather particular people": [1941] 2 K.B. 377.

[98] *Haseldine* v. *Daw & Son Ltd.* [1941] 2 K.B. 343, 377, *per* Goddard L.J. See the full review of authorities in *Herschtal* v. *Stewart and Ardern Ltd.* [1940] 1 K.B. 155.

[99] *Kubach* v. *Hollands* [1937] 3 All E.R. 907; *Holmes* v. *Ashford* [1950] 2 All E.R. 76.

expected.[1] There is an increasing tendency in practice for manufacturers to warn consumers of subsequently discovered defects.[2] Such "recall notices" are therefore now quite common,[3] and are of obvious importance in protecting the public.

(ii) *Opportunity used, but unsuccessfully*

What is the position if an intermediate examination has been carried out, but so carelessly that it fails to reveal the defect? It was once held that the manufacturer is exonerated in such circumstances,[4] but the prevalent view now is that the manufacturer is not in general excused[5] by the fact that an intermediary has failed to perform his duties properly.[6] Thus an architect who carelessly plans a building or supervises a demolition operation may be liable to any lawful visitor to the premises, and is not entirely exempt[7] from liability merely because the builders or demolition contractors[8] or a public authority[9] have inspected the plans or the site.

(iii) *Successful intermediate examination*

The general principle is that if the plaintiff has discovered the defect for himself he is without remedy, because in such a case he has in truth failed to prove that the defendant caused the damage.[10] This is the explanation of *Farr* v. *Butters Bros.*,[11] a case which seems to have caused some difficulty. The defendant crane-manufacturers sent out a crane in parts to be assembled by the buyers. Their foreman, an experienced man, realised that it was defective but nevertheless assembled and worked it and was killed. The defendants were held not liable; the plaintiff had deliberately incurred the risk. This interpretation of *Donoghue* v. *Stevenson* has not in theory been affected by the Law Reform (Contributory Negligence) Act: if there is a probability of intermediate examination the defendant owes no duty, and so there are no damages to be reduced.[12] But in practice the courts look at the matter broadly and seem to be ready to reduce the damages.[13] Moreover it is clear that the general principle does not apply when it could reasonably be contemplated that the plaintiff, despite his knowledge of the defect, might yet reasonably incur the risk. Thus in *Denny* v. *Supplies and*

---

[1] *London Graving Dock Co.* v. *Horton* [1951] A.C. 737, 750.
[2] See Miller and Harvey, *Consumer Trading Law Cases and Materials*, p. 159.
[3] See Russell, "Product recall: weighing up the risks," L.S. Gaz. March 28, 1990.
[4] *Buckner* v. *Ashby and Horner Ltd.* [1941] 1 K.B. 321; *Holmes* v. *Ashford* [1950] 2 All E.R. 76.
[5] He was in *Taylor* v. *Rover Co. Ltd.* [1966] 1 W.L.R. 1491.
[6] *Power* v. *Bedford Motor Co.* [1959] I.R. 391; *Clay* v. *A. J. Crump & Sons Ltd.* [1964] 1 Q.B. 533.
[7] There may be claims for contribution or indemnity; see below, Chap. 20.
[8] *Clay* v. *A. J. Crump & Sons Ltd.* [1964] 1 Q.B. 533.
[9] *Voli* v. *Inglewood Shire Council* (1963) 110 C.L.R. 74.
[10] *Grant* v. *Australian Knitting Mills* [1936] A.C. 85, 105; *Conole* v. *Red Bank Oyster Co. Ltd.* [1976] I.R. 191, 196.
[11] [1932] 2 K.B. 606.
[12] *Cathcart* v. *Hull* [1963] N.Z.L.R. 333.
[13] *Jull* v. *Wilson and Horton* [1968] N.Z.L.R. 88.

Transport Co.[14] the defendants sent out a barge loaded with timber so badly stowed that the plaintiff, who realised the danger, was injured while unloading it in the course of his employment. There was no practicable alternative course of action open to him for it was shown that there is no safe way of unloading badly stowed timber.[15] It was held that the plaintiff's opportunity of inspection did not break the chain of causation. There is no magic in a warning, and a danger is not removed by the mere process of the plaintiff gazing at it.[16] The basic question is whether, as in the case of visitors to dangerous premises, the plaintiff is really and truly free to act on his knowledge.[17]

(5) "And with the knowledge that the absence of reasonable care in the preparation or putting up of the products"

Reasonable care must be taken to ensure not only that the product itself is safe but also that any container or package in which it is sent out is suitable for its purpose.[18] Reasonable care must also be taken to ensure that any labels or instructions which accompany the article and are necessary for its proper use are so worded as to ensure that the article can be used with safety.[19] For sometimes an article of the highest standard of construction may be rendered dangerous by some misrepresentation which accompanies it—*e.g.* a steam boiler when the figures on the pressure gauge have been misplaced.[20]

(6) "Will result in injury to the consumer's life or property"

The principle enunciated by Lord Atkin was limited to cases where physical injury to person or property had been caused. But in recent times a number of decisions had the effect of calling this position into question by allowing recovery of the cost of repairing a defective product before it had actually injured anyone,[21] and in *Junior Books Ltd.* v. *Veitchi Ltd.*[22] a majority of the House of Lords permitted recovery in tort for a product that was merely defective in itself. While such economic loss may indeed be reasonably foreseeable, the result was equivalent to saying that there is a warranty in tort as well as in contract that an article is reasonably fit for its purpose. In the 1990 case of *Murphy* v. *Brentwood*

---

[14] [1950] 2 K.B. 374.
[15] This clearly distinguishes the case from *Farr* v. *Butters Bros.*, where there was no evidence of any legal or economic obligation on the plaintiff to work the crane until the defect had been remedied.
[16] *A. C. Billings & Sons Ltd.* v. *Riden* [1958] A.C. 240.
[17] *Rimmer* v. *Liverpool City Council* [1985] Q.B. 1, 14.
[18] *Donoghue* v. *Stevenson* [1932] A.C. 562, 595, 616, which must be taken to have overruled *Bates* v. *Batey & Co.* [1913] 3 K.B. 351, though Horridge J. (who had decided it) thought not in *Pattendon* v. *Beney* (1933) 50 T.L.R. 10. Pollock ((1934) 50 L.Q.R. 28) said that the opinions of the Law Lords had brought *Bates* v. *Batey & Co.* "well within the classical precept, 'Put that case out of your books, for it is not law.' "
[19] *Blacker* v. *Lake and Elliot* (1912) 106 L.T. 533, 541; *Kubach* v. *Hollands* [1937] 3 All E.R. 907; *Watson* v. *Buckley* [1940] 1 All E.R. 174; *Holmes* v. *Ashford* [1950] 2 All E.R. 76.
[20] *Hindustan S.S. Co. Ltd.* v. *Siemens Bros. & Co. Ltd.* [1955] 1 Lloyd's Rep. 167.
[21] *Anns* v. *Merton London Borough Council* [1978] A.C. 728; *Batty* v. *Metropolitan Realisations Ltd.* [1978] Q.B. 554.
[22] [1980] A.C. 520.

District Council,[23] however, this trend was put emphatically into reverse by the House of Lords and the traditional limitation was insisted upon. Although the House in so holding overruled one of its own earlier decisions[24] the decision in *Junior Books* itself has not been formally overruled, and the unusual circumstances making for a close proximity between the parties in that case may mean that its special facts put it into an exceptional category. In general, however, it is now clear once more that a claim in respect of defective or unsuitable, as distinct from dangerous, products should be brought only in contract and not in tort.[25]

(7) "Owes a duty to take that reasonable care"

The onus of proving negligence rests on the plaintiff. There has been some dispute whether he can pray in aid the maxim *res ipsa loquitur*. In principle there seems to be no reason why he should not be permitted to do so.[26] Thus in *Grant* v. *Australian Knitting Mills* (in which the defendants showed that their factory was the most up to date possible and that they had sold over a million similar garments without complaint) the Judicial Committee said: "If excess sulphites were left in the garment, that could only be because someone was at fault. The appellant is not required to lay his finger on the exact person in all the chain who was responsible, or to specify what he did wrong. Negligence is found as a matter of inference from the existence of the defects taken in conjunction with all the known circumstances."[27] It is submitted that this is the better opinion, having been followed in a number of cases,[28] and supported by the Law Commission.[29]

Date at which duty arises

For the purposes of the law relating to limitations of actions, it may be necessary to ascertain the moment of time at which the duty arises. It seems that the duty arises at the stage of manufacture and is a continuing duty, although the plaintiff's cause of action does not accrue until he has suffered damage[30] which is more than minimal.[31] The manufacturer's duty is a continuing one in the sense that if later research discloses a defect hitherto unknown, he should do what is reasonable to

---

[23] [1991] 1 A.C. 398.
[24] *i.e. Anns* v. *Merton London Borough Council* [1978] A.C. 728.
[25] For further discussion see above, Chap. 9.
[26] *Contra*, Lord Macmillan in [1932] A.C. 562, 622.
[27] [1936] A.C. 85, 101. It will be recalled that Lord Macmillan was a member of the Board.
[28] *Cassidy* v. *Ministry of Health* [1951] 2 K.B. 343, 359; *Mason* v. *Williams and Williams Ltd.* [1955] 1 W.L.R. 549; *Lockhart* v. *Barr*, 1943 S.C. 1, *Hill* v. *Crowe Ltd.* [1978] 1 All E.R. 812 and *Martin* v. *Thorn Ltd.* [1978] W.A.R. 10. The case of *Daniels* v. *White & Sons* [1938] 4 All E.R. 258 (manufacturers of lemonade containing carbolic acid excused when they proved "a fool-proof method" of cleaning and filling the bottles and adequate supervision) is not now followed in England.
[29] See Law Com. No. 64, §§ 39–45.
[30] *Watson* v. *Winget Ltd.*, 1960 S.C. 100, and below, Chap. 25.
[31] *Cartledge* v. *Jopling & Sons Ltd.* [1963] A.C. 758. For undiscoverable damage, see below, Chap. 25.

cure that defect, or even perhaps cease to market the product.[32] If there is indeed a duty to issue warning notices, or to recall the product, then this may be an exception to the general rule that there is no liability for omissions.

§12.5. LIABILITY UNDER THE CONSUMER PROTECTION ACT 1987, PART I[33]

The European Community (EC) Directive on Product Liability was adopted by the Council of the EC in 1985. It ended a long-standing controversy[34] by providing for a regime of strict liability for damage caused by defective products. In pursuance of its obligation, as a member of the EC, to make its laws conform to the Directive, the UK Government secured the passing of the Consumer Protection Act in 1987. During its passage through the House of Lords Government spokesman stated that the Act was designed to implement, "no more and no less," the EC Directive.[35] But whether the Act actually succeeds in fully implementing the Directive, and fulfilling the obligations of the U.K., is a matter of some controversy.[36] The main provisions of the Act will now be considered.

(1) Strict liability

Liability under the Act is, ostensibly at least, not to be based on fault. Section 2(1) provides that when any damage is caused wholly or partly by a defect in a product, every producer of the product "shall be liable for the damage." So causation rather than negligence is intended to be the primary criterion. Producers are defined so as to include importers—an advantage for consumers when goods are brought in to the United Kingdom from some overseas point of manufacture. Products include agricultural produce provided it has "undergone an industrial process."

(2) Damage

Damage is defined by section 5 of the Act so as:
   (i) to be limited to death or personal injury or any loss or damage to any property (including land) exceeding the sum of £275[37] so economic loss is apparently excluded;

---

[32] *Wright* v. *Dunlop Rubber Co. Ltd.* (1973) 13 K.I.R. 250.

[33] Newdick, (1987) 104 L.Q.R. 288.

[34] See, *e.g.* in addition to the EC Directive, the Report of the English and Scottish Law Commissions on Liability for Defective Products: Law. Com. No. 82 (Cmnd. 6831, 1977); The Royal Commission on Civil Liability and Compensation for Personal Injury (Pearson) (Cmnd. 7054, 1978), Chap. 22; the Strasbourg Convention on Products Liability (Council of Europe).

[35] For debates, see the H.L. Hansard for December 8, 1986; January 19, 1987; March 19, 1987; and the H.C. Hansard for April 27, 1987 and May 13, 1987.

[36] The European Commission has expressed concern that the wording of the Act with respect to the so-called development risks or "state of the art" defence in s.4(1)(*e*) may be significantly more generous to defendants than the equivalent Article 7(*e*) of the Directive.

[37] This figure is a threshold, *i.e.* those whose loss exceeds it recover in full while those whose loss is below it recover nothing.

(ii) not to extend to loss of or damage to the product itself[38];

(iii) not to extend to loss or damage to the whole or any part of any product which has been supplied with the product in question comprised in it[39]:

(iv) not to extend to property which is not of a kind "ordinarily intended for private use, occupation or consumption" and is not "intended by the person suffering the loss or damage mainly for his own private use, occupation or consumption" (section 5(3)).

It is also important to note that liability is non-excludable by contract, notice or otherwise (section 7) and that the Act does not abrogate the existing common law on products liability, discussed earlier in this chapter, which will therefore continue to apply where appropriate (see section 2(6) of the Act).

(3) The definition of a defect

According to section 3 of the Act there is a defect in a product if the safety of the product "is not such as persons generally are entitled to expect." All the circumstances are to be considered, including in particular the get-up of the product; the date when it was supplied, the use which might be expected to be made of it, and any instructions or warnings issued.

(4) The defences available

The Act specifically incorporates the provisions of the Law Reform (Contributory Negligence) Act 1945.[40] It will also be a defence that the product was supplied otherwise than by way of the defendant's business, e.g. by way of gift.[41]

But the most significant defence provided by the Act, and certainly the one which has caused the most controversy, is that sometimes called the "development risks," or the "state of the art," defence.

The defence means that "the state of scientific or technical knowledge at the relevant time was not such that a producer of products of the same description as the product in question might be expected to have discovered the defect if it had existed in his products while they were under his control" (section 4(1)(e)).

Government spokesmen assured Parliament during the passage of the Act that the defence "was essential for the innovative character of British industry," although it was conceded that the defence was not permitted at all in France, Belgium or Luxembourg, or in Germany for pharmaceutical products.

The Government also stated that it would not be easy to make out the defence, in that the producer would have to prove something more than testing difficulties, or that he had simply followed the procedures

---

[38] This accords with the common law position as recently restored by *Murphy* v. *Brentwood District Council* [1991] 1 A.C. 398.

[39] This accords with the common law position as reflected in *Aswan Engineering Co.* v. *Lupdine* [1987] 1 W.L.R. 1.

[40] s.6(4).

[41] See s.4(1)(c).

adopted by other manufacturers. The comment may be allowed that this is not what the section says. It may also be noted that the defendant has expressly been given an important bargaining factor, the use, or even threatened use of which, may increase the length and expense of litigation.

CHAPTER 13

THE RULE IN RYLANDS *v*. FLETCHER AND LIABILITY FOR FIRE

§ 13.1. Rule in Rylands *v*. Fletcher[1]

The hazards arising from a highly developed technological society are often regulated by statute—*e.g.* the Nuclear Installations Act 1965 and the Environmental Protection Act 1990. The Pearson Commission[2] recommended that strict liability should be imposed by statute on controllers of unusually hazardous things (*e.g.* explosives) or of operations carrying a risk of serious casualties (*e.g.* dams and bridges). As new things and operations displayed extraordinarily dangerous[3] characteristics, they could be brought under the statute by statutory instrument. There is, however, little prospect of these recommendations being enacted in the foreseeable future. But there does exist a well-established common law principle, developed by the nineteenth century judiciary and closely related to the law of nuisance, which provides for strict liability in certain limited circumstances involving special danger. This doctrine, known as the rule in *Rylands* v. *Fletcher*,[4] is probably the best-known example of strict[5] liability recognised by our law—one of the chief instances in which a man acts at his peril and is responsible for accidental harm, independently of the existence of either wrongful intent or negligence. The rule may be formulated thus:

The occupier of land who brings and keeps upon it anything likely to do damage if it escapes is bound at his peril to prevent its escape, and is liable for all the direct consequences of its escape, even if he has been guilty of no negligence.[6]

In *Rylands* v. *Fletcher* the two defendants[7] constructed a reservoir upon their land,[8] in order to supply water to their mill, and upon the site chosen for this purpose there was a disused and filled-up shaft of an old coal mine, the passages of which communicated with the adjoining mine of the plaintiff. Through the negligence of the contractors or engineers by whom the work was done (and who were not the

---

[1] See Prosser, *Topics* Chap. III; Newark, "Non-natural user and *Rylands* v. *Fletcher*" (1961) 24 M.L.R. 557; *Civil Liability for Dangerous Things and Activities* (Law Com. No. 32, 1970).

[2] Cmnd. 7054, Chap. 31.

[3] Since 1977 this is the term preferred by the *Restatement of Torts, Second*, instead of the former "ultra-hazardous".

[4] (1868) L.R. 3 H.L. 330.

[5] Winfield suggested ("The Myth of Absolute Liability" (1926) 42 L.Q.R. 37, 51) that "strict" was a better term than "absolute" in view of the admitted exceptions to the rule, and this is now recognised as the appropriate term in English law: *Read* v. *J. Lyons & Co.* [1945] K.B. 216, 226.

[6] *St. Anne's Well Brewery Co.* v. *Roberts* (1928) 140 L.T. 1, 6; *Hale* v. *Jennings Bros.* [1938] 1 All E.R. 579, 582, 584; *Read* v. *J. Lyons & Co. Ltd.* [1945] K.B. 216, 247; *Vaughn* v. *Halifax-Dartmouth Bridge Commission* (1961) 29 D.L.R. (2d) 523, 525.

[7] John Rylands and Jehu Horrocks.

[8] They seem to have been in occupation as lessees.

employees of the defendants) this fact was not discovered, and the danger caused by it was not guarded against. When the reservoir was filled, the water escaped down the shaft and thence into the plaintiff's mine, which it flooded, causing damage estimated at £937.

In a judgment which has always been recognised as one of the masterpieces of the Law Reports, Blackburn J., for the Court of Exchequer Chamber, held the defendants (who had not themselves been negligent) liable, and the House of Lords dismissed their appeal. Blackburn J. said[9]:

> "The question of law therefore arises, What is the obligation which the law casts on a person who, like the defendants, lawfully brings on his land something which, though harmless while it remains there, will naturally do mischief if it escapes out of his land? It is agreed on all hands that he must take care to keep in that which he has brought on the land and keeps there, in order that it may not escape and damage his neighbours: but the question arises whether the duty which the law casts upon him under such circumstances is an absolute duty to keep it at his peril or is, as the majority of the Court of Exchequer have thought, merely a duty to take all reasonable and prudent precautions in order to keep it in, but no more . . .
>
> We think that the true rule of law is that the person who for his own purposes brings on his lands and collects and keeps there anything likely to do mischief if it escapes, must keep it in at his peril, and if he does not do so is prima facie answerable for all the damage which is the natural consequence of its escape. He can excuse himself by showing that the escape was owing to the plaintiff's default; or, perhaps, that the escape was the consequence of *vis major* or the act of God; but as nothing of the sort exists here, it is unnecessary to inquire what excuse would be sufficient."[10]

§ 13.2. Origin and Nature of Rule[11]

It is important to distinguish between the immediate and the more remote origins of the rule in *Rylands* v. *Fletcher*.

Immediate origins

The fundamental phrase in Sir Colin Blackburn's judgment is that which runs: "the person who for his own purposes brings on his lands and collects and keeps there anything likely to do mischief if it escapes." The basis of liability is the artificial accumulation of things

---

[9] *Fletcher* v. *Rylands* (1866) L.R. 1 Ex. 265, 279.

[10] This sentence is significant: it shows that Blackburn J. himself recognised the possibility of exceptions to his general rule, so that liability may be strict but not absolute: see note 5, above.

[11] Newark, "Non-Natural User and *Rylands* v. *Fletcher*" (1961) 24 M.L.R. 557; Prosser, *Topics*, Chap. III; Linden, "Whatever Happened to *Rylands* v. *Fletcher*?" in Klar (ed.), *Studies in Canadian Tort Law* (1978), p. 287; Simpson, "Legal Liability for Bursting Reservoirs: The Historical context of *Rylands* v. *Fletcher*" (1984) 13 J.L.S. 209.

not in or on the land by the ordinary course of nature. This can be clearly seen if we distinguish three cases of damage done by water:

(i) rain falls on the defendant's land, and the resultant water passes off by natural gravitation on to the plaintiff's premises. The defendant is not responsible, as there is no liability under *Rylands* v. *Fletcher* for things naturally on the land1[12];

(ii) water accumulates itself on the defendant's land in the ordinary course of nature, and is released on to the plaintiff's land by the defendant carrying on his normal operations in a reasonable way. Thus in *Smith* v. *Kenrick*[13] it was held that the plaintiff had no cause of action when water which had accumulated itself in a natural pool or reservoir flowed into the plaintiff's mine as a result of the ordinary mining operations of the defendant; and

(iii) water is accumulated artificially by the defendant for his own purposes and then flows on to the plaintiff's land. Here the defendant is liable. The distinction between the *Smith* v. *Kenrick* type of case and the *Rylands* v. *Fletcher* type of case is that between the escape of water naturally present on the defendant's land and the escape of water artificially accumulated there. The reasons of policy for such a distinction were clearly stated by Blackburn J.:

> "It seems but reasonable and just that the neighbour, who has brought something on his own property which was not naturally there, harmless to others so long as it is confined to his own property, but which he knows to be mischievous if it gets on his neighbour's, should be obliged to make good the damage which ensues if he does not succeed in confining it to his own property. But for his act in bringing it there no mischief could have occurred, and it seems but just that he should at his peril keep it there so that no mischief may accrue, or answer for the natural and anticipated consequences. And upon authority, this we think is established to be the law whether the things so brought be beasts, or water, or filth, or stenches."

Remoter origins of the rule

(i) *Historical*

The historical background of the rule in *Rylands* v. *Fletcher* was fourfold. In early law a landowner had four remedies against his neighbour whose use of his land injuriously affected him in the exclusive enjoyment of his property; the action of trespass where the injury was direct, the assize of nuisance in which the primary object of the proceedings was abatement, the action upon the case "upon the custom of the realm" for harm done by the spread of fire, and the action of cattle-trespass. To none of these actions (except perhaps that for the escape of fire[14]) was it a good defence to prove that the defendant was without

---

[12] This always used to be considered indisputable, but the law appears to be changing with regard to a defendant's liability for things naturally on his land; see below, § 13.6.

[13] (1849) 7 C.B. 515.

[14] See below, § 13.11.

fault. Blackburn J. did not intend to make new law[15] in *Rylands* v. *Fletcher*; he made a generalisation which covered the cases of absolute liability which had survived the general "moralisation" of the law in the eighteenth and nineteenth centuries. In the language of Wigmore, these cases of liability without fault "wandered about, unhoused and unshepherded, except for a casual attention, in the pathless fields of jurisprudence, until they were met by the master-mind of Mr. Justice Blackburn, who guided them to the safe fold where they have since rested. In a sentence epochal in its consequences this judge coordinated them all in their true category."[16]

(ii) *Social*

Some attention has also been given to the social or economic background of the case. No doubt the decision (like all decisions) is to some extent rooted in the society which gave it birth,[17] but there seems no foundation for the belief that Sir Colin Blackburn and the ten other judges who took part in the three stages of the case were influenced, consciously or unconsciously, by a desire to propitiate the dominant landed gentry of the time, who, it is alleged, regarded the right of exclusive dominion over the land as paramount to its commercial exploitation.[18] The decision has also been attributed to the growth of collectivism,[19] but there is no real evidence for this hypothesis either.

The future

The rule in *Rylands* v. *Fletcher* has been narrowly interpreted by the courts[20] and has not in practice been widely applied outside the context, largely influenced by the law of nuisance, in which it was first developed.[21] Today, however, the extension of strict liability to cover, on a less restrictive basis, things and activities which involve special danger (*i.e.* a more than ordinary risk of accident or a risk of more than

---

[15] This was Blackburn J.'s own opinion: "I wasted much time in the preparation of the judgment in *Rylands* v. *Fletcher* if I did not succeed in showing that the law held to govern it had been law for at least 300 years"; *Ross* v. *Fedden* (1872) 26 L.T. 966, 968.

[16] "Responsibility for Tortious Acts" (1894) 7 Harv.L.Rev. 441, 454. But Lord Simon has said that "it appears to me logically unnecessary and historically incorrect to refer to all these instances as deduced from one common principle." *Read* v. *Lyons* [1947] A.C. 156, 167.

[17] See the shrewd comment from Texas in *Turner* v. *Big Lake Oil Co.* (1936) 128 Tex. 155, 96 S.W. (2d) 221, quoted below, § 13.4.

[18] This was the view put forward by Bohlen (*Studies*, pp. 368–369), but effectively criticised by Molloy, "*Fletcher* v. *Rylands*—A Re-Examination of Juristic Origins" (1941) 9 U. Chi.L.Rev. 266 and Pound, "The Economic Interpretation and The Law of Torts," (1940) 53 Harv.L.Rev. 365, 383. It might be added that Rylands and Horrocks had developed their mill and reservoir with the consent of their lessor, the Earl of Wilton—a member of the family of Grosvenor, famous not only for the extent of their acres but also for the efficient commercial development of them.

[19] Dicey, *Law and Public Opinion in England* (2nd ed.), pp. 259 *et seq.*; see criticism by Buxton, "The Negligent Nuisance" (1966) 8 Malaya L.R. 1, 7.

[20] See, especially, *Read* v. *Lyons* (J.) & Co. [1947] A.C. 156.

[21] For an interesting discussion of a respect in which the narrow interpretation of the rule represented a lost opportunity see Spencer, "Motor-cars and the Rule in *Rylands* v. *Fletcher*" [1983] C.L.J. 65.

ordinary damage if accidents in fact result) would be regarded by many as highly desirable. As has already been pointed out, the Pearson Commission recommended[22] that there should be a statutory scheme of strict liability with power to add by statutory instrument new things or processes to that list.

Relationship to other torts

(i) *Nuisance*

Historically the relationship between the rule in *Rylands* v. *Fletcher*, and the law of nuisance, is clearly a close one. The authorities relied on by the plaintiffs in the case itself were almost entirely drawn from this branch of the law.[23] Bramwell B., dissenting in the Court of Exchequer, thought that the defendants could be held liable in nuisance,[24] and his judgment was effectively adopted by Blackburn J. on appeal. He could see no distinction between the man "whose mine is flooded by the water from his neighbour's reservoir" and the man "whose cellar is invaded by the filth of his neighbour's privy, or habitation is made unhealthy by the fumes and noisome vapours of his neighbour's alkali works": each "is damnified without any fault of his own."[25] He proceeded to compare the present case with several actions which had been brought "against the occupiers of some alkali works at Liverpool for the damage alleged to be caused by the chlorine fumes of their works"— clearly actions in nuisance. Those occupiers had been held liable. "There is no difference in this respect between chlorine and water; both will, if they escape, do damage, the one by scorching, the other by drowning."[26]

In the House of Lords, Lord Cairns L.C. fully accepted Blackburn J.'s judgment in the Exchequer Chamber and held that the case was indistinguishable from *Baird* v. *Williamson*,[27] a nuisance case. The case was to be distinguished from *Smith* v. *Kenrick*,[28] another nuisance case in which the defendants had avoided liability because of a defence of "ordinary use." To construct a reservoir was not an ordinary use, just as pumping up water was not an ordinary use in *Baird's* case[29]; consequently, the ordinary principles of nuisance applied, and the defendants were liable for allowing the water "to pass off into the close of the plaintiff."[30] Lord Cranworth's judgment was also expressly founded on nuisance principles.

The preponderance of subsequent interpretation also, it is submitted, supports the view that the rule in *Rylands* v. *Fletcher* is but an example of a nuisance action. Windeyer J. in the High Court of Australia in *Ben-*

---

[22] Cmnd. 7054, Chap. 31.
[23] *Smith* v. *Kenrick* (1849) 7 C.B. 515; *Aldred's Case* (1610) 9 Co. Rep. 576; *Tenant* v. *Goldwin* (1704) 2 Ld. Raym. 1089; *Williams* v. *Groucott* (1863) 4 B. & S. 149, 157; 122 E.R. 416, 419.
[24] 3 H. & C. 774, 789.
[25] (1866) L.R. 1. Ex. 265, 280.
[26] *Ibid*. 285–286.
[27] 15 C.B.(N.S.) 376; 143 E.R. 831.
[28] (1849) 7. C.B. 515.
[29] 15 C.B.(N.S.) 376; 143 E.R. 831.
[30] L.R. 3 H.L. 330, 339.

ning v. *Wong*[31] saw the doctrine as merely "a special form of the ancient cause of action for nuisance." He said further that the distinctions tabulated for students of law by the writers of textbooks "between actionable nuisances of traditional kinds and *Rylands* v. *Fletcher* actions" were not fundamental. Sir John Salmond, in his judicial capacity, held that "the actual or apprehended escape into [the plaintiff's] land from that of the defendant of a dangerous thing kept by the defendant—namely an artificial heap of soil" gave rise to an action in nuisance.[32] In *Read* v. *J. Lyons & Co. Ltd.*, the doctrine of *Rylands* v. *Fletcher* was said to derive "from a conception of mutual duties of adjoining or neighbouring landowners" and as "in harmony with a strictly analogous branch of the law, the law of nuisance."[33] There are also many other cases to like effect.[34]

(ii) *Trespass*

Some judges,[35] have regarded the action under the rule in *Rylands* v. *Fletcher* as in the nature of trespass, the underlying idea being that a man releases some force brought by him onto his own property, which gets beyond his control and injures his neighbour. But the opposite view was favoured in *Rigby* v. *Chief Constable of Northamptonshire*,[36] since in most cases under the rule the injury done to the plaintiff is consequential and not direct.

(iii) *Negligence*

Other writers[37] have regarded the rule in *Rylands* v. *Fletcher* as a branch of the law of negligence. But it is perfectly clear that a man may be liable under the rule even though neither he nor anyone else has been guilty of any negligence in allowing the escape.[38] It is equally clear that he may be liable though he has done no unlawful act in introducing the dangerous thing onto his land. In practice the importance of the distinction can be seen from the fact that if the plaintiff states his claim on the principle of *Rylands* v. *Fletcher* he need plead only the escape; whereas if he states his claim in negligence he must plead and prove negligence. It has been suggested that these cases can be regarded as a

---

[31] (1969) 43 A.L.J.R. 467, 484; see too the judgment of Barwick C.J., especially at p. 471.

[32] *Knight* v. *Bolton* [1924] N.Z.L.R. 806, 808. "A heap of earth" was one of the very instances of liability cited by Blackburn J. And see the 6th ed. of this book, pp. 257 *et seq.*, where *Rylands* v. *Fletcher* was clearly seen as coming within the law of nuisance.

[33] [1947] A.C. 156, 173, 182.

[34] *Rickards* v. *Lothian* [1913] A.C. 263, 275; *Eastern and South African Telegraph Co.* v. *Cape Town Tramways Co.* [1902] A.C. 381, 394; *Musgrove* v. *Pandelis* [1919] 2 K.B. 43, 47, 49, 51; *J. P. Porter Co. Ltd.* v. *Bell* [1955] 1 D.L.R. 62, 64; *Shell-Mex & B.P. Ltd.* v. *Belfast Corporation* [1952] N.I. 72, 75.

[35] *e.g.* Stirling L.J. in *Foster* v. *Warblington U.C.* [1906] 1 K.B. 648, 672; Parker J. in *Jones* v. *Llanwrst U.C.* [1911] 1 Ch. 393, 403 and Astbury J. in *Hoare & Co.* v. *McAlpine* [1923] 1 Ch. 167, 175.

[36] [1985] 1 W.L.R. 1242, 1255. (Taylor J.)

[37] Thayer "Liability Without Fault" (1916) 29 Harv.L.Rev. 801.

[38] *Att.-Gen.* v. *Cory Bros.* [1921] A.C. 521, 539, 544. It is no defence that the defendant did not know of the dangerous character of that which he was keeping: it is no defence that there was no reason why he should know: *West* v. *Bristol Tramways* [1908] 2 K.B. 14, 16.

special instance of negligence, where the law exacts a degree of diligence so high as to amount practically to a guarantee of safety.[39] But, if the concept of "duty of care" is to be meaningful, the defendant must always have the opportunity of meeting the standard required; it must never be the case that, because damage has occurred, one *automatically* assumes that the duty has been breached. By contrast, in *Rylands* v. *Fletcher*, care or the lack of it continues to be an irrelevant factor.[40] On the other hand, the apparent reluctance of the courts in recent years to look with favour upon strict liability has in some cases led to defences being held available to a *Rylands* v. *Fletcher* action in such a way as to produce, in certain circumstances, a situation in which "the claim based on *Rylands* v. *Fletcher* merges into the claim in negligence."[41]

§ 13.3. THE PLAINTIFF

Who may sue

This problem was much discussed by the House of Lords in *Read* v. *J. Lyons & Co. Ltd.*[42] The appellant was injured by an explosion in the respondents' munitions factory while performing her duties as an inspector of the Ministry of Supply. She neither alleged nor proved negligence on the respondents' part. "Boldly she averred and by her counsel maintained the averment before this House, that he who lawfully carries on the business of manufacturing high-explosive shells upon his premises, is, without proof of negligence, liable to any person lawfully upon those premises who suffers damage by reason of an explosion. For, she said, high-explosive shells are 'dangerous things' and the respondents knew it."[43] Her contention was unanimously repudiated. That high-explosive shells are "dangerous things" was admitted, but "the strict liability recognised by this House to exist in *Rylands* v. *Fletcher* is conditioned by two elements which I may call the condition of "escape" from the land of something likely to do mischief if it escapes, and the condition of "non-natural use" of the land.[44] The

---

[39] *Donoghue* v. *Stevenson* [1932] A.C. 562, 611–612; *Haseldine* v. *Daw & Sons Ltd.* [1941] 2 K.B. 343, 355–356.

[40] *West* v. *Bristol Tramways* [1908] 2 K.B. 14, 16; *Att.-Gen.* v. *Cory Brothers* [1921] 1 A.C. 521, 539, 544; *Benning* v. *Wong*, 43 A.L.J.R. 467, 487.

[41] *Perry* v. *Kendricks Transport* [1956] 1 W.L.R. 85 (Jenkins L.J.).

[42] [1947] A.C. 156, 170. "Nothing could be simpler than the facts in this appeal; nothing more far-reaching than the discussion of fundamental legal principles to which it has given rise": Lord Macmillan.

[43] [1947] A.C. 156, 179, *per* Lord Simonds. In the Court of Appeal her case was based not only on the rule in *Rylands* v. *Fletcher* but also on absolute liability for the "miscarriage of ultra-hazardous activities carefully carried on" formulated in 3 *Restatement of the Law of Torts* s.519. The Court held that English law did not recognise this doctrine. "Ultra-hazardous" has now been replaced by the phrase "extraordinarily dangerous" in the *Restatement*.

[44] [1947] A.C. 156, 167, *per* Lord Simon. The need for an "escape" was re-emphasised in *J. Doltis Ltd.* v. *Isaac Braithwaite & Sons Ltd.* [1957] 1 Lloyd's Rep. 522.

House reserved its opinion on the question of non-natural use,[45] for the case could be disposed of by denying that there had been an escape. The rule in *Rylands* v. *Fletcher* was said to be no more than "a principle applicable between occupiers in respect of their land."[46] Lord Simonds held that the position was exactly analogous with the law of nuisance, where only he who had suffered an invasion of some proprietary or other interest in land had a lawful claim.[47]

It is not suggested that the action in *Rylands* v. *Fletcher* is limited to adjacent freeholders; the action in nuisance is not so limited. An "occupier" has been defined as one who has "some right or interest in land beyond that of a mere gratuitous licensee."[48] Thus, lessees[49] and licensees in exclusive occupation, including occupation of the sub-soil,[50] can maintain an action in *Rylands* v. *Fletcher* as in nuisance. Dicta in two English decisions favour the view that even a non-occupier, who has no interest in the land of any kind at all, can invoke the rule.[51] It is submitted, however, that the better view (recently reaffirmed in New Zealand) is that "liability under *Rylands* v. *Fletcher* requires proof of interference with the use of the land of another."[52] If *Rylands* v. *Fletcher* were seen as a general action to redress harm caused by extra-hazardous activities it would obviously be illogical to insist on the plaintiff's having an interest in land. But, rightly or wrongly, the courts refused to extend the doctrine very far beyond its historical confines,[53] and it is now far too late to do so. Coherent reform of the law on strict liability can now only be achieved by legislation; the recommendations of the

---

[45] For this, see below, § 13.4.

[46] *Ibid.* 173, *per* Lord Macmillan, 186 *per* Lord Uthwatt. But it appears that the *defendant* need not necessarily be the occupier of the land *from which* the escape takes place, at least if it is from the highway: *Rigby* v. *Chief Constable of Northamptonshire* [1985] 1 W.L.R. 1242, 1255. See also *Read* v. *Lyons* [1947] A.C. 156, 183, *per* Lord Simonds.

[47] *Ibid.* 182. Weak *obiter dicta* to the contrary in earlier cases must be considered overruled by these unequivocal speeches from their Lordships: *Miles* v. *Forest Rock Granite Co. (Leicestershire) Ltd.* (1918) 34 T.L.R. 500; *Shiffman* v. *The Grand Priory in the British Realm of the Venerable Order of the Hospital of St John of Jerusalem* [1936] 1 All E.R. 557 (both actually decided in negligence). Certainly neither case is binding on any court now: *cf. Halsey* v. *Esso Petroleum Co. Ltd.* [1961] 2 All E.R. 145, 152.

[48] *Benning* v. *Wong*, 43 A.L.J.R. 467, 494, *per* Windeyer J. The plaintiff was an occupier, and the remarks of Barwick C.J. and Menzies J. were carefully so confined (*ibid.* 467, 477). Wider *obiter dicta* to the effect that, even had the plaintiff not been an occupier, he would still have been able to sue (*ibid.* 494) were not assented to by the other members of the High Court.

[49] *Farrer* v. *Nelson* (1885) 15 Q.B.D. 258; *Federic* v. *Perpetual Investments Ltd.* (1968) 2 D.L.R. (3d) 50, 52.

[50] *Hale* v. *Jennings Brothers* [1938] 1 All E.R. 579; *Charing Cross Electricity Supply Co.* v. *Hydraulic Power Co.* [1914] 3 K.B. 772; *Eastern and South African Telegraph Co.* v. *Cape Town Tramways Co.* [1902] A.C. 381; *Vaughn* v. *Halifax-Dartmouth Bridge Commission* (1961) 29 D.L.R. (2d) 523, 525 (licensee not in exclusive possession, therefore no action).

[51] *Perry* v. *Kendricks Transport Ltd.* [1956] 1 W.L.R. 85 (*obiter dicta* on this point, as case turned on defence of "act of a stranger"); *British Celanese Ltd.* v. *A. H. Hunt (Capacitors) Ltd.* [1969] 2 All E.R. 1252, 1258, *per* Lawton J. (again *obiter dicta*, as plaintiff was in fact occupier).

[52] *N.Z. Forest Products Ltd.* v. *O'Sullivan* [1974] N.Z.L.R. 80, 83.

[53] See § 13.2.

Pearson Commission, already referred to,[54] provide an example of the kind of approach which could be adopted.

Personal injuries

In a number of cases, including several decided by the Court of Appeal, it has been held or stated that damages for personal injury may be recovered[55] under the rule in *Rylands* v. *Fletcher*. On the other hand several members of the House of Lords in *Read* v. *Lyons* appeared to doubt whether such an award was possible,[56] and the analogy with private nuisance, in which no case actually awarding such damages apparently exists, would also point against recovery. But as far as damage to chattels is concerned, Blackburn J. himself allowed an occupier to recover for such damage under the rule in *Rylands* v. *Fletcher*[57] although he was equally clear that a non-occupier had no such claim.[58] A possible view is that a similar position holds good with respect to personal injuries, *i.e.* that the distinction turns on the character of the claimant and not on the character of his injuries. Thus the High Court of Australia has recently held that an occupier may recover for personal injuries.[59] Nevertheless the fact that no plaintiff in England appears actually to have received such an award in any case reported since *Read* v. *Lyons*, combined with what might be regarded as the arbitrariness of allowing occupiers of land in certain circumstances to enjoy a strict liability regime for the recovery of personal injuries when other plaintiffs have to prove negligence, favours the conclusion that such damages are not recoverable. It is submitted that this is indeed the better view. Of course the proposed statutory reforms in this area proposed by the Pearson Commission would, if implemented, be expressly intended to provide compensation for personal injuries.[60]

§ 13.4. NON-NATURAL USE OF LAND[61]

Blackburn J.'s statement, basing liability on the defendant's artificial accumulation of the thing in question, was expressly approved in the

---

[54] *Supra*, § 13.2.

[55] See, *e.g. Hale* v. *Jennings Bros.* [1938] 1 All E.R. 579; *Perry* v. *Kendrick's Transport* [1956] 1 W.L.R. 85.

[56] See [1947] A.C. 156, 173 (Lord Macmillan), 180–181 (Lord Simmonds), 178 (Lord Porter).

[57] *Jones* v. *Festinog Ry. Co.* (1868) L.R. 3 Q.B. 733. A similar decision is *Halsey* v. *Esso Petroleum Co. Ltd.* [1961] 1 W.L.R. 683. See also *Vaughn* v. *Halifax-Dartmouth Bridge Commission* (1961) 29 D.L.R. (2d) 523 and *British Celanese Ltd.* v. *A. H. Hunt (Capacitors) Ltd.* [1969] 2 All E.R. 1252.

[58] *Cattle* v. *Stockton Waterworks Co.* (1875) L.R. 10 Q.B. 453; followed by Widgery J. in *Weller* v. *Foot and Mouth Disease Research Institute* [1966] 1 Q.B. 569.

[59] *Benning* v. *Wong* (1969) 43 A.L.J.R. 467.

[60] Cmnd. 7054–I, para. 1651.

[61] See Stallybrass, "Dangerous Things and Non-Natural User of Land" (1929) 3 Camb.L.J. 376; Newark, "Non-Natural User and *Rylands* v. *Fletcher*" (1961) 24 M.L.R. 557.

House of Lords.[62] But difficulty has arisen because Lord Cairns, probably unconsciously,[63] laid down another principle, distinguishing the natural from the non-natural user of land, and holding that in the latter case only was the liability absolute. This is to substitute a different principle from that adopted by Blackburn J. Its advantage is that it converts a rigid into a flexible rule, and enables the court by determining what is or is not a natural user of land to give effect to its own view of social and economic needs.[64] Its disadvantage is that it has produced a bewildering series of decisions on the meaning of non-natural use. What is the natural use of land? Is it natural to build a house on it,[65] or to light a fire?[66] Is it natural to keep cattle on land?[67] This must be one of the oldest methods of using land but in Blackburn J.'s view it is quite logical to impose strict liability[68] because the cattle have been artificially collected. But in Lord Cairns' view it is necessary to say that cattle-keeping is non-natural. Again, it has been held not to be natural to spray crops with herbicide from an aircraft[69]: the activity of destroying weeds is as old as nature itself, but it seems odd today to insist that the hoe should be the only method used. Finally, since, contrary to earlier authorities, it is now the law that there is liability in nuisance for things naturally on the land,[70] the distinction is even less helpful.

Although such unreal and impracticable distinctions are not creditable to the development of English Law,[71] there is an abundance of authority in support of this qualification upon the generality of the

---

[62] (1868) L.R. 3 H.L. 330, 340. Only two Law Lords, Lord Cairns and Lord Cranworth (who died seven days after judgment had been delivered on July 17) are reported as having been present, although three peers are required to form a quorum in the House of Lords. No satisfactory explanation of this curious fact has been found: Heuston, Note (1970) 86 L.Q.R. 160. But the importance of the decision as an example of judge-made law is unquestionable. As J. M. Landis wrote (*Harvard Legal Essays* (1934) p. 213): "Had Parliament in 1868 adopted a similar rule, no such permeating results to the general body of Anglo-American law would have ensued. All this would be true, though the Act had been preceded by a thorough and patient inquiry by a Royal Commission into the business of storing large volumes of water and its concomitant risks, and even though the same Lords who approved Mr. Fletcher's claim had in voting 'aye' upon the measure given reasons identical with those contained in their judgments."

[63] Lord Cairns merely seems to have been attempting to restate in his own words Blackburn J.'s point that it was the accumulation or collection by the defendant which was the basis of liability. What Blackburn J. had in mind was the distinction between "natural water" and "artificial water," which is not the same as the distinction between ordinary and extraordinary user.

[64] It has even been said that there are two rules in *Rylands v. Fletcher*: *Porter (J.P.) Co. Ltd. v. Bell* [1955] 1 D.L.R. 62, 66.

[65] Yes, according to *Wilkins v. Leighton* [1932] 2 Ch. 106, 111.

[66] Yes, if it is an ordinary household fire in a grate; *J. Doltis Ltd. v. Isaac Braithwaite & Sons Ltd.* [1957] 1 Lloyd's Rep. 522.

[67] Even though not indigenous to this country: *e.g.* Friesian cattle: *Western Silver Fox Ranch v. Ross and Cromarty C.C.*, 1940 S.C. 601.

[68] As was done in *Noonan v. Hartnett* (1950) I.L.T.R. 41.

[69] *Michalchuk v. Ratke* (1966) 57 D.L.R. (2d) 269.

[70] See *Leakey v. National Trust* [1980] Q.B. 485.

[71] *Mason v. Levy Auto Parts Ltd.* [1967] 2 Q.B. 530, 543.

rule,[72] in particular the decision of the Privy Council in *Rickards* v. *Lothian*,[73] which was itself expressly approved in *Read* v. *Lyons*.[74] It has been held to be a natural use of land to bring water into a cistern in a house,[75] but not industrial water (*i.e.* water under pressure),[76] or water stored in bulk, as in *Rylands* v. *Fletcher* itself.[77] So the laying of gas pipes by a landlord for the supply of gas to dwelling-houses owned by him is a natural and not a non-natural use of his property,[78] and so is wiring for domestic use or for purposes of trade,[79] or the manufacture of electrical or electronic components.[80] On the other hand, there is some authority that electricity[81] is within the principle of *Rylands* v. *Fletcher*, at least when carried in bulk as distinct from use for ordinary domestic purposes.[82] So also within the principle are the collection in a sewer of a large quantity of noxious and inherently dangerous sewage,[83] or the storage of a motor-vehicle with a tank full of petrol in a garage,[84] or even with a tank which has been emptied.[85] It is probably not a non-natural use of land to make munitions on it, at any rate when it is done "at the government's request in time of war for the purpose of helping to defeat the enemy."[86]

"Extraordinary," "exceptional," "abnormal," are words that are sometimes used in substitution for "non-natural" and they suggest the true principle underlying the doctrine. It is a question of fact, subject to

---

[72] See the cases cited in 3 Camb.L.J. 390–397, and add *Howard* v. *Furness Houlder* [1936] 2 All E.R. 786; *Tilley* v. *Stevenson* [1939] 4 All E.R. 207; *Hale* v. *Jennings Bros.* [1938] 1 All E.R. 584; *Eastern Asia Navigation Co. Ltd.* v. *Fremantle Harbour Trust Commissioners* (1951) 83 C.L.R. 353.

[73] [1913] A.C. 263.

[74] [1947] A.C. 156, 169, 186.

[75] *Rickards* v. *Lothian* [1913] A.C. 263; *Crown Diamond Paint Co. Ltd.* v. *Acadia Ltd.* [1952] 2 D.L.R. 541.

[76] *Charing Cross Electricity Supply Co.* v. *Hydraulic Power Co.* [1914] 3 K.B. 772. Contrast *Peters* v. *Prince of Wales Theatre Ltd.* [1943] K.B. 73.

[77] "This basis of the English rule is to be found in the meteorological conditions which obtain there. England is a pluvial country, where constant streams and abundant rains make the storage of water unnecessary for ordinary or general purposes. . . . In Texas we have conditions very different from those which obtain in England. . . . The country is almost without streams; and without the storage of water from rainfall in basins constructed for the purpose, or to hold waters pumped from the earth, the great livestock industry of West Texas must perish.": *Turner* v. *Big Lake Oil Co.* (1936) 128 Tex. 155, 96 S.W. (2d) 221, 225–226, *per* Cureton C.J.

[78] *Miller* v. *Addie & Son's Collieries*, 1934 S.C. 150.

[79] *Collingwood* v. *Home and Colonial Stores* [1936] 3 All E.R. 200.

[80] *British Celanese Ltd.* v. *A. H. Hunt (Capacitors) Ltd.* [1969] 1 W.L.R. 959.

[81] *National Telephone Co.* v. *Baker* [1893] 2 Ch. 186, approved (*obiter*) by Lord Simon of Glaisdale in *F.A. and A.B. Ltd.* v. *Lupton* [1972] A.C. 634, 659.

[82] *Northwestern Utilities* v. *London Guarantee Co.* [1936] A.C. 108.

[83] *Smeaton* v. *Ilford Corporation* [1954] Ch. 450, 472.

[84] *Musgrove* v. *Pandelis* [1919] 2 K.B. 43. But is it really a non-natural use of land to build a garage upon it? See *Collingwood* v. *Home and Colonial Stores* [1936] 3 All E.R. 200, 209; *Read* v. *J. Lyons & Co. Ltd.* [1947] A.C. 156, 176. And is there not a difference (recognised by the practice of insurance companies) between petrol in the tank of a car and petrol in a separate drum? So liability was rightly imposed in *Mulholland and Tedd Ltd.* v. *Baker* [1939] 3 All E.R. 253.

[85] *Perry* v. *Kendrick's Transport Ltd.* [1956] 1 W.L.R. 85.

[86] *Read* v. *J. Lyons & Co. Ltd.* [1947] A.C. 156, 169–170, 173–174.

a ruling of the judge whether the particular object can be dangerous or the particular use can be non-natural, and in deciding this question all the circumstances of the time and place and practice of mankind must be taken into consideration so that what might be regarded as dangerous or non-natural may vary according to those circumstances.[87] So today the collection of toxic waste on a rubbish tip, which escapes from it in solution in percolating water, and poisons water on the plaintiff's premises, is probably unlawful at common law[88] as well as by statute.[89]

§ 13.5. DANGEROUS THINGS

To what "things" does the rule in *Rylands* v. *Fletcher* apply? The language of Blackburn J. is very wide—"anything likely to do mischief if it escapes." Subsequent decisions have equated the expression with "dangerous things."[90] Most things are likely to do mischief if they escape, however, and an attempt to identify attributes which can be described as those of inherent dangerousness is likely to be as unproductive in this context as in the pre-*Donoghue* v. *Stevenson* law of negligence.[91] Certainly an examination of all the cases in which the rule in *Rylands* v. *Fletcher* has been held to apply does not carry us very far. Chemicals, fire and electricity are usually treated as falling under the rule; water, trees, chimney stacks and motor-cars sometimes do and sometimes do not come under it.

Foreseeability of harm

It would seem that it is necessary for the defendant to have knowledge, or means of knowledge, of the dangerous propensity. In *Rylands* v. *Fletcher* itself, Blackburn J. said that liability arose only if the thing brought on to the property was known to be mischievous.[92] In later cases based on the principle, the courts have held that knowledge of the harm was a pre-requisite of liability[93] and have used as a guide "the common experience of mankind."[94] Perhaps the most satisfactory interpretation of these expressions in modern terms is to treat the whole concept of "dangerousness" as but another way of saying that harm must have been in some sense foreseeable. That a thing is "dangerous" simply means that it is generally accepted as having the potential to cause damage[95] and that is equivalent to a finding that harm is a foreseeable consequence of its escaping. There is no reason in principle why a tort of strict liability (in the sense that negligence need not be

---

[87] *Read* v. *J. Lyons & Co. Ltd.* [1947] A.C. 156, 176, 188.
[88] *Disposal of Solid Toxic Wastes* (H.M.S.O. 1970, para. 117); *Gertsen* v. *Toronto Municipality* (1973) 41 D.L.R. (3d) 641.
[89] See below, § 13.10.
[90] See Stallybrass (1929) 3 Camb.L.J. 378; *Northwestern Utilities Ltd.* v. *London Guarantee Co.* [1936] A.C. 108, 118 and *Hale* v. *Jennings Bros.* [1938] 1 All E.R. 579.
[91] Above § 12.2.
[92] L.R. 1 Ex. 265, 280.
[93] *e.g. Imperial Furniture Pty. Ltd.* v. *Automatic Fire Sprinklers Ltd.* [1967] 1 N.S.W.R. 29, 38.
[94] *Crowhurst* v. *Amersham Burial Board* (1878) 4 Ex.D. 5, 12; *Sullivan* v. *Creed* [1904] 2 Ir.R. 317, 325; *West* v. *Bristol Tramways Co.* [1908] 2 K.B. 14, 21.
[95] *Mulholland & Tedd Ltd.* v. *Baker* [1939] 3 All E.R. 253, 256.

established) is incompatible with a concept of foreseeability.[96] The possibility of escape need not be foreseeable, nor can a defendant in *Rylands* v. *Fletcher* rely on a defence of reasonable precautions which might be available in a negligence action. Indeed in practice, since most things are likely to do mischief if they escape, a plaintiff able to prove escape and relevant damage is unlikely to fall at the "dangerous thing" hurdle. The fluid concept of non-natural user[97] of land, which is separate from that of the "dangerous thing," is much more likely to provide the defendant with a means of avoiding liability.

§ 13.6. Things Naturally on Land

It was once thought that a defendant could not be liable even in nuisance if the thing which escaped was the product of natural forces or had accumulated itself on the defendant's land. Thus in *Giles* v. *Walker*[98] it was held that the occupier of land was not liable when he ploughed up forest land and in consequence a large crop of thistles sprang up and the thistledown was blown onto the neighbouring land.[99] But in *Leakey* v. *National Trust*[1] it was held that developments in negligence and nuisance have eroded the decision in *Giles* v. *Walker*. Such a defendant may now be held liable in negligence[2] or in nuisance.[3]

In theory this is presumably the position today under *Rylands* v. *Fletcher* as well. It must be remembered, however, that to have things naturally on land will prima facie constitute an ordinary and reasonable, as distinct from non-natural, use of land for the purposes of the rule. A defendant may, however, incur liability in nuisance for their escape unless his failure to prevent it was reasonable in all the circumstances.[4]

§ 13.7. Where the Plaintiff Consents or Defaults

The *Rylands* v. *Fletcher* principle is subject to a number of important exceptions, there being particular classes of cases in which the occupier is either not liable at all, or not liable in the absence of negligence. When stated without the exceptions, it is a rule of absolute liability, but there are so many exceptions to it that it has been said to be doubtful whether there is much of the rule left.[5] The rule is not applicable to the escape of things brought or kept upon his premises by the defendant with the consent of the plaintiff. In such cases the defendant is not

---

[96] Carroll, 8 Ir.Jur. 208, 222–223.

[97] Above, § 13.4.

[98] (1890) 24 Q.B.D. 656.

[99] "It may be that the court was disinclined to regard thistledown as sufficiently noxious to be dignified as a nuisance, and in 1890 agriculture was perhaps the least regarded of British industries.": *Davey* v. *Harrow Corporation* [1958] 1 Q.B. 60, 72, *per curiam*.

[1] [1980] Q.B. 485.

[2] *French* v. *Auckland City Corporation* [1974] 1 N.Z.L.R. 340 (decision same whether in nuisance or negligence).

[3] *Morgan* v. *Khyatt* [1964] 1 W.L.R. 475.

[4] See above, Chap. 5.

[5] *St. Anne's Well Brewery Co.* v. *Roberts* (1928) 140 L.T. 1, 6.

liable except for negligence.[6] Although not limited to such cases,[7] this exception finds its chief application in those situations in which the different storeys of a building are in the occupation of different persons, and the occupant of a lower storey complains of the damage done by the escape of water from an upper storey. The water has been collected or brought there for the mutual benefit and with the express or implied consent of both parties; there is therefore no sufficient reason why the risk of accident should lie upon the upper rather than upon the lower occupant, and the only duty is one of reasonable care.[8] The same principle would doubtless apply to an escape of gas or any other deleterious substance[9] which is there with the consent and for the mutual benefit of the occupants. In most of these cases the benefit of the water or other thing is common to both parties, but the mutual benefit, though an important element in showing that there was consent, is not decisive. It has been said that the exception really depends upon the fact that the defendant has taken the premises as they are and must put up with the consequences.[10] But it is hard to reconcile this assertion with the established rule that it is no defence that the plaintiff came to the nuisance.[11]

Default

The rule is not applicable where the escape was owing to the plaintiff's default, as was specifically recognised by Blackburn J. himself.[12] Again, if the plaintiff is a trespasser on land he cannot complain of the things he may find there, nor if he goes out of his way to encounter danger can he blame the defendant for any harm he may suffer.[13] So also where the damage would not have occurred but for some special or non-natural user of the plaintiff's property the defendant will not be liable under this rule.[14]

§ 13.8. The Act of a Stranger

The rule in *Rylands* v. *Fletcher* is not applicable to damage done by the act of a stranger. Thus if a trespasser lights a fire on my land I am not liable if it burns my neighbour's property,[15] unless with knowledge or

---

[6] *Att.-Gen.* v. *Cory Bros. & Co.* [1921] 1 A.C. 521, 539.

[7] *Kiddle* v. *City Business Properties Ltd.* [1942] 1 K.B. 269, 274.

[8] *Akerib* v. *Booth Ltd.* [1960] 1 W.L.R. 454, 458 (reversed on another ground [1961] 1 W.L.R. 367). Since claims will therefore fail in the absence of negligence it follows that "Like 'every dog is allowed his first bite' so every basin is allowed its first overflow": *Hawkins* v. *Dhawan and Mishiku* [1987] 2 E.G.L.R. 157, 158.

[9] *Collingwood* v. *Home and Colonial Stores* [1936] 3 All E.R. 200 (domestic electric wiring).

[10] *Prosser (A.) & Son Ltd.* v. *Levy* [1955] 1 W.L.R. 1224.

[11] See above Chap. 5.

[12] *Fletcher* v. *Rylands* (1868) L.R. 1 Ex. 265, 279–280; quoted above, § 13.1.

[13] *Postmaster-General* v. *Liverpool Corporation* [1923] A.C. 587. In *Miles* v. *Forest Rock Granite Co.* (1918) 34 T.L.R. 500, the Court of Appeal appear to have held that a plaintiff who persisted in walking along a highway in spite of warnings of a coming explosion from blasting operations and was injured by a piece of stone was none the less able to recover. *Sed quaere.*

[14] *Eastern and South African Telegraph Co.* v. *Cape Town Tramways* [1902] A.C. 381; *Western Silver Fox Ranch* v. *Ross and Cromarty County Council*, 1940 S.C. 601.

[15] *Balfour* v. *Barty-King* [1957] 1 Q.B. 496, 504.

presumed knowledge of its existence I have failed to extinguish it within a reasonable time.[16] So in *Box* v. *Jubb*[17] the defendants were held not responsible for damage done through an overflow from their reservoir, when that overflow was caused by an act of a third person who emptied his own reservoir into the stream which fed that of the defendant. And in *Rickards* v. *Lothian*[18] it was held by the Judicial Committee that the occupier of an upper storey of a block of flats was not liable for damage done to the occupier of a lower storey by the escape of water from a lavatory, when the escape was caused by the malicious act of a third person. In this context malicious means a conscious or deliberate[19] act which could not reasonably have been foreseen. It has been held that sky-larking at a fair is "just the kind of behaviour that ought to have been anticipated. People go there in a spirit of fun."[20] The onus is on the defendant to show affirmatively that the escape was due to the deliberate or conscious act of a stranger over whom he had no control and against whose acts he could not reasonably be expected to have taken precautions.[21]

But it should be noted that an occupier may be liable in negligence for the acts of strangers even though he escapes liability under the rule in *Rylands* v. *Fletcher*. When the stranger's act is of a kind which ought to have been anticipated and guarded against the occupier will be liable for a failure to take reasonable care. Thus in *Northwestern Utilities* v. *London Guarantee and Accident Co.*[22] the appellants, who were carrying gas at high pressure under the streets of Edmonton, Alberta, were held liable when an hotel insured by the respondents was destroyed owing to the escape of gas due to a leak caused by the operations of third persons, since those operations were conspicuous and ought to have been foreseen and guarded against. But "They left it all to chance,"[23] and were thereby guilty of negligence.[24]

It does not clearly appear, however, who is a stranger within the meaning of this rule. The term certainly includes a trespasser, and also any person who, without entering on the defendant's premises at all, wrongfully and without the defendant's authority causes the escape of dangerous things from those premises.[25] It is equally clear that the term stranger does not include any person employed or authorised by the

---

[16] *Goldman* v. *Hargrave* [1967] 1 A.C. 645.
[17] (1879) 4 Ex.D. 76.
[18] [1913] A.C. 263.
[19] *Northwestern Utilities* v. *London Guarantee Co.* [1936] A.C. 108, 119. Cf. *Dominion Natural Gas Co.* v. *Collins* [1909] A.C. 640, 647 ("the conscious act of another volition": Lord Dunedin); *Smith* v. *G.W. Ry.* (1926) 42 T.L.R. 391; *Philco Radio Ltd.* v. *Spurling* [1949] 2 All E.R. 882; *Perry* v. *Kendricks Transport Ltd.* [1956] 1 W.L.R. 85, 90.
[20] *Hale* v. *Jennings Bros.* [1938] 1 All E.R. 579, 585.
[21] *Northwestern Utilities* v. *London Guarantee Co.* [1936] A.C. 108, 120: *Prosser (A.) & Sons Ltd.* v. *Levy* [1955] 1 W.L.R. 1224.
[22] [1936] A.C. 108. See the article by Lord Wright (who delivered the judgment of the Judicial Committee) in his *Legal Essays*, Chap. 5, and Goodhart, "The Third Man" [1951] C.L.P. 177.
[23] [1936] A.C. 108, 127.
[24] *Shell-Mex and B.P. Ltd.* v. *Belfast Corporation* [1952] N.I. 72 is a similar case.
[25] *Box* v. *Jubb* (1879) 4 Ex.D. 76. It also includes an employee acting in a place to which he is forbidden access: *Stevens* v. *Woodward* (1881) 6 Q.B.D. 318, 321.

defendant to deal in any way with dangerous things on his land; for the acts of such a person, even though he is an independent contractor, and even though he acts in excess or disregard of his authority, the occupier is liable.[26] But what shall be said of persons lawfully upon the defendant's land with his permission, but without authority to bring upon it, or to deal with, dangerous things—for example, the members of his family, his employees, his guests, or licensees permitted to use the land? It is submitted that the occupier is liable for the acts of all such persons in bringing or keeping dangerous things on the premises, or in meddling with such things already on the premises[27] unless it can be said that in all the circumstances the occupier had no control over the activities of the person in question.[28]

§ 13.9. ACT OF GOD

Shortly after *Rylands* v. *Fletcher* itself was decided it was held that the rule which it embodied was not applicable to damage caused by the act of God. The authority for this limitation, the possibility of which was recognised by Blackburn J. himself in his judgment,[29] is the decision of the Court of Appeal in *Nichols* v. *Marsland*.[30] The defendant was in possession of certain artificial pools formed by damming a natural stream. The embankments and weirs were well and carefully constructed and were adequate for all ordinary occasions. A very violent storm, however—described by witnesses as the heaviest within human memory—broke down the embankments, and the rush of water down the stream carried away certain bridges, in respect of which damage the action was brought. It was held, notwithstanding *Rylands* v. *Fletcher*, that the defendant was not liable, inasmuch as the jury had found that there was no negligence on the part of anyone and that the accident was due directly to the act of God.

In *Greenock Corporation* v. *Caledonian Railway Co.*,[31] on the other hand, decided by the House of Lords on very similar facts, the defence was unsuccessful, even though rain fell in "a heavy, it may be an extraordinary and it may be an unprecedented, spate."[32] The two decisions are difficult to reconcile, and the later case in effect casts considerable doubt upon the correctness of the earlier.[33] Indeed *Nichols* v. *Marsland* is believed to be the only reported case in which act of God proved successful as a defence to an action under the rule in *Rylands* v. *Fletcher*. Moreover it has been powerfully argued that the duty of protection

---

[26] *Hale* v. *Jennings Bros.* [1938] 1 All E.R. 579, 583; *Balfour* v. *Barty-King* [1957] 1 Q.B. 496, 504.

[27] This may be inferred by analogy from such cases as *Beaulieu* v. *Finglam* (1401) Y.B. 2 Hen. IV, f. 18, pl. 6, and *Lawrence* v. *Jenkins* (1873) L.R. 8 Q.B. 274. But see *Whitmores Ltd.* v. *Stanford* [1909] Ch. 427, 438.

[28] *Perry* v. *Kendricks Transport Ltd.* [1956] 1 W.L.R. 85, 90; *Behrens* v. *Bertram Mills Circus Ltd.* [1957] 2 Q.B. 1, 22.

[29] *Fletcher* v. *Rylands* (1866) L.R. 1 Ex. 265, 280.

[30] (1876) 2 Ex. D. 1.

[31] [1917] A.C. 556.

[32] *Ibid.* 580.

[33] See [1917] A.C. 556, 575, 580–581.

imposed by the rule should not be limited to foreseeable events, otherwise there would be no difference between strict liability and negligence.[34] But erosion of strict liability in favour of the fault principle is evident in cases decided under other aspects of the rule, and a possible view is that the purpose of the defence of act of God has been taken over nowadays by the concept of foreseeability of harm. Nevertheless it would be premature to suppose that *Rylands* v. *Fletcher* has become indistinguishable from negligence in this respect. Paradoxically, in view of *Nichols* v. *Marsland* being regarded as having weakened the strict liability, it may be that the concept of act of God serves to highlight the difference, albeit only one of degree, between the two torts. In so far as the law admits of differing degrees of foreseeability,[35] it is submitted that *Rylands* v. *Fletcher* still differs from negligence in being more reluctant to admit that a natural occurrence was so freakishly rare that it should be permitted to exonerate a defendant on grounds of unforeseeability.[36] Those who create exceptional risks must be under a heavier duty with respect to extraordinary hazards.

§ 13.10. STATUTORY AUTHORITY

Sometimes a statute imposes strict liability for the escape of dangerous things, *e.g.* the Reservoirs Act 1975, in respect of accumulated water, or the Nuclear Installations Acts 1965 and 1969, in respect of the escape of ionising radiations.[37] Again an International Convention has attempted to regulate responsibility for oil pollution on the high seas.[38] The problem of toxic waste is a real one today. The basic statutory framework for pollution control is now to be found in the provisions of the Environmental Protection Act 1990. More generally, the relationship between statutes and the rule in *Rylands* v. *Fletcher* is obscured by the fact that Acts which authorise or require the performance of dangerous activities are often silent about the application of the rule. It has sometimes been said that a local authority exercising statutory duties (*e.g.* of sewage disposal) is altogether outside the rule in *Rylands* v *Fletcher*.[39] But in principle the better view would seem to be that local authorities, or other bodies exercising statutory powers or duties, are within the rule unless the statute expressly or impliedly exempts them. At the same time, however, it may well be right to construe the statute in a manner favourable to the defendant in such cases, and the courts indeed appear

---

[34] Goodhart [1951] C.L.P. 177.
[35] *cf. Overseas Tankship (U.K.) Ltd.* v. *Miller Steamship Co.: The Wagon Mound (No. 2)* [1967] 1 A.C. 617.
[36] *cf. per* Bramwell B. in *Ruck* v. *Williams* (1858) 3 H. & N. 308, 318.
[37] Note that s.12 channels liability on to the licensee of the site: no other person can be sued. The scope of the statutory liability was considered in *Merlin* v. *British Nuclear Fuels* [1990] 2 Q.B. 557.
[38] See Ingram, "Oil Pollution and *Rylands* v. *Fletcher*" (1971) 121 N.L.J. 183.
[39] See Denning L.J. in *Pride of Derby and Derbyshire Angling Association* v. *British Celanese* [1953] Ch. 149, 189. *Contra* Evershed M.R. at 176.

to adopt such a policy.[40] Thus in *Green* v. *Chelsea Waterworks Co.*[41] a main belonging to the defendant company burst, and the water flooded the plaintiff's premises. It was held by the Court of Appeal that the company, being authorised by Act of Parliament to lay the main, and having a statutory duty to maintain a continuous supply of water, and having been guilty of no negligence, was not liable in damages to the plaintiff.[42] The governing principle is that statutory powers are meant to be exercised. The defence of statutory authority is further considered below.[43]

§ 13.11. LIABILITY FOR FIRE[44]

At common law

Liability for damage done by the spread of fire was established many centuries before the rule in *Rylands* v. *Fletcher* was formulated. The usual remedy was trespass upon the case for negligently allowing one's fire to escape in contravention of the general custom of the realm. The allegation was that the defendant *tam negligenter custodivit ignem suum* that the plaintiff's property was burnt. Difficulty has arisen over both parts of this phrase.

Tam negligenter. Whatever this meant, it was not negligence in the modern sense.[45] There is some authority[46] that the common law held an occupier absolutely liable for damage done by fire, but also some authority the other way.[47] It is unlikely that the matter will ever need to be settled. The Act of 1774 clearly assumes that liability was not, but ought to be, based on fault.

Ignis suus. As there must also be an escape of the fire from the defendant's premises to some place or thing outside those premises,[48] the courts seem to be anxious to equate this form of liability with nuisance and *Rylands* v. *Fletcher.* So it has even been held that the defendant is liable in his capacity as occupier of premises, and not on the ground of ordinary negligence.[49] It must be remembered that more than one per-

---

[40] *Northwestern Utilities Ltd.* v. *London Guarantee and Accident Co.* [1936] A.C. 108; *Smeaton* v. *Ilford Corporation* [1954] Ch. 450 (but note that the successful defendant paid the plaintiff "a substantial sum" to abandon his appeal to the H.L.—*Law Journal* (1954), p. 619).

[41] (1894) 70 L.T. 547.

[42] See also *Dunne* v. *North-Western Gas Board* [1964] 2 Q.B. 906.

[43] See below, § 22.7.

[44] See Newark, "The Accidental Fires Act (Northern Ireland)" (1945) 6 N.I.L.Q. 134 (the scope of which is wider than the title of the article suggests); Ogus, "Vagaries in Liability for the Escape of Fire" [1969] C.L.J. 104.

[45] *Hargrave* v. *Goldman* (1964) 110 C.L.R. 24, 56.

[46] *Collingwood* v. *Home and Colonial Stores Ltd.* [1936] 3 All E.R. 200, 203; *Mulholland and Tedd Ltd.* v. *Baker* [1939] 3 All E.R. 253, 255; and above, § 13.2.

[47] *Turberville* v. *Stampe* (1697) 1 Ld. Raym. 264 (in which Holt C.J. clearly assumed that liability was based on negligence); *Commissioner for Railways* v. *Wise Bros. Pty.* (1947) 75 C.L.R. 59.

[48] *Doltis Ltd.* v. *Braithwaite Ltd.* [1957] 1 Lloyd's Rep. 522; and above, § 13.3.

[49] *Sturge* v. *Hackett* [1962] 1 W.L.R. 1257.

son may be the occupier of premises.[50] The occupier is liable for fires negligently started or spread by his servants, contractors or lawful visitors.[51] But he is not liable for a fire started by an act of God[52] or a stranger whose activities cannot be controlled, although they may have been foreseen[53]—such a fire is not *ignis suus*.

Under statute

The Fires Prevention (Metropolis) Act 1774,[54] which substantially re-enacted an Act of 1707 (6 Anne c. 31), provides "that no action, suit, or process whatever shall be had, maintained, or prosecuted against any person in whose house, chamber, stable, barn, or other building, or on whose estate any fire shall . . . accidentally begin, nor shall any recompense be made by such person for any damage suffered thereby, any law, usage or custom to the contrary notwithstanding." Some of the difficulties which have arisen may be noted.

"in whose house . . . or on whose estate." The Act's protection will not, therefore, apply when a steam-engine is used on the highway.[55]

"any fire." It is almost certain that the Act is not limited to fires caused by lightning or spontaneous combustion, but extends to fires intentionally lit which then spread accidentally from the defendant's premises. Otherwise the scope of the Act would be so limited as to be almost useless.[56]

"shall . . . accidentally begin." One possible interpretation of this phrase is that it abolished all liability for accidental fires, whether they are due to negligence or not.[57] But it was held in *Filliter* v. *Phippard*,[58] which has been approved in the Judicial Committee,[59] that the statute extends only to fires caused by mere chance, or incapable of being traced to any cause,[60] and that fires due to negligence are still a source of liability.[61] So are fires due to a nuisance created by the landlord or those for whom he is responsible.[62]

"begin." In *Musgrove* v. *Pandelis*[63] it was further held that the statute confers no protection even if the fire begins without negligence, pro-

---

[50] *H. & N. Emanuel Ltd.* v. *Greater London Council* [1971] 2 All E.R. 835.
[51] *H. & N. Emanuel Ltd.* v. *Greater London Council* [1971] 2 All E.R. 835.
[52] *Hargrave* v. *Goldman* (1964) 110 C.L.R. 24, 56.
[53] *Holderness* v. *Goslin* [1975] 2 N.Z.L.R. 46.
[54] s.86. This Act, despite its title is not limited to London: *Filliter* v. *Phippard* (1847) 11 Q.B. 347. In Ireland, similar provisions are contained in the Accidental Fires Act 1943.
[55] *Mansel* v. *Webb* (1919) 88 L.J.K.B. 323.
[56] Holdsworth, H.E.L., Vol. xi, p. 608.
[57] The opinion of Blackstone: Bl.Comm., Vol. i, p. 431.
[58] (1847) 11 Q.B. 347.
[59] *Goldman* v. *Hargrave* [1967] 1 A.C. 645.
[60] As in *Collingwood* v. *Home and Colonial Stores* [1936] 3 All E.R. 200.
[61] The onus is on the plaintiff to prove negligence: *Mason* v. *Levy Auto Parts of England Ltd.* [1967] 2 Q.B. 530.
[62] *Spicer* v. *Smee* [1946] 1 All E.R. 489; *Williams* v. *Owen* [1955] 1 W.L.R. 1293.
[63] [1919] 2 K.B. 43.

vided that the spread of it which did the mischief complained of was due to negligence. The fire which accidentally begins, within the meaning of the statute, is the fire which actually does the mischief and not the fire in its initial and harmless stage.[64] Hence, since the statute there can be no liability for accidental fire only if there is no negligence on the part of anyone concerned. The present law is a rule of vicarious liability for the negligent acts of all persons except mere strangers—not a rule of absolute liability for accidents for which no one is to blame. Thus there was no liability when, in the absence of any evidence of negligence, such as the fire being too large for the grate, the ordinary domestic fire of a lodger spread from the fireplace and damaged the house.[65]

"nor shall any recompense be made by such person." At common law it was well established that an occupier was liable for his employees[66] acting within the scope of their employment,[67] or guests,[68] or those who had entered his house by his leave or knowledge,[69] and in this respect the statute of 1774 as interpreted by *Filliter* v. *Phippard* is probably merely declaratory of the common law. It is also settled that an occupier is responsible for an escape of fire caused by the negligence of his independent contractor.[70] Although an occupier has no right to control the mode in which a contractor performs his task,[71] he yet has control over him in the sense that he has invited him onto the premises and can require him to leave.[72] An occupier will not, however, be responsible for the acts of a mere stranger over whom he has no control, such as a trespasser[73]—unless with knowledge of the fire started by the stranger, he has failed to extinguish it within a reasonable time.[74]

"any law, usage or custom . . . notwithstanding." It follows from this phrase that an innkeeper is entitled to the protection of the Act, and is not under his strict common law liability.[75] But in *Musgrove* v. *Pandelis*[76] it was held that the statute did not afford a good defence when the rule in *Rylands* v. *Fletcher* applied. Such a fire did not "accidentally begin." In so holding the Court of Appeal went very far.[77] In *Musgrove* v. *Pandelis* the defendant's motor-car caught fire in his garage, over which the

---

[64] *Sturge* v. *Hackett* [1962] 1 W.L.R. 1257; *Goldman* v. *Hargrave* [1967] 1 A.C. 645, 665.
[65] *Sochacki* v. *Sas* [1947] 1 All E.R. 344.
[66] *Beaulieu* v. *Finglam* (1401) Y.B. 2 Hen. IV, f. 18, pl. 6. Yet note that the Act 6 Anne c. 31, imposed on the employee by whose negligence the fire began a fine of £100, to be distributed amongst the victims. This is very unlike the modern notion of vicarious liability.
[67] *Eriksen* v. *Clifton* [1961] N.Z.L.R. 705.
[68] *Boulcott Golf Club Inc.* v. *Engelbrecht* [1945] N.Z.L.R. 556.
[69] *Turberville* v. *Stampe* (1697) 1 Ld.Raym. 264; *Balfour* v. *Barty-King* [1957] 1 Q.B. 496.
[70] *H. & N. Emanuel Ltd.* v. *Greater London Council* [1971] 2 All E.R. 835.
[71] See below, Chap. 21.
[72] *Balfour* v. *Barty-King* [1957] 1 Q.B. 496.
[73] *Balfour* v. *Barty-King* [1957] 1 Q.B. 496, 504.
[74] *Goldman* v. *Hargrave* [1967] 1 A.C. 645. See above, § 5.6.
[75] *Williams* v. *Owen* [1955] 1 W.L.R. 1293.
[76] [1919] 2 K.B. 43. See too *Mulholland & Tedd Ltd.* v. *Baker* [1939] 3 All E.R. 253, 256; *Mackenzie* v. *Sloss* [1959] N.Z.L.R. 533.
[77] *Mason* v. *Levy Auto Parts of England Ltd.* [1967] 2 Q.B. 530, 541.

plaintiff occupied rooms which were burnt out. It was held that a motor-car with its tank full of petrol was a mischievous thing within the rule in *Rylands* v. *Fletcher* and that therefore the defendant must make good the loss. Although it may be doubted whether the rule in *Rylands* v. *Fletcher* was correctly applied to the facts of this case,[78] the decision has been followed.[79] But the *Musgrove* v. *Pandelis* principle has been restated so as to impose liability only when (i) the defendant brought onto his land things likely to catch fire, and kept them there in such conditions that, if they did ignite, the fire would be likely to spread to the plaintiff's land, and (ii) he did these things in the course of some non-natural use of the land.[80]

Who may sue

The right of action is not limited to the adjoining occupier. "If I happen to be on somebody else's land at a time when a fire spreads to that land and my motor-car or property is destroyed, I have just as much right against the person who improperly allows the fire to escape from his land as the owner of the land on which I happen to be."[81]

Who may be sued

Primarily liability rests upon occupancy or control of premises, rather than on the fact that the defendant has failed to control "his fire" (*ignis suus*).[82]

Reform

It will be observed that the protection conferred by section 86 is very limited—at least as the section has been interpreted—and it may well be that the time is fast approaching when section 86 should be repealed. There is no justification today for fire being treated any differently from any other dangerous thing on one's land, and social conditions have changed dramatically in two important respects since 1774: an occupier can now insure himself (and nearly always does) against damage to others and to himself caused by the spread of fire, and modern fire fighting techniques and equipment make it relatively easy to confine a fire within a limited area. There is now little risk of an "accidental" fire destroying streets of houses, and the occupier of the house from which the fire spreads being liable to dozens of occupiers.

---

[78] See above, § 13.4.

[79] *Mulholland and Tedd Ltd.* v. *Baker* [1939] 3 All E.R. 253; *Balfour* v. *Barty-King* [1956] 1 W.L.R. 779.

[80] *Mason* v. *Levy Auto Parts of England Ltd.* [1967] 2 Q.B. 530.

[81] *Sochacki* v. *Sas* [1947] 1 All E.R. 344, 345, *per* Lord Goddard C.J.

[82] *Sturge* v. *Hackett* [1962] 1 W.L.R. 1257. If the Court of Appeal in this case had adopted the latter view, the liability of the defendant's insurers would have been limited to £10,000, and not extended to £100,000. Liability for fires caused by the escape of sparks or cinders from locomotives is now governed by the Railway Fires Acts 1905 and 1923, which provide that railway companies shall be liable, notwithstanding their statutory authority, to the extent of £200 at the most, for the damage done to agricultural land or crops by the escape of sparks or cinders from locomotive engines.

CHAPTER 14

LIABILITY FOR ANIMALS

§ 14.1. Different Forms of Liability[1]

"The law of torts has grown up historically in separate compartments, and . . . beasts have travelled in a compartment of their own."[2] At common law the responsibility of the owners of animals for damage done by them developed along two main lines, one a branch of the law of trespass, and the other a branch of the law which imposes upon the owner of a dangerous animal or thing a duty to take measures to prevent it from doing damage.[3] In addition, a man may be involved in liability for damage caused by his animal under the general principles of negligence or nuisance. Finally, the Animals Act 1971 has made major changes in England, but the common law relating to trespass and the *scienter* action has been simplified rather than abandoned, and so must be discussed.

§ 14.2. Strict Liability for Dangerous Animals

From the fourteenth century an action on the case provided a remedy for harm done by savage or dangerous animals. The action was commonly known by the convenient although inelegant title of "the *scienter* action."[4] For liability was dependent upon proof that the defendant knew or ought to have known of the animal's dangerous character.[5] But the law at an early date decided that certain animals were in their nature so dangerous to mankind that the keeper of them could not be suffered to say that he did not know of their character. *Scienter* was in such a case to be conclusively presumed. Hence under this branch of the law there are two classes of animals: (1) animals *ferae naturae, e.g.* a tiger or a gorilla, which are obviously of a dangerous nature, although individual animals may be more or less tamed; (2) animals *mansuetae naturae, e.g.* a dog, a cow, or a horse, which have in individual cases given indications of the development of a vicious or dangerous disposition. The Law Commission, upon whose Report the Animals Act 1971 is founded,

---

[1] See Williams, *Liability for Animals* (Cambridge, 1939); Report of the Committee on the Law of Civil Liability for Damage done by Animals (Cmd. 8746 (1953)); Law Commission Working Paper No. 13 (H.M.S.O., 1967); North, *The Modern Law of Animals* (1971). It is worth noting that no English court is entitled to look at Law Commission No. 13 to interpret any ambiguous provision of the Act of 1971. A clause in the Bill, supported by three Law Lords, which would have given such power, was deleted by the House of Commons on the ground that its effect would be to reduce the authority of Parliament and inflate that of the Law Commission.

[2] *Read* v. *Lyons* [1947] A.C. 156, 182, *per* Lord Simonds.

[3] *Buckle* v. *Holmes* [1926] 2 K.B. 125, 128.

[4] See Jackson, "On the Origins of Scienter" (1978) 94 L.Q.R. 85.

[5] *Quod defendens quendam canem ad mordendum oves consuetum scienter retinuit*: so ran the form of the old writ (1 Roll.Abr. 4).

approved the basic distinction between dangerous and non-dangerous animals. Accordingly the Act reformulates the principles of strict liability for the keeping of dangerous animals. First, section 1 of the Act provides that the sections which follow replace "the rules of the common law imposing a strict liability in tort for damage done by an animal on the ground that the animal is regarded as *ferae naturae* or that its vicious or mischievous propensities are known or presumed to be known." Secondly, section 2 replaces the rules of the *scienter* action by the following provisions:

(1) Where any damage is caused by an animal which belongs to a dangerous species, any person who is a keeper of the animal is liable for the damage, except as otherwise provided by this Act.

(2) Where damage is caused by an animal which does not belong to a dangerous species, a keeper of the animal is liable for the damage, except as otherwise provided by this Act, if—

> (*a*) the damage is of a kind which the animal, unless restrained, was likely to cause[6] or which, if caused by the animal, was likely to be severe[7]; and
>
> (*b*) the likelihood of the damage or of its being severe[8] was due to characteristics of the animal which are not normally found in animals of the same species or are not normally so found except at particular times or in particular circumstances; and
>
> (*c*) those characteristics were known to that keeper or were at any time known to a person who at that time had charge of the animal as that keeper's servant or, where that keeper is the head of a household, were known to another keeper of the animal who is a member of that household and under the age of sixteen.

Some of the problems raised by these complex provisions will now be considered.

(1) What animals are included

The Act does not define "animal" (as distinct from "livestock"), but probably the term includes birds, reptiles and insects, but not bacteria.[9] The Act distinguishes between animals of a dangerous species[10] and other animals. This distinction is not to be found in nature, but is of crucial importance to the lawyer, for upon it depends the question whether the relevant provision is section 2(1) or section 2(2). Under section 2(2) there will only be liability if the keeper of the animal has knowledge of its dangerous characteristics, whereas such knowledge is not necessary under section 2(1). It is a question of law whether a particular species of animal is dangerous, and it is irrelevant what the

---

[6] The C.A. has held that it is sufficient to prove that the event was such as might happen: *Smith* v. *Ainger* [1990] C.L. 500.

[7] So the defendant was liable for a dog which "weighed about 10 stones and had big teeth and a large mouth": *Curtis* v. *Betts* [1990] 1 W.L.R. 459, 469.

[8] The C.A. has also given a wide interpretation to this obscure phrase: it means simply "the damage": *Curtis* v. *Betts* [1990] 1 W.L.R. 459, 463, 469.

[9] North, *Animals*, p. 22, n. 5.

[10] Which s.6 defines to include subspecies and variety.

characteristics of the particular animal are. "The reason why this is a question of law and not a question of fact is because it is a matter of which judicial notice has to be taken. The doctrine has from its formulation proceeded upon the supposition that the knowledge of what kinds of animals are tame and what savage is common knowledge. Evidence is receivable, if at all, only on the basis that the judge may wish to inform himself."[11] Thus it is a rule of law, and not a mere proposition of fact, that it is not natural for a dog to bite mankind. "The law," said Sir John Holt C.J.,[12] "takes notice that a dog is not of a fierce nature, but rather the contrary."

The Act in section 6(2) defines a dangerous species as follows:

A dangerous species is a species—

   (a) which is not commonly domesticated in the British Islands[13]; and

   (b) whose fully grown animals normally have such characteristics that they are likely, unless restrained, to cause severe damage or that any damage they may cause is likely to be severe.

It may be predicted that such general phrases as "commonly domesticated" and "severe damage" will give rise to many difficulties of interpretation.

(2) Nature of liability

At common law the principle was that he who kept a dangerous animal kept it at his peril.[14] This rule was too well established to be challenged.[15] Similarly liability under section 2(1) of the Act is strict.[16] The liability is for "any damage" caused by an animal of a dangerous species: it is irrelevant that the particular animal is in fact tame, or was acting out of fright rather than viciously.[17] It would seem to follow that the test of remoteness of damage is not reasonable forseeability but directness of consequence.

(3) Liability for non-dangerous species

When damage is done by a dangerous animal its keeper is liable without proof that the animal had a tendency to do such damage, or (if the animal had such a tendency) that the defendant knew of it. But when damage is done by an animal of a non-dangerous species, section 2(2) of the 1971 Act requires (in effect) that the plaintiff must show that

---

[11] *Behrens* v. *Bertram Mills Circus Ltd.* [1957] 2 Q.B. 1, 15, *per* Devlin J. Yet Scrutton L.J. thought that "a judge should not rely on his general knowledge about such matters, even though some judges know a good deal about horses": *Glanville* v. *Sutton* [1928] 1 K.B. 571, 575.

[12] *Mason* v. *Keeling* (1699) 12 Mod. 332, 335.

[13] *e.g.* a camel: *Tutin* v. *Mary Chipperfield Promotions Ltd.* N.L.J., September 4, 1980.

[14] *Gould* v. *M'Auliffe* [1941] 1 All E.R. 515, 519, affirmed [1941] 2 All E.R. 527.

[15] *May* v. *Burdett* (1846) 9 Q.B. 101.

[16] But not absolute: the defences are discussed below, § 14.3.

[17] A point already settled by *Behrens* v. *Bertram Mills Circus* [1957] 2 Q.B. 1, 17.

the animal had certain abnormal characteristics, and that its keeper had knowledge, actual or constructive, of those characteristics.

(i) *Abnormal characteristics*

At common law it was uncertain whether it must be proved that the animal's vicious tendency was contrary to the nature of animals of that class. In the past liability has been imposed for bulls charging, horses kicking, and dogs chasing pheasants. But the need for proof of an unnatural tendency was emphatically affirmed by the Court of Appeal in *Fitzgerald* v. *E.D. and A.D. Cooke Bourne (Farms) Ltd.*,[18] in which it was held that there was no liability in *scienter* for personal injuries inflicted by a young filly which was following its own natural propensities, which were also those of fillies as a class, by galloping up to and prancing round lawful visitors to a field. The court may well have been unduly tender to owners of horses,[19] and much of its reasoning seems to be based on an anthropomorphic conception of animals. But a dog cannot reason like a human being, and there is something bizarre in seeking the *mens rea* of a pony. So it should be enough to prove that a horse has been unpredictable and unreliable in its behaviour as distinct from having a vicious tendency to harm people.[20]

(ii) *Knowledge*

Three different situations are covered by section 2(2)—the knowledge of the keeper himself, or of his servant, or of a member of his household under the age of 16 who is also a keeper of the animal.[21] The Act does not define "knowledge," so presumably the common law is still relevant. If so, it is not necessary to prove that the animal has on any previous occasion actually done the kind of harm complained of; it is enough that it has sufficiently manifested a tendency to do such harm, and that the defendant was aware of the fact.[22] But it is necessary to prove knowledge that the animal is prone to do or has done the particular kind of damage complained of. If a horse bites a man the keeper's knowledge is not established by proving that the horse was known to bite other horses.[23] On the other hand, if the animal is known to have a propensity to attack people (in the sense explained above) it is immaterial that it does so from non-vicious motives—*e.g.* an over-friendly large dog which hugs the plaintiff.[24]

---

[18] [1964] 1 Q.B. 249.
[19] Diplock L.J. said that it would be "an intolerable burden" on horse-owners to impose liability.
[20] As in *Wallace* v. *Newton* [1982] 1 W.L.R. 375 (in which the name of the "nervous and unreliable" horse was Lord Justice).
[21] So the knowledge of a minor who occasionally takes the household pet for a run will not necessarily be ascribed to the head of the household.
[22] *Barnes* v. *Lucille Ltd.* (1907) 96 L.T. 680. So the common maxim "Every dog is entitled to its bite" is no more accurate law than "Trespassers will be prosecuted."
[23] *Glanville* v. *Sutton & Co. Ltd.* [1928] 1 K.B. 571.
[24] *Fitzgerald* v. *Cooke (E.D. and A.D.) Bourne (Farms) Ltd.* [1964] 1 Q.B. 249, 259.

(4) Who is liable

Liability under either subsection of section 2 of the 1971 Act is placed on a "keeper" of the animal. Section 6(3) of the Act provides that: a person is a keeper of an animal if—

(*a*) he owns the animal or has it in his possession; or

(*b*) he is the head of a household of which a member under the age of 16 owns the animal or has it in his possession;

and if at any time an animal ceases to be owned by or to be in the possession of a person, any person who immediately before that time was a keeper thereof by virtue of the preceding provisions of this subsection continues to be a keeper of the animal until another person becomes a keeper thereof by virtue of those provisions.

But where an animal is taken into and kept in possession for the purpose of preventing it from causing damage or of restoring it to its owner, a person is not a keeper of it by virtue only of that possession.

§ 14.3. Defences to Action Under Section 2 of the Animals Act

The following defences are available:—

(1) Contributory negligence and fault of the plaintiff

Section 5(1) provides that there is no liability under section 2 for damage which is due wholly to the fault of the person suffering it. If the damage is due partly, as distinct from wholly, to the fault of the plaintiff, then sections 10 and 11 enable the apportionment provisions of the Law Reform (Contributory Negligence) Act 1945 to be applied.

(2) Plaintiff a trespasser

It was formerly a good defence that the plaintiff, when injured by the animal, was trespassing upon the defendant's premises where the animal was kept, unless it was kept there with the deliberate purpose of injuring him.[25] The Act in section 5(3) now provides that a person is not liable for any damage caused by an animal kept on any premises or structure[26] to a person trespassing there, "if it is proved either—

(*a*) that the animal was not kept there for the protection of persons or property[27]; or

(*b*) (if the animal was kept there for the protection of persons or property) that keeping it there for that purpose was not unreasonable."

It has been held not to be unreasonable to keep a savage dog in a built-up area to protect scrap metal,[28] but the events in that case occurred before the passage of the Guard Dogs Act 1975, which imposed certain restrictions on the keeping of such animals.

If for any reason the claim is not brought under section 2—*e.g.*

---

[25] *Sarch* v. *Blackburn* (1830) 4 C. & P. 297; above, § 11.9.

[26] This probably includes an aircraft or motor-car; see above, § 11.1.

[27] But some animals—*e.g.* dogs—are kept both for companionship and for protection.

[28] *Cummings* v. *Grainger* [1976] 1 Q.B. 397.

because the defendant is not the occupier of the premises trespassed upon—the ordinary principles of negligence will apply.[29]

(3) Volenti non fit injuria

The maxim *volenti non fit injuria* was no less applicable to dangerous animals than to other dangerous things of which the plaintiff has agreed to run the risk.[30] So a person who intervened in a dog-fight might be met with this defence.[31] Section 5(2) of the Act now specifically provides that a person is not liable under section 2 for any damage suffered by a person who has voluntarily accepted the risk thereof. So, in accordance with the settled rules on the matter,[32] it has been held that the defendant must prove more than the fact that the plaintiff knew there was a dangerous dog loose.[33] Further, by section 6(5) when a person employed as a servant by a keeper of an animal incurs a risk incidental to his employment he shall not be treated as accepting it voluntarily.

(4) Act of third person

How far, if at all, it was a good defence that the immediate cause of the damage complained of was the unlawful act of a third person in letting the animal loose or inciting it to mischief cannot be regarded as being definitely decided before the Act. In *Baker* v. *Snell*[34] the question was much discussed by a Divisional Court and by the Court of Appeal, but there was such a conflict of judicial opinion that it is difficult to determine what the case decided or to regard it as authority. But in *Behrens* v. *Bertram Mills Circus Ltd.*[35] Devlin J. held that the judgments of Sir Herbert Cozens-Hardy M.R. and Farwell L.J. in *Baker* v. *Snell* were authority for the proposition that the wrongful act of a third party is no defence, and the Law Commission[36] was of the same opinion for the reason that the act of a third party is one of the circumstances against which the person creating the risk should take precautions. As the Act does not mention this defence in section 5, it must be assumed to have disappeared. The possible defence of act of God must also have gone.

§ 14.4. LIABILITY FOR DOGS

Section 3 provides that "where a dog causes damage by killing or injuring livestock, any person who is a keeper[37] of the dog is liable for the damage, except as otherwise provided by this Act."

---

[29] See below, § 14.7.
[30] *Behrens* v. *Bertram Mills Circus Ltd.* [1957] 2 Q.B. 1.
[31] *Smith* v. *Shields* (1964) 108 S.J. 501.
[32] See below, § 22.3.
[33] *Cummings* v. *Grainger* [1976] 1 Q.B. 397.
[34] [1908] 2 K.B. 352, 825. For a remarkably outspoken criticism, see Beven, "Responsibility at Common Law for the Keeping of Animals" (1909) 22 Harv.L.Rev. 465; Pollock, "The Dog and the Potman: or 'Go it, Bob!' " (1909) 25 L.Q.R. 317.
[35] [1957] 2 Q.B. 1.
[36] Law Com. No. 13, § 24.
[37] Not the owner, as under the previous Dogs Act.

This section replaces the provisions of the Dogs Acts 1906 to 1928. By section 11 "livestock" means "cattle, horses, asses, mules, hinnies, sheep, pigs, goats and poultry, and also deer not in the wild state and, while in captivity, pheasants, partridges and grouse."

It will be noted that liability under this section is quite independent of the proof of knowledge or negligence on the part of the keeper of the dog. It is peculiarly revealing of the Englishman's scale of values, or else of the influence of the farmers' lobby on Parliament, that sheep should be better protected than human beings from dogs.[38] Finally, section 9 of the Act provides a statutory defence to an action for killing or causing injury to a dog if the defendant was acting, or had reasonable grounds for believing he was acting, for the protection of livestock. The Guard Dogs Act 1975 displays a different legislative policy. The Act (s.1) provides that a person shall not use, or permit the use of, a guard dog[39] on any premises unless a competent handler is present and a warning notice is exhibited at the entrance. But although breach of section 1 is a criminal offence, section 5(1) specifically provides that it shall not confer a civil right of action.[40] Finally, in practice it may be the best course to apply to a magistrates' court under the Dogs Act 1871, s.2 for an order for the destruction of a dangerous dog.

§ 14.5. Liability for Straying Livestock

We now pass to the second branch of the law relating to liability for harm done by animals. Cattle-trespass was one of the oldest grounds of liability in English law. Although a form of strict liability, it was acceptable to the farming community as a simple method of allocating responsibility for relatively minor damage.[41] But it has now been abolished by section 1(1) of the Act, and replaced by the following provisions in section 4(1). Where livestock belonging[42] to any person strays[43] on to land in the ownership or occupation of another[44] and—

> (a) damage is done by the livestock to the land or to any property on it which is in the ownership or possession of the other person[45]; or
>
> (b) any expenses are reasonably incurred by that other person in keeping the livestock while it cannot be restored to the person to whom it belongs or while it is detained in pursuance of section 7 of this Act, or in ascertaining to whom it belongs;

the person to whom the livestock belongs is liable for the damage or expenses, except as otherwise provided by this Act.

---

[38] *Hughes* v. *Williams* [1943] K.B. 574, 580.

[39] The breed of such a dog is irrelevant: the Act concentrates on its function.

[40] Still, an occupier in breach of the Act would hardly be acting reasonably for the purpose of s.5(3) of the Animals Act 1971.

[41] Law Com. No. 13, paras. 62–63.

[42] Under s.4(2) livestock belongs to the person in whose possession it is: so the owner out of possession cannot be sued.

[43] Note that the Act does not require a trespass: so it is doubtful whether *Ellis* v. *Loftus Iron Co.* (1874) L.R. 10 C.P. 10 is still law.

[44] But not from the highway on to that land (s.5(5)).

[45] So there is no liability for personal injuries.

§ 14.6. Defences to Action for Straying Livestock

As section 4(1) provides that the person in possession of straying live-stock is liable for them "except as provided by this Act," it follows that the common law defences to cattle-trespass have been abolished. Thus the act of a third party, which was a defence both in England[46] and in Ireland,[47] is now inapplicable to a claim under section 4. The only defences recognised by the 1971 Act are the following.

(1) Plaintiff's own default

In section 5(1) it is specifically provided that a person is not liable under section 4 for any damage which is wholly due to the fault of the person suffering it. But section 5(6) provides that "the damage shall not be treated as due to the fault of the person suffering it by reason only that he could have prevented it by fencing; but a person is not liable under that section where it is proved that the straying of the livestock on to the land would not have occurred but for a breach by any other person, being a person having an interest in the land, of a duty to fence."

(2) Contributory negligence

If the plaintiff's damage is due partly, as distinct from wholly, to his own negligence, the apportionment provisions of the Law Reform (Contributory Negligence) Act 1945 seem to apply by virtue of sections 10 and 11 of the 1971 Act.

(3) Straying from the highway

The Act in section 5(5) specifically recognises the well-established rule[48] that the occupier of premises adjoining a highway is presumed to have accepted the risks incidental to the passage of ordinary traffic along that highway.

§ 14.7. Detention and Sale of Trespassing Livestock

The common law remedy of distress damage feasant[49] is expressly abolished by section 7(1). In its place section 7(2) to (6) provide a right to detain the livestock and to sell it at the end of 14 days. The animal must be adequately fed and watered. The right of detention ceases after 48 hours unless within that time notice of the detention is given to the police, and to the person to whom the livestock belongs, if he is known, or if there is a tender of amends. The Act provides in section 7(5) for the disposition of the proceeds of the sale, which must be at a market or

---

[46] *Sutcliffe* v. *Holmes* [1947] K.B. 147.
[47] *Moloney* v. *Stephen* [1945] Ir.Jur.Rep. 37.
[48] *Tillett* v. *Ward* (1882) 10 Q.B.D. 17.
[49] See below, § 26.4.

public auction, in order to obtain a fair price. The grant of a power of sale, which did not exist in distress damage feasant, is to be welcomed, but there is something odd about giving the occupier of a suburban house the right to detain and feed a trespassing pony. It might be simpler to drive it away.

§ 14.8. Liability in Negligence

Apart altogether from the doctrines of cattle-trespass and *scienter* there was at common law the ordinary liability in negligence for the keeping of animals.[50] This was confirmed by the Court of Appeal in *Draper* v. *Hodder*,[51] decided after the Animals Act 1971 became law, but on events which had occurred in 1968. The infant plaintiff had been savaged by a pack of Jack Russell terriers which had escaped from the defendant's land. Apart from the fact that it was impossible to prove which of the dogs had inflicted the injuries there was no evidence that any of these terriers had ever attacked a human being, so there could not be liability under the *scienter* action. But in view of evidence that Jack Russell terriers are dangerous when in a pack and allowed to roam free, the defendant was held liable in negligence for failing to take precautions against a foreseeable risk. Liability based on negligence is quite distinct from the statutory strict liability under the Animals Act 1971—the defendant may be different, the duty is different, and so is the test of remoteness of damage. But before the Act of 1971 there was one important common law exception to the general principle of liability in negligence.

Fences. In *Searle* v. *Wallbank*[52] the House of Lords affirmed the long-standing rule that the owner or occupier of land adjoining the highway is under no duty to users of the highway to prevent his domestic animals not known to be dangerous from straying on to the highway. This rule was founded upon our ancient social conditions and was in no way related to, or liable to be qualified by, such matters as the relative levels of fields and highway, the nature of the highway, or the amount of traffic upon it.[53] Such an occupier might incur criminal liability under the Highways Act 1980, s.105,[54] but there is no civil liability for breach of that statutory duty.[55] In particular there was no ground for a distinction

---

[50] *Fardon* v. *Harcourt-Rivington* (1932) 146 L.T. 391, 392, *per* Lord Atkin. "One can perhaps with hindsight deduce from the language of the speeches in *Fardon* v. *Harcourt-Rivington* how *Donoghue* v. *Stevenson* was likely to be decided": *Draper* v. *Hodder* [1972] 2 Q.B. 556, 578, *per* Roskill L.J.

[51] [1972] 2 Q.B. 556. The H.L. refused leave to appeal.

[52] [1947] A.C. 341.

[53] *Brock* v. *Richards* [1951] 1 K.B. 529, 534.

[54] But the penalty was only 25p a head (with a maximum of 150p) and Sir Carleton Allen knew "of one offender—a serious menace to his neighbourhood—with eighty-four convictions, punishable each time with 5s. only": *Law in the Making* (7th ed.), p. 301. His activities were stopped only when he was bound to keep the peace in the sum of £25: (1961) 77 L.Q.R. 27.

[55] *Davies* v. *Davies* [1975] Q.B. 172.

between town and country.[56] It also followed that since there was no duty to maintain a fence at all, it could not be a breach of duty to maintain one which was imperfect.[57] Although protests against this rule may be found in the reports from 1699[58] to 1963,[59] a number of private members' Bills to change the law failed to secure enactment.[60] Finally section 8 of the Animals Act 1971 put an end to the privileged position of the farmer and imposed a duty to take care to prevent damage from animals straying on to the highway. This duty was created, not by imposing a statutory duty of care on the land-owner, but by abolishing the rule in *Searle* v. *Wallbank*. In section 8(1) the Act provides that "so much of the rules of the common law relating to liability for negligence as excludes or restricts the duty which a person might owe to others to take such care as is reasonable to see that damage is not caused by animals straying on to a highway is hereby abolished." So it will be for the tribunal of fact to give due weight to such circumstances as the nature of the land and of the adjoining highway, and of the type of animal. But Parliament recognised that it might be unreasonable to subject the occupiers of unfenced land, such as is usual in the north of England, to ordinary liability in negligence. So section 8(2) of the Act provides that

where damage[61] is caused by animals[62] straying from unfenced[63] land to a highway a person who placed them on the land shall not be regarded as having committed a breach of the duty to take care by reason only of placing them there if—

(*a*) the land is common land, or is land situated in an area where fencing is not customary, or is a town or village green; and

(*b*) he had a right to place the animals on that land.[64]

§ 14.9. LIABILITY FOR NUISANCE

Actions for nuisance caused by animals do not require lengthy consideration. It might well have been held that obstruction of a highway by an animal was a nuisance but the cases have almost all been decided on the basis of negligence.[65] But a dog with a long loose lead running

---

[56] *Gomberg* v. *Smith* [1963] 1 Q.B. 25, 40; *Ellis* v. *Johnstone* [1963] 2 Q.B. 8, 26.

[57] *Searle* v. *Wallbank* [1947] A.C. 341, 361; *Brock* v. *Richards* [1951] 1 K.B. 529, 535.

[58] *Mason* v. *Keeling*, 1 Ld.Raym. 606. In (1699) 12 Mod. 332, 333 counsel is reported as saying "It is hard that one should have a remedy for the least trespass done in his land, and none for a trespass done thus to the person by wounding or maiming."

[59] *Ellis* v. *Johnstone* [1963] 2 Q.B. 8, 27.

[60] The Supreme Court of Canada refused to follow *Searle* v. *Wallbank* in *Fleming* v. *Atkinson* (1959) 18 D.L.R. (2d) 81, 113, but the High Court of Australia held that such a change is a matter for the legislature: *State Government Insurance Commission* v. *Trigwell* (1979) 53 A.L.J.R. 656.

[61] As defined in section 11, includes the death of or injury to, any person (including any disease and any impairment of physical or mental condition).

[62] There is no statutory definition of animals, as distinct from livestock, so there is now a duty to prevent dogs, cats, and even poultry, from straying.

[63] "Fencing" includes the construction of any obstacle designed to prevent animals from straying.

[64] See *Davies* v. *Davies* [1975] Q.B. 172.

[65] See above, § 14.7.

about by itself in the streets of London is a nuisance.[66] If animals escape on to a highway in such numbers as to amount to an obstruction there also may be liability in nuisance. It is a question of fact in each case: 24 cows on an Irish country road have been held to be a nuisance,[67] but not two sheep on a country road in South Australia.[68] It is necessary to rely upon nuisance when there is no escape or no negligence, or when the animal is not livestock within the definition in section 11 of the Animals Act 1971—*e.g.* it is a cat or a dog. The stench of pigs,[69] the barking of dogs,[70] and the crowing of cockerels[71] have each been held to constitute a nuisance.

In general, there is no liability for the escape of noxious animals naturally on the defendant's land, such as rats,[72] rabbits[73] or deer.[74] These decisions may be open to review in the light of the tendency to impose liability for the escape of things naturally on the land if the defendant has behaved unreasonably.[75] In any event, if for the purpose of sport or otherwise, a man purposely accumulates rabbits or game upon his land, he is probably liable for all damage done by them to neighbouring proprietors.[76] So if he keeps bees[77] in an unreasonable number[78] or manure in such unreasonable quantities as to attract flies[79] or, it seems, rats[80] he will be liable in nuisance.

§ 14.10. LIABILITY IN OTHER TORTS

As with negligence[81] and nuisance,[82] liability for other torts is unaffected by the 1971 Act. So it has long been settled that trespass to the person can be committed through the agency of an animal, as when the defendant sets his dog onto the plaintiff[83]; again trespass to goods is committed if I train my dog to take another's golf balls.[84] Again a lawful

---

[66] *Pitcher* v. *Martin* [1937] 3 All E.R. 918.

[67] *Cunningham* v. *Whelan* (1917) 52 I.L.T.R. 67.

[68] *State Government Insurance Commission* v. *Trigwell* (1979) 53 A.L.J.R. 656.

[69] *Aldred's Case* (1610) 9 Co. 57b.

[70] There may also be criminal liability under a local by-law, as in *Morrissey* v. *Galer* [1955] 1 W.L.R. 110, or under the Public Health Act 1936, s.92.

[71] *Leeman* v. *Montagu* [1936] 2 All E.R. '1677 (but the cockerels sounded like "a football crowd cheering a cup-tie").

[72] *Stearn* v. *Prentice Bros.* [1919] 1 K.B. 394.

[73] *Pratt* v. *Young* (1952) 69 W.N.(N.S.W.) 214.

[74] *Brady* v. *Warren* [1900] 2 I.R. 632.

[75] See above, § 13.6.

[76] *Farrer* v. *Nelson* (1885) 15 Q.B.D. 258, 260; *Seligman* v. *Docker* [1949] Ch. 53.

[77] Sir K. Swan, *A Receiver of Stolen Property* (Middle Temple, 1956), is a monograph on bees and the law. Much information will also be found in *Stormer* v. *Ingram* (1978) 21 S.A.S.R. 93 (bees are not cattle) and *Tutton* v. *A.D. Walter Ltd.* [1986] Q.B. 61 (bees are not trespassers and may be owed a duty of care).

[78] *O'Gorman* v. *O'Gorman* [1903] 2 I.R. 573.

[79] *Bland* v. *Yates* (1914) 58 S.J. 612.

[80] *Stearn* v. *Prentice Bros.* [1919] 1 K.B. 394.

[81] See above, § 14.7.

[82] See above, § 14.8.

[83] *Scott* v. *Shepherd* (1773) 3 Wils. 403, 408.

[84] *Manton* v. *Brocklebank* [1923] 2 K.B. 212, 219.

visitor to premises may apparently base his claim on the rules relating to the liability of occupiers[85] rather than on the Animals Act, and so may a trespasser if the case is not covered by section 5(3) of the Act. It is possible that there might be liability under the principle in *Rylands* v. *Fletcher*[86] for the escape of a tiger[87] or a fox.[88]

---

[85] *Kavanagh* v. *Stokes* [1942] I.R. 596.
[86] See above, Chap. 13.
[87] *Behrens* v. *Bertram Mills Circus Ltd.* [1957] 2 Q.B. 1, 22.
[88] *Brady* v. *Warren* [1900] 2 I.R. 632, 651.

CHAPTER 15

DOMESTIC RELATIONS

§ 15.1. Introductory

In this chapter we shall consider those tortious acts which are an injury neither to the person, nor reputation, nor physical property, but are based on a wrongful interference with a man's relations with others, for example, his wife, his children or those with whom he holds a contract. For a man may be damnified by the death of another person,[1] by the loss of his wife's consortium, by the seduction of his daughter, by the deprivation of the work of his servants or by the non-fulfilment of contractual obligations due to him from another. If the law had been developed on a rational basis without reference to the accidents of history it might have been expected that a fundamental distinction would have been taken between intentional and careless invasions of the security of existing domestic and contractual relations. On the one hand, it would have been natural to find a remedy given to one who had suffered loss from a wilful act done with the object and effect of depriving him of the benefits which he enjoyed from a relationship with another, at least whenever the deprivation was permanent, and whether the relationship was with a spouse, parent, child, employer, servant, partner, or contractor. For the general principle is that violation of a legal right committed knowingly gives a cause of action unless there is some reason to the contrary.[2] On the other hand, it would have been surprising to find a remedy given to one who had suffered such a loss as the result of an act not done with the object (although having the effect) of depriving him of the advantages of the continuance of the relationship in question. The only exception might have been the case of a family deprived of its bread-winner. For it is equally clear that the general principle is that the mere fact that an injury to A prevents a third party getting from A a benefit which he would otherwise have obtained does not invest the third party with a right of action against the wrongdoer.[3] This rational approach has not been adopted, either by the courts or by Parliament. The vagaries of English legal development produced a situation in which the interest which one person had in the continuance of his existing relationship (whether domestic or contractual) with another was protected by the law in a way which was at once surprisingly wide and surprisingly narrow. We shall consider in turn the relations of (1) master and servant, (2) parent and child, and (3) husband and wife, and

---

[1] "Whenever a man dies, if he is a man of an active type, it has repercussions, great or small, on all those with whom he has been previously concerned": *Burgess* v. *Florence Nightingale Hospital for Gentlewomen* [1955] 1 Q.B. 345, 355, *per* Devlin J.

[2] See above, § 2.1.

[3] *Att.-Gen. for New South Wales* v. *Perpetual Trustee Co. Ltd.* [1955] A.C. 457, 484. See also above, § 9.6.

346

in respect of each relationship we shall consider the actions for (1) loss of services, (2) enticement, and (3) harbouring.

§ 15.2. MASTER AND SERVANT[4]

(1) Action per quod servitium amisit

Until the action was abolished by the Administration of Justice Act 1982, s.2(c)(i), it was a tort actionable at the suit of a master to take away, imprison, or cause bodily harm to his servant, if (i) the act was a tort as against the servant, and (ii) the master was thereby deprived of his servant's services. Note that no action lay if the servant was killed by the defendant, as distinct from being injured[5]—one of the many anomalies which disfigured this area of the law. From the earliest days of the common law the master had an action of trespass against the wrongdoer whose battery or other wrongful act had brought about the loss of the services of his servant (*per quod servitium amisit*). It is significant that the action was originally in trespass and not in case: for although the act complained of must have been wrongful as against the servant himself,[6] it was also regarded as being a direct invasion of the interest of a proprietary nature which the master had either in the servant himself or in the services which were the fruit of the relationship between them.[7]

(2) Enticement of a servant

At an early date a remedy by way of an action on the case was developed when a stranger had deprived a master of his servant not by force, but by persuasion. In the absence of lawful justification it was a tort actionable at the suit of a master to induce his servant to leave his employment wrongfully or to induce him by illegal means, such as fraud or intimidation, to leave his employment even rightfully, or to conspire to do so. The action was available even though employer and employed did not stand in the strict relation of master and servant. This was established in *Lumley* v. *Gye*.[8] The plaintiff was the lessee and manager of a theatre. Miss Johanna Wagner, an artiste of some distinction, had agreed with the plaintiff to sing in his theatre for a definite term and during that term not to sing elsewhere. The defendant, "knowing the premises, and maliciously intending to injure the plaintiff," before the expiration of the term enticed and procured Miss Wagner to refuse to perform. A majority of the Court of Queen's Bench held that the defendant was liable in damages to the plaintiff. The action for enticement was not limited to such menial servants as were

---

[4] See 11th Report of the Law Reform Committee (Cmnd. 2017, 1963); Law Commission Working Paper No. 19 (1968).

[5] *Admiralty Commissioners* v. *S.S. Amerika* [1917] A.C. 38. For the reason, see below, § 24.4.

[6] In the action by a parent for the seduction of his child this would never (and in the actions for enticing and harbouring or procuring breach of contract not necessarily) have been the case.

[7] *Inland Revenue Commissioners* v. *Hambrook* [1956] 2 Q.B. 641.

[8] (1853) 2 E. & B. 216.

comprehended by the Statute of Labourers.[9] "The plaintiff's cause of action against the opera singer lay in contract, and the plaintiff's cause of action against the defendant lay in tort. But both the opera singer and the defendant were joint wrongdoers participating in an unlawful common design."[10]

(3) Harbouring a servant

It was actionable knowingly to continue to employ the servant of another, though the person so continuing to employ the servant did not procure him to leave his master or know when he engaged him that he was the servant of another.[11] The action lay even when the relationship was not strictly one of master and servant.[12]

But now the Administration of Justice Act 1982, s.2(c)(iii) provides that no person shall be liable in tort on the ground only of enticement of a servant or harbouring a servant.

§ 15.3. PARENT AND CHILD

At common law no parent had, as such, any right in respect of his child of such sort that an action for damages lay against any other person for a violation of that right. The only right which a parent had as such was a right to the possession and custody of his child during minority. The remedy for the infringement of this right was not an action for damages against the person who deprived him of his child but the recovery of possession either by means of a writ of habeas corpus or by an application to the Family Division to exercise its power in respect of the guardianship of infants.[13] Nor, conversely, had a child any action for any loss which he may have suffered from interference with his relationship with his parents (apart from that provided by the Fatal Accidents Act, 1976). The law, however, gave to a parent in his fictitious capacity as employer an action for damages if he had been deprived of the services of his child by any tort committed as against that child. But this action was abolished by the Administration of Justice Act 1982, s.2(b).

It was once actionable in England to induce a child under age but capable of service to leave his or her parent against the latter's will, or not to return home, having so left, unless there was some justification.[14] But this cause of action was abolished by the Law Reform (Miscellaneous Provisions) Act 1970, section 5. The Administration of Justice Act 1982, s.2(c)(ii) also provides that no person shall be liable in tort on

---

[9] Note that it was not by reason of any wrong done to Miss Wagner that the plaintiff suffered damage. The decision is also the basis of the rule that it is a tort maliciously to procure a breach of contract: see below, § 16.3.

[10] *C.B.S. Songs Ltd.* v. *Amstrad plc* [1988] A.C. 1013, 1058, *per* Lord Templeman.

[11] *Jones Bros. (Hunstanton) Ltd.* v. *Stevens* [1955] 1 Q.B. 275.

[12] *De Francesco* v. *Barnum* (1890) 63 L.T. 514 (a different action from that reported in (1890) 45 Ch.D. 430).

[13] The preceding three sentences were approved by Gibson and Stuart-Smith L.JJ. in *F.* v. *Wirral Metropolitan Council* [1991] 2 W.L.R. 1132, 1169, 1173.

[14] *Evans* v. *Walton* (1867) L.R. 2 C.P. 615; *Lough* v. *Ward* [1945] 2 All E.R. 338.

the ground only of having deprived another of the services of his female servant by raping or seducing her.

§ 15.4. HUSBAND AND WIFE

Injuries to the husband

For many years the interest which a husband has in the companionship and services of his wife was protected against the interference of strangers in four distinct ways, but three of these were abolished by the Law Reform (Miscellaneous Provisions) Act 1970, ss.4 and 5, and the fourth by the Administration of Justice Act 1982, s.2(*a*).

(i) *Action for loss of services*

Until the Act of 1982 it was a tort actionable at the suit of a husband to take away, imprison, or do physical harm to his wife, if (i) the act was wrongful as against the wife, and (ii) the husband was thereby deprived of her society or services. Any tortious act, therefore, committed against the wife was actionable at the suit of her husband, if he could prove that he was thereby deprived for any period of her society or services (*per quod consortium amisit* or *servitium amisit*). It will be noted that the husband's remedy was not limited to cases where he has been deprived of his wife's *consortium* by reason of the defendant's enticement, although the tort was often called by that name. This action depended on entirely different principles from those on which the action of enticement was founded. The latter was founded (or at any rate justifiable) on the principle that the violation of a legal right committed knowingly is a cause of action[15]; the former was a relic of the proprietary rights a husband was once thought to possess in his wife.[16] If the matter had arisen for decision in this century the courts would almost certainly have refused to give an action to the husband merely for loss of *consortium* due to the negligence of a third party.[17]

(ii) *Harbouring a wife*

It was actionable to harbour the wife of another, after a request by the husband to deliver her up,[18] although the defendant did not procure her to leave her husband or know when he took her in that she was the

---

[15] *Best* v. *Samuel Fox Ltd.* [1952] A.C. 716, 729.
[16] Petruchio's remarks in *The Taming of the Shrew*, III, ii, vividly express the attitude of the common law:

"I will be master of what is mine own:
She is my goods, my chattels; she is my house,
My household stuff, my field, my barn,
My horse, my ox, my ass, my any thing;
And here she stands, touch her whoever dare;
I'll bring mine action on the proudest he
That stops my way in Padua."

[17] *Best* v. *Samuel Fox Ltd.* [1952] A.C. 716, 733.
[18] *Spencer* v. *Relph* [1969] N.Z.L.R. 713.

wife of another,[19] provided that loss of *consortium* was proved.[20] It was held "on principles of humanity" to be a defence that owing to the husband's conduct the wife was justified or (perhaps) was honestly believed by the defendant to be justified in leaving her husband.[21] But the tort was abolished by the Law Reform (Miscellaneous Provisions) Act 1970, s.5.

(iii) *Enticement*

The same Act has also abolished the tort of enticement in England, which was committed when the defendant, without lawful justification, induced the plaintiff's wife to leave him or to remain away from him against his will.[22]

(iv) *The action for "criminal conversation"*

An action formerly lay against one who had committed adultery[23] with the wife of the plaintiff. It was known as an action for criminal conversation.[24] The wife's consent was irrelevant. The action was distinct from that of enticement: one may commit adultery without enticing a wife away from her husband. The action was no doubt a necessity when divorce could only be obtained by Act of Parliament: as Parliament was not a tribunal suitable for trying allegations of adultery it was reasonable to require the petitioner to establish the truth of his allegations before a court of law. The action might also have been justified on the ground that the plaintiff was in substance complaining of the invasion of the privacy of his marriage, and the insult thereby caused to his honour as a husband. But when the Divorce Court was established in 1857 the reason for the action disappeared and it was accordingly abolished in England. After 1857 a husband's claim for damages for adultery was made by way of petition in matrimonial proceedings, whether accompanied by a petition for divorce or not. However, this procedure in its turn became unpopular, but as the common people of England saw no reason why a wealthy seducer of a poor man's wife should not pay for what he had done[25] the Law Commission felt it could

---

[19] *Winsmore v. Greenbank* [1745] Willes 577.

[20] *Winchester v. Fleming* [1958] 1 Q.B. 259. So if the wife would not have returned to her husband in any event the plaintiff cannot recover: *Spencer v. Relph* [1969] N.Z.L.R. 713.

[21] *Place v. Searle* [1932] 2 K.B. 497, 513, 517. Even under the old writ of ravishment the defendant was not liable if he conducted the wife on a pilgrimage or took her into his house when she was "in danger of being lost in the night or of being drowned with water": Brooke, abridg. *s.v. Trespass*, pll. 207, 213.

[22] *Smith v. Kaye* (1904) 20 T.L.R. 261.

[23] A.I.D. is probably not adultery: *Maclennan v. Maclennan* 1958 S.C. 105.

[24] *Norfolk (Duke of) v. Germaine* (1692) 12 St.Tr. 929 is the first reported action of this kind. The plaintiff alleged that the defendant had "by lascivious conversation" committed adultery with the duchess, and claimed £100,000 damages. The jury were severely reprimanded by Holt C.J. for awarding £66 13s. 4d.

[25] So one Labour M.P. opposed the abolition of the action as being "an open sesame to some rich philanderer, who would be able to cruise past the factory gates in his leather upholstered Rolls-Royce and importune away the prettiest wife at the works": Standing Committee C, February 11, 1970, col. 38.

not recommend its abolition,[26] although Parliament finally effected this by the Law Reform (Miscellaneous Provisions) Act 1970, s.4.

Injuries to the wife

(i) *Enticement and harbouring*

No action will lie against another woman by a wife for adultery committed with her husband.[27] But at common law she could sue for enticement,[28] although not for harbouring.[29] But the 1970 Act has also abolished these claims.

(ii) *Loss of consortium*

A married woman has no right of action against a person who by a negligent act or omission has deprived her of her husband's society or services. This claim was put forward (apparently for the first time) in *Best v. Samuel Fox Ltd.*,[30] in which the plaintiff's husband had, by reason of the defendant's negligence, suffered injuries the effect of which was to deprive the plaintiff of the opportunity of having normal marital relations. It was argued that in modern conditions it was anomalous to grant such an action to the husband and refuse it to the wife. But the House of Lords held that the real anomaly today was the husband's right of action for loss of his wife's *consortium* and that there was no reason for extending such an anomaly. The decision in *Best v. Fox* cannot be evaded by suing in negligence.[31] On the other hand, for the death of her husband a wife, if dependent, may claim compensation under the Fatal Accidents Act.[32]

§ 15.5. DEATH OF RELATIVES[33]

At common law it was not a civil wrong to cause the death of a human being.[34] So although a husband could sue at common law for any wilful or negligent harm done to his wife whereby he was temporarily deprived of her society or services, he could not sue in respect of that permanent deprivation which he suffered by reason of her death. A father's rights in respect of his children were similarly limited. Thus in

---

[26] Law Com. No. 19, paras. 91–92.
[27] *Newton* v. *Hardy* (1933) 149 L.T. 165.
[28] *Best* v. *Samuel Fox Ltd.* [1952] A.C. 716, 729–730.
[29] *Winchester* v. *Fleming* [1958] 1 Q.B. 259.
[30] [1952] A.C. 716.
[31] *Marx* v. *Att.-Gen.* [1974] 1 N.Z.L.R. 164.
[32] See below, § 24.9.
[33] See Holdsworth, H.E.L., 3rd ed., iii, pp. 331–336, 576–583; Report of Law Revision Committee (Cmd. 4540 (1934)).
[34] *Baker* v. *Bolton* (1808) 1 Camp. 493. The reporter of Lord Ellenborough's decisions at Nisi Prius was the future Lord Campbell, who in his *Life* (ii, p. 215), after paying tribute to the high judicial qualities of the Chief Justice, said "When I arrived at the end of my fourth and last volume, I had a whole drawer full of 'bad Ellenborough law.'" If Lord Campbell had put *Baker* v. *Bolton* into that drawer he would have earned the gratitude of later generations—though then he would not have given his name to a statute.

Osborn v. *Gillett*[35] a father sued at common law[36] for the death of his daughter, who had been negligently run over and killed by the defendant. The defendant pleaded that the deceased had been killed on the spot and therefore that the plaintiff had not been deprived of the services of his daughter otherwise than by her death; and it was held that the plea was good. Had the death ensued after an interval only, the plaintiff would have had a good cause of action for loss of service during that interval,[37] but none in respect of the death. In *Jackson* v. *Watson and Sons Ltd.*,[38] however, it was decided that this rule does not apply in an action for breach of contract, but is limited to cases of pure tort. But when the breach of a contract made with the plaintiff results in the death of some third person in whose life the plaintiff has an interest, the damages recoverable in an action of contract will, it seems, include any pecuniary loss resulting, not too remotely, from that death. Thus in *Jackson* v. *Watson* itself, a husband, in an action for breach of warranty in a contract of sale, recovered damages (independently of the Fatal Accidents Act) for the death of his wife caused by eating certain poisonous food sold to him by the defendants.

We shall see[39] that the Law Reform (Miscellaneous Provisions) Act 1934, abolished the effect of the maxim *actio personalis moritur cum persona*. But that rule is entirely distinct from the rule in *Baker* v. *Bolton*, which deprives other persons than the deceased of any remedy where they have suffered damage as the result of the death. The latter rule seems to be based, in so far as it refers to inability to recover for the loss of services by the infliction of death, on the principle that a trespass is merged in a felony, a reason inadequate in Lord Ellenborough's time, and now obsolete. It is probable that it was introduced into the law owing to a confusion of the *actio personalis* maxim with the former rule[40] that no action will lie for a tort which is also a felony until the felon has been prosecuted, a rule which will not support the doctrine in its present wide form. But although the rule may be both unjust and technically unsound, it is the present law of England, for it was affirmed by the House of Lords in *Admiralty Commissioners* v. *S.S. Amerika*.[41] "We can only regard the decision as perhaps the strongest illustration which we have in our books of the manner in which *communis* error sometimes *facit jus*."[42] Although its abolition was recommended by the Law Revision Committee[43] the Government felt it would be difficult to allow

---

[35] (1873) L.R. 8 Ex. 88.

[36] It does not appear from the report why the action was not brought under the Fatal Accidents Act. Under this Act damages could in such a case be recovered to the extent of the value of the daughter's gratuitous services to her father: *Berry* v. *Humm & Co.* [1915] 1 K.B. 627.

[37] As in *Baker* v. *Bolton* itself.

[38] [1909] 2 K.B. 193.

[39] Below, § 20.10.

[40] See below, § 20.10.

[41] [1917] A.C. 38.

[42] Holdsworth, H.E.L., Vol. iii, pp. 336, 667.

[43] Cmd. 4540 (1934) s.15(e).

an employer to recover for the death of his servant without also making provision for the converse situation.[44] We shall deal later with the statutory exceptions to the rule in *Baker* v. *Bolton* created by the Fatal Accidents Acts 1846 to 1959,[45] now consolidated in the Fatal Accidents Act 1976.

---

[44] Hutton, "Mechanics of Law Reform" (1961) 24 M.L.R. 18, 23.
[45] See below, § 24.9.

CHAPTER 16

THE ECONOMIC TORTS[1]

§ 16.1. The Decision in Allen v. Flood

The fundamental case is *Allen* v. *Flood*.[2] Flood and Taylor were ship-wrights who had a daily contract of employment with the Glengall Iron Company. Some iron men who also worked for the company objected to the employment of the plaintiffs, believing them, probably wrongly, to have worked on iron at another ship-yard, and Allen, a trade union official acting on their behalf, informed the company's manager that unless Flood and Taylor were dismissed the men would "knock off work," or "be called out." (It was uncertain exactly which phrase he used.) Flood and Taylor thereupon were lawfully dismissed by the Glengall Company at the end of the day. Kennedy J. awarded the plaintiffs damages and his judgment was upheld by the Court of Appeal, which held that it was a tort (1) maliciously to procure the lawful dismissal of another, and (2) maliciously to procure another to abstain from making a contract. A majority of the House of Lords held that the Court of Appeal was wrong on both points, and that Flood and Taylor had no cause of action against Allen. No unlawful act had been committed by him: he had not introduced or procured the breach of any contract. Nor had he entered into any conspiracy. The fact that his motives might have been malicious made no difference. "At the end of the day all that *Allen* v. *Flood* decides is that where there is no element of combination so far as the individual is concerned what he does is either lawful or unlawful; if it is unlawful it is not saved by good intentions, and if it is lawful it is not made unlawful by reason of malice on his part."[3]

It was also settled in *Allen* v. *Flood* that so far as a single defendant is concerned there is a chasm between inducing a breach of contract and inducing a person not to enter into a contract.[4] The common law does not protect mere expectancies as distinct from promised advantages. Perhaps the clearest illustration of the conduct which might be actionable if such a tort existed is to be found in the American case of *Tuttle* v. *Buck*,[5] in which the plaintiff, who had carried on his hairdressing business in a small town for many years, incurred the enmity of the defendant, a wealthy man, who deliberately set up a rival establishment in the same town with the object and effect of driving the plaintiff out of business by under-cutting his rates. The court held that an action lay.

---

[1] See Burns, "Tort Injury to Economic Interests" (1980) 50 Can. Bar Rev. 103; Carty, "Intentional Violation of Economic Interests" (1988) 104 L.Q.R. 250.
[2] [1898] A.C. 1.
[3] Lord Gardiner Q.C., *arguendo*, in *Rookes* v. *Barnard* [1963] 1 Q.B. 623, 645.
[4] *Rookes* v. *Barnard* [1964] A.C. 1129, 1168, 1234.
[5] (1909) 107 Minn. 145; 119 N.W. 946.

In other words, what the plaintiff is trying to establish in a case like *Tuttle* v. *Buck* is "*Quinn* v. *Leathem* without the conspiracy."[6] Sir John Holt in 1705 and Sir William Erle in 1869 suggested that such an action might lie[7] and the following Law Lords have at various times and in various words contemplated the likelihood of such an action: Lord Lindley in *Quinn* v. *Leathem*[8]; Lord Loreburn in *Conway* v. *Wade*[9]; Lords Cave, Atkinson and Sumner in *Sorrell* v. *Smith*[10]; and Lord Devlin in *Rookes* v. *Barnard*.[11] On the other hand Lord Dunedin described this view as "the leading heresy,"[12] and Lord Donovan in *Stratford and Son Ltd.* v. *Lindley*[13] also opposed it. Dicta of Lord Diplock may be cited both for[14] and against.[15] But the draftsman of the second limb of section 3 of the Trade Disputes Act 1906,[16] clearly assumed that deliberate interference with trade, business or employment without lawful justification might be held to be a tort.[17] If it be said that this view is untenable since section 13(2) of the Trade Union and Labour Relations Acts 1974 and 1976,[18] the reply is that the position was uncertain in 1906 and Parliament was putting in a provision which would be necessary if the law as interpreted by the courts went one way[19] but unnecessary if it went the other way.

Indeed, since 1906 Parliament has consistently made it clear that certain immunities must be given to those who induce breaches of contracts in the course of trade disputes, although at different times different meanings have been given to the terms "contracts" and "trade disputes." Yet there is much to be said for the view that if *Allen* v. *Flood* had gone the other way the courts would have had a useful weapon against intolerable conduct.[20] So much of the complex legislation on race relations would have been unnecessary.[21] It is too definite to say

---

[6] Lord Devlin's memorable phrase in *Rookes* v. *Barnard* [1964] A.C. 1129, 1216.
[7] *Keeble* v. *Hickeringill* (1705) 11 East 573n. 575; Erle, *Trade Unions* (1869), p. 12. This was also the view of six of the eight High Court judges summoned to advise in *Allen* v. *Flood* [1898] A.C. 1. It is worth remembering that of the 21 judges before whom *Allen* v. *Flood* was argued, no fewer than 13 thought that such an action lay, and only eight were in favour of the trade union official who was the successful defendant, but as six of those eight were Lords of Appeal their opinions prevailed.
[8] [1901] A.C. 495, 537. See also below, § 16.4.
[9] [1909] A.C. 506, 511.
[10] [1925] A.C. 700, 713, 739.
[11] [1964] A.C. 1129, 1215.
[12] *Sorrell* v. *Smith* [1925] A.C. 700, 719.
[13] [1965] A.C. 269, 340.
[14] *Merkur Island Shipping Corporation* v. *Laughton* [1983] 2 A.C. 570, 609–610, cited below, § 16.2.
[15] *Lonrho Ltd.* v. *Shell Petroleum Co. Ltd. (No. 2)* [1982] A.C. 173, 189–190 (hereafter *Lonrho (Oil)*).
[16] See below, § 17.1.
[17] See [1964] A.C. 1129, 1177, 1216, and Hoffmann in (1965) 81 L.Q.R. 116, 133–134, on the parliamentary history of the section.
[18] See below, § 17.1.
[19] *i.e.* by recognising "*Quinn* v. *Leathem* without the conspiracy."
[20] See Heydon, *Economic Torts*, p. 28.
[21] Under the Race Relations Act 1976 damages may be assessed *as if* a tort has been committed, but the statute is obscure: *Alexander* v. *Home Office* [1988] 1 W.L.R. 968.

that outside the area of industrial disputes *Allen* v. *Flood* is only of academic interest.[22]

So far as is possible to find a common element in all the cases on trade competition it seems to be that the defendant has used a third person to harm the plaintiff.[23] "Pressure is at the heart of this branch of tort."[24] "This is not surprising. One can bloody one's neighbour's nose unaided, but to ruin him usually requires assistance; the defendant in the economic torts is commonly Iago, not Jehu."[25] It is important to note that the defendant has not usually procured the third party to commit any tort; if he had done this, there would be no problem, for the defendant and the third party would be joint tortfeasors.

§ 16.2. CAUSING LOSS BY UNLAWFUL MEANS[26]

There is general agreement that a new tort has been invented or discovered during the past two decades.[27] The tort is described in different ways—causing loss by unlawful means, wrongful interference with trade or business, or interference with the right to trade. Until a definition, as distinct from a description, emerges from the judgments, the tort may have to be called innominate. A definition may be latent in a dictum of Lord Diplock which asserts that the tort of causing loss by unlawful means is a genus of which the nominate specific torts—*e.g.* inducement of breach of contract—are only examples.[28] Apparently the same act may give rise to two or more specific torts—*e.g.* inducement of breach of contract and interference with trade.[29] But a specific tort must be proved: conduct does not become unlawful simply by calling it unfair. "There is no tort of unfair trading."[30] The world is a very unfair place.[31] On the other hand, an intent to injure the plaintiff need not be proved, as it must in one of the two forms of the related tort of conspiracy.[32] It is enough to prove an intent to do a wrongful act which foreseeably must injure the plaintiff. Presumably also this genus tort will authorise the creation of new specific torts, the possibility of which is

---

[22] In any event, the decision may be justifiable from the standpoint of policy. So Pollock thought it was correct "for a world of people who mostly get muddled over subtle distinctions, and think them unjust whenever they can't understand" (Pollock-Holmes *Letters*, Vol. I, pp. 84–85).

[23] See Silkin *arguendo* [1963] 1 Q.B. 623, 652.

[24] *Morgan* v. *Fry* [1968] 2 Q.B. 710, 738, *per* Russell L.J. So in *Rookes* v. *Barnard* the defendant Fistal said in evidence "We secured our desires by pressure" (Printed Case, p. 39).

[25] Weir, Note [1964] C.L.J. 225, 227.

[26] See Carty, "Intentional Violation of Economic Interests" (1988) 104 L.Q.R. 250.

[27] See various judicial statements in *Lonrho plc* v. *Fayed* [1990] 2 Q.B. 479, 487–489; [1991] 3 W.L.R. 188, 194–198 (hereafter *Lonrho (Harrods)*); *Associate British Banks* v. *T.G.W.U.* [1989] 1 W.L.R. 939, 952, 963, 965.

[28] *Merkur Island Shipping Corporation* v. *Laughton* [1983] 2 A.C. 570, 609–610. As Lord Diplock took a conservative view of the judicial function in the law of torts, this statement is significant.

[29] *Mercury Communications Ltd.* v. *Scott-Garner* [1984] Ch. 37, 56; *Associated British Ports* v. *T.G.W.U.* [1989] 1 W.L.R. 939, 952.

[30] *Associated Newspapers plc* v. *Insert Media Ltd.* [1990] 1 W.L.R. 900, 909, *per* Mummery J.

[31] *Swedac Ltd.* v. *Magnet Southern plc* [1989] F.S.R. 243, 249. See above, § 2.2.

[32] *Lonrho (Harrods)* [1991] 3 W.L.R. 188.

hinted at in some judgments—*e.g.* the torts of unfair competition,[33] economic duress,[34] and harassment.[35]

The requirement of unlawful means, which stems from the basic decision in *Allen* v. *Flood*,[36] imposes an arbitrary and illogical limit on the development of a rational general principle to explain this part of the law. But until *Allen* v. *Flood* can be distinguished by the House of Lords on some ground,[37] the law must be expounded on the basis that an essential part of the description or definition of the generic tort is that, apart from the anomalous case of conspiracy, the defendant should have used unlawful means to damage the plaintiff. Means are unlawful either at common law or under statute.

At common law the phrase unlawful means includes acts which can be indexed under one of the conventional rubrics (battery, libel, nuisance), and have not been protected under the Trade Disputes Act 1906 and the subsequent amending legislation.[38] But problems will arise if the scope of one of those torts is widened, as when intimidation was held to include threats to break a contract.[39]

Statutory unlawful means cannot be defined with precision. Since the decision of the House of Lords in *Lonrho (Oil)*[40] it is clear that the breach of a statutory duty cannot be relied on as unlawful means for the purpose of this tort unless it is also actionable at the suit of the plaintiff.[41] In *Lonrho* the claim failed although the defendant's acts were deliberate and positive and also serious offences under legislation prohibiting the importation of goods into Rhodesia. But that legislation did not confer any rights on the public in general or any particular class of it.[42] So a criminal act, deliberately done, which has the (intended) result of causing economic loss to another, and is outside the area of trade disputes, gives no remedy to the wronged party.[43]

§ 16.3. INDUCEMENT OF BREACH OF CONTRACT[44]

Intentionally and without lawful justification to induce or procure anyone to break a contract made by him with another is a tort action-

---

[33] *Cadbury-Schweppes Ltd.* v. *Pub Squash Co. Ltd.* [1981] 1 W.L.R. 193, 200–201. (But a strong tribunal expressly refused to recognise the tort.)

[34] *Universe Tankships Inc. of Monrovia* v. *I.T.W.F.* [1983] A.C. 366, 400. But the majority of the Law Lords thought that duress gave rise only to claims in restitution.

[35] *Thomas* v. *N.U.M.* [1986] Ch. 20, 64. But the existence of this tort was denied in *News Group Newspapers Ltd.* v. *S.O.G.A.T. 1982* [1987] 1 R.L.R. 180, 206.

[36] [1898] A.C. 1.

[37] *e.g.* that the decision was arrived at by a complex process: see above, § 16.1.

[38] For these provisions, see below, § 17.1.

[39] *Rookes* v. *Barnard* [1964] A.C. 1129. See below, § 16.6.

[40] [1982] A.C. 173.

[41] *Associated British Ports* v. *Transport and General Workers Union* [1989] 3 W.L.R. 939, 955, 981, 986.

[42] So as to be actionable under the traditional rules which permit an individual to sue for breach of statutory duty: see above § 10.1.

[43] See Harman J. in *Shelley* v. *Cunane* [1983] 9 F.S.R. 390.

[44] See Carty, "Intentional Violation of Economic Interests" (1988) 104 L.Q.R. 250.

able at the suit of that other, if damage has resulted to him.[45] In practice today the courts seem to be more willing to grant injunctions in such cases than they were in the past.[46] The tort had its origin in the action for enticing away the servant of another. In *Lumley* v. *Gye*[47] it was held that such an action lay even when the contract, the breach of which had been procured, was not one of service in the strict sense of the term. It was, however, for some time believed that the principle so established was confined to cases where (i) the defendant's action was malicious, and (ii) the contract in question was one to render exclusive personal services for a fixed period. But now it is perfectly well established that the scope of the action is not limited in either of these ways. Indeed, the modern cases indicate that the tort has become so broad as to be better described as unlawful interference with contractual relations.

(1) The unlawful intention

Proof of malice in the sense of spite or ill-will is unnecessary. "I think," said Lord Macnaghten,[48] "the decision [in *Lumley* v. *Gye*] was right, not on the ground of malicious intention—that was not, I think, the gist of the action—but on the ground that a violation of a legal right committed knowingly is a cause of action, and that it is a violation of legal right to interfere with contractual relations recognised by law, if there be not sufficient justification for the interference." It is no justification for the defendant to say that he had an honest doubt whether he was interfering with the plaintiff's contract,[49] or that he had acted without malice,[50] or in good faith,[51] or that the breach was really for the plaintiff's benefit, if he had only properly understood the position.[52] It is enough to show that the defendant did an act which must damage the plaintiff: it need not be proved that he intended it to do so.[53]

(2) The contracts protected

The principle in *Lumley* v. *Gye* protects contracts which involve a continuous course of dealing as well as those to do a particular act.[54] Nor is the principle any longer confined to inducements to break contracts of service. Thus in *Temperton* v. *Russell*[55] certain builders had contracted with the plaintiffs to purchase from him their building materials. The defendants, officials of a trade union which wished to bring pressure to bear upon the plaintiff, procured the builders to break these contracts

---

[45] *James McMahon Ltd.* v. *Dunne* (1965) 99 I.L.T.R. 45, 49; *Becton, Dickinson Ltd.* v. *Lee* [1973] I.R. 1, 45.

[46] *Swiss Bank Corporation* v. *Lloyd's Bank Ltd.* [1979] 2 All E.R. 853, 871.

[47] (1853) 2 E. & B. 216.

[48] *Quinn* v. *Leathem* [1901] A.C. 495, 510.

[49] *Swiss Bank Corporation* v. *Lloyd's Bank* [1977] 2 All E.R. 853.

[50] *Greig* v. *Insole* [1978], W.L.R. 302, 332.

[51] *Pratt* v. *British Medical Association* [1919] 1 K.B. 244, 265–266.

[52] *South Wales Miners' Federation* v. *Glamorgan Coal Co. Ltd.* [1905] A.C. 239, 246.

[53] See the dicta in *Lonrho (Harrods)* [1990] 2 Q.B. 479, 492, impliedly approved by the H.L. in [1991] 3 W.L.R. 188.

[54] *National Phonograph Co. Ltd.* v. *Edison-Bell Phonograph Co. Ltd.* [1908] 1 Ch. 335, 367–368.

[55] [1893] 1 Q.B. 715.

by threatening them with labour trouble if they refused to do so. The Court of Appeal held the defendants liable.[56]

The decision was of great significance in that it also foreshadowed the many contemporary cases on "secondary action"—*i.e.* interfering with the commercial contracts of the primary party to a trade dispute by disrupting the employment contracts of his supplier. The court in *Temperton* v. *Russell* was of the opinion that it was actionable to induce persons not to enter into contracts with the plaintiff, but in this it was wrong. "So far from thinking it a small step from one decision to the other, I think there is a chasm between them."[57] In short, the principle in *Lumley* v. *Gye* protects promised advantages and not mere expectancies.[58] But to this proposition there is a qualification: if the plaintiff's contract has been breached by the defendant, the court can, by way of injunction,[59] restrain interference not only with that contract but also with any other similar contract which he may make in the future.[60] This is justifiable because what is restrained is a breach of contract, whether to take place now or in the future, which is not the same as ordering a person not to make a contract.[61]

(3) The breach procured

It has been held that no action will lie for the inducement of the breach of a contract which is void, *e.g.* a wagering contract,[62] or one which is in restraint of trade.[63] Probably no action lies for breach of a contract which is not void but only unenforceable.[64] It has been suggested that no action will lie for inducement of the breach of a contract which is determinable at pleasure, for (unless illegal means have been used) in such case there has been in truth no breach at all,[65] but as the gist of the action is the intentional violation of contractual rights this view may be too simple. For if a union official induces a supplier not to fulfil his primary obligations under a contract with an employer, the official may be liable to the employer in tort, even though the supplier is protected from his secondary obligation to pay damages by a *force majeure* clause,[66] or the contract is regarded by the parties to it as suspended rather than broken.[67] It was once said that the breach procured

---

[56] Today the defendants might have protection under the Employment Act 1980, s.17: see below, § 17.1.

[57] *Allen* v. *Flood* [1898] A.C. 1, 121, *per* Lord Herschell. Trade competition, however ruthless, is not in itself wrongful: see above, § 16.1.

[58] So interference with the economic advantages to be gained from a contract, as distinct from interference with the contract itself, is not actionable: *R.C.A. Ltd.* v. *Pollard* [1983] Ch. 135, 149.

[59] *Acrow Ltd.* v. *Rex Chainbelt Inc.* [1971] 1 W.L.R. 1676.

[60] *Torquay Hotel Co. Ltd.* v. *Cousins* [1969] 2 Ch. 106.

[61] *Midland Cold Storage Ltd.* v. *Steer* [1972] Ch. 630.

[62] *Joe Lee Ltd.* v. *Dalmeny* [1927] 1 Ch. 300.

[63] *Greig* v. *Insole* [1978] 1 W.L.R. 302.

[64] *Smith* v. *Morrison* [1974] 1 W.L.R. 659.

[65] *McManus* v. *Bowes* [1938] 1 K.B. 98, 127.

[66] *Merkur Island Shipping Corporation* v. *Laughton* [1983] 2 A.C. 570, 608.

[67] *Daily Mirror Newspapers Ltd.* v. *Gardner* [1968] 2 Q.B. 762.

must be one which goes to the root of the contract in question,[68] but this is now not accepted,[69] especially since the law has moved so far as to hold that a direct and deliberate interference with a contract may be tortious even though no breach has been caused.[70]

Interference without breach

A deliberate interference with contractual relations is actionable if it prevents or hinders[71] one of the parties to that contract from performing his primary obligations under it,[72] even though he is not thereby in breach of it.[73] To that extent a direct and deliberate interference with the trade or business of another is now a distinct tort.[74]

But a contract which has been rendered less valuable to either or both of the parties to it by reason of the deliberate acts of a third party will not necessarily involve that third party in civil liability. So if a recording company makes a contract with a pop star to record and sell his performance the intention of both parties is that nobody else shall record those performances. The contract will obviously be much less valuable to both parties if such an illicit recording ("boot-legging") is made. Yet English law gave no tortious remedy against the boot-legger. Now the Copyright Designs and Patents Act 1988, ss.185–188, gives a remedy to the recording company.

Knowledge. But the plaintiff is favoured in that he is not obliged to prove that the defendant knew the precise terms of the contract breached[75]: it is enough if the defendant's knowledge is sufficient to entitle the court to say that he has knowingly[76] or recklessly[77] procured a breach.[78] The result is to hold that it is enough for the plaintiff to prove an intent on the defendant's part to bring the contract to an end.[79] So constructive knowledge of the terms of the contract breached may suffice, in the sense that it may be enough to show common knowledge of the way in which business is conducted,[80] at least when the plaintiff's application is for an interlocutory injunction.[81]

---

[68] *De Jetley Marks* v. *Greenwood (Lord)* [1936] 1 All E.R. 863, 872.

[69] *D.C. Thomson & Co. Ltd.* v. *Deakin* [1952] Ch. 646, 664, 689–690.

[70] *Torquay Hotel Co. Ltd.* v. *Cousins* [1969] 2 Ch. 106, 138.

[71] *David Dimbleby & Sons Ltd.* v. *National Union of Journalists* [1984] 1 W.L.R. 427.

[72] *e.g.* if the defendant increases the plaintiff's costs of performing a contract to keep a highway in repair by dumping rubbish upon it.

[73] *Torquay Hotel Ltd.* v. *Cousins* [1969] 2 Ch. 106, 138.

[74] *Merkur Island Shipping Corporation* v. *Laughton* [1983] 2 A.C. 570, 608.

[75] *Torquay Hotel Co. Ltd.* v. *Cousins* [1969] 2 Ch. 106, 139; *Acrow Ltd.* v. *Rex Chainbelt Inc.* [1971] 1 W.L.R. 1676, 1682, *Brekkes* v. *Cattel* [1972] Ch. 105, 114; *Midland Cold Storage Ltd.* v. *Steer* [1972] Ch. 630, 644–645.

[76] So it might be prudent for an employer threatened with industrial action to send the third party a copy of the relevant contract, as in the *Merkur Island* case: [1983] 2 A.C. 570.

[77] *Emerald Construction Co. Ltd.* v. *Lowthian* [1966] 1 W.L.R. 691, 701.

[78] *Stratford (J.T.) & Son Ltd.* v. *Lindley* [1965] A.C. 269, 332.

[79] *Greig* v. *Insole* [1978] 1 W.L.R. 302.

[80] *James McMahon Ltd.* v. *Dunne* (1965) 99 I.L.T.R. 45 ("timber does not enter the Port of Dublin like manna from Heaven").

[81] *Daily Mirror Newspapers Ltd.* v. *Gardner* [1968] 2 Q.B. 762.

(4) The inducement or procurement

The classic exposition of the law on this point[82] has stood for 40 years, and there is therefore no point in going back to the earlier cases.[83] The law is that, subject to the important immunities given by section 13 of the Trade Union and Labour Relations Act 1974, as amended by the Employment Acts 1980 and 1982, the necessary ingredients of an actionable interference with contractual rights will exist in the following cases:

(1) When a third party, with knowledge of the contract and the intent to procure its breach, directly persuades or procures or induces one of the parties to that contract to break it. This is the most obvious form of actionable interference and is well illustrated by *Lumley* v. *Gye* itself[84] or by the cases in which there is unlawful picketing. An intent to injure the plaintiff, as distinct from interfering with his contract, need not be shown.[85]

(2) When a third party, instead of acting on the mind of the contract-breaker, physically detains him[86] or otherwise renders it impossible for him to perform his contract, *e.g.* by breaking his essential tools or machinery.[87] On such facts the contract-breaker will himself have an action for assault or intimidation. These acts must, of course, be done with knowledge of the contract and intent to bring about its breach. In these cases of direct disablement the means used need not be intrinsically unlawful,[88] as they must be when the inducement is indirect.[89]

(3) When a third party and the contract-breaker deal together in a manner which the third party knows to be inconsistent with the contract, *e.g.* when A pays for and takes delivery of a new car from B, knowing that it is offered to him in breach of a covenant against the resale of new cars.[90] (In this case the tort of conspiracy will probably also have been committed.) The contract-breaker may himself be a willing party to the breach: it is the interference with existing contractual relations which in the essence of the tort, not the inducement to break them.[91] The tort is only committed if the inconsistent dealing is begun, or continued, after the third party has notice of the contract.[92]

---

[82] In an unreserved judgment by Jenkins L.J. in *D.C. Thomson Ltd.* v. *Deakin* [1952] Ch. 646, 690–699.

[83] *Merkur Island Shipping Corporation* v. *Laughton* [1983] 2 A.C. 570, 608.

[84] (1853) 2 E. & B. 216.

[85] *Edwin Hill & Partners* v. *First National Finance Corp.* [1989] 1 W.L.R. 225, 234; *Lonrho (Harrods)* [1991] 3 W.L.R. 188.

[86] As if Gye had kidnapped Johanna Wagner: Weir [1964] C.L.J. 225, 228.

[87] *D.C. Thomson Ltd.* v. *Deakin* [1952] Ch. 646, 678, 695–696.

[88] *Esso Petroleum Ltd.* v. *Kingswood Motors Ltd.* [1974] 1 Q.B. 142, 155.

[89] See the distinction drawn between direct and indirect interference in *Greig* v. *Insole* [1978] 1 W.L.R. 302, 334.

[90] *B.M.T.A.* v. *Salvadori* [1949] Ch. 556 (a decision of "that extremely clever judge, Roxburgh J.": *Esso Ltd.* v. *Ministry of Defence* [1990] Ch. 163, 165, *per* Harman J.).

[91] *Sefton (Earl)* v. *Tophams Ltd.* [1964] 1 W.L.R. 1408; [1965] Ch. 1140. The appeal to the H.L. was on another point: [1967] 1 A.C. 50.

[92] *D.C. Thomson Ltd.* v. *Deakin* [1952] Ch. 646, 694.

(4) Again, so far from persuading or inducing or procuring one of the parties to the contract to break it, the third party may commit an actionable interference with the contract, against the will of both and without the knowledge of either, if, with knowledge of the contract, he does an act which, if done by one of the parties to it, would have been a breach. Of this type of interference the case of *G.W.K. Ltd.* v. *Dunlop Rubber Co. Ltd.*[93] affords a striking example.

(5) In the preceding four cases Jenkins L.J. was considering direct interference. For the fifth, and final, example he considered indirect interference, which is actionable only if unlawful means are used. In *Thomson* v. *Deakin* itself there was indirect interference with the principal contract by direct interference with the contracts of employment of those who were intended to perform the principal contract, but the plaintiff failed to prove a causal link between the inducement and the damage. It had not been proved that the employment contracts had in fact been broken, so as to disrupt performance of the supply contracts. But in theory action lies when a third party, with knowledge of the contract and intent to secure its breach or to interfere with its performance,[94] definitely and unequivocally persuades, induces or procures the servant of one of the parties to break his contract of employment, provided that the breach of the commercial contract forming the alleged subject of interference in fact ensues as a necessary consequence of the breach of the contract of employment.[95] It must be clearly shown that the effect of the withdrawal of the services of the particular servant concerned was to render it quite impracticable for the contract-breaker to perform his contract.[96] So "general exhortations issued in the course of a trade dispute, such as 'Stop supplies to X,' 'Refuse to handle X's goods,' 'Treat X as "black," ' and the like,"[97] will not usually constitute a sufficient inducement to be actionable (even if the other requisites are present), for the persons moved by such advocacy might well respond in a perfectly lawful way. So if the interference or disablement is indirect, it must be distinctly shown that unlawful means were advocated with the intent of interfering with the performance of a particular contract.[98]

Advice distinguished from inducement

It will be noticed that the tort is variously described as "procuring" or "inducing" a breach of contract or "interfering with contractual rela-

[93] (1926) 42 T.L.R. 376 and 593 (removal of rival's tyres from the car at motor show).

[94] As in *Merkur Island Shipping Corporation* v. *Laughton* [1983] 2 A.C. 570, 608 (a case in which there was actionable interference, albeit at three or four removes from the principal contract).

[95] The plaintiff succeeded in proving this in *Stratford & Son Ltd.* v. *Lindley* [1965] A.C. 269, 333, which is the leading case on indirect or secondary boycotts.

[96] *D.C. Thomson Ltd.* v. *Deakin* [1952] Ch. 646, 682, 696.

[97] *D.C. Thomson Ltd.* v. *Deakin* [1952] Ch. 646, 696, *per* Jenkins L.J.

[98] *Acrow Ltd.* v. *Rex Chainbelt Inc.* [1971] 1 W.L.R. 1676, 1681.

tions." Do these expressions cover mere advice? In the first place it is clear that the advice or inducement to be actionable must have been acted upon.[99] Secondly, the better view is that merely to give advice or information[1] is not inducement. So there is no liability when a trade union official advises a customer of the employer in dispute that he should consider his business relations with that employer in the light of the dispute, or a physician advises a patient to break a contract of service for his health's sake.[2] This advice will not constitute an inducement even if it calls attention to the possible dangers of continuing the contract in question—e.g. that a supplier's men may be called out if he maintains his contract with the employer in dispute. There must be an inducement in the strict sense—that is to say, the intentional creation of some inducing cause or reason for the breach of contract: for example, to induce a servant to leave his employment by an offer of higher wages, or by a threat to inflict some harm upon him, legal or illegal, if he continues in it. To induce a breach of contract means to create a reason for breaking it; to advise a breach of contract is to point out the reasons which already exist. The former is certainly actionable: the latter is probably innocent.[3]

"Threats"

Another difficulty arises from the word "threat." A threat is a preintimation of proposed action of some kind, and everything depends upon whether the action proposed (with, it is understood, the object and effect of injuring the plaintiff) is lawful or not. At one time there was a tendency to distinguish between a threat on the one hand and a notice or warning on the other hand, so that if a trade union official says "all my members have decided to embark upon this course of action," it would be a question whether he was just acting as a messenger or uttering a threat. But it is now generally agreed that this distinction is unhelpful.[4] A threat is not *per se* unlawful. The distinction between unlawful and lawful threats is drawn according to the nature of the act threatened and not according to the nature of the threat. One might give proper notice of termination of a contract in the most violent language: conversely, an announcement of an intention to call out all the workers in a vital industry may be couched in subdued tones.[5] The conclusion is

---

[99] *Read* v. *Friendly Society of Stonemasons* [1902] 2 K.B. 732, 737.

[1] *Torquay Hotel Co. Ltd.* v. *Cousins* [1969] 2 Ch. 106, 125.

[2] This was the opinion of the Royal Commission on Trade Unions (Donovan Commission), 1968, Cmnd. 3623, para. 891.

[3] See *De Stempel* v. *Dunkels* [1938] Ch. 352, 366, in which Simonds J. expressed an opinion opposed to that in the text.

[4] *Hodges* v. *Webb* [1920] 1 Ch. 70. But see Lords Reid, Evershed and Hodson in *Rookes* v. *Barnard* [1964] A.C. 1129, and Lord Reid *arguendo* in *Stratford (J.T.) & Son Ltd.* v. *Lindley*, *The Times*, July 2, 1964.

[5] So in *Dimbleby & Sons Ltd.* v. *National Union of Journalists* [1984] 1 W.L.R. 67, 71, the union official addressed its members in words which were "gentle and reassuring—almost avuncular."

that if one may do something, one may threaten to do it. A threat is usually made by, or on behalf of, a number of people, but a threat by one important employee may be very effective.

It has been said that the threat must be a coercive one—*i.e.* coupled with some demand, so that if my gardener tells me he is not going to dig my potatoes that is only an announcement and not a threat unless he couples it with, say, a demand for higher wages.[6] But this view seems to rest upon the now outmoded difference between a threat and an announcement or warning. It is certainly clear that the threat may be either an "if" threat or an "unless" one. There is no difference between saying that one will break one's contract if an employer does something, and saying that one will break one's contract unless he does something.[7]

(5) The defence of justification

There is uncertainty about the very existence of this defence. Some have taken the view that an illegal act can never be justified.[8] Others think there is an analogy with conspiracy, or with qualified privilege in defamation. This seems to be the majority view. If so, to induce a threat of contract is not actionable if there is in the circumstances of the case a legal justification for the inducement. What amounts to a justification is a question to which no precise answer can be given.[9] It was said by (Sir Robert) Romer L.J.[10] in a passage often approved,[11] that most attempts to give a complete and satisfactory definition would probably be mischievous and that it must be left to the good sense of the tribunal to analyse the circumstances of the particular case. In so doing regard might be had to the nature of the contract broken; the position of the parties to the contract; the grounds for the breach; the means employed to procure the breach; the relation of the person procuring the breach to the person who breaks the contract; and to the object of the person in procuring the breach.[12] This broad approach has naturally produced problems. Presumably it would be a good justification if, in inducing a breach of contract made by A with the plaintiff, the defendant was doing nothing more than insisting on the performance of another and inconsistent contract previously made between himself and A.[13] But the breach by B of his contract with A cannot properly be held to justify or excuse A in procuring C to break an independent contract with B.[14]

---

[6] Lord Denning M.R. in *Stratford (J.T.) & Son Ltd. v. Lindley* [1965] A.C. 269, 287.

[7] [1965] A.C. 269, 292.

[8] *Read v. Friendly Society of Operative Stonemasons* [1902] 2 K.B. 732, 738.

[9] There is a full review of the cases in *Pete's Towing Services Ltd. v. Northern Industrial Union* [1970] N.Z.L.R. 32, 49.

[10] *Glamorgan Coal Co. v. South Wales Miners' Federation* [1903] 2 K.B. 545, 574–575.

[11] *Edwin Hill & Partners v. First National Finance Corp.* [1989] 1 W.L.R. 225, 229–230.

[12] *Dirassar v. Kelly, Douglas Ltd.* (1966) 59 D.L.R. (2d) 452, 481–482.

[13] *Pratt v. British Medical Association* [1919] 1 K.B. 244, 265.

[14] *Smithies v. National Association of Operative Plasterers* [1909] 1 K.B. 310, 341.

Moral duty

There are dicta[15] which suggest that where the defendant is acting under the pressure of moral duty he may possibly be justified, as, for example, when the claims of family relationship or guardianship demand an interference amounting to protection.[16] But it is significant that there are apparently only two reported cases in which a breach has been so justified. In one, *Brimelow* v. *Casson*,[17] the conduct of the plaintiff had been "utterly disgraceful,"[18] in that he had paid the chorus girls in his theatrical company such low wages that they had been driven to prostitution. In the other case a defendant was justified in procuring a breach in order to expose the "absolutely nonsensical mumbo-jumbo" of the plaintiff scientologists which was capable of injuring the public's health.[19] Lord Denning suggested[20] that union officials taking industrial action against members of a break-away union would be justified if those persons "were really trouble-makers who fomented discord." But other dicta assert that it is no sufficient justification that the defendant was acting as an altruist, seeking only the good of another and careless of his own advantage[21] or that he was performing a public service.[22] It has been held that it is no justification that an association has a duty cast upon it to protect the interests of its members and has acted in pursuance of that duty.[23] If the decision had gone the other way, every official of a trade union who procured a breach of contract in the course of a trade dispute would be protected independently of the Trade Union and Labour Relations Act 1974, s.13(2).[24]

Inducement by servant

Notwithstanding the general rule, a servant or agent acting on behalf of his employer or principal within the scope of his employment or authority is not liable in tort for inducing or procuring a breach of contract by his employer or principal. For in such a case the servant is not really an intervener or interferer in the contractual relationship but only the *alter ego* of one of the parties to it. If, for example, a company acting by its directors breaks its contract, the only remedy of the other party is to sue the company for breach of contract; he cannot sue the directors for the tort of inducing that breach.[25] But the possibility of procuring an injunction against a servant to restrain him from procuring his

---

[15] *South Wales Miners' Federation* v. *Glamorgan Coal Co.* [1905] A.C. 239, 249; *Camden Nominees* v. *Forcey* [1940] Ch. 352, 366.

[16] *Midland Bank Trust Co. Ltd.* v. *Green* [1979] 3 All E.R. 28, 42. But this may perhaps be better explained as an instance of advice as distinct from inducement.

[17] [1924] 1 Ch. 302.

[18] *Pritchard* v. *Briggs* [1980] Ch. 338, at 416, *per* Goff L.J.

[19] *Church of Scientology* v. *Kaufman* [1973] R.P.C. 627, 635.

[20] *Morgan* v. *Fry* 2 Q.B. 710, 729.

[21] *Read* v. *Friendly Society of Stonemasons* [1902] 2 K.B. 88, 97.

[22] *Camden Nominees* v. *Forcey* [1940] Ch. 352, 366.

[23] *South Wales Miners' Federation* v. *Glamorgan Coal Co.* [1905] A.C. 239.

[24] See below, § 17.1.

[25] *D.C. Thomson Ltd.* v. *Deakin* [1925] Ch. 646, 680–681; *Rutherford* v. *Poole* [1953] V.L.R. 130. See, however, *de Jetley Marks* v. *Greenwood (Lord)* [1936] 1 All E.R. 863, 872.

employer to break his contract with his own customer has certainly been considered.[26]

(6) Remedies

This is a tort in which the swift and peremptory remedy of an injunction may be more valuable than damages.[27] But the Trade Union and Labour Relations Act 1974, T.U.L.R.A. s.17 provides that an *ex parte* injunction shall not be granted in respect of acts connected with a trade dispute unless all reasonable steps have been taken to ensure that the party to be enjoined has been notified of the application. In 1975 a further provision was introduced by the Employment Protection Act for, as the Act states, the avoidance of doubt.[28] Thus subsection (2) of section 17 provides that where an application is made to a court for an interlocutory injunction and the other party claims that he acted in contemplation or furtherance of a trade dispute, the court shall, in exercising its discretion whether or not to grant the injunction,[29] have regard to the likelihood of that party succeeding at the trial of the action in establishing a defence under sections 13–15 of T.U.L.R.A. The phrase "have regard to" has caused difficulties. A High Court judge who refused an injunction because there was "a high degree of probability that the defence will succeed" was held by the House of Lords to have exercised his discretion correctly.[30] But there are dicta of the Law Lords which indicate that the court has a residual discretion to grant an injunction despite the fact that the defence may succeed at the trial, so that the conduct enjoined is ultimately held to have been lawful. But it would require an altogether exceptional case before such an injunction could be granted—*e.g.* where the consequences to the employer or to third parties or to the public or the nation might be disastrous if it were refused.[31] If the case is a suitable one for the grant of an interim injunction to preserve the status quo until trial, then the defendant may be restrained from interfering with future contracts as well as existing ones, for the plaintiff is entitled to carry on business in the usual way until trial of the action.[32]

§ 16.4. Conspiracy[33]

The tort of conspiracy exists when two or more persons agree to commit an act which would be lawful if done by one person but which is

---

[26] *Bowles & Son* v. *Lindley* [1965] 1 Lloyd's Rep. 207.

[27] The Donovan Commission (Cmnd. 3623, para. 848) noted that because violation of an injunction might be followed by imprisonment for contempt of court, it was as serious a penalty as that likely to follow from a criminal prosecution.

[28] The doubt arose from the decision in *American Cyanamid Co.* v. *Ethicon* [1975] A.C. 396 (see below, § 25.2) which lessened the burden of proof on an applicant for an injunction. He need not show that he has a strong case: an arguable case will do.

[29] The discretion is that of the trial judge, and so cannot be reviewed on appeal unless he hs misdirected himself in law: *Duport Steels Ltd.* v. *Sirs* [1980] 1 W.L.R. 142, 163, 171.

[30] *Duport Steels Ltd.* v. *Sirs* [1980] 1 W.L.R. 142.

[31] *Duport Steels Ltd.* v. *Sirs* [1980] 1 W.L.R. 142, 166, 171.

[32] *Torquay Hotel Co. Ltd.* v. *Cousins* [1969] 2 Ch. 106.

[33] See Sales, "The Tort of Conspiracy and Civil Secondary Liability" [1990] C.L.J. 491.

intended by the conspirators to do damage to the plaintiff, and such damage is in fact caused. The tort also exists when two or more agree to commit some recognised nominate tort,[34] *e.g.* assault, inducement of breach of contract, or intimidation, with resultant damage to the plaintiff. It is possible that the tort and the crime have a common origin in the time of Edward I. But the tort, unlike the crime, requires not only the combination to two or more to harm the plaintiff, but also concerted action taken in pursuance of that combination.

Although no branch of torts has a higher proportion of decisions of the House of Lords (six are discussed in the following pages) the scope of the tort is as obscure as its history. Its very existence was doubted by Salmond, who asserted that all the cases on conspiracy were really examples of the tort of intimidation.[35] But this view has not been accepted since it was described by Lord Dunedin as "the leading heresy."[36] The scope of the tort was exhaustively considered by the Court of Appeal in 1989 after "a massive citation of authority,"[37] but the fundamental question why conduct by two should be actionable when the same conduct by one is not has not yet been satisfactorily answered. It was once thought that a group of persons might be more powerful than an individual, but this 19th century answer "makes no sense in 20th century trading conditions,"[38] when a multi-national conglomerate (a single juristic person) may dispose of immense political and financial power.

Although the first significant House of Lords decision was a century ago,[39] one should start with the contrast between *Allen* v. *Flood*[40] and *Quinn* v. *Leathem.*[41] As we have seen, *Allen* v. *Flood* clearly established that, with the element of conspiracy absent, the motives of a single defendant are immaterial, so that he is not liable for damage caused intentionally or malevolently to the economic (or other) interests of the plaintiff. But when the element of conspiracy is present, all is different. So in *Quinn* v. *Leathem* the plaintiff was a butcher who had a dispute with the trade union of which the defendants were officials, with respect to the employment of certain workmen who did not belong to the union. The defendants requested the plaintiff to discharge these men, but he refused. Whereupon, with a view to compelling him to do so, the defendants compelled the plaintiff's chief customer to cease to deal with him, by threatening that otherwise they would call out that customer's workmen. The jury found that the defendants had maliciously con-

---

[34] But not simply the breach of a criminal statute: *Lonrho Ltd.* v. *Shell Petroleum & B.P. Ltd. (No. 2)* [1982] A.C. 172 (hereafter *Lonrho (Oil)*). See below, § 16.6.

[35] See (6th ed.), pp. 576–578.

[36] *Sorrell* v. *Smith* [1925] A.C. 700, 715.

[37] *Metall and Rohstoff A.G.* v. *Donaldson, Lufkin and Jenette Inc.* [1990] 1 Q.B. 391, 449 (hereafter *Metall*). In *Lonrho (Harrods)* [1991] 3 W.L.R. 188 the H.L. disapproved many of the dicta in *Metall*.

[38] *Metall* [1990] 1 Q.B. 391, 402–403, *per* Gatehouse J.

[39] *Mogul S.S. Co. Ltd.* v. *McGregor, Gow & Co. Ltd.* [1892] A.C. 25. The tort "is a modern invention altogether": *Midland Bank Trust Co. Ltd.* v. *Green* [1982] Ch. 529, 539, *per* Lord Denning M.R.

[40] [1898] A.C. 1. See above, § 16.1.

[41] [1901] A.C. 495.

spired to induce the plaintiff's customers not to deal with the plaintiff.[42] It was held that the plaintiff was entitled to sue the defendants for damages for the loss which he had sustained through the withdrawal of his customer. It is doubtful if a similar decision on these facts would be arrived at today, for neither the judges nor a Belfast jury at the end of the nineteenth century could be expected to appreciate the importance of the "closed shop" in trade union organisation.[43] But the effect of *Quinn* v. *Leathem* was almost immediately neutralised by the Trade Disputes Act 1906, s.1,[44] which provided that conduct by two should only be actionable if it would have been wrongful if done by one—and *Allen* v. *Flood* was accepted as establishing that one person could do these acts with impunity.

Forty years later in *Crofter* a unanimous House of Lords re-stated the law. It was held that, on the assumption that there were two distinct forms of conspiracy, the combination between the defendants with the object and effect of injuring the plaintiffs[45] was not actionable because the predominant purpose of the defendants was the promotion of their own (varied) interests. But the principle in *Quinn* v. *Leathem*, as distinct from its application to a particular set of facts, was not affected by the decision in *Crofter*, as another unanimous House of Lords recognised after another forty years in *Lonrho (Oil)*.[46] Lastly (for the moment) in 1991 another unanimous House of Lords[47] approved the long-standing professional opinion that there were two distinct forms of the tort of conspiracy.[48] So the current law is stated in an often cited dictum: "There are, as is well known, two sorts of conspiracies, the *Quinn* v. *Leathem* type which employs only lawful means but aims at an unlawful end, and the type which employs unlawful means."[49] These will be considered in turn.

§ 16.5. The First Type of Conspiracy

This is the *Quinn* v. *Leathem* type. Since *Crofter* the law is clear. A combination[50] wilfully to do an act causing damage to another in his trade or other interests is unlawful, and if damage is in fact caused is action-

---

[42] The malice lay in the fact that the defendants had refused a reasonable compromise, and stipulated that the men "must walk the streets for a year." But today it might be appreciated that from a union point of view it would be harmful to its bargaining power to give the impression that non-members could regain the advantages of membership simply by paying back-dues and fines.

[43] In *Crofter Hand-Woven Harris Tweed Co. Ltd.* v. *Veitch* [1942] A.C. 435 (hereafter *Crofter*) the H.L. in effect reversed *Quinn* v. *Leathem* by holding that a "closed shop" was a legitimate form of union activity: *Hadmor Productions Ltd.* v. *Hamilton* [1983] 1 A.C. 191, 228.

[44] See now T.U.L.R.A. 1974, s.13.

[45] Who were up-to-date manufacturers driven out of business by an embargo on their supplies imposed by a combination between old-fashioned manufacturers and a trade union.

[46] [1982] A.C. 173, 189.

[47] *Lonrho (Harrods)* [1991] 3 W.L.R. 188, 195–198.

[48] See below, n. 60.

[49] *Rookes* v. *Barnard* [1964] A.C. 1129, 1204, *per* Lord Devlin. (Approved in *Lonrho (Harrods)* [1991] 3 W.L.R. 188, 194).

[50] It is not necessary to prove a *contract*: an agreement or combination is enough.

able as a conspiracy.[51] There is liability if the conspirators know all the facts and act with the necessary intention even if they do not appreciate that they are acting unlawfully.[52]

Terminology

The usual expressions "conspiracy to injure" and "intent to injure" are misleading. Strictly speaking "injury" means an actionable wrong, and "damage" means loss or harm occurring in fact, whether actionable as an injury or not. There is also confusion between "motive" and "intention." It is better to use the terms "purpose" or "object."[53]

The purpose or object of the defendants

Before *Crofter* some had thought that a combination to do damage to another was not actionable unless it was inspired by malice or malevolence. But it is now clear that the predominant intent to injure is not to be equated with spite, vindictiveness or malevolence, although these will often be present. The correct proposition is that if there is a predominant intent to injure, and resultant damage, the conspiracy is actionable unless there is some justification. Such justification will be found if the combination is proved or admitted to be inspired by self-interest.[54] The pursuit of selfish ends provides in law, whatever may be the case in morals, its own justification.[55] Even the fact that the damage so inflicted is disproportionately severe does not necessarily involve liability. On the other hand, it is not a legitimate purpose of a combination to demonstrate dislike of the religious or racial opinions of the plaintiff,[56] or to punish him for the sake of punishment,[57] or to continue a boycott after a dispute has ended.[58]

Burden of proof

There are conflicting dicta.[59] Some put the burden of proving absence of justification on the plaintiff, others put the burden of proving its presence on the defendant. The former view is consistent with the analogy between the crime and the tort of conspiracy (the plaintiff must prove *mens rea*), but the latter is more consistent with the general principle that harm intentionally inflicted is wrongful unless justification is shown, as well as with the general reluctance to require a plaintiff to prove a negative.

---

[51] *Canada Cement La Farge Ltd.* v. *British Columbia Lightweight Aggregate Ltd.* (1983) 145 D.L.R. (3d) 385, 394.

[52] *Pritchard* v. *Briggs* [1980] Ch. 388.

[53] *Crofter* [1942] A.C. 435, 442–444. The case also contains many dicta on the issues which may arise if the motives of the parties are mixed.

[54] So in *Lonrho (Oil)* it was conceded that the combination between the defendants was to forward their own commercial interests.

[55] *Crofter* [1942] A.C. 435, 450, 469–471, 496.

[56] As in *Scala Ballroom (Wolverhampton) Ltd.* v. *Ratcliffe* [1958] 1 W.L.R. 1057.

[57] As in *Huntley* v. *Thornton* [1957] 1 W.L.R. 321 ("ruffled dignity" of trade union leaders).

[58] As in *Hutchison* v. *Aitchison* (1970) 9 K.I.R. 69.

[59] [1942] A.C. 435, 447–457, 471, 488, 495.

§ 16.6. THE SECOND TYPE OF CONSPIRACY

A second type of actionable conspiracy exists when two or more combine to injure a third person by unlawful means—*e.g.* the commission of a crime or a tort. In such a case it is immaterial that the object of the conspirators in using those means may be legitimate.[60] After much uncertainty, which was caused mainly by an elliptical passage in the speech of Lord Diplock in *Lonrho (Oil)*,[61] it was unanimously held by the House of Lords in *Lonrho (Harrods)*[62] that proof of a predominant intention to injure the plaintiff was not an essential component of this cause of action. *Lonrho (Oil)* did not lay down the rule which the Court of Appeal in *Metall* thought it did.

In *Lonrho (Oil)* the two corporate defendants had agreed to do and had done acts which were unlawful, intentional and positive, and which had caused economic loss to the plaintiffs. The acts so done were the importation by rail into Rhodesia from South Africa of large quantities of refined oil in breach of an English statutory order which had made such conduct criminal and provided serious penalties for it. The plaintiff's damage consisted of the loss of the profits which would have been made at their refinery in Rhodesia if crude oil had been imported by a pipe-line running to it from the coast of Mozambique. That mode of importation had been closed by a naval blockade ordered by the British Government in fulfilment of its policy of sanctions against the illegal regime in Rhodesia. The plaintiff company failed because it could not prove (i) that the statutory prohibitions had been imposed for its benefit, and (ii) that the acts of the defendants had been done with the intention of injuring it. Although the second restriction imposed on the tort by *Lonrho (Oil)* is no longer law, the first still exists and may be important. That restriction is that when the damage-causing acts are unlawful solely because they are in breach of a criminal statute, then the complex rules relating to actionable breaches of statutory duty must be satisfied.[63] Briefly, such acts are not unlawful means unless the court considers that the nature and context of the particular statute makes it appropriate that the plaintiff should be permitted to sue for breach of the duties which it imposes. The statute in *Lonrho (Oil)* could not be so construed, for its object was to carry out a governmental policy of bring-

---

[60] The two preceding sentences appeared in each edition of this textbook from the 15th (1969), p. 511, to the 19th (1987), p. 419, and were conceded by a unanimous Court of Appeal in *Metall* [1990] 1 Q.B. 391, 452, to represent correctly professional thinking in those years.

[61] [1982] A.C. 173, 187–188. The C.A. in *Metall* [1990] 1 Q.B. 391, 459, did concede that "Even a speech by Lord Diplock is not to be construed like a statute," but still took eight pages of the Law Reports to analyse what Lord Diplock had said in one and a half pages. (In *Lonrho (Harrods)* [1991] 3 W.L.R. 188 the H.L. stated that the C.A.'s analysis was erroneous. In another context Sir William Wade wrote: "A solitary judgment in a single case is not an ideal instrument for proclaiming radical and sweeping changes. In his later years Lord Diplock was inclined to yield to the temptation to restate whole branches of the law in his own terms" (Wade, *Administrative Law* (6th ed.), p. viii).

[62] [1991] 3 W.L.R. 188, 195–198.

[63] See above, Chap. 10.

ing down a treasonable régime,[64] and not to protect the plaintiff's business interests. If the plaintiff cannot escape from that restriction, then he must sue on the substantive torts (if any) for which the conspirators are jointly and severally liable as joint wrongdoers. Normally this will enable justice to be done, although conspiracy has some procedural advantages which other torts do not have.[65]

§ 16.7. INTIMIDATION[66]

The wrong of intimidation includes all those cases in which harm is inflicted by the use of unlawful threats whereby the lawful liberty of others to do as they please is interfered with.[67] This wrong is of two distinct kinds, for the liberty of action so interfered with may be either that of the plaintiff himself or that of other persons with resulting damage to the plaintiff. In other words, the defendant may either intimidate the plaintiff himself, and so compel him to act to his own hurt, or he may intimidate other persons, and so compel them to act to the hurt of the plaintiff. There is an analogy with fraud and injurious falsehood, in the former of which the defendant may deceive the plaintiff himself, but in the latter deceive other persons to the plaintiff's injury. Whichever of these two forms is taken by the tort, it is now possible that the tort is only an example of the wider wrong of intentionally causing loss by unlawful means.[68]

(1) Intimidation of the plaintiff himself

(i) By illegal acts

It is an actionable wrong intentionally to compel a person, by means of a threat of an illegal act, to do some act whereby loss accrues to him.[69] The threats must be made seriously and taken seriously.[70] For example, an action will lie at the suit of a trader who has been compelled to discontinue his business by means of threats of personal violence made against him by the defendant with that intention,[71] or by a creditor who has been threatened by his debtor that the latter will pay nothing unless the former accepts a lesser sum in full settlement.[72] So where A uses force to prevent B from carrying out his contract with C, A can be sued for intimidation by B and for procurement of breach of contract by C.[73]

---

[64] In fact the régime survived until 1979.
[65] e.g. the acts and admissions of one conspirator are admissible evidence against the other(s): *Derby & Co. Ltd.* v. *Weldon (No. 5)* [1989] 1 W.L.R. 1244, 1254.
[66] See Hughes, "Liability for Loss Caused by Industrial Action" (1970) 86 L.Q.R. 181; Burns, "Tort Injury to Economic Interests" (1980) 50 Can. Bar. Rev. 103.
[67] See the similar definition in *Pete's Towing Services Ltd.* v. *Northern Industrial Union* [1970] N.Z.L.R. 32, 41.
[68] See above, § 16.1.
[69] *Allen* v. *Flood* [1898] A.C. 1, 17; *The Tubantia* [1924] P. 78, 93; *Cory Lighterage Ltd.* v. *T.G.W.U.* [1973] 1 W.L.R. 792, 814; *Huglich* v. *Hale* [1973] 2 N.Z.L.R. 279, 285.
[70] *News Group Newspapers Ltd.* v. *SOGAT 1982* [1987] I.C.R. 180, 204.
[71] *Rookes* v. *Barnard* [1964] A.C. 1129, 1205, expressly approving the passage in the text.
[72] *D. & C. Builders Ltd.* v. *Rees* [1966] 2 Q.B. 617, 625.
[73] *Williams* v. *Hursey* (1959) 103 C.L.R. 30, 77.

(ii) *By legal acts*

But it is clear that the threat complained of must be a threat to do an act which is in itself illegal. No threat to exercise one's legal rights can amount to a cause of action, even if made for the purpose of intimidation or coercion, and even if inspired by malicious motives. So if one party to a contract asserts what he reasonably considers to be his rights arising under a contract, as distinct from threatening to break that contract, the other party should contest that assertion by suing for breach of contract.[74] To decide otherwise would mean overruling a clear decision of the House of Lords,[75] or at least distinguishing it on some ground which is not obvious. This has many consequences. English law permits a wealthy company to drive its competitors out of the field by under-cutting prices to an uneconomic level,[76] or an essential employee to threaten to leave unless his wages are substantially increased, or another employee, whom he dislikes, is lawfully dismissed.[77] In such cases it makes no difference that the threat is couched in menacing and disagreeable language: for if one may lawfully do a thing, one may threaten to do it.[78] But, as we have seen, it may be different if two or more are involved.

(2) Intimidation of other persons to the injury of the plaintiff

In certain cases it is an actionable wrong to intimidate other persons with the intent and effect of compelling them to act in a manner or to do acts which they themselves have a legal right to do which cause loss to the plaintiff: for example, the intimidation of the plaintiff's customers whereby they are compelled to withdraw their custom from him[79] or the intimidation of an employer whereby he is compelled to discharge his servant, the plaintiff. There are at least two cases in which such intimidation may constitute a cause of action:

- (i) When the intimidation consists in a threat to do or procure an illegal act;
- (ii) When the intimidation is the act, not of a single person, but of two or more persons acting together in pursuance of a common intention.[80]

Intimidation by threats of illegal act

Any person is guilty of an actionable wrong who, with the intention and effect of intimidating any other person into acting in a certain manner to the harm of the plaintiff, threatens to commit or procure an illegal act. Illegal acts now include breaches, or threatened breaches, of con-

---

[74] *Central Canada Potash Co. Ltd.* v. *Government of Saskatchewan* (1978) 88 D.L.R. (3d) 609, 639–640.

[75] *Allen* v. *Flood* [1898] A.C. 1. See above, § 16.1.

[76] See above § 16.4.

[77] See the example given in *Allen* v. *Flood* [1898] A.C. 1, 138–139. But the other servant might have an action for intimidation.

[78] See above, § 16.2.

[79] "Picketing" in a trade dispute is considered in detail below, § 17.1.

[80] *Rookes* v. *Barnard* [1964] A.C. 1129, 1205.

tract, as well as those which are criminal or tortious.[81] On the other hand, it is not necessary to prove a predominant intent to injure, as it is in the (anomalous) tort of conspiracy.[82] The existence of this form of intimidation was emphatically affirmed by the House of Lords in *Rookes v. Barnard*.[83]

The threat in *Rookes v. Barnard* was that strike action on the part of all AESD men employed by BOAC would occur within three days unless the plaintiff was withdrawn from the design department. The plaintiff was a non-unionist; although once he had been a shop steward in AESD, and the defendants Barnard and Fistal were two fellow-employees of BOAC, union members, and Silverthorne, the local trade union official, who was not himself under a contract of employment with BOAC. The threat made by the defendants was a wrongful act, being in breach of the no-strike agreement made between BOAC and the union.[84] So there were threats of wrongful acts aimed and directed at the plaintiff's employment with the object and result of causing its termination, for BOAC were so impressed by the threat that they responded to it by giving Rookes one week's notice of dismissal. At the trial the jury found for the plaintiff, and awarded him £7,500 damages. The magnitude of this award showed how seriously the plaintiff's fellow-citizens regarded the interference with his right to work.[85] On appeal, the House of Lords ordered a new trial on the issue of damages,[86] but otherwise upheld the verdict. The House of Lords held that the defendants' threat constituted the tort of intimidation and that the defendants were not protected by section 3 of the Trade Disputes Act 1906,[87] for the acts of the defendants were not immune from action "on the ground *only* that they interfered with the trade business or employment of the plaintiff," since they also constituted the tort of intimidation.[88]

If the party intimidated does not respond to the threat, then the plaintiff cannot sue,[89] for the plain reason that he has not been damaged. The damage to the plaintiff must be linked to the coercion of the threatened party. This meets the case where the threat is whimsical—for example, the office boy who threatens to leave unless the chairman of the com-

---

[81] *Cory Lighterage Ltd. v. T.G.W.U.* [1973] 1 W.L.R. 792.

[82] *Lonrho (Harrods)* [1991] 3 W.L.R. 195–198.

[83] [1964] A.C. 1129.

[84] A no-strike clause is unusual. Normally employees who go on strike either terminate their own contracts of employment or commit anticipatory breaches of them which the employer can treat as amounting to repudiation.

[85] The jury panel was drawn from those living near London Airport.

[86] The proceedings were eventually settled for £4,000. The plaintiff has published his own account of the case: Rookes, *Conspiracy* (London, 1966). His leading counsel has also recorded his memory of the plaintiff: "I don't care for bearded pacifists, and told him I didn't think an English jury would, either, and I forecast much lower damages than he was later awarded. But the enemy were so unattractive in the witness box that we easily beat the £1,500 paid into court": Sir Neville Faulks, *A Law unto Myself* (1978), p. 96.

[87] See now below, § 17.1.

[88] It is not too clear why Silverthorne was held liable; he had no contract to threaten to break. Perhaps it was because he was a party to a conspiracy: *Morgan v. Fry* [1968] 2 Q.B. 710, 729.

[89] *Morgan v. Fry* [1968] 2 Q.B. 710, 724.

pany is removed,[90] or the case where the person threatened is brave enough to stand up to the threat, as was Mr. Stratford in *Stratford & Sons Ltd.* v. *Lindley.*[91] The decision certainly shows the willingness of the courts to treat economic loss in the same way as physical loss and is in general justifiable on the ground that intimidation of any kind is highly objectionable and that there is no reason to limit the unlawful acts which constitute the wrong to those which are criminal or tortious as distinct from those which are breaches of contract.[92]

Actionable threats are not limited to cases of trade disputes though doubtless they are its most common illustration. For a lessor who threatened breaches of, say, the covenant for quiet enjoyment in a lease with the object of damaging one of the tenant's friends or relations would be liable.[93] The unlawful means which constitute the tort may also extend to cover threats of vexatious litigation,[94] or the entry into an agreement which is contrary to the public interest.[95]

The defence of justification

It is uncertain what justification, if any, might be held a defence.[96] It is hard to see how an act which is admittedly illegal can ever be justified. On the other hand, justification is allowed as a defence to two other intentional torts—conspiracy and inducement of breach.[97]

---

[90] *Rookes* v. *Barnard* [1963] 1 Q.B. 623, 666–667.
[91] [1965] A.C. 269.
[92] [1964] A.C. 1129, 1219.
[93] [1964] A.C. 1129, 1187.
[94] *Allen* v. *Flood* [1898] A.C. 1, 105.
[95] *Brekkes* v. *Cattel* [1972] 1 Ch. 105.
[96] Lord Devlin alone mentioned this defence in [1964] A.C. 1129, 1206.
[97] See Collins M.R. in *Read* v. *Friendly Society of Stonemasons* [1902] 2 K.B. 732, 738; and *Morgan* v. *Fry* [1968] 1 Q.B. 521, 548.

CHAPTER 17

TRADE DISPUTES[1]

§ 17.1. The Trade Union and Labour Relations Acts 1974 and 1976[2] and the Employment Acts 1980 to 1990[3]

This complex body of legislation follows the scheme of the Trade Disputes Act 1906 in giving certain immunities to unions and their members from common law liabilities. The later Acts disapplied the immunities in certain cases. For example, E.A. 1988, s.10 removes the immunity from liability granted by T.U.L.R.A. 1974, s.13 from all industrial action taken to enforce or support union membership. So a closed shop cannot be defended by union pressure, and an employee cannot be fairly dismissed for non-membership of a union.

The immunity or protection given to a union must be carefully distinguished from that given to its members or officials. So far as the union itself is concerned, section 14 of T.U.L.R.A., as amended by section 15 of E.A., gives immunity in some cases.[4] So far as the members or officials are concerned, the statutes give certain immunities or protections to those who do certain acts in the contemplation or furtherance of a trade dispute. The immunities or protections in question are mainly given by section 13 of T.U.L.R.A., which must be reproduced in full.

(1) An act done by a person in contemplation or furtherance of a trade dispute shall not be actionable in tort on the ground only—

> (a) that it induces another person to break a contract or interferes or induces another person to interfere with its performance; or
>
> (b) that it consists in his threatening that a contract (whether one to which he is a party or not) will be broken or its performance interfered with or that he will induce another person to break a contract or to interfere with its performance.

(2) For the avoidance of doubt it is hereby declared that an act done by a person in contemplation or furtherance of a trade dispute is not actionable in tort on the ground only that it is an interference with the trade, business or employment of another person, or with the right of another person to dispose of his capital or his labour as he wills.

(3) [This subsection has been repealed by section 17(8) of the Act of 1980.]

(4) An agreement or combination by two or more persons to do or procure the doing of any act in contemplation or furtherance of a trade dispute shall not be actionable in tort if the act in question is

---

[1] See Kidner, "Lessons in Trade Union Law Reform" (1982) 2 *Legal Studies* 34; Elias and Ewing, "Economic Torts and Labour Law" [1982] C.L.J. 321.

[2] Cited as T.U.L.R.A.

[3] Cited as E.A.

[4] For details, see below, § 20.5.

one which, if done without any such agreement or combination, would not be actionable in tort.

It will be observed that the draftsman was set the task of reversing or nullifying the effect of four well-known decisions, namely *Lumley* v. *Gye*,[5] *Torquay Hotel* v. *Cousins*,[6] *Rookes* v. *Barnard*[7] and *Quinn* v. *Leathem*,[8] and of quietening certain doubts which had arisen from dicta in a fifth, *Allen* v. *Flood*.[9] In addition, section 15 reverses *Lyons & Sons* v. *Wilkins*.[10] Each of these problems will now be considered.

(1) The reversal of Lumley v. Gye and Torquay Hotel v. Cousins

A detailed analysis of section 13(1) is required.

"An act done by a person"

The protection is not limited to trade unions or their members. On the other hand, trade unions no longer have the total immunity from any action in tort which they were held to possess under section 4 of the Trade Disputes Act 1906, which is now repealed.

"In contemplation or furtherance"

Until the decision of the House of Lords in *Express Newspapers Ltd.* v. *McShane*[11] there was much division of opinion about the meaning of these words. But in *McShane* it was laid down by a majority of the Law Lords that the test was subjective and not objective, as the Court of Appeal had thought.[12] It was the policy of the Act to exclude industrial disputes from judicial review.[13] It followed that, if there was a trade dispute within the section, and that was an issue over which courts still retained some control, then an act done as against a customer or a supplier of the party in dispute with the union might be protected, if the doer of the act honestly believed that it would further the cause of the union. In *Duport Steels Ltd.* v. *Sirs*[14] the House of Lords again emphatically reaffirmed the subjective interpretation established in *McShane* in preference to the objective interpretation favoured by the Court of Appeal in a series of decisions.

"Of a trade dispute"

Although the scope of judicial review has been limited by the House of Lords in *McShane* and *Sirs* it has not been entirely excluded. There

---

[5] (1853) 2 E. & B. 216. See above, § 16.3.
[6] [1969] 2 Ch. 106.
[7] [1964] A.C. 1129. See above, § 16.6.
[8] [1901] A.C. 495. See above, § 16.4.
[9] [1898] A.C. 1. See above, § 16.1.
[10] [1899] 1 Ch. 11. See above, § 5.10.
[11] [1980] A.C. 672.
[12] "Subsequent events and subsequent comments have shown convincingly that the four in the majority in the House of Lords made the wrong choice. Yet, as they had the last word, no one can gainsay it": *R.* v. *Crown Court (Sheffield)* [1980] Q.B. 530, at 539, *per* Lord Denning M.R.
[13] *N.W.L. Ltd.* v. *Woods* [1979] 1 W.L.R. 1294.
[14] [1980] 1 W.L.R. 142.

must be some objective event or situation before there can be a statutory trade dispute. So if the dispute has in truth ceased to exist months ago it cannot be revived simply by asserting that it still exists.[15]

T.U.L.R.A. and E.A. provide an elaborate definition of "trade dispute." By section 29(1) it means a dispute between employers and their workers, which "relates wholly or mainly to" seven different matters, e.g. terms and conditions of employment, matters of discipline, or the membership of a union. So that the courts are entitled to inquire whether there is a genuine connection between the dispute and the matters listed.[16] By section 29(2) disputes between workers and a Minister of the Crown are to be treated as a trade dispute, and so also, by section 29(3), are certain disputes as to matters occurring outside the United Kingdom.

"Shall not be actionable in tort"

The words "in tort" were not included in the corresponding section of the 1906 Act, under which it was held that the court was precluded from granting an injunction as well as awarding damages. An employee who breaks his contract of service may still be sued *in contract* by his employer, but a strike after due notice is not a breach of contract.[17]

The immunity granted by s.13(1) of T.U.L.R.A. is removed when secondary action takes place otherwise than in the cause of peaceful picketing, and action which is primary action relating to one trade dispute cannot be secondary action relating to another trade dispute (E.A. 1990, s.4).

"On the ground only"

This phrase, which also appeared in the 1906 Act, is very difficult to construe.[18] After much argument it was held in *Rookes* v. *Barnard*[19] that section 3 of the 1906 Act did not prevent actions if they were based on some ground other than inducement of breach of contract, or interference with business—*e.g.* slander, deceit or intimidation.[20] Although *Rookes* v. *Barnard* was reversed by the Trades Disputes Act 1965, whose provisions are re-enacted in section 13(1)(*b*) of T.U.L.R.A., the interpretation which it gave to "on the ground only" seems to be correct.

"That it induces another person to break a contract or interferes or induces another person to interfere with its performance"

The wide meaning given to "induces" in modern cases has already been considered.[21]

---

[15] *Hutchison* v. *Aitchison* (1970) 9 K.I.R. 69.

[16] *Universe Tankships* v. *I.T.F.* [1983] 1 A.C. 366, 386–387, 392.

[17] This has been settled since *Allen* v. *Flood* [1898] A.C. 1. See above, § 16.1. But the statutory protection is limited to actions *in tort*: a claim for restitution may lie: *Universe Tankships* [1983] A.C. 366, 385.

[18] Lord Reid in *Rookes* v. *Barnard* [1964] A.C. 1129, 1172.

[19] [1964] A.C. 1129.

[20] See above, § 16.6.

[21] See above, § 16.4.

"A contract" is a much wider term than that used in the Acts of 1906 and 1974, "a contract of employment." Parliament therefore clearly intended to protect breaches of commercial contracts procured in the course of an industrial dispute. On the other hand, breaches of statutory duty are not protected by the subsection so that in some cases it has been argued that such breaches have been committed with resultant liability for interference with business by unlawful means.[22]

Protection is also extended to one who "interferes with the performance of a contract." This is a notable parliamentary recognition of the judicial broadening of the scope of the principle in *Lumley* v. *Gye* to cover not only inducing breach of contract but also preventing the performance of it.[23] Similarly, section 13(1)(*h*) re-enacts section 1(1) of the 1965 Act, with equally broad meanings given to the concepts of contract, threats, and prevention of performance. But then Parliament decided to deal with the problem of secondary blacking or secondary boycotts by removing or lifting the immunities given by section 13(1) of T.U.L.R.A. when breach of a commercial contract was induced or procured by impermissible secondary action. In effect secondary action was allowed (and so the immunities given by section 13(1) continued in force) when the purpose of the secondary action was directly to disrupt the supply of goods and services between the employer in dispute and his first customer or supplier.[24] This was provided by the Employment Act 1980, s.17(1)–(3). Secondary action which does not satisfy the requirements of these subsections does not enjoy the protection of section 13(1) of T.U.L.R.A. as when action is taken because an employee has been dismissed, but that dismissal is not unfair because the employee was taking part in an unofficial industrial dispute (E.A. 1990, s.4). The complexity of these provisions has taxed the powers of comprehension of even the most skilled and experienced judges.[25] Anyone who has to tread a path through this legislative maze should do so in four stages.[26] Stage 1 is to determine whether the plaintiff has established what would have been a cause of action before T.U.L.R.A. Stage 2 is to ask whether that cause of action has been removed by T.U.L.R.A. Stage 3 is to ask whether the immunity so removed has been restored by E.A. Stage 4 is to ask whether the action in question has been authorised by a ballot held in accordance with the Trade Union Act 1984, s.10. Under E.A. 1988, s.1 a union member may seek a restraining court order when unballoted industrial action is proposed.

---

[22] See, *e.g. Barretts & Baird (Wholesale)* v. *Institution of Professional Civil Servants* [1987] I.R.L.R. 3.

[23] See *Merkur Island Shipping Corporation* v. *Laughton* [1983] 2 A.C. 570.

[24] But this purpose is frustrated if an intermediary or buffer company has been inserted between the primary employer and its customers or suppliers: see *Dimbleby & Sons Ltd.* v. *N.U.J.* [1984] 1 W.L.R. 427. The H.L. gave leave to appeal because it was the first case in which "damages and injunctions were sought against a trade union itself and not merely personally against its office-holders."

[25] In *Hadmor Productions Ltd.* v. *Hamilton* [1983] 1 A.C. 191, 205, Lord Denning M.R. said "It is the most tortuous section I have ever come across. . . . Some species of secondary action are given immunity by sub-sections (3), (4) and (5), but these are so confusing that I cannot attempt to summarise them."

[26] See *Merkur Island Shipping Corporation* v. *Laughton* [1983] 2 A.C. 570, 604.

Unlawful industrial action may now result in severe financial penalties. So in the Wapping Dispute in 1986, a union (SOGAT 82) which failed to obey an order of the High Court restraining certain unlawful industrial action was in one day fined £250,000 for contempt of court and its assets ordered to be sequestered.

(2) Allen v. Flood approved

The second subsection of section 13 of T.U.L.R.A. apparently gave the parliamentary death-blow to the residual tort of interference with business relations, which has had judicial support for two centuries.[27] But as section 13(2) was itself repealed by section 19(1) of the Employment Act 1982, some of the former doubts have been revived. Probably the object of the repeal was to enable a plaintiff alleging unlawful secondary action under section 17(1) to sue—otherwise there would have been no tort.

(3) The reversal of Quinn v. Leathem

It will be seen that subsection (4) of section 13 of T.U.L.R.A., which substantially re-enacts section 1 of the 1906 Act, restricts the bringing of an action of conspiracy to cases in which the acts in question would also be actionable if done by one person instead of by two or more. But it will be recalled that the courts had largely evaded the strict logic of *Quinn* v. *Leathem* by conceding that the defendants' objects were not unlawful if their intention was to advance their own lawful interests.[28] Still the 1974 Act is valuable because it disposes of an awkward doubt which arose out of dicta in *Rookes* v. *Barnard*—namely, whether threats by employees to break their own contracts of employment might not be unlawful means sufficient to found a charge of conspiracy.

(4) The reversal of Lyons v. Wilkins

At common law the torts of assault or nuisance or intimidation may be committed by watching or besetting or obstructing the access to premises, at least if done in a violent or menacing way.[29] There is, therefore, no general legal right to demonstrate or picket in support of a political or economic or social cause.[30] English law does not recognise "consumer picketing." But in the 1906 Act a certain degree of protection was given to peaceful picketing in the course or furtherance of a trade dispute. The 1971 Act made some changes, and then there were further changes in the Acts of 1974, 1980, 1982 and 1990.

After all these repeals, amendments and re-enactments, the relevant provisions are now contained in section 16 of the 1980 Act which reads as follows:

---

[27] See above, § 16.1.
[28] See above, § 16.5.
[29] *Thomas* v. *N.U.M.* [1986] Ch. 20.
[30] *Hubbard* v. *Pitt* [1976] Q.B. 142.

(1) It shall be lawful for a person[31] in contemplation or furtherance of a trade dispute[32] to attend—

    (*a*) at or near his own place of work,[33] or

    (*b*) if he is an official of a trade union, at or near the place of work of a member of that union whom he is accompanying and whom he represents,[34]

for the purpose only[35] of peacefully obtaining or communicating information, or peacefully persuading any person to work or abstain from working.[36]

(2) If a person works or normally works—

    (*a*) otherwise than at any one place, or

    (*b*) at a place the location of which is such that attendance there for a purpose mentioned in subsection (1) above is impracticable,

    his place of work for the purposes of that subsection shall be any premises of any employer from which he works or from which his work is administered.

(3) In the case of a worker who is not in employment and whose last employment was terminated in connection with a trade dispute, or the termination of his employment was one of the circumstances giving rise to a trade dispute, subsection (1) above shall in relation to that dispute have effect as if any reference to his place of work were a reference to his former place of work.

(4) A person who is an official of a trade union by virtue only of having been elected or appointed to be a representative of some of the members of the union shall be regarded for the purposes of subsection (1) above as representing only those members; but otherwise an official of a trade union shall be regarded for those purposes as representing all its members. Finally, section 16(2) provides that nothing shall prevent an act done in the course of picketing from being actionable in tort unless it is done in the course of attendance declared lawful by the above provisions.

---

[31] It is noteworthy that from 1906 to 1980 the statutory protection was given to "one or more persons."

[32] The meaning of this phrase is discussed above.

[33] The "attendance" may be "at or near" but not "in": so a "sit-in" is a trespass. But a picket at the entrance to a business park, 0.7 miles from the place of work, is protected: *Rayware Ltd.* v. *Transport and General Workers Union* [1989] 1 W.L.R. 675. The section in effect legalises the use of the highway for purposes which would otherwise be trespassory as against the owner of the subsoil: *British Airports Authority* v. *Ashton* [1983] 1 W.L.R. 1079, 1089. Note that picketing of an employer's house, or even of another workplace of that employer (or an associated company) is not protected: *News Group Newspapers Ltd.* v. *S.O.G.A.T. 1982* [1987] I.C.R. 180—nor is picketing at the home of another employee: *Thomas* v. *N.U.M.* [1986] Ch. 20.

[34] These words attempt to place some limits on the presence of extraneous elements on the picket-line—*e.g.* "flying pickets."

[35] Picketing which is neither informational nor persuasive may therefore be wrongful—*e.g.* as intimidation or battery. There is no right to stop a vehicle bringing in supplies or other workers: *Broome* v. *D.P.P.* [1974] A.C. 587.

[36] If the picketing really is peaceful in the sense explained above, then these words will protect conduct which might otherwise be actionable as an inducement of a breach of contract.

The contemporary position can be seen in *Thomas* v. *N.U.M.*[37] The plaintiffs, who included miners who were known to have returned to work during a strike, sought injunctions against a union and some of its officers.[38] Crowds of 50 to 70 attended daily at colliery entrances, and shouted abuse as the vehicles containing the plaintiffs passed in and out. There was also evidence that the homes and places of education of the plaintiffs had been picketed, which the defendants did not attempt to justify. The court held that the torts of assault, nuisance and interference with contract had not been committed,[39] but as the presence of pickets in such members was intimidatory and a harassment of the plaintiffs in their right to go to work, an injunction was granted to restrain the union from organising pickets in numbers exceeding six[40] at colliery entrances. An injunction to restrain the union from organising secondary picketing was refused. There was no evidence that the union had persistently organised mass secondary picketing, which would have been unlawful. It is important to note that the court did not hold that a union was automatically in breach of its own rules if it authorised a tort in the course of industrial action.

---

[37] [1986] Ch. 20.

[38] Since 1980 the former immunity of a union has been modified: see below, § 20.5.

[39] Not assault, as plaintiffs in a convoy of vehicles were safe from battery; not nuisance, as plaintiffs had suffered no special damage; not interference with contract, as NCB's primary obligations not disturbed. Plaintiffs also argued ([1986] Ch. 20, 39) that two further statutory torts had been committed—watching and besetting, and intimidation, but these were not judicially recognised.

[40] This was the figure recommended as a sensible number for a picket line by the Code of Practice issued in 1980 by the Secretary of State.

CHAPTER 18

DECEIT AND INJURIOUS FALSEHOOD

§ 18.1. Elements of Deceit

Wrongs of fraud or misrepresentation are of two essentially distinct kinds—first, the wrong of deceiving the plaintiff so that he causes harm to himself by his own mistaken act, and, secondly, the wrong of deceiving other persons so that they by their mistaken acts cause harm to the plaintiff. The first of these injuries may be called, in a narrow and specific sense of the term, the wrong of Fraud or Deceit; the second has no recognised distinctive title, and in default of a better designation it will here be called the wrong of Injurious Falsehood. We proceed to consider the former of these.

The tort of deceit consists in the act of making a wilfully false statement with intent that the plaintiff shall act in reliance on it, and with the result that he does so act and suffers harm in consequence.[1] As we have seen,[2] the origin of the tort can be clearly traced to the decision in *Pasley* v. *Freeman*.[3] There are four main elements in this tort: (1) there must be a false representation of fact; (2) the representation must be made with knowledge of its falsity; (3) it must be made with the intention that it should be acted on by the plaintiff, or by a class of persons which includes the plaintiff, in the manner which resulted in damage to him; (4) it must be proved that the plaintiff has acted upon the false statement, and has sustained damage by so doing.[4]

§ 18.2. The False Representation of Fact

Here three points are to be noted. First, the false statement may be made either by words or by conduct. Any conduct designed to deceive another by leading him to believe that a certain fact exists is equivalent in law, as in morals, to a statement in words that that fact does exist. Thus it is a fraud to obtain goods on credit in Oxford by wearing without right an undergraduate's cap and gown.[5]

Secondly, the defendant must have made a positive false statement; a mere passive non-disclosure of the truth, however deceptive in fact, does not amount to deceit in law. In the absence of a contractual duty to speak (as with the duty of disclosure required in a contract of insurance)

---

[1] *Bradford Building Society* v. *Borders* [1941] 2 All E.R. 205, 211.

[2] Above, § 2.1.

[3] (1789) 3 T.R. 51. "I am old enough to remember when this species of action came into use," said Sir Vicary Gibb C.J. (b. 1751) in *Ashlin* v. *White* (1816) Holt 387, 388, "It was dexterously intended to avoid the Statute of Frauds." Although this particular loophole was stopped by Lord Tenterden's Act 1828 (see below, § 18.6), the action of deceit flourished and is now of general application.

[4] *Diamond* v. *Bank of London & Montreal Ltd.* [1979] Q.B. 333, 349.

[5] *R.* v. *Barnard* (1837) 7 C. & P. 784.

no such duty can arise in tort.[6] The law leaves the parties to the contractual scheme which they have accepted even if the refusal to disclose has been deliberate and dishonest.[6a] This principle, however, is subject to four qualifications:

(1) The non-disclosure of a part of the truth may make the statement of the residue positively false. It is permissible to tell the whole truth, or to tell none of it, but it is not always possible to tell merely part of it without falling into positive falsehood.[7]

(2) Active concealment of a fact is equivalent to a positive statement that the fact does not exist. By active concealment is meant any act done with intent to prevent a fact from being discovered: for example, to cover over the defects of an article sold with intent that they shall not be discovered by the buyer has the same effect in law as a statement in words that those defects do not exist.[8]

(3) As it is an actionable fraud to leave uncorrected a false statement which is ultimately acted on by the plaintiff to his detriment,[9] it follows that if the defendant makes a statement which he believes to be true and he afterwards discovers that it is false before it has been acted on by the plaintiff, or if he makes a statement which is true when made but becomes false to his knowledge before it has been acted on,[10] it is his duty to disclose the truth.[11] In such a case a person who is not the maker of the statement may also be liable, either if he is vicariously responsible for the acts of the representor[12] or if he deliberately and knowingly uses the delusion created by the fraud in the injured party's mind in order to profit by it.[13]

(4) In certain cases there is a statutory duty of disclosure, the breach of which is apparently an actionable fraud. For example, there is a statutory duty to disclose certain matters in a company prospectus.[14]

Thirdly, the misrepresentation must be a false statement of fact, and not a mere broken promise. If the words of the defendant amount to a mere promise, they cannot be the basis of an action of tort, and impose no liability on him unless they conform to all the requirements of a valid contract. There is no such thing known to the law as a promise

---

[6] *Banque Keyser S/A v. Skandia (U.K.) Insurance Co. Ltd.* [1990] Q.B. 665, 774.

[6a] *Bank of Nova Scotia v. Hellenic Mutual Ltd.* [1990] Q.B. 665, 800.

[7] *Arkwright v. Newbold* (1881) 17 Ch.D. 301, 318.

[8] *Horsfall v. Thomas* (1862) 1 H. & C. 90.

[9] *Northern Bank Finance Ltd. v. Charlton* [1979] I.R. 149, 166.

[10] The tort becomes complete only when the misrepresentation—not having been corrected in the meantime—is acted upon by the misrepresentee: if false when made but true when acted upon there is no misrepresentation: *Briess v. Woolley* [1954] A.C. 333, 353. Although no action will lie until damage has been suffered (which may be after the act induced) the tort is complete in the sense that this is the moment relevant to an inquiry into its falsity: see *Diamond v. Bank of London & Montreal Ltd.* [1979] Q.B. 333.

[11] *Brownlie v. Campbell* (1889) 5 App.Cas. 925, 950. The question was left open by Lord Porter in *Bradford Building Society v. Borders* [1941] 2 All E.R. 205, 228, but the matter seems settled by *Briess v. Woolley* [1954] A.C. 333.

[12] *Briess v. Woolley* [1954] A.C. 333.

[13] *Bradford Building Society v. Borders* [1941] 2 All E.R. 205, 208.

[14] Companies Act 1985, s.67.

which is not good enough for a contract, but the breach of which is actionable as a tort.[15] The term fact, however, is used to include everything except a promise. Thus a statement of opinion, if wilfully false, is actionable as a tort.[16] So an expression of opinion concerning a present or future event may be a representation of fact if it implies that it is an opinion presently held.[17] "It may be that in the first instance the description of an object is a matter of opinion; but, if everyone's opinion about it is agreed, the description achieves sufficient certainty to become a fact."[18] Similarly there seems no real reason to doubt that an action will lie for a fraudulent misrepresentation of law.[19] So also an action of tort will lie for a false representation of intention.[20] An unfulfilled promise to do a thing is actionable as a contract or not at all; a false statement of intention to do a thing may be actionable as a tort. Thus in *Edgington* v. *Fitzmaurice*,[21] the directors of a company were held liable for fraud in borrowing money on behalf of the company on a false statement of the purpose to which the loan was to be applied. "The state of a man's mind," said Bowen L.J., "is as much a fact as the state of his digestion."[22]

§ 18.3. Knowledge of the Statement's Falsity

A false statement is not actionable in deceit, as distinct from in negligence,[23] unless it is wilfully false, This was established by the House of Lords in the leading case of *Derry* v. *Peek*.[24] The facts were that the directors of a tramway company which had authority to use steam power with the consent of the Board of Trade, believing, honestly but unreasonably, that this consent would be given as a matter of course, issued a prospectus in which it was stated that they had the right to use steam power without reference to any condition. In reliance on this statement the plaintiff took shares in the company. The promoters were held not liable in damages, on the ground that there was no proof that the error was fraudulent.

Dishonest belief essential

When, then, is a statement false within the meaning of the rule in *Derry* v. *Peek*? The test is the existence of a genuine belief in the truth of the statement. It is not necessary for liability that the defendant should

---

[15] *Jordan* v. *Money* (1954) 5 H.L.C. 185.

[16] *Anderson* v. *Pacific Insurance Co.* (1872) L.R. 7 C.P. 65, 69.

[17] *Bisset* v. *Wilkinson* [1927] A.C. 177, 182.

[18] *Armstrong* v. *Strain* [1951] 1 T.L.R. 856, 860, *per* Devlin J.

[19] *West London Commercial Bank* v. *Kitson* (1884) 13 Q.B.D. 360.

[20] And also a criminal prosecution since the Theft Act 1968.

[21] (1885) 29 Ch.D. 459.

[22] 29 Ch.D. 459, 483. It is not actionable fraud, however, for a seller or buyer to obtain an advantageous bargain by falsely stating that he is not prepared to take less or give more for the property than a certain sum. In such a case the plaintiff can show no legal damage; he has lost a better bargain, indeed, but he has lost nothing to which he had any legal right: *Vernon* v. *Keys* (1810) 12 East 632.

[23] See above, § 9.7.

[24] (1889) 14 App.Cas. 337.

have known it to be false; it is sufficient if he did not genuinely and honestly believe it to be true. Every statement is explicitly or implicitly a statement as to the belief of the speaker, and if that belief does not exist the statement is knowingly and wilfully false.[25]

It is sometimes said that it is sufficient for liability that the statement should be made recklessly. The term recklessly, however, must here be taken to be used to indicate the absence of any genuine belief—the presence of conscious ignorance of the truth of the matter.[26] Recklessness, in the sense of gross negligence, is no ground of liability. Although an absence of reasonable grounds for believing a statement to be true is not in itself a ground for liability, it is important evidence that no such belief really exists and therefore that the defendant is guilty not of negligence but of fraud.[27]

If a statement is ambiguous, it must be taken in the sense in which the defendant himself meant it—that is to say, in the sense in which he intended that it should be understood by the plaintiff. It is not legitimate for the court to construe the statement as it thinks it ought to have been construed by a reasonable man.[28] If both the representor and the representee in fact intended and understood, respectively, the statement to bear a certain meaning, the representor cannot then say that a reasonable man would have understood it in another sense.[29] On the other hand, it is immaterial that the objective meaning is more natural, and that the plaintiff understood the statement in that sense and was deceived by it; for in such a case the defendant is guilty of negligence only, and not of fraud. This may be very hard on the plaintiff, particularly if the defendant "is not the sort of man who worries too much about what he wrote last week when writing a letter this week."[30]

§ 18.4. INTENT THAT STATEMENT SHALL BE ACTED ON

A false statement is not actionable, whatever damage may result from acting in reliance on it, unless it was made with intent that the plaintiff should act in reliance on it in the manner in which he did act. He who tells lies is not responsible to the whole world for the consequences of them.[31] The only person entitled to rely on a statement and to act accordingly is he who is intended to rely on it and to act upon it by the person making it. All others accept it at their own risk, and if they come to harm, must blame their own credulity only. On the other hand, it is not necessary that the false statement should be made directly to the

---

25 *Smith* v. *Chadwick* (1884) 9 App.Cas. 187, 203.

26 *Martin* v. *Ryan* [1990] 2 N.Z.L.R. 209, 231.

27 *Derry* v. *Peek* 14 App.Cas. 337, 375. For the protection afforded by legal advice, see *Delaney* v. *Keogh* [1905] 2 I.R. 267, 290; and for the burden of proof to be discharged by the plaintiff, see *Hornal* v. *Neuberger Products Ltd.* [1957] 1 Q.B. 247.

28 *Akerhielm* v. *De Mare* [1959] A.C. 789. There are, indeed, several dicta to the contrary, but they are prior to *Derry* v. *Peek* and must now be treated as unsound. See Devlin J. in *Armstrong* v. *Strain* [1951] 1 T.L.R. 856, 871.

29 *Woodhouse Cocoa Ltd.* v. *Nigerian Produce Marketing Co. Ltd.* [1972] A.C. 741.

30 *Gross* v. *Lewis Hillmann Ltd.* [1970] 1 Ch. 445, 465.

31 *Banque Keyser S.A.* v. *Skandia Insurance Co. Ltd.* [1990] 1 Q.B. 665, 790.

plaintiff[32] with intent that any specific individual should be deceived and act in reliance on it.[33] Nor need there be an intention to cause loss to the plaintiff; the only necessary intent is that the plaintiff shall be deceived and shall act in a certain way; and if, as the natural and probable result of so acting, any damage is suffered by him, the defendant is responsible for it, whether he meant that damage to ensue or not.[34]

It is not enough, therefore, that it is the natural and probable consequence of the false statement that the plaintiff will rely and act on it, if this was not the intention of the defendant. It would seem on principle, however, that it is enough if the defendant's apparent intention was that the plaintiff should act on his statement, whatever his real and concealed intention may have been.[35] If the defendant makes a wilfully false statement, which the plaintiff naturally and reasonably believes to be made to him with intent that he shall act in reliance on it in a certain manner, and he does so act, it would seem right that the defendant should be estopped from alleging that his apparent intention was not his real intention.[36]

"Materiality"

If the statement is actually relied on, it is no defence that the plaintiff was negligent or foolish in doing so, or that he had a full opportunity of discovering the truth for himself. Consent is no defence. Every man has in law a right to believe and act on all lies told him by others with intent to deceive him.[37] Nor is it any defence to say that the representation is not "material," or would not have induced a reasonable man. The true question is whether the statement was a real inducement to the plaintiff: a representation may be material as between the parties, though not to a normal man.[38]

§ 18.5. DAMAGE TO THE PLAINTIFF

No action will lie for a false statement unless the plaintiff did in fact rely and act upon it. A mere attempt to deceive is not actionable.[39] It is sufficient, however, that the false statement was one of the reasons which

---

[32] *Commercial Banking Co. of Sydney Ltd.* v. *Brown & Co.* (1972) 46 A.L.J.R. 297.

[33] *Andrews* v. *Mockford* [1896] 1 Q.B. 372.

[34] *Edgington* v. *Fitzmaurice* (1885) 29 Ch.D. 459, 482.

[35] *Polhill* v. *Walter* (1832) 3 B. & Ad. 114.

[36] (1873) L.R. 9 Q.B. 34.

[37] *Pearson* v. *Dublin Corporation* [1907] A.C. 351. Nor is it any defence that the plaintiff's agent knew of the falsity of the statement, if the plaintiff himself did not: *Wells* v. *Smith* [1914] 3 K.B. 722.

[38] *Nicholas* v. *Thompson* [1924] V.L.R. 554, 566, 578.

[39] *Horsfall* v. *Thomas* (1862) 1 H. & C. 90. "It is common knowledge that the well-known case of *Peek* v. *Derry* very nearly never got beyond the court of first instance, because Sir Henry Peek could not be induced to say that he relied upon the statements in the prospectus. It was only by the most skilful management of counsel that he was ultimately got to say that he took the shares relying on the statement in the prospectus": *Horwood* v. *Statesman Publishing Co. Ltd.* (1929) 141 L.T. 54, 58, *per* Scrutton L.J. ("a matchless commercial lawyer": *Banque Keyser S.A.* v. *Skandia Insurance Co. Ltd.* [1990] 1 Q.B. 665, 790, *per* Steyn J.).

induced the plaintiff to act as he did.[40] Nevertheless, if the plaintiff, although he relied on the statement, would have acted as he did even had the statement not been made, he will have no cause of action.[41] In such a case he has suffered no damage by the fraud. But it is worth noting that the damage need not necessarily have been suffered at the moment at which the plaintiff acted on the statement.[42] In this tort the test of remoteness of damage is directness and not reasonable foresight.[43] In an action for fraudulent misrepresentation on a sale of land or goods the usual measure of damages is the difference between the price paid and the fair market value at the time of the contract, for to permit the plaintiff to recover for the loss of prospective gains would be to equate him with a buyer suing for breach of contract.[44] But it is market value without reference to the cost of production of the goods.[45]

§ 18.6. EXCEPTIONS TO RULE IN DERRY v. PEEK

The rule in *Derry* v. *Peek* is subject to nine exceptions or qualifications.

(1) Liability under Hedley Byrne v. Heller

The scope of liability in negligence for careless statements which cause financial loss has already been considered.[46]

(2) Physical harm

The rule in *Derry* v. *Peek* does not apply to cases in which physical harm to person or property is caused by dangerous chattels or premises negligently represented to be safe. A distinct category of the law of torts is applicable.[47] There is also authority that an action will lie if physical harm results from careless statements made in other circumstances.[48]

(3) Contractual duty

When there is a contractual relation between the plaintiff and defendant which involves a contractual duty to use care in the making of statements, the rule in *Derry* v. *Peek* is excluded.[49] A person may take on himself by contract a duty which the common law does not impose upon him. It should be noticed, however, the even where there is a contractual duty of careful statement the rule in *Derry* v. *Peek* is excluded only in favour of the person with whom the contract is made and not in

---

[40] *Paul and Vincent Ltd.* v. *O'Reilly* (1913) 49 I.L.T.R. 89.
[41] *Macleay* v. *Tait* [1906] A.C. 24. The question, however, seems mainly academic, for the wrongdoer has no right to institute a conjectural inquiry as to what would have happened if certain things had been said which were in fact not said, or had been said differently: *Smith* v. *Kay* (1859) 7 H.L.C. 750, 759.
[42] *Diamond* v. *Bank of London & Montreal Ltd.* [1979] Q.B. 333.
[43] *Doyle* v. *Olby (Ironmongers) Ltd.* [1969] 2 Q.B. 158. See below, § 23.2.
[44] *Foster* v. *Public Trustee* [1975] N.Z.L.R. 24.
[45] *Smith Kline & French Laboratories Ltd.* v. *Long* [1989] 1 W.L.R. 1.
[46] See above, § 9.7.
[47] See above, Ch. 12.
[48] See above, § 9.7 n. 27.
[49] See, for example, *De la Bere* v. *Pearson Ltd.* [1908] 1 K.B. 280.

favour of third persons who are injured by negligent statements made in breach of it.[50]

(4) Fiduciary relationship

When there has been a breach of a special duty recognised in equity, whether arising from the fiduciary relationship of the parties or the special circumstances of the case, the defendant will be liable for "constructive fraud," even though he has no fraudulent intention. In such a case no damages can be given for tort, but the plaintiff will be given an indemnity for the loss he has suffered—an equitable remedy.[51] So in *Nocton* v. *Ashburton*[52] a mortgagee claimed to be indemnified against the loss which he had sustained by having been improperly advised and induced by the defendant, acting as his confidential solicitor, to release a part of a mortgage security, whereby the security had become insufficient. Although the solicitor had not been guilty of fraud the House of Lords held that that did not preclude the plaintiff from obtaining relief on the footing of a breach of duty arising from the fiduciary relationship. A similar relationship exists between a bank and its customers, whether actual or potential.[53]

(5) Warranty of authority

Every person who purports to act as the agent of another is deemed in law to have entered into an implied contract of warranty of authority with any person who contracts or otherwise deals with him in reliance on his authority. If, therefore, the agent misrepresents the existence or extent of his authority, he is liable in damages for any loss thereby suffered by those who have dealt with him, the rule in *Derry* v. *Peek* being excluded by the existence of a contract implied in law.[54]

(6) Estoppel

The rule as to estoppel by representation is not affected by *Derry* v. *Peek*, and may in certain cases so operate as to impose liability in damages for a false statement which is not fraudulent. A company, for example, which registers a forged transfer of shares is liable by way of estoppel to a purchaser who buys the shares in reliance on the share

---

[50] *Dickson* v. *Reuter's Telegram Co.* (1877) 3 C.P.D. 1.

[51] See Sealy, "Some Principles of Fiduciary Obligation" [1963] C.L.J. 119, 137–139.

[52] [1914] A.C. 932. On May 20, 1914, Pollock wrote to Holmes: "Haldane [L.C.] asked me last week to a tobacco talk of *Derry* v. *Peek* and the possibility of minimising its consequences. The Lords are going to hold that it does not apply to the situation created by a positive fiduciary duty such as a solicitor's, in other words, go as near as they dare to saying it was wrong, as all Lincoln's Inn thought at that time": Pollock-Holmes, *Letters* (Ed. M. Howe), Cambridge University Press (1941), Vol. i, p. 215.

[53] *Woods* v. *Martins Bank Ltd.* [1959] 1 Q.B. 55, 72. See above, § 9.7.

[54] *Collen* v. *Wright* (1857) 8 E. & B. 647; "Seen in retrospect, *Collen* v. *Wright* looks like a curious island. If it had asserted liability for negligent, as well as fraudulent, misrepresentation of authority, it could hardly have escaped immersion by *Derry* v. *Peek*. But, because it placed the liability in the particular case on so high a ground, the flood swept past it and it escaped and grew": Mr. Justice Fullagar, "Liability for Representations at Common Law" (1951) 25 Austr.L.J. 278, 283.

certificate so issued, for the company is estopped from denying the truth of that certificate, and therefore the title of the plaintiff.[55]

(7) Statutory duty

In certain cases a duty of giving correct information is imposed by statute. Immediately after the decision in *Derry* v. *Peek* Parliament passed the Directors' Liability Act 1890, which gave a right of action for damages to persons who had suffered damage as the result of acting upon incorrect statements negligently inserted in a prospectus issued by the promoters or directors of a company. This statute has now been repealed and its provisions re-enacted in section 67 of the Companies Act 1985.

(8) Principal's liability for fraud of agent

The judgments of the Court of Appeal in *London County Freehold Properties Ltd.* v. *Berkeley Property Co. Ltd.*[56] suggest that there may be yet another exception to the rule in *Derry* v. *Peek*. In order to understand the problem it is necessary to see how far a principal is liable for the frauds of his agent. The principal is clearly liable if he expressly authorises an agent to make a statement which the agent believes to be true but which the principal knows to be false,[57] or if he purposely employs an agent who is ignorant of the true facts hoping he will give false information. He may also be liable if he deliberately stands by and allows his innocent agent to make deceitful statements.[58] Nor can it be doubted that the principal is liable if the agent knowingly makes a false statement in the course of his employment. This is so even though the false statement reaches the third party who acts on it to his detriment either through the principal himself[59] or through the agency of a fellow servant,[60] and even though either of them honestly believes the statement to be true. For in such a case the false representation is made by the agent just as truly as if it had been sent through the post or by the hand of a messenger.[61]

But what is the position if one agent innocently makes a false representation and the principal (or another agent) knows the facts which make the representation false but does not know or have any reason to believe that the agent will make the representation? The language used in the *London County Freehold Properties* case was wide enough to suggest liability even in such a case, but the following year Atkinson J.

---

[55] *Re Bahia and San Francisco Ry.* (1868) L.R. 3 Q.B. 584.

[56] [1936] 2 All E.R. 1039.

[57] *Ludgater* v. *Love* (1881) 44 L.T. 694. If the agent also knows it is false, then they are joint tortfeasors.

[58] *Gordon Hill Trust Ltd.* v. *Segall* [1941] 2 All E.R. 379, 390.

[59] *Pearson & Son Ltd.* v. *Dublin Corporation* [1907] A.C. 351, as explained in *Anglo-Scottish Beet Sugar Corporation Ltd.* v. *Spalding U.D.C.* [1937] 2 K.B. 607, 619–621.

[60] *London County Properties* case, as explained by Atkinson J. in the *Anglo-Scottish Beet Sugar Corporation* case in a judgment described by Singleton L.J. as "a masterly analysis of it, and of the authorities on the subject": *Armstrong* v. *Strain* [1952] 1 K.B. 232, 243.

[61] *Pearson* v. *Dublin Corporation* [1907] A.C. 351, 367.

said[62] that the decision had been based on a finding of fraud against the defendant's property manager, Jasper Addis, who had supplied the information which was conveyed to the plaintiff by another agent of the company, one De Rees, who honesty believed it to be true. In 1951 the point came before Devlin J. in *Armstrong v. Strain.*[63] He found himself unable to adopt the interpretation of Atkinson J. and preferred to follow the apparently inconsistent decision of the Court of Appeal in *Gordon Hill Trust Ltd.* v. *Segall.*[64] Devlin J. pointed out that ever since *Derry v. Peek* it had been necessary to find actual fraud or dishonesty— conscious knowledge of the falsity of the statement—on the part of the defendant, and it was precisely this finding of conscious knowledge which it was impossible to make in the case of an innocent division of ingredients.[65] But in the Court of Appeal the view of Atkinson J. was preferred, Singleton L.J. saying[66] that the *London County Freehold* case "should not be treated as an authority except and in so far as the decision was based on the fraud of Addis." Although the court would thus seem to have denied that there was any inconsistency between its own previous decisions, and so absolved itself from considering in detail the criticisms of the doctrine that the elements of fraud may be collected from the various agents of the defendant, it is clear from the whole tenor of the judgments that that doctrine is no longer supported by any convincing reasoning.[67]

(9) The Misrepresentation Act 1967[68]

One of the objects of this Act is to remove certain bars to rescission for innocent misrepresentation in the law of contract. But another object is to extend the tort of deceit by enabling a person who has entered into a contract as a result of a misrepresentation made to him by another party to that contract to recover damages for his loss if the party making the misrepresentation would have been liable in damages if that misrepresentation had been made fraudulently. In effect there is now a statutory duty not to state matters of the kind in question. Further, the

---

[62] *Anglo-Scottish Beet Sugar Corporation* case [1937] 2 K.B. 607, 624.

[63] [1951] 1 T.L.R. 856. By a strange coincidence, Sir Patrick Devlin, when a junior at the common law Bar, had written an article ("Fraudulent Representation" (1937) 53 L.Q.R. 344) containing penetrating criticism of the *London County Freehold* case (in which he had been counsel for the unsuccessful defendants: see 155 L.T. 190 (not in [1936] 2 All E.R. 1039)). Much of the reasoning in this article (to which "I was not unnaturally referred") finds a place in his judgment.

[64] [1941] 2 All E.R. 379. "I find it impossible to believe that the Court of Appeal would convict of fraud a man whom the trial judge had acquitted without making it plain that they were doing so"—[1951] 1 T.L.R. 856, 862. But on appeal Singleton L.J. said that Devlin J. had been misled by "the somewhat nebulous way in which the judgments in the case are expressed"—[1952] 1 K.B. 232, 243.

[65] [1951] 1 T.L.R. 856, 872.

[66] [1952] 1 K.B. 232, 244.

[67] See in particular the explanation of the judgment of (Sir Mark) Romer L.J. in the *London County Properties* case given by (Sir Charles) Romer L.J. in *Armstrong v. Strain* [1952] 1 K.B. 232, 248.

[68] See the elaborate and highly critical analysis by Treitel and Atiyah, "The Misrepresentation Act 1967" (1967) 30 M.L.R. 369.

statutory duty is one of strict liability.[69] The Act has been unpopular with conveyancers. Thus the Law Society's Conditions of Sale, and also the National Conditions, attempt to exclude its operation[70] in various ways. The clauses in question do not attempt to exclude liabilities or remedies; rather they attempt to prevent some or all pre-contract statements obtaining, or retaining, the status of representations. Finally, the Act in no way affects the decision in *Hedley Byrne*—the plaintiff in that case had not "entered into a contract after misrepresentation had been made to him by another party thereto" (s.2(1)).

§ 18.7. Representations as to Credit

There is one kind of false statement which is no ground of action unless made in writing—namely, a representation as to the credit of a third person. This exception is established by the Statute of Frauds Amendment Act 1828, s.6, commonly known as Lord Tenterden's Act, by which it is provided that "No action shall be brought whereby to charge any person upon or by reason of any representation or assurance made or given concerning or relating to the character, conduct, credit, ability, trade, or dealings of any other person, to the intent or purpose that such other person may obtain credit, money, or goods upon [*sic*],[71] unless such representation or assurance be made in writing signed by the party to be charged therewith." The purpose of this enactment was to prevent the evasion of the fourth section of the Statute of Frauds 1677 (which requires a guarantee to be in writing), by suing on a verbal guarantee in an action of tort instead of contract, and alleging that the defendant had made a false and fraudulent representation as to the credit or financial ability of the debtor.[72] A writing, therefore, has been made essential for the tort as well as for the contract.[73] But Lord Tenterden's Act applies only to actions of tort based on fraudulent misrepresentations, not to actions for breach of contract,[74] or for the breach of some other duty of care in making representations,[75] such as the duty of care established by the decision in *Hedley Byrne* v. *Heller*.[76]

The signature of an agent is not sufficient for the Act requires the personal signature of the defendant himself.[77] But in view of modern developments of the law relative to corporate activities, it has been held

---

[69] *Diamond* v. *Bank of London & Montreal Ltd.* [1979] Q.B. 333.

[70] For exclusion clauses in general, see below, § 22.2.

[71] The word "upon" is nonsensical, and evidently represents some clerical error in the Act. It has been suggested that the word "credit" has been accidentally transposed, and should follow the word "upon" so that the phrase would read "may obtain money or goods upon credit." Other suggestions are that "upon" is a mistake for "thereupon" or that "it" should be inserted after "upon." See *Lyde* v. *Barnard* (1836) 1 M. & W. 101.

[72] See above, § 18.1.

[73] *Lyde* v. *Barnard* (1836) 1 M. & W. 101, 114.

[74] *Banbury* v. *Bank of Montreal* [1918] A.C. 626.

[75] *Anderson (W.B.) & Sons Ltd.* v. *Rhodes Ltd.* [1967] 2 All E.R. 850.

[76] [1964] A.C. 465. See above, § 9.7, for the scope of this principle.

[77] *Swift* v. *Jewsbury* (1874) L.R. 9 Q.B. 301.

that the signature of a duly authorised agent of a company acting within the scope of his authority is the signature of the company.[78]

Lord Tenterden's Act is not to be read literally in accordance with the vague and unrestricted generality of its terms, but is on the contrary to be restrictively construed by reference to the known object of the legislature and the known mischief which it was intended to prevent.[79] This has produced some curious distinctions. So the Act applies only to those cases in which the defendant's representations have been made for the purpose of inducing the plaintiff to give credit to a third person.[80] Where, on the other hand, the plaintiff is induced by the defendant's representations to act in some other way than that of giving credit to a third person, Lord Tenterden's Act is not applicable, even though those representations may fall within the letter of the Act as relating to character, conduct, ability, trade or dealings of that third person. Thus, if the defendant has induced the plaintiff to buy the goodwill of A's business by fraudulent statements as to the nature, prosperity and prospects of that business, the defendant will plead in vain that those statements were not in writing signed by him. Again, since *Hedley Byrne* v. *Heller* it is clear that a fraudulent oral representation is not actionable in tort, while a negligent representation is so actionable.[81] But Lord Tenterden's Act is a good defence even though the intent of the defendant in inducing the plaintiff to give credit to the third person was thereby to obtain a pecuniary advantage for himself, as for example the payment of a debt owing to him by that third person. The statute looks to the immediate intent with which the false representation was made, not to the ulterior motive of the person who makes it.[82]

§ 18.8. Injurious Falsehood: Slander of Title and Slander of Goods[83]

We proceed now to the consideration of the second form of actionable misrepresentation—namely, Injurious Falsehood.[84] The wrong of deceit consists, as we have seen, in false statements made to the plaintiff himself whereby he is induced to act to his own loss. The wrong of injurious falsehood, on the other hand, consists in false statements made to other persons concerning the plaintiff whereby he suffers loss through the action of those others. The one consists in misrepresentations made to the plaintiff, the other in misrepresentations made concerning him.

It may also be stated as a general rule that it is an actionable wrong maliciously to make a false statement respecting any person or his property with the result that other persons deceived thereby are induced to

---

[78] *U.B.A.F. Ltd.* v. *European American Banking Corporation* [1984] Q.B. 713.

[79] *Banbury* v. *Bank of Montreal* [1918] A.C. 626, 691.

[80] *Diamond* v. *Bank of London & Montreal Ltd.* [1979] Q.B. 333.

[81] *Anderson (W.B.) & Sons Ltd.* v. *Rhodes (Liverpool) Ltd.* [1967] 2 All E.R. 850.

[82] *Clydesdale Bank Ltd.* v. *Paton* [1896] A.C. 381.

[83] See Prosser, "Injurious Falsehood: the Basis of Liability" (1959) 59 Col.L.Rev. 425.

[84] Salmond's term hs been generally accepted, although the draftsman of the Defamation Act 1952, s.3, described the tort as Malicious Falsehood, a term which is also used in the Faulks Report (Cmnd. 5909, Chap. 22).

act in a manner which causes loss to him.[85] This wrong of injurious falsehood is to be distinguished not only from the wrong of deceit, but also from that of defamation, to which it is analogous, but from which it is distinct. Both in defamation and in injurious falsehood the defendant is liable because he has made a false and hurtful statement respecting the plaintiff; but in one case the statement is an attack upon his reputation, and in the other it is not. The distinction is clearly made in the following quotation[86]: "Thus the malicious publication in a newspaper to the effect that Y, the famous pop-singer, had commenced his novitiate with a closed order of monks would not lower him in the esteem of right-thinking people—quite the reverse possibly—but would lose him engagements and therefore money, and therefore be actionable at his suit." It should be noted that no action lies for such a statement unless it has been made maliciously: here, as in some other branches of the law of torts, carelessness alone, however gross, does not suffice to establish liability.[87] Thus one who has his application for employment refused as the result of an inaccurate (but not dishonest) medical report has no remedy in this tort against the careless doctor.[88]

Examples of injurious falsehood

The earliest cases concern oral aspersions on the plaintiff's title to land. Later the law was extended to cover written aspersions on the title to property other than land, and then to cover disparagement of quality as distinct from title. An example of "slander of title" in the narrow sense occurs when a sale by auction is defeated or prejudiced by an adverse claim made to the property by the defendant, or when the plaintiff's trade is affected by a false charge that the goods offered by him for sale are an infringement of a patent or copyright.[89] Another example of the wrong of injurious falsehood is a false and malicious depreciation of the quality of the merchandise manufactured and sold by the plaintiff.[90] No action, however, will lie for any statement, however false or malicious, which is nothing more than a statement by one trader that his goods are better than those of a rival. This is a special exception to the general rule of liability for injurious falsehood—an exception established to prevent traders from using litigation as a means of advertisement.[91] It is otherwise, however, with a specific allegation of some defect in the plaintiff's goods, even though made by a rival with the view to promoting the sale of his own.[92] But an action for injurious falsehood lies not only in cases of slander of title, slander of

---

[85] *Ratcliffe* v. *Evans* [1892] 2 Q.B. 524, 527.

[86] From the Report of the Younger Committee on Privacy (Cmnd. 5012 (1972)), App. 1, para. 8.

[87] See below, § 18.10.

[88] Liability in negligence might be imposed since *Ross* v. *Caunters* [1980] Ch. 297.

[89] *Royal Baking Powder Co.* v. *Wright, Crossley & Co.* (1901) 18 R.P.C. 95.

[90] *White* v. *Mellin* [1895] A.C. 154. Note that words which merely disparage a man's goods without in any way casting reflections on his personal or trading character do not give rise to an action for libel: *Alcott* v. *Millar's Karri Forests Ltd.* (1905) 91 L.T. 722.

[91] *White* v. *Mellin* [1895] A.C. 154.

[92] *Alcott* v. *Millar's Forests Ltd.* (1905) 91 L.T. 722.

goods and passing off, but in analogous cases where damage has been wilfully done without just cause or excuse. So in *Kaye* v. *Robertson*[93] an interlocutory injunction was granted to restrain a tabloid newspaper from publishing an "interview" with the plaintiff which was falsely stated to have been obtained with his consent.

Remedies

It should be remembered that the tort of injurious falsehood is one of those in which the remedies of injunction and declaratory judgment may be more appropriate than an action for damages. In particular, the court has power to make a declaration as to the defendant's title in an action for slander of title or goods, even though such slander has not been proved, when the court thinks it appropriate to state its conclusion upon the title of the plaintiff which the defendant has challenged.[94]

§ 18.9. Conditions of Liability

These were stated as follows by Lord Davey: "To support such an action it is necessary for the plaintiffs to prove (1) that the statements complained of were untrue; (2) that they were made maliciously—*i.e.* without just cause or excuse; (3) that the plaintiffs have suffered special damage thereby."[95]

(1) Falsity

The statement must be untrue. This requirement has already been fully considered.

(2) Malice

Lord Davey defined malice as the absence of just cause or excuse. But it is now apparently settled that malice in the law of slander of title and other forms of injurious falsehood means some dishonest or otherwise improper motive.[96] The onus of proof is on the plaintiff.[97] A bona fide assertion of title, however, even though mistaken, if made for the protection of one's own interest or for some other proper purpose, is not malicious.[98]

---

[93] (1991) 18 F.S.R. 62.

[94] *Reuter (R.J.) Co. Ltd.* v. *Mulhens* [1954] Ch. 50.

[95] *Royal Baking Powder Co.* v. *Wright Crossley & Co.* (1901) 18 R.P.C. 95, 99.

[96] See *Balden* v. *Shorter* [1933] Ch. 427, 430; *London Ferro-Concrete Co. Ltd.* v. *Justicz* (1951) 68 R.P.C. 261, 265; *Loudon* v. *Ryder (No. 2)* [1953] Ch. 423, 428.

[97] *London Ferro-Concrete Co. Ltd.* v. *Justicz* (1951) 68 R.P.C. 261.

[98] *Greer's Ltd.* v. *Pearman & Corder Ltd.* (1922) 39 R.P.C. 406, 417; see also *Serville* v. *Constance* [1954] 1 W.L.R. 487, (1954) 71 R.P.C. 146 (better report). Newark, "Malice on Actions on the Case for Words" (1944) 60 L.Q.R. 336, came to the conclusion that the plaintiff need prove no more than that the words were spoken with intent to disparage, and that malice need only be proved if the defendant raises a privilege, *e.g.* by claiming a title in himself.

(3) Damage

The common law required the plaintiff to prove special damage as the action was case and not trespass. In 1948 the Porter Committee[99] stated: "The necessity of furnishing proof of special damage has rendered this type of action rare in the extreme: but statements of these kinds may cause very serious damage which, owing to technical rules of evidence, it is impossible to prove strictly as special damage. In the result, the injured person is left without any remedy for the loss which he has suffered." Thus when the plaintiff proved that the *Daily Mail* had published a statement that his house was haunted ("by a little old man creeping about the house") he failed because he was unable to prove special damage.[1] This defect has now been remedied by the Defamation Act 1952. Section 3 provides that it shall not be necessary to allege or prove special damage if the words[2] upon which the action is founded are calculated to cause pecuniary damage to the plaintiff and are published in writing or other permanent form,[3] or if they are calculated to cause pecuniary damage to the plaintiff in respect of any office, profession, calling, trade or business held or carried on by him at the time of publication.

§ 18.10. INJURIOUS FALSEHOOD: PASSING OFF[4]

The legal and economic basis of this tort is to provide protection for the right of property which exists not in a particular name, mark or style but in an established business, commercial or professional reputation or goodwill. So to sell merchandise or carry on business under such a name, mark, description, or otherwise in such a manner as to mislead the public into believing that the merchandise or business is that of another person is a wrong actionable at the suit of that other person. This form of injury is commonly, though awkwardly, termed that of *passing off* one's goods or business as the goods or business of another and is the most important example of the wrong of injurious falsehood. The gist of the conception of passing off is that the goods are in effect telling a falsehood about themselves, are saying something about themselves which is calculated to mislead.[5] The law on this matter is designed to protect traders against that form of unfair competition which consists in acquiring for oneself, by means of false or misleading devices, the benefit of the reputation already achieved by rival traders. Normally the defendant seeks to acquire this benefit by passing off his goods as and for the goods of the plaintiff in one or more of the modes

---

[99] Cmnd. 7536 (1948), para. 51.

[1] *Barrett* v. *Associated Newspapers Ltd.* (1907) 23 T.L.R. 666. By a strange coincidence, the Supreme Court of Canada dealt with a similar allegation in the same year: *Manitoba Free Press Co.* v. *Nagy* (1907) 39 S.C.R. 340.

[2] This includes broadcast statements.

[3] The Faulks Committee (Cmnd. 5909, § 594) recommends the abolition of the distinction between written and spoken words.

[4] Morison, "Unfair Competition and 'Passing-off' " (1956) 2 Sydney L.Rev. 50; Cornish, "Unfair Competition" (1972) 12 J.S.P.T.L. 126.

[5] *Draper* v. *Trist* [1939] 3 All E.R. 513, 517–518.

specified later. But in the *Champagne* case[6] it was held that the law governing trade competition is wide enough to prevent a person attaching to his product a name or description with which it has no natural connection in order to make use of the reputation and goodwill gained by a product genuinely indicated by that name and description. This principle was approved by the House of Lords in the *Dutch Advocaat* case,[7] so that the scope of the tort has been widened.

The wrong of passing off is not confined to cases of the sale of goods but assumes many forms, of which the following are the most important:

(1) A direct statement that the merchandise or business of the defendant is that of the plaintiff

Thus it is an actionable wrong to seek to sell a publication by falsely putting the name of a well-known author on the title-page.[8]

(2) Trading under a name so closely resembling that of the plaintiff as to be mistaken for it by the public

Thus in *Hendriks* v. *Montagu*[9] the Universal Life Assurance Society obtained an injunction preventing a company subsequently incorporated from carrying on business under the name of the Universe Life Assurance Association. In these days of international trade it is not necessary for the plaintiff company to prove it has obtained its goodwill by trading within the jurisdiction.[10]

(3) Selling goods under a trade name already appropriated for goods of that kind by the plaintiff, or under any name so similar thereto as to be mistaken for it

A trade name means a name under which goods are sold or made by a certain person and which by established usage has become known to the public as indicating that those goods are the goods of that person. A trade name is opposed to a merely descriptive name—namely, one under which the goods are sold, but which indicates merely their nature, and not that they are the merchandise of any particular person.[11] The principle is not confined to purely commercial matters, for "if a man, be he musician, portrait painter or writer of articles in newspapers, gets to be known under a particular name, that name becomes

---

[6] *J. Bollinger* v. *Costa Brava Wine Co. Ltd.* [1960] Ch. 262. The result of this decision has been said to be the creation of "a new-fangled tort called 'unfair competition' ": *Vine Products Ltd.* v. *Mackenzie & Co. Ltd.* [1969] R.P.C. 1, 28. But a strong tribunal refused to decide this point in *Cadbury-Schweppes Pty. Ltd.* v. *Pub Squash Pty. Ltd.* [1981] 1 W.L.R. 193, and Mummery J. has tersely stated that "There is no tort of unfair trading": *Associated Newspapers plc* v. *Insert Media Ltd.* [1990] 1 W.L.R. 900, 909.

[7] *Erven Warnink BV* v. *Townend (J.) & Sons Ltd.* [1979] A.C. 731.

[8] *Byron (Lord)* v. *Johnston* (1816) 2 Mer. 29. But the bare unauthorised use of another's name without more (*e.g.* that it is a libel) is not actionable: *Tolley* v. *Fry* [1930] 1 K.B. 467. 478. See above, § 8.2.

[9] (1881) 17 Ch.D. 638.

[10] *Maxims Ltd.* v. *Dye* [1977] 1 W.L.R. 1155.

[11] *British Vacuum Cleaner Co.* v. *New Vacuum Cleaner Co.* [1970] 2 Ch. 312.

inevitably part of his stock-in-trade, and apart from some special contract or anything of that kind, he is entitled to say that it is his name, and that anyone who adopts or causes the adoption of that name by some other person is inflicting on him an injury."[12] But "It is established beyond argument that under the law of England a man is not entitled to exclusive proprietary rights in a fancy name *in vacuo*."[13] The activities of the defendant must have misled the public into confusing his profession, business or goods with those of the plaintiff.[14] It may be that misappropriation of personality is on the verge of recognition as a distinct tort.[15]

(4) Selling goods with the trade mark of the plaintiff or any deceptive imitation attached thereto

A trade mark is at common law any mark habitually attached by a trader to goods manufactured or sold by him in order to indicate that they are his merchandise, and by established usage known to the public as possessing that significance. The statute law as to the infringement of registered trade marks does not exclude or supersede this common law protection.

(5) Imitating the get-up or appearance of the plaintiff's goods so as to deceive the public

When there is anything so characteristic in the get-up or appearance of the plaintiff's goods that it identifies those goods as the merchandise of the plaintiff, any deceptive adoption or imitation of that get-up or appearance is subject to the same rules as the deceptive adoption or imitation of his trade name or trade mark. So when the plaintiffs had sold lemon-juice in plastic lemon containers since 1956 it was held that in effect they had a monopoly in such containers as the defendant had not taken sufficient steps to distinguish his containers from those of the plaintiffs.[16] A tort (perhaps a form of misrepresentation analogous to passing off) is also committed where the defendant knowingly uses unauthorised articles in the performance of some service or process which has acquired a brand or fancy name by reason of the use in it of the plaintiff's branded articles—*e.g.* a "Jamal hair wave" means not a particular style but a process performed with certain materials.[17] The *Champagne* case[18] extended the tort beyond cases in which the defendant claims that his goods or services are identical with those of the plaintiff. Champagne properly means French champagne, which is associated with being "drunk at the gayest parties and in distinguished

---

[12] *Hines* v. *Winnick* [1974] Ch. 708, 713, *per* Vaisey J.

[13] *McCulloch* v. *May Ltd.* [1947] 2 All E.R. 845, 849, *per* Wynn-Parry J. (The plaintiff, who was well known as "Uncle Mac" of the BBC Children's Hour had no common field of activity with the defendants, who distributed "Uncle Mac's Puffed Wheat.")

[14] *Sim* v. *J. Heinz & Co. Ltd.* [1959] 1 W.L.R. 313.

[15] See above, § 3.2.

[16] *Reckitt & Coleman Ltd.* v. *Borden Inc.* [1990] 1 W.L.R. 491.

[17] *Sales Affiliates Ltd.* v. *Le Jean Ltd.* [1974] Ch. 295.

[18] *J. Bollinger* v. *Costa Brava Wine Co. Ltd.*[1960] Ch. 262.

circles"[19]: it was therefore wrong for the defendant to market his product under the name "Spanish champagne." The principle has been further extended to cover cases in which the name by which the genuine product is known has no geographical connotation, but has a definite and distinctive meaning,[20] or in which the defendant imitates the descriptive material which has become attached to the plaintiff's product by reason of an advertising campaign.[21]

Basis of passing-off action

The courts have wavered between two conceptions of a passing-off action—as a remedy for the invasion of a quasi-proprietary right in a trade name or trade mark, and as a remedy, analogous to the action on the case for deceit, for invasion of the personal right not to be injured by fraudulent competition. The true basis of the action is now held to be that the passing off injures the right of property in the plaintiff, that right of property being his right to the goodwill of his business.[22] Indeed, talk about deceit tends to obscure the essential fact that the plaintiff himself has not been deceived: his complaint is that the defendant by his misrepresentations has deceived other persons and that that deception is injuring the plaintiff's trade.[23] It is sufficient in all cases to prove that the practice complained of is calculated (that is to say, likely) to deceive.[24]

The remedies of the plaintiff in an action for passing off are (1) an injunction, and (2) either damages or an account of profits, at the plaintiff's option. The uncertainty as to the conception underlying the action has led to uncertainty as to the requirement of proof of damage. Damage or likelihood of damage to property is the gist of all such actions according to most authorities.[25] Probably it is sufficient to prove that the practice complained of is of such a nature that it is likely in the ordinary course of business to deceive the public.[26] Indeed, it seems that the essence of the tort lies in the misrepresentation that the goods in question are those of another; an offer to sell, as distinct from an actual sale, may be enough to constitute an actionable wrong.[27] This is sufficient for an injunction in equity and even for nominal damages at common law. In considering whether deception is probable, account is to be taken, not of the expert purchaser, but of the ordinary ignorant and unwary member of the public.[28] On the other hand, it is not enough that a thoughtless person may unwarrantably jump to a false conclusion. In cases of fraud the onus of proving likelihood of damage is not heavy; the court will readily assume that the defendant will suc-

---

[19] [1961] R.P.C. 116, 125.
[20] *Erven Warnink BV v. Townend (J.) & Sons Ltd.* [1979] A.C. 731 ("Dutch Advocaat").
[21] *Cadbury-Schweppes Pty. Ltd. v. Pub Squash Pty. Ltd.* [1981] 1 W.L.R. 193, 204.
[22] *Reckitt & Coleman Properties Ltd. v. Borden Inc.* [1990] W.L.R. 491, 510, 516.
[23] *J. Bollinger v. Costa Brava Wine Co. Ltd.* [1960] Ch. 262, 275.
[24] *Draper v. Trist* [1939] 3 All E.R. 513, 517.
[25] *Reckitt & Coleman Properties Ltd. v. Borden Inc.* [1990] 1 W.L.R. 491, 510, 516.
[26] *Reddaway v. Bentham Hemp Spinning Co.* [1892] 2 Q.B. 639, 644.
[27] *Spalding & Bros. v. A.W. Gamage Ltd.* (1915) 32 R.P.C. 273; (1918) 35 R.P.C. 101.
[28] *Reckitt & Coleman Properties Ltd. v. Borden Inc.* [1990] W.L.R. 491, 510, 516.

ceed in accomplishing that which he has set himself to accomplish; but where there is no fraud the onus is a heavy one.[29] Indeed, it may be that nothing more than nominal damages, if even those, can be given for an innocent passing off.[30]

§ 18.11. Confusion through Use of Similar Names

A name originally merely descriptive, and therefore *publici juris*, may by exclusive use in connection with the plaintiff's goods acquire a secondary sense as the trade name of those goods, and will then become subject to the ordinary rule as to trade names; so that the use of it by other persons ceases to be *publici juris*, and is actionable unless they take specific precautions to prevent deception. So in *Reddaway* v. *Banham*[31] it was found by a jury that the term "camel-hair belting" had by long and exclusive association with the plaintiffs' manufacture come to mean, not merely belting made from camel hair, but belting made by the plaintiffs. "The whole merit of that description, its one virtue for Banham's purposes, lies in its duplicity. It means two things. At Banham's works, where it cannot mean Reddaway's belting, it may be construed to mean belting made of camel's hair; abroad, to the German manufacturer, to the Bombay mill-owner, to the up-country native, it must mean Reddaway's belting; it can mean nothing else. I venture to think that a statement which is literally true, but which is intended to convey a false impression, has something of a faulty ring about it; it is not sterling coin; it has no right to the genuine stamp and impress of truth."[32] Hence it was held that the term could not be used by other persons unless they took adequate precautions against deceiving the public by means of it. The burden, however, of proving this secondary sense is not a light one. The courts will not be easily persuaded to sanction such appropriation of words which belong to the common stock of our language.[33]

A name which is originally a trade name may through general use cease to indicate specifically the merchandise of any particular person and so may become merely descriptive and *publici juris*. Thus Liebig's Extract of Meat no longer means a material prepared by Liebig or his assigns.[34] In such a case the onus is reversed: it is for the defendant to show that the work-mark has entirely lost its original meaning and that no purchaser can be deceived by its use.[35]

Use of own name

The application of the rule as to passing off to cases in which the instrument of deception is the use by the defendant of his own personal

---

[29] *Society of Motor Manufacturers and Traders* v. *Motor Manufacturers', etc., Insurance Co.* [1925] Ch. 675, 686, 689.
[30] *Draper* v. *Trist* [1939] 3 All E.R. 513, 518, 525, 528.
[31] [1896] A.C. 199.
[32] [1896] A.C. 199, 218–219, *per* Lord Macnaghten.
[33] *Reckitt & Coleman Ltd.* v. *Borden Inc.* [1990] 1 W.L.R. 491, 516.
[34] *Liebig's Extract of Meat Co.* v. *Hanbury* (1967) 17 L.T.(N.S.) 298.
[35] *Havana Cigar and Tobacco Factories Ltd.* v. *Oddenino* [1924] 1 Ch. 179.

name is obscure. It would appear, however, that subject to certain qualifications an individual is entitled to trade under his own name regardless of the fact that his business may be thereby confused with a business of some other person bearing the same or a similar name. Nor does it make any difference in such a case that a trader using his own name is well aware of the fact that his business will be confused with that of a rival trader, and intends to take the advantage which such confusion will confer upon him.[36] This can be very inconvenient, but not necessarily wrongful. "There is a great deal to be said in favour of a man who engages in any pursuit using therein his own name. If the accomplished but rather disreputable Lord Chancellor of King James was the author of the tragedy of *Hamlet*, as some misguided people think, he would have saved the world much discussion if he had published it under the name of Bacon, or St. Albans, or Verulam, instead of allowing it to appear in the name of one of the best-known men in London of the time."[37] It is different if he intends to deceive and not merely to confuse.[38]

A surname is not a man's legal property, and if a man is called by some other than his real name he may acquire his second name by reputation.[39] In such a case he will not be restrained from using it honestly. So in *Jay's Ltd. v. Jacobi*[40] the defendant, who was manageress of a ladies' outfitters' shop, had been known to everyone for 15 years as Miss Jay, and it was held that she had acquired that name by reputation and was entitled to trade under it so long as she acted honestly, even though the similarity of the name to that of the plaintiffs might occasionally lead to the goods of the one being mistaken for those of the other.

But a man is not entitled to use his own name dishonestly in order that his goods may be passed off as and for the goods of another.[41] But in order to deprive him of the right there must be evidence of dishonesty outside the mere use of the name, for example, a resemblance in the manner of the display of the name, or the concealment of that part of the name which differs from the plaintiff's by the use of smaller characters.[42] Although an individual trader is entitled to trade under his own name, even though he thereby gets the benefit of the reputation of a rival trader of the same name, an incorporated company has not the same right to use the names of its shareholders. By the Companies Act 1985, ss.26–29, a company is prevented from being registered with a name which in the opinion of the Registrar of Companies is undesir-

---

[36] *Burgess v. Burgess* (1953) 3 De G.M. & G. 896 (on which Lord Macnaghten once remarked that "The judgment of Turner L.J. though eclipsed in public favour by the brilliancy and point of his colleague's language is an accurate and masterly summary of the law": *Reddaway v. Banham* [1896] A.C. 199, 220).

[37] *Dickson v. Dickson* [1909] 1 I.R. 185, 202, *per* Holmes L.J.

[38] *Parker-Knoll Ltd. v. Knoll International Ltd.* [1962] R.P.C. 265.

[39] *Massam v. Thorley's Cattle Food Co.* (1880) 14 Ch.D. 748, 760. No specific formality seems to be required to change one's surname, but a Christian name may (apart from statute) be changed only at confirmation and, possibly, on adoption: *Re Parrott* [1946] Ch. 183.

[40] [1933] Ch. 411.

[41] *Croft v. Day* (1843) 7 Beav. 84.

[42] *Brinsmead's Case* (1913) 29 T.L.R. 237, 238.

able. Independently of this statutory provision, a company must select a name which is not calculated to deceive, and it is no excuse for choosing a deceptive name that a shareholder to whom that name belongs might lawfully use it in his own business.[43] The rule as to passing off is not to be extended to cases in which there is no appropriation by one man of the trade reputation or custom of another, but merely some other form of loss or inconvenience caused by the deception of the public. In the absence of actual fraud no action will lie in such a case. Thus, in *Day* v. *Brownrigg*[44] the plaintiff and defendant occupied adjoining villas, and the defendant changed the name of his residence, and gave it the same name as that of the plaintiff. An injunction to prevent this was refused, although it was proved that inconvenience would result to the plaintiff through the confusion thus caused. Had the parties been rival traders the result might have been different.

§ 18.12. IMMATERIAL PROPERTY

The forms of immaterial property known to our law are patents, copyright, registered trade marks, and the various franchises which may be vested in private persons, such as markets and ferries. A violation of any of these rights of property is an actionable tort. The law as to these matters is, however, too special in its nature to call for examination here.

---

[43] *Tussaud* v. *Tussaud* (1890) 44 Ch.D. 678.
[44] (1878) 10 Ch.D. 294.

CHAPTER 19

WRONGFUL PROCESS OF LAW

§ 19.1. Liability of the Officers of Superior Courts

A judge of one of the superior courts is absolutely exempt from all civil liability for acts done by him in the execution of his judicial functions.[1] His exemption from civil liability[2] is absolute, extending not merely to errors of law and fact, but to the malicious, corrupt, or oppressive exercise of his judicial powers.[3] For it is better that occasional injustice should be done and remain unredressed under the cover of this immunity than that the independence of the judicature and the strength of the administration of justice should be weakened by the liability of judges to unfounded and vexatious charges of error, malice, or incompetence brought against them by disappointed litigants—"otherwise no man but a beggar, or a fool, would be a judge."[4] The remedy for judicial errors is some form of appeal to a higher court, and the remedy for judicial oppression or corruption is a criminal prosecution or the removal of the offending judge; but in neither case can he be called on to defend his judgment in an action for damages brought against him by an injured litigant. Nor is the Crown vicariously liable for his acts,[5] as judicial error is not a tort. It is possible that there is liability under the European Convention on Human Rights.[6]

Acts beyond jurisdiction

When, however, the illegal act complained of is beyond the limits of the defendant's jurisdiction, it is not definitely settled whether a superior judge is free from liability; or whether, as in the case of inferior judges, he is civilly responsible for such an excess of jurisdiction. This much is clear: in order to establish exemption as regards proceedings in an inferior court the judge must prove that he had jurisdiction,[7] whereas the plaintiff must prove want of jurisdiction in the case of proceedings in a superior court.[8] Probably, however, the exemption is

---

[1] Immunity from actions for defamation has already been considered: above, § 8.10. In this section we consider actions of trespass for invasions of personal or proprietary interests as the result of an unauthorised or erroneous decision, *i.e.* unlawful arrest or imprisonment or unlawful distress.

[2] It will be recalled that the Habeas Corpus Act 1679, s.9 provides that a High Court judge who unlawfully refuses to issue a writ of habeas corpus during the vacation is liable to pay a penalty of £500 to the person detained.

[3] *Anderson* v. *Gorrie* [1895] 1 Q.B. 668; *Tughan* v. *Craig* [1918] 1 I.R. 245.

[4] *Arenson* v. *Casson, Beckman Rutley & Co.* [1977] A.C. 405, at p. 440, *per* Lord Fraser.

[5] *Maharaj* v. *Att.-Gen. of Trinidad* [1979] A.C. 385.

[6] A Belgian criminal who was criticised by a judge obtained substantial compensation for remarks which were such "as to disturb the serenity of the atmosphere during the proceedings": *Boeckmans* v. *Belgium* (No. 1727/62).

[7] *Carratt* v. *Morely* (1841) 1 Q.B. 18.

[8] *Peacock* v. *Bell* (1667) 1 Saund. 73.

absolute even in this case.[9] This is justifiable not merely on grounds of public policy but also as a deduction from the principle that a superior court always has power to determine the limits of its own jurisdiction: it follows that an erroneous conclusion as to the ambit of its jurisdiction is merely an abuse of its jurisdiction and not an act outside its jurisdiction.[10] Protection is also extended to the acts of one whose appointment as a judge is in fact a nullity: the principle appears to be that the acts of a person holding the office of judge *de facto* and with colour of right are unimpeachable in any way.[11] But it is well settled that the protection accorded to judicial acts is not extended to ministerial acts of a judicial officer.[12]

§ 19.2. LIABILITY OF OFFICERS OF INFERIOR COURTS

Judges of an inferior court possess the same immunity as judges of the superior courts so long as they do not exceed their jurisdiction.[13] There are many dicta, however, to the effect that justices of the peace (and therefore, presumably, other judicial officers whose courts are not of record) are liable for the malicious exercise of their judicial powers even within the limits of their jurisdiction. But in the first case to reach the House of Lords in which the liability of magistrates was considered, three Law Lords stated emphatically that this head of liability was obsolete.[14] This view was adopted by the Courts and Legal Services Act 1990, s.108(2), which specifically states that there is no liability for acts done within jurisdiction.

Liability for excess of jurisdiction

A judge of an inferior court was civilly liable at common law for any act done by him in excess of his jurisdiction and in the nature of a trespass against the person or property of the plaintiff or otherwise a cause of damage to him.[15] The Courts and Legal Services Act 1990, s.108(2) now provides that the plaintiff must prove "bad faith" before liability can be established for acts done outside jurisdiction. It should be noted that it is not the mere making of the order in excess of or without jurisdiction which gives rise to the cause of action in trespass, but the acts done against the plaintiff in consequence of that order, *e.g.* his committal to prison or the levying of a distress against his goods.[16] One who is aggrieved by an invalid order is not permitted to have the option either of appealing it or of obeying it and then suing the judge for damages.[17]

---

[9] But an emphatic *obiter dictum* in *Re McC.* [1985] A.C. 528, 540 asserts that "if the Lord Chief Justice himself, on the acquittal of a defendant charged before him with a criminal offence, were to say: 'That is a perverse verdict,' and thereupon proceed to pass a sentence of imprisonment, he could be sued for trespass": *per* Lord Bridge of Harwich.

[10] *Sirros* v. *Moore* [1975] 1 Q.B. 118, 139.

[11] *Re Aldridge* (1893) 15 N.Z.L.R. 361.

[12] *Ferguson* v. *Kinnoull (Earl of)* (1842) 9 Cl. & F. 311, 312.

[13] *Sirros* v. *Moore* [1975] 1 Q.B. 118.

[14] *Re McC.* [1985] A.C. 528.

[15] *Re McC.* [1985] A.C. 528.

[16] *Re McC.* [1985] A.C. 528.

[17] *O'Connor* v. *Isaacs* [1956] 2 Q.B. 288, 302.

The distinction thus drawn between an excess of jurisdiction and a wrongful act within the limits of jurisdiction is one which it is easier to state in general terms than to define with accuracy or apply with precision. It may probably he said, however, that a judge may exceed his jurisdiction in three ways:

(i) When he has no power to deal with the kind of matter brought before him: as when a county court judge tries an action of libel other than an action remitted to him by the High Court or an action in which jurisdiction has been given by consent.

(ii) When he has no power to deal with the particular person concerned: for example, because that person has not been properly summoned before him, or is not resident within the local jurisdiction of the court.

(iii) When, although there is jurisdiction over the matter and the person, the judgment or order given or made in the matter is of a kind which he has no power to give or make: as if he imprisons instead of fining, or imprisons for a longer period than the law permits.[18]

In all these cases the judge is liable as for an excess of jurisdiction. When, on the other hand, he has power to give the kind of judgment which he has given against the person complaining of it, he is not liable merely because his judgment is erroneous in law or in fact, or because there has been some irregularity of procedure. Such an error or irregularity is merely a wrongful exercise of jurisdiction, not an excess of it.[19]

§ 19.3. LIABILITY OF PARTIES

Having considered the liability of magistrates and judges in the case of wrongful legal proceedings, it remains to deal with the liabilities of the parties to these proceedings. This matter must be considered under two heads—(1) proceedings instituted maliciously; (2) proceedings instituted erroneously and irregularly. Formerly there was a third head—proceedings maintained by parties with no interest, or maintained for a share of the fruits of the action. But the torts of maintenance and champerty have been abolished by the Criminal Law Act 1967, s.14(1).

Proceedings instituted maliciously[20]

It is an actionable wrong to institute certain kinds of legal proceedings against another person maliciously and without reasonable and probable cause. The tort clearly has some affinities with defamation and false imprisonment, but there are also differences.[21] It differs from defamation not only in having an earlier and distinct historical origin but also in affording protection to the plaintiff's interest in the security of his person and property as well as his reputation. The tort differs from

---

[18] See the examples given in *Re McC.* [1985] A.C. 528.

[19] *Cave* v. *Mountain* (1840) 1 M. & G. 257.

[20] For the history of this action, see Harper, "Malicious Prosecution, False Imprisonment, and Defamation" (1937) 15 Tex.L.Rev. 157; Fridman, "Compensation of the Innocent" (1963) 26 M.L.R. 481.

[21] *Reid* v. *Webster* (1966) 59 D.L.R. (2d) 189, 201.

false imprisonment, as we have seen,[22] in that the acts of a court of justice cannot be imputed to the litigant at whose suit they have been done: the litigant can be charged only with having maliciously and without reasonable cause exercised his right of setting a court of justice in motion. The tort is commonly called malicious prosecution, but the word "prosecution" has a wider meaning than in the criminal law and, conversely, not all proceedings which are technically prosecutions are capable of founding an action for malicious prosecution.[23] The chief classes of proceedings to which this rule applies are the following:

(1) Malicious criminal prosecutions

It is the wrong known as malicious prosecution to institute criminal proceedings against anyone if the prosecution is inspired by malice and is destitute of any reasonable cause. The offence charged need not be an indictable one.[24] As it is an action on the case damage must be proved. Unfortunately there is doubt about the definition of damage. As far back as 1701 Sir John Holt C.J. said[25] that there were three sorts of damage which would maintain the action: (1) "The damage to a man's fame, as if the matter whereof he is accused be scandalous"; (2) damage to the person; (3) damage to property, "as where he is forced to expend his money in necessary charges, to quit himself of the crime of which he is accused." As to (1), it has been held by the Court of Appeal;[26] that the test is whether the charge is necessarily and naturally defamatory of the plaintiff, or, in other words, whether the statement that the plaintiff was charged with the offence in question is capable of a non-defamatory meaning. This is a very severe test. It has been held[27] that a conviction for pulling a communication cord on a train without reasonable cause does not damage the "fair fame" of the person charged, because he might have done so for a number of reasons—e.g. because he had left valuable property behind on the platform. Paradoxically, a charge of failing to pay a tram-car fare has been held such an offence,[28] apparently because it necessarily involves fraud.[29] The decisions are open to review on the ground that they misunderstand Sir John Holt's test: what he really meant was whether an oral imputation of the crime would have amounted to a slander actionable *per se*.[30]

As to (2), damage to the person, the courts have in this instance interpreted *Savile* v. *Roberts* in an unexpectedly wide way, by holding that it covers any crime punishable with imprisonment in the first instance, even though the plaintiff has not in fact been imprisoned.[31]

As to (3), damage to property, mere proof of financial loss is not

[22] Above, § 7.2.
[23] See below, § 19.4.
[24] *Reid* v. *Webster* (1966) 59 D.L.R. (2d) 189.
[25] *Savile* v. *Roberts* (1698) 1 Ld.Raym. 374.
[26] *Wiffen* v. *Bailey* [1915] 1 K.B. 600.
[27] *Berry* v. *British Transport Commission* [1962] 1 Q.B. 306.
[28] *Rayson* v. *South London Tramways Co.* [1893] 2 Q.B. 304.
[29] *Wiffen* v. *Bailey* [1915] 1 K.B. 600.
[30] See Diplock J. in *Berry* v. *British Transport Commission* [1961] 1 Q.B. 149, 166.
[31] *Wiffen* v. *Bailey* [1915] 1 K.B. 600. Note the analogy with slander actionable *per se*.

enough. But the difference between party and party costs and solicitor and client costs is sufficient damage to found an action.[32]

(2) Malicious bankruptcy and liquidation proceedings

A similar liability attaches to him who maliciously and without reasonable cause petitions to have another person adjudicated a bankrupt,[33] or to have a company wound up as insolvent.[34]

(3) Malicious arrest

Similarly it is an actionable injury to procure the arrest and imprisonment of the plaintiff by means of judicial process, whether civil or criminal, which is instituted maliciously and without reasonable cause.[35] Although no action lies against a witness for giving false evidence,[36] the plaintiff is not debarred from bringing an action for wrongful arrest by reason only of the fact that a step in procuring the arrest consisted of evidence given in court in the course of another person's trial.[37] This species of wrong is to be distinguished from false imprisonment. False imprisonment is the act of the defendant himself or of a merely ministerial officer put in motion by him.[38]

(4) Malicious execution against property

On the same principle it is an actionable wrong maliciously and without reasonable and probable cause to issue execution against the property of a judgment debtor.[39] Both malice and want of reasonable and probable cause must be proved: the former relates to motive, the latter to intention.[40]

(5) Malicious civil proceedings

It was once thought that to institute or maintain an ordinary civil action (not extending to any arrest or seizure of property) is not a tort, however unfounded, vexatious and malicious it may be.[41] The reason alleged for this rule is that the advancement of a false case for the purpose of sustaining a claim or defence is not the cause of any damage of which the law can take notice—perhaps because the costs awarded to the successful party are regarded as sufficient compensation.[42] To what classes of civil proceedings this exemption applies is far from clear. Will an action lie at the suit of a solicitor whom the defendant has mali-

---

[32] *Berry* v. *British Transport Commission* [1962] 1 Q.B. 306.
[33] *Johnson* v. *Emerson* (1871) L.R. 6 Ex. 329.
[34] *Quartz Hill Gold Mining Co.* v. *Eyre* (1883) 11 Q.B.D. 674.
[35] *Foth* v. *O'Hara* (1959) 15 D.L.R. (2d) 332, 336.
[36] *Hargreaves* v. *Bretherton* [1959] 1 Q.B. 45.
[37] *Roy* v. *Prior* [1971] A.C. 470.
[38] See above, § 7.3.
[39] *Clissold* v. *Cratchley* [1910] 2 K.B. 244.
[40] *Horner* v. *Irwin & Son Ltd.* [1972] N.I. 202, 205.
[41] *Metall* [1990] 1 Q.B. 390, 466. It has also been held that no action lies for conspiracy to give perjured evidence: *Hargreaves* v. *Bretherton* [1959] 1 Q.B. 45.
[42] But in *Metall* it was admitted that such costs might not always be adequate: [1990] 1 Q.B. 390, 469.

ciously endeavoured to have struck off the roll? If malicious proceedings in bankruptcy are, as we have seen, a good cause of action, there seems no reason founded on history or public policy why a similar conclusion should not be drawn with respect to other civil proceedings.[43] Again, there seems to be no reason why an action should not lie for the institution of unfounded and malicious proceedings before a court-martial,[44] or some administrative or domestic tribunal. The adverse decision of such a body may cause serious damage to the reputation or livelihood of the party accused.

(6) Abuse of the process of the court

Even those who doubt the existence of a tort entitled "malicious civil proceedings" admit that a tort is committed[45] when one party uses a legal process, whether civil or criminal, against another primarily to accomplish a purpose for which it has not been designed.[46] Such behaviour does not necessarily involve the presentation of a false case. The action may have been brought or continued with an ulterior purpose—e.g. to bring pressure on the other party to grant a lease,[47] or to surrender some item of property which he is entitled to retain.[48] The plaintiff in this form of the tort need not show that the suit has terminated in his favour, or that it was instituted without reasonable or probable cause[49]—indeed he may be unable to do so just because the defendant has successfully polluted the fountain of justice.

§ 19.4. ESSENTIALS OF MALICIOUS PROSECUTION

In order that an action shall lie for malicious prosecution or the other forms of abusive process which have been referred to, the following conditions must be fulfilled:

(1) The proceedings must have been instituted or continued by the defendant;

(2) He must have acted without reasonable and probable cause;

(3) He must have acted maliciously;

(4) The proceedings must have been unsuccessful—that is to say, must have terminated in favour of the plaintiff now suing.

We shall deal with these requirements in their order.

---

[43] *Dorene Ltd.* v. *Suedes (Ireland) Ltd.* [1981] I.R. 312. An action will lie for procuring a search warrant to be issued maliciously and without reasonable and probable cause: *Calveley* v. *Chief Constable of Merseyside* [1989] Q.B. 136, 147.

[44] In *Fraser* v. *Balfour* (1918) 87 L.J.K.B. 1116 the H.L. held that the question was still open. The question is fully discussed by McCardie J. in *Heddon* v. *Evans* (1919) 35 T.L.R. 642 (fuller report in R. O'Sullivan, *Military Law and the Supremacy of the Civil Courts*, 1921).

[45] As did the C.A. in *Metall* [1990] 1 Q.B. 391, 462. The tort "has an ancient lineage": *Dorene Ltd.* v. *Suedes (Ireland) Ltd.* [1981] I.R. 312, 315.

[46] *Speed Seal Ltd.* v. *Paddington* [1985] 1 W.L.R. 1327, 1335.

[47] As in *Dorene Ltd.* v. *Suedes (Ireland) Ltd.* [1981] I.R. 312, 315.

[48] As in the leading case of *Grainger* v. *Hill* (1838) 4 Bing.N.C. 212.

[49] *Metall* [1990] 1 Q.B. 391, 468.

(1) Institution of proceedings

The proceedings complained of by the plaintiff must have been instituted by the defendant—that is to say, he must be the person who put the law in motion against the plaintiff. It is not necessary, however, that he should be a party to the proceedings. Thus an action for malicious abuse of process will lie against the solicitor who in his client's name has set the law in motion against the plaintiff.[50] But it should be exceptional for a third party to be liable: public policy requires that a member of the public who supplies information to the police should feel safe in doing so.[51] Probably the police continue to be prosecutors even after the setting-up of the Crown Prosecution Service by the Prosecution of Offences Act 1985 for the Crown Prosecution in essence takes over a prosecution started by another. Laying an information before a magistrate is sufficient to found an action, even though the information is withdrawn before a summons or a warrant has been issued.[52]

(2) Want of reasonable and probable cause

No action lies for the institution of legal proceedings, however malicious, unless they have been instituted without reasonable and probable cause.[53] This is a difficult part of the law[54] and two points may be noted at the outset. First, the burden of proving absence of reasonable and probable cause is on the plaintiff, who thus undertakes the notoriously difficult task of proving a negative.[55] Further, if the defendant denies it, it is not the practice to require him to give particulars of his denial.[56] Secondly, the existence of reasonable and probable cause is a question for the judge and not for the jury.[57] This anomalous rule was established as a precaution against erroneous verdicts for the plaintiff— *per doubt del lay gents.* Still, all preliminary questions of fact on which this issue depends are for the jury. Thus if the defendant alleges that he prosecuted the plaintiff because of information received from a third person, it is for the jury to say whether that information was really received by the defendant and (if the question is relevant) whether it was really believed by him, and it is for the judge to decide whether, if it was so received and believed, it constituted a reasonable ground for

---

[50] *Johnson v. Emerson* (1871) L.R. 6 Ex. 329.

[51] *Commercial Union Assurance Co. Ltd. v. Lamont* [1989] 3 N.Z.L.R. 187.

[52] It has been held that the proceedings need not have reached a stage when they can be accurately described as a prosecution: it is enough if damage to the plaintiff may result: *Mohammed Amin v. Bannerjee* [1947] A.C. 322.

[53] *Williams v. Taylor* (1829) 6 Bing. 183, 186, *per* Tindal C.J.: "Malice alone is not sufficient, because a person actuated by the plainest malice may none the less have a justifiable reason for prosecution."

[54] An attempt to avoid the difficulties by alleging the distinct tort of misfeasance in a public office (see above, § 3.2) failed in *McDonagh v. Metropolitan Police Commissioner* [1990] C.L. 400.

[55] *Abrath v. N.E. Ry.* (1883) 11 Q.B.D. 440. Otherwise in false imprisonment: *Hicks v. Faulkner* (1878) 8 Q.B.D. 167, 170.

[56] *Stapeley v. Annetts* [1970] 1 W.L.R. 70.

[57] *Lister v. Perryman* (1870) L.R. 4 H.L. 521. So also in false imprisonment: *Hailes v. Marks* (1861) 7 H. & N. 56.

the prosecution.[58] This division of functions between judge and jury may be effected at the discretion of the judge in one of two ways. He may either direct the jury to find the facts specially and then decide for himself on the facts so found whether there was reasonable and probable cause, or he may tell the jury that if they find the facts to be such and such then there is reasonable and probable cause, and if they find the facts to be otherwise then there is none, thus leaving the jury to find a general verdict on this hypothetical direction.[59]

Reasonable and probable cause means a genuine belief, based on reasonable grounds, that the proceedings are justified. The terms reasonable and probable are synonyms. *Probabilis causa* was an expression which was not unknown in classical Latin and became familiar in medieval usage.[60] *Probabilis* means primarily provable—hence capable of being put to the test—hence reliable, approved, right, good, justifiable. *Probabilis causa* means a good reason—a ground of action which commends itself to reasonable men.[61] The defendant is not required to believe that the accused is guilty: it is enough if he believes there is reasonable and probable cause for prosecution.[62] He need only be satisfied that there is a proper case to lay before the court.[63] In *Hicks v. Faulkner*[64] Hawkins J. said, "I should define reasonable and probable cause to be an honest belief in the guilt of the accused, based upon a full conviction, founded on reasonable grounds, of the existence of a state of circumstances which, assuming them to be true, would reasonably lead any ordinary prudent and cautious man, placed in the position of the accused, to the conclusion that the person charged was probably guilty of the crime imputed."[65] It is a degree of presumption which is hard to define in words, but in practice is quite comprehensible.[66] The prosecutor must himself honestly believe in the case which he is making: it may not be enough that he is acting (if a police officer) on the instructions of his superiors,[67] or in blind reliance on the opinion of counsel.[68] But if a

---

[58] *Herniman* v. *Smith* [1938] A.C. 305, 317–318. Since this is an inference of fact, the judge necessarily has to determine it without any guidance from precedent, for each case depends on its own facts, and his task might therefore be thought to be a difficult one. Yet Lord du Parcq said: "A judge is frequently set the task of deciding whether there was 'reasonable and probable cause' for an action and I have heard no complaint that the question is too vague to be answered with accuracy"—*Tyne Improvement Commissioners* v. *Armement Anversois S/A* [1949] A.C. 326, 353.

[59] *Abrath* v. *N.E. Ry.* (1883) 11 Q.B.D. 440, 458.

[60] See references in 6th edition of this work, p. 590.

[61] *Robinson* v. *Keith*, 1936 S.C. 25, 48.

[62] *Tempest* v. *Snowden* [1952] 1 K.B. 130, 135.

[63] *Glinski* v. *McIver* [1962] A.C. 726, 758.

[64] (1878) 8 Q.B. 167, 171.

[65] Lord Atkin, in a judgment concurred in by other members of the House, said he knew of no better statement that this: *Herniman* v. *Smith* [1938] A.C. 305, 316. But Sir Raymond Evershed M.R. remarked that "If that is the meaning of the question 'Was there reasonable and probable cause,' it is no wonder that it is a question not to be left to a jury": *Tempest* v. *Snowden* [1952] 1 K.B. 130, 135.

[66] *R.* v. *Brixton Prison Governor, ex p. Armah* [1968] A.C. 192, 252.

[67] *Glinski* v. *McIver* [1962] A.C. 726, 756, 769.

[68] *Abbott* v. *Refuge Assurance Co. Ltd.* [1962] 1 Q.B. 432, 456; *Glinski* v. *McIver* [1962] A.C. 726, 745.

private person honestly states his complaint to a responsible police officer, who advises him to prosecute, he will be protected.[69]

The question whether the defendant possessed such an honest belief should not be left to the jury in every case, but only if it is in dispute and the plaintiff leads some evidence of its absence.[70] If it were asked in every case it would put every police officer at the mercy of an accused who happened to be acquitted.[71] When honest belief is in issue the question left to the jury should be in the form "Did the defendant honestly believe in the charges he was making?"[72] The question should not contain any reference to reasonable grounds for belief. For to ask the jury whether the defendant had an honest belief that he had reasonable and probable grounds for prosecuting is to ask them a question (albeit one of fact) which it is for the judge alone to answer.[73]

Grounds for belief

Further, even if the defendant honestly believed the proceedings to be justified there is no reasonable and probable cause unless this belief was based on reasonable grounds. This question is to be determined by the facts actually known to the defendant at the time when he laid the information and subsequently proceeded with the prosecution, not to the facts as they actually existed.[74] So facts unknown to the prosecutor do not prevent the facts which were known to him from constituting reasonable and probable cause.[75] When a person embarks upon a prosecution without any evidence at all or with evidence on which no reasonable jury would convict, then (whatever his state of mind) there is strong evidence that he had no reasonable and probable cause.[76] Further, one who continues a prosecution, which has been instituted with reasonable and probable cause, after he has discovered facts which indicate that it is groundless may well be held to have no reasonable and probable cause for continuing unless he at least informs the court of the facts which have been discovered. It may be inferred from *Herniman v. Smith*,[77] in which the point was allowed to go by default, that it is not enough in itself to establish a reasonable or probable cause that the plaintiff was committed for trial or even that he was convicted by a court at first instance and subsequently acquitted on appeal. This seems good sense, for, though these facts would be weighty evidence of a reasonable and probable cause, they should not be conclusive.

---

[69] *Malz v. Rosen* [1966] 1 W.L.R. 1008.
[70] *Glinski v. McIver* [1962] A.C. 726, 744, 768.
[71] *Dallison v. Caffery* [1965] 1 Q.B. 348, 368.
[72] *Glinski v. McIver* [1962] A.C. 726, 761, 767.
[73] *Tempest v. Snowden* [1952] 1 K.B. 130.
[74] *Herniman v. Smith* [1938] A.C. 305, 315. The question of reasonable and probable cause is one which the court has to determine objectively on the evidence before it: *Tims v. John Lewis & Co. Ltd.* [1951] 2 K.B. 459, 472. But the prosecutor need not test every fact: "His duty is not to ascertain whether there is a defence but whether there is reasonable and probable cause for a prosecution"—[1938] A.C. 305, 319, *per* Lord Atkin.
[75] *Herniman v. Smith* [1938] A.C. 305; *Wright v. Sharp* (1947) 176 L.T. 308.
[76] *Tims v. John Lewis & Co. Ltd.* [1951] 2 K.B. 459, 472–474 (reversed on another point [1952] A.C. 676).
[77] [1938] A.C. 305. See Winfield, Note (1937) 53 L.Q.R. 12.

(3) Malice

No action will lie for the institution of legal proceedings, however destitute of reasonable and probable cause, unless they are instituted maliciously—that is to say, from some wrongful motive.[78] Malice and absence of reasonable and probable cause must unite in order to produce liability. So long as legal process is honestly used for its proper purpose, mere negligence or want of sound judgment in the use of it creates no liability; and, conversely, if there are reasonable grounds for the proceedings (for example, the probable guilt of an accused person) no impropriety of motive on the part of the person instituting these proceedings is in itself any ground of liability. Therefore it is necessary to distinguish between honesty of belief and honesty of motive; the former is relevant to the question of reasonable and probable cause, the latter to the question of malice.[79]

Malice means the presence of some improper and wrongful motive—that is to say, an intent to use the legal process in question for some other than its legally appointed and appropriate purpose.[80] It can be proved either by showing what the motive was and that it was wrong, or by showing that the circumstances were such that the prosecution can only be accounted for by imputing some wrong or indirect motive to the prosecutor[81]: for example, prosecuting a person for theft in order to deter others from committing similar depredations,[82] the levying of blackmail, or the coercion of the accused in respect of some unconnected matter, such as the obtaining of compensation or restitution from the accused (the civil law, not the criminal, being the appropriate instrument for this purpose). Again, a prosecution is not malicious merely because inspired by anger for the injury suffered,[83] for this is one of the motives on which the law relies to secure the prosecution of offenders against the criminal law.[84]

Burden of proof

The burden of proving malice lies on the plaintiff; and, subject to two qualifications, the question is one for the jury and not, like that of reasonable and probable cause, one for the judge.[85] The first of these qualifications is that the question whether any particular motive is a proper or improper motive for the proceeding in question is a matter of law for the determination of the judge. Malice is any motive of which the law disapproves, not any motive which is displeasing to a jury. The jury has merely to decide whether the motive exists. The second qualification is that there must be some reasonable evidence of malice, other-

---

[78] *Williams* v. *Taylor* (1829) 6 Bing. 183, 186.
[79] *Horner* v. *Irwin & Son Ltd.* [1972] N.I. 202, 204.
[80] *Dorene Ltd.* v. *Suedes (Ireland) Ltd.* [1981] I.R. 312.
[81] *Brown* v. *Hawkes* [1891] 2 Q.B. 718, 722.
[82] *Stevens* v. *Midland Counties Ry.* (1854) 10 Ex. 352, 356.
[83] As distinct from anger at some other activity of the accused—*e.g.* his perjured evidence in other proceedings: *Glinski* v. *McIver* [1962] A.C. 726.
[84] *Brown* v. *Hawkes* [1891] 2 Q.B. 718, 722.
[85] *Mitchell* v. *Jenkins* (1833) 5 B. & Ad. 588.

wise the case will be withdrawn from the jury.[86] Want of reasonable and probable cause is itself in certain cases sufficient evidence of malice to go to a jury.[87] Nevertheless, a jury is not at liberty in all cases to infer malice from want of reasonable cause. Want of reasonable cause is sufficient evidence of malice in those cases only in which it is sufficient evidence that there was no genuine belief in the accusation made. If it appears that there was such a belief, the plaintiff must produce some independent evidence of malice, and cannot rely on the absence of reasonable cause. On the other hand, malice is in general never evidence of want of reasonable cause,[88] unless the same fact supplies evidence both of malice and of absence of reasonable and probable cause, as where it is established that when the defendant instituted the prosecution he knew that the plaintiff was innocent.[89] For a prosecutor may be inspired by malice and yet have a genuine and reasonable belief in the truth of his accusation.[90]

(4) Termination of the proceedings in favour of the plaintiff

No action for malicious prosecution will lie until or unless the prosecution or other proceeding has terminated in favour of the person complaining of it. No person, for example, who has been convicted on a criminal charge can sue the prosecutor for malicious prosecution even though he can prove that he is an innocent man and that the accusation was a malicious and unfounded one.[91] Even if the prosecution or other proceeding is still pending, the same rule applies. "It is a rule of law that no one shall be allowed to allege of a still depending suit that it is unjust."[92] But if the prosecution has actually determined in any manner in favour of the plaintiff it matters nothing in what way this has taken place. There need not have been any acquittal on the merits. What the plaintiff requires for his action is not a judicial determination of his innocence but merely the absence of any judicial determination of his guilt. Thus it is enough if the prosecution has been discontinued,[93] or if the accused has been acquitted by reason of some formal defect in the indictment[94] or if a conviction has been quashed,[95] even if for some technical defect in the proceedings.[96] Conversely, if the proceedings have actually determined against the plaintiff it is immaterial that the judgment cannot be attacked by way of appeal.[97] This rule applies not only to malicious prosecution but to all malicious proceedings which

---

[86] *Brown* v. *Hawkes* [1891] 2 Q.B. 718.
[87] [1891] 2 Q.B. 718, 723.
[88] *Johnstone* v. *Sutton* (1886) 1 T.R. 510, 544.
[89] *Mitchell* v. *John Heine & Sons Ltd.* (1938) 38 S.R.(N.S.W.) 466.
[90] *Glinski* v. *McIver* [1962] A.C. 726, 782.
[91] *Basebé* v. *Matthews* (1867) L.R. 2 C.P. 684.
[92] *Gilding* v. *Eyre* (1861) 10 C.B.(N.S.) 592, 604, *per curiam*.
[93] *Casey* v. *Automobiles Renault of Canada* (1965) 54 D.L.R. (2d) 600. Probably this principle governs a decision of the Crown Prosecutor under the Prosecution of Offences Act 1985, s.23(4).
[94] *Wicks* v. *Fentham* (1791) 4 T.R. 247.
[95] *Herniman* v. *Smith* [1938] A.C. 305, 315.
[96] *Casey* v. *Automobiles Renault of Canada* (1965) 54 D.L.R. (2d) 600, 605–606.
[97] *Metropolitan Bank* v. *Pooley* (1885) 10 App.Cas. 210.

involve the judicial determination of any question at issue. Thus no action will lie for maliciously procuring the plaintiff to be adjudicated a bankrupt, until and unless the adjudication has been set aside.[98] But the rule does not apply to proceedings which can be classified as an abuse of the process of the court, which is apparently a distinct tort[99]—yet it is hard to see why it is not the genus of which malicious prosecution is a species.

§ 19.5. Erroneous and Irregular Proceedings

Having considered the liability of litigants for the malicious abuse of legal process, it remains to consider how far they are responsible for mere errors and irregularities of procedure in the absence of any malice. The rule is that no action will lie against any person for procuring an erroneous decision of a court of justice. This is so even though the court has no jurisdiction in the matter and although its judgment or order is for that or any other reason invalid. A court of justice is not the agent or servant of the litigant who sets it in motion so as to make that litigant responsible for the errors of law or fact which the court commits.[1] Every party is entitled to rely absolutely on the presumption that the court will observe the limits of its own jurisdiction and decide correctly on the facts and the law.[2] But a party who has actually misled the tribunal by his fraud or malice may be liable, and there is even authority for saying that one who prefers a charge to a magistrate (even though in vague language and by way of suspicion) is liable for the ulterior consequences and may not say they were due to the mistake or indiscretion of the tribunal he has set in motion.[3]

No action will lie against any person for issuing execution or otherwise acting in pursuance of a valid judgment or order of a court of justice even though it is erroneous and even though it is afterwards reversed or set aside for error.[4] A valid judgment, however erroneous in law or fact, is a sufficient justification for any act done in pursuance of it. The remedy of an aggrieved litigant is some form of appeal whereby the judgment may be reversed or set aside and not an action for damages against those who enforce or act on the judgment while it stands. If, however, any litigant executes any form of legal process which is invalid for want of jurisdiction, irregularity, or any other reason, and in so doing he commits any act in the nature of a trespass to person or property he is liable therefor in an action of trespass and it is not necessary to prove any malice or want of reasonable or probable cause. This is an application of the fundamental principle that mistake, however honest or inevitable, is no defence for him who intentionally interferes with the person or property of another.[5] But a distinction is to

---

[98] *Everett v. Ribbands* [1952] 2 Q.B. 198.
[99] *Speed Seal Products Ltd. v. Paddington* [1985] 1 W.L.R 1327.
[1] See above, § 7.3.
[2] (1848) 12 Q.B. 871.
[3] *Fitzjohn v. Mackinder* (1860) 8 C.B.(N.S.) 78.
[4] *Williams v. Williams* [1937] 2 All E.R. 559.
[5] *Painter v. Liverpool Oil Gas Light Co.* (1836) 3 Ad. & E. 433.

be drawn between process which is wholly void and process which is merely voidable. Process which is void is no defence at all and an action will lie without taking any steps to set it aside.[6] But when process is merely voidable it is a sufficient justification until it has been set aside; though when it has been set aside it becomes void *ab initio* and an action will thereupon lie for acts done in pursuance of it.

---

[6] *Brooks* v. *Hodgkinson* (1859) 4 H. & N. 712.

CHAPTER 20

PARTIES

§ 20.1. THE CROWN

The law on this topic was greatly changed by the Crown Proceedings Act 1947. At common law the procedure by way of petition of right generally provided a remedy against the Crown in cases of breach of contract and possibly also enabled real or personal property to be recovered. But it was impossible to sue the Crown in tort, either for wrongs which it had expressly authorised or for wrongs committed by its servants in the course of their employment.[1] Nor was it possible to sue the head of the department or other official superior of the wrong-doer, for all the servants of the Crown were and are fellow-servants and do not stand to each other in the relationship of master and servant.[2] The individual wrongdoer was, of course, liable and could not plead the commands of the king or state necessity as a defence.[3] These rules became highly unsatisfactory when the Crown became one of the largest employers of labour and occupiers of property in the country. Various devices were available to ensure that substantial justice was done. These became unnecessary when the Crown Proceedings Act 1947 was passed.

Section 2(1) of the Act provides as follows:

"Subject to the provisions of this Act, the Crown shall be subject to all those liabilities in tort to which, if it were a private person of full age and capacity, it would be subject:

    (a) in respect of torts committed by its servants or agents;

    (b) in respect of any breach of those duties which a person owes to his servants or agents at common law by reason of being their employer[4]; and

    (c) in respect of any breach of the duties attaching at common law to the ownership, occupation, possession or control of property."[5]

Proceedings are instituted against the appropriate Government

---

[1] *Trawnik* v. *Lennox* [1985] 1 W.L.R. 532.

[2] *Pearce* v. *Secretary of State for Defence* [1988] A.C. 755, 791. Superior servants of the Crown were in no special position in this respect; it is a general principle of the common law: see below, § 21.3.

[3] *Entick* v. *Carrington* (1765) 19 St.Tr. 1029. This is still the law. For the defences of act of State and statutory authority, see §§ 20.2, 22.7. It has, however, been held that neither the Crown nor its individual servants are liable in negligence for acts or omissions by H.M. Forces in active operation against the enemy: *Nisbet Shipping Co.* v. *The King* (1951) 4 D.L.R. 636.

[4] See below, § 21.10.

[5] The Crown is bound by the Occupiers' Liability Act 1957 (see s.6).

Department (to be selected from a list published by the Treasury), or, if there is doubt about this, against the Attorney-General.

Although the Act appears to have given rise to very few difficulties there are a few points which may be mentioned in detail.

(1) Torts committed by servants or agents

First, it is notable that the proviso to section 2(1) states that the Crown is not liable unless the act or omission of the servant or agent would (apart from the provisions of the Act) have given rise to a cause of action against him. The object of this proviso may have been to ensure that the Crown could avail itself of any defence open to the primary wrongdoer. Secondly, the liability of the Crown for the torts of its officers (a term which includes any servant or Minister of the Crown) is restricted to cases where the officer is appointed by it directly or indirectly and was at the material time paid in respect of his duties as an officer of the Crown wholly out of the Consolidated Fund, moneys provided by Parliament,[6] or a fund certified by the Treasury as equivalent.

The police

One consequence of section 2(1) is to exclude liability for the police, for the funds out of which they are paid are not (even in the case of the Metropolitan Police) provided wholly by Parliament.[7] In any case a constable is not a servant of the Crown in such a sense that the ordinary law of master and servant determines the relationship of the parties.[8] But although a constable is a servant neither of the Crown, nor of the police authority, nor of the chief constable, the Police Act 1964, s.48, provides that the chief officer of police of any area shall be liable in respect of torts committed by constables under his control in the performance of their functions in like manner as a master is liable in respect of torts committed by his servants in the course of their employment.[9] The chief constable is a joint tortfeasor with the delinquent constable, but the police fund is automatically charged with the payment of any damages or costs awarded against a chief constable. Thirdly, the 1947 Act provides[10] that the Crown is not liable for anything done by any person while discharging responsibilities of a judicial nature vested in him, or any responsibilities which he has in connection with the execution of judicial process. Fourthly, there may be difficulty in ascertaining which of the numerous persons, organs and institutions necessary for the government of the United Kingdom today are Crown servants, in the

---

[6] This means moneys paid out of the Consolidated Fund on the authority of the annual Consolidated Fund Acts or Appropriation Acts instead of on the authority of permanent legislation.

[7] Nor are they the servants of the police authority which appoints, pays and dismisses them (*Fisher* v. *Oldham Corporation* [1930] 2 K.B. 364): for the reasons for this, see below, § 172.

[8] *Att.-Gen. for N.S.W.* v. *Perpetual Trustee Co.* [1955] A.C. 457.

[9] See Williams, "Suing Policemen" (1989) 139 New L.J. 1664.

[10] s.2(5). The judicial officer himself has certain immunities: above, § 19.1.

absence of a clear provision in the enabling statute.[11] In particular, questions have arisen as to the status of the public corporations. In *Tamlin* v. *Hannaford*[12] the Court of Appeal held that the British Transport Commission was not a servant or agent of the Crown.

(2) Breach of statutory duty

Section 2(2) imposes on the Crown liability for breach of statutory duty[13] when the duty is binding both on persons other than the Crown and on the Crown itself. If the statute expressly states that it binds the Crown (*e.g.* the Factories Act 1961, s.173) no problem arises. If the statute is silent there may be difficulty, for the Act preserves the common law principle of construction that the Crown is not bound by a statute in the absence of express words or necessary implication.[14]

(3) Her Majesty's Forces and the Post Office

Although the general object of the Act is to place the Crown in the same position as a private subject it is plain that the Crown cannot in all respects be treated in exactly the same way as a private employer. Hence H.M. Forces and the Post Office occupy a special status.

(i) H.M. Forces[15]

By section 10(1) the Crown was exempt from liability in tort for death or personal injury caused by a member of the armed forces when on duty to another member of the armed forces, provided that the latter was either on duty or was on any land, premises, ship or vehicle being used for the purpose of the armed forces of the Crown, and the Minister of Pensions certified that the death or injury would be treated as attributable to service for pension purposes.[16] It should be noted that the exemption from liability was extended to the actual wrongdoer himself unless the court was satisfied that the act or omission complained of was not connected with the performance of his duties. By section 10(2) the Crown was also exempted from liability in tort for death or personal injury suffered by a member of the armed forces in consequence of the nature or condition of any land, premises, ship, aircraft or vehicle being used for the purpose of the armed forces or in consequence of the nature or condition of any equipment or supplies used for that purpose if the Minister of Pensions certified that the death or injury would be attribu-

---

[11] It has, however, been settled since *Mersey Docks Trustees* v. *Gibbs* (1866) L.R. 1 H.L. 93 that the mere fact that a body has been created by statute for public purposes does not mean that it is a servant or agent of the Crown.

[12] [1950] 1 K.B. 18.

[13] See above, §§ 10.01–10.05.

[14] The Crown is generally regarded as bound by the Fatal Accidents Acts 1846 to 1908 and the Law Reform (Miscellaneous Provisions) Act 1934, s.1.

[15] The Crown Proceedings (Armed Forces) Act 1987, s.4 repeals s.10 of the 1947 Act.

[16] See *Bell* v. *Secretary of State* [1985] 2 W.L.R. 248.

table to service for pension purposes. Any individual officer of the Crown at fault was also exempted.[17]

(ii) *The Post Office*

Under the Post Office Act 1969, as amended by the British Telecommunications Act 1981, the Post Office is not longer to be regarded as a servant or agent of the Crown, but is constituted as a separate public authority. Nevertheless the Act of 1969 retains some of the privileges which the former law conferred on the Post Office. Thus section 29(1) provides that no proceedings shall lie in tort[18] against the Post Office in respect of any loss or damage suffered by any person in respect of acts or omissions in the postal or telecommunications services. Further, section 29(2) provides that no officer or servant of the Post Office shall be subject to any civil liability, except at the suit of the Post Office, for any act for which the Post Office itself is not liable.[19] On the other hand, by section 30 the Post Office is under a certain measure of liability for the loss of or damage to[20] certain packets.

§ 20.2. ACTS OF STATE

It is a fundamental principle of English law that the Crown or its servants must be prepared to justify before the ordinary courts the legality of any act which interferes with the person or property of the subject. The justification must be found in some distinct rule of common law or statute: there is no principle which permits the Crown in time of peace to act for the public good as it thinks best. This was established in *Entick* v. *Carrington*.[21] The action was one of trespass for breaking and entering the plaintiff's house and seizing his papers.[22] The defendants pleaded that they had acted in obedience to warrants issued by the Secretary of State. The Court of Common Pleas held that there was no legal justification for such warrants. "And with respect to the argument of state necessity," said Sir Charles Pratt C.J. in his famous judgment, "the common law does not understand that kind of reasoning." But the

---

[17] The exemption of the actual wrongdoer has been criticised on the ground that it is contrary to general principles. But if this had not been done there would probably have been a revival of the practice of suing the individual wrongdoer in the hope that the Crown would stand behind him. Injustice may, however, arise in the not unlikely case of a member of the armed forces being killed or injured by the combined negligence of a fellow-member of the armed forces and a civilian in circumstances covered by s.10(1). In such a case the civilian will be liable for the whole of the plaintiff's damage without any right of contribution or indemnity from the service tortfeasor. We shall see that this is not the only example of such a situation: below, § 21.2.

[18] This prohibition cannot be evaded by suing in bailment: *American Express Ltd.* v. *British Airways Board* [1983] 1 W.L.R. 701.

[19] It is less easy to see why the individual wrongdoer has been rendered exempt in this case. It seems that if a postmaster tore up a customer's unregistered letter before his eyes the customer would be without remedy.

[20] This covers financial loss or damage: *Building and Civil Engineering Holidays Scheme Management Ltd.* v. *Post Office* [1966] 1 Q.B. 247.

[21] (1765) 19 St.Tr. 1029.

[22] It is characteristic of English law that an important constitutional principle should be established in an ordinary action of tort.

defence of act of State is available when the plaintiff is a non-resident and the wrong complained of is suffered elsewhere than in British territory,[23] and done by the authority, precedent or subsequent, of the Crown. A British subject owes allegiance to the Crown in whatever part of the world he may be; it seems therefore that the Crown cannot plead act of State as against him,[24] wherever the wrong may have been committed.[25] On the other hand, those who owe no allegiance to the Crown may, save in British territory, be dealt with by the Crown as it pleases. Thus in *Buron v. Denman*[26] the defendant, the commander of a British man-of-war, had destroyed certain property of an alien slave-trader on the coast of Africa in circumstances that would have given a good cause of action to a British subject. It was held, however, that inasmuch as the act of the defendant had been ratified by the British Government, it was an act of State for which no action would lie at the suit of an alien. In such cases if redress is to be obtained it must be through diplomatic channels. The Crown or its servant is really contending not that the act is innocent but that the plaintiff has chosen to proceed before a tribunal which has no jurisdiction to inquire into the matter.

The rule in *Buron v. Denman* has no application in time of peace to injuries inflicted within the Queen's dominions. An alien friend resident within those dominions owes temporary allegiance to the Queen and has the same legal protection as a British subject against acts committed by or on the authority of the Crown. Thus in *Johnstone v. Pedlar*[27] the respondent was an American citizen who resided in Dublin (before the establishment of the Irish Free State) and sympathised actively with Irish nationalism. After serving a sentence of imprisonment for illegal drilling he successfully sued the appellant, the Chief Commissioner of Police, to recover a sum of money which had been found on him at the time of his arrest and the seizure of which had been subsequently adopted as an act of State by the Chief Secretary for Ireland. The decision might have been different if the Crown had actually withdrawn its protection on the ground of his treasonable activities. Similarly, if an alien friend, though resident abroad, owns property in England his title thereto will have the same protection, even against the Crown, as if it belonged to a British subject.[28] An alien enemy, on other hand, possesses no rights against the Crown. His residence within the realm by the express or tacit licence of the Crown gives him legal protection against private persons,[29] and the courts are open to him, but

---

[23] *Buron v. Denman* (1848) 2 Ex. 167.

[24] *Walker v. Baird* [1892] A.C. 491. Note that the plaintiff was within British territory.

[25] The preceding sentence was approved by Lord Denning M.R. and Winn L.J. in the C.A., and by Lord Pearce in the H.L., in *Att.-Gen. v. Nissan* [1968] 1 Q.B. 286, 339, 347; [1970] A.C. 179, 225.

[26] (1848) 2 Ex. 167. The defendant was a younger son of Lord Denman, at that time C.J.Q.B., who was himself an ardent opponent of the slave trade. The decision was approved in *Buttes Oil & Gas Co. Ltd. v. Hanmer (No. 3)* [1982] A.C. 888.

[27] [1921] 2 A.C. 262.

[28] *Commercial and Estates Co. of Egypt v. Board of Trade* [1925] 1 K.B. 271, 290, 297.

[29] *Johnstone v. Pedlar* [1921] 2 A.C. 262, 283.

probably he remains none the less at the mercy of the Crown, which may do with him and with his property as is thought fit.[30]

§ 20.3. FOREIGN SOVEREIGNS, AMBASSADORS AND PUBLIC OFFICIALS

A foreign sovereign is not personally liable in the English courts for any tort committed by him, unless he has waived his immunity.[31] The only remedy for injuries done by him is by way of diplomatic action on the part of the British Government. It makes no difference that the wrongful act is committed in England. A foreign sovereign does not by residing in British territory waive his privilege or submit himself to the jurisdiction of the local courts. Nor does it make any difference that the wrongful act is done by the sovereign in this private capacity.[32] The only exception to this broad principle of immunity is that trading transactions are not protected since the State Immunity Act 1978.

Diplomatic immunity

The object of the Diplomatic Privileges Act 1964 is to replace the old law on the privileges and immunities of diplomatic representatives in the United Kingdom. The new law is mainly contained in the Schedule to the 1964 Act, which gives the force of law to the relevant provisions of the Vienna Convention on Diplomatic Relations 1961.

The main change made by the Act is to adopt the continental practice of dividing the members of a diplomatic mission into three classes:

(1) Members of the diplomatic staff, who will have full personal immunity, civil and criminal, with three exceptions:

    (*a*) a real action relating to private immovable property situated in the territory of the receiving state, unless he holds it on behalf of the sending state for the purpose of the mission;

    (*b*) an action relation to succession in which the diplomatic agent is involved as executor, administrator, heir or legatee as a private person and not on behalf of the sending state;

    (*c*) an action relating to any professional or commercial activity exercised by the diplomatic agent in the receiving state outside his official functions:

(2) members of the administrative and technical staff, who enjoy full immunity for official acts, but who are liable civilly (but not criminally) for acts performed outside the course of their duties;

(3) members of the service staff, who enjoy immunity for official acts, but are liable civilly and criminally for acts performed outside the course of their duties.

It can thus be seen that for the first time the courts will have power to determine whether an act committed by a member of a diplomatic mission was performed in the course of his duties. An important practical result is that an embassy chauffeur who is involved in a traffic accident will no longer be entitled as of right to have the writ in any

---

[30] *R. v. Bottrill* [1947] K.B. 41.
[31] *The Cristina* [1938] A.C. 485, 490.
[32] *Mighell v. Sultan of Johore* [1894] 1 Q.B. 149.

proceedings against him set aside, for the court will have power to determine whether he was acting within the scope of his employment.

§ 20.4. Corporations[33]

(1) Capacity to be sued

Inasmuch as a corporation is an artificial person distinct in law from its members, it is not capable of acting *in propria persona*, but acts only through its agents or servants. All the acts, and therefore all the wrongful acts, of a body corporate are in fact the acts of its agents or servants, though imputed in law to the corporation itself. But this does not mean that the liability of a body corporate is therefore in all cases a vicarious liability for the acts of other persons. A distinction can be drawn between the personal and the vicarious liability of a corporation in much the same way as is done with the liability of natural persons.[34] So it has always been assumed that a corporation is personally liable for breach of the duties which an employer owes at common law to his servants.[35]

The existence and extent of the liability of a corporation in actions of tort were at one time a matter of doubt, due partly to technical difficulties of procedure and partly to the theoretical difficulty of imputing wrongful acts or intentions to fictitious persons.[36] It is now well settled, however, that the liability of a corporation for the torts committed by its agents or servants is governed by the same rules as those which determine the liability of any other principal or employer. This liability extends, moreover, to wrongs of malice or fraud, no less than to wrongs of other descriptions. Thus a corporation can be sued for malicious prosecution, or for malicious libel on a privileged occasion, or for fraudulent misrepresentation,[37] no less than for trespass, conversion, or negligence.[38]

Ultra vires torts

It was sometimes said that the liability of a corporation for the acts of its agents or servants existed only where the scope of the authority or employment of those agents or servants was within the legal limits of the corporation's powers, and that if a corporation went beyond the limits set by law for its activities, and entered upon any business or undertaking which was *ultra vires*, it could not be made liable for torts committed by its agents or servants in the course of that business or undertaking.[39] But practical convenience and common sense made the

---

[33] Atiyah, *Vicarious Liability*, Chap. 34.
[34] See below, § 21.2.
[35] See below, § 21.10.
[36] *Abrath* v. N.E. Ry. (1886) 11 App.Cas. 247, 250–251.
[37] Usually actions of deceit are brought against one or more of the directors or other persons responsible for the misrepresentation; for their liability remains although the claim against the company may be barred by (*e.g.*) the fact that it has gone into liquidation.
[38] *Citizens' Life Assurance Co.* v. *Brown* [1904] A.C. 423.
[39] Goodhart, *Essays*, p. 90.

courts reluctant to accept the logic of this agreement. For "A corporation is an abstraction. It has no mind of its own any more than it has a body of its own; its active and directing will must consequently be sought in the person of somebody who for some purposes may be called an agent, but who is really the directing mind and will of the corporation, the very ego and centre of the personality of the corporation. That person may be under the direction of the shareholders in general meeting; that person may be the board of directors itself,"[40] or it may be the managing director or general manager[41] or other person having authority from the board of directors to conduct the company's business.[42] So in *Campbell v. Paddington Corporation*[43] a metropolitan borough, in pursuance of a formal resolution of its council, erected a stand in a highway which was a public nuisance. It was held that the corporation was liable, although they had no legal right to erect the stand. Accordingly, the true principle is the following: Every act done, authorised, or ratified on behalf of a corporation by the supreme governing authority of that corporation, or by any person or body of persons to whom the general powers of the corporation are delegated, is for the purpose of the law of torts the act of the corporation itself, whether *intra vires* or *ultra vires* of the corporation, and the corporation is liable accordingly for that act or for any tort committed in respect of it by any agent or servant of the corporation within the scope of his authority or employment. This sensible solution is almost certainly correct since the Companies Act 1985, s.35 (as amended), abolishes the *ultra vires* doctrine in relation to dealings between the company and third parties.

Liability of members

The members of a corporation are not as such liable for torts committed by the corporation. For the purposes of the law of torts, no less than for those of the law of contracts or of property, a body corporate is a personality distinct from its members; and just as a member is not responsible for the debts contracted by a corporation, so also he is not responsible for torts committed by it. From this undoubted principle the very doubtful inference has sometimes been drawn that the members of a corporation are not liable for torts committed by it, even if they have themselves acted as the agents by whom the corporation has so acted.[44] But it is undoubted law that the servants or agents by whom a corporation commits a tort are themselves personally liable to the same extent as any other servants or agents who commit torts in the service or on behalf of their principals or employers. It is difficult, therefore, to understand why the corporators themselves, if they act as the agents of

---

[40] *Lennard's Carrying Co. v. Asiatic Petroleum Co.* [1915] A.C. 705, 713, *per* Lord Haldane.

[41] *Fanton v. Denville* [1932] 2 K.B. 309, 329.

[42] *Rudd v. Elder Dempster & Co. Ltd.* [1933] 1 K.B. 566, 594. Welsh "The Criminal Liability of Corporations" (1946) 62 L.Q.R. 345 demonstrates that the criminal law has developed on similar lines.

[43] [1911] 1 K.B. 869.

[44] e.g. by Kelly C.B. in *Mill v. Hawker* (1874) L.R.Ex. 309, 321. On appeal to the Exchequer Chamber no opinion was expressed on this point, the court being apparently divided.

the corporation, should not be equally liable for any wrongful acts so committed by them.

In any case, it is clear that a corporation is liable to its members for the torts of its agents to the same extent as it is liable to strangers. To this there is one anomalous exception: an action of deceit will not lie against a company at the suit of a shareholder until his allotment of shares has been rescinded.[45]

(2) Capacity to sue

In general a corporation may sue for any tort (*e.g.* malicious presentation of a winding-up petition)[46] in the same way as an individual. The only qualifications are (i) the tort must not be of a kind which it is impossible to commit against a corporation—*e.g.* assault or false imprisonment; (ii) in case of defamation, it must be shown that the defamatory matter reflects upon the corporation itself, and not merely on its officers or members,[47] and also that it is of such a nature that its tendency[48] is to cause actual damage to the corporation in respect of its property or business.[49] Actual loss need not be shown if the libel has a tendency to damage the trading reputation of the plaintiff corporation.[50] An action of libel will lie at the suit of a trading corporation charged with insolvency or with dishonest or incompetent management.[51] It was once held that a non-trading corporation, such as a local government authority, could not sue for libel charging it with corruption and bribery[52] but later it was held that such a body is entitled to have its reputation as well as its property protected.[53]

§ 20.5. UNINCORPORATED BODIES

Trade unions

Until 1901 it was generally agreed that a corporation and an individual or individuals were the only entities known to the common law who could sue or be sued. But in that year, in *Taff Vale Ry.* v. *Amalgamated Society of Railway Servants*[54] it was held by the House of Lords that a registered trade union, though not a corporate body, was a legal entity having sufficient of the characteristics of a juristic person to enable it to be sued in tort for the wrongful acts of its officials. The decision was in effect reversed by section 4 of the Trade Disputes Act 1906, which

---

[45] *Houldsworth* v. *City of Glasgow Bank* (1880) 5 App.Cas. 317.
[46] *Quartz Hill Gold Mining Co.* v. *Eyre* (1883) 11 Q.B.D. 674.
[47] *Bognor Regis U.D.C.* v. *Campion* [1972] 2 Q.B. 169.
[48] *Irish People's Assurance Co.* v. *Dublin City Assurance Co.* [1929] I.R. 25.
[49] *D. & L. Caterers Ltd.* v. *D'Ajou* [1945] K.B. 364.
[50] *Company of Proprietors of Selby Bridge* v. *Sunday Telegraph Ltd.* [1966] C.L.Y. 6973.
[51] *Metropolitan Saloon Omnibus Co.* v. *Hawkins* (1859) 4 H. & N. 87.
[52] *Manchester (Mayor of)* v. *Williams* [1891] 1 Q.B. 94.
[53] *Bognor Regis U.D.C.* v. *Campion* [1972] 2 Q.B. 169. Recently the C.A. has reverted to the older view: *Derbyshire County Council* v. *Times Newspapers plc*, *The Independent*, February 21, 1992.
[54] [1901] A.C. 426. Somewhat similar reasoning enabled liability to be imposed on an unregistered union for the wrongful acts of shop stewards in *Heatons Transport (St. Helens) Ltd.* v. *Transport & General Workers' Union* [1973] A.C. 15.

granted complete immunity to a trade union for all tortious acts committed on its behalf. Then the 1906 Act was repealed by the Trade Union and Labour Relations Act 1974, s.14.

Section 14 of the 1974 Act was itself repealed by the Employment Act 1980, s.15, which displayed an entirely new legislative policy towards trade unions (and employers' associations). In effect the principle in *Taff Vale* was revived: trade unions were not above the law,[55] but to be treated as natural persons, so that while acting in the course or furtherance of a trade dispute (as narrowly redefined by the Employment Act 1982, s.29) they were to be entitled to the same immunities or protections (again narrowly redefined by the E.A. 1982, s.13) as natural persons so acting.

But while trade unions were thus, after 75 years, brought back within the rule of law, it was conceded that they could not in all respects be treated exactly as natural persons. First, when proceedings within section 13 of the 1974 Act (*e.g.* for conspiracy or inducement of breach of contract) are brought against a union, it shall be liable only if the act in question has been authorised or endorsed by the union—a phrase which is given an exhaustive statutory definition (E.A. 1982, s.15(2)–(6) as amended by the Employment Act 1990, s.6). Secondly, section 16 limits the amount of damages which may be awarded against a union successfully sued.[56] But the maximum amount is still substantial (£250,000); there is no limit on costs; and there is also no limit on fines or sequestration of assets for breach of an injunction or other court order.[57] Thirdly, adopting a recommendation made by the Dunedin Commission in 1906, certain union funds—*e.g.* the provident benefit fund—are protected from legal process (section 17). Fourthly, not all torts committed on the authority of a union are necessarily outside its own rules.[58]

Formerly it was thought that as a trade union is a legal entity it has the correlative right to sue in its registered name.[59] But as the 1974 Act, s.2(1), expressly provides that a trade union shall not be treated as a corporate body, it has been held that a union cannot be a plaintiff in a libel action.[60]

Other unincorporated entities

It is uncertain how far the principle in the *Taff Vale* case applies to the many heterogeneous bodies known to English law. It has been held to

---

[55] To use Lord Macnaghten's phrase in *Quinn* v. *Leathem* [1901] A.C. 426, 438.

[56] But this very limitation may make it easier to obtain an interlocutory injunction on the ground that damages will be an inadequate remedy: see below, § 25.2.

[57] See *Dimbleby & Sons Ltd.* v. *N.U.J.* [1984] 1 W.L.R. 427, 431. In the miners' dispute with the Coal Board in 1985/1986, the N.U.M. lost many millions of its assets in satisfying such claims, as did SOGAT 82 in the Wapping Dispute of 1986. The financial risks to a union of an unprotected strike are vividly shown by *Falconer* v. *A.S.L.E.F.* [1986] I.R.L.R. 331 (railway traveller stranded by unballoted strike recovers damages).

[58] *Thomas* v. *N.U.M.* [1986] Ch. 20.

[59] *National Union of General and Municipal Workers* v. *Gillian* [1946] K.B. 81; *Willis* v. *Brooks* [1947] 1 All E.R. 191; *B.M.T.A.* v. *Salvadori* [1949] Ch. 556.

[60] *Electrical and Plumbing Union* v. *Times Newspapers* [1980] Q.B. 585.

cover a registered Friendly Society,[61] and a Trustee Savings Bank,[62] but not an ordinary members' club which is neither incorporated nor proprietary. In some cases it may be possible to prove that the actual wrong-doer was the servant or agent of a particular member or members (*e.g.* the committee[63]); in other cases it may be possible to obtain a representation order under R.S.C., Ord. 15, r. 12, provided that the members whose names appear on the writ are persons who may fairly be taken to represent the body of club members, and that they and all the other club members have the same interest in the action.[64]

§ 20.6. MINORS[65]

(1) Capacity to be sued

A person under full age may now be described as a minor instead of as an infant,[66] as used to be customary before the age of majority was lowered from 21 to 18 years by the Family Law Reform Act 1969, s.1. A minor[67] is in general liable for his torts in the same manner and to the same extent as an adult. In certain other branches of the law liability is excluded by the fact that the defendant is below a certain age. Thus a child under 10 years of age is exempt from all responsibility for crimes committed by him. A child between the ages of 10 and 14 is presumed to be incapable of criminal intent, though this presumption may be rebutted by proof to the contrary. A person under the age of 18 is in general free from liability for breach of contract.

In the law of torts, however, there are no similar rules of exemption. For over 500 years it has been assumed that a child of any age may be sued for trespass[68] to land or goods,[69] or to the person,[70] at least if he is old enough to form an intention to do the necessary act,[71] and will be held liable in damages just as if he were an adult.[72] The youth of the defendant is not however in all cases wholly irrelevant. For it may be evidence of the absence of the particular mental state which is an essential element in the kind of tort in question. Thus, if an action is based on

---

[61] *Longdon-Griffiths* v. *Smith* [1951] 1 K.B. 295.
[62] *Knight and Searle* v. *Dove* [1964] 2 Q.B. 631.
[63] As in *Brown* v. *Lewis* (1896) 12 T.L.R. 455 (members of committee of Blackburn Rovers Football Club personally liable for defective stand). But the general rule is that membership of a committee does not imply any duty of care towards the members: *Robertson* v. *Ridley* [1989] 1 W.L.R. 872.
[64] *Campbell* v. *Thompson* [1953] 1 Q.B. 445.
[65] See Bohlen, "Liability in Tort of Infants and Insane Persons" (1924) 23 Mich.L.Rev. 9, *Studies*, Chap. 11.
[66] Family Law Reform Act 1969, s.12.
[67] A person reaches majority on the commencement of the 18th anniversary of his natal day: Family Law Reform Act 1969, s.9.
[68] See Baker and Milsom, *Sources of English Legal History* (1986), p. 326.
[69] *O'Brien* v. *McNamee* [1953] I.R. 86 (child of seven liable in trespass for burning plaintiff's haystack).
[70] *McHale* v. *Watson* (1966) 115 C.L.R. 199.
[71] *Tillander* v. *Gosselin* (1966) 60 D.L.R. (2d) 18 (three-year-old child not liable).
[72] *Walmsley* v. *Humenick* [1954] 2 D.L.R. 232, 239.

malice or on some special intent, the fact that the defendant is extremely young is relevant as tending to disprove the existence of any such malice or intent.[73] Similarly, in order to make a child liable for negligence, it must be proved that he failed to show the amount of care reasonably to be expected from a child of that age. It is not enough that an adult would have been guilty of negligence had he acted in the same circumstances. This, indeed, seems never to have been decided,[74] but it would seem implied in the decisions on the contributory negligence of children.[75] The precise age of the child may be of importance. "At some stages in life one year's difference in age matters nothing; but in youth and early manhood when knowledge is rapidly blossoming, a twelve-month is a very long time."[76] In general the principle is that a minor who is incapable of forming a culpable intention or of realising the probable consequences of his conduct is relieved from liability in those cases in which fault is essential to liability, but that whenever liability is imposed irrespective of fault he is fully liable as a normal adult.[77]

It sometimes seems to be assumed that it is not worthwhile suing a minor in tort, because he may have no assets out of which to satisfy the judgment. Apart from the fact that this assumption may be untrue in the affluent society, it is worth remembering that a judgment debtor now without funds may acquire them later, and that he may be sued on the judgment, or execution may be issued on it, up to six years from its date, or even after that period with the leave of the court.[78] If judgment is given against a minor, and if, as is usual, it is made payable by instalments, it is an abuse of the process of the court for him to lodge his petition in bankruptcy.[79]

Tort and contract

When the act of a minor is both a tort and a breach of contract, is he liable for the tort, notwithstanding that the contract is not binding on him,[80] or does his exemption from an action for breach of contract protect him against an action for the tort also? Here the law has seen some development. By the middle of the seventeenth century it was settled that if an action against an infant was in truth founded on contract the plaintiff could not convert it into an action of tort lest "touts les infants

---

[73] Note the cases holding that in trespass intention or negligence must be shown: above, § 7.4.

[74] Though in *Williams* v. *Humphrey* (*The Times*, February 20, 1975) it was held that a boy aged 15 years and 11 months was to be judged by the same standard as an adult, and the defendant was ordered to pay £13,352 damages for personal injuries suffered by the plaintiff as a result of being pushed into a swimming pool.

[75] See also the law relating to infant entrants on premises, above, § 11.7.

[76] *Kerry* v. *Carter* [1969] 1 W.L.R. 1372, at 1377, *per* Edmund Davies L.J.

[77] *Walmsley* v. *Humenick* [1954] 2 D.L.R. 232, 239; *McHale* v. *Watson* (1966) 115 C.L.R. 199, 205, 233.

[78] R.S.C., Ord. 46, r. 2.

[79] *Re A Debtor* [1967] Ch. 590.

[80] Since the Minors' Contracts Act 1987, a contract which is disadvantageous to a minor is in general not binding on him.

in Angleterre serront ruine."[81] In the eighteenth century "Lord Mansfield, indeed, frequently said, that this protection was to be used as a shield, and not as a sword; therefore If an infant commit an assault, or utter slander, God forbid that he should not answer for it."[82] But the courts still would not permit the plaintiff to sue in tort for what was in truth a breach of contract. So in *Jennings* v. *Rundall*[83] the infant defendant was held not liable for riding too hard a mare which he had hired from the plaintiff. But in 1863 "a far stronger and more learned court"[84] made the distinction, which is now accepted law, between acts which were merely wrongful modes of performing the contract and acts which were outside the contract altogether. In *Burnard* v. *Haggis*[85] the defendant, an undergraduate of Trinity College, Cambridge, under the age of majority, hired a mare for riding, but in breach of an express term in his agreement he used her for jumping and so injured her. It was held that the defendant was liable in tort, notwithstanding the fact that it was at the same time the breach of a void contract. So if an infant bailee refuses to redeliver the chattel bailed, contrary to an express term of the contract of bailment, he can be sued for conversion.[86] In such a case the infant has gone outside the four corners of the contract, or to put it in another way, has committed a breach of a fundamental term of the contract which determines the bailment and constitutes an independent trespass.[87]

There is, however, an important exception to the rule that a minor is liable for his torts. If a minor fraudulently pretends to be of full age, whereby the plaintiff is induced to contract with him, the contract is not for that reason binding on the minor, nor is he estopped from pleading his infancy.[88] Neither can the plaintiff sue in tort for the deceit. This was clearly established by the Court of Appeal in *R. Leslie Ltd.* v. *Sheill*.[89] "At the time of the transaction in question," said Lord Sumner,[90] "the appellant was an infant. He succeeded in deceiving some money-lenders by telling them a lie about his age, and so got them to lend him £400 on the faith of his being adult. Perhaps they were simpler than money-lenders usually are: perhaps the infant looked unusually mature. At any rate, when they awoke to the fact that they could not enforce their bargain and sought to recover the £400 paid, charging him

---

81 *Johnson* v. *Pye* (1665) 1 Sid. 258. The garbled Law-French of Restoration reports is a well-known oddity. In the collateral report in 1 Keb. 905 Sir John Keeling C.J. is reported to have said that if the action were allowed "the whole foundation of the common law will be shaken."
82 *Jennings* v. *Rundall* (1799) 8 T.R. 335, 336–337, *per* Lord Kenyon C.J. ("Where Lord Mansfield led, Lord Kenyon C.J. followed, though he was not a judge who followed blindly": *Government of India* v. *Taylor* [1955] A.C. 591, 605, *per* Viscount Simonds.)
83 (1799) 8 T.R. 335.
84 Pollock, *Revised Reports*, iv, 5.
85 (1863) 14 C.B.(N.S.) 45 (Erle C.J., Willes, Byles and Keating JJ. "What Erle C.J. and Willes J. twice and Byles J. once stated to be the law in 1864 cannot be lightly disregarded in 1973": *Henriksens Rederi A/S* v. *Rolimpex* [1974] Q.B. 233, at 262, *per* Roskill L.J.
86 *Ballett* v. *Mingay* [1943] K.B. 281.
87 Compare the cases on exemption clauses, below, § 22.2.
88 *Levene* v. *Brougham* (1909) 25 T.L.R. 265.
89 [1914] 3 K.B. 607.
90 [1914] 3 K.B. 607, 611.

with fraud, the jury found that the appellant had been guilty of fraud, and he does not now complain of the verdict. . . . It is not a pretty story to begin life with, and one might have expected that the appellant's chief anxiety would have been to live it down, but money is money, and I suppose that £400 is more than he cares to pay, or rather to repay, if he can avoid it." The court allowed the infant's appeal. Although a minor who procures a contract by fraudulent representation that he is of age is not liable either on the contract or in tort, he is nevertheless liable under the Minors' Contracts Act 1987, s.3(1), to restore any property or other advantage thereby obtained by him.

Parents not responsible for their children's torts[91]

A father[92] is not as such liable for the torts of his children, even while they are under age and living in his house, and even though he has control over them.[93] Nor is a father, as such, liable to a child: the blood relationship does not of itself impose a duty of care.[94] It is to be observed, however, that a child may be his father's servant, so as to bring the father within the rule as to employers' liability. If a father sends his son on an errand with a motor-car, he will answer for his son's negligence in driving; but he will answer for him, not as being his father, but as being his employer.[95] Secondly, a father may be liable for his own personal negligence in affording or allowing his child an opportunity of doing mischief. So in *Newton* v. *Edgerley*[96] a father was held liable when he supplied his 12-year-old son (who was "young for his years") with a .410 rifle without giving him proper instructions for handling it and an accident occurred. On the other hand, in *Goreley* v. *Codd*[97] a father was held not liable when he entrusted a .22 rifle to his son aged 15 years with adequate instructions. The son (together with the 16-year-old plaintiff[98]) was at a special school, but the evidence showed that the son's "considerable retardation" related only to "book-learning" and not to his ability to handle a gun. Now the plaintiff in such a case would be in an even stronger position, for the Firearms Act 1968, s.24, makes it a criminal offence to give an air weapon to a person under 14 years, or for him to accept it. The Act also places severe restrictions upon the use or possession of air weapons by young persons except under supervision. Breach of these provisions might give rise to an action for breach of statutory duty,[99] and could always be relied upon as evidence of negligence.[1] In any event, it will not necessarily be a defence to plead that

---

[91] The Children Act 1989 refers to "parental responsibility", but not in relation to the law of tort.

[92] Presumably the same rule applies to a mother (or indeed any person *in loco parentis*) in the absence of a father.

[93] See below, § 21.3.

[94] *Hahn* v. *Conley* (1971) 126 C.L.R. 276.

[95] *Gibson* v. *O'Keeney* [1928] N.I. 66.

[96] [1959] 1 W.L.R. 1031.

[97] [1967] 1 W.L.R. 19.

[98] Who obtained judgment against the infant defendant personally for £1,000.

[99] See above, Chap. 10.

[1] *Hinds* v. *Direct Supply Co. Ltd.* [1966] C.L.Y. 5210.

the child was warned to be careful, for everyone knows that even well-behaved children sometimes disobey their parents' warnings.[2] In some American cases[3] parents have been held liable for assaults committed by children known to have the habit of attacking people: this "vicious child" doctrine has not yet been applied in England, though a reasonably prudent parent may be personally, as distinct from vicariously, liable if he fails to take reasonable care to prevent small children escaping on to the highway, and injuring users of it,[4] or to control such children when they have been brought onto the highway,[5] or are passengers in a vehicle.[6]

Finally, it should be remembered that the Criminal Injuries Compensation Board may award to a victim of a minor's wrongdoing a sum sufficient to make an action in tort unnecessary. The Board assumes jurisdiction even if the child is under the age of 10, and so not criminally responsible.

(2) Capacity to sue

Apart from the procedural rule that he must sue by his next friend[7] a minor is in this respect no different from an adult. It has even been decided that an infant may sue its own parent for negligence.[8] But in one respect an infant plaintiff in tort may be in an unfavourable position: he may be held to be *volens* to the wrongful act of the defendant, even though a contract not to sue would not have been for his benefit, and so not binding on him.[9]

Pre-natal injuries[10]

The common law was uncertain,[11] but now the Congenital Disabilities (Civil Liability) Act 1976, s.1, provides that a person responsible for an occurrence affecting the parent of a child, causing the child to be born disabled, will be liable to the child if that person would have been liable in tort to the parent affected. Liability is thus derivative. There are various exceptions and qualifications—*e.g.* there is no liability for a pre-conceptional occurrence if the parents accepted the particular risk. This action ("wrongful birth") by the parents for damage to themselves resulting from the child's birth must be distinguished from the action brought by a child for damage to itself arising from the fact of birth

---

[2] *Newton* v. *Edgerley* [1959] 1 W.L.R. 1031.

[3] Prosser, Torts, § 123.

[4] *Carmarthenshire County Council* v. *Lewis* [1955] A.C. 549.

[5] *McCallion* v. *Dodd* [1966] N.Z.L.R. 710.

[6] *Curley* v. *Mannion* [1965] I.R. 543 (children known to be in habit of opening off-side door).

[7] Usually his parent: Ord. 80, r. 2.

[8] *McCallion* v. *Dodd* [1966] N.Z.L.R. 710. This is certainly the assumption behind the Congenital Disabilities (Civil Liability) Act 1976, ss.1 and 2, which specifically provide that a mother is not liable to her own disabled child, except when she drives a motor-vehicle negligently.

[9] *Buckpitt* v. *Oates* [1968] 1 All E.R. 1145.

[10] See Symmons, "Policy Factors in Actions for Wrongful Birth" (1987) 50 M.L.R. 269.

[11] But in some cases an action lay: *B.* v. *Islington Health Authority* [1991] 2 W.L.R. 501.

("wrongful life"). Such an action for "wrongful life" did not exist before the Act,[12] and almost certainly does not exist now.

§ 20.7. MENTAL DISORDER[13]

There is not much English authority as to the liability of mentally disordered or insane persons for their torts. On principle, however, we may say with some confidence that insanity is not in itself any ground of exemption. The object of the law of torts is compensation and not punishment,[14] so there is nothing illogical in holding an insane person civilly responsible. If insanity is no defence to a charge of cruelty in matrimonial proceedings,[15] there is no reason why it should be a defence in tort. Still insanity may be relevant, for, like infancy, it operates (if at all) as evidence that the mental state requisite to create liability is not present. It is probable that the M'Naughten Rules[16] do not provide the test of insanity for the civil as distinct from the criminal law.[17] In any event, it is necessary to distinguish between different species of wrongs:

(1) In wrongs based on malice or on some specific intent, like malicious prosecution, malicious libel on a privileged occasion, or deceit, insanity may be a good defence as disproving the existence of any such malice or intent.

(2) In wrongs of voluntary interference with the person, property, reputation, or other rights of other persons, such as trespass, assault, conversion, or defamation, it is no defence that the defendant was under an insane delusion as to the existence of a sufficient legal justification. If he knew the nature and quality of his act it is no defence that he did not know that what he was doing was wrong, whatever the position may be in the criminal law.[18] An insane person, therefore, who converts another's property to his own use under the delusion that it is his own, or who publishes a defamatory statement under the belief that it is true, is just as liable as if he were sane.[19] If, however, the insanity of the defendant is of so extreme a type as to preclude any genuine intention to do the act complained of, there is no voluntary act at all, and therefore no liability.[20] Mischief done by an epileptic in one of his paroxysms, or by a fever patient in his delirium, or by a somnambulist in his sleep is presumably not actionable.[21]

---

[12] *McKay* v. *Essex Health Authority* [1982] Q.B. 1166.

[13] See Fridman, "Mental Incompetency" (1963) 79 L.Q.R. 502, (1964) 80 L.Q.R. 84.

[14] *White* v. *White* [1950] P. 39, 58. See above, § 2.2.

[15] *Williams* v. *Williams* [1964] A.C. 698.

[16] (1843) 10 Cl. & F. 200.

[17] *Williams* v. *Williams* [1964] A.C. 698.

[18] *Morriss* v. *Marsden* [1952] 1 All E.R. 925 (person of unsound mind liable for assault and battery), cited with apparent approval by Lord Pearce in *Williams* v. *Williams* [1964] A.C. 698, 751.

[19] *Vaughan* v. *Ford*, 1953 (4) S.A. 486 (anonymous letters sent by a person with emotional age of child of 8).

[20] *Tindale* v. *Tindale* [1950] 4 D.L.R. 363.

[21] *Morriss* v. *Marsden* [1952] 1 All E.R. 925, 927.

(3) In wrongs of strict liability there is no reason why insanity should be any defence, unless it is of so extreme a nature as to deprive the act in question of its voluntary quality.

(4) In wrongs dependent upon negligence the conduct of the defendant must be judged by reference to his knowledge or means of knowledge. Insanity, therefore, may be relevant as evidence that the necessary knowledge or means of knowledge did not exist. It has been held that automatism is no defence to an action for negligence in operating a motor-vehicle, unless it is so extreme as to render the defendant's acts completely involuntary.[22]

§ 20.8. MARRIED PERSONS

(1) Actions between spouses

Since August 1, 1962, each of the parties to a marriage has had the like right of action in tort against the other as if they were not married. This change was effected by section 1 of the Law Reform (Husband and Wife) Act 1962, in consequence of the recommendations of the Law Reform Committee.[23] The only restriction is that when an action in tort is brought by one party to the marriage against the other party during the subsistence of the marriage the court may stay the action if (a) it appears that no substantial benefit[24] would accrue to either party from a continuance of the proceedings, or (b) the question could be more conveniently disposed of under section 17 of the Married Women's Property Act 1882, which provides for settlement of disputes between husband and wife as to the ownership or possession of property. A judge of the High Court or of the county court is empowered, on application by summons, to make in such a case such an order as he thinks just. Elaborate changes in this area were made by the Matrimonial Causes Act 1973, ss.21–26.

(2) Liability of a wife to third persons

Since the Law Reform (Married Women and Tortfeasors) Act 1935, s.1, a married woman may be sued for her torts, and is subject to the law relating to bankruptcy and to the enforcement of judgments and orders in all respects as if she were a *femme sole*. Before that Act any damages

---

[22] *Roberts v. Ramsbottom* [1980] 1 All E.R. 7.

[23] Ninth Report (Cmnd. 1268 (1961)). Actions between spouses were once thought to be unseemly and undesirable, but the modern practice of insurance (compulsory in some cases) has had its effect on some traditional ideas: "The growth of liability insurance has to a great extent changed the effect of a law-suit between relatives, or even friends, from the traditional friction to the closest sort of amicable co-operation. Nothing draws two people together like a mutual desire to get something out of one's insurance carrier": Larson, "A Problem in Contribution" (1940) 3 Wis.L.Rev. 467, 499.

[24] On second reading in the House of Lords the Government spokesman said this phrase was intended to mean benefit of financial value to the parties, and not that it should include ethical or moral values: 241 H.L.Deb., 5s., col. 1104 (Viscount Colville of Culross).

recovered against her could be levied only out of her separate property not restrained from anticipation and she could not be made bankrupt unless she was carrying on a separate trade.

(3) Liability of a husband for his wife's torts

The Act of 1935 made a still bigger change in the position of the husband. At common law a husband was liable to be joined with his wife in all actions for torts committed by her during the subsistence of the marriage and the House of Lords decided[25] that this liability had not been taken away by the Married Women's Property Act 1882. But as the Act of 1882 had deprived the husband of all his interest *jure mariti* in his wife's separate property and earnings out of which he might have satisfied a claim for his wife's wrongdoing it became his hard fate to continue to bear the burden of his wife's wrongdoings when he had been relieved of the means which would have assisted him to bear it.[26] This injustice has now been remedied. Under the Act of 1935[27] the husband of a married woman is not, by reason only of his being her husband,[28] liable in respect of any tort committed by her whether before or after the marriage, or to be sued or made a party to any proceeding brought in respect of any such tort. Section 4(2)(c) also provides that nothing in the Act "prevents a husband and wife from rendering themselves, or being rendered, jointly liable in respect of any tort, contract, debt, or obligation, and of suing and being sued either in tort or in contract or otherwise, in like manner as if they were not married." It is now settled that a conspiracy between husband and wife is capable of giving rising to tortious liability.[29]

§ 20.9. PRISONERS AND BANKRUPTS

Criminals, even when undergoing imprisonment, have the same rights of action for torts as a man with a blameless life. Those who break the law remain the Queen's subjects—they are not her enemies. Of course, the imprisonment itself (if lawful) does not found an action for false imprisonment, and certain acts done by the prison authorities, which would otherwise constitute assault or battery will not be such against one in lawful detention.[30]

---

[25] *Edwards* v. *Porter* [1925] A.C. 1.

[26] In *Newton* v. *Hardy* (1933) 149 L.T. 165 the plaintiff recovered damages for the enticement of her husband by the wife of the defendant, who was himself entirely innocent.

[27] s.3.

[28] So he will be liable where he has authorised the tort on the general principle of liability for an agent: *Barber* v. *Pigden* [1937] 1 K.B. 664.

[29] *Midland Bank Trust Co. Ltd.* v. *Green (No. 3)* [1979] Ch. 496. The Court of Appeal ([1982] Ch. 529) approved the judgment of Oliver J., who later wrote (*The Green Saga*, p. 15): "The question . . . whilst great fun to decide, was really susceptible of only one answer in modern conditions, and merely clears an interesting historical anomaly out of the way. It rates no more than a footnote in text-books on the law of tort."

[30] *R.* v. *Deputy Governor of Parkhurst Prison* [1990] 3 W.L.R. 1210, 1269.

Bankrupts

(1) Liability

The Insolvency Act 1986, s.382[31] provides that liability in respect of a tort committed before the bankruptcy is a bankruptcy debt. And under the Law Reform (Miscellaneous Provisions) Act 1934[32] where the plaintiff has a right of action in tort against the estate of a deceased wrongdoer, and that estate is insolvent, he may prove in the administration of the estate for unliquidated damages.

(2) Power to sue

Where a right of action exists for a tort committed against the bankrupt a distinction is taken. A right of action in respect of a tort which results in injuries mainly to the person of the bankrupt does not pass to the trustee.[33] On the other hand, a right of action which results in injuries mainly to the estate of the bankrupt passes to the trustee. Where the tort results in injuries both to the estate and also to the person of the bankrupt, the right of action for the tort, in so far as it results in injuries to the estate,[34] will pass to the trustee: in so far as it results in injuries to the person of the bankrupt, it will remain in him. In such a case the trustee and bankrupt can either bring separate actions or join as plaintiffs in one action in which case the damages will be assessed under two separate heads.[35]

§ 20.10. EXECUTORS AND ADMINISTRATORS

The question whether a cause of action survives the death of the person injured must be carefully distinguished from the question whether the act of causing the death of a person gives any right of action for damages to his relatives. The former question is that which is considered in this section: the latter will be dealt with later in connection with the provisions of the Fatal Accidents Act.[36]

Until 1934, subject to important exceptions, no executor or administrator could sue or be sued for any tort committed against or by the deceased in his lifetime. This was the purport of the maxim of the common law *actio personalis moritur cum persona*—a personal action dies with the parties to the cause of action. An action for a tort had to be begun and concluded in the joint lifetime of the wrongdoer and the person injured.[37] But sweeping changes were made by the Law Reform

---

[31] The Act consolidates the law on the topic.

[32] s.1(6).

[33] *Beckham* v. *Drake* (1849) 2 H.L.C. 579. In such a case the bankrupt may spend the damages, if he recovers any, in the maintenance of himself and his family: *Ex p. Vine* (1878) 8 Ch.D. 364.

[34] *Wenlock* v. *Moloney* [1965] 1 W.L.R. 1236.

[35] *Wilson* v. *United Counties Bank* [1920] A.C. 102.

[36] Below, § 24.9.

[37] *Ronex Properties Ltd.* v. *John Laing Construction Ltd.* [1983] Q.B. 598.

(Miscellaneous Provisions) Act 1934.[38] Before that Act it was often said to be cheaper to kill than to maim or cripple.[39] This defect in the law became particularly noticeable with the growth of motor traffic. A person injured in a collision due to the negligence of another might (even after the Road Traffic Act 1930 had made it compulsory to insure against third-party risks) find himself left without remedy because the negligent party had himself been killed in the accident. The Law Reform Act in section 1(1) lays down the general rule that in future on the death[40] of any person all causes of action subsisting against or vested in him shall survive against, or, as the case may be, for the benefit of, his estate. A claim for contribution made under the Law Reform (Married Women and Tortfeasors) Act 1935 survives under that Act.[41] But there is no survival of causes of action for defamation.[42] The Act does not, however, abolish the common law rule that it is no tort to cause the death of another. It does not make the infliction of death into a new tort: death is only the event which is required to enable an existing cause of action to descend to the personal representatives.[43]

§ 20.11. Joint and Several Tortfeasors[44]

(1) Who are joint tortfeasors

Where the same damage is caused to a person by two or more wrongdoers those wrongdoers may be either joint or independent tortfeasors. Persons are to be deemed joint tortfeasors within the meaning of this rule whenever they are responsible for the same tort—that is to say, whenever the law for any reason imputes the commission of the same wrongful act to two or more persons at once. This happens in at least three classes of cases—namely, agency,[45] vicarious liability,[46] and common action, i.e. where a tort is committed in the course of a common action, a joint act done in pursuance of a concerted purpose.[47] In order

---

[38] See the interesting account of the genesis of the Act by the First Parliamentary Counsel (Sir Noël Hutton) in "Mechanics of Law Reform" (1961) 24 M.L.R. 18.

[39] But see *H. West & Son Ltd.* v. *Shephard* [1964] A.C. 307, 342.

[40] This includes suicide: *Pigney* v. *Pointers Transport Services* [1957] 1 W.L.R. 1121.

[41] *Ronex Properties Ltd.* v. *John Laing Construction Ltd.* [1983] Q.B. 598.

[42] s.1(1). It is not clear why this should be so. Defamation may cause much more harm to the next of kin than an assault, and it is hard to see why the death of the defamer should deprive the plaintiff of his damages, or the terminally ill be given a general licence to defame. The reason given by the Law Revision Committee 1934 (Cmd. 4540, p. 7) that "the presence of the plaintiff or of the defendant may be of the greatest importance" is unconvincing, as the Faulks Committee thought (Cmnd. 5909, § 417.

[43] This was an essential step in the reasoning in *Rose* v. *Ford* [1937] A.C. 826, which has now been reversed by the Administration of Justice Act 1982, s.1.

[44] The leading work is Williams, *Joint Torts and Contributory Negligence*. Many of the ideas expressed in this book were given legislative form in ss.11–33 of the Irish Civil Liability Act 1961, which is still in several respects superior to the English legislation on the same problems.

[45] See below, § 20.14.

[46] See below, § 21.2. A master is always treated as a joint tortfeasor with the servant for whom he is vicariously liable (*Jones* v. *Manchester Corporation* [1952] 2 Q.B. 852, 870), although it is difficult to see why this should be so: *Semtex Ltd.* v. *Gladstone* [1954] 1 W.L.R. 945, 949; *Treacy* v. *Robinson & Son* [1937] I.R. 255, 266.

[47] *Brooke* v. *Bool* [1928] 2 K.B. 578, 585.

to be joint tortfeasors there must be a concurrence in the act or acts causing damage, not merely a coincidence of separate acts which by their conjoined effect cause damage.[48] The *injuria* as well as the *damnum* must be the same.[49] So that if the presence of a particular mental intent is necessary to constitute liability each tortfeasor must be proved to have that intent.[50] This may give rise to special problems when qualified privilege is pleaded as a defence in libel.[51] But there are many cases in which the same damage is caused by independent and separate wrongful acts of several persons, as where a plaintiff sustains a single damage from the combined negligence of two motor-car drivers, who are not engaged in a common design (*e.g.* racing on the road).[52] A handler of stolen goods is not necessarily, therefore, a joint tortfeasor with the thief.[53]

(2) Nature of liability

"If a number of persons jointly participate in the commission of a tort, each is responsible, jointly with each and all of the others, and also severally, for the whole amount of the damage caused by the tort, irrespective of the extent of his participation."[54] This is to say, the person injured may sue any one of them separately for the full amount of the loss; or he may sue all of them jointly in the same action, and even in this latter case the judgment so obtained against all of them may be executed in full against any one of them.[55] So when the court assesses the damages to be awarded against joint tortfeasors sued in the same action only one sum is to be awarded.[56] But if the tortfeasors were independent or separate "the person damnified might sue them one by one and recover from one alone or from such as he chose to execute judgment against, provided that he did not recover more than the greatest sum awarded or, against any defendant, more than was awarded in the action against him."[57] In the next section we shall consider how far there is any right of contribution or indemnity between the tortfeasors.

(3) Effect of judgment

At common law a judgment obtained against one joint wrongdoer released all the others, even though it was not satisfied, and even though the defendant did not then know of the existence of the other

---

[48] *The Koursk* [1924] P. 140, 159.
[49] *The Koursk* [1924] P. 140, 156.
[50] *Gardiner* v. *Moore* [1969] 1 Q.B. 55, 91.
[51] See above, § 8.18.
[52] *Drinkwater* v. *Kimber* [1952] 2 Q.B. 281, 292.
[53] *Toome Eel Fishery (N.I.) Ltd.* v. *Cardwell* [1966] N.I. 1, 29.
[54] *Dougherty* v. *Chandler* (1946) 46 S.R.(N.S.W.) 370, 375, *per* Jordan C.J.
[55] In practice this explains why in construction cases there are often several defendants (builders, architects, and local authority): see *Peabody Donation Fund* v. *Sir Lindsay Parkinson & Co. Ltd.* [1985] A.C. 210, 230.
[56] *Wah Tat Bank Ltd.* v. *Chan* [1975] A.C. 507.
[57] *Wimpey (George) & Co. Ltd.* v. *British Overseas Airways Corporation* [1955] A.C. 169, 181, *per* Lord Porter.

tortfeasors. The tort was merged in the judgment.[58] This rule was completely abolished[59] by the Law Reform (Married Women and Tortfeasors) Act 1935, s.6(1)(a). This has now been repealed and replaced by the Civil Liability (Contribution) Act 1978, s.3. This provides that judgment recovered[60] against any person liable in respect of any debt or damage shall not be a bar to an action, or to the continuance of an action against any other person jointly liable with him in respect of the same debt or damage. The result is that an unsatisfied judgment against one tortfeasor is no longer a bar to recovery against another tortfeasor, whether that unsatisfied judgment arose out of a single action against the tortfeasors resulting in separate judgments,[61] or out of successive separate actions against the tortfeasors.[62]

But section 4 provides that if successive actions are brought, the plaintiff may not recover costs in any but the first action unless the court decides there was reasonable ground for bringing the subsequent action. The Act of 1935, but not that of 1978, also provided[63] that if more than one action was brought in respect of the same damage by or on behalf of the person by whom it was suffered, against tortfeasors liable in respect of the damage (whether as joint tortfeasors or otherwise) the sums recoverable under the judgments given in those actions by way of damages should not in the aggregate exceed the amount of the damages awarded by the judgment first given. The effect of the disappearance of this rule is that a plaintiff in a second action can now recover more than he recovered in the first action—e.g. if he has under-estimated his damage at the time of the first action. The sanction against abuse of this process is the power given by section 4 to deprive such a plaintiff of his costs.[64]

(4) Release

The release of one joint wrongdoer releases all the others, even though this was not the intention of the parties, the reason being that the cause of action, which is one and indivisible, having been released, all persons otherwise liable thereto are consequently released.[65] This rule is equally applicable to a release under seal and to a release by way of accord and satisfaction.[66]

A mere covenant or other agreement not to sue one of the joint wrongdoers must, however, be distinguished from an actual release given to him, whether by deed or by accord and satisfaction.[67] An

---

[58] *Brinsmead* v. *Harrison* (1871) L.R. 7 C.P. 547. This rule never applied to independent tortfeasors.

[59] *Wah Tat Bank Ltd.* v. *Chan* [1975] A.C. 507, 518.

[60] So that if there is a release of one tortfeasor there is apparently no right of action against the other or others. *Aliter* in cases of contribution between tortfeasors: below § 20.12.

[61] As in *Bryanston Finance Ltd.* v. *de Vries* [1975] 1 Q.B. 703.

[62] As in *Wah Tat Bank Ltd.* v. *Chan* [1975] A.C. 507.

[63] s.6(1)(b).

[64] See Lord Scarman (extra-judicially) in (1978) 395 H.L.Deb. col. 252.

[65] *Duck* v. *Mayeu* [1892] 2 Q.B. 511, 513.

[66] *Thurman* v. *Wild* (1840) 11 A. & E. 453.

[67] "An arid and technical distinction without any merits," *per* Lord Denning M.R. in *Bryanston Finance Ltd.* v. *de Vries* [1975] Q.B. 703, 723.

agreement not to sue does not, like a release, destroy the cause of action, but merely prevents it from being enforced against the particular wrongdoer with whom the agreement was made.[68] A transaction which is in form an actual release, whether by deed or by accord and satisfaction, will be construed as being merely an agreement not to sue, if it contains an express or implied[69] reservation of the right to proceed against the other wrongdoers. For this reservation would otherwise be wholly ineffective.

§ 20.12. CONTRIBUTION[70]

"How some rules of law arose is not always known. For instance, except for the fact that in 1799 Lord Kenyon C.J. laid it down categorically in *Merryweather* v. *Nixan*[71] that there was no contribution between joint tortfeasors, no one has ever discovered whence the rule came, but it remained the law till abrogated by the Law Reform (Married Women and Tortfeasors) Act 1935."[72] That Act provided that where damage is suffered by any person as a result of a tort (whether a crime or not), any tortfeasor liable in respect of that damage may recover contribution from any other tortfeasor who is, or would if sued have been, liable in respect of the same damage, whether as a joint tortfeasor or otherwise. The 1935 Act did not cover a wrongdoer who was not a tortfeasor—*e.g.* one guilty of a breach of contract or trust—but this has now been done by the Civil Liability (Contribution) Act 1978, s.6(1). So the legislation now provides for two cases—the normal one in which the plaintiff sues the two (or more) persons responsible for his damage in the same action,[73] and the exceptional one in which he decides to proceed against only one of them. If the latter course is followed, the defendant is entitled to claim against any other person not made a party to the action (the third party), and the third party then becomes a party to the action with the same rights in respect of his defence against any claim made against him, and otherwise, as if he had been sued by the defendant.[74]

Under the pre-1978 law there were two problems which caused great difficulties. The first was whether a tortfeasor who had settled the claim made against him, with or without an admission of liability, was

---

[68] *Duck* v. *Mayeu* [1892] 2 Q.B. 511.

[69] *Gardiner* v. *Moore* [1969] 1 Q.B. 55.

[70] See Williams, *Joint Torts and Contributory Negligence* (1951), Chap. 6; Law Commission Report on Contribution, Law Com. No. 79, 1977.

[71] (1799) 8 T.R. 186.

[72] *Carmarthenshire C.C.* v. *Lewis* [1955] A.C. 549, 560, *per* Lord Goddard C.J., "whose knowledge of the history of the common law was profound": *per* Lord Diplock in *Bremer Vulkan Schiffbau* v. *South Indian Shipping Ltd.* [1981] A.C. 909, 978.

[73] Hence contribution may be ordered between several concurrent tortfeasors—*e.g.* two motorists, not engaged in a common design, whose combined negligence injures the plaintiff: *Pride of Derby and Derbyshire Angling Association Ltd.* v. *British Celanese Ltd.* [1952] 1 All E.R. 1326.

[74] See Ord. 16 for the machinery of contribution.

entitled to claim contribution.[75] The second was whether contribution could be recovered from a defendant who had been sued to judgment and held not liable (either on the merits, or because of some procedural defence peculiar to him), even if he would have been held liable if he had been sued at some other time or in some other way.[76] Since 1978 a person claiming contribution must be liable in an action, actual or hypothetical, brought in England or Wales (s.1(6)). But it is also clear from section 1(4) that a wrongdoer who enters into bona fide settlement or compromise with the plaintiff may claim a contribution "without regard to whether or not he himself is or ever was liable in respect of the damage, provided, however, that he would have been liable assuming that the factual basis of the claim against him could be established." It is immaterial that the person claiming contribution has ceased to be liable (*e.g.* by payment or by virtue of a compromise) since the time when the damage occurred (s.1(2)). Furthermore, by section 1(3), a person is liable to make contribution "notwithstanding that he has ceased to be liable[77] in respect of the damage in question since the time when the damage occurred,[78] unless he ceased to be liable by virtue of the expiry of a period of limitation or prescription which extinguished the right on which the claim against him in respect of the damage was based."[79] Thus, where the plaintiff effects a bona fide compromise (not amounting to a release) with one of two or more wrongdoers and then brings an action against the other(s), the first is liable to make contribution to that other (and can himself claim contribution in respect of any payment made under the compromise) unless such liability has ceased through effluxion of time.

An important qualification to section 1(3) is effected by section 1(5), which provides that a judgment given[80] in any action brought by the person who suffered the damage in question against any person from whom contribution is sought shall be conclusive in the proceedings for contribution as to any issue[81] determined by that judgment in favour of the person from whom contribution is sought.

Contracts of indemnity. Nothing in the 1978 Act affects any express or implied contractual or other right to indemnity which would be

---

[75] As the great majority of tort claims are settled (see above, § 2.1.), this was of great practical importance. But it has been held that the 1978 Act does not cover a case where the plaintiff's *costs* are paid, without any admission of liability as to *damages*: *Eastwood* v. *Ryder* [1990] C.L. 3117.

[76] In *Wimpey (George) & Co. Ltd.* v. *B.O.A.C.* [1955] A.C. 169 it was held that he could not.

[77] For whatever reason: *Nottingham Health Authority* v. *Nottingham City Council* [1988] 1 W.L.R. 903.

[78] This reverses the decision in *George Wimpey & Co. Ltd.* v. *B.O.A.C.* [1955] A.C. 169.

[79] But conversion is the only tort in which the plaintiff's rights, as distinct from his remedy, is barred by the Limitation Act: see above, § 6.10.

[80] In any part of the United Kingdom.

[81] Probably this means "any issue as to the merits": if it means "any issue, including one of limitation" then *Wimpey* is still law.

enforceable apart from the Act, or, conversely, renders enforceable any agreement for indemnity which would not be enforceable at common law.[82]

At common law an insured person cannot himself recover from his insurers if the contract purports to indemnify him against the consequences of his own intentional criminal act.[83] It is also settled that a contract to indemnify another against the consequences of committing a tort is unlawful, unless either the act to be done is not obviously tortious, or the party to be indemnified has been induced to commit it by the fraudulent statement of the other.[84] The policy of protecting the victims of traffic accidents has also led to decisions whereby a contract of insurance is valid in respect of claims made by innocent third parties even though the circumstances of the accident gave rise to criminal liability (*e.g.* manslaughter) on the part of the insured motorist.[85] The Act of 1978, by section 2(2), specifically gives the court power to order a complete indemnity. The result is "that if A considers he has against B a right of indemnity or contribution under a contract enforceable under the law as it was before the passing of the Bill, he can sue on that contract and in doing so will neither require nor receive any help from the Bill: if he considers that apart from the contract he has a right of contribution against B under the Bill, he can add an alternative claim for cash contribution. In the event of his contract being held valid he will get what the contract provides for; in the event of its being held invalid, he will get under the Bill such amount, if any, as the court thinks he ought to have."[86]

Libel. Contracts of indemnity are common in the world of publishing.[87] The Law Reform Committee upon whose recommendations[88] the Act of 1935 was based gave as one instance of the hardship of the common law case of *W.H. Smith & Son* v. *Clinton*.[89] In that case the plaintiff agreed to publish a newspaper for the defendants, one of the terms being that the defendants should give the plaintiffs a letter of indemnity against claims arising out of the publication of libellous matter in the newspaper. A libel was published, and the plaintiffs were unsuccessful in their action on the letter of indemnity to recover the damages which they had paid to the person libelled, for they well knew that matter published was libellous. They might still be unable to recover on

---

[82] See s.7(3) of the 1978 Act, which in substance reproduces part of s.6 of the 1935 Act.
[83] *Gardner* v. *Moore* [1984] A.C. 548.
[84] *W.H. Smith & Sons* v. *Clinton* (1908) 99 L.T. 840, 841.
[85] *Gardner* v. *Moore* [1984] A.C. 548.
[86] An extract from an unpublished memorandum on the 1935 Bill by its draftsman, Sir Granville Ram, K.C.B., K.C.
[87] But there is no customary implied term that a book is not libellous: *Eastwood* v. *Ryder* [1990] C.L. 3117.
[88] Cmd. 4637.
[89] (1908) 99 L.T. 840.

the letter of indemnity,[90] but they might take proceedings for such contribution as might be found to be just and equitable.

Implied indemnities—(1) A wrongdoer cannot recover contribution from an innocent person whom he has led into the commission of a tort. For a principal must indemnify his agent for all liability incurred by him in consequence of the act authorised being (without the knowledge of the agent) an illegal one. This principle is of the widest general application.[91] Thus an auctioneer is entitled to be indemnified by a client who has instructed him to sell goods to which, as it subsequently appeared, he had not title.[92] There are also many statutes which empower local authorities to indemnify their employees.[93]

(2) It is the converse of the former principle that a wrongdoing servant is obliged to indemnify his master who has been held vicariously responsible for the tort.[94] Hence a servant who has been sued in respect of some tort committed in the course of his employment cannot claim an indemnity from his innocent master.

Assessment of contribution

The framers of the Act of 1935 borrowed the principles of the Maritime Conventions Act 1911,[95] in determining the measure of contribution, and provided[96] that in proceedings against any person for contribution the amount of the contribution recoverable should be such as may be found by the court to be just and equitable having regard to the extent of that person's responsibility for the damage. The assessment must be made[97] having regard to the parties who are before the court: the negligence or contributory negligence of a party not before the court cannot be considered.[98] There has been some controversy whether the Act contemplates that damages should be apportioned on the basis of causation or on the basis of the respective degrees of fault or culpability of the parties,[99] or by combining the concepts of causation and blameworthiness.[1] This third approach is in accord with the prac-

---

[90] The Defamation Act 1952, s.11, provides only that agreements for indemnity in respect of liability for libel shall not be unlawful unless at the time of publication the person claiming to be indemnified knows that the matter is defamatory and does not reasonably believe there is a good defence to an action brought upon it.

[91] *Secretary of State v. Bank of India Ltd.* [1938] 2 All E.R. 797, 801.

[92] *Adamson v. Jarvis* (1827) 4 Bing. 66.

[93] e.g. the Town and Country Planning Act 1971, s.4(6).

[94] *Lister v. Romford Ice and Cold Storage Co. Ltd.* [1957] A.C. 555. See below, § 21.10.

[95] See below, § 22.10.

[96] s.6(2).

[97] The trial judge should deal with the question of contribution at the end of the trial: *Calvert v. Pick* [1954] 1 W.L.R. 456. Only in very exceptional cases should an appeal court interfere with the judge's apportionment: *The MacGregor* [1943] A.C. 197.

[98] *Maxfield v. Llewellyn* [1961] 1 W.L.R. 1119.

[99] This view was adopted in *Weaver v. Commercial Process Co.* (1947) 63 T.L.R. 466 and is approved by Williams, *Joint Torts*, pp. 157–158; Chapman (1948) 64 L.Q.R. 26 ("Causation itself is difficult enough; degrees of causation would really be a nightmare").

[1] *Madden v. Quirk* [1989] 1 W.L.R. 702, 707.

tice under the contributory negligence legislation,[2] though it may give rise to difficulties in cases involving breaches of totally different kinds of duties.[3]

Limitation. As the right of contribution is not a cause of action in tort but is a right *sui generis* the limitation period available in contribution proceedings was once held to be six years. But now in England the Limitation Act 1980, s.10, provides that where a tortfeasor becomes entitled to a right to recover contribution in respect of any damage from another tortfeasor, no action to recover contribution shall be brought after the end of two years from the date on which the right accrued to the first tortfeasor. This may still be hard on a defendant called upon to defend contribution proceedings brought many years after the accident. There is a saving (s.10(3)) for cases of fraud, disability and mistake. Section 10(2) provides that the date on which the right to recover contribution accrued shall be ascertained as follows:

(*a*) if the tortfeasor is held liable in respect of that damage by a judgment given in any civil proceedings, or an award made on any arbitration, the relevant date shall be the date on which the judgment is given, or the date of the award, as the case may be;

(*b*) if, in any case not falling within the preceding paragraph, the tortfeasor admits liability in favour of one or more persons in respect of that damage, the relevant date shall be the earliest date on which the amount to be paid by him in discharge of that liability is agreed by or on behalf of the tortfeasor and that person, or each of those persons, as the case may be;

and for the purposes of this subsection no account shall be taken of any judgment or award given or made on appeal in so far as it varies the amount of damages awarded against the tortfeasor.

§ 20.13. PERSONS JOINTLY INJURED

Where two or more persons possess a right of action in respect of one and the same injury—as, for example, a trespass or other wrong to the property of co-owners, or a libel on a firm of partners in the way of their business—is it necessary that those persons should all join in one and the same action, or can one of them sue without the others? Now the non-joinder of persons jointly injured is no bar to an action by one or some of them. The only effect of such a non-joinder is that the court may, in its discretion, order the other persons so jointly injured to be joined as parties to the action, either as plaintiffs or (if they will not consent) as defendants. Where two or more persons have suffered a joint, but not a several, injury, a release granted by one of them will, in the absence of fraud, destroy the whole cause of action, and operate as a bar to an action by any of the others.

---

[2] See below, § 22.11.
[3] See 129 N.L.J. 509.

§ 20.14. PRINCIPAL AND AGENT

Usually an agent, as distinct from a servant, is engaged to perform a particular task, and has authority to do whatever is required for that purpose but has no general authority. But whether he is a servant or an agent the test of vicarious liability is the same: was he acting on behalf of, or within the scope of the authority conferred by, the master or principal?[4] Any person who authorises or procures a tort to be committed by another is responsible for that tort as if he had committed it himself: *Qui facit per alium facit per se.* Principal and agent, therefore, are jointly and severally liable as joint wrongdoers for any tort authorised by the former and committed by the latter. This is one way in which the employer of an independent contractor can be held liable[5] for a tort committed by the contractor. It must be clearly shown that the principal gave to the agent express or implied authority to commit the acts complained of. So the Transport and General Workers' Union was held responsible for certain activities of certain shop stewards in the docks at Liverpool and Hull.[6] Those shop stewards were not the servants of the union but still had authority to take the industrial action complained of, which was in accordance with union policy.

Ratification

If one person commits a tort while acting on behalf of another, but without his authority, and that other subsequently ratifies and assents to the act so done, he thereby becomes responsible for it, just as if he had given a precedent authority for its commission.[7] When an illegal act done by one person on behalf of another but without his authority would have been legal had it been done with his authority, it becomes legal *ab initio* if he subsequently ratifies it.[8] An act may be thus justified by ratification, even after the commencement of an action against the agent; but the ratification must in all cases have taken place at a time when the principal still retained the power of lawfully authorising the act to be done.[9] The following conditions must be fulfilled:

(1) The wrongful act must have been done on behalf of the principal. No man can ratify an act which was done, not on his behalf, but on behalf of the doer himself.[10] In the case of contracts it has been decided[11] that there can be no ratification unless the agent not merely contracts on behalf of the principal, but also avows that intention at the time. Possibly the same rule applies to torts also.[12] But the necessary

---

[4] *Heatons Transport (St. Helens) Ltd.* v. *Transport and General Workers' Union* [1973] A.C. 15, 99.

[5] *Jolliffe* v. *Willmet & Co.* (1970) 114 S.J. 619.

[6] *Heatons Transport (St. Helens) Ltd.* v. *Transport and General Workers' Union* [1973] A.C. 15.

[7] *Wilson* v. *Tumman* (1843) 6 M. & G. 236, 242.

[8] *Buron* v. *Denman* (1848) 2 Ex. 167.

[9] *Bird* v. *Brown* (1850) 4 Ex. 786.

[10] *Eastern Construction Co.* v. *National Trust Co.* [1914] A.C. 197, 213.

[11] *Keighley, Maxsted & Co.* v. *Durant* [1901] A.C. 240.

[12] *Keighley, Maxsted* v. *Durant* [1901] A.C. 240, 260.

avowal need not be expressed in words, but may sufficiently appear from the conduct of the parties and the facts of the case. It cannot be necessary for a railway official who arrests a passenger for defrauding the railway company to state in terms that he does so on behalf of the company.

(2) The principal must know the nature of the act which has thus been done on his behalf, unless, indeed, he is content to dispense with any such knowledge and to approve and sanction the acts of the agent whatever they may be.[13] It is sufficient, however, if the principal has such knowledge of the nature of the act as would have sufficed to make him liable had he actually authorised it or done it himself. Mistake or ignorance is no greater defence to a principal who gives an authority subsequent than to one who gives an authority precedent.[14]

§ 20.15. PARTNERS

By the Partnership Act 1890, ss.10 and 12, it is provided that partners are jointly and severally liable for each other's torts committed in the ordinary course of the business of the firm. Thus in *Hamlyn* v. *Houston & Co.*[15] a firm was held liable for the act of one of the partners who, on behalf of the firm, induced by bribery a servant of the plaintiff to commit a breach of his contract of service. Whether the act of a partner is one done in the course of the business of the firm is a question to be determined on the same considerations as those which determine the responsibility of a master for the acts of his servant. As liability is joint and several, it follows that there can be no judgment against the partnership or any one of the partners if the actual tortfeasor has some substantive defence peculiar to himself,[16] although the courts do not favour such a plea.[17]

---

[13] *Freeman* v. *Rosher* (1849) 13 Q.B. 780.
[14] *Hilbery* v. *Hatton* (1864) 2 H. & C. 822.
[15] [1903] 1 K.B. 81.
[16] *Kliendienst* v. *Kliendienst & Sons* (1959) S.R.(N.S.W.) 150. See further below, § 21.2.
[17] *Meekins* v. *Henson* [1964] 1 Q.B. 472.

CHAPTER 21

VICARIOUS LIABILITY

This term does not indicate a distinct tort, but rather a process by which one person can be held liable for a recognised tort committed by another.

§ 21.1. MASTER AND SERVANT[1]

A master is jointly and severally liable for any tort committed by his servant while acting in the course of his employment. This is by far the most important of the various cases in which vicarious responsibility or vicarious liability[2] is recognised by the law. Vicarious liability[3] means that one person takes or supplies the place of another so far as liability is concerned.[4] Although the doctrine has its roots in the earliest years of the common law, it was Sir John Holt (1642–1710) who began the task of adapting medieval rules to the needs of a modern society, and his work was continued by the great Victorian judges. By the beginning of the twentieth century it was firmly established that the master's liability was based, not on the fiction that he had impliedly commanded his servant to do what he did, but on the safer and simpler ground that it was done in the scope or course of his employment or authority. Today it has been developed so far "that it would be a good deal safer to keep lions or other wild animals in a park than to engage in a business involving the employment of labour."[5]

Some different theories

It will never be possible, or perhaps even desirable, to expound a theory which will at once explain and justify all aspect of the doctrine,[6] although it has long been accepted as necessary and beneficial.[7] The combined effect of all the reasons may be overwhelming, though one or more in isolation may be unconvincing. The maxim *respondeat superior* does not explain why the superior should answer; it does not enshrine a principle, but announces rather a result[8]—namely, that the employer

---

[1] Atiyah, *Vicarious Liability* is the leading monograph. See also Glanville Williams, "Vicarious Liability" (1956) 72 L.Q.R. 522; "Liability for Indpendent Contractors" [1956] C.L.J. 180. The terms master and servant have an old-fashioned sound today, and so are gradually being replaced by employer and employee, but it would be needless pedantry to rewrite the language used in the older reports.

[2] The ordinary speech of lawyers draws no distinction between these two phrases—perhaps mistakenly: see Hart, "Varieties of Responsibility" (1967) 83 L.Q.R. 346.

[3] A term which Pollock claimed he had invented: *Pollock-Holmes Letters*, vol. i, p. 233.

[4] *Launchbury* v. *Morgans* [1971] 2 Q.B. 245, 253.

[5] *Kay* v. *I.T.W. Ltd.* [1968] 1 Q.B. 140, 155 *per* Danckwerts L.J.

[6] Atiyah, *Vicarious Liability*, Chap. 2, considers nine theories.

[7] Few dissenting voices have been raised, though Lord Bramwell (always a sturdy individualist) opposed it in 1877: C. 285, p. 46.

[8] *Kilboy* v. *South-Eastern Fire Area Joint Committee*, 1952 S.C. 280, 287.

ought to pay.[9] The maxim *qui facit per alium facit per se*, although often cited with approbation,[10] is similarly unhelpful.[11] The truth is that "a mixture of ideas has inspired many unconvincing judicial efforts to find a common basis for the maxim. What was once presented as a legal principle has degenerated into a rule of expediency, imperfectly defined, and changing its shape before our eyes under the impact of changing social and political conditions."[12] But there is one idea which is to be found in the judgments from the time of Sir John Holt[13] to the present day,[14] namely, public policy. As Lord Brougham[15] said: "The reason that I am liable is this, that by employing him I set the whole thing in motion; and what he does, being done for my benefit and under my direction, I am responsible for the consequences of doing it." In short, vicarious liability is based on "social convenience and rough justice."[16] This is an adequate explanation of the doctrine, subject to the qualification that the master may be liable even though the act or default is not for his benefit, and even though he has expressly prohibited it.[17] In all this there is no doubt that the courts have been much influenced by the fact that the master is usually more able than the servant to satisfy claims by injured persons and can pass on the burden of liability by way of insurance.[18] There is also some evidence to show that the imposition of strict liability on the master results in the prevention of accidents: the master takes more care than he would otherwise have done.[19]

§ 21.2. The Nature of Vicarious Liability

There has been some discussion about the nature of the doctrine of vicarious liability, as well as of the reason for it.[20] The orthodox view assumes that the master is vicariously liable for the servant only when the servant himself would be liable. "In every case . . . the first question is to see whether the servant was liable. If the answer is yes, the second question is to see whether the employer must shoulder the servant's liability."[21] This is the view which was adopted in the Crown Proceed-

---

[9] *Morgans* v. *Launchbury* [1973] A.C. 127, 135.

[10] As by two Law Lords in *Morgans* v. *Launchbury* [1973] A.C. 127, 140.

[11] *Moynihan* v. *Moynihan* [1975] I.R. 192, 200.

[12] *Kilboy* v. *South-Eastern Fire Area Joint Committee*, 1952 S.C. 280, 285, *per* Lord Cooper.

[13] See *Hern* v. *Nichols* (1700) 1 Salk. 289, in which he said, "seeing somebody must be a loser by this deceit, it is more reason that he, that employs and puts a trust and confidence in the deceiver, should be a loser than a stranger." In *Armagas Ltd.* v. *Mundogas S.A.* [1986] A.C. 717, 735, 768, 780 some doubts were expressed.

[14] *Nettleship* v. *Weston* [1971] 2 Q.B. 691, 700; *Rose* v. *Plenty* [1976] 1 W.L.R. 141, 147–148.

[15] *Duncan* v. *Finlater* (1839) 6 Cl. & F. 894, at 910.

[16] *I.C.I. Ltd.* v. *Shatwell* [1965] A.C. 656, 686, *per* Lord Pearce.

[17] See below, § 21.6.

[18] *Launchbury* v. *Morgans* [1971] 2 Q.B. 245, 254.

[19] See above, § 10.3.

[20] See literature cited above, § 21.1.

[21] *Young* v. *Edward Box & Co.* [1951] 1 T.L.R. 789, 793, *per* Denning L.J. In later cases Denning L.J. departed from this simple view (below, note 29), but later readopted it: *Rose* v. *Plenty* [1976] 1 W.L.R. 141, 143.

ings Act 1947, s.2(1),[22] and which has been approved judicially.[23] So in the normal case there has been only one tort, but as it has been committed in the course of employment the master is jointly responsible for it.[24] But four exceptional cases have caused difficulties, and given rise to an unorthodox theory.

(1) There is some authority for the proposition that the employer may be liable even if the conduct of no single employee is tortious if the conduct of a number of the employees can be regarded as a composite tort.[25] But it is difficult to see how innocence can be added to innocence to produce guilt.[26]

(2) Sometimes the servant has not committed a tort (or at any rate an actionable tort) but the master is still responsible. Thus in *Broom v. Morgan*[27] the defendant, the licensee of the "Bird in Hand" public house, West End Lane, Hampstead, employed both the plaintiff and her husband. The plaintiff was injured as a result of her husband's negligent act committed in the course of his employment, and the Court of Appeal held that she was entitled to hold the defendant vicariously responsible for it, even though she could not have sued her husband as the law then stood.[28] It has been said that such a decision (and indeed all decisions on vicarious liability) can be explained on the ground that it is the acts or omissions and not the torts of the servant which the law attributes to the employer: the true question is said to be whether the employer himself has broken his own personal duty to the plaintiff.[29] But *Broom v. Morgan* itself is explicable on the simple ground preferred by the majority of the Court of Appeal— an immunity from suit conferred upon A cannot be taken advantage of by B.[30] It would be different if the servant was under no duty at all, as distinct from enjoying an immunity from suit in respect of an admitted duty: in such a case the master is entitled to share the servant's exemption.[31] In so far as the new theory purports to supply a general basis for the doctrine of vicarious liability it is open to the following objections. First, it would revive the notion (forgotten since the mid-nineteenth century)

---

[22] See above, § 20.1.

[23] *Staveley Iron and Chemical Co. Ltd. v. Jones* [1956] A.C. 627; *I.C.I. Ltd. v. Shatwell* [1965] A.C. 653; *Byrne v. Ireland* [1972] I.R. 241, 280.

[24] Above, § 20.14.

[25] *W. B. Anderson & Sons Ltd. v. Rhodes (Liverpool) Ltd.* [1967] 2 All E.R. 850.

[26] See above, § 18.6.

[27] [1953] 1 Q.B. 597.

[28] See above, § 18.6.

[29] See Uthwatt J. in *Twine v. Bean's Express Ltd.* [1946] 1 All E.R. 202, and Denning L.J. in *Broom v. Morgan* [1953] 1 Q.B. 597 and *Jones v. Staveley Iron Co. Ltd.* [1955] 1 Q.B. 474: his views were not approved by the H.L. in [1956] A.C. 627, or by Fullagar J. (*contra*, Taylor and Kitto JJ.) in *Darling Island Stevedoring Co. v. Long* (1957) 97 C.L.R. 36, or Windeyer J. in *Parker v. Commonwealth* (1965) 112 C.L.R. 295.

[30] There are authorities analogous to *Broom v. Morgan*. Thus, an employer is vicariously liable for an assault by his servant although the servant had procured a certificate of dismissal under the Offences Against the Person Act 1861, s.45. See *Dyer v. Munday* [1895] 1 Q.B. 742.

[31] *I.C.I. Ltd. v. Shatwell* [1965] A.C. 656, 686.

that the master is liable because he commanded (expressly or impliedly) his servant to do the act: the modern view is based on the fact that the act was done in the course of the employment. Secondly, it would mean that master and servant would never be joint tortfeasors: each would have committed a distinct tort. Thirdly, it would mean that the master would be free from liability in many cases in which he is now held responsible. For his duty could not (save in some rather exceptional cases) be a strict one: it could only be a duty to take reasonable care. Hence it would be a defence for him to show that he had taken reasonable care to select an apparently competent servant—a defence which has never been allowed within modern times.[32] There seems to be no reason to depart from the traditional theory.

(3) There is authority for saying that if the tort in question is solely the breach of a duty imposed directly upon the servant himself either by common law[33] or statute[34] the master is not vicariously liable for it: he will be liable, it is said, only if he has committed (as he may have) a breach of some duty laid upon him personally, or has intervened in the matter with express orders to the servant. These dicta seem to have introduced an unnecessary subtlety and refinement into the law. They seem to be based upon the obsolete and misleading notion that vicarious liability depends upon the existence of the master's power to control the way in which the work is done: the true theory, however, is that the relationship of master and servant of itself gives rise to the liability, and that the right of control is only one factor in determining whether the relationship exists.[35]

(4) Sometimes an injured person will be in the position of being able to allege that the defendant is liable to him on two distinct grounds—first, as vicariously responsible for the tort of his servant; secondly, as personally responsible for a breach of some obligation laid directly on him.[36] So it seems that a hospital authority is not only vicariously responsible for those in its service but also under a primary obligation to take reasonable care to provide proper treatment.[37] There is an increasing tendency to

---

[32] Nor could the decision in *Armstrong v. Strain* [1952] 1 K.B. 232 (above, § 18.6) be reconciled with the new view. *Contra*, Williams (1956) 72 L.Q.R. 531–532.

[33] As with a police officer's power of arrest: *Att.-Gen. for N.S.W. v. Perpetual Trustee Co.* [1955] A.C. 457.

[34] As with a sanitary inspector's power to seize diseased animals: *Stanbury v. Exeter Corporation* [1905] 2 K.B. 838. The similar point raised in *England v. National Coal Board* [1953] 1 Q.B. 724 has been settled by the Mines and Quarries Act 1954, s.159. See also *Stapley v. Gypsum Mines Ltd.* [1953] A.C. 663, 685. There is no clear English decision, but the High Court of Australia has decided that the master is not liable: *Darling Island Stevedoring Co. Ltd. v. Long* (1957) 97 C.L.R. 36.

[35] So far as Crown servants are concerned, the point is provided for by the Crown Proceedings Act 1947, s.2(3): *The Truculent* [1952] P. 1.

[36] As in *Fairline Shipping Corporation v. Adamson* [1975] Q.B. 180 (managing director and his company).

[37] See the dicta of the C.A. in *Wilsher v. Essex Area Health Authority* [1987] Q.B. 730, 778, and below, § 21.3.

hold directors of companies under a personal liability in tort.[38] But these duties are distinct in their nature and origin, and serious confusion may arise from a failure to keep them separate.[39] So a plaintiff who pleads that the defendant is vicariously liable may not be permitted to amend his claim to one based on personal responsibility.[40]

In order that the doctrine of vicarious liability may apply, there are two conditions which must co-exist:

(a) The relationship of master and servant must exist between the defendant and the person committing the wrong complained of;
(b) The servant must in committing the wrong have been acting in the course of his employment.

We shall consider each in turn.

§ 21.3. Who is a Servant?

Agents and servants

A servant may be defined as any person employed by another to do work for him on the terms that he, the servant, is to be subject to the control and direction of his employer in respect of the manner in which his work is to be done.[41] If we use the term agent to mean any person employed to do work for another, we may say that agents are of two kinds, distinguishable as servants and independent contractors. It is for the first kind of agent only that his employer is responsible under the rule which we are now considering. When the agent is an independent contractor, his employer is not, in general, answerable for the torts either of the contractor himself or of his servants. But when the agent is a servant, his employer will answer for all torts committed in the course of the employment, whether or not the employer has obtained any benefit thereby.[42]

It is sometimes said that there may be vicarious liability for the torts of agents, and the cases in which car-owners have been held liable for the negligence of drivers who could not be described as servants in any normal sense of that term[43] certainly support this view. But the main reason why this view cannot be accepted is that it would entail that every independent contractor was an agent.[44] In any event both the House of Lords[45] and the Court of Appeal[46] have asserted that the long-established difference between the liability for the acts of a servant and

---

[38] *Thomas Saunders Partnership v. Harvey, The Independent*, May 5, 1989.
[39] See *Staveley Iron and Chemical Co. Ltd. v. Jones* [1956] A.C. 627.
[40] *Esso Petroleum Co. Ltd. v. Southport Corporation* [1956] A.C. 218. See above, § 1.1.
[41] This definition can "hardly be bettered," according to MacKinnon L.J. in *Hewitt v. Bonvin* [1940] 1 K.B. 188, 191.
[42] The preceding paragraph was cited by Rowell C.J. in *T. G. Bright & Co. Ltd. v. Kerr* [1937] 2 D.L.R. 153, 165, with the remark that "Greatly as I respect any statement of law contained in Salmond, this statement does not appear to me to be adequate or exhaustive." But on appeal ([1939] 1 D.L.R. 193) three judges said Rowell C.J. was wrong.
[43] As in *Morgans v. Launchbury* [1973] A.C. 127.
[44] Atiyah, *Vicarious Liability*, Chap. 9.
[45] *Morgans v. Launchbury* [1973] A.C. 127.
[46] *Heatons Transport v. T.G.W.U.* [1972] 3 W.L.R. 73 (not considered in H.L.).

the liability for the acts of an agent has not been abrogated by social changes in the fields of car ownership and industrial relations. It is for Parliament and not for the courts to change the fundamental principles of the common law.

Servant distinguished from independent contractor

What, then, is the test of this distinction between a servant and an independent contractor? The distinction is important not only for the doctrine of vicarious liability but also in relation to the legislation governing tax and social security benefits and unfair dismissal.[47] The test is the existence of a right of control over the agent in respect of the manner in which his work is to be done. A servant is an agent who works under the supervision and direction of his employer; an independent contractor is one who is his own master. A servant is a person engaged to obey his employer's orders from time to time; an independent contractor is a person engaged to do certain work, but to exercise his own discretion as to the mode and time of doing it—he is bound by his contract, but not by his employer's orders.[48] Thus my chauffeur is my servant; and if by negligent driving he runs over someone in the street, I am responsible. But the cabman whom I engage for a particular journey is not my servant; he is not under my orders; he has made a contract with me, not that he will obey my directions, but that he will drive me to a certain place: if an accident happens by his negligence, he is responsible and not I.[49] So I am responsible for the domestic servants in my house, but I am not responsible for a skilled man whom I engage to do a certain job in my house—for example, to paint it, or to mend a window. (Nor, as we shall see, am I responsible to him for the safety of my premises to the same degree as I am to a servant.)[50]

This may be put in another way by drawing a distinction between one employed by a master under a contract of service (a servant) and one engaged by a principal under a contract for services (an independent contractor). "The distinction between a contract for services and a contract of service can be summarised in this way: In the one case the master can order or require what is to be done, while in the other case he can not only order or require what is to be done but how itself it shall be done."[51] This right of control has always been accepted[52] as a necessary, but not a sufficient,[53] mark of a contract of service. Other marks of a

---

[47] *Massey* v. *Crown Life Co. Ltd.* [1978] 1 W.L.R. 676.
[48] *Honeywill and Stein* v. *Larkin* [1934] 1 K.B. 191, 196.
[49] *Performing Right Society* case [1924] 1 K.B. 762, 768; *Hamelin* v. *Canada Egg Products Ltd.* (1966) 56 W.W.R. 14, 18. "The late Mr. Southmayd, of New York, though he possessed a fine carriage and horses, used always to drive in a hired conveyance for this reason": Baty, *Vicarious Liability*, p. 33n. Note that the proprietors of cabs are responsible for the negligence of the drivers to whom they are hired (in London, under the London Hackney Carriages Act 1843; elsewhere, under the Town Police Clauses Act 1847), even though the relationship is really that of bailor and bailee.
[50] See below, § 21.10.
[51] *Collins* v. *Hertfordshire C.C.* [1947] K.B. 598, 615, *per* Hilbery J.
[52] At least since *Yewens* v. *Noakes* (1880) 6 Q.B.D. 530, 532–533.
[53] *Ready Mixed Concrete (South East) Ltd.* v. *Minister of Pensions* [1968] 2 Q.B. 497—a decision of MacKenna J. which has been consistently followed.

contract of service are (i) the master's power of selection of his servant, (ii) the payment of wages or other remuneration, (iii) the master's right of suspension or dismissal. One should also consider who owns the tools or equipment, and "what in modern parlance is called economic reality."[54] To put it in another way, a contractor is one who is in business on his own account.[55]

Yet it cannot be doubted that a contract of service may exist although one or more of these elements is absent altogether or present only in an unusual form. In particular it is now accepted that the degree of control exercised by the employer over the servant is no longer the decisive factor.[56] Thus, although the right of control is present, the contract may be some other kind of contract (*e.g.* one of carriage) if its provisions, taken as a whole, are inconsistent with its being a contract of service.[57] The mere fact that A has control over B does not make B the servant of A—otherwise a parent would be responsible for his child,[58] and a superior servant for his subordinates.[59] The House of Lords[60] and the Privy Council[61] have reserved the right to restate the elements of a contract of service in the light of modern industrial conditions,[62] for the powers of the Government to control or direct entry into employment and the restrictive practices of trade associations and trade unions may affect materially the position of an employer as it was formerly understood.[63]

The right of control

One criticism of this distinction between a contract of service and a contract for services is that there are many contracts which are undoubtedly contracts of service but in which the master does not or cannot control the way in which the work is done: the captain of a ship[64] and the house surgeon at a hospital are each under a contract of service but each would greet with some astonishment a direction from his employer stating how a particular task was to be performed. Indeed in many cases the employer lacks the technical skill necessary to give such a direction. Or, even though he may have the skill, he may not have the time, as would be the case in fast-moving modern traffic, even if the employer were the most skilled of drivers and was sitting beside his servant.[65] Or, as is so often the case in industrial accidents, the employer may be a limited company incapable of controlling anybody except through its own superior servants or agents.[66] The significant fact may be the

---

[54] *Argent v. Minister of Social Security* [1968] 1 W.L.R. 1749, 1760, *per* Roskill J.
[55] *Lee Tin Sang v. Chung Chi-Keung* [1991] 2 W.L.R. 1173, 1176.
[56] *Kilboy v. S.E. Fire Area Joint Committee*, 1952 S.C. 280, 285–286.
[57] *Global Plant Ltd. v. Secretary of State* [1972] 1 Q.B. 139, 150.
[58] See above, § 20.4.
[59] See below, § 21.4.
[60] *Short v. Henderson (J.W.) Ltd.* (1946) 62 T.L.R. 427, 429.
[61] *Montreal v. Montreal Locomotive Works Ltd.* [1947] 1 D.L.R. 161, 169.
[62] See *Ferguson v. Dawson Ltd.* [1976] 1 W.L.R. 1213.
[63] *Re Hughes* [1966] 1 W.L.R. 1369, 1374–1375.
[64] But a ship's pilot is an independent professional man: *Esso Petroleum Ltd. v. Hall Russell Ltd.* [1989] A.C. 643.
[65] *Union SS. Co. v. Colville* [1960] N.Z.L.R. 100, 109.
[66] For their position, see § 21.4.

employer's right to control his insurance rather than to control his agent.[67] But although the distinction may ultimately rest on economic theories no longer fashionable, and even though it may be conceded that control is not as determinative as it was once thought,[68] the distinction is still real.[69] An employer may well be unable or unwilling to give specific orders to a skilled man, thinking it best to allow him to carry out the task in his own way,[70] but that will not necessarily relieve the employer from liability. It does not follow that because in any particular case it has not been found necessary to exercise a paramount authority that that authority does not exist.[71] There may well be such an authority in relation to incidental or collateral features of the employment. As Lord Porter said in *Mersey Docks and Harbour Board* v. *Coggins and Griffith (Liverpool) Ltd.*,[72] "the ultimate question is not what specific orders, or whether any specific orders, were given but who is entitled to give the orders as to how the work should be done." Indeed, in this very case, where the issue was whether the general or special employer was vicariously liable for the negligence of a driver of a crane, the driver had said in evidence: "I take no orders from anybody." That, as Lord Simonds remarked, was "a sturdy answer which meant that he was a skilled man and knew his job and would carry it out in his own way. Yet ultimately he would decline to carry it out in the appellants' way at his peril, for in their hands lay the only sanction, the power of dismissal."[73]

Hospital cases. These principles have been much discussed in a series of cases dealing with the liability of hospital authorities for their staff. In *Gold* v. *Essex C.C.*[74] the Court of Appeal stated the modern view and held a hospital authority liable for the negligence of a radiographer employed under a full-time contract of service. The position of the permanent medical staff was considered in *Collins* v. *Hertfordshire C.C.*,[75] where the defendants were held liable for the negligence of a resident

---

[67] *Nottingham* v. *Aldridge* [1971] 2 Q.B. 739, 749.

[68] *Whittaker* v. *Minister of Pensions* [1967] 1 Q.B. 156, 167.

[69] "It is often easy to recognise a contract of service when you see it, but difficult to say wherein the difference lies. A ship's master, a chauffeur, and a reporter on the staff of a newspaper are all employed under a contract of service; but a ship's pilot, a taxi-man, and a newspaper contributor are employed under a contract for services. One feature which seems to run through the instances is that, under a contract of service, a man is employed as part of the business, and his work is done as an integral part of the business; whereas, under a contract for services, his work, although done for the business, is not integrated into it but is only accessory to it": *Stevenson, Jordan and Harrison Ltd.* v. *Macdonald* [1952] T.L.R. 101, 111, *per* Denning L.J.

[70] "A good leader of men (and an employer is a leader of men) leaves to his men as much discretion as he can, otherwise unforeseen circumstances will upset the best laid plan": *Winter* v. *Cardiff R.D.C.* [1950] 1 All E.R. 819, 823, *per* Lord Oaksey. See also below, § 21.4.

[71] *Samson* v. *Aitchison* (1911) 30 N.Z.L.R. 160, 165.

[72] [1947] A.C. 1, 17.

[73] *Ibid.* 20.

[74] [1942] 2 K.B. 293; Lord Denning had been counsel for the plaintiff: see (1959) 5 J.S.P.T.L. 85.

[75] [1947] K.B. 598 (lethal cocaine injected instead of harmless procaine).

house-surgeon employed under a contract of service, and by the Court of Appeal in *Cassidy* v. *Ministry of Health*.[76] In the latter case the plaintiff's hand was rendered useless by the negligent post-operational treatment afforded by the full-time employees (assistant medical officer, house-surgeon and nurses) of the hospital authority, each of whom was employed under a contract of service. The fact that these employees were exercising professional care and skill was held to be no defence. There can be no doubt that the principle of these cases applies to hospital authorities such as regional hospital boards and hospital management committees, and that they will accordingly be liable for any negligence established against their permanent medical staff.[77]

It is said to be uncertain whether there is liability for a visiting or consulting surgeon or physician (although in *Roe* v. *Minister of Health*[78] the Court of Appeal was prepared to impose liability for the acts of a part-time specialist anaesthetist), as such a person is not employed under a contract of service so as to attract the operation of the doctrine *respondeat superior*. But it seems that there is no need to pray in aid of that doctrine. Under the National Health Service Acts, a hospital authority is itself under a duty to provide treatment and not merely to make arrangements for treatment by and at the sole risk of independent specialist contractors.[79] This duty, the scope of which in any particular case is a question of fact, is one which cannot be delegated, and the professional man who performs it does so as the agent of the hospital authority (unless he has been selected and employed by the patient himself).[80] Hence the word "consultant" is now rather a title denoting the holder's place in the hospital staff than a term denoting his relationship with the hospital authority.[81] The courts today will hold that the hospital is also liable for the acts of its nurses done in the operating theatre on the orders of the surgeon.[82]

Gratuitous service[83]

One person may be the servant of another although employed not continously, but for a single transaction only, and even if his service is gratuitous or *de facto* merely, provided that the element of control is present. The relationship of master and servant is commonly a continuing engagement in consideration of wages paid; but this is not essen-

---

[76] [1951] 2 K.B. 343.

[77] *Macdonald* v. *Glasgow Western Hospitals Board of Management*, 1954 S.C. 453. It is also generally accepted that the hospital authority and not the Minister of Health is the proper defendant even though the hospital authority is carrying on the services of the Crown: *Pfizer Corporation* v. *Minister of Health* [1965] A.C. 512. This is the assumption of circular H.M. (54) (issued by the Ministry of Health), which contains detailed provisions for the conduct of such actions, in so far as they may affect the various possible parties—doctors, hospital authorities, and medical defence societies.

[78] [1954] 2 Q.B. 66.

[79] See the dicta of the C.A. in *Wilsher* v. *Essex Area Health Authority* [1987] Q.B. 730, 778 (the point was not considered in the H.L.).

[80] *Razzell* v. *Snowball* [1954] 1 W.L.R. 1382.

[81] *Razzell* v. *Snowball* [1954] 1 W.L.R. 1382, 1386.

[82] *Cassidy's Case* [1951] 2 K.B. 343, 361–362.

[83] See Osborough, "The Vicarious Liability of the Vehicle Owner" (1971) 6 *Irish Jurist* 77.

tial. The service may be merely gratuitous, as when a child acts *de facto* as the servant of his father.[84] But this must not be taken too far. The owner of a dog is hardly liable if a friend takes it for a walk and a pedestrian trips over the lead carelessly held.[85] Nor is a householder liable if a guest, as distinct from a hired domestic help, carelessly pours hot tea over a fellow-guest,[86] for it must always be remembered that the mere existence of a right of control is not sufficient to found liability. Otherwise a parent would always be responsible for the torts of his child,[87] or the Crown for the torts of its prisoners.[88]

Vehicle owners

The owner[89] of a motor-vehicle who asks or permits another to drive it may find that the fact of ownership very easily gives rise to an inference that the driver was his servant or agent.[90] The right of control which is the test of the existence of a contract of service may be deduced from the fact that the owner of the motor-car remains in it while allowing another to drive,[91] even though the speed of modern traffic or his own intoxicated state[92] may render his right of control meaningless.

The social desirability of compensating persons injured in traffic accidents led to an extension of the concept of gratuitous service. Some courts even favoured the view that the owner of a family car should be held responsible for the negligent driving of any member of the household whom he permitted to drive it. So the Court of Appeal once held a wife, owner of a Jaguar, responsible for an accident when her husband used the car for a "night-out," and asked a friend to drive him home when he became intoxicated.[93] But this decision was unanimously reversed by the House of Lords.[94] Such a change in the basic concept of vicarious liability must be made by Parliament and not by the courts. Until the law has been so changed in England,[95] it is clear that in order to fix vicarious liability on the owner of a car in such a case it must be shown that the driver was using it for the owner's purposes, under delegation of a task or duty.[96] Mere permission to use the vehicle is not enough to establish vicarious liability. Nor is it enough to show, as was once thought,[97] that the owner had an interest or concern in the safe use of the vehicle, for every bailor can be said to have an interest in the safety of the article lent. Still, the fact that the journey is at the owner's

---

[84] *Johnson* v. *Lindsay* [1891] A.C. 371, 377. See the cases on volunteers below, § 22.5.
[85] *Nottingham* v. *Aldridge* [1971] 2 Q.B. 739, 749.
[86] *Contra, Moynihan* v. *Moynihan* [1975] I.R. 192.
[87] See above, § 20.6.
[88] See above, § 20.1.
[89] In the economic rather than the legal sense. Nobody has yet sought to make a finance company liable for its vehicles let on hire-purchase.
[90] *Rambarran* v. *Gurrucharran* [1970] 1 W.L.R. 556.
[91] *Samson* v. *Aitchison* [1912] A.C. 844; *The Trust Co.* v. *De Silva* [1956] 1 W.L.R. 376.
[92] As in *Morgans* v. *Launchbury* [1973] A.C. 127.
[93] *Launchbury* v. *Morgans* [1971] 2 Q.B. 245.
[94] [1973] A.C. 127.
[95] The Irish Parliament made the change as long ago as 1933.
[96] [1973] A.C. 127, 135, 140.
[97] *e.g.* in *Ormrod* v. *Crosville Motor Services Ltd.* [1953] 1 W.L.R. 409.

request[98] is some evidence that the driver was acting as the owner's agent. It may be helpful to ask whether the proposal for the use of the car emanated from the owner or from the driver.[99] But it is not necessary for the plaintiff to prove a contract, as distinct from a casual social agreement.[1] Conversely, the mere fact that the car is being used for the owner's purposes, but without his consent, will not involve him in responsibility.[2]

§ 21.4. Employee with Two Employers[3]

An employee may have two or more employers at the same time in respect of different employments. Nobody can have two *de jure* employers, but he can have a general (*de jure*) and a special (*de facto*) employer.[4] In particular an employer may lend or hire his servant to another person for a certain transaction so that *quoad* that employment he becomes the servant of the person to whom he is so lent, though he remains for other purposes the servant of the lender. When a servant is sent by his employer to do work for another, it is a question depending on the construction of the contract between the general and the special employer, whose servant he may be.[5] If there is no contract, then it is a question of fact, depending on the nature of the arrangement and the degree of control exercised over the servant. When a servant has thus two employers, the responsibility for a tort committed by him lies exclusively upon the employer for whom he was working when he did the act complained of. It must lie on one or the other; for the law does not recognise a several liability in two principals who are unconnected,[6] although it would certainly simplify the task of the plaintiff if it did, and the normal law relating to joint tortfeasors applied.[7] The question may be important in modern industrial conditions, when the servants of an employer and the servants of his contractors and sub-contractors often work together on the same task—for example, a large new building. As in general an employer is not liable for the torts of his contractor's servants (and never for their acts of collateral negligence[8]), a person injured by such a tortious act will be obliged, if he wishes to proceed against the main employer, to prove that he has become the temporary master of the delinquent servant of his own contractor.[9] This may be important for the injured party, as the main contractor may be as solvent as the sub-contractor is insolvent,[10] but it may not be easy to prove

---

[98] As in *Ormrod v. Crosville Motor Services Ltd.* [1953] 1 W.L.R. 409.

[99] *Carberry v. Davies* [1968] 1 W.L.R. 1103.

[1] *Morgans v. Launchbury* [1973] A.C. 127, 140.

[2] *Nottingham v. Aldridge* [1971] 2 Q.B. 739.

[3] Atiyah, *Vicarious Liability*, Chap. 18.

[4] *Esso Petroleum Ltd. v. Hall Russell Ltd.* [1989] A.C. 643, 683.

[5] See *Arthur White Ltd. v. Tarmac Civil Engineering Ltd.* [1967] 1 W.L.R. 1508 for a contract which did transfer liability from the general to the special employer.

[6] *Laugher v. Pointer* (1826) 5 B. & C. 547, 558; *Treacy v. Robinson & Son* [1937] I.R. 255, 266.

[7] Atiyah, *Vicarious Liability*, p. 156.

[8] See below, § 20.13.

[9] He may be able to frame his claim in another way—*e.g.* for breach of the duty owed by an occupier of premises.

[10] See above, § 1.4.

such a transfer[11] in view of the decision of the House of Lords in *Mersey Docks and Harbour Board* v. *Coggins and Griffith (Liverpool) Ltd.*[12]

The appellant board owned a number of mobile cranes, each driven by a skilled workman engaged and paid by them, which they were accustomed to let out on hire. The respondents, master stevedores, hired one of these cranes so driven to load a ship. The contract provided that the driver should be the servant of the hirers. In the course of the loading a third party was injured through the driver's negligence. At the time of the accident the stevedores had the immediate direction and control of the operations to be executed by the crane-driver—*e.g.* the power to order him to pick up and move a particular piece of cargo. But they had no power to direct the driver how to manipulate the crane or its controls. It was held that the appellant board as the driver's general employers were responsible for his negligence.

In such a case a heavy burden of proof rests on the general or permanent employer to shift his prima facie responsibility for the negligence of servants employed and paid by him on to the hirer who for the time being has the advantage of the particular service rendered.[13] No universal test can be laid down, although it may be helpful to ask whether the servant was transferred or only the use and benefit of his work.[14] "Who is paymaster, who can dismiss,[15] how long the alternative service lasts, what machinery is employed,[16] have all to be kept in mind."[17] If an employer sends out a skilled man to work for another, the general rule is that he remains the servant of the general employer.[18] The question will often be answered by asking who has the right to control the way in which the work is to be done.[19] The hirer (as in the *Mersey Docks* case) may often have control over the task to be performed but not over the way in which it is to be done.[20] The hirer may, of course, intervene to give a specific order which is in fact obeyed by the workman, and if damage then results he will in general be liable as a joint tortfeasor with the workman, but this is not by reason of any relationship of master and servant.[21] Nor is it conclusive as against the injured third party that

---

[11] See *McArdle* v. *Andmac Roofing Co. Ltd.* [1967] 1 W.L.R. 356.

[12] [1947] A.C. 1.

[13] Indeed the burden is so heavy that it has not been discharged in any reported case in this century: *Bhoomidas* v. *Singapore Harbour Authority* [1978] 1 All E.R. 956.

[14] *Ready Mixed Concrete Ltd.* v. *Yorkshire Traffic Area Licensing Authority* [1970] 2 Q.B. 397, 405.

[15] This is not conclusive: *Garrard* v. *Southey & Co.* [1952] 2 Q.B. 174, 180.

[16] There may be a distinction between a case where a complicated piece of machinery and a driver are lent and a case where labour only (and not necessarily of a skilled character) is transferred. In the former case it may be more difficult to assume that the general employer intended to allow the hirer to direct the manner in which a valuable piece of machinery should be operated: *Garrard* v. *Southey & Co.* [1952] 2 Q.B. 174, 179; *Denham* v. *Midland Employers Mutual Assurance Ltd.* [1955] 2 Q.B. 437.

[17] *Mersey Docks* case [1947] A.C. 1, 17, *per* Lord Porter.

[18] *Savory* v. *Holland and Hannen and Cubitts (Southern) Ltd.* [1964] 1 W.L.R. 1158.

[19] Yet see Lord Wright in *Century Insurance Co.* v. *Northern Ireland Road Transport Board* [1942] A.C. 509, 517. The fact that he who has the right of control may not have the requisite technical knowledge to give an order is irrelevant: see above, § 21.3.

[20] See *Lynch* v. *Palgrave, Murphy Ltd.* [1964] I.R. 150.

[21] *Mersey Docks* case [1947] A.C. 1, 12.

(again as in the *Mersey Docks* case) the two employers have made a contract stating whose servant the employee is to be on the particular occasion: servants cannot be transferred from one service to another without their consent.[22] Such a contract may determine the liability of the employers *inter se*[23] but it has only an indirect bearing on the question which of them is to be regarded as master of the workman on a particular occasion.[24] But it may be easier to assume a transfer of employment when the plaintiff is not a third party, but the workman himself, who is claiming that he has been injured by reason of the hirer's failure to fulfil some duty owed by an employer to his servants—*e.g.* the duty to provide a safe system of work.[25]

Superior servant not responsible for subordinates

A superior servant is not the master of the inferiors who are under his control, and he is not responsible for their torts.[26] Thus the directors of a company are not responsible for the torts committed by inferior servants of the company, although those servants are appointed and controlled by the directors, and even though the directors are the sole directors and sole shareholders in the company.[27] Any other decision would destroy the whole object of the Companies Act, which is that the limited liability of a company should be substituted for the unlimited liability of individuals, so that enterprise and adventure may be encouraged. But it would offend common sense and justice to treat the director of a company more kindly than the servant who takes his orders from the director. So an officer of a company, such as a chairman or managing director, is capable of being a joint tortfeasor with the company itself if he procures or directs the commission of a tort.[28] The company might then also be vicariously responsible for his wrongful acts.[29] It has become increasingly common so to join individual directors in actions against their companies.[30] This is particularly important when so many professional persons have been permitted by Parliament to practise as limited liability companies.

§ 21.5. THE COURSE OF EMPLOYMENT

A master is not responsible for a wrongful act done by his servant unless it is done in the course of his employment. It is deemed to be so

---

[22] *Ibid.* 14. Such a transfer may well involve difficult questions of insurance benefits, and this increases the strength of the presumption against it: *Denham* v. *Midland Employers Mutual Assurance Ltd.* [1955] 2 Q.B. 437.

[23] *Arthur White Ltd.* v. *Tarmac Civil Engineering Ltd.* [1967] 1 W.L.R. 1508.

[24] *Herdman* v. *Walker (Tooting) Ltd.* [1956] 1 W.L.R. 209; *The Panther and the Ericbank* [1957] P. 143.

[25] *Johnson* v. *J. H. Beaumont Ltd.* [1953] 2 Q.B. 184; *Gibb* v. *United Steel Companies Ltd.* [1957] 1 W.L.R. 668.

[26] See above, § 20.1.

[27] *C. Evans Ltd.* v. *Spritebrand Ltd.* [1985] 1 W.L.R. 317, 319.

[28] *C. Evans Ltd.* v. *Spritebrand Ltd.* [1985] 1 W.L.R. 317, 330.

[29] *Yuille* v. *B. & B. Fisheries (Leigh) Ltd. and Bates* [1958] 2 Lloyd's Rep. 596.

[30] See *Fairline Shipping Corpn.* v. *Adamson* [1975] 1 Q.B. 180, and *Thomas Saunders Partnership* v. *Harvey, The Independent,* May 5, 1989.

done if it is either (1) a wrongful act authorised by the master, or (2) a wrongful and unauthorised mode of doing some act authorised by the master.[31] Although there are few decisions on the point, it is clear that the master is responsible for acts actually authorised by him[32]: for liability would exist in this case, even if the relation between the parties was merely one of agency, and not one of service at all.[33] But a master, as opposed to the employer of an independent contractor, is liable even for acts which he has not authorised, provided they are so connected with acts which he has authorised that they may rightly be regarded as modes—although improper modes—of doing them. In other words, a master is responsible not merely for what he authorises his servant to do, but also for the way in which he does it. If a servant does negligently that which he was authorised to do carefully, or if he does fraudulently that which he was authorised to do honestly, or if he does mistakenly that which he was authorised to do correctly, his master will answer for that negligence, fraud or mistake.[34] On the other hand, if the unauthorised and wrongful act of the servant is not so connected with the authorised act as to be a mode of doing it, but is an independent act, the master is not responsible: for in such a case the servant is not acting in the course of his employment, but has gone outside it.[35]

As is often the case, the principle is easy to state but difficult to apply. All that can be done is to provide illustrations on either side of the line. In a borderline case the plaintiff may be helped by the onus of proof.[36] Once it is conceded that the servant was doing something in his working hours, on his employers' premises, and that his act had a close connection with the work which he was employed to do, then the onus[37] shifts to the employers to show that the act was one for which they were not responsible. It should also be noted that the courts today are reluctant to dissect the servant's employment into its component parts—*e.g.*

---

[31] *Poland v. Parr (John) & Sons* [1927] 1 K.B. 236, 240; *Warren v. Henlys Ltd.* [1948] 2 All E.R. 935, 937; *Ilkiw v. Samuels* [1963] 1 W.L.R. 991, 997, 1002, 1004; *Reilly v. Ryan* [1991] I.L.R.M. 449, 451.

[32] *Kooragang Investments Pty. Ltd. v. Richardson & Wrench Ltd.* [1982] A.C. 462, 472.

[33] See above, § 20.13.

[34] *Barwick v. English Joint Stock Bank* (1867) L.R. 2 Ex. 259, 266. He will be liable in an action on the case, even if a trespass is an incident in the wrong done: *Goh Choon Seng v. Lee Kim Soo* [1925] A.C. 550.

[35] The preceding paragraph constitutes "the well-known passage in Salmond on Torts" (*Keppel Bus Co. v. Ahmad* [1974] 1 W.L.R. 1082, 1084), which has been "much quoted and approved" (*General Engineering Ltd. v. Kingston and St. Andrew Corporation* [1989] 1 W.L.R. 69, 72). See also *Canadian Pacific Ry. v. Lockhart* [1942] A.C. 591, 599; *Warren v. Henlys Ltd.* [1948] 2 All E.R. 935, 938; *London County Council v. Cattermoles (Garages) Ltd.* [1953] 1 W.L.R. 997, 998; *Hamilton v. Farmers' Ltd.* [1953] 3 D.L.R. 382, 386; *Kirby v. National Coal Board*, 1958 S.C. 514, 533, 540; *Daniels v. Whetstone Entertainments Ltd.* [1962] 2 Lloyd's Rep. 1, 5 ("cannot be bettered": *Ilkiw v. Samuels* [1963] 1 W.L.R. 991; *Att.-Gen. v. Hartley* [1964] N.Z.L.R. 785, 801; *Kay v. I.T.W. Ltd.* [1968] 1 Q.B. 140, 153–154; *Stone v. Taffe* [1974] 1 W.L.R. 1575, 1582; *Armagas Ltd. v. Mundogas S.A.* [1986] A.C. 717, 737, 763 ("the test which has found most favour"); *Irving v. Post Office, The Times* (April 18, 1987).

[36] This is doubted by Edmund Davies L.J. in *Chapman v. Oakleigh Animal Products Ltd.* (1970) 8 K.I.R. 1063, 1071.

[37] In the sense of the evidential burden, as distinct from the legal burden, which throughout rests on the plaintiff.

loading, driving and unloading a vehicle. A broad approach is now preferred.[38]

(i) Outside the course of employment

In *General Engineering Services Ltd.* v. *Kingston & St. Andrew Corporation*[39] the plaintiff's premises were completely destroyed by a fire
which could have been extinguished if the defendants' firemen had not
deliberately delayed their arrival at the fire in order to bring pressure on
their employers in an industrial dispute. "Such conduct was the very
negation of carrying out some act authorised by the employer, albeit in
a wrongful and unauthorised mode."[40] On the other hand it has been
held that a servant who is authorised to drive a motor-vehicle, and who
permits an unauthorised person to drive it in his place, may yet be acting within the scope of his employment.[41] The act of permitting another
to drive may be a mode, albeit an improper one, of doing the authorised
work. The master may even be responsible if the servant impliedly, and
not expressly, permits an unauthorised person to drive the vehicle, as
where he leaves it unattended in such a manner that it is reasonably
foreseeable that the third party will attempt to drive it, at least if the
driver retains notional control of the vehicle.[42]

A master is not responsible for the negligence or other wrongful act of
his servant simply because it is committed at a time when the servant is
engaged on his master's business, or because it is committed while
using the tools or equipment provided by the master. It must be committed in the course of that business, so as to form a part of it, and not
be merely coincident in time with it. On this principle, in *Hensmans* v.
Clarity Cleaning Co.[43] one who was employed to clean a telephone was
not authorised to use it for his own long-distance calls. A similar rule
applies when a servant invites another on to his employer's property,[44]
or to engage in some dangerous activity.[45]

(ii) Within the course of employment

We may contrast the decision of the House of Lords in *Century Insurance Co.* v. *Northern Ireland Road Transport Board*,[46] in which the driver

---

[38] *Rose* v. *Plenty* [1976] 1 W.L.R. 141.

[39] [1989] 1 W.L.R. 69.

[40] [1989] 1 W.L.R. 69, 73, *per* Lord Ackner. When the Chief Fire Officer was asked why he
had let the building burn down, he replied: "We are on a go-slow, and even if my
mother was in there it would have to burn down. I want my raise of pay."

[41] *Ilkiw* v. *Samuels* [1963] 1 W.L.R. 991. The contrary decision in *Beard* v. *London General
Omnibus Co.* [1900] 2 Q.B. 530 dates from an era when few could drive motor-vehicles.

[42] *Fulwood House Ltd.* v. *Standard Bentwood Chair Ltd.* [1956] 1 Lloyd's Rep. 160.

[43] [1987] I.C.R. 749.

[44] As in *Twine* v. *Bean's Express* [1946] 1 All E.R. 202 (motor vehicle).

[45] As in *Hillen* v. *I.C.I. (Alkali) Ltd.* [1936] A.C. 65 where the crew of a barge invited stevedores to unload cargo in a dangerous and prohibited way. Lord Atkin said: "The owner
of a barge does not clothe the crew with apparent authority to use it or any part of it for
purposes which are known to be extraordinary and dangerous. The crew could not
within the scope of their employment convert it into a dancing hall or drinking booth.
They could not invite stevedores to work the engines or take part in the navigation."

[46] [1942] A.C. 509.

of a petrol lorry, whilst transferring petrol from the lorry to an under-ground tank, struck a match to light a cigarette and threw it on the floor, and thereby caused a fire and an explosion which did great damage. It was held that his employers were liable. His negligence was negligence in the discharge of his duties. Though the act of lighting his cigarette was done for his own comfort and convenience and was in itself both innocent and harmless, it could not be regarded in abstraction from the circumstances and was a negligent method of conducting his work. A similar case in which the decision went the other way was *Hilton v. Thomas Burton (Rhodes) Ltd.*[47] Four workmen were permitted to use their employers' van to go to work on a demolition site in the country. After half a day's work they decided to knock off and go to a café seven miles away for tea. When they had almost reached the café they changed their minds and started back again. On that journey one of them was killed through the negligent driving of another. The employer was not vicariously responsible, as the men were "on a frolic of their own."[48] Accidents occurring while the employee is going to or return-ing from his work-place continue to trouble the courts.[49]

Implied and ostensible authority[50]

There is a difference between implied authority and ostensible auth-ority. The servant's act may be an authorised act for the purposes of vicarious liability even if it is done solely for his own purposes if in the circumstances the permission of the master can be implied. Ostensible authority is different; it may be held to exist if, whatever the true state of affairs, the stranger has been misled by appearances. So as a general rule a servant has an implied authority upon an emergency to endeav-our to protect his master's property if he sees it in danger or has reason-able ground for thinking that he sees it in danger.[51] In an emergency a servant may be impliedly authorised to do an act different in kind from the class of acts which he is expressly authorised or employed to do. So in *Poland v. John Parr & Sons,*[52] where a carter, whilst off duty, seeing his employers' wagon apparently being robbed by boys, in order to prevent the theft struck one of the boys, who in consequence was run over and lost his leg, the employers were held liable.

In *Lloyd v. Grace, Smith & Co.*[53] the House of Lords in effect decided that the scope of an agent's employment is not limited to the rightful performance of his duties, but may be extended to his apparent or ostensible authority. So a modern company secretary is no longer a

---

[47] [1961] 1 W.L.R. 705.
[48] This phrase, which goes back to Parke B. in *Joel v. Morrison* (1834) 6 C. & P. 501, 503, is often used as a rough test of liability. It is restated in the complex English prose of today in *Harrison v. Michelin Tyre Co. Ltd.* [1984] C.L.Y. 2345.
[49] In *Smith v. Stages* [1989] A.C. 928 the H.L. laid down some elaborate guidelines which illustrate rather than resolve the difficulties.
[50] See Atiyah, *Vicarious Liability*, Chaps. 20–24.
[51] *D'Urso v. Sanson* [1939] 4 All E.R. 26. A similar rule applies to claims for industrial injury benefit under the Social Security Act 1975, s.54.
[52] [1927] 1 K.B. 236.
[53] [1912] A.C. 716.

mere clerk but an officer with extensive duties and responsibilities, who can be regarded as having ostensible authority to hire cars to meet the company's customers,[54] and the duties of a modern solicitor extend far beyond legal advice and assistance.[55]

But if there is no dealing with the servant, and so no question of "holding out,"[56] the question simply is whether actual (or implied) authority exists.[57] Again, if there is a "one-off transaction" outside the scope of actual or implied authority, the employer will not be liable simply because the employee falsely stated that he had authority.[58]

§ 21.6. EFFECT OF EXPRESS PROHIBITION

Even express prohibition of the wrongful act is no defence to the master at common law,[59] if that act was merely a mode of doing what the servant was employed to do.[60] Thus in *Limpus* v. *London General Omnibus Co.*[61] the defendant company was held liable for an accident caused by the act of one of its drivers in drawing across the road so as to obstruct a rival omnibus. It was held to be no defence that the company had issued specific instructions to its drivers not to race with or obstruct other vehicles: the driver whose conduct was in question was engaged to drive and the act which did the mischief was a negligent mode of driving for which his employers must answer, irrespective of any authority or of any prohibition.[62] The question has often arisen when the servant, in breach of an express prohibition, gives a lift in a motor-vehicle which he is employed to drive, and the person to whom he gives the lift[63] is injured as a result of his negligence. Thus in *Rose* v. *Plenty and Co-operative Retail Services Ltd.*[64] the first defendant was a milkman employed by the second defendants, who expressly prohibited him from using children in the performance of his duties. Nevertheless the milkman permitted the plaintiff, a 13-year-old boy, to ride on the milk float to assist him in the delivery of milk—and, indeed, had paid him to do so. As these acts were done for the purpose of the employers' business, they were held vicariously responsible for the milkman's negligence in driving the float.[65] There may also be liability in the case of a stray passenger, picked up by a driver to whom no con-

---

[54] *Panorama Developments (Guildford) Ltd.* v. *Filelis Furnishing Fabrics Ltd.* [1971] 2 Q.B. 711.
[55] *United Bank of Kuwait Ltd.* v. *Hammond* [1988] 1 W.L.R. 1051, 1063, 1066.
[56] See below, § 21.7.
[57] *Kooragang Investments Pty Ltd.* v. *Richardson & Wrench Ltd.* [1982] A.C. 462, 474.
[58] *Armagas Ltd.* v. *Mundogas S.A.* [1986] A.C. 717.
[59] It may also be no defence to a claim for industrial injury benefit under the Social Security Act 1975, s.52.
[60] *London County Council* v. *Cattermoles (Garages) Ltd.* [1953] 1 W.L.R. 997, 1005.
[61] (1862) 1 H. & C. 526.
[62] "The law casts upon the master a liability for the act of his servant in the course of his employment; and the law is not so futile as to allow a master, by giving secret instructions to his servant, to discharge himself from liability": *per* Willes J. 1 H. & C. 526, 539.
[63] In North America such a person is called a rider.
[64] [1976] 1 All E.R. 97.
[65] Note that the plaintiff also recovered judgment for £600 against the milkman personally.

trary instruction had been given,[66] or if the plaintiff could show that the defendants had acquiesced in their servant's breaches of his instructions.[67] The question also arises in cases in which the servant deviates from the route prescribed by the master and an accident occurs during the deviation. If the deviation constitutes an unauthorised *journey*, then the servant is "on a frolic of his own."[68] But if the deviation is no more than an unauthorised *route*, then it is a question of fact and degree whether the deviation is sufficiently substantial to put it outside the course of employment.[69] Further illustrations are unnecessary, for in every case it is a question of fact whether a servant is acting within the scope of his employment.[70]

§ 21.7. WHICH TORTS GIVE RISE TO LIABILITY

The liability of a master extends to assault,[71] or arson[72] or trespass[73] no less than to negligence. It was long supposed that where the fraud or other wilful wrongdoing of the servant was committed for his own benefit and not on his master's behalf, his master was not responsible. It was, however, decided by the House of Lords in *Lloyd* v. *Grace, Smith & Co.*,[74] that this was not so. The facts, as recounted by Lord Macnaghten,[75] were that "in the office of Grace, Smith & Co., a firm of solicitors in Liverpool of long standing and good repute, the appellant, Emily Lloyd, a widow woman in humble circumstances, was robbed of her property. It was not much, just a mortgage for £450 bequeathed to her by her late husband, and two freehold cottages at Ellesmere Port which she had bought herself without legal assistance for £540 after her husband's death. But it was all she had; and after the order of the Court of Appeal reversing a decision in her favour pronounced by Scrutton J., who tried the case with a special jury, she was compelled to appeal to this House as a pauper."[76] The "robbery" was committed by the solicitor's managing clerk, who had induced Mrs. Lloyd, a client of the firm, to transfer a mortgage to him by fraudulently misrepresenting the nature of the deed of assignment, and thereupon obtained and misappropriated the mortgage moneys. The solicitor was held liable to his

---

[66] *Twine* v. *Bean's Express Ltd.* [1946] 1 All E.R. 202, 205.
[67] *Conway* v. *Wimpey (George) Ltd.* [1951] 2 K.B. 266, 274–275. cf. *Young* v. *Box (Edward) Ltd.* [1951] 1 T.L.R. 789. These cases show an alternative approach to the problem: the plaintiff in such a case is a trespasser on the defendants' vehicle (and none the less so because the driver may have induced him to believe he was not) and so unable to recover from the employers (as distinct from the driver). But now that trespassers are more favoured these decisions have less authority: *Rose* v. *Plenty* [1976] 1 W.L.R. 141.
[68] *Joel* v. *Morison* (1834) 6 C. & P. 501, 503, *per* Parke B.
[69] *A. & W. Hemphill Ltd.* v. *Williams* [1966] 2 Lloyd's Rep. 101.
[70] *Marsh* v. *Moores* [1949] 2 K.B. 208, 215.
[71] See Rose, "Liability for an Employee's Assaults" (1977) 40 M.L.R. 420.
[72] *Photo Production Ltd.* v. *Securicor Ltd.* [1980] A.C. 827, 846, 852.
[73] *League Against Cruel Sports* v. *Scott* [1986] Q.B. 240.
[74] [1912] A.C. 716.
[75] "To generations who have passed their lives in the law his is truly *clarum et venerabile nomen*": *Public Trustee* v. *I.R.C.* [1960] A.C. 398, 409, *per* Viscount Simonds.
[76] [1912] A.C. 716, 727.

client for the fraud although it was committed in the office[77] solely for the benefit of the fraudulent servant himself. The House held that so long as a servant is acting within the scope of his employment, his employer is liable for all frauds committed by that servant, whether for the benefit of the employer or for his own profit. The employer is similarly liable even though the fraud involves a forgery and even though the victim of the fraud is not a client but a third person who is damnified by relying on the apparent or ostensible authority possessed by the clerk.[78] But in the first case to reach the House of Lords since 1912, it was said that "dishonest conduct was of a different character from blundering attempts to promote the employer's business interests,"[79] and ostensible authority for such conduct was not to be readily implied.

Malice of servant[80]

The mere fact that the servant has acted out of personal vengeance or malice or resentment or by way of a practical joke[81] will not necessarily exonerate the master provided that the act was within the scope of his employment. But this proviso is important, for the courts have shown a distinct reluctance to hold an employer liable for aggressive acts committed by a servant even though they are generated by the latter's employment. So there has been no liability for an assault on a passenger committed by an ill-mannered bus conductor.[82] So when a patron of a dance-hall was assaulted twice by a steward[83] in the course of ejecting unruly persons, first inside the hall and secondly outside it, it was held that the second assault, as distinct from the first, was an act of private retribution for which the employers were not liable.[84]

But although a principal is liable for the fraud or malice of his agent, an innocent agent is not liable for the fraud or malice of his principal—there is no doctrine of *respondeat inferior*.[85]

Bailments

The liability of a master for thefts committed by his servant of property bailed to the master or otherwise committed to his charge was once a matter of doubt. It used to be believed that a bailee was not responsible for the loss of the property by theft, even though the thief was the bailee's own servant, unless the bailee had given occasion for the theft by his own negligence or by that of some other servant employed to

---

[77] At least it can be said in his favour that he followed the old-fashioned view that solicitors should not run after clients but do their business in their office: see *United Bank of Kuwait Ltd.* v. *Hammond* [1988] 1 W.L.R. 1051, 1056.

[78] *Uxbridge Permanent Benefit Building Society* v. *Pickard* [1939] 2 K.B. 248.

[79] *Armagas Ltd.* v. *Mundogas S.A.* [1986] A.C. 717, 780, *per* Lord Keith of Kinkel.

[80] See Rose, "Liability for an Employee's Assaults" (1977) 40 M.L.R. 420.

[81] *Hudson* v. *Ridge Manufacturing Co. Ltd.* [1957] 2 Q.B. 348.

[82] *Keppel Bus Co.* v. *Ahmad* [1974] 1 W.L.R. 1082.

[83] Aggression is to be expected from such a person, who is not employed "for his intelligence or beauty": *Lehnert* v. *Nelson* [1947] 4 D.L.R. 473, 475.

[84] *Daniels* v. *Whetstone Entertainments Ltd.* [1962] 2 Lloyd's Rep. 1, 10.

[85] *Egger* v. *Chelmsford (Viscount)* [1965] 1 Q.B. 248.

take care of the property.[86] But this belief is a heresy since the Court of Appeal held in *Morris v. Martin (C.W.) & Sons Ltd.*[87] that the responsibility of the bailee must depend on whether the servant by whom the theft is committed is one to whom the charge or custody of the thing stolen has been entrusted by his master. If such a servant[88] steals the thing entrusted to him, he is acting nevertheless in the course of his employment—he is doing fraudulently what he is employed to do honestly—and his employer is liable for the loss of the goods. So in *Morris v. Martin* a firm of cleaners to whom a furrier had sent the plaintiff's mink stole were liable for the theft of the stole by an employee[89] whose duty it was to clean it. It will be a question of fact whether the employment merely provided an opportunity for the theft, when there will be no liability,[90] or was part of the task on which the servant was engaged in which there will be liability.[91] But if the theft is committed by a servant to whom the property has not been entrusted, the theft is outside the scope of his employment, and the master is not responsible unless he has been negligent in the selection of the servant or the theft has been induced by his own negligence or by the negligence of some other servant to whom the charge of the property has been committed.[92] The distinction between personal and vicarious liability is one which may be helpful here as elsewhere.[93]

Improper use of master's property

The same principle applies when a servant makes unauthorised use not amounting to larceny of property which has been bailed to his employer—for example, a garage-hand who takes out for his own purposes a motor-car left with his employers for repair and damages it. In such a case, it will be no defence to an action by the bailor for the employer to plead that the servant was "on a frolic of his own"[94] if that servant was one to whom the charge or custody of the car has been entrusted, for in such a case there will have been a breach of the implied term of the bailment to use reasonable care in the custody of the goods.[95] But there can be little doubt that such a plea would be a good defence if the plaintiff was a bystander or other person injured by the servant's careless driving; in such a case the bailment is irrelevant.[96] For

---

[86] *Cheshire v. Bailey* [1905] 1 K.B. 237.
[87] [1966] 1 Q.B. 716.
[88] The employment of a known thief may prevent the employer from relying on an exemption clause: *W. J. Lane v. Spratt* [1970] 2 Q.B. 480.
[89] The employee might himself have been sued in conversion: *Fairline Corporation v. Adamson* [1975] Q.B. 180, 190.
[90] *Armagas Ltd. v. Mundogas S.A.* [1986] A.C. 717, 782.
[91] *Hensmans v. Clarity Cleaners Ltd.* [1987] I.C.R. 749.
[92] *Morris v. C. W. Martin & Sons Ltd.* [1966] 1 Q.B. 716. The decision has been approved both by the Privy Council (*Port Swettenham Authority v. T. W. Wu Ltd.* [1979] A.C. 580, 591) and the House of Lords (*Photo Production Ltd. v. Securicor Transport Ltd.* [1980] A.C. 827.)
[93] See below, § 21.10.
[94] *Joel v. Morison* (1834) 6 C. & P. 501, 503, *per* Parke B.
[95] *Morris v. C. W. Martin & Sons Ltd.* [1966] 1 Q.B. 716.
[96] *Adams (Durham) Ltd. v. Trust Houses Ltd.* [1960] 1 Lloyd's Rep. 380, 385–386.

a master is not responsible for the negligence of his servant in the unauthorised use of his master's property for the servant's own purposes.[97] This rule has been applied on many occasions when harm has been done by the negligent driving of servants while using their master's vehicle for their own ends.[98]

Permission is not authority

On the same principle, a master is not responsible for the negligence of his servant while engaged in doing something which he is permitted to do for his own purposes, but not employed to do for his master. I am liable only for what I employ my servant to do for me, not for what I allow him to do for himself.[99] If I permit my servant for his own ends to drive my car, I am not liable for his negligence in doing so.[1] In this respect he is not my servant, but a mere bailee to whom I have lent my property; and there is no more reason why I should answer for his conduct in such a matter than why I should answer for that of my friends or my children to whom, without personal negligence on my own part, I lend or entrust property that may be made the instrument of mischief. In such a case, much may depend on whether the act was performed in the master's interests or supposed interests,[2] or was reasonably incidental to the servant's duties.[3]

§ 21.8. THE DOCTRINE OF COMMON EMPLOYMENT

Formerly a master was not responsible for negligent harm done by one of his servants to a fellow-servant engaged in a common employment with him. This rule was abolished, after many years of criticism, by the Law Reform (Personal Injuries) Act 1948, but some account of its history and nature is necessary. The rule is generally, but perhaps mistakenly,[4] traced back to *Priestley* v. *Fowler*.[5] The doctrine was based on a fictitious implied term in the contract of service to the effect that the servant agreed to run the risks naturally incident to his employment, and that one of these risks was that of harm due to the negligence of a fellow-servant. The doctrine became complex and subtle with the passing years. In particular, it could no longer be stated in the simple form that one servant could not claim damages from his master for the negligence of a fellow-servant. Two conditions had to be filled before the doctrine could apply: (1) the servant injured and the servant causing the injury must have been fellow-servants—*i.e.* they must be servants of the same

---

[97] See *Hensmans* v. *Clarity Cleaners Ltd.* [1987] I.C.R. 949 (no liability for servant employed to clean a telephone who used it to make international calls costing £1,400.)

[98] See, *e.g. Hilton* v. *Thomas Burton (Rhodes) Ltd.* [1961] 1 W.L.R. 705; *Jones* v. *McKie and Mersey Docks and Harbour Board* [1964] 1 W.L.R. 960.

[99] *Hilton* v. *Thomas Burton Ltd.* [1961] 1 W.L.R. 705.

[1] *Britt* v. *Galmoye* (1928) 44 T.L.R. 294.

[2] See above, § 21.5.

[3] See above, § 21.6.

[4] Newark, "Bad Law" (1966) 17 N.I.L.Q. 469, 477.

[5] (1837) 3 M. & W. 1.

master; (2) they must at the time of the accident have been engaged in a common work.

Curtailment and abolition[6]

The story of how the doctrine of common employment was gradually limited in scope and eventually abolished is an interesting one. Legislation and judicial decision have combined with each other to complicate the story: the effect of neither can really be understood in isolation from the other.[7] The important decision of the Court of Appeal in *Groves v. Wimborne (Lord)*[8] made it plain that common employment was no defence when the cause of action was based on the breach of a statutory duty imposed on the employer.[9] The doctrine was at last abolished by the Law Reform (Personal Injuries) Act 1948, with effect from July 5, 1948. Section 1(3) of that Act provides that any provision contained in a contract of service or apprenticeship or agreement collateral thereto which would have the effect of excluding or limiting any liability of the employer in respect of personal injuries[10] caused to the person employed or apprenticed by the negligence of persons in common employment[11] with him shall be void.

§ 21.9. THE NATIONAL INSURANCE ACTS

The Workmen's Compensation Act 1897 adopted a new approach. The Act provided compensation for a workman injured in the course of his employment even though no negligence on the part of his employer or anyone else could be shown. The basis of the workman's claim was not negligence or fault but accident. It was assumed that the employer would insure against this liability and pass on the premium to the public by way of increased prices.[12] The scope of the Act was widened by subsequent legislation which was in turn replaced by the National Insurance (Industrial Injuries) Act 1946 and later legislation. The National Insurance Acts have now been consolidated in the Social Security Act 1975, which establishes a basic scheme of contributions and benefits.

---

[6] Howells, "*Priestley v. Fowler* and the Factory Acts" (1963) 26 M.L.R. 367.
[7] As Lord Devlin observed (41 M.L.R. at 506), the English judges "outpaced Parliament" in the provision of remedies for workmen.
[8] [1898] 2 Q.B. 402.
[9] See the interesting (extra-judicial) remarks of Lord Reid in 248 H.L.Deb., 5s., col. 1338.
[10] The doctrine never seems to have applied in cases of other torts (*e.g.* assault, defamation).
[11] The phrase "common employment" appears in the section, and for that reason alone it is still necessary to know something of the old law.
[12] It is worth noting that Lord Bramwell in his dissenting speech in *Smith v. Baker & Sons* [1891] A.C. 325, 340, said: "I am not certain it would not be a good thing to give a person injured as the plaintiff was a right to compensation, perhaps from the state, even where there was no blame in the master; even where there was blame in the servant. Men would not wilfully injure themselves, and then compensation would be a part of the cost of the work." This point (made, incidentally, by one who was a sturdy exponent of Victorian individualism) has been developed at much greater length by some modern writers: see above, § 2.5.

(1) Insurable employment

The Act covers all those employed in Great Britain under a contract of service or apprenticeship, written or oral, express or implied. There is not (as there was under the Workmen's Compensation Acts) any upward limit on the amount of earnings. This very large class is the main category of insured persons. Self-employed persons are also covered.

(2) Risks insured against

Work-related accidents continue to receive the preferential treatment to which they have been entitled since 1892, although there is an increasing tendency to bring these accidents within the ordinary social security system. A person in insurable employment is entitled to benefit if he suffers personal injury by accident arising out of and in the course of his employment, and he is also insured against any prescribed disease or prescribed personal injury not so caused by accident but which is a disease or injury due to the nature of that employment. The terms "personal injury," "accident," and "arising out of and in the course of such employment" were taken over from the Workmen's Compensation Acts. They had been the subject of a vast number of judicial decisions, and it was thought "better to stick to the devil we know than to fly to the devils we know not of."[13] Once the insured person has shown that the accident arose in the course of the employment he is relieved (in the absence of evidence to the contrary) from proving that it arose out of the employment (s.50). The Act (ss.52–55) specifically brings within the employment four cases which would normally be outside it.

(3) Contributions

A proportion is paid by the employer and another proportion by the workman. A further contribution is provided by Parliament. So in effect the state and not the employer is the insurer.

(4) Benefits

The term "compensation" is not used. The unemployment and sickness benefit, now "statutory sick pay," and disablement benefit to which the claimant is entitled is not "compensation" or "damages" at common law but money payable under a statutory scheme of insurance. Benefits are not related to contributions.

(5) Administration

This has been taken away from the ordinary courts and vested in the Secretary of State. Claims to injury benefit are made in the first instance to the local insurance officer; from him an appeal may be taken to a local appeal tribunal and thence to the National Insurance Commissioner.

---

[13] 414 H.C.Deb. (5th ser.), col. 270.

§ 21.10. MASTER'S COMMON LAW DUTIES TO SERVANTS[14]

Before the end of the nineteenth century the courts themselves intervened to mitigate the severity of the doctrine of common employment. The doctrine went no further than to imply in the contract of employment a term by which the servant agreed to bear the risks arising from the negligence of a fellow-servant who had been selected with due care by the master. The doctrine did not mean that the servant impliedly agreed to hold the master immune from liability for the consequences of the master's own personal negligence. The common law has always held the master to be under an obligation to take reasonable care for his servant's safety. The nature of the duty was expounded by Lord Herschell in *Smith* v. *Charles Baker & Sons*[15] in words which have been consistently cited with approval: "It is quite clear that the contract between employer and employed involves on the part of the former the duty of taking reasonable care to provide proper appliances, and to maintain them in a proper condition, and so to carry on his operations as not to subject those employed by him to unnecessary risk." Those words are important both in prescribing the positive obligation and in negativing by implication anything higher.[16]

Four points may be made about the scope and nature of the duty which they impose on the employer. First, there are several judicial warnings against interpreting the duty too strictly.[17] Secondly, the duty in question is apparently capable of being pleaded either in contract or in tort. There are conflicting judicial dicta on the matter.[18] The normal practice is to sue in tort. But the court cannot impose a duty in tort if the express or implied terms of the contract of employment negative such a duty.[18a]

Thirdly, the duty is imposed upon the master himself, and if he entrusts the performance of it to another instead of performing it himself he is liable for the negligence of that other.[19] The duty remains personal to the master even though he is obliged by statute to entrust to a duly qualified person the task of providing a safe system of work and is forbidden to interfere in the working himself.[20] It was once held that an employer who buys from a reputable source a tool with a latent defect not discoverable by reasonable care which injures an employee had fulfilled his duty to take reasonable care for his safety.[21] But this decision was reversed by the Employer's Liability (Defective Equipment) Act

---

[14] See Fleming, "Tort Liability for Work Injury," Vol. 15 of the *International Encyclopaedia of Comparative Law* (1975).

[15] [1891] A.C. 325, 362.

[16] *Davie* v. *New Merton Board Mills Ltd.* [1959] A.C. 604, 620.

[17] *Buckingham* v. *Daily News Ltd.* [1956] 2 Q.B. 534.

[18] So the House of Lords has said both that the duty is tortious (*Davie* v. *New Merton Board Mills Ltd.* [1959] A.C. 604) and that it is contractual (*Lister* v. *Romford Ice Co. Ltd.* [1957] A.C. 555). The various dicta are surveyed in *Matthews* v. *Kuwait Bechtel Corporation* [1959] 2 Q.B. 57.

[18a] *Reid* v. *Rush & Tompkins plc* [1990] 1 W.L.R. 212.

[19] *McDermid* v. *Nash Dredging & Reclamation Co. Ltd.* [1987] A.C. 906, 911, 919.

[20] *Wilsons and Clyde Coal Co.* v. *English* [1938] A.C. 57, 81.

[21] *Davie* v. *New Merton Board Mills Ltd.* [1959] A.C. 604.

1969, s.1, which imposes strict liability on an employer providing defective equipment[22] for the purposes of his business, and an employee[23] in consequence suffers personal injury.[24] In such a case, if the defect[25] is attributable wholly or partly to the fault of a third party (whether identified or not), the injury shall be deemed to be also attributable to negligence on the part of the employer. The employer may then recover from the manufacturer—who may still be sued directly by the employee. The employer is obliged to insure under the Employers' Liability (Compulsory Insurance) Act 1969.

Fourthly, it has been customary ever since *Wilsons and Clyde Coal Co. v. English*[26] to expound these duties under the threefold heading of the provision of a competent staff of men, adequate material, and a proper system of work. But it is only for convenience of exposition that the simple duty to take reasonable care is regarded as having three different facets.

(1) Competent staff of men

This duty still exists, though it is usually of little importance since the abolition of the defence of common employment has made an employer liable for the negligence of the plaintiff's fellow-servants. But an employer has been held personally liable for practical jokes or bullying[27] by the plaintiff's fellow-servants.

(2) Proper plant, appliances and premises

"The providing of proper plant," said Sir Arthur Channell in *Toronto Power Co. v. Paskwan*,[28] "as distinguished from its subsequent care, is especially within the province of the master rather than of his servants. . . . It is true that the master does not warrant the plant, and if there is a latent defect which could not be detected on reasonable examination, or if in the course of working plant becomes defective and the defect is not brought to the master's knowledge and could not by reasonable diligence have been discovered by him, the master is not liable, and further, a master is not bound at once to adopt the latest improvements and appliances." Although the duty is not only to provide proper plant but also to maintain it, it is not broken by a merely temporary failure to keep in order or adjust the plant or appliances.

The duty to provide and maintain safe premises is similar. It extends as well to the servant's working place as to the means whereby the ser-

---

[22] As defined in s.1(3), includes any plant and machinery, vehicle aircraft and clothing. A ship of 90,000 tons is included: *Coltman v. Bibby Tankers Ltd.* [1988] A.C. 276.

[23] As defined in s.1(3). Note that a self-employed person is excluded.

[24] As defined in s.1(3), this includes loss of life, any impairment of a person's physical or mental condition, and any disease.

[25] It is the defect, and not the injury, which must be attributed to the third party's fault.

[26] [1938] A.C. 57.

[27] *Hudson v. Ridge Manufacturing Co. Ltd.* [1957] 2 Q.B. 348.

[28] [1915] A.C. 734, 738. ("One of the most eminent judges before whom I ever had the good fortune to practise": *R. v. Kritz* [1950] 1 K.B. 82, 87, *per* Lord Goddard C.J.).

vant has to reach it.[29] The duty is to make the place of work as safe as reasonable care and skill will permit[30]; it is probably not as high as the obligation under the Factories Act 1961 to provide safe premises and means of access.[31] Neither the statutory nor the common law duty is broken if the place of work becomes unsafe through some transient or exceptional condition.[32]

(3) Safe system of work

The duty covers all acts which are normally and reasonably incidental to the day's work.[33] The most valuable analysis of the scope of the duty is to be found in the judgment of Lord Justice-Clerk Aitchison in *Wilsons and Clyde Coal Co.* v. *English*[34]: "Broadly stated, the distinction is between the general and the particular, between the practice and method adopted in carrying on the master's business of which the master is presumed to be aware and the insufficiency of which he can guard against, and isolated or day-to-day acts of the servant of which the master is not presumed to be aware and which he cannot guard against; in short, it is the distinction between what is permanent or continuous on the one hand and what is merely casual and emerges in the day's work on the other hand." For such a casual departure from the system the employer is not liable. It has been made plain[35] that the duty to provide a safe system may arise in relation to an isolated task which may never have to be repeated in exactly the same way—*e.g.* the loading and unloading of ships. So all the circumstances relevant to that servant must be considered by a prudent employer, including the gravity of the injury which he may suffer if an accident occurs.[36]

As the standard of care required is no higher than that to be expected of an ordinary prudent employer the defendant will usually succeed if he shows that his system of protection is in accordance with the general practice in that particular trade,[37] or with the relevant statute or statutory regulations.[38] One common difficulty arises from the fact that men often disregard a system which has been established for their own protection. Their folly may be due either to inexperience or over-confidence. The employer must then consider the situation and do what is reasonable to ensure that a suitable system of protection is not only devised but also kept in operation: he cannot expect his workmen to lay down and operate a system for themselves.[39] "Workmen are not in the position of employers. Their duties are not performed in the calm

---

[29] *Hurley* v. *Sanders & Co. Ltd.* [1955] 1 All E.R. 833, 835 (this point is not reported in [1955] 1 W.L.R. 470).

[30] *Naismith* v. *London Film Productions Ltd.* [1939] 1 All E.R. 794, 798.

[31] *Latimer* v. *A.E.C. Ltd.* [1953] A.C. 643, 658.

[32] *O'Reilly* v. *National Rail and Tramway Appliances Co.* [1966] 1 All E.R. 499.

[33] *Davidson* v. *Handley Page Ltd.* [1945] 1 All E.R. 235 (washing teacups).

[34] 1936 S.C. 883, 904.

[35] *Colfar* v. *Coggins and Griffith (Liverpool) Ltd.* [1945] A.C. 197, 202.

[36] *Paris* v. *Stepney Borough Council* [1951] A.C. 367.

[37] See above, § 9.13.

[38] See above, Chap. 10.

[39] *McDermid* v. *Nash Dredging Co. Ltd.* [1987] A.C. 906, 909.

atmosphere of a boardroom with the advice of experts. They have to make their decisions on narrow window sills and other places of danger, and in circumstances in which the dangers are obscured by repetition."[40] Thus in *General Cleaning Contractors Ltd.* v. *Christmas*[41] the House of Lords held that it was not a safe system to employ window-cleaners to work outside high self-locking windows on a sill 6¼ inches wide and 27 feet above the ground without giving them any orders to keep one sash open or any appliance to prevent both sashes closing. The case shows clearly that in cases where perils are involved which thought or planning might avoid or lessen, it may not be enough for the employer to entrust that thought or planning to the skill and experience, however great, of the man who carries out the work.[42] But there certainly are cases in which an employer is entitled to rely on a skilled man being sensible enough to avoid a danger of which he has been warned.[43] The relationship between employer and skilled workman is not equivalent to that of a nurse and imbecile child,[44] or matron and patient,[45] or schoolmaster and pupil.[46]

Proof

The plaintiff is not obliged in every case to plead and prove an alternative system of work which would have been safe; in some cases it may be prudent for him to do so,[47] but in others it may be enough for him to allege that the system provided was dangerous and that a prudent employer would have done better.[48] But the onus is on the plaintiff to prove causation,[49] and this may be difficult when the fault complained of is one of omission.[50]

Contributory negligence[51]

It must be remembered that a great deal of work which has to be done is dangerous, and if it is not really practicable for the master to diminish or eliminate the danger then the risk of it is a necessary incident of the employment and a risk which the servant is paid to take.[52] Again, a servant who is aware that the work is dangerous and knows of the precautions which should be taken to avert the danger but yet does nothing may be guilty of contributory negligence and have to bear some of the loss himself. In actions under the Factories Act the courts

---

[40] *General Cleaning Contractors Ltd.* v. *Christmas* [1953] A.C. 180, 189, *per* Lord Oaksey.
[41] [1953] A.C. 180.
[42] *Barcock* v. *Brighton Corporation* [1949] 1 K.B. 339, 343 ("A system of work is not devised by telling a man to read the regulations and not to break them.")
[43] See *Qualcast (Wolverhampton) Ltd.* v. *Haynes* [1959] A.C. 743.
[44] *Smith* v. *Austin Lifts Ltd.* [1959] 1 W.L.R. 100, 105.
[45] *Haynes* v. *Qualcast Ltd.* [1958] 1 W.L.R. 225, 230.
[46] *Withers* v. *Perry Chain Co. Ltd.* [1961] 1 W.L.R. 1314, 1320.
[47] *Vickers* v. *B.T.C. Docks Board* [1964] 1 Lloyd's Rep. 275.
[48] *Dixon* v. *Cementation Co. Ltd.* [1960] 1 W.L.R. 746.
[49] *McWilliams* v. *Sir William Arrol Ltd.* [1962] 1 W.L.R. 295.
[50] See above, § 9.15.
[51] See below, § 22.11.
[52] *Hurley* v. *Sanders & Co. Ltd.* [1955] 1 All E.R. 833, 836.

have adopted a lenient standard by which to judge whether the workman is guilty of contributory negligence: for as the purpose of imposing the absolute statutory obligation is to protect the workman against those very acts of inattention which may constitute contributory negligence, too strict a standard would defeat the object of the statute. But this doctrine cannot be used so as to require any modification in the standard of care required of a workman in a simple case of common law negligence, where there is no evidence of repetitive work being performed under strain or for long hours at dangerous machines.[53]

Servant working on premises of third party

The protection afforded by the law to one who is directed by his employer to work on premises occupied by a third party is not as clear as might be wished. First, the servant may possibly have a claim against some other contractor working on the premises who by his misfeasance has created a source of danger.[54] Secondly, it may be possible for him to establish that the occupier is in such close control of the situation as to have become his temporary employer, so as to owe him the duty which we have already expounded.[55] But at present the courts do not favour such claims.[56] Thirdly, the servant will be a lawful visitor of the occupier and so will be entitled to the common duty of care under the Occupiers' Liability Act 1957.[57]

But until the Occupiers' Liability Act the rule was that an invitee who continued his work or activities with knowledge of the danger which ultimately caused him injury was without remedy against the occupier.[58] So in order to safeguard workmen, it was held that a master who sent his men out to work on another's premises was still subject to his common law obligation to take reasonable care for their safety by providing a safe system of work on those premises[59] as distinct from seeing that the premises themselves were safe.[60] But fine distinctions are now to be avoided: the three headings under which it is customary to consider the liability of a master to his servant are really only manifestations of the fundamental duty to take such care as is reasonable in the circumstances.[61] In some circumstances a warning of the danger may be enough[62]; in other cases the employer may be obliged to take positive steps to protect the employee, and in such cases the fact that the servant knowingly incurs the risk only goes to the question of his contributory negligence.[63] The cases have produced the rather curious result[64] that a

---

[53] *Staveley Iron and Chemical Co. Ltd.* v. *Jones* [1956] A.C. 627.
[54] See above, § 11.3.
[55] Above, § 21.4.
[56] *Savory* v. *Holland and Hannen and Cubitts (Southern) Ltd.* [1964] 1 W.L.R. 1158.
[57] See above, § 11.4.
[58] *London Graving Dock Co. Ltd.* v. *Horton* [1951] A.C. 737.
[59] *General Cleaning Contractors Ltd.* v. *Christmas* [1953] A.C. 180.
[60] *Cilia* v. *James (H.M.) & Sons (A Firm)* [1954] 1 W.L.R. 721.
[61] *Wilson* v. *Tyneside Window Cleaning Co. Ltd.* [1958] 2 Q.B. 110, 121.
[62] *Smith* v. *Austin Lifts Ltd.* [1959] 1 W.L.R. 100, 117.
[63] *A. C. Billings & Sons Ltd.* v. *Riden* [1958] A.C. 240.
[64] See, *e.g. Savory* v. *Holland and Hannen and Cubitts (Southern) Ltd.* [1964] 1 W.L.R. 1158.

skilled man working on the premises of a third party is not very well protected. For the more skilled he is the less likely is he to be the temporary servant of the occupier, and if the latter is sued for breach of the common duty of care he can plead that he is entitled to expect that a skilled man will guard against the normal risks of his calling.[65] It seems that if the person injured in such a case is a "labour-only" independent contractor and not a workman, he is not owed the *Smith* v. *Baker* duty.[66] A householder is entitled to expect that a self-employed window-cleaner will take his own precautions against risks customarily incidental to his work, such as ill-balanced weights or loose plywood.[67]

§ 21.11. Summary

What effect have these changes had on the legal relationship of master and servant? First, it is plain that though the benefits payable under social security are greatly superior to those provided by the Workmen's Compensation Acts, there are still very many cases where a servant injured in the course of his employment will wish to institute proceedings at common law. For the damages awarded by the courts (even after the deductions described above have been made) will often exceed the benefits made available by the Department of Social Security. Secondly, it seems that the threefold obligation of *Wilsons'* case is now capable of being expressed more simply and truly as a duty to take reasonable care for the servant's safety. The reason for drawing a distinction between a failure to take reasonable care to provide proper plant and a safe system of work (for which the master was personally responsible) and an isolated act of negligence by a fellow-servant (for which the master was not) has disappeared with the defence of common employment itself.[68] But the duty which a master owes to take reasonable care for the safety of his servant cannot be delegated to another person who is not an employee: the employer remains personally responsible.[69] The distinction between the duty owed by a master personally and the vicarious liability which rests upon him as master may also be important if the defendant is a corporation, for the responsibility for the proper discharge of its duties lies squarely on the board of directors in the light of the knowledge which it has or ought to have from the personnel of the company.[70]

§ 21.12. Servant's Duties to Employer

One who is under a contract of service owes to his employer a number of different duties:

---

[65] See above, § 11.4.

[66] *Jones* v. *Minton Construction Co. Ltd.* (1973) 15 K.I.R. 309.

[67] *Smith* v. *Austin Lifts Ltd.* [1959] 1 W.L.R. 100, 115. (Note that the employers in this case had on four different occasions warned the occupier that the premises were unsafe.)

[68] *Smallwood* v. *Lamport and Holt Lines Ltd.* [1959] 2 Lloyd's Rep. 213. 225.

[69] *McDermid* v. *Nash Dredging Ltd.* [1987] A.C. 966.

[70] *Wright* v. *Dunlop Rubber Co. Ltd.* (1972) 13 K.I.R. 255.

(1) Duty to take reasonable care

There is an implied term in the contract of service that the servant will take reasonable care not only of his master's property entrusted to him but also generally in the performance of his duties.[71] It seems that this duty is to be thought of as an implied contractual obligation rather than as a particular example of the tort of negligence.[72] Hence if the servant breaks this obligation his employer has a cause of action for breach of contract to recover damages for such loss as is not too remote a consequence of the breach. The damage which the master has suffered may be either physical[73] or financial—e.g. the sums which the master, as vicariously responsible for his servant's torts, has paid to third parties injured by such a tort committed in breach of the implied contractual obligation.[74] Thus in *Lister* v. *Romford Ice and Cold Storage Co. Ltd.*[75] the appellant and his father were employed by the respondents. One day Lister junior, in the course of his duties as a lorry driver, knocked down Lister senior, who was acting as his mate. Lister senior recovered damages for his personal injuries from the respondents, as being vicariously liable for the tort of Lister junior. The respondents' insurers, in virtue of their right of subrogation and of an express term in the policy of insurance, then instituted proceedings against the appellant (in the name but without the knowledge of the respondents) to recover the damages and costs which had been paid to his father. The House of Lords, by a bare majority, held that the respondents, whose rights were of course neither greater nor less than if they had not been insured, were entitled to succeed. The House refused to accept the appellant's argument that a term should be implied in his contract of service to the effect that he was entitled to the benefit of any insurance taken out by his employers.

There may be difficulty if a master who has himself been negligent pursues a claim for breach of implied contractual duty against his negligent servant.[76] Unless the servant can plead that the claim should be made under the 1935 Act,[77] it is hard to see how the damages can be less than 100 per cent.

(2) Duty to indemnify at common law

The ancient rule of the common law (now abolished) that one wrongdoer could not seek indemnity or contribution from another[78] was confined to cases in which the person seeking redress must be presumed to have known that he was committing an illegal act. If he were personally

---

[71] *Century Insurance Co. Ltd.* v. *N.I.R.T.B.* [1942] A.C. 509, 519.

[72] *Lister* v. *Romford Ice and Cold Storage Co. Ltd.* [1957] A.C. 555.

[73] In *Digby* v. *General Accident Fire and Life Assurance Coporation Ltd.* [1943] A.C. 121, Merle Oberon, the film actress, recovered £5,000 damages from her own chauffeur for injuries caused by his negligent driving.

[74] The implied obligation extends no further than those acts which the servant is actually employed to do: *Harvey* v. *O'Dell Ltd.* [1958] 2 Q.B. 78.

[75] [1957] A.C. 555.

[76] As in *Jones* v. *Manchester Corporation* [1952] 2 Q.B. 852.

[77] See above, § 20.11.

[78] See above, § 20.11.

free from any blame, it seems that he could sue the other for redress. So an agent would be entitled to indemnity if he reasonably believed that the act was one which his principal could authorise. It seems clear on principle, also, that in all cases of vicarious liability the person held vicariously liable for the tort of another must have a right of indemnity as against that other.[79] Thus a master who has paid for the negligence of his servant can doubtless sue that servant for indemnity, at least if it is just and equitable that he should do so.[80]

(3) Statutory duty to provide indemnity or contribution

It has now been settled that as master and servant are joint tortfeasors the former is entitled to claim contribution or indemnity from the latter to such extent as the court thinks just and equitable in accordance with the provisions of the Law Reform (Married Women and Tortfeasors) Act 1935.[81] Thus if the negligence of the employer himself (or one of his other servants) has contributed to the damage the employer will be able to recover only a contribution and not an indemnity.[82] Similar rules govern those cases in which a principal is liable for the torts of his independent contractors.[83] In practice an indemnity of 100 per cent. seems to be commonly given in the ordinary case of vicarious liability, even though the claim at common law fails for one reason or another.[84]

§ 21.13. Independent Contractors[85]

The general rule is that although an employer is responsible for the negligence and other wrongdoing of his servant, he is not responsible for that of an agent who is not a servant but an independent contractor.[86] There are, however, certain cases in which an employer is liable for the

---

[79] *Jones* v. *Manchester Corporation* [1952] 2 Q.B. 852, 865; *Semtex Ltd.* v. *Gladstone* [1954] 1 W.L.R. 945, 948; *Romford Ice Co.* v. *Lister* [1956] 2 Q.B. 180, 199 (on appeal see [1957] A.C. 555, 570); *Overmyr Co. of Canada Ltd.* v. *Transfer Ltd.* (1975) 65 D.L.R. (3d) 717, 721.

[80] *Morris* v. *Ford Motor Co. Ltd.* [1973] Q.B. 792.

[81] The relevant cases are cited in note 79. See also Jolowicz, 'Right to Indemnity between Master and Servant" [1956] C.L.J. 101; Jolowicz (1959) 22 M.L.R. 71, 189; Williams, "Vicarious Liability and Master's Indemnity" (1957) 20 M.L.R. 220. Some grave issues of policy raised by these decisions are discussed in the Report of an Inter-departmental Committee (H.M.S.O., 1959; Gardiner, (1959) 22 M.L.R. 652), which discovered that there was "a gentleman's agreement" amongst insurance companies not to take advantage of the *Lister* case, unless the evidence clearly indicated collusion or wilful misconduct on the part of the employee. The medical profession (always a strongly organised body) secured the consent of the Minister of Health to an agreement under which hospital authorities will invoke the Act against negligent doctor servants only when the doctor is not assisted by one of the professional medical defence societies: Circular H.M. 54 (32).

[82] As in *Jones* v. *Manchester Corporation* [1952] 2 Q.B. 852.

[83] *Burnham* v. *Boyer* [1936] 2 All E.R. 1165; *Daniel* v. *Rickett, Cockerell & Co. Ltd.* [1938] 2 K.B. 322.

[84] *Harvey* v. *O'Dell Ltd.* [1958] 2 Q.B. 78.

[85] See Williams, "Liability for Independent Contractors" [1956] C.L.J. 180; McKendrick, "Vicarious Liability and Independent Contractors—a Re-examination" (1990) 53 M.L.R. 770.

[86] *Rivers* v. *Cutting* [1982] 1 W.L.R. 1146, 1149–1150.

acts of an independent contractor.[87] Although the tendency of development is in the direction of extending rather than restricting this liability, the advantages of departing from the traditional distinction are not very obvious. It is worth noticing that many of the decisions in favour of liability come from the time before it was clearly established[88] that a careless contractor might himself be liable directly to the injured party, and that an employer today usually stipulates for an indemnity from the contractor.[89] On the other hand, there has been a marked increase in the number of self-employed persons, or persons in "a-typical employment," who a generation ago would have been regarded as servants. But "sub-contracting" in the building industry has given rise to great evils: financially irresponsible contractors, and their employers, may leave an injured person without remedy. So there was a distinct tendency to hold that the developer of a housing estate cannot delegate his duties to men of straw or shell companies, but this is now doubtful.[90]

The liability of the employer of an independent contractor is not properly vicarious: the employer is not liable for the contractor's breach of duty; he is liable because he has himself broken his own duty.[91] He is under a primary liability and not a secondary one.[92] Hence it is misleading to think of the law on this point as a general rule of non-liability subject to a more or less lengthy list of exceptions. The real question is whether the defendant is, in the circumstances of the particular case, in breach of a duty which he owes to the plaintiff. If the plaintiff proves such a breach it is no defence to say that another has been asked to perform it. The performance of the duties, but not the responsibility for that performance, can be delegated to another. This seems to be all that is meant by the oft-repeated phrase "non-delegable duties."[93]

When a duty exists

The main difficulty in this branch of the law is to discover when the law will impose such a duty. One thing can, however, be said with confidence: the mere fact that the work entrusted to the contractor is of a character which may cause damage to others unless precautions are taken is not sufficient to impose liability on the employer.[94] There are

---

[87] *Salsbury* v. *Woodland* [1970] 1 Q.B. 324, 347.

[88] In *Donoghue* v. *Stevenson* [1932] A.C. 562. See above, § 9.2.

[89] See an example of an indemnity clause in *Hosking* v. *De Havilland Aircraft Co. Ltd.* [1949] 1 All E.R. 540, 542.

[90] "As a matter of social policy this may be entirely admirable . . . As a matter of legal principle, however, I can discover no basis on which it is open to the court to embody this policy in the law.": *D. & F. Estates Ltd.* v. *Church Commissioners for England* [1989] A.C. 177, 209, *per* Lord Bridge of Harwich. See also the argument of counsel in [1989] A.C. at 189–190.

[91] *Daniel* v. *Rickett, Cockerell & Co. Ltd.* [1938] 2 K.B. 322, 325.

[92] It is hardly necessary to add that the contractor himself will normally be liable to the injured party—in theory: in practice the contractor is often without assets, as in *Salsbury* v. *Woodland* [1970] 1 Q.B. 324.

[93] *Cassidy* v. *Ministry of Health* [1951] 2 K.B. 343, 363; *McDermid* v. *Nash Dredging Ltd.* [1987] A.C. 906, 909.

[94] *Hughes* v. *Percival* (1883) 8 App.Cas 443, 446.

few operations entrusted to an agent which are not capable, if due precautions are not observed, of being sources of danger and mischief to others; and if the principal was responsible for this reason alone, the distinction between servants and independent contractors would be practically eliminated from the law.[95] If I employ a contractor to manufacture explosives for me, I am hardly responsible if an explosion happens because of the negligence of his servants in the course of manufacture.[96] So a head contractor on a building site is not necessarily responsible because a sub-contractor breaks his statutory[97] or common law duties.[98] Here, as elsewhere in the law of negligence, it is not enough to establish liability to show that a reasonable man could have foreseen damage as a result of the defendant's acts. It may be helpful if we draw a distinction between two classes of duty—(1) a duty to take reasonable care, and (2) a duty to see that care is taken.[99] In the former there is in general no liability for the default of an independent contractor, in the latter there is.

(1) Duty to take reasonable care

The normal duty imposed by the law of negligence is no higher than one of reasonable care. As always, it is a question of fact in each case whether reasonable care has been taken. But it is certainly material to consider whether what has to be done is something which forms part of the obligor's ordinary trade or business. If the act or process in question is one which involves technical skill or knowledge, then the ordinary man will discharge his duty by entrusting its performance to an apparently competent contractor.[1] A good example is the duty owed by those who take motor-vehicles on to a highway. It is no more than a duty to take reasonable care to avoid injury to other users of the highway. So if the owner of such a vehicle entrusts its repair to an apparently competent contractor, he is not liable[2] if, as a result of the contractor's careless work, a wheel comes off and injures a passer-by.[3]

On the other hand the principal may be liable when due care is not taken to see that the agent is properly qualified for the performance of the task so committed to him, or where proper instructions are not given to him in order to enable him to avoid the dangers incidental to the work.[4] For it is important not to give an undue advantage to the

---

[95] *Cape Breton* v. *Chappells Ltd.* (1962) 36 D.L.R. (2d) 58, 73; *Salsbury* v. *Woodland* [1970] 1 Q.B. 324, 337.

[96] *Rainham Chemical Works Ltd.* v. *Belvedere Fish Guano Co.* [1921] 2 A.C. 465, 491.

[97] *Donaghey* v. *Boulton and Paul Ltd.* [1968] A.C. 1.

[98] *D. & F. Estates Ltd.* v. *Church Commissioners* [1989] A.C. 177, 184.

[99] See *The Pass of Ballater* [1942] P. 112, 117.

[1] *Riverstone Meat Co. Pty. Ltd.* v. *Lancashire Shipping Co. Ltd.* [1960] 1 Q.B. 536, 580–582.

[2] *Stennett* v. *Hancock* [1939] 2 All E.R. 578, 581 (which also decides that he is not obliged to inquire whether the repairer has done his work properly).

[3] But the contractor himself may well be liable under the principles in *Donoghue* v. *Stevenson* [1932] A.C. 562; see above, § 9.2.

[4] *Robinson* v. *Beaconsfield R.D.C.* [1911] 2 Ch. 188.

ignorant employer who confides all his affairs to independent contractors.[5]

Exceptions

There are, however, two cases in which it was generally assumed that an employer was liable for the defaults of his contractor, even though the obligation imposed on him belonged to the category of negligence rather than of strict liability.

(a) *Duty to invitees.* Before the Occupier's Liability Act 1957, it seemed that an occupier was, in general, liable to his invitees under the rule in *Indermaur v. Dames* for the default of his independent contractor.[6] Now the Occupiers' Liability Act 1957, s.2(4), puts the matter almost[7] beyond doubt. It provides that where damage is caused to a visitor by a danger due to the faulty execution of any work of construction, maintenance or repair[8] by an independent contractor employed by the occupier, the occupier is not to be treated "without more" as answerable for the danger if in all the circumstances he has acted reasonably in choosing and supervising the contractor.[9]

(b) *Employer's duty to employees.* It is now settled[10] that the duty which a master owes to his servants to take reasonable care of their safety cannot be avoided by entrusting its performance to a contractor, at least if the duty is to be performed on the master's own premises, and would normally be so performed by one of his own servants, and the negligent workmanship is discoverable by reasonable inspection. The Employer's Liability (Defective Equipment) Act 1969, s.1 imposes liability on an employer for breach of its provisions when the defect is attributable to the fault of a third party. But as those provisions are limited to cases in which injury has been caused by the supply of defective equipment, the common law will still govern cases in which an independent contractor has been entrusted by the employer with the performance of some task which injures the employee.

(2) Duty to see that care is taken

In some cases the law imposes a duty irrespective of negligence. Where the act which the contractor is employed to do is one of the kind which the employer does at his own peril—so that the existence of neg-

---

[5] *Sumner* v. *William Henderson & Sons Ltd.* [1964] 1 Q.B. 450, 471. Perhaps this is the justification for *Cynat Products Ltd.* v. *Landbuild Ltd.* [1984] 3 All E.R. 513, 523 (defendant builders said to be under "a primary duty which they could not delegate").

[6] *Thomson* v. *Cremin* (1941) [1953] 2 All E.R. 1185, 1188, 1191–1192; [1956] 1 W.L.R. 103n. This case is also reported (*sub nom. Cremin* v. *Thomson*) in (1941) 71 Ll.L.R. 1.

[7] See above, § 11.6.

[8] Note that the draftsman has omitted the words "or other like operation," which occur in the recommendation of the Law Reform Committee: Cmd. 9305, p. 34. See also above, § 11.3.

[9] *AMF International Ltd.* v. *Magnet Bowling Ltd.* [1968] 1 W.L.R. 1028.

[10] *McDermid* v. *Nash Dredging Co. Ltd.* [1987] A.C. 906, in which the H.L. brushed aside some doubts in the C.A.

ligence is immaterial—it is no defence that the cause of the mischief was the negligence of an independent contractor by whose agency the act was done.[11] If an employer is under a duty to a person or class of persons, he is liable if that duty is not performed and damage thereby results, and cannot evade that liability by delegating the performance of the duty to an independent contractor. Whether there is such a duty will depend upon whether the employer as a reasonable man ought to foresee that the persons who suffer damage are likely to be affected by the performance of the independent contractor's acts,[12] provided always that the case falls within one of the following recognised categories of duty.

(i) Statutory duties and powers

When an absolute duty is laid by statute upon an individual or class of individuals, the performance of it cannot be delegated to an independent contractor to enable liability to be evaded.[13] This principle applies whether the duty is owed to the public or only to a section of the public.[14] The carrier of goods by sea does not fulfil his statutory obligation to use due diligence even if he employs a competent ship repairer and has his work inspected by a Lloyd's surveyor in the usual way.[15] The duties imposed by the Factories Act 1961 to fence dangerous machinery[16] and to provide safe means of access[17] are of this kind, but not the duties imposed on local authorities in respect of the approval of building plans under the Public Health Act 1961, s.4.[18] The courts are moving in the direction of holding that the duties imposed on hospital authorities are also of this character.[19] It is possible that an employer who exercises statutory powers through the agency of a contractor is responsible for that contractor's defaults.[20]

(ii) Common law duties

(a) *Public nuisance.* Such a duty is imposed when a person employs a contractor to do in a highway (or perhaps in any place to which there is a public right of access or entry)[21] some dangerous act other than the ordinary use of the highway for the purposes of passage or traffic,[22] or when a person, having done such an act in the highway, delegates to a contractor the work of taking the precautions necessary to prevent mischievous consequences. Such employment or delegation is permissible only on the terms of warranting the public against the negligence of the

---

[11] *Balfour* v. *Barty-King* [1956] 1 W.L.R. 779, 783.
[12] *Savage* v. *Wilby* [1954] 3 D.L.R. 204, 206–207.
[13] *The Pass of Ballater* [1942] P. 112, 117.
[14] *Mulready* v. *J. H. & W. Bell Ltd.* [1953] 2 Q.B. 117.
[15] *Riverstone Meat Co. Pty. Ltd.* v. *Lancashire Shipping Co. Ltd.* [1961] A.C. 807.
[16] *Groves* v. *Wimborne (Lord)* [1898] 2 Q.B. 402.
[17] *Hosking* v. *De Havilland Aircraft Co. Ltd.* [1949] 1 All E.R. 540.
[18] *Murphy* v. *Brentwood District Council* [1990] 3 W.L.R. 414.
[19] See above, § 20.1.
[20] *Darling* v. *Att.-Gen.* [1950] 2 All E.R. 793.
[21] *Pickard* v. *Smith* (1861) 10 C.B.(N.S.) 470 (railway station platform).
[22] When there is liability only for personal negligence; above, § 21.3.

contractor so entrusted with the work. The duty covers work done in the space above or below, but not near or alongside, the highway.[23] This duty, which was well established at common law,[24] is recognised by the Highways Act 1980, s.58, which provides that in an action for damage arising from non-repair of highways or bridges it shall not be relevant to prove that the highway authority had arranged for a competent person to carry out or supervise the maintenance of the part of the highway to which the action relates, unless it is also proved that the authority had given proper instructions with regard to the maintenance of the highway and that the instructions had been carried out.

(b) *Hazardous operations.* There is liability under the rule in *Rylands* v. *Fletcher* for the acts of an independent contractor.[25] The principle is the same in the case of escape of fire,[26] or of damage done by a savage animal.[27] Again, in the case of extra-hazardous acts, that is, acts which, in their very nature, involve special danger to others, an obligation may be imposed upon the ultimate employers to take special precautions which they cannot delegate by having the work carried out by independent contractors. Thus in *Honeywill and Stein Ltd.* v. *Larkin Bros.*[28] it was held that the plaintiffs, who employed the defendants to take flash-light photographs in a cinema, were liable to the owners of the cinema for a fire caused by the defendants in carrying out the work.[29] But later cases[30] are opposed to the imposition of liability, and it can hardly be regarded as in accordance with the views of the Law Lords in *Read* v. *J. Lyons & Co. Ltd.*,[31] which emphasise fault rather than strict liability.

(c) *Private nuisance.* We have already seen that an occupier is responsible for the acts of his independent contractor which cause a nuisance to the highway or interfere with his neighbour's right of support.[32] A similar conclusion was arrived at in *Matania* v. *National Provincial Bank*,[33] in which the nuisance complained of was dust and noise caused by building operations on an extensive scale.

(d) *Bailees.* A bailee for reward, such as a warehouseman, may have attributed to him the negligence of a contractor employed to guard the

---

[23] *Salsbury* v. *Woodland* [1970] 1 Q.B. 324.

[24] *Clements* v. *Tyrone C.C.* [1905] 2 I.R. 415, 542 (survey of authorities by Palles C.B.).

[25] The best authority for this proposition is *Rylands* v. *Fletcher* itself. See above, § 13.10.

[26] *Spicer* v. *Smee* [1946] 1 All E.R. 489; *Balfour* v. *Barty-King* [1957] 1 Q.B. 496.

[27] See above, § 14.1.

[28] [1934] 1 K.B. 191.

[29] But "extra-hazardous," a phrase of American origin, has now been replaced by "extraordinarily dangerous" in the U.S.A. itself: see above, § 13.10, n. 43.

[30] See the full survey of the cases in *Stevenson* v. *Brodribb Sawmilling Pty. Ltd.* (1986) 60 A.L.J.R. 194, which concludes that the doctrine of extra-hazardous acts is an example of personal rather than vicarious liability.

[31] [1947] A.C. 156. See above, § 13.3.

[32] Above, § 5.6. An example is *Alcock* v. *Wraith* [1991] E.G.C.S., 137.

[33] [1936] 2 All E.R. 633.

subject of the bailment.[34] If the bailment is of valuable goods for carriage, there is no implied right to sub-contract.[35]

(e) *Shipowners.* It is settled that negligence by a ship's pilot renders the shipowner, and not the pilot's general employer (*e.g.* a harbour authority), liable to the injured third party.[36]

Collateral negligence[37]

An employer is never liable for the collateral or casual negligence of his independent contractor. It is not always easy to decide whether the negligent act in a particular case is collateral or not. Thus in *Padbury* v. *Holliday and Greenwood Ltd.,*[38] where one of the sub-contractors' workmen placed a tool on a window-sill, not in the ordinary course of the work which the contractors were employed to do, and the casement having been blown to by the wind the tool fell and injured the plaintiff, it was held that this was collateral negligence and the ultimate employers were not liable. On the other hand, in *Holliday* v. *National Telephone Co.,*[39] where, owing to the negligence of a plumber employed as an independent contractor to do work in a public street, molten solder was scattered by the explosion of a benzoline lamp, judgment was given for the defendant in the court below on the express ground that the negligence of the plumber was merely collateral. Nevertheless the Court of Appeal disagreed with this view and gave judgment for the plaintiff, holding that the negligence was in the very act which the plumber was employed to perform.

Probably the rule as to collateral negligence means nothing more than that the negligence required to impose liability upon the employer of an independent contractor must be negligence committed in the doing of the act itself which he is employed to do, and that negligence in other operations which, though connected with that work, are not themselves part of the work which he has contracted to do is not sufficient.[40] The negligence is central, not casual or collateral.[41] The employer is exempt from liability, not so much because the act done cannot be foreseen or guarded against, but because it is outside the scope of the duty imposed on the employer. If this is all that "collateral negligence" means, it is only an obscure way of saying that an employer is only liable for acts which are within the scope of the contractor's authority—which is obvious, but unhelpful in any particular case.

---

[34] *British Road Services Ltd.* v. *A. V. Crutchley & Co. Ltd.* [1968] 1 Lloyd's Rep. 271.
[35] *Garnham, Harris and Elton Ltd.* v. *Alfred W. Ellis (Transport) Ltd.* [1967] 2 All E.R. 940.
[36] *Esso Petroleum Co. Ltd.* v. *Hall Russell & Co. Ltd.* [1989] A.C. 643.
[37] Atiyah, *Vicarious Liability*, Chap. 33.
[38] (1912) 28 T.L.R. 492.
[39] [1899] 2 Q.B. 392. See also *Thompson* v. *Anglo-Saxon Petroleum Co. Ltd.* [1955] 2 Lloyd's Rep. 363—one of the few modern reported cases in which collateral negligence has been successful as a defence.
[40] *McDonald* v. *Associated Fuels* [1954] 3 D.L.R. 775, 779.
[41] To use the terminology of *McDermid* v. *Nash Dredging Co. Ltd.* [1987] A.C. 906, 919.

CHAPTER 22

MISCELLANEOUS DEFENCES

§ 22.1. Necessity[1]

In some cases even damage intentionally done may not involve the defendant in liability when he is acting under necessity to prevent a greater evil. The precise limits of the defence are not clear, for it has affinities with certain other defences, such as an act of God, self-help, duress, or inevitable accident. It is distinguishable from self-defence on the ground that this presupposes that the plaintiff is prima facie a wrongdoer: the defence of necessity contemplates the infliction of harm on an innocent plaintiff.[2] The defence, if it exists, enables a defendant to escape liability for the intentional[3] interference with the security of another's person[4] or property[5] on the ground that the acts complained of were necessary to prevent greater damage to the community or to another or to the defendant himself. The distinction is between public and private necessity.[6] The use of the term necessity serves to conceal the fact that the defendant always has a choice between two evils. This is what distinguishes the defence of necessity from that of impossibility. Here, as elsewhere in the law of torts, a balance has to be struck between competing sets of values and no more can be done here than to indicate the factors relevant to such a choice. So there is some authority that the subject as well as the Crown has a right and a duty at common law to justify a trespass or other tort on the ground of necessity in the defence of the realm, but such a right has been said to be obsolescent. "No man now, without risking an action against him in the courts, could pull down his neighbour's house to prevent the fire spreading to his own; he would be told that he ought to have dialled 999 and summoned the local fire brigade."[7]

---

[1] See Williams, "The Defence of Necessity" [1953] C.L.P. 216; Glazebrook, "The Necessity Plea in English Criminal Law" [1972] Camb.L.J. 87; Bates, "Consenting to the Necessary" (1972) 46 A.L.J.R. 73.

[2] But if A so parks his car that B cannot move his, would not B be justified in breaking A's window to release the brake? See *Proudman* v. *Allen* [1954] S.A.S.R. 336.

[3] It is inconceivable that the careless invasion of another's interests should be defensible on the ground of necessity.

[4] Examples of this are rare: our law does not recognise "protective custody" or enforced therapy: see above, § 7.4, and below, § 22.3. But see *Leigh* v. *Gladstone* (1909) 29 T.L.R. 139 (forcible feeding of hunger-striker permissible: but perhaps the case, which has been much criticised, illustrates rather the proper use of discipline).

[5] *London Borough of Southwark* v. *Williams* [1971] Ch. 734.

[6] *Re F. (Mental Patient: Sterilisation)* [1990] 2 A.C. 1, 74.

[7] *Burmah Oil Co.* v. *Lord Advocate* [1965] A.C. 75, 165, *per* Lord Upjohn. Nor is it permissible for the driver of a fire-engine to ignore traffic signals: *Buckoke* v. *Greater London Council* [1971] Ch. 655. The Fire Services Act 1947, s.30(1) in effect gives the defence of necessity to a *criminal* charge of trespass.

Again, it seems plain that "the safety of human lives belongs to a different scale of values from the safety of property. The two are beyond comparison and the necessity for saving life has at all times been considered a proper ground for inflicting such damage as may be necessary upon another's property."[8] So in the course of medical or surgical treatment to which the patient's consent has been obtained there may suddenly arise an emergency which puts the patient's life at risk. In such a case the degree of necessity may obviate the need to obtain consent to further treatment, at least if it is broadly of the same character.[9] When the defendant has acted in protection of a private rather than a public interest it seems that the law was once stricter than it now is. "For the rule that the property in question must be actually under attack has been substituted the more generous rule that it must be in real or imminent danger; and for the absolute criterion that the act of trespass must be shown—in the light of subsequent events—to have been necessary for the preservation of the property has been substituted the more relative standard of reasonable necessity, viz. that any reasonable man would, in the circumstances of the case, have concluded that there was no alternative to the act of trespass if the property endangered was to be preserved."[10] Thus in Cope v. Sharpe[11] the defendant committed certain acts of trespass on the plaintiff's land in order to prevent the spread of heath-fire to land over which the defendant's master had shooting rights.[12] It was shown that the fire never in fact damaged the property of the defendant's master and would not have done so even if the preventive measures had not been taken. The Court of Appeal, however, held that the defendant was entitled to succeed: the risk to his master's property had been real and imminent, and a reasonable person, placed in the defendant's position, would have acted as he had done. It has since been laid down both by the courts[13] and by Parliament[14] that the principle in Cope v. Sharpe affords a general justification for acts of trespass.

It is uncertain whether the defence of necessity is available if the defendant has acted in good faith otherwise than for the protection of property—e.g. if out of mercy he kills a dog which has been run over,[15] but on principle the defendant should be protected.

---

[8] *Southport Corporation v. Esso Petroleum Ltd.* [1953] 3 W.L.R. 773, 779, *per* Devlin J. On appeal, see [1956] A.C. 218, 235, 392.

[9] See Lord Goff in *Re F. (Mental Patient: Sterilisation)* [1990] 2 A.C. 1, 75. The other Law Lords were more cautious, for if necessity alone was the test, many incompetents might be deprived of treatment which would be beneficial, though not exactly necessary, for them to receive. See also below, § 21.3.

[10] *Cresswell v. Sirl* [1948] 1 K.B. 241, 247, *per* Scott L.J. For criticism of the phrase "reasonably necessary" see *Re Naylor Benzon Mining Co.* [1950] Ch. 567, 575.

[11] [1912] 1 K.B. 496.

[12] Note that the defendant was not a mere volunteer, as he was in *Carter v. Thomas* [1893] 1 Q.B. 673 (well-intentioned entrant on another's premises to extinguish a fire at which firemen were already working held a trespasser).

[13] *Rigby v. Chief Constable of Northants* [1985] 1 W.L.R. 1242, 1254.

[14] See the Animals Act 1971, s.9, which gives protection, subject to numerous conditions, to one who kills or injures a dog which is worrying livestock.

[15] See *Workman v. Cowper* [1961] 2 Q.B. 143.

But the defence of necessity is not in general favoured by the courts.[16] "The good samaritan is a character unesteemed by the English law."[17] It is important that people should not interfere with the person or property of others without due sense of responsibility, particularly as the obligation to pay compensation for any damage done is uncertain. The obligation to compensate certainly binds the Crown acting under its prerogative,[18] but how much further it extends is doubtful. There is some authority that any rescuer of life, as distinct from property, is entitled to be reimbursed his expenditure, particularly if he is a professional man. In any case, the defence is hardly available if the predicament in which the defendant found himself was brought about by his own negligence.[19]

§ 22.2. EXEMPTION CLAUSES AND DISCLAIMERS

Exemption clauses

Although parties to a contract are in general free to make what bargain they please, the courts lean against clauses which purport to exempt a party from the liability which would otherwise fall on him.[20] Parliament too disapproves of such clauses. So the operator of a public service vehicle is not able by contract to limit his liability in respect of the death of, or bodily injury to, any passenger other than one travelling under a free pass.[21] Formerly the owner of a private vehicle was entitled to exclude liability to a passenger by means of an aptly worded notice,[22-23] but the Road Traffic Act 1988, s.149(3) annuls all such notices or agreements. So too the duties owed under the Dangerous Premises Act 1972 are non-excludable. These trends were generalised by the Unfair Contract Terms Act 1977. Section 2 provides that liability for death or personal injury resulting from negligence cannot be excluded by businesses, while such exclusion or restriction of liability by all persons for other loss or damage is subject to the test of reasonableness. In Smith v. Eric S. Bush (A Firm)[24] the House of Lords unanimously held that the requirement of reasonableness imposed by the Unfair Contract Terms Act cannot be excluded, however wide the terms of the exemption clause. All exclusion clauses or notices must be reasonable. On the facts it was not reasonable for a firm of valuers employed by a building society to value a modest house to impose on the purchaser the risk of

---

[16] *The Goring* [1987] Q.B. 687, 708, 713. So that when it was attempted to defend a nuisance caused by noisy building operations on the ground that they were necessary to save time and money, Bennett J. said: "I cannot help being reminded of a line I remember in *Paradise Lost*: 'So spake the Fiend, and with necessity, the tyrant's plea, excused his devilish deeds.' ": *Andreae* v. *Selfridge & Co. Ltd.* [1936] 2 All E.R. 1413, 1422.

[17] Lord Devlin, *Samples of Lawmaking* (1962), p. 90.

[18] *Burmah Oil Co. Ltd.* v. *Lord Advocate* [1965] A.C. 75.

[19] *Rigby* v. *Chief Constable of Northants* [1985] 1 W.L.R. 124, 125.

[20] *Spurling (J.) Ltd.* v. *Bradshaw* [1956] 1 W.L.R. 461.

[21] Public Passenger Vehicles Act 1981, s.29.

[22-23] As in *Birch* v. *Thomas* [1972] 1 W.L.R. 294.

[24] [1990] 1 A.C. 831.

loss arising from the valuer's incompetence.[25] The common understanding of all parties in such a situation is that the report will be relied
upon by both parties to the mortgage: the purchaser is not in a position
to pay for another report himself.

Even if an exemption clause has been validly inserted in a contract,
the courts have held that general words in such a clause will not ordinarily exempt the party seeking to rely on them from liability for his
own negligence or that of his servants, unless the only scope for the
operation of the clause is the negligence of that party or his servants.[26]
But it is generally accepted that the words "howsoever caused" are
wide enough to exclude liability for negligence.[27] The question whether
a party who has been guilty of a fundamental breach of contract can rely
on an exemption clause was much discussed until finally the House of
Lords held that there was no rule of law requiring any particular construction of the contract in issue.[28] Nor in general can such a clause be
relied on by a negligent servant of the contractor: there is no doctrine of
vicarious immunity.[29] But apparently if there is a valid contract not to
sue the servant, then even though the servant could not take advantage
of such a contract, an action against him may be stayed by the court as a
fraud on the employer.[30] Where but for the contract there would be a
concurrent liability in tort and contract the contract may give express
protection to what would otherwise be a tort. The plaintiff cannot then
disregard any limitations of liability under the contract by alleging a
wider liability in tort.[31]

Disclaimers

A disclaimer may be defined as a non-contractual exclusion clause
The common law does not usually permit one who is under a duty of
care to disclaim responsibility for his actions regardless of the wishes of
others.[32] So it is impossible to disclaim liability for a dishonest statement made with intent that another shall act on it.[32a] Statutes—e.g. the
Road Traffic Act 1988, s.149(3)—also sometimes prohibit disclaimers of
liability.[33] Disclaimers in a business context, like exclusion clauses,

---

[25] Although no distinction should be made between valuers who are contractors and
those who are in-house employees, it might be reasonable to distinguish between an
ordinary suburban house and a large development, where "breathtaking sums of
money may turn on professional advice against which it would be impossible for the
adviser to obtain adequate insurance cover and which would ruin him if he were to be
held personally liable": [1990] A.C. 831, 858, per Lord Griffiths.

[26] White v. Warwick (John) & Co. Ltd. [1953] 1 W.L.R. 1285.

[27] White v. Blackmore [1972] 2 Q.B. 651.

[28] Photo Production Ltd. v. Securicor Transport Ltd. [1980] A.C. 827.

[29] Scruttons Ltd. v. Midland Silicones Ltd. [1962] A.C. 446.

[30] Gore v. Van der Lann [1967] 2 Q.B. 31.

[31] This simple proposition has had to be reasserted recently: see above, § 2.1.

[32] "Thus, to take an absurd illustration, it would obviously be irrelevant for a driver sued
in negligence to say that he had displayed a sign on the top of his car, 'No liability
accepted for any collision—keep out of the way' " Harris v. Wyre Forest District Council
[1988] Q.B. 835, 853, per Kerr L.J.

[32a] Commercial Banking Co. of Sydney Ltd. v. Brown & Co. (1972) 46 A.L.J.R. 297.

[33] See below, § 22.3.

must now satisfy the requirement of reasonableness imposed by the Unfair Contract Terms Act 1977.[34] But the Occupiers' Liability Act 1957 gave statutory permission for an occupier to disclaim the common duty of care which he owes to lawful visitors, and the disclaimer was effective even though the defence of consent was inapplicable.[35] Now, however, the Unfair Contract Terms Act 1977, as amended by the Occupiers' Liability Act 1984, s.2 enables an occupier to limit or exclude liability to recreational or educational visitors if (in effect) they are not being charged a fee for entry by a business occupier.

§ 22.3. Volenti Non Fit Injuria[36]

No injury is done to one who consents. This maxim had its origin in the process by which Roman law validated the act of a free citizen selling himself into slavery. In the nineteenth century it somehow found its way into the law of torts, in which it applies both to intentional and accidental harms.[37] It might be more helpful if a distinction was drawn between consent (as a defence to intentional harms) and assumption of risk (as a defence to negligent harm).

(1) Intentional harms: consent

No act is actionable as a tort at the suit of any person who has expressly or impliedly assented to it: *volenti non fit injuria*. No man can enforce a right which he has voluntarily waived or abandoned.[38] The maxim applies to intentional acts which would otherwise be tortious: consent, for example, to an entry on land or goods[39] which would otherwise be a trespass, or consent to physical harm which would otherwise be a battery, as in the case of involuntary contacts in a crowded street.[40] The only exception appears to be the tort of deceit.[41] So the maxim affords a defence to a physician or surgeon for an act done in the course of medical or surgical treatment, accepted as proper by a responsible body of professional opinion.[42] If the practice of the medical profession is disputed, then the court must decide on the standard of care. The defendant must establish that the plaintiff's consent was fully and freely given, but he need not tell the patient everything (unless "specifically asked"[43]). The North American doctrine of "informed consent" is not accepted in England.

What is the position if medical or surgical treatment is given to a per-

---

[34] *Smith v. Eric S. Bush (A Firm)* [1990] A.C. 831.
[35] *White v. Blackmore* [1972] 2 Q.B. 651. See above, § 11.4.
[36] See Atiyah, "Causation, Contributory Negligence, and *Volenti Non Fit Injuria*" (1965) 43 Can. Bar Rev. 609; Dias, "Consent of Parties and *Voluntas Legis*" [1966] Camb.L.J. 75; Jaffey, "*Volenti Non Fit Injuria*" [1985] C.L.J. 87.
[37] *O'Hanlon v. Electricity Supply Board* [1969] I.R. 75, 90.
[38] *Chapman v. Ellesmere* [1932] 2 K.B. 431, 463; *Buckpitt v. Oates* [1968] 1 All E.R. 1145, 1148; *Freeman v. Home Office (No. 2)* [1984] Q.B. 524, 538.
[39] *Leitch v. Leydon* [1931] A.C. 90, 109.
[40] See above, § 7.1.
[41] See above, § 18.4.
[42] See above, § 9.12.
[43] *Sidaway v. Governors of Bethlehem Royal Hospital* [1985] A.C. 871, 898.

son who, for any reason, temporary or permanent, lacks the capacity to give, or to communicate, consent to that treatment? There was no clear answer to that question until the decision of the House of Lords in *Re F.* *(Mental Patient: Sterilisation)*,[44] and even now there are uncertain areas. In *Re F.* it was held that the lawfulness of the treatment depended on whether it was in the best interests of the patient, not on whether the defences of necessity or implied consent could be made out. In a difficult case—and surely most such cases are difficult—it was suggested to be desirable to obtain a declaratory judgment in the Family Division. This is as near as English law comes to recognising paternalism: traditionally it has emphasised the integrity of the human body, and the right of each individual to decide what to do with it.[45]

If the person subjected to medical treatment is under the age of majority (now 18), the defendant may be protected by the Family Law Reform Act 1969, s.8(1). This provides that the consent of a minor who has attained the age of 16 to surgical, medical or dental treatment[46] which, in the absence of consent, would constitute a trespass to his person,[47] shall be as effective as it would be if he were of full age. The same Act, in section 8(3), provides that consents at common law retain whatever validity they have, so the House of Lords has held that a child under 16 can consent to medical treatment, including contraceptive advice and treatment, if the child has "sufficient understanding and intelligence" to comprehend what is proposed.[48] A number of guidelines have been laid down to determine whether a girl under 16 is competent to make such a decision. In wardship proceedings the court may even over-ride the preference of a competent minor.[48a]

(2) Accidental harms: assumption of risk

The maxim applies, in the second place, to consent to run the risk of accidental harm which would otherwise be actionable as due to the negligence of him who caused it. There is some authority for saying that the maxim means a waiver by the plaintiff of an admitted breach of duty, but the better view is that consent here means the agreement of the plaintiff, express or implied, to exempt the defendant from the duty of care which he would otherwise have owed.[49]

It follows that if the defendant owes to the plaintiff no duty of care at

---

[44] [1990] 2 A.C. 1, 171 ("a startling fact"). The widespread belief in the medical profession that the spouse or next-of-kin of a patient had the power to consent to treatment was almost certainly mistaken.

[45] See above, § 22.1.

[46] As defined in s.8(2), is probably limited to therapeutic procedures. It is doubtful if a minor over 16 can validly consent to a transplant or to a blood donation.

[47] Note this interesting parliamentary recognition of the difference between Trespass and Case: see above, §§ 1.2, 7.1.

[48] *Gillick* v. *West Norfolk A.H.A.* [1986] A.C. 112, 169–170.

[48a] *Re R.* [1991] 3 W.L.R. 592.

[49] *Buckpitt* v. *Oates* [1968] 1 All E.R. 1145, 1148; *McGinlay* v. *British Railways Board* [1983] 1 W.L.R. 1427, 1434. It is sometimes said that the law of negligence assumes the principle of *volenti* to be inapplicable: *Dann* v. *Hamilton* [1939] 1 K.B. 509, 517, but in *Morris* v. *Murray* [1991] 2 Q.B. 6, the C.A. held that *volenti* could be a defence to negligence.

all, no question of *volenti non fit injuria* arises. The Court of Appeal has held that spectators at games and sporting events assume the risk of any harm caused by the players unless it results from intentional or reckless conduct.[50] It would seem to follow that no participant in a game is owed the ordinary duty of care by any other participant. But the better view is that it is a question of fact in each case whether a duty exists, and that the rules of the game are a relevant but not a conclusive factor in deciding whether the defendant has taken reasonable care, or whether the plaintiff has consented to the risk.[51] So it would be relevant that the defendant was a competitor in a race in which he was expected to go "all out" to win.[52] But if the person sued is the occupier of the premises a duty of care to spectators and players may exist, although the defendant may find it easy to prove that the visitor willingly accepted the risk.[53]

If there is an express agreement to exempt the defendant from the consequences which would ordinarily follow from his negligent act no difficulty arises, except that it should be remembered that such contracts are construed strictly as against the party claiming the benefit of the exemption,[54] and that sometimes they are prohibited by statute. So Parliament has expressly provided that agreements by which businesses purport to exclude or restrict liability for death or personal injury resulting from negligence shall be void.[55] Exclusions or restrictions of liability by businesses for other heads of loss or damage must satisfy the test of reasonableness.[56] Conversely, Parliament may expressly provide that there is no liability for any particular damage suffered by a person who has voluntarily accepted the risk thereof.[57]

Otherwise it is in each case a question of fact whether a real consent to the assumption of the risk without compensation can be deduced from all the circumstances of the case.[58] The issue is whether the plaintiff has consented to run the risk, or consented to the lack of care which produces the risk, at his own expense.[59] For the issue is not whether the plaintiff voluntarily and rashly exposed himself to the risk of injury, but whether he agreed that if injury befell him the loss should be on him and not on the defendant.[60] The true question in every case is: did the

---

[50] *Wooldridge* v. *Sumner* [1963] 2 Q.B. 43. This case is open to serious criticism both on the law and the facts (see Goodhart, Note (1962) 78 L.Q.R. 490), has been distinguished in *Wilks* v. *Cheltenham Home Guard Motor Cycle Club* [1971] 1 W.L.R. 668, and can hardly be reconciled with *Condon* v. *Basi* [1985] 1 W.L.R. 8.

[51] *Condon* v. *Basi* [1985] 1 W.L.R. 866.

[52] *Wilks* v. *Cheltenham Home Guard Motor Cycle Club* [1971] 1 W.L.R. 668.

[53] *Simms* v. *Leigh Rugby Football Club Ltd.* [1969] 2 All E.R. 923.

[54] See *Wooldridge* v. *Sumner* [1963] 2 Q.B. 43, 66.

[55] Unfair Contract Terms Act 1977, s.2(1).

[56] Unfair Contract Terms Act 1977, s.2(2). See above, § 22.2.

[57] As in the Animals Act 1971, s.5(2). So a plaintiff who trespasses knowing that a savage Alsatian dog is running loose has no remedy: *Cummings* v. *Granger* [1977] Q.B. 397.

[58] *Merrington* v. *Ironbridge Metal Works Ltd.* [1952] 2 All E.R. 1101, 1103.

[59] *Kelly* v. *Farrans Ltd.* [1954] N.I. 41, 45.

[60] *Car and General Insurance Corporation Ltd.* v. *Seymour* [1956] 2 D.L.R. 369, 371–372; *Wilson* v. *Darling Island, etc. Co.* (1955) 95 C.L.R. 43, 82.

plaintiff give a real consent to the assumption of the risk without compensation; did the consent really absolve the defendant from the duty to take care?[61] It is not necessary that his consent should have been given in a *contract* under seal or supported by consideration[62]: any acts or statements from which free consent can be deduced will be sufficient for the purposes of the law of torts.[63] So if the plaintiff has in fact consented, it is irrelevant that he is a minor[64] or an alien.[65] Conversely, the defence of *volenti* cannot be successful if the plaintiff has clearly shown that he does not accept the legal risk of injury falling on him—*e.g.* by asking whether the defendant is insured,[66] or by treating a disclaimer as a joke.[67]

Three more points may be noticed. First, many of the cases in which the maxim has been considered have been cases of master and servant,[68] in which special considerations apply[69]—so much so that the defence has almost disappeared in such cases,[70] unless the claim is for breach of a statutory duty imposed directly on a fellow-workman.[71] The employer is entitled to the benefit of such an implied consent by the plaintiff workman.[72]

Secondly, the traditional form of the question (*i.e.* did the plaintiff assume the risk?) tends to disguise the fact that the defendant is setting up acceptance of the risk as a term of the undertaking, the burden of proof of which lies on him.[73]

Thirdly, the maxim may extend to a bargain to accept *future* negligent acts on the part of the defendant—a licence to commit a tort, in other words. Such a bargain or licence might be capable of arising in cases of passengers accepting lifts from drunken drivers of motor vehicles[74] or aircraft,[75] but if the act relied upon to establish consent precedes the negligence, the plaintiff is unlikely to have acquired full knowledge of the extent as well as the nature of the risk.[76] Still, the defence is certainly available in such a case,[77] for the essence of it is not so much assent to the infliction of injury as assumption of the risk of it.[78]

---

[61] *Seymour's* case [1956] 2 D.L.R. 369, 378; *Lehnert* v. *Stein* (1962) 36 D.L.R. (2d) 159, 164.
[62] *Bennett* v. *Tugwell* [1971] 2 Q.B. 267.
[63] *Wilson* v. *Darling Island, etc. Co.* (1955) 95 C.L.R. 43, 82.
[64] *Buckpitt* v. *Oates* [1968] 1 All E.R. 1145.
[65] *Geier* v. *Kujawa* [1970] 1 Lloyd's Rep. 364.
[66] As in *Nettleship* v. *Weston* [1971] 2 Q.B. 691.
[67] As in *McComiskey* v. *McDermott* [1974] I.R. 75.
[68] Also considered below, § 22.4.
[69] *Merrington* v. *Ironbridge Metal Works Ltd.* [1952] 2 All E.R. 1101, 1103.
[70] *I.C.I. Ltd.* v. *Shatwell* [1965] A.C. 656, 680, 686.
[71] *O'Hanlon* v. *Electricity Supply Board* [1969] I.R. 75, 90.
[72] *I.C.I. Ltd.* v. *Shatwell* [1965] A.C. 656.
[73] *Multinational Gas Ltd.* v. *Multinational Gas Services Ltd.* [1983] Ch. 258, 282.
[74] *Dann* v. *Hamilton* [1939] 1 K.B. 509.
[75] *Morris* v. *Murray* [1991] 2 Q.B. 6.
[76] As in *White* v. *Blackmore* [1972] 2 Q.B. 651.
[77] As in *Morris* v. *Murray* [1991] 2 Q.B. 6, 17, where "the wild irresponsibility" of the joint venture was such that the plaintiff knew the pilot of the aircraft had consumed the equivalent of 17 whiskies.
[78] *Burnett* v. *British Waterways Board* [1973] 1 W.L.R. 700.

Intoxicated drivers

One particular difficulty arises when injuries are suffered by a passenger in a motor-car driven by a person intoxicated by drink or drugs. A solution might have been found by holding that a special relationship exists whenever a passenger is aware of facts which show that the driver cannot be expected to drive other than dangerously.[79] But the courts have been reluctant to assert that an intoxicated driver owes no duty to his passenger, and have preferred to use the concepts of contributory negligence or *volenti* to defeat an unmeritorious claim. In *Dann v. Hamilton,*[80] the plaintiff, who voluntarily chose to travel by motor-car though she knew the driver was under the influence of drink and though she could have made her journey by omnibus, was injured in an accident caused by the driver's drunkenness. The defence of *volenti* was held to be capable of arising out of the relationship of the parties, although the plaintiff succeeded on the facts.[81] In any event, the Road Traffic Act 1988, s.149(2) provides, in effect, that the defence of *volenti* is not available in respect of any liability required to be covered by a policy of insurance.

§ 22.4. KNOWLEDGE NOT CONSENT

Mere knowledge of an impending wrongful act, or of the existence of a wrongfully caused danger, does not in itself amount to consent, even though no attempt is made by the plaintiff to prevent or avoid that act or danger. Consent involves an express or implied agreement that the act may be rightfully done or the danger rightfully caused. The maxim of the law is *volenti non fit injuria*, not *scienti non fit injuria*.[82] Thus in *Brunswick (Duke of) v. Harmer*[83] the plaintiff successfully sued for libel, although the only publication was the sale of a copy of the libellous paper to a person whom the plaintiff himself had instructed to buy it for the very purpose of enabling an action to be brought.

The same principle applies to the other branch of the maxim *volenti non fit injuria*, relating to the consent to run the risk of accidental harm. Accordingly a servant who knowingly works on dangerous premises or with defective plant or tools is not for that reason *ipso facto* debarred

---

[79] *Nettleship* v. *Weston* [1971] 2 Q.B. 691.
[80] [1939] 1 K.B. 509, 517–518. The case has been much criticised (Goodhart, Note (1971) 87 L.Q.R. 444), but is binding on the C.A.: *Morris* v. *Harvey* [1991] Q.B. 6, 12.
[81] Although the defence of contributory negligence was not raised in (1953) 69 L.Q.R. 317 Lord Asquith of Bishopstone explained why not), it might be available on such facts: *Owens* v. *Brimmell* [1976] 3 All E.R. 765. But it is difficult to see that in such a case the damage is caused partly by the fault of the plaintiff himself: the cause of the accident will be the same whether the plaintiff knew of the driver's drunkenness or not, unless the plaintiff was encouraging the driver's reckless conduct, as in *Pitts* v. *Hunt* [1991] 1 Q.B. 24. *Contra, Dawrant* v. *Nutt* [1961] 1 W.L.R. 253, but as Pollock would have said, this case "cannot be law as reported."
[82] *Thomas* v. *Quartemaine* (1887) 18 Q.B.D. 685, 696, *per* Bowen L.J.
[83] (1849) 14 Q.B. 185. For another aspect of this decision, see above, § 8.7.

from suing his employer when an accident happens.[84] The question is not whether he knew of the danger, but whether in fact he agreed to run the risk, in the sense that he exempted his employer from his duty not to create the danger, and agreed that if injury happened the loss should be on him and not on his employer. Knowledge of the danger may be evidence of such an agreement, but it is nothing more.[85] This principle was established by the House of Lords in the leading case of *Smith* v. *Charles Baker & Sons*,[86] and has never since been doubted. It received express recognition in the Unfair Contract Terms Act 1977, s.2(3), which states: "Where a contract term or notice purports to exclude or restrict liability from negligence a person's agreement to or awareness of it is not of itself to be taken as indicating his voluntary acceptance of any risk."

X

Other effects of knowledge

But there may be cases in which knowledge of the danger, even if it does not prove an agreement to undertake the risk within the rule in *Smith* v. *Baker*, may nevertheless be relevant to the success of the plaintiff's action for two other reasons:

(1) It may negative the existence of any negligence on the part of the defendant in causing that danger;

(2) It may establish the existence of contributory negligence on the part of the plaintiff.

In the first place, there are certain cases in which he who causes a danger fulfils his legal duty of care by giving notice of that danger to the persons whom it affects. Thus, he who lends a chattel gratuitously is probably not bound to do anything more than disclose the existence of any dangerous quality of which he actually knows and of which the borrower does not know.[87]

In the second place, there are cases in which the act of the plaintiff in knowingly running a risk created by the defendant's wrongful act amounts to contributory negligence on his own part. The assessment will depend on whether the conduct of the plaintiff was reasonable, having regard to the magnitude of the risk and the urgency of the occasion. A certain amount of risk I am entitled to face, even with full knowledge, rather than submit to being deprived of my liberty of action by the wrongful act of another. In *Clayards* v. *Dethick*,[88] the plaintiff, a cab-driver, occupied certain stables in Gower Mews, Gower Street, and the defendant wrongfully dug a trench along the passage which afforded the only outlet from the mews to the street. The plaintiff attempted to lead out one of his horses along the passage and over the heaps of soil which the defendant had excavated, and while doing so

---

[84] But "in these days of trade unions and shop stewards I very much doubt if there are many cases in which a workman would be placed in such a position": *Horton* v. *London Graving Dock Ltd.* [1949] 2 All E.R. 169, 171, *per* Lynskey J.

[85] *Neilsen* v. *Redel* [1955] 1 D.L.R. 125, 132.

[86] [1891] A.C. 325.

[87] See above, § 12.2.

[88] (1848) 12 Q.B. 439.

the horse fell into the trench and was injured. It was held that the defendant was liable; for the plaintiff was not bound to submit to be thus deprived of the use of his stables. "The whole question was, whether the danger was so obvious that the plaintiff could not with common prudence make the attempt."[89] This principle was reaffirmed by the House of Lords in *A. C. Billings & Sons Ltd.* v. *Riden.*[90] In any event, no risk can be made the ground of a charge of contributory negligence if the defendant himself requested or ordered or authorised the act of the plaintiff[91] in running the risk.

Summary

Before the Law Reform (Contributory Negligence) Act 1945, the courts did not often distinguish very clearly between the defences of *volenti non fit injuria* (or assumption of risk), remoteness of damage, and contributory negligence, for it was seldom necessary for them to do so. But today it is of great importance to keep them distinct, for while *volenti non fit injuria* and remoteness of damage still afford a complete defence there is now power to apportion the loss in cases of contributory negligence. In any event the various concepts are entirely distinct. For a plaintiff may be guilty of contributory negligence if he did not know but ought to have known of the danger which confronted him. But he can never be held to have been *volens* unless it is shown that he had full knowledge of the nature and extent of the risk.[92] Again, a plaintiff may be, and usually is, guilty of contributory negligence when he is careless for his own safety, but he may be truly *volens* even when he is exercising the utmost care for his own safety.[93]

§ 22.5. REALITY OF CONSENT

The consent must be a real consent.[94] It can hardly be doubted that consent obtained by duress (actual violence or threats of violence to the person of the plaintiff) is no real consent. If a person commits suicide, or injures himself in an unsuccessful attempt to commit suicide, he has inflicted the injury on himself, and he, or his estate, can be met by the defence of *volenti*—unless the balance of his mind was disturbed, when it is quite unrealistic to regard him as truly consenting.[95] But it is probably not enough for the plaintiff to show that his consent was given reluctantly, or under the mistaken belief that the defendant was legally entitled to act as he did.[96] If the mistake was induced by the fraud of the defendant, however, it vitiates the consent. It is true that in *Hegarty* v.

---

89 (1848) 12 Q.B. 439, *per* Patteson J. ("who, of course, was a judge of very great experience and learning": *Davies* v. *Property Corporation Ltd.* [1929] 2 K.B. 222, 228, *per* Talbot J.).

90 [1958] A.C. 240.

91 As in *Bowater* v. *Rowley Regis Corporation* [1944] K.B. 476.

92 *I.C.I. Ltd.* v. *Shatwell* [1965] A.C. 656, 672.

93 *Prior* v. *Kyle* (1965) 52 D.L.R. (2d) 272, 281.

94 *Chatterton* v. *Gerson* [1980] 3 W.L.R. 1003.

95 *Kirkham* v. *Anderton* [1990] 2 Q.B. 283.

96 *Latter* v. *Braddell* (1881) 50 L.J.Q.B. 448.

Shine[97] the plaintiff was unsuccessful in an action for assault against her paramour, who had infected her with venereal disease, but the decision of the Irish Court of Appeal was based partly on the ground that the defendant's non-disclosure of his disease was not such a fraud as to vitiate consent, and partly on the ground that *ex turpi causa non oritur actio*.[98] Again, a man cannot be said to give a real consent if he acts under the compulsion of a legal duty. Thus it is the duty of a servant to protect his master's premises from fire. If in so doing he runs risks he is not a volunteer, and, if he is injured, he will have a remedy against him whose negligence caused the fire.[99] A man cannot be said to be "willing" unless he is in a position to choose freely; and freedom of choice predicates the absence from his mind of any feeling of constraint interfering with the freedom of his will.[1]

Rescue cases[2]

The "rescue cases" hold that the same principle applies if the plaintiff has acted under a moral duty. In *Haynes* v. *Harwood*[3] the Court of Appeal laid it down that "the doctrine of the assumption of risk does not apply where the plaintiff has, under an exigency caused by the defendant's wrongful misconduct, consciously and deliberately faced a risk, even of death, to rescue another from imminent danger of personal injury or death, whether the person endangered is one to whom he owes a duty of protection, as a member of his family, or is a mere stranger to whom he owes no such special duty."[4] In that case the defendant's servant had left his van and horses unattended in a crowded street. The horses bolted when a boy threw a stone at them. The plaintiff was a police constable on duty inside a police station; he saw that if nothing was done a woman and children were in grave danger, and at great personal risk managed to stop both horses, but in so doing suffered serious personal injuries. He was entitled to damages. As the negligent act preceded the alleged consent, the case would have been a model one for the application of the maxim had not the court been able to find an exception to it.

The principle is the same when the plaintiff is under no legal duty[5] to

---

[97] (1878) 4 L.R.Ir. 288.

[98] On this maxim, see below, § 22.6.

[99] *D'Urso* v. *Sanson* (1939) 4 All E.R. 26. He may also be entitled to benefit under the Social Security Act 1975, s.54.

[1] *Bowater* v. *Rowley Regis Corporation* [1944] K.B. 476, 479; *Merrington* v. *Ironbridge Metal Works Ltd.* [1952] 2 All E.R. 1101.

[2] Mannie Brown, "A Study in Negligence" (1932) 10 Can. Bar Rev. 556; Linden, "Rescuers and Good Samaritans" (1971) 34 M.L.R. 241; Binchy, "The Good Samaritan" (1974) 25 N.I.L.Q. 147.

[3] [1935] 1 K.B. 146, followed in *Ogwo* v. *Taylor* [1988] A.C. 431 (fireman).

[4] *Per* Greer L.J., 157, citing the language of Goodhart, "Rescue and Voluntary Assumption of Risk" (1935) 5 Camb.L.J. 192, 196.

[5] The fact that the plaintiff is under a legal duty to act in the emergency which has arisen is no reason for excluding him from the rescue principle: *Ogwo* v. *Taylor* [1988] A.C. 431, 443.

effect the rescue, for example, a passer-by who is injured while rescuing a little girl from the danger of being run over by a lorry,[6] or a doctor who descends a gas-filled well to attempt to rescue two workmen overcome by fumes.[7] The principle is that if one person by his negligence causes another to be in a position of danger, he should have regard to the probability that a third person, acting bravely and promptly and subjugating any timorous over-concern for his own well-being or comfort, may attempt a rescue.[8] No distinction appears to be drawn between the rescuer who acts instinctively and the one who takes time for reflection before he encounters the risk.[9] It has even been held that a first rescuer who bungles his attempt may be liable to a second rescuer.[10] In some cases it may be argued that a plaintiff who has shown supreme courage has been "unreasonably brave," but the courts do not favour such a plea,[11] although it is possible for a rescuer's damages to be reduced on the ground of his contributory negligence.[12]

The principle also covers cases where the risk had been incurred to save property belonging to the rescuer himself[13] or to a third party,[14] or even to the defendant.[15] It is material to consider in every case whether or not it is life or property which is in danger. It is material to consider the relationship of the plaintiff who intervenes in the matter to the property in peril or to the person in peril. It is relevant to consider the degree of danger and risk, and so forth.[16] It is possible that the rescuer of property owes a duty of care to its owner.[17] The rescuer also owes to the rescued a duty to effect the rescue with reasonable care.[18]

The principle also covers cases where the person rescued, who is the defendant in the action brought by the rescuer, has been put in peril by his own negligence, and not by that of another.[19] The principle even extends to cases where the person rescued has himself no cause of action at all, for example, because he is a trespasser or has waived his rights by a contract.[20] For the duty of care owed to a rescuer is an original one; it is not derived from or secondary to any duty owed to the

---

[6] *Gregory* v. *Miller, The Times,* February 9, 1933; *Morgan* v. *Aylen* [1942] 1 All E.R. 489.
[7] *Baker* v. *T. E. Hopkins & Sons Ltd.* [1959] 1 W.L.R. 966.
[8] *Baker* v. *T. E. Hopkins & Sons Ltd.* [1959] 1 W.L.R. 966, 976, 977.
[9] *Haynes* v. *Harwood* [1935] 1 K.B. 146, 158–159, 164.
[10] *Horsley* v. *MacLaren* (1972) 22 D.L.R. (3d) 545.
[11] *Ogwo* v. *Taylor* [1988] A.C. 431, 447.
[12] *Harrison* v. *British Railways Board* [1981] 3 All E.R. 679.
[13] *Hutterley* v. *Imperial Oil Co. and Calder* (1956) 3 D.L.R. (2d) 719.
[14] *Russell* v. *McCabe* [1962] N.Z.L.R. 392.
[15] *Hyett* v. *G.W. Ry.* [1948] 1 K.B. 345.
[16] *Hyett* v. *G.W. Ry.* [1948] 1 K.B. 345, 347–348.
[17] *The Tojo Maru* [1972] A.C. 242.
[18] *The Ogopogo* [1970] 1 Lloyd's Rep. 257.
[19] *Baker* v. *T. E. Hopkins & Sons Ltd.* [1958] 1 W.L.R. 993, 1004.
[20] *Videan* v. *British Transport Commission* [1963] 2 Q.B. 650, 669. It is a little difficult to follow the reasoning whereby the Court of Appeal held that the defendants ought to have foreseen that a stationmaster would attempt to rescue an infant on the lines (the infant being the stationmaster's son), yet need not have foreseen the presence of that infant himself.

rescued person by another,[21] but is an example of the "neighbour principle" in *Donoghue* v. *Stevenson*. So it is settled that the rescuer is not deprived of remedy merely because the risk which he runs is not the same as that run by the party rescued. Indeed, the very fact of rescue involves unexpected things happening.[22] But the defendant, whether the person rescued or another, must first be proved to have been at fault. There is no liability when the defendant's negligence has not imperilled the person whose rescue the plaintiff attempted.[23]

Sometimes the courts have preferred to treat the rescue cases as raising a problem in the law relating to remoteness of damage.[24] Is the intervention of the rescuer an act which breaks the causal sequence of events set in motion by the defendant's initial act of negligence? But "If what is relied upon as *novus actus interveniens* is the very kind of thing which is likely to happen if the want of care which is alleged takes place, the principle embodied in the maxim is no defence. The whole question is whether . . . the accident can be said to be 'the natural and probable result' of the breach of duty."[25] "In answering the question it is helpful but not decisive to consider which of these events were deliberate choices to do positive acts and which were mere omissions or failures to act, which acts or omissions were innocent mistakes or miscalculations and which were negligent having regard to the pressures and gravity of the emergency and the need to act quickly."[26]

Volunteers

It is suggested that the true principle should be that one who interferes wilfully and officiously in another's affairs takes the risk of all injuries which are not inflicted in deliberate disregard of his presence. Such a person is a mere volunteer with no claim to better treatment than a trespasser.[27] This principle, however, has no application where (1) the relationship of master and servant is in fact established between the parties, or (2) the plaintiff had volunteered to save the property of another in an emergency,[28] or (3) the plaintiff had a common interest in the matter with the defendant,[29] or (4) where the defendant was in all the circumstances of the case under a duty to take reasonable care for the plaintiff's safety. Such a duty may be established when the defendant invites the plaintiff to assist him in some job of work, even though the plaintiff stands to gain nothing from it.[30]

---

[21] *Videan* v. *British Transport Commission* [1963] 2 Q.B. 650.
[22] *Chadwick* v. *British Railways Board* [1967] 1 W.L.R. 912.
[23] *Horsley* v. *MacLaren* (1972) 22 D.L.R. (3d) 545.
[24] As in *Knighley* v. *Johns* [1981] 1 W.L.R. 349.
[25] *Haynes* v. *Harwood* (1935) 1 K.B. 146, 156, *per* Greer L.J.
[26] *Knightley* v. *Johns* [1982] 1 W.L.R. 349, 366, *per* Stephenson L.J.
[27] This would be in accord with the refusal of the law of contracts to recognise the *negotiorum gestor* of Roman law. In our law liabilities are not to be forced on people behind their backs.
[28] *Cutler* v. *United Dairies Ltd.* [1933] 2 K.B. 297, 306–307.
[29] *Lomas* v. *Jones* [1944] K.B. 4.
[30] *Fitzgerald* v. *G.N.R. (I.) Ltd.* [1947] N.I. 1—a full review of the cases by MacDermott J.

§ 22.6. PLAINTIFF A WRONGDOER[31]

This is a rather obscure corner of the law. Confusion has been increased by the use of the maxim *ex turpi causa non oritur actio*, which originally had its proper field of application in the law of contract,[32] but has been extended to cases in which the plaintiff has been guilty of a crime or a tort, or even simply of conduct which "affronts public conscience."[33] There is also an overlap with the defences of consent and contributory negligence and no duty on the grounds of public policy.[34] So in *Murphy v. Culhane*[35] the Court of Appeal held that the defendant, who had pleaded guilty to the manslaughter of the plaintiff's husband, was entitled to raise all these defences in a civil action because the deceased had initiated the affray which led to his death. Meanwhile at common law it is settled that if an act is in itself a criminal act it does not cease to be criminal because the person to whose detriment it is done consents to it. "No person can license another to commit a crime."[36] Thus no person can lawfully consent to his own death, so that killing a man in a duel is murder. Nor can anyone lawfully consent to bodily harm, save for some reasonable purpose: for example, a proper surgical operation or manly sports.[37]

It is not so clear whether consent in such cases is a good defence to a civil action, although it is submitted that on principle it ought to be, provided that the wrongful act is a step in the execution of the common illegal purpose, and not totally unconnected with it. So no action for negligence lies by a passenger in a vehicle against the driver of it, if the parties were joint participants in "a reckless, irresponsible and idiotic" piece of driving, involving "moral turpitude of a high degree."[38] It may be different if the driver has, to the passenger's knowledge, simply been disqualified from driving. On the other hand, "if A and B are proceeding to the premises which they intend burglariously to enter, and before they enter them, B picks A's pocket and steals his watch, I cannot prevail on myself to believe that A could not sue in tort."[39] In such a case the appropriate principle is that the mere fact that the plaintiff is a wrongdoer is no defence.[40] Some other examples of this principle may be offered. One who is a trespasser on land cannot be maltreated with impunity by the occupier,[41] and one who is in breach of the obligations

---

[31] See Crago, "The Defence of Illegality in Negligence Actions" (1964) 4 M.U.L.R. 534; Fridman, "The Wrongdoing Plaintiff" (1972) 18 McGill L.J. 276.

[32] *Smith* v. *Jenkins* (1970) 119 C.L.R. 379, 410.

[33] *Kirkham* v. *Anderton* [1990] 2 Q.B. 283, 291.

[34] As in *Pitts* v. *Hunt* [1991] 1 Q.B. 24, in which all the authorities are reviewed.

[35] [1977] Q.B. 94.

[36] *R.* v. *Donovan* [1934] 2 K.B. 498, 507.

[37] *Bravery* v. *Bravery* [1954] 1 W.L.R. 1169.

[38] *Pitts* v. *Hunt* [1991] 1 Q.B. 24, 51.

[39] *National Coal Board* v. *England* [1954] A.C. 403, 428, per Lord Asquith of Bishopstone. If the plaintiff in *Donoghue* v. *Stevenson* had stolen the bottle of ginger-beer, would she have been successful? It is suggested that she would, because historically, causally, and morally, there is no significant relationship between the theft and the damage.

[40] *Green* v. *Costello* [1961] N.Z.L.R. 1010.

[41] Above, § 11.9.

for ensuring safety imposed by the Factories Act, or the Mines and Quarries Act, is not debarred from suing although his damages may be reduced on the ground of contributory negligence.[42] It would be helpful if a statute briefly provided that it shall not be a defence merely to show that the plaintiff is in breach of the civil or criminal law.

§ 22.7. STATUTORY AUTHORITY[43]

When a statute authorises a certain act to be done by a certain person, which would otherwise be unlawful and actionable, no action will lie at the suit of any person for the doing of that act. For such a statutory authority is a statutory indemnity, taking away all legal remedies provided by the law of torts for persons injuriously affected. No compensation is obtainable save that, if any, which is expressly provided by the statute itself. The principle is not confined to statutory duties, whereby the defendant is obliged to act, but also extends to statutory powers.[44] This defence of statutory authority has its most important application in actions of nuisance, but it is one of general application throughout the whole sphere of civil liability. The statutory authority and indemnity extends not merely to the act itself but also to all its necessary consequences.[45] When the legislature has authorised an act, it must be deemed also to have authorised by implication all inevitable results of that act; for otherwise the authority to do the act would be nugatory. So that when the Gulf Oil Refining Act 1965 authorised a company to acquire land for a refinery it by necessary implication authorised the use of such a refinery, which otherwise would have been "nothing more than a visual adornment to the landscape in an area of natural beauty."[46] The test of the necessity of a consequence is the impossibility of avoiding it by the exercise of due care and skill.

> "The onus of proving that the result is inevitable is on those who wish to escape liability for nuisance, but the criterion of inevitability is not what is theoretically possible but what is possible according to the state of scientific knowledge at the time, having also in view a certain common-sense appreciation, which cannot be rigidly defined, of practical feasibility in view of situation and of expense."[47]

But once it is established that the interference exceeded that which would inevitably have resulted from the works authorised the statutory immunity is lost. In *Tate & Lyle Ltd.* v. *Greater London Council*[48] the defendants, acting under statutory authority, erected ferry terminals in

---

[42] *National Coal Board* v. *England* [1954] A.C. 403.

[43] See also above, § 9.14, and Craig, "Compensation in Public Law" (1980) 96 L.Q.R. 413.

[44] *London, Brighton and South Coast Railway Co.* v. *Truman* (1886) 11 App.Cas. 45.

[45] Where the statute is one conferring a power, then the wider the discretion the greater will be the scope for contending that harm inflicted was unnecessary: *Metropolitan Asylum District Managers* v. *Hill* (1881) 6 App.Cas. 193.

[46] *Allen* v. *Gulf Oil Refining* [1981] A.C. 1004, 1014, *per* Lord Diplock.

[47] *Manchester Corporation* v. *Farnworth* [1930] A.C. 171, 183, *per* Lord Dunedin. See *Provender Millers* v. *Southampton C.C.* [1940] Ch. 131, 136–140, 150.

[48] [1983] 2 A.C. 509.

the River Thames. The design adopted caused excessive siltation of the river bed thereby interfering with the public right of navigation causing the plaintiffs to suffer damage. A different design was available which would have minimised the siltation. The House of Lords held that reasonable care would have led to the adoption of this other design and found for the plaintiffs. Thus where avoidable interference has been caused this will often be due to negligence, which the statute will be deemed not to have authorised and for which liability will be imposed.[49] If the avoidable interference does not involve carelessness on the defendant's part the position is less clear. But the courts seem to lean against the imposition of liability for torts of strict liability upon those acting under statutory authority.[50] Some authorising statutes expressly preserve the liability of statutory undertakers for "nuisance," but without indicating whether this is meant to include situations in which the defendants have not been at fault. In practice, however, the courts are reluctant to construe such provisions so as to impose liability on statutory undertakers where all proper precautions have been taken but interference equivalent to nuisance has nevertheless occurred.[51]

Discretionary powers

The imposition of ordinary negligence liability upon those acting under statutory authority, whose carelessness simply causes them to forfeit the protection they would otherwise have enjoyed, needs to be distinguished from a recently developed body of doctrine whereby a special kind of negligence liability may be imposed upon those exercising discretionary powers. In these cases the existence of the statutory power itself provides the basis for an allegation of carelessness which could not have been made without it.

It has long been clear that if a statute imposes a duty, then a breach of that duty may be actionable in tort subject to certain tests and rules of construction.[52] But if there was a statutory power or discretion it was formerly held that there could be no complaint about its exercise until the plaintiff suffered more harm than if nothing at all had been done.[53] In *Anns* v. *Merton London Borough Council*,[54] however, the law was restated.[55] No change was propounded in the accepted principles governing actions for breach of statutory duties. But if the case involved a statutory power, then a further distinction was to be drawn between policy or planning decisions and operational decisions. According to dicta in the Privy Council this distinction:

---

[49] *Geddis* v. *Proprietors of Bann Reservoir* (1878) 3 App.Cas. 430, 455, *per* Lord Blackburn.
[50] *Dunne* v. *North-Western Gas Board* [1964] 2 Q.B. 806.
[51] *Department of Transport* v. *North West Water Authority* [1984] A.C. 336; *Smeaton* v. *Ilford Corporation* [1954] Ch. 450. *Cf. Midwood & Co.* v. *Manchester Corporation* [1905] 2 K.B. 597.
[52] See Chap. 10, above, for the complex law on this matter.
[53] *East Suffolk Rivers Catchment Board* v. *Kent* [1941] A.C. 140.
[54] [1978] A.C. 728.
[55] See also *Fellows* v. *Rother D.C.* [1983] 1 All E.R. 513, 522 (Goff J.).

"is expressive of the need to exclude altogether those cases in which the decision under attack is of such a kind that a question whether it has been made negligently is unsuitable for judicial resolution, of which notable examples are discretionary decisions on the allocation of scarce resources or the distribution of risks."[56]

So in *Anns* itself, which concerned building control, the question of how many, if any, building inspectors should be appointed was a matter of policy for which the council were responsible only to the electors. But the question whether there was carelessness in carrying out an inspection was an operational matter for which the council would be vicariously responsible if the plaintiff could prove his case by interrogatories or otherwise. As a matter of general principle this particular aspect of the decision in *Anns* would not appear to have been affected by the overruling of that case on another point in *Murphy v. Brentwood District Council.*[57] In practice, however, its utility is likely to be substantially reduced since pure economic loss, which is the kind of harm negligent public authorities are perhaps most likely to cause, is no longer to be recoverable in tort as a result, indeed, of the overruling of *Anns* itself in its other context. Nevertheless cases involving personal injury or damage to property can arise,[58] so this area of the law remains a significant one.

The position is that policy decisions are a matter of public law alone, but while operational decisions *may* give rise to a common law duty of reasonable care they will not necessarily do so.[59] Indeed whether the statutory framework permits the imposition of such a duty cannot be answered simply by an invocation of the neighbour principle. A closer analysis of the alleged carelessness, and of the particular statute in question, will be required before the relevant degree of proximity can be discovered. Thus the House of Lords[60] and the Privy Council[61] have demonstrated that claims will fail if scrutiny of the statute conferring the power indicates that general public benefit, rather than compensation for specific individuals, was its purpose.[62] Moreover other recent decisions, also at the highest level, have emphasised the undesirability of unduly inhibiting the work of those discharging public responsibilities, such as the police[63] or Ministers of the Crown,[64] by causing

---

[56] *Rowling v. Takaro Properties Ltd.* [1988] A.C. 473, 501.

[57] [1991] 1 A.C. 398. See above, Chap. 9.

[58] See *Home Office v. Dorset Yacht Co. Ltd.* [1970] A.C. 1004. See also *Hill v. Chief Constable of West Yorkshire* [1989] A.C. 53.

[59] *Rowling v. Takaro Properties Ltd.* [1988] A.C. 473.

[60] See *Peabody Donation Fund Governors v. Sir Lindsay Parkinson & Co. Ltd.* [1985] A.C. 210.

[61] See *Yuen Kun-yeu v. Att.-Gen. of Hong Kong* [1988] A.C. 175.

[62] It is possible that *Anns* itself would now be decided differently even on this point, *i.e.* if a case on similar facts were to recur involving, say, personal injury so that the plaintiff did not fall at the first hurdle of the economic loss point. The House of Lords reserved its opinion on this question in *Murphy v. Brentwood District Council* [1991] 1 A.C. 398, 457 (Lord Mackay), 463 (Lord Keith), 479 (Lord Bridge), 492 (Lord Jauncey).

[63] *Hill v. Chief Constable of West Yorkshire* [1989] A.C. 53 (House of Lords).

[64] *Rowling v. Takaro Properties Ltd.* [1988] A.C. 473 (Privy Council).

them to be constantly in fear of negligence actions even in largely operational, and hence justiciable, situations.[65]

§ 22.8. CONTRIBUTORY NEGLIGENCE: PRELIMINARY[66]

Contributory negligence once comprised one of the most difficult branches of the law. Fortunately, however, the Law Reform (Contributory Negligence) Act 1945, and several decisions of the highest courts, have introduced a straightforward and comprehensive body of principles in place of a mass of subtle arguments and tedious refinements. The present law embodies two distinct principles which do not always harmonise. The doctrine that if the plaintiff's act was the proximate cause of the damage the plaintiff could not recover was a well-established principle of medieval law. In the sixteenth and seventeenth centuries the conception of negligence as a ground of liability worked its way into the common law. Therefore a practice grew up of alleging that a plaintiff could not recover because he was debarred by his own negligence. So we find a penal theory of contributory negligence.[67] In the same way it is common to speak of a plaintiff as being "guilty" of contributory negligence. But the penal theory is inconsistent with the application of the law by the courts. A plaintiff may have been ever so negligent at some stage of the proceedings, but he will be able to recover if his negligence did not contribute to the accident, even if his negligence was criminal. On the other hand, the doctrine of contributory negligence is more than an application of the rule as to remoteness of damage. For if a third party is injured the negligence of each—both the plaintiff and the defendant—is treated as a cause of the accident: each is liable to the third party.[68] Nor is the defence of contributory negligence an application of the maxim *volenti non fit injuria*, although the two principles have often been confused.[69] The defence of contributory negligence confesses and avoids a prima facie liability, it excludes the idea of deliberation, and relies upon the failure of the plaintiff to exercise reasonable care. Of the defence that the plaintiff has consented to run the risk, none of these three statements is true.

§ 22.9. CONTRIBUTORY NEGLIGENCE: THE COMMON LAW

"The rule of law," said Lord Blackburn,[70] "is that if there is blame causing the accident on both sides, however small that blame may be on one

---

[65] There appears to be a greater readiness to impose liability upon public bodies in Canada: see the decisions of the Supreme Court in *Just* v. *British Columbia* [1989] 2 S.C.R. 1228 and *City of Kamloops* v. *Nielsen* [1984] 2 S.C.R. 2.

[66] Further information: Williams, *Joint Torts and Contributory Negligence*; Fleming, "Comparative Negligence At Last" (1976) 64 Calif.L.Rev. 239.

[67] See *Wakelin* v. *L.S.W. Ry.* (1886) 12 App.Cas. 41, 45.

[68] *Grant* v. *Sun Shipping Co.* [1948] A.C. 549, 563–564. See the cases on the doctrine of identification, below, § 22.13, and the valuable brochure published in Tasmania in 1936 entitled *Negligence, Contributory Negligence and Damage Sustained by a Third Party*, and written by the Hon. Mr. Justice Clark of the Tasmanian Supreme Court.

[69] See also above, § 22.4.

[70] *Cayzer, Irvine & Co.* v. *Carron Co.* (1884) 9 App.Cas. 873, 881.

side, the loss lies where it falls." Thus in *Butterfield* v. *Forrester*[71] the defendant wrongfully obstructed a street in Derby by placing a pole across it, and the plaintiff rode along the street "at eight o'clock in the evening of August, when they were just beginning to light candles," but while there was still sufficient light to notice the obstruction, and coming into collision with the pole he was thrown from his horse and injured. It was held that he had no cause of action, as he could, notwithstanding the defendant's negligence, have avoided the accident by the use of due care.

Principle in Davies v. Mann

It soon became apparent however, that there were cases where there was so substantial a difference between the position of the two parties at the material time that, although the accident would not have occurred without the plaintiff's negligence, it would not be fair or reasonable to regard him as the author of his own wrong. This is the fundamental (though seldom openly expressed) idea behind a series of cases which begin with *Davies* v. *Mann*.[72] In this case the plaintiff negligently left his donkey, with its legs tied, in the highway. The defendant, driving his waggon and horses "at a smartish pace," crashed into the animal and killed it. It was held that the defendant was liable. "Although the ass may have been wrongfully there," said Parke B.,[73] "still the defendant was bound to go along the road at such a pace as would be likely to prevent mischief. Were this not so, a man might justify the driving over goods left on a public highway, or even over a man lying asleep there, or the purposely running against a carriage going on the wrong side of the road." In this case the expression "contributory negligence" was not used, nor is it clear whether the defendant did or did not see the ass; he probably did see it but too late.[74]

Salmond invents the last opportunity rule

The doctrine laid down in these cases with the object of mitigating the harshness of the original common law rule has often been called (although not in the cases themselves) the doctrine, or rule, of the "last opportunity," the "last clear opportunity," or the "last clear chance." Indeed, the first person to use the term appears to have been Salmond himself. Writing in 1912[75] he summarised the effect of the cases at that time in the following words[76]: "*Ex hypothesi* in all cases of contributory negligence the defendant has been guilty of negligence which caused

---

[71] (1809) 11 East 60. This case is commonly cited as the source of the doctrine but the term "contributory negligence" is not used in it and the conception can be traced further back.

[72] (1842) 10 M. & W. 546.

[73] *Ibid.* 549. ("Probably the most acute and accomplished lawyer this country ever saw": *Brinsmead* v. *Harrison* (1871) L.R. 7 C.P. 547, 554, *per* Blackburn J.).

[74] This is the accepted view. Rand J. thought he did not: *Bruce* v. *MacIntyre* [1955] 1 D.L.R. 785, 787.

[75] 3rd ed., pp. 39–43; 6th ed., pp. 40–42.

[76] Which were cited with approval by the High Court of Australia in *Alford* v. *Magee* (1952) 84 C.L.R. 437, 456.

the accident: therefore in all cases he could by the exercise of reasonable care have avoided the accident; and therefore . . . he is liable notwithstanding the contributory negligence of the plaintiff. Clearly, therefore, something more than a mere opportunity of avoiding the accident by reasonable care is required in order to bring the rule in *Davies* v. *Mann* into operation. . . . Subject to certain qualifications, it would seem that the true test is the existence of the *last* opportunity of avoiding the accident. . . . "

This admirable passage is open to discussion on two points. First, it necessarily required modification in later editions in order to accommodate the strange case of *British Columbia Electric Ry.* v. *Loach.*[77] From *Loach's* case it appears that a last opportunity which the defendant would have had but for his own negligence is equivalent in law to one which he actually had.[78]

Secondly, Salmond's use of the phrase "the last opportunity" was understood as suggesting that such an opportunity must have been always available to one or other of the parties, although "this is clearly remote from what the author meant."[79] The fallacy of the notion that the test of the last opportunity was a rule of law applicable over the whole field of contributory negligence can be demonstrated most readily by reference to the very common case of a highway collision between two modern fast-moving vehicles, for here the maximum period of time available to either party for avoiding the accident is seldom as much as a few seconds. Yet it was in just such a case that the House of Lords was invited to say that Humphreys J. had misdirected a Cambridge special jury by refusing to leave to them the issue of the last opportunity and asking them instead to answer the simple question: whose negligence was it that substantially caused the injury?[80] But the House held that in the circumstances of that case (a crossroads collision between a car and a motorcycle) that was a sufficient direction.[81] Henceforward this interpretation of the rule of last opportunity became increasingly suspect and finally it was abandoned in *The Boy Andrew (Owners)* v. *St. Rognvald (Owners).*[82]

---

[77] [1916] 1 A.C. 719.

[78] Few decisions given by so eminent a tribunal (Lord Sumner delivered the judgment of a Board composed of himself, Lord Haldane and Lord Parker of Waddington) have given rise to so much criticism. "The truth is that no one knows precisely what is settled": Williams, *Contributory Negligence*, p. 234.

[79] *Alford* v. *Magee* (1952) 85 C.L.R. 437, 457.

[80] *Swadling* v. *Cooper* [1931] A.C. 1.

[81] Yet it should be noticed that the jury returned to court and told the judge that they did not understand it. (This lends point to the remarks of du Parcq L.J. in *Gibby* v. *East Grinstead Gas Co.* [1944] 1 All E.R. 358, 363: "Unless the trial had taken place in a university city and it had happened that the jury was composed mainly of philosophers and logicians, I doubt if a discussion of theories of causation would have either assisted or interested them.") The jury's difficulty was no doubt caused by the fact that although the question was perfectly sensible they could not (as the law then stood) return a sensible answer to it. For if they replied: "They both caused it," as they would rightly wish to do, and did, the plaintiff would recover nothing—as in fact happened. See Monteith, Note (1949) 65 L.Q.R. 318.

[82] [1948] A.C. 140, 148–149. (In [1947] 2 All E.R. 350, *sub nom.* (more correctly) *Admiralty Commissioners* v. *North of Scotland and Orkney and Shetland Steam Navigation Co.*).

Conclusion[83]

A number of other judicial statements of high authority[84] have made it clear that the rule of last opportunity, in this incorrect sense of the term, suffered a demise quite independently of the Act of 1945.[85] Indeed, it may well be that in this sense the rule was never really law at all, for it seems to have been adopted in no case of good authority in any jurisdiction in the Commonwealth. As the High Court of Australia has said[86]: "It is a sound 'rule,' only if it is framed in the terms in which it was originally framed by Salmond, and if it is recognised that it does not cover the whole ground. If it is expanded in a hopeless attempt to meet cases to which it is inappropriate, and subjected to innumerable refinements, it becomes not merely unsound but unintelligible." The last opportunity rule as such no longer exists in England.[87]

§ 22.10. CONTRIBUTORY NEGLIGENCE: IN ADMIRALTY

Before the Law Reform (Contributory Negligence) Act 1945 is discussed it may be helpful to indicate the rules of maritime law governing collisions at sea. For although by section 3(1) of the Law Reform (Contributory Negligence) Act that Act does not apply to any claim to which section 1 of the Maritime Conventions Act 1911 applies, the principles to be applied at common law are now the same as those applied in admiralty. The Maritime Conventions Act enabled the court to apportion the loss according to the degree to which each party was in fault, but the court had first to decide whether the fault of either vessel had contributed to the loss or damage suffered. This problem was in general solved by applying the principles familiar to the courts of common law: "The legal doctrine of causation in admiralty law was not different from the rule at common law—it merely differed in respect of the consequences."[88]

---

[83] See the full survey by Casswell, "Avoiding Last Clear Chance" (1990) 69 Can.B.R. 129.

[84] Speaking of the period after *Swadling* v. *Cooper*, Lord du Parcq said: "But the 'rule of the last opportunity' still haunted the courts. I well remember the pained expression which used to appear on the faces of some counsel when, as a comparatively young judge, I irreverently expressed doubts about its existence. I might have been Betsy Prig questioning the existence of Mrs. Harris, 'Have I know'd Mrs. Harris five-and-thirty year,' said Mrs. Gamp, 'to be told at last that there ain't no such person living?' Perhaps Betsy Prig was not the only unbeliever, certainly I was not, and now the daring statement of the Law Revision Committee that 'there is no such rule' has been adopted and authoritatively affirmed by Viscount Simon *ex cathedra* in the House of Lords. . . . How much has been swept away with the debris of the rule—what a mass of verbal refinements, of logic-chopping, of the results of pointless microscopical research!": *Aspects of the Law* (Holdsworth Club, 1948), p. 22.

[85] *Davies* v. *Swan Motor Co.* [1949] 2 K.B. 291, 318, 321; *Jones* v. *Livox Quarries Ltd.* [1952] 2 Q.B. 608, 615.

[86] *Alford* v. *Magee* (1952) 85 C.L.R. 437, 460.

[87] *Chisman* v. *Electromatic (Export) Ltd.* (1969) 6 K.I.R. 456, 458–459; *Lloyd's Bank* v. *Budd* (1982) R.T.R. 80, 83.

[88] *Davies* v. *Swan Motor Co.* [1949] 2 K.B. 291, 310, *per* Bucknill L.J.

The principle in The Volute

The "rule of last opportunity," in the erroneous sense which has already been explained, was, however, never accepted in admiralty. There was no place for it. It had been invented by the courts of common law as an exception to their general rule that the contributory negligence of the plaintiff defeated his claim, but since the Court of Admiralty did not recognise that rule there was no need for the exception. All this was made plain in the memorable speech of Viscount Birkenhead L.C. in *The Volute*,[89] which received the rare distinction of warm approval from the other members of the House.[90] Lord Birkenhead said:

> "Upon the whole I think that the question of contributory negligence must be dealt with somewhat broadly and upon common-sense principles as a jury would probably deal with it. And while no doubt, where a clear line can be drawn, the subsequent negligence is the only one to look to, there are cases in which the two acts come so closely together, and the second act of negligence is so much mixed up with the state of things brought about by the first act, that the party secondly negligent, while not held free from blame under the *Bywell Castle* rule,[91] might, on the other hand, invoke the prior negligence as being part of the cause of the collision so as to make it a case of contribution."

§ 22.11. CONTRIBUTORY NEGLIGENCE: THE ACT OF 1945[92]

The Law Reform (Contributory Negligence) Act 1945, by section 1(1), provides as follows: "Where any person suffers damage[93] as the result partly of his own fault[94] and partly of the fault of any other person or persons, a claim in respect of that damage shall not be defeated by reason of the fault of the person suffering the damage, but the damages

---

[89] [1922] 1 A.C. 129, 144.

[90] "I regard the judgment to which we have just listened as a great and permanent contribution to our law on the subject of contributory negligence, and to the science of jurisprudence": Lord Finlay (with whom Lord Shaw concurred) at 145. But it has been said that the speech was really written by Lord Phillimore, and that Lord Finlay's effusive praise was in truth subtle denigration: Lord Wright (1950) 13 M.L.R. 17; Goodhart, 7 J.S.P.T.L. 181. The speech (whatever its source) has been consistently cited with approval.

[91] For this rule, see below, § 22.12.

[92] See Taggart, "Contributory Negligence" (1977) 3 Auckland Univ.L.Rev. 140; Fagelson, "The Last Bastion of Fault?" (1979) 42 M.L.R. 646; Hudson, "Contributory Negligence as a Defence to Battery" (1984) 4 L.S. 332; Chandler, "Contributory Negligence and Contract" (1989) 40 N.I.L.Q. 152.

[93] "Includes loss of life and personal injury": s.4. The word has been held to cover a case in which the plaintiff's lack of care contributes to the extent of his injury rather than to the accident: *O'Connell* v. *Jackson* [1972] 1 Q.B. 270 (failure to wear crash helmet).

[94] "Means negligence, breach of statutory duty or other act or omission which gives rise to a liability in tort or would, apart from this Act, give rise to the defence of contributory negligence": s.4. The definition has been extended to liability for animals: see the Animals Act 1971, ss.10 and 11. As the Act expressly contemplates that a plaintiff in breach of some statutory duty imposed upon him may yet recover part of his damages, the defence of *ex turpi causa non oritur actio* cannot be raised in such a case: see above, § 22.6.

recoverable in respect thereof shall be reduced to such extent as the court thinks just and equitable having regard to the claimant's share in the responsibility for the damage: . . . " Although the statutory definition of fault seems to authorise a reduction of damages because the plaintiff has been guilty of a tort *or* of contributory negligence, in the great majority of cases it has been assumed that contributory negligence must be proved against the plaintiff, and not just (say) a breach of statutory duty.[95] The court cannot of its own motion reduce the plaintiff's damages: the defence of contributory negligence must be pleaded.[96] If the defendant does not plead contributory negligence, and there seems to be some reluctance to do so outside the area of personal injuries, then the court may be tempted to distort the scope of the relevant duty to do justice.[97] On the other hand in personal injuries cases the defence is often pleaded as a matter of routine and without any real justification. In such a case the plaintiff should request further and better particulars of the defence.

Scope of defence. It is probable that the provisions of the Act are not limited to those cases in which the defendant is charged with negligence, "as though the negligences belong to the same pack and one trumps the other."[98] This would seem to follow from the definition of "fault" in section 4. The rules on contributory negligence therefore apply to actions for breach of statutory duty,[99] nuisance,[1] and also to actions for breach of the duties owed by occupiers of dangerous premises.[2] On the other hand the Act has been interpreted narrowly, in the sense that the requirement that the defence could have been pleaded "apart from this Act" (s.4) has been held to mean that the defence cannot be pleaded (and so damages apportioned) in claims based on assault or battery.[3] This may be only an illustration of the general principle that contributory negligence is irrelevant to an intentional tort such as intimidation or conspiracy.[4] Secondly, whatever the position at common law, the defence is not available in actions based on trespass to goods or conversion.[5] Thirdly, the defence does not apply to claims based purely on breach of contract.[6] It seems that the defendant in an action for breach of a duty imposed by a contract cannot plead that the

---

[95] See *Westwood* v. *Post Office* [1974] A.C. 1.
[96] *Fookes* v. *Slayton* [1978] 1 W.L.R. 1293.
[97] This may be what happened in the difficult *Peabody* case: see [1985] A.C. 210, 231.
[98] *Caswell* v. *Powell Duffryn Collieries Ltd.* [1940] A.C. 152, 165, *per* Lord Atkin.
[99] As under the Animals Act 1971.
[1] *Trevett* v. *Lee* [1955] 1 W.L.R. 113, 121.
[2] See § 11.4.
[3] See above, § 7.4.
[4] *Dellabarra* v. *Northern Storemen and Packers Union* [1989] 2 N.Z.L.R. 731.
[5] The Torts (Interference with Goods) Act 1977, s.12(1) specifically so provides. See above, § 6.7.
[6] There was curious uncertainty about this elementary point until the decision of the C.A. in *Forsikringsaktieselskapet Vesta* v. *Butcher* [1989] A.C. 852 (the decision was not challenged in the H.L.). But as Sir Roger Ormrod said ([1989] A.C. 852, 879), if contributory negligence had been a defence to a contractual claim before 1945, the reports would have been full of references to it.

plaintiff is guilty of contributory negligence unless the contractual duty is coterminous with a tortious one.[7] It is curious that a plaintiff in an action for personal injuries should be able to recover in full if he proves a breach of contract not dependent on fault, but is liable to have his damages reduced if he proves a tort, especially as a plaintiff now has the option of suing either in contract or in tort.

Section 1(3) of the 1945 Act incorporates the law relating to apportionment of liability between joint tortfeasors.[8] This means that when a collision has been caused by the fault of two parties, and a third party also suffers damage, partly as the result of his own fault and partly as the result of the faults of the first two parties, the plaintiff's conduct should be weighed against the totality of the defendants' conduct. There is then one judgment against the tortfeasors separately. After this has been done, the court should turn to the contribution proceedings, in which there is one sum forming the subject-matter of several judgments.[9]

§ 22.12. BASIS OF APPORTIONMENT

When a court has decided, according to the principles already discussed, that the case is one in which it is proper to apportion the loss between the parties, the result is that the claimant's damages are "reduced to such extent as the court thinks just and equitable having regard to the claimant's share in the responsibility for the damage."[10] There may be sub-apportionments in respect of subsequent heads of damage properly traceable to the original disaster.[11]

There has been some discussion whether the apportionment is to be made on the basis of responsibility or of fault. It is significant that (unlike the Maritime Conventions Act 1911) the Act of 1945 does not contain the word "cause."[12] While responsibility (or fault) is not to be equated with causation, it does flow from causation in the sense that it is settled[13] that if there is no causation there is no tort.[14] But if there is causation, so that the plaintiff is contributorily negligent, then his damages must be reduced by some proportion. The Act requires that the damages "shall be reduced," so the court cannot refuse to make any

---

[7] The Law Commission has this difficult subject under review.

[8] See above, § 20.12.

[9] Fitzgerald v. Lane [1989] A.C. 328. So a plaintiff guilty of contributory negligence does not have to carry the risk of the insolvency of one of the co-defendants.

[10] s.1.(1).

[11] The Calliope [1970] P. 172.

[12] "That Act, with which I had some slight connection as a member of the Law Revision Committee, carefully avoided all references to the word 'causation.' While it was being finally prepared by Lord Simon, the then Lord Chancellor, I discussed it with him, and he emphasised that he was not going to allow any idea of causation to confuse the issue": Goodhart, "Appeals on Questions of Fact" (1955) 71 L.Q.R. 402, 413–414. Simon himself wrote to Winfield on June 14, 1945: "of course the law as to what constitutes contributory negligence is not altered by my Bill at all; it is the effect of it upon the rights of the parties which is changed" (Simon Papers).

[13] See above, § 9.2.

[14] O'Sullivan v. Dwyer [1971] I.R. 275, 284.

reduction merely because it thinks it just and equitable to do so.[15] It is necessary to consider not only the causative potency of a particular act but also its blameworthiness.[16] So if a pedestrian is struck by a motorist while crossing the road, and both driver and pedestrian have a clear view of each other, while the causative factors of the accident are in one sense equal, nevertheless the motorist may be held much more to blame than the pedestrian, who is going at perhaps three miles per hour and has to look both sides as well as forwards.[17] But culpability here, as elsewhere in the law of torts,[18] means not so much moral blameworthiness as a departure from the standard of care of the reasonable man.[19] For it would be as misleading to place the whole emphasis on "fault" as it would be to place it on "causation."[20] The court must also consider a third factor—namely, what is "just and equitable."[21] Hence the precise percentage by which the award is reduced is a question of fact in each case. The respective faults are not to be assessed according to some mathematical computation, but by looking at the matter broadly.[22] But it is wrong to assess the plaintiff's contributory negligence, even if massive, at 100 per cent., for the plaintiff's negligence is contributory to that of the defendant.[23] Conversely, there is no rule that the plaintiff's contributory negligence cannot be assessed at less than 10 per cent., although in practice minute percentages are rare.[24] The combined percentages must, of course, total 100 per cent. and not some lesser figure.[25]

The following additional points should be noticed.

(1) By section 1(2) the court should find and record the total damages which would have been awarded if the claimant had not been at fault.[26]

(2) An appellate court, in a case in which the findings of fact are not disputed,[27] will interfere with the apportionment made at the trial only when it is clearly wrong: it will not interfere merely because its members might themselves have made a different apportionment.[28] This principle is easy to state, but in practice its application varies from time to time. At one time the House of Lords was ready to alter apportionments even though one or more of the Law Lords agreed with the trial judge,[29] and this

---

[15] *Boothman* v. *British Northrop Ltd.* (1972) 13 K.I.R. 112, 122.
[16] *Keaney* v. *British Railways Board* [1968] 1 W.L.R. 879, 893; *Froom* v. *Butcher* [1976] Q.B. 286, 292.
[17] *Baker* v. *Willoughby* [1970] A.C. 467.
[18] See above, § 2.6.
[19] *O'Sullivan* v. *Dwyer* [1971] I.R. 275, 286.
[20] See Lamb Q.C., *arguendo* in *Stapley's* case [1953] A.C. 663, 670.
[21] *Turner* v. *Ford Motor Co. Ltd.* [1965] 1 W.L.R. 948, 953–954.
[22] *Gregory* v. *Kelly* [1978] R.T.R. 426.
[23] *Pitts* v. *Hunt* [1991] 1 Q.B. 24. Yet in factory accident cases the C.A. has taken a different view: *Jayes* v. *IMI (Kynoch) Ltd.* [1985] I.C.R. 155.
[24] *Capps* v. *Miller* [1989] 1 W.L.R. 839, 849.
[25] *Black* v. *McCabe* [1964] N.L. 1.
[26] *Kelly* v. *Stockport Corporation* [1949] 1 All E.R. 893.
[27] For the powers of an appellate court in this respect, see above, § 9.15.
[28] *Sigurdson* v. *British Columbia Electric Ry.* [1955] A.C. 291.
[29] *Stapley* v. *Gypsum Mines Ltd.* [1953] A.C. 663; *National Coal Board* v. *England* [1954] A.C. 403.

made the Court of Appeal less restrained.[30] Later that court emphatically rebutted the suggestion that it was ready to alter the trial judge's attribution. "If there is any widespread belief to that effect at the Bar, it should be discarded."[31] But more recently the court has reverted to its earlier position, and stated that it has the same attitude to apportionment as it has to damages.[32]

(3) Costs may be[33] apportioned between the parties on the same basis as the loss.

Finally, it must be conceded that there is some unreality about these rules, as only a minute percentage of personal injury cases proceeds to trial. The practising lawyer may do better to heed the following advice[34]:

"It is sometimes helpful to compromise by accepting a higher percentage of contributory negligence but with the insurer's representative agreeing to the more generous valuation proposed by the plaintiff's solicitor, with the result that the client ends up with the same amount of money and the insurer's representative is able to report that he has negotiated a settlement with a high degree of contributory negligence."

§ 22.13. What Negligence is Contributory

Such then are the main causes of the confusion which has prevailed in the law of contributory negligence. With them present to our minds we will endeavour to state the governing principles of this defence, leaving aside for the moment any question arising out of *Davies* v. *Mann*. The present law may be summarised in the following propositions.

(1) Plaintiff need not owe any duty to defendant

The question of contributory negligence does not depend upon any breach of duty as between the plaintiff and the defendant.[35] This is a significant exception to the general principle that the question whether the plaintiff's conduct amounts to contributory negligence is to be decided according to the same principles as the question whether the defendant's conduct amounts to negligence. To this extent contributory negligence is subjective, whereas primary negligence is objective. All that the defendant is obliged to prove is that the plaintiff failed to take reasonable precautions for his own safety in respect of the particular danger which in fact occurred, so that he thereby contributed to his own injury.[36] So a plaintiff motor cyclist who fails to wear a crash helmet is not thereby in breach of any common law duty to the defendant,

---

[30] *McArdle* v. *Andmac Ltd.* [1967] 1 W.L.R. 356.
[31] *Brown* v. *Thompson* [1968] 1 W.L.R. 1003, 1009, *per* Winn L.J.
[32] *Kerry* v. *Carter* [1969] 1 W.L.R. 1372, 1376.
[33] *Smith* v. *Smith (W.H.) & Sons Ltd.* [1952] 1 All E.R. 528.
[34] In Pritchard, *Personal Injury Litigation* (4th ed.), p. 31.
[35] *Nance* v. *British Columbia Electric Ry. Co.* [1951] A.C. 610. It is strange that this company should have been the unsuccessful party to an appeal in three of the leading cases on contributory negligence.
[36] *Moor* v. *Nolan* (1960) 94 I.L.T.R. 153.

as distinct from a breach of statutory duty, but yet he may be held guilty of contributory negligence.[37] The same is true of a passenger in a vehicle who fails to use a seat belt, for, in determining what is contributory negligence, the court is entitled to look to the cause of the damage as well as the cause of the negligence.[38] This, however, is not to say that in all cases the plaintiff who is guilty of contributory negligence owes to the defendant no duty to act carefully. Such a duty will normally be owed in most cases of highway collisions.[39]

(2) Inoperative negligence to be distinguished from contributory negligence

These difficult problems never arise unless it is proved, not merely that both parties were negligent, but that the negligence of each of them was a contributory cause of the accident.[40] The plaintiff may have been negligent, but unless that negligence was an operative cause of the accident none of the problems connected with contributory negligence arise. He may have been drunk, but if the defendant would have equally run him down had he been sober there is no question of contributory negligence.[41] In such a case the negligence of the plaintiff did no more than account for his being in a place where the negligence of the defendant operated.[42] The governing principle is that the plaintiff's failure to exercise reasonable care for his own protection does not amount to contributory negligence in respect of damage unless that damage results from the particular risk to which his conduct has exposed him.[43] Therefore, no question of operative contributory negligence arises in a case where the defendant proves only that the plaintiff has failed to take precautions against a foreseeable danger which has not occurred and that those precautions, if taken, would have been effective to protect him against the unforeseeable danger which in fact occurred.[44] A motorist who drives straight across a light-controlled crossing against the red light and knocks down a pedestrian who has begun to cross in reliance on the lights but without looking over his right shoulder cannot be heard to say that the pedestrian is thereby guilty of contributory negligence as against him, though such conduct on the part of the pedestrian might attract that description if he had been knocked down by a motorist lawfully turning left with the green light in his favour.[45] The statement that the plaintiff must be shown to have failed to take proper precautions for his own safety against the particular danger which in fact occurred does not mean that the particular form in which the danger manifested itself should actually have

---

[37] *Capps v. Miller* [1989] 1 W.L.R. 839.

[38] *Froom v. Butcher* [1976] Q.B. 286.

[39] *Nance v. British Columbia Electric Ry. Co.* [1951] A.C. 601, 611.

[40] See Lord Simon in the *Boy Andrew* case [1948] A.C. 140, 148—where each ship admitted she was to blame but maintained her negligence was not even a cause of the collision.

[41] *Woods v. Davison* [1930] N.I 161 (H.L.).

[42] *Moor v. Nolan* (1960) I.L.T.R. 153, 159.

[43] *Jones v. Livox Quarries Ltd.* [1952] 2 Q.B. 608.

[44] *Moor v. Nolan* (1960) 94 I.L.T.R. 153.

[45] *Moor v. Nolan* (1960) 94 I.L.T.R. 153.

occurred to his mind. It is sufficient if it is a danger of a particular class whose occurrence he should anticipate and take reasonable precautions to guard against.[46]

(3) The plaintiff's right to rely on the care of others[47]

In many cases the plaintiff is entitled to assume that there is no danger. So a workman is entitled to assume that his employer has complied with his statutory duties.[48] If an accident happens in such a case, the defendant will not be heard to say that the plaintiff might have avoided it by care, because no such care was obligatory on him.[49] There is in general no duty to anticipate that another will be negligent, and to avoid the effects of that negligence by anticipation.[50] So both the pedestrian[51] and the motorist[52] are entitled to proceed more or less upon the assumption that the drivers of all the other vehicles will do what it is their duty to do, namely, observe the rules regulating the traffic of the streets. But there is a distinction between legal duties and the common courtesies of the road. So a driver who flashes his lights at another who is waiting to come out of a side-road does not thereby undertake any duty to that other: he merely means "Come forward, I am waiting for you."[53] Yet there are some cases where a prudent man will guard against the possible negligence of others when experience shows such negligence to be common.[54] Experience shows this to be particularly common on the highway—a driver is not bound to anticipate folly in all its forms, but he is not entitled to put out of consideration the teachings of experience as to the form those follies commonly take.[55] So a driver entering a light-controlled crossing with the green light in his favour is not entitled to assume that no other driver will enter against the red light.[56]

(4) The doctrine of alternative danger: the "dilemma principle"

Where the plaintiff is perplexed or agitated or deceived by being exposed to danger by the wrongful act of the defendant, it is sufficient if he shows as much judgment and self-control in attempting to avoid that danger as may reasonably be expected of him in the circumstances. Although the reasonable man is cool and collected and remembers to take precautions for his own safety even in an emergency,[57] what is

---

[46] *Moor* v. *Nolan* (1960) 94 I.L.T.R. 153, 160–161.
[47] See also above, §§ 9.10–9.11.
[48] *Westwood* v. *Post Office* [1974] A.C. 1.
[49] *Grant* v. *Sun Shipping Co.* [1948] A.C. 549, 567.
[50] *Compania Mexicana* v. *Essex Transport Co.* (1929) 141 L.T. 106, 115.
[51] "The passenger is not bound to look out for mats on the highway. He may look at the stars if he likes": *De Teyron* v. *Waring* (1884) 1 T.L.R. 414, *per* Lord Coleridge C.J.
[52] *Toronto Railway Co.* v. *King* [1908] A.C. 260, 269.
[53] *Clarke* v. *Winchurch* [1969] 1 W.L.R. 69.
[54] *Grant* v. *Sun Shipping Co.* [1948] A.C. 549, 567.
[55] *L.P.T.B.* v. *Upson* [1949] 155, 173.
[56] *Doyle* v. *H. F. Murray Ltd.* [1967] I.R. 390.
[57] *Ghannan* v. *Glasgow Corporation*, 1950 S.C. 23, 28 ("It will not do to equate the reasonable man to the young man in a hurry"—*per* Lord Cooper.)

done or omitted to be done in "the agony of the moment" cannot fairly be treated as negligence[58] unless the plaintiff's trade or calling is such that a certain degree of aptitude for dealing with dangerous situations may be expected of him. The courts do not demand of the plaintiff the care of a superman,[59] but only that of a man of ordinary nerve and presence of mind. So in *Jones* v. *Boyce*,[60] in a coach accident, the plaintiff was placed by the negligence of the defendant in a perilous alternative—to jump or not to jump. He jumped and was injured. Had he kept his seat he would have escaped. But he was able to recover from the defendant, for he had acted reasonably and not from a rash apprehension of danger. So a lady locked in a public lavatory is entitled to make reasonable efforts to escape from her predicament.[61] The same rule is applied in cases of collisions at sea and is known as the rule in *The Bywell Castle*.[62] On the other hand, it must be remembered that such an emergency does not last for ever.[63]

So also a plaintiff is not necessarily guilty of contributory negligence simply because he has knowledge of a danger which the defendant has wrongfully created, but chooses to run the risk rather than to forgo the exercise of his liberty of action.[64] Similarly if the plaintiff is invited or ordered by the defendant to run the risk in question he cannot be held guilty of contributory negligence in doing so.[65] This doctrine has been further extended to cover the case of a plaintiff acting under the compulsion of a legal or moral duty.[66]

(5) Contributory negligence of children and persons under disability

The governing principles here are in theory the same as for the standard of care to be expected of a defendant.[67] But in practice a subjective approach is often adopted, which takes into account the deficiencies or idiosyncrasies of the plaintiff. In the case of a child of tender years there must be some age up to which the child cannot be expected to take any precautions for his own safety.[68] In cases where contributory negligence is alleged against a child, it is the duty of the trial judge to rule, in each particular case, whether the plaintiff, having regard to his age and mental development, may properly be expected to take some precautions for his own safety and consequently be capable of being guilty of contributory negligence. Having ruled in the affirmative, it becomes a question of fact for the jury, on the evidence, to determine whether he has fallen short of the standard which might reasonably be expected

---

[58] *Jones* v. *G.W. Ry.* (1930) 144 L.T. 194, 201.
[59] *U.S. Shipping Board* v. *Laird Line Ltd.* [1924] A.C. 286, 292.
[60] (1816) 1 Starkie 493.
[61] *Sayers* v. *Harlow U.D.C.* [1958] 1 W.L.R. 623.
[62] (1879) 4 P.D. 219.
[63] *Richman* v. *Railway Executive* (1950) 83 Ll.L.R. 409, 411.
[64] *Billings (A.C.) & Sons Ltd.* v. *Riden* [1958] A.C. 240. See above, § 22.4.
[65] *Yarmouth* v. *France* (1889) 19 Q.B.D. 647.
[66] *Haynes* v. *Harwood* [1935] 1 K.B. 146. See above, § 22.5.
[67] See above, § 9.10.
[68] *Gough* v. *Thorn* [1966] 1 W.L.R. 1387, 1388.

from him having regard to his age and development.[69] In practice the courts are not anxious to penalise a child who is unusually intelligent or well informed. Certainly an ordinary 13-year-old girl is not necessarily guilty of contributory negligence if she crosses the road at the signal of a halted lorry-driver without pausing to see if a vehicle is wrongly overtaking the lorry on the far side.[70]

(6) Contributory negligence in factory cases[71]

It has been laid down in a series of cases arising out of claims made under the Factories Act that it is not every error of judgment or heedlessness or inadvertence which amounts to contributory negligence. A similar principle has long existed in actions by servants against employers for breach of the common law duty of care.[72] Therefore when the defendant has been guilty of a flagrant and continuous breach of the regulations, and an accident happens which is of the nature intended to be guarded against by the regulations, then the court "must be careful not to emasculate that regulation by the side-wind of apportionment."[73] On the other hand, a plaintiff workman may have a high percentage of blame attributed to him if his carelessness has been very great.[74]

(7) Contributory negligence of plaintiff's servants and agents

The contributory negligence of a servant of the plaintiff is a good defence, in the same cases and to the same extent as that of the plaintiff himself, whenever the plaintiff would have been responsible for that negligence of his servant had harm ensued from it. In other words, the rule that the negligence of a servant in the course of his employment is imputed to his master is applicable when the master is a plaintiff no less than when he is a defendant.[75] It should be remembered that one spouse may be the servant or agent of the other. Hence if a husband is a passenger in a motor-car which is being driven by his wife as his servant or agent, and a collision occurs as a result of the combined negligence of the wife and a third party in which the husband is injured, the damages which may be awarded to him for his personal injuries may be reduced by the amount to which she is at fault.[76] Presumably the same principle applies to other forms of vicarious liability.[77]

---

[69] *Macnamara* v. *E.S.B.* [1975] I.R. 1, 18.

[70] *Gough* v. *Thorne* [1966] 1 W.L.R. 1387.

[71] See Fagelson, "The Last Bastion of Fault" (1979) 42 M.L.R. 646.

[72] See above, § 21.10.

[73] *Mullard* v. *Ben Line Steamers Ltd.* [1970] 1 W.L.R. 1414, 1418, *per* Sachs L.J.

[74] *Jayes* v. *I.M.I. (Kynoch) Ltd.* [1985] I.C.R. 155 ("a crazy thing to do").

[75] The Law Reform (Contributory Negligence) Act 1945 does not expressly provide for this situation, but it cannot have been intended to alter the well-settled law on this point. In *Mallett* v. *Dunn* [1949] 2 K.B. 180, it was assumed that the Act applied in a case of imputed negligence.

[76] *Lampert* v. *Eastern National Omnibus Co.* [1954] 1 W.L.R. 1047.

[77] *The Bernina* (1888) 13 App.Cas. 1, 16.

The doctrine of identification

(i) Passengers

The contributory negligence of an independent contractor or other agent of the plaintiff for whom he is not responsible, on the other hand, is no bar to the plaintiff's action. If a taxi-cab hired by the plaintiff comes into collision with another vehicle by the negligence of both drivers, and the plaintiff is hurt, he can recover damages not only from his own driver but also from the other.[78] It was for some time, indeed, believed that this was not so, and that the negligence of the driver of a vehicle was imputed to the passenger with the result that the passenger lost his remedy against third persons. This unreasonable doctrine, sometimes known as "the doctrine of identification," was exploded (to use the traditional legal word) by the House of Lords in *Mills* v. *Armstrong, The Bernina*.[79]

(ii) *Children in the charge of adults*

It was once thought that a child in the charge of an adult was so far "identified" with that adult as to disentitle it from suing for personal injuries caused by the negligence of the adult and a third party.[80] In *Oliver* v. *Birmingham and Midland Omnibus Co.*,[81] in which the plaintiff, aged four years, was injured due to the combined negligence of his grandfather (in whose care he was) and the defendants, it was held that since *The Bernina* this doctrine was no longer law. The fact that the child is in the charge of an adult may, however, in certain cases exempt the defendant from a duty which would otherwise exist of care towards the child—the defendant being entitled to assume that the child will be duly protected by its adult guardian, and therefore is not in danger.[82]

On the other hand two recent examples of statutory recognition of identification should be noted. Under the Fatal Accidents Act 1976, s.5 a dependant is identified with his deceased's contributory negligence. So also a child is identified with the contributory negligence of its parents in respect of a pre-natal occurrence which causes it to be born disabled (the Congenital Disabilities (Civil Liability) Act 1976, s.1(7)). So an infant with AIDS born to a drug-dominated household may have its damages reduced.

---

[78] *France* v. *Parkinson* [1954] 1 W.L.R. 581.
[79] (1888) 13 App.Cas. 1. Nor is the bailor of a chattel precluded by the contributory negligence of his bailee from recovering damages from a third person by whose negligence the chattel has been injured or destroyed: *Wellwood* v. *King (Alexander) Ltd.* [1921] 2 I.R. 274. The C.A. assumed this to be the law in *France* v. *Parkinson* [1954] 1 W.L.R. 581.
[80] *Waite* v. *North Eastern Ry.* (1858) E.B. & E. 719. See the full discussion of the case in a valuable booklet by Mr. Justice Clark, *Contributory Negligence and Damage Sustained by a Third Party* (Tasmania, 1936).
[81] [1933] 1 K.B 35. The principle of this decision applies to other persons incapable of looking after themselves—*e.g.* the very old: [1933] 1 K.B. 35, 41.
[82] See above, § 11.7, for an example.

(8) Burden of proof

The burden of proving the negligence of the plaintiff and that it contributed to the damage in such a way as to exonerate the defendant wholly or partially lies upon the defendant.[83] The defendant must always establish such contributory negligence as will amount to a defence: it is not true that the onus of establishing that the defendant failed to take advantage of a last opportunity rests upon the plaintiff.[84]

§ 22.14. Principle in Davies v. Mann Today

It has already been seen that "the rule of last opportunity," in the sense of an inflexible rule of law applicable over the whole field of contributory negligence, had become obsolete even before the Act of 1945.[85] This does not mean that the plain and sensible principle expounded in *Davies* v. *Mann* has also become obsolete. Just as there is room for it in admiralty after the Act of 1911, so there is room for it at common law after the Act of 1945. For, as Lord Birkenhead went to such pains to emphasise in *The Volute*, the mere fact that a collision has occurred in consequence of the blameworthy conduct of two vessels does not necessarily imply that the loss must automatically be distributed between the parties in some proportion. It might be possible to find "a sufficient separation of time, place or circumstance" to enable "a clear line to be drawn" between the faults of the two parties. The same principle now applies at common law.[86] Hence it is still the law that sole liability may be imputed to one party even though the misdoings of both are relevant to the cause of the accident.[87] It will be convenient to examine the application of this principle to different situations of fact.

(1) Collisions between two moving objects

It has already been seen that in admiralty it is seldom possible to draw "a clear line" in cases of this kind.[88] The position is similar in the case of collisions on land between two modern fast-moving vehicles.[89] So in *France* v. *Parkinson*,[90] in which two motor-cars proceeding along cross-roads of equal status had come into collision at the centre of the crossing, it was said that there was a prima facie case of negligence against both drivers.

(2) Collisions between moving and stationary objects

The perennial temptation to turn decisions on facts into rules of law should be resisted here as elsewhere. In particular there is no rule that

---

[83] *Heranger SS. Co.* v. *Diamond SS. Co.* [1939] A.C 94, 104.
[84] *Alford* v. *Magee* (1952) 85 C.L.R. 437, 463.
[85] Above, § 22.9.
[86] *Stapley* v. *Gypsum Mines Ltd.* [1953] A.C. 663, 681.
[87] *Sigurdson* v. *B.C. Electric Ry.* [1953] A.C. 291, 304.
[88] Above, § 22.10.
[89] *Alford* v. *Magee* (1952) 85 C.L.R. 437, 465.
[90] [1954] 1 W.L.R. 581. Contrast the difficulties which arose on similar facts in *Swadling* v. *Cooper* [1931] A.C. 1 (above, § 22.9).

one who erects or maintains a danger in a public place must necessarily have attributed to him the greater share of fault for an accident than the person who collides with it.[91] Still, it may be possible to draw a clear line between the respective faults in such a case. Time and knowledge are factors which are critical but not necessarily decisive.[92]

(3) Principle applies to non-highway cases

The fact that the cases which have so far been discussed have concerned actions for personal injuries arising out of traffic accidents does not mean that the principle in *Davies* v. *Mann* is limited to such cases. This is clearly shown by *Stapley* v. *Gypsum Mines Ltd.*,[93] an action for personal injuries arising out of a mining accident.

---

[91] *Carroll* v. *Clare County Council* [1975] I.R. 221, 228.
[92] *Sigurdson* v. *B.C. Electric Ry. Co.* [1953] A.C. 291.
[93] [1953] A.C. 663.

CHAPTER 23

DAMAGES: GENERAL PRINCIPLES

Remedies for torts are of two kinds, being either judicial or extrajudicial—remedies by way of an action at law, and remedies by way of self-help. The various forms of extrajudicial remedy, such as distress, the retaking of property, and the abatement of a nuisance, will be considered in another chapter, and we are here concerned with the other class alone. The remedies obtainable for a tort by means of an action are of three chief kinds—damages, injunction,[1] and specific restitution of property.[2] The first of these is the ordinary and characteristic remedy.

§ 23.1. Damages

Damages are classified in several ways.

(1) Nominal, contemptuous or real

Nominal damages are a small sum of money[3] awarded not by way of compensation for any actual loss suffered, but merely by way of recognition of the existence of some legal right vested in the plaintiff and violated by the defendant. Real damages, on the other hand, are those which are assessed and awarded as compensation for damage actually suffered by the plaintiff, and not simply by way of mere recognition of a legal right violated. Damages are not nominal merely because they are very small. If actual damage, however small, is proved, and damages, however small, are awarded in respect of it, such damages are real and not nominal. Nominal damages must also be distinguished from contemptuous or derisory damages: the former term is appropriate in a case where the plaintiff is not concerned with his actual loss (if any), but brings his action with the sole and proper object of establishing his right; the latter term indicates that in the opinion of the jury the action should not have been brought at all, and display this opinion by awarding "the smallest coin of the realm."[4] In the latter case the court may refuse to award the plaintiff his costs.

When nominal damages recoverable

It follows accordingly that nominal damages are recoverable only in the case of torts which are actionable *per se*. If such a right is violated the law presumes damage and an action will lie even though no damage at

---

[1] See § 25.2., below.
[2] See § 6.12., above.
[3] In 1939 the sum was £2; in 1986 it was £20: *Rae* v. *Yorkshire Bank* [1988] F.L.R. 1, 2.
[4] As in *Pamplin* v. *Express Newspapers Ltd.* [1988] 1 W.L.R. 116 ($\frac{1}{2}$ p). But where loss of liberty is concerned there is no room for contemptuous damages: *Pike* v. *Waldrum* [1952] 1 Lloyd's Rep. 431, 455; *Hook* v. *Cunard Steamship Co. Ltd.* [1953] 1 All E.R. 1021. And see also § 2.4.

all has in fact been suffered by the plaintiff. This is the case in all types of trespass, whether to land, goods or the person, and in some actions on the case, as in libel and in certain cases of slander. Thus in *Ashby* v. *White*,[5] Sir John Holt C.J. held that an elector had a right of action against a returning officer who wrongfully and maliciously rejected his vote at an election, even though the candidate for whom he intended to vote was elected. "So if a man gives another a cuff on the ear, though it cost him nothing, no not so much as a little diachylon,[6] yet he shall have his action, for it is a personal injury. So a man shall have an action against another for riding over his ground, though it did him no damage: for it is an invasion of his property and the other has no right to come there."[7] So again in *Constantine* v. *Imperial London Hotels*[8] the plaintiff, a famous West Indian cricketer, was held entitled to nominal damages of five guineas because the defendants wrongfully refused to receive him into one of their hotels to which he wished to go, though they provided him with lodging in another of their hotels.

(2) Real damages

But in many cases the plaintiff's only right is not to be caused damage by the defendant, and in such a case he must prove actual damage. Damage then is the gist of the action. Thus, for example, damage must be proved in an action of negligence, and indeed in the great majority of actions on the case. Where the damages are real it becomes necessary to determine what is the measure of damages in each case.[9] The general English rule today is that damages are compensatory, whether in contract or in tort. The function of damages is therefore to put the person whose right has been invaded in the same position as if it had been respected.[10] It is well settled, at least in the economic torts, that the basic question is, what has the plaintiff lost, not what can the defendant pay.[11]

It is sometimes said that the general principle of assessment is *restitutio in integrum*. But this cannot always be applied to actions in tort. "If by somebody's fault I lose my leg and am paid damages, can anyone in his senses say that I have had *restitutio in integrum*?"[12] There are some kinds of damage for which no true compensation can be given in this world by any amount of money, no matter how elaborate an arithmetical computation is employed. This is particularly so with claims for loss of amenities and pain and suffering. Yet the courts are obliged to do the best they can. In such cases the plaintiff is entitled to fair and reason-

---

[5] (1703) 2 Ld.Raym. 938. The principle of this case is unaffected by the protection given to returning officers by the Representation of the People Act 1983, s.23.
[6] Plaster.
[7] 2 Ld.Raym. 938, 955. (Yet note that in *Ashby* v. *White* itself the damages which the plaintiff recovered were real and not merely nominal.)
[8] [1944] K.B. 693.
[9] In the sense explained below, § 23.2.
[10] *The Albazero* [1977] A.C. 774, 841.
[11] *General Tyre and Rubber Co. Ltd.* v. *Firestone Tyre Co. Ltd.* [1975] 1 W.L.R. 819, 824.
[12] *Admiralty Commissioners* v. *S.S. Valeria* [1922] 2 A.C. 242, 248, *per* Lord Dunedin.

able, as distinct from perfect, compensation, assessed in the light of previous awards in respect of comparable damage.[13] It might be better to say that such sums are "an acknowledgement of regret for having caused a hurt that is imponderable rather than a compensation properly so called,"[14] or if the legislature fixed a definite sum to which the relatives would be entitled by way of *solatium*, as it has now done by the Administration of Justice Act 1982, s.3. So again with libel, in which the rules are so flexible that is seems better to say that the plaintiff is awarded damages *because* his reputation has been injured rather than *for* that injured reputation.[15]

(3) General or special

General damages are compensation for general damage; special damages for special damage. General damage is that kind of damage which the law presumes to follow from the wrong complained of and which, therefore, need not be expressly set out in the plaintiff's pleadings. Special damage, on the other hand, is damage of such a kind that it will not be presumed by the law and it must therefore be expressly alleged in those pleadings so that the defendant may have due notice of the nature of the claim. Thus in the case of a collision between two ships due to the negligence of the defendant, the plaintiff will be able to recover general damages for the loss of the use of his ship during the repairs,[16] even if it be not used for trading or profit.[17] "What right," asked Lord Halsbury L.C. in *The Mediana*,[18] "has a wrongdoer to consider what use you are going to make of your vessel? . . . Supposing a person took away a chair out of my room and kept it for twelve months, could anybody say you had a right to diminish the damages by showing that I did not usually sit in that chair, or that there were plenty of other chairs in the room?"

(4) Compensatory, aggravated and exemplary[19]

Compensatory damages are awarded as compensation for, and are measured by, the material loss suffered by the plaintiff. A distinct category is that of aggravated damages, which may be awarded when the motives and conduct of the defendant aggravate the injury to the plaintiff. Insult and injured feelings are a proper subject for compensation.[20] So a substantial sum was awarded for an "insolent and high-

---

[13] *Fletcher* v. *Autocar and Transporters Ltd.* [1968] 2 Q.B. 322.
[14] *M'Leish* v. *Fulton & Sons*, 1955 S.C. 46, 49, *per* Lord Carmont.
[15] See above, § 8.25.
[16] *Carslogie Steamship Co.* v. *Royal Norwegian Government* [1952] A.C. 292.
[17] *The Hebridean Coast* [1961] A.C. 545.
[18] [1900] A.C. 113, 117. See also *Stoke-on-Trent City Council* v. *Wass (W. & J.) Ltd.* [1988] 1 W.L.R. 1406, and above, § 6.12.
[19] Gandhi, "Exemplary damages in the law of tort" (1990) 10 L.S. 182.
[20] *Archer* v. *Brown* [1985] Q.B. 401.

handed trespass" by an inquiry agent.[21] In such a case damages are at large precisely because the "real" damage cannot be ascertained: it is not a matter of determining the "real" damage and adding to that a sum by way of aggravated damages.[22] Yet another distinct category is that of exemplary damages, which reflect the jury's view of the defendant's outrageous conduct. Aggravated damages are given for conduct which shocks the plaintiff: exemplary damages for conduct which shocks the jury, and may serve the useful function of deterring others as well as punishing the defendant.[23]

There has been considerable dispute about both the nature of and the conditions for the award of exemplary damages. Salmond thought that exemplary damages were a sum of money awarded in excess of any material loss or by way of *solatium* for an insult or other outrage to the plaintiff's feelings that is involved in the injury complained of.[24] It seems clear that Salmond thought of exemplary damages as being part of aggravated compensatory damages, or, conversely, as not being punitive or vindictive. Salmond also asserted that the sole condition for the award of such damages was conscious wrongdoing in contumelious disregard of another's rights.[25]

Unfortunately it is no longer possible in England to uphold either branch of Salmond's statement. As a result of two cases in the House of Lords it is plain not only that exemplary damages are criminal, vindictive, or punitive in nature, but also that they are not to be awarded merely because of contumelious disregard of another's rights, but only in very restricted categories of cases. This was laid down in *Rookes* v. *Barnard*,[26] and re-asserted by five out of seven Law Lords in *Cassell & Co. Ltd.* v. *Broome*.[27] Many courts in other jurisdictions have thought this considerable pruning operation was too severe.[28] Nevertheless there are strong logical arguments against exemplary damages[29]—they bring a criminal element into the civil law without the safeguards of criminal procedure; they lead to excessive awards, and are an unmerited windfall for the plaintiff.[30] It must also be remembered that an obligation to pay a large sum by way of compensatory damages has itself a

---

[21] *Jolliffe* v. *Willmet & Co.* (1970) 114 S.J. 619.
[22] *McCarey* v. *Associated Newspapers Ltd.* [1965] 2 Q.B. 86. See above, § 8.25.
[23] So it is irrelevant that the defendant is insured: *Lamb* v. *Cotogno* (1987) 61 A.L.J.R. 549.
[24] See *Australian Consolidated Press Ltd.* v. *Uren* [1969] 1 A.C. 590, 636–637.
[25] His views on this point have the approval of the High Court of Australia: *Uren* v. *John Fairfax & Sons Pty. Ltd.* (1967) 117 C.L.R. 118, 150, 154.
[26] [1964] A.C. 1129.
[27] [1972] A.C. 1027.
[28] Appellate tribunals in Australia, Canada, Ireland and New Zealand have refused to follow *Rookes* v. *Barnard* and have insisted on retaining a wider power to award exemplary damages: see *Lamb* v. *Cotogno* (1987) 61 A.L.J.R. 549; *Vogel* v. *C.B.C.* [1982] 3 W.L.R. 97; *Taylor* v. *Beere* [1982] 1 N.Z.L.R. 81; *Conway* v. *Irish National Teachers Organisation* [1991] I.L.R.M. 497.
[29] So the Faulks Committee (Cmnd. 5909, § 360) recommended their abolition.
[30] So if the defendant is already in prison there is no reason to punish him twice by awarding such damages against him: *Archer* v. *Brown* [1985] Q.B. 401.

punitive element in it, as has the English rule that costs follow the event.[31]

But even opponents have recognised that exemplary damages showed a continued vitality,[32] perhaps because the ordinary citizen feels that a defendant ought to be made to pay for insolent or outrageous conduct.[33]

The English principles relating to the award of exemplary damages[34] are now therefore as follows. First, exemplary damages are not to be awarded merely because the tort has been committed with a contumelious disregard of the plaintiff's rights.[35] Secondly, however, exemplary damages may[36] be awarded in three categories of cases (which are considered below), provided always that both aggravated and compensatory damages are inadequate, and that a full and careful direction is given to the jury.[37] Thirdly, when there are two or more defendants, the total sum awarded by way of exemplary damages must not exceed that to be awarded against the least blameworthy,[38] save that it may be possible to find some way of giving separate judgments against joint tortfeasors.[39]

Finally, the Privy Council has held[40] that when exemplary damages are awarded they need not be specified separately from the amount of compensatory damages awarded. It is not easy to fit this decision into any coherent theory, or even with judicial practice in other cases on assessment.

Which Torts? One Law Lord stated[41] that as the object of *Rookes* v. *Barnard*[42] was to restrict the award of exemplary damages, they should not be awarded in respect of torts for which they had not previously been awarded. This is logical, but the courts seem to prefer the dictum of another Law Lord,[43] which does not automatically rule out other

---

[31] *Cassell & Co.* v. *Broome* [1972] A.C. 1027, 1095, 1114. (A case in which there were "grave libels perpetrated quite deliberately and without regard to their truth by a young man and a firm of publishers interested solely in whether they would gain by the publication of this book.") The unsuccessful appellants (who had not raised the issue) were required to pay damages of £40,000 (compensatory, £15,000; exemplary, £25,000), with costs calculated at more than £60,000. Eventually the H.L. ordered the costs of the appeal to be halved: [1972] A.C. 1136.

[32] Lord Wilberforce in [1972] A.C. 1027, 1114.

[33] It is significant that even in a jurisdiction where a no-fault compensation scheme exists, there is still a place for exemplary damages: *Donselaar* v. *Donselaar* [1982] 2 N.Z.L.R. 97.

[34] This term is to be preferred to "vindictive" or "punitive": [1972] A.C. 1027, 1073, 1124; *Conway* v. *I.N.T.O.* [1991] I.L.R.M. 497, 509.

[35] [1972] A.C. 1027, 1080, 1082.

[36] *Holden* v. *Chief Constable of Lancashire* [1987] Q.B. 380.

[37] *Riches* v. *News Group Newspapers Ltd.* [1986] Q.B. 246 (a case in which there were 10 plaintiffs, and the jury became thoroughly confused by the judge's direction, although it was conceded "that any judge would be thankful not to have to direct a jury on this issue," p. 268.)

[38] See [1972] A.C. 1027, 1063, 1081, 1118.

[39] *X.L. Petroleum* v. *Caltex Oil Ltd.* (1985) 59 A.L.J.R. 352.

[40] *Att.-Gen. of St. Christopher* v. *Reynolds* [1980] A.C. 637, 662.

[41] *Cassell & Co. Ltd.* v. *Broome* [1972] A.C. 1027, 1131, *per* Lord Diplock.

[42] [1964] A.C. 1129.

[43] *Cassell & Co. Ltd.* v. *Broome* [1972] A.C. 1027, 1114, *per* Lord Wilberforce.

intentional torts[44] from the scope of exemplary damages. So there are decisions awarding exemplary damages for nuisance[45] and the "relatively new tort of unlawful racial discrimination."[46] Indeed, the oppressive or malicious execution of a court order (though not a tort) might justify the award of such damages.[47]

The categories

First. Oppressive, arbitrary or unconstitutional action by servants of the government may justify such an award.[48] Today a wide interpretation is to be given to the term "government,"[49] but outrageous action by the private bully is to be dealt with by the award of aggravated, rather than exemplary, damages.[50] Nor does every unlawful act by a police officer entitle the plaintiff to such damages.[51] It is noteworthy that what is decisive here is not the conduct of the defendant, or even the character of the plaintiff, but simply the defendant's status as a public official. A citizen with no reputation to lose who had been wrongly imprisoned might get only a small sum by way of compensatory damages: but the courts may also rightly award him a sum which will deter flagrant injustices.[52]

Second. Aggravated damages will not do justice when the defendant's conduct has been calculated by him to make a profit for himself which may well exceed the compensation payable to the plaintiff. The facts of *Cassell* v. *Broome* were such that it was "a forlorn hope" for the appellants to argue that they were not within this second category.[53] An arithmetical calculation is not required—the profit motive is a factor and not a condition.[54] Again when a tenant has been unlawfully evicted in an outrageous way exemplary damages have been awarded in England.[55]

Third. A statute may occasionally permit such an award—*e.g.* the Reserve and Auxiliary Forces (Protection of Civil Interests) Act 1951, (s.13(2)). The Copyright, Designs and Patents Act 1988, s.96, permits the

---

[44] *e.g.* deceit, which is the paradigm case for exemplary damages: see *Mafo* v. *Adams* [1970] 1 Q.B. 548.
[45] *Guppy's Ltd.* v. *Brookling* (1984) 269 E.G. 846, But no court has yet given such an award for the tort of negligence.
[46] *Alexander* v. *Home Office* [1988] 1 W.L.R. 918, 975.
[47] *Columbia Pictures Inc.* v. *Robinson* [1987] Ch. 38, 87.
[48] *Kelly* v. *Faulkner* [1973] N.I. 31.
[49] *Bradford City Council* v. *Aropa* [1991] 2 W.L.R. 1327.
[50] [1972] A.C. 1027, 1078, 1134.
[51] *Holden* v. *Chief Constable of Lancashire* [1987] Q.B. 380.
[52] [1972] A.C. 1027, 1134. So John Wilkes, a man of imperfect character, was awarded £4,000 against Lord Halifax in 1769 (19 St.Tr. 1466). Even then the sum was so much less than expected "that the jurymen were obliged to withdraw privately for fear of being insulted."
[53] See [1972] A.C. 1027, 1059. Of the 11 judges who heard this case, 10 agreed that, assuming the second category existed, and assuming that the jury had been properly directed on it, the facts justified an award within this category.
[54] [1972] A.C. 1027, 1079, 1130.
[55] *Drane* v. *Evangelou* [1978] 1 W.L.R. 455.

award of "additional damages" when the plaintiff's statutory rights have been infringed in aggravating circumstances.

"Parasitic" damages

It sometimes happens that damage which is in itself *damnum sine injuria* is caused by an act which, by reason of some other kind of damage also caused by it to the same person, is wrongful and actionable at the suit of that person. For example, a building which wrongfully obstructs the ancient lights of an adjoining building may at the same time obstruct other windows in that building which have not yet acquired legal protection.[56] In such cases the damages recoverable for the wrongful act include compensation for the whole loss so caused, even though part of that loss is in itself *damnum sine injuria*.[57] Again the protection of privacy, or redress for purely economic loss carelessly caused,[58] is often dependent on some other cause of action, such as trespass to land or goods. This has been aptly called the "parasitic" element in damages.[59] But it must be admitted that the status of the doctrine is somewhat doubtful, for it has been both approved[60] and disapproved[61] in appellate courts.

§ 23.2. Remoteness of Damage: Introduction[62]

A plaintiff who has suffered damage in consequence of the act of the defendant may be disentitled to recover compensation:
(1) Because the defendant's act was not wrongful at all;
(2) Because the plaintiff is not the person to whom the defendant owed the duty which he has violated;
(3) Because the damage is not of a kind recognised by the law;
(4) Because the damage has been caused in a manner which the law does not recognise as a sufficient ground of liability.
These four cases will be considered in their order.

(1) Damnum sine injuria

This is the case when there is *damnum* suffered by the plaintiff, but no *injuria* committed by the defendant, either against the plaintiff or

---

[56] *Oldham* v. *Lawson* [1976] V.R. 208.

[57] See also *Campbell* v. *Paddington Corporation* [1911] 1 K.B. 869 (loss of a view).

[58] *S.C.M. Ltd.* v. *Whittall Ltd.* [1971] 1 Q.B. 337.

[59] Street, *Foundations of Legal Liability*, Vol. i, p. 461. At p. 470 he says: "The treatment of any element of damage as a parasitic factor belongs essentially to a transitory stage of legal evolution. A factor which is today recognised a parasitic will, forsooth, tomorrow be recognised as an independent basis of liability."

[60] *Scott* v. *Goulding's Fertilisers Ltd.* [1973] I.R. 200, 203, 204.

[61] *Spartan Steel and Alloys Ltd.* v. *Martin & Co. (Contractors) Ltd.* [1973] 1 Q.B. 27, 35.

[62] The leading monograph is Hart and Honoré, *Causation in the Law* (2nd ed., Oxford 1985). See also J. C. Smith, *Liability in Negligence* (1984) Chap. 8, which proposes a test said to be supported by the decisions in over 90 per cent. of the reported cases. The periodical literature is vast, but pre-*Wagon Mound* publications are now only of historical interest. The more valuable post-1960 articles are Cooke, "Remoteness of Damage and Judicial Discretion" [1978] C.L.J. 288; Stapleton, "Law, Causation and Commonsense" (1988) 8, O.J.L.S. 111.

against any other person. The plaintiff's interests are not protected against conduct of this kind. Illustrations from cases which have already been discussed[63] are damage done by way of competition in trade; or by the withdrawal of underground water.

(2) Damnum suffered by one person and injuria by another

In the second class of case there is both *damnum* and *injuria*, but the *damnum* is suffered by one person and the *injuria* by another. He who does a wrongful act is liable only to the person whose rights are thereby violated. He is not bound to make compensation to all persons who, in the result, suffer harm from his wrongdoing. The *damnum* and *injuria* must be united in the same person. This is illustrated by the problem of the unforeseeable plaintiff in the tort of negligence.[64]

(3) Damnum of a kind not recognised by law

The third class of case is that in which, although the defendant's act is wrongful, and although the duty violated by him was a duty towards the plaintiff, nevertheless the damage resulting to the plaintiff is not recoverable, because it is not the kind of damage which it is the purpose of the law to prevent or to give redress for.[65] Thus at common law, before the Fatal Accidents Acts 1846 to 1959, no damages could be recovered for the death of a human being. The protection of human life was left to the criminal law.

(4) Damnum too remote

It remains to consider the fourth and last class of case in which damage is irrecoverable. In this class of case the plaintiff fails because the chain of causation connecting the defendant's act with the damage resulting it is of such a nature that the law for some reason refuses to regard it as sufficiently continuous for liability. Damage of this kind is said to be too remote. Between the defendant's act and the plaintiff's damage some third factor has intervened. Thus when a casualty officer at a hospital failed to see and examine a patient who complained of vomiting, the doctor was said to be "negligent." Yet it was held that his negligence had not *caused* the death of the patient, which was due to arsenical poisoning which could not have been detected and cured in time in any event.[66] But there may be responsibility for another's tort under the doctrine of vicarious liability without the master (as distinct from the servant) having been proved to have caused the wrong.

Common sense and causation

This doctrine of remoteness of damage is one of very considerable obscurity and difficulty.[67] Questions of causation "have vexed the best

---

[63] See also above, § 1.3. 1–4.
[64] See above, § 9.9.
[65] See above, § 10.1.
[66] *Barnett* v. *Chelsea Hospital Management Committee* [1969] 1 Q.B. 428.
[67] See Watkins L.J. in *Lamb* v. *Camden L.B.C.* [1981] 1 Q.B. 625, 644.

of human intellects for 2,400 years."[68] Yet "In the varied web of affairs, the law must abstract some consequences as relevant, not perhaps on ground of pure logic but simply for practical reasons."[69] There are many judicial statements praising the value of common-sense principles and stating that in any case the question of issue can be determined by applying common-sense to the facts of the particular case.[70] There are also many judicial warnings against too ready a reliance on "philosophy,"[71] or the "grave danger of being led astray by scholastic theories of causation and their ugly and barely intelligible jargon."[72] Some judges and writers go so far as to say that it is impossible to characterise any principles on which common sense proceeds. "This seems a counsel of despair which we should hesitate to accept. . . . Common sense is not a matter of inexplicable or arbitrary assertions, and the causal notions which it employs, though flexible and complex and subtly influenced by context, can be shown to rest, at least in part, on stateable principles; though the ordinary man who uses them may not, without assistance, be able to make them explicit."[73] Nor should it be assumed (as it seems sometimes to have been done) that philosophy is equivalent to that department of it called metaphysics: much can be learnt from the empiricists of the past and their influential descendants of the present day.[74]

An attempt has been made to state more explicitly those common-sense principles of causation according to which the courts have consistently said that causal questions must be decided.[75] These principles cannot provide conclusive answers to the complex causal questions which the courts are sometimes obliged to answer, but serve rather as an organising framework within which a choice may be made according to whatever considerations of policy the law may consider to be relevant. At the outset it should be noted that a question as to the cause of an event may lead to answers which vary according to the context of the inquiry. "A car skids while cornering at a certain point, turns turtle, and burst into flames. From the car-driver's point of view, the cause of the accident was cornering too fast, and the lesson is that one must drive

---

[68] *Arnott* v. *O'Keeffe* [1977] I.R.I., 19, *per* Kenny J.

[69] *Liesbosch Dredger* v. *Edison* [1933] A.C. 449, 460, *per* Lord Wright. See also *Monarch Steamship Co.* v. *A/B Karlshamns Oljefabriker* [1949] A.C. 196, 226.

[70] *Banque Keyser S.A.* v. *Skandia (U.K.) Insurance Co. Ltd.* [1990] Q.B. 665, 717, 814.

[71] As in the following quotation: "The common law of this country has been built up, not by the writings of logicians or learned jurists, but by the summings-up of judges of experience to juries consisting of plain men, not usually students of logic, not accustomed to subtle reasoning, but endowed, so far as my experience goes, as a general rule, with great common sense, and if an argument has to be put in terms which only a school-man could understand, then I am always very doubtful whether it can possibly be expressing the common law": *Smith* v. *Harris* [1939] 3 All E.R. 960, 967, *per* du Parcq L.J.

[72] *Overseas Tankship (U.K.) Ltd.* v. *Morts Dock and Engineering Co. Ltd. (The Wagon Mound)* [1961] A.C. 388, 419.

[73] Hart and Honoré, *Causation in the Law*, (2nd ed.), p. 26.

[74] Even a Law Lord has said that he used the term philosopher "in no disparaging sense, for what is a philosopher but who one, *inter alia*, reasons severely and with precision?": *Stapley* v. *Gypsum Mines Ltd.* [1953] A.C. 663, 687, *per* Lord Asquith of Bishopstone.

[75] Hart and Honoré, *Causation in the Law*, Chap. 2.

more carefully. From the county surveyor's point of view, the cause was a defective road surface, and the lesson is that one must make skid-proof roads. From the motor-manufacturers' point of view, the cause was defective design, and the lesson is that one must place the centre of gravity lower."[76] The conclusion is that the word "cause" can hardly be defined, but is one "to which converging limits can be assigned in its context as concrete cases come to be decided."[77]

So the basic principle in the common-sense notion of cause is that "*the cause*" is one condition selected from a complex set of conditions which, according to known generalisations, are together jointly sufficient for the occurrence of the consequence in question. For, even though the road surface is defective, a car will not skid unless certain other conditions are satisfied—*e.g.* the car must be of a certain weight and construction and be moving at a certain minimum speed.[78] Within this jointly sufficient set of conditions common sense (like the law) distinguishes mere conditions from causes, and the principal criterion for this distinction lies in the contrast between (1) a voluntary human action and other conditions, (2) an abnormal contingency (*e.g.* an act of God or a coincidence) and other conditions. The legal distinctions of *novus actus interveniens*, superseding cause, and proximate cause may be defined in terms of these contrasts. It should be noted that although either an abnormal contingency or a voluntary human act may negative causal connection, there are differences between them. Thus an abnormal contingency only negatives causal connection if it intervenes in time between the wrongful act and the consequence; whereas a voluntary act may negative causal connection even though it precedes in time both the wrongful act and the harm.

Finally, it is worth noting that the broad open question "What is the cause of this event?" is more suited to those inquiries in which we are seeking to discover the explanation of how or why some contingency happened. But when an explanation has been provided (or when none is needed) the more circumscribed question "Given this wrongful act (or other designated event) and given this loss or harm, is the latter the consequence of the former?" is appropriate. To ask the question in this way makes it plain that we are not seeking to understand what has happened but to allocate responsibility. This form of question is also helpful when we are considering a case which raises the issue of *novus actus interveniens*, for it makes it plain that the real problem is whether some third factor (which may be the act or omission of a human being, or the act of an animal, or a natural event or state of affairs) prevents the attri-

---

[76] Collingwood, "The Idea of Cause" (1938) Aristotelian Society Proceedings 85 (cited in (1953) 69 L.Q.R. 433). Note some words of Lord Porter, written before he became a judge (5 Camb.L.J. 189): "The fact is that judges like the rest of us are human and, where for a particular decision accuracy is not essential, will use several words in the same sense or one in several. It is not by pressing the meaning attributed to a word in one or two instances that its true meaning can be obtained."

[77] *Commissioner of Customs and Excise* v. *Top Ten Promotions Ltd.* [1969] 1 W.L.R. 1163, 1178, *per* Lord Wilberforce.

[78] It should be remembered that the jointly sufficient set of conditions may include negative conditions—*e.g.* the failure to give the appropriate signal—as well as positive ones.

bution of a given harm to a given action or contingency as its consequence.

Some conclusions

Before investigating this difficult topic more fully, it may be convenient to state briefly four propositions which both on principle and authority seem to be indisputable.

First, an event may be the consequence of several causes. Until the Law Reform (Contributory Negligence) Act 1945 altered the law, there was a tendency to believe that there could not have been more than one effective cause of any single event. This error has been exposed.[79] It is now accepted that an act can be an effective cause of damage even if it is preceded, accompanied or followed by another act (whether intentional or negligent) of the injured party or a third party.[80] It is still necessary to avoid the fallacy of assuming that because one cause might have brought about a certain event therefore more than one cause could not have done so.[81]

Secondly, the doctrine of remoteness of damage applies not merely to wrongs of negligence, but to wrongs of all kinds, whether wilful, negligent, or of strict liability. Even a wilful wrongdoer is not liable *ad infinitum* for all the consequences which in fact flow from his wrongful act.

Thirdly, on the other hand, a consequence cannot be held too remote if it was actually intended by the wrongdoer.[82] The defendant is held responsible for all those consequences which he actually desired and intended to inflict upon the plaintiff, however remote may be the chain of causation by which he effected his purpose.[83]

Fourthly, remoteness of damage (what items?) must be distinguished from assessment of damages (what loss?). The former concept deals with the heads or items of recoverable loss. The latter deals with the arithmetical computation of the money which will compensate for that loss.

§ 23.3. Tests of Causation

A number of different tests of causation have been proposed. We shall now consider in detail the more important judicial and extra-judicial suggestions.

(1) Different kinds of cause

Various qualifying adjectives have been attached to the word "cause" to determine whether the consequence is too remote. Thus it has been said by some that damage is too remote unless the act of the defendant is the real, by some the effective, by some the substantial cause of it,[84]

---

[79] *Cork* v. *Kirby MacLean Ltd.* [1952] 2 All E.R. 402, 406.
[80] *O'Dowd* v. *Secretary of State* [1983] N.I. 210, 214.
[81] *Stapley* v. *Gypsum Mines Ltd.* [1953] A.C. 663, 665.
[82] *Quinn* v. *Leathem* [1901] A.C. 495, 537.
[83] *Jones* v. *Fabbi* (1973) 37 D.L.R. (3d) 27, 35.
[84] *Gray* v. *Barr* [1971] 2 Q.B. 554.

whilst others have distinguished the *causa causans* from the *causa sine qua non*.[85] The question has been much, and fruitlessly, discussed in cases on the assessment of damages for personal injuries. Is the tort the *causa causans* of the payment of a pension[86] or an insurance benefit,[87] or the remarriage of a widow to a man who turns out to be a kind step-father.[88]

(2) The chain of causation

Others again have said that the test of remoteness is whether the chain of causation has been interrupted or broken by some independent intervening cause: that a defendant remains liable for all consequences until such an interruption or breach frees him from further liability. Such is, however, the language of metaphor,[89] and the metaphor is not completely satisfactory. It cannot mean that the chain of causation is broken or interrupted in fact; for in that case the damage would not be a consequence of the defendant's act at all. The meaning can only be that, though the chain of causation remains unbroken in fact, it is deemed in law to have been interrupted so as to save the defendant from further liability for ensuing damages. But this is the very question for determination.

(3) The test of proximate cause

Another test sometimes proposed is that of proximate cause. But this might suggest that only the cause which is latest in time is significant, whereas the proximate cause, in the sense of the dominant or efficient cause, is not necessarily the one which operates last.[90] "The old flint-lock musket required a flash in the pan to ignite the powder and drive out the bullet, but death due to penetration by the bullet would not

---

[85] *Weld-Blundell* v. *Stephens* [1920] A.C. 956, 984; *Holling* v. *Yorks Traction Co.* [1948] 2 All E.R. 662, 664. "Dominant," "immediate" and "precipitating" are other adjectives which have been judicially used: *Minister of Pensions* v. *Chennell* [1947] K.B. 250; *Howgate* v. *Bagnall* [1951] 1 K.B. 265.

[86] No, according to *Payne* v. *Railways Executive* [1952] 1 K.B. 26, 36.

[87] No, according to *Bradburn* v. *G.W. Ry.* (1874) L.R. 10 Ex. 1.

[88] Yes, according to *Mead* v. *Clark, Chapman & Co. Ltd.* [1956] 1 W.L.R. 76.

[89] Other metaphors which have been judicially used refer to conduit pipes, transmission gears, nets, rivers and streams. "It was his hand that let the tiger out of the cage," said Oliver J. of an employee who switched on a dangerous machine to clean it: *Williams* v. *Sykes and Harrison Ltd.* [1955] 1 W.L.R. 1180, 1189. Geoffrey Lane J. preferred "he who first put a match to the blue touch-paper": *Electrochrome Ltd.* v. *Welsh Plastics Ltd.* [1968] 2 All E.R. 205, 208. The main objection to metaphors about causation is that they foster a confused conception of a cause as something which, like a human being or a moving thing, may exert more or less power at different times. Despite the main criticisms of metaphors they continue to be used. "The instrument most effective to move the mind seems to be the lucky metaphor. Perhaps the main business of the lawyer in this matter of causation is simply the finding of that metaphor which is capable of moving the mind to see in the event (which is probably neutral in itself) the pattern which he desires to be seen there": Hamson [1954] C.L.J. 41.

[90] *Gray* v. *Barr* [1971] 2 Q.B. 554, 566–567.

naturally be described as death by fire."[91] It is a fallacy to suppose that the last cause is the sole cause.[92] There may even be two dominant or proximate causes.[93]

(4) The doctrine of equivalence of conditions

A number of writers have asserted that all the necessary conditions of an event are equally entitled to be called the causes of that event: every event is the result of a "cone of causation" stretching back to the beginning of the world. It follows that these writers are obliged not only to deny the existence of the distinction between causes and mere conditions (a distinction which is, as we have seen, embedded in the structure of common-sense thinking about causation) but also to assert that when a court selects one out of the multiplicity of necessary conditions as "the cause" of an event its decision is based upon some irrational and inexplicable ground of policy. But this doctrine has not been accepted by the courts.[94]

(5) The test of reasonable foreseeability

There was always some authority[95] for the proposition that a wrongdoer is liable only for damage which was intended by him or which, though not intended, was the natural and probable consequence[96] of his wrongful act. This test of reasonable foreseeability, having been decisively rejected by the Court of Appeal in *Re Polemis*,[97] was as decisively accepted and restored to favour by the Judicial Committee in *Overseas Tankship (U.K.) Ltd.* v. *Morts Dock and Engineering Co. Ltd.*,[98] an appeal from the Full Court of the Supreme Court of New South Wales. (This case is generally known as *The Wagon Mound*, the name under

---

[91] *Boiler Inspection and Insurance Company of Canada* v. *Sherwin-Williams Company of Canada* [1951] A.C. 319, 337, *per* Lord Porter. Yet Prosser said: "I doubt that all the manifold theories of the professors really have improved at all upon the old words 'proximate' and 'remote,' with the idea they convey of some reasonable connection between the original negligence and its consequences": *Topics*, p. 242.

[92] *Miller* v. *South of Scotland Electricity Board*, 1958 S.C.(H.L.) 20, 39.

[93] *Wayne Tank and Pump Co. Ltd.* v. *Employers' Liability Assurance Corporation Ltd.* [1974] 1 Q.B. 57, 61, 67.

[94] "The argument in the old fable in which the loss of a kingdom is traced back to an originating and ultimate cause in the loss of a single nail from a horse's shoe does not commend itself to me as adaptable to this case": *Norris* v. *William Moss & Sons Ltd.* [1954] 1 W.L.R. 346, 351, *per* Vaisey J. And nobody has suggested that the farrier should be liable in damages for the defeat: *Banque Keyser Ullmann S.A.* v. *Skandia (U.K.) Insurance Co. Ltd.* [1991] 2 A.C. 249, 280.

[95] It rested mainly upon dicta of Pollock C.B. in two cases decided upon the same day, May 8, 1850—*Rigby* v. *Hewitt*, 5 Ex. 240, 243, and *Greenland* v. *Chaplin*, 5 Ex. 243, 248. These dicta were of an extremely non-committal character, and were not agreed to by the other members of the court, but were accepted by Pollock's grandson in successive editions of his *Torts* and by Salmond as a correct statement of the law.

[96] For the meaning of this phrase, see above, § 23.3.

[97] [1921] 3 K.B. 560.

[98] [1961] A.C. 388.

which it is reported in the courts below.[99]) We shall consider first the decision in *Re Polemis* and then the decision in *The Wagon Mound*.

(6) The test of direct consequences[1]

The Court of Appeal in *Re an Arbitration between Polemis and Furness, Withy & Co.*[2] rejected the supposed rule that a wrongdoer is only responsible for the natural and probable consequences of his act. The court held that the probability of evil consequences is a test of whether the defendant was negligent or not; but if he was negligent, he is liable for the direct physical consequences whether probable or not. In that case Messrs. Polemis and Boyazides, the owners of the Greek steamship *Thrasyvoulos*, chartered the ship to Furness, Withy and Company, who loaded in the hold a quantity of petrol[3] in tins. During the voyage the tins leaked, and in consequence there was a considerable quantity of petrol vapour in the hold. At Casablanca in Morocco it became necessary for the Arab stevedores, servants of the charterers, to shift some of the cases, and for this purpose they placed a number of heavy planks at the end of the hatchway for use as a platform. While a sling containing the cases was being hoisted, the rope was negligently allowed to come into contact with these planks and to displace one of them, which fell into the hold. The fall of the plank was immediately followed by an outbreak of fire in the hold caused by the ignition of the petrol vapour by a spark struck by the falling plank. The ship was totally destroyed by fire.

The shipowners then claimed the value of the ship from the charterers, who relied, by way of defence, on the excepted perils clause in the charter-party, which was in the customary form, "act of God, the King's enemies, loss or damage from fire on board . . . excepted." The reply to this was that an excepted perils clause has no effect if the peril in question has been brought about by the negligence of the charterers or their servants. This was the issue referred to arbitration, and at first sight it might seem that the claim had little or nothing to do with the tort of negligence. The claim was upon a contract (a charterparty), and the issue was the simple one whether the negligence (in the sense of carelessness), of the defendants disentitled them from relying on the exemption clause.[4] But the charterers expressly pleaded that the damage was too remote,[5] and so the case was regarded as one of tort before Sankey J. and the Court of Appeal. The experienced arbitrators[6] from whom the appeal was brought found as a fact that the causing of a spark could not reasonably have been anticipated from the falling of the plank, though some (unspecified) damage to the ship might reasonably have

---

[99] [1958] 1 Lloyd's Rep. 575 (Kinsella J.); [1959] 2 Lloyd's Rep. 697 (Full Court).

[1] See Davies, "The Road From Morocco: *Polemis* Through *Donogue* to No-Fault" (1982) 45 M.L.R. 534.

[2] [1921] 3 K.B. 560.

[3] Described in some reports as benzine—a foreign term for petrol.

[4] *The Wagon Mound* [1959] 2 Lloyd's Rep. 697, 706.

[5] See McNair, "This *Polemis* Business" (1931) 4 Camb.L.J. 125, where the pleadings and the judgment of Sankey J. are set out in full. (This point seems to have escaped Manning J. in *The Wagon Mound*.)

[6] W. Clifton, A. F. Wootten, and Stuart Bevan, K.C.

been anticipated.[7] A strong Court of Appeal[8] unanimously held the charterers liable to the owners for the loss, which amounted to nearly £200,000. For to allow the plank to fall into the hold was in itself an act of negligence, inasmuch as it would not improbably cause some damage to the ship or cargo. The charterers, therefore, being guilty of negligence, were held liable for the direct consequences of that negligence, though in nature and magnitude those consequences were such as no reasonable man would have anticipated.[9]

Impecuniosity

Some light was later thrown upon the meaning of direct cause by the decision of the House of Lords in 1932 in *Liesbosch Dredger (Owners)* v. *Edison (Owners)*.[10] In that case a dredger was sunk owing to the negligence of *Edison*. The owners of the dredger required it for the performance of a contract, delay in the completion of which exposed them to heavy penalties. Owing to want of funds they could not purchase a dredger to take the place of the *Liesbosch*, and were forced to hire one at an exorbitant rate. It was held that the increased loss which the plaintiffs suffered due to their impecuniosity could not be recovered. The decision has never been fully accepted.[11] In particular it is hard to reconcile it with the principle that it is the plaintiff's duty to mitigate his loss, which should entitle an impecunious plaintiff to borrow money to mitigate that loss. Indeed, if that loss has been caused by the deceit of the defendant, it is "a brazen argument"[12] for him to say it should fall on the plaintiff. It has been said that the decision is an authority for the proposition that the principle of *Re Polemis* is limited to direct consequences to the particular interest of the plaintiff which has been invaded,[13] but in *The Wagon Mound*[14] the Judicial Committee said it was not easy to see why such a distinction should be drawn or where the line was to be drawn.

End of Polemis

The principle of *Re Polemis* could claim the support of some of the most eminent common lawyers: from Sir William De Grey C.J. in 1773,[15]

---

[7] Goodhart says that this finding "was obviously incorrect": *Essays*, p. 146n.

[8] Bankes, Scrutton and Warrington L.JJ. ("I always like, if I can, to find authority from Scrutton L.J., who was one of the greatest judges of my time": *Kemshead* v. *British Transport Commission* [1958] 1 W.L.R. 173, 174, *per* Lord Goddard C.J.).

[9] It is interesting that both counsel for the unsuccessful appellants, the future Lords Wright and Porter, later independently accepted that decision as correct; see Porter, 5 Camb.L.J. 176; Wright (1951) 14 M.L.R. 393.

[10] [1933] A.C. 449. Lord Wright, whose speech in this case was concurred in by the other Law Lords, later published some further reflections on the case in *Legal Essays*, pp. 96–123.

[11] See *Perry* v. *Sidney Phillips & Son* [1982] 1 W.L.R. 1297, 1307; *Archer* v. *Brown* [1985] Q.B. 401, 417.

[12] *Archer* v. *Brown* [1985] Q.B. 401, 417.

[13] So Lord Wright himself in *Bourhill* v. *Young* [1943] A.C. 92, 110 and Tilley, 33 Mich.L.R. 829, 847–851.

[14] [1961] A.C. 388, 424.

[15] *Scott* v. *Shepherd* (1773) 2 W.Bl. 892, 899.

through Channell B, and Blackburn J. in 1871,[16] down to Lord Sumner in 1920,[17] there is clear authority to support the view that the defendant is liable for all the direct and immediate consequences of his wrongful act[18]—although, as we have seen, there is also authority the other way. But in the years after 1922 it appeared as if the courts were trying to avoid a direct decision on the merits of *Re Polemis* by holding that there was no duty because the damage to this particular plaintiff was not reasonably foreseeable,[19] or that the defendant, although under a duty to take care, had observed the requisite standard in the particular case.[20]

But in 1960 the issue was squarely raised before the Judicial Committee of the Privy Council in *The Wagon Mound*[21] on appeal from New South Wales.

§ 23.4. THE WAGON MOUND: REASONABLE FORESEEABILITY

The facts of this case have already been set out.[22] The Judicial Committee considered whether the appellants, the charterers of the SS. *Wagon Mound*,[23] were liable for the consequential damage of the destruction of the wharf by fire, as the courts of New South Wales had (reluctantly) held them to be. The Judicial Committee reversed the courts below and found that the appellants were not responsible for the fire because the damage in question was not reasonably foreseeable. The Judicial Committee held that the decision in *Re Polemis* should no longer be regarded as good law and that the test of direct consequences was therefore inappropriate. The Judicial Committee stated that the decision in *Re Polemis* was objectionable on the ground that "it does not seem consonant with current ideas of justice or morality that for an act of negligence, however slight or venial, which results in some trivial foreseeable damage the actor should be liable for all consequences however unforeseeable and however grave, so long as they can be said to be 'direct.' It is a principle of civil liability, subject only to qualifications which have no present relevance, that a man must be considered to be responsible for the probable consequences of his act. To demand more of him is too harsh a rule, to demand less is to ignore that civilised order requires the observance of a minimum standard of behaviour."[24] Yet it might be asked why it is "consonant with current ideas of justice or

---

[16] *Smith* v. *L. & S.W. Ry.* (1871) L.R. 6 C.P. 14, 21. Yet Pollock (*Torts*, p. 29n.) thought "Blackburn and Willes JJ. would have been shocked beyond measure by *Polemis'* case."

[17] *Weld-Blundell* v. *Stephens* [1920] A.C. 956, 984. It should be noted that Lord Sumner used the test of direct consequences to limit liability and not to extend it: he thought that what had happened was foreseeable but not direct.

[18] So Atkin L.J. said in *Hambrook* v. *Stokes Bros.* [1925] 1 K.B. 141, at 156 that *Re Polemis* "laid down no new law."

[19] As in *Bourhill* v. *Young* [1943] A.C. 92.

[20] As in *Woods* v. *Duncan* [1946] A.C. 401.

[21] [1961] A.C. 388.

[22] See above, § 9.10.

[23] So called after a little known battle at Wagon Mound, New Mexico.

[24] [1961] A.C. 388, 422.

morality" that the innocent plaintiff should have to suffer without compensation the loss of his wharf.[25]

The authority of the decision

The decision in *The Wagon Mound*, according to the strict doctrine of precedent, is binding only upon some[26] tribunals in the Commonwealth, and is of only persuasive authority[27] in the final appellate tribunal in the United Kingdom. Yet in the House of Lords it has been assumed,[28] and in the Court of Appeal,[29] and in the High Court,[30] expressly stated, that *Polemis* is no longer law, and that *The Wagon Mound* is the governing authority. It may turn out that the controversy has little practical effect. For an increasingly favoured interpretation of the *Wagon Mound* cases is that they establish that the tortfeasor is liable for any damage which he can reasonably foresee, however unlikely it may be, unless it can be brushed aside as far fetched.[31] Such a test is not so different from the rejected direct consequences rule of *Re Polemis*—a decision which was probably correct on its facts.[32]

In this state of uncertainty it may be helpful to indicate a number of situations in which it seems clear that the principle in *The Wagon Mound* does not operate. One can often best judge the significance of a decision by observing what is excluded from it. The principle that reasonable foreseeability is the test of remoteness does not apply:

(1) When the tort is one of strict liability

The Judicial Committee itself recognised this exception so far as the rule in *Rylands* v. *Fletcher* was concerned,[33] and so has a later decision.[34] Probably in liability for dangerous animals[35] the test of remoteness is directness and not foresight. It is possible that libel,[36] and trespass to chattels,[37] are other exceptions.

(2) When the claim is under the Fatal Accidents Act

It is obvious that the test of remoteness here is not foresight. The question simply is whether the defendant has caused harm of a kind for

---

[25] *Shulhan* v. *Peterson, Howell and Heather Ltd.* (1966) 57 D.L.R. (2d) 491.
[26] So it has not been followed in Saskatchewan: *Shulhan* v. *Peterson, Howell and Heather Ltd.* (1966) 57 D.L.R. (2d) 491.
[27] The judgment in *The Wagon Mound* is rather ambiguous. In one place it expressly recognises that there are tribunals for which *Re Polemis* is still binding authority: in another it talks about "overruling" that case: see [1961] A.C. 388, 415, 420.
[28] *Hughes* v. *Lord Advocate* [1963] A.C. 837.
[29] *Doughty* v. *Turner Manufacturing Co. Ltd.* [1964] 1 Q.B. 518, 528, 532.
[30] *Smith* v. *Leech Brain & Co. Ltd.* [1962] 2 Q.B. 405.
[31] *Koufos* v. *Czarnikow* [1969] 1 A.C. 350, 422.
[32] See Lord Reid in [1967] 1 A.C. 617, 643, and *Kimber (David) T.V. Sound Ltd.* v. *Kaiapoi B.C.* [1988] N.Z.L.R. 376, 379.
[33] [1961] A.C. 388, 426–427.
[34] *British Celanese Ltd.* v. *A. H. Hunt (Capacitors) Ltd.* [1969] 1 W.L.R. 959.
[35] See above, §§ 14.2, 14.5.
[36] *Morgan* v. *Odhams Press Ltd.* [1971] 1 W.L.R. 1239.
[37] *Mayfair Ltd.* v. *Pears* [1987] 1 N.Z.L.R. 459.

which the law gives compensation. One who has deprived a family of its bread-winner cannot plead that he reasonably supposed he injured a bachelor of independent means.[38]

(3) When the claim is for breach of a strict statutory duty

The cases show that in actions for (say) the failure to fence dangerous machinery securely foresight of the consequences is irrelevant.[39]

(4) When the claim is for fraud

In an action for the tort of deceit the defendant must pay for all the actual damage of whatever character[40] directly flowing from the fraudulent inducement.[41]

(5) When the damage which has occurred, although foreseeable, is not damage of a kind against which it was the duty of the defendant to guard

The leading case of *Gorris* v. *Scott*[42] is perhaps the clearest example of this exception.

(6) When the defendant cannot be said to have caused the damage, although that damage was in face foreseeable, and a duty was owed to the particular plaintiff[43]

The *Wagon Mound* cases have laid it down that the plaintiff must prove foreseeability as well as causation. So there has been a tendency to emphasise foreseeability and to forget causation. But causation must still be proved. Thus in *Performance Cars Ltd.* v. *Abraham*[44] the defendant was held not liable when his car negligently collided with the plaintiff's Rolls-Royce for which the plaintiff claimed the cost (£75) of a re-spray for at the time of the accident the Rolls already needed such a re-spray as the result of a previous collision with a third party. Contrariwise, it is settled by *Baker* v. *Willoughby*[45] that a tortfeasor's liability remains unaffected by a later tortious event causing the same or greater damage to the plaintiff so long as the original tort remains one cause of the damage.[46] This is but an illustration of the established principle that successive torts causing the same damage give rise to joint and several liability.

---

[38] *Haber* v. *Walker* [1953] V.R. 339. See below, § 24.9.
[39] See above, § 10.2.–10.3.
[40] *Shelley* v. *Paddock* [1980] Q.B. 348.
[41] *Northern Bank Finance Co. Ltd.* v. *Charlton* [1979] I.R. 149.
[42] (1874) L.R. 9 Ex. 125. See above, § 10.1.
[43] See McGregor, "Variations on an Enigma" (1970) 33 M.L.R. 378.
[44] [1962] 1 Q.B. 33.
[45] [1970] A.C. 467.
[46] But a later supervening natural illness is not causally connected with the first injury: *Jobling* v. *Associated Dairies Ltd.* [1982] A.C. 794.

(7) When the damage which has been caused in damage of the same type or kind that might have been foreseen, but is greater in amount than could have been foreseen

This is perhaps the most important exception to the *Wagon Mound* principle. That principle requires that the type of damage must have been reasonably foreseeable; it does not require that the amount of that damage must have been foreseeable.

(i) *Type of damage must be foreseen.* It has been made plain that the precise details of the accident, or the exact concatenation of circumstances, need not be foreseen.[47] It is sufficient if the type, kind, degree, category or order of harm could have been foreseen in a general way.[48] The question is, was the accident a variant of the perils originally brought about by the defendant's negligence?[49] The law of negligence has not been fragmented into a number of distinct torts.[50]

(ii) *Amount of damage need not be foreseen.* If the damage which occurs is damage of the type or kind which ought to have been foreseen, in the sense explained in the preceding paragraph, then it is immaterial that the extent or amount of the damage was unforeseeable. As we have already seen,[51] there is a distinction between remoteness of damage and measure of damages, and the principle of foreseeability is applicable only to the former head. Indeed, once actionable injury has been established, compensation is rarely, if ever, just a valuation of that injury, but is rather a valuation of the harm suffered as a result of that injury.[52]

The "egg-shell skull" rule. This seventh exception, to the effect that the amount of damage not to be foreseen, is illustrated by the well-established rule that, at least so far as the physical[53] condition of the victim is concerned, abnormal circumstances existing at the time of the wrongful act do not negative causal connection. So if the consequences of a slight personal injury are aggravated by the state of health of the person injured, the wrongdoer is nonetheless liable to the full extent,[54] though he had no knowledge of that state of health and no reason to suspect

---

[47] *Hughes* v. *Lord Advocate* [1963] A.C. 837 (liability for fire caused by an explosion as distinct from a conflagration: see above, § 9.11). A similar principle governs cases of pure economic loss: *Banque Keyser S.A.* v. *Skandia (U.K.) Insurance Co. Ltd.* [1990] Q.B. 665, 763–765.

[48] *Doughty* v. *Turner Manufacturing Co. Ltd.* [1964] 1 Q.B. 518 (eruption of liquid by chemical change not a variant of the perils from the foreseeable risk of splashing: see above, § 9.11).

[49] *Bradford* v. *Robinson Rentals Ltd.* [1967] 1 W.L.R. 337, 344–345 (frostbite unusual, but a foreseeable variant of the perils of the English winter).

[50] In *Reeves* v. *Carthy* [1984] I.R. 348, at 367, Griffin J. said that the preceding paragraph "concisely and conveniently summarised this branch of the law."

[51] Above, § 23.1.

[52] *Wieland* v. *Cyril Lord Carpets Ltd.* [1969] 3 All E.R. 1006, 1009.

[53] Or perhaps even financial (*The Despina R.* [1977] 1 Lloyd's Rep. 618, 620), or emotional (*Malcolm* v. *Broadhurst* [1970] 3 All E.R. 508, 511).

[54] *Dulieu* v. *White* [1901] 2 K.B. 669, 679.

it.[55] So in the leading case of *Smith v. Leech Brain & Co. Ltd.*[56] it was held that if a victim of a negligent act suffers from a pre-cancerous condition which is activated by that act, the wrongdoer is responsible for all the disastrous consequences. This is always known as the "egg-shell skull" rule, although there appears to be only one case in which the plaintiff in fact suffered from this peculiar disability.[57] After a period of uncertainty, it has now been held in England,[58] Scotland,[59] Ireland,[60] New Zealand[61] and Canada[62] that *The Wagon Mound* did not affect the "egg-shell skull" rule. Although the rule is usually advantageous to the plaintiff, the facts of *Performance Cars Ltd. v. Abraham*[63] show that it may work to the advantage of the defendant.

The same rule applies when damage has been done to chattels. So we have it on the authority of Sir James Shaw Willes that a case was "tried before me at Newcastle spring assizes, 1859, in which a chemist who sold ointment to rub sheep with was held liable to pay to their owner the whole of their value, £2,000 and upwards, it having killed them; and yet it was hard that a man who could only make a profit of a few pence should be held responsible for so heavy a loss."[64] Again, if a chemical is supplied which is liable to explode on contact with water, and that hazard and consequent damage to property are reasonably foreseeable, then it matters not that the magnitude of the former and the extent of the latter were not so foreseeable.[65]

§ 23.5. EFFECT OF AN INTERVENING ACT

It remains to consider how far, if at all, the general principles of remoteness of damage are affected by the circumstance that the damage has been brought about by some overwhelming supervening event which is of such a character that it relegates into history matters which would otherwise be looked on as causative factors.[66] Such an event or act is often called a *novus actus interveniens*.[67] In discussing this difficult subject it will be helpful to recall that it is beyond question that human

---

[55] *Robinson v. Post Office* [1974] 1 W.L.R. 1176.

[56] [1962] 2 Q.B. 405.

[57] *Wilson v. Birt (Pty.), Ltd.*, 1963 (2) S.A. 508.

[58] *Smith v. Leech Brain & Co. Ltd.* [1962] 2 Q.B. 405.

[59] *McKillen v. Barclay Curle & Co. Ltd.* 1967 S.L.T. 41.

[60] *Burke v. John Paul & Co. Ltd.* [1967] I.R. 277.

[61] *Stephenson v. Waite Tileman Ltd.* [1973] 1 N.Z.L.R. 152.

[62] *Winteringham v. Rae* (1965) 55 D.L.R. (2d) 108.

[63] [1962] 1 Q.B. 33, cited in previous sub-head.

[64] *Mullett v. Mason* (1866) L.R. 1 C.P. 559, 561.

[65] *Vacwell Engineering Co. Ltd. v. B.D.H. Chemicals Ltd.* [1971] 1 Q.B. 88, 110 (on appeal, [1971] 1 Q.B. 111n).

[66] *R. v. Anderson and Morris* [1966] 2 Q.B. 110, 120.

[67] du Parcq L.J. thought that we could get on equally well without this phrase: *Ingram v. United Automobile Services* [1943] 2 All E.R. 71, 73, but, like the metaphor "chain of causation," it is a conveniently compendious expression and hallowed by long usage. "It has often been said that Latin phrases cannot help to solve problems of causation, but they are sometimes so convenient a label that the careful avoidance of them becomes an inverted kind of pedantry"; *Hogan v. Bentinck West Hartley Collieries (Owners) Ltd.* [1949] 1 All E.R. 588, 596, *per* Lord Normand.

action does not *per se* sever the connected sequence of acts.[68] There are two main views as to the proper test of causation in such a case. The one is that of foreseeability or probability, the other is that of isolation. It is in dealing with the effect of a *novus actus interveniens* that the divergence between these two views is most marked.

(1) The foreseeability or probability test

This test involves two propositions: first, if a consequence which actually results from the defendant's tort is a probable or foreseeable consequence, then the defendant may be liable; secondly, if a consequence which actually results from the defendant's tort is an improbable or unforeseeable consequence, then the defendant is not liable. If the *novus actus interveniens* is unforeseeable, it is much easier to recognise it as entirely independent and so efficient in its own effects that it should properly be regarded as having relegated the original act to an event of merely historical significance.[69] But if the *novus actus* is foreseeable, the defendant may be responsible, for it is often easy to foresee unreasonable conduct, as will be shown below.

(2) The isolation test

The isolation test is best expressed in the words of Lord Sumner in *Weld-Blundell* v. *Stephens*.[70] "In general (apart from special contracts and relations and the maxim *Respondeat superior*), even though A is in fault, he is not responsible for injury to C, which B, a stranger to him, deliberately chooses to do. Though A may have given the occasion for B's mischievous activity, B then becomes a new and independent cause. It is hard to steer clear of metaphors. Perhaps one may be forgiven for saying that B snaps the chain of causation; that he is no mere conduit pipe through which consequences flow from A to C, no mere moving part in a transmission gear set in motion by A; that in a word he insulates A from C." According to Lord Sumner[71] it is even immaterial that the intervening act is the probable consequence of the defendant's own wrongful act. This, undoubtedly, is a hard saying. Salmond was therefore reluctant to accept Lord Sumner's dictum as a correct statement[72] and in view of the criticisms passed upon the dictum by the Judicial Committee in *The Wagon Mound (No. 1)*[73] and by the Court of Appeal in *Slipper* v. *B.B.C.*[74] his reluctance would seem to have been justified.

---

[68] *The Oropesa* [1943] P. 32, 37; *Woods* v. *Duncan* [1946] A.C. 401, 442.

[69] *Iron and Steel Holdings and Realisation Agency* v. *Compensation Appeal Tribunal* [1966] 1 W.L.R. 480.

[70] [1920] A.C. 956, 986. "Lord Sumner was a reputed master of explicit language and clear thought. Few could say so precisely what they meant, and no one was less likely to say what he did not mean": *The People* v. *Kirwan* [1943] I.R. 279, 315, *per* Black J.

[71] *Weld-Blundell* v. *Stephens* [1920] A.C. 956, 988.

[72] See 6th ed., (s.36). Yet it should not be forgotten that these statements of Lord Sumner followed a passage in which he had given at least half-a-dozen examples of cases where a defendant would be held responsible despite the intervening act of some third party.

[73] [1961] A.C. 388, 417.

[74] [1991] Q.B. 283.

§ 23.6. LIABILITY WHERE INTERVENING ACT FORESEEABLE

There are undoubtedly many decisions which are expressed to rest upon the principle that damage which is the foreseeable or probable consequence of the defendant's wrongdoing is imputable to him notwithstanding an intervening act. The only qualification is that human actions are less easily foreseeable than a sequence of rational inanimate reactions.[75]

It must always be question of fact in each case whether the intervening act or omission was foreseeable, but the cases fall into five categories.

(1) Novus actus intentionally procured by defendant

Clearly the defendant will be liable wherever he has actually authorised or instigated the intervening act, or omission.[76] Salmond will also be liable if he has intentionally induced or procured the intervening act by putting the necessary means, opportunity, or inducement in the way of him who does it. But it is difficult to accept this extension in view of the decision in *C.B.S. Songs Ltd.* v. *Amstrad Electronics plc*,[77] in which manufacturers of hi-fi recording systems were held not liable to copyright owners for infringing acts by purchasers of these systems.

(2) Where the novus actus is a natural and probable result of the breach of duty

Greer L.J. in *Haynes* v. *Harwood*[78] said: "If what is relied upon as *novus actus interveniens* is the very kind of thing which is likely to happen if the want of care which is alleged takes place, the principle embodied in the maxim is no defence. The whole question is whether or not, to use the words of the leading case, *Hadley* v. *Baxendale*,[79] the accident can be said to be 'the natural and probable result' of the breach of duty." This statement has been cited with approval on several occasions in the Court of Appeal.[80] Thus in *Stansbie* v. *Troman*[81] a householder was obliged to leave a painter working alone in his house. The painter also left the house for about two hours to obtain some wallpaper and (although warned by the householder to shut the front door when he left the house) left the door unlocked. The painter was held liable for the loss of jewellery stolen by a third party who had entered the house in his absence, because this was just the kind of thing which was likely to happen. It has also long been settled that if a person collects a crowd to the annoyance of his neighbours that may constitute a nuisance, and that it is unnecessary to show that it was his object to create a nuisance,

---

[75] *Knightley* v. *Johns* [1982] 1 W.L.R. 349, 364.

[76] It should be noted that a deliberate omission is just the same in quality as an act of commission. It is a voluntary act: *Harnett* v. *Bond* [1924] 2 K.B. 517.

[77] [1988] A.C. 1013.

[78] [1935] 1 K.B. 146, 156.

[79] (1854) 9 Ex. 341.

[80] *Knightley* v. *Johns* [1982] 1 W.L.R. 349, 359.

[81] [1948] 2 K.B. 48. *Cobb* v. *Great Western Ry.* [1894] A.C. 419 (no liability for pick-pockets in overcrowded carriage) is not now treated as law.

or that it was the inevitable result of his act. It is sufficient to show that the collecting together of the crowd was, according to the common experience of mankind, the probable consequence of his act. So liability has been imposed where a crowd has collected in consequence of an interesting shop-window,[82] a theatrical success,[83] and a racecourse.[84] There has been much litigation on the question of whether the acts of vandals or squatters can be attributed to the occupiers of property on which they are resident. The courts have held that the occupier (often a local authority in an inner city area) is not responsible, not because the vandalism is not foreseeable, but because policy forbids the imposition of a duty.[85] The plaintiff need not prove that the defendant ought to have foreseen every step in the chain of events leading to the accident.[86]

Defamation no exception

Until recently it was thought that damage caused by the republication of a defamatory statement by an independent third party must always be ascribed to that party and not to the original publisher. But a unanimous Court of Appeal has held that there is no such exception to the general principles of *novus actus interveniens*. It is always a question of fact whether the republication was the foreseeable consequence of the original publication.[87]

(3) Where the intervening actor is not fully responsible

Again the chain of causation is not broken and the consequence is direct if the *novus actus interveniens* is the act of some person who is not fully responsible for his acts, and whose lack of responsibility should have been foreseen, such as a child,[88] or a workman in a factory whose senses have been dulled by routine work.[89]

The doctrine of "alternative danger"

One of the most familiar examples of this branch of the law is of a person acting in a state of excusable alarm produced by the defendant's own wrongful act.[90] Thus in *Scott v. Shepherd*[91] the defendant threw a lighted squib into the market-house at Milborne Port on a fair-day. The squib fell upon the stall of Yates, who sold gingerbread; one Willis, in order to prevent injury to himself and the goods of Yates, instantly

---

[82] *R. v. Carlile* (1834) 6 C. & P. 636, in which it was questioned whether the beautiful daughter of Mr. Very, a Regent Street confectioner, whose shop was daily beset by admiring crowds, might not have been an indictable nuisance.

[83] *Barber v. Penley* [1893] 2 Ch. 447 (*Charley's Aunt*).

[84] *Dewar v. City and Suburban Racecourse Co.* [1899] 1 I.R. 345.

[85] *P. Perl Ltd. v. Camden L.B.C.* [1984] Q.B. 342. See above, § 9.9.

[86] *Wieland v. Cyril Lord Carpets Ltd.* [1969] 3 All E.R. 1006, 1009. See above, §§ 9.4., 23.4.

[87] *Slipper v. B.B.C.* [1991] 1 Q.B. 283.

[88] *Latham v. Johnson* [1913] 1 K.B. 398, 413.

[89] See above, § 22.12.

[90] The doctrine of "alternative danger," as it is sometimes called, is also important in the law relating to contributory negligence: see above, § 22.13.

[91] (1773) 2 W.Bl. 892. The plaintiff in this leading case was the grandfather of C. P. Scott, the famous editor of the *Manchester Guardian*.

picked up the squib and threw it across the market-place; it landed upon the stall of one Ryal, who also sold gingerbread, and who in his turn threw the squib to another part of the market-house. On this occasion the squib burst in the plaintiff's face and destroyed one of his eyes. A majority of the Court of Common Pleas held that the defendant was responsible in trespass. "It has been urged that the intervention of a free agent will make a difference; but I do not consider Willis and Ryal as free agents in the present case, but acting under a compulsory necessity for their own safety and self-preservation."[92]

It has been said[93] to be desirable to limit the application of this principle to those cases in which the danger is personal danger and the plaintiff or third person has taken "instant action on the first alarm," where the choice has been automatic and without reflection. But the better view is that the doctrine extended to cases in which the plaintiff or third person had acted reasonably and "not unnaturally" and to cases in which the danger was danger to property.[94]

(4) Where the intervening act is done in pursuance of a duty

On the same principle the consequence is direct where the intervening act is that of a person acting under the compulsion of a legal or even only a moral duty. The commonest example is the rescue cases, which we have already discussed.[95] The action of the rescuer follows naturally and properly in the natural sequence of events from the act of the wrongdoer.[96]

(5) Where the intervening act is done in defence of rights

Again, the chain of causation is not treated as broken when the intervening act is that of a person acting in the exercise or defence of his rights and without intention to injure others.[97] So it is a foreseeable consequence of obstructing a highway that some passer-by may lawfully attempt to abate the nuisance and in so doing create a source of danger.[98]

Acts done to minimise damage

It is the duty of the plaintiff to minimise damage, so no act which he does reasonably with that object in view will break the chain of causation.[99] The duty to mitigate damage is really an application of the

---

[92] (1773) 2 W.Bl. 892, 900, *per* De Grey C.J. The dissenting judgment of Blackstone J. was based on the view that the acts of Willis and Ryal were not such a direct and immediate consequence of Shepherd's original act as to render him liable in *trespass*, as distinct from *case*. Denning L.J. said he agreed with Blackstone J.: the *Esso Petroleum Case* [1954] 2 Q.B. 182, 196.

[93] *Singleton Abbey (Owners)* v. *Paludina (Owners)* [1927] A.C. 16, 28.

[94] *Sutherland* v. *Glasgow Corporation*, 1951 S.C. 1.

[95] Above, § 22.5.

[96] *The Gusty* [1940] P. 159, 165.

[97] A good illustration of the principle is *Clayards* v. *Dethick* (1848) 12 Q.B. 439, the facts of which are given above, § 22.4.

[98] *Cunningham* v. *McGrath Bros.* [1964] I.R. 209.

[99] *McKew* v. *Holland and Hannen and Cubitts (Scotland) Ltd.* [1969] 3 All E.R. 1621.

broad principle of contributory negligence, so that the plaintiff cannot recover damages for an aggravation or prolongation of his injuries which is due to his own neglect or wilful default.[1] "If a man suffering from a sprained leg wishes to win a prize in a high-jumping competition and proceeds to endeavour to win it and thereby makes his leg so much worse that it takes an additional six months to recover, he is only entitled to damages for such part of his suffering as was not due to such heedless conduct."[2] Conversely, any profits earned as a result of the mitigating acts must be brought into account against the loss caused by the wrongful act.[3]

Refusal to accept professional advice or treatment[4]

So also a refusal by the plaintiff to accept medical advice or treatment (even when given by the defendant's doctors) may in all the circumstances be unreasonable and so damages should be assessed as if he had undergone the treatment and it had been successful.[5] Similarly, if the medical attention which the plaintiff receives aggravates his existing injury or causes a new injury, the defendant will probably not be liable if such injury is properly attributable to the actionable negligence of the surgeon or doctor, or some chemical or physical freak occurrence.[6] The erroneous advice of counsel does not break the chain of causation resulting from a solicitor's negligence.[7] On the other hand, the defendant will be liable if the original injury still subsists, although in an aggravated form, after an operation prudently advised and properly carried out.[8] Again, if the owner of a damaged chattel (not being a unique object) insists on having it repaired at a cost greatly in excess of the market replacement value, he has not taken reasonable steps to mitigate the damage.[9] But in criminal law it has been held that the wrongdoer must take his victim as he finds him. So it does not lie in the mouth of the assailant to say that his victim's religious beliefs, which inhibited him from accepting certain kinds of treatment, were unreasonable.[10]

§ 23.7. Currency of Award[11]

It is now possible for an English court to award damages in some currency other than sterling. In the case of tort, damages may be calculated in the currency in which the loss was effectively felt or borne by the plaintiff, having regard to the currency in which he generally oper-

---

[1] [1969] 3 All E.R. 1621, 1623.
[2] *Jones* v. *Watney, Combe, Reid & Co. Ltd.* (1912) 28 T.L.R. 399, 400.
[3] *The World Beauty* [1970] P. 145.
[4] See Hudson, "Refusal of Medical Treatment" (1983) 3 L.S. 50.
[5] *Selvanayagam* v. *University of West Indies* [1983] 1 W.L.R. 585.
[6] As in *Alston* v. *Marine and Trade Insurance Co. Ltd.* 1964 (4) S.A. 112, in which the plaintiff suffered a stroke after eating cheese following the administration of the drug parstellin.
[7] *Cook* v. *Swinfen* [1967] 1 W.L.R. 457.
[8] *Hogan* v. *Bentinck West Hartley Collieries (Owners) Ltd.* [1949] 1 All E.R. 588, 596, 607.
[9] *Darbishire* v. *Warran* [1963] 1 W.L.R. 1067.
[10] *R.* v. *Blaue* [1975] 1 W.L.R. 1411.
[11] See Knott, "Foreign Currency Judgments in Tort" (1980) 43 M.L.R. 18.

ates.[12] This is really no more than an application of the general principle of reasonable foreseeability.

§ 23.8. Contract and Tort[13]

A large number of conflicting dicta exist on the relationship of the rules governing remoteness of damage in contract and in tort. All must now be read in the light both of the two *Wagon Mound* cases[14] and also of the decision of the House of Lords in *Czarnikow Ltd.* v. *Koufos*.[15] It is clear that the measure of damages in contract is not the same as in tort.[16] Beyond that, all is obscure, and there has been judicial complaint about a "sea of semantic exercises."[17] So the following analysis is tentative.

In contract the rule is that the plaintiff can recover for loss which the defendant, when he entered into the contract, ought to have contemplated as a reasonable man was of a very substantial degree of probability or was not unlikely to result from a breach. The plaintiff cannot recover, as he can in tort, for loss which is a serious possibility or a real danger. The reason for this distinction between contract and tort is that in contract, if one party wishes to protect himself from a risk which to the other party would appear unusual, he can direct that other's attention to it before the contract is made. But in tort there is no such opportunity available to the injured party, and so the tortfeasor cannot complain if he has to pay for some very unusual but still foreseeable damage which results from his wrongdoing. Therefore liability in tort is normally wider than liability in contract—but not necessarily so, for the parties to a contract may expressly agree that there shall be liability for some remote and quite unforeseeable head of damage. So damages for the tort of deceit are quite different from damages for breach of warranty.[18] Thus in deceit it is settled that a plaintiff cannot recover damages for loss of his bargain: he is only entitled to be put in the position which he would have been in had the representation not been made. Yet in an action for breach of contract he is entitled to be put in the same position as if the representation had been true or fulfilled.

---

[12] *The Despina R* [1979] A.C. 685.
[13] See Harris, *Remedies in Contract and Tort* (1988), pp. 225–227.
[14] Above, §§ 23.2.–23.4.
[15] [1969] 1 A.C. 350. Note that the leading judgment was delivered by Lord Reid, who had also sat in both *Wagon Mound* appeals.
[16] *Czarnikow Ltd.* v. *Koufos* [1969] 1 A.C. 350, 385, 411, 413, 422.
[17] *Parsons Ltd.* v. *Ingham Ltd.* [1978] 2 Q.B. 791, 802, *per* Lord Denning M.R.
[18] *Doyle* v. *Olby (Ironmongers) Ltd.* [1969] 2 Q.B. 158; *East* v. *Maurer* [1991] 1 W.L.R. 401.

CHAPTER 24

DAMAGES FOR PERSONAL INJURY AND DEATH

§ 24.1. Actions for Injuries to the Person

The award of damages in respect of losses arising out of personal injury and death is a topic of considerable complexity.[1] Some of the difficulty is due to the absence of any coherent philosophy behind the different sources of compensation to accident victims in the welfare state. Tort is not the only, nor the main, source of compensation today for social security (D.S.S. benefits) must be taken into account.[2] Within torts the cases on damages reveal a striking discordance of views on the most elementary matters. Because of the great mass of reported cases it is not possible to do more here than indicate the broad general principles governing the matter. In each case the proper computation is a question of fact.[3] Hence it is for the judge in his discretion to decide whether he will permit counsel to refer to decisions showing the amount awarded in similar cases, but in practice such citations are increasingly frequent.[4] It is often discussed whether the governing principle is that of *restitutio in integrum*, or whether the defendant is only obliged to give the plaintiff fair compensation. The truth appears to be that each of these principles of assessment has its own proper sphere of operation. There is no criterion which is universally valid over the whole field of damages.

One classification distinguishes pecuniary loss from non-pecuniary loss. Another classification is between special damages and general damages. Special damages can be defined as pecuniary loss actually suffered up to the date of the trial—*e.g.* loss of earnings, and general damages are then the other heads of loss—*e.g.* pain and suffering and future pecuniary loss. Special damage must be pleaded and proved[5]; general damage is implied.[6] The principle of *restitutio in integrum* is appropriate to pre-trial and future loss of income: so far as actual or prospective pecuniary loss is concerned the amount of compensation can

---

[1] The outstanding general survey is in Atiyah, *Accidents, Compensation and the Law* (4th ed., 1987). See also Kemp and Kemp, *The Quantum of Damages in Personal Injury Claims*; (note that this is a different work from Kemp, *Damages for Personal Injury and Death*); Munkman, *Damages for Personal Injuries and Death*; McGregor on Damages Chap. 33; the *Report on Personal Injury Litigation—Assessment of Damages* Law Com. No. 56, 1973), and the Pearson Report (Cmnd. 7054), §§ 343–614. A useful guide for the solicitor is Pritchard, *Personal Injury Litigation*.

[2] See the magisterial survey by Fleming, *International Encyclopedia of Comparative Law*, vol. xi (1971).

[3] *Waldon* v. *War Office* [1956] 1 W.L.R. 51.

[4] The proper course is for counsel to inquire whether the court wishes to have assistance. The practitioner is careful to avoid the trap into which the student so often falls—citing a mass of cases without being asked to do so.

[5] *Domsalla* v. *Barr* [1969] 1 W.L.R. 630.

[6] *British Transport Commission* v. *Gourley* [1956] A.C. 185, 206.

be assessed with a degree of accuracy which will go far towards putting the injured person in the same position as he would have been in had he not sustained the wrong. But the principle of fair and reasonable compensation is more appropriate to the non-pecuniary heads of damage such as pain and suffering.[7] Money cannot renew a shattered human frame.[8] Still, the law has said that this is a head of damage for which monetary compensation can be awarded and so the court must do the best it can in the light of such comparable cases as it may consider to be of assistance to it.[9]

Again, there is dispute whether the object of an award of damages is to compensate the plaintiff or punish the defendant. In England the main object is compensation which is fair and adequate but not perfect.[10] So awards of exemplary damages have been cut down[11] and within the field of compensatory damages the plaintiff must bring into account some collateral benefits.[12]

§ 24.2. PRE-TRIAL PECUNIARY LOSS

Pre-trial pecuniary loss (sometimes called special damages) must be pleaded and provided.[13] In general there are two distinct heads—expenses and loss of earnings. These will be considered separately.

Expenses

The plaintiff is entitled to recover all expenses actually and reasonably incurred as a result of the accident before the date of the trial.[14] This will enable him to recover for such items as loss of, or damage to, clothing, medical expenses,[15] the cost of lost board and lodging,[16] and nursing expenses.[17] But if the plaintiff has been maintained at the public expense in any hospital, nursing home or other institution, any saving to him should be set off against any loss of income.[18] But damages for private medical care are still recoverable. A literal application of *Gourley*[19] might seem to require the *deduction* of living expenses from the total award on the ground that the plaintiff would have had to maintain himself anyway. So it has been held that it would be proper to take

---

[7] *The Mediana* [1900] A.C. 113, 116.
[8] *West & Son Ltd.* v. *Shephard* [1964] A.C. 326, 345.
[9] *Wright* v. *British Railways Board* [1983] 2 A.C. 773.
[10] *West (H.) & Son Ltd.* v. *Shephard* [1964] A.C. 326, 346.
[11] See *Rookes* v. *Barnard* [1964] A.C. 1129.
[12] See below, § 24.4.
[13] *British Transport Commission* v. *Gourley* [1956] A.C. 185, 206.
[14] Expenses which may crystallise in the future should be claimed as general damages: *Shearman* v. *Folland* [1950] 2 K.B. 43, 51.
[15] Sometimes the value of necessary services voluntarily furnished to the plaintiff can be recovered; *Gage* v. *King* [1961] 1 Q.B. 188, but it is no longer necessary for a kind relative to make a contract before nursing the plaintiff: see *Donnelly* v. *Joyce* [1974] Q.B. 454, for it is the plaintiff's loss of capacity which creates the need for those services, and that loss has been caused by the defendant.
[16] *Liffen* v. *Watson* [1940] 1 K.B. 556.
[17] *Shearman* v. *Folland* [1950] 2 K.B. 43.
[18] Administration of Justice Act 1982, s.5.
[19] See below, § 24.4.

into account expenditure which would have been incurred in maintaining the victim (but not his dependants) at the appropriate standard.[20] Deductions for expenses saved are not in practice a significant element in the calculation.

Loss of earnings

It is settled that the plaintiff is entitled to damages for the loss of the earnings or profits which would normally have accrued to him up to the date of the judgment.[21] But what he is entitled to claim is the loss of what would have been in his pay-packet—*i.e.* the net amount after deduction of income tax[22] and social security contributions,[23] or unemployment benefit.[24] Normally the amount can be calculated easily by multiplying the plaintiff's weekly wage or salary by the number of weeks during which he was incapacitated by his injuries.[25] The existence of inflation makes it important to take into account any increases in remuneration.

§ 24.3. FUTURE PECUNIARY LOSS

Nature of the award

The main component of a claim for future pecuniary loss is, almost invariably, loss of income or, in fatal cases, lost dependency.[26] As these sums can merely be estimated, being prospective, they are claimed as general damages. The use of the "multiplier" is the favoured method of assessing the sum: the plaintiff's net annual loss is multiplied by a figure chosen so as to produce an overall sum which is intended to provide, by withdrawals of both interest and capital, compensation for the lost income in the years ahead. The multiplier should not be confused with the number of working years which would have been left to the plaintiff if he had not been injured, since allowance is made for contingencies such as illness, which might have struck him in any event, as well as for the fact that the plaintiff in a sense receives his compensation in advance as a lump sum. In practice the multiplier hardly ever exceeds 18, even in the case of young plaintiffs. The actuarial method of calculation is not favoured by the courts, except as a check or guide.[27] A plaintiff may sometimes be awarded damages for loss of earning *capacity, i.e.*

---

[20] *Harris* v. *Empress Motors Ltd.* [1984] 1 W.L.R. 212.

[21] But for the position with respect to deduction of D.S.S. benefits, see below, § 24.4.

[22] *British Transport Commission* v. *Gourley* [1956] A.C. 185.

[23] *Cooper* v. *Firth Brown Ltd.* [1963] 1 W.L.R. 418.

[24] *Parsons* v. *B.N.M. Laboratories Ltd.* [1964] 1 Q.B. 95.

[25] See the calculation in *Harris* v. *Bright's Asphalt Contractors Ltd.* [1953] 1 Q.B. 617. This sum may have to be reduced if there is any possibility that, apart from his injuries, the plaintiff might for some reason have been unable to earn the same wages: *Rouse* v. *Port of London Authority* [1953] 2 Lloyd's Rep. 179, 184. But if the injured plaintiff is a person legally entitled to be paid wages by his employer during the period of incapacity, he cannot claim under this head, for he has not sustained any loss as a result of the defendant's wrong: *Receiver for Metropolitan Police District* v. *Croydon Corporation* [1957] 2 Q.B. 154.

[26] See below, § 24.9.

[27] *Taylor* v. *O'Connor* [1971] A.C. 115.

a potential handicap in the job-market in the future.[28] After some doubt the prevailing view appears to be that this is to be regarded as a factor to be taken into account in assessing damages for loss of earnings, rather than as a separate head of damage.[29] Nevertheless it is still sometimes seen as presenting special problems, especially where the plaintiff is a young child.[30]

Disadvantages of the lump sum

The award of damages for future pecuniary loss as a lump sum necessarily requires the court, when making its assessment, to make assumptions or guesses about a number of factors, including the likely duration of the plaintiff's incapacity, his chances for promotion or increase in earnings, and the future rates of return on invested capital.[31] The court has to be wrong on only one of these assumptions for the plaintiff to be extensively over-compensated or under-compensated. There is no opportunity for making a correction subsequently. The Pearson Commission acknowledged these drawbacks in lump sum awards for future pecuniary loss and recommended by a majority that, in cases of death or serious and lasting injury, the plaintiff ought to be able to take his damages in the form of periodic payments. These payments would be administered by the defendant's insurer (where he was injured), and would be revalued annually in line with the movement in average earnings. The awards would also be subject to review by the courts, but such a review would be confined to changes in the plaintiff's pecuniary loss brought about by changes in his medical condition. The recommendation has not been implemented but a limited reform has mitigated some of the disadvantages of the lump sum where there is a chance of a serious disease, or deterioration[32] in the plaintiff's condition, developing in the future. The Administration of Justice Act 1982, s.6 added a new provision, s.32A, to the Supreme Court Act 1981 enabling "provisional damages" to be awarded in such cases whereby the plaintiff may be able to return to the court for an additional award if circumstances so warrant.[33] A longer-established procedure for mitigating the disadvantage of the lump sum is the split trial whereby the determination of *quantum* is postponed to a later date than the hearing on liability.[34]

Structured settlements[35]

Although the courts have no power to order the payment of damages in the form of periodic payments such payments have become increas-

---

[28] *Moeliker* v. *A. Reyrolle & Co.* [1977] 1 W.L.R. 132.

[29] See the Report of the Pearson Commission (Cmnd. 7054), § 337–338.

[30] *Croke* v. *Wiseman* [1982] 1 W.L.R. 71.

[31] See the analysis in Atiyah's *Accidents, Compensation and the Law*, (4th ed., Cane ed.). Ch. 7.

[32] See *Willson* v. *Ministry of Defence* [1991] 1 All E.R. 638.

[33] For the procedural details see R.S.C., Ord. 37.

[34] See R.S.C., Ord. 33. For the assessment of interest on awards in such cases see *Thomas* v. *Bunn* [1991] 1 A.C. 362. For interest on awards generally, see below, § 24.6.

[35] See Allen, "Structured Settlements" (1988) 104 L.Q.R. 448.

ingly common when negotiated as "structured settlements" in cases settled out of court. As a result of an agreement between the Inland Revenue and the Association of British Insurers such agreements have tax advantages, and they can be very beneficial to claimants.[36]

Lost years

Should a plaintiff be entitled to damages for his loss of earnings in the years for which he would normally have lived but for his injuries? In accordance with the principle that a plaintiff is entitled to be compensated for loss of anything having a money value, an affirmative answer was given by the House of Lords in *Pickett* v. *British Rail Engineering Ltd.*[37] But the *Pickett* case gave rise to its own problems when it was held that a claim for the lost years survived for the benefit of the estate.[38] This opened up the possibility of substantial claims for damages against wrongdoers if the deceased had left his estate to persons other than his dependants. So now the Administration of Justice Act 1982, s.4 prohibits the recovery of any damages for loss of income[39] in respect of any period after a person's death,[40] if that claim is made by the person's estate, as distinct from the injured party himself while he is still alive. Therefore not all heads of damages available to a victim are available to his estate. A deduction must also be made for the deceased's living expenses.[41]

Inflation[42] and taxation

The controlling view is that inflation should not be taken into account in the assessment of damages for future pecuniary loss largely in the (not wholly realistic) belief it can be offset by prudent investment, so that the problem "is taken care of in a rough and ready way."[43] This approach was confirmed by four members of the House of Lords in *Lim* v. *Camden Health Authority.*[44] In one case the House of Lords was prepared to concede that there could be exceptional cases where it might be appropriate to increase the multiplier[45] to allow for the effect of high rates of taxation on a very substantial award, but in the more recent case

---

[36] In one settlement announced in the summer of 1991 a brain-damaged road-accident victim stands to receive £14 million if he lives to be 80. A conventional lump-sum award would have been only around £1 million: see *The Times*, July 13, 1991.

[37] [1980] A.C. 136, overruling the much-criticised decision in *Oliver* v. *Ashman* [1962] 2 Q.B. 210.

[38] *Gammell* v. *Wilson* [1982] A.C. 27.

[39] Does this phrase cover, say, the chance of acquiring an inheritance?

[40] If death occurred after January 1, 1983.

[41] For the mode of calculation, see *Harris* v. *Empress Motors* [1984] 1 W.L.R. 132.

[42] See Fleming, "The Impact of Inflation on Tort Compensation" (1978) 26 Am.Jo. of Comp. Law 51.

[43] *Cookson* v. *Knowles* [1979] A.C. 556, 571, *per* Lord Diplock.

[44] [1980] A.C. 174. See especially *per* Lord Scarman at p. 193. But Lord Scarman also once said that "in truth, of course, judicial awards of damages follow, but rarely keep pace with, inflation": *Pickett* v. *British Rail Engineering* [1980] A.C. 136, 173.

[45] *Cookson* v. *Knowles* [1979] A.C. 556.

of *Hodgson* v. *Trapp*[46] the House refused to sanction such an adjustment in the case before it and even appeared to doubt the likelihood of cases occurring in which increasing the multiplier for this purpose would be appropriate.[47]

Cost of care

With advances in medical science very seriously injured accident victims often survive, but remain permanently disabled and in need of constant care and attendance for the rest of their lives. The cost of such care is a recognised head of damages, and a plaintiff is under no obligation to mitigate his loss by using the National Health Service instead of private medical facilities.[48] Often he will be cared for at home by a parent or spouse and the value of such services is recoverable by the plaintiff.[49]

§ 24.4. Offsets

Taxation liabilities[50]

In *British Transport Commission* v. *Gourley*[51] the House of Lords held that in assessing damages for loss of personal earnings in cases of personal injury the tax which the plaintiff would have had to pay had he continued to receive those earnings must be taken into account. On the facts of the *Gourley* case itself this meant that the plaintiff recovered £6,695 instead of £37,720. This decision at first seemed novel and inequitable to many; it was not easy to see why the courts should tax when the Revenue did not,[52] particularly when the beneficiary was not the Revenue but the defendant's insurance company. But the decision is no more than a logical application of the settled principle that damages are intended to put the plaintiff in the same position as he would have been in had he not received the injury. Damages are intended to compensate the plaintiff for that which he has lost, and in assessing the value of what has been lost to him it would be unrealistic for the court to close its eyes to the incidence of taxation. It is true that the court may be called upon to make elaborate calculations, but the courts are not unfamiliar with complex arithmetical computations, and the estimate "will be none the worse if it is formed on broad lines, even

---

[46] [1989] A.C. 807 overruling the majority decision of the Court of Appeal in *Thomas* v. *Wignall* [1987] Q.B. 1098.

[47] See *per* Lord Oliver in [1989] A.C. 807, 835.

[48] Law Reform (Personal Injuries) Act 1948, s.2(4). The Pearson Commission recommended that this provision should be repealed and the use of private facilities subjected to a reasonableness test: Report, para. 341.

[49] *Donnelly* v. *Joyce* [1974] Q.B. 454.

[50] The Law Commission's Report (Law Com. No. 56, 1973).

[51] [1956] A.C. 1985. See Bishop and Kay, "Taxation and Damages: the Rule in Gourley's case" (1987) 104 L.Q.R. 211.

[52] [1957] A.C. 403, 410.

though it may be described as rough and ready."[53] *Gourley* has been followed in Ireland,[54] and in Australia,[55] but not in Canada.[56]

Various other criticisms have been made of the decision in *Gourley*.[57] One is that it is wrong that the defendant should profit from the fact that the plaintiff is in a high tax bracket. The answer to this is that the defendant can hardly be supposed to have selected on purpose a plaintiff who was a large taxpayer. Another criticism is that a person whose earning capacity is wholly or partially destroyed thereby loses a capital asset, and as it is[58] a fundamental principle of English revenue law that a capital asset is not taxable, it should follow that the compensation which replaces that asset is also tax-free. But while it is true that a man's skill and experience are in the nature of capital assets, all that was done in *Gourley* was to value those assets by the income which they are likely to produce, and that income was affected by the predictable factor of taxation. In short, the Law Lords in *Gourley* faced the realities of life and refused to be misled by maxims such as *res inter alios acta*.[59] There is no reason why someone who has lost a net sum should receive a gross sum. A logical application of the principle that potential liabilities must be taken into account means that a plaintiff may be compelled to disclose particulars of his tax position,[60] and to give credit for a tax rebate.[61]

Collateral benefits

If a plaintiff receives collateral benefits of any kind in compensation for an injury, it might be thought that his damages in tort ought to be correspondingly reduced; otherwise, he will be over-compensated, for the aim of the law is simply to restore him as near as possible to the position he would have been in but for the accident. But the law has not insisted on such a reduction in all cases, usually for overriding policy reasons. Various benefits will now be considered in turn.

(i) Loss insurance

Benefits received under a contract of insurance are not deducted from damages for personal injury.[62] The rationale is that the beneficiary has

---

[53] [1956] A.C. 185, 203, *per* Earl Jowitt.
[54] *Glover* v. *B.L.N. Ltd.* [173] I.R. 432.
[55] *Cullen* v. *Trappell* (1980) 29 A.L.R. 1.
[56] *The Queen* v. *Jennings* (1966) 57 D.L.R. (2d) 644.
[57] But it is significant that neither the Law Reform Committee (Seventh Report, Cmnd. 501 (1958)) nor the Law Commission (Law Com. No. 56, 1973), wished to recommend a reversal of *Gourley*.
[58] Or was until the introduction of the Capital Gains Tax, which, significantly, does not apply to awards for personal injuries.
[59] So Lord Reid (who had sat in *Gourley*) in *Parry* v. *Cleaver* [1970] A.C. 1, 15.
[60] *Phipps* v. *Orthodox Unit Trusts* [1958] 1 Q.B. 314.
[61] *Hartley* v. *Sandholme Iron Co.* [1975] Q.B. 600.
[62] *Bradburn* v. *Great Western Railway Co.* (1874) L.R. 10 Ex. 1. As regards damages following death, the Fatal Accidents Act 1976, s.4(1) specifically provides that insurance money shall not be taken into account.

paid for this policy, and it would not be right to deprive him of his benefit under this contract.[63]

(ii) Payments by an employer

Occupational sick pay diminishes the plaintiff's loss, and so should be taken into account in assessing damages.[64] This applies whether or not the plaintiff has been injured at work so that his employer is also the defendant. Thus in *Hussain* v. *New Taplow Paper Mills*[65] the House of Lords reduced on this ground the damages awarded against the plaintiff's employer, and rejected a contention that the fact that the defendants had insured against their contractual liability to provide sick pay meant that the insurance policy had indirectly been paid for by the plaintiff himself, in lieu of higher wages, and that its proceeds should therefore have been treated as equivalent to those of a health insurance policy taken out by the plaintiff directly. There was no evidence that the plaintiff's wages would have been higher if the policy had not been taken out.[66] Where a plaintiff was made redundant following an accident at work a redundancy payment made to him by the defendants, his employers, was deducted.[67]

(iii) Occupational pensions

In *Parry* v. *Cleaver*[68] the House of Lords held that a disability pension, whether or not discretionary and whether or not contributory, should be left out of account in assessing the plaintiff's lost earnings. The majority argued that a disability pension should be regarded as a form of loss insurance, which was in large measure paid for—either directly in the form of contributions, or indirectly in lieu of higher wages—by the beneficiary himself. The minority view was that an occupational disability pension should be regarded as a benefit provided by the employer, analogous to sick pay. The Pearson Commission thought neither view exactly reflected the realities of occupational pensions provision, but on balance thought it nearer the truth to regard such pensions as benefits provided by the employee.[69] This view was reaffirmed in the 1991 case of *Smoker* v. *London Fire and Civil Defence Authority*[70]

---

[63] The Law Commission and the Pearson Commission recommended no change in the law: Law Com. No. 56, s.151; Pearson Report, ss.513–516.

[64] *Metropolitan Police Receiver* v. *Croydon Corporation* [1957] 2 Q.B. 154. The Pearson Commission recommended that sick pay should not be taken into account where the plaintiff is by his contract of service under a contractual obligation to refund it from damages or where it was advanced by his employer as a loan on the express understanding that it would be repaid if damages were recovered: Report, paras. 513–516.

[65] [1988] A.C. 514.

[66] But the Court of Appeal distinguished *Hussain's* case in a situation in which the defendant employer had simply taken out an accident insurance policy for the benefit of employees unrelated to any contractual liability for sick pay. The proceeds of such a policy were treated as equivalent to personal benevolence and not deducted: *McCamley* v. *Cammell Laird Shipbuilders* [1990] 1 W.L.R. 963.

[67] *Colledge* v. *Bass Mitchells & Butlers* [1988] I.C.R. 125.

[68] [1970] A.C. 1.

[69] Pearson Report, ss.517–521; see too Law Com. No. 56, s.152.

[70] [1991] 2 A.C. 502.

when a unanimous House of Lords, which had been invited to overturn *Parry* v. *Cleaver*, refused to do so and chose instead to emphasise the correctness of the earlier decision.

However, disability pensions should be taken into account in assessing damages for loss of a retirement pension—for example, where the plaintiff, after completing his service, would have received a full retirement pension rather than a lower disability pension.

Where part of the plaintiff's wages normally go to pay pension scheme contributions any damages for lost earnings will be reduced to reflect his net income after the payment of such contributions, provided that his failure to make contributions while off sick after the accident would not in practice reduce his pension entitlement.[71] Otherwise he would have the best of both worlds: the entitlement without payment of the contributions. But in the perhaps more usual situation where a reduction in entitlement will have occurred the plaintiff is obviously entitled to damages to compensate for this.

(iv) Social security benefits

The Social Security Act 1989 made a radical change in the law relating to the relationship between damages and social security benefits. Formerly the court was obliged by section 2(1) of the Law Reform (Personal Injuries) Act 1948 to offset against damages for loss of income due to personal injury one-half of the social security benefits for five years. This odd provision, which will continue to apply to cases in which the damages are less than £2,500, and also to all cases concerning accidents which occurred before January 1, 1989, reflected a compromise between those who favoured full deduction and those who did not. It was much criticised, not least because only the tortfeasor benefited from the deductions: the state did not itself receive back the value of the benefits which it had paid out. The new Act[72] provides that the value of such social security benefits as are listed in Regulations[73] made under it are to be deducted *in full*, for a period of five years following the date of the accident, from the total sum of damages awarded for personal injury including both pecuniary and non-pecuniary loss. The offsets are thus no longer confined to damages for lost earnings.[74] The tortfeasor is required to obtain a certificate from the Department of Social Security of the value of benefits paid, or likely to be paid, to the plaintiff over the relevant period. The sum will then be deducted from the award (or out-

---

[71] *Dews* v. *National Coal Board* [1988] A.C. 1.

[72] Social Security Act 1989, s.22 and Sched. 4.

[73] See the Social Security (Recoupment) Regulations 1990 (S.I. 1990 No. 322) and related Amendment Regulations (S.I. 1990 No. 1558). The following benefits are listed: income support and family credit, attendance allowance, disability benefits and mobility allowance, statutory sick pay and unemployment benefits.

[74] It is to be noted that the new scheme involves rejection of the Pearson Commission's elaborate recommendation that benefits should be classified into three different categories, corresponding to the various differing pecuniary and non-pecuniary heads of tort damages, and then deducted in assessing the corresponding portion of the tort award: see the Report, ss.467–495.

of-court settlement) and the tortfeasor will himself be obliged to reimburse the Department of Social Security the relevant amount.[75]

§ 24.5. NON-PECUNIARY LOSS

By definition, money cannot make good a non-pecuniary loss. Yet
damages are recoverable for it in almost all tort systems. Even under the
New Zealand accident compensation scheme, lump sum compensation
is payable for non-pecuniary loss. The Pearson Commission concluded
that there is a place for damages for non-pecuniary loss, although it
stressed that the main aim of any compensation system should be to
make good pecuniary loss.

There are two main categories of non-pecuniary loss: pain and suffering is one while loss of amenities of life is the other. A former third separate category, shortened expectation of life, has since 1982 effectively
been subsumed by statute within the pain and suffering category.
Damages for loss under the two categories are usually made in a single
sum. The figure assessed[76] is arbitrary,[77] but that does not mean it is
unjust, for a known conventional figure enables settlements to be made,
and so the evil of litigation is avoided. After an exhaustive review of
this difficult subject, the Law Commission was unable to arrive at any
conclusion, except to say that "the only helpful question that we think
can be asked is not whether the damages awarded are 'right' but who
ought to decide what these arbitrary amounts should be."[78] The Pearson Commission rejected the idea of a legislative tariff providing a scale
of damages. The Commission, however, recommended that no damages
should be recoverable for non-pecuniary loss suffered during the first
three months after the date of injury: the rationale was to eliminate the
bulk of small claims, while continuing to allow damages to those suffering lasting pain and loss of amenity.[79] The recommendation has not
been implemented.

Pain and suffering

It is well established that, given clear evidence of reasonably pro-
longed suffering, damages are recoverable in English courts[80] both for
past, and likely future, pain and suffering. Since the concept is necess-

---

[75] The Government expects to save £55 million per annum in this way.

[76] "Assessment" is the term more appropriate than "calculation" for non-pecuniary loss,
as such loss is incapable of precise measurement.

[77] Atiyah commented, "All such damage awards could be multiplied or divided by two
overnight and they would be just as defensible or indefensible": *Accidents, Compensation and the Law*, (3rd ed.), p. 213.

[78] Law Com. No. 56, s.20.

[79] Pearson Report, paras. 373–389. The Commission estimated that this change would
result in a saving equivalent to almost one-fifth of all tort compensation for personal
injury.

[80] It was not always so. Pollock C.B. once said, "In my personal judgment, it is an
unmanly thing to make such a claim": *Theobald* v. *Railway Passengers Assurance Co.*
(1862) 15 Jur. 583, 586. Such awards apparently seldom exist in the socialist-based legal
systems of what were formerly known as Eastern Bloc countries.

arily a subjective one[81] there can be no award for pain and suffering where the plaintiff has been, and will remain, permanently unconscious since it is assumed that patients in such a state do not experience pain.[82] But unless the plaintiff is actually in a coma he will usually be taken to have some awareness of his condition.[83] Moreover even patients in that state will recover damages for loss of amenity.[84]

Loss of expectation of life

Prior to 1982 there existed a claim for damages for loss of expectation of life. An unexpected and unintended by-product of the Law Reform (Miscellaneous Provisions) Act 1934 was that this additionally became recoverable on an objective basis by the estates of persons who had been killed outright instead of merely by plaintiffs who continued to live albeit with a shorter life expectancy than they had hitherto enjoyed.[85] In practice awards took the form of a largely conventional sum[86] which, shortly before its abolition, stood at a little over £1,000.[87] When Parliament finally eliminated this somewhat bizarre head of damage it emphasised that the much more rational claim by living plaintiffs for damages in respect of their *knowledge* of their predicament would not be affected. Thus the Administration of Justice Act 1982, s.1(1) now provides that in an action for personal injuries:

(*a*) no damages shall be recoverable in respect of any loss of expectation of life caused to the injured person by the injuries; but

(*b*) if the injured person's expectation of life has been reduced by the injuries, the court, in assessing damages in respect of pain and suffering caused by the injuries, shall take account of any suffering caused or likely to be caused to him by awareness that his expectation of life has been so reduced.

When abolishing the claim for loss of expectation of life as such Parliament also recognised that it had often indirectly had the legitimate effect of compensating close relatives of a deceased person for their bereavement. This took the form of an addition by section 3 of the Administration of Justice Act 1982 to the Fatal Accidents Act 1976, and is dealt with below.[88]

Loss of amenities of life[89]

The courts may award substantial damages for loss of amenity or loss of faculty.[90] This can be called loss of enjoyment, as distinct from loss of

---

[81] Suffering has been described as the subjective appreciation of objective pain: *Cutts* v. *Chumley* [1967] 1 W.L.R. 742.

[82] *West (H.) & Son Ltd.* v. *Shephard* [1964] A.C. 326.

[83] *Lim* v. *Camden Health Authority* [1980] A.C. 174.

[84] See below.

[85] *Rose* v. *Ford* [1937] A.C. 826. For a fuller account of the background, which is now only of historical interest, see previous editions of this book.

[86] *Benham* v. *Gambling* [1941] A.C. 157.

[87] *Gammell* v. *Wilson* [1982] A.C. 27.

[88] See § 24.11.

[89] Ogus, "Damages for Lost Amenities" (1972) 35 M.L.R. 1.

[90] The latter term was preferred in *Andrews* v. *Freeborough* [1967] 1 Q.B. 1.

expectation, of life. But these damages can only be fair and adequate compensation: no sum could be perfect compensation for a grave injury. The nature of the injury itself is the main factor taken into account, and the courts strive to maintain a broadly "objective" approach by making conventional awards in similar cases in order to facilitate out-of-court settlements. Nevertheless the circumstances of the particular plaintiff will be relevant. The court will look at all the facts of the case, and endeavour to give fair compensation not only for the injury itself but also for all its unpleasant consequences.[91] A young and active person who has been blinded or crippled will recover substantial damages. And in a 1981 case a plaintiff who, when aged 21 months, had been so severely injured that he would never speak or see, and who was paralysed in all four limbs, was awarded £35,000 under this head.[92] Equally a successful professional woman of 36 whose life had been totally transformed was held in 1979 to be entitled to at least £20,000.[93] In another case the Court of Appeal indicated that, on 1985 values,[94] £75,000 was an appropriate guideline figure for what was described as "a typical middle-of-the-road case of tetraplegia."[95]

Unconscious plaintiffs

If the plaintiff has actually been deprived of the amenities of life, the fact that he cannot appreciate this loss, or that he cannot use or enjoy the damages awarded to him, is held to be no ground for reducing the amount of the award. This is consistent with the generally "objective" approach adopted by the court. Thus in *West (H.) and Son Ltd.* v. *Shephard*[96] the plaintiff had been rendered at least partially unconscious and totally paralysed as a result of the defendant's negligence. The House of Lords refused, albeit by a bare majority, to interfere with a substantial award[97] for loss of amenities. Her "grave and sombre deprivation"[98] entitled her to substantial compensation: unconsciousness was relevant only in respect of those heads of damage which can be felt or appreciated—*e.g.* pain and suffering.[99] The basis of awards is therefore that something of value has been lost, not that plaintiffs have been deprived of their subjective happiness. Life is worth living quite apart from any happiness or pleasure it may bring. Although the decision in *West (H.) and Son Ltd.* v. *Shephard* was unanimously approved by the House of Lords in 1979,[1] after full consideration of the various objections to it, their Lordships urged that this area needed consideration by the legis-

---

[91] *West (H.) & Son Ltd.* v. *Shephard* [1964] A.C. 326, 349, 365.
[92] *Croke* v. *Wiseman* [1982] 1 W.L.R. 71.
[93] *Lim* v. *Camden Health Authority* [1980] A.C. 174.
[94] It is important to note the date of the decision when comparing cases in this area since they reflect money values at the date of the trial and, although not formally indexed, they thereby keep broadly in line with inflation: *Wright* v. *British Railways Board* [1983] 2 A.C. 773, 785, *per* Lord Diplock.
[95] *Housecroft* v. *Burnett* [1986] 1 All E.R. 332, 338, *per* O'Connor L.J.
[96] [1964] A.C. 326.
[97] £17,500 in 1963.
[98] [1964] A.C. 326. 351, *per* Lord Morris.
[99] *Wise* v. *Kaye* [1962] 1 Q.B. 638.
[1] *Lim* v. *Camden Health Authority* [1980] A.C. 174.

lature. The Pearson Commission recommended that awards for non-pecuniary loss should no longer be made to unconscious plaintiffs, but their recommendation has not been implemented.[2]

§ 24.6. INTEREST

Interest is compensation for not getting the right amount of money at the right time. Since the Administration of Justice Act 1979, s.22[3] empowered a court to award interest on damages for which judgment was given, it became usual for trial judges to itemise their awards, as interest has to be awarded, at different rates, upon the sums given for the different heads of damages. The decisions of the House of Lords in *Pickett* v. *British Rail Engineering Ltd.*[4] and *Wright* v. *British Railways Board*[5] lay down the following rules:

Special damages—interest at half the appropriate rate from the date of accident to the date of trial. The appropriate rate is that which is payable on the court special account (previously known as short-term investment account). As from November 1989 that rate is 14.25 per cent.

Loss of future earnings—no interest should be awarded, as the money in question is neither ascertainable nor due until the date of the judgment. On the contrary, there must be a discount for the early receipt of a lump sum.

Pain, suffering and loss of amenities—interest is awarded (but at only 2 per cent.) from the date of service of the writ to the date of trial. So issuing a writ but not serving it merely loses interest.

Fatal Accidents Act cases—interest at half rate on the pecuniary loss from the date of death to the date of trial. No interest is given for future loss.

These rules are of considerable practical importance because R.S.C., Ord. 22, r. 1(8) provides that no payment into court is fully effective unless it includes interest. So interest due up to the date of payment in must be taken into account in deciding whether the plaintiff has obtained a judgment which beats that payment in.

§ 24.7. FUNCTIONS OF AN APPELLATE COURT

In former times personal injury actions were tried by jury. This created much uncertainty with respect to the assessment of damages and made the attainment of a degree of consistency an almost impossible objective. This was because the law prohibited the jury from being informed about comparable cases and also because the Court of Appeal, which is able to rehear the case on an appeal from a judge alone, had no such

---

[2] Report, paras. 393–398.
[3] See now the Supreme Court Act 1981, s.35A and R.S.C., Ord. 29, rr. 9 to 18.
[4] [1980] A.C. 136.
[5] [1983] 2 A.C. 773.

power of correction on an appeal from the verdict of a jury but was able only to set aside such a verdict if satisfied that the amount of damages was out of all proportion to the circumstances of the case.[6] Although trial by jury has been retained for personal injury actions in some other common law jurisdictions,[7] it has in practice disappeared in England. In 1965 a five-member Court of Appeal held that the need to pursue uniformity in levels of award rendered trial by jury inappropriate for personal injury actions in normal circumstances.[8] Since that decision there has been only one reported instance of a personal injury action being ordered to be tried by jury.[9] In 1981 section 69(3) of the Supreme Court Act, while still leaving a discretion as to the mode of trial, effectively reinforced the presumption in favour of trial by judge alone in personal injury cases. This provision was considered by the Court of Appeal in 1991 which held that the circumstances would have to be very exceptional before the court would order trial by jury in such a case.[10] The jury is therefore no longer a factor in the assessment of damages.

Since the award will be that of the judge alone, any appeal will be by way of rehearing on damages as on all other issues, but generally there is so much room for legitimate difference of opinion that the appellate court will be slow to interfere. It must be satisfied either that the judge, in assessing the damages, applied a wrong principle of law (as by taking into account some irrelevant factor or leaving out of account some relevant one): or, short of this, that the amount awarded is either so inordinately low or so inordinately high that it must be a wholly erroneous estimate of the damage.[11] It has been said that the court would interfere if it said to itself "Good gracious me—as high as that."[12] In exceptional circumstances the Court of Appeal may take account of facts occurring after the date of the judgment.[13]

§ 24.8. SURVIVAL ACTIONS: PERSONAL REPRESENTATIVE AS PLAINTIFF

If a person dies as a result of injuries tortiously inflicted upon him by the defendant his estate can, by virtue of the Law Reform (Miscellaneous Provisions) Act 1934,[14] recover damages in respect of both the

---

[6] *Davies* v. *Powell Duffryn Associated Collieries Ltd.* [1942] A.C. 601, 616. As a result, however, of the Courts and Legal Services Act 1990, s.8 the Court of Appeal is no longer to be so restricted and, in cases (such as defamation) where juries are still used in civil actions, will henceforth be able to substitute its own figure of damages for that of the jury instead of merely ordering a retrial.

[7] *e.g.* the U.S.A.

[8] *Ward* v. *James* [1966] 1 Q.B. 273.

[9] *Hodges* v. *Harland & Wolff Ltd.* [1965] 1 W.L.R. 525.

[10] *H.* v. *Ministry of Defence* [1991] 2 Q.B. 103. A case in which exemplary damages are sought might be exceptional for this purpose: *ibid.*

[11] *Nance* v. *British Columbia Electric Ry.* [1951] A.C. 601, 613.

[12] *McCarthy* v. *Coldair Ltd.* [1951] 2 T.L.R. 1226, 1229, *per* Denning L.J. If it is said that the award is unreasonable, this means, not that the court below was unreasonable, but that having regard to the relevant principles of assessment, the court below has arrived at a result not reasonably in accord with those principles: *M'Leish* v. *Fulton & Sons*, 1955 S.C. 46, 50.

[13] *Mulholland* v. *Mitchell* [1971] A.C. 66.

[14] At common law the rule had been that a person's causes of action died with him.

pecuniary and non-pecuniary losses suffered by the deceased.[15] The damages recoverable do not, however, include damages for lost income during the lost years.[16] Section 4 of the Administration of Justice Act 1982 amended section 1(2)(*a*) of the Law Reform (Miscellaneous Provisions) Act 1934 to reverse a decision of the House of Lords[17] which had held that damages for such lost income, which had been held recoverable by the slightly earlier decision of the House of Lords in *Pickett* v. *British Rail Engineering*,[18] could be recovered by the estates of deceased persons as well as by living plaintiffs whose life expectancy had been reduced. If this amendment had not been enacted tortfeasors could in some cases have found themselves liable twice over for the same lost income: once to the estate under the 1934 Act and once to the deceased's dependants under the Fatal Accidents Act. It seems that today the only scope for Law Reform Act damages in injury cases is where there is an interval between the injury to the plaintiff and his death, the estate being confined to the recovery of losses suffered by the deceased during that period. Even in this category there will be no claim if the interval, during which the suffering of the deceased is alleged by the estate to have occurred, was so brief as to have been in reality part of the death itself. In *Hicks* v. *Wright*,[18a] which was the second of the two cases arising out of the 1989 Hillsborough football stadium disaster to reach the House of Lords,[18b] it was held that the terror suffered by the deceased victims in the seconds leading up to their deaths by crushing did not give rise to an actionable head of loss.

✷ § 24.9. DEPENDENCY ACTIONS: THE FATAL ACCIDENTS ACT 1976

The rule that no person has any legally protected interest in the life of another has been to a great extent derogated from by statute, but it still remains the general principle, the Fatal Accidents Acts 1846 to 1959, now consolidated in the Fatal Accidents Act 1976, having merely established exceptions to it. Section 1 of the 1976 Act, as amended by the Administration of Justice Act 1982, s.3, provides: "If death[19] is caused[20] by any wrongful act, neglect, or default, which is such as would (if death had not ensued) have entitled the person injured to maintain an action and recover damages in respect thereof, the person who would have been liable if death had not ensued shall be liable to an action for

---

[15] The position is different in Ireland where the Civil Liability Act 1961, s.7 prohibits the estate from recovering damages for pain and suffering, or loss of expectation of life or personal injury.

[16] Exemplary damages, and bereavement damages (see below, § 24.11) are also excluded.

[17] *Gammell* v. *Wilson* [1982] A.C. 27.

[18] [1980] A.C. 136, see above, § 24.3.

[18a] [1992] 2 All E.R. 65.

[18b] For the other case, *Copoc* v. *Wright* [1991] 4 All E.R. 907, see above § 9.8.

[19] There is no limitation as to the place of the wrong or of the death, or as to the nationality or domicile of the parties: *The Esso Malaysia* [1975] Q.B. 198.

[20] Foresight is irrelevant in an action under the Fatal Accidents Act: causation alone is the test: *Haber* v. *Walker* [1953] V.R. 339.

damages, notwithstanding the death of the person injured."[21] The action is brought in the name of the executor or administrator for the benefit of certain near relatives of the deceased, if those relatives have suffered a pecuniary loss in consequence of his death. The following points on the interpretation of the Act should be noted:

(1) What relatives are covered

The relatives whose interests are thus protected are, by section 1(3), the following: husband, wife,[22] and any of the deceased's ascendants or descendants, and any person treated by the deceased as his parent, or treated by him (within a marriage to which the deceased was a party[23]) as his child. The class of dependants also includes any person who is, or who is the issue of, a brother, sister, uncle, or aunt of the deceased person. By section 1(5) illegitimate children are for the purposes of the Acts to be deemed to be children, any relationship by affinity is to be treated as a relationship by consanguinity, and any relationship of the half-blood as of the whole blood. Posthumous children also come under the Act.[24]

(2) The action

Only one action is to be brought in the name of the deceased's personal representative,[25] giving full particulars of the person for whose benefit the action is brought.[26] The action must be brought within three years after the date of death, or the date of the knowledge of the person for whose benefit the action is brought, whichever is the later.[27] The action is brought by the executor or administrator of the deceased on behalf of the relatives; but if there is no executor or administrator, or if he does not commence an action within six months, any relative entitled to the protection of the Act may sue in his own name on behalf of himself and the others.

(3) Damages not part of the deceased's estate

The amount recovered is not part of the estate of the deceased so as to be liable for debts. The executor or administrator recovers it, not in his ordinary capacity as the personal representative of the deceased, but in a special capacity in right of the relatives.[28]

---

[21] It has been held that an action will lie if the deceased committed suicide as a result of insanity caused by the defendant's negligence: *Pigney* v. *Pointers Transport Services* [1957] 1 W.L.R. 1121.

[22] Former wives or husbands are now included, as also is "any person living with the deceased as husband or wife." Probably such common-law spouses will be awarded lower sums because of the possibility of maintenance-free separation had the deceased survived: see s.3(4) of the Act.

[23] See s.1(3)(f).

[24] *The George and Richard* (1871) L.R. 3 A. & E. 466.

[25] Fatal Accidents Act 1976, s.2(3).

[26] s.2(4). See *Cooper* v. *Williams* [1963] 2 Q.B. 567.

[27] Limitation Act 1980, s.12(1). The court has a discretionary power to allow a time-barred action to proceed.

[28] *Marginson* v. *Blackburn B.C.* [1939] 2 K.B. 426.

(4) Deceased himself must have been able to sue

There is no right of action unless the deceased himself could have sued had he been merely injured by the defendant's act and not killed. Therefore, if he has in his lifetime, in the interval between the accident and his death, accepted full compensation from the defendant and so extinguished his right of action, his relatives cannot sue in respect of his death, nor can they if he has obtained judgment against the defendant. Compensation must be claimed by victims within three years, but if it is claimed too soon the result may therefore be disastrous for the deceased's family.[29] The same rule applies if the deceased agreed to take the risk of the accident on himself so as to exclude any right of action in accordance with the maxim *volenti non fit injuria*,[30] or if at the time of his death the Limitation Acts have already run against him. If the deceased has been guilty of contributory negligence, the Fatal Accidents Act 1976, s.5 provides that the damages awarded under that Act may be reduced proportionately, and the same rule applies by analogy if a plaintiff dependant has been guilty of contributory negligence.[31] But the contributory negligence of one dependant does not affect the rights of another.[32]

(5) A new cause of action

Nevertheless the cause of action conferred upon the relatives of the deceased by the Act is a new cause of action and not merely a continuance of that which was formerly vested in the deceased himself.[33] The measure of damages may be very different from that which would have been recoverable by the deceased in respect of his injuries if he had lived: the relatives recovering substantially for the loss of their bread-winner.[34] This is strikingly illustrated by the fact that if the period of limitation under the Limitation Act 1980 was not complete as against the deceased at the date of his death, it cannot be completed afterwards so as to bar the claim of the relatives under the Act. This claim is subject to its own period of limitation as fixed by the Act itself and commencing on the death of the deceased, and is not subject to the provision of the Limitation Act affecting the claim of the deceased himself.

§ 24.10. ASSESSMENT OF DAMAGES UNDER THE FATAL ACCIDENTS ACT

The Act provides (s.3) that such damages may be awarded as are proportioned to the injury resulting from the death to the dependants respectively. In this difficult task the courts often find help in the principles enunciated by Lord Wright in *Davies* v. *Powell Duffryn Associated*

---

[29] *Griffiths* v. *Dudley (Earl of)* (1882) 9 Q.B.D. 357.
[30] *British Columbia Electric Ry.* v. *Gentile* [1914] A.C. 1034, 1042.
[31] *Mulholland* v. *McCrea* [1961] 1 N.I. 135.
[32] *Dodds* v. *Dodds* [1978] Q.B. 543.
[33] *The Vera Cruz* (1883) 10 App.Cas. 59, 70.
[34] Unless their bread was being won by criminal means: *Burns* v. *Edman* [1970] 2 Q.B. 541.

Collieries Ltd.[35] The starting point is the amount of wages which the deceased was earning, the ascertainment of which to some extent may depend upon the regularity of his employment. Then there is an estimate of how much was required or expended for his own personal and living expenses. The balance will give a datum or basic figure, called the multiplicand, which will generally be turned into a lump sum by taking a certain number of years' purchase.[36] That sum, however, has to be taxed down by having due regard to uncertainties. In making the assessment the court can look at events since the accident to see whether contingencies have become certainties. "The court should never speculate where it knows."[37] But at the end of the day arithmetic may have to be mitigated by common sense, for it is an assessment and not a calculation which is being made.[38]

Some particular applications of these principles must be mentioned:

(1) The multiplier

The estimate of the probable length of the deceased's earning period should be the basis for the computation of the plaintiff's loss. This will serve to fix the upper and the lower limits of his claim, for it is impossible to compute the loss on a strictly arithmetical or actuarial basis.[39] The multiplier is not intended to reflect the number of years the dependency would have continued, for this might result in over-compensation for the dependants.[40] Hence no definite figure can be chosen as a multiplier which will give a correct result in all cases: the court has a discretion in the matter. But probably 16 years' purchase is near the upper limit. Unlike personal injury cases, where the date for the selection of the multiplier is that of the trial,[41] in fatal accident cases it is the date of the death.[42] Whatever figure is chosen ought not to be materially reduced by reason of the hazardous nature of the deceased's occupation in life.[43] If the award is split into two parts, namely the loss from the date of the death to trial, and the future loss, the multiplier may also have to be split.[44] In 1971 Parliament provided that in assessing the damages payable to a widow in respect of the death of her husband there should not be taken into account the remarriage of the widow or her prospects of remarriage.[45] This provision had its origin in understandable judicial distaste for the task of estimating such prospects.

---

[35] [1942] A.C. 601, 617.

[36] Now called the multiplier.

[37] *Curwen v. James* [1963] 1 W.L.R. 748, 753, *per* Harman L.J.

[38] *Daniel v. Jones* [1961] 1 W.L.R. 1103.

[39] *Nance v. British Columbia Electric Ry.* [1951] A.C. 601, 614–617.

[40] *Taylor v. O'Connor* [1971] A.C. 115.

[41] See above, § 24.3.

[42] *Graham v. Dodds* [1983] 1 W.L.R. 808. A majority decision of the Court of Appeal has held, however, that in certain cases the multiplier may be adjusted to take into account facts as they were known at the date of the trial: *Corbett v. Barking Havering and Brentwood Health Authority* [1991] 2 Q.B. 408.

[43] *Bishop v. Cunard White Star Ltd.* [1950] P. 240, 248.

[44] *Cookson v. Knowles* [1979] A.C. 556.

[45] See now the Fatal Accidents Act 1976, s.3(3), as amended by the Administration of Justice Act 1982, s.3.

Nevertheless it has been much criticised, mainly on the ground that it can lead to gross over-compensation, especially where it obliges the court to disregard a remarriage to a wealthy new partner which has actually taken place.[46] Since 1982, however, it seems in effect to be subsumed within a wider principle favouring dependants whereby benefits received by them are to be disregarded generally.[47] There are many other factors which may serve to increase or decrease the multiplier or the multiplicand[47A]. The courts usually fix the multiplier after taking contingencies into account and not before. One particular contingency which has caused difficulty is that of inflation. The present English view is that neither the multiplier nor the multiplicand should be increased to take account of inflation, save in exceptional cases.[48] The dependants must rely on prudent investment to provide them with such protection as it is capable of affording.[49]

(2) The dependency: the multiplicand

There is no right of action on behalf of any relative who cannot show some financial loss in consequence of the death of the deceased. There is, however, a sufficient financial loss if the claimant can show some reasonable expectation of pecuniary benefit from the continuance of the deceased's life.[50] The dependency begins to run from the date of the death[51]; and if there is a substantial chance, as distinct from a mere possibility, that the dependant suffered financial loss from the death, then that chance must be evaluated.[52] But a widow who is in receipt of a pension cannot claim compensation for loss of the chance of a post-retirement pension.[53]

Damages can be assessed under two distinct heads.[54] First, in respect of the sums which the deceased would probably have applied out of his income to the maintenance of his dependants; and secondly, in respect of such portion of any additional savings which he might have accumulated during the period for which, but for the accident, he would have lived. Tax must be taken into account.[55]

On the other hand, the fact that the dependant has private means is

---

[46] See the Law Commission Report No. 56 (1973), para. 247, the Pearson Commission, para. 411, and Atiyah, *Accidents, Compensation and the Law* (4th ed.), p. 157.
[47] See the Fatal Accidents Act 1976, s.4 (inserted by the Administration of Justice Act 1982, s.3) as explained in *Stanley* v. *Saddique* [1992] 1 Q.B. 1.
[47A] Including the possibility of divorce: see *Martin* v. *Owen, The Times*, May 21, 1992, C.A.
[48] *Young* v. *Percival* [1975] 1 W.L.R. 17. Nor should any attention be paid to the speculations of academic economists: *Mitchell* v. *Mulholland (No. 2)* [1972] 1 Q.B. 65.
[49] *Lim* v. *Camden Health Authority* [1980] A.C. 174, 193.
[50] *Baker* v. *Dalgleish Steam Shipping Co.* [1922] 1 K.B. 361.
[51] *K.* v. *J.M.P. Co. Ltd.* [1976] Q.B. 85.
[52] *Davies* v. *Taylor* [1974] A.C. 207, 212.
[53] *Auty* v. *National Coal Board* [1985] 1 W.L.R. 784 ("A man who is dead today cannot die tomorrow.") If, however, allowances received by the widow do not constitute a pension they will be regarded as "benefits," within s.4 of the Act, and hence ignored, even if they come from the same fund as her former husband's pension: *Pidduck* v. *Eastern Scottish Omnibuses* [1990] 2 All E.R. 69.
[54] *Nance* v. *B.C. Electric Ry.* [1951] A.C. 601, 614.
[55] *British Transport Commission* v. *Gourley* [1956] A.C. 185.

irrelevant, except in so far as it shows the amount of pecuniary benefit received from the deceased.[56] Nor is it necessary that any benefit should have been actually received from the deceased during his lifetime.[57] The benefit must be derivable, however, from the claimant's relationship to the deceased, and not merely from a contract between them, as where husband and wife are in partnership together in some trade or profession.[58] But a merely speculative possibility of pecuniary benefit is not enough.[59] When the dependant himself dies subsequently to the death of the person in respect of whose death the action is brought but before judgment, the shortness of his tenure of life before dependence was terminated must be taken into account in determining the amount to be awarded.[60]

Funeral expenses may be recovered if they have been incurred by the parties for whose benefit the action is brought.[61]

Loss of wife and mother

A husband can recover damages for the death of his wife in respect of the loss of the pecuniary value of her domestic services, and the law interprets the term "services" widely—a wife and mother does not normally work set hours.[62] A child can recover for the loss of his or her mother's services. The commercial cost of hiring a nanny usually forms the basis of the calculation, although regard has to be had to the fact that a healthy child needs less looking after as he or she gets older.[63] If the child acquires an adoptive mother this will extinguish any claim for loss of the services of the deceased natural mother from the date of the adoption.[64]

(3) The deductions

The complex former law on this subject has been replaced by a provision of sweeping simplicity in the Fatal Accidents Act 1976, s.4. In assessing damages in respect of a person's death in an action under this Act, benefits which have accrued or will or may accrue to any person from his estate or otherwise as a result of his death shall be disregarded. The provision is not confined to direct pecuniary benefits but encompasses any form of material benefit. Thus a child's claim for loss of the services of an unreliable natural mother is not to be reduced by virtue of

[56] *Sheils* v. *Cruickshank* [1953] 1 W.L.R. 533.
[57] *Taff Vale Ry.* v. *Jenkins* [1913] A.C. 1.
[58] *Burgess* v. *Florence Nightingale Hospital for Gentlewomen* [1955] 1 Q.B. 349. *Aliter* if the wife has been employed by the husband's one-man company: *Malyon* v. *Plummer* [1964] 1 Q.B. 330.
[59] *Barnett* v. *Cohen* [1921] 2 K.B. 461.
[60] *Williamson* v. *Thornycroft & Co.* [1940] 2 K.B. 658.
[61] Fatal Accidents Act 1976, s.3(5).
[62] *Regan* v. *Williamson* [1976] 1 W.L.R. 305.
[63] *Spittle* v. *Bunney* [1988] 1 W.L.R. 847.
[64] *Watson* v. *Willmott* [1991] 1 Q.B. 140.

the fact that he subsequently acquires a stepmother who provides a much higher standard of parental care.[65]

(4) The apportionment

When all necessary deductions from the starting sum have been made, the resulting total is usually apportioned amongst the family, taking the family as a unit, when claims are made in respect of more than one dependant,[66] although each dependant is entitled to an individual judgment for a separate sum. The actual apportionment is no concern of the defendant. The court has power to control the investment and release of the sum awarded as damages when minors are dependants[67] although it has no such power in respect of Law Reform Act damages, or of the widow's own damages since the Law Reform (Miscellaneous Provisions) Act 1971, s.5. After the 1971 Act the courts will often assess separately each child's damages. The sums so awarded can then be placed under the control of the court.

§ 24.11. BEREAVEMENT DAMAGES

In 1982 Parliament introduced an award new to English law in the form of "a claim for damages for bereavement."[68] A fixed sum, which in 1991 was raised to £7,500, is payable for the benefit of the spouse of the deceased or of his parents if he was a minor and unmarried. But children are not entitled to such damages for the loss of their parent, apparently because they are regarded as adequately compensated by their dependency action under the Fatal Accidents Act.

---

[65] *Stanley* v. *Saddique* [1992] 1 Q.B. 1. C.A. But the Court of Appeal has held that where a father, who was himself the defendant tortfeasor in respect of a road accident in which his wife had died, gave up work to look after their infant daughter his services were *not* a benefit accruing from the death so that s. 4 of the 1976 Act did *not* apply and the value of the father's services *would* be taken into account: *Hayden* v. *Hayden, The Times,* April 6, 1992.

[66] *Bishop* v. *Cunard White Star Ltd.* [1950] P. 240.

[67] R.S.C., Ord. 80, r. 12. The average life of a fund in court is five years. Does this mean that awards are too low, or that dependants are extravagant? The Pearson Commission found that only one-fifth of the recipients of damages made any attempt to treat the money as capital as distinct from income.

[68] See the Fatal Accidents Act 1976, s.1A (an entirely new provision inserted by the Administration of Justice Act 1982, s.3).

CHAPTER 25

REMEDIES: MISCELLANEOUS MATTERS

§ 25.1. Successive Actions on the Same Facts

More than one action will not lie on the same cause of action; therefore all damages resulting from the same cause of action must be recovered at one and the same time. The rule is designed to prevent the oppressive and vexatious litigation that might result if an injured person were at liberty to divide his claim and sue in successive actions for different portions of the loss sustained from a single cause of action. Thus in *Fitter* v. *Veal*[1] the plaintiff, after recovering damages for an assault and battery, discovered that his injuries were more serious than was at first supposed, and he found it necessary to submit to a surgical operation; whereupon he brought a second action for additional damages. But it was held that he had only one cause of action, which had been wholly extinguished by the judgment recovered in the first action. The application of this rule is not excluded or affected by the fact that when the first action was brought the damage in respect of which the second action is brought had not yet accrued to the plaintiff.[2] But if the damage in either action was unknown to him he may be able to obtain an extension of time under the Limitation Act 1980.[3]

If, however, there are two distinct causes of action, and not merely two distinct heads of damage, successive actions will lie in respect of each of them. This happens in the following classes of cases:

    (1) When the same act amounts to a violation of two distinct rights;
    (2) When the defendant has committed two distinct acts, even though in violation of the same right;
    (3) When the cause of action is a continuing one;
    (4) (Probably) When the wrong is only actionable on proof of actual damage and it produces damage at different times.

(1) Violation of distinct rights

When the wrongful act of the defendant has violated two distinct rights vested in the plaintiff, a separate action will lie to recover the damage suffered in respect of each of these rights. Thus in *Brunsden* v. *Humphrey*[4] the plaintiff, a cabdriver, having already recovered compensation in the county court for damage done to his cab by a collision with the defendant's van, was held entitled by a majority of the Court of Appeal to bring a second action in the High Court in respect of personal

---

[1] (1701) 12 Mod. 542; (*sub tit. Fetter* v. *Beale*) 1 Ld.Raym. 339, 692, approved in *Cartledge* v. *E. Jopling & Sons Ltd.* [1963] A.C. 758, 780. But it is possible that the Civil Liability (Contribution) Act 1978, s.4 has indirectly altered the law in this area: see above, § 20.12.
[2] *Derrick* v. *Williams* [1939] 2 All E.R. 559. but now the Supreme Court Act 1981, s.32A permits a provisional award of damages: see above, § 24.3.
[3] See below, § 25.4.
[4] (1884) 14 Q.B.D. 141.

injuries suffered by him in consequence of the same accident. So a plaintiff who has already sued for damages in a personal capacity can subsequently bring another action for damages arising from the same wrongful act in a representative character.[5] To justify two actions, however, there must be two distinct rights violated; it is not enough that the same act amounts to two distinct violations of the same right. Thus separate actions will not lie for two different personal injuries received from the same act of negligence or assault, as when the plaintiff has his leg broken, and also his arm.[6] The arguments in favour of the rule in *Brunsden* v. *Humphrey* are that there may be issues of identity or justification or measure of damages in one action which are irrelevant in the other, and that the notion of separate rights or interests is familiar in negligence. The arguments against[7] are that a cause of action now means a factual situation which gives a right to the plaintiff, that a single factual situation cannot be split up into several legal situations, and that repetition and technicality in litigation are not to be encouraged. In any event, the rule in *Brunsden* v. *Humphrey* relates to action estoppel. A different problem (issue estoppel) arises when the question is whether a plaintiff is bound by a judgment relating to the same facts in an earlier action to which he was not a party or privy.[8]

(2) Distinct wrongful acts

So also two actions will lie when the defendant has committed two distinct wrongful acts, even against the same person in violation of the same right. Thus if he has on two different occasions entered upon the plaintiff's land, the plaintiff is not bound to sue for both these trespasses at once, but may bring separate actions for each of them. On the same principle, if the same libellous statement is published to two or more persons at different times, a separate action will lie for each publication.[9]

(3) Successive actions for continuing injuries

When the act of the defendant is a continuing injury, its continuance after the date of the first action is a new cause of action for which a second action can be brought, and so from time to time until the injury is discontinued. An injury is said to be a continuing one so long as it is still in the course of being committed and is not wholly past. Thus the wrong of false imprisonment continues so long as the plaintiff is kept in confinement; a nuisance continues so long as the state of things causing the nuisance is suffered by the defendant to remain upon his land; and a trespass continues so long as the defendant remains present upon the plaintiff's land. In the case of such continuing injury an action may be

---

[5] *Marginson* v. *Blackburn B.C.* [1939] 2 K.B. 426; *Randolph* v. *Tuck* [1962] 1 Q.B. 175.
[6] *Conquer* v. *Boot* [1928] 2 K.B. 336, 340.
[7] See *Cahoon* v. *Franks* (1967) 65 D.L.R. (2d) 274.
[8] See *Shaw* v. *Sloan* [1982] N.I. 393 for an exhaustive survey by the N.I.C.A.
[9] See above, § 8.7. Any vexatious or oppressive exercise of this right will be restrained by the court in the exercise of its discretionary power to prevent the abuse of legal process, or by a refusal to award costs in the second action.

brought during its continuance, but damages are recoverable only down to the time of their assessment in the action.[10] Prospective damages for any further continuance of the injury are not recoverable by way of anticipation, for *non constat* that the defendant will not discontinue the wrong forthwith. This is so however permanent the source of the mischief may be, and however improbable it may be that the defendant will discontinue it: as when he has built a house which blocks the ancient lights of the plaintiff. There will be time enough to sue for future damage when it accrues.[11] Nor does it make any difference in this respect that the known probability of the future continuance of the injury has diminished the present saleable value of the property affected by it.[12]

If the continuing injury is actionable *per se*, as in the case of trespass, or if it is the cause of fresh damage from day to day, as in the case of an obstruction of ancient lights, successive actions will lie *de die in diem* until the defendant chooses to relief himself from this burden of litigation by discontinuing his wrong. If, on the other hand, a continuing injury is of a kind which is actionable only on proof of actual damage, and the damage caused is intermittent, as in the case of withdrawal of support, a new action will lie only when some new damage accrues. A continuing injury to property is actionable at the suit of a plaintiff whose title did not accrue until after the commencement of the injury, and such a plaintiff may recover damages in respect of the continuance of the act since the accrual of his title. Thus, he who buys land may sue for a continuing trespass or nuisance which existed at the time of his purchase.[13] Notwithstanding these rules as to the measure of damages in continuing injuries, when an action is brought for an injunction against such an injury, damages may be given in substitution for an injunction; such damages are given in full satisfaction for all future damage which may arise from a continuance of the injury complained of, and therefore no subsequent action will lie in respect thereof.[14]

(4) Successive actions for wrongs actionable only on proof of damage

Where the act of the defendant is actionable *per se*, there is no doubt that all damage, both actual and prospective, may and must be recovered in one action. But where the act of the defendant is not actionable *per se*, but is actionable only if it produces actual damage, and it produces damage twice at different times, is there one cause of action, or are there two? Both on principle and on authority[15] it seems that when an act is actionable only on proof of actual damage, successive actions will lie for each successive and distinct accrual of damage.[16] So a purchase of a defective building may recover for some of the

---

[10] Ord. 37, r. 6.
[11] *Darley Main Colliery Co. v. Mitchell* (1886) 11 App.Cas. 127.
[12] *West Leigh Colliery Co. v. Tunnicliffe and Hampson Ltd.* [1908] A.C. 27.
[13] *Konskier v. B. Goodman Ltd.* [1928] 1 K.B. 421.
[14] See below, § 25.2.
[15] *Maberley v. Peabody & Co.* [1946] 2 All E.R. 192.
[16] *O'Keefe v. Walsh* [1903] 2 I.R. 681, 700.

damage which he has suffered, even though similar damage is not recoverable as having occurred outside the limitation period.[17] But where the damage sued for in the second action is not in reality distinct from that sued for in the first, but is merely a part of it or consequential upon it, it cannot be recovered. In other words, compensation for the first damage includes compensation for all the ulterior consequences of that damage whether already accrued or not, but it does not include compensation for entirely distinct damage accruing from the defendant's act independently of the damage first sued for.[18]

Accord and satisfaction

An accord and satisfaction is a destruction of the cause of action, just as a judgment is, and therefore it is equally a bar to any later action founded on the same cause of action, even though for further damage.[19] Yet if it can be shown that the real agreement between the parties was not to destroy the whole cause of action, but merely to pay and receive compensation for the damage accrued up to that time, that agreement will be effective, and an action will lie for any further damage.

§ 25.2. Injunctions

Under the Supreme Court Act 1981, s. 37(1) all Divisions of the High Court have had power to issue injunctions whenever it shall appear to the court to be just and convenient that such order should be made. There are well established judicial limitations on this jurisdiction,[19a] but it is still very wide. So a creditor may obtain what is known as a *Mareva*[20] injunction to restrain a debtor removing assets out of the jurisdiction whether the defendant is resident within the jurisdiction or not.[21] Or there may be an *Anton Piller* order giving the plaintiff a power of entry and search for material which it is in the interests of justice to preserve until trial—*e.g.* videos containing bootlegged material or essential documents.[22] Such an order may be made *ex parte*—indeed, it may be essential to avoid giving notice to the defendant if the subject-matter is to be preserved.[23]

Injunctions are either prohibitory or mandatory. A prohibitory injunction is an order restraining the defendant from committing or repeating an injurious act—for example, a trespass to land or the erec-

---

[17] *Johnson* v. *Mount Albert B.C.* [1979] 2 N.Z.L.R. 234, 243.

[18] *Bowen* v. *Paramount Builders Ltd.* [1977] 1 N.Z.L.R. 394, 424.

[19] *Bristow* v. *Grout* [1986] 11 C.L. 363.

[19a] *Pickering* v. *Liverpool Post plc* [1991] 2 W.L.R. 513, 524.

[20] *Mareva Compania Naviera S.A.* v. *International Bulkcarriers* [1975] 2 Lloyd's Rep. 509. The jurisdiction is now statutory: see the Supreme Court Act 1981, s.37(3).

[21] For the conditions to be satisfied by the plaintiff, see the exhaustive monograph by Hoyle, *The Mareva Injunction* (1985).

[22] *Anton Piller K.G.* v. *Manufacturing Processes Ltd.* [1976] Ch. 55.

[23] On the other hand, two well-informed critics have said that the draconian character of the order and the width of the judicial discretion mean that "an exceptional device intended to avoid injustice has become almost a routine method of creating it": Dockray and Laddie, "Piller Problems" (1990) 106 L.Q.R. 600, 620.

tion of a building which would obstruct the plaintiff's lights. A mandatory injunction is an order requiring the defendant to do some positive act for the purpose of putting an end to a wrongful state of things created by him—for example, an order to pull down a building which he has already erected to the obstruction of the plaintiff's lights.[24] A mandatory injunction ought to be in such terms that the person against whom it is granted knows exactly what he has to do.[25] Injunctions, whether prohibitory or mandatory, may also be either interlocutory or perpetual. An interlocutory (or interim) injunction is one issued provisionally before the hearing of an action, in order to prevent the commission or continuance of an alleged injury in the meantime,[26] pending an inquiry into the case and a final determination of the right of the plaintiff to a perpetual injunction.

Onus of proof. It was once thought that an applicant for an interlocutory injunction had to show that he had a prima facie case. But in *American Cyanamid Co. v. Ethicon Ltd.,*[27] an action for the infringement of a patent, the House of Lords laid down a more complex set of guidelines, which should not, however, be construed as limiting the wide discretion given by the Supreme Court Act 1981, s.37(3). The court should first consider whether damages would be an adequate remedy. If yes, then normally no interlocutory injunction should be granted. But if there is doubt as to the adequacy of damages,[28] the court, if satisfied that there is a serious question to be tried[29] should then consider any other factors relevant to the question whether the balance of convenience favours the grant of an injunction—*e.g.* the uncompensatable harm and inconvenience which may be suffered by the plaintiff if the injunction is refused. In effect the plaintiff is entitled to an injunction of his claim is neither frivolous nor vexatious. But these guidelines have not settled all problems.[30] They have not apparently affected the practice in defamation actions, and were modified in labour disputes by the Trade Union and Labour Relations Act 1974, s.17(2).[31] That section is still in force, although the definition of a trade dispute has been much modified by the Employment Acts 1980 and 1982.[32]

Categories of injunctions. Injunctions are made either against the continuance of an injury, against the repetition of one, or against the commission of one. The commonest and most important case is the first of

---

[24] See *Kelsen v. Imperial Tobacco Co. Ltd.* [1975] 2 Q.B. 334, above, § 4.3.

[25] *Redland Bricks Ltd. v. Morris* [1970] A.C. 652.

[26] *Hampstead and Surburban Properties Ltd. v. Diomedous* [1969] 1 Ch. 248.

[27] [1975] A.C. 396.

[28] *e.g.* because the defendant is an immigrant worker: *De Falco v. Crawley B.C.* [1980] 1 All E.R. 913, 922.

[29] "If he can establish that, then he has, so to speak, crossed the threshold": *R. v. Secretary of State for Transport, ex p. Factortame Ltd. (No. 2)* [1991] 1 A.C. 603, 671 *per* Lord Goff.

[30] *NWL Ltd. v. Woods* [1979] 1 W.L.R. 1294.

[31] See above, § 17.1.

[32] *Dimbleby & Sons Ltd. v. N.U.J.* [1984] 1 W.L.R. 427, 431.

these; and an injunction is the ordinary and most effective remedy in all cases of continuing wrongs—for example, a nuisance. Even when the injury is not continuing, however, an injunction may be granted if there is any sufficient reason to believe that the conduct will be repeated—for example, a trespass under a claim to a right of way. It is no answer to a claim for an injunction to restrain a trespass that no damage has been done to the plaintiff.[33]

Indeed, it is possible to say that every tort is redressible by an injunction except assault and battery,[34] negligence,[35] false imprisonment, and malicious prosecution. But an interlocutory injunction to restrain the publication of a libel will be granted only in the clearest cases (and probably not at all when justification or fair comment[36] or perhaps even privilege,[37] are pleaded), in which any jury would say the matter was defamatory, and in which, if the jury did not so find, their verdict would be set aside on appeal as unreasonable.[38] So in *Bestobell Paints Ltd.* v. *Bigg*[39] the defendant posted a notice on his shabby house. "These premises have been painted with Carson's paint." A claim for an interlocutory injunction was refused when the defendant stated that he would plead justification at the trial. But the reluctance to grant an interlocutory injunction in libel does not exist when the claim is for a permanent injunction after trial.[40]

But even if no complete injury or cause of action for damages yet exists, an injunction may be obtained in a *quia timet* action to prevent the commission of an injury in the future; as when the defendant threatens or intends to erect a building which will obstruct the plaintiff's lights.[41]

No injunction will be granted in a case in which obedience to the order is impossible.[42] For there are cases in which a defendant is liable in law for the continuance of a wrongful state of things, and yet has no power to put an end to it. In such a case, unless the court grants an injunction but suspends its operation for such time as may seem necessary to enable the defendant to comply with the order,[43] the plaintiff's only remedy is damages. Suspending the operation of an injunction is a well-established practice when the defendant is a local authority, but in other cases the practice is not so clear.[44]

---

[33] *Patel* v. *Smith (W.H.) Ltd.* [1987] 1 W.L.R. 853.
[34] Unless the case is very exceptional: *Egan* v. *Egan* [1975] Ch. 218, 221.
[35] *Miller* v. *Jackson* [1977] Q.B. 966, 980.
[36] *Wallersteiner* v. *Moir* [1974] 1 W.L.R. 991.
[37] *Harakas* v. *Baltic Exchange Ltd.* [1982] 1 W.L.R. 958.
[38] So held by the C.A. in *Kaye* v. *Robertson* (1991) 18 F.S.R. 62, 67. There is an exception when the publication is part of a conspiracy to inflict damage on the plaintiffs: *Gulf Oil Ltd.* v. *Page* [1987] Ch. 327.
[39] *Mount Cooke Group Ltd.* v. *Johnstone Motors Ltd.* [1990] 2 N.Z.L.R. 488, 501.
[40] (1975) 119 S.J. 678.
[41] *Redland Bricks Ltd.* v. *Morris* [1970] A.C. 652.
[42] *Harrington (Earl)* v. *Derby Corporation* [1905] 1 Ch. 205, 220.
[43] *Pride of Derby and Derbyshire Angling Association Ltd.* v. *British Celanese Ltd.* [1953] Ch. 149.
[44] *Trenberth* v. *National Westminster Bank* (1979) 123 S.J. 388.

Damages in lieu of injunction[45]

Since Lord Cairns' Act 1858,[46] the court has had jurisdiction, in all cases in which it might grant an injunction, to award damages either in addition to or in substitution for such an injunction. This jurisdiction seems to be at once wider and narrower than that of the High Court under the Judicature Act. It is wider in that damages can be given when they have not been asked for; narrower, in that they can only be given in a case where an injunction could be given. The discretion of the court to depart from the general rule of restraining an injury by injunction, and to compel a plaintiff to accept pecuniary satisfaction for his wrongs, is in theory unfettered. But "Ever since Lord Cairns' Act, the Court of Chancery has repudiated the notion that the legislature intended to turn that court into a tribunal for legalising wrongful acts; or, in other words, the court has always protested against the notion that it ought to allow a wrong to continue simply because the wrongdoer is able and willing to pay for the injury he may inflict."[47]

"In my opinion," said A. L. Smith L.J. in Shelfer's case,[48] "it may be stated as a good working rule that (i) if the injury to the plaintiff's legal rights is small, (ii) and is one which is capable of being estimated in money, (iii) and is one which can be adequately compensated by a small money payment, (iv) and the case is one in which it would be oppressive to the defendant to grant an injunction: then damages in substitution for an injunction may be given." These principles have been cited with approval "time and time again"[49] although their application to the facts of a particular case may cause difficulty,[50] and it may be that they do not apply to an action for trespass as distinct from nuisance.[51] The onus of proving special circumstances which would justify the award of damages is on the defendant.[52] At least three matters may be taken into account by the court, namely, (1) the magnitude of the injury complained of, (2) the conduct of the parties, and (3) the interests of the defendant and the public.

(i) *Magnitude of the injury*

On this principle injunctions have been refused in the case of merely temporary or intermittent nuisances,[53] and in the case of repeated trespasses committed under a claim of right but causing no damage,[54] and

---

[45] See Jolowicz, "Damages in Equity—A Study of Lord Cairns' Act" [1975] C.L.J. 224.
[46] Although the Act has been repealed the jurisdiction so created is preserved by the Supreme Court Act 1981, s.50.
[47] *Shelfer* v. *City of London Electric Lighting Co.* [1895] 1 Ch. 287, 315, 316, *per* Lindley L.J.
[48] [1895] 1 Ch. 287, 322.
[49] *Kennaway* v. *Thompson* [1981] Q.B. 88, 93.
[50] *Redland Bricks Ltd.* v. *Morris* [1970] A.C. 652.
[51] *Woollerton and Wilson Ltd.* v. *Costain Ltd.* [1970] 1 W.L.R. 411.
[52] *McKinnon Industries Ltd.* v. *Walker* [1951] 3 D.L.R. 577, 581, *per* Lord Simonds.
[53] *Swaine* v. *G.N. Ry.* (1864) 4 De G.J. & S. 211.
[54] *Behrens* v. *Richards* [1905] 2 Ch. 614.

in cases where the interest of the plaintiff in the property affected was about to determine.[55]

(ii) *Conduct of the parties*

If a plaintiff has knowingly stood by and made no objection while the defendant has in ignorance invaded his rights (as by erecting a building which obstructs an easement of light or a right of way), no injunction will be granted to him.[56] Conversely, if the defendant has himself acted with wilful and high-handed disregard of the plaintiff's rights, an injunction may be granted.[57]

(iii) *Effect on interests of defendant or of the public*

When the damage done or apprehended is substantial, and there is nothing in the conduct of the plaintiff sufficient to render him undeserving of this remedy, an injunction may be granted even though its effect will be to inflict upon the defendant or upon the public at large a loss that is greater than any benefit so conferred upon the plaintiff. The court will not sanction, in the interest of individuals or of the public, any substantial invasion of private rights, even on the terms of paying full compensation for the injury so inflicted.[58] So Lord Sumner, dissenting, doubted[59] "whether it is complete justice to allow the big man, with his big building and his enhanced rateable value and his improvement of the neighbourhood, to have his way, and to solace the little man for his darkened and stuffy little house by giving him a cheque that he does not ask for."

When damages are awarded in substitution for an injunction in pursuance of the discretionary jurisdiction conferred by Lord Cairns' Act, such damages are given in respect of the future, and not merely, as at common law, in respect of damages already done in the past. Such an award of damages amounts, therefore, to a legalisation of the apprehended mischief; the defendant has thereby purchased a right to do the act in respect of which an injunction was asked, and in respect of which damages have been given instead. Further, it should be noted that a bare majority of the House of Lords has held[60] that the court has power to award damages in lieu of an injunction in a *quia timet* action when no actual harm or complete cause of action for damages already exists. The curious result of this decision is that a court of equity has power to award damages when a court of law could not. But apart from these exceptional cases the Act does not provide for the assessment of damages on any new basis.[61] The measure of damages is the same under Lord Cairns' Act as at common law, although in some cases

---

[55] *Jacomb v. Knight* (1863) 3 De G.J. & S. 533.
[56] *Gaskin v. Balls* (1879) 13 Ch.D. 324.
[57] *Sefton (Earl) v. Tophams Ltd.* [1964] 1 W.L.R. 1408.
[58] *Kennaway v. Thompson* [1981] Q.B. 88.
[59] *Leeds Industrial Co-operative Society v. Slack* [1924] A.C. 851, 872.
[60] *Leeds Industrial Co-operative Society v. Slack* [1924] A.C. 851.
[61] *Johnson v. Agnew* [1980] A.C. 367.

under the Act the time at which such damages are assessed may be the date of the judgment rather than the date of the breach.

§ 25.3. THE LIMITATION ACTS 1939 TO 1980[62]

The public policy behind the Statutes of Limitation has been clear since 1603. A time must come when defendants can relax and know that actions against them are time-barred.[63] But the statutes are complex and so are the cases. Litigation about litigation is highly technical. We can start with the Limitation Act 1939, which, as amended by the Law Reform (Limitation of Actions, etc.) Act 1954, simplified the law. Unfortunately the law again became complex, partly because of the Limitation Act 1963, which attempted to settle some difficulties by establishing a machinery which was at once flexible and elaborate,[64] and partly because of some decisions which took an unexpectedly benevolent view of the plaintiff's rights. Two more complex statutes, the Limitation Act 1975 and the Limitation Amendment Act 1980, became necessary. Then all these statutes were consolidated by the Limitation Act 1980,[65] which came into force on May 1, 1980. Then some decisions on the question of latent damage made necessary the passage of yet another statute, the Latent Damage Act 1986, which inserted two new sections into the 1980 Act. It has been calculated that no less than nine limitation periods can arise between the same parties out of the same set of facts.

By the Limitation Act 1980, s.2 no action founded on tort shall be brought after the expiration of six years from the date on which the cause of action accrued. By section 11 the limitation period for actions for damages in respect of personal injuries was reduced to three years. By section 33 new time limits for various types of personal injuries actions were prescribed, subject to an overriding power given to the court.[66]

When time begins to run

In calculating whether time (whether the period be six or three years) has run against the plaintiff, the day on which the accident happened is

---

[62] Report of the Law Commission, Cmnd. 4532 (1970); Twenty-first Report of the Law Reform Committee, Cmnd. 6923 (1977); Twenty-fourth Report of the Law Reform Committee, Cmnd. 2390, 1984; Davies, "Limitations of the Law of Limitation" (1982) 98 L.Q.R. 249.

[63] *Pirelli General Cable Works Ltd.* v. *Oscar Faber & Partners* [1983] A.C. 1, 6.

[64] The Act "has a strong claim to the distinction of being the worst drafted Act on the statute book": *Central Asbestos Co. Ltd.* v. *Dodd* [1973] A.C. 518, 529, *per* Lord Reid. But Lord Reid never had to consider the Rehabilitation of Offenders Act 1974.

[65] The Act must be pleaded: the court will not of its own motion take notice that the claim is statute-barred: *Ronex Properties Ltd.* v. *John Laing Construction Ltd.* [1983] Q.B. 398. But on the other hand, "it must be borne in mind that insurance companies are not philanthropic institutions, and if they have the opportunity to take a limitation point or to strike out a claim for want of prosecution or some other technical reason, they will do so. It is not in the interests of insurers to remind solicitors of limitation periods. They will happily negotiate until the limitation period has passed then politely enquire the date on which the writ was issued": [1985] *Law Society's Gazette* 2323.

[66] See below, § 25.4.

excluded from the computation,[67] but the day on which the writ was issued is included.[68] In any event, it is important to observe that although the writ must be issued within the prescribed period, another year can elapse before it need be served.[69] So in practice the period of limitation may be seven or four, not six or three, years. These periods may be too long. Although there is power to strike out an action for want of prosecution, the delay must have been inordinate and inexcusable,[70] and normally the plaintiff will cure his default by issuing a new writ.

The period of limitation begins to run at the time when the cause of action accrued, *i.e.* "the earliest time at which an action could be brought."[71] Therefore, when a wrongful act is actionable *per se* without proof of actual damage, the statute runs from the time at which the act was committed—as in libel,[72] assault, or interference with goods. This is so even though the resulting damage does not happen or is not discovered until a later date; for such damage is not a new cause of action, but merely an incident of the old one.[73]

When, on the other hand, the wrong is not actionable without actual damage the period of limitation does not begin to run until that damage happens: as in the case of negligence,[74] fraud,[75] or wrongful interference with an easement[76] of support.[77]

Latent damage: personal injuries

It was formerly held that once damage had occurred the cause of action accrued and that time began to run against the plaintiff even though he was unaware of the damage,[78] or even though the defendant was unknown or untraceable.[79] This gave rise to grave injustice, *e.g.* in some cases of pneumoconiosis, in which substantial injury to the lungs may be suffered years before it can be discovered. A committee reported[80] in favour of a change in the law, and the Limitation Act 1963,

---

[67] *Marren* v. *Dawson, Bentley & Co. Ltd.* [1961] 2 Q.B. 135.

[68] *Trow* v. *Ind Coope (West Midlands) Ltd.* [1967] 2 Q.B. 899. In *Jones* v. *Swansea City Council* [1990] 1 W.L.R. 1453 the plaintiff issued her writ five years and 364 days after the date on which her cause of action arose.

[69] R.S.C., Ord. 6, r. 8(2). It is only in exceptional cases that the court will extend this period for a writ which has not been timeously served: *Waddon* v. *Whitecroft Scovill Ltd.* [1988] 1 W.L.R. 309.

[70] *Department of Transport* v. *Chris Smaller Ltd.* [1989] 2 W.L.R. 578.

[71] *Sevcon Ltd.* v. *Lucas C.A.V. Ltd.* [1986] 1 W.L.R. 462, 467.

[72] *Brunswick (Duke of)* v. *Harmer* (1849) 14 Q.B. 185. See above, § 22.4.

[73] *Cartledge* v. *E. Jopling & Sons Ltd.* [1963] A.C. 758.

[74] *Moore (D.W.) Co. Ltd.* v. *Ferrier* [1988] 1 W.L.R. 267.

[75] Otherwise there might be great injustice in "a clock fraud"—one so timed as to explode and damage the plaintiff more than six years later: *Barber* v. *Houston* (1885) 18 L.R.Ir. 475, 481.

[76] *Backhouse* v. *Bonomi* (1861) 8 H.L.C. 503. As to the period of limitation when distinct damage results at different times from the same wrongful act, see above, § 25.1.

[77] *Long* v. *Western Propellers Ltd.* (1967) 65 D.L.R. (2d) 147, 149.

[78] *Cartledge* v. *Jopling & Sons Ltd.* [1963] A.C. 758.

[79] *R.B. Policies at Lloyd's* v. *Butler* [1950] 1 K.B. 76.

[80] Cmnd. 1829 (1961).

ss.1 and 2[81] made the change recommended. But these changes in turn revealed defects,[82] and on the advice of another committee further changes were made by the Limitation Act 1975, now re-enacted by sections 11, 14 and 33 of the 1980 Act.[83] There is no power to lift an accrued bar with retrospective effect.[84]

Latent damage: other cases

Until 1986 it was uncertain how far absence of knowledge may suspend the running of time when the damage alleged is damage to house property. While it became clear in the 1970s that the former rule that the cause of action arose at the date of construction, or perhaps on the date of the conveyance of a building,[85] was no longer accepted in the House of Lords,[86] it was not at first possible to go beyond Lord Wilberforce's statement that the cause of action arises when the state of the property constitutes present or imminent danger to the occupier's person or property,[87] although it was generally believed that the courts were moving in the direction of starting the limitation period at the point of discoverability. The problem was so difficult that Lord Hailsham of St. Marylebone L.C., told the House of Lords that it was premature to express a solution in the Limitation Act 1980.[88] While the implications of this statement were being considered by the Law Reform Committee, to whom the issue had been referred, the House of Lords in December 1982 reversed the trend towards discoverability by holding unanimously[89] that in cases of latent damage to buildings the cause of action will accrue when damage occurs, no sooner[90] and no later, and irrespective of discoverability. It was also held that if time runs against one owner, it runs against all his successors in title. Two years later the Law Reform Committee was able to report,[91] making recommendations for reform, and two years later again these were accepted by Parliament in the Latent Damage Act 1986.

So now section 14A of the 1980 Act (inserted by the 1986 Act) provides a new time limit for actions in respect of latent damage not involving personal injuries. The relevant period is either six years from the date on which the cause of action accrued, or three years from the date on which the plaintiff knew or ought to have known facts about the damage, whichever is the later. There is no judicial power to override

---

[81] Which received the royal assent on July 31, 1963, only six months after the decision in *Cartledge* v. *Jopling*. Law reform can be speedy.

[82] See *Central Asbestos Co.* v. *Dodd* [1973] A.C. 518.

[83] For the complex details, see below, § 25.4.

[84] *Arnold* v. *C.E.G.B.* [1988] A.C. 228.

[85] Put forward in *Dutton* v. *Bognor Regis Building Co.* [1972] 1 Q.B. 373.

[86] *Anns* v. *Merton B.C.* [1978] A.C. 728.

[87] [1978] A.C. 728, 760.

[88] H.L.Deb. Vol. 400, col. 1234 (October 20, 1979).

[89] In *Pirelli General Cable Works Ltd.* v. *Oscar Faber and Partners* [1983] 2 A.C. 1.

[90] An exception was contemplated when "the defect is so gross that the building is doomed from the start" ([1983] 2 A.C. 1, 16). No judge or commentator was quite certain what this meant (see *Ketteman* v. *Hansel Properties Ltd.* [1987] A.C. 189, 205 but the question is irrelevant after the Latent Damage Act 1986.

[91] Twenty-fourth Report, Cmnd. 9390, 1984.

the statutory period, as there was under the Limitation Act 1975. The discretionary power had been much criticised as leading to uncertainty in an area in which certainty is of great public importance. So it was thought that a period of three years from the date of (presumed) knowledge was long enough to protect potential plaintiffs.

On the other hand, an indefinite postponement of the date of discoverability was capable of giving rise to injustice to potential defendants. So section 14B provides an overriding time limit ("the long stop") of 15 years from the date of the defendant's breach of duty. The long stop cannot be invoked if the defendant has been guilty of fraud or wilful concealment.

Even after the 1986 Act there will be problems for both plaintiffs and defendants. It may be hard for a plaintiff to prove that damage has not occurred until a particular date (whatever that date may be) in order to prevent time running against him. It may also be hard for a defendant to prove that a plaintiff had knowledge of significant damage (the statutory provisions on this point are extremely complex[92]) so as to start time running against him. But no law reform measure could entirely eliminate these problems, and the seventh statute of limitations to be enacted within 50 years probably strikes the best possible balance.

The 1986 Act is favourable to plaintiffs in two respects. First, it provides (section 3) that where property the subject of latent damage is acquired by successive owners, a fresh cause of action in respect of any negligence shall accrue to each owner on the date on which he acquires his interest in the property. Secondly, section 14A applies to "any action for damages for negligence," and so is not limited to construction cases, but also covers, for example, a case where, *e.g.* the plaintiff has suffered economic loss by acting on careless professional advice.[93]

Disability

If when a cause of action accrued, the person to whom it accrued was under a disability, the action may be brought within six years from the date when he ceased to be under a disability or died, whichever event first occurred.[94] In the case of an action for personal injuries[95] the period is three years from the cesser of the disability or death. A minor has therefore a statutory right of which he cannot be deprived by the court to delay the issue of his writ until three years after his 18th birthday, however long that may be after the accident.[96] A person is unsound of mind if he is a person who, by reason of mental disorder within the meaning of the Mental Health Act 1983, is incapable of managing his affairs as a reasonable man would have done.[97]

These disabilities must exist at the time when the cause of action first

---

[92] They are analogous to, though not identical with, those in s.33 of the 1980 Act, for which see below, § 25.4.
[93] *Bell* v. *Peter Browne & Co.* [1990] 3 W.L.R. 510.
[94] Limitation Act 1980, s.28(1).
[95] Below, § 25.4.
[96] *Tolley* v. *Morris* [1979] 1 W.L.R. 592.
[97] Limitation Act 1980, s.38(3).

arises. If the statute has once commenced to run, the subsequent insanity of the plaintiff or the fact that the claim has passed to a person under a disability[98] will not have any effect.[99] When a person is under successive disabilities, *e.g.* insanity supervening on infancy, time does not run against him until the last of the disabilities has come to an end provided that there is no interval between any of the disabilities.[1] But, when a right of action which has accrued to a person under a disability accrues on his death to another person under a disability, no further extension of time is allowed.[2]

Fraud

The Limitation Act 1980, s.32(1) provides that when the action is based upon the fraud of the defendant or any fact relevant to the plaintiff's cause of action has been deliberately concealed from him by the defendant,[3] or the action is for relief from the consequences of a mistake, time does not run until the plaintiff has discovered the fraud, concealment or mistake, or could with reasonable diligence have discovered it. A defendant guilty of deliberate concealment cannot take advantage of the "long-stop" provisions of the 1986 Act. But the bona fide purchaser of property for valuable consideration or any person claiming through him[4] is not to be prejudiced by this provision.[5]

§ 25.4. SPECIAL PERIODS OF LIMITATION[6]

The general limitation period of six years established by the Limitation Act 1939 has been both extended and contracted by different statutes. It has been extended to 30 years by the Nuclear Installations Act 1965, s.15. It has been contracted by other statutes in five special cases:

    (1) personal injuries;
    (2) accidents at sea and in the air;
    (3) actions arising out of death;
    (4) contribution between tortfeasors;
    (5) defamation.

(1) Personal injuries

The primary limitation period

Section 2(1) of the Law Reform (Limitation of Actions, etc.) Act 1954, now section 11(3) of the 1980 Act, amended the Limitation Act 1939 by reducing from six years to three years the period of limitation for

---

[98] Limitation Act 1980, s.28(1).

[99] *Rhodes* v. *Smethurst* (1840) 6 M. & W. 351.

[1] *Borrows* v. *Ellison* (1871) L.R. 6 Ex. 128.

[2] Limitation Act 1980, s.28(3).

[3] By s.32(2) the concept of concealment has been extended to cover deliberate concealment of a breach of duty in circumstances in which it is unlikely to be discovered.

[4] *Eddis* v. *Chichester Constable* [1969] 2 Ch. 345.

[5] See the elaborate provisions of s.32(3) and (4).

[6] See Law Reform Committee, 20th Report, Cmnd. 5630 (1974), and also the 21st and 24th Reports (1977 and 1984).

actions for damages for negligence, nuisance or breach of duty (whether the duty exists by virtue of a contract or of a provision made by or under a statute or independently of any contract or any such provision), where the damages claimed by the plaintiff for the negligence, nuisance or breach of duty consist of or include damages in respect of personal injuries to any person. The reason for this change is that it is desirable in the interests of justice that actions for personal injuries should be brought to trial quickly, while the evidence is still fresh in the minds of parties and witnesses. The Court of Appeal has held[7] that the words "breach of duty" are wide enough to include causes of action for personal injuries which are framed in trespass as distinct from case. This is to be welcomed on the ground that it is undesirable that a plaintiff should be able to avoid the three-year period of limitation by taking advantage of the technicalities of the forms of action. Still, on the other side it may be said that the distinction between trespass and case has not yet been expressly abolished,[8] that the Limitation Acts have not impliedly done so, and that a plaintiff is entitled to the period of limitation appropriate to his cause of action until Parliament otherwise determined. So if the action is for breach of contract for failing to effect an insurance policy to cover personal injuries, the period is six years and not three.[9]

The effect of knowledge: latent damage

The simple three-year rule has become complex as the result of two efforts by Parliament to provide a solution for the problem of latent damage. The Limitation Act 1975, s.1, did some complicated legislative surgery on the body of the 1939 Act by inserting four new sections, numbered 2A–2D, after section 2,[10] and these have been re-enacted in section 33 of the 1980 Act. The Latent Damage Act 1986, s.1 inserts similar sections (sections 14A and 14B) in the 1980 Act to deal with latent damage not involving personal injuries. Section 11 redefines the moment at which time begins to run against a plaintiff, and then section 33 gives the court power to "disapply"[11] the primary period, as so re-defined, if it thinks it equitable to do so.

So it is necessary to set out much of section 11. It runs as follows:

11.—(1) This section applies to any action for damages for negligence, nuisance or breach of duty (whether the duty exists by virtue of a contract or of provision made by or under a statute or independently of any contract or any such provision) where the damages claimed by the plaintiff for the negligence, nuisance or breach of duty consist of or include damages in respect of personal injuries to the plaintiff or any other person.

(2) None of the time limits given in the preceding provisions of this Act shall apply to an action to which this section applies.

---

[7] *Letang* v. *Cooper* [1965] 1 Q.B. 232; *Long* v. *Hepworth* [1968] 1 W.L.R. 1299.
[8] See above, § 1.2.
[9] *Ackbar* v. *C.F. Green & Co. Ltd.* [1975] Q.B. 582.
[10] *Firman* v. *Ellis* [1978] Q.B. 886, 910.
[11] To use the verb recognised by the draftsman but not by the Oxford English Dictionary.

(3) An action to which this section applies shall not be brought after the expiration of the period applicable in accordance with subsections (4) or (5).[12]

(4) Except where subsection (5) applies, the period is three years from—

    (a) the date on which the cause of action is accrued, or

    (b) the date of knowledge (if later) of the person injured.

(5) If the person injured dies before the expiration of the period in subsection (4) above, the period applicable as respects the cause of action surviving for the benefit of the estate of the deceased by virtue of section 1 of the Law Reform (Miscellaneous Provisions) Act 1934 shall be three years from—

    (a) the date of death, or

    (b) the date of the personal representative's knowledge, whichever is the later.

Further, section 14(1) provides that references to a person's date of knowledge are references to the date on which he first had knowledge of the following facts—

    (a) that the injury in question was significant, and

    (b) that the injury was attributable in whole or in part to the act or omission which is alleged to constitute negligence, nuisance or breach of duty, and

    (c) the identity of the defendant, and

    (d) if it is alleged that the act or omission was that of a person other than the defendant, the identity of that person and the additional facts supporting the bringing of an action against the defendant,

and knowledge that any acts or omissions did or did not, as a matter of law, involve negligence, nuisance or breach of duty is irrelevant.[13]

(2) For the purposes of this section an injury is significant if the person whose date of knowledge is in question would reasonably have considered it sufficiently serious to justify his instituting proceedings for damages against a defendant who did not dispute liability and was able to satisfy a judgment.

(3) For the purposes of this section a person's knowledge includes knowledge which he might reasonably have been expected to acquire—

    (a) from facts observable or ascertainable by him, or

    (b) from facts ascertainable by him with the help of medical or other appropriate expert advice which it is reasonable for him to seek,

but a person shall not be fixed under this subsection with knowledge of a fact ascertainable only with the help of expert advice so long as he has taken all reasonable steps to obtain (and, where appropriate to act on) that advice.

---

[12] This covers a case in which more than one injury arises from the same act: *Bristow* v. *Grout* [1986] 11 C.L. 363.

[13] So it is knowledge of the facts, not of the law, which is critical.

Sections 14 and 14B make similar provision for cases of latent damage to property.

The disapplication provisions of section 33

The power to "disapply" the complex provisions set out above may be exercised, "if it appears to the court that it would be equitable to allow an action to proceed." As has been observed, the result is that "we have uncertainty deliberately built into the law on top of the minute detail provided."[14] The basic question which arose was whether the court's discretion was to be exercised only in exceptional cases. In favour of such a view was the existence of six guide-lines in the section itself, and the fact that the Law Reform Committee, on whose Report[15] the Act was based, had so recommended. But it has twice been held by the House of Lords that section 33 should not be read in any restrictive sense so as to apply only to exceptional cases.[16]

So that if the plaintiff has been guilty of extreme delay in notifying the defendant of the claim against him, the court can take that delay into account whether it occurred before or after the expiry of the limitation period,[17] although normally there is no power to dismiss an action for want of prosecution before the expiry of the statutory period.[18]

(2) Accidents at sea and in the air

By the Maritime Conventions Act 1911, s.8, a period of limitation of two years is imposed upon claims in respect of damage to a vessel or her cargo, or in respect of loss of life or personal injuries suffered by any person on board a vessel, caused by the fault of any other vessel.[19] Under the same Act the period within which the owners of the vessels involved may enforce their right of contribution in cases of loss of life or personal injuries is one year from the date of payment. These periods may, however, be extended by the court in certain circumstances.[20] By the Carriage by Air Act 1962, s.5(1), a two-year limitation period applies to such proceedings against air-carriers as are governed by that Act.

(3) Statutes connected with death

(i) Death of injured party

Claims under the Fatal Accidents Act 1976 have a special period of three years under the Limitation Act 1980, s.12. As to survival actions, the ordinary six- or three-year period applies. It runs from the accrual of the cause of action as if no death had occurred. But if the deceased could

---

[14] W. L. Dale, *Legislative Drafting—A New Approach* (1978), p. 216.

[15] Cmnd. 5630, 1974.

[16] *Simpson* v. *Norwest Holst Southern Ltd.* [1980] 1 W.L.R. 968; *Donovan* v. *Gwentoys Ltd* [1990] 1 W.L.R. 472.

[17] *Donovan* v. *Gwentoys Ltd.* [1990] 1 W.L.R. 472.

[18] *Birkett* v. *James* [1978] A.C. 297. *Aliter* if the action has been commenced with the leave of the court: *Biss* v. *Lambeth B.C.* [1978] 1 W.L.R. 382.

[19] See *The Alnwick* [1965] P. 357.

[20] See Cmnd. 5334, § 29.

have applied to the court for leave to bring the action out of time then his estate will have a similar right.

(ii) *Death of wrongdoer*

Under section 1(3) of the 1934 Act no proceedings in respect of a cause of action in tort could be taken against the estate of a deceased person unless either the proceedings were pending at the date of his death or the proceedings were taken not later than six months after his personal representatives took out representation.[21] But the "six-months rule" was criticised by the Law Commission[22] on the ground that a plaintiff might be seriously prejudiced if the tortfeasor was unknown to him, and died at the time of the accident or shortly thereafter, or even if known, the death occurred before a writ had been served. It therefore proposed the total repeal of the "six-months rule," leaving all claims against estates to be governed by the general law of limitations. Parliament accepted this recommendation, and by the Proceedings Against Estates Act 1970, s.1, repealed section 1(3) of the 1934 Act.

Where the cause of action, as in the case of disturbance of the right of support, does not arise until the damage has been suffered, the Act of 1934 expressly provides[23] that if the wrongdoer dies before or at the same time as the damage is suffered, there shall be deemed to be subsisting against him such cause of action as would have subsisted if he had died after the damage was suffered.

(4) Contribution between tortfeasors

The limitation period is two years under the Limitation Act 1980, s.10. The statutory right to contribution is not based upon a breach of any obligation owed to the claimant in the contribution action by the respondent in that action. The right is *sui generis*, and passes to the personal representatives of a deceased claimant.[24]

(5) Defamation

Section 57 of the Administration of Justice Act 1985 amends the Limitation Act 1980 by adding a section 4A, which reduces the limitation period for actions for libel and slander from six to three years. The section gives the High Court a discretion to extend the time-limit where a prospective plaintiff did not find out about the relevant facts until the time-limit had expired.

---

[21] The Law Reform (Limitations of Actions) Act 1954, ss.4, 8(3), and Sched., repealed the former additional requirement of the 1934 Act that the cause of action must have arisen not earlier than six months before the death of the wrongdoer. This provision remains familiar to all who have read what is, perhaps, the best of all detective stories with a legal setting, Cyril Hare's *Tragedy at Law*.

[22] Law Com. No. 19 (Cmnd. 4010, 1969).

[23] s.1(4). "Damage" in this subsection means injury: *Post Office* v. *Official Solicitor* [1951] 1 All E.R. 522.

[24] *Ropex Properties Ltd.* v. *John Laing Construction Ltd.* [1983] Q.B. 398.

§ 25.5. FELONIOUS TORTS[25]

At common law the rule was that when a tort was also a felony, no action could be brought in respect of the tort until the defendant had been prosecuted for the felony or a reasonable excuse had been shown for his not having been prosecuted.[26] But the rule has been abolished by the Criminal Law Act 1967, s.1. It is now possible to sue a thief for unlawful interference with goods before he has been prosecuted.

§ 25.6. ASSIGNMENT OF RIGHTS OF ACTION[27]

The assignment of a right of action for damages for a tort is in general illegal and void. The rule is based on fundamental considerations of public policy, and is designed to prevent the oppressive litigation that would result if a right of action for damages were recognised as a marketable commodity capable of purchase by way of a commercial speculation ("champerty"). The rule applies to torts of all kinds, whether they are injuries to property or to the person or otherwise, and has not been affected by the abolition of criminal and tortious liability for champerty and maintenance by the Criminal Law Act 1967, ss.13 and 14. But there is an increasing tendency to uphold assignments when the assignee has a legitimate and genuine interest in the subject-matter of the suit,[28] at least if that interest is of a commercial character.[29] So the rule is not applicable in the following six cases:

(1) Where the right assigned has some other source than an illegal act. It is on this principle that rights arising under a contract are assignable, as opposed to rights arising from the breach of a contract. On the same principle, there should be no objection to the assignment of a judgment debt even in an action of tort, or to the assignment of money agreed to be paid by way of settlement of a claim in tort. (2) The rule does not prevent the assignment of property merely because it is the subject of litigation and cannot be recovered without an action.[30] (3) Where a trustee in bankruptcy assigns the bankrupt's choses in action, even though they arise *ex delicto*, and even though the assignment is back to the bankrupt himself.[31] (4) The rule does not prevent the subrogation of an insurer to the rights of the assured, even though these rights are rights of action for damages for a tort, nor the subsequent express assignment of the assured's rights to the insurer.[32] (5) The rule does not apply to any other case in which the assignee has any lawful interest in the subject-matter sufficient to exclude the doctrine of maintenance—for example, an assignment by a trustee to his beneficiaries of a right of action for an injury to the trust estate. (6) The rules does not prevent the assignment

---

[25] See Pannam "The Felonious Tort Rule" (1965) 39 Austr.L.J. 164.

[26] *Smith* v. *Selwyn* [1914] 3 K.B. 98.

[27] See Tan, "Champertous Contracts and Assignments" (1990) 106 L.Q.R. 656.

[28] See *Trendtex Trading Corporation* v. *Credit Suisse* [1980] A.C. 679.

[29] *Brownton Ltd.* v. *Edward Moore Inbucom Ltd.* [1985] 3 All E.R. 499.

[30] *Dawson* v. *G.N. Ry.* [1905] 1 K.B. 260, 271.

[31] "The position of the trustee in bankruptcy is fascinating": [1980] Q.B. 629, 648.

[32] *Compania Colombiana de Seguros* v. *Pacific S.N. Co.* [1965] 1 Q.B. 101.

of the fruits of an action in tort, *i.e.* an assignment of the damages to be recovered in such an action—even though the assessment is made before the action has commenced or before judgment has been recovered.[33] This is not the assignment of an existing cause of action. It is merely the equitable assignment of future property defined or identified by reference to such a cause of action.

§ 25.7. WAIVER OF TORTS[34]

In certain cases when the defendant has by means of a tort become possessed of a sum of money at the expense of the plaintiff, the plaintiff may at his election waive the tort. He may sue either for damages for the tort, or in restitution for money had and received by the defendant to the use of the plaintiff. This is so, for example, if the defendant wrongfully takes by trespass or obtains by fraud the money of the plaintiff.[35] So also if the plaintiff's goods are wrongfully converted and sold by the defendant the plaintiff may choose between an action in tort for wrongful interference with goods and an action in restitution for the price so received by the defendant.[36] It is obvious that in these cases there is no real waiver as where the forfeiture of a lease is waived by the receipt of rent. "If I find that a thief has stolen my securities and is in possession of the proceeds," said Lord Atkin,[37] "when I sue him for them I am not excusing him; indeed, he may be in prison upon my prosecution." The waiver is as fictitious as the contract. The phrase "waive the tort" is a picturesque one and as a pleasing sound and was (perhaps for that reason) regarded by the old common lawyers with affection,[38] but it is inaccurate. What is waived is not the tort but the right to recover damages for it. It is clear that there are some torts to which the doctrine of waiver cannot be applied, for example, defamation and assault.[39] The torts which it has been held can be waived are those of conversion, trespass to land or goods, deceit and the action for extorting money by threats. There are authorities which, if they could be relied on, would justify us in laying down a general rule to the effect that whenever the defendant has by his tort acquired a profit of any sort (whether it is the receipt of money or not) the tort may be waived, and an action of restitution brought to compel payment of a pecuniary equivalent for that profit. The fundamental concepts in this part of the law need re-examination: why should a plaintiff in a restitution action be in a better position because a tort has been committed against him?

---

[33] *Glegg* v. *Bromley* [1912] 3 K.B. 474.

[34] See Hedley, "The Myth of Waiver of Tort" (1984) 100 L.Q.R. 653.

[35] *Neate* v. *Harding* (1851) 6 Ex. 349.

[36] *Rodgers* v. *Maw* (1846) 15 M. & W. 444, 448.

[37] [1941] A.C. 1, 29.

[38] One of them was sufficiently moved to express his feelings in verse:

"Thoughts much too deep for tears subdue the Court
When I assumpsit bring, and god-like waive a tort."
—J. L. Adolphus, "The Circuiteers: an Eclogue": (1885) 1 L.Q.R. 232.

[39] *United Australia* case [1941] A.C. 1, 12.

Effect of election

In those cases in which the waiver of a tort is permitted the two causes of action are not cumulative but alternative. The plaintiff must make his election between them. Anything, therefore, which exhausts or extinguishes one of the causes of action destroys the other also. Accordingly, when the plaintiff's goods have been converted and sold and he obtains judgment in an action for money had and received he cannot thereafter resort to an action of conversion; and this is so even though the damages recoverable in conversion would far exceed the price for which the defendant sold the goods and for which judgment has been obtained against him.[40] But the mere commencement of an action in restitution is no bar to a subsequent action in tort: such an action is not a waiver of the tort but merely a choice of one of two alternative remedies, and it is judgment alone in the first action which constitutes a bar to the second.[41]

When election to be made

Confusion has arisen from failure to distinguish between (1) election between inconsistent rights, and (2) election between alternative remedies. If a man is entitled to one of two inconsistent rights, when with full knowledge[42] he has done an unequivocal act showing that he has chosen the one, he cannot afterwards pursue the other[43]; which after the first choice is by reason of the inconsistency no longer his to choose. The commencement of an action is only evidence from which an election may be inferred: it is not conclusive.[44] Otherwise a plaintiff who issued a writ against one of two tortfeasors in order to prevent time running out would find that he was barred from proceeding against the other. When the plaintiff's failure to elect becomes embarrassing to the defendant and the court he may be compelled to make his election during the trial.[45] But where there are alternative remedies on the same set of facts the plaintiff need not make his election until he applies for judgment.[46] It need hardly be necessary to add that if the same act constitutes two different torts the bringing of an action for both of them is no waiver of either.

§ 25.8. FOREIGN TORTS[47]

The technological revolution of the twentieth century has made this subject important. A defective product may be manufactured in one country, assembled in another, sold in a third, and cause damage in a

---

[40] *Rice* v. *Reed* [1900] 1 Q.B. 54; *Re Simms* [1934] Ch. 1.
[41] *United Australia Ltd.* v. *Barclays Bank Ltd.* [1941] A.C. 1. And if there are two tortfeasors an unsatisfied judgment against one is no bar to proceedings against the other.
[42] [1941] A.C. 1, 30.
[43] *Re United Railways of the Havana and Regla Warehouses Ltd.* [1961] A.C. 1007, 1065.
[44] *Clarkson Booker Ltd.* v. *Andjel* [1964] 2 Q.B. 775.
[45] *British Ry. Traffic Co.* v. *Roper* (1939) 162 L.T. 217.
[46] *Mahesan* v. *Malaysia Government Housing Society Ltd.* [1979] A.C. 374.
[47] The literature is almost as voluminous as on negligence. The most penetrating analysis is that by P. B. Carter, "Choice of Law in Tort and Delict" (1991) 107 L.Q.R. 405.

fourth. Two issues must be kept distinct. One is whether a writ can be served outside the jurisdiction in respect of damage of a tortious character sustained within it (the most convenient forum problem). The other is whether a defendant who has been properly served with a writ in England can be sued here in respect of a tort committed wholly within another jurisdiction (the double actionability problem).

(1) Most convenient forum

Under R.S.C., Order 11, rule 1(1)(*f*) a plaintiff is entitled to ask the leave of the court to serve a writ out of the jurisdiction if "the claim is founded on a tort and the damage was sustained, or resulted from an act committed, within the jurisdiction." This "long-arm jurisdiction" has become more flexible since Order 11 was amended in 1987 to take account of the changes made by the Civil Jurisdiction and Foreign Judgments Act 1982. If the court is satisfied that some substantial and efficacious damage was sustained in England, then it need not consider the double actionability problem,[48] but can at once decide whether England is a more appropriate forum than the foreign court in the interests of justice and of the parties.[49]

(2) Double actionability

If the alleged tort is found to be in substance committed in a foreign country (even though the defendant happens to be resident in England), then the court should follow *Boys* v. *Chaplin*,[50] and impose liability only if each of two conditions is satisfied. First, that the relevant acts would have given rise to liability in tort if they had been committed in England, and secondly, that the alleged tort would be actionable in the country where it was committed.[51] Although these conditions are now interpreted more flexibly than before, it is not easy for a plaintiff to surmount the double hurdle which they set in his way, and some courts now favour a doctrine known as "the proper law of the tort."[52]

Trespass

At common law no action lay in respect of trespass to land situated out of England.[53] But this rule was abolished by the Civil Judgments Act 1982, s.30, which gives the English court jurisdiction over trespass to, or any other tort affecting, immovable property in another jurisdiction, unless the proceedings are "principally concerned with" the ownership or possession of that property.

---

[48] *Metall* [1990] 1 Q.B. 391, 446.
[49] *Attock Cement Co. Ltd.* v. *Romanian Bank for Foreign Trade* [1989] 1 W.L.R. 1147, 1156.
[50] [1971] A.C. 356, in which the H.L. reformulated the rules laid down by Willes J. in his classic judgment in *Phillips* v. *Eyre* (1870) L.R. 6 Q.B. 1.
[51] See the C.A. in *Metall* [1990] 1 Q.B. 391, 446.
[52] In effect approved in *Grehan* v. *Medical Incorporated* [1986] I.R. 528, but not accepted in *Boys* v. *Chaplin* [1971] A.C. 356.
[53] *Hesperides Hotels Ltd.* v. *Muftizade* [1979] A.C. 508.

CHAPTER 26

EXTRAJUDICIAL REMEDIES

It is not necessary in all cases that a man should resort to judicial proceedings in order to seek protection or redress in respect of injuries threatened or committed against him. In many instances the law grants him liberty to help himself by his own act and strength. We shall deal in this chapter with self-redress; with self-defence and the prevention of trespass we have already dealt.[1]

§ 26.1. Re-entry on Land[2]

He who is wrongfully dispossessed of land is not bound to proceed for its recovery by action at law,[3] for he may retake possession of it by his own act, if he can do so peaceably and without the use of force.[4] Even if he has obtained a judgment for possession he may still enter at his own risk without the aid of the sheriff.[5] A forcible entry, however, even by a person lawfully entitled to the possession, was an indictable misdemeanour under the Statutes of Forcible entry 1381, 1429 and 1623.[6] These statutes have been repealed by the Criminal Law Act 1977, s.13, and replaced by a number of specific criminal offences—*e.g.* under section 6 it is an offence without lawful authority to use or threaten violence to secure entry into premises against the known opposition of someone on the premises. There is an exception for a "displaced residential occupier."[7] Before the Act of 1977 it was established that forcible entry upon a person wrongfully in possession by a person entitled to the possession has, although a criminal offence, no civil injury for which the wrongdoer so ejected had any remedy.[8] If in the course of a forcible entry an assault is committed upon the occupier or other person defending the possession, or damage is done to chattels upon the premises, will an action for damages lie in respect of this independent injury, although none lies for the entry and eviction itself? After some conflict of opinion the Court of Appeal in *Hemmings* v. *Stoke Poges Golf Club*[9]

---

[1] Above, § 7.4.

[2] See Law Commission Report (Law Com. No. 76), 1974, which is the basis of the Criminal Law Act 1977, and Prichard, *Squatting* (1981).

[3] Unless the premises have been let as a dwelling under a tenancy which is not a protected tenancy within the meaning of the Protection for Eviction Act 1977, when a court order is required by s.3 of the Act.

[4] *Taunton* v. *Costar* (1797) 7 T.R. 431.

[5] *Aglionby* v. *Cohen* [1955] 1 Q.B. 558.

[6] This "is the reason for the perenially comic spectacle, so dear to playwrights and novelists, of the patient or crafty bailiff trying to obtain entry without strong hand or multitude of people": Allen, *The Queen's Peace*, p. 48.

[7] So an occupier who is not within this category cannot apparently use force to recover his property unless the person in occupation is a squatter (or other trespasser), for such a person has never obtained possession: *McPhail* v. *Persons Unknown* [1973] Ch. 447.

[8] *Pollen* v. *Brewer* (1859) 7 C.B.(N.S.) 371.

[9] [1920] 1 K.B. 720.

held that it would not. So long as no more force was used than was justifiable at common law for the ejection of a trespasser[10] or the removal of his goods, the fact that the entry was a breach of the Statutes of Forcible Entry did not expose the true owner to an action for trespass to person or goods.[11] It is uncertain how far these rules are still law.

§ 26.2. Recaption of Chattels[12]

Any person entitled to the possession of a chattel may retake the chattel either peaceably or by the use of reasonable force from any person who has wrongfully taken or detained it from him. Such a retaking, even though forcible, is neither a civil injury nor a criminal offence.[13] As to the amount of force which is permissible, and as to the necessity of a precedent request,[14] the defence and recaption of chattels is presumably governed by the same rules as the ejectment of trespassers upon land.[15] The remedy of forcible recaption is not limited to cases of the wrongful taking of chattels, but extends to all cases of the wrongful possession of them.[16] Under the Copyright, Patents and Designs Act 1988, ss.95–100, there is power to order the delivery up and seizure of articles which have infringed copyright—e.g. videos and cassettes.

It is a matter of some doubt how far the right of retaking the chattels will serve to justify an entry on the land on which they are situated. It is clear that if the occupier of the land has himself wrongfully taken and placed the goods there, the owner of them may enter and take them.[17] A similar rule applies if the occupier has permitted a wrongdoer to leave goods on the land.[18] But what if the occupier is in no way responsible for the presence of the goods on his land, but merely refuses to give them up, or to allow the owner to enter and take them; as in the case of a lessee who gives up possession of the land, but leaves a chattel behind him, and then seeks to recover it? This is a question that has more than once come before the courts, but has not succeeded in obtaining a definite answer.[19] The Law Reform Committee suggested that the deciding

---

[10] See above, § 7.4.

[11] *Aglionby v. Cohen* [1955] 1 Q.B. 558, 562.

[12] See Branston, "Forcible Recaption of Chattels" (1912) 28 L.Q.R. 263, and the 18th Report of the Law Reform Committee (Cmnd. 4774 (1971)), paras. 116–126.

[13] *Blades v. Higgs* (1865) 11 H.L.C. 621.

[14] The need for a prior request was not accepted in *Whatford v. Carty* [1960] C.L.Y. 3258.

[15] See above, § 7.4.

[16] *Blades v. Higgs* (1861) 10 C.B.(N.S.) 713, 720. It has been doubted whether it extends to a mere wrongful detention of a chatel lawfully acquired: *Devoe v. Long* [1951] 1 D.L.R. 203.

[17] *Austin v. Dowling* (1870) L.R. 5 C.P. 534, 539.

[18] *Huet v. Lawrence* (1948) S.R. (Qd.) 168.

[19] As the authorities stand the position seems to be as follows. A man may enter another man's land to retake his own chattels if they came there (1) by accident, e.g. if a fruit tree grow in a hedge and the fruit fall on to another's land: *The Case of Thorns* (1466) Y.B. 6 Edw. IV, 7, p. 18; *Mitten v. Faudrye* (1626) Poph. 16.1; (2) by the felonious act of a third party: *Higgins v. Andrewes* (1619) 2 Roll.Rep. 55. But it is not enough to prove that his property was on the land without proving the circumstances in which it came there: *Anthony v. Haney* (1832) 8 Bing. 186; still less does it suffice to justify the entry if the property came there by his own act—for example, by way of bailment. In such a case it has been held that the owner of the chattels may enter to retake them only if (1) the

factor should be whether the person retaking his chattel has acted reasonably in entering on another's premises or in using any degree of force.[20] It is settled[21] that a man who has hived bees has no right if they swarm to follow them on to another man's land, for when they get there they once more become *ferae naturae* and are the property of no one until they are again hived.

§ 26.3. ABATEMENT OF NUISANCE

It is lawful for any occupier of land, or for any other person by the authority of the occupier, to abate (*i.e.* to terminate by his own act) any nuisance by which that land is injuriously affected. Thus the occupier of land may without notice cut off the overhanging branches of his neighbour's trees,[22] or sever roots which have spread from those trees into his own land.[23] In these cases the abator can act without leaving his own land, but subject to certain requirements as to prior notice, which will be considered later, the right also extends to the cases in which it is necessary for the abator to enter upon the land of the other party.[24] In abating a nuisance any unnecessary damage done is an actionable wrong, and therefore, where there are two ways of abating a nuisance, the less mischievous is to be followed.[25] The right of abatement is alternative to damages. If the nuisance is abated, no damages can be obtained in respect of the injury suffered.[26] It is sometimes said that the law does not regard the right of abatement with favour,[27] but this seems too strong. There is no reason to encourage litigation to deal with such trivial nuisances as overhanging branches.[28] But as an abatement may give rise to a breach of the peace, caution is desirable.[29]

It seems to be assumed that there is no right of entry and abatement in a case in which, although an actionable nuisance exists, an injunction against the continuance of it could not be obtained. If, for example, a

---

occupier's right of possession has been validly determined, and (2), no breach of the peace is committed: *Devoe* v. *Long* [1951] 1 D.L.R. 203. The occupier is not liable merely because he refuses to hand the chattels back to their owner; *Capital Finance Co. Ltd.* v. *Bray* [1964] 1 W.L.R. 323. He is not liable unless he has exercised dominion over the chattel: *British Economical Lamp Co.* v. *Empire, Mile End* (1913) 29 T.L.R. 386, 387; *Ellis* v. *Noakes* (1930), [1932] 2 Ch. 98, 104.

[20] Cmnd. 4774 (1971), para. 126. But the Law Commission disagree—see Working Paper No. 54 (1974).

[21] *Kearry* v. *Pattinson* [1939] 1 K.B. 471.

[22] *Lemmon* v. *Webb* [1895] A.C. 1.

[23] *Butler* v. *Standard Telephones* [1940] 1 K.B. 399. He may not, however, appropriate to his own use the things so severed, and if he does so, he is liable in conversion for their value: *Mills* v. *Brooker* [1919] 1 K.B. 555.

[24] See Law Commission Working Paper No. 78, *Rights of Access to Neighbouring Land* (1980).

[25] *Lagan Navigation Co.* v. *Lambeg Bleaching Co.* [1927] A.C. 226, 245.

[26] *Baten's Case* (1610) 9 Co.Rep. 53b.

[27] *Lagan Navigation Co.* v. *Lambeg Bleaching Co.* [1927] A.C. 226, 244.

[28] So when there was a dispute about a boundary fence, "The plaintiff consulted her own solicitors who advised her to exercise self-help and pull up the fence which Mr. Kenworthy had erected and throw it back on to the Kenworthys' land, which she did": *Re Basham, decd.* [1986] 1 W.L.R. 1498, 1502.

[29] *R.* v. *Chief Constable of Devon and Cornwall* [1982] Q.B. 458, 473.

house is built which obstructs ancient lights, but to so small an extent or under such circumstances that no mandatory injunction would be granted to pull the house down, it cannot be supposed that the owner of the obstructed light is nevertheless at liberty to attain the same end by the exercise of his right of abatement.[30] Strangely enough, however, there may apparently be a right of entry and abatement where there is no action for damages for the nuisance. So no damages can be obtained against a defendant who has allowed a tree to overgrow his boundary, unless it is the cause of actual damage[31]; for damage is of the essence of nuisance. But there is no reason to suppose that the right of the neighbour to cut the encroaching roots and branches is subject to any such limitation.[32]

Necessity of notice before abatement

It is clear that there are at least two cases in which no notice is required:
  (1) When there is no entry on the land of the other party—e.g. cutting roots and branches.[33]
  (2) In case of emergency—i.e. where the nuisance threatens such immediate harm to person or property that the delay involved in giving notice would be unreasonable.[34]

It seems clear also that there are four cases in which notice must be given:
  (1) When the nuisance was committed, not by the present occupier, but by a predecessor in title.[35]
  (2) When the occupier is not responsible for the creation or continuance of the nuisance.[35a]
  (3) When the abatement involves the demolition of a house which is actually inhabited.[36]
  (4) When the more mischievous of the two ways of abating a nuisance is followed.[37]

Whether notice is required in other cases is a question to which no certain reply can be given. In *Lemmon* v. *Webb*[38] there is an obvious

---

[30] This is discussed in *Lane* v. *Capsey* [1891] 3 Ch. 411.

[31] *Smith* v. *Giddy* [1904] 2 K.B. 448; *Lemmon* v. *Webb* [1894] 3 Ch. 1, 11. If damage has been caused, an injunction may also be obtained: *McCombe* v. *Read* [1955] 2 Q.B. 429.

[32] Salmond regarded this as going further than a mere right of abating a nuisance—as simply a part of the occupier's exclusive right of possession, and of doing as he pleases with his own. But the overhanging branches and the encroaching roots are until severance realty, and realty which is the property of the owner of the tree: *Mills* v. *Brooker* [1919] 1 K.B. 555. An overhanging roof or cornice has been held to be a nuisance to the land it overhangs because of the necessary tendency to discharge rainwater upon it: *Baten's Case* (1610) 9 Co.Rep. 53b.

[33] *Lemmon* v. *Webb* [1894] 3 Ch. 1; [1895] A.C. 1.

[34] *Jones* v. *Williams* (1843) 11 M. & W. 176, 182; *Lemmon* v. *Webb* [1894] 3 Ch. 1, 13.

[35] *Jones* v. *Williams* (1843) 11 M. & W. 176.

[35a] *Jones* v. *Williams* (1843) 11 M. & W. 176.

[36] *Davies* v. *Williams* (1851) 16 Q.B. 546.

[37] *Lagan Navigation Co.* v. *Lambeg Bleaching Co.* [1927] A.C. 226, 245.

[38] [1895] A.C. 1.

inclination to state the rule in the general form that in all cases of entry and abatement notice is required except in case of emergency.

Abatement of public nuisance

It is lawful for any person to abate a public nuisance to a highway, so far as it is necessary to enable him to exercise his right of way thereon, or right of access thereto. Thus if a fence is unlawfully erected across a highway or a gate wrongfully locked, any member of the public may in the exercise of his right of way remove the fence or break open the gate.[39] And this is so even though the obstruction has been erected in the exercise of a bona fide but unfounded claim or right. Probably this right of abatement exists only when the abator can prove that he has sustained such special damage as is required to confer upon him a private right of action.[40] The right of abating a nuisance on a highway extends only to nuisances of commission, and not to those of omission so as to entitle any member of the public to undertake the repair of a highway or the creation thereon of a permanent structure such as a bridge, which he may consider necessary for the convenient exercise of his right of passage. Such acts must be done by those who are charged with the common law or statutory duty of repairing or constructing highways.[41]

§ 26.4. DISTRESS DAMAGE FEASANT[42]

It is lawful for any occupier of land to seize any chattels which are unlawfully upon his land and have done or are doing damage there, and to detain them until payment of compensation for the damage done. This right is known as that of distress damage feasant. Normally the things so distrained were cattle or other trespassing animals, but the Animals Act 1971, s.7, has abolished the right to seize and detain any animal by way of distress damage feasant, and substituted a new remedy which gives the occupier a power of sale.[43] But distress damage feasant still exists, and it is established that the right extends to all chattels animate or inanimate.[44] So an occupier is not obliged to return a cricket ball which has broken his window-pane. Distress damage feasant differs from other forms of distress in that it is a remedy which can be exercised out of hand, at any time of the day or night.[45] The right of distress damage feasant is vested, in general, only in the occupier of land. Mere use without exclusive possession is, it may be assumed, as insuf-

---

[39] *Webb* v. *Stansfield* [1966] C.I.Y. 2590 (opening door of car parked in front of garage: in such a case the defence of necessity may also be available: see § 22.1., but not that of distress damage feasant: see § 26.4).

[40] *Campbell Davys* v. *Lloyd* [1901] 2 Ch. 518, 524.

[41] *Campbell Davys* v. *Lloyd* [1901] 2 Ch. 518.

[42] See the exhaustive discussion of this topic in Williams, *Animals*, pp. 1–123.

[43] See above, § 14.6.

[44] *Ambergate Ry.* v. *Midland Ry.* (1853) 2 E. & B. 793.

[45] *E.g.* a locomotive engine: *Watkinson* v. *Hollington* [1944] K.B. 16.

ficient to confer this right as it is to confer the right to eject a trespasser or to sue in an action of trespass.[46]

Limits of right of distress

(i) *Object's presence must be wrongful*

The thing distrained must be unlawfully on the land—*i.e.* it must be there under such circumstances that an action for damages will lie against the owner or some other person responsible for it.[47]

(ii) *Actual damage*

There must be actual damage done by the thing distrained; for it is rightly taken and detained only as a security for the payment of compensation, and where there is no damage done there can be no compensation due.[48] But the damage need not be done to the land itself or to things forming part of the freehold, such as crops. It is sufficient if damage is done on the land to the property or, presumably, the person of the occupier.[49]

(iii) *Object must still be on land*

The thing must be seized while still on the land. There is no right of following it, even in fresh pursuit, and even if it is purposely removed by its owner in order to avoid distress.[50] It does not seem that the thing distrained need have been caught *flagrante delicto* doing damage, but if the same thing comes more than once upon the same land it cannot be distrained or detained on a subsequent occasion in respect of damage done by it on a former visit.[51]

(iv) *No right of sale*

The right of distress damage feasant includes no right of sale, but merely a right to retain the thing until adequate compensation is made. Formerly the law was the same in the case of distress for rent also, but the statutes which confer a power of sale on landlords have left unaffected the common law as to distress damage feasant. But the right of the occupier is to detain only until compensation is paid for the damage done. It is the duty of the owner to form an estimate of the amount of the damage, and to make a tender of this sum, however extortionate the

---

[46] *Burt* v. *Moor* (1793) 5 T.R. 329.

[47] *Tillet* v. *Ward* (1882) 10 Q.B.D. 17.

[48] *R.* v. *Howson* (1966) 55 D.L.R. (2d) 582, 596—mere trespass by wrongfully parked car does not justify distress, though the removal of the car may be justified under abatement of nuisance (see § 26.3.) or necessity (see § 22.1.). So that unless a technical trespass can be construed as damage the legality of "wheel-clamping" by a private occupier must be doubtful though in criminal law the motorist has no excuse for destroying the clamp: *Lloyd* v. *D.P.P.* [1992] 1 All E.R. 982.

[49] *Boden* v. *Roscoe* [1894] 1 Q.B. 608.

[50] *Clement* v. *Milner* (1800) 3 Esp. 95.

[51] *Vaspor* v. *Edwards* (1701) 12 Mod. 658, 660.

demand made by the distrainor.[52] Things distrained damage feasant may at the option of the distrainor be kept by him on the premises where they were seized, or kept in his own custody elsewhere, or impounded by him in a public pound.[53] By the Protection of Animals Act 1911, s.7, he is bound to provide animals impounded by him with food and water.

(v) *Alternative to action*

The exercise of the right of distress damage feasant suspends the right of action for the damage complained of, so long as the detention of the property continues. Distress and action are alternative remedies which cannot be concurrently pursued. If, however, the property distrained perishes or is lost without the distrainor's fault, he is remitted to his right of action, and so also if the property is restored to the owner.

---

[52] *Sorrell* v. *Paget* [1950] 1 K.B. 252, 265. In this case the distrainor's demand was for a sum as "salvage." Although "salvage by land is a legal chimera" (Asquith L.J.) this did not excuse the wrongdoer from making a tender.

[53] *Vaspor* v. *Edwards* (1701) 12 Mod. 658, 664. "As a public institution the pound was commonly referred to in our literature of a hundred years and more ago. I hope that a good many people recollect that in, perhaps, the most celebrated of English novels, Mr. Pickwick was removed by Captain Boldwig to the village pound under the imputation of being a drunken plebeian": *Searle* v. *Wallbank* [1947] A.C. 341, 350, *per* Lord Maugham.

INDEX